CLASSICAL AND MEDIEVAL LITERATURE CRITICISM

Guide to Gale Literary Criticism Series

For criticism on	Consult these Gale series
Authors now living or who died after December 31, 1999	*CONTEMPORARY LITERARY CRITICISM (CLC)*
Authors who died between 1900 and 1999	*TWENTIETH-CENTURY LITERARY CRITICISM (TCLC)*
Authors who died between 1800 and 1899	*NINETEENTH-CENTURY LITERATURE CRITICISM (NCLC)*
Authors who died between 1400 and 1799	*LITERATURE CRITICISM FROM 1400 TO 1800 (LC)* *SHAKESPEAREAN CRITICISM (SC)*
Authors who died before 1400	*CLASSICAL AND MEDIEVAL LITERATURE CRITICISM (CMLC)*
Authors of books for children and young adults	*CHILDREN'S LITERATURE REVIEW (CLR)*
Dramatists	*DRAMA CRITICISM (DC)*
Poets	*POETRY CRITICISM (PC)*
Short story writers	*SHORT STORY CRITICISM (SSC)*
Black writers of the past two hundred years	*BLACK LITERATURE CRITICISM (BLC)* *BLACK LITERATURE CRITICISM SUPPLEMENT (BLCS)*
Hispanic writers of the late nineteenth and twentieth centuries	*HISPANIC LITERATURE CRITICISM (HLC)* *HISPANIC LITERATURE CRITICISM SUPPLEMENT (HLCS)*
Native North American writers and orators of the eighteenth, nineteenth, and twentieth centuries	*NATIVE NORTH AMERICAN LITERATURE (NNAL)*
Major authors from the Renaissance to the present	*WORLD LITERATURE CRITICISM, 1500 TO THE PRESENT (WLC)* *WORLD LITERATURE CRITICISM SUPPLEMENT (WLCS)*

ISSN 0896-0011

Volume 38

CLASSICAL AND MEDIEVAL LITERATURE CRITICISM

Excerpts from Criticism of the Works of World
Authors from Classical Antiquity through the
Fouteenth Century, from the First Appraisals
to Current Evaluations

Jelena O. Krstović
Editor

Detroit
New York
San Francisco
London
Boston
Woodbridge, CT

STAFF

Lynn M. Spampinato, Janet Witalec, *Managing Editors, Literature Product*
Jelena Krstović, *Editor*
Mark W. Scott, *Publisher, Literature Product*

Elisabeth Gellert, *Associate Editor*
Patti A. Tippett, Timothy J. White, *Technical Training Specialists*
Kathleen Lopez Nolan, *Managing Editor, Literature Content*
Susan M. Trosky, *Director, Literature Content*

Maria L. Franklin, *Permissions Manager*
Edna Hedblad, Kimberly F. Smilay, *Permissions Specialists*
Erin Bealmear, Sandy Gore, Keryl Stanley, *Permissions Assistants*

Victoria B. Cariappa, *Research Manager*
Tracie A. Richardson, *Project Coordinator*
Andrew Guy Malonis, Barbara McNeil, Gary J. Oudersluys, Maureen Richards, Cheryl L. Warnock, *Research Specialists*
Tamara C. Nott, *Research Associate*
Timothy Lehnerer, *Research Assistant*

Dorothy Maki, *Manufacturing Manager*
Stacy Melson, *Buyer*

Mary Beth Trimper, *Composition Manager*
Evi Seoud, *Assistant Production Manager*
Gary Leach, *Composition Specialist*

Mike Logusz, *Graphic Artist*
Randy Bassett, *Image Database Supervisor*
Robert Duncan, *Imaging Specialist*
Pamela A. Reed, *Imaging Coordinator*

Library of Congress Catalog Card Number 88-658021
ISBN 0-7876-4380-7
ISSN 0896-0011
Printed in the United States of America

10 9 8 7 6 5 4 3 2 1

Contents

Preface

S ince its inception in 1988, *Classical and Medieval Literature Criticism* (*CMLC*) has been a valuable resource for students and librarians seeking critical commentary on the works and authors of antiquity through the fourteenth century. The great poets, prose writers, dramatists, and philosophers of this period form the basis of most humanities curricula, so that virtually every student will encounter many of these works during the course of a high school and college education. Reviewers have found *CMLC* "useful" and "extremely convenient," noting that it "adds to our understanding of the rich legacy left by the ancient period and the Middle Ages," and praising its "general excellence in the presentation of an inherently interesting subject." No other single reference source has surveyed the critical reaction to classical and medieval literature as thoroughly as *CMLC*.

Scope of the Series

CMLC provides an introduction to classical and medieval authors, works, and topics that represent a variety of genres, time periods, and nationalities. By organizing and reprinting an enormous amount of critical commentary written on authors and works of this period in world history, *CMLC* helps students develop valuable insight into literary history, promotes a better understanding of the texts, and sparks ideas for papers and assignments.

Each entry in *CMLC* presents a comprehensive survey of an author's career, an individual work of literature, or a literary topic, and provides the user with a multiplicity of interpretations and assessments. Such variety allows students to pursue their own interests; furthermore, it fosters an awareness that literature is dynamic and responsive to many different opinions. Early commentary is offered to indicate initial responses, later selections document changes in literary reputations, and retrospective analyses provide the reader with modern views. The size of each author entry is a relative reflection of the scope of the criticism available in English.

An author may appear more than once in the series if his or her writings have been the subject of a substantial amount of criticism; in these instances, specific works or groups of works by the author will be covered in separate entries. For example, Homer will be represented by three entries, one devoted to the *Iliad,* one to the *Odyssey,* and one to the Homeric Hymns.

CMLC continues the survey of criticism of world literature begun by Gale's *Contemporary Literary Criticism* (*CLC*), *Twentieth-Century Literary Criticism* (*TCLC*), *Nineteenth-Century Literature Criticism* (*NCLC*), *Literature Criticism from 1400 to 1800* (*LC*), and *Shakespearean Criticism* (*SC*).

Organization of the Book

A *CMLC* entry consists of the following elements:

- The **Author Heading** cites the name under which the author most commonly wrote, followed by birth and death dates. Also located here are any name variations under which an author wrote, including transliterated forms for authors whose native languages use nonroman alphabets. If the author wrote consistently under a pseudonym, the pseudonym will be listed in the author heading and the author's actual name given in parenthesis on the first line of the biographical and critical information. Uncertain birth or death dates are indicated by question marks. Single-work entries are preceded by a heading that consists of the most common form of the title in English translation (if applicable) and the original date of composition.

- The **Introduction** contains background information that introduces the reader to the author, work, or topic that is the subject of the entry.

- A **Portrait of the Author** is included when available.

- The list of **Principal Works** is ordered chronologically by date of first publication and lists the most important works by the author. The genre and publication date of each work is given. In the case of foreign authors whose works have been translated into English, the list will focus primarily on twentieth-century translations, selecting those works most commonly considered the best by critics. Unless otherwise indicated, dramas are dated by first performance, not first publication. Lists of **Representative Works** by different authors appear with topic entries.

- Reprinted **Criticism** is arranged chronologically in each entry to provide a useful perspective on changes in critical evaluation over time. The critic's name and the date of composition or publication of the critical work are given at the beginning of each piece of criticism. Unsigned criticism is preceded by the title of the source in which it appeared. All titles by the author featured in the text are printed in boldface type. Footnotes are reprinted at the end of each essay or excerpt. In the case of excerpted criticism, only those footnotes that pertain to the excerpted texts are included. Criticism in topic entries is arranged chronologically under a variety of subheadings to facilitate the study of different aspects of the topic.

- A complete **Bibliographical Citation** of the original essay or book precedes each piece of criticism.

- Critical essays are prefaced by brief **Annotations** explicating each piece.

- An annotated bibliography of **Further Reading** appears at the end of each entry and suggests resources for additional study. In some cases, significant essays for which the editors could not obtain reprint rights are included here. Boxed material following the further reading list provides references to other biographical and critical sources on the author in series published by Gale.

Cumulative Indexes

A **Cumulative Author Index** lists all of the authors that appear in a wide variety of reference sources published by the Gale Group, including *CMLC*. A complete list of these sources is found facing the first page of the Author Index. The index also includes birth and death dates and cross references between pseudonyms and actual names.

Beginning with the second volume, a **Cumulative Nationality Index** lists all authors featured in *CMLC* by nationality, followed by the number of the *CMLC* volume in which their entry appears.

Beginning with the tenth volume, a **Cumulative Topic Index** lists the literary themes and topics treated in the series as well as in *Nineteenth-Century Literature Criticism, Twentieth-Century Literary Criticism,* and the *Contemporary Literary Criticism* Yearbook, which was discontinued in 1998.

A **Cumulative Title Index** lists in alphabetical order all of the works discussed in the series. Each title listing includes the corresponding volume and page numbers where criticism may be located. Foreign-language titles that have been translated into English are followed by the titles of the translation—for example, *Slovo o polku Igorove (The Song of Igor's Campaign)*. Page numbers following these translated titles refer to all pages on which any form of the titles, either foreign-language or translated, appear. Titles of novels, dramas, nonfiction books, and poetry, short story, or essay collections are printed in italics, while individual poems, short stories, and essays are printed in roman type within quotation marks.

Citing *Classical and Medieval Literature Criticism*

When writing papers, students who quote directly from any volume in the Literary Criticism Series may use the following general format to footnote reprinted criticism. The first example pertains to material drawn from periodicals, the second to material reprinted from books.

T. P. Malnati, "Juvenal and Martial on Social Mobility," *The Classical Journal* 83, no. 2 (December-January 1988): 134-41; reprinted in *Classical and Medieval Literature Criticism,* vol. 35, ed. Jelena Krstović (Farmington Hills, Mich.: The Gale Group, 2000), 366-71.

J. P. Sullivan, "Humanity and Humour; Imagery and Wit," in *Martial: An Unexpected Classic* (Cambridge University Press, 1991), 211-51; excerpted and reprinted in *Classical and Medieval Literature Criticism,* vol. 35, ed. Jelena Krstović (Farmington Hills, Mich.: The Gale Group, 2000), 371-95.

Suggestions are Welcome

Readers who wish to suggest new features, topics, or authors to appear in future volumes, or who have other suggestions or comments are cordially invited to call, write, or fax the Managing Editor:

Managing Editor, Literary Criticism Series
The Gale Group
27500 Drake Road
Farmington Hills, MI 48331-3535
1-800-347-4253 (GALE)
Fax: 248-699-8054

Acknowledgments

The editors wish to thank the copyright holders of the excerpted criticism included in this volume and the permissions managers of many book and magazine publishing companies for assisting us in securing reproduction rights. We are also grateful to the staffs of the Detroit Public Library, the Library of Congress, the University of Detroit Mercy Library, Wayne State University Purdy/Kresge Library Complex, and the University of Michigan Libraries for making their resources available to us. Following is a list of the copyright holders who have granted us permission to reproduce material in this volume of *CMLC*. Every effort has been made to trace copyright, but if omissions have been made, please let us know.

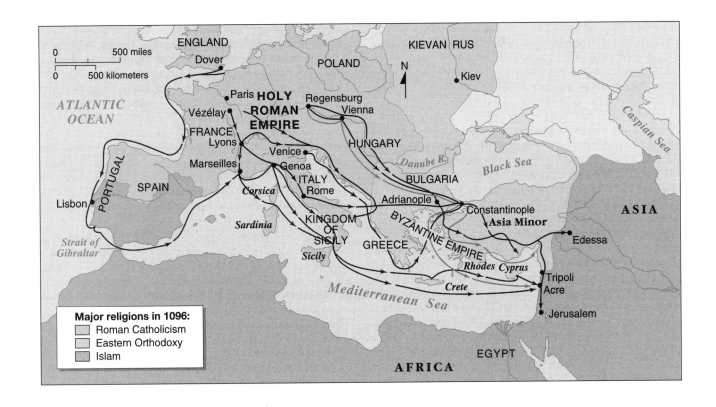

Major religions in 1096:
- Roman Catholicism
- Eastern Orthodoxy
- Islam

The Crusades

INTRODUCTION

The Crusades were military excursions made by Western European Christians during the late eleventh century through the late thirteenth century. The proclaimed purpose of the Crusades, which were often requested and encouraged by papal policy, was to recover the city of Jerusalem as well as other eastern locations of religious pilgrimage (all located in an area referred to as the Holy Land by Christians) from the control of the Muslims. During the mid-eleventh century, Muslim Turks conquered Syria and Palestine, causing concern among Western Christians. The year 1095 marks the beginning of the Crusades. At this time, Pope Urban II preached a sermon at the Council of Clermont in which he proposed that Western European noblemen and their armies join ranks with the Eastern Christian Byzantine Emperor and his forces in order to mount an attack against the Muslim Turks. Between 1097 and 1099, these combined forces of the First Crusade destroyed the Turkish army at Dorylaeum, conquered the Syrian city of Antioch, and captured Jerusalem. The military achievements of the First Crusade have been at-

tributed to the weak and isolated nature of the Muslim forces. Following the First Crusade, however, they became more united thereby gaining strength, and began attacking the Crusaders' strongholds. In 1145, a Second Crusade was instigated. German and French forces suffered serious casualties and failed to regain the lost ground. After the failed Second Crusade, the Muslim leader Saladin and his Egyptian troops struck many of the Crusaders' strongholds in 1187; that year, Jerusalem was again captured by Muslim forces. The Third Crusade, proclaimed by Pope Gregory VIII, set out after Jersusalem was taken. This Crusade failed to regain the city; however, Crusaders did manage to conquer some of Saladin's holdings along the Mediterranean coastline. In the early thirteenth century, a Fourth Crusade was organized but was beset with financial troubles, leading to the diversion of the Crusaders from the original destination of Egypt to Constantinople, which was conquered by the Turks. The Fifth Crusade, lasting from 1217 to 1221, attempted to capture Cairo, but failed. In 1228, the excommunicated Holy Roman Emperor Frederick II led a diplomatic campaign to the Holy Land and negotiated a treaty that returned Jerusalem to the Crusaders and offered a ten-year guarantee against attack. After

1

the Muslims recaptured Jerusalem in 1244, King Louis IX of France organized another Middle Eastern expedition, which resulted in his capture in 1250. The strongholds of the Crusaders began to fall to new enemies and despite a few minor expeditions, the crusading movement dwindled to an end.

Critics and historians have approached this period of history in a variety of ways, analyzing the details of the historical records, the literature produced during this time, and the attitudes of Christians toward the Crusades, as well as the forces which influenced people to join the crusading movement. George W. Cox has studied the precursors to the Crusades, demonstrating the relationship between the pilgrimages to the Holy Land that preceded the Crusades and the Crusades themselves. Other critics, such as G. P. R. James, have focused on the history of a particular Crusade. James has analyzed the developments leading to and the events of the Second Crusade, commenting in particular on the social changes that influenced it. Like James, Aziz S. Atiya has concentrated his examination on a specific era of the crusading movement. Atiya argues that the spirit of the Crusades did not die out at the end of the thirteenth century, but continued into the fourteenth and fifteenth centuries. While many critics examine the Crusades from the viewpoint of the Western Christian Crusaders, Robert Lee Wolff and Harry W. Hazard have traced the history of the Crusades from the point of view of the Byzantine empire, examining the contribution of the Byzantine rulers to the military and political developments wrought by the Crusades. Another area of critical interest is the source material from which our knowledge of the Crusades is derived. Oliver J. Thatcher and Steven Runciman are two of the scholars who have evaluated such sources. Thatcher concentrates on the Latin sources, and he assesses the historical value of extant letters and eyewitness accounts. Runciman offers an overview of Greek, Latin, Arabic, Armenian, and Syrian sources.

While Thatcher, Runciman, and others study the contemporary sources of the Crusades for historical accuracy, other critics consider these sources—as well as the poetry, songs, and chronicles of the Crusades—in light of their literary and social value. August C. Krey has studied contemporary accounts of the First Crusade, such as the anonymous *Gesta* (c. 1099-1101), commenting on the form, content, and style of such works. For example, Krey has observed that the lack of literary allusions and limited vocabulary of the *Gesta* suggest that the author had acquired a low level of education. Palmer A. Throop has examined the poetry and songs written during the thirteenth century, demonstrating the way in which these verses represent the subtle opposition of their authors to the papal policies on crusading. Similarly, Michael Routledge has analyzed the "crusade songs," observing in particular the usage of the vernacular in French and German songs of the time. Routledge points to such songs as the entertainment of common and illiterate people during the years of the first four Crusades. The epic poetry of the time is also a source of interest for critics. Alfred Foulet has studied two epic cycles, one written (or at least begun) toward the end of the twelfth century, and the other composed during the 1350s. Foulet discusses the form and content of these epic cycles, notes their similarities, and comments on their literary value. Compared to other contemporary works, such as William of Tyre's *Historia rerum in partibus transmarinis gestarum,* these epic cycles have little historical value, Foulet maintains. The letters written during the Crusades have also been found by critics to be quite revealing. S. D. Goitein has examined such a letter composed during the summer of 1100. What the letter offers, Goitein explains, is a likely reason for the lack of Jewish narrative on the First Crusade.

Another field of scholarly interest is the search for contemporary evidence of propaganda used to influence the attitudes of Christians toward the Crusades. Dana Carleton Munro has argued that papal sermons and policies encouraged the crusading movement by portraying the Muslims as heathens and worshippers of false gods and idols. Carl Erdmann has studied the development of the crusading movement during the second half of the eleventh century, observing how rhetoric about ecclesiastical aims and warfare became increasingly commingled, which allowed a very general conception of the Crusade to become transformed into the specific form of a Crusade to Jerusalem. Religious forces encouraged the Crusades in another manner as well, observes Colin Morris. The popes, Morris has argued, were aware of the persuasive power of visual imagery, particularly on the illiterate. Therefore, in addition to the preaching of the Crusades in sermons, songs, and liturgy, papal policy encouraged the Crusades through placards carried to advertise a particular Crusade, and through the art and architecture of churches and halls.

REPRESENTATIVE WORKS

Anonymous
Gesta (anonymous chronicle) 1099-1101

Benedetto and Leonardo Accolti
De bello a Chistianis contra Barbaros gesto pro Christi sepulchro et Judaea recuperandis libri tres (anonymous history) 1452

Fulcher of Chartres
Historia Hierosolymitana (anonymous history) 1105

Guillaume le Clerc
Le Besant de Dieu (anonymous satire) 1226-27

William of Tyre
Historia hierosolymitana; or Historia rerum in partibus transmarinis gestarum (anonymous history) 1549

HISTORY OF THE CRUSADES

G. P. R. James (essay date 1854)

SOURCE: "Chapter X" in *The History of Chivalry*, Harper & Brothers, 1854, pp. 214–32.

[In the following essay, James offers an overview of the history of the Second Crusade, which began in 1145. James notes the societal developments that occurred between the First and Second Crusades, and provides an account of the martial developments and ultimate failure of the Second Crusade.]

The loss of Edessa shook the kingdom of Jerusalem; not so much from the importance of the city or its territory, as from the exposed state in which it left the frontier of the newly established monarchy. The activity, the perseverance, the power of the Moslems had been too often felt not to be dreaded; and there is every reason to believe, that the clergy spoke but the wishes of the whole people, when in their letters to Europe they pressed their Christian brethren to come once more to the succour of Jerusalem. Shame and ambition led the young Count of Edessa to attempt the recovery of his capital as soon as the death of Zenghi, who had taken it, reached his ears. He in consequence collected a large body of troops, and on presenting himself before the walls during the night, was admitted, by his friends, into the town. There he turned his whole efforts to force the Turkish garrison in the citadel to surrender, before Nourhaddin, the son of Zenghi, could arrive to its aid. But the Saracens held out; and, while the Latin soldiers besieged the castle, they found themselves suddenly surrounded by a large body of the enemy, under the command of Nourhaddin. In this situation, they endeavoured to cut their way through the Turkish force, but, attacked on every side, few of them escaped to tell the tale of their own defeat. Nourhaddin marched over their necks into Edessa, and, in order to remove for ever that bulwark to the Christian kingdom of Jerusalem, he caused the fortifications to be razed to the ground.

The consternation of the people of Palestine became great and general. The road to the Holy City lay open before the enemy, and continual applications for assistance reached Europe, but more particularly France.

The state of that country, however, was the least[1] propitious that it is possible to conceive for a crusade. The position of all the orders of society had undergone a change since the period when the wars of the Cross were first preached by Peter the Hermit; and of the many causes which had combined to hurry the armed multitudes to the Holy Land, none remained but the spirit of religious fanaticism and military enterprise. At the time of the first crusade, the feudal system had reached the acme of its power. The barons had placed a king upon the throne. They had rendered their own dominion independent of his, and though they still acknowledged some ties between themselves and the monarch—some vague and general power of restraint in the king and his court of peers—yet those ties were so loose, that power was so undefined in its nature, and so difficult in its exercise, that the nobles were free and at liberty to act in whatever direction enthusiasm, ambition, or cupidity might call them, without fear of the sovereign, who was, in fact, but one of their own body loaded with a crown.

The people, too, at that time, both in the towns and in the fields, were the mere slaves of the nobility; and as there existed scarcely a shadow of vigour in the kingly authority, so there remained not an idea of distinct rights and privileges among the populace. Thus the baronage were then unfettered by dread from any quarter; and the lower classes—both the poorer nobility, and that indistinct tribe (which we find evidently[2] marked) who were neither among the absolute serfs of any lord, nor belonging to the military caste—were all glad to engage themselves in wars which held out to them riches and exaltation in this world, and beatification in the next; while they could hope for nothing in their own land but pillage, oppression, and wrong; or slaughter in feuds without an object, and in battles for the benefit of others.

Before the second crusade was contemplated, a change—an immense change had operated itself in the state of society. Just fifty years had passed since the council of Clermont: but the kings of France were no longer the same; the royal authority had acquired force[3]—the latent principles of domination had been exercised for the general good. Kings had put forth their hands to check abuses, to punish violence and crime; and the feudal system began to assume the character, not of a simple confederation, but of an organized *hierarchy*,[4] in which the whole body was the judge of each individual, and the head of that body the executor of its sentence. Louis VI., commonly called Louis the Fat,[5] was the first among the kings of France who raised the functions of royalty above those of sovereignty, and the distinction between the two states is an important one. The former monarchs of France, including Philip I., under whose reign the first crusade was preached, had each been but sovereigns, who could call upon their vassals to serve them for so many days in the field, and whose rights were either simply personal, that is to say, for their own dignity and benefit, or only general so far as the protection of the whole confederacy from foreign invasion was implied. Louis the Fat, however, saw that in the kingly office was comprised both duties and rights of a different character; the right of punishing private crime,[6] and of opposing universal wrong; the duty of maintaining public order, and of promoting by one uniform and acknowledged power the tranquillity of the whole society and the security of each individual. The efforts of that prince were confined and partial, it is true;[7] but he and his great minister, Suger, seized the just idea of the monarchical form of government, and laid the basis of a well-directed and legitimate authority.

This authority, of course, was not pleasing to the barons, whose license was thus curtailed, Their views, therefore, were turned rather to the maintenance of their own unjust privileges, than to foreign adventures. At the same time, the nobles found themselves assailed by the classes below them, as well as by the power above, and the people of the towns were seen to struggle for the rights and immunities so long denied to them. The burghers had,[8] indeed, been permitted to labour in some small degree for themselves. Though subject to terrible and grievous exactions, they had still thriven under the spirit of commerce and industry. Their lords had sometimes even recourse to them for assistance. The greater part, though of the servile race, had been either freed, or were descended from freed men; and the baron of the town in which they lived, though cruel and tyrannical, was more an exacting protector than a master. At length—the precise time is unknown—the people of the cities began to think of protecting themselves; and, by mutual co-operation, they strove at once to free themselves from the tyranny of a superior lord, and to defend themselves against the encroachments of others. The word *commune*[9] was introduced, and each town of considerable size hastened to struggle for its liberty. At first the horror and indignation of the nobles were beyond all conception; but the spirit of union among them was not sufficiently active to put down that which animated the commons.

Each lord had to oppose his revolted subjects alone; and after long and sanguinary contests,[10] sometimes the baron, the bishop, or the abbot succeeded in subjugating the people; sometimes the burghers contrived, by perseverance, to wring from the nobles themselves a charter which assured their freedom.

This struggle[11] was at its height, at the time when the fall of Edessa and the growing power of the Moslems called Europe to engage in a second crusade; but the barons at that moment found their privileges invaded both by the crown and the people; and the latter discovered that they had rights to maintain in their own land—that they were no longer the mere slaves to whom all countries were alike—that prospects were opened before them which during the first crusade they hardly dreamed of—that the swords which had before been employed in fighting the quarrels of their lords at home, or raising them to honour and fame abroad, were now required to defend their property, their happiness, and the new station they had created for themselves in society. Thus the period at which aid became imperatively necessary to the Christians at Jerusalem, was when France was least calculated to afford it. Nevertheless, the superstition of a king and the eloquence of a churchman combined to produce a second crusade; but in this instance it was but a great military expedition, and no longer the enthusiastic effort of a nation, or a great popular movement throughout the whole of the Christian world.

One of the strongest proofs of this fact[12] is the scantiness of historians on the second crusade, and the style in which those that do exist, speak of its operations. It is no longer the glory of Christendom that they mention, but the glory of the king; no more the deliverance of the Holy Land, but merely the acts of the monarch.

In pursuance of the general plan of extending the dominion of the crown, which had been conceived by Louis VI., and carried on with such infinite perseverance by his great minister Suger, Louis VII., the succeeding monarch, on hearing of the election of the Archbishop of Bourges by the chapter of that city, without his previous consent, had declared the nomination invalid, and proceeded to acts of such flagrant opposition to the papal jurisdiction, that the church used her most terrific thunders to awe the monarch to her will. Thibalt, Count of Champagne, armed in support of the pope's authority, and Louis instantly marched to chastise his rebellious vassal. Thibalt was soon reduced to obedience, but the anger of the monarch was not appeased by submission; for, even after the town of Vichy had surrendered, he set fire to the church, in which nearly thirteen hundred people had taken refuge, and disgraced his triumph by one of the direst pieces of cruelty upon record. A severe illness, however, soon followed, and reflection brought remorse. At that time the news of the fall of Edessa was fresh in Europe; and Louis, in the vain hope of expiating his crime, determined to promote a crusade, and lead his forces himself to the aid of Jerusalem.

Deputies were speedily sent to the Pope Eugenius, who willingly abetted in the king's design, and commissioned the famous St. Bernard, Abbot of Clairvaux, to preach the Cross through France and Germany. St. Bernard possessed every requisite for such a mission.[13] From his earliest years he had been filled with religious enthusiasm; he had abandoned high prospects to dedicate himself entirely to an austere and gloomy fanaticism; he had reformed many abuses in the church, reproved crime wherever he found it, and raised the clerical character in the eyes of the people, too much accustomed to behold among his order nothing but vice, ignorance, and indolence. He was one of the most powerful orators of his day, endowed with high and commanding talents of many kinds; and in his controversy with the celebrated Abelard, the severe purity of his life and manners had proved most eloquent against his rival. Thus, when after repeated entreaties[14] he went forth to preach the crusade, few that heard him were not either impressed by his sanctity, persuaded by his eloquence, or carried away by his zeal: and thus, notwithstanding the unfavourable state of France,[15] a multitude of men took the symbol of the Cross, and prepared to follow the monarch into Palestine. In Germany the effects of his overpowering oratory were the same. Those who understood not even the language that he spoke, became awed by his gestures and the dignified enthusiasm of his manner, and devoted themselves to the crusade, though the tongue in which it was preached was unknown to them. Wherever he went his presence was supposed to operate miracles, and the sick are reported to have recovered by his touch, or at his command; while all the legions of devils, with which popish superstition peopled the atmosphere, took flight at his approach. For some time Conrad, Emperor of Germany, suffered[16] St. Bernard to call the inhabitants of his dominions to the crusade without taking any active part in his proceedings, but at length the startling eloquence of the Abbot of Clairvaux reached even the bosom of the monarch, and he declared his intention of following the Cross himself. At Vezelai Louis VII. received the symbol: but the most powerful obstacle that he found to his undertaking was the just and continued opposition of his minister,[17] Suger, who endeavoured by every means to dissuade the monarch from abandoning his kingdom. All persuasions were vain; and having committed the care of his estates to that faithful servant,[18] Louis himself, accompanied by Eleonor, his queen, departed for Metz, where he was joined by an immense multitude of nobles and knights, among whom were crusaders from England[19] and the remote islands of the northern sea. Ambassadors from Roger, King of Apulia, had already warned Louis of the treachery of the Greeks, and besought him to take any other way than that through the dominions of the emperor; but the French monarch was biassed by other counsels, and determined upon following the plan before laid down.

The Emperor of Germany was the first[20] to set out, and by June reached Constantinople in safety, followed by a large body of armed men, and a number of women whose gay dress, half-military, half-feminine, gave the march the appearance of some bright fantastic cavalcade.

The King of France, having previously received[21] at St. Denis, the consecrated banner as a warrior, and the staff and scrip[22] as a pilgrim, now quitted Metz, and proceeded by Worms and Ratisbon. Here he was met by envoys from the Emperor of the East, charged with letters so filled with flattery and fair speeches, that Louis is reported to have blushed, and the Bishop of Langres to have observed—

    Timeo Danaos et dona ferentes.

Here,[23] too, the French beheld, for the first time, the custom of an inferior standing in the presence of his lord. The object of the emperor was to obtain from Louis a promise to pass through his territories without violence, and to yield to him every town from which he should expel the Turks, and which had ever belonged to the Grecian territory.

Part of this proposal was acceded to, and part refused; and the army marched on through Hungary into Greece. The progress of the second crusade was of course subject to the same difficulties that attended that of the first, through a waste and deserted land; but many other obstacles no longer existed—the people of the country were more accustomed to the appearance of strangers;[24] the army was restrained by the presence of the king; and the whole account of the march to Constantinople leaves the impression of a more civilized state of society than that which existed at the period of the first crusade. We meet with no massacres, no burning of towns, no countries laid waste: and though there are to be found petty squabbles between the soldiers and the townspeople, frays, and even bloodshed; yet these were but individual outrages, kindled by private passions, and speedily put down by the arm of authority.

The Germans[25] were less fortunate on their way than the French, and some serious causes of quarrel sprung up between them and the Greeks, in which it is difficult to discover who were the chief aggressors. The Greeks call the Germans[26] barbarians, and the Germans accuse the Greeks of every kind of treachery; but it appears evident,[27] that Conrad himself was guilty of no small violence on his approach to Constantinople. A most magnificent garden had been laid out at a little distance from that capital, filled with every vegetable luxury of the day, and containing within its walls vast herds of tame animals, for whose security woods had been planted, caverns dug, and lakes contrived; so that the beasts which were confined in this vast prison might follow their natural habits, as if still at liberty. Here also were several buildings, in which the emperors were accustomed to enjoy the summer: but Conrad, with an unceremonious freedom, partaking not a little of barbarism, broke into this retreat, and wasted and destroyed all that it had required the labour of years to accomplish. Manuel Comnenus, who now sat on the throne of Constantinople, beheld, from the windows of his palace, this strange scene of wanton aggression; and sent messengers[28] to Conrad, who was connected with him by marriage,[29] desiring an interview. But the Greek would not trust himself out of the walls of his capital, and the German would not venture within them, so that a short time was passed in negotiation; and then Conrad passed over the Hellespont with his forces, relieving the eastern sovereign from the dread and annoyance of his presence. Manuel, however, furnished the German army with guides to conduct it through Asia Minor; and almost all accounts attribute to the Greek the design of betraying his Christian brethren into the hands of the infidels. After passing the sea, the troops of Conrad proceeded in two bodies,[30] the one under the Emperor, and the other under the Bishop of Freysinghen; but the guides with which they had been provided led them into the pathless wilds of Cappadocia, where famine soon reached them. At the moment also when they expected to arrive at Iconium,[31] they found themselves attacked by the army of the infidels, swelled to an immense extent by the efforts of the sultaun of the Seljukian Turks, who, on the first approach of the Christian forces, had spared no means to ensure their destruction. The heavy-armed Germans[32] in vain endeavoured to close with the light and agile horsemen of the Turkish host. The treacherous guides had fled on the first sight of the infidels, and the enemy hovered round and round the German army, as it struggled on through the unknown deserts in which it was entangled, smiting every straggler, and hastening its annihilation by continual attacks. Favoured by the fleetness of their horses, and their knowledge of the localities, they passed and repassed the exhausted troops of the emperor,[33] who now endeavoured to retrace his steps under a continued rain of arrows. No part of the army offered security. The famous Count Bernard, with many others, was cut off fighting in the rear; the van was constantly in the presence of an active foe; and the emperor himself was twice wounded by arrows which fell in the centre of the host. Thus, day after day, thousands on thousands were added to the slain; and when at length Conrad reached the town of Nice, of seventy thousand knights, and an immense body of foot, who had followed him from Europe, scarcely a tenth part were to be found in the ranks of his shattered army.

That he was betrayed into the hands of the Turks by the guides furnished by the emperor no earthly doubt can be entertained; nor is it questionable that Manuel Comnenus was at that time secretly engaged in treaty with the infidels. It is not, indeed, absolutely proved that the monarch of Constantinople ordered or connived at the destruction of the Christian forces; but every historian[34] of the day has suspected him of the treachery, and when such is the case it is probable there was good cause for suspicion.

In the mean while, Louis the younger led the French host to Constantinople, and, unlike Conrad, instantly accepted the emperor's invitation to enter the city with a small train. Manuel received him as an equal, descending to the porch of his palace to meet his royal guest. He, of course, pretended to no homage from the King of France, but still his object was to secure to himself all the conquests which Louis might make in the ancient appendages of Greece, without acting himself against the infidels.

To force the French monarch into this concession, he pursued a plan of irritating and uncertain negotiations, not at all unlike those carried on by his predecessor Alexius,[35] towards the leaders of the former crusade. In the midst of these, however, it was discovered that Manuel had entered into a secret treaty with the Turks; and, indeed, the confidence which the deceitful Greeks placed in the promises of the crusaders forms a singular and reproachful comment on the constant and remorseless breach of their own. There were many of the leaders of the French who did not scruple to urge Louis to punish by arms the gross perfidy of the Greek emperor; and, by taking possession of Constantinople, to sweep away the continual stumbling-block by which the efforts of all the crusades had been impeded. Had Louis acceded to their wishes, great and extraordinary results would, no doubt, have been effected towards the permanent occupation of the Holy Land by the Christian powers; but that monarch was not to be seduced into violating his own good faith by the treachery of another, and after having, on the other hand, refused to aid Manuel in the war which had arisen between him and Roger, King of Apulia, he crossed the Bosphorus, and

passed into Asia Minor. Thence advancing through Nicomedia,[36] Louis proceeded to Nice, and encamped under the walls of that city. Here the first reports reached him of the fate of the German army, for hitherto the Greeks had continued to fill his ears with nothing but the successes of his fellows in arms. For a time the news was disbelieved, but very soon the arrival of Frederic, duke of Suabia, charged with messages from the German monarch, brought the melancholy certainty of his defeat.

Louis did all that he could to assuage the grief of the Emperor Conrad,[37] and uniting their forces, they now marched on by the seacoast to Ephesus. Here, however, Conrad, mortified at a companionship in which the inferiority of his own troops was painfully contrasted with the multitude and freshness of the French, separated again from Louis; and, sending back the greater part of his army by land, took ship himself and returned to Constantinople, where he was received both with more distinction and more sincerity, on account of the scantiness of his retinue, and the disasters he had suffered.

In the mean while, the French proceeded on their way, and after travelling for some days without opposition, they first encountered the Turks on the banks of the Meander.[38] Proud of their success against the Germans, the infidels determined to contest the passage of the river; but the French knights, having found a ford, traversed the stream without difficulty, and routed the enemy with great slaughter. The loss of the Christians was so small, consisting only of one knight,[39] who perished in the river, that they as usual had recourse to a miracle, to account for so cheap a victory.

Passing onward to Laodicea they found that town completely deserted, and the environs laid waste; and they here heard of the complete destruction of that part of the German army which had been commanded by the Bishop of Freysinghen.[40] In the second day's journey after quitting Laodicea, a steep mountain presented itself before the French army, which marched in two bodies, separated by a considerable distance. The commander of the first division, named Geoffroy de Rancun,[41] had received orders from the king, who remained with the rear-guard, to halt on the summit of the steep, and there pitch the tents for the night. That Baron, unencumbered by baggage, easily accomplished the ascent, and finding that the day's progress was considerably less than the usual extent of march, forgot the commands he had received, and advanced two or three miles beyond the spot specified.

The king, with the lesser body of effective troops and the baggage, followed slowly up the mountain, the precipitous acclivity of which rendered the footing of the horses dreadfully insecure, while immense masses of loose stone gave way at every step under the feet of the crusaders,[42] and hurried many down into a deep abyss, through which a roaring torrent was rushing onward towards the sea. Suddenly, as they were toiling up, the whole army of the Turks, who had remarked the separation of the division, and watched their moment too surely, appeared on the hill above. A tremendous shower of arrows instantly assailed the Christians. The confusion and dismay were beyond description: thousands fell headlong at once down the precipice, thousands were killed by the masses of rock which the hurry and agitation of those at the top hurled down upon those below; while the Turks, charging furiously all who had nearly climbed to the summit, drove them back upon the heads of such as were ascending.

Having concluded,[43] that his advance-guard had secured the ground above, Louis, with the cavalry of his division, had remained in the rear, to cover his army from any attack. The first news of the Turkish force being in presence was gathered from the complete rout of the foot-soldiers, who had been mounting the hill, and who were now flying in every direction. The king instantly sent round his chaplain, Odon de Deuil, to seek for the other body under Geoffroy de Rancun, and to call it back to his aid; while in the mean time he spurred forward with what cavalry he had, to repel the Turks and protect his infantry. Up so steep an ascent the horses could make but little progress, and the Moslems, finding that their arrows turned off from the steel coats of the knights, aimed at the chargers, which, often mortally wounded, rolled down the steep, carrying their riders along with them. Those knights who succeeded in freeing themselves from their dying steeds were instantly attacked by the Turks, who, with fearful odds on their side, left hardly a living man of all the Chivalry that fought that day. The king even, dismounted by the death of his horse, was surrounded before he could well rise; but, catching the branches of a tree, he sprang upon a high insulated rock, where, armed with his sword alone, he defended himself, till the night falling freed him from his enemies. His situation now would have been little less hazardous than it was before, had he not luckily encountered a part of the infantry who had remained with the baggage. He was thus enabled, with what troops he could rally, to make his way during the night to the advance-guard, which had, as yet, remained unattacked. Geoffroy de Rancun had nearly been sacrificed to the just resentment of the people, but the uncle of the king, having been a participator in his fault, procured him pardon; and the army, which was now reduced to a state of greater discipline than before, by the Grand Master of the Templars,[44] who had accompanied it from Constantinople arrived without much more loss at Attalia.[45] Here the Greeks proved more dangerous enemies than the Turks, and every thing was done that human baseness and cunning could suggest, to plunder and destroy the unfortunate crusaders.

Much discussion now took place concerning their further progress, and the difficulties before them rendered it necessary that a part of the host should proceed by sea to Antioch. The king at first determined that that part should be the pilgrims on foot; and that he himself with his Chivalry would follow the path by land. The winter season, however, approaching, the scanty number of vessels that could be procured, and the exorbitant price which the Greeks demanded for the passage of each man—being no

less than four marks of silver[46]—rendered the transport of the foot impossible. Louis, therefore, eager to reach Jerusalem, distributed what money he could spare among the pilgrims, engaged at an enormous price a Greek escort and guide to conduct them by land to Antioch, left the Count of Flanders to command them, and then took ship with the rest of his knights. The Count of Flanders soon found that the Greeks, having received their reward, refused to fulfil their agreement, and the impossibility of reaching Antioch without their aid being plain, he embarked and followed the king.

The unhappy pilgrims, who remained cooped up beneath the walls, which they were not permitted to enter, on the one hand, and the Turkish army that watched them with unceasing vigilance, on the other, died, and were slaughtered by thousands. Some strove to force their passage to Antioch by land, and fell beneath the Moslem scimitar. Some cast themselves upon the compassion of the treacherous Greeks, and were more brutally treated than even by their infidel enemies. So miserable at length became their condition, that the Turks themselves ceased to attack them, brought them provisions and pieces of money, and showed them that compassion which their fellow-christians refused. Thus, in the end, several hundreds attached themselves[47] to their generous enemies, and were tempted to embrace the Moslem creed. The rest either became slaves to the Greeks, or died of pestilence and famine.

In the mean while, Louis and his knights[48] arrived at Antioch, where they were received with the appearance of splendid hospitality by Raimond, the prince of that city, who was uncle of Eleonor, the wife of the French monarch. His hospitality, however, was of an interested nature: Antioch and Tripoli hung upon the skirts of the kingdom of Jerusalem as detached principalities, whose connexion with the chief country was vague and insecure. No sooner, therefore, did the news of the coming of the King of France reach the princes of those cities, than they instantly laid out a thousand plans for engaging Louis in extending the limits of their territories, before permitting him to proceed to Jerusalem. The Prince of Antioch assuredly had the greatest claim upon the king, by his relationship to the queen;[49] and he took every means of working on the husband, by ingratiating himself with the wife. Eleonor was a woman of strong and violent passions,[50] and of debauched and libertine manners, and she made no scruple of intriguing and caballing with her uncle to bend the king to his wishes. The Archbishop of Tyre, who was but little given to repeat a scandal, dwells with a tone of certainty upon the immoral life of the Queen of France, and says, she had even consented that her uncle should carry her off, after Louis had formally refused to second his efforts against Cesarea.

However that may be, her conduct was a disgrace to the crusade; and Louis, in his letters to Suger, openly complained of her infidelity.

The king resisted all entreaties and all threats, and, equally rejecting the suit of the Count of Tripoli,[51] he proceeded to

Jerusalem, where the emperor Conrad, having passed by sea from Constantinople, had arrived before him. Here the whole of the princes were called to council; and it was determined that, instead of endeavouring to retake Edessa, which had been the original object of the crusade, the troops of Jerusalem, joined to all that remained of the pilgrim armies, should attempt the siege of Damascus. The monarchs immediately took the field, supported by the knights of the Temple and St. John, who, in point of courage, equalled the Chivalry of any country, and in discipline excelled them all. Nourhaddin and Saphaddin, the two sons of the famous Zenghi, threw what men they could suddenly collect into Damascus, and hastened in person to raise as large a force as possible to attack the Christian army. The crusaders advanced to the city, drove in the Turkish outposts[52] that opposed them, and laid siege to the fortifications, which in a short time were so completely ruined, that Damascus could hold out no longer. And yet Damascus did not fall. Dissension, that destroying angel of great enterprises, was busy in the Christian camp. The possession of the still unconquered town[53] was disputed among the leaders. Days and weeks passed in contests, and at length, when it was determined that the prize should be given to the Count of Flanders, who had twice visited the Holy Land, the decision caused so much dissatisfaction, that all murmured and none acted. Each one suspected his companion; dark reports and scandalous charges were mutually spread and countenanced; the Templars were accused of having received a bribe from the infidels; the European monarchs[54] were supposed to aim at the subjugation of Jerusalem; the conquerors were conquered by their doubts of each other; and, retiring from the spot where they had all but triumphed, they attempted to storm the other side of the city, where the walls were as firm as a rock of adamant.

Repenting of their folly, they soon were willing to return to their former ground, but the fortifications had been repaired, the town had received fresh supplies, and Saphaddin, emir of Mousul, was marching to its relief. Only one plan was to be pursued. The siege was abandoned, and the leaders,[55] discontented with themselves and with each other, retreated gloomily to Jerusalem.

The Emperor of Germany set out immediately for Europe; but Louis, who still hoped to find some opportunity of redeeming his military fame, lingered for several months; while Eleonor continued to sully scenes, whose memory is composed of all that is holy, with her impure amours. At length the pressing entreaties of Suger induced the French monarch to return to his native land. There he found the authority he had confided to that great and excellent minister had been employed to the infinite benefit of his dominions—he found his finances increased and order established in every department of the state;[56]—and he found, also, that the minister was not only willing, but eager, to yield the reins of government to the hand from which he had received them.—During the absence of the king, his brother, Robert of Dreux, who returned before him, had endeavoured to thwart the noble Abbot of St. De-

nis, and even to snatch the regency from him; but Suger boldly called together a general assembly of the nobility of France, and intrusted his cause to their decision. The court met at Soissons, and unanimously supported the minister against his royal opponent; after which he ruled, indeed, in peace; but Robert strove by every means to poison the mind of the king against him; and it can be little doubted, that Louis, on his departure from Palestine, viewed the conduct of Suger with a very jealous eye.

The effects of his government, however, and the frankness with which he resigned it, at once did away all suspicions. The expedition was now over but yet one effort more was to be made, before we can consider the second crusade as absolutely terminated.

Suger had opposed the journey of the king to the Holy Land, but he was not in the least wanting in zeal or compassionate enthusiasm in favour of his brethren of the east.[57] Any thing but the absence of a monarch from his unquiet dominions he would have considered as a small sacrifice towards the support of the kingdom of Jerusalem; and now, at seventy years, he proposed to raise an army at his own expense, and to finish his days in Palestine.—His preparations were carried on with an ardour, an activity, an intelligence, which would have been wonderful even in a man at his prime; but, in the midst of his designs, he was seized with a slow fever, which soon showed him that his end was near. He saw the approach of death with firmness; and, during the four months that preceded his decease, he failed not from the bed of sickness to continue all his orders for the expedition, which could no longer bring living glory to himself. He named the chief whom he thought most worthy to lead it; he bestowed upon him all the treasures he had collected for the purpose; he gave him full instructions for his conduct, and he made him swear upon the Cross to fulfil his intentions. Having done this, the Abbot of St. Denis waited calmly the approach of that hour which was to separate him from the living; and died, leaving no one like him in Europe.

With his life appears to have ended the second crusade, which, with fewer obstacles and greater facilities than the first, produced little but disgrace and sorrow to all by whom it was accompanied.[58]

Notes

1. Mills says, "The news of the loss of the eastern frontier of the Latin kingdom reached France at a time peculiarly favourable for foreign war." It will be seen that I have taken up a position as exactly the reverse of that assumed by that excellent author as can well be conceived; but I have not done so without much investigation, and the more I consider the subject, the more I am convinced that the moment when the feudal power was checked by the king and assailed by the communes, was not the most propitious to call the nobility to foreign lands—that the moment in which the burghers were labouring up hill for independence, was not a time

for them to abandon the scene of their hopes and endeavours—and that the moment when a kingdom was torn by conflicting powers, when the royal authority was unconfirmed, and the nobility only irritated at its exertion, was not the period that a monarch should have chosen to quit his dominions.

2. A curious essay might be written on the classes or castes in Europe of that period. It is quite a mistaken notion which some persons have entertained, that the only distinctions under the monarch, were noble and serf. We find an immense class, or rather various classes, all of which consisted of freemen, interposed between the lord and his slave. Thus Galbertus Syndick, of Bruges, in recounting the death of Charles the Good, Count of Flanders, A.D. 1130, mentions not only the burghers of the town, but various other persons who were not of the noble race, but were then evidently free, as well as the Brabançois or Cotereaux, a sort of freebooting soldier of that day. Guibert of Nogent, also, in his own life, and Frodoardus, in the history of Rheims, refer to many of whose exact station it is difficult to form an idea.

3. Rouillard, Histoire de Melun: Vie de Bouchard.

4. I know that I use this word not quite correctly, but I can find none other to express more properly what I mean.

5. Suger in vit. Ludovic VI.

6. Galbert in vit. Carol.

7. Suger in vit. Ludovic VI.

8. Chron. Vezeliac.

9. Guibert Nog. in vit. s.

10. Chron. Vezeliac.

11. Gesta regis Ludovici VII.

12. The only two I know who accompanied this crusade, and wrote any detailed account of it, are Odon de Deuil, or Odo de Diagolo, and Frisingen, or Freysinghen. It is an extraordinary fact, that the Cardinal de Vitry makes no mention of the second crusade.

13. William of St. Thierry, Mabillon.

14. Geoffroi de Clairvaux; Continuation of the Life of St. Bernard.

15. Odo of Deuil.

16. Mabillon.

17. Guizot.

18. A.D. 1147.

19. Odon de Deuil.

20. William of Tyre.

21. Odon de Deuil.

22. See note X.

23. It appears from the passage of Odo of Deuil which mentions the curious servility, as he designates it, of the Greeks never sitting down in the presence of a superior till desired to do so, that the French of that day were not quite so ceremonious as in that of Louis XIV.

24. Odo of Deuil.

25. Nicetas.

26. Cinnamus, cited by Mills.

27. Odon de Deuil.

28. Ibid.

29. Manuel Commenus had married Bertha, and Conrad, Gertrude, both daughters of Berenger the elder, Count of Sultzbach.

30. Odon de Deuil.

31. William of Tyre; Odon de Deuil.

32. The Pope, in his exhortation to the second crusade, had not only regulated the general conduct of the crusaders, and formally absolved all those who should embrace the Cross, but he had given minute particulars for their dress and arms, expressly forbidding all that might encumber them in their journey, such as heavy baggage, and vain superfluities, and all that might lead them from the direct road, such as falcons and hunting-dogs. "Happy had it been for them," says Odo of Deuil, "if, instead of a scrip, he had commanded the foot pilgrims to bear a cross bow, and instead of a staff, a sword."

33. Odo of Deuil; Will. Tyr.

34. Will. Tyr: Odon de Deuil; Gest. Ludovic VII: Nicetas.

35. Odon de Deuil.

36. Will. Tyr.; Odon de Deuil.

37. Odon de Deuil; Freysinghen; William of Tyre.

38. William of Tyre.

39. Odon de Deuil.

40. Odo of Deuil always calls Otho, Bishop of Freysinghen, brother of the Emperor Conrad. He was, however, only a half-brother; his relationship being by the mother's side.

41. Will. Tyrens lib. xvi.; Odon de Deuil.

42. Odon de Deuil; Will. Tyr.

43. Odon de Deuil.

44. Odon de Deuil.

45. William of Tyre.

46. Odon de Deuil.

47. Ibid.

48. William of Tyre; Vertot.

49. Gest. Ludovic. regis; William of Tyre; Vertot.

50. Vertot, a learned man and a diligent investigator, speaks of Eleonor in the following curious terms: "On pretend que cette princesse, peu scrupuleuse sur ses devoirs, et devenue éprise d'un jeune Turc baptisé, appellé Saladin, ne pouvait se résoudre à s'en séparer, &c." These reports of course gave rise to many curious suppositions, especially when Richard Cour de Lion, Eleonor's son by her second marriage, went to war in the Holy Land. On his return to France, Louis VII. instantly sought a plausible pretext for delivering himself from his unfaithful wife without causing the scandal of a public exposure of her conduct. A pretence of consanguinity within the forbidden degrees was soon established, and the marriage was annulled. After this Eleonor, who, in addition to beauty and wit, possessed in her own right the whole of Aquitain, speedily gave her hand to Henry II. of England, and in the end figured in the tragedy of Rosamond of Woodstock.

51. William of Tyre; Vertot.

52. Gest. regis Ludov. VII.

53. Vertot.

54. William of Tyre; Col. script. Arab.; Vertot.

55. William of Tyre; Freysinghen, reb. gest. Fred.; Gest. reg. Lud. VII.

56. Guil. Monach. in vit. Suger. Ab. Sanct. Dion.; Gest. reg. Lud. VII.

57. Guil. Monach. in vit. Sug.

58. All the writers of that day attempt to excuse St. Bernard for having preached a crusade which had so unfortunate a conclusion. The principles upon which they do so are somewhat curious. The Bishop of Freysinghen declares, that it was the vice of the crusaders which called upon their heads the wrath of Heaven; and, to reconcile this fact with the spirit of prophecy which elsewhere he attributes to the Abbot of Clairvaux, declares that prophets are not always able to prophesy.—*Freysing. de rebus gestis Fred. Imperat.* Geoffroy of Clairvaux, who was a contemporary, and wrote part of the Life of St. Bernard, would fain prove that the crusade could not be called unfortunate, since, though it did not at all help the Holy Land it served to people heaven with martyrs.

Oliver J. Thatcher (essay date 1901)

SOURCE: "Critical Work on the Latin Sources of the First Crusade," in *Annual Report of the American Historical Association for the Year 1900,* Volume I, Washington Government Printing Office, 1901, pp. 499–509.

[In the following essay, Thatcher discusses and ranks the contemporary Latin sources of the First Crusade and comments on what these sources reveal about the reality of that Crusade.]

When dealing with the history of the crusades in the class room I have always met with great surprise, not to say incredulity, on the part of many students. The legends about Peter the Hermit and Godfrey of Bouillon have not only occupied a prominent place in text-books, but also have done yeoman service as homiletic material in illustrating various Christian virtues. It is no wonder, therefore, that these legends have a firm place in the minds of the youth of the land, who are surprised and shocked when told that these stories are untrue. They wish to know how it is possible for so false accounts to have got into circulation and to have found credence. And how do we now know that they are false? Such questions find their answer in a history of the History of the First Crusade. I have thought that it might not be unprofitable to repeat here, briefly and in a popular form, the substance of the answer I have given my classes. The brief time allowed by your committee makes all elaboration impossible.

There had been no critical study of the first crusade until in 1837, Leopold Ranke, in the University of Berlin, set for the members of his seminar the task of examining its sources. Their investigations, while not exhaustive, led to unexpected discoveries. It was left to one of the members of the class, Heinrich von Sybel, to continue the study, the results of which he published in 1841 in his History of the First Crusade.

Leaving aside the accounts which are to be found in Arabic, Armenian, and Greek, von Sybel limited himself to a critical study and comparison of the Latin sources. While his general conclusions were, in the main, correct, his judgments have been considerably modified by later investigators, such as Hagenmeyer, Kugler, Riant, Kuehn, Klein, and others.

I. The sources of the first rank are not numerous. Without presuming to settle pending controversies in an offhand manner, they may be said to consist, first, of the extant letters of the crusaders to their friends at home. These letters, written while on the march, have a peculiar interest and value. There is no complete critical edition of them, but Riant has given a good account of them in his Inventaire Critique des Lettres Historiques des Croisades, 1880. The text of the most important but least known letters is added.

II. In addition to these letters, the sources of the first rank consist, in the second place, of four writings by eyewitnesses, by men who themselves took part in the crusade.

1. Of these four writings, probably the most valuable is a history of the crusade by an Italian knight. Owing to the fact that his name is unknown he is always quoted as the Anonymous. Up to the end of 1098 he was in the service of Boëmund. He then attached himself to Raymond of Toulouse, with whom he made the rest of the journey to Jerusalem. His account has something of the nature of a diary, giving evidence of having been composed, not all at once, after the crusade was over, but in sections, at various times during the progress of the crusade. It faithfully

reflects the varying temper and moods of the crusaders. The author seems to have completed his work toward the end of the year 1099. His manuscript, or at least a copy of it, was left at Jerusalem, where it was afterwards often consulted and copied by pilgrims from the west. In 1889–90 Heinrich Hagenmeyer published an excellent critical edition of this work, making of it a mine of information about the first crusade.

2. Of these four writings by eyewitnesses the second in importance is a history of the crusade by a priest, named Raymond of Aguilers, who went as a chaplain of Raymond, Count of Toulouse, the leader of the troops from southern France. This account is valuable and interesting for a reason which I shall point out at the end of this paper.

3. The third eyewitness, Fulcher of Chartres, also a priest, threw in his lot with Baldwin, who left the main army before it reached Antioch to seek his fortune farther to the east. Fulcher is our principal source for the career of Baldwin in the Euphrates Valley and in Edessa. This is also in the nature of a diary and was continued by its author to the year 1125.

4. The work of the fourth eyewitness, Tudebod, also a priest, is of less value than the other three, because he was content to copy them and to add little of importance on his own authority.

III. This exhausts the sources which are strictly of the first rank, but not much inferior to them are to be reckoned two writings, not by eyewitnesses, but by men who went to the East soon after the crusade was ended. They form a class by themselves. They are, first, a brief history of the crusade by Ekkehard, known as the abbot of the little monastery of Urach on the Upper Main River. In the year 1101 Ekkehard made a pilgrimage to Jerusalem. Being of more than ordinary intelligence and judgment he made use of every opportunity while in the East to learn of eyewitnesses all he could about the crusade. On his return to his home he set down the results of his investigations in his valuable little history of the crusade. Hagenmeyer has also published an edition of this with an excellent commentary.

The other writing of this class is by a certain Radulf of Caen, who in 1107 joined Boëmund and soon afterwards went to the East and served for several years under Tancred at Antioch. He committed to writing the reminiscences, or "table talk" of Tancred, adding whatever interesting items he could obtain from other sources. As one of the leaders of the crusade Tancred was able to give Radulf much important information of an almost official character.

In the letters of the crusaders and in these six writings named we have essentially the Latin sources of the first crusade. For all the later writers (such as Baldrich of Dole, Guilbert of Nogent, Henry of Huntingdon, and many others) have in the main either copied, abridged, or fused them. The additions which such writers have made are relatively unimportant. Of the one exception, however, I shall speak later.

Now, if on the basis of these sources the history of the crusade were written, it would bear little resemblance to what for seven hundred years was believed to have been its history. In the first place, in this true history the Pope, Urban II, appears as the originator of the crusade. It was in response to his call at Clermont, in 1095, that the West took up arms and marched to the siege of Jerusalem. The stories about Peter the Hermit, his pilgrimage to Jerusalem, his visions there, his visit to the Patriarch of Jerusalem, his journey to the Pope at Rome, his successful appeals to Urban to preach a crusade, and Peter's commanding position as one of the great preachers and leaders of the crusade, all are found to be without the least foundation in fact. Not from Peter the Hermit, but from Alexius, the Emperor at Constantinople, Urban received the impulse to call the West to arm itself and march against the infidel.

2. In the second place, the rôle which Peter the Hermit actually did play is shown to have been an inglorious one. After the council of Clermont, in which the crusade had been determined on and proclaimed, along with many others, and perhaps without a direct commission from the Pope, Peter began to preach the crusade. In response to his appeal he was joined by several hundred worthless men and corrupt women, the most of them without arms. In their ignorance they believed that the miraculous power of the cross would put the Turks to flight. By being the first on the ground they would be the first to recover the holy places and would have the first chance to enrich themselves with the booty. In these vain hopes Peter and his motley band hastily set out for the East. As crusaders they felt themselves freed from all ordinary obligations and restrictions. While on the march they lived by plundering. On their arrival in Constantinople they behaved in the most shameless manner. They helped themselves to whatever they wished; they stole the lead from the roofs of the churches and sold it; they even set fire to the city. The Emperor, Alexius, was disappointed and disgusted. He had been promised reenforcements; he had hoped for an army; he had received only a band of marauders. Seeing the danger of their presence in the city, Alexius quickly set them across the Bosporus, and they began their mad march into the interior of Asia Minor. Peter soon lost all control over them and, with curses upon them, he returned to Constantinople, leaving them to their fate. They continued their journey, but were soon attacked by the Turks and destroyed. When the crusaders reached Constantinople Peter joined them. When he had first set out from Europe his name had been in the mouth of all; but now, in consequence of his failure, he became the laughingstock of the army and the butt of their jokes.

3. In the third place, the crusading army is seen to have had no unity. There was no one who was regarded as the leader of the whole movement, as the commander of all

the troops. Each of the many leaders or princes led his own men, acted for himself and largely on his own responsibility. Godfrey of Bouillon, instead of having command of the whole army, as the later legends say, really played only a secondary rôle.

4. In the fourth place, the motives of these leaders are discovered to have been of the most worldly sort. They were, almost without exception, adventurers, soldiers of fortune, seeking an opportunity to enrich themselves and to get possession of some little kingdom or principality where they might establish an independent power for themselves. And when such an opportunity presented itself they seized it with avidity and deserted the crusade. Thus Boëmund got possession of Antioch and refused to go on to Jerusalem. Baldwin left the army and went to make his fortune at Edessa. It was through no lack of effort that Tancred failed to find a suitable place to establish himself in power. And Raymond of Toulouse was so bent on settling by the way that nothing but the burning of his tents by the crusaders and the desertion of his troops could compel him to go on to Jerusalem.

5. In the fifth place, this ambition of the leaders is seen to have made them bitterly hostile to each other. The troops of Tancred engaged in a desperate battle with those of Baldwin. Boëmund and Raymond of Toulouse made war on each other, and so fierce did their hostility become that Raymond spent the rest of his life in a prolonged though unsuccessful effort to destroy Boëmund.

6. In the sixth place, the success of the crusade is found to have been, in fact, very small. The so-called Kingdom of Jerusalem was confined almost to the city walls. When the crusade was over and the city had been, in reality, thrust upon Godfrey, there remained with him probably not 2,000 fighting men. The weakness of such a principality is apparent. Nothing but the internal quarrels of the Mohammedans made it possible for Godfrey, with this mere handful of men, to maintain himself in the heart of a hostile country. As it was, he led a most precarious existence and held fast to Jerusalem more through the weakness of the enemy than by his own strength.

We are thus confronted with several questions which, of course, can be here touched on only in the briefest manner. Why was the true history of the crusade so quickly forgotten? Why did Peter the Hermit rob the Pope of the glory of having caused the crusade? What clothed the leaders with sanctity and heroism and caused their selfish careers to be forgotten? What raised Godfrey of Bouillon into the position of commander of the whole crusading army, gave him the character of a saint, and exalted his humble rule into a magnificent kingdom?

I can here only indicate in a general way where the answers to these questions are to be sought. It must be said, first of all, that the crusade made a most profound and lively impression on Europe. Being a new and unique movement, it shook Europe as she had probably never been shaken before. It took hold of what we may call the popular imagination of the time and stirred it into eager creative activity. This popular imagination, by way of naive interpretation and invention, informed the ignorance, satisfied the pride, and appeased the curiosity of the west. Within a few years it had woven about the crusade and its leaders so thick a web of story, legend, and romance that their true history was completely obscured.

The purpose of the crusade, the recovery of the holy places, lifted it into an atmosphere of sanctity and heroism in which every crusader appeared with the halo of a saint and hero combined.

From the very first, poets began to handle the history of the crusade in an imaginative way. In fact, the crusaders themselves made a beginning of this. They composed many couplets and songs to cheer themselves while on the march, and especially during the long siege of Antioch. A daring deed, an amusing mishap, a ridiculous situation—in short, a great variety of incident—would furnish some rhymester a theme on which to exercise his wit, imagination, and skill in versification. These verses naturally displayed a wide range of sentiment. Along with praise, they contained coarse wit, rough humor, and biting irony. Of the latter, Peter the Hermit came in for a large share. The camp evidently took great delight in treating him in a mock heroic way. For his brief popularity he now paid with a long period of humiliation, the object of jeers and gibes. But even these resulted eventually in his glorification. For when these songs were carried to the west their character was not perceived by those who had not been with the crusade. To the undiscerning westerners, ready to believe the wildest things, such songs appeared to be sober statements of facts. They passed for history. Western poets then began their work, and, within a few years after the end of the crusade, there were several poems in existence dealing with one or another of its phases. Early in the twelfth century a certain knight, named Gregory, wrote a history of the crusade, in verse. In Antioch there was a fugitive poem in circulation which was known as "The Song of the Poor." It dealt largely with Peter the Hermit and embodied many of the camp songs just spoken of. It would be difficult to say which prevailed in it, the heroic or the mock heroic. Raymond, then Prince of Antioch, caused it to be reduced to writing. In its original form it no longer exists, but much of it seems to have been incorporated by a certain pilgrim, named Richard, in his poem, "The Siege of Antioch." Godfrey of Bouillon and Boëmund are Richard's heroes. This poem by Richard was taken by Graindor of Douay and made the basis for his poem, "The Song of Antioch," which became so widely known. It existed in many editions, for additions were made to it wherever it circulated. It is purely a work of the imagination.

These poems were recited all over Europe and regarded as the real history of the crusade. In the presence of their wealth of imagery and detail the meager and simple accounts of eyewitnesses were forgotten.

The cause of the glorification of Godfrey of Bouillon is not far to seek. Since he was put in charge of the Holy Grave, the most sacred object in the world, it is but natural that the West should have developed the most extravagant ideas about his character, his sanctity, and his ability. They reasoned that, if he had not possessed the most transcendent qualities of heart and mind, he would not have been chosen to so honorable a position. Poets sang his praises, and, by a natural association of ideas, connected him with the story of the Holy Grail and the Knight with the Swan.

Since this popular imagination and the poetic spirit began, from the first, to enlarge on the facts and to add to them, it follows that every later work on the crusade contains more and more that is legendary. How quickly these stories and legends took the place of the truth may be seen from the work of Albertus Aquensis, written, probably, about 1125. It contains a well-developed legend about Peter the Hermit.

It remained for William, who, in 1174, was made archbishop of Tyre, to perpetuate this legendary material by incorporating it in his famous history of the crusading movement. We are interested here only in William's ability as an historian. In common with his age he believed all that was written. He was master of a fine Latin style; he could narrate with great facility. He gathered his materials from all quarters, and, instead of sifting them, he used them all. Two or three varying accounts of the same event he skillfully wove into one. His work, being an interesting, pleasing, and complete narrative of the crusade, easily displaced all other accounts, and, for six hundred years, was the source from which the world drew all its knowledge of the first crusade. It was Von Sybel who deposed him from his high position when he published his book in 1841.

Although much has been done, there is still a good deal of preparatory work to be done before a perfectly satisfactory history of the first crusade can be written. Leaving out of account the Greek and Oriental sources, I must confine my remarks to the Latin. For the letters of the crusaders the work of Riant is, perhaps, sufficient. Hagenmeyer has published an excellent commentary on the "Gesta" of the anonymous knight and on Ekkehard's work. There is need of similar commentaries on the accounts of Raymond of Aguilers, Fulcher, Tudebod, and Radulf. These would all be comparatively easy but fruitful tasks.

Of all the other sources only the work of Albert presents any great difficulties. Von Sybel thought very lightly of Albert; Kugler, in trying to rehabilitate him, has probably gone too far in the opposite direction; Kuehn has taken a middle ground. The last word on the subject has not yet been said. It is to be hoped that some one will now take his work in hand and give us a critical edition of it, paying special attention to the analysis and identification of its sources.

Closely akin to this and having some bearing on the subject, although it is, in my judgment, rather a literary topic, would be a similar study of the poems dealing with the crusade.

One of these preparatory studies would be extremely interesting and valuable on another account. The priest, Raymond of Aguilers, was at the head of a band of swindlers who made gain by playing on the credulity, superstitions, and religious simplicity of the crusaders. It was he who, with the aid of a few accomplices, planned and executed the fraud of discovering the holy lance in Antioch. Having been charged with this, he wrote his account of the crusade as his defense, but while trying to clear himself he has unwittingly betrayed his guilt. In addition to valuable information about the crusade his book would furnish the basis for an instructive chapter in the history of mediæval fraud.

George W. Cox (essay date c. 1906)

SOURCE: "Causes Leading to the Crusades," in *The Crusades,* Scribner, Armstrong and Co., 1906, pp. 1–19.

[*In the following essay, Cox reviews the events preceding Pope Urban II's call for a Holy War in 1095, focusing on the ongoing pilgrimages to Palestine and their relationship to the call-to-arms of the Crusades.*]

The Crusades were a series of wars, waged by men who wore on their garments the badge of the Cross as a pledge binding them to rescue the Holy Land and the Sepulchre of Christ from the grasp of the unbeliever. The dream of such an enterprise had long floated before the minds of keen-sighted popes and passionate enthusiasts: it was realized for the first time when, after listening to the burning eloquence of Urban II. at the council of Clermont, the assembled multitude with one voice welcomed the sacred war as the will of God. If we regard this undertaking as the simple expression of popular feeling stirred to its inmost depths, we may ascribe to the struggle to which they thus committed themselves a character wholly unlike that of any earlier wars waged in Christendom, or by the powers of Christendom against enemies who lay beyond its pale. Statesmen (whether popes, kings, or dukes) might have availed themselves eagerly of the overwhelming impulse imparted by the preaching of Peter the Hermit to passions long pent up; but no authority of pope, emperor, or king, could suffice of itself to open the floodgates for the waters which might sweep away the infidel. In this sense only were men stirred, whether at the council of Piacenza in 1094, or in that of Clermont, to a strife of a wholly new kind. If Urban II. gave his blessing to the missionaries who were to convert the Saracens at the point of the sword, the papal benediction had been given nearly thirty years before at the instigation of Hildebrand to the expedition by which the Norman William hoped to crush the free English people and usurp the throne of the king whom they had chosen.

But the movement of the Norman duke against England was merely the work of a sovereign well awake to his own interest and confident in the methods by which he chose to promote it. Under the sacred standard sent to him by Pope Alexander II. he gathered, indeed, a motley host of adventurers; but the religious enthusiasm by which these may have fancied themselves to be animated had reference chiefly to the broad acres to which they looked forward as their recompense. The great gulf which separated such an undertaking from the crusade of the hermit Peter lay in the conviction, deep even to fanaticism, that the wearers of the Cross had before them an enterprise in which failure, disaster, and death were not less blessed, not less objects of envy and longing, than the most brilliant conquests and the most splendid triumphs. They were hastening to the land where their Divine Master had descended from his throne in heaven to take on Himself the form of man—where for years the everlasting Son of the Almighty Father had patiently toiled, healing the sick, comforting the afflicted, and raising the dead, until at length He carried his own Cross up the height of Calvary, and having offered up his perfect sacrifice, put off the garments of his humiliation when the earthquake shattered the prison-house of his sepulchre. For them the whole land had been rendered holy by the tread of his sacred feet: and the pilgrim who had traced the scenes of his life from his cradle at Bethlehem to the spot of his ascent from Olivet, might sing the *Nunc dimittis*, as having with his own eyes seen the divine salvation.

Thus the crusade preached by Peter the Hermit, and solemnly sanctioned by Pope Urban, was rendered possible by the combination of papal authority with an irresistible popular conviction. That papal authority was the necessary result of the old imperial tradition of Rome; the popular conviction was the growth of a tendency which had characterized every religion professed by Aryan or Semitic nations; and both these causes were wholly unconnected with the teaching of Christ and of his disciples, as it is set before us in the New Testament. Far from ascribing special sanctity to any one spot over another, the emphatic declaration that the hour was come in which men should worship the Father not merely in Jerusalem or on the Samaritan mountain, proclaimed a gospel which taught that all men in all places are alike near to God in whom they live, move, and have their being. If we turn to the narrative which relates the Acts of the Apostles, we shall find not a sign of the feeling which regards Bethlehem, Jerusalem, or Nazareth, the Sea of Galilee, or the banks of the Jordan, as places which of themselves should awaken any enthusiastic or passionate feeling. The thoughts of the disciples, if we confine ourselves to this record, were absorbed with more immediate and momentous concerns. Before their generation should pass away, the Son of Man would return to judgment, and the dead should be summoned from their graves to his awful tribunal. Hence any vehement longing for one spot of earth over another was wretchedly out of place for those who held that the time was short, and that it behooved those who had wives to be as though they had none, those that bought as though they possessed not, and those that wept and rejoiced as though they wept and rejoiced not. Nay, more, with a feeling almost approaching to impa-

tience, the great apostle of the Gentiles could put aside the yearnings of a weaker sentiment and declare that although he had known Christ in the flesh, yet henceforth he would so know Him no more.

The image, therefore, of the great founder of Christianity was for him purely spiritual. In the letters which he wrote to the churches formed by his converts there is not a sign that the thought or the sight of Bethlehem or Nazareth would awaken in him any deeper feeling than places wholly destitute of historical associations. If he speaks of Jerusalem, he never implies that it had for him any special sanctity. His mission was to preach a faith altogether independent of time and place, and not only not needing but even rejecting the sensuous aid afforded by visible memorials of the Master whom he loved.

Such was the Christianity of St. Paul; and with such weapons it went forth to assail and throw down the strongholds of heathenism. Three centuries later we behold Christianity dominant as the religion of the Roman Empire; but in its outward aspect and in its practical working it has undergone a vast and significant change. It cannot be supposed that this change was wrought at once by the mere fact of its recognition by the temporal power. The endless debates, which fill the history of early Christianity, on the relations of the Persons of the Trinity and on the mystery of the Incarnation, may in some degree have helped to fix the minds of men on the land where the Saviour had lived, and on the several scenes of his ministry; but this alone would never have sufficed to work the revolution which Christianity has manifestly undergone, even before we reach the age of Constantine. The victory won over heathenism, if not merely nominal, was at best partial. The religion of the empire knew nothing of the One Eternal God, who demands from all men a spontaneous submission to his righteous law, and bids them find their highest good in his divine love. That religion rested on the might of the Capitoline Jupiter and the visible majesty of the Emperor; but the real influences which were at work from the first to modify the Christianity of St. Paul lay in the lower strata of society, in the modes of thought and feeling prevalent among the masses who furnished the converts of the first two or three centuries. In these converts we cannot doubt that there was wrought a real change,—a change manifest chiefly in the conviction that the divine law is binding on all, and that the state of things in the Roman world was unspeakably shameful. In the Jesus whom Paul preached they beheld the righteous teacher who condemned the iniquities of godless rulers and a corrupt people, the avenger of their unjust deeds, the loving Redeemer in whose arms the weary and heavy-laden might find rest, the awful Judge who should be seen at the end of the world on his great white throne, with all the kindreds of mankind awaiting their doom before Him. The personal human love thus kindled in them turned only into a different channel thoughts and feelings which it would need centuries to root out.

These thoughts and feelings had been fed by that tendency to localize incidents in the supposed history of gods or heroes which is the most prominent characteristic of all heathen religions; and of the vast crowd of these heathen religions or superstitions there was, if we may trust the statements of Roman writers, scarcely one which had not its adherents and votaries at Rome. Here were gathered the priests and worshippers of the Egyptian Isis, the virgin mother of Osiris, the god who rose again after his crucifixion to gladden the earth with his splendour; here might be seen the adorers of the Persian sun-god Mithras, born at the winter solstice, and growing in strength until he wins his victory over the powers of darkness after the vernal equinox. But this idea of the death and resurrection of the lord of light was no new importation brought in by the theology of Egypt or Persia. The story of the Egyptian Osiris was repeated in the Greek stories of Sarpedon and Memnon, of Tithonos and Asklepios (æsculapius), of the Teutonic Baldur and Woden (Odin). The birthplace of these deities, the scenes associated with their traditional exploits, became holy spots, each with its own consecrating legends, and not a few attracting to themselves vast gatherings of pilgrims.

It was not wonderful therefore that the worshippers of these or other like gods should, on professing the faith of Christ, carry with them all that they could retain of their old belief without utterly contradicting the new; that his nativity should be celebrated at the time when the sun begins to rise in the heavens, and his resurrection when the victory of light over darkness is achieved in the spring. The worshipper of the Egyptian Amoun, the ram, carried his old associations with him when he became a follower of the Lamb of God; and the burst of light which heralded the return of the Maiden to the Mourning Mother in the Greek mysteries of Eleusis was reproduced in the miracle still repeated year by year by the patriarch of Jerusalem when he announces the descent of the sacred fire in the sepulchre of Christ.

Thus for the Christians of the third century, if not of the second, Judæa or Palestine became a holy land; and with the growth of devotion to the human person of Christ grew the feeling of reverence for every place which He had visited and every memorial which He had left behind Him. The impulse once given soon became irresistible. Every incident of the gospel narratives was associated with some particular spot, and the certainty of the verification was never questioned by the thousands who felt that the sight of these places brought them nearer to heaven and was in itself a purification of their souls. They could follow the Redeemer from the cave in which He was born and where the Wise Men of the East laid before Him their royal offerings, to the mount from which He uttered his blessings on the pure, the merciful, and the peacemakers, and thence to the other mount on which He offered his perfect sacrifice for the sins of the whole world. The spots associated with his passion, his burial, his resurrection, called forth emotions of passionate veneration which were intensified by the alleged discovery of the cross on which He had suffered, together with the two crosses on which the thieves had been condemned to die. If the presence of

the tablet containing the title inscribed by Pontius Pilate still left it uncertain to which of the crosses that tablet belonged, and to which therefore the homage of the faithful should be paid, all doubt was removed when a woman at the point of death on whom the touch of two of these crosses had no effect was restored to strength and youth by the touch of the third.

The splendid churches raised by the devout zeal of Constantine and his mother Helena over the cave at Bethlehem and the sepulchre at Jerusalem became for the Christians that which the sacred stone at Mecca and the tomb of the prophet at Medina became afterwards for the followers of Islam; nor can we be surprised if the emperor whose previous life had been marked by special devotion to the Greek and Roman sun-god transferred the characteristics of Apollon (Apollo) to the meek and merciful Jesus whose teaching to the last he utterly misapprehended. The purpose which drew to Palestine the long lines of pilgrims, which each year increased in numbers, was not the mere aimless love of wandering which is supposed to furnish the motive for Tartar pilgrimages in our own as in former ages. The Aryan, so far as we know, was never a nomadic race; but we can understand the eagerness even of a stationary population to undertake a long and dangerous journey, if the mere making of it should insure the remission of their sins. Nothing less than this was the pilgrim led to expect, who had traversed land and sea to bathe in the Jordan and offer up his prayers at the birthplace and tomb of his Master. A few men, of keener discernment and wider culture, might see the mischiefs lurking in this belief, and protest against the superstition. Augustine, the great doctor whose 'Confessions' have made his name familiar to thousands who know nothing of his life or teaching, might bid Christians remember that righteousness was not to be sought in the East nor mercy in the West, and that voyages are useless to carry us to Him with whom a hearty faith makes us immediately present. In these protests he might be upheld by men like Gregory of Nyssa and Jerome; but Jerome, while he dwelt on the uselessness of pilgrimage and the absurdity of supposing that prayers offered in one place could be more acceptable than the same prayers offered in another, took up his abode in a cave at Bethlehem, and there discoursed to Roman ladies, who had crossed the sea to listen to his splendid eloquence. Heaven, he insisted, was as accessible from Britain as from Palestine: but his actions contradicted his words, and his example exercised a more potent influence than his precept. The purely spiritual faith on which Jerome laid stress was as much beyond the spirit of the age as the moral feelings of a later age were behind those of the woman who in the crusade of St. Louis was seen carrying in her right hand a porringer of fire, and in her left a bottle of water. With the fire she wished, as Joinville tells us, to burn paradise, with the water to drown hell, so that none might do good for the reward of the one, nor avoid evil from fear of the other, since every good ought to be done from the perfect and sincere love which man owes to his Creator, who is the supreme good. Such a tone of thought was in ludicrous discord with the temper which brought

Jerome himself to Bethlehem, and which soon began to fill the land with those who had nothing of Jerome's culture and the sobriety which in whatever degree must spring from it.

The contagion spread. From almost every country of Europe wanderers took their way to Palestine, under the conviction that the shirt which they wore when they entered the holy city would, if laid by to be used as their winding-sheet, convey them (like the carpet of Solomon in the Arabian tale) at once to heaven. An enterprise so laudable roused the sympathy and quickened the charity of the faithful. The pilgrim seldom lacked food and shelter, and houses of repose or entertainment were raised for his comfort on the stages of his journey as well as in the city which was the goal of his pilgrimage. Here he was welcomed in the costly house which had been raised for his reception by the munificence of Pope Gregory the Great. If he died during his absence, his kinsfolk envied rather than bewailed his lot: if he returned, he had their reverence as one who had washed away his sins, and still more perhaps as one who had brought away in his wallet relics of value so vast and of virtue so great that the touch of them made the journey to Palestine almost a superfluous ceremony. Wherever these pilgrims went, these fragments of the true cross might be found; and the happy faith of those who gave in exchange for them more than their weight in gold never stopped to think that the barren log which was supposed to have produced them must in truth have spread abroad its branches wider than the most magnificent cedar in Libanus. Nor probably, even in the earliest ages, was the traffic consequent on these pilgrimages confined to holy things. The East was not only the cradle of Christianity, but a land rich in spices and silks, in gold and jewels: and the keen-sighted merchant, looking to solid profits on earth, followed closely on the steps of the devotee who sought his reward in heaven.

The first interruption to the peaceful and prosperous fortunes of pilgrims and merchants was caused by one of the periodical ebbs and flows which for nearly seven hundred years had marked the struggle between the powers of Persia and of Rome. The kings of the restored Persian kingdom had striven to avenge on the West the wrongs committed by Alexander the Great, if not those even of earlier invaders; and the enterprise which Khosru Nushirvan had taken in hand was carried on forty years later by his grandson Khosru (Chosroes) II. Almost at the outset of his irresistible course Jerusalem fell, nor was it the fault of the Persians that the great churches of Helena and Constantine were not destroyed utterly by fire. Ninety thousand Christians, it is said, were put to death: but, according to the feeling of the age, a greater loss was sustained in the carrying off of the true cross into Persia. From Palestine the wave of Persian conquest spread southward into Egypt, and the greatness of Khosru seemed to be unbounded, when from an unknown citizen of Mecca he received the bidding to acknowledge the unity of the Godhead and to own Mahomed as the prophet of God. The Persian king tore the letter to pieces, and the man of

Mecca, whose successors were to carry the crescent to Jerusalem and Damascus, to the banks of the Nile and the mountains of Spain, warned him that his kingdom should be treated as he had treated his letter.

For the present the signs of this catastrophe were not to be seen. The Roman emperor was compelled to sign an ignominious peace and to pay a yearly tribute to the sovereign of Persia. But Heraclius (Herakleios) woke suddenly from the sluggishness which marked the earlier years of his reign. The Persians were defeated among the defiles of Mount Taurus, and the destruction of the birthplace of Zoroaster offered some compensation for the mischief done to the churches of Helena and Constantine. Two years later the Roman emperor carried his arms into the heart of the enemy's land; and during the battle of Nineveh, in which he won a splendid victory, he slew with his own hands the Persian general Rhazates. Khosru fled across the Tigris; but he could not escape from the plots of his son, and his death in a dungeon ended the glories of the Sassanid dynasty, under whom the Persian power had, in the third century of our era, revived from the death sleep into which it had sunk after the conquests of Alexander.

With Siroes, the son and murderer of Khosru, the Roman emperor concluded a peace which not merely delivered all his subjects from captivity, but repaired the loss which the church of the Holy Sepulchre had sustained by the theft of the true cross. The great object of pilgrimage was thus restored to Jerusalem, and thither Heraclius (Herakleios) during the following year betook himself to pay his vows of thanksgiving. With the pageant which marked this ceremony the splendour of his reign was closed. Before his death the followers of Mahomed had deprived him of the provinces which he had wrested from the Persians.

Eight years only had passed after the visit of Heraclius (Herakleios) to Jerusalem, when the armies which had already seized Damascus advanced to the siege of the Holy City. A blockade of four months convinced the patriarch Sophronios that there was no hope of withstanding the force of Islam: but he demanded the presence of the caliph himself at the ratification of the treaty which was to secure a second sacred capital to the disciples of the Prophet. After some debate his request was granted; and Omar, who on the death of Abubekr had been chosen as the vicegerent of Mahomed, set out from Medina on a camel, which carried for him his leathern water-bottle, his bags of corn and dates, and his wooden dish.

The terms imposed by the caliph sufficiently marked the subjection of the Christians, but they imposed no severe hardships and perhaps showed a large toleration. The Christians were to build no new churches, and they were to admit Mahomedans into those which they already had, whether by day or by night. The cross was no longer to be seen on the exterior of their buildings or to be paraded in the streets. The church-bells should be tolled only, not rung. The use of saddles and of weapons was altogether

us in sparse, short quotations in later writers. There are only three works of real value.

Ibn al-Qalānisī of Damascus wrote, in the years 1140-60, a history of his native city from the time of the Turkish invasions to his own day. The title of the work, the *Mudhayyal Tarikh Dimashq* (the 'Continuation of the Chronicle of Damascus') shows that it was intended as a sequel to the chronicle of the historian Hilal. But whereas Hilal aimed at giving the history of the world, Ibn al-Qalānisī was only interested in Damascus and its rulers. He spent his life in the chancery of the Damascene court, rising to be its chief official. He was therefore well-informed; and except when the reputations of his masters were at stake he seems to have been accurate and objective.[25]

Ibn al-Athir of Mosul wrote his *Kamil at-Tawarikh* ('Sum of World History') at the beginning of the thirteenth century. But his careful and critical use of earlier sources makes him an authority of primary importance, though his entries are usually very brief.[26]

Kemal ad-Din of Aleppo wrote his unfinished chronicle of Aleppo and his Encyclopaedia half a century later still. But he too made full use of earlier sources, and in his Encyclopaedia he cites them by name. Of these lost sources the most to be regretted is the history of the Frankish invasion by Hamdān ibn Abd ar-Rahīm of Maaratha, of which even in Kemal ad-Din's time only a few pages survived. Ibn Zuraiq of Maarat al-Numan, who was born in 1051 and played a part in the events of the Crusade, left a history of his times also only known from a few extracts; and al-Azimi of Aleppo, born in 1090, left an account of northern Syrian history at the time of the Crusade, of which a slightly larger number of extracts still exist.[27]

4. ARMENIAN

There is one invaluable Armenian source covering the period of the First Crusade, the *Chronicle* of Matthew of Edessa. The work deals with the history of Syria from 952 to 1136 and must have been written before 1140. Matthew was a naïve man with a hatred for the Greeks and no great love for those of his compatriots who were Orthodox in religion. Much of his information about the Crusade must have been derived from some ignorant Frankish soldier; but about events in his native city and its neighbourhood he was very fully informed.[28]

Later Armenian chroniclers, such as Samuel of Ani and Mekhitar of Airavanq, writing at the end of the twelfth century, and Kirakos of Gantzag and Vartan the Great, in the thirteenth century, treat only briefly of the First Crusade. They seem to have made use of Matthew and of a lost history written by a certain John the Deacon, whom Samuel praises highly and who showed special animosity not only against the Emperor Alexius but also against his mother, Anna Dalassena.[29]

5. SYRIAC

The only surviving Syriac work to treat of the First Crusade is the chronicle of Michael the Syrian, Jacobite Patriarch of Antioch from 1166 to 1199, who passes very briefly over the period before 1107. He made use of earlier Syriac chronicles that are now lost as well as of Arabic sources. His information is of little value till he reaches his own lifetime.[30]

Though some of the primary histories of the Crusade have been individually edited, the only collection of sources is the great *Recueil des Historiens des Croisades,* published in Paris from 1844 onwards. This includes Latin and Old French, Arabic, Greek and Armenian texts, with translations into French of the Greek and eastern writers. Unfortunately except for the last (fifth) volume of the Latin texts, published some years after the rest of the *Recueil,* the editing of the manuscripts has been careless. There are also many arbitrary lacunae; and the translations are not always accurate. Nevertheless the collection remains indispensable for the student of the Crusades.

Notes

1. The latest edition of Anna Comnena is published in the *Collection Budé* and edited by Leib, with a full introduction and notes. *Anna Comnena,* by Mrs Buckler, gives a detailed critical study of the *Alexiad.* There is an English translation of the *Alexiad,* by E. A. S. Dawes (London, 1928).

2. Both edited in the Bonn *Corpus Scriptorum Historiae Byzantinae.*

3. Ed. in Sathas, *Bibliotheca Graeca Medii Aevi,* vol. VII.

4. Theophylact's letters are given in *M.P.G.* vol. CXXVI.

5. Ed. in the *Recueil des Historiens des Croisades.* There is room for a good critical edition.

6. The edition by Hagenmeyer, which is fully annotated, has superseded that in the *Recueil.*

7. Ed. in the *Recueil.* See Cahen, *La Syrie du Nord,* p. 11 n. 1.

8. Ed. in the *Recueil.*

9. See Cahen, *loc. cit.* Sicard's chronicle no longer exists.

10. The latest edition is Bréhier's, under the title of *Histoire Anonyme de la Première Croisade.* The notes in Hagenmeyer's edition, *Anonymi Gesta Francorum* (Heidelberg, 1890) are still useful.

11. Ed. in the *Recueil.* See Cahen, *op. cit.* pp. 8-9.

12. Ed. in the *Recueil.* See Cahen, *loc. cit.*

13. Ed. in the *Recueil.* See Cahen, *loc. cit.*

14. Ed. in the *Recueil.* See Cahen, *loc. cit.*

15. Ed. in the *Recueil.* See Cahen, *loc. cit.*

16. Extracts of Hugh and Henry are published in the fifth volume of the *Recueil.* The *Expeditio Contra Turcos* is published with Tudebod in the third volume.

17. The edition in the fifth volume of the *Recueil* is far better than that of Hagenmeyer (*Fkkehard von Aura*, Leipzig, 1888).

18. Ed. in the *Recueil*.

19. Ed. in the *Recueil*. There is a large literature about Albert, of which the most important works are those of Krebs, Kügler, Kuhne and Beaumont (see Bibliography). See also von Sybel, *Geschichte des ersten Kreuzzuges*, 2nd ed. (preface), and Hagenmeyer, *Le Vrai et le Faux sur Pierre l'Hermite*, especially pp. 9 ff.

20. Ed. in the *Recueil*. See Prutz, *Wilhelm von Tyrus*, and Cahen, *op. cit.* pp. 17-18.

21. Ed. in the fifth volume of the *Recueil*.

22. Extracts are published by Hagenmayer in vol. II of the *Archives de l'Orient Latin*.

23. For the epics, see Hatem, *Les Poèmes Epiques des Croisades*, defending a Syrian origin for the poems, and the summary in Cahen, *op. cit.* pp. 12-16.

24. The best edition of these letters is in Hagenmeyer, *Die Kreuzzugsbriefe*. A fuller collection is to be found in Riant, *Inventaire des Lettres historiques*.

25. For Ibn al-Qalānisī, see the preface to Gibb's translation of the passages of the *Damascus Chronicle* that refer to the Crusades (see Bibliography). The full text in Arabic is published by Amedroz (Leyden, 1908).

26. The full text of Ibn al-Athir's works is published in Arabic in 14 volumes by Tornberg (Leyden, 1851-76). Relevant passages are published in *R.H.C. Occ.*

27. There is no good edition of Kemal ad-Din. Passages relative to the Crusades, from 1097 to 1146, are fully given in the *Recueil*.

28. A French translation was published from the MSS. by Dulaurier in 1858 and extracts of the Armenian text with French translation in *R.H.C.Arm.* The full Armenian text was published in Jerusalem in 1868. I have not been able to obtain it, and have therefore used the translation by Dulaurier, checking it where possible with the extracts in Armenian in the *Recueil*.

29. Extracts of these historians are published in the *Recueil*.

30. Trans. and publ. by Chabot.

Aziz S. Atiya (essay date 1962)

SOURCE: "The Crusade in the Later Middle Ages" in *Crusade, Commerce and Culture,* Indiana University Press, 1962, pp. 92–119.

[In the following essay, Atiya argues that while many critics cite the late thirteenth century as the end of the Crusades, following the "tragic exit of the Franks from Palestine," the crusading movement in fact continued into the fourteenth and fifteenth centuries.]

INTRODUCTION

Crusading historiography, as already stated, has recently been subject to considerable revision and emendation, and older concepts have given way to new schools of thought. Until the last few decades, historians identified the span of the Crusade movement with the duration of the Latin kingdom of Jerusalem on the Asiatic mainland. Inaugurated by Urban II's memorable speech at Clermont-Ferrand in 1095, the holy war presumably ended with the tragic exit of the Franks from Palestine in 1291–92. This cataclysmic view of the Crusade has been repudiated in the light of cumulative research in the field; and in the present chapter an attempt will be made to outline the fate of the movement after the fall of Acre on the Syrian coast to the Egyptians toward the close of the thirteenth century. Notwithstanding ostensible changes in its basic motives, the continuance of the Crusading movement in the later Middle Ages will be proved beyond any shadow of doubt from a quick survey of the events. Strictly speaking, the fourteenth century was the age of the later Crusade in its fuller sense. Afterward in the course of the fifteenth century, the Crusade began to lose its real significance and ended in becoming a forlorn cause without hope of resuscitation.

The first half of the fourteenth century, extending roughly from 1292 to 1344, abounds in propagandist literature for the resumption of the Crusade. The second half of the century, lasting from 1344 to 1396, is a period of successive Crusading campaigns in the East. That century witnessed a number of monumental changes in the delineation of the traditional frontiers of Crusading terrain. Hitherto, holy war had been confined to the area of the Near East. In the later Middle Ages it reached distant horizons beyond the Holy Land in almost every direction. Though lacking in the qualities of vigor and valor, and in the sensational achievements of the early Crusaders, the fourteenth-century movement left its impression on the annals of mankind by the spectacular opening of the way to Cathay. The exploratory adventures of the Latin missionary at the court of the Mongol kingdom of Khān Bāliq [Khanbalik or Cambaliech, otherwise Peking in subsequent history.] signalled a revolution in the geographical lore of the Middle Ages. The idea of collaboration with the Mongols, after their conversion to Christinaity, in the struggle against the Mamluk sultans of Egypt and Syria has sometimes been described as the "Mongol" or "Tartar Crusade." This became a major feature in the propagandist literature of the time, and the idea was espoused by Popes and kings. The enlargement of the map of the Old World was, in a sense, a byproduct of the Later Crusade.

Though the final goal of the whole movement remained the acquisition of the Holy Land, the fourteenth-century Crusaders appear to have pursued their quests by devious ways, through attacking or sacking other ostensibly more important centers in the Muslim Empire, which, it was thought, should first be enfeebled and impoverished before making any serious landing on the shores of Palestine. As will be seen, the new Crusades were conducted against Anatolia, Egypt, North Africa, and the Balkans rather than the Holy Places.

The seizure of Acre in 1291 by the Muslims, like the fall of Jerusalem earlier in 1187, and the collapse of Constantinople later in 1453, provided Europeans with a rude reminder of the sad state of the East. Other reminders were the wandering or "mendicant" kings from countries of the Near East. Peter I de Lusignan, called "athleta christi" by his chancellor, Philippe de Mézières, spent almost three years (1362–65) roaming from court to court throughout the continent of Europe soliciting aid for his bellicose projects. King Leo VI of Armenia, a disconsolate refugee without a crown, died childless in 1393 in Paris. Between 1399 and 1401 Manuel II Palaeologus left Byzantium on a tour of Western Europe to implore the Holy Pontiff and the strong monarchs of France and England for effective relief for his imperial city, long battered by a succession of Ottoman sieges and assaults. Even after the extinction of the Eastern Empire and the downfall of that great city, an imperial pretender by the name of Thomas Palaeologus took refuge at Rome in 1461. The Crusade, however, had become a defensive rather than offensive movement in the course of the fifteenth century.

FOURTEENTH-CENTURY PROPAGANDISTS AND MISSIONARIES

The fourteenth century was the real age of propaganda for the Crusade, notably in its early decades. This was the natural reaction of the European conscience to a situation which was steadily becoming desperate in the Levant. The failure of the Crusaders to save the Latin kingdom of Jerusalem and defend the city of Acre was one of the most poignant features of the time, and Europe had to search for the reasons of its discomfiture in the face of Islam. This accounts for the avalanche of propagandist literature which marked that era. In reality, the promoters of the idea of the Crusade seem to have come from all classes of medieval society and included Popes, kings, men of the sword and of the pen, ministers of state and of religion, and an endless stream of pilgrims returning from the holy city with fervent tales to tell about the East. Theorists pondered, not only over the reconquest of the birthplace of Christ, but also over the most effective manner whereby it could be retained in the hands of Christians after the reinstatement of the lost kingdom of Jerusalem.

A certain Thaddeo of Naples, an eyewitness of the Acre catastrophe in 1291, inaugurated the movement with a tract called "Hystoria," in which he described the fate of this last bastion of Latin Christianity on the shores of Palestine. His exhortations for union among all the princes of Catholic Christendom under the leadership of the Church Militant to save "our heritage" were in full conformity with the official policy of the Papacy. Nicholas IV (1288–92), his contemporary, actually planned a "passagium generale" in collaboration with Charles II of Anjou (d. 1309), whose interest in the project was enhanced by his claim to the crown of the Latin kingdom of Jerusalem. Even before the fall of Acre, a Franciscan by the name of Fidenzio of Padua advised Pope Nicholas on the details and plan of the projected campaign in a work entitled "Liber Recuperationis Terre Sancte." The maritime blockade of the Muslim Empire, the problem of military bases in Armenia and Syria, naval and land forces, routes to the East, and other important subjects were discussed by the author on the assumption that Acre was still in Christian hands, a fact which minimized the value of some aspects of his counsel. Nevertheless, the pontificate of Nicholas IV did witness the birth of a new phase in the literary and diplomatic propaganda for the Crusade.

The propagandist output of the time is bewildering in its dimensions, and a severe measure of selectivity must necessarily be observed in the treatment of some of its representative or outstanding landmarks. Perhaps the most novel approach to the subject was that ascribed to a Catalan by the name of Raymond Lull, born in 1232 and stoned to death by infuriated Muslims on the shores of North Africa in 1315 or 1316. Lull was one of the most extraordinary personalities of his age or any age. A poet, a philosopher, a writer of at least several hundred books, and the author of a new system of philosophy based on the unity of knowledge as demonstrated in his work entitled "Arbor Scientiae," he was also one of the earliest Orientalists, who mastered the Arabic tongue and even composed Arabic poetry. Though he began his life by promoting a new plan of Crusade in his "Liber de Fine," it soon dawned upon him that it might be more appropriate if he tried to win the Muslims over to Christ, and that by thus saving their souls from perdition, he would eventually bring the Holy Land and the whole world of Islam into the fold of the faithful without violence or the spilling of blood. To him, therefore, the study of Arabic and Islamic theology was a vehicle for the preaching of Christianity, and he became the apostle of missionary work among Muslims. Thrice he crossed over to North Africa with this perilous quest in view. In the first voyage he formulated his debates with a certain ibn 'Ammār, the grand mufti of Tunis, in a treatise called "Disputatio Raymundi Christini et Hamar Sarraceni." In the second, he was immediately seized by the Tunisian authorities and kept behind bars until his deportation by the lenient Muslim governor. In the third, he earned his much-desired crown of martyrdom when he was stoned by an intolerant mob outside the Algerian seaport of Bugia (the Arabic Bijayah), when he had reached the advanced age of eighty-two; his body was recovered by Genoese mariners and deposited in the cathedral of his native town of Las Palmas on the island of Majorca.

At the same time the traditional Crusading spirit was being nurtured at the court of France, where Philip IV (1285–1314), after humiliating Pope Boniface VIII (1294–1303) in Rome and establishing the Papacy within his realm at Avignon, envisioned the extension of French hegemony over most of the world. Among other things, he wished to install one of his sons at the head of a new Eastern Empire incorporating Byzantium, the Holy Land, and the Mamluk sultanate of Egypt. Apparently he regarded himself as the rightful heir to the universal leadership of the Holy Pontiffs, with the Crusade as the basic element of his foreign policy. Consequently his court harbored men who flourished on feeding royal aspirations with propagandist documents of the highest interest. Notable among them were two famous French jurisconsults, namely, Pierre Dubois and William of Nogaret. Eminent men of action, too, such as James de Molay, grand master of the Templars, Fulk de Villaret, grand master of the Hospitallers of St. John of Jerusalem, Henry II de Lusignan, Latin king of Cyprus, and Benito Zaccharia, the Genoese admiral of the French navy, came to solicit cooperation in executing the French monarch's plans.

The prevailing ideas at his court are best represented in Dubois's remarkable treatise "De Recuperatione Terre Sancte." A medieval publicist of the highest order, Dubois worked out a set of rules for universal governance with his imperious master as the central figure in authority. Political discord among the princes of the West must be eradicated, preferably by persuasion, but if necessary by force. A European tribunal consisting of three high clerics and three laymen should be set up for international arbitration, and economic sanctions could be imposed on recalcitrant states. The right of appeal to the Papacy was maintained; but the Popes must continue to live in France within the French monarch's sphere of influence, as they had done since the beginning of the Babylonian Captivity at Avignon. Church fiefs should be administered by the king, and the ecclesiastical hierarchy must return to the original rule of poverty. The Orders of the Templars and Hospitallers were to be merged into one organization, and their vast revenues confiscated for use in financing Eastern campaigns. The constitution of the Holy Roman Empire was to be transformed into an hereditary regime with a French prince at its head. The crown of Egypt and the Holy Land after the reconquest would be conferred upon Philip's second son. Details of the new reformed military government of the East were provided, and missionary work among the so-called dissident Eastern Christians, as well as the Muslims, was to be undertaken by scholars conversant with Oriental languages. The keynote to this incongruous patchwork of ideas was evidently the implementation of the Crusade to confirm French supremacy over the rest of the world.

Dubois was a propagandist with preconceived ideas and no personal experience in the field. Of a totally different character was another propagandist, Marino Sanudo the Elder (Il Vecchio) (1274–c. 1343). A rational thinker, Sanudo spent a lifetime in the Levant and was a descendant of the Venetian ducal dynasty of Naxos in the Archipelago. He was a man of great acumen and immense knowledge of an area in which he had travelled far and wide. During his comprehensive peregrinations he managed to collect a tremendous mass of concrete data about the countries of the Near East in the form of accurate descriptions, figures, and statistics. In fact, Sanudo could claim the title of the first statistician in European history.

His argument was preeminently based on economic considerations. If the sultan of Egypt were to be deprived of his chief source of revenue, which was trade, he would ultimately fall into a state of material and military bankruptcy. Consequently the Crusaders could defeat his armies and reconquer and retain the Holy Land without much difficulty. The trade emporia of the Mamluk Empire were the terminal points of the Eastern spice and pepper trade, ardently sought by the maritime powers of southern Europe. They paid a heavy toll to the enemy of the Cross for the acquisition of these articles. In addition to the enrichment of the sultan's coffers from these dues, Genoa and other Italian communes supplied him, in partial exchange, with war material and slaves from the markets of Caffa and elsewhere destined to swell the Mamluk battalions. Marino Sanudo recorded his reactions to this paradoxical position and his thoughts on the solution of the Western predicament in a monumental work entitled "Secreta Fidelium Crucis," of which the first edition was dedicated to Pope Clement V in 1309 and the second to King Charles IV of France.

After a detailed inquiry, he prescribed a ban on trade with Muslim territories on pain of excommunication and even of interdict. Further, a strict maritime blockade should be organized under papal leadership to watch over the execution of that ban until the resources of Egypt were completely drained and its army starved of men and war material. He estimated that three years would bring about the desired results. Though the plan received the Holy Pontiff's immediate support, it was ultimately defeated by two main circumstances: first the issue of papal dispensations to some Venetian ships to resume trade with the enemy; and second, perfidious Genoese smuggling of war material and slaves to the Egyptian markets in exchange for valuable staples and special trade privileges.

It would be futile to attempt a full parade of the fourteenth-century propagandists. Nevertheless, we should not overlook one principal idea, that of alliance with the Tartars for more effective Crusading against Islam. This new feature captivated the Western imagination and gave rise to the Latin mission to Tartary, with immense consequences for Crusading. Started during the pontificate of Innocent IV (1243–54) and the reign of St. Louis (1226–70), king of France, the most spectacular phase in the Catholic mission to Cathay may well be associated with the names of John of Monte Corvino and Oderic of Pordenone. John had, of his own volition and without any noise, made his way to the kingdom of Khān Bāliq and is said to have baptized 5,000 souls at Peking in 1304, built two churches and even translated the Psalms and the New Testament into the language of his congregation. A decade later he was joined by Oderic, who had rounded the continent of Asia by way of Iran, India, and the islands of Indonesia; Oderic returned to Avignon in 1330, completely exhausted, to die at Udine in the following year. Meanwhile, in recognition of his triumph, John was appointed archbishop of Sultaniya and the Far East by the Pope, who also despatched seven bishops suffragan to assist him in that vast new diocese. He died in 1328, and his last successor, John of Florence, was murdered at an unknown place in the heart of China during 1362. The knell of Roman Catholicism was tolled in medieval China; but the idea of joint action with the Mongols was later revived by Christopher Columbus, who wanted to reach India by the western route. The New World barred his way, and the discovery of America changed the whole face of history and of the Crusade.

AGE OF THE LATER CRUSADE

The outcome of sustained propaganda over a number of decades was the resumption of holy warfare in a series of campaigns of varying intensity during the latter half of the fourteenth century. The first chapter in these wars was the Aegean Crusade, in which the Holy League composed of Venice, Cyprus, and the Hospitallers, under the leadership of Pope Clement VI, succeeded in wresting Smyrna from Turkish hands in 1344. It remained in the Hospitallers' custody until Timur overthrew its Christian garrison in 1402, and the Turks ultimately took over the reigns of government in the whole of Anatolia, after the withdrawal of the Mongols from the Peninsula.

The new Latin foothold on the Asiatic mainland, though insignificant, was hailed in Europe as the beginning of the end of the Islamic Empire. Thanksgiving processions and popular celebrations were held in numerous cities of the West, and the Avignonese Pope Clement VI invited Edward III of England and Philip VI of France to reap the benefit of this auspicious Christian victory in the East by joining arms for decisive action against their common enemy, instead of continuing their internecine strife in the Hundred Years' War. The position appeared to be pregnant with magnificent possibilities for a definitive Crusade, and Christendom lived in the expectation of a second Godfrey of Bouillon to lead its forces into the field.

At that time, an unknown and unhappy feudatory from the southeast of France by the name of Humbert II, dauphin de Viennois, espoused the cause of the Crusade and persuaded the Pope to grant him the title of "Captain-General of the Crusade against the Turks and the Unfaithful to the Holy Church of Rome" on condition that he should equip five galleys with twelve bannerets, 300 knights, and 1,000 arbalesters for fighting in the East, where he was to remain for at least three years. Humbert had lost his only son and heir and had become inconsolable. He had formerly quarrelled with the Church, and only the Pope's personal clemency had rescued him from the sentence of excommunication. The Crusade offered him opportunities for drowning his sorrow over the loss of his son and atoning for his past sins against Holy Church.

So he renounced his hereditary rights over the Dauphiné, which consequently devolved on the French Crown, [The Dauphiné was given by the French king to his heir, who became identified with the title of dauphin after that time.] and devoted himself to the service of the Holy Pontiff in the new cause.

Humbert's Crusade, a continuation of the Aegean campaign, was planned by the Pope first to relieve the Genoese at their mercantile colony of Caffa in the Crimea, which was beleaguered by the Tartars, and then to attack the Turks in Anatolia. The former dauphin, sailing from Marseilles in August 1345, crossed Lombardy after disembarking at Genoa to resume the voyage with his troops from Venice to Negropontis. Unable to risk the hazardous passage through the Marmora, he became involved in the petty squabbles and local differences of the Latin principalities of the Archipelago and only engaged in minor skirmishes with Turkish mariners in the Aegean and later at Smyrna. His subservience to papal command in practically all details enhanced his indecision, and the news of his wife's decease cast new shadows of hopelessness on his life. In the summer of 1347 he decided to become a Dominican friar and was absolved from his military obligations by the Pope, who bestowed upon him the honorific title of Latin patriarch of Alexandria and nominated him archbishop of Paris later in 1354. He died at the relatively early age of forty-three, while proceeding through southern France toward his new archdiocese after an unsuccessful career.

The first real "passagium generale" was reserved for the Lusignan kings of Cyprus, whose island was destined by its geographical and political position to become the meeting place of all Crusaders and of most Latin merchants. In this they were encouraged by the seizure of some outposts on the southern Anatolian coast, including Gorigos and Adalia in 1361. It was then that three champions of the idea of the Crusade were assembled on Cyprus: King Peter I de Lusignan (1359–69); Peter de Thomas (d. 1366), the Latin patriarch of Constantinople and apostolic legate for the East since 1362; and Philippe de Mézières (d. 1405), who became chancellor of the Cypriot kingdom and was one of the most celebrated propagandists of the age. Philippe spent his latter years writing extensively to promote his newly established military order of religion, which he called the "Militia Passionis Jhesu Christi." He dreamed of the creation of a unified military brotherhood throughout Europe under the banner of his novel Militia, which should incorporate all other military orders together with the feudal contingents of Europe as the only remaining hope for the reconquest of the Holy Land.

For the present, he accompanied the king of Cyprus during part of his European peregrinations lasting from 1362 to 1365 and extending from Poland to France and from England to Venice, in order to raise funds and recruits for his forthcoming project of Crusade. The various European detachments thus assembled were enjoined to converge in the waters of Rhodes, and Peter I sailed from Venice in

June 1365 to lead a fleet totalling 165 vessels against an unknown target beyond the sea. The secret of his objective was closely kept by the king and his chief consultants— Peter de Thomas and Philippe de Mézières—for fear of Venetian or Genoese treachery in alerting the enemy. Their direction toward Alexandria was divulged only as the naval squadrons attained the high seas. They came within sight of the city on Thursday, October 9, 1365, and they landed on the shore of its western harbor on the following day. The storming and the sack of the city lasted seven fateful days with immeasurable consequences.

This occurred in the reign of Sultan Sha'bān (1363–76), who was only a boy of eleven, while the city governor, ibn 'Arrām, was in the Hijaz performing pilgrimage. The Mamluk court was torn asunder by disaffection, and the atabek Yalbogha, who acted as guardian of the sultanate, could with difficulty marshal enough manpower to press onward to Alexandria. Even then, he had to circle his way around the edge of the western desert, owing to the Nile flood in the Delta. As soon as the Egyptian army came within sight in the Mareotis area, the bulk of the Christian occupation forces evacuated the city on October 16, without making any earnest attempt at the defense of their conquest, contrary to the command of the king and against the advice of Peter de Thomas and Philippe de Mézières. Once they had completed the pillage of the city's treasures and set on fire its public buildings and principal warehouses, their only concern was to sail back to Cyprus in safety with their rich booty. Thus ended the tragedy of the most successful of all fourteenth-century Crusading adventures; the Egyptians could never forget its vandalism, for which the Cypriots had to pay a heavy price in the following century.

However, the immediate result of that untoward event was the promotion of another Crusade. News of the ephemeral triumph at Alexandria, as in the case of preceding campaigns in the Levant, soon circulated in the West, and Pope Urban V urged the faithful to pursue these occurrences to a successful conclusion. The most serious response to his call came from Amedeo VI, count of Savoy, who had previously taken the Cross with King Peter de Lusignan at Avignon from the Pope's own hand. His preconceived plan to go to Cyprus was changed by marriage between members of his dynasty and the Palaeologi. The course of his expedition was deflected to fighting for Byzantium against the Turkish invaders and some of their Balkan Christian allies and vassals. Sailing from Venice in June 1366 at the head of his own feudal militia, Amedeo VI was joined by an army of mercenaries from Italy, Germany, France, and England, meeting him at Coron in the Morea, whence a total of fifteen galleys advanced on Gallipoli, their first objective. That little peninsula, in Ottoman possession since the reign of Sultan OrKhān (1326–60), proved to be invaluable to the Turks both as a landing-place and as a base for expansionist operations in the Balkan Peninsula. Its garrison was surprised by the Crusaders, and its recapture in August was a serious blow to the Turks. Afterward the count went to Constantinople, where

he discovered that his cousin, Emperor John V Palaeologus, had been taken prisoner by King Shishman of Bulgaria. So he was constrained to campaign for the deliverance of the Emperor, rather than reap the fruit of his recent brilliant acquisition from the Turks. After penetrating Bulgaria from the Black Sea as far as Varna, he successfully negotiated the liberation of the captive Emperor. By the end of 1366 his material resources were running out, and he was forced to retire to Constantinople, where John reimbursed him with 15,000 florins in exchange for ceding the conquered territory; this sum helped the count to pay off his mercenaries and ultimately dismiss them before the middle of 1367.

The next Crusade took place in 1390 against the kingdom of Tunis. A joint expedition was organized by the Genoese commune and the kingdom of France for different motives. Whereas the Genoese aimed to chastize the Barbary corsairs who had been harassing their merchant ships in the waters of the western Mediterranean, the French nobility, under the leadership of Duke Louis II of the house of Bourbon, cherished the idea of walking in the footsteps of St. Louis against the Muslims in Tunisia. Under the auspices of the Hafsid kings of Tunis, Muslim Moorish pirates had nestled in the strong town of al-Mahdiya, known in the French sources as the Cité d'Auffrique. It was agreed between the allied Crusading parties that Genoa should provide the expedition with a whole fleet fully equipped with an army of seamen, while the duke furnished the land forces consisting of feudal nobility, knights, men-at-arms, and squires. Pope Clement VII blessed the project and officially declared the Crusade, while gentlemen from France, England, Hainault, and Flanders swelled the ducal numbers to 15,000 strong. The Genoese totaled 6,000 of whom 2,000 were redoubtable arbalesters and men-at-arms, the rest being proved mariners, under Admiral Giovanni Centurione d'Oltramarino, whose first target was the island of Conigliera sixteen leagues off the African coast, within easy reach of the sea town of al-Mahdiya.

There the Christian ships reassembled after a rough passage, and the council of war decided the tactical procedure before setting siege to the city. Once on African soil, they became exposed to guerilla attacks from the joint armies of the kingdoms of Tunis, Bugia, and Tlemsen; the latter systematically avoided a pitched battle with superior contingents. The Europeans, on the other hand, used all manner of modern devices of warfare in their attempt to storm the city walls and gates, including one of the earliest examples of the use of gunpowder. Nevertheless, they remained unable to achieve their final goal; and the practical Genoese, seeing the difficulties with which they were beset, began secretly to negotiate a unilateral settlement with the enemy, who was approaching the point of exhaustion. A ten-year truce was approved together with a cessation of piratical practices, and the king of Tunis agreed to pay an annual tribute over fifteen years for peacefully retaining al-Mahdiya, as well as an immediate indemnity of 25,000 ducats to be divided between the commune and the duke. In the end, the council of war was summoned to ratify the proffered treaty, even against the will of the duke, who declared that he would be the last Crusader to board a galley. They finally returned home in October 1390, after the astute Genoese merchants had used the French as their cat's-paw for the solution of one of their major problems.

The greatest and indubitably the most disastrous of all fourteenth-century Crusading campaigns was still to come in 1396 in the face of the rising tide of Ottoman expansion in Eastern Europe. The new menace was sighted within the confines of Hungary, and was reported in 1395 at the French court by Nicholas of Kanizsay, archbishop of Gran and treasurer of Hungary, on behalf of King Sigismund, who solicited help from the West. It was around that date that Philippe de Mézières wrote his hitherto unpublished Epistle to Richard II (1377–1399) of England by order of Charles VI (1380–1422) of France, promoting peace between their two countries and urging unity of action in the East.

But eyes were fixed on the richest man in Europe, Philip the Bold, duke of Burgundy (1363–1404), for an effective initiation of the movement. Philip, who was eager to have his son and heir, John de Nevers, the future John the Fearless, knighted in the field of battle while fighting the infidels, readily espoused the new cause and appointed John to command of the Franco-Burgundian contingents. Both the Avignonese Pope, Benedict XIII (1394–1415), and the Roman Pope, Boniface IX (1389–1404), issued bulls endorsing the Crusade, each within his own jurisdiction; and the most elaborate and lavish preparations were undertaken for a universal "passagium." Men of the highest distinction from France, such as John le Meingre, dit Boucicaut, marshal of the realm, Admiral John de Vienne, Enguerrand de Coucy, Philip and Henry de Bar, Guy and Guillaume de la Trémouille, and many others hastened to enroll under Nevers's banner, together with their feudal retainers and mercenary troops.

The response was even more general. German auxiliaries came under the Count Palatine, Ruprecht Pipan, count of Katznellenbogen, Count Hermann II of Cilly, and Burgrave John III of Nuremberg. John Holland, earl of Huntingdon, and John Beaufort, son of the duke of Lancaster, also joined at the head of a detachment of a thousand English knights. Further volunteers were recruited from Spain and Italy, while a Veneto-Genoese fleet was joined by the Hospitallers' galleys on its way to the Danube. King Sigismund of Hungary, who later became Holy Roman Emperor from 1410 to 1437, contributed the main bulk of the armed forces from his own realm, and other groups came from Austria, Bohemia, Poland, and notably from Wallachia. Not since the First Crusade had such a truly great army been assembled. The total has been estimated at 100,000, and their rendezvous was Buda, where the first general council of war was held in the midsummer of 1396 to draw up procedures and tactics.

Sigismund wisely favored defensive tactics, which he knew from past experience to be more effective in battle with the Turks. But the Western leaders deprecated his advice, for, in Froissart's words, they came "to conquer the whole of Turkey and to march into the Empire to Persia, . . . the Kingdom of Syria and the Holy Land." [Froissart, Jean: *Chroniques,* ed. by Kervyn de Lettenhove, XV, Brussels 1870-77, 242. Cf. Atiya: *The Crusade in the Later Middle Ages,* London 1938, 441; and *The Crusade of Nicopolis,* London 1934, 55-56 and 180 n.] So lightly did they take their enterprise, and so confusing and misleading was their knowledge of Eastern geography!

The united hosts marched along the Danube as far as Orsova, where they crossed the river at the famous Iron Gate into Bulgaria, then under Turkish suzerainty. In seizing the towns of Widdin and Rahova, the Crusaders displayed no discrimination between hostile Turkish garrisons and friendly Orthodox Christian natives. On September 10 they received their first formidable check at the sturdy fortifications of the city of Nicopolis, situated on a hill overlooking the Danube to the north and a plain to the south. It was decided to set siege to Nicopolis from the land, while the galleys of the Venetians, Genoese, and Hospitallers encircled the city from the river. The siege lasted fifteen days, during which little or no constructive action was taken and the time was wasted in debauchery, orgies, and gambling.

In contrast to this was the position in the Turkish camp. On hearing the news of the Christian advent, Sultan Bayezid I (1389–1402) speedily called off a siege which he had been setting against Constantinople, summoned all his Asiatic and European troops, and marched to the relief of Nicopolis with about 100,000 men under his highly disciplined command. He reached the outlying hills on the south side of the plain in the neighborhood of Nicopolis on September 24, organized his army with great military cunning in a fortified position near the hilltop, and awaited the pitched battle which occurred on the following day.

Sigismund's appeal for placing the Hungarians, who were conversant with Turkish methods of warfare, and the Wallachians, whose loyalty was doubtful, in the van facing the enemy, while the French and foreign legions were saved in the rear for the decisive blow, was rejected outright by the impetuous French, who accused the Hungarian monarch of attempting to rob them of the glory of a great day. Bayezid's irregular light calvary (akinjis) formed the first Ottoman mobile line of battle, concealing behind them an extensive field of pointed stakes which separated them from the next line of foot-archers (janissaries and azebs), up the hill. The French and foreign knights on horseback had no difficulty in routing the first line of mounted Turks, who fled to the rear and reorganized their corps beyond the stakes and the archers. Confronted with the barrier of stakes, however, many Christians descended from their horses under showers of arrows, to uproot the stakes in order to make way for the rest of the mounted attackers. This, too, they soon accomplished, and they further inflicted heavy slaughter on the Turks after fierce hand-to-hand fighting. Then they pursued their fleeing victims upward to the hilltop, which they attained in a state of complete exhaustion, believing that to have been the end of a good day.

To their horror, it was only the beginning of the end, for they saw beyond the skyline Bayezid's picked cavalry (sipahis), together with his vassal Serbs under Stephen Lazarovitch, totalling some 40,000 in complete array ready to begin a fresh phase of the battle. The deadly massacre was reversed, and the pursuers became pursued; the survivors were carried into captivity. In the meantime, the riderless horses discarded by the French earlier in the battle, stung by Turkish arrows, stampeded in confusion to the rear across the plain and were regarded by both Hungarians and Wallachians as a sure sign of the discomfiture of their allies. The latter took to flight and Sigismund, grand master of Rhodes, and the burgrave of Nuremberg barely managed to save their skins by boarding a Venetian ship which floated downstream, as the Ottomans began to make their appearance later in the day amid the remaining Christians.

As the sounds of battle were quelled, however, and the sultan had time to look around the field, he was alarmed at his own losses, which were estimated at 30,000, and he displayed his wrath in the cold-blooded massacre of 3,000 prisoners of war on the following day. Bayezid discovered among these captives Jacques de Helly, whom he had previously employed in his eastern campaigns and who understood Turkish. Through Jacques' intercession, the French nobility, including John de Nevers, Enguerrand de Coucy, Philip d'Artois, Guy de la Trémouille, and others, were saved from decapitation and held as precious hostages pending payment of a ransom of 200,000 gold florins. The news of this catastrophe overwhelmed Europe with deep sorrow and dismay; and the grim fate of the chivalry of the West at Nicopolis marked the end of one chapter and the beginning of another in the relations between the East and the West. The prospect for the Crusade became dimmer every day, and the Turk had to be accepted as a member of the European common-wealth of nations despite his race and religion.

After the great calamity which befell the Christian chivalry at Nicopolis, the nations of Western Europe became more and more unwilling to embark on hazardous adventures to overthrow the power of Islam and put an end to Turkish domination. The great propagandist upheaval of the early century began to subside, although we still encounter some writers clamoring for resumption of the Crusade. Most outstanding among these was Philippe de Mézières, who spent the later years of his life in a retreat at the Abbey of the Celestines in Paris, writing several voluminous works of high interest in defense of the old cause. After the defeat of 1396 in Bulgaria, he took up his pen to compose a penetrating epistle entitled "Épistre lamentable et consolatoire," which he addressed to the duke of Burgundy.

De Mézières tried to analyze the causes of and prescribe the remedies for the downfall of the Christians in the East.

He explained that the root of Christian impotence was imbedded in the lack of the four virtues of good governance—Order, Discipline, Obedience, and Justice. Instead of these, society was ruled by the three vicious daughters of Lucifer—Vanity, Covetousness, and Luxury. The "Summa Perfectio," declared Mézières, could be attained only by the adoption of his "Nova Religio Passionis," which provided for the redemption of the birthplace of Christ. This organization or military order of religion was the sole road leading to a successful Crusade, that is, if the old cause could be resuscitated. Meanwhile, it should be noted that de Mézières aptly described himself as an old pilgrim and an old dreamer, an echo of bygone days.

THE FIFTEENTH CENTURY

The complete discomfiture and humiliation of the hosts of Europe, and the massacre of the flower of Western chivalry in the Balkans, rudely awakened the Christian potentates to the stark realities of the Crusades and their futility as an implement for the solution of East-West relations. Furthermore, the fifteenth century resounded with other momentous problems of immediate consequence nearer home which distracted public attention from the old cause. The reopening of the Hundred Years' War between England and France, with its devastating ferocity, on the one hand, and the Conciliar Movement to end the Great Schism of the Church in the West on the other, were issues which consumed public attention throughout Western Europe.

Nevertheless it would be a serious error to contend that the Crusade, both as idea and as action, was extinct. Although the movement had already started to lose its universal character, vestiges could be traced in a series of localized struggles to arrest Ottoman expansion in Eastern Europe and the Levant. In the first place, Burgundy, which bore the brunt of the heavy ransom paid to Sultan Bayezid I for the deliverance of the Nicopolis prisoners of war, became the center of deliberations for revenge. This yielded a new harvest of propagandist literature, which remained confined to the realm of theory. In the second place, the principalities of East Central Europe, led by the kingdom of Hungary, became the real bulwark of Christendom; and resistance in that area has frequently been termed the Hungarian Crusade. In the third place, the mid-century was characterized by the heroic but hopeless aspirations for the defense of the imperial city of Constantinople, which was almost continuously beleaguered by the Turks until the extermination of the Byzantine Empire. Afterward, practically all wars of defense fought against the Ottomans were conducted under the misnomer of Crusade.

Duke Philip the Good of Burgundy still entertained thoughts of leading the holy war, but preferred to proceed with the utmost caution and deliberation in order to avoid another disaster. For a perfect understanding of the position of his adversary, he commissioned two ambassadors in succession to go to the lands beyond the sea and attempt to gather original information about the Islamic polity in an intelligence report coupled with their recommendations. The first of these two was Ghillebert de Lannoy, who spent the years 1420–23 in the Near East, and the second was Bertrandon de la Broquière, whose embassy lasted from 1432 to 1439. While de Lannoy devoted most of his time and attention to Egypt and the Holy Land, de la Broquière, after performing pilgrimage to Jerusalem and the holy places as far as Sinai, retraced his steps to the north, where he conducted his inquiry on Armenia, Anatolia, Byzantium, and above all the Balkan territories subject to the Grand Turk. He visited the court of Sultan Murad II (1421–51) at Adrianople and remarked that the Turks were more friendly to the Latins than the Greeks were. He described the Turkish armies and armor as well as the whole Ottoman military system for the enlightenment of the duke.

Another propagandist of a different character, also from among the adherents of the Burgundian court, was Bishop Jean Germain, chancellor of the Order of the Golden Fleece, who compiled a political discourse to prove that the general position was still more favorable to the Christians than to the Muslims and that it was not yet too late for Crusading. Jean Germain wrote in 1452, on the eve of the downfall of Constantinople. He seemed to underline the shadowy religious union of the Christian East with Rome, concluded at the Council of Ferrara-Florence in 1439, which according to his estimate would bring to the Crusader ranks 200,000 combatants from Armenia, 50,000 from Georgia, some recruits from the Greek empires of Constantinople and Trebizond, the "Jacobites of Ethiopia," Russia, and "Prester John of India." The rosy picture he painted for Christian leaders was of secondary importance, since its author derived his arguments from wishful thinking rather than original knowledge. He had no direct acquaintance with the East and compiled his material from sundry sources.

The flickering ray of hope for the defense of Christendom was largely forthcoming from the hard-pressed peoples of East Central Europe in what has been described as the Hungarian Crusade, while reinforcements from the West grew less every day. The pivotal figure in this conflict was John Hunyadi (1444–56,), regent of Hungary and voyavode of Transylvania, whose heroic career passed into legend in contemporary Balkan annals. His spirited attacks on the Turks almost brought Murad II's reign (1421–51) to a disastrous end. The story began with the sultan's irruptions of the year 1438 into Transylvania across the Danube, as far as the strong city of Hermannstadt to the north and as far as the gates of Belgrade in Serbia to the west. It was at this precarious juncture that Hunyadi emerged on the scene in a coalition with Ladislas, king of Poland (1434–44) and also of Hungary since 1440, as well as George Brankovitch, despot of Serbia (1427–56).

At first each of the three leaders conducted hostilities against the Turkish battalions independently within his own realm. When Murad repeated the invasion of Transyl-

vania in 1442, he was again beaten at Hermannstadt, leaving behind him 20,000 dead. In fury, he made a third and desperate attempt on the city and suffered the same consequences. Hunyadi captured 5,000 Turkish prisoners of war and 200 Ottoman standards. The myth of Turkish invincibility seemed shattered, and the voyavode, hitherto on the defensive, was further encouraged to take the offensive south of the Danube by the arrival of a number of detachments of Latin Crusaders under Cardinal Julian Cesarini in 1443. Again, joined by King Ladislas and John Brankovitch, John Hunyadi sallied into Serbia and scored a new triumph by routing the Turks at Nish, before he seized the Bulgarian capital, Sofia. Even the Albanians, who were Murad's sworn vassals, became so emboldened by these momentous victories that they seceded from Turkish suzerainty and declared open revolt under John Castriota, better known as Scanderbeg. On July 15, 1444 Murad was constrained to sign the Treaty of Szegedin with the coalition leaders. By its terms, George Brankovitch was reinstated in Serbia, a ransom of 60,000 gold ducats was paid by the sultan for the liberation of his captive sons-in-law, and a ten-year truce was approved; but it was later broken under pressure from Cardinal Cesarini. In the end, the despairing sultan decided to abdicate and disappeared from the scene of strife into the interior of Anatolia.

Hopes were revived in the West on hearing of the new triumphs. Duke Philip the Good of Burgundy (1419–67) received an embassy from the Byzantine Emperor, John VIII (1425–48), to court his support at Châlons-sur-Saône; and he consequently equipped four galleys under Geoffroy de Thoisy and Martin Alphonse, while Pope Eugenius IV (1431–47) contributed ships under the command of his own nephew, Francesco Condolmieri, to fight the Turks. The Crusading fire was rekindled, and Cardinal Cesarini's position was strengthened in persuading Hunyadi to break a truce held to be null and void in principle since it was concluded with an infidel. Moreover, the voyavode was promised the crown of Bulgaria on the final liberation of that country from the Turkish yoke.

The first great objective of the joint forces was the strong coastal town of Varna on the Black Sea. On the way, the Christian fleet from the West helped in the relief of the Hospitallers of St. John, who were under siege by the Egyptians in their island fortress of Rhodes during 1444. Afterward, the men-of-war proceeded directly to the Black Sea, to join the siege of the strong city of Varna, already surrounded on the land side and heavily battered by the coalition contingents under the command of the intrepid Hunyadi. Another shattering victory was within sight, when suddenly the old sultan emerged from his retreat at the head of 40,000 picked men whom the perfidious Genoese had transported from Asia to Europe for gain and the promise of trade privileges. During the mortal fighting which ensued outside Varna, both Ladislas and Cardinal Cesarini fell, leaving the weight of the defense operations solely on Hunyadi's shoulders. The Poles and Latins were demoralized by their leaders' sudden disappearance from the field, and the Hungarians faced extermination by an invincible enemy. Hunyadi had no choice but to take to flight on November 10, 1444 to save the remnants of his exhausted army.

Nevertheless, the Albanian rebellion continued to rage under the indomitable Scanderbeg; until, in 1448, Hunyadi reassembled another army of 24,000 men and crossed the Danube at the Iron Gate to invade Serbia. Murad was waiting for him with a superior army of 150,000. They met on the old field of Kossovo-Polye, where the heroism of Hunyadi and his desperate followers did not save them from disaster. Their numerical inferiority, the incoherence and absence of concerted tactics between the Albanians and the Hungarians, the doubtful loyalty of the Wallachians, and the exhaustion of ammunition in the hands of the German and Bohemian infantry, rendering their fearful gunfire utterly ineffective—all these were factors culminating in the tragedy of the Second Battle of Kossovo (October 17–19, 1448), which ended the Hungarian Crusade with irreparable rout.

Perhaps the only positive result of this painful chapter in Crusading history was the prolongation of the agonies of the tottering Byzantine Empire by a few more years. Even before the downfall of Constantinople in 1453, the sultan's suzerainty over the imperial city had in some way or other been tacitly recognized by most members of the imperial family. On John VIII's death in 1448, his three brothers appealed to Murad II for arbitration on their right of succession to the imperial throne, and the sultan's choice fell on Constantine Dragases, the last Emperor destined to defend the city with his life. The defense of this last bulwark of Eastern Christendom, in which a few detachments from the Christian West participated, was described by some contemporaries as a Crusade. Nevertheless, the story of the triumphant entry of Sultan Muhammad II (1451–81) into Constantinople, at midday on April 29, 1453, must be regarded as the consummation of the Turkish Counter-Crusade, and as such will be treated elsewhere in this book.

Although long foreseen and even expected, the final downfall of Constantinople to the Ottomans in 1453 was received throughout Christian Europe with utter bewilderment and great embitterment. The flight of many Greek personalities for refuge in the West became a living reminder of the fateful events in progress in Eastern Europe. The last of the Palaeologi, Thomas, brother of Constantine Dragases, ultimately settled down at the Roman Curia in 1461, taking with him the head of the Apostle Andrew, one of the priceless relics which he had saved from desecration. Pope Pius II (Aeneas Sylvius Piccolomini, 1458–64), who had previously associated himself with the moribund cause as a staunch propagandist for holy war, now espoused the cause of the imperial pretender and took the Cross himself. He invited all European monarchs to join him in a new universal Crusade for the recovery of Byzantium and the reconquest of the Holy Land. The only response to his call came from Philip the

Good, who promised to follow the Holy Pontiff with 6,000 men. A little later, the Burgundian duke requested respite for a year and laid the blame on Louis XI's machinations against his duchy. As a matter of fact, Pius II himself was a very sick man at the time, and the whole project was ultimately buried with him on his decease in 1464. His successor to the tiara, Paul II (1464–71), was less ambitious and more practical. He decided to relegate the funds accumulated for the Crusade to Hungary and Venice as a contribution toward the cost of their intermittent wars with the Turks.

The call to Crusade was fading into a distant cry, though its echoes lingered in the minds of Western princes as late as the seventeenth century. Pope Innocent VIII (1484–92), attempting in vain to renew the plan of an expedition against the Turks, was heartened by the advent of Bayezid II's brother and rival Djem as a fugitive in Rome. Innocent VIII conceived the possibility of inciting rebellion in Turkey in favor of his protégé, but it is said that he was persuaded by the sultan's agents to give up the project, with Djem's body yielded in return for a prize of 300,000 gold ducats.

Alexander VI (1492–1503) succeeded Innocent and became the chief actor in this mysterious tragedy, in conjunction with King Charles VIII of France (1483–98). The Holy Pontiff surrendered his hostage to the king, and finally we hear of Djem's unnatural death in the course of 1495. The sultan was thus relieved of this menace, and immediately he resumed his irruptions into Hungary, Croatia, Moldavia, and even as far as remote Poland, until the peace treaty of 1503 provided Europe with a breathing space for some seventeen years. Both the Popes and the Western monarchs adopted a passive attitude and stood on the defensive, awaiting fearfully the next step to be taken by the Supreme Porte. ["Al-Bāb al-'Ālī" in Arabic and Turkish, equivalent to the "lofty gate," otherwise the "Supreme Porte" of the sultanate at the height of its power.] In the year 1515 Pope Leo X (1513–21) did indeed consider the renewal of hostilities against the Ottoman Empire in conjunction with King Francis I (1515–47) of France and Emperor Maximilian I (1493–1519) of the Holy Roman Empire, but their plan remained in the realm of discussion. Perhaps the only positive action of the period occurred when Emperor Charles V (1519–56) granted the Hospitallers a new abode on the island of Malta (1530) after their expulsion from Rhodes by Sultan Sulaiman the Magnificent (1520–66). Subsequently, a number of imperial detachments descended on Algiers in 1541, and again on the shores of al-Mahdiya in 1550, to chastise the Barbary corsairs. On the other hand, these minor successes scored by the Emperor induced his antagonist, Francis I, to swing French policy toward the conclusion of the alliance of 1536 with the Supreme Porte, marking the birth of the famous Capitulations. Only at the gates of Vienna (1529) and in the waters of Lepanto (1571) was Europe able to arrest the progress of Turkish invasions.

Henceforward, the Turkish was became more or less localized in Central Europe; and in the following century we hear of the deliverance of Jerusalem only occasionally, as a mere dream. Cardinal Richelieu (1585–1642) and the famous French diplomat Father Joseph (1577–1638) spoke about the Holy Land and how to save it. Ferdinand I of Tuscany went a little further when he landed on the island of Cyprus in the course of 1607–08 and tried to arouse the discontented Turkish subjects for joint action against their lord, Sultan Ahmed I (1603–17). The attempt yielded no practical results and Ferdinand himself died shortly afterward in 1609. It was in these years that a certain Father Giovanni Dominelli, an Italian priest living in Cairo, wrote what may be regarded as the last propagandist document outlining a project for saving Jerusalem and the holy places. He argued that the times were eminently suited for landing in Palestine since the sultan was engaged in fighting on several fronts in the continents of Asia and Europe, while his men silently harbored the spirit of insubordination and his Christian subjects were biding their time and chance for insurrection in order to throw off their heavy yoke of servitude. Father Dominelli's faint voice passed unheeded in a changing world, and Crusading days were mere memories.

James A. Brundage (essay date 1962)

SOURCE: "Proclamation of the Crusade" in *The Crusades: A Documentary Survey*, The Marquette University Press, 1962, pp. 14–23.

[*In the following essay, Brundage offers a brief account of the events directly preceding Pope Urban II's Council of Clermont sermon. An eyewitness report of the Pope's sermon directly follows.*]

I

The fruitless efforts of Pope Gregory VII to secure military forces to fight in the East failed in stemming the Turkish threat to Byzantium. Turkish advance into Byzantine territory in Asia Minor continued apace after 1074 and the consequences for Byzantium were nearly disastrous. Provincial governors and army commanders, one after another, revolted against the governments of successive emperors at Constantinople, while the Normans, who had already ousted the Byzantines from their colonies in southern Italy and Sicily, added to the difficulties of the Greek emperors by invading the Empire's Balkan provinces. Chaos threatened to overwhelm the only powerful Christian government in the eastern Mediterranean when, in 1081, as the result of still anothe revolt, the most promising of Byzantium's military leaders, the youthful Alexius Comnenus, seized the throne.[1]

The thirty-seven years of Alexius' reign were to see a gradual stabilization of the Empire's frontiers, the expulsion of the Normans from the Balkans, a halt put to the Turkish invasions, and a regeneration of the internal administration of the Empire. But Alexius, for all his great ability and administrative capacity, could not undertake, unaided, a counteroffensive against the Turks. He was able to stabilize the empire's frontiers, but he was unable to advance back into the territories which the Turks had captured in the decades prior to his accession to the Byzantine throne. Alexius had perforce to endure, since he could do nothing else about it, the presence of a Turkish sultan at Nicaea, less than a hundred miles from Constantinople itself.

The military commitments of Byzantium were heavy: there was a long Danube border which must be guarded against persistent threats by various enemies, including Oghuz, Kuman, and Pecheneg Turks, Bulgars, and Slavs. The Norman invasion of the Balkans, although successfully repulsed after more than five years of fighting, made it imperative for the Empire to remain on guard against further aggression from that quarter. And in Asia Minor, where Byzantium had already lost all but a handful of coastal towns, there was a long, ill-defined frontier to guard against a treacherous, ever threatening foe.

In 1095 Alexius determined to appeal again, as Michael Dukas had done twenty years before, for military aid from Western Christendom. His petition was prompted by his hope of securing from the West the troops he needed so badly, both to guard his present positions and to take the offensive against the Seljuk Turks who now controlled Asia Minor. One obvious avenue of approach for a Byzantine emperor searching for Western assistance was through the Pope, the spiritual leader of the West.[2] Accordingly, Alexius dispatched ambassadors to seek out the reigning Pontiff, Pope Urban II, a former disciple and colleague of Pope Gregory VII.

In March of 1095, Rome was held by the anti-Pope, Clement III, while Pope Urban II was presiding over an ecclesiastical council at Piacenza, in northern Italy. It was there that the Byzantine ambassadors caught up with him and presented their messages. Urban seems to have been greatly impressed by the urgency of the Byzantine requests. The ambassadors were called upon to address the council, which is said to have numbered 4,000 clerics and more than 30,000 laymen.[3] The Emperor's envoys urged upon their auditors the fearful picture of a Moslem conquest of all the East, up to the very walls of Constantinople. There is good reason to believe that they stressed to their audience the fact that Jerusalem and the Lord's Sepulcher were being defiled by pagan hands. This latter fact was presented to the council as one of the principal reasons why united Christian efforts against the Turks were of major importance and of great urgency.[4] Pope Urban II was apparently as impressed by the envoys' personal pleas as he was by the message they bore and he is said to have addressed the council himself in support of their claims.[5]

II

The claims and arguments advanced at Piacenza for Western intervention in the East doubtless led the Pope to ponder the situation there and to reflect upon the part the Papacy might play in channeling military aid to Byzantium. We have no record of Urban's thoughts during the spring and summer of 1095 as he journied through northern Italy from Piacenza to Vercelli, to Milan, Como, and Asti,[6] but the lines along which his mind travelled are fairly obvious.

For decades the papacy had been on uneasy terms with the patriarchs of the East. Could Western response to these recent Eastern pleas for military aid be turned to good account in strengthening papal discipline over the churches of that area? For decades, too, the papacy had encouraged the Christian reconquest of Spain and to that end had granted spiritual privileges to those who took part in the wars against the Moslems. Could this technique also be applied to abate the peril which was taking shape in the East? For nearly a century the papacy had encouraged efforts to promote civil peace in Europe, to limit private feudal warfare in the West. Could a Western military expedition to the East contribute in some way to the achievement of these ends? Perhaps most pressing of all, there was the history of the past twenty years in Europe, the record of a consuming internecine strife between Empire and Papacy. Would not a successful military venture in the East, under papal auspices and papal leadership, tend to bolster papal prestige and power against the Western enemies of the Papacy? And if such a military expedition were to be organized, when, where, and how should the work begin? These and similar questions may well have occupied the pontiff's attention in the months between the closing of the Council of Piacenza and August 1095, when he entered France.

By August 15, when he was at Le Puy, Urban must have settled on some tentative plans, for from there he dispatched a summons to the French hierarchy to meet with him in council at Clermont on November 18. Urban spent the month of September travelling in Provence; October saw him in Burgundy, consecrating the high altar of the new basilica at the monastery of Cluny where he had once been a monk. By November 14, Urban had reached Clermont, in company with the bishop of that city, who had worked so strenuously preparing for the meetings of the council that he died on the night of Urban's arrival.

The sittings of the Council of Clermont opened formally on Sunday, November 18, 1095. The membership of the council is variously estimated. Whatever the exact figures may have been, it is clear that the council was attended by several hundred archbishops, bishops, abbots, and other ecclesiastical dignitaries, drawn mainly from southern France. Ten days were devoted to purely ecclesiastical business, concerned for the most part with disciplinary reforms within the church. Finally it was announced that on Tuesday, November 27, the Pope would address a general gathering of both the clergy and the laity. At this meeting Pope Urban announced publicly for the first time the details of the plan which had been maturing in his mind for six months or more. An eyewitness reports his words[7] as follows:

The Sermon of Pope Urban II at Clermont[8]

In the year of the Incarnation of our Lord 1095, a great council was held in the Auvergne region of Gaul, in the city of Clermont. Among those present at the council were the Roman bishops and cardinals and Pope Urban II. This famous council was also attended by a great number of bishops and princes from both Gaul and Germany. When the ecclesiastical business of the gathering had been disposed of, the lord Pope went out to a wide and spacious field, since the crowds could not easily be accommodated in any building. There the pope addressed the whole gathering in these words:

"Frenchmen! You who come from across the Alps; you who have been singled out by God and who are loved by him—as is shown by your many accomplishments; you who are set apart from all other peoples by the location of your country, by your Catholic faith, and by the honor of the Holy Church; we address these words, this sermon, to you!

"We want you to know the melancholy reasons which have brought us among you and the peril which threatens you and all the faithful. Distressing news has come to us (as has often happened) from the region of Jerusalem and from the city of Constantinople; news that the people of the Persian kingdom, [That is, the Seljuk Turks who had taken over the Baghdad caliphate.] an alien people, a race completely foreign to God, 'a generation of false aims, of a spirit that broke faith with God,'[9] has invaded Christian territory and has devastated this territory with pillage, fire, and the sword. The Persians have taken some of these Christians as captives into their own country; they have destroyed others with cruel tortures. They have completely destroyed some of God's churches and they have converted others to the uses of their own cult. They ruin the altars with filth and defilement. They circumcize Christians and smear the blood from the circumcision over the altars or throw it into the baptismal fonts. They are pleased to kill others by cutting open their bellies, extracting the end of their intestines, and tying it to a stake. Then, with flogging, they drive their victims around the stake until, when their viscera have spilled out, they fall dead on the ground. They tie others, again, to stakes and shoot arrows at them; they seize others, stretch out their necks, and try to see whether or not they can cut off their heads with a single blow of a naked sword. And what shall I say about the shocking rape of women? On this subject it would, perhaps, be worse to speak than to keep silent. These Persians have so dismembered the kingdom of the Greeks and have sequestered so much of it that it would be impossible to cross the conquered territory in a two month journey.

"Who is to revenge all this, who is to repair this damage, if you do not do it? You are the people upon whom God has bestowed glory in arms, greatness of spirit, bodily agility, and the courage to humble the 'proud locks'[10] of those who resist you.

"Rise up and remember the manly deeds of your ancestors, the prowess and greatness of Charlemagne, of his son Louis, and of your other kings, who destroyed pagan kingdoms and planted the holy church in their territories. You should be especially aroused by the fact that the Holy Sepulcher of the Lord our Savior is in the hands of these unclean people, who shamefully mistreat and sacrilegiously defile the Holy Places with their filth. Oh, most valiant knights! Descendants of unconquered ancestors! Remember the courage of your forefathers and do not dishonor them!

"But if your affection for your beloved children, wives, and parents would hold you back, remember what the Lord says in the Gospel: 'He who loves father or mother more than me is not worthy of me.'[11] 'Everyone who has left house, or brothers, or father, or mother, or wife, or children, or lands, for my name's sake, shall receive a hundredfold, and shall possess life everlasting.'[12] Do not allow any possession or any solicitude for family affairs to detain you.

"This land in which you live, surrounded on one side by the sea and on the other side by mountain peaks, can scarcely contain so many of you. It does not abound in wealth; indeed, it scarcely provides enough food for those who cultivate it. Because of this you murder and devour one another, you wage wars, and you frequently wound and kill one another. Let this mutual hatred stop; let these quarrels abate; let these wars cease; and let all these conflicts and controversies be put to rest. Begin the journey to the Holy Sepulcher; conquer that land which the wicked have seized, the land which was given by God to the children of Israel and which, as the Scripture says, 'is all milk and money.'[13]

"Jerusalem is the navel of the world, a land which is more fruitful than any other, a land which is like another paradise of delights. This is the land which the Redeemer of mankind illuminated by his coming, adorned by his life, consecrated by his passion, redeemed by his death, and sealed by his burial. This royal city, situated in the middle of the world, is now held captive by his enemies and is made a servant, by those who know not God, for the ceremonies of the heathen. It looks and hopes for freedom; it begs unceasingly that you will come to its aid. It looks for help from you, especially, because, as we have said, God has bestowed glory in arms upon you more than on any other nation. Undertake this journey, therefore, for the remission of your sins, with the assurance of 'glory which cannot fade'[14] in the kingdom of heaven."

When Pope Urban had said these and many similar things in his urbane sermon, those who were present were so moved that, as one man, all of them together shouted: "God wills it! God wills it!" When the venerable pontiff heard this, he turned his eyes toward heaven and gave thanks to God. He then waved his hand for silence, and said:

"Dearly beloved brethren! We have seen today that, as the Lord says in the Gospel, 'Where two or three are gathered together in my name, I am there in the midst of them.'[15] If the Lord God had not been present in your minds, you would not all have cried out the same thing, for although all of you shouted, your cries had but one origin. I tell you, therefore, that God placed this shout in your breasts and that God brought it out. Since this shout came from God, let it be your battle cry. When you make an armed attack on the enemy, let all those on God's side cry out together, 'God wills it! God wills it!'

"We do not ask or advise that elderly or feeble persons or those who are unable to bear arms should undertake this journey. No women should set out unless they are accompanied by their husbands, brothers, or legal guardians. Such persons are more a hindrance than an aid, more burdensome than useful. Let the rich help the poor; let them also, as their means allow, bring experienced soldiers with them to the war. Priests or clerics of whatever kind are not to come without the permission of their bishops, for the journey will be of no profit to them if they go without their bishops' authorization. [The Pope's meaning is that priests who went on Crusade without the approval of their bishops would not receive the indulgence which they would otherwise gain.] Nor, indeed, should laymen begin the pilgrimage without their priest's blessing.

"Whoever shall decide to make this holy pilgrimage and shall take a vow to God, offering himself as 'a living sacrifice, consecrated to God and worthy of his acceptance,'[16] shall wear the sign of the Lord's cross, either on his forehead or on his breast. When, after fulfilling his vow, he shall wish to return home, let him place the cross on his back, between his shoulders. By this twofold action such men will fulfill that command of the Lord which he uttered in the Gospel: 'He who does not take up his own cross and follow after me is not worthy of me.'"[17]

When all these things were done, one of the Roman cardinals, Gregory by name, said the "confiteor" for the whole crowd, which now knelt on the ground. All of them, beating their breasts, begged absolution for their misdeeds. When the absolution had been given, the blessing followed; when the blessing was finished, the crowd was given leave to go home.

[Trans. James A. Brundage]

On the day following this scene, a final conference of the council was held at Clermont. At this meeting the details of the organization of the expedition were arranged. The Bishop of Le Puy, Adhemar, whom Urban had visited the previous August, was selected as Papal legate to lead the Crusade as Urban's personal representative. It was probably also at this meeting that arrangements were made to set August 15, 1096 as the official starting date for the expedition. This would give the bishops time to preach and to enlist recruits for the expedition; it would also give the knights who were to take part sufficient time to settle their affairs at home before setting out on the journey.

Pope Urban spent the next eight months in France, attending to ecclesiastical business[18] there and, probably, gathering recruits himself for the glorious expedition which he had announced at Clermont. On August 15, 1096, the date set for the official beginning of the expedition, Urban was crossing the Alps on his way back to Italy, secure in the knowledge that the Crusade was well under way.

Notes

1. The fundamental source for the history of the reign of Alexius Comnenus (and, incidentally, for the Greek view of the First Crusade) is the *Alexiad*, by Alexius' daughter, Anna Comnena. The best edition

is that by Bernard Leib, which includes the Greek text with a French translation and copious notes in three volumes (Paris: Les Belles Lettres, 1937-1945). There is an English translation by E. A. S. Dawes (London: Kegan Paul, French, Trubner and Co., 1928). The best general treatment of the reign of Alexius is that by Ferdinand Chalandon, *Essai sur le règne d'Alexius I Comnène (1081-1118)* (Paris: A. Picard, 1900). There is an interesting study by Georgina Buckler entitled *Anna Comnena* (Oxford: Oxford University Press, 1929), which treats of a great many aspects of eleventh and twelfth century Byzantine life. There are also numerous short treatments in English of Alexius' life and work in the several general histories of Byzantium, e.g., Norman H. Baynes and H. St. L. B. Moss, *Byzantium: An Introduction to East Roman Civilization* (Oxford: Clarendon Press, 1948); Charles Diehl, *Byzantium, Greatness and Decline* (New Brunswick: Rutgers University Press, 1957); Jack Lindsay, *Byzantium into Europe* (London: The Bodley Head, 1952); George Ostrogorsky, *History of the Byzantine State* (New Brunswick: Rutgers University Press, 1957); A. A. Vasiliev, *History of the Byzantine Empire, 324-1453,* (2d English edition; 2 vols; Madison: University of Wisconsin Press, 1958).

2. The relationship between Byzantium and the Papacy at this period was complex and often is rather puzzling. The "schism" of 1054 is regarded by most recent writers as a much less clear-cut and decisive break between Rome and Constantinople that it had been considered in the past. Certainly the ties between the Eastern and Western churches were tenuous in 1095, but there is little reason to believe that Alexius and Urban II regarded one another as hopeless heretics or irretrievable schismatics. Cf. George Every, *The Byzantine Patriarchate* (London: Society for Promoting Christian Knowledge, 1947); Peter Charanis, chapter, "The Byzantine Empire in the Eleventh Century," in Setton, *Crusades,* I, 177-219; Runciman, *Crusades,* I, 93-105; Yves Congar, "Neuf cents ans après; notes sur le 'schisme oriental,'" in *1054-1954, L'Église et les églises* (2 vols.; Chevetogne: Editions de Chevetogne, 1954-1955), I, 3-95.

3. If these figures were divided by ten or fifteen, they would probably represent the council's numbers more accurately. The figures quoted are those given by Bernold of Constance, *Chronicon, MGH, SS,* V, 462.

4. See Peter Charanis, "A Greek Source on the Origin of the First Crusade," *Speculum,* XXIV (1949), 93.

5. Bernold of Constance, *Chronicon, MGH, SS,* V, 462; cf. D. C. Munro, "Did the Emperor Alexius I. Ask for Aid at the Council of Piacenza, 1095?" *AHR,* XXVII (1921-1922), 731-33.

6. Urban's travels between Piacenza and Clermont are summarized in C. J. Hefele and H. Leclercq,

Histoire des Conciles (11 vols. in 22; Paris: Letouzey et Ané, 1907-1952), V^1, 396-99. For Urban's plans for the Crusade, see Frederick Duncalf, "The Pope's Plan for the First Crusade," Munro, in *Essays,* pp. 44-56; A. C. Krey, "Urban's Crusade—Success or Failure?" *AHR,* LIII (1947-1948), 235-50; Augustin Fliche, "Les origines de l'action de la papauté en vue de la Croisade," *Revue d'Histoire Ecclésiastique,* XXXIV (1938), 765-75.

7. Urban II's address at Clermont was reported by four contemporary writers: Fulcher of Charters, Baldric of Dol, Guibert of Nogent, and Robert the Monk. Of these four, Robert the Monk, whose report is translated here, was the only one to make a definite claim that he was present, although it is reasonable to assume that the others were there also. There are numerous discrepancies between the various accounts of the sermon; these have been analyzed by D. C. Munro, "The Speech of Pope Urban II. at Clermont, 1095," *AHR,* XI (1905-1906), 231-42. English translations of the four accounts have been printed by Munro in *Translations and Reprints from the Original Sources of European History* (Philadelphia: University of Pennsylvania Press, n.d.). I, no. 2.

8. Robert the Monk, *Historia Hierosolimitana,* I, 1-3 (*RHC, Occ.,* III, 727-730).

9. Ps. 77:8.

10. 77:22.

11. Matt. 10:37.

12. Matt. 29:29.

13. Exod. 3:8.

14. I Peter 5:4.

15. Matt. 18:20.

16. Rom. 12:1.

17. Luke 14:27; Matt. 10:38.

18. The Pope's business in France was mainly concerned with routine administrative affairs. The seventy-five letters which he wrote during the eight months following the Council of Clermont are principally concerned with confirming grants to monasteries, dedicating churches, awarding privileges, and deciding appeals which were referred to him as chief arbiter of the ecclesiastical courts. Setton, *Crusades,* I, 250-52; P. Jaffé *et al.* (eds.,) *Regesta pontificum Romanorum ab condita ecclesia ad annum post Christum natum MCXCVIII* (2 vols.; Graz: Akademische Druck-und Verlagsanstalt, 19-56), No. 5592-5667.

Zoé Oldenbourg (essay date 1965)

SOURCE: "The Reckoning" in *The Crusades,* translated by Anne Carter, Pantheon Books, 1965, pp. 551–78.

[*In the essay that follows, Oldenbourg provides an overview of the history of the early Crusades, examining, in particular, the social effects of the warfare.*]

LEGENDS AND DISASTERS

The Crusades have been glorified, discussed, decried, and judged by historians in many different ways, but they remain a great episode in the history of Western Christendom. A close examination reveals them as an extremely complex phenomenon, and yet, unlike most great historical movements, they grew out of an idea which was simple enough in itself. In spite of everything, the Crusades are still the symbol of a glorious, disinterested—and even chimerical—undertaking. Since the eighteenth century there has been no shortage of detractors to insist that in these holy wars there was little enough altruism and on the contrary a great many atrocities, to say that the whole affair was a piece of brigandage giving free rein to the basest instincts on the pretext of religious zeal, and to assert that only fanatics and narrow-minded nationalists could still approve of the principle of this succession of battles and massacres carried out in the name of Christ. (It is worth remembering here Simone Weil's remark that the Crusades were "the basest" of wars.)

As a military operation, the Crusades were a failure. Western Christendom lost Jerusalem ninety years later, after it had unwittingly helped to bring about the reunification of Islam in the Near East, had strengthened the warlike ardor of the Moslem world, had first weakened and then ruined the Empire of Byzantium and in so doing increased the danger from the Turks and Mongols. They were, however, a considerable moral triumph for the West, which is a good deal, and they were also an indirect source of both material and cultural wealth as a result of prolonged contact between the Western world and the East. The Crusades were part of a general movement in the West, an expansion which was then only beginning but which, in the course of several hundred years, was to assume altogether unexpected proportions.

The Crusades can be treated to a process of "demythification," as it should perhaps be called, but nonetheless they form an integral part of the myth of the Christian, barbarian West, all-conquering, unashamedly militarist, adventurous, and accustomed to confusing heroism with prowess in battle. The greatness of this conquering adventure, which was in other respects a failure, lay in the name of Jerusalem. Jerusalem delivered and Jerusalem lost: these are still significant pointers to the growing self-awareness of the Latin West. There was Jerusalem and there was an uninterrupted series of disasters: wars, massacres, murders, pillage, and devastation. The far from negligible benefits which the West obtained from the Crusades have also been used to explain and justify them in the history books. The Crusades are known to have involved a fantastic waste of human life, and it is this angle which deserves to be considered now.

It is a notorious fact that the Crusades were responsible for an immense amount of bloodshed, and the appalling massacre of the people of Jerusalem is enough to discredit the Crusades as "holy wars" forever. But the earliest victims of the Crusades were the Jews of Metz, Mainz, Worms, Prague, and Speyer in 1096, more than a thousand men, women and children and possibly even several thousand. Next were the Hungarians, Serbs, and Greeks who lived in the regions through which the bands of Crusaders passed, and then the inhabitants of the district around Chrysopolis in Asia Minor, all of whom were Christians. These crimes were expiated to the full and more, and the Crusaders who indulged in this orgy of violence were nearly all exterminated like wild beasts, some in Hungary and others near Nicaea in Asia Minor. "When the bodies of all the warriors who had been slain, which lay all around, were brought together they made, I will not call it a great heap nor yet a mound, nor even a hill, but as it were a high mountain of considerable size."[1] The "high mountain" may only have existed in Anna Comnena's imagination, but the dead numbered more than twenty thousand and not all of them were murderers; there were many women, children, old men, and sick among them, and their numbers, in Europe as well as in Asia, were far greater than those of their victims.

The regular armies, from Lorraine, Normandy, Provence, and France, who set out along the road to Asia Minor in 1096 were lucky enough to distinguish themselves by great victories and to reach Jerusalem. But contemporary accounts, with their endless recital of the misfortunes which befell the armies one after another, might have been written to discourage volunteers who were anxious to imitate the Crusaders' exploits. The holy war made many more martyrs than it did conquering heroes.

THE FIRST CRUSADE

After their victory at Nicaea, where they had been robbed of the fruits of their victory by the Greeks' agreement with the Sultan, the Crusaders narrowly escaped being wiped out at Dorylaeum when they were confronted by such multitudes of Turks that "all the hills, all the valleys, and all the plains, inside and out," were covered with enemy troops. The Turks ground their teeth, uttering resounding cries and demoniacal yells, and attacked ferociously, retreating and returning to the attack and overrunning the Crusaders' camp in a succession of waves so terrifying that their defeat could only be explained by God's help. "Who is wise enough to describe the sagacity, the war-like talents and valor of these Turks?"[2] For a long time the Crusaders withstood the terrifying charges, the hell of howling warriors, the thunder of galloping horses, the whistle of bows, and the dense, murderous hail of arrows and javelins. We are not told how many were the dead and wounded, and no one had time to count them. The foot soldiers crouched on the ground with their long shields and spears while the cavalry charged, and the women were "a great help," running into the front line and carrying drinks to the fighting men. There was victory, pursuit, and vast spoils of "gold and silver, horses, asses, camels, sheep, oxen, and many other things."

But the march was hard. They traveled for hundreds of miles through an arid landscape in high summer under a burning sun. They had to climb mountains (called by the chroniclers "the Mountain of the Devil"—the Anti-Taurus) "so steep and narrow, none dared go before the others on the path that was up the side. The horses plunged into the ravines, and one pack animal dragged down the others." Men and women died of heat stroke, thirst, and exhaustion and fell from precipices, while those who lagged behind were slain by the Turks. It took the army four months to cross Asia Minor in the heat of a summer such as the pilgrims had never seen in their own countries. Then there was the long siege outside Antioch, in winter, with icy, torrential rains. For lack of adequate shelter, they camped in the freezing wind, sleeping in muddy water, while the poor died of exhaustion and hunger finished off the sick who were already half dead with cold. Historians merely remark that "too many" pilgrims died.

The battles went on with their almost ritual exchange of severed heads: heads of Turks and heads of Franks, brandished on the ends of spears, flung from one camp to another, and carried as presents to the leaders. Then there were the heads of prisoners which Bohemond had roasted, to make people believe that he ate them, and the three hundred heads which the Franks sent to St. Symeon to the ambassadors of the Caliph of Egypt, who were the Seljuks' enemy. Victories were as bloody for the victors as for the vanquished. In one engagement at the gates of Antioch on March 6, "the swift waves of the river [Orontes] were red with the blood of the Turks."[3] Corpses were piled in heaps on the bridge. Antioch was captured and the Turkish garrison massacred. Kerbogha, the atabeg of Mosul, arrived to relieve the besieged, cut his way into the city, and slaughtered the Frankish garrison guarding the bridge. Then, when the fighting was over, the famine, epidemics, and despair came once again.

"Anyone who found a dead dog or cat ate it with relish. . . . There were to be seen knights and sergeants, who had been so brave and strong and valiant in all warlike enterprises, become so weak and wasted that they went about the streets leaning on sticks, their heads bowed, begging for bread."[4] If knights were reduced to this condition, it is not hard to guess what the state of the poor people must have been.

Even the most experienced minds, the leaders who had most accurately calculated the difficulties of the undertaking beforehand, must have felt that things were getting out of hand; only the physical impossibility of giving up the war which had begun so badly (in spite of its initial success) compelled the army to persevere in its design of conquest. Some deserted, and more would probably have done so if flight in disorder through hostile desert country had not been more dangerous than carrying on with the war. Even Peter the Hermit attempted to flee. When Count Stephen of Blois fled with his knights and placed himself under the protection of the *basileus's* armies, he is known to have told them that the Crusaders had certainly been annihilated by Kerbogha already and that it was useless to go to their assistance. He was probably so crushed and the whole adventure seemed so cruel and absurd that he secretly hoped it was true. Stephen had to pay dearly for his defection, but at least, as the richest man in France, he had the means to escape with the maximum chance of getting out alive. The bulk of the army, which stayed where it was, was saved by the miracle of the Holy Lance.

It was now a case of conquer or die. At Antioch, as at Dorylaeum, it was the energy of despair which worked the miracle and won the Franks immortal renown. Contemporary accounts make it clear how much of this access of almost mystical exaltation was due to the fierce refusal to admit defeat, to crude fighting spirit and to sheer heroism. The Crusaders' luck—if luck it can be called—in the critical situations in which they were always finding themselves always lay in their comparative weakness.

It can be estimated that about a quarter of the army which crossed the Bosporus set out again from Antioch on the road to Jerusalem. The proportion of those who deserted is unknown, but most of them, if they were not murdered on the spot, ended up as slaves. The number of dead must have been immense, and historians console themselves with the assurance that all these pilgrims had become martyrs and were even now praying God for their comrades, from the ranks of the celestial hosts which fought invisibly alongside God's soldiers. To any other army, losses like these would have meant defeat and the end of the war. But the Crusaders could not go home, or even sue for peace. A peace concluded at Antioch, for example, would have resulted in the immediate disintegration of the army and a retreat with heavier losses even than those already sustained. The Turks, though their courage was reputed to be without equal, could afford to be routed because they had somewhere to flee to.

The Frankish army moved on toward Palestine, weakened, reduced, desperate, and formidably inured to suffering and all the fiercer because of it. After what they had been through, God's soldiers had nothing more to fear and nothing more to lose. Neither the chronicles nor historical *chansons de geste* can convey what life in the Crusader camp must have been like, a mixture of misery and heroism, compounded of mud, blood, sweat, and tears. Occasionally, when a siege proved particularly severe, historians mention the intolerable smell exhaled by the dead and dying, the swarms of black flies, and the polluted food. For men at the end of their tether, cramped together in a narrow space, these things could be the cause of unbearable wretchedness, but the smells, flies, and vermin were at any rate ordinary, everyday plagues. Filth was everywhere in these camps, where water was always rationed in hot weather, where the animals had to be watered first, and where victuals and fodder were a perpetual source of anxiety. Men, horses, pack animals, and animals intended for slaughter trailed along the roads in convoys miles long and camped on broad open spaces surrounded by ditches, filling the air with the heavy stench forces. The few survivors of these sacrificial armies found themselves in the Holy Land. They had the consolation of having accomplished the pilgrimage to Jerusalem and of placing their swords at the service of the Holy Sepulcher. No blame attached to these leaders for having escaped, practically alone, from an escapade in which all their soldiers and all the civilians who had set out under their protection had lost their lives. They were like the survivors of some natural disaster, and in a tragedy of such magnitude any who managed to escape were regarded as fortunate rather than cowardly.

They were men who had lived through a hell of hunger, thirst, heat, and Turkish arrows. First the arrows, and then the sabers, slicing off heads by the dozen; thousands of bleeding corpses and living men trampled underfoot by the charging horsemen. Bishops and counts could be seen running away on foot, half-naked, dragging themselves for days on end through rocky, waterless mountains to arrive, half-dead from exhaustion, at the gates of the nearest Christian city. Hugh of Vermandois, the brother of King Philip I, who was wounded in the battle of Heraclea, reached Tarsus in this condition and died there. William IX of Aquitaine was luckier: he managed to make his way back home, where he earned himself a reputation as a troubadour which eclipsed his exploits and misfortunes in the Holy Land. How many of the less illustrious escaped is unknown, but all historians state that their number was very small.

In Syria, where the Crusaders were dealing with adversaries less formidable than Kilij Arslan and the Danishmendites, war was possible, and they made war. The Egyptian armies came up the coast and attacked what was left of the first Crusading army. Baldwin I was a man to defend his own lands. Once again it was a case of conquer or die. "If you are killed you will have a martyr's crown. If you are victorious, immortal glory. All desire for flight is useless: France is too far away!" Accompanied by the True Cross, which was carried by the Bishop Gerard, the King, at the head of his knights, hurled himself against forces ten times greater than his own. At Ramleh he lost his best companions, Bervold and Geldemar Carpenel, who fell with all their men, but he won the victory. Eight months later there was another massacre of Frankish knights and a total rout. Hugh of Lusignan, Geoffrey of Vendôme, Stephen of Blois, to mention only the greatest of them, were killed there. "There had not been such a slaughter of knights in Syria before—and the power of Christendom in that land was greatly weakened thereby. Those who knew the land best were more shaken than the rest, and considered fleeing from the country because it was too dangerous to stay there," wrote William of Tyre. And this was in 1102, three years after the capture of Jerusalem. There was talk of two hundred knights slain, and although this is a ludicrous figure when compared to the strength of the great Crusading armies, for Frankish Syria it was enormous. It was indeed dangerous to stay, but they stayed all the same.

They not only stayed—those in Jerusalem and in the north, in Antioch, Edessa, and the Lebanon—they indulged in the luxury of making war among themselves. Not very often, indeed, but as often as was physically possible for them. There was no longer any great army, but there were always newcomers and seasonal reinforcements. Ten years after the great departure for the First Crusade, there was already a kernel of Franks in Syria who considered themselves at home there and were fighting for lands which were already their own. Some had lost friends and brothers there; others, like Baldwin I, their wives and children, and all shared in the pride of possessing the most glorious land in all the world because it was the holiest. They had other reasons, too, for being attached to it.

THE HOLY LAND

It was a beautiful country, though too hot for men who came from Normandy and Flanders, and with some regions, like parts of Judaea and Galilee, that were barren enough. But there were also provinces like the coastal plain, the plain of the Jordan, and the lands around the Orontes that were so providentially fertile that three harvests could be gathered in one year and men could grow not only corn and vines and apples but other fruits, unknown in Europe, such as oranges and lemons, many varieties of vegetables, and sugar cane. There were also the forests of the Lebanon and Banya, which produced the finest woods for building and were well stocked with game, and the prairies of Jordan and the coast of Lebanon. As good landowners, the Franks prized all this. They appreciated and admired the comforts and beauty of the cities, and the superb fortifications and defense works, which excited them so much that they began covering the land with castles.

With its wooded hills, calm white villages and cypress groves, stony tracks where donkeys passed to and fro laden with stone jars and baskets of olives, and broad roads along which the great caravans traveled, this land with its bluest of blue skies and cold, starry nights was a land a man could love, and would have loved even if it had not been the birthplace of Jesus Christ.

The original inhabitants—those of the cities, at any rate—were more or less roughly dispossessed. In Edessa and Antioch they were left where they were, but oppressed. In Jerusalem, and also in Caesarea, the other Palestinian city which suffered a massacre, they were wiped out. Moslems were expelled from other cities along the coast: Jaffa, Tripoli, Beirut, and Tyre lost their Moslem populations and only the poor remained. Every time a city fell there was murderous fighting, especially on the side of the attackers, but the brunt of the attack was shared by the Italian sailors who had well earned the privileges they obtained. The Crusaders gained a good deal of wealth from the spoils of victory, and a man who had not owned "so much as one village" might find himself in the East "the lord of a city." Fulcher of Chartres was telling the truth, but he forgot to mention that these fortunate ones were the minority and that most of the warrior pilgrims, far from becoming lords of anything at all, simply became "martyrs." There were not such vast numbers of cities or even villages in the East waiting to be picked up by adventurers from Europe.

In those first ten years the knights, eager for land and for glory, conquered as many strongholds as their means allowed and then established a summary plan of campaign: the next aim was to increase the possessions already acquired by seizing the coastal cities and the lands immediately bordering on Palestine and the states of Antioch and Edessa. They must not venture too far because it was necessary to live in peace with their stronger neighbors, or at least not to have them as enemies all the time.

This state of constant warfare was not too much of a strain for the Frankish knights. They were doing their job and they simply had more opportunity of exercising their trade in the East than in Europe, where even so, private wars had long since become a public scourge. Here they could fight with a clear conscience because the Church, far from condemning their wars as fratricidal, proclaimed them agreeable to God. They also got comparatively more profit out of their wars, since in non-Christian lands the rights of pillages were more loosely applied. They very quickly established a *modus vivendi* which reduced the profits gained from the holy war to the same proportions as those of any other war, but there were always a few fortresses left to conquer on the borders—or at least, so men might hope.

THE CHIVALRY

As long as the Frankish kingdom endured, these wars, whether great or small, were extremely murderous. Moreover—something which was not the case in Europe—they were very nearly as lethal to the cavalry as to the infantry.

The Frankish warriors in the East had not given up their heavy armor: experience had shown that it was their best asset. To men less tough it might have seemed an instrument of torture when they had to fight in the heat of summer. Worn in a heat that was almost unendurable even for men very lightly clad, a shirt of mail, steel helmet, and iron greaves—all of which were naturally padded inside for protection against blows—must have been a test which only men of exceptional strength and trained to the wearing of armor from their earliest youth could have borne for long. Their helmets were protected by plumes of feathers, their hauberks by tunics of fine cloth, but even so this costume was a good deal warmer than that worn by Eastern warriors, of whom even the wealthy wore only a light coat of mail beneath their white woolen cloaks. The Frankish knight's shield and lance were much bigger and heavier than those of the enemy. Their battle chargers, protected by leather caparisons padded with horsehair and reinforced with metal plates, carried a hundred pounds of metal on their backs, as well as the weight of a man.

A knight, said al-Imad—who even after ninety years of Frankish presence in the East was still astonished by the fact—was practically invulnerable. Arrows, javelins, and sword cuts were all powerless against him. There was therefore good reason for the assertion that one single Frankish knight was worth ten Moslem horsemen: he could take ten times as many blows and still stand firm when others would have been killed outright. However, as al-Imad noted, there was another side to the coin. Once the knight was off his horse he was helpless, because he could not move fast enough to escape swiftly: "The horse must be wounded or killed before the rider can be unseated." (The Moslems' spears were not strong enough to knock a man off his horse, whereas this happened frequently in Western battles or tourneys.) It was easier to kill a horse than a man, but it must be said that the combatants were reluctant to kill horses and only did so in the last extremity. Horses were the most valuable of all booty, and especially a horse capable of carrying the weight of a knight and enduring the strain, noise, and terror of a battle. But if in the end the horse fell, then the knight was half-disarmed and easily captured. Indeed, it is even somewhat unfair to blame some of these invulnerable cavaliers for not fighting to the death. Arrows and swords slid harmlessly off their armor and it took an exceptional ferocity to get killed if the enemy was determined to take one alive. It was easier to beat the knights down and then tie them up than it was to kill them.

Many were killed in battle. Massacres of prisoners were fairly infrequent—there was an impressive one after the battle of the *Ager Sanguinis,* and occasional others after the storming of castles, but never in any systematic fashion. Saladin's policy toward the warrior monks from 1187 onward was an exception to the rule, and before that date neither Templars nor Hospitalers had been executed. If a knight had money, he was usually able to obtain his release from captivity on payment of a ransom (except during the reign of Nur ed-Din, who was not keen on restoring enemy combatants to freedom). The same was true of eminent Moslem prisoners. Poor prisoners of war became slaves, but they were not compelled to abjure their faith, or only in cases where it was judged the equivalent of capital punishment, and then in most cases the Frankish prisoners preferred death. Those who died rather than surrender were many. A man might live through thirty battles only to fall at last in the thirty-first, and even generals rarely died in their beds.

Not one of the kings of Jerusalem was killed in battle: the King's person was regarded as sacred and was the object of special protection, even in the thick of the fight, while the enemy had more to gain from taking the King alive than from killing him. Only Baldwin I died as a result of wounds, and these he got during a raid against the Bedouin, who cared little for his royal rank. Baldwin II was twice taken prisoner but was never seriously wounded. He lived to a respectable age. Fulk I, it will be remembered, died while still at the height of his powers, as a result of a hunting accident, and his two sons, Baldwin III and Amalric I, died young, of illness. Baldwin IV was already doomed by his leprosy to a short life, and was probably finished off by a fever which shortened his agony. All of them, however, were excellent soldiers.

Of the princes of Antioch, only Tancred died of illness. Roger of Salerno was killed at the *Ager Sanguinis* and Bohemond II in Cilicia, Raymond of Poitiers perished at Fons Murez, and all three fell with the greater part of their knights, when it would probably have been possible for them to ransom themselves later if they had surrendered, since the value of their heads was common knowledge. Only two counts ruled over Edessa. Joscelin I died as a result of an accident which occurred while he was supervising mining operations, and Joscelin II died as a prisoner of Nur ed-Din. Of the rulers of the county of Tripoli, only Bertrand of Toulouse died a natural death, after he had been in the Holy Land for three years. Raymond of Saint-Gilles died—when he was over sixty—of the aftereffects of injuries received in a fire; William-Jordan of Cerdagne was killed by an arrow, possibly on Bertrand's orders; Pons, Bertrand's son, was killed when fleeing across country after a defeat, and his son, Raymond II, was killed by the Assassins. Raymond III, the last of the line, died after the fall of Jerusalem, of grief more than sickness. This, in the circumstances, amounts to a natural death, but one even sadder than that of Roger of Salerno or Raymond of Poitiers.

There were leaders, like the two last-named princes, who died in despair at having led their armies to disaster, an emotion not unlike the despair of the old Roman generals who flung themselves on their swords rather than face dishonor. Baldwin I, who escaped alone after his defeat at Ramleh in 1102 to build up a fresh army, may have shown a greater courage because his passionate love for his kingdom was stronger than any other feeling. The Franks' courage was proverbial and generally admired, because the knights had the cult of honor and in the Holy Land this cult had grown to remarkable proportions because of the stimulant provided by the presence of the infidel.

THE MYSTIQUE OF WAR

Usama compared the courage and ferocity of the Franks to that of wild beasts, and this was also the way in which Europeans once tried to explain the fearlessness of the "savage" African and Indian warriors. In fact, it is well known that nothing could be less animal than the courage of primitive peoples. It is a courage built up painfully in the course of prolonged initiation trials in which the future warriors are conditioned from childhood to endure what are sometimes real tortures, and also a careful psychological training aimed at overcoming fear in all its forms and exalting the ability to resist pain. The training of a medieval warrior was certainly more rudimentary, with less of ritual and "magic" about it, since Christianity had proscribed as impious anything which might have survived of pagan practices of this kind among the Germans and Scandinavians, but the training still existed. It was hard, and to the adolescent of noble birth the idea of sanctity was inseparable from that of courage itself and of physical

endurance for its own sake. It is an undeniable fact that the impulse of the Crusades provided a most valuable stimulant for this, so to speak, natural warrior mystique, a fact which has already been noted earlier in this book. Much has been said about chivalric piety and the piety of the Crusaders, a piety which often found its supreme expression in courage. It is worth noting that knights in the Holy Land were probably no more pious than those in Europe, but they were in general braver.

It can be assumed that they were less reluctant to shed "pagan" blood than Christian, but the history of wars in Europe teaches us that no one was afraid of shedding Christian blood and that the rough warriors of the eleventh and twelfth centuries were not unduly fearful of incurring damnation by splitting their countrymen's skulls. The Crusades brought to war an atmosphere of poetry and greatness, and even of purity and sacrifice, which was lacking elsewhere.

It is a fact that the ambitions of the Crusading leaders and their vassals were quite bluntly terrestrial, and even the pious Fulcher of Chartres does not hesitate to present the Crusade as a profitable undertaking primarily on a material level. It would be idle to assume that in this army of volunteers, the leaders were all ambitious vulgarians while the bulk of the knights—who, rich or poor, belonged to the same social class as their leaders—were made up of pure soldiers of Christ. There were good and bad in the army, men like Emich of Leisingen as well as those like Hugh of Payens, and the testimony of historians and of the *chansons de geste* seems to indicate that when it came to fighting, all of them allowed themselves to be carried away by a warlike frenzy which transformed them into heroes of the faith and candidates for martyrdom. It is not easy for us to imagine how much this civilization, which was based on the love of war, had in it of serious and deeply human exaltation. The Moslems of the period were amazed, even though they had their own traditional warrior mystique, perhaps because they had thought they were dealing with ignorant savages.

But the strength of the Franks did not lie only in their armor and their strategy. They did belong to a genuine civilization, suddenly and deeply aware of its own existence, and confronting the East with its own particular weapons because it had no others. It was a civilization which already possessed a rich past of traditions, moral values, myths, and dreams.

The *chanson de geste*—which was not intended for an educated elite—exalts suffering and death above victory. Any people or social class whose vision of the world is essentially tragic has already reached a high degree of moral maturity. The *Song of Roland,* which was written (or at least written down) at the time of the Crusades, without being the story of a Crusade properly speaking, tells us a great deal more about chivalry than the historians do. The hero, formidable to his enemies but gentle and humble with his friends, is "clear of face, broad of shoulder and narrow of hips"; he is prodigiously strong and possesses a horse of exceptional worth, glittering armor, and a miraculous sword studded with relics. He is the saint of a new kind of paradise. Saint Maurice, and to an even greater extent Saint George, with his shining armor and his white horse, are this knight's brothers in arms. Yet these heroes are not loved for their strength but for their weakness.

Roland has certainly slain a hundred, four hundred of the enemy; with the single blow of his fist he can shatter steel helmets, make the eyes start from men's heads and their brains spill. All this is necessary to sustain his reputation. But what matters is that he is ultimately vanquished. He can do no more; he drags himself along, bleeding, with his brains dripping over his ears, until he faints from weakness. Dying, he seeks out the bodies of his comrades, weeps and laments and prays for their souls, overcome with tenderness and pity. He dies, holding his glove up to God and remembering all the lands he has conquered. And if the angels do come at last to find his soul and carry it to paradise, there is nothing joyous in this ending. His friends, including Charlemagne himself, come and bow down over his corpse, but they have come too late. They sob and tear their hair, mourning for the youth and strength of those who are no more: nothing can ever repair such a loss. Vengeance comes, but it is a poor and useless thing; the beauty of the tale lies in its being the story of a great misfortune.

They are stories of passionate love, but for what? Is it for war? Yes, insofar as war is the symbol of the ultimate test, the greatest grief. The funeral passages of the *chansons de geste* have the value of an exorcism. No one wanted to share the lot of Roland and his twelve peers, whose heroic death was lived again in imagination by generations of warriors and released superfluous reserves of emotion. The death of Roland was the moral justification for all war and gave the rudest soldier a sense of the spiritual grandeur of his calling. One could kill, plunder, rape, and burn villages: the lofty figure of Roland was there to remind men that the warrior—especially when he was a soldier of Christ—carried within him a power of redemption through suffering and a mystical purity.

This note of passionate feeling recurs in all warlike civilizations, and is further strengthened among Christian warriors by a dangerous equivocation. The dying hero is unconsciously imitating the Passion of Christ, and struck down, wounded and bleeding, reduced to a glorious wreck of a human being, he comes closer in his agony to the crucified God. The hero's prestige benefitted from the intensity of feeling which surrounded a God "who suffered for our sins," and it was not for nothing that of all the companions of Charlemagne the most popular was Roland, of whom nothing is known except that he was defeated and killed at Roncevaux. Yet Charlemagne's armies had infinitely more victories than defeats.

Thus armed with a pathetic and purifying concept of heroism, the knights of the twelfth century always had good

reasons for fighting. Faith was one form of a warrior's honor. In the *Chanson d' Antioch,* we find Bohemond's brother Guy exclaiming when he hears the news—false, but he does not know that—of the destruction of the Crusading army: "God, if You have permitted this, no one will serve You any more, for there would be no more honor in Your service!" God had a duty to be a faithful suzerain and protect His vassals. His soldiers had to fight for Him because, all-powerful though He was, He could not reconquer a land He wished to possess by His own means; the land had to be given to Him. The Crusaders' piety also contained a deep need for loyalty and submission, a need which had long been unsatisfied and which, in imagination, fell back on the person of Charlemagne, the great Charles, the good, the wise, the strong, the very incarnation of God the Father and the God of Battles.

In Germany, the dream of the great empire and the sovereign emperor sought for its incarnation in the German emperors, whose power often remained hypothetical and bitterly disputed. In France there was, not the shadow of an emperor, but a king who was much too weak to challenge the memory of Charlemagne, however faintly. God was the undisputed Emperor (and God is generally given the title of Emperor in all the *chansons de geste*) and more remote even than Charlemagne, but living and powerful to all eternity. He was the perfect *seigneur* in whose service was glory.

In practice, it was not easy to serve Him, because He was not there to be seen riding at the head of His army and giving orders. The authority of the real leaders of the Crusade was precarious and constantly open to question. But God's soldiers felt that they were raised to a dignity which placed them above other soldiers, while the cross sewn on their garments as a sign of their divine protection and calling was loved because through it a man belonged to God, as the slave belonged to his master. They believed that its purifying virtues could sometimes absolve them from the worst of crimes. The only crime it would never absolve was cowardice.

A real and obsessional horror of cowardice can be discerned in all the texts of the period, whether they are the work of clerics or laymen. Courage is the great virtue with which all others have to fall into line, and it is clear that medieval man, and the medieval knight in particular, lived under a moral law of a highly individual kind. It was not altogether Christian, although it contained elements of Christianity, but was based on a stoicism, even an asceticism, that was altogether warlike and on the cult of honor. The old Germanic paganism, which had apparently been defeated and forgotten, was exacting its revenge.

The audiences who listened to the *chansons de geste* found Roland's pride in refusing to sound his horn to call for help perfectly natural, although culpable. Roland was afraid of seeming a coward and so bringing dishonor on his whole family. Similar motives prevented even the least brave from retreating so much as an inch in battle. Rather than draw back they would be killed where they stood. Frankish defeats in Syria were more often followed by massacres of the chivalry than by flight or rout (although the Franks were not bent on suicide and on occasion they did flee or surrender). In general, their endurance seemed to the Moslems something miraculous, as also did their fury in battle.

Once they were taken prisoner, they were quite docile, like people who know the game is lost. They were not like the warriors of antiquity who would fall back, in the last resort, on putting an end to their own lives rather than face dishonor, because their religion forbade suicide. Al-Fadil did, however, witness the suicide of a Templar in command of the castle of Beit al-Ahzan. Seeing that his castle had been stormed and set on fire, "when the flames reached his side . . . he flung himself into the fiery abyss, fearless of the burning heat, and from this fire he immediately entered another [that of hell]."[6] One rash or ill-considered word could send a whole body of fighting men to certain death. ("Do you then love your blond head so much . . . ?" In 1187, when the kingdom was in deadly peril, the deliberate waste of a hundred and fifty Templars was a criminal act, but a knight who had been challenged to go and get himself killed was beyond the help of reason.)

Admittedly, this kind of knightly pride was more suitable for knights of the Temple or the Hospital than it was for laymen, because the soldier monks had nothing to lose. They had already bound themselves by the most terrible of oaths never to draw back or calculate the number of the enemy. An utter disregard for death had been elevated to a point of dogma with them, and these men, far from being the most Christian of fighters, were the most abandoned to a completely pagan exultation in combat. The doubts that their religion was later to arouse have been seen. When they were accused of heresy, at a time when after the evacuation of the last Frankish ports in Syria the military orders had lost the reason for their existence, the Templars did not actually make any precise admissions. Their ritual and their rule were such as to forge men of steel, hardened against all fear, even that of hell (this could have been the meaning of the mysterious abjuration of Christ imposed upon the postulant). A knight might have to fight in a state of mortal sin, and no consideration should make him draw back from death. Such heretical doctrines as there may have been in the teachings of the Temple came from a logical twisting of the warrior mystique which was already to be seen in the *chansons de geste*. Ismailian influences provided a new element in this mystique: the brothers of the sect of the Ismailians were also dedicated to death as to a bride, and whether or not they were raised to their state of mystical exaltation by the use of hashish they were ready to die—and to die on the orders of their leader—as if this were a supreme beatitude and an end in itself. So strong was the cult of ritual death in the fulfillment of duty (in this case murder) that mothers were seen celebrating the heroic death of their sons as a triumph, and putting on mourning when they learned that their sons had escaped from the enemy instead of standing still and wait-

ing for death. The Templars, who were after all Christians, were somewhat less fanatical and did not share this cult of murder and longing for death. But they too systematically cultivated a spirit of extravagance and indifference to danger which made them at once useful and dangerous to the kingdom.

By a fairly natural coincidence, the Frankish knights of Syria found themselves in very much the same situation as Roland and his peers—with this difference: that there was no treachery involved and no invincible Emperor to come to their rescue at the mere sound of a horn. Always there were the countless hordes of the enemy, the pagans who came from beyond the mountains in their tens of thousands, and always the same anxiety: ". . . and we were only a small company." According to the situation, they had to refuse battle and stand on the defensive, close together like a wall, or charge headlong forward. The famous charges of the Franks were prodigies of calculated risk, and to train men to this state of discipline took all the moral and physical strength of the knights. Like professional sportsmen they were obliged to keep constantly in training. They were men who spent their whole lives, between the ages of fifteen and sixty, in fighting or in practicing for future fights, and their relaxations seldom lasted long.

War in this country did not stop for the winter, because the winters were not very severe and all months were good for war. Given the frequency of battles, every knight might reasonably expect to be killed in the end, and those who were taken prisoner were not always certain of their release. The wealthiest ransomed themselves sooner or later. Many ended their days as slaves or shut up in dungeons. After Hattin a certain number of the combatants were released on payment of a ransom, but the majority— more than ten thousand of them—were never able to ransom themselves. There were poor knights among them, squires and sergeants, and soldiers of the citizen militia. Al-Imad describes the melancholy processions of tens and hundreds of men roped together in columns being led to Damascus at the same time as the "heads of Christians as numerous as watermelons," and sold in the market very cheap because there were so many of them that no one knew what to do with them. Abu Shama writes: "One of the fakirs accompanying the army had as his share of the booty a prisoner whom he exchanged for a pair of sandals which he needed. And when someone remarked on such a bargain with astonishment, he replied, 'I wanted people to remark on it and to say: these Christian slaves were so numerous and so cheap that one of them was sold for a pair of sandals. Praise be to God!'"[7]

The Slaves

How many of these Christian prisoners were there, between 1096 and 1192? In Asia Minor in 1101 there were a very great many, and these were largely women and children, the men having been killed on the spot. Women who were still young, adolescents, small children—anyone who could be useful was taken. The old and the sick were generally not worth the trouble. The victors divided their spoils, keeping pretty women and attractive children for their own pleasure, while the remainder were scattered around the markets and bought like cattle for domestic purposes.

Children were not worth much: a tenth of the price of a man and a fifth of that of a woman; they were long-term goods which had to be fed and trained, and there was a risk that they might die before they could be useful. Children were of course converted automatically to Islam. The Moslems believed they could do no less than save their souls. Many probably became excellent Moslems and excellent servants, forgetting their mother tongue and distinguished from their fellows only by their lighter hair and eyes. If they lived, children were better value than adults because they had no regrets for their lost liberty or their native land. Even children still at the breast were bought. (In 1191 Saladin bought back a baby of three months and returned it to its Frankish mother who, in her delight, put it to her breast at once. The purchaser would have been obliged to procure a nurse for his little slave.)

Women were generally employed in domestic work, or were put to work in textile workshops or at spinning and other skills if they were young enough to learn a trade. If they were still in their teens, or very pretty, they might be bought for a rich man's harem, becoming the slaves of their master's wives, and there was even a chance that they might become favorites themselves. Several thousand Frankish women were sold in 1101, and captives were obviously taken in the various campaigns throughout the century. Many were captured from Conrad III's army in 1147, and the men of this army were also taken and sold. There were also the defeated of Hattin and the fifteen thousand poor Franks from Jerusalem.

Slavery, for adults, was a living death. Families were broken up, unless a wealthy and kindhearted purchaser thought of buying a whole family. Usually they were divided beforehand by the slave merchant, who had nothing to gain from keeping the small family units in his caravan. It was more practical to group people according to their price and the purpose for which they would be used.

The slaves were evaluated according to their abilities, their trade, or their physical strength. One legend has it that a Christian bishop who was a talented sculptor suffered martyrdom for refusing to carve an "idol," when he would have been able to earn a great deal of money if he had shown himself a docile workman. In fact Moslems had no use for carved idols, but slaves who had any skill in a particular art were expected to use it, and frequently were well rewarded for doing so. Young, strong men were used in building work (the same was true of Moslem prisoners of war in Frankish Syria), and their lot was no harder than that of any other laborers, because workmen were always very poorly paid. Slaves were fed and housed, and in

theory their masters were not entitled to inflict serious bodily harm on them. But in practice a slave was dead to society; he had no appeal against his master and was severely punished if he ran away.

Slavery as an institution was so deeply rooted in custom that no one thought of finding it unfair. In the West it had practically died out, but the Franks became accustomed to it very quickly in the East. There were slave markets in every Frankish city, and the King of Jerusalem's armies captured and sold into slavery the inhabitants of conquered strongholds. Moreover, the Franks themselves practiced slavery to a certain extent. The great lords had slaves among their servants, and prisoners of war were sometimes sent to forced labor, though for a limited time. The institution never became an accepted habit with Frankish society. The slave trade was a business like any other, and professionals in the traffic were not interfered with in the exercise of their trade. (Moreover, slavery was too powerful an institution for the government to attempt to suppress it.) But it may be said that the Franks regarded it as simply a local custom to be respected but not necessarily adopted.

The reason the Franks had such a bad reputation as slaves—and they were notorious for adapting to slavery very badly—was that they came from a land where people were not sold in the marketplaces. (This is not to say that any of the other peoples were easily resigned to it; the few details mentioned, almost in passing, by Arab chroniclers do however suggest that the Franks, who were perhaps more demonstrative than the Orientals, showed their misery in a more obvious fashion, and the cases already quoted, which are reported by Usama, show that this revulsion from slavery was not unduly frequent.)

The fact was that no idea of degradation was necessarily attached to the word "slave" in the East. Relations between master and slave, even including the actual buying and selling, were a part of normal human relations and too thoroughly accepted in everyday life to arouse any rebellion.

A slave who was chosen as a concubine might well be honored and treated with respect even though she remained a slave, and an able and conscientious slave could become a friend of his master. To have been sold as a result of some misfortune or a defeat in battle was not necessarily shaming, and strictly speaking the purchaser was not acquiring the persons themselves but only a right to their labor.

The only form of slavery officially practiced in our own day is the use of prisoners of war for forced labor, which is a custom as old as the world. Systems of concentration camps and other forms of slavery rest on the principle of disciplinary sanctions against individuals guilty of some infringement of the law (even when this infringement is imaginary and simply intended to justify the practice of forced labor). In the Middle Ages, this aspect of slavery also existed: people who were unable to pay their debts and insolvent criminals who had been sentenced to a fine could be sold as slaves. It can even be said that the conditions of factory workers, miners, and even of workers on the land in our own era is sometimes not very far removed from slavery, because there can be no real freedom for a badly paid man who is completely dependent on his employer and condemned for life to a basically servile condition. Slaves who had lived on one estate for generations had their own families, their own living accommodation, and work assured, and could feel perfectly free so long as they did not want to move away. It was different for a man who had once been free: his was then primarily a social fall.

To foreigners, slavery meant a total and hopeless uprooting and the cruelest mental torment for families who were separated. Consequently slavery, which was generally accepted by law and approximated in time of peace to a system of ensuring cheap labor, became in time of war the most terrible of all misfortunes.

Ever since the Turkish invasions, the East had been permanently at war. In the eleventh and twelfth centuries, the number of Armenians, Greeks, Arabs, Syrians, and Franks who were sold into slavery as a result of the various armies' campaigns was immense, the equivalent of an entire nation of "displaced persons." To these unfortunates were added the travelers captured by pirates and robbers on the great highways, who were nearly as numerous as the war victims. These, since they were bound by no rules of war but simply by the whims of professionals in the traffic, were even more irremediably lost than the rest. A general in war could be held responsible for his prisoners and they could be ransomed from him (it will be remembered that Manuel Comnenus succeeded in negotiating with Nur ed-Din for the release of six thousand Christian prisoners of war, the majority of whom had been slaves for more than ten years). No one could get back the victims of a pirate, whose trade was in any case illegal and whose victims had long been sold to slave traders who were half pirates themselves. This was merchandise of whose origins everyone preferred to claim ignorance.

It is hard to imagine the condition of these vast numbers of Western pilgrims, travelers, and Crusaders being moved in a series of forced marches across the country, examined, bought, and taken to mines, farmyards, harems, or middle-class homes in a country whose language they did not understand and whose climate and customs were completely strange to them. There was a reasonable chance that they might sometimes come across a fellow countryman, but they were frequently cut off from all contact with their past lives. Those who were not young or clever, and learned only the rudiments of Arabic, lost even their language and were doomed to a gradual process of debasement.

Their ethnic type and their ignorance of the language made escape almost impossible for them, and in any case, there was little chance of escape when there were hundreds of miles to be traveled on foot. Christian slaves were sent into provinces as far as possible from the Frankish states or into big cities with a well-organized police force. The women spent the rest of their days carrying jars of water from the well to the house or scrubbing floors—like pack animals, mute and anonymous, waiting for their ration of food and rest at night on the bare ground in some outhouse. For the younger and prettier, if they were lucky enough to escape the brutality of the soldiery on the actual battlefield, the attentions of their master became a happiness which, at whatever cost, at least saved them from a slow process of decay. A woman chosen as a concubine, even an inferior one, was treated with honor, and she rose even higher in the hierarchy of the harem if she had children.

(It is a curious thought that popular legend made the Margravine Ida of Austria the mother of Zengi. This great lady, who was as pious as she was gallant, would probably have preferred a place among the ranks of the martyrs for the faith. She disappeared without trace and was probably slain or trampled to death in the battle, and her mutilated body, robbed of its rich clothes, left a prey to the vultures and jackals somewhere among the great heap of bodies of men and horses. The poor woman might well have turned in what, for want of a better word, might be called her grave with indignation to hear herself—one of the first ladies of Germany—transformed by posterity into a Moslem's concubine. It is not easy to imagine the Moslems bestowing such a dubious honor on the memory of a great Arab princess. It is a fact that the Franks showed little jealousy of the honor of their women. But the legend of the Margravine was an unconscious popular comfort: the fathers, husbands, and brothers of each of these vanished women could console themselves with the hope, the only one that remained to them, that she had escaped the worst and that she was living somewhere rich, honored, and happy and the mother of fine children, even if they were pagans . . . and that it was Frankish women who were giving the enemy their bravest warriors.)

Slaves judged beautiful enough to deserve a happy life were rare; girls and young women were sold to brothels, luxury class or otherwise, and there they did not live long. Perhaps the fate of those vigorous matrons who were capable of hard work was not so unenviable after all. Young boys, if they were pretty, were also destined for their masters' pleasure. Neither the Turks nor the Arabs had any prejudice against homosexuality (frowned on by pious men but sanctioned by custom and widely practiced). Great chieftains—Zengi in particular—surrounded themselves with pages and minions, and caliphs and sultans had their male as well as their female favorites. There was a strong chance of a child slave finding a master with a fondness for boys. If he was intelligent, or had a good voice, or was gentle and considered suitable to serve in the harem, he was also a likely candidate for castration.

Frankish children of all ages—and there were many in the Crusading armies of 1101 and among the civilian captives during the hundred years of the war—mingled gradually

with the great mass of slaves from all countries. Even today there are probably Turks and Arabs who are among their descendants, and totally unaware of the tiny drop of Western blood in their veins. For adults, especially men over thirty, there was no hope, because unless they were highly qualified craftsmen they were condemned to a life of hard work, treated little better than animals, with nothing to do but dream regretfully of their native land, so far away and so very different. A few slaves did obtain their freedom, but they were a small minority. When the Emperor Manuel preferred to ransom six thousand Christians instead of capturing Aleppo, it cannot have been the liberated prisoners who thought of accusing him of treason to Christendom.

Reynald of Châtillon remained a prisoner for sixteen years: a record for an important person. As Prince of Antioch he did not live in a dungeon underground, or work in the mines, but was able to lead a fairly comfortable existence. Even so, for a man devoured by his insatiable passion for action, those sixteen years must have been years of torture. Baldwin II spent six years of his life in captivity; Raymond III of Tripoli, eight years; Joscelin II, nine years—until his death. There is no way of knowing how many knights died in captivity, but they were many, especially among the military orders, which did not pay ransoms. Moreover, some Turkish chieftains like Nur ed-Din did not let their prisoners go even on payment of a ransom. If there had been no news of a man for seven years, he was regarded as dead and his wife was allowed to remarry, but some of these living dead did come back. The knight Gauffier already mentioned was captured by the Egyptians

in 1103 and came back after thirty-four years, having been released without a ransom (who would have paid it? Everyone thought he was dead) because he was old and there seemed to be no point in keeping him any longer. Ordinary soldiers who either managed to escape or were released by kindly masters also came back like this from time to time and, if they were not too old, went back to the army or took ship for Europe.

There is no record of these thousands of adventures, fantastic, tragic, or merely ordinary because they were so frequent, or even sometimes improbably lucky, which happened in the course of a century of Crusades to tens of thousands of pilgrims. Those lucky enough to make their way back to their countrymen told their adventures, and their family and friends remembered them. But people in the East had heard it all before, and in Europe there were so many tall stories going about that it was not easy to tell truth from lies. Most of these lost men—and lost women—had no one to tell their stories to and ended their days on farms and in workshops, dead to their families long before their actual deaths.

Notes

1. Anna Comnena, *Alexiad,* IV, ch. 6.

2. *Anonymi Gesta Francorum* (ed. Bréhier), p. 53.

3. *Ibid.,* p. 94.

4. William of Tyre, *R.H.C.Occ.,* I, p. 254.

5. *Anonymi Gesta Francorum,* p. 203.

6. Quoted by Abu Shama, *R.H.C.Or.,* IV, p. 208.

7. Imad ed-Din, quoted by Abu Shama, *R.H.C.Or.,* IV, p. 289.

Joan M. Hussey (essay date 1969)

SOURCE: "Byzantium and the Crusades 1081–120" in *A History of the Crusades, Vol. II: The Later Crusades, 1189–1311,* edited by Kenneth M. Setton, University of Wisconsin Press, 1969, pp. 123–51.

[*In the following essay, Hussey offers a brief history of the Crusades from the point of view of the Eastern Christian Byzantine empire, discussing the conflicts that arose between the Eastern Christian rulers and the Western European Christian Crusaders.*]

The middle part of the eleventh century was a watershed in the history of the Byzantine empire. It is only necessary to compare the successful expansion of the frontier under Basil II and his determined onslaught on the aristocracy with the straitened circumstances of Alexius I Comnenus and the steady growth in the power of the great military families. The period of transition was characterized by a bitter struggle between the civil and military parties. The accession of Alexius Comnenus in 1081 marked the end of a half century which had seen a swift succession of inefficient or ill-fated rulers. He, his son, and his grandson among them ruled for almost a hundred years. But even their statesmanship could only check the ring of hostile powers, and at home they often had to accept, and use, precisely those elements which some of their greatest predecessors had been most anxious to curb. Indeed, from the end of the eleventh century and throughout its precarious existence in the later Middle Ages, the two decisive factors which molded the history of the empire were the predominance of the military aristocracy, to which the Comneni belonged, and the steady growth of feudal and separatist elements. The inevitable corollary was the impossibility of restoring the systems of government and defense which had been the twin pillars of the middle Byzantine empire. Effective central administration and the farmer-soldier as the mainstay of the armed forces virtually vanished with the death in 1025 of the greatest Macedonian emperor, Basil II. After the follies of the civil party, it was left to rulers drawn from a wealthy landed family to use what resources were available, and it was only by reason of Comnenian statesmanship that the empire, during most of the twelfth century at any rate, was able to hold its own among the rising Slav and Latin powers and to check the various Moslem potentates.

The way in which the young but astute Alexius Comnenus came to the throne in 1081 has already been traced.[1] With the help of his own native wits and the support of his family, including his redoubtable mother Anna Dalassena, he weathered "the stormy waters of government" which threatened him. But the first ten years of his reign revealed difficulties which were to recur throughout the twelfth century. At home the treasury was short of money, while recruitment for the navy and army slackened seriously. Abroad Alexius' authority was challenged on all sides, for he was ringed by enemies in Asia Minor, in the Balkans and beyond, and in Italy. Much of Anatolia was in the hands of the Selchükid Turks, and the empire was thus deprived of an important source of manpower and wealth. The native recruitment of its army and of its navy suffered accordingly, and, further, its trade, as well as its defense, was adversely affected by the decline of its maritime strength, at a time when the Italian powers were developing apace.

It was indeed from the west, from the Normans and later the growing Italian maritime cities, that Alexius' most dangerous foes were to come. In the months immediately succeeding his coronation, imperial defense and imperial diplomacy were concentrated against the Norman Robert Guiscard, whose flagrant and persistent attacks on Byzantine territory bore out Anna Comnena's belief that he "desired to become Roman emperor",[2] Between Alexius' accession in April 1081 and the arrival of the First Crusade in 1096, the Comnenian came to terms with the Selchükid ruler of Rūm, Sulaimān, thus temporarily stabilizing the position in Anatolia. He made various diplomatic moves in the west, seeking help against Guiscard. He enlisted the naval support of Venice and obtained mercenaries from Sulaimān. He kept a wary eye on the Balkans and fomented revolts in the Norman lands in Italy. Though Guiscard's unexpected death in 1085 was opportune for Alexius and was followed by Norman withdrawal from Greek territory, it entailed no more than a truce in the duel between Constantinople and the Latins; in the immediate future Bohemond, the son of Guiscard, was to carry on his father's aggressive and ambitious policy.

This early period of Alexius' reign revealed certain important factors which no Byzantine ruler could afford to neglect. In particular, the various minor principalities in the Balkans were potential enemies whose defection might turn the balance; overwhelming disaster might threaten from the roving Pecheneg or Kuman tribes beyond the Danube; maritime help was required, even at the cost of ever-increasing trading privileges, thus piling up economic problems and the ill-will of the native Greeks towards the Italian cities, first Venice, and then Pisa and Genoa. In the east, the diplomatic situation at this time was perhaps more favorable than in the west or in the Balkans. The death of Sulaimān of Rūm, the partition of the sultanate, and the mutual hostility of the emirs had considerably eased the position and, as always, the precarious balancing of forces in the Moslem world gave scope of which Byzantine diplomacy was quick to take advantage.

This situation had been exploited to the full by the resourceful Alexius. It was, however, radically changed by the coming of the western crusaders, for Greek and Latin aims were marked by fundamental differences. It is unlikely that Alexius invited the crusade by appealing to Urban II[3]; the Byzantine need was for mercenaries or auxiliaries under imperial control to be employed as required, whether in the Balkans or in Asia Minor. Latin concentration on Syria, and particularly Palestine, the natural goal of the devout crusader, and the refusal of the westerners to put the needs of Byzantine foreign policy before their own individual ambitions inevitably led to mounting hostility between eastern and western Christendom during the twelfth century.

The advent of the Latin crusaders and their establishment in the eastern Mediterranean may have influenced, but did not dominate, Alexius' policy at home and abroad. The more detailed account of the first few crusades[4] has already demonstrated Comnenian adaptability and clearsighted recognition of the real danger, never far below the surface, of a western attack on Constantinople itself. Alexius' exaction of homage and fealty, and of an oath to restore former Byzantine territory, and his genuine coöperation with western military leaders, particularly in providing essential supplies and guides, show his understanding of the feudal tie and its obligations, and his determination to control and direct the adventure. He reaped his reward in western Asia Minor, where land was regained, but with the capture of Antioch in 1098 and the astute maneuvering of his enemy, the Norman Bohemond, he received his first real check. Antioch, though uncontestably Byzantine and recently in imperial hands, became the center of a virtually independent principality ruled by Guiscard's son. The kingdom of Jerusalem and the county of Edessa were farther off, and for various reasons not of such immediate concern to Constantinople.

During the years 1096-1108 Alexius had to reckon with open Norman aggression directed from both Antioch and Italy, and with an insidious propaganda campaign against Byzantium in the west, of which Bohemond was almost certainly one of the main instigators. Fickle, malicious, courageous, tenacious, Bohemond in Syria quarreled with his fellow crusaders and with the emperor, and was worsted by the Turks. He was forced to return to Italy to seek help; there he spread the story that the crusaders had been betrayed by the Byzantines, and even suggested the conquest of Constantinople, a feat at which he himself aimed in his renewed attack on Greece in 1107, when he landed at Avlona. But he had no more success than his father, and was defeated by Alexius. By the treaty of Devol (Deabolis; 1108) Bohemond had to recognize the overlordship of Alexius and his son John, and to promise to hold Antioch as a fief and to give military service to the emperor. He also swore that "there shall never be a patriarch of our race, but he shall be one whom your Majesties shall appoint from among the servants of the great church of Constantinople",[5] for the appointment of a Latin patriarch (Bernard of Valence) to the ancient see of Antioch had caused great offense in Byzantium. Tancred, who was at the time acting for his uncle in the principality, refused to implement this treaty, and Antioch long continued to be a center of opposition to Constantinople. But Alexius had at least checked Bohemond and guarded his western approaches.

The defeat of Bohemond indicated the steady increase of Alexius' strength. His prestige grew commensurately. He held the balance between the Serbian principalities of Zeta and Rascia in the Balkans; in 1104 he married his son and heir John to a Hungarian princess, thus recognizing the increasing importance of Hungary in Balkan and Adriatic politics; he organized campaigns against the Selchükids in Anatolia. Although he excelled at playing off one power against another, his weapons were not only diplomatic ones. Indeed diplomacy alone would not suffice to build up the military and naval strength of the empire, and imperial attention and astuteness were therefore also constantly directed towards the improvement of internal affairs.

Amid fundamental changes which distinguish the Comnenian from earlier periods, the old Byzantine conception of the imperial office still remained unchallenged, as the *Alexiad* demonstrates. At home Alexius was a vigorous administrator and a keen churchman, aware of his responsibilities in both secular and spiritual spheres. His support of orthodoxy and of the church was unwavering. In acute financial difficulties in the early years of his reign, he had incurred ecclesiastical displeasure by pawning certain church treasures. Differences over property did not, however, sour his good relations with the church. Alexius led the campaigns against heresy, chiefly Bogomilism,

already entrenched in the Balkans and now creeping into the capital itself. It is even possible that the emperor's mother Anna Dalassena became tainted with heresy.[6] Though armed with military force as well as powerful theological arguments, even Alexius could not root out the insidious dualist heresy which exploited national feeling in Bulgaria against the imperial conquerors and their churchmen, and various forms of dualism lingered on in the Balkans long after 1204. Alexius was more successful with the theological aberrations of intellectuals, and the philosopher and scholar John Italus, for instance, was made to recant his "errors" from the pulpit of Hagia Sophia.[7]

Monasticism received full imperial support. Alexius regulated life on Mt. Athos, and encouraged reform and new foundations on and around Patmos, and elsewhere. His wife, the empress Irene, did likewise; the regulations for her house in Constantinople reveal everyday life in an ordinary nunnery, as well as the foundress's practical nature. The careful detail found in monastic charters, or ecclesiastical reports, or recorded in the *Alexiad,* admirably illustrate the imperial sense of values. However precarious the foreign situation, however imminent the threat of invasion or treachery, no Byzantine emperor could afford to neglect what was universally regarded as one of his most important responsibilities.

Alexius' main administrative concern was with problems of finance and defense. Both had been inefficiently dealt with by his more immediate predecessors. Though he did not introduce radical changes in policy—the taxes for instance continued to be farmed out, thus increasing the taxpayers' burden—he did to some extent attempt to check the debasement and inflation which had been chronic from the mid-eleventh century onwards.[8] He ruled that a nomisma should have the value of four silver coins (miliaresia), only a third of its original value, thus effecting a devaluation the impact of which extended to the poorest classes. The population was also burdened with obligatory labor services and billeting. By these acts Alexius contrived to extract for the treasury the maximum revenue, and the government found some relief from its financial straits and could build up its military and naval defenses.

The mainstay of the Byzantine army in Alexius' day was no longer the native soldier-farmer with his small heritable military holding, though the Comneni did from time to time settle prisoners of war on the land in this way. Cecaumenus's continuator, who wrote at the beginning of Alexius' reign, speaks at length on military matters. It is noticeable that he says a good deal about mercenaries, who had become a particularly vital element in the Byzantine army in the eleventh century, and on whom Alexius had at first largely to rely. He also drew on levies, particularly of lightarmed infantry, from the great secular and ecclesiastical estates. Of particular importance for the future was the device of granting an estate for a specific time in return for military service. The first known grant in *pronoia* is found in the mid-eleventh century, but it is not until Alexius' reign that a military obligation can be traced. The grantee, or *pronoiar,* became known as a rule as the "soldier" (*stratiotes*). Equipped and mounted and accompanied by his contingent of troops, he was of a different social class from the small farming militia. As long as the estate was held by him in pronoia he enjoyed its revenues, and the taxes and dues of the peasant tenants (*paroikoi*) were now collected by him. This financial aspect constituted one of the main attractions of the grant, which at this time was usually made for life while title and disposition remained with the state.

Alexius also made use of the *charistikion,* a device by which monastic property was handed over, in the past usually by ecclesiastical authorities, to the care of a private person. In this way the property was developed, the monastic community was guaranteed an income sufficient for their needs, and any excess went to the *charistikarios.* Alexius found this a convenient way of rewarding individuals and the practice increased during his reign, though the grant remained, as before, without specific conditions. As a method for promoting a more economic development of monastic lands it was sometimes defended by churchmen, but was also sometimes condemned, for it was obviously open to abuse.

The establishment of the Comnenian dynasty in 1081 had marked the triumph of the great military families after their long struggle with the civil aristocracy in the eleventh century. Alexius, true to his upbringing and party, chose to build on those elements which the strongest rulers of the middle Byzantine period had tried to check. He was as statesmanlike and as capable an emperor as Romanus Lecapenus or Basil II, but he was sufficiently realistic to accept the fact that in changing circumstances he could only recognize and use the landed families. Such a development at a time when Latin feudal states were established in the east, when western crusaders thronged to and fro through the empire, and when the Byzantine court was so often linked by marriage and friendship to Frankish families, has sometimes given rise to the view that it owed much to western feudalism. Recent research has shown, however, that Byzantine feudalism was in many ways the product of its own internal forces and was not a Frankish import,[9] though naturally the influx of Latin crusaders familiarized the Byzantines with many of the customs of western feudalism.

Thus Alexius' domestic and foreign policy was characterized by the growing ascendancy of the military aristocracy. The success with which he maintained Byzantine prestige abroad in the face of major threats on all fronts, particularly from the Normans, and upheld the imperial tradition in church and state, should not blind the historian to those fundamental changes at work within the polity which were ultimately to undermine the imperial authority and to strengthen local and separatist elements.

In essentials the situation remained unaltered throughout the reigns of Alexius' son John II (1118-1143) and his grandson Manuel I (1143-1180). Thus to some extent the policies of John and Manuel were predetermined for them. The main concern of the Comnenian house was the problem of finding some *modus vivendi* with the Normans of Sicily, and then, after the failure of direct male heirs in the Norman house, with the German emperors, Frederick Barbarossa and his son Henry VI, who married the heiress of the Sicilian kingdom and planned the conquest of Constantinople. Generally speaking, the policies of John and Manuel Comnenus were distinguished by variations in emphasis and orientation rather than by fundamental differences. John concentrated more on the east, but was unexpectedly cut short in the midst of his career; Manuel had a more original western policy and a longer reign, but was inevitably alive to eastern problems, if only because Mediterranean politics were now an inescapable factor in European diplomacy. Indeed, events during the sixty-odd years covered by the reigns of these two impressive rulers highlight the startling changes introduced by the crusading movements and by the steady development of western states and Balkan powers.

John Comnenus was the finest of the three Comnenim though his fame has perhaps suffered from lack of any particular contemporary historian of his own. He was a mild and moderate man in his personal life, but an austere disciplinarian in military matters, and his principles and statesmanship continued the best traditions of his house and enabled him to maintain the imperial position. There is a comparative dearth of material for reconstructing the domestic policy of his twenty-five years. John found time to interest himself in the trial of heretics, and, with his wife, the Hungarian Piriska ("Irene"), to promote hospitals and social welfare through a splendid monastic foundation. His agrarian policy was that of his father and was dictated by military needs: he settled prisoners of war (such as the Pechenegs and Serbs) on small farms in return for military service, and continued to grant lands in pronoia for the same reason. For the most part he was a military emperor, who used both diplomacy and force in his successful exploitation of the advantages secured by his father.

John thought in terms of allies and recognition in the west and in the Balkans, and of an offensive in the east. In the Balkans two factors were of importance—the rise to power of the Serb principality of Rascia and the growing encroachment of Hungary south of the Danube. Where he could not hope for direct control—in Hungary, in Rascia, and in Zeta—John intervened in disputed elections. Although Rascia, as also Bosnia, was drawn into the orbit of Hungarian influence—the ruler (župan) of Rascia had married his daughter Helena to Bela the Blind, king of Hungary (1131-1141)—Constantinople on the whole outweighed the Magyars, especially when it came to war, and in 1128 forced Hungary to make peace. Further, after 1131 Byzantium was helped by the understanding between Bela II of Hungary and the pro-Byzantine Conrad III of Germany, and no doubt by Hungary's realization that its Dalmatian ambitions would inevitably antagonize Venice, in which case it might be advisable to have an ally in its powerful Byzantine neighbor.

Byzantium for its part was not averse to reducing the power of Venice, which had been extended in Dalmatia during the later years of Alexius' reign. Venice had applied to John on his accession for a renewal of the trading privileges in the empire which had brought it great wealth, though also great unpopularity. John's attempt to reduce Venetian influence resulted in attacks on Byzantine territory, particularly the islands, during the years 1122-1126. Finally he judged it expedient to make peace and in 1126 renewed the privileges granted by his father. He had to recognize that Venetian enmity would damage his position in Italy. He did, however, attempt to establish good relations with Venice's rivals, Pisa and Genoa. Pisa, which was being approached by Roger II of Sicily, was courted by a Byzantine embassy in 1136, followed by the confirmation of the trading privileges which had been granted it by Alexius Comnenus. The Genoese, who were to play so important a role in the later empire, also wished for a share in imperial trade, and they appear to have been in Constantinople in 1142 for purposes of negotiation.

At the opening of John's reign affairs in Germany and Italy were not unfavorable to him. Emperor Henry V of Germany and pope Gelasius II were at loggerheads and Apulia was rent by feuds. But when Roger II united the Norman lands in southern Italy and Sicily in 1127 and was crowned king in 1130, danger threatened. John sought to counter this by a rapprochement with the German rulers, first Lothair II, who followed Henry in 1125, and then his successor, Conrad III. Throughout he also kept in touch with the popes, who were precariously placed between the Normans and the Germans; he approached first Calixtus II in 1124, and then Honorius II in 1126,[10] with the prospect of ecclesiastical reunion. In particular, he suggested an understanding whereby the pope would have the spiritual, and the "Roman" (Byzantine) emperor the secular, supremacy, though the actual wording of this famous letter is so vague as to defy precise elucidation (which was perhaps what was intended).

With his position to some extent safeguarded by his network of alliances in the west, John in 1136 judged it opportune to attempt the extension of his authority in the east by striking at both Moslem and Christian powers. His goal was full control of Antioch and the implementation of the treaty of Devol which his father had made with Bohemond in 1108. Apart from constant vigilance towards his Selchükid neighbors at Iconium (Konya), John's more particular concern in Anatolia at this time was the rising power of the Dānish-mendids, who had in 1125 captured Melitene. They had penetrated into Cilicia, compelling the Roupenids to pay tribute, and moving still further south had defeated the Normans of Antioch, killing Bohemond II in 1130. It was therefore necessary for John Comnenus to safeguard his own frontiers in Paphlagonia and to check the Dānishmendids as a preliminary to the advance south which he himself was planning, and with this in view, during the years 1132-1134 he undertook campaigns in the neighborhood of Kastamonu against the emir Gümüshtigin Ghāzī. John's position was eased by the death of the powerful Gümüshtigin Ghāzī about 1134. Towards the end of 1136 he advanced against the Christian Armenians who had settled in the Taurus and Anti-Taurus districts and took the offensive against the Roupenids of Lesser Armenia, the principality which stood between his domains and the crusading kingdoms. Its ruler Leon I fled to the mountains in 1137 but was captured in the following year and sent to Constantinople. John was thus able to turn his full attention to Antioch.

His intervention was opportune for various reasons. In both Jerusalem and Antioch the throne had passed in 1131 to the female line; problems of succession were already threatening to weaken the Latin principalities. In Antioch at any rate there was a proByzantine party who realized the wisdom of a firm alliance with Constantinople, all the more so since in the north Zengi, the regent (*atabeg*) of Mosul, was daily growing in power. By August 1137 John had reached Antioch, and Raymond of Poitiers, the husband of the Norman princess Constance, was compelled to swear allegiance. A year later John made a solemn entrance into the city. Even so, the Byzantine, and indeed the Christian, cause was weakened by lack of Latin support. It was largely for this reason that John had been unable to make any real headway against the Moslems in northern Syria earlier in 1138, and later in the year he judged it wiser to leave Antioch, where riots were being stirred up against the Greeks.

Afraid of papal and Sicilian activities in the west, as well as the Dānishmendids in Anatolia, John returned to Constantinople in 1138. Here he renewed his links with Germany and negotiated a marriage between Bertha of Sulzbach, the sister-in-law of Conrad III, now undisputed king, and his son Manuel. After further campaigns against the Dānishmendids, he again turned his attention towards Antioch. Cinnamus suggests that John, who had every reason to distrust the Latins, now intended to create a frontier principality, consisting of Adalia, Antioch, and Cyprus, for his son Manuel,[11] or he may possibly have had in mind the revival of the old duchy of Antioch,[12] only on a wider basis. Byzantine intentions were bitterly resented by an influential party among the Latin knights and clergy in Antioch. Both laity and clergy clearly had everything to lose if John's demand in 1142 for the surrender of the entire city was met. Therefore the prince of Antioch repudiated the agreement of 1137, ostensibly on the ground that he could not dispose of his wife's inheritance. John clearly intended to force the issue. He wintered near Mamistra (1142-1143), and from a letter he wrote to king Fulk of Jerusalem, we may surmise that he hoped to extend his authority southwards as soon as he had taken control in Antioch. But in the spring of 1143 he died of a septic wound.

Thus Christian feuds and John's untimely death prevented any effective drive against the Moslems, and in the next year Zengi captured Edessa, thus provoking the ill-fated Second Crusade.

Before he died John had had his youngest son Manuel, who was with him in Cilicia, acclaimed emperor. Manuel

Comnenus was exceedingly tall, with a complexion so dark that his enemies taunted him with being like a negro. He possessed great physical strength and endurance and could hold his own with the best of the western knights (though it seemed odd to his subjects that he should even wish to do so). He had charm of manner and was a gracious host; he had too the family taste for letters and had read widely, though his mind was vivacious and lively rather than profound or deeply intellectual, and, as the discerning Cinnamus remarked, he tried to make up for inadequacies in logic and dialectic by being exceedingly quick witted.[13] Both Greek and Latin contemporary writers testify to his medical knowledge, which he did not hesitate to use, as for instance when he set Baldwin's arm when it was broken on a hunting expedition.

Manuel was removed by two generations from the days of the First Crusade, and he got on with westerners in a way which would have seemed unbecoming to his grandfather Alexius, still more to his earlier predecessors. His mother was a Hungarian, his first wife the German Bertha of Sulzbach (renamed Irene by the Greeks), his second the Norman princess Maria of Antioch. His little son Alexius was betrothed to a daughter of the French Louis VII. Half a century had witnessed great changes in the eastern Mediterranean, and political and economic circumstances, as well as imperial marriages and friendships, had brought an influx of Latins into all parts of the Byzantine empire, thus sowing seeds of future trouble. It has even been suggested that Manuel sought to renew the internal vigor of Byzantium by deliberately introducing Latin elements into the empire.[14] At the same time he was essentially Byzantine: he would concede nothing to the west insofar as his imperial position was concerned, for like any true medieval "Roman" emperor he regarded himself as the heir of a long line stretching back to Caesar Augustus.

Manuel's outlook and needs determined his policy at home and abroad. He had to establish his somewhat unexpected succession to the throne and secure allies among the western powers. And he even went a step further by aiming at active rehabilitation of Byzantine authority in the west. His ceaseless diplomatic moves, like those of other powers interested in the Mediterranean, were characterized by a fluidity, a readiness to consider offers from any quarter, a reluctance to close any door, which created a constantly shifting situation, though the main trends are clearly discernible.[15]

Like Alexius and John, Manuel knew that his interests conflicted with those of Sicily. At the very start of his reign in 1143 he was apparently willing to consider a rapprochement with Roger II, who had asked for a Greek princess to wed his son, but this plan fell through. The first major phase of Manuel's Italian policy was primarily one of military intervention, and concluded with his defeat in Sicily in 1158; after this he changed his methods somewhat, confining himself on the whole to diplomatic weapons. Throughout he sought to continue his father's alliance with the German ruler, Conrad III, who shared his

hostility to Roger. In 1147 the Second Crusade forced a temporary suspension of their plans. Conrad had taken the cross and was moving east, leaving his ally Manuel isolated in the west and exposed to attack, as well as faced with the passage of crusading armies through his lands. Roger of Sicily, now hostile to Manuel, was trying to rouse the French king, Louis VII, and was himself plotting against the Byzantine emperor. Manuel was able to take little part in the disastrous expedition[16]: he was engaged with Roger, who had attacked Corfu and the Morea (1147) at a time when Manuel might reasonably be supposed to have concentrated his forces in the east to aid the crusaders. Manuel had to safeguard his eastern borders by making a treaty with Mas'ūd, the Selchükid ruler at Iconium, and by getting Venetian help against the Normans at the cost of still further trading privileges. The Normans were driven out, but they took with them an enormous booty and a number of captured Greek silk weavers. At the same time Manuel reinforced his alliance with Conrad when the latter journeyed through the Byzantine empire on his return from the Second Crusade.

By the treaty of Thessalonica (1148) it was evidently agreed that Manuel had some claim on Italian territory. The text itself has not survived, but the account of Cinnamus states that the emperor reminded Conrad of what he had previously undertaken to do, "to restore to Irene [his kinswoman Bertha of Sulzbach] her dowry, Italy . . ."[17] However the word "Italia" may be interpreted—and it has been suggested that it might mean the whole of Italy—it would certainly include the southern Italian lands of Apulia and Calabria. A joint expedition proposed against Roger did not materialize. Manuel's preparations were held up by a Serbian revolt fostered by Hungary and by Venetian intrigues; Conrad was hampered by Welf troubles fomented by Roger, who had by now gained papal recognition and had signed a truce with Eugenius III. But fortunately for Manuel any active western league against Byzantium foundered on the papal fear of increasing Roger's power and the steady pro-Byzantine policy of Conrad. Both Conrad and Manuel were planning an expedition in Italy for 1152, when Conrad died in the February of that year.

The new German ruler, Frederick Barbarossa, managed to come to an understanding with the pope (1153) whereby both agreed that no land in Italy was to be ceded to Manuel, "the king [*rex*] of the Greeks". Undeterred, Manuel still hoped to win Barbarossa over and to continue his western offensive by means of both diplomacy and force. When it suited his plans, the German emperor was, indeed, willing to negotiate with Manuel; there were a number of diplomatic approaches between the two courts, and Frederick even considered taking a Byzantine wife. On Roger's death in 1154 Manuel took advantage of opposition to William I of Sicily, and, without German assistance, he launched his attack. His forces and those of his allies at first gained ground. Frederick I, newly crowned in 1155, evidently wished to assist Manuel, or at least to have some share in the project, but he could not get the support of his vassals and had to go north, not returning to Italy until

1158. Manuel's successes in Apulia aroused the hostility of Venice, and William grew in strength. The Greeks were trapped and badly defeated at Brindisi. Pope Hadrian IV, who had been wooed by Manuel, had judged it expedient to come to terms with William in June 1156. In Germany Frederick was cooling off, and a Byzantine embassy to his court in 1157 had no success. In 1158 Manuel had to sign a thirty years' truce with William, and he evacuated his troops from Italy.

By now Manuel must have realized the difficulties caused by Frederick's imperial ambitions, and perhaps also the hazardous nature of military action in a country where, in spite of lavish expenditure of money, he could count on no secure base and no sure ally. He did not abandon his western policy, but henceforth he concentrated on diplomacy which, if more cautious than formerly, yet still showed his resourcefulness and determination. The flow of embassies and correspondence between Constantinople and the western powers was unceasing. Manuel tried to utilize the rift between the papacy and Barbarossa, negotiating first with Hadrian and then with his successor Alexander III. From 1159 to October 1177 there were cordial relations between Alexander and Manuel and discussion of the terms on which the Byzantine emperor might receive the imperial crown from the pope. Manuel offered financial aid and ecclesiastical reunion. At this time Alexander feared Barbarossa, who was supporting an anti-pope; hence his negotiations with Constantinople, Sicily, and France. But with the formation of the Lombard League, the pope became less dependent on Manuel, and after the treaty of Venice (1177) and the defeat of Manuel at Myriokephalon, any real hope for a Byzantino-papal understanding faded out.

From the outset Manuel had responded to pope Alexander III's overtures, and had also hoped for the support of Louis VII in a concerted attack against Frederick in 1163, which however came to nothing. He then turned to the project of a marriage alliance with Sicily. William I had died in May 1166 and his heir was a boy of thirteen, William II. According to Romuald Guarna of Salerno, Manuel proposed that the Norman should marry his daughter Maria, who was then his heiress (his son Alexius was not born until 1169). She was already betrothed to Bela (III) of Hungary, but apparently Manuel was prepared to throw over this arrangement and its advantages, possibly as a counter-move to Frederick Barbarossa's fourth expedition to Italy in that year (1166), and perhaps with the hope of being himself crowned by the pope as sole emperor should the kingdom of Sicily be united to the Byzantine empire. But the marriage proposal came to nothing, possibly because the news of Maria's betrothal to Bela had become known, though no specific explanation is given, only the cryptic phrase "for various reasons". Later on, after 1170, a second attempt was made, and negotiations were so far carried through that the young William II went to Taranto to meet a bride who never came. It was a humiliating experience for the Norman, all the more so if he realized that Manuel

may have changed his plans because he thought that there might be a possibility of marrying Maria to the heir of Frederick I.

Throughout the second phase of Manuel's western policy (1158-1180) he was also involved in constant negotiation with the various Italian cities, particularly Venice, Pisa, and Genoa. Venice had always had substantial commercial interests in the east; the rapid rise of Pisa and Genoa now introduced rivals and provided Constantinople with alternative allies, particularly in the Genoese. Support could be bought only by trading concessions, as Alexius and John Comnenus had found; further, it was impossible to satisfy one party without arousing the dangerous hostility of others, and in any case the privileged position of foreign merchants within the empire was bitterly resented by the Greeks themselves. Hence the mounting tension in Manuel's reign, and a radical change in relations which was one of the underlying causes of the Fourth Crusade. Common distrust, first of Roger II, and then of Barbarossa, had for a time united Venice and Constantinople. But Venetian suspicion had been aroused by Byzantine activities in Italy, and partially successful designs on Dalmatia, as well as by the concessions granted to their Italian rivals; treaties were made with Genoa in 1169 and with Pisa in 1170.[18] Venetians within the empire had long been hated for their arrogance and envied for their wealth. In 1162 they had taken part in an attack on the Genoese in Constantinople which had annoyed Manuel, who was at that time trying to win Genoese support. He himself may still have resented the Venetian parody of him at the time of Corfu's recapture from the Normans in 1148, when the Venetians had a mock Byzantine ceremony in which the part of the emperor was played by a huge negro. And it is suggested by a Venetian source that his anger had been aroused by his failure to receive the active support of Venice against the Normans, whose ruler he had alienated by withholding the promised Byzantine bride. Thus the accumulated resentment of the native Greek populace coincided with reasons of policy which may have contributed to the carefully planned attack.

On March 12, 1171, all Venetians in the empire were arrested and their goods confiscated. The doge, Vitale Michiele, had to send a fleet to attack Dalmatia and the Greek islands, though he was favorably disposed toward Byzantium and wanted to maintain diplomatic relations. Manuel now realized the danger of an alliance between Venice and Sicily, and began negotiations with Venice. Nicetas Choniates says that he restored Venetian privileges and paid them compensation and made peace,[19] but Venetian sources suggest that the treaty was probably not concluded or relations restored until the following reign, that of Andronicus I.[20] Even then Venetian resentment remained.

In the Balkans and Hungary Manuel scored successes. Rascia, inclined to be independent and open to approach from Latin powers, such as Sicily, had put up irritating opposition, particularly under Stephen Nemanya, who became "župan" in either 1166 or 1167. Stephen approached Hungary and Germany, and tried to stir up trouble in Dalmatia, where Manuel had restored imperial control in 1166. He was finally subdued in 1172 and had to play a humiliating part in Manuel's triumphal entry into Constantinople.

In Hungary, as elsewhere, Manuel took his father's policy a step further. He not only intervened to his own advantage in disputed successions, but went so far as to have in mind the acquisition of the whole country. He proposed a novel solution to end the long hostility between Hungary and Constantinople. After endless diplomacy, he agreed to recognize Stephen III as king in return for his brother and heir Bela as hostage. Bela was to have Hungary's Croatian and Dalmatian lands as appanage, and was to marry Manuel's heiress Maria. The treaty of 1164 was executed only after further fighting, but by 1167 Manuel had Dalmatia, Croatia, Bosnia, and Sirmium. He planned to make Bela his heir, and gave him the name of Alexius and the title of despot. He thus hoped to secure Hungary and incorporate it into the empire, a plan similar to that which he entertained from time to time with regard to Sicily.

The situation changed with the birth of his son in 1169. The betrothal of Bela and Maria was dissolved, and Bela was reduced to the rank of a caesar and married to Agnes of Châtillon, the daughter of Constance of Antioch. With Greek support, Bela succeeded to the Hungarian throne in 1173, and as long as Manuel lived he was loyal to Byzantium, making no attempt to regain lost territory until after 1180. Manuel had thus gained some measure of security in the Balkans and in the north, as well as considerable territory.

In the east, before he was really hampered by Frederick Barbarossa, Manuel successfully developed his father's policy.[21] He asserted his suzerainty, first over the Armenian prince Toros II in Cilicia in 1158, and then over Reginald of Antioch in 1159, where the crowning symbol of his victory was to be the restoration of a Greek, Athanasius, to the ancient patriarchate in 1165. He was on particularly friendly terms with Baldwin III of Jerusalem, and anxious to prevent the encirclement of the crusading principalities by a single Moslem power. Manuel may have foreseen that any drastic reduction of crusading prestige and territory might turn the Latins towards his own lands. But neither his overtures to the ruler of Aleppo, Nūr-ad-Dīn, nor his expeditions with Amalric of Jerusalem against Egypt, could stay the rise of Saladin. Moreover the death of Nūr-ad-Dīn in 1174 affected the political situation in Anatolia, as well as in Syria and Egypt.

Manuel's position in Anatolia had to some extent been safeguarded by the tension between the rival Moslem powers, the Selchükids at Iconium and the Dānishmendids. The eastern ambitions of the former had been kept in check by Nūr-ad-Dīn's support of the Dānishmendids. Now dissident Moslem elements looked to Constantinople for help. Manuel, aware of the Selchükid sultan's quiet consolida-

tion of his position, turned to his own frontier defenses on the marches of Iconium. He refused the overtures of Kilij Arslan II and led an expedition against him in 1176. Showing marked lack of generalship he allowed himself to be trapped in the pass of Myriokephalon, and was prevented from headlong flight only by the firm refusal of his officers to countenance this. What might well have been a wholesale massacre was checked by Kilij Arslan, who again offered terms. Manuel's prestige and that of the Christians in Syria was shaken by this defeat, though his generals still carried on intermittent warfare against Moslem penetration into the Maeander valley. Manuel himself may have felt that his earlier policy towards Iconium, in particular the treaty of 1161,[22] had been mistaken and perhaps opportunist. He had obtained an ally, but only at the cost of permitting the steady growth of a Moslem principality on his very borders. Nicetas Choniates says that the sultan of Rūm observed that the worse the "Romans" were treated, the more splendid were the presents which their emperor gave.[23]

It might be pointed out that the difficulties with Iconium had been fomented by Frederick Barbarossa, at heart an enemy of the empire, who revealed his real plans in a letter to Manuel after Myriokephalon in which he announced himself as the heir of the Roman emperors with authority over the "rex Grecorum" and the "regnum Greciae".

The rise of Frederick Barbarossa and the dramatic humiliation of Myriokephalon should not be allowed to obscure Manuel's achievements and his statesmanship. His diplomacy was marked by a bold attempt to adapt a traditional policy to changing circumstances. His conception of imperial authority might have been held by any Byzantine ruler, but its execution had certain original features, such as his project for uniting the thrones of Hungary and Constantinople in the person of his prospective son-in-law Bela-Alexius, or of Sicily and Constantinople by a marriage alliance with William II (and possibly, earlier, with Roger II), demonstrating by this latter move a flexibility of outlook with regard to the Norman problem. The main threat to the empire was from the western, rather than the Moslem, powers. Manuel did at least succeed in postponing during his lifetime a fresh crusade, which would perhaps have struck its first blow at Constantinople, as in 1204, and if successful in the east would in any case have weakened Byzantine influence there. Almost his last move, the marriage of his son Alexius to Agnes of France, was an attempt to stay the hand of Louis VII, who, with pope Alexander III, was contemplating a new crusade. To condemn Manuel for not having concentrated exclusively on strengthening his position in Anatolia and Syria would be completely to misunderstand the practical needs of Byzantium.

The internal life of the empire at this time shows no marked break with the days of the earlier Comneni. Its main features were concentration on needs of defense, the steady growth in the use of grants in pronoia and of the power of the landowner, and the continuity of the normal activities of a cultured society. As under John Comnenus, the army was well organized and well disciplined. Recruitment presented serious problems. Manuel tried to increase the free population by liberating those who had become enslaved and by settling prisoners of war within the empire. A good many troops were provided by the system of grants in pronoia. Mercenaries were an important element, whether hired on a purely temporary basis, or provided by the various enrolled corps, or furnished by vassals or allies, such as the Serbs or the Selchükids. Nicetas Choniates says that the navy was somewhat diminished by Manuel's policy of allowing the islands and littoral to pay ship-money in lieu of maritime service and duties,[24] but even so, Byzantium was in a stronger position than in Alexius' day, when it had to rely almost exclusively on Venetian maritime assistance.

Foreign policy, however directed, had always been an expensive item in the Byzantine budget. But though burdens fell heavily on the poorer classes, Byzantium was by no means impoverished. In spite of the territorial contraction of the eleventh century and loss of customs revenue by reason of privileges granted to foreign merchants, there were still strong reserves, and lucrative trade was carried on in the great commercial centers of the empire, such as Thessalonica and Constantinople. The riches of Byzantium were the surprise and envy of all visitors; Benjamin of Tudela reports that the Greeks went about looking like princes.[25]

The fundamental difference between this period and that of the middle Byzantine state was however the gradual weakening of the central authority, particularly by reason of grants made to individuals. This was not so acute in Manuel's day as after 1204, but even under him the use of the pronoia had become an established feature of Byzantine administration. The strictly limited and non-heritable character of the grant was in the course of time to be gradually modified, so that the property became more like the western fief handed down from father to son. The grant carried with it the right to collect taxes from the tenants (paroikoi) on the estate, as well as any other duties owed. This system had become so accepted a part of the Byzantine social structure that by the end of the twelfth century it seemed quite normal to speak of all land as being either heritable or in pronoia. It was used of other than landed wealth, and was not reserved for Greeks alone. When Nicetas Choniates spoke of some of the pronoiars as being "half barbarian", he may have been thinking of the steppe peoples settled in the Balkans whose wealth was not in land but in herds and flocks, or even of the Latin knights, such as Renier of Montferrat, to whom Manuel granted what his brother Boniface refers to as "a feudum".[26]

Manuel's reign saw a marked strengthening of the feudal element. Though not hostile to monasticism or the church, Manuel furthered the interests of secular landlords at the expense of ecclesiastical estates when in 1158 he forbade monasteries to add to their land or to the number of their paroikoi, and did not permit alienation of property except to the senatorial and the military (i.e. the pronoiar) classes. Nicetas Choniates remarked on the liberality with which he assigned paroikoi to the pronoiars. But at the same time Manuel did attempt to control the movement of labor and the financial rights of the exchequer. So in confirming the claim to an estate, the imperial charter would give the number of its paroikoi, and new paroikoi could be acquired only if they were without obligations to the fisc, and then only up to a permitted number. The struggle to retain control over the state paroikoi (demosiakoi), which is evident as early as the tenth century, was not abandoned by the Comneni, though in the end, as the Palaeologian period was to show, feudal and separatist forces were to triumph at the expense of the central authority.

Manuel's activities at home included administrative and ecclesiasticla reform. His chrysobulls and rulings deal with subjects ranging from the reorganization of the secular courts in order to expedite justice to decisions on points of ecclesiastical discipline and ownership of church property.[27] For instance, he forbade bishops to linger long in the capital and charged the civil authorities with the responsibility of seeing that they returned to their dioceses. He and his family were generous patrons of monasticism, but like others before him, he made it clear that the proper home of the monk was in the remote countryside and not in the crowded city.

Manuel took a lively and characteristic part in the theological discussions and problems of his day. Disputes over the nature of the sacrifice of the mass, or of the Trinity, divided Byzantine circles, and Manuel's views were not always those of orthodoxy. He evidently fancied his powers of persuasion, and almost abused his imperial position in his attempt to win supporters over to his point of view. Both inclination and political considerations fostered a certain flexibility in Manuel's outlook. He was for instance anxious for a rapprochement between the Orthodox and dissident churches, and embassies went backwards and forwards between Constantinople and Armenia. They were fruitless, for in both churches a solid block of conservative opinion prevented any form of compromise. By his tolerant attitude towards Moslems, Manuel roused vigorous and open protest. His suggestion that his visitor, the sultan of Iconium, should accompany him in the procession to Hagia Sophia was regarded as wholly unsuitable. His view that the abjuration exacted from Moslems could be worded in a more acceptable form did however prevail, and instead of anathematizing the God of Mohammed the convert was required only to condemn Mohammed, his doctrine, and his successors. It is not surprising that Manuel's contemporaries did not always find his views on theological matters acceptable, and it was even considered after his death that he ought to be condemned as a heretic.[28] No taint of this kind could however cling in respect of his policy towards the various forms of the Bogomil, Massalian, and Paulician heresies which persisted within and without the empire. In Constantinople in 1143 two bishops, and then a monk Niphon, were condemned as Bogomils. They had all worked in Anatolia, and evidently the sect was particularly prevalent in Cappadocia. It was also strong in the Balkans, especially Macedonia and Bulgaria.[29] Manuel could do comparatively little to purge these heretical movements. They gained added strength from underlying Slav antagonism to Byzantine, and later Frankish, rule, and were an important factor in adding to the complexity of the situation in the Balkans at the time of the Fourth Crusade.

During the years 1081-1180 the Comnenian house had given the empire three outstanding rulers whose statesmanship and personality blinded contemporaries and later historians to the fundamental nature of the changes at work in Byzantine society and in neighboring polities. Manuel left a minor heir, Alexius II, whose mother was the Latin Maria of Antioch. Hatred of the strong Latin element in the empire had already been shown during Manuel's reign, though directed in 1171 against the Venetian traders. Political circumstances, marriage alliances, Manuel's personal friendships, all helped to bring a flood of westerners into the empire, and long-pent-up hatred against "the accursed Latins" broke out in May 1182, when the people of Constantinople made an indiscriminate attack on all foreigners in the city.

At this point Manuel's cousin Andronicus Comnenus was already preparing to take control. An element of instability and restlessness in his character and an underlying antagonism toward Manuel had prevented him from giving service to the empire or settling on his estates; wandering from court to court, Moslem and Christian alike, he had toured the Near East for a number of years, living on his personality and charm. Now he returned to seize his opportunity and to show that he had views of his own on the nature of imperial rule. The reaction against Maria of Antioch and the Latin elements served his purpose. In May 1182 he was accepted by the city, and in September 1183 was crowned co-emperor with Alexius II. So far this was normal procedure, but Andronicus had an impetuous, violent streak in his make-up. Autocratic and dominating, impatient and impulsive, he could not refrain from the elimination, first of Maria, and then of Alexius, though not of Alexius' widow, the little French princess Agnes ("Anna"), whom he married.

Andronicus instituted a vigorous campaign against administrative corruption and the power of the aristocracy. He tried to protect the lower classes against the extortions of tax collectors, government officials, and landlords, so that those who had rendered unto Caesar what was Caesar's could sleep at ease in the shade of their trees.[30] Thus good salaries were to be paid, suitable men were to be appointed, and the sale of offices was prohibited. For various reasons Andronicus was biased against the aristocracy. Their power and their privileges were incompatible with his conception of imperial autocracy and the well-being of his subjects. The bulls of 1158 and 1170[31] which permitted alienation of imperial grants of land only to the senatorial or military class were revoked in December 1182 in the early months of Andronicus's regency.[32] His anti-Latin bias might have gained some support from the aristocracy, but it was more than outweighed by his open hostility to their own privileged position. The widespread practice of grants, whether in pronoia, or of charistikion, had gone too far to be successfully challenged.

There was strong opposition to Andronicus, who met conspiracy and risings with violence and executions. As external troubles once more threatened, the reaction in his favor rapidly turned to hostility. He lost the support of the military families on whom the empire now depended, and he had no effective weapon with which to ward off attacks from without and revolts from within. Hungary took the offensive and regained Dalmatia and parts of Croatia and Sirmium; Stephen Nemanya shook off his allegiance; in 1185 the Normans of Sicily took Corfu and other islands and advanced to capture Thessalonica. Centrifugal tendencies within the empire were evidenced by Isaac Comnenus, who proclaimed himself independent ruler of Cyprus. Andronicus had tried to stave off western attack by approaching the papacy and by allying with Venice and with Saladin. But news of the dramatic fall and sack of Thessalonica and fear of suffering a similar fate led the people of Constantinople to dethrone and kill Andronicus, the last emperor of the Comnenian house.

The rulers of the dynasty of the Angeli had not the character or qualities of the Comneni. Their policy represented a compromise: it was aristocratic, but not pro-Latin. The difficulties of the empire during the years 1185-1204 were aggravated, but not caused, by the ineffectiveness of the Angeli. Internally the old abuses in the administration reappeared—the sale of offices, the extortions of the tax collector, the oppression and predominance of the landowner. The themes had increased in number despite loss of territory[33]; the provincial governor was overshadowed by the local magnate, thus heralding one of the distinctive features of Byzantium in the Palaeologian age.

Had Isaac II been a statesman of the caliber of John Comnenus he would still have been tried to the utmost. As it was he showed that he was not a mere nonentity. He had to deal first with Norman aggression and then with Hohenstaufen hostility and the Third Crusade. The most pressing problem, once the Normans had been driven from Thessalonica and Durazzo and their fleet recalled from the Sea of Marmara, was in the Balkans, where the discontented Bulgarian provinces were ripe for rebellion and every small Slav principality was easy prey for western mischief-makers. Bulgaria had never wholly acquiesced in its incorporation in the empire in 1018. Religious and political discontent simmered throughout the eleventh and twelfth centuries and came to the surface in the troubled days following the death of Manuel Comnenus. The situation was successfully exploited by two local magnates, Peter and Asen, who successfully reëstablished an independent kingdom and called themselves the *imperatores* (tsars) of the whole of Bulgaria and Vlachia. Fierce controversy has raged around the question of their own ethnic origins, whether Bulgar, Vlach, or Kuman, for in the foundation of the Second Bulgarian empire all three racial groups took part,[34] and the Kumans, for instance, were an important element in the new kingdom. Isaac had already tried to win the support of Hungary by the treaty of 1185 and by his marriage to the Hungarian princess Margaret. He now struggled against centrifugal forces in the Balkans, and after the treachery of his general Alexius Branas, himself led military expeditions during 1186-1187. But he had to accept the situation, and in 1186 Asen was crowned tsar by Basil, the newly established archbishop of Tirnovo. Stephen Nemanya of Rascia made himself "grand župan" of Serbia in 1186, and continued to build up his power at Byzantine expense; he supported the Bulgarian rebels. Imperial authority in the Balkans was therefore being constantly undermined, a situation which the western leaders of the Third Crusade were quick to exploit.

Thus weakened by civil war and campaigns in the Balkans, and without strong military leadership, Byzantium was in no position to control the new crusade or to counter Hohenstaufen ambitions.[35] With the continual deterioration of the crusading position in Syria and Palestine and the comparative failure of the Third Crusade, attention was more and more focussed on the Byzantine empire. Political hostility, keen commercial rivalries, and even the schism between the two churches created a situation in which a concerted western attack on the empire seemed only a question of time. The Third Crusade was a convenient cloak for the ambitions of Frederick Barbarossa, whose son was betrothed to the heiress of the Sicilian kingdom. Frederick traveled through Hungary and the Balkans. He had in 1188 negotiated with Byzantium on the subject of his passage through its territory,[36] but he was also in touch with the sultan at Iconium, and was regarded by both Serbia and Bulgaria as a desirable ally, particularly in view of the understanding between Hungary and Constantinople. Both the "grand župan" and the Bulgarian tsar were willing to submit to Frederick and to attack Constantinople.

Isaac could hardly afford to support the Latin crusading cause, and in the early summer of 1189 he renewed the treaty which Andronicus had made with Saladin, probably in 1185. Frederick prepared to take the offensive against Isaac, who had no diplomatic finesse and mishandled the situation. Philippopolis and Adrianople were occupied by the Germans, who then approached Constantinople. Frederick had already written to his son Henry telling him to bring a fleet to attack the city by sea. Constantinople awaited its fate, fearing that, like Thessalonica, it would be captured and looted. Isaac had no option but to accept Frederick's terms, and in February 1190 he agreed to the treaty of Adrianople, which granted the Germans transport and shipping and Byzantine hostages. Thus Barbarossa had very nearly anticipated events of 1204; he had certainly demonstrated the weakness of the Byzantine government. Meanwhile he crossed into Asia Minor and shortly afterwards his untimely death removed a dangerous enemy.

His western fellows in the Third Crusade, Richard the Lion-hearted of England and Philip Augustus of France, reached the Holy Land, but achieved little for the Christian cause there. But an event of significance for eastern Mediterranean politics in the later Middle Ages was Richard's conquest of the strategic island of Cyprus, then under the independent control of the Byzantine, Isaac Comnenus. From Richard it passed first to the Templars, and then in 1192 to Guy of Lusignan and his dynasty.

Temporarily freed from the German danger, Isaac hastened to retrieve the position in the Balkans. In the autumn of 1190 he defeated the Serbs and came to terms with Stephen Nemanya. The "grand župan" was allowed to retain certain of his conquests and was given the title of sebastocrator and the emperor's niece Eudocia as wife for his son Stephen. Though Isaac could not subdue the Serbian ruler as Manuel had done, in true Byzantine fashion he did at least try to retain him in the hierarchy of princes under the "Roman" basileus. Bulgaria proved more difficult to tame and Byzantine expeditions were defeated. Isaac was undertaking a fresh campaign with Hungarian help when his brother Alexius III deposed and blinded him, and ascended the throne on April 8, 1195.

Isaac has been, perhaps unfairly, denounced as "utterly ineffectual".[37] Faced with contemporaries of the caliber of Frederick Barbarossa, Henry VI, Stephen Nemanya, Peter and Asen, and Saladin, he could not hope to hold his own. But unwise and impetuous and shortsighted as he was, particularly in his internal policy, his military expeditions and his diplomatic activity do at least show him attempting to retrieve Byzantine prestige in the Balkans with Hungarian assistance, or trying to safeguard Byzantine interests in the east by coming to an understanding with Saladin. Indeed Isaac's negotiations with Saladin reveal the essential rift between the Latins and Greeks and the futility of hoping for any measure of unity in the Christian ranks.

Isaac's successor, Alexius III Angelus, ruled from April 8, 1195, to July 17-18, 1203. His weakness and greed lost the empire what little prestige it still enjoyed, and played directly into the hands of the western and Balkan powers. Already in 1195 Barbarossa's son the German emperor Henry VI, now ruler of Sicily, had demanded from Isaac II the cession of the Greek territory occupied by the Normans under William II of Sicily. The marriage of his brother Philip of Swabia to Irene, the daughter of the deposed Isaac II, provided Henry with a fresh weapon which he did not hesitate to use in his bold policy of attack. Henry planned a new crusade to conquer Constantinople and the empire before passing on to Syria and Palestine. Alexius in his fear tried to meet Henry's demands for heavy tribute, by levying what was known as the "German" tax, though this would doubtless have afforded only a temporary breathing space. Henry, in spite of papal opposition, continued to strengthen his position and was recognized by the rulers of Cyprus and of Cilician Armenia. The danger was averted only by his unexpected death in 1197.

Meanwhile Byzantine weakness had been further exposed by the advances made by Serbia and Bulgaria, both of which now judged it expedient to turn to Rome and to Hungary rather than to Constantinople. In both countries Constantinople had opportunities to extend its influence, but failed to do so. Stephen of Serbia, who was married to Alexius III's daughter Eudocia, in vain sought Byzantine help against his brother Vukan, who succeeded in temporarily gaining control of the government in 1202 with papal and Hungarian help, though only at the price of acknowledging Rome's supremacy and Hungary's suzerainty. The "ban" (ruler) of Bosnia, Kulin, strengthened his position by similar action. In Bulgaria civil war had broken out, and the throne was gained by Ioannitsa (Kaloyan), who had lived in Constantinople as a hostage. But even he, significantly, looked to Rome and not to Byzantium, and in 1204 he was crowned king by the Bulgarian archbishop Basil, who had just been consecrated primate by Innocent III's legate, cardinal Leo.

It needed only Venetian ambition to give direction to the hostile forces waiting to take advantage of Byzantine difficulties. The dismemberment of the empire would ensure the maritime supremacy of Venice, which in the course of the twelfth century had from time to time been threatened by Byzantine imperial policy and by the antagonism of the Greek people. The Fourth Crusade could have presented no surprise in western diplomatic circles. In fact, the internal condition of the empire did in several respects favor such an attack. In the past scholars have stressed the weakness of the dynasty of the Angeli and the hostility and greed of Byzantium's Latin enemies. But in reality a prime cause in determining the course of events was the fundamental change in the character of the empire from the eleventh century onwards. This was largely due to separatist and centrifugal forces which were continually undermining the central authority; such forces were enormously accelerated by the method of land holding based on grants in pronoia which bore a marked similarity to the western feudal system.

Thus weakened, the empire was no match for its western enemies. When Alexius III considered the strength of the crusading host, actually bent on restoring his imprisoned and blinded brother to his throne, he fled with what portable funds he could lay hands on. Nicetas Choniates, who disliked him, said that he was too cowardly to attempt any defense of the city as his son-in-law Theodore Lascaris wished.[38] And so Isaac II was again placed on the throne with his son Alexius IV as co-emperor. But it was an impossible position for the unfortunate Angeli: the hovering Latins continually pressed them for funds which they could not easily raise, while the populace resented and feared the influence of the westerners. Both Greek and Latin sources tell of continual tension and of constant clashes and skirmishes which came to a climax on January 1, 1204, with the Greek attempt to send fire-ships against the Venetian fleet. "This, then, was the way in which Alexius repaid us for all that we had done for him," wrote Villehardouin.[39] The Greeks, for their part, reproached Al-

exius IV for his failure to control the crusaders; terrified of his own people, the young emperor even thought of admitting the French and Italians into the palace of the Blachernae for his own defense. At this, Alexius Ducas "Mourtzouphlus", another son-in-law of Alexius III, promptly seized the throne in late January 1204. He had Isaac and Alexius IV imprisoned and was himself proclaimed as Alexius V. Isaac died shortly afterwards and Alexius IV was probably strangled.

Alexius IV, understandably enough, had been favorably disposed towards the Latins. Alexius V, on the other hand, did at least attempt to keep them in check, and he set about fortifying the city against the inevitable attack. The very severity of his discipline made enemies. The Latins were by no means at one among themselves, but expediency and ambition determined Boniface and the other leaders to support the intentions of the doge. The empire was partitioned in advance (March 1204) and the city taken by assault on April 13.[40] Mourtzouphlus' troops fought with determination to stave off the repeated attacks made from the crusading ships in the Golden Horn, but his camp was finally broken up and he fled from the city and joined his father-in-law at Mosynopolis. Alexius III treacherously had him blinded; he was caught by the crusaders and finally killed by being hurled from the column of Theodosius in Constantinople. Alexius III fared somewhat better than he deserved: he fell into the hands of Boniface of Montferrat, then took refuge in Epirus with the despot Michael I, who had ransomed him, and finally, after fomenting trouble in Asia Minor, was captured by his son-in-law Theodore Lascaris in 1210; he ended his days in a monastery in Nicaea. It was here that Theodore Lascaris had established his base after the fall of the city, and with courage and astuteness he was now rebuilding the shattered Byzantine state.

Notes

1. See volume I of this work, chapter VI.

2. Anna Comnena, *Alexiad,* I, xii, 5 (ed. Leib, I, 44).

3. See G. Ostrogorsky, *History of the Byzantine State,* p. 321; a different view is to be found in volume I of this work, p. 219.

4. See volume I, chapters VIII-X, XIV.

5. Anna Comnena, *Alexiad,* XIII, xii, 20 (ed. Leib, III, 134).

6. See S. Runciman, "The End of Anna Dalassena," *Mélanges Henri Grégoire,* I (Brussels, 1949), 517-524.

7. On possible political implications of John Italus' trial, see Joannou, *Christliche Metaphysik,* I, 26-29.

8. See P. Grierson, "The Debasement of the Bezant in the Eleventh Century," *Byzantinische Zeitschrift,* XLVII (1954), 386, "It was left for Alexius I Comnenus to restore a 'hyper-pure' gold nomisma and to build up out of the debased nomismata a system of fractional coinage whose intricacies we

still only very imperfectly understand." On this controversial and difficult subject see also Ostrogorsky, *Byzantine State,* pp. 327-328.

9. See G. Ostrogorsky, *Pour l'histoire de la féodalité byzantine* (Brussels, 1954); cf. A. A. Vasiliev, *History of the Byzantine Empire* (Madison, 1952), pp. 563 ff. (on Byzantine feudalism).

10. Some scholars suggest the years 1139 and 1141 in Innocent II's pontificate. See Lamma, *Comneni e Staufer,* I, 28.

11. John Cinnamus, *Historia,* I, 10 (*CSHB,* p. 23).

12. Cf. Chalandon, *Les Comnène,* pp. 184-185. For an adverse judgment on John's accomplishments, see volume I, chapter XIII, pp. 445-446.

13. John Cinnamus, *Historia,* VI, 2 (*CSHB,* p. 253).

14. See Lamma, *Comneni e Staufer,* passim.

15. This lack of any fixed political system is one of the main themes of Lamma, *Comneni e Staufer.*

16. See volume I, chapter XIV; on Roger's moves, see above, chapter I, pp. 11-15.

17. John Cinnamus, *Historia,* II, 19 (*CSHB,* p. 87); Dölger, *Regesten,* no. 1374.

18. Dölger, *Regesten,* nos. 1488, 1497, 1498, 1499.

19. Nicetas Choniates, *Historia; De Manuele Comneno,* V, 9 (*CSHB,* p. 225).

20. Cf. Ostrogorsky, *Byzantine State,* p. 346.

21. See volume I, chapter XVII, and below, chapter XIX.

22. Dölger, *Regesten,* no. 1444.

23. Nicetas Choniates, *Historia; De Manuele Comneno,* III, 9 (*CSHB,* p. 163).

24. Nicetas Choniates, *Historia; Manuele Comneno,* I, 3 (*CSHB,* p. 75).

25. Benjamin of Tudela, *Reisebeschreibungen* (ed. L. Grünhut and M. N. Adler, 2 vols., Jerusalem and Frankfurt a. M., 1903-1904), II, 17-18.

26. Nicetas Choniates, *Historia; De Manuele Comneno,* VII, 4 (*CSHB,* p. 273): see Ostrogorsky, *Pour l'histoire de la féodalité byzantine,* pp. 28-31 and p. 53.

27. See Dölger, *Regesten, passim.*

28. John Cinnamus, *Historia,* VI, 2 (*CSHB,* pp. 251 ff.), and Nicetas Choniates, *Historia; De Manuele Comneno,* VII, 5 (*CSHB,* pp. 274 ff.); cf. Chalandon, *Les Comnène,* pp. 644 ff.

29. See D. Obolensky, *The Bogomils,* pp. 219 ff., and V. Grumel, *Les Actes des patriarches,*1., fasc. 3 (especially on chronology).

30. See Nicetas Choniates, *Historia; De Manuele Comneno,* VII, 2 (*CSHB,* pp. 265-268).

31. Dölger, *Regesten,* nos. 1333 and 1398, but on the dating see Ostrogorsky, *Byzantine State,* p. 348, note 6.

32. Dölger, *Regesten,* no. 1553.

33. Dölger, *Regesten,* no. 1647.

34. Cf. Ostrogorsky, *Byzantine State,* p. 358, note 4, and see in general R. L. Wolff, "The Second Bulgarian Empire: Its Origin and History to 1204," *Speculum,* XXIV (1949), 167-206.

35. See above, chapters II and III, for details of the Third Crusade.

36. Dölger, *Regesten,* no. 1581; cf. above, chapter III, pp. 90-91.

37. Runciman, *Crusades,* II, 429.

38. Nicetas Choniates, *Historia (CSHB),* p. 720.

39. Geoffrey of Villehardouin, *La Conquéte de Constantinople,* chap. 220.

40. See below, chapter V, pp. 184-185.

Abbreviations

AHR	*American Historical Review,* I (1895) and ff.
BAS	Michele Amari, *Biblioteca arabo-sicula,* versione italiana, 2 vols., Turin and Rome, 1880-1881.
CSHB	*Corpus scriptorum historiae byzantinae,* eds. B. G. Niebuhr, Imm. Bekker, and others, 50 vols., Bonn, 1828-1897.
FSI	*Fonti per la storia d'Italia,* 91 vols., Rome, 1887-1946 (?).
Hist. Zeitschr.	*Historische Zeitschrift,* I (1859) and ff.
MGH	*Monumenta Germaniae historica,* eds. G. H. Pertz, T. Mommsen, and others, Reichsinstitut für ältere deutsche Geschichtskunde, Hanover, 1826 and ff. [*SS = Scriptores,* etc.].
MGH, SSRG	*Monumenta Germaniae historica . . . Scriptores rerum germanicarum,* new series, 10 vols., 1922 and ff.
PG	*Patrologiae graecae cursus completus . . . ,* ed. J.-P. Migne, 161 vols., Paris, 1857 and ff.
PL	*Patrologiae latinae cursus completus . . . ,* ed. J.-P. Migne, 221 vols. Paris, 1844 and ff.
RHC	*Recueil des historiens des croisades,* Académie des inscriptions et belles-lettres, Paris, 16 vols. in fol., 1841-1906:
Arm.	*Documents arméniens,* 2 vols., 1869-1906.

Grecs	*Historiens grecs,* 2 vols., 1875-1881.
Lois	*Assises de Jérusalem,* 2 vols., 1841-1843.
Occ.	*Historiens occidentaux,* 5 vols., 1841-1895.
Or.	*Historiens orientaux: Arabes,* 5 vols., 1872-1906.
RHGF	*Recueil des historiens des Gaules et de la France,* ed. Martin Bouquet [1685-1754] and others, 24 vols. in fol., Paris, 1738-1904.
RISS	*Rerum italicarum scriptores . . . ,* ed. L. A. Muratori [1672-1750], 25 vols. in 28, Milan, 1723-1751; new edition by G. Carducci and V. Fiorini, Città di Castello, 1900 and ff.
ROL	*Revue de l'Orient Latin,* 12 vols., Paris, 1893-1911.
Rolls Series	*Rerum britanicarum medii aevi scriptores: The Chronicles and Memorials of Great Britain and Ireland during the Middle Ages,* 244 vols., London, 1858-1896.

Bibliography

The main Greek historical sources are: Anna Comnena, *Alexiad* (the best edition is by A. Reifferscheid, 2 vols., Leipzig, 1884; there are also *CSHB,* 2 vols., Bonn, 1839, 1872, and ed. B. Leib, 3 vols., Paris, 1937-1945, with translation; English translation by E. Dawes, London, 1928); John Zonaras, *Epitome historiarum* (3 vols., *CSHB,* 1841-1897; ed. L. Dindorf, 6 vols., Leipzig, 1868-1875); John Cinnamus, *Historia* (*CSHB,* Bonn, 1836); Nicetas Choniates (wrongly called Acominatus), *Historia* (*CSHB,* Bonn, 1835). These texts are also in Migne, *Patrologia graeca.* The rise of the Comnenian house is also dealt with by the historians of the period before 1081, for which see volume I of the present work, chapter VI. There are several world chronicles of little value—Michael Glycas (*CSHB,* Bonn, 1836); Constantine Manasses (*CSHB,* Bonn, 1836); Joel (*CSHB,* Bonn, 1836); and Ephraem (*CSHB,* Bonn, 1840). The capture of Thessalonica in 1185 is described by Eustathius, metropolitan of Thessalonica (*CSHB,* Bonn, 1842, after Leo Grammaticus; German translation by H. Hunger in *Byzantinische Geschichtsschreiber,* ed. E. Ivanka, vol. III, Vienna, 1955).

The most important of the numerous occasional pieces, letters, and poems are: Theophylact of Ochrida, *Epistolae* (*PG,* vol. 126); Theodore Prodromus, *Scripta* (*PG,* vol. 133, and various critical editions scattered in periodicals; see details in G. Moravcsik, *Byzantinoturcica,* 2 vols., rev. ed., Budapest, 1958, pp. 522 ff.); Eustathius of Thessalonica, *Opuscula* (ed. G.L.F. Tafel, Frankfurt,

1832), and *PG,* vols, 135-136; Nicetas Choniates, ed. K. Sathas, ... I (1872), and ed. E. Miller, in *RHC, Grecs,* II; Michael Choniates, *Opera* (ed. Sp. P. Lampros, 2 vols., Athens, 1879-1880), and in G. Stadtmüller, *Michael Choniates Metropolit von Athen* (*Or. Christ. Analecta,* XXXIII, Rome, 1934).

Documents, secular and ecclesiastical, are cited in F. Dölger, *Regesten der Kaiserurkunden des oströmischen Reiches,* part II: *1025-1204* (Munich, 1925), and in V. Grumel, *Les Actes du patriarcat de Constantinople,* I, fasc. 3: *Les Regestes de 1043 à 1206* (1947). Reference should also be made to F. Dölger, *Byzantinische Diplomatik* (Ettal, 1956), and to G. Moravcsik, *op. cit.,* which is an indispensable bibliographical guide to the Greek sources.

Reference to Latin and oriental sources will be found in the relevant chapters in this volume. Brief references to the more important Slavic sources may be found in G. Ostrogorsky, *History of the Byzantine State* (Oxford, 1956), *passim,* which gives the best short survey both of the sources and of the historical background, with bibliography to the end of 1954.

The most substantial secondary authority is still F. Chalandon, *Essai sur le regne d'Alexis I Comnène (1081-1118)* (Paris, 1900); *Les Comnène: Jean II Comnène (1118-1143) et Manuel Comnène (1143-1180)* (Paris, 1912); and *Histoire de la domination normande en Italic et en Sicile* (2 vols., Paris, 1907); Chalandon's work sometimes needs to be modified in the light of recent research, often scattered in periodicals. Other studies on political aspects are: H. v. Kap-Herr, *Die abendländische Politik Kaiser Manuels mit besonderer Rücksicht auf Deutschland* (Strassburg, 1881); F. Cognasso, "Partiti politici e lotte dinastiche in Bisanzio alla morte di Manuele Comneno," *Memorie della R. Accademia della Scienze di Torino,* ser. 2, LXII, 1912), and *idem,* "Un imperatore bizantino della decadenza: Isacco II Angelo," in *Bessarione'* XIX (1915), 29-60; W. Ohnsorge, "Ein Beitrag zur Geschichte Manuels I. von Byzanz," *Brackmann Festschrift* (1931).

On social, intellectual, and ecclesiastical life see: C. Diehl, *La Société byzantine à l'époque des Comnènes* (Paris, 1919); J. M. Hussey, *Church and Learning in the Byzantine Empire 867-1185* (Oxford, 1937); L. Oeconomos, *La Vie religicuse dans l'empire byzantin au temps des Comnènes et des Anges* (Paris, 1918); P. E. Stephanou, *Jean Italos, philosophe et humaniste* (Rome, 1949); D. Obolensky, *The Bogomils* (Cambridge, 1948); and P. Joannou, *Christliche Metaphysik,* I (Ettal, 1956).

On the administrative and economic side, fresh ground has been broken by the brilliant work of G. Ostrogorsky, *Pour la féodalité byzantine* (Brussels, 1954), and *Quelques problèmes d'histoire de la paysannerie byzantine* (Brussels, 1956). See also P. Charanis, "The Monastic Properties and the State in the Byzantine Empire," *Dumbarton Oaks Papers,* IV (1948), 51-118, and E. Stein, "Untersuchungen zur spätbyzantinischen

Verfassungs- und Wirtschaftsgeschichte" in *Mitteilungen zur osmanischen Geschichte,* II (1923-1925), 1-62. An indispensable study for diplomatic relations, particularly during the years 1143-1185, is P. Lamma, *Comneni e Staufer: ricerche sui rapporti fra Bisanzio e l'occidente nel secolo XII* (Studi storici, fasc. 14-18 and 22-25, 2 vols., Rome, 1955-1957).

LITERATURE OF THE CRUSADES

Fulcher of Chartres (essay date c. 1095-97)

SOURCE: "Prologue to *A History of the Expedition to Jerusalem, 1095–1127*" in *A History of the Expedition to Jerusalem,* translated by Frances Rita Ryan, edited by Harold S. Fink, University of Tennessee Press, 1969, pp. 56–59.

[In the following prologue, Fulcher outlines the story that will be told in his A History of the Expedition to Jerusalem *and describes the Crusade as a "pilgrimage in arms."]*

HERE BEGINNETH MASTER FULCHER'S PROLOGUE
TO THE WORK WHICH FOLLOWS

It is a joy to the living and even profitable to the dead when the deeds of brave men, especially those fighting for God, are read from written records or, retained in the recesses of the memory, are solemnly recited among the faithful.[1] For those still living in this world, on hearing of the pious purposes of their predecessors, and how the latter following the precepts of the Gospels spurned the finest things of this world and abandoned parents, wives, and their possessions however great, are themselves inspired to follow God and embrace Him with enthusiasm [Matth. 12:29; Marc. 10:29; Luc. 18:29; Matth. 16:24; Marc. 8:34; Luc. 9:23]. It is very beneficial for those who have died in the Lord when the faithful who are still alive, hearing of the good and pious deeds of their forebears, bless the souls of the departed and in love bestow alms with prayers in their behalf whether they, the living, knew the departed or not.

2. For this reason, moved by the repeated requests of some of my comrades, I have related in a careful and orderly fashion the illustrious deeds of the Franks when by God's most express mandate they made a pilgrimage in arms to Jerusalem in honor of the Savior. I have recounted in a style homely but truthful what I deemed worthy of remembrance as far as I was able or just as I saw things with my own eyes on the journey itself.[2]

3. Although I dare not compare the above-mentioned labor of the Franks with the great achievements of the Israelites or Maccabees or of many other privileged people whom God has honored by frequent and wonderful miracles, still I consider the deeds of the Franks scarcely less inferior since God's miracles often occurred among them. These I have taken care to commemorate in writing. In what way do the Franks differ from the Israelites or Maccabees? Indeed we have seen these Franks in the same regions, often right with us, or we have heard about them in places distant from us, suffering dismemberment, crucifixion, flaying, death by arrows or by being rent apart, or other kinds of martyrdom, all for the love of Christ. They could not be overcome by threats or temptations, nay rather if the butcher's sword had been at hand many of us would not have refused martyrdom for the love of Christ.

4. Oh how many thousands of martyrs died a blessed death on this expedition! But who is so hard of heart that he can hear of these deeds of God without being moved by the deepest piety to break forth in His praise? Who will not marvel how we, a few people in the midst of the lands of our enemies, were able not only to resist but even to survive? Who has ever heard of the like? On one side of us were Egypt and Ethiopia; on another, Arabia, Chaldea and Syria, Assyria and Media, Parthia and Mesopotamia, Persia and Scythia. Here a great sea[3] separated us from Christendom and by the will of God enclosed us in the hands of butchers. But His mighty arm mercifully protected us. "Blessed indeed is the nation whose God is the Lord" [Psalm. 32:12].

5. The history which follows will tell both how this work was begun and how, in order to carry out the journey, all the people of the West freely devoted to it their hearts and hands.

HERE ENDETH THE PROLOGUE

Notes

1. The Prologue appears in most manuscripts of the second redaction, which was begun in 1124, and, oddly enough, in MS I (Br. Museum, King's Library 5 B XV) of the first redaction. Hagenmeyer suggests that the Prologue was written between 1118-20, at about the same time as a reference to the Maccabees that occurs in Book II, chap. liv, and after the death of Baldwin I in 1118 but before 1120, the last date in MS K (*HF* 115, note 1).

2. Fulcher's characterization of his style as "homely" is a reminder that he came from Chartres, then famous for its classical studies. Fulcher must have been aware of this and indeed often quoted classical authors. He used medieval rather than classical Latin and apparently was a little sensitive about it. He also reveals at this point that he was an eyewitness to the First Crusade.

3. The Mediterranean.

August C. Krey (essay date 1921)

SOURCE: "The Accounts of Eye Witnesses and Participants" in *The First Crusade,* Peter Smith, 1921, pp. 1–21.

[In the following essay, Krey analyzes the eyewitness chronicles and letters of the First Crusade, maintaining that they have primarily been examined as sources for literature, not as literary productions. Krey then examines the style and language of these accounts.]

It is now more than eight hundred years since Christian Europe was first aroused to arms in an effort to wrest the Holy Land from the hands of the Infidel, and yet the interest in those expeditions still persists. Scarcely a generation has passed without demanding a fuller and fresher account of the Crusades for its own perusal. Sober historians have sought earnestly to answer the call, but, voluminous as their work has been, the fanciful poet and novelist have succeeded in keeping a pace in advance. It would require many pages to list only the titles of the books and articles which the last generation alone has produced. Apparently the subject will not cease to appeal to the interest of the world so long as the history of Syria remains a treasured memory. And the story of the first and most successful Christian effort to retake possession of the Holy Land will continue to be read with feeling by the descendants, blood and spiritual, of those first Crusaders. It seems, therefore, not out of place to make available for the English reader the story of that expedition as related by the men who witnessed it and participated in it.

I. General Importance of the Chronicles

Modern writers have viewed the Crusades with varying opinion. Scholarly enthusiasts have seen in them "the first great effort of mediaeval life to go beyond the pursuit of selfish and isolated ambitions; . . . the trial feat of the young world essaying to use, to the glory of God and the benefit of many, the arms of its new knighthood."[1] Others, like Gibbon, more cynical in their attitude, have seen in them only the mournful spectacle of hundreds of thousands of human beings led on to inevitable slaughter by a spirit of ignorant fanaticism.[2] However varied the opinion on the wisdom and the expediency of the undertaking, there is less room for difference in regard to the importance of the movement as a phase in the development of European civilization. The highly localized life of the eleventh century, in which the immediate horizon so often served to limit men's vision of knowledge, was shaken from end to end. Not all who started on this expedition to the Holy Land ever reached the other end of Europe, to be sure, but even these saw for the first time strange cities and men and returned home, if not with glory, certainly with more experience than they had had before. As for the thousands who finally succeeded in overcoming the almost superhuman obstacles involved in the conquest of the holy places, what wonders did they not have to relate! Individuals and occasional bands of pilgrims had journeyed over the same route before the Crusaders, but they were relatively so few that their experiences were absorbed within their own limited localities and left few traces. The First Crusade, however, enlisted people of all classes, of both sexes, and every age, drawing them from practically all parts of Christian Europe. As the first bands proceeded through

district after district, others caught the spirit and started after them. And thus the narrow highways were choked with a constant stream of Crusaders, some hurrying eastward, others returning home. Nor did the movement cease with the capture of Jerusalem. Ten years later there were Crusaders still going East in answer to Urban's call for the First Crusade, while the actual possession of the Holy City by the Crusaders afforded the necessary impetus for a steady stream of pilgrims between West and East. With the pilgrim and the Crusader went also the merchant, courier, minstrel, and adventurer. Thus wayfaring, with all its attendant good and evil, became a habit over all of Europe. What this exchange of ideas and wares meant transcends statistics and must be looked for in the accelerated progress of Europe which followed, in the so-called Renaissance of the Twelfth Century.

Quite apart from the Crusade itself, the eye-witness accounts of the expedition have a peculiar value for the student of history as the first fairly full description of European society since the fall of the Roman Empire in the West. It is difficult to find in the period between the fifth and twelfth centuries any writings which describe contemporary life and society. Einhard's *Life of Charlemagne* is the striking exception. Just as the meagre *Germania* of Tacitus has been remorselessly tortured into a confession of Germanic civilization, frequently made to serve all centuries from the prehistoric to the eighth, and even beyond, so Einhard, with but little help, has been pressed into equally heroic service for the eighth and ninth centuries. The next two centuries, for lack of a Tacitus or an Einhard, have been constrained to linger under the infamy of the name "Dark Ages." This darkness, however, is effectively dispelled at the end of the eleventh century, largely through these chronicles of the First Crusades, while the steadily swelling volume of writings thereafter obviates the danger for succeeding ages. The religious character of the Crusades drew the sympathetic attention of clerical writers, the only writers of the time. All that the leaders did on this journey "of the Lord," whether petty or great, trivial or important, was thought worthy of commemoration for the benefit of posterity. Under the circumstances, the varied composition of the crusading host was particularly fortunate. Practically the only classes of Europe not personally represented on the Crusade were Emperor and King, Pope and Archbishop. In other words, that portion of society which alone was deemed worthy of attention in the ordinary brief annals and chronicles of the time was absent, and those who detailed the story of the expedition lavished their enthusiasm upon ordinary nobles, knights, and foot soldiers, even the poor being accorded a generous measure of notice. These accounts, accordingly, present a picture of society in which the relationship of all classes, ecclesiastical and lay, masculine and feminine, is portrayed in its intimate aspects. Although ordinary affairs are at times slighted, the extraordinary recur so frequently and with such variety as to make the inference of the ordinary fairly easy. The descriptions are so full and touch so many activities of society that they illumine not only the civilization of the time, but also cast considerable light on the preceding and following periods. As a result, it has been a common practice for master historians to initiate their apprentices into the study of European history through the accounts of the First Crusade.

The literary value of these writings is rather indirect than otherwise. They have afforded apparently inexhaustible material for literature, but as literary productions themselves have been only lightly appraised. Nevertheless, they are fair specimens of the writings of that time, and, as such, they deserve some consideration in a comprehensive history of literature. Some of them, such as the letters of Stephen of Blois and Anselm of Ribemont, have a charm which entitles them to much higher consideration. Here and there in the chronicles the authors soar to fairly great heights. It would be difficult to find anywhere a more graphic description of deep despair than is presented by the anonymous author of the *Gesta* in his account of the reception by Alexius and his army of the fate of the Crusaders at Antioch. In like manner, the fanciful account of the interview of Kerbogha and his mother before Antioch may be ranked with many a better known piece of imagery. In general, however, the literary merit of the following accounts consists chiefly in their vivid realism, which the very crudeness of expression only serves to accentuate. The hopes and fears, mournful sorrows and exultant joys, the profound despair and terror of the army, as it marched through one trial after another, are described with the awful earnestness and sincerity of men who have actually shared these experiences. It is this quality which causes the chronicles themselves to be read with interest long after their material has been adorned with finer language by more skilful writers.

II. THE DISTRIBUTION OF NEWS

But the absence of a polished literary finish was not wholly due to a lack of skill on the part of the writers. It was partly due, also, to the fact that these writings were intended for the information of the contemporary world. They were the newspapers of the time and in this they mark a distinct advance in the art of disseminating current information. Hitherto, writing had been almost exclusively confined to the Latin language and, hence, to churchmen. The few exceptions in vernacular tongues before the twelfth century have been deservedly treasured as rare monuments of philology. In the Latin writings only such matters as were of interest to the clergy were accorded much consideration. Theological writings, Scripture, the writings of the Church Fathers, books of Church service, textbooks for the schools, and treatises on kindred subjects constituted the chief themes for writers. Laws of kingdoms and meagre entires in monastic annals composed the major portion of secular information committed to writing. Occasionally the career of some ruler was chronicled in panegyric fashion, usually because of some past or expected favor to the Church. Even the histories of nations—e.g., *The History of the Franks* by Gregory of Tours, or *The Ecclesiastical History of England* by the Venerable Bede—were ecclesiastical histories, in which the purely secular played but an incidental part.

The written description of contemporary events for contemporary men was left to letters. But in the narrow life of the time people were rarely so far removed from their friends that they found it necessary to resort to such means for exchanging information. The churchmen, whose organization radiated from Rome, and whose training had made them more familiar with the art of writing, alone employed letters to any great extent. Here again, however, ecclesiastical and scholastic matters received the preponderant share of attention, though often current bits of general interest were included. These latter items might be transmitted to Church gatherings and, doubtless, were frequently so treated. But for the most part the news of the day was passed orally from neighbor to neighbor, or wider areas were momentarily linked together by the tales of some warfaring minstrel or other traveller. As the monasteries and castles were most famous for their hospitality, so these were the best informed centers of the time.

The Crusade, however, created abnormal conditions. Most of the people who went on the expedition did so with the expectation of returning home after the fulfillment of their purpose. As a result, the social interests of the local communities were suddenly expanded even to Palestine itself. Since, moreover, there were few regions of western Europe which did not furnish some of their people for the cause, many different lines of interest focused themselves upon the army and were constantly crossing one another. Secular Europe was no longer limited by a local horizon; it was ever eager for news, and more news, from the East. Neighborhood gossip could serve only as a local distributing agency in this work. Wayfarers were eagerly accosted for news and probably supplied the localities with much real information. But where the interest was great and so constant, the temptation to expand small items to magnificent proportions was too great to be resisted, and many a glib-tongued impostor exchanged the fabrication of his fertile imagination for full fare and comfortable lodging. Some of these wild tales found their way into writing and were transmitted to a credulous posterity with all the authority which the written page could lend. Authentic information—and even the common world was soon forced to discriminate between kinds—had to be obtained through more assured channels. The service of couriers, long known to the official world, was expanded to meet the need.

III. LETTERS

In the earlier stages of the march it was a relatively easy matter to detach squires or foot-soldiers and send them back with messages and news. This continued even to the time when the army left Nicaea; thereafter this method became impracticable, if not quite impossible. Chance meetings with ships from the West then offered almost the only opportunity to exchange greetings, and, as the accounts show, these opportunities occurred but rarely. Letters alone could be used under such circumstances. It was, therefore, fortunate that the expedition represented a union of ecclesiastical and secular interests, for the churchmen, priests, or clerics lent themselves willingly to the task of drawing up letters—in Latin, of course. The churchmen in the West, upon receiving these letters, copied them and rapidly passed on the information to the waiting world. Such letters, even when addressed to individuals, were regarded as common property, unless they were carefully sealed, and their contents were widely diffused, usually at Church gatherings of some sort. How eagerly the congregations everywhere must have looked forward to such meetings for news from relatives, friends, and acquaintances, gone so long and so far away!

These letters,[3] of which fourteen are here translated and distributed at their appropriate places in the narrative, constitute the most important sources of our knowledge of the events which they describe. The authors are all men of prominence and responsibility. Two of the letters are from popes. One is from the Emperor Alexius. Five are from the leaders of the Crusade and may be regarded as official reports of progress, while the remaining four, though also the works of leaders, are of a more personal nature. The two letters of Stephen of Blois to his wife, Adele, are among the literary gems of the period. In addition to the responsible character of their writers, the letters have the further merit of greater proximity both of time and place to the events which they narrate. The emotions of the moment grip the writers irresistibly, beyond the power of epistolary formality to efface and thus lend a vividness which the later chronicles sometimes lack. Our chief regret is that there are not more of them.

IV. CHRONICLES

The interest of the world in the events of the First Crusade could not be satisfied by letters alone. Numerous motives combined to keep this interest inflamed. Patriotic pride in the achievements of countrymen, natural enjoyment of the marvelous and adventurous, the continued need of both men and money to insure the permanence of the conquest, and, no less, the pardonable pride of the Crusaders themselves in preserving the memory of their deeds—all these influences tended to the telling and the retelling of the story. Book-making in itself offered little inducement, for the absence of publishing houses and the lack of copyright laws denied prospective authors hope either of fame or wealth. Publishing, if the multiplication of copies by the laborious process of hand-writing may be so called, was done chiefly in the scriptoria of monasteries or episcopal schools. But parchment was expensive, and only the clerics could write. Ordinarily the military exploits of contemporary men seemed too ephemeral to justify description. However, the Crusade was a different matter in that its exploits, though largely military and material, nevertheless had a deep religious significance. Urban's remark at Clermont, that the recovery of the Holy Land would be a deed comparable to those of the Maccabees, was not forgotten. The thought that he was really adding a chapter to Sacred History served to carry more than one writer over depressing periods of discouragement to the

successful completion of his history of the expedition. These varied motives, both sacred and profane, combined to inspire the composition of the following detailed accounts of the First Crusade.[4]

The first complete account of the Crusade which has come down to us is commonly known as the *Gesta*. Its author has attained some measure of distinction as the Anonymous. What is known to him, therefore, rests solely upon the inferences to be drawn from his work. He accompanied the Italian Norman prince, Bohemund, from the siege of Amalfi to the capture of Antioch. From there he went to Jerusalem with the general band under Raymond's leadership, whether with Raymond himself or, which is more likely, with Tancred or Robert of Normandy, who were associated with Raymond, is not clear. His book was written before the close of 1101, for Ekkehard saw and used a copy of it at Jerusalem in that year. So much may be stated fairly positively; the rest is only inferential, for in his book personal references are singularly few. There is no preface or dedication, no parting remark to the reader. However, certain expressions, certain modifications of the Latin which he employs, betray a high degree of familiarity with the verbal habits of southern Italy, while his constant laudation of Bohemund, even though he abandoned him after the capture of Antioch, tends to confirm the belief that his home was in that region. He may have been a Norman; if so, he left Normandy long before the First Crusade. His somewhat secular point of view in regard to events, occasional impersonal remarks upon the clergy, or participation in battle, have led modern critics to the belief that he was a knight, though his lack of intimacy with the leaders would indicate that he was a lesser knight. The style of his work and the general lack of literary allusions do not bespeak a very high degree of education. His use of language is that of an amateur, and his vocabulary is decidedly limited. Unable adequately to describe the achievements of the various crusaders, he strains the superlative degree of his adjectives so constantly that occasionally he finds it necessary to lapse into the simple positive as a means of actual distinction. The Bible is practically the only work which he quotes. His real piety is sustained both in his book and in his own career, as is indicated by the fact that he chose to go on to Jerusalem, instead of remaining with his leader at Antioch. What he lacks elsewhere is greatly outweighed by his judgment in evaluating the relative importance of events, his restraint in preventing intimate details from obscuring the perspective of his story, his unusual fairness and impartiality toward the rival Christian leaders, as well as toward his Turkish foes, and a certain native instinct for the dramatic apparent throughout the book. Guibert, Balderic, and Robert the Monk all criticized his style, but unwittingly paid him the lavish compliment of incorporating nearly the whole of his work in their "literary" accounts of the expedition. The great historical value of the work rests not only in the fact that it was written by an eye-witness and participant, but also upon the fact that it was probably composed from time to time on the journey and finished immediately after the battle of Ascalon in September 1099, the last event which it mentions. It is the first full account of the Crusade still extant, and almost every other history of the First Crusade is based either directly or indirectly upon it. Six MS copies of it still remain, and all of the material has been preserved in one form or another in the later accounts of the Crusade.

The second chronicle listed, on the other hand, does not at all efface its author, for the preface sets forth the authorship and the purpose in full:

"To my Lord Bishop of Viviers and to all the orthodox, from Pontius of *Balazun* and Raymond, Canon of Puy; greeting, and a share in our labor.

"We have concluded that we ought to make clear to you and to all who dwell across the Alps the great deeds which God in the usual manner of His love performed, and did not cease constantly to perform, through us; especially so, since the unwarlike and the fearful left us and strove to substitute falsehood for the truth. But let him who shall see their apostasy shun their words and companionship! For the army of God, even if it bore the punishment of the Lord Himself for its sins, out of His compassion also stood forth victor over all paganism. But since some went through Slavonia, others through Hungary, others through Longobardy, and yet others by sea, it would be tedious for us to write about each. Therefore we have omitted the story of others and have taken it as our task to write about the Count, the Bishop of Puy, and their army."

Pontius of *Balazun,* a knight in the Provençal army, was killed at Archas, and Raymond was thus left to complete the task alone. Raymond had been elevated to the priesthood while on the Crusade and had become the chaplain of Count Raymond of Toulouse, who was the wealthiest leader on the expedition. The expense of compiling the book was, therefore, a trivial matter. His intimacy with Count Raymond and with Bishop Adhemar gave him access to much information not available to such writers as the Anonymous. Critics have been exceedingly harsh in their condemnation of both the form and the content of the book. They condemn it as crude, bigoted, intensely partisan, and a mass of confused and credulous mysticism. Partisan it undoubtedly is, for Raymond was writing to correct a probable impression conveyed by the returning Crusaders both as to the bravery of the Provençal host and the validity of the Holy Lance, especially the latter. He himself had been among the first to accept the visions of Peter Bartholomew, had participated in the digging for the Lance, and even the apparently adverse judgment of the Ordeal was not sufficient to shake his faith in it. A large part of his work, therefore, is a brief in defense of the Lance, in support of which he adduces vision after vision and numerous witnesses. The rest of his book is devoted to the part played by Count Raymond, Bishop Adhemar, and the Provençal host in the Crusade. All this is true, but it cannot be said in justice that he is totally blind to the faults of either leader or people. To the historian the book is second in importance only to the *Gesta,* for it was the work of an eye-witness, written possibly no earlier than 1102, though undoubtedly on the basis of notes taken during the journey. It must be regarded as an independent account, even though, as Hagenmeyer conjectures, its author may have used details from the *Gesta* to correct his own account. For what may be termed the sociological aspects of the Crusade, Raymond's history is the most valuable of all the accounts. Six MS copies of the work are extant.

The third account of the Crusade as a whole was written by Fulcher of Chartres, whose career can be traced more fully than that of any other eye-witness chronicler of the Crusade. Born probably at Chartres in 1059, he was trained for the service of the Church, and when the Council of Clermont was held in 1095 he was a priest either at Chartres or at Orleans. The enthusiasm which swept over the land claimed him, as it did so many of his countrymen, so that when the army of Stephen of Blois moved from Chartres, late in 1096, Fulcher was one of the band. He was with Stephen's army until October, 1097, when he became the chaplain of Baldwin, Godfrey's brother. From this time until Baldwin's death in 1118 he remained in that capacity, closely associated with the energetic leader. As a result, he was present neither at the siege of Antioch nor at that of Jerusalem, being then at Edessa, which place he did not leave until late in 1099, when he made a pilgrimage to Jerusalem with Baldwin and Bohemund. When Baldwin was summoned to take the reins of government upon the death of Godfrey, Fulcher accompanied him to Jerusalem, where he remained until the time of his own death in 1127 or 1128.

His *Historia Hierosolymitana,* of which only the portion relating events actually witnessed by Fulcher on the First Crusade is here translated, was written upon the urgent solicitation of his friends. It first appeared in 1105, and the welcome then accorded it encouraged him to go on with it. The latter part of his work takes the form of an annalistic account of the Latin Kingdom of Jerusalem, for the early history of which it is undoubtedly the most important single source of information. He seems to have revised the earlier portions of his history at least twice, and the final version ends somewhat abruptly with the mention of a plague of rats in the year 1127. Fulcher apparently had a more extensive literary training than either of the two preceding writers. His fondness for quotation has been charged against him as an affectation by modern critics, but, as a fault, it mars only the latter portion of his work, written when he was quite old. On the whole, his book is free from either partisanship or bias. He seems to have been interested chiefly in describing the events as they occurred, with possibly an additional desire to attract soldiers from the West to the support of the needy Latin state in Syria. He displays a strong interest in nature and describes strange plants, animals, and natural phenomena in a naïve manner. His interest in the intrigues of the lords, both lay and ecclesiastical, is very slight, but the general welfare of the people he views with all the kindly concern of a simple French curé. As a whole, the book is exceedingly valuable and very soon was widely read and copied.

It was second only to the *Gesta* as a mine for exploitation by later writers on the Crusade. More than fifteen MS copies of the original are still extant.

Of the writings which contribute eye-witness testimony to but a portion of the history of the Crusade, the *Alexiad,* by Anna Comnena, is one of the most important. The writer was the daughter of Alexius, and, though she was barely fourteen years of age when the Crusaders came to Constantinople, it may be assumed that the presence of so many rude strangers in the imperial city made a most vivid impression on her mind. Both Anna and her husband, Nicephorus Briennius, had been highly educated, and when the palace intrigue in which they were both concerned proved unsuccessful and she was shut up in a convent by her brother's order, she undertook to complete the history which her husband had begun. Forty years after the first Crusaders had passed through Antioch she began her task. In the meantime there had been various bands of Crusaders from the West. Bohemund had taken Antioch in defiance of the Emperor and had even made war upon him. The relations of Alexius with Count Raymond of Toulouse had undergone changes, and many other events relating to the Latins and the Crusades had occurred. Thus, with so much to confuse her memory, her chronology is uncertain, her statement of fact often inaccurate, and her style highly rhetorical and affected. Never very certain of the identity of the Latin leaders, as she herself confesses, she calls them all counts and confuses one group with another in hopeless fashion. Nevertheless, her work is exceedingly valuable as a presentation of the Byzantine attitude toward the Latins, and her conception of her father's feeling toward the Westerners can probably be relied upon as correct. A MS copy of the account, corrected by Anna herself, is preserved at Florence. Other fragments also remain.

It is necessary to include in the list of eye-witness accounts of the First Crusade the work by Peter Tudebode, a priest of Civray.[5] This work, once regarded as the original of the *Gesta,* has been dethroned from that position by recent criticism. It is almost a verbatim copy of the latter, with portions added from the account of Raymond of Agilles, together with a very few personal remarks and observations. He speaks of the death of his brother in Antioch and his own share in the funeral services. His account differs from that of the *Gesta* primarily in the change of adjectives qualifying Raymond of Toulouse and Bohemund, for Tudebode was a follower of Count Raymond. However, this policy is not consistently maintained. At best, the work may be regarded as an eye-witness corroboration of the *Gesta.* It was written after both the account by the Anonymous and by Raymond had been composed, and sometime before 1111, after which date it was quoted by other writers. Four MS copies are preserved.

Ekkehard of Aura, who is still regarded as one of the greatest of the German historians of the Middle Ages, was a monk at Corvey when the First Crusade was preached. He accompanied a later band of crusaders in 1101 as far as Constantinople by land, and by sea from there to Joppa.

At Jerusalem he saw a copy of the *Gesta,* which he made a basis for his own history. This work he wrote for the Abbot of Corvey in 1112, after he himself had become Abbot of Aura. The language and the style of this book reveal a greater familiarity with classical authors than is shown by any of the preceding accounts of the Crusade. Its value rests chiefly upon his eye-witness account of the Crusade of 1101, and his brief items about the Peasants' Crusade, of which no direct chronicle has come down to us. Only the latter material has been included in the following translation. Six MS copies of the work are extant.

Raoul de Caen, a Norman knight too young to accompany the Crusaders of 1096, enlisted in the army which Bohemund assembled in 1107. He reached Syria and entered the service of Tancred, then prince of Antioch, whom he served until the latter's death. In his early years he had received instruction in letters from Arnulf, who became Patriarch of Jerusalem after 1112. He was an accomplished knight and seems to have enjoyed the friendship of Tancred. During the first five years of this relationship he learned much about the First Crusade, especially Tancred's view of events. He also visited Jerusalem and there conversed with his former teacher, Arnulf, now the Patriarch, to whom he dedicated his work, the *Gesta Tancredi.* Though an important source of information, this work is not, strictly speaking, an eye-witness account. It is a panegyric of the Norman princes of Antioch and is very hostile to the Emperor Alexius and to Count Raymond. It deals with the history of the First Crusade and of Tancred up to 1105, and its chief value lies in the reflection of the Norman point of view. It also contains some information not afforded by other writers. The Latin is polished and adorned with numerous passages and quotations from classical authors. Raoul writes chiefly in prose, but he sometimes attempts to soar to poetic form in describing unusually great achievements. On the whole, Patriarch Arnulf had reason to be proud of his former pupil's achievement. The book was written sometime between Tancred's death in 1112 and that of Arnulf in 1118. A single MS copy is preserved at the Royal Library of Brussels. His account of the Holy Lance, in which he takes an opposite view from Raymond, is here translated in full. Other material from the work is included in the notes.

The value of the account by Albert of Aix has been much disputed. Little is known of the author, who is said to have been a canon of the church of Aix-la-Chapelle about the middle of the twelfth century. By his own confession he never visited the Holy Land himself. Nevertheless, he wrote a history of the First Crusade and the Latin Kingdom of Jerusalem down to the year 1120, of which twelve MS copies exist. The date of this writing has, therefore, been placed somewhere between 1120 and the middle of the century. He obtained his information, he says, from the oral and written testimony of participants. Much of the material is palpably legendary; more of it, however, seems entirely probable and stands the test of comparison with well established accounts. The work contains so much not treated by other writers and, therefore, incapable of corroboration that its value must stand or fall with the reader's attitude toward the author. It has been conjectured that much of the material was taken from a Lorraine chronicle now lost, an explanation plausible enough, though thus far not substantiated. At any rate, his items of information cannot be ignored, and they may be of full value. Until further evidence is discovered, the question cannot be settled positively.[6] Only excerpts on the Peasants' Crusade and Godfrey's march to Constantinople are here translated from Albert.

The other three works included in this translation because their authors were present at the Council of Clermont may be grouped together as literary histories. None of the writers accompanied the expedition, but each wrote a history of the whole Crusade, thus illustrating the deep interest of the people of Europe in the subject. All three were churchmen of high position, and each sought to rewrite the crude account of the *Gesta* in more literary form. They succeeded in varying degree, but their names are remembered, while that of the original author has been irretrievably lost. Robert the Monk is generally identified as the monk chosen Abbot of Saint-Remi of Rheims in 1094, and later forced to retire to the priory of Senuc. His work was written at the request of Bernard, Abbot of Marmoutier, sometime before 1107. It adds little to the *Gesta,* but was very popular in the twelfth century. More than eighty MS copies of it are still extant. Balderic, Abbot of Bourgeuil, and Archbishop of Dol after 1107, added little more than Robert to the *Gesta* account. His work was written after 1107 and was also quite popular. Seven MS copies remain. The best of these three accounts is that of Guibert, who was Abbot of Nogent from 1104 to 1121. He composed his book between 1108 and 1112 and dedicated it to Lisiard, Bishop of Soissons. Guibert was one of the leading scholars of his time, well versed in classical lore, which he used to adorn his accounts of the Crusade. He was also fairly well informed about matters in northern France. His additions to the *Gesta* contain many valuable items about the crusading leaders from that region. Four MS copies of his work are preserved.

V. Terminology.

In the translation of these accounts a conscious effort has been made to reproduce as nearly as possible the style and manner of expression of the original. Though the writers all used the same language, they employed different words and idioms to describe the same occurrences, even the ordinary incidents of life. Under the circumstances, it was felt that too much would be lost if the expressions were all translated in the standard idiom of today. The person of the twentieth century who is interested in the manners and customs of that time will find enough pleasure and profit in this treatment, it is hoped, to repay him for whatever confusion the variety of expressions may create. A brief explanation of some of the more distinctive habits in the terminology of the period may be of use.

1. *Names of persons and places.*

The names of the same persons and the same places are spelled in many different ways not only by the different writers, but often, too, by the same writer. While this is more true of Eastern persons and places, it is, also, quite generally true with regard to the West, a revelation of how much of the world was strange to the people of eleventh century Europe. It must be remembered, however, that dictionaries, gazetteers, and similar works of reference, which greet the twentieth century person at every turn, were virtually unknown, while newspapers and other periodicals, which serve to standardize so much of life today, did not then exist. Almost the only common descriptions of the world known at that time were those contained in either the classical writings or in those of the Church fathers. It is not strange, therefore, to find the names of old Roman provinces and cities applied to places by some of the more highly educated writers, such as Ekkehard, Raoul, or Guibert. Less trained writers—and most of our writers fall within this category—had to trust chiefly to their powers of hearing and their ability to reproduce in writing what they heard. They had to follow their own rules of phonetic spelling and, considering the difficulties under which they labored, their results deserve genuine admiration. In order to avoid undue confusion, a uniform spelling has been adopted for the names of places which have been identified. In most cases the mediaeval name has been employed, but where the modern equivalent is much better known that form has been chosen.

The identification of the places mentioned by the writers presents considerable difficulty at times. It would be asking almost too much to expect the chroniclers to recall vividly and correctly both the name and exact location of all the strange places which they mention five or more years after they had passed through them. Important towns and places in which they spent some time, or with which they were able to associate some dramatic event, are usually located quite accurately; other lesser places cannot always be positively identified. All places mentioned whose location can be identified appear on the accompanying maps. The others, whose location is uncertain, have been italicized.

Names of persons, such as Robert, Godfrey, Baldwin, and Stephen were common enough, and little variation occurs. But Adhemar, papal leader of the expedition, seems to have had a baffling name, probably due to its similarity to a variety of names. As a result, his name appears as Haymarus, Aimarus, Ademarus, or Adhemarus, or not at all. Guibert, in describing the Pope's appointment of a vicar for the Crusade, confesses that he does not know his name, an interesting comment on the isolation of the time. His use of the name later may be an indication that he was using his original too closely, for the author of the *Gesta,* too, was ignorant of the name until later in the expedition. For the purposes of this translation, however, the names of the Western leaders are standardized. This is not the case with Oriental names, the unusual character of which occasioned the chroniclers a great deal of trouble. The name of the Turkish ruler of Antioch may be cited as a typical instance. The common spelling of his name today is Yagi-Sian or Iagi-Sian. It appears in the accounts, however, wth the Latin ending as Aoxian-us, Cassian-us, Caspian-us, and even Gracianus. Fulcher, who coined the first of these, succeeded remarkably well on the whole. In the case of less prominent men who are mentioned only once or twice, the variations have caused considerable confusion, leading even to the belief that they were different persons—e.g., Godfrey of Lastours, who appears as Gulferrus de Daturre, Golprius *de turribus,* and Gosfridus de Dasturs. This example seems to indicate the beginning of the use of surnames, but it is probably fortunate for the reader that the movement had not yet developed far. The efforts of the Crusaders to distinguish between the numerous Raymonds, Roberts, Stephens, Baldwins, and Godfreys, are of interest as early factors in the movement which led to the growth of heraldry and the multiplication of names.

2. *Expressions of time.*

The reader will doubtless be impressed by the absence in the chronicles of precise and minute statements of time, which are such a marked feature of modern industrial life. The year seems to have been of little account as a basis for reckoning time, for the author of the *Gesta* mentions it only once during the whole narrative which extends over a period of four years, and Raymond of Agilles scarcely more often. The more learned Fulcher uses it, to be sure, but rather as an ornament than because he feels the need of such a measure of time. The great festival days of the Church constituted the chief standards of time, and here, thanks to the influence of the Church, we find a fairly uniform practice among the writers. The necessity of determining the variable date of Easter compelled the Church to keep a calendar, while the custom of regulating the ordinary affairs of life with reference to the chief festival days of the Church had long since become an established habit of Christian Europe. The old Roman Calendar, too, continued to exert some influence despite the efforts of the Church to supplant it with a Christian scheme. As a result, the days of the month are reckoned both by Kalends, Nones, and Ides, and by the numerical count of days from the incoming or outgoing month. Days of the week bear the old Roman names and the canonical enumeration from the Lord's Day, as well. Time of day is expressed usually by means of the canonical hours, Matins, Prime, Terce, Sext, None, Vespers, and Compline, though such expressions as cock-crow, earliest dawn, and sunrise also occur. Time of day, and day of year are sometimes noted by the psalms and prayers customary at those times. Local variations in reckoning the beginning of the year and seasons, or in expressing dates by festivals of loyal saints, a practice quite common in the West, appear rather infrequently in these accounts.[7]

3. *Numbers.*

The figures used by mediaeval writers in stating numbers of people have baffled modern investigators. In order to discover the actual numbers involved, it has become almost a rule to divide the figures of the chroniclers by ten. Perhaps it would be fairer to regard almost all numbers over one thousand as figures of speech, intended only to convey the impression of a very large number. Roman numerals alone were in use, and neither the average writer nor the average reader of the period had very much training in arithmetic. It was certainly a difficult task to describe, if not a more difficult task to decipher, a very uneven number of six figures in Roman numerals. Quite aside from the mere mechanical difficulty of the task, few, if any persons, had had experience in dealing with large numbers. Neither commercial, ecclesiastical, nor military establishments dealt accurately in very large amounts or numbers at this time. As a result, when these chroniclers found themselves in the midst of the vast host which composed the crusading army they were struck with amazement. Nothing in their previous experience afforded them a satisfactory basis for estimating the size of the army. The numbers implied in their frequent resort to the term "countless" and "innumerable," or "as the sands of the sea," and "as the leaves of autumn," are probably almost as accurate as the numerals which they employ. The actual number of persons who took part in the First Crusade cannot be fixed with any certainty. Army rosters were not yet in use. It is, furthermore, extremely doubtful whether even among the better organized bands, such as those of Raymond and Godfrey, the leaders themselves knew exactly how many persons were in their following. The more adventurous knights were constantly digressing in smaller or larger companies from the main line of march; the more timid were dropping behind or deserting; and new enthusiasts were joining the march at almost every halting place. Thus the total number in the army fluctuated from day to day. Fulcher's statement that if all who had signed themselves with the cross had been present at Nicaea, there would have been six million, instead of six hundred thousand, armed men is probably more accurate in its proportions than in its actual figures. A modern estimate of the number in the army as it left Nicaea, ingeniously computed from the length of time required to cross a certain bridge in Asia Minor, is 105,000 persons.[8] The combined army was then at its maximum size. It dwindled rapidly thereafter, and the figures offered by the chroniclers themselves became more and more accurate, so that when Fulcher reports the number of Crusaders left to garrison Jerusalem as a few hundred, his statement may be accepted without great question.

If they had so much difficulty in describing their own numbers, little surprise need be felt at their estimate of the enemy's forces. After chronicling battles against the Turks and Saracens for almost thirty years, Fulcher reaches the following conclusion: "As to the number of dead or wounded in this or any other battle, it is not possible to determine the truth, for such great numbers cannot be computed by anyone, except approximately. Often when different writers deceive, the reason for their deception is to be attributed to adulation; for they try to enhance the glory of the victors and to extol the valor of their own land for people present and to come. From this it is very clear why they so foolishly and falsely exaggerate the number of dead among the enemy, and minimize, or remain entirely silent, about their own loss." This critical attitude, however, was not taken by the earlier writers, not even by Fulcher himself in the period with which this translation deals.

4. *Money and prices.*

Europe was still dealing largely on a basis of natural economy when the First Crusade started on its way. Money was regarded rather as a luxury than as a matter of general need, and even ordinary state obligations were discharged in kind rather than coin. Indeed, there was no standard coin in the West, and coinage was a right exercised by all the great feudal vassals. There were expressions of value common to all Europe—e.g., the *liber,* or pound, which equalled 20 *solidi,* or shillings, which equalled 240 *denarii,* or pennies; and a *marc* which equalled two-thirds of a liber, or 160 *denarii.* But when these terms were applied to coins in actual circulation, their meaning varied with the character of the coin involved. The coin in most general use was the *denarius,* or penny. This was usually of silver, but might be made of an alloy, or sometimes of copper alone. A large and a small *denarius* were known, the latter often called an *obol.* The intrinsic value of the coin varied somewhat according to the particular mint at which it was coined, weight constituting, on the whole, the safest method of determining value. Raymond mentions seven different *denarii* from a limited region of the West as current in the army. Variation was caused by debasement through coin-clipping and kindred practices, which, however, appear to have been less common at this time than later. In view of such facts, generalizations about monetary matters are exceedingly hazardous. However, it is usually safe to assume when Western coins are mentioned that *denarii* are meant. *Solidi, liberi,* and *marci* are moneys of account, convenient in expressing large sums of *denarii.* The ordinary silver *denarius* weighed from 20 to 24 gr. as compared with the American dime which weighs 38.5 gr. In the East the Crusaders met with gold coins, the *besant* and *perperus* of Constantinople, and the gold *besant* of the Saracens. The *besant* of Constantinople weighed about 65 gr. as compared with the American gold coinage, which weighs about 25 gr. per dollar. The *perperus,* called also *purpuratus, yperperus, yperperon,* and *perpre,* is less well known. Its value, as stated by the author of the *Gesta,* was equal to 15 *solidi,* or 180 *denarii.* The gold *besant* of the Saracens, a Latin term for the Arabian *dinar,* was about equal in weight and intrinsic value to the *besant* of Constantinople. In seeking the modern equivalents of these coins, it is necessary to bear in mind the relative value of gold and silver in the middle ages. Another coin encountered in the East was the *tartaron,* which appears to have been a cheap copper coin of somewhat varying value.

From an economic point of view the First Crusade must be regarded as one of the most important factors in transforming the basis of European exchange from the natural to the monetary. The change was by no means complete with the end of the Crusades, but a long step had been taken toward that goal when the first of these expeditions was launched. Money was necessary to defray the ordinary living expenses on the march, and the Crusaders resorted to almost every conceivable device to obtain it. They tortured Jews, melted plate, mortgaged their possessions, and sold their goods for ridiculously small sums. Money, ordinarily scarce, rose in value until, as Albert recounts, one peasant sold seven sheep for a single *denarius.* Normally, a *denarius* was the equivalent of a workman's dinner, but the Crusade created abnormal conditions. Unfortunately, this abnormal state of affairs accompanied the Crusaders along their whole line of march, for just as their arrangements for departure caused the exchange value of money to soar, so the arrival of so many people at one town or another caused the limited food supply to take on incredible prices. Occasionally, in time of famine, food rose to almost impossible heights, so that the peasant who exchanged his seven sheep for one *denarius* in the Rhine country might have exchanged his *denarius,* in turn, for a single nut at Antioch during its siege by Kerbogha. The student of economics will be able to find many such equations in the following pages. The Crusaders had unwittingly become steady victims of the law of supply and demand, but for lack of such knowledge they blamed their misfortunes upon the cupidity of the Armenians and Greeks. Thus, however, they learned to esteem the possession of money, and in Saracen territory they lost few opportunities to secure it either as tribute, extortion, or plain robbery. Sometimes they even burned the dead bodies of their foes to obtain the coins which they believed these people had swallowed or secreted about their bodies. Actual money and its value was one of the most important contributions of the returning Crusaders to Western life, so much so that the *besant* of Constantinople and the Saracen *besant* became well known coins in Europe.

5. *Military arrangements.*

A definite organization of the army as a whole did not exist. The Pope's representative, Adhemar, who met all of his charges at Nicaea for the first time, was social and ecclesiastical head of the expedition until his death at Antioch, August 1, 1098. For military purposes, the Crusaders chose Stephen of Blois as their leader on the march across Asia Minor, and, after his withdrawal, Bohemund acted in that capacity for a time. Little real authority, however, was accorded these leaders, except for the brief period of Kerbogha's siege, when Bohemund was entrusted with full powers. Ordinarily, matters of policy were decided at a council of all the leaders, both lay and ecclesiastical. For all practical purposes, each band was almost a separate army in itself, and even within each band matters were usually decided by a common council. Leaders of the separate bands frequently had to resort to all the arts of persuasion at their command in order to keep their many-minded and impulsive vassals in leash. Eloquence, entreaty, offers of pay, and even threats were used time and time again. The feudal oath of allegiance of vassal to over-lord was the only basis of obedience, but the conditions under which the campaign was conducted were so different from those of the West as to render the ordinary feudal obligations quite inadequate. As a result, adventurous knights frequently went off on raiding expeditions without regard for the wishes of their lords, and companies of knights for these forays were formed from many different bands. Disorganization was further increased by the presence of great numbers of non-combatants. Persons of both sexes and all ages had attached themselves to the army from various motives—serfs to perform menial tasks; peasants with their families seeking improvement, material, social, or spiritual; women, wives of Crusaders, or mere adventurers; pious pilgrims of all ages; and clergy, both regular and secular. At Nicaea this multitude probably largely outnumbered the fighting men, and, as a rule, they were a great hindrance to the army.

The fighting men were of two classes—the mounted and armored knight, and the more or less armored foot-soldiers. At first the mounted knights were probably all of noble birth, but, as the exigencies of the campaign multiplied, this condition was changed. At times noble knights were compelled to ride on oxen or other beasts, or to proceed on foot, and, again, ignoble foot-soldiers found mounts and suits of armor. In the course of time, many of the latter proved themselves worthy of knighthood, so that by the time the army reached Jerusalem a great number of the so-called knights were not of noble birth.

The knight, protected by his breastplate and his suit of chainmail, and equipped with shield, lance, and two-edged sword, was the mainstay of the army. His squires, also mounted, usually accompanied the knight in battle. The foot-soldiers, whose chief weapons were the cross-bow and javelin, were used both to break up the line of the enemy in the opening charge and to dispose of the dismounted enemy after the main charge of the knights. Noncombatants were of some service in refreshing the fighters with drinks, caring for the wounded, and helping to collect the spoils. The clergy played an important part by administering the sacrament before battle and offering up prayers during the course of the fighting. Such was the practice against an enemy in the open field. The tactics of the Turks, however, caused some modifications. This foe, usually mounted on swift horses and armed with dangerous small bows, insisted upon encircling the Crusaders without coming to close quarters. Their arrows, which they shot quickly and in profusion, were calculated to shatter the ranks of the Crusaders and usually did great damage to the less heavily armored foot-soldiers. If this device failed to open up the ranks, they scattered in feigned flight, hoping thus to draw the Crusaders after them in disorganized pursuit, when it was an easy matter to turn and cut them down. The Emperor Alexius gave the Crusaders some very valuable advice on these matters. Actual experience proved an even more effective teacher, so that the Crusaders regularly placed a strong line at their rear

and on the flanks, as well as in front, and did not pursue the enemy until they were actually in rout.

To the Westerners siege warfare was less well known than open fighting. In most of Western Europe there was little of the heavy masonry of Roman days, such as had never gone out of use in the East. The Italians had had relatively more experience than the people north of the Alps, but both had much to learn. The military engineers of Constantinople gave the Crusaders some important lessons in siege-craft at Nicaea. The development of more powerful hurling engines for both stones and arrows became a necessity. These were of two kinds: the *ballistae,* used to shoot large arrows or bolts with great force, and the *Petraria,* which hurled large stones. The motive power was provided by the torsion of twisted ropes or the sudden release of a heavy counter-poise, and great ingenuity was exercised to increase their force. During the whole expedition, however, they were not developed sufficiently to make any considerable impression upon the walls. They were chiefly effective in clearing the walls of defenders, which facilitated other siege operations. Battering rams of various kinds were also used, and, as a protection for the manipulators, mantlets made of wattled stakes were constructed. Undermining the walls was an operation also resorted to, but the most effective devices in overcoming strongly fortified towns were the great movable towers and the blockade. The first was used successfully both at Marra and Jerusalem, the latter at Nicaea and Antioch. These are fully described in the text (see pages 256, 205, 105). Scaling ladders of wood were of subsidiary value, but played a part at Marra and Jerusalem and especially at Caesarea. In all these operations there was a great demand for skilful engineers, as well as for unskilled labor. It is significant that Greek engineers were employed at Nicaea and Antioch, Italian at Antioch and Jerusalem. The Westerners had much to learn, it is true, but that they were quick to do so is shown not only by their success at Jerusalem, but also by the stronger castles and fortifications which appeared in Western Europe during the twelfth century.

Notes

1. Bishop Stubbs, quoted by George L. Burr in the *American Historical Review* for April, 1901, page 439.

2. Gibbon: *Decline and Fall of the Roman Empire,* Chapters LVIII-LXI.

3. The following fourteen letters have been translated from the Latin texts edited by Hagenmeyer in his *Epistulae et Chartae . . . Primi Belli Sacri:*

   II. Urban II to all the faithful assembling in Flanders. Written about the end of Decembe, 1095. Pages 42-43.

   IV. Stephen of Blois to his wife, Adele. Written from Nicaea, June 24, 1097. Pages 100-101; 107-109.

   VI. Simeon, Patriarch of Jerusalem, and Adhemar, Bishop of Puy, to the faithful of the northern regions. Written from Antioch, October, 1097. Page 132.

VIII. Anselm of Ribemont to Manasses, Archbishop of Rheims. Written from Antioch about the end of November, 1097. Pages 106-107; 129.

IX. The Patriarch of Jerusalem to all the bishops of the West. Written from camp at Antioch, January, 1098. Pages 142-144.

X. Stephen of Blois to his wife, Adele. Written from Antioch, March 29, 1098. Pages 131-132, 155-157.

XI. Alexius to Oderisius, Abbot of Monte Casino. Written from Constantinople, June, 1098. See Chapter III, n. 26. Pages 110-111.

XII. Bohemund, son of Robert Guiscard, Raymond, Count of St. Gilles, Duke Godfrey, and Hugh the Great, to all the faithful in Christ. Written from Antioch, either October, 1097(?) or April-July, 1098. Pages 130-131.

XV. Anselm of Ribemont to Manasses, Archbishop of Rheims, July, 1098. Pages 157-160; 189-191.

XVI. Bohemund, Raymond, Count of St. Gilles, Godfrey, Duke of Lorraine, Robert, Count of Normandy, Robert, Count of Flanders, and Eustace, Count of Boulogne to Pope Urban II. Written from Antioch, September 11, 1098. Pages 160-161; 192-195.

XVII. The Clergy and people of Lucca to all the faithful. Written from Lucca, October, 1098. Pages 161-162; 191-192.

XVIII. Daimbert, Archbishop of Pisa, Duke Godfrey, Raymond of St. Gilles, and the whole army in the land of Israel to the Pope and all the faithful in Christ. Written from Laodicea, September, 1099. Pages 275-279.

XIX. Pascal II to all the archbishops, bishops and abbots of Gaul. Written about the end of December 1099. Page 279.

XX. Manasses, Archbishop of Rheims to Lambert, Bishop of Arras. Written from Rheims, November or December, 1099. Pages 264-265.

4. The following are the accounts contained in this book:

1. *Anonymi Gesta Francorum et aliorum Hierosolymitanorum.* Translated in full from Hagemeyer's edition. To read in the order of the original, see pages 28, 57, 71, 57, 80, 62, 93, 98, 101, 113, 118, 120, 123, 125, 132, 136, 144, 151, 163, 169, 174, 182, 195, 204, 214, 223, 212, 249, 256, 262, 265.

2. *Historia Francorum qui ceperunt Jerusalem,* by Raymond of Aguilers. Translated in full from the text in the *Recueil des Historiens des Croisades, Historiens Occidentaux,* III. To read in the order of the original see pages 8, 64, 97, 103, 116, 124, 126, 134, 139, 147, 153, 168, 173, 176, 182, 173, 185, 197, 207, 217, 224, 243, 250, 257, 262, 268.

3. *Historia Hierosolymitana,* by Fulcher of Chartres. Translated in part from Hagenmeyer's edition.

Preface: I, chapters 1-14, 33-34; II, chapter 6 *passim;* III, chapter 37 *passim.* To read in the order of the original see pages 24, 26, 28, 40, 24, 44, 45, 56, 61, 67, 99, 104, 105, 116, 118, 119, 121, 272.

4. *The Alexiad,* by Anna Comnena. Translated in part from the edition by Reifferscheid. Vol. II, Book X; chapters 5-6 *passim;* 7; 9 *passim;* 10; 11 *passim;* Book XI; chapters 2-3 *passim;* pages 70, 76, 86, 94, 99, 109.

5. *Historia de Hierosolimitano Itinere,* by Peter Tudebode. Only the variations from the *Gesta* are indicated and are to be found in the notes. The edition used was that of the *Rec. Occid.* III. See also Molinier: *Sources de l'histoire de France,* nos. 2115-2116.

6. *Hierosolymita,* by Ekkehard, Abbot of Aura. Translated in part from Hagenmeyer's edition, chapters VII-XIII. See pages 41, 46, 53.

7. *Gesta Tancredi,* by Raoul de Caen. Translated in part from the text in *Rec. Occid.* III; chapters 99-103, 108-109. See page 237.

8. *Liber Christianae expeditionis pro ereptione, emundatione, restitutione Sanctae Hierosolymitanae,* by Albert of Aix. Translated in part from the text in the *Rec. Occid.* IV. Included in this translation are I, chapters 2, 6-8, 15-24, 26-30, *passim;* II, chapters 1-17 *passim.* It has been thought necessary to translate only the gist of the matter contained in most of the chapters, as Albert was not, strictly speaking, an eye witness. Pages 48, 54, 57, 73, 80.

9. *Hierosolymitana Expeditio,* by Robert the Monk. The report of Urban's speech at Clermont, as contained in *Rec. Occid.* Vol. III, Book I, chapters 1-2, has alone been translated. Page 30.

10. *Historia Hierosolymitana* by Balderic, Archbishop of Dol. Urban's speech at Clermont; contained in *Rec. Occid.* IV, Book I, chapters 4-5, has alone been translated. Page 33.

11. *Gesta Dei per Francos,* by Guibert, Abbot of Nogent. Here the speech of Urban and the description of Peter the Hermit, contained in *Rec. Occid.* IV, Book II, chapters 4-6, have alone been translated. Pages 36-47.

5. "He who first wrote this should be believed, since he was on the expedition and saw it with the eyes of his body—to wit, Peter Tudebode of Civray." See Tud. XIV: 6.

6. For a more detailed discussion of this point, see Kugler: *Analekten zur Kritik Albert's von Aachen,* and the summary of the discussion in Molinier: *Les sources de l'histoire de France,* no. 2126.

7. For a comprehensive treatment of mediaeval chronology, consult Grotefend: *Taschenbuch der Zeitrechnung,* or Giry: *Manuel de Diplomatique.*

8. Delbrück: *Geschichte der Kriegskunst,* III, pp. 228-29.

Palmer A. Throop (essay date 1940)

SOURCE: "Independent Criticism" in *Criticism of the Crusade: A Study of Public Opinion and Crusade Propaganda,* N.V. Swets & Zeitlinger, 1940, pp. 26–68.

[*In the following essay, Throop examines the songs and poetry written and performed in opposition to the Crusades and papal policy.*]

The political difficulties encountered by Gregory X in launching his crusade can hardly be realized unless one knows that there had grown up during the thirteenth century a profound distrust of papal motives. The hostility and cynical indifference revealed in the memoirs submitted to Gregory X were nothing new in 1274. Long before this the papacy had received violent criticisms of its crusade policy, and, unlike Gregory's memoirs, such criticism had been entirely unsolicited. From the beginning of the thirteenth century to the time of Gregory X one may find the severest indictments of the Church for promoting war among Christians, wars dignified by the names of crusades.[1]

Some of the most bitter accusations came just a few years before the pontificate of Gregory X; some were made at the very time he was requesting memoirs from the clergy. However, not one of the extant reports received by Gregory X mention these condemnations of the papacy as the Judas who had betrayed the Holy Sepulchre. Consequently a study of these criticisms, most of them coming from laymen writing in the vernacular, will serve to show the limitations of the memoirs and how they failed in this most important respect to fulfil Gregory's request that hostility to the Church should be reported from all walks of life. A tailor, a merchant, a judge, court poets, and simple knights expressed their views with more force than courtesy. Not only were these critics from all of the literate classes, they were from many different regions of Europe. Spain, Italy, southern and northern France are all well represented. It must therefore be kept in mind that this literature is more than individual expression. It indicates wide-spread opinion with political and even religious implications.

These bold critics who ascribed to the papacy itself the reverses which overtook the Holy Land during the thirteenth century declared that the Vicar of Christ waged war against his own enemies in Europe, not against Christ's enemies in the East. As early as the eleventh century there had been denunciations of the pope for offering spiritual rewards to armies fighting his European foes. In the eleventh century, however, when Leo IX and Gregory VII were endeavoring to make theocracy a political reality, objections had revolved about the question of how far armed force was consonant with Christianity.[2] Although this vital question was still raised in the thirteenth century[3], the crusade ideal preached by Urban II in 1095 shifted the center of controversy. Urban insisted that Christian should no longer wage war against Christian:

all forces should combine against the Moslem, the enemy of all Christians[4]. This ideal, upheld in general by the popes of the twelfth century, fell into increasing neglect during the thirteenth[5]. Christian crusaded against Christian, while the Saracen triumphed in the Holy Land.

This change of policy brought a storm of denunciation in Old French and Provençal poetry. Furthermore, much of this poetry was written with the clear intent of spreading distrust of the papacy. Such lyrics, it should be remembered, were written to be sung[6] and thus influenced a far wider circle than the educated few. The Provençal *sirventés* in particular was composed for a large audience. It was frequently adapted to the melody and strophe form of a familiar song: the words could then be spread more rapidly because they could be more easily remembered.[7] The *sirventés* was always a polemic, often concerned with some question of public life, and usually written in the interest of some lord or political faction.[8] For this reason it is by far the most instructive genre from the historical point of view. It undoubtedly represents in many cases the determined attempt of some individual or group to control public opinion.[9] In short, the Provençal *sirventés* must always carry the suspicion of propaganda and its historical interest is increased, not lessened, by this suspicion.

The earliest criticism of the pope for his neglect of the Holy Land is in a Provençal *sirventés* composed by the troubadour Giraut de Bornelh in the late twelfth century.[10] Moved by the loss of Jerusalem in 1187 and irritated by Gregory VIII's lack of action in the face of this disaster,[11] Giraut condemned in general terms both temporal rulers and the pope:

> Many desire an emperor's throne who ill protect our faith and the pope sleeps between tierce and nones so soundly that I see no lords rise up against the Saracens. Rather they consider him an enemy who says a word about it.[12]

In the next stanza, however, Giraut deserts this fine impartiality and placed all the blame on the pope. "Jesus Christ", he wrote, "wore a crown of thorns to save mankind: the pope basely abandons His Sepulchre."[13] His very concision carried a sting. Again and again this complaint of papal indifference to the Holy Land was echoed in the thirteenth century.

Certainly the thirteenth-century Church was quite aware of the dangerous influence of these anti-papal songs. To sing one in public was an offense that came under the jurisdiction of the inquisition, an offense that this authority punished severely. For example, a burgher of Toulouse, Bernart Raimon Baranhon, was convicted by the inquisition of having sung Guillem Figueira's *sirventés* against Rome in the presence of many. The inquisitors also found incriminating his possession of the *Bible* of Guyot de Provins.[14]

These poets whose works the inquisition considered so dangerous were among the earliest and most violent critics of papal crusade policy. Both protested against the first great diversion of a crusade from the Holy Land, the fourth crusade (1204), which captured Constantinople and set a precedent for yet other crusades against the Greeks.[15] Guyot de Provins, a Cluniac monk, wrote in Old French a satire on the Church, known as *La Bible,*[16] which accused the papacy of avarice and, in this connection, pointedly inquired why the crusades were directed only against the Greeks.[17] Somewhat later the Provençal tailor and troubadour Guillem Figueira repeated this accusation that greed was the motivating force of the crusade against the Greeks. The violence of Figueira's *sirventés* may be better understood when one realizes that it was written in Toulouse in 1229 while the town was beseiged by crusaders sent by the pope to crush the Albigensian heretics[18]. He declared:

> Deceitful Rome, avarice ensnares you, so that you shear the wool of your sheep too much. May the Holy Ghost, who takes on human flesh, hear my prayer and break your beak, O Rome! You will never have a truce with me because you are false and perfidious with us and with the Greeks.[19]
>
> . . . Rome, you do little harm to the Saracens, but you massacre Greeks and Latins. In hell-fire and ruin you have your seat, Rome.[20]

These charges against the papacy are not wholly justifiable. Innocent III was outraged by the diversion of the crusade he had organized to combat the Saracen.[21] Yet once Constantinople was captured and the Latin Empire created, the popes felt the necessity of promoting crusades against the schismatic Greeks, who stubbornly refused to acknowledge the Latin rite and planned attacks upon their conquerors[22]. It would be extremely difficult to prove that these crusades were motivated solely by greed. The significant fact remains, however, that they took many resources, military and financial, that would otherwise have gone to aid the Holy Land[23]. Ugly suspicions had been aroused.

The failure of the fifth crusade helped spread such suspicions. This expedition had made a good beginning with the capture of Damietta in Egypt, but the crusaders soon lost the important city.[24] Many found at fault the papal legate Pelagius, whose head-strong conduct and squabbles with other leaders were widely discussed. A Frenchman, Huon de Saint-Quentin, writing shortly after the disaster in Egypt (1221),[25] placed the full blame of the failure upon the Church, and ascribed clerical avarice as the fundamental cause.[26] He bluntly declared that the papal legate had betrayed John of Brienne, the chief secular leader of the crusade; the legate was, in his opinion, wholly responsible for the loss of Damietta.[27]

From the evidence of yet other contemporaries of the fifth crusade, it appears that the conduct of the pope's representative aroused a great deal of indignation. Huon's views are repeated by three poets writing in Old French: Moniot,[28] Gautier de Coincy,[29] and Guillaume le Clerc de Normandie. Of these Guillaume le Clerc is the most explicit. In his satire *Le Besant de Dieu,* written in 1226 or 1227,[30] he declared:

> Because of the legate who governed and led the Christians, everyone says in truth, we lost that city through folly and sin. We should be greatly reproached. For when the clergy take the function of leading knights, certainly that is against law. But the clerk should recite aloud from his Scripture and his psalms and let the knight go to his great battlefields. Let him [the clerk] remain before his altars and pray for the warriors and shrive the sinners. Greatly should Rome be humiliated for the loss of Damietta.[31]

From this revealing passage it is clear that direct papal control of an army was greatly resented. Indeed, in pointing out the ancient distinction between the duties of priest and warrior, Guillaume seems to be maintaining that it is against canon law. Furthermore, from Guillaume's expression "everyone says in truth," and from the number of independent critics, one may risk the conclusion that a large body of opinion in French speaking provinces was becoming increasingly distrustful of the Church's guidance of the crusades.

Among Provençal poets, embittered by the Albigensian crusade then devastating their land, the loss of Damietta was commented upon with far more acerbity. Guillem Figueira in his terrible *sirventés* against Rome observed:

> Rome, you know well that your base cheating and folly caused the loss of Damiette. Evil leader, Rome! God will strike you down because you govern too falsely through money, O Rome of evil race and evil compact.[32]

With similar rancor two knights of Tarascon, the collaborators Tomier and Palazi[33], jeer at the papal legate in Provence[34] for his indifference to the fate of Damietta:

> Our cardinal takes his ease, cheats, and lives in fine houses. May God strike him down for it! But he cares very little about the disaster of Damietta.[35]

The Church, however, found a defender of its leadership in a poetess of Languedoc, Gormonda de Montpellier. This lady, refuting the charges made by Figueira in his *d'un sirventes far,* insisted that it was not the cardinal legate who caused the loss of Damietta, but the folly of vile men.[36] Pope Honorius III made a more specific defense by accusing Frederick II of bringing about the failure of the expedition through his many empty promises which kept the crusaders waiting in vain for his aid.[37] The same accusation may also be found in a *sirventés* written by a crusader, Peirol, upon the point of returning home from Damietta.[38] This troubadour, one of the few to engage actively in a crusade, shamed the emperor for the breach of his crusade vow and the neglect of his duty.[39]

There is a great deal to justify the contentions of Peirol and the pope, but justly or unjustly, the loss of Damietta had brought a wide distrust of the Church's leadership.

Even when one discounts the attacks of Figueira, Tomier and Palazi, enemies of the pope writing during the fury of the Albigensian crusade, there still remains a body of protest in Old French that is far from negligible. The papal direction of the crusades was being boldly questioned.

All of these criticisms, however, are mild and innocuous when compared to the vitriolic abuse heaped upon the papacy for directing a crusade against the Albigensian heretics. Provence and Languedoc had long been hot-beds of heresy, a fact which one troubadour attributed to the corruption of the Church.[40] The usual ecclesiastical threats and punishments failed to prevent the spread of heresy, so Alexander III felt it necessary to declare a crusade against the heretics in 1179 at the Third Lateran Council.[41] Yet it was not until 1209, during the pontificate of Innocent III, that the crusade took on serious proportions. Alarmed by the growing strength of the heresy, the popes of the early thirteenth century determined to stamp it out by force of arms. The same spiritual rewards were offered as those gained on the crusade against the Saracen[42]. The holy war was brought within the borders of Western Europe. Naturally, the severest critics of this shift in crusade aims were the troubadours, whose rich and beautiful country was devastate by French crusaders. They made very serious charges: the pope was using the crusade to stir up neighbor against neighbor while the real enemy, the Moslem, was left undisturbed in the Holy Land.

One may easily doubt this pious enthusiasm for the Holy Land. The troubadours were not as a rule burdened by their religious aspirations. They frequently wrote with levity of sacred things; sometimes they did not stop at sacrilege. Raimon Jordan preferred a night with his beloved to all paradise.[43] Bertran d'Alamanon rejoiced when told of the coming of Antichrist because this evil power would enable him to possess a resisting beauty.[44] Guillem Ademar approved of a crusade solely on the grounds that it took the jealous husband away and left the lover undisturbed with his lady.[45] Indeed, the troubadours rarely went on crusades, much preferring southern pleasures to the dangers of an expedition overseas.[46] Although they eloquently urged the faithful to take the cross, their crusade zeal was usually confined to poetry,[47] poetry for which they may have received material rewards.[48]

Although one may suspect the crusade ardor of the Provençaux, there is no doubting the sincerity of their hatred of the papacy which had brought the horrors of war to their beloved country. One troubadour, Perdigon, dared use his talents in behalf of the invading crusaders and was, as a consequence, driven forth and exiled by his compatriots.[49] This shows clearly enough that when the troubadours protested against the crusade in Languedoc and Provence they were voicing the anger and disgust of their fellow countrymen.[50] The fact that they did not protest as heretics,[51] denying all rights to the pope, but as zealous Christians who had the interest of the Holy Land at heart, lent great emphasis to their censure. Their devotion to the Holy Sepulchre was a most effective weapon against the detested papacy. It enabled them to object to the Albigensian crusade on pious grounds.

It is not surprising, therefore, to find that the Provençal knights Tomier and Palazi objected to the Albigensian crusade in 1216 precisely on the score that the cause of the Holy Land was being neglected.

> He who abandons the Holy Sepulchre has no sincere faith in God. Certainly the clergy and the French care very little about the shame inflicted upon Him. Yet God will be revenged upon those whose rapacity has cut the roads and closed the ports which lead to Acre and Syria.[52]

Similar expressions of disgust with the papacy's neglect of the Holy Sepulchre are to be found in two poems of Guillem Rainol.[53] There is evidence that such charges were quite justifiable. The Christians in the Holy Land sent messengers to Innocent III to protest that the indulgences granted for the Albigensian crusade endangered aid for the Holy Sepulchre.[54] Certainly the zeal shown by the papacy for the crusade against the heretic was a contributing factor to the interminable delay of Innocent III's projected crusade against the Saracen. For example, Honorius III, Innocent's successor, thought it was better to use money destined for the Holy Land in the interest of the Albigensian crusade.[55]

The Holy Land, it seems, was deprived of warriors as well as money; for, if one is to believe William of Tudela, the French fought the Albigensians with far more enthusiasm than the Saracens.[56] The Provençaux had no difficulty explaining such crusade zeal. Their property was the reward of victorious crusaders.[57] What the local nobility, insisting upon their loyalty to the Church, thought of a crusade that stripped them of their lands is vividly expressed by the anonymous poet who continued the *Chanson de la croisade contre les Albigeois* after William of Tudela.[58] Having come to the Fourth Lateran Council to protest against the spoliation of his lands, the Count of Foix pleaded his case with fiery eloquence before Innocent III himself.[59] Accused of heresy and the murder of crusaders by Folquet de Marseille, a troubadour who had attained the high rank of Bishop of Toulouse, the count replied that he had never hurt any true pilgrim, but he rejoiced that he had put out the eyes, cut off the feet, hands and fingers,[60] of the false traitors and perjurers who assumed the cross for his distruction. His only regret was that some had escaped. As for his accusor the Bishop of Toulouse, he was a traitor to God and his compatriots. He composed lying songs and slanderous sayings for the destruction of those who sang or recited them. When he had been a jongleur, the nobility had maintained him with gifts. Now that he was Bishop of Toulouse no one dared defend whatever he attacked. The whole earth was flaming with the conflagration he had lit. He had caused the destruction, body and soul, of more than five hundred thousand.[61] By his acts, words, and conduct he seemed Antichrist rather than a papal legate.[62]

It is interesting to note that, according to this same anonymous poet, the crusaders themselves were critical of the behavior of the clergy. After the French had been repulsed from Beaucaire in 1216, their leader Simon de Montfort gathered together the bishops to ask them to explain the failure of God's army.[63] Finding their explanations unsatisfactory, one knight, Foucaut de Berzi, marvelled at the fashion in which the clergy granted absolution without penance. A bishop explained in vain that whoever fought the heretics, even though guilty of mortal sin, had done his penance. This Foucaut refused to believe and insisted that the crusaders' defeat at Beaucaire was caused not only by their sins, but by the "preaching of the clergy" as well.[64]

When Simon de Montfort had his head crushed by a stone which hit just "where it was necessary" during the seige of Toulouse,[65] the poet reported that the Bishop of Toulouse wished to consider the fallen leader a saint and a martyr, but that the Count of Soissons objected because he had died without confession.[66] However, it seems that the bishop had his way in the end; for an epitaph was made celebrating the crusader's pious virtues, an epitaph that stirred the author of the *Chanson* to the most terrible indictment of the Albigensian crusade. There could be no more eloquent condemnation of the abuse of the holy war than his stinging reproach of the Church for promising to the greedy and blood-thirsty the greatest spiritual rewards:

> And the epitaph relates, to one who can read it, that he (Simon de Montfort) is a saint and a martyr, and that he is destined to rise at the last day and to inherit and enjoy the marvelous bliss of heaven, and to wear the crown and to sit in the kingdom (of heaven). And I have heard it said that it may well be so: if by killing men, by shedding blood, by destroying souls, by consenting to murders, by following evil counsels, by starting conflagrations, by destroying barons, by bringing the nobility to shame, by seizing lands, by advancing the wicked, by kindling evil, by extinguishing good, by killing women and destroying children, one can gain Jesus Christ in this world, one should wear a crown and shine in heaven![67]

As the popes continued in their determined effort to destroy the Albigensian heretics, the Provençal poets were in no way cowed by increasing hardships and brutalities. Rather they were stirred to deeper indignation at the Church for promoting war within Christendom. During the siege of Avignon in 1226 Tomier and Palazi composed another *sirventés* much more violent than the one they had written ten years before. Obviously intended to maintain the morale of the Provençaux during the conflict with the French crusaders, this poem has a martial and catchy refrain which must have made it effective propaganda.[68] All restraint has disappeared. The Tarascon poets now contended that whoever betrayed the Holy Land by joining the "false crusade" was guilty of heresy:

> We shall have mighty aid—I have faith in God—with which we shall conquer the French; of an army which does not fear God, God soon takes his vengeance.

> Seignors, we are certain and confident of mighty aid.

> Many a person prepares himself to come with a false crusade, but he shall have to flee without (having the time to light) his campfires. For by hitting hard, one easily conquers the rabble.

> Seignors, we are certain and confident of mighty aid.

> They have deprived the Sepulchre of help and strength—those who have taken the cross against us, and that is heresy. The false fools shall ill enjoy the silver[69] thus acquired.

> Seignors, we are certain and confident of mighty aid.[70]

It is obvious that Tomier and Palazi have here exceeded the bounds of orthodoxy: to accuse the Church of heresy is to confess oneself a heretic. The tailor Figueira likewise proved himself a heretic by denying the orthodoxy of the Albigensian crusade. Writing in 1228, when the war was drawing to its bloody end,[71] he denied the validity of indulgences offered for the conquest of his native land, indulgences, he implied, that worked to the detriment of the Holy Sepulchre.

> Rome, truly I know without doubt that with the trickery of false pardons you delivered to torment the barons of France. And you killed the good King Louis[72] with your false preaching—you drew him out of Paris.

> Rome, you do little harm to the Saracens, but you massacre Greeks and Latin. In hell fire and ruin you have your seat, Rome. God give me no share in the indulgence nor in the pilgrimage of Avignon.

> Rome, it is most true that you offer too eagerly the false pardons against Toulouse. You bite hands like a mad-dog, Rome, sower of discord. But if the brave count[73] lives two years more, France will feel the pain of your trickery.[74]

Another poem written in the same desperate year of 1228 reflects not heresy, but the deep contempt and hatred the crusade had inspired. Folquet de Romans, viewing the ruin about him, concluded that the clergy, whose duty it was to maintain virtue, were the worst of a bad world. He declared:

> They prefer war to peace, malice and sin please them so much. I would have enjoyed going on the first crusade, but nearly all I see of this one [the Albigensian] repels me.[75]

Not only the Provençaux, whose rage is quite understandable, criticized the spectacle of a holy war in Europe while the Moslem was left in peace. Poets writing in Old French did not hesitate to condemn the Albigensian crusade as most unchristian and repellent to God. Nor is there any reason to doubt the sincerity of their testimony: the French gained, not lost, by the Albigensian crusade.

One of the first protests in Old French against the holy war in Languedoc may be found in a vigorous lyric, ascribed to Moniot. The poet referred to the defeats of Amauri de Montfort, son of the hated Simon, citing his failure in 1219 as clear evidence that the crusade was against God's will.[76] Guillaume le Clerc had similar doubts of God's approval. He wondered what God would say to the French knights who went on the crusade, many of whom were as sinful as those against whom they waged war.[77] In another passage of *Le Besant de Dieu* Guillaume le Clerc reproved the papacy with a restraint that is more telling than the violence of the troubadour Guillem Figueira:

> Rome should not, I think, if one of her sons has fallen into error and wishes to rectify it, send upon him an elder brother to destroy him. Rather should she summon, talk gently, and admonish him than waste his country. When the French go against the people of Toulouse, whom they consider heretics, and when the papal legate leads and guides them, that is not at all right in my opinion.[78]

One should note that together with Guillaume le Clerc's disapproval of the use of force against heretics there appears the same strong dislike of a papal legate's command on an army which he expressed while commenting upon the loss of Damietta.[79] It is quite true that the papacy's direct control of the army was much in evidence during the Albigensian crusade before the King of France assumed active leadership.[80]

Similar disgust with papal crusade policy was voiced by Huon de Saint-Quentin, who felt that early crusading ideals were betrayed by the crusade against the heretic in Europe. Like the troubadours, he protested that the Albigensian crusade was ruinous to the cause of the Holy Land.

> The river, the Sepulchre, the cross all cry with one voice that Rome plays with false dice. It appeared well in Albi . . .[81]

That these criticisms in Old French may be representative of a much larger body of opinion is shown by the evidence of Roger of Wendover, a monk of St. Albans who wrote shortly after the conquest of Avignon.[82] Roger related that when King Louis VIII took the cross for a renewal of the Albigensian crusade in 1226 and the Roman legate began to preach, very many entered upon the crusade more because of fear of the king or the desire to curry favor with the legate than for their "zeal for justice". Many considered it a sin to attack a true Christian, and had been very unfavorably impressed by the harshness of the papal legate at the Council of Bruges, where the offer of the Count of Toulouse to submit himself and his territory to an investigation of faith had been summarily refused.[83] After Avignon had been taken through a most unedifying ruse which involved the breach of solemn oaths, Roger of Wendover concluded that from the death, sorrow, and bitterness resulting from this crusade, it was obviously an unjust war, inspired by greed rather than zeal to exterminate heresy.[84] This opinion, of course, may have been the result of seeing the French king use the crusade as a means of political aggrandizement. Possibly it indicates English dislike of the French monarchy as well as criticism of the Church for permitting such exploitation of the holy war.

There were some, however, who rose to defend the Church's crusade against the heretic and their defense completely substantiates the critics' contention that the Albigensian crusade had injured the crusade in the Holy Land. For example, Gormonda de Montpellier, who answered Guillem Figueira's violent attack upon the Church with a *sirventés* no less violent, did not deny the charge that the Church had neglected the crusade against the Saracen for the sake of crushing heresy. On the contrary, she justified the policy by insisting that the wretched heretics were worse than Saracens and with false hearts.[85] In reply to the charge of "false indulgences", she declared that whoever wished to be saved should take the cross to defeat the "false heretics",[86] concluding with the pious wish that Guillem Figueira should be tortured and put to death for having dared criticize the Church.[87]

During the last rebellion of the Albigensians in 1244, Lanfranc Cigala, a Genoese judge[88] writing in Provençal, took the same position as Gormonda in regard to the relative evil of heretic and Saracen. Although critical of papal crusade policy for other reasons,[89] he felt that the holy war against heresy was necessary. Addressing the Count of Provence, he wrote:

> Count of Provence, the Sepulchre would soon be freed if your means corresponded to the esteem you inspire . . . But I do not have the heart to urge you to cross (the sea), because there is need for your valor to defend the Church from its attackers. On the other side of the sea there are not Turks who are worse.[90]

The statements of Gormonda de Montpellier and Lanfranc Cigala were not aberrations of bigoted zealots. They may be fully justified by papal bulls and theological reasoning. During the thirteenth century the popes had to contend with heretics throughout Europe and they found the crusade a most potent weapon in enforcing religious unity. The Albigensian crusade had set them an example they found expedient to follow.[91] During these wars the questions inevitably arose as to which should have precedence, the crusade against the Saracen in the Holy Land or the heretic in Europe. Innocent III was forced to make his decision during the course of the Albigensian crusade, and it served as a precedent for his successors.

Deeply concerned for the welfare of the Holy Land, Innocent III hesitated at first, it would seem, to offer spiritual rewards equivalent to those granted for the crusade against the Moslem. Perhaps one can measure his increasing fear of heresy by the increasingly generous indulgences offered for the Albigensian crusade, indulgences which in 1208 were finally greater than those offered for the crusade in the Holy Land.[92] It was precisely in 1208 that Innocent III declared that the heretics were worse than Saracens,[93] the opinion echoed by Gormonda de Montpellier and Lanfranc Cigala. The actions of later popes were consistent with this view. Honorius III helped finance the Albigensian crusade from funds collected for the Holy Land.[94] In a bull of 1254 Innocent IV declared that if necessary he would detain crusaders leaving for the Holy Land and send them against the heretics in Europe since it was much better to defend the faith at home than in the distant East.[95]

The theological basis for this position was stated later[96] by Thomas Aquinas in his *Summa Theologica.* Unbelievers who had once accepted the faith, such as heretics and apostates, could be forced even by bodily compulsion into submission to the true Church. On the contrary, compulsion should not be used against the infidels who had never had the true faith; wars were waged against them only to keep them from hindering the Christian faith.[97] Death was a just penalty for the heretic, who endangered the salvation of others.[98] From such conclusions it is not difficult to see that when heresy was more threatening at home than the mere hindrance of Christianity overseas, a crusade against the heretic was of more vital importance to the Church than the crusade against the Moslem. Nothing was more imperative than religious unity. From the very inception of the Albigensian crusade, the declared purpose of the war against heresy had been the preservation of the faithful from error spread by the heretic.[99]

After the Albigensian heresy was crushed, denunciation of papal crusade policy grew rather than diminished. The papacy of the thirteenth century was intent upon making theocracy a political reality and used with increasing frequency the crusade against rebellious rulers and cities. The holy war flourished in Europe, not in the Orient. This policy of offering indulgences for war against recalcitrant princes was not at all new. Indeed, the origins of the crusade were closely connected with eleventh-century theocratic theory.[100] But it remained for Innocent III to give new impetus to the Church's determination to dominate in the political as well as the religious sphere. It was he who offered full crusade indulgence to recover the vassal state of Sicily from Markwald in 1199.[101] It was he who declared that Christians rebelling against the Church were "worse than Saracens" because they stood in the way of the recovery of the Holy Sepulchre.[102] By preaching a crusade against a defiant ruler, he could call into being an army anywhere in Europe to uphold the political suzerainty of the Church.[103] Throughout the thirteenth and fourteenth centuries the popes followed Innocent's example and proclaimed crusades against their enemies,[104] either charging their opponents with heresy or declaring that they obstructed the recovery of the Holy Land. The former accusation could be made all the more easily in that anyone who failed to submit to the Church after a year of excommunication was suspected of heresy.[105]

Such crusades were a dreaded weapon in the hands of a politically ambitious papacy and those antagonistic to papal aims were always ready to present the holy war in Europe as a perversion of the crusading motive. Thus their criticism gives an excellent insight into the bitterness of the Guelf-Ghibelline struggle and the decaying prestige of a papacy too inclined to use spiritual weapons for apparently secular aims. This sort of censure began when the pope preached a crusade against the excommunicated Frederick II, while that formidable enemy of theocracy was

recovering the Holy Sepulchre and establishing claims of overlordship in the East.[106]

The crusade against Frederick was preached as the Albigensian holy war was ending. It is not surprising, therefore, to find the Provençal Guillem Figueira railing at the pope for his war on the emperor in his excoriating *sirventés* against Rome. Just as Figueira had denied the validity of indulgences granted for the crusade against the cities of Languedoc,[107] he similarly labelled the indulgences for the crusade against the emperor as unreasonable and invalid.[108] He questioned the pope's authority for permitting violence against Christians in passages that lack nothing in the way of sharpness:

> Rome, you have killed many people without reason and I am not pleased that you hold to a wicked way. You close the door to salvation.
>
> . . . Rome, the evil one says of you strikes home; for you through mockery have Christians martyred. But in what book, Rome, do you find that one should kill Christians?[109]

After the crusaders had conquered his native land, Figueira fled to Italy where he became a protégé of Frederick II,[110] and loudly proclaimed the necessity of peace between the two heads of Christendom as essential for the success of the crusade in the Holy Land.[111] It is quite probable that his *sirventés* against Rome already reflected Frederick's propaganda. The emperor's widely-circulated manifesto to Christian princes written after his excommunication has many points in common with Figueira's *D'un sirventes far.*[112] And there is yet additional evidence that Figueira was repeating current criticism made by enemies of the Church. A pilgrim gave to Roger of Wendover a letter addressed to Frederick by one of his followers in Sicily and the chronicler quotes this epistle in full. In this suspiciously accessible letter[113] Frederick is informed that his friends were most astonished to see the pope sending an army against his possessions and even the clergy wondered how the pope's conscience permitted him to make war on Christians.[114]

Although Frederick made his peace with the pope in 1230, it was only to consolidate his power more firmly in Italy.[115] Considering circumstances propitious in 1236, the emperor began an attack on Lombardy in spite of the pope's exhortation to go on a crusade overseas. With truly diabolical cleverness Frederick pointed to many heretics in northern Italy, especially Milan, and using the pope's own reasoning, declared it would be most ill-advised for him to go to the Holy Land and leave unpunished the false Christians worse than any Saracen.[116] It was not long, however, before Frederick found himself suspected of heresy, and the inevitable crusade against him soon followed.[117]

The second phase of the struggle between the pope and Frederick II began just as a crusade was about to depart for the Orient. As one of the greatest powers in the West, the emperor seemed to some the proper leader, but now that he was a declared enemy of the Church the pope was determined that Frederick should not repeat his astonishing crusading exploits of 1228 to the detriment of papal prestige. Consequently, the French crusaders already gathered together at Lyons were threatened with excommunication if they dared accept the leadership of Frederick II.[118] This caused deep resentment among the French, who in their fury at the pope's prohibition to leave Lyons for their crusade, almost attacked the papal legates.[119] Much of the army having dispersed, Thibaut IV, Count of Champagne, finally led the remnant of crusaders on this futile expedition.[120] Thibaut was a poet as well as a warrior and has expressed the general suspicions of his compatriots in a crusade song. Times were, he declared, bad indeed when one beheld excommunicated those who had right on their side.[121] Thibaut was no exception. Many French nobles were sympathetic with Frederick's cause.[122]

Not all contemporary poets agreed with Thibaut. Just as the Church had a Provençal defender who justified its crusade against the heretic, it now found a troubadour who considered the crusade against Frederick II praiseworthy. Uc de Saint Circ, who spent part of his life wandering in Lombardy,[123] where Frederick was none too popular, described the emperor as a monster of heresy, believing in neither immortality nor paradise.[124] Frederick, he charged, planned to humiliate France and the Church.

> That is why (he pointed out) the Church and the king should send us an army of crusaders to enable us to go into Apulia and conquer Frederick II; for whoever does not believe in God should not reign.[125]

When Frederick found himself again the object of a crusade, his sympathies for suffering Christians seem to have been marvelously quickened. Although he continued to deplore heresy in northern Italy and called the pope the protector of heretics,[126] he now found it expedient to proclaim a war against the infidel. In 1241 he addressed a letter to Christian princes in which he instructed the pope upon his high duty to Christendom. He complained that Innocent IV preached a crusade against him, "an arm and advocate of the Church" rather than against the invading Tartars or the Saracens in the Holy Land.[127]

Throughout the remaining desperate battle between papacy and empire, the Ghibelline adherents of the Hohenstaufen piped the same tune: the crusade against a Christian ruler was a betrayal of the Holy Sepulchre. They, like the earlier troubadours, enjoyed reading the pope a lesson on his obligations to the Christians in Palestine, and, as in the case of the earlier troubadours, their zeal for the Holy Sepulchre must not always be taken seriously.[128] Upon one occasion, at least, the partisans of the emperor sought to use the pope's own weapon of a holy war in Europe. The deacon and chapter of Passau preached quite successfully a so-called crusade against the papal legate in 1240. Many took the cross, certain of their salvation in fighting the pope.[129] This irony of ironies, a crusade against the pope's representative, speaks eloquently of the degeneration of

crusading motives by the middle of the thirteenth century. During the tremendous struggle between pope and emperor the crusade became a convenient military resource, a means of seeking fresh recruits. It is doubtless for this reason that in the Ghibelline town of Ratisbon any one found wearing the cross was immediately condemned to death.[130]

One of the greatest Provençal satirists of the thirteenth century, Peire Cardenal, expressed his eloquent scorn at the sight of the holy war becoming a mere pawn in the complex battle for political domination. The clergy, he maintained, pretended to be shepherds while they were really butchers. They were wolves in sheep's clothing devouring the simple.[131] To Cardenal the papal monarchy and the coercive measures used to build it up were anathema.

> Kings, emperors, dukes, counts, nobles, and knights with them used to rule the world; now I see authority possessed by the clergy by means of robbery, treachery, hypocrisy, force, and preaching; and they are indignant at any one who does not give his all to them; and they will get all, however long it is delayed.[132]

Nor did Cardenal disguise his contempt for the laity who let themselves be so duped. Upon hearing a command from the clergy he sneered, the laity "will draw their swords towards heaven and get into the saddle".[133] If only the clergy order it, the credulous fools will go to pillage their neighbor's territory.[134] His intense hatred of the clergy for this abuse of their influence hardly knows bounds. In his poem *Atressi cum per fargar* he does not mince words in damning the Church for stirring up war among Christians.

> The clergy send knights to carnage. When they have given them bread and cheese, they place them where one covers them with wounds. They [the clergy] protect their own swinish flesh from every blade, but they do not complain if the brains of others are scattered abroad.

> They are so full of evil cunning that with the gloveless hands of others they take rebellious cat in order that they themselves may suffer no harm. But when they are at their porringers, they are all the equal of Roland.[135]

In Peire Cardenal's none-too-modest opinion, it was precisely this worldly ambition of the Church that hindered any new crusade against the Saracen. Mohammedan leaders, he observed sarcastically, had no need to fear that abbot or prior would come to attack them or seize their lands. The clergy much preferred remaining in Europe to devise means of getting possession of the world and ruining Frederick II.[136]

Peire Cardenal's accusation that the Church was sacrificing the Holy Land for the crusade against Frederick II is well substantiated by the pope himself. As in the case of the crusade against the Albigensian heretics, the question arose as to the relative importance of the holy war in the East and the holy war in Europe. Again the papacy followed the policy of promoting the crusade in Palestine. Louis IX of France tried in vain to reconcile Innocent IV with Frederick II, who had, it appeared, offered to spend the rest of his life fighting in the Holy Land.[137] In 1241 Innocent IV empowered his legate in Hungary to free crusaders from their oath to go to the Holy Land if they would join in the crusade against Frederick II.[138] In 1247 the pope stated that his crusade policy with great clarity. Writing to the papal legate in the Empire, he declared that in the circumstances it was more useful and pleasing to God to fight Frederick II, the rebellious emperor, than to undertake a crusade against the Moslem. The defeat of Frederick would profit the Holy Land while his triumph would not help it.[139]

The Genoese Lanfranc Cigala clearly perceived how greatly the cause of the Holy Land was injured by such a policy. The loss of Jerusalem in 1244 had dramatically revealed the weakness of the Christian States in the Orient.[140] Cigala placed the blame for this disaster directly upon the battle between papacy and emperor. The war between these two great powers, he maintained, had made impossible the first requisite of a successful crusade, peace among Christian states. Nor did they show, he added, any indication of wanting peace. "I will not say", he commented, "which is at fault. May God inspire the guilty one with better intentions or have him suddenly die.[141] His ending, however, completely belied this admirable impartiality. "Pope", he declared, "I believe you make war or peace as it profits you; for if you continue your usual course, the Holy Sepulchre will not be saved by you".[142]

The suspicions thus frankly expressed by Lanfranc Cigala were greatly intensified after the failure of Louis IX's first crusade in 1250. Some rejoiced over the failure, interpreting it, doubtless, as a check to papal prestige.[143] Some despaired to the point of doubting Christianity.[144] Others expressed their distrust of the Church while voicing their sorrow over the calamity. A troubadour, Austorc d'Aurillac, wailed the loss of Louis IX's magnificent army and in a frenzy of exasperation exclaimed: "Curse Alexandria, curse the clergy, curse the Turks. . . ." He then expressed the wish that Frederick might go on a crusade and make an alliance with the French against the perfidious clergy. He ended his diatribe by observing that Saint Peter held to the right way, but that the pope now wandered from it when he and his clergy did evil to many for the sake of money.[145]

One finds ample confirmation that those using the vernacular were reflecting popular discontent. Matthew Paris reported that the French were most indignant over the failure of Louis IX's crusade. They ascribed his defeat to the pope because he had refused to make peace with Frederick II and thus dispersed the strength of Christendom. They considered it the pope's fault that the Orient was inundated with Christian blood; his was the blame that so much blood had been uselessly spilt in Germany and Italy.[146] Frederick II himself, it goes without saying,

did not let the opportunity pass of condemning the pope for the disaster, pointing out how Innocent IV had supported the crusade against him to the detriment of the holy war overseas.[147] A careful scrutiny of the pope's crusade policy makes this charge difficult to refute,[148] although no one should take seriously Frederick's tone of pious horror.

The crusade against the Hohenstaufen did not cease with the death of Frederick in 1250. The papacy was determined to destroy the formidable dynasty root and branch. The holy war was preached most zealously against Frederick's legitimate son Conrad IV.[149] The crusade against Manfred, Frederick's illegitimate son who had seized power in Sicily, was pursued with equal vigor. Manfred was formally accused of heresy and of alliance with the Saracens[150]—the charge previously brought against Frederick II. This accusation had good foundation in fact. Both Frederick and Manfred had sought the aid of Saracens,[151] but whether such an alliance was cause or effect of papal animosity remains a moot question in the history of the complex struggle. Justifiable as the crusades against the Hohenstaufen were on theocratic grounds, their continuation precisely at the time St. Louis was courageously endeavoring to bring victory out of defeat in the Holy Land presented a striking contrast in crusade aims that inevitably aroused a storm of protest.

Perhaps the best evidence of the extraordinary discontent in France may be perceived in the uprising known as the Pastoureaux, led by a mysterious "master of Hungary" who preached against the clergy and the papal curia. The avowed purpose of this mass movement was the rescue of Louis IX in the Holy Land. Hysterical bands of agricultural and town workers, disapproved by the Church, marched through France viciously attacking priests and monks while on their way to kill the Saracen. At first tacitly approved by the queen mother, Blanche of Castile, the Pastoreaux finally became so disorderly that they were dispersed.[152] There is no doubt, however, that Blanche of Castile shared the resentment of the lower classes for the papacy's apparent neglect of her son. Of exemplary piety, she nevertheless listened sympathetically when the French nobles denounced the pope's new crusade against Conrad. The pope, they said, was stirring up new, internal wars among Christians in Christian territory while he consigned Louis IX to oblivion in Palestine. Blanche at once ordered the confiscation of the property of all in the royal domain who had taken the cross against Conrad, declaring: "Let those who fight for the pope be supported from the pope's own means, and let them go, never to return". The nobles followed the same procedure in their own lands.[153]

In Germany as well as France there were expressions of indignation at the crusade against Conrad. The Bishop of Mainz protested that it was not the duty of priests to kindle war, but to reestablish peace.[154] Henry of Embrun (Hostiensis), who accompanied the papal legate to Germany in 1251, related in his *Summa Aurea* that he met many who considered a crusade against a Christian ruler most unjust—an opinion Henry refuted by pointing to the close analogy between the conduct of heretics and rebellious Christians, both more sinful than Saracens.[155]

The resentment in France and Germany, however, was mild in comparison to the fury of the Italian Ghibellines. Composed in the very arena of the political crusades, the poetry of the Italian troubadours reflects the desperate struggle most vividly. One can assume with more certainty that the opinion they expressed was personal, since the Italian troubadours after the death of Frederick II found few princely patrons. Instead of being dependents at a court, the troubadours were self-supporting Italian burghers who cultivated Provençal and used this sharp-edged language in their bitter political feuds.[156] The pope was not spared; even gutter abuse was disdained as a weapon against him. For example, Bonifacio de Castellana in a *sirventés* of 1251-52 accused the clergy of endeavoring to disinherit Conrad in order to make gifts to their bastards.[157] Others railed at the Church for its war on Manfred.[158] Many of these attacks are composed in the same bellicose style used against ordinary secular rulers and contain no reproach for neglect of the Holy Land.[159] Yet the mistake should not be made of considering such censure entirely a matter of partisan politics. In distant England when the papal legate proclaimed the crusade against Manfred in 1255, the people jeered and laughed at the changeability of preachers who now promised them the same heavenly reward for the shedding of Christian blood they had formerly promised for the destruction of the Saracen.[160]

That the Provençaux had not forgotten their old enmity may be seen from a poem of Bertran d'Alamanon written after Frederick II's death and before 1265.[161] This Provençal knight charged the pope with keeping the office of emperor vacant in order to receive bribes for his support of claimants. The Empire thus brought him more money than if he owned it outright, Bertran shrewdly observed. The issue, in Bertran's opinion, could only be decided by letting the claimants fight until one finally attained victory. The conqueror might rest assured that the pope would crown him without difficulty; for the clergy always obeyed a powerful master and then worked for his ruin when they saw his power declining. If this plan did not please the contestants, Bertran added, they could do a hundred times better by going on a crusade against the Saracens.[162] The pope, he cuttingly added, would give out indulgences generously for the crusade, but little of his money.[163]

There is evidence to confirm Bertran d'Alamanon's insinuation that the Holy Land did not have the complete financial support of the papacy. The war against the Hohenstaufen as it entered the last phase strained every resource. An army had to be organized and maintained for Charles of Anjou, whom the papacy had invited into Italy to carry on the war against Manfred. After Manfred was defeated in 1266 and Charles had successfully seized southern Italy, a second crusade was organized against Corradino, who inherited the claims of his father Conrad IV and came to Italy to recapture former Hohenstaufen possessions.[164] Protesting against the pope's holy war against him, Corradino echoed his grandfather Frederick II: "See", he wrote "the cross of the Saviour turned against Christians".[165]

It was during this last battle between pope and Hohenstaufen that the most despairing comment was made by an inhabitant of the Holy Land itself. Ricaut Bonomel, a Templar in Palestine, hopeless and resentful because of constant losses, held the pope largely responsible for these disasters in the Holy Land.

> The pope bestows many indulgences for the war of Lombardy in favor of Charles and the French, while for us here [in the Holy Land] he shows great avarice since he redeems our cross for money. Whoever wishes to change the war in the Holy Land for the war in Lombardy has permission from our legate, because they [the clergy] sell God and indulgences for money.
>
> French Lords, Alexandria has done you more harm than Lombardy; for here [in the Orient] the Turks have robbed us of power, taken us, conquered us, and sold us for money.[166]

This accusation that the pope commuted crusade vows for money and that he permitted the substitution of the crusade vow against the Hohenstaufen for the crusade vow against the Saracen is indisputable. Clement IV in 1265 permitted the conversion of crusade vows for the Holy Land to vows for the holy war in Italy,[167] and it is quite possible that Ricaut Bonomel referred specifically to this papal decision.[168] However, such substitution had been a part of crusade policy long before 1265. Innocent IV had permitted them during his war with Frederick II,[169] and had also used money gathered from crusade vow redemptions for the war against the emperor rather than the crusade in the Holy Land.[170] In 1255 Henry III of England was allowed to change his original crusade vow to one against Manfred, and then released from this vow upon the payment of a large sum of money, used in the Italian crusade.[171]

While Ricaut Bonomel was complaining in Palestine of crusade vow redemptions, the troubadours in Italy were not silent. They raged against the Church and Charles of Sicily in their usual virulent style.[172] Shortly before the hated Charles defeated and killed Corradino in the crusade of 1268, Calega Panza, a Genoese cloth merchant with commerical interests in the Orient,[173] joined in the chorus of denunciation. In a passage similar to the arraignment of Simon de Montfort's epitaph found in the *Chanson de croisade contre les Albigeois*[174] Calega Panza vented his wrath upon the Church for betraying his conception of Christian ideals by promoting a crusade against Christians.

> He who wishes to kill or live by rapine can quickly and easily attain salvation. He has only to murder a hundred Christians; and whoever should strive to kill a thousand would have a higher place in paradise. You have abandoned the [right] way, the precepts God made pure and holy, and Moses who wrote the commandments.[175]

Calega Panza likewise pointed out that the crusade in the Holy Land was being sacrificed to the crusade in Italy. He exclaimed:

> Ah unfaithful [clergy]! You have Tuscany and Lombardy massacred and pay no attention to Syria. You make a truce with the Turks and Persians to kill here French and Germans.[176]

Nor was it only overseas, Calega Panza insisted, that the Church was conciliatory to the Mohammedans while preaching crusades against Christians. The Greeks and Latins could get no truce from Charles of Sicily (Anjou), although this warrior of the pope made a truce with the Saracens of Lucera in Italy, where they were permitted to worship Mohammed as much as they pleased: there were no churches and monasteries. He wondered that the pope should endanger the true faith by such toleration.[177]

A somewhat more dispassionate critic writing at about the same time[178] may be found in Guillem Fabre, a burgher of Narbonne. After condemning the quarrels among princes as a hindrance to the crusade, he revealed his Ghibelline sympathies by declaring:

> He who is our head, placed to govern our faith, merits even greater blame. In fact, although the greater part of the known world obeys him, he did not command a crusade against the perfidious wretches who hold the Holy Land before the present discord occurred and before the world became bad; for [if he had done this] I believe that all the great who maintain hatred would now be there [in the Holy Land] doing good.[179]

After the defeat of the last Hohenstaufen there was a lull in the storm of criticism. Indeed, following the death of Clement IV in 1268 the Holy See was vacant for almost three years[180] and there was no pope to reproach. During this time Louis IX was preparing his second crusade against the Saracens. This ill-fated expedition which attempted the capture of Tunis ended in failure and Louis' death. Again a cry of despair and doubt arose,[181] but reproaches were not addressed directly to the papacy which was still vacant at the time of the disaster (1270).

It is most ironical that when Gregory X appeared in 1271 to fulfill the wishes of Calega Panza and other critics by devoting himself wholeheartedly to the cause of the Holy Land, he found himself checked on all sides by the incredulity and suspicion they had expressed. The papacy had aroused such distrust during the thirteenth century by its use of the crusades that Gregory X's sincere appeal to forget selfish interests for the sake of a crusade against the Saracen met little response. By reversing the policy of his predecessors and centering everything upon the recovery of the Holy Land, Gregory X was confronted with the necessity of pacifying a war-torn Europe, thoroughly suspicious of papal aims.[182]

The distrust which made Gregory's crusade plans seem futile in the midst of tangled Guelf-Ghibelline hostilities[183] was expressed bluntly by Folquet de Lunel, a troubadour patronized by Alfonso of Castile, the Ghibelline claimant to the Emperorship.[184]

> It would be a good thing to summon the pope before some one higher than he is, since he gives King Alfonso nothing, King Charles (of Sicily) everything. Also it is time to free Henry[185] and the Empire should no longer remain vacant. Then the pope with all the kings that have received baptism should go to Syria to revenge Jesus Christ.[186]

These charges of Folquet de Lunel are not at all justifiable, but they illustrate admirably the suspicions with which Gregory had to contend, suspicions aroused by the crusade policy of the thirteenth century popes. Gregory X had no desire to favour Charles of Sicily unduly,[187] nor did he deny favors to Alfonso X,[188] nor did he wish to keep the Empire vacant,[189] nor was there anything he desired more than the crusade recommended by Folquet. The old Ghibelline charge of betrayal of the Holy Land had by now become a cliché, a valuable criticism which made the Ghibelline more pious than the pope. Yet as banal and unfair as these accusations were, one must realize that Gregory's tactics might well seem suspect to contemporaries witnessing the continued ferocity of the Guelf-Ghibelline struggle. The Ghibellines had seen former popes make brave statements about saving the Holy Land only to behold the commutation of crusade vows against the Saracen to crusade vows against the Ghibellines. The openly avowed suspicions of Folquet de Lunel must have appeared quite reasonable to those hostile to the papacy.

Yet it would be a mistake to consider that all of this suspicion of the crusade with which Gregory had to contend throughout his pontificate came entirely from partisan politics. Certainly much of the criticism in Old French was inspired by moral conviction rather than political expediency. The French did not suffer from the Albigensian crusade and yet Guillaume le Clerc revealed that there existed a religious conception outraged by the use of force instead of persuasion in the destruction of heresy. Nor is there any reason for doubting the moral integrity of Huon de Saint Quentin, Moniot, and Gautier de Coincy.

On the other hand, the Provençaux and the Italians using Provençal had obvious worldly reasons for hating the papal monarchy and all its works. Undoubtedly many of them were Ghibelline propagandists more concerned with damning the pope than saving the Holy Sepulchre. Yet their criticism is none the less significant. Their protests show to what extent the papacy was losing control of public opinion in its firm determination to establish theocracy. Doubtless theocracy was a high ideal, but the means used to make it a reality conflicted dramatically with the twelfth century conception of an internally peaceful Christendom united against the Moslem. The papacy had once been able to unify Europe with the crusading ideal; the pope had been the great arbiter of international affairs by virtue of his leadership in the cause of the Holy Sepulchre.[190] But the papacy could not unify Europe with claims to secular overlordship and when it strove to enforce these claims by means of a crusade, it inevitablyl aid itself open to suspicion and contempt. This growing distrust, voiced for the most part by the laity, has been traced in Old French and Provençal literature. As expressions of laymen opposed to ecclesiastical domination and as attempts to turn public opinion against Church policy, these criticisms are a striking manifestation of the increasing secularization of European ideals.[191] Gregory's crusade zeal was no longer in harmony with the spirit of the times.

It is strange that none of the extant memoirs submitted to Gregory X reported these suspicions of the papacy's crusade policy. Yet the protests which had been voiced with growing vehemence during the thirteenth century were still being made[192] Furthermore, these criticisms of the papacy had been exceedingly wide-spread, coming from all parts of Europe: the Empire, England, France, Italy, and Spain. In this case the authors of the memoirs failed to carry out Gregory's command that hostility to the Church be reported from those in all walks of life. Clearly, this deep-rooted suspicion which found increasingly violent expression during the thirteenth century makes more intelligible the ultimate failure of Gregory X's crusade plans.

Notes

1. It is a curious fact that in the thirteenth century nearly all criticisms of this sort written in the vernacular came from France, Italy, and Spain. Of the poets writing in German, it seems that only Walther von der Vogelweide and Freidank criticized the papacy, but even these writers did not offer the sort of criticism discussed in this chapter, namely, that the papacy had misdirected the crusades. It is true Walther von der Vogelweide accused the papacy of fostering civil war in the Empire while taxing it and draining it of silver. See *Ahî, wie kristenliche nû der bâbest lachet,* ed. K. Lachman, *Die Gedichte Walthers von der Vogelweide* (Berlin, 1875), p. 34. He also called the pope the "new Judas" and declared the clergy had become warriors. See *Wir klagen alle* and *Ich saz ûf eine steine,* ed. K. Lachman, pp. 38 and 8, 9. Yet Walther made no reference to the harm done the Holy Land by the papacy's political ambitions; he was concerned with the harm done his fatherland. Even in the poem in which he expressed his doubt that the money gathered for the Holy Land would ever reach there, he did not state that the money would be used for a crusade in Europe. See *Sagt an, hêr Stoc, hat iuch der bâbest her gesendet,* ed. K. Lachman, p. 34.

   Freidank's accusations, although involving the crusades, were of another tenor. Freidank expressed his profound disillusion as an ex-crusader. As a partisan of Frederick II, he had a bad opinion of the pope and Syrian Christians, but he no more than Walther von der Vogelweide criticized the papal crusades for political ends. See Freidank, *Bescheidenheit,* ed. H. E. Bezzenberger (Halle, 1872), 208-16.

2. For a thorough study of this matter, see Carl Erdmann, *Die Entstehung des Kreuzzugsgedankens* (*Forschungen zur Kirchen- und Geistesgeschichte,* VI: Stuttgart, 1935), particularly p. 212 ff. See also Carl Mirbt, *Die Publizistik im Zeitalter Gregors VII* (Leipzig, 1894), pp. 456-462.

3. See Humbert of Romans, *Opus tripartitum, loc. cit.,* p. 191.

4. D. C. Munro, 'The Speech of Urban II at Clermont,' *American Historical Review,* XI (1905-06), 239.

5. There are relatively few instances in the twelfth century of indulgences issued as a reward for fighting the pope's European enemies. See Otto Volk, *Die abendländischhierarchische Kreuzzugsidee,* (Halle, 1911), p. 52.

6. The melodies of some of these lyrics have been put into modern notation and edited. See J. Bédier and P. Aubry, *Les chansons de croisade avec leurs mélodies* (Paris, 1909); E. Lommatzsch, *Provenzalisches Liederbuch* (Berlin, 1917); J. Beck, *Les chansonniers des troubadours et des trouvères* (*Corpus cantalenarum medii aevi,* series 1, I, II: Paris, 1927).

7. E. Levy, *Guilhem Figueira* (Berlin, 1880), p. 21.

8. A. Jeanroy, *La poésie lyrique des troubadours* (Paris, 1934), II, 174 ff. See also E. Levy, *op. cit.* p. 20.

9. Diez considered the *sirventés* an expression of public opinion. Jeanroy has pointed out that this conception must be accepted with reservations: the *sirventés* was written to form public opinion. He observes: "La plupart [des troubadours] étaient les protégés de personnages plus ou moins importants, dont ils sont nécessairement les interprètes, parce qu'ils étaient précisément payés pour cela . . . En quelque sens qu'on la tranche, les sirventés n'en conservent pas moins un vif intérêt: s'ils ne sont pas les reflets de l'opinion publique, ils ont pu contribuer à la former. Le fait que les princes en ont fait composer pour défendre leur politique, que parfois ils ont répondu ou fait répondre à ceux où ils étaient attaqués, nous prouve qu'il y avait réellement là, au sentiment général, un moyen d'action que l'histoire n'a pas le droit de négliger. See A. Jeanroy, *op. cit.,* II, 175, 176.

10. Jeanroy considers the *sirventés Talls gen prezich'e semona* (no. 67) of doubtful authorship, although, unfortunately, he does not give his reasons. See Jeanroy, *op. cit.,* II, 57, note 2. A. Kolsen, the editor of Giraut de Bornelh, together with Maus and Vossler, considers it authentic. See A. Kolsen, *Sämtliche Lieder des Trobadors Giraut de Bornelh* (Halle, 1935), II, 119. Certainly the content of the poem, particularly the phrase "Tals quer d'emperi corona" of stanza V, would indicate the interregnum of the thirteenth century. However, Kolsen's authority, based upon literary similarities to

undoubted compositions of the twelfth century troubadour, has here been accepted.

11. A. Kolsen, *op. cit.,* II, 119.

12. Giraut de Bornelh, *Tals gen prezich' e sermona,* ed. A. Kolsen, *op. cit.* (Halle, 1910), I, 428, 430. See stanza V.

13. Giraut de Bornelh, *op. cit.,* I, 430. Stanza VI.

14. A. Jeanroy, *op. cit.,* II, 225, and note 1.

15. L. Bréhier, *L'église et l'Orient au moyen âge: les croisades,* p. 144 ff.

16. Carl Voretzsch, *Einführung in das Studium der altfranzösischen Literatur* (3rd edition, Halle, 1925), p. 349.

17. *La Bible de Guiot de Provins,* ed. J. Orr, *Les Oeuvres de Guiot de Provins* (Manchester, 1915), p. 34.

18. V. de Bartholomaeis, *Poesie provenzali storiche relative all' Italia (Istituto storico italiano: fonti per la storia d'Italia, scrittori secoli XII-XIII,* LXXII: Rome, 1931), II, 98, note.

19. Guillem Figueira, *D'un sirventes far,* ed. V. de Bartholomaeis, *op. cit.,* II, 98, 99, See stanza III.

20. *Ibid.,* p. 99. Stanza VII.

21. A. Luchaire, *Innocent III: la question d'Orient,* pp. 114, 115.

22. L. Halphen, *L'essor de l'Europe (Peuples et civilisations,* VI: Paris, 1932), p. 427 ff.

23. L. Bréhier, *op. cit.,* pp. 174, 188.

24. *Ibid.,* pp. 194-197.

25. Dated by G. Paris, 'L'auteur de la Complainte de Jerusalem,' *Romania,* XIX (1890), 294-296.

26. Huon de Saint Quentin, *Rome, Jherusalem se plaint,* ed. K. Bartsch and A. Horning, *La langue et la littérature françaises,* cols. 373, 374.

27. *Ibid.,* col. 379.

28. Moniot, *Bien mostre Dieus apertement,* ed. A. Jeanroy and A. Langfors, *Chansons satiriques et bachiques du XIIIᵉ siècle (Les classiques français du moyen âge,* XXIII: Paris, 1921), no. 6, p. 10.

29. Gautier de Coincy, *Vie de Sainte Léocade,* ed. E. Barbazan, M. Méon, *Fabliaux et contes des poètes français* (Paris, 1808), I, 300.

30. K. Voretzsch, *Altfranzösischen Literatur,* 406.

31. Guillaume le Clerc, *Le besant de Dieu,* ed. E. Martin (Halle, 1869), p. 73. See verses 2547-64.

32. Guillem Figueira, *D'un sirventes far,* ed. V. de Bartholomaeis, *Poesie provenzali,* II, 99. Stanza V.

33. Possibly these two knights of Tarascon were brothers. See A. Jeanroy, *op. cit.,* I, 431.

34. De Bartholomaeis has identified the cardinal referred to as Tomier and Palazi as Romano Bonaventura of Rome, appointed as papal legate in Provence February 25, 1225. See V. de Bartholomaeis, *op. cit.,* II, 57, note.

35. Tomier and Palazi, *De chantar farai,* ed. V. de Bartholomaeis, *op. cit.,* II, 57. Probably written while Louis VIII of France was laying siege to Avignon. See V. de Bartholomaeis, *op. cit.,* II, 57. Stanza VIII.

36. Gormonda de Montpellier, *Greu m'es a durar,* ed. V. de Bartholomaeis, *op. cit.,* II, 107, 108. Dated 1228-1229. *Ibid.,* p. 106.

37. F. Rocquain, *La cour de Rome et l'esprit de réforme avant Luther* (Paris, 1895), II, 16.

38. See V. de Bartholomaeis, *op. cit.,* II, 11, 12, note lxxiv.

39. Peirol, *Pos flum Jordan ai vist el Monumen,* ed. V. de Bartholomaeis, *op. cit.,* II, 13, 14. Stanzas IV, V.

40. Peire Vidal, writing around 1193-94, observed:

   The pope and the false doctors have put Holy Church in such distress that God is angered. They are so mad and sinful that the heretics have arisen. Peire Vidal, *A per pauc de chantar n'om lais,* ed. J. Anglade, *Les poésies de Peire Vidal (Les classiques français du moyen âge,* XI: Paris, 1913), pp. 101, 102. See stanza II.

41. H. Pissard, *La guerre sainte en pays chrétien* (Paris, 1912), pp. 27, 29.

42. N. Paulus, *Geschichte des Ablasses im Mittelalter* (Paderborn, 1923), II, 27, 28.

43. V. Lowinsky, 'Zum geistlichen Kunstlied in der altprovenzalischen Literatur,' *Zeitschrift für französisiche Sprache und Literatur,* XX (1898), 164, 165.

44. Bertran d'Alamanon, *Pos anc nous valc amors, seigner Bertran,* ed. J. J. Salverda de Grave, *Le troubadour Bertran d'Alamanon (Bibliothèque méridionale,* series 1, VII: Toulouse, 1902), 118.

45. Guillem Ademar, *No pot esser sofert ni atendut,* ed. M. Raynouard, *Choix des poésies des troubadours* (Paris, 1818), III, 197, 198.

46. K. Lewent, *Das altprovenzalische Kreuzlied,* pp. 95-100.

47. Provençal crusade songs really begin with the third crusade (although there are a few which antedate this event, such as the works of Marcabrun) and become less and less frequent as the thirteenth century progressed. A very few belong to the fourteenth century. See K. Lewent, *op. cit.,* p. 76 ff.

48. Politics and personalities play such an important part in Provençal crusade songs that they are to be considered as polemical *sirventés* for which the poet was rewarded. See V. Lowinsky, *loc. cit.,* p. 166. Cf. A. Jeanroy, *La poésie lyrique des troubadours,* II, 175 ff.

49. F. Diez, *Leben und Werke der Troubadours* (2nd edition, Leipzig, 1882), p. 441.

50. It should be noted that some of the troubadours lamented the ruin of their country without criticizing the war as an abuse of the crusades. They said bitter things concerning the greed of the Church, the inquisition, and the French; they attacked the Kings of Aragon and England for not supporting them strongly against their enemies, etc. Such criticisms, unless they are connected with condemnation of papal crusade policy, have not been considered here. For general discussions of the troubadours during the Albigensian crusade, see J. Anglade, *Histoire sommaire de la littérature méridionale au moyen âge* (Paris, 1929), pp. 85-98, and A. Jeanroy, *op. cit.,* II, 212-229.

51. Guillem Figueira, whose *sirventés* was condemned by the inquisition, must be considered a heretic. Jeanroy has noted the similarity between Figueira's invectives and those current among the heretics: ecclesiam romanam meretricem . . . matrem fornicationum, etc. See A. Jeanroy, *op. cit.,* II, 220, note 1. Although one may suspect other Provençaux of heresy, there is rarely enough evidence in their poetry to justify the accusation. One could criticize and even fight against the pope without being a heretic.

52. Tomier and Palazi, *Si col flacs molins torneja,* ed. A. Jeanroy, 'Un sirventés en faveur de Raimon VII,' *Bausteine zur romanischen Philologie, Festgabe für A. Mussafia* (Halle, 1905), p. 631.

53. K. Lewent, *Das altprovenzalische Kreuzlied,* p. 44, note 2.

54. Innocent III, Letter to Simon de Montfort, Ep. XII (1209), 123, ed. Migne, P.L., CCXVI, col. 153.

55. A. Molinier, 'Catalogue des actes de Simon et d'Amauri de Montfort,' B.E.C., XXXIV (1873), 183.

56. William of Tudela, *Chanson de la croisade albigeoise,* ed. E. Martin-Chabot (*Classique de l'histoire de France au moyen âge,* Paris, 1931), I, laisse 47, p. 112. William of Tudela, a member of the clergy, approved of the Albigensian crusade, and wrote the first part of the *Chanson* between 1210 and 1213. See preface, p. xi.

57. The Church claimed the right of offering the property of heretics to the orthodox who helped extirpate heresy. In the sixteenth century this right came to be known as the *exposition en proie,* but in the thirteenth century expressions such as *terram exponere catholicis occupandam* were used. See H. Pissard, *La guerre sainte en pays chrétien* (Paris, 1912), pp. 37-40, 114, 115.

58. The anonymous poet who describes this scene wrote between June 25, 1218 and the summer of 1219. His poem stops abruptly after he describes the renewal of the siege of Toulouse by the French prince. An opponent of the crusade, it is possible that he was killed during the seige. See P. Meyer, *La chanson de la croisade contre les Albigeois* (Paris, 1875), I, lx, lxi.

59. P. Meyer is of the opinion that the poet was a witness of this dramatic episode at the Fourth Lateran Council and conjectures that he came to Rome with one of the Provençaux nobles, possibly the Count of Toulouse or the Count of Foix. The poet describes the protests of both these counts in some detail. The tone of this account is quite deferential to Innocent III, although violent against Simon de Montfort and the crusade, See P. Meyer, *op. cit.,* pp. lxvii to lxxv.

60. The crusaders multilated the Provençaux in the same fashion. In an anonymous collection of anecdotes to be used in sermons there is an account of how Folquet, Bishop of Toulouse, was once preaching and described heretics as wolves and the orthodox as sheep. He was interrupted by a heretic whose nose had been cut off and whose eyes had been put out by command of Simon de Montfort. The heretic showed his mutilation and inquired if the bishop had even seen a wolf so bitten by a sheep. The bishop replied that the Church had dogs to protect its sheep, and that the heretic had been properly bitten by a good and strong dog. See A. Lecoy de la Marche, *Anecdotes historiques d'Etienne de Bourbon* (Paris, 1877), pp. 23, 24, note 3.

61. This estimate, of course, cannot be accepted. It is another example of the medieval love of generous, round numbers.

62. *Chanson de la croisade contre les Albigeois,* ed. P. Meyer, lines 3285-3327, I, 146, 147.

63. The poet reported many expression of doubt from the crusaders after a defeat. Simon de Montfort cried out against God and accused the clergy of betraying him. See *Chanson,* lines 7049-7055, I, 292; lines 7286-7297, I, 300-301; lines 8215-26, I, 333. God was also bitterly reproached by the crusaders after the death of Simon. See *Chanson,* lines 8459-68, I, 342; lines 8741-54, I, 353.

64. *Chanson,* lines 4330-47, I, 188, 189.

65. *Ibid.,* line 8450, I, 342.

66. *Ibid.,* lines 8524-32, I, 344-45.

67. *Ibid.,* lines 8683-96, I, 354. See part CCVIII.

68. V. de Bartholomaeis gives convincing evidence that this *sirventés* of Tomier and Palazi, *De chantar farai,* was composed while Louis VIII of France was marching on Avignon. He has noted the propagandistic aspects of the poem, observing that it must have been composed to be sung on public squares. See *Poesie provenzali storiche,* II, 54, 55, note.

69. The interpretation of V. de Bartholomaeis has been accepted here. The word "Argenza" is used as a

pun, meaning both silver and the district around Beaucaire. *Ibid.,* II, 56, note 46.

70. Tomier and Palazi, *De chantar farai, loc. cit.,* II, 55, 56. Stanzas II, III, and VI.

71. V. de Bartholomaeis, *op. cit.,* II, 99, notes.

72. Louis VIII, who died October 1226 of dysentery, probably contracted at the siege of Avignon. See A. Luchaire, *Histoire de France,* ed. E. Lavisse (Paris, 1911), III, part 1, 293.

73. A reference to Raymond VII of Toulouse. See F. Diez, *Leben und Werke der Troubadours,* p. 456, note 4.

74. Guillem Figueira, *D'un sirventes far,* ed. V. de Bartholomaeis, *op. cit.,* II, 99, 100. Stanzas VI, VII, X.

75. Folquet de Romans, *Quan cug chantar,* ed. R. Zenker, *Die Gedichte des Folquet von Romans* (*Romanische Bibliothek,* XII: Halle, 1896), p. 59. Dated 1228. *Ibid.,* pp. 22-24. Stanza II.

76. Moniot(?), *Bien mostre Dieus apertement,* ed. A. Jeanroy, A. Lanfgors, *Chansons satiriques et bachiques du XIIIᵉ siècle* (*Les classiques français du moyen âge,* XXIII: Paris, 1921), p. 10.

77. Guillaume le Clerc, *Le besant de Dieu,* ed. E. Martin, verses 2485-90, pp. 71, 72.

78. *Ibid.,* verses 2387-99, p. 69.

79. *Ibid.,* verses 2547-64, p. 73.

80. H. Pissard, *La guerre sainte en pays chrétien,* pp. 47-49, 63-68.

81. Huon de Saint-Quentin, *Rome, Jherusalem se plaint,* ed. K. Bartsch, A. Horning, *La langue et la littérature françaises,* col. 375. Writing after 1221. See G. Paris, 'L'auteur de la Complainte de Jerusalem,' *Romania,* XIX (1890), 294-96.

82. Roger of Wendover began writing around 1231. See H. G. Hewlett, preface to *Flores historiarum* (Rolls series, LXXXIV: London, 1886), I, vii.

83. *Ibid.,* (London, 1887), II, 305, 306.

84. *Ibid.,* 314, 315.

85. Gormonda de Montpellier, *Greu m'es a durar,* ed. V. de Bartholomaeis, *op. cit.,* II, 108.

86. *Ibid.,* p. 111.

87. *Ibid.,* p. 112.

88. F. Diez, *op. cit.,* pp. 458, 459.

89. See *infra* p. 56.

90. Lanfranc Cigala, *Si mos chans fos de joi,* ed. G. Bertoni, *I trovatori d'Italia* (Modena, 1915), p. 352. K. Lewent dates this poem 1244. See *Das altprovenzalische Kreuzlied,* p. 36. Stanza VI.

91. For example, Gregory IX preached a crusade against the Lucifernians and Stedigners in Northern Europe; he launched another against the Catharists in Bosnia.

Innocent IV repeatedly preached the crusade against the Waldensians in Italy. See N. Paulus, *Geschichte des Ablasses im Mittelalter,* II, 27, 28.

92. In 1198 for aid against the heretics Innocent III offered an indulgence equivalent to that offered for a pilgrimage to Rome or Compostella. In 1204 and 1207 he offered indulgences equivalent to those for the crusade in Palestine. In 1208 and 1209 he offered indulgence to any one who would give at least forty days service, the usual feudal military obligation. See N. Paulus, *op. cit.,* I, 208. In addition to these spiritual rewards there was also tempting material recompense: the property of heretics was confiscated and distributed among the faithful crusaders. See H. Pissard, *op. cit.,* p. 37.

93. Innocent III, Letter to Philip of France, Ep. 28, anno XI (1208), ed. Migne, P.L., CCXV, col. 1359.

94. A. Molinier, 'Catalogue des actes de Simon et d'Amauri de Montfort,' B.E.C., XXXIV (1873), 183.

95. N. Paulus, *op. cit.,* II, 27, 28.

96. Thomas Aquinas' *Summa theologica* was begun between 1267 and 1273. See M. de Wulf, *History of Medieval Philosophy* (London, 1926), II, 7.

97. Thomas Aquinas, *Summa theologica* (Rome, 1928), III, 100, 101. 'Utrum infideles compellendi sint ad fidem,' II, ii, quest. x, art. viii.

98. *Ibid.,* p. 111, 112. 'Utrum haeretici sint tolerandi,' II, ii, quest. xi, art. iii.

99. H. Pissard, *op. cit.,* p. 31 ff.

100. C. Erdmann, *Die Entstehung des Kreuzzugsgedankens,* chaps. IV, V, p.107 ff.

101. H. Pissard, *op. cit.,* pp. 122-25.

102. After John of England had taken the cross, Innocent III made this declaration in his excommunication of rebellious barons: Pejores proculdubio Saracenis existentes, cum illum conantur a regno depellere, de quo potius sperabatur, quod deberet succurrer Terrae Sanctae. See Roger de Wendover, *Flores historiarum,* II, 152. Sub anno 1215. For a repetition of this statement, see *Ibid,* II, 168. Sub anno 1216.

103. H. Pissard, *op. cit.,* p. 141 ff.

104. The most important of these crusades were against Frederick II and his sons, but there were many others. The popes sometimes directed a crusade against a rebellious city, sometimes against a leader of the opposition. For example, Honorius III preached a crusade against Pisa; Gregory IX preached one against Ezzelino of Romano and another against Viterbo; a crusade was preached against Simon de Montfort as a rebel against the Church's vassal Henry III of England; similarly Martin IV preached a crusade against Peter of Aragon in 1282 after the Sicilian Vespers; Boniface waged a holy war against the Colonna family; John

XXII against the Visconti of Milan. See N. Paulus, *op. cit.,* II, 29, 30. Also H. Pissard, *op. cit.,* pp. 121-42.

105. H. Pissard, *op. cit.,* pp. 108-110.

106. L. Bréhier, *L'église et l'Orient au moyen âge: les croisades,* p. 197 ff.

107. Guillem Figueira, *D'un sirventes far,* ed. V. de Bartholomaeis, *op. cit.,* II, 99, 100. Stanzas VI, VII.

108. *Ibid.,* II, 102, 103. Stanza XIX.

109. *Ibid.,* II, 100. Stanzas VIII, IX.

110. A. Jeanroy, *La poésie lyrique des troubadours,* I, 378, 379.

111. Guillem Figueira, *Del preveire major,* ed. E. Levy, *Guilhem Figueira* (Berlin, 1880), p. 31. Dated between 1244 and 1249. *Ibid.,* p. 6.

112. V. de Bartholomaeis, *op. cit.,* I, liii, liv.

113. It seems quite obvious that this letter, addressed to Frederick in the East but circulating freely in England, was intended to stir up opinion against the pope.

114. Roger of Wendover, *Flores historiarum,* II, 358-60. Sub anno 1229.

115. L. Halphen, *L'essor de l'Europe,* p. 348 ff.

116. Matthew Paris, *Chronica majora,* III, 375. Sub anno 1236.

117. F. Graefe, *Die Publizistik in der letzten Epoche Kaiser Friedrichs II* (*Heidelberger Abhandlungen zur mittleren und neueren Geschichte,* XXIV: Heidelberg, 1909), pp. 38-40.

118. R. Röhricht, 'Die Kreuzzüge des Grafen Theobald von Navarra und Richard von Cornwallis nach dem Heiligen Land,' *Forschungen zur deutschen Geschichte,* XXVI (1886), 70.

119. Matthew Paris, *Chronica majora,* III, 614, 615. Sub anno 1239.

120. Arbois de Jubainville, *Histoire des ducs et des comtes de Champagne* (Paris, 1864), IV, i, 306-12.

121. Thibaut IV de Champagne, *Au tans plains de felonie,* ed. J. Bédier, *op. cit.,* pp. 181, 182.

122. F. Graefe, *op. cit.,* pp. 229-236.

123. A. Jeanroy, *op. cit.,* II, 162, note 5.

124. Uc de Saint Circ, *Un sirventes voill far,* ed. A. Jeanroy, J. J. Salverda de Grave, *Poésies d'Uc de Saint Circ* (*Bibliothèque méridionale,* series 1, XV: Toulouse, 1913), no. xxiii, p. 96.

125. Uc de Saint Circ, *Un sirventes voill far, loc. cit.,* pp. 97, 98. Stanza V.

126. F. Graefe, *op. cit.,* pp. 20, 21, note 20.

127. Matthew Paris, *Chronica majora,* IV, 116, 117, 119.

128. One should note that during both of Frederick II's struggles with the papacy there were troubadours who took his part, urged an attack upon Milan, etc., without mentioning the Holy Land. For an account of Frederick's partisans, see A. Jeanroy, *op. cit.,* II, 233, 234.

129. N. Paulus, *Geschichte des Ablasses im Mittelalter,* II, 27, note 1.

130. Raynaldus, *Annales ecclesiastici,* sub anno 1248, no. 11.

131. Peire Cardenal, *Le clerc si fon pastor,* ed. C. L. E. Appel, *Provenzalische Chrestomatie* (Leipzig, 1930), no. 76, p. 113. Stanza I.

132. Peire Cardenal, *loc. cit.,* Stanza II.

133. Peire Cardenal, *Un sirventes trameterai per message,* ed. C. Fabre, 'Estève de Belmont,' *Annales du Midi,* XXI (1909), 22, 23. This poem is dated 1237-38. *Ibid.,* p. 25.

134. Fabre shows that there is historical basis for the charge that the Church favored the invasions of the places mentioned by Cardenal. *Ibid.,* p. 23, note 2.

135. Peire Cardenal, *Atressi cum per fargar,* ed. C. Fabre, 'Estève de Belmont,' *Annales du Midi,* XXI (1909), 23, 24.

136. Peire Cardenal, *Li clerc si fon pastor,* ed. C. L. E. Appel, *loc. cit.,* p. 113. F. Fabre dates this poem 1245 on the grounds that at the First Council of Lyons in 1245 the clergy concerned themselves more with the war on Frederick than with the crusade of Lous IX of France. F. Fabre, *op. cit.,* p. 25, note 1. There is, however, no mention of Louis IX or his crusade in the poem. K. Vossler prefers the date of 1230, giving very weak reasons for doing so. See K. Vossler, 'Peire Cardenal, ein Satiriker aus dem Zeitalter der Albigenserkriege,' *Sitzungsberichte der Bayerischen Akademie der Wissenschadften, Philosophische-Philologische und Historische Klasse* (1916), pp. 179, 180. There is no evidence for dating *Li clerc si fon pastor* other than the reference to the Church's struggle with Frederick II, which may indicate either the earlier quarrel of 1227-30 or the later contest of 1239-50. Yet from conclusive evidence recently presented by F. Fabre that Peire Cardenal was still writing in 1271-72, it seems more probable that the troubadour referred to the later struggle between the pope and Frederick. For F. Fabre's proof of Cardenal's literary activity in 1271-72, see 'Un sirventés de Cardinal, encore inédit en partie (1271-72),' in *Miscellany of Studies in Romance Languages and Literature Presented to L. E. Kastner* (Cambridge, 1932), p. 225 ff.

137. Matthew Paris, *Chronica majora,* IV, 524.

138. N. Paulus, *Geschichte des Ablasses im Mittelalter,* II, 28.

139. N. Paulus, *op. cit.,* II, 28.

140. L. Bréhier, *op. cit.,* p. 211.

141. Lanfranc Cigala, *Si mos chanz fos de ioi ni de solatz,* ed. G. Bertoni, *I trovatori d'Italia,* pp. 350, 351. Stanza II.

142. *Ibid.,* p. 352, Stanza VII.

143. F. Wilken, *Geschichte der Kreuzzüge* (Leipzig, 1832), VII, 299, 300.

144. Salimbene reported an intense revulsion of feeling after the failure of Louis IX's crusade. When Dominicans and Franciscans (always great crusade preachers) went begging, the people called other beggars and offered their alms in the name of Mohammed, who had proved himself stronger than Christ. Salimbene, *Chronica,* M.G.H.SS., XXXII, 225. Cf. H. Prutz, *Kulturgeschichte der Kreuzzüge* (Berlin, 1883), p. 273.

145. Austorc d'Aurillac, *Ai Dies! per qu'as facha tan gran maleza,* ed. A. Jeanroy, 'Le troubadour Austorc d'Aurillac et son sirventés sur le septième croisade,' *Mélanges Chabaneau: Romanische Forschungen,* XXIII (1907), 83.

146. Matthew Paris, *Chronica majora,* V, 172, 173.

147. J. L. A. Huillard-Bréholles, *Historia diplomatica Friderici Secundi* (Paris, 1858), VI, 774.

148. E. Berger has carefully examined the question as to how much the political crusade against Frederick II injured the interests of Louis IX's crusade against the Moslem. His study, based upon the papal registers of Innocent IV, shows clearly that the pope sacrificed the welfare of Louis IX's expedition to the success of the crusade against Frederick. See *Les registres d'Innocent* IV, ed. E. Berger (*Bibliothèque des écoles françaises d'Athènes et de Rome,* series 2: Paris, 1887), II, clvi-clxix.

149. A. Potthast, *Regesta Pontificum Romanorum* (Berlin, 1875), II, 1170, no. 14170. Letter of Innocent IV, dated February 5, 1251. See also *ibid.,* p. 1173, no. 14204. Dated February 19, 1251. Innocent IV declared that the papacy would never permit any descendant of Frederick to have kingdom or empire. *Ibid.,* p. 1177, no. 14258. Dated March 29, 1251.

150. H. Pissard, *op. cit.,* p. 134.

151. R. Röhricht, *Beiträge zur Geschichte der Kreuzzüge* (Berlin, 1878), II, 284, 285, note 42.

152. E. Berger, *Histoire de Blanche de Castille, reine de France* (Paris, 1895), pp. 392-401.

153. Matthew Paris, *Chronica majora,* V, 259-61. Sub anno 1251.

154. H. Pissard, *op. cit.,* pp. 132, 133.

155. N. Paulus, *op. cit.,* II, 30.

156. V. de Bartholomaeis, *op. cit.,* I, lxi.

157. Bonifacio de Castellana, *Era, pueis yverns es el fil,* ed. V. de Bartholomaeis, *op. cit.,* II, 177. Stanza V.

158. For example, see Raimon de Tors, *Ar es ben dretz,* ed. V. de Bartholomaeis, *op. cit.,* II, 212-14, and an anonymous *sirventés, Ma voluntatz me mou guerr' e trebalh,* ed. V. de Bartholomaeis, *loc. cit.,* pp. 205-208.

159. For a good discussion of these political *sirventés,* see A. Jeanroy, *op. cit.,* II, 234-37, and V. de Bartholomaeis, *op. cit.,* I, lxiii-lxv.

160. Matthew Paris, *Chronica majora,* V, 522. Sub anno 1255.

161. J. J. Salverda de Grave, *Le troubadour Bertran d'Alamanon* (*Bibliothèque méridionale,* series 1, VII: Toulouse, 1902), pp. 57, 58.

162. Bertran d'Alamanon, *D'un sirventes mi ven gran voluntatc,* ed. J. J. Salverda de Grave, *op. cit.,* pp. 54-56.

163. *Ibid.,* p. 57.

164. L. Halphen, *op. cit.,* p. 478.

165. H. Pissard, *op. cit.,* p. 134.

166. Ricaut Bonomel, *Ir' e dolors s'es e mon cors assezo,* ed. V. de Bartholomaeis, *op. cit.,* II, 223, 224. Stanza VI. Dated 1265. *Idem.,* note.

167. A. Potthast, *Regesta Pontificum Romanorum,* II, 1544, no. 19050. Dated March 5, 1265.

168. See V. de Bartholomaeis, *op. cit.,* II, 224, note.

169. E. Berger, *Registres d'Innocent IV,* II, clxvii ff.

170. *Ibid.,* p. clxvi.

171. R. Röhricht, *Beiträge zur Geschichte der Kreuzzüge,* II, 284, note 41.

172. There were many Italian troubadours who did not add the betrayal of the Holy Land to their other charges. For an excellent discussion of Charles of Sicily (Anjou) and Provençal poetry in Italy, see V. de Bartholomaeis, *op. cit.,* I, lxv-lxxviii.

173. *Ibid.,* I, lxxxviii.

174. Lines 8683-96. See *supra.*

175. Calega Panza, *Ar es sazos c'om si deu alegrar,* ed. V. de Bartholomaeis, *op. cit.,* II, 252. Stanza III.

176. *Ibid.,* 250, 251. Stanza I.

177. *Ibid.,* 254, 255. Stanza VIII. Jeanroy points out the possibility of a truce between Charles of Sicily and the Saracens of Lucera, but considers the charge that the pope had a part in it an absurd exaggeration. See A. Jeanroy, 'Un *sirventés* contre Charles d' Anjou,' *Annales du Midi,* XV (1903), 160, 161. Calega Panza also made the accusation that Charles of Sicily (Anjou) treated Christians more cruelly than he himself had been treated by the Saracens when they held him prisoner in 1250. The Italian chronicler Malavolti made the same reproach. A. Jeanroy, *loc. cit.,* p. 155.

178. There is no way of dating exactly Guillem Fabre's poem *Pus dels majors princeps.* It is known, however, that he lived during the late thirteenth

century. J. Anglade conjectures that he wrote *Pus dels majors princeps* around 1269. See J. Anglade, *Deux troubadours narbonnais: Guillem Fabre, Bernard Alanhan* (Narbonne, 1905), p. 30. This dating is unconvincing, however, as Guillem Fabre refers to a pope and there was no pope in 1269. It seems more probable that the poem was written during the pontificate of Clement IV (1265-68) when the Guelf-Ghibelline struggle was very intense.

179. Guillem Fabre, *Pus dels majors princeps,* ed. J. Anglade, *loc. cit.,* p. 27.

180. L. Halphen, *L'essor de l'Europe,* p. 480.

181. See chapter VI.

182. A. Hirsch-Gereuth, *Studien zur Geschichte der Kreuzzugsidee nach der Kreuzzüge* (Munich, 1897), p. 24 ff.

183. A good summary of this complicated political struggle may be found in an account by C. W. Previté-Orton, *Cambridge Medieval History* (New York, 1929), VI, 183 ff.

184. Diez concluded that the pope referred to in Folquet de Lunel's poem *Al bon rey qu'es reys de pretz* was Gregory X, and dated it between April 1272 and September 1273. See F. Diez, *Leben und Werke der Troubadours,* pp. 478, 479. Salverda de Grave disputed Diez's dating and preferred the date 1269, since it was in this year that Alfonso X of Castile first demanded the release of his brother Henry, whose captivity is mentioned in the poem. See J. J. Salverda de Grave, *Le troubadour Bertran d'Alamanon,* pp. 58, 59. Salverda de Grave is obvious ly mistaken, however, as there was no pope in 1269 and Folquet de Lunel's poemis largely concerned with criticism of a pope. Diez's dating must be accepted as correct.

185. This Henry, a brother of Alfonso X of Castile, was held prisoner by Charles of Anjou. See F. Diez, *op. cit.,* p. 479.

186. Folquet de Lunel, *Al bon rey qu'es reys de pretz,* ed. M. Raynouard, *Choix des poésies des troubadours* (Paris, 1819), IV, 240, 241. Stanza VI.

187. C. W. Previté-Orton, *op. cit.,* pp. 193, 194.

188. Gregory X was quite willing to grant Alfonso crusade tithes for the crusade against the Saracens of Spain and Africa, a crusade which would benefit Alfonso directly. See A. Hirsch-Gereuth, *op. cit.,* p. 57.

189. *Ibid.,* pp. 26-28.

190. A. Luchaire, *Innocent III: la question d'Orient,* pp. 3, 4.

191. Out of this welter of popular resentment crystallized reasoned systems of political thought contesting the superiority of the Church. Pierre Dubois declared in the early fourteenth century that the papacy should be stripped of all its temporal power in the interest of the Holy Sepulchre. See his *De recuperatione Terre Sancte,* ed. C. V. Langlois (*Collection de textes pour servir à l'étude et à l'enseignement de l'histoire,* IX: Paris, 1891), p. 25, no. 33; p. 33, no. 40. When John XXII preached a crusade against the Italian Ghibellines and Louis of Bavaria, Marsilius of Padua denounced this use of the holy war for temporal ends and argued that the crusade was one of the many abuses that could best be remedied by the absorption of the Church by the State. See the *Defensor Pacis,* ed. C. W. Previté-Orton, (New York, 1928), dictio ii, capitulum xxvi, 15, 16, pp. 415-18.

192. After the fall of Acre in 1291 and the complete victory of the Saracens, the papacy continued to be blamed for the disastrous losses in the Holy Land along with the Hospitalers, the Templars, and the sins of Christendom. For example, see Rostaing Berenguier, *Pos de sa mar man cavalier del Temple,* ed. P. Meyer, 'Les derniers troubadours de Provence,' B.E.C., XXX (1869), 497, 498. For a brief account of similar criticism of the crusading orders to be found in the work of crusade theorists, see L. Bréhier, *op. cit.,* p. 255 ff. Dante is the most eminent of the many later critics of the papacy who denounced the neglect of the Holy Land. See *Inferno,* xxvii, lines 85-90; *Paradiso,* ix, 124-26; xv, 142-45.

Abbreviations

A.A.S.S., Acta Sanctorum, Bollandists.

A.F.H., Archivum Franciscanum Historicum.

A.H.R., American Historical Review.

B.E.C., Bibliothèque de l'Ecole des Chartes.

B.E.F.A.R., Bibliothèque des Ecoles françaises d'Athènes et de Rome.

Bouquet, Rerum Gallicarum et Francicarum Scriptores (Recueil des historiens des Gaules et de la France).

Mansi, S.C.C., Sacrorum Conciliorum Nova et Amplissima Collectio.

M.G.H., SS., Monumenta Germaniae Historica, Scriptores.

Migne, P.L., Patrologia Latina.

M.I.O.G., Mittheilungen des Instituts für oesterreichische Geschichtsforschung.

M.O.P.H., Monumenta Ordinis Praedicatorum Historica.

R.H.C., Occ., Recueil des Historiens des Croisades, Occidentaux.

W.Z.G.K., Westdeutsche Zeitschrift für Geschichte und Kunst.

John I. LaMonte (essay date 1941)

SOURCE: An Introduction to *The Crusade of Richard Lion Heart,* translated by Merton Jerome Hubert, Columbia University Press, 1941, pp. 4–27.

[*In the following essay, LaMonte studies two accounts of the Crusade of Richard the Lion-Hearted (the Third Crusade) and suggests that both works are derivatives of "a common basic form of the narrative."*]

The poem here presented has unusual value both for the historian and for the student of medieval literature. Of all the accounts of the Crusade of Richard written down by those who lived through it, the *Estoire de la guerre sainte* of Ambroise and the *Itinerarium regis Ricardi* provide the most complete and circumstantial narratives that we now possess. They furnish, indeed, the major part of our factual knowledge of that ill-fated expedition. The evidence of an eyewitness is always precious, doubly so in the case of medieval events, for which only meager records were kept or have survived. On the face of it, the *Estoire de la guerre sainte* is the work of such an eyewitness, and many scholars have taken it at its face value. As will be set forth later in this Introduction, the present editors consider it to be a second-hand version, based directly on the account of one who had seen the events he described. We have reason to believe, however, that the existing text follows the original with so large a degree of exactitude and was written at so short an interval after the end of the crusade as to possess an evidential value only slightly inferior to that of a first-hand account.

IMPORTANCE OF THE POEM

As a piece of literary craftsmanship, the poem stands almost unique, occupying a transitional position between the fiction of the heroic *chansons de geste* and the prose narratives of men such as Villehardouin and Joinville. Whatever we may think of the theories of the origin of the epic set forth by the late Joseph Bédier and those who have followed in his footsteps, we may fairly assume that the medieval man accepted as fact the tales of Charlemagne and William of Orange and Doon of Mayence which furnish the matter for the *chansons de geste.* The poets usually took pains to cite their authorities and to surround their fictions with something like an air of verisimilitude. Nevertheless, they told of events that were presumed to have occurred three or four hundred years before they were born: they were, in substance, ancient history.

In the *Estoire,* on the other hand, we have a writer who told, in metrical form, a tale of happenings that were fresh in the minds of the living men who heard or read his words. For those who had no Latin, here was a great chapter of contemporary history. Here was a war correspondent, who told in the vernacular the very latest episodes in the struggle to throttle Islam and keep western Europe safe for Christianity. He wrote in verse, because he was a jongleur, trained in the art of writing, and verse was the natural and traditional way of telling a story meant to be read aloud. He told more than the march of armies, the succession of rulers, and the quarrels of dynasties. He told something of how ordinary men lived and felt, ate, drank, and slept. After him came Villehardouin and Joinville, aristocrats and soldiers, who told their stories in prose because they were men of action unskilled in writing poetry. With them history in the vulgar tongue came into being. Whereas before there had existed, on the one hand, the Latin chronicle giving the bare bones of political and military events, and on the other the *chanson de geste,* with its mass of tradition, legend, propaganda, and fancy, we now have the beginnings of historiography in the modern sense of the term.

SOURCE OF THE POEM AND ITS RELATION TO THE ITINERARIUM RICARDI

The *Estoire de la guerre sainte* was first brought to light when Gaston Paris published his edition of the text, with elaborate critical material, in 1897. For centuries it had lain unnoticed or unrecognized in the Vatican Library,[1] while historians of the crusades accepted as authoritative the Latin prose chronicle, the *Itinerarium regis Ricardi,* which gives a parallel, but not quite identical, account of the events that both record. After a study of the two works Gaston Paris presented in his Introduction certain conclusions concerning the author of the poem and the originality of his work, which have been partially confirmed and partially refuted by later research.

The author of the poem names himself Ambroise at various points in his narrative.[2] Gaston Paris concludes that this Ambroise was present in person at most of the events of the third crusade which he relates and that his account must be accepted as that of an eyewitness except for that portion of the story which deals with the siege of Acre prior to the arrival of Richard of England and Philip of France upon the scene. The poet specifically disclaims any personal knowledge of this particular sequence of events, which he nevertheless relates on the authority of another in a long interpolated section of the poem (lines 2387-4568). This section contains the material of Book I of the *Itinerarium.*[3]

The great French scholar, basing his argument on various bits of internal evidence which further investigation has corrected in detail, but not in substance, deduced the following facts: Ambroise was neither knight, man-at-arms, nor priest. Well-read in the French poetry of his day, to which he refers at many points,[4] he knew little or nothing of Latin literature. He was in all probability a jongleur or professional poet. He was of Norman origin, and the frequency of his allusions to otherwise unknown personages from the region surrounding Evreux justifies the assumption that he was himself a native of that region.[5] The Vatican manuscript, the only one known to have been preserved, appears to have been written in England about the end of the thirteenth century,[6] and while its definitely Anglo-Norman characteristics do not prove conclusively that the original was composed in that tongue, no evidence has been adduced to the contrary.

Thus far Gaston Paris's reasoning may be accepted with confidence. His conclusions regarding the originality of the poem and its relation to the *Itinerarium Ricardi* rest, however, upon assumptions that are more convenient than convincing. Briefly, the situation is that we are confronted with two texts, a Latin prose chronicle and an Old French narrative poem, which present, with one exception, accounts of the third crusade so closely parallel in word and phrase that a relation of some sort between them is obvious and incontravertible. The exception consists of the excursus in the *Estoire* previously referred to, containing the account of the siege of Acre before the arrival of the kings of England and France. Of this excursus we need here note only that while the parallelism of the two works is less striking than elsewhere, a relation is nevertheless perfectly apparent.

Before the discovery and publication of the *Estoire de la guerre sainte,* the *Itinerarium Ricardi* had been accepted as the original work of one Richard, a canon, who personally took part in the crusade and wrote at the request or under the direction of the prior of Holy Trinity in London. This in spite of the fact that the *De expugnatione Terrae Sanctae per Saladinum libellus,* one of the few pieces of evidence available, states beyond any possibility of misunderstanding that the work was translated from the French.[7] Stubbs, editor of the standard edition of the *Itinerarium,*[8] writing in 1864, affirms categorically: "It is impossible that the work should be a translation."[9] He marshals an array of arguments to demonstrate that the author of the *Libellus* must have been mistaken or deluded, conceding at the most that if any translating took place it would have been merely a putting into formal Latin of rough notes in the vulgar tongue made during the course of the campaign.[10]

Gaston Paris, rescuing from oblivion the long-buried poem of Ambroise, concluded that here was the work from which the English cleric had translated the *Itinerarium, ex gallica lingua.* Dismissing or refuting in detail Stubbs's arguments—which are indeed something less than objective in nature—he asserted that in any case a further discussion of them had become futile now that we have discovered the original French work which Richard of Holy Trinity had put into Latin.[11] Richard, he declared, was a downright plagiarist, who set forth deliberately to delude posterity into believing that he had shared the hardships and the glory of the crusade and was an eyewitness of the events he described.

He argues substantially as follows. First, the Latin text contains numerous traces of rhyming words, of which some are found in various equivalent couplets of Ambroise's poem, and others, particularly certain pairs of proper names, must have been in portions of the poem that have been lost through the carelessness of copyists. Second, the Latin text of Richard presents certain errors or

inconsistencies which are explicable only on the theory that Richard misunderstood the French text on which he worked and, in one case, was so unfamiliar with Old French epic literature that he was led into a ludicrous mistake concerning Agoland, one of the well-known characters of that literature. Most important of all, perhaps, asserts Gaston Paris, the words and phrases of Richard's text that have no equivalent in the French poem, reveal themselves on examination to be purely rhetorical ornamentation. They add nothing of fact to the narrative, being in substance the kind of florid exhibition of literary skill and erudition with which the medieval clerk loved to bedazzle his readers. It is inconceivable, affirms the critic, that a poet should translate this sort of fancywork into the simple and direct narrative verse that we find in the *Estoire.* On the other hand, it is not merely logical, but a matter of frequent occurrence, that a learned Latinist should embellish the bare simplicity of a composition in the vulgar tongue with such literary flowers as he considered necessary to give it dignity.

In dismissing thus summarily the portions of Richard's text that have no equivalent in the *Estoire,* Gaston Paris either neglects or explains away in unsatisfactory fashion a variety of evidence which his own comparison of the two works places before the reader's eye. Richard does, in point of fact, supply numerous bits of information that can by no stretch of the imagination be termed rhetorical ornament. Such are—to choose only a few among many—the detailed itinerary of King Richard from Tours to Vézelay and from Vézelay to Lyons (Bk. II, chs. viii and x), the interview between King Richard and Tancred in Sicily (Bk. II, ch. xxii), a quarrel between Pisans and Genoese (Bk. II, ch. xxv), details concerning the geography of Crete (Bk. II, ch. xxvii), the names of the three bishops present at the king's marriage (Bk. II, ch. xxxv), an account of a trip made by the king to inspect the fortifications of Gaza and the Daron (Bk. V, ch. xix), and a large number of precise dates. This list might be greatly lengthened.

Gaston Paris accounts for the presence of this additional material in the *Itinerarium* by asserting that it was either (1) derived from some official itinerary of King Richard, (2) added by the author of the Latin work from his own personal information or other sources not specified, or (3) originally present in the French poem, but omitted or lost by copyists who transmitted the text to posterity. While it is true that in some cases these explanations lie within the realm of possibility, it is equally true that they rest on conjecture rather than proof.

Mention should also be made of the fact that Ambroise includes some material for which the *Itinerarium* has no equivalent. We may mention, for instance, details concerning the messengers sent by Tancred to King Richard and the names of the churchmen who arranged terms of peace between the two rulers (lines 1007 ff.), a mention of the lofty ancestry of Guy de Lusignan (lines 1722 ff.), an urgent invitation from King Philip to King Richard (lines 1879-1906), and various others.

Kate Norgate, writing in 1910, subjected the problem to further analysis.[12] While Gaston Paris had fixed on 1196 as the probable date for the composition of the French poem, Miss Norgate brought forth evidence that it should be dated between September, 1203, and November, 1207. Her proof, based on Ambroise's references in present and past tense to various personages of the crusade, may not carry conviction to those who are familiar with the laxity of tense usage in Old French. Nevertheless she makes a fairly convincing case. After studying in similar fashion the *Itinerarium,* which has come down to us in three manuscripts, she concludes:

> The *Itinerarium* in the earliest of the three forms now extant was not completed till after 6 April 1199, and the conclusion in manuscript C was added probably not earlier than 1202. But one passage in lib. i was written *before September 1192;*[13] and it is chronologically possible that the whole work, except the conclusion as it stands in manuscript C, may have been written before that date.[14]

Certain passages inconsistent with this conclusion, she notes, may have been inserted later. In fine, there is no reason for rejecting her statement that "the *Estoire* and the *Itinerarium* were composed within a short distance of time the one from the other," but that the chronological evidences "are insufficient to decide which of the two works *in its original form,* is the earlier."

After refuting Gaston Paris's dismissal of Richard of Holy Trinity as a shameless plagiarist, Miss Norgate then goes on to elaborate—but, to our way of thinking, not to prove—a theory according to which both Richard and Ambroise took part in the crusade and were in fact friends and fellow men-of-letters.[15] While Miss Norgate has made valuable contributions to the solution of the problem, the body of evidence she has gathered seems insufficient to justify an inference which may best be expressed in her own words:

> A Norman poet, Ambrose by name, and an English clerk who is supposed to have been Richard "de Templo," canon of Holy Trinity in London, went through the crusade together as comrades and friends. While it was in progress "Richard" took notes—whether in French or Latin—of the experiences which befell one or both of them in particular, and the host in general; and also of what information he could collect about the siege of Acre down to the time of their arrival there. He worked up a portion of these notes into fairly complete liberary form before the close of the crusade. In after years he worked out the whole of them into the form in which his book has come down to us. But meanwhile, probably, before doing this—possibly while both men were still in the Holy-Land—he had lent the rough draft of his work to his Norman friend, to serve as the basis of another record of the crusade, which the latter writer intended to compose in the form of an historical *chanson.* So far as the substance of the narrative was concerned, Ambrose had only to translate his comrade's notes, perhaps from Latin into French, perhaps only from prose into verse, making such additions, omissions, and alterations as might be suggested to him by his own judgment and his own independent memory of the events recorded, and, for the introductory history, of what he too had picked up from those who had been earlier on the scene of action. On the other hand, Richard's work would also receive additions and alterations from its author when he came to revise it for publication. But it evidently never received a final revision from him; and thus certain imperfections and confusions—such as the blunder about Agoland, the confusion about Garnier of Naplouse, and that about the ransom of William de Préaux—which were no doubt in his original notes, jotted down "in the camp," amid "the din of war which left him no leisure to think quietly"—remained uncorrected and were repeated by scribe after scribe from one copy to another.

The more carefully one scrutinizes these two works, the more clearly one perceives two things: first, the poem of Ambroise cannot be a translation from the *Itinerarium;* second, the *Itinerarium* cannot be a translation from Ambroise. Yet the two books are obviously and undeniably related in some fashion. The present editors reached the conclusion that both works had their origin in a common source, now lost, and were delighted to find that Mr. J. G. Edwards, in a scholarly and penetrating study, had propounded the same theory.[16] He had also presented a certain amount of evidence to support a conjecture that the unidentified author of the lost original wrote in French, and probably in prose; we believe that the first of these conjectures is a likely one, but that the second rests on evidence that is rather tenuous.

For a complete statement of Mr. Edwards's position we refer the reader to his essay, of which we venture to include here only a summary of certain outstanding portions. One of the critical points, for instance, consists of the two references to Agoland, the Saracen king who appears in the Old French *chanson de geste* named Aspremont. The *Estoire* refers to the city of Messina as:

> E bien et bel assise vile,
> Car el siet el chief de Sezille,
> Desus le Far, encontre Rise
> Que Agoland prist par s'emprise.[17]

This indicates an accurate knowledge of the contents of the Aspremont, that is, Agoland *seized Reggio by force.* The parallel passage of the *Itinerarium* speaks of Messina as "situ amoena et plurimum commodo, in confinio Siciliae et Risae quae illi famoso Agolando dicitur olim fuisse pro servitio suo collata."[18] This can mean only that the writer considered Reggio to have been bestowed on Agoland as a fief in reward for services rendered and therefore believed Agoland to have been a Christian baron. According to Gaston Paris this meant that the author of the *Itinerarium* misunderstood and mistranslated the *Estoire de la guerre sainte.* According to Miss Norgate the priest who wrote the *Itinerarium,* unversed in secular literature, picked up on the spot and misinterpreted some fragment of legend transmitted by word of mouth, whereas

Ambroise, seeing the error in his friend's notes, quietly and discreetly corrected it in his text.

The difficulty with both these explanations emerges when they are studied in the light of the second reference to Agoland. In Book V, chapter xxi, Richard of Holy Trinity writes of "the most powerful Agoland, who, with a great force of Saracens almost invincible to men without the aid of God, had reached Reggio, a city of Calabria."[19]

It is perfectly obvious that the writer of these words here accurately represents as a Saracen the same Agoland to whom he had previously referred in terms applicable only to a Christian. But he did not get the information from the *Estoire,* whose lines, incorrectly described by Gaston Paris as more explicit than the previous passage, contain no suggestion whatsoever of the Moslem origin of Agoland. They read as follows:

> E quant il mena l'ost par Rome
> Quant Agolant par grant emprise
> Fu par mer arivé a Rise
> En Calabre la riche terre.[20]

In other words, the priest who wrote the first passage misstated a fact which he then correctly stated in the second passage. He did not get that fact from Ambroise. Mr. Edwards's cogently argued conclusion can hardly be improved:

> A further conclusion follows. Taken together, these passages about Agoland do much more than prove a negative. As the writer of the *Itinerarium* does not realize in one place that Agoland was a Saracen, and yet in a later passage correctly describes him as a Saracen, he must have been prompted in the later passage. Yet he was not prompted by the *Estoire.* Consequently he must have been prompted by something else. Gaston Paris was therefore following a sound instinct when he remarked upon the "contradiction" implicit between these two passages. How is this "contradiction" to be explained? How is it possible that a writer should both know and not know the same fact? The most natural explanation in this case seems to be the one which normally accounts for the same phenomenon in other writers. One is driven to the conclusion that the compiler of the *Itinerarium* was not an original author, but was reproducing an original author whose allusions, if they happened not to be clear in themselves, he did not always understand. It was presumably by this original author that the writer of the *Itinerarium* was prompted when he correctly described Agoland, in his second reference, as a leader of the Saracens.[21]

A similar confusion on the part of the author of the *Itinerarium* appears in the references to Garnier de Naplouse. At one point (p. 267) he clearly considers that Garnier de Naplouse and the Master of the Hospital were two separate and distinct persons. A little later (p. 371) he refers to Garnier de Naplouse as Master of the Hospital. Thus, observes Mr. Edwards, he seems both to know and not to know the same fact. Obviously, too, such inadvertencies as these and others pointed out by Mr. Edwards are hardly compatible with the hypothesis that Richard of Holy Trinity worked out his book on the basis of rough notes made during the course of the campaign.

A matter to which Miss Norgate gives much careful attention, but which Mr. Edwards passes over lightly, is the considerable number of passages in the *Estoire de la guerre sainte* where the poet refers to an unidentified written source for his material, using phrases such as "si dist l'estoire," "ço dist li livres," "si com testemoine la letre" and the like. Miss Norgate considers the frequency of such phrases as corroborative evidence of her theory that Ambroise was translating from the *Itinerarium.*[22] On this point, three observations should be made. First, as she has herself noted, such formulae are the common stock in trade of the medieval jongleurs, who attempted thereby to lend some kind of authenticity to their most fantastic tales—"I saw it written down, it must be true." Their frequency, not very remarkable after all in a poem of more than twelve thousand lines, in no way proves that Ambroise was translating from the Latin. Secondly, it is obvious that the *Estoire* was written to be recited aloud rather than read. The poet addresses himself at intervals, not to his *readers,* but to his *hearers,* and minstrels reciting to an audience were particularly given to the habit of quoting written authority. It is worthy of note that in the prologue to the *Itinerarium*[23] Richard of Holy Trinity twice refers, not to a *lector,* but to an *auditor;* a fact which, Mr. Edwards conjectures, may be explained by the theory that the words in question represent an echo of something that appeared in the prologue of the original French work which Richard was translating. Thirdly, and perhaps most important, the presence of such phrases as "ço dist li livres" is entirely compatible with the hypothesis which we believe to be the true one, that is, that both works derive from a common original.

In the opinion of the present translators, certain other factors lend additional probability to this hypothesis. First, while the main body of the narrative runs along in parallel and almost identical fashion in the two works, each writer omits a number of specific facts which the other includes. We have already mentioned some of these facts; it has not seemed desirable to overburden this Introduction with a complete list of them. The *Itinerarium* is particularly rich in exact dates which the *Estoire* fails to mention.[24] No doubt the poet found, as did the present translator, that dates fit awkwardly into verse. In any case, we suggest that each writer omitted details in the common source which he considered unessential and that the author of the *Estoire* in particular omitted facts that were hard to rhyme.

In the second place, disregarding the excursus of lines 2387-4568, there are numerous points where the two writers actually *differ* in their statement of facts. Leaving out those which seem either inconsequential or easily explicable by a slight corruption of the manuscript, there remain such matters as the following. The *Estoire* states that after the collapse of the Rhone bridge at Lyons the army crossed in small boats (*bargetes*); the *Itinerarium* declares that a bridge of boats was built.[25] In recounting the terms of the treaty made with King Tancred of Sicily, each writer includes certain provisions of the pact which the other passes over in silence.[26] The same observation is true of the agreement made between Guy de Lusignan and Conrad de Montferrat.[27] It is not unreasonable to deduce that in these two cases each writer chose those of the terms of peace which he thought most important. Here an omission constitutes a difference, for obvious reasons. Where the *Estoire* names as Gilbert Taleboz a knight whom the Latin calls Gerardus Taleboz, we suggest that the divergence arose from differing interpretations of an abbreviation in the original text.[28] The same cause may have led both writers astray in the matter of the duke of Burgundy's Christian name, which they record as Henricus and Henri, whereas it actually was Hugh.[29] The author of the *Itinerarium* has clearly misread either an abbreviation or a French word when he gives "medium autumnum" for a date which the *Estoire* correctly states as mid-August ("mi aust").[30] Mr. Edwards has commented effectively upon this latter passage, as well as upon the curious line where the pilgrims in their visit to Jerusalem are said by the Latin writer to have rested "juxta montem," where the French text has "dejoste un mur"[31] (beside a wall). These matters are insignificant at first glance, but, as Mr. Edwards points out, their very insignificance gives them interest. They are so inconsequential that one cannot conceive of them as representing a correction of one writer by the other; one can easily conceive of them, however, as representing varying interpretations of an identical basic text. Miss Dorothy Bovée has called attention to another textual variation that points in the same direction, though she has not drawn from it what seems to us the obvious inference: the *Itinerarium* describes the lance of a powerful Saracen emir as being "duabus nostris grossiorem" (heavier than two of ours); the *Estoire* states that "que dous groisseurs n'aveit en France" (in all France there are not to be found two lances that are heavier).[32] In these passages, it will be noted, both the Latin and the French are so crystal-clear that it is impossible to imagine their misinterpretation by anybody who knew enough to translate either one. But if both worked from an original that was less lucid, the divergence at once becomes understandable.

In discussing the references to Agoland and to Garnier de Naplouse we pointed out that the author of the *Itinerarium* was led into errors of fact. Several other such errors appear in his narrative. He relates, for instance, an interview between King Richard and Tancred that took place at Catania, which he says is located midway between Messina and Palermo.[33] No one familiar with the geography of Sicily could make such a blunder. The three cities lie on the coast—Catania almost due south from Messina, Palermo almost due west from Messina. The *Estoire* makes no mention of such an interview.

Even more striking perhaps are the passages in which Richard of Holy Trinity at three separate points refers to Saladin's withdrawal to Daron—which he locates in the mountains—and to his activities there.[34] As a glance at the map will reveal, Daron lies, not among the hills, but on the seacoast, many miles away from the scene of activities indicated by everything in the context. Ambroise correctly locates the action in each of these three cases at Toron of the Knights.[35] The learned editor of the *Itinerarium,* writing of course before the discovery of the *Estoire,* found himself perplexed by the obvious inconsistency in the Latin text and explained it in words which suggest that he was not too well satisfied with his own explanation.[36]

Of the remaining differences between the two narratives, we include here three which seem not to have attracted Mr. Edwards's attention. The Earl of Leicester took part in a skirmish in which he was hard pressed by the Saracens, who hemmed him in on every side. Ambroise uses the phrase: "Qui l'avoient entr'els noié," in which the figurative sense of the verb *noyer* is made obvious by the accompanying "entr'els."[37] The Latin writer apparently took the drowning to be literal, though the combatants had obviously gone well past the only stream mentioned in the context, for he renders the idea in words that admit of no other interpretation: "In ipso flumine propemodum in turba submergerent."[38]

At a point shortly after the episode just mentioned the Christian leaders deliberate on the wisdom of attacking Jerusalem; the Templars, Hospitalers, and Pulani, who had most accurate knowledge of local conditions, advised against such attack, for reasons which both writers set forth in some detail. At the end of the argument, the Latin text makes the amazing assertion that their counsel was not heeded: "Sed adhuc consilium eorum non omnino exauditur," although everything in the remainder of his narrative shows clearly that the advice was not merely heeded but also followed.[39] The *Estoire* contains no such statement, which we believe to be founded, like others, upon a misinterpretation of an original text.

In the accounts of King Richard's illness provided by the two writers we note the curious fact that while the canon of Holy Trinity attempts a diagnosis of the *cause* of the malady—in terms little more illuminating to us than they would have been to the patient—the French jongleur contents himself with recording the *symptoms,* of which the Latin work makes no mention whatsoever. The two texts read as follows:

> Gravissimam incurrit aegritudinem, quae vulgo Arnoldia vocatur, ex ignotae regionis constitutione, cum eius naturali complexione minus concordante.[40]

> Mais le reis Richarz iert malades
> E aveit boche e levres fades
> D'une emferté que Deu maudie
> Qu'en apele leonardie.[41]

It seems to us probable that the original account mentioned both the symptoms and the supposed causes of the illness, while the authors of our surviving texts recorded what each one thought most pertinent.

We cannot conclude this study of the differences between the *Estoire de la guerre sainte* and the *Itinerarium* without inviting the reader's attention to the frequent cases involving numerals. There are about a score of such cases. In eleven of them the two works give different numbers; in the remainder one text gives a number, while the other does not. Sometimes one gives a larger figure; sometimes the other. Sometimes the difference is slight, as in the case of King Richard's fleet, which Ambroise credits with one hundred and seven ships, whereas the Latin says one hundred and eight.[42] Sometimes it is enormous: where Ambroise affirms that three thousand crusaders died of illness and famine at Acre during the siege and afterward, Richard of Holy Trinity puts the casualties from this source at three hundred thousand.[43] Some of the divergences are explicable on the theory that the writers, or one of them, misread or misinterpreted Roman numerals in the hypothetical original; in other cases it is hard to see how this can have been possible. The present translators find themselves obliged to fall back on the explanation that one writer or the other chose at various points to exaggerate or to minimize, for reasons of his own. While this explanation is not illuminating, it is as reasonable as any.

Of the evidence adduced by Mr. Edwards and by ourselves in support of the theory that the two works in question derive from a common basic form of the narrative, we believe that although no single item of testimony would suffice in itself to verify the hypothesis, the very considerable number of clues all pointing in the same direction does encourage a strong presumption. To put the matter from a slightly different point of view, we consider demonstrably untenable the theory that the *Estoire de la guerre sainte* was either the source of the *Itinerarium,* as Gaston Paris would have it, or derived from the *Itinerarium* as Miss Norgate believes. No one could maintain for a moment that the two are independent. By a process of elimination we conclude that our theory provides the only possible explanation of the facts.

The nature of the lost original must remain a matter for conjecture. Mr. Edwards finds reason to believe that it was written in French and probably in prose. His reasons are good enough to suggest such a conclusion, but hardly adequate to prove it. In the main, we incline to agree with him, and we would add to what he has said the interesting and suggestive fact that of the large number of proper names appearing in the Latin text of the *Itinerarium* a noteworthy proportion are written in the French form rather than in the Latin form which they would naturally have taken had the original been composed in that tongue. If the basic text was indeed an Old French prose history, it was a landmark in literature, the first piece of historical prose writing in the French language, antedating by a considerable period the familiar narrative of Villehardouin.

LITERARY QUALITIES OF THE POEM

If we are correct in postulating a lost original, probably in French prose, from which the existing text of the poem derives, one deduction is inescapable: the writer of the *Estoire de la guerre sainte* followed his model very closely.

The amazingly close parallelism of the *Estoire* and the *Itinerarium* permits of no other conclusion. Consequently any estimate of the literary merit of the poet whose work we actually possess must apply in large measure to the man from whom he drew his material. Since we cannot evaluate a work which we do not possess, we must content ourselves with a consideration of the poem that has survived. Whether it was the author of the manuscript in the Vatican or his predecessor who bore the name Ambroise is beyond our power to determine, but for purposes of convenience we have used that name in our commentary as referring to the man who first wrote the story. While our observations on style and content are founded on a study of the present text, we make the reservation that they may more accurately describe the shadowy figure whose labor furnished the matter for that text.

Gaston Paris has presented excellent reasons for believing that the poet was not noble, priest or soldier, but in all probability a professional poet or jongleur attached to the army of King Richard. Further research has fortified the hypothesis that he came from the Evreux district in Normandy, upon whose knights and men-at-arms he lavishes particular praise for their valor and steadfastness. It is precisely because Ambroise was one of the "lesser folk" of the host that he was able to give us so precious an account, not merely of events, but of the mental and spiritual background of events. He pictures the soul of the crusader, with all its curious mélange of confusion and lucidity. Seldom does he reach greater heights of eloquence than in his descriptions of the joy of the host at some battle won or at the prospect of reaching Jerusalem, or than in his pictures of the despair that beset the pilgrims when they found themselves forced to turn back from the Holy City. Accepting the reasons given by Richard for refusing to advance on Jerusalem and criticizing those who disagreed with his royal master, he nevertheless lamented the decision that closed to the pilgrims the road to the Sepulchre.

He was not privy to the councils of the leaders of the crusade, though at times he recounts their deliberations with all the assurance of one who had participated in them. This, however, will not greatly impress anyone who knows how in any army the vaguest and falsest rumors take on authoritative precision as they spread among the rank and file. The long exhortation of the priest to Richard to remember his past fame and glories undoubtedly grew out of awed stories circulated in the camp about the temerity of the man who dared thus address the Lion Heart. Furthermore, Ambroise tells what went on in the inner circles of Saladin's councils of war with exactly the same confidence that marks his descriptions of what the Christian generals said and thought; the orations which he attributes to the Saracen emirs are, of course, nothing but the imagination and wishful thinking of the crusaders, who pictured their enemies as saying the things which, in the opinion of the Christian army, they ought to have thought and said.

Ambroise never refers to himself as participating personally in a battle. He does, however, affirm that he marched among the second group of pilgrims who visited the Holy Places of Jerusalem after the truce with Saladin, and he tells of the emotion that came over him as he trod in the footsteps of the Saviour. At this climactic or anticlimactic moment of the crusade he speaks with the sincerity and directness of one who had witnessed the event. But this same sincerity, this same tone of the eyewitness, runs throughout most of the work and gives the reader a strong conviction that he is listening to one who knew whereof he spoke.

For all its tone of earnestness, the poet's work is nevertheless very uneven in quality. For pages he will amble tranquilly along, guided by the *musa pedestris,* presenting his array of fact in matter-of-fact manner, with no tinge of enthusiasm, emotion, or poetic fire. He speaks simply and directly, to be sure, but not with the stark majesty that makes the *Chanson de Roland* so magnificent. He gives us, in rhyming couplets, a straightforward chronicle of events—no more and no less. His flow of imagery is sparse, seldom going beyond the commonplace of the medieval trouvère. In a battle arrows and spears fill the air like a heavy snowfall in winter, the victors pursue the vanquished like the wolf pursuing the hapless flock of sheep—these clichés and others of the same banality mark the limits of our poet's command of figurative language.

His accounts of battle scenes appear particularly tedious to the modern reader, though the poet evidently reveled in them with that peculiar sadistic joy that the medieval writer seems to derive from the moving accident on flood and field. One ought in all fairness to note that while one fight seems very like another, with the streaming flags and shining armor, the clouds of arrows and impetuous charges, the mighty blows and the heaps of corpses, the poet does nevertheless manage to give a lucid and presumably accurate narrative of the tactics, the disposition of troops, and the varying tides of fortune. These passages do not lack vividness, nor are they without value for the military historian, who can determine the facts with a little effort. What they do lack is a sense of perspective. A minor skirmish in which a few score men participate on each side takes on in Ambroise's narrative all the grandiose proportions of the battle of Arsur or the recapture of Jaffa. The frequency with which such skirmishes appear in the story robs them of most of their dramatic quality.

Ambroise was not an especially observant traveler. His descriptions of the topography, climate, and architecture of what was to him a new and exotic country seem comparatively meager. He mentions some of the Holy Places visited in Jerusalem, he tells the legendary stories about the walls and towers of Ascalon, he introduces here and there incidental details taken from popular legends or the *chansons de geste,* but in this respect he cannot compare with Robert de Clari, who avidly accumulated information about the wonderful things he saw in Constantinople. The summer heat and dust, the venomous insects and the heavy rains, all these are mentioned by Ambroise, to be sure, but only incidentally, only as the background against which

the human drama of the crusade was being played. One feels that in themselves they held slight interest for the chronicler, though it may be that they are simply dwarfed by the surpassing magnitude of the spiritual adventure which meant so much to him.

The poet can however be dramatic and colorful on occasion. Woven into the fabric of his tale are sections of swift and skillful verse, purple patches that glow with the fire of faith or of indignation. Such are, for instance, his account of the collapse of the Rhone bridge, the surrender and humiliation of Isaac of Cyprus, the heroism of Jacques d'Avesnes, the assassination of Conrad of Montferrat, and the rhythmic invective hurled at Conrad for his aloofness from what Ambroise believed to be the cause of righteousness. His description of the pilgrims' march through France on their way to the seacoast and of their reception by the populace has astonishing vigor and pathos.

Layman though he was, few clerics could outdo him in his passionate devotion to the cause of Christendom—a devotion that has all the prejudice of the simply pious soul. He shares, naturally enough, the common medieval view that the paynim suffer from the basic wrongness and wickedness of the unbaptized, a view which the *Chanson de Roland* expresses in the ingenuous formula: "Christians are right, paynim are wrong." Whatever the Saracens do is evil, except in those circumstances—unhappily too numerous—where God chooses them as instruments whereby to punish the corruption of Christianity that has strayed from the paths of virtue. But for all that, the poet cannot suppress his unwilling admiration for their skill at arms and for the chivalry of Saladin. If such a man had only been a Christian, he laments, if he had not been a worshiper of false gods, what a man he would have been!

THE HISTORICAL VALUE OF AMBROISE

Having already given our reasons for judging that the *Itinerarium* and the *Estoire* were both based on a common lost original, we shall take the liberty in this section to consider the two as a single work and to attempt an estimate of the historical value of the original, which we have arbitrarily and for convenience called Ambroise. We have shown throughout our notes the variants and divergencies between the *Estoire* and the *Itinerarium,* and they may be summarized by stating that while the *Itinerarium* is in general more precise as to chronology and more inclusive as to proper names, there are several incidents which are given in greater detail by the *Estoire.* But as historical documents they have much the same validity, and we shall here essay to evaluate their narrative in comparison with other independent sources.

Ambroise, as we have already pointed out, cannot be called the best single source for the entire third crusade, but it is certainly the best source for the crusade of Richard. The events in Syria which led up to the crusade are treated very broadly and not too accurately by the *Estoire,* while the *Itinerarium,* which follows the Latin Continuator of

William of Tyre, is more detailed, but not much more reliable. For a complete account of the crusade probably the best single source would be the *Eracles,* the Old French Continuator of William.[44] Ambroise virtually omits the expedition of Frederick Barbarossa; more attention is given it in the *Itinerarium,* where several chapters are derived from the Latin Continuator, than in the *Estoire,* but both are quite brief. Further, Ambroise's account of the crusade of Philip Augustus is incidental to the crusade of Richard; his knowledge of Cyprus, apart from the details of its conquest, seems very slight. But Ambroise does give the best account of the campaigns in Palestine, of the fighting at Messina and in Cyprus, and of the incidents in the camp before Acre.

It is not our purpose here to analyze in detail the history of Ambroise, but a very brief comparison of his work with the other major sources of the crusade adds to our appreciation of the historical significance of our chronicle. The other chief occidental accounts are those of the *Eracles,* the *Gesta*-Hoveden (which are virtually the same), Diceto, Devizes, and Rigord; while for the siege of Acre and the events before the arrival of Richard supplementary information may be found in the accounts of Haymarus and the *Libellus.* Of the oriental sources by far the most important is Beha ed Din, but Ibn al Athir, Abu Chamah, Ibn Kallikan, and Abulfaraj Bar Hebraeus all supply details. For the background of Syrian history the *Libellus* and the *Eracles* are the most informative; Ambroise appears at his worst in this connection. But Ambroise admits frankly that what he tells of these matters he knows only from the writings of others and that he has no personal knowledge thereof. The discoloration of his account by his personal prejudices will be discussed below, but it must be stated here that Ambroise is not the source to which one should turn for information on the internal history of the kingdom of Jerusalem.

Neither is Ambroise the best authority for the history of Richard in France and in England before the crusade. Diceto, Devizes, and the *Gesta*-Hoveden all provide many more details on the doings in the West, and all are better sources both for the preparations for the crusade and for the events in France and England during Richard's absence. But for the march of the crusaders and the war in Sicily, Ambroise is of the first importance. Here he writes about what he himself saw. In no other account is the narrative so vivid and lively. Hoveden is much more full and exact as to chronology, but his story lacks the freshness and spirit of Ambroise's. Hoveden wrote from sources which enabled him to quote treaties, ordinances, and the decisions of councils with a knowledge which Ambroise lacked, but, though Hoveden is the more exact, Ambroise is by far the more vivid. The forest may not be seen as clearly, but the trees are much more distinct and have greener foliage.

For the conquest of Cyprus Ambroise gives us by far the most detailed account. Here again the facts recorded are actions in which Ambroise himself may have participated, or which, at least, he saw taking place around him. He does not know the regulations Richard established for the administration of the island, which Hoveden gives, but he tells more stirringly of the fighting and the capture of Isaac.

For the scenes at the siege of Acre, Ambroise again depended upon others for information. Here we have clearly camp gossip—incidents retold from tent to tent. Ambroise's chronology is most defective in this part; there is little sequence in the order of battles, but the heroism of individuals, the suffering of the host, the alternate joy and despair of the pilgrims are told vividly and dramatically. After Richard's arrival the chronology improves, and Ambroise's account of the end of the siege equals any other.

True, he omits any considerable discussion of many details which we know from other sources. He was concerned solely with reciting the *gestes* of Richard, and irrelevant events, distracting from this single purpose, are subordinated even more in the *Estoire* than in the *Itinerarium.* Philip's voyage home, which receives so much attention in Hoveden, is omitted altogether. Ambroise is telling the deeds of the Lion Heart; he does not bother with the lesser acts of smaller folk. The *Eracles,* the *Libellus,* and Haymarus give more connected accounts of the siege; Ambroise by far the most personal.

It is in his story of the campaigns of Richard in Palestine that Ambroise is unique and unexcelled. Only in Beha ed Din, who like Ambroise concerns himself only with the deeds of his hero, can one find an equally good account of these campaigns. The details of the marches and battles, the heroic struggles, the joys and agonies of the pilgrims as fortune smiled or frowned upon them, are recorded by Ambroise colorfully, vividly, and sympathetically. The negotiations for truces were not known, and so remain largely unmentioned unless they became so noticeable that the whole camp speculated on them. Ambroise was merely one of the mass of pilgrims who followed where their lord led them, unknowing why and only able to speculate about the motives which prompted the decisions made. He explains such decisions with naïve simplicity: treason, bad faith, selfishness, were for him more acceptable motives than those reasons of state and strategy which prompted the leaders.

We have already observed that Ambroise colors his entire narrative with a strong personal bias. He writes as the avowed partisan of Richard and of all Richard's friends and protégés. This is especially noticeable in his treatment of Guy de Lusignan and Conrad de Montferrat. It is so strong as to render almost wholly false his account of the history of Jerusalem before the beginning of the siege of Acre. Ambroise gained his information of these events entirely at second hand and apparently entirely from partisans of Guy. He never understood the psychology or the problems of the Syrian Franks. Ambroise expressed perfectly the attitude of the western crusader as opposed to that of the Syrian colonists. To him all Saracens were

enough, but also with some virtues. The fortunes of war were observed more dispassionately by the eastern Christians; we do not find them reveling in the number of Saracens slain as did Ambroise.

These Syrian Franks knew personally the situation in the East; they judged events from the political viewpoint, and the good of their kingdom more than the zeal for the Cross governed their judgments. To these men, who knew and understood the issues involved, Raymond of Tripoli and Conrad de Montferrat were the heroes of the story, not the villains; it was to Ambroise, prejudiced and ill informed, that they appeared as base traitors and wicked scoundrels. When one considers the unanimity with which all the greater barons of Frankish Syria, men who had the greatest stake in the land, supported Raymond and Conrad; when one studies the record of the court party under Guy and Renaud de Châtillon; when one forgets religious prejudice and considers only political exigency, he cannot but realize that Raymond and Conrad represented and led the party which comprised the ablest, soundest, most far-seeing elements in the kingdom of Jerusalem. Ambroise cursed Conrad for his diversion of supplies from the camp before Acre to his city of Tyre; he did not in the least appreciate the fact that the defense of Tyre must have been the first consideration of the native Franks, in whose opinions the siege of Acre was a venture in which they could have but little hope of success, while the preservation of Tyre was the essential cornerstone in the defense of the kingdom. Ambroise forgot, or did not know, that in Tyre were the refugees from all the cities of the kingdom taken by Saladin; he ignored the fact that it was on the rock of Conrad's resistance at Tyre that the wave of Moslem conquest was broken; he condemned as treason in Conrad the negotiations with Saladin for the preservation of part of the kingdom as a vassal state—yet he had no criticism for Richard when the king subsequently offered almost identical terms to the sultan after he had come to realize the impossibility of a complete reconquest. Guy de Lusignan had amply demonstrated political and military incompetence; the lords of Syria had no confidence in him and refused to accept his leadership, trusting rather to Conrad, whose prowess had been ably evidenced at Tyre. But it never occurred to Ambroise that the Franco-Syrian lords were anything other than traitors and false when they supported the party opposed to Richard, or that Philip Augustus could have shown greater political acumen in supporting the marquis than did Richard in assisting Guy. The history of Richard's reign, as evidenced by his treatment of John and by some of his appointments, reveals the inability of the king to judge character or competence. Ambroise never suspected this, nor did he seem to feel any inconsistency either in his own statements or in his hero's policy when he finally accepted Conrad as king of Jerusalem. The villain suddenly became the ally of the hero and was recognized by all as the best man for the position to which he aspired; the false marquis became overnight the favored candidate for the throne. This change of front, which Richard accepted as he grew to learn the needs of the country and the impossibility of further supporting the

"pagan cattle," and he reveled, almost sadistically, in descriptions of their slaughter and discomfiture. Even though he mentioned instances of the generosity and chivalry of Saladin and Saphadin, he spoke of them most unflatteringly and piously invoked God's curse against the whole Moslem breed. He did not record miracles, nor did he recount tales of the intervention of saints in behalf of the Christian army as did some of the chroniclers of the first crusade; but he did see in the sufferings of the Christians the evidences of God's wrath at the unworthy actions of the people; and the tribulations of Jerusalem were to him the direct result of the impiety of her inhabitants.

In contrast to Ambroise we must consider the accounts of Ernoul and of the *Eracles,* both written by Frankish settlers in Syria. They represent the "colonial" as distinguished from the "crusader" viewpoint, and they disagree with Ambroise in their whole interpretation of the events which led up to the crusade. While to them the Saracens were the enemy, there can be found in them none of that hatred which inspired the western writers. They wrote of the Saracens as an Englishman of that time would have written of the French or as a modern Englishman would write of the Italians: enemy neighbors with vices surely incompetent and unpopular Lusignan, Ambroise recorded without a word of explanation.

It must be remembered that throughout the history of the crusaders' states there were many indications that the native Franks were able to get along better with their Saracen neighbors than they were with their Christian allies from the West. When Conrad offered vassalage to Saladin, he thought of ending the war which was ruining the country without offering chance of success. He recognized that honorable vassalage was preferable to a ruined kingdom devastated by years of fruitless warfare. Richard himself finally accepted this point of view; certainly Conrad's offers were not more treasonable than Richard's suggestion that the kingdom of Jersualem be reconstructed as a vassal state, its king to perform homage to Saladin and provide troops for his army, especially when we remember Richard's proposal that his sister marry Saphadin and that the kingdom be given to them jointly.

Richard was not a fool. During the campaigns in Palestine he learned much: he discovered the impossibility of a complete reconquest of the kingdom; he came to realize that the baronial party knew what it was about when it preferred Conrad; and he grew to appreciate the possibility of honorable agreements between men of different faiths. Richard developed the colonial attitude; himself chivalrous and a master of the art of war, he was able to recognize these qualities in his great antagonist. Ambroise never learned these things; but he accepted the decisions of his king blindly and without question.

In our notes we have endeavored to indicate these prejudices of our author and to correct the narrative from facts derived from the eastern sources.

With all its prejudice and partisanship, with all its piety and blood-thirstiness, with all its epic redundancy and exaggeration, the account of Ambroise remains nevertheless finer than any other account of the crusade of Richard and also one of the most significant documents extant in revealing the mind and spirit of the crusaders—those men who threw themselves heart and soul into futile and disastrous warfare, enduring hardship and discouragement for the sake of a religious and chivalric ideal. But the *Estoire* is more than that; it is the epic, the saga, of the *gestes* of one of Christendom's most romantic and colorful figures.

Notes

1. For an account of early references to the MS see Gaston Paris's Introduction, pp. ii-vi.

2. Lines 728, 2401, 3226, 3734, 4560, *et al.*

3. The excursus on the earlier history of Jerusalem and the earlier stages of the siege of Acre were derived according to Ambroise's own statement from some earlier existent book. What this was we cannot say. The first book of the *Itinerarium* was derived from the Latin Continuator of William of Tyre if we can credit the very convincing argument of Marianne Salloch (*Die lateinische Fortsetzung Wilhelms von Tyrus,* diss. Greifswald, 1934). But, as Miss Salloch points out, the parts of the *Itinerarium* which are derived from this source are precisely those in which it does not resemble the *Estoire*. The narrative history of the *Itinerarium* follows the Latin Continuator, but the chapters dealing with the incidents of the siege (*Itinerarium,* Bk. I, chs. xlvii-lx, 97-115) and those cursing the Marquis for his desertion of the army and the sufferings of the pilgrims (chs. lxvi-lxxxi, 124-37), while not found in the Latin Continuator, are identical with the parallel passages in the *Estoire*. It is evident that the *Estoire* did not depend on the Latin Continuator, but that both the *Estoire* and the *Itinerarium* did derive these passages from some other still unknown source, which must have been an eyewitness account of the siege.

4. See lines 516, 1388, 4665, 8479-93, *et al.*

5. See J. H. Round in *English Historical Review,* XVIII (1903), 475-81.

6. Gaston Paris, Introduction, p. vi.

7. "Quorum seriem itineris et quae in itinere gesserunt, seu ex qua occasione rex Phillippus repatriavit, si quis plenius nosse desiderat, legat librum quem dominus prior Sanctae Trinitatis Londoniis *ex Gallica lingua in Latinam tam eleganti quam veraci stilo transferri fecit.*" *Libellus* in Stevenson *Radulphi de Coggeshall,* p. 257.

8. *Chronicles and Memorials of the Reign of Richard I.* Vol. I, *Itinerarium Perigrinorum et gesta Regis Ricardi.* Edited . . . by William Stubbs (London, 1864). For convenience this work will be referred to as the *Itinerarium.*

9. *Ibid.,* p. lviii.

10. *Ibid.,* p. lxiv.

11. Introduction, pp. lix ff.

12. *English Historical Review,* XXV (1910), 523 ff. This article is based on notes made by T. E. Archer, but it embodies Miss Norgate's conclusions.

13. Italics hers.

14. *Op. cit.,* p. 526.

15. As Dorothy Bovée (*The Sources of the Third Crusade*) has pointed out, it is extraordinary, if such a relationship existed between the two writers, that neither one so much as mentions the name of the other.

16. "The *Itinerarium regis Ricardi* and the *Estoire de la Guerre Sainte,*" in *Historical Essays in Honor of James Tait* (Manchester, 1933), pp. 59-77.

17. Lines 513-18.

18. Bk. II, ch. xi.

19. "Illi potentissimo Agolando, Roma transiens . . . qui cum manu validissima, et nisi Deo opitulante,

hominibus pene invincibili, Saracenorum, applicuerat apud Rysam civitatem Calabriae."

20. Lines 8490-93.

21. Edwards, *op. cit.,* p. 63.

22. She has noted twenty-eight of them; *op. cit.,* p. 538.

23. Page 4. Miss Bovée has noted another such reference: "audientibus iis etiam qui interfuerant, audenter protestamur."—pp. 439-40.

24. See Edwards's appendix, p. 75.

25. *Estoire,* lines 450 ff.; *Itinerarium,* p. 152.

26. *Estoire,* lines 998 ff.; *Itinerarium,* p. 169.

27. *Estoire,* lines 5041 ff.; *Itinerarium,* p. 235.

28. *Estoire,* line 4719; *Itinerarium,* p. 217.

29. *Estoire,* line 10653; *Itinerarium,* p. 395.

30. *Estoire,* line 5570; *Itinerarium,* p. 244.

31. *Estoire,* line 11969; *Itinerarium,* p. 434.

32. Bovée: *op. cit.,* p. 74; *Estoire,* line 6026; *Itinerarium,* pp. 256-57.

33. "Eadem autem civitas Catinensium medio spatio sita est inter Messanam et Palermam." *Itinerarium,* p. 171. Miss Bovée has noted this error: *op. cit.,* p. 68.

34. Pages 298, 301, 303.

35. Lines 7462, 7551, 7613.

36. "It is possible and very probable, that our author in this passage has confounded Daron and Netroun, (*le darun* and *le toron*) the position among the mountains not answering well to the former place. It is of course impossible to be exact in these points, as, in the case of so large and encumbered armies as both the contending hosts were, there might be miles between the rear and the van."—*Op. cit.,* p. 298*n.*

37. *Estoire,* line 7518. The word "noyé" recurs with the same meaning in lines 10014-15:

> "Car cil de la nostre partieEsteient si entr'els noié"

Here the Latin correctly renders: "nostri . . . inter hostes prae multitudine eorum quasi absconderentur."—p. 374.

38. *Itinerarium,* p. 300.

39. *Itinerarium,* p. 306. See our note to line 7716, *infra,* p. 301.

40. *Itinerarium,* p. 214.

41. *Estoire,* lines 4605 ff. See our note on these lines, *infra,* p. 196.

42. *Ibid.,* line 311; *Itinerarium,* p. 440.

43. *Estoire,* line 12245; *Itinerarium,* p. 440.

44. For titles and editions of authors cited here, see our Bibliography.

S. D. Goitein (essay date 1952)

SOURCE: "Contemporary Letters on the Capture of Jerusalem by the Crusaders,"*The Journal of Jewish Studies,* Vol. III, No. 4, 1952, pp. 162–77.

[*In the following essay, Goitein attempts to explain the dearth of Jewish accounts of the First Crusade. After examining a letter written in 1100, Goitein theorizes that the lack of Jewish narratives about the victory of the Franks in Jerusalem stems from the fact that local inhabitants viewed the event as one of "only passing importance," offering little opportunity for the type of "heroic sacrifice" worthy of literary narration.*]

So far, not a single Jewish literary source, bearing on the capture of Jerusalem by the Crusaders, has come to light. The absence of a narrative on this event does not seem to be natural, for the Jews living around the eastern shores of the Mediterranean did not completely lack historical interest. They possessed family chronicles and compositions describing special events, both called *Megilloth* (Scrolls). A number of such Scrolls of the eleventh and the beginning of the twelfth centuries are still preserved, such as the " 'Ahima'az Scroll," the chronicle of a pious, learned, and very influential family which was active in Southern Italy, Egypt, and some adjacent countries; the "Misraim Scroll" of 1012, describing events in the early days of the mad Fatimid Caliph al-Hakim, when he was still regarded as a Messiah-like prince of justice; the Scroll of the priestly family of 'Ebhyathar, which flourished in Palestine shortly before the Crusades; and finally the story of 'Obadyah the Proselyte, a Norman knight of noble descent, who embraced Judaism in 1102 and travelled in Syria, Irak, and Egypt in search of the expected Messiah. From a new fragment of the 'Obadyah Scroll recently found by the present writer, it appears clearly that some literary accounts of the bloody persecutions of Jewish communities in Western and Southern Germany in 1096 had reached the East. It is not, therefore, the lack of a literary tradition that would account for the absence of a Jewish narrative of the First Crusade in the East.

Not less astonishing is the fact that not a single Jewish document, bearing directly on the capture of Jerusalem by the Crusaders, has made its appearance so far. It is true that in general "very little contemporary correspondence has survived" even in Europe, and "no official charters or documents of the period" from the Saracene side have come down to us.[1] However, hundreds of documents of this period, from various Mediterranean countries, have been preserved in the Geniza of Old Cairo, and it is, therefore, rather odd that no document bearing on such decisive an event as the capture of Jerusalem has been found.

This complete silence has usually been explained by the fate which befell the Jewry of Jerusalem at the time of the conquest. According to a notice preserved by the Muslim polyhistor Ibn al-Djauzi, which has been known to

European writers for over a hundred years, but which in its turn was taken from another Muslim historian, Ibn al-Qalanisi (died 1160), the Crusaders drove the Jewish inhabitants of the town into the synagogue and burnt them there together with the building.[2] Thus it was believed that the capture of Jerusalem by the Crusaders resulted in the total extermination of its Jewish population, which would explain the complete silence of Jewish sources. However, as B. Dinaburg has pointed out, a different picture of the fate of the Jews in Jerusalem is conveyed to us by Latin chronicles.[3] Although the Jews had taken an active part in the defence of the town,[4] they were not annihilated, but many of them, who were assembled round the Dome of the Rock, were commanded, together with poor native Christians, to clean the town of corpses of the slain. A number of Jews were sold, on Tancred's command, as was customary with war prisoners, and were deported as far as Apuleia in Southern Italy.[5] Many of these were, however, thrown into the sea or beheaded on the way.

A fuller account of what actually happened in Jerusalem is contained in a Geniza document preserved in the Taylor-Schechter Collection of the Cambridge University Library, T-S 20.113, an English translation of which is given at the end of this paper. The document is a letter, written, as usual, in Hebrew characters, but mostly in the Arabic language; it lacks the beginning, and its script is faded or torn in various places. This state of the manuscript explains perhaps why it has escaped hitherto the attention of the many scholars, who have perused the precious treasures of the Taylor-Schechter Collection, and I am particularly obliged to Dr. Teicher, the editor of this Journal, who drew my attention to this difficult, but highly important, document.

As the beginning is missing, neither the place, from which the letter was sent, nor the names or the whereabouts of the persons to whom it was addressed, have been preserved. These, however, can be fairly safely reconstructed from its contents. The three men who signed the letter, no doubt the heads of the community of Ascalon (1. 40-44),[6] must have been in Egypt at this time, because they refer to the place, from which they are writing, as the country in which they are foreigners (1. 29; 1. 19, verso) and to which the refugees were coming from Palestine either by sea (1. 29) or on camels (1. 36). This place could hardly have been Alexandria, since they mention this town expressly (1. 15); but always refer to the place where they are staying as "here." In addition, there can be little doubt that they were addressing one of the two big Jewish communities in Egypt, either Alexandria or Cairo, for the sums, mentioned in the letter, are far larger than those collected by the provincial congregations on similar occasions.[7] The very deferential tone of the letter shows, further, that it was addressed to prominent people, leaders of a big community. Thus it is safe to assume that the authors of the letter sojourned in Damietta or another town in Eastern Egypt. We shall show later that the letter was actually sent to Alexandria.

One might ask for what reason have the authors of the letter left their native town of Ascalon and endeavoured with all their might to evacuate from there also captives who had been ransomed from the Franks. Ascalon was, in fact, taken by the Crusaders only as late as 1153. However, at the time when the letter was written, it looked as if the fall of the town were only a question of time. It is known that, after the defeat of the Egyptian army in August, 1099, the Governor of Ascalon—the same Iftikhar who had capitulated in Jerusalem—was prepared to hand over the town to the Franks, and that it was solely the rivalry between Godfrey of Bouillon and Raymond of Toulouse which caused the Muslim commander to withdraw his offer. Under these circumstances it is perfectly understandable that, at that time, Ascalon was regarded by the Jews as a zone of utmost danger.

The letter was written after Passover (1. 34), *i.e.*, in the summer of 1100. It had been preceded by other letters, which announced the arrival of groups of refugees (1. 32-33). As the writers repeatedly mention their own contributions towards the relief work (1. 1-2; 1. 16, verso), they themselves were clearly not refugees, but must have left Ascalon in an orderly way.

The purpose of the letter was to raise money for paying back the debts incurred by the Ascalon community in connection with the disaster which had befallen the Jerusalem congregation. Besides the expenses on medicine, food, and clothes for the ransomed people, a hundred dinars had been spent for the ransom itself and for the purchase of two hundred and thirty volumes, a hundred codices, and eight Thora Scrolls that had been looted by the Crusaders. As a special messenger was to convey the letter, the authors refrained from making detailed communications (1. 31, verso). Nevertheless, quite a full picture of the fate of the Jews of Jerusalem, both immediately after the fall of the city and during the subsequent months, emerges from our letter. However, for a correct interpretation of its contents one should always bear in mind that other communications which had preceded it are no longer available. But notwithstanding this it is clear that only in the spring of 1100, when almost all the captives, who could be ransomed had reached Ascalon or even Egypt, was it possible to make a complete survey of what had actually happened. We shall try now to reconstruct the facts as far as our letter allows.

Jerusalem, as is well known, was attacked and taken on July 15, 1099, from two directions, from the North by Godfrey and Tancred with their Lotharingians and Flandrians, and from the South by Raymond of Toulouse with his French knights. In both areas there were Jewish quarters: in the South, not far from the so-called Wailing Wall, and in the North in the vicinity of the Damascus Gate.[8] Raymond was blamed for making prisoners and selling them to Ascalon, thus preferring money to "religious" considerations, and it was he who received the capitulation of Iftikhar, the Egyptian commander of the so-called Citadel of David, and gave him a safe-conduct for himself and his men.

The information contained in our letter is to be interpreted against this background. A small number of Jews, probably army agents[9] and people with useful connections, succeeded in leaving the city in the company of the Governor (l. 26); others escaped after having been captured (l. 27); the majority, however, of those who remained alive and had been made prisoners were ransomed—most probably from captivity in Raymond's hands. According to a long-established rule, the ransom of a free man, whether Muslim, Christian, or Jew, was fixed at 33 dinars, a comparatively high sum. Such was the amount at the time of the famous geographer al-Maqdisi of Jerusalem (985 A.D.) and the same amount is recorded in Jewish sources throughout the eleventh century.[10] Had this usage been adhered to in the case of the captives of Jerusalem, only a comparatively small number of them would have been ransomed. The writers of our letter see a special sign of God's mercy in the fact that this time a far smaller ransom had to be paid (l. 44-48). This was hardly due to the ignorance on the part of the Crusaders of the customary ransom fee; most probably military considerations induced them to get rid at any price of the embarrassing number of prisoners, before meeting the Fatimid army in the open field. The number of persons thus ransomed must have been rather considerable, for at the time when our letter was written, after various groups of ex-captives had already arrived in Egypt (including the main group conducted there by an Alexandrian worthy [l. 13-17, 33-37]), there still remained at Ascalon over twenty persons (l. 9, verso).

Not all the prisoners could be ransomed. Since Jerusalem was taken by various Christian commanders, it is not surprising to find that the treatment of the local population was far from uniform. According to Baldricus, as mentioned above, it was Tancred who took Jewish prisoners; but, as Baldricus adds, many of these were murdered—a fact echoed in our letter (l. 10). Others were purposely detained and these finally embraced the Christian faith (l. 23). There was, in particular, the interesting case of a man known as "the son of the Tustari's wife,"[11] who was urged to become a Christian priest after a high ransom had been offered or even payed for him.

There is another detail which deserves special attention: the very great number of books, originally synagogue property, which were sold by the Crusaders to the Jewish relief committee of Ascalon (l. 38-39). The Cairo Geniza has preserved various lists of the property of the synagogues of Fostat (Old Cairo), which enable us to make comparisons. In 1075 the synagogue of the Palestinian Jews there possessed twenty-eight codices and eighteen Thora Scrolls, part of which belonged to the synagogue of Dumuh (a place of pilgrimage outside Cairo) and another part to the synagogue of the Iraqian Jews.[12] The latter possessed in 1080 only twenty-five codices. In 1181, however, the Iraqians alone still possessed more or less the same number (most of which from recent acquisitions or donations), but the synagogue of the Palestinians possessed in 1186 over fifty codices, including the famous co-

dex of the Bible called *Taj* (the Crown),[13] which ultimately found its way to Aleppo, and another similarly precious codex, called "The Brother of the Taj," details of which are to be found in Hebrew MS. Oxford 2876, fol. 23 (to be published by me shortly).

The figures just given are significant in many respects. They show, first, that Jerusalem was still at the time of the conquest by the Crusaders a place of Jewish learning, or at least of comparatively many Jewish books, although the Academy of Talmudic Studies had been transferred to Tyre many years before. Secondly, it now becomes evident that the Crusaders, after the fall of the town, proceeded to loot rather systematically. At least they did not burn a synagogue without first removing its library and its Thora Scrolls, which, of course, represented money. Thirdly, we can see now how books from Jerusalem found their way to Cairo (and probably also to Alexandria). As I understand, Dr. Teicher is going to deal with this point in a special paper, and I shall refrain from commenting on it further.

Our letter alludes to another important detail, in regard to which the behaviour of the various conquerors of the city was different. It says (l. 24-25) that those known as *Ashkenazim*, Germans, did not force or violate[14] women, as the others did. In order to understand this statement properly, one has to consider, as mentioned above, that various groups of ransomed prisoners had reached Egypt before our letter was written. Among these, there were no doubt women who had undergone that trial. According to the Jewish Law a wife of a priest, *kohen,* who had been violated, must be divorced by her husband. Most probably such cases had occurred; hence the problem of violated women was one of public concern. The bulk of the captives, as we have surmised above, were ransomed from Raymond and his Frenchmen shortly after the fall of Jerusalem. It appears, thus, obvious to assume that these captives reported cases of violated women. Prisoners made by the Lotharingians and Flandrians were, however, redeemed at a later period and reached in trickles Ascalon and subsequently Egypt. This explains why the notice about the different behaviour of the Christian conquerors of Jerusalem finds its place in a letter written as late as the summer of 1100.

The sufferings of the captives did not end with their ransom. They ceased to be "prisoners" and became "refugees."[15] The limited means of the small community of Ascalon were hardly sufficient for the ransom of the people and of the books and for supplying medical and other assistance. Many of the ransomed perished on their way to Egypt, partly also because of the severe winter (l. 29-31). Even the Crusaders, who came from northern countries suffered, as is known from Latin sources, very severely. Those prisoners who succeeded in reaching Egypt became the victims of an outbreak of the plague and other epidemic diseases, which reached their peak at that time—a detail to which we shall have to refer again when discussing another document dealing with the conquest of Jerusalem by the Crusaders.

The letter is written in a dignified and almost eloquent language, and leaves a favourable impression of its writers and recipients as well as of the other persons mentioned in it. We see the old Jewish tradition of conquering disaster with charity as strong at that time as it has been in our own days. Particular mention is made of Abu' l-Fadl Sahl, son of Yusha', son of Sha'ya, an influential agent of the Sultan, who succeeded, by able negotiations, in ransoming all those "whom it was possible to liberate" (l. 13-18), and who, besides granting a loan to the public relief fund, undertook at his own expense to bring a group of refugees to Egypt—a costly affair, since the Jews did not travel on Saturday (this meant, of course, extra pay for the Bedouin camel drivers), and the time was Passover, which required the provision of special food (l. 34).

It would lead us too far to discuss here the interesting passage concerning the raising of funds (l. 21-35, verso). As in our own days, charity was not left entirely to the discretion of each individual. Thus, in a similar situation, when Jewish captives from Byzantium were brought by Saracene pirates to Alexandria in 1027, the Jewish authorities ordered a public fast, the closure of shops, and a compulsory attendance at the synagogues, where indeed the whole Jewish population, including the women and the Moroccan merchants present in the town, contributed their share.[16]

The cryptic remark that the rich and wealthy in the city of the recipients of the latter had become impoverished seems to find its explanation in a passage of the second document (translated below, l. 40-41), where it is said that owing to the continued plague and other diseases which ravaged Alexandria (in the years 1095-1098) the rich had become poor in that town. It would appear, therefore, that our letter was addressed to Alexandria; and this is in conformity with the high praise given repeatedly in the letter to the addressees that they were the first and the most eager to help—a praise which would have been somewhat out of place had it been destined for Cairo, the leading community of the country.

We are turning now to a second document referring to the capture of Jerusalem by the Crusaders. It is preserved in the Bodleian Library, Hebr. MS. b11 (Catalogue No. 2874), fol. 7. This is a letter sent from Egypt to North Africa or Spain by a pilgrim who had set out from his country more than five years before 1099, in order "to behold" Jerusalem but was detained in Alexandria, owing to the dangers of the constant warfare in Palestine. In fact, hardly one out of a whole company which had tried to reach Jerusalem succeeded in coming back (l. 12-17). The wars between the Fatimids and the various factions of the Seldjuks are well known from Muslim sources; still it is interesting to see how they affected everyday life in the years preceding the arrival of the Crusaders.

There was no peace in Egypt either. After the death of the Caliph al-Mustansir on January 10, 1094, al-Afdal, the almighty viceroy, placed on the throne the Caliph's younger son, al-Musta'li, instead of the elder Nizar, who,

however, succeeded in making himself acknowledged in Alexandria. Al-Afdal twice laid siege to this town, until it acquiesced in rendering homage to al-Musta'li. To these events the writer of our letter alludes in 1. 17-22, from which one can gather how successfully Fatimid propaganda influenced the local population. The writer describes the new Caliph[17] as a prince of justice, the like of whom never has existed in the world—just as the Misraim Scroll of 1012 had done in respect of al-Hākim[18]—and he, although a foreigner in Egypt and a Jew, repeatedly calls him *our* "Sultan." His expectation that the just and energetic ruler would conquer Jerusalem was fulfilled, and therefore he moved from Alexandria to Cairo in order to set out from there to the Holy Land. Before, however, he could do so, the Franks arrived and captured the city.

It seems that our letter was written approximately at the same time as the document discussed before, because the situation is the same: a number of captives had already been ransomed, while others were still in the hands of the Crusaders "in all parts of the world"; this is in conformity both with the remark in the letter of the elders of Ascalon that some captives were brought to Antiochia, and with the information of Baldricus that many captives were sent to Apuleia in Southern Italy. The writer, on the one hand, complains that so far the general expectation that "the Sultan" would attack and wipe out the Franks has not yet been fulfilled, and, on the other hand, he is convinced that "*this*" year"—as he says—the armies would meet in battle. With *this* year he obviously means either the Muslim year 493, which began on November 17, 1099, or the corresponding Jewish year, which started a few weeks earlier. It is most probable that he wrote in the spring of 1100, shortly before the campaigning period opened. He hopes—but seems to be not completely confident about it—that the Fatimid army would rout the Franks and drive them out of Jerusalem, in which case he would be the first to set out for the Holy City in order to fulfil his vow of pilgrimage. He was not, however, prepared to wait much longer, for he was old and longed to go back to his homeland and "the inheritance of his fathers."

To my mind, this simple letter is a precious historical document, as it reflects very tangibly the mood of the subjects of the Fatimid Caliph in the year following the capture of Jerusalem. On the one hand, the wholesale slaughter at the time of the conquest had achieved the result intended.[19] Our writer says that the Crusaders killed *all* the Muslims and Jews, although he himself refers to different groups of surviving captives; he, like everybody else, was deeply impressed by the reports about the murder of the civil population. On the other hand, after Jerusalem had changed its lords several times in the course of a single generation—the Fatimids had conquered it less than one year before the Crusaders—it was only natural that everybody should have expected that the city would soon be wrested again from the Crusaders' hands. We see here again the efficient Fatimid propaganda machine at work, which, in order to disarm the indignation of the people about the loss of Jerusalem, was spreading, from time to time, the rumour that the Sultan was setting out with his troops against the Franks. On the whole, one clearly perceives that at this early period it was by no means realised that the Franks had come to stay for such a long period.

Again the writer's report about the plague and the other diseases which wasted Alexandria during four successive years (1095-1098) and destroyed its wealth and a great part of its population, is not without historical interest. The plague broke out again early in 1100 and affected also the Crusaders.[20] It may be, indeed, worth while to investigate whether Egypt was not weakened by these epidemics during the years preceding the arrival of the Franks so that she became unable to put up an effective resistance.

Having reviewed the contents of these new documents concerning the capture of Jerusalem by the Crusaders, we are now in a position to answer the question put at the beginning of this article, *i.e.,* why the fall of the Holy City, unlike the happenings in Western and Southern Germany in the year 1096, found no literary expression in Jewish sources. The victory of the Franks was, apparently, regarded by the local population as an event of only passing importance.[21] It meant disaster for the inhabitants of Jerusalem, but there was no opportunity for heroic sacrifice and "Sanctification of the Name (of God)," as was the case in Germany. It was a case for charity and relief work, not for heroism. Heroism may give rise to literary expression, relief work breeds reports. Indeed, the report of the elders of Ascalon, discussed above, with its decent and warmhearted account of the relief work done, is, so far, the most eloquent response of Oriental Jewry to the challenge of the fall of Jerusalem in 1099, which has come down to us.

. . . . .

The original text of the documents which are given here in English translation is published, together with a detailed philological commentary, in Zion, *Vol. XVII.*

I take this opportunity to extend my sincerest thanks to the Librarians of the Cambridge University Library and of the Bodleian Library in Oxford for their kindness in allowing me to examine and publish these documents. I am also indebted to Professor D. H. Baneth for the important comment he has made on the Arabic of the text, and likewise to Professor S. Halkin and Mr. H. Blank for revising the English translations.

Document No. 1

[Cambridge University Library MS. Hebr. T-S 20.113. Proper names are printed in italics.]

(Recto)

(1) We thank the Most High who gave us the opportunity of fulfilling this pious deed, and granted to you to take a (2) share in it with us. We spent the money for the ransom of some of the captives, after due consideration (3) of the instructions contained in your letter, that is, we send what was available to those who [had already been ransomed(?)].

(4) We did not fail to reply to what you had written us, (5) and indeed we answered, but we were seeking a man who would bring our reply to you. Afterwards it happened that these illnesses came upon us; (6) plague, pestilence, and leprosy, which filled our minds with anxiety, that (7) we ourselves or some of our relatives might be stricken with disease. A man whom we trust went from here and must have explained to you (8) the position with respect to the sums you had sent: that they reached us safely and that they were spent in the manner indicated [in your letter].

(9) News still reaches us that among those who were redeemed from the *Franks* and remained (10) in *Ascalon* some are in danger of dying of want. Others remained in captivity, and yet others were killed (11) before the eyes of the rest, who themselves were killed afterwards with all manner of tortures; [for the enemy murdered them] in order to give vent to his anger on them. (12) We did not hear of a single man of Israel who was in such plight without exerting ourselves to do all that (13) was in our power to save him.

The Most High has granted opportunities of relief and deliverance to individual fugitives, (14) of which the first and most perfect instance—after the compassion of Heaven—has been the presence in *Ascalon* of the honourable shaykh *'Abu' l-Fadl Sahl* (15) *son of Yusha' son of Shay'a* (may God preserve him), an agent of the Sultan (may God bestow glory upon his victories), (16) whose influence is great in *Alexandria* where his word is very much heeded. He arranged matters wisely and took great pain in securing the ransom; (17) but it would require a lengthy discourse to explain how he did it. But he could only ransom some of the people and had to leave the others. In the end, (18) all those who could be ransomed from them [the Franks] were liberated, and only a few whom they kept remained in their hands, including (19) a boy of about eight years of age, and a man, known as [?] *the son of* (20) *the Tustari's wife.* It is reported that the Franks urged the latter to embrace the Christian faith of his own free will (21) and promised to treat him well, but he told them, how could he become a Christian priest and be left in peace by them [the Jews], who had disbursed (22) on his behalf a great sum. Until this day these captives remain in their [Franks] hands; as well as those who were taken to *Antioch,* but these are few; (23) and not counting those who abjured their faith because they lost patience as it was not possible to ransom them, and because they despaired of being permitted to go free.

(24) We were not informed, praise be to the Most High, that the accursed ones who are called *'Ashkenazim* (Germans) violated (25) or raped women, as did the others.

Now, among those who have reached safety (26) are some who escaped on the second and third days following the battle and left with the governor who was granted safe conduct; (27) and others who, after having being caught by the *Franks,* remained in their hands for some time and escaped in the end; these are but few. (28) The majority consists of those who were ransomed. To our sorrow, some of them ended their lives under all kind of suffering and affliction. (29) The privations which they had to endure caused some of them to leave for this country (30) without food or protection against the cold, and they died on the way. (31) Others in a similar way perished at sea; and yet others, after having arrived here safely, became exposed to a "change of air"; they came at the height of the plague, and a number of them died. We had, at the time, reported the arrival (33) of each group.

And when the aforementioned honoured shaykh arrived, he brought a group (34) of them, *i.e.,* the bulk of those who had reached *Ascalon;* he spent the Sabbath and celebrated Passover with them (35) on the way in the manner as is required by such circumstances. He contracted a private loan for the sum (36) that he had to pay the camel drivers and for their maintenance on the way, as well as the caravan guards and for other expenses, after (37) having already spent other sums of money, which he did not charge to the community. All this is in addition to the money that (38) was borrowed and spent in order to buy back two hundred and thirty volumes, a hundred codices (39) and eight Torah Scrolls. All these are communal property and are now in *Ascalon* (40).

The community, after having disbursed about five hundred dinars for the actual ransom of the individuals (40 interlinear), for maintenance of some of them and for the ransom, as mentioned above, of the sacred books (41) remained indebted for the sum of two hundred dinars. This is in addition to what has been spent (42) on behalf of those who have been arriving from the beginning until now, on water and other drinks, medical treatment, (43) maintenance and, in so far as possible, clothing. If it could be calculated how much this has cost over such a long period, (44) the sum would indeed be great.

Had the accepted practice been followed, that is, of selling three Jewish captives (in the margin) (45) for a hundred [dinars], the whole available sum would have been spent (46) for the ransom of only a few. However, the grace of the Lord, may His name be exalted, (47) and His ever-ready mercy, has been bestowed upon these wretched people, (48) the oppressed, the captives, the poor and indigent, (49) who may, indeed, groan, lament, and cry out (50) as it is written [Ps. xliv, 12-13]: "Thou hast given us like sheep appointed for meat, and hast scattered us among the heathen. (51) Thou sellest Thy people for nought and dost not increase Thy wealth by their price." (52) And we ourselves may say [Is. i, 9]: "Except the Lord of Hosts had left unto us (53) a very small remnant, we should have been as Sodom, and we should have been like unto Gomorrah." (54) We declare that all the silver which we have weighed [*i.e.,* the money we have spent] in this catastrophe, from the beginning (55) until now is but light and insignificant in relation to its magnitude (56) and the greatness of the sorrow it has entailed.

(57) Some adduce as an excuse the impoverishment of (58) this class of financial magnates and property holders (59) . . . and (?) the harshness of the winter season (60) . . . and . . . enfeebled it.

(Verso)

(1) We could not refrain ourselves from reporting what we know and the outcome of what we have done in this juncture, (2) for we are convinced that you, just like ourselves, regret and mourn for those who have died (3) and strive for the preservation of those who are alive; especially since your determination to distinguish yourselves was clearly shown (4) and the loftiness of your aspiration and generosity became apparent. You were the first and the most consistent (5) in the fulfilment of this "good deed" which you were granted to perform, and which gained for you great superiority over the other communities (6) as well as much honour. Thus, you may be, indeed, compared with that class of people to whom it was assigned to perform generous deeds (7) and to strive to do praiseworthy acts, as it is written [Deut. xxxiii, 21]: "And he came with the heads of the people, he executed the justice of the Lord, and his judgments (8) with Israel."

We have already indicated that we remained in debt of over two hundred dinars, apart from the moneys that are (9) required for the maintenance of the captives who remained in *Ascalon*—they number more than twenty (10) persons—for their transfer and other needs until they arrive here. (11) Among those who are in *Ascalon* is the honoured elder *'Abi al-Khair Mubarak* the son of (12) the teacher *Hiba b. Nisan* (may God protect him for a long time). It is well known how much he is revered, wise, (13) God-fearing, and endowed with high virtues; he is bound by an old vow not to benefit in anything from charity (14) together with the whole of the community, but only from what is explicitly destined for him by name. [He should be enabled] (15) to come here, after [you] our Lords, elders and masters—may God preserve your happiness—(16) have graciously offered us the sum needed for cancelling the debt incurred for the ransom of our and your brethren. Gird now your loins together with us (17) in this matter, and it will be accounted for you as a mark of merit in the future, as it has been in the past . . . (18) the generous deed which you began, by helping us to lighten our burden and by assisting us (19) with your generosity in order to put us back on our feet, for we have no one in this country to whom we could write (20) as we are writing to you. It is proper that we should turn to you and cause you some disturbance. (21) The main tenor of this letter ought to be read out to your [entire] community, after you have announced that (22) everyone must attend [the meeting]. For the benefit will [thus] be complete and general, both to those who pay and to those who receive payment. (23) For it is unlikely that there should lack among the public those who had made a vow, or those who had undertaken an obligation to perform "holy deeds" which have not yet been determined; such should, then, be invited (24) to contribute as much as may be seen fitting. Or there may be those who had previously intended to make contribution to charity, or others may wish (25) to make a specific contribution to one cause rather than to another. In this manner you will achieve your purpose, and deal with us (26) in your accustomed generosity and excellent manner . . . (27) . . . and you will deserve, through this charitable act, to acquire "both worlds." (28) Only rarely does such a juncture present itself, in which "commerce"* is beneficial and "business" [*i.e.,* The heavenly reward for contributions to charity.] entirely profitable. We do not call your attention to (29) such a matter in order to remind you of the duty of doing it, but . . . (30) your own lofty [virtues] are the strongest urger and reminder.

We dispatched a messenger to you and what (31) he will tell you about the details of this misfortune exempts us from discoursing on it at a greater length. We (32) beg of you, may God preserve you in long life, to deal with him kindly until he returns; and concerning that which (33) God may cause him [to collect] amongst you—may God preserve you—if you could write out for him a bill of exchange (34), it would make things easier for him, since he is but a messenger, and speed up his return. If this cannot be done, arrange that an exact statement (35) of how much has been collected be made, and have your letter sent through him [the messenger] and mention the sum in it. The God of Israel, etc. . . .

(There follow nine lines with complimentary phrases in Hebrew.)

(In the margin)

(1) The writer of the above, the pained, sorrowful, and grieving *Yesha'ya ha-Kohen b. Masliah the Enlightened* (2) sends respectful greetings to all the gentlemen, and begs them to accept his apology. (3) They are not unaware of what he has gone through from the time he took leave of them until this day.

(To the left of preceding lines)

(1) *David b. R. Shelomo b. R.* . . . (2) sends his greeting to your excellencies (3) and begs you to note . . . (4) *al-Fadl Abu.* . . .

(To the right of the first signature, in Arabic characters)

(1) *Hanina b. Mansur b. 'Ubayd (peace be on him)* reserves for the venerable lords and masters, may God preserve their excellencies, (2) the best greeting and most excellent salutation and attention; expresses his longing for them and begs them to take note of the contents of this letter. Peace.

DOCUMENT NO. 2

[Bodleian Library, Oxford, Heb. MS. b11 (Catalogue, No. 2874) fol. 7. The Hebrew or Aramaic words and phrases of the original are printed here in italics.]

IN YOUR NAME, YOU MERCIFUL.

(2) If I attempted to describe my longing for you, my Lord, my brother *and cousin,* (3)—may God prolong your days and make permanent your honour, success, happiness, health, (4) and welfare; and [. . .] subdue your enemies—all the paper in the world would not suffice. My longing will but increase (5) and double, just as the days will grow and double. May *the Creator of the World* presently (6) make us meet together in joy when I return under His guidance to my homeland *and to the inheritance of my Fathers* in complete (7) happiness, *so that we rejoice and be happy through His great mercy* (8) *and His vast bounty; and thus may be His will!*

You may remember, my Lord, that many years ago (9) I left our country to seek God's mercy and help in my poverty, (10) to behold Jerusalem and return thereupon. However, when I was in Alexandria (11) God brought about circumstances which caused a slight delay. Afterwards, however, (12) "the sea grew stormy," and many armed bands made their appearance in Palestine; (13) "*and he who went forth and he who came had no peace,*" so that hardly one survivor out of a whole group (14) came back to us from Palestine and told us that scarcely anyone could save himself (15) from those armed bands, since they were so numerous and were gathered round (16) . . . every town. There was further the journey through the desert, among (17) [the bedouins] and whoever escaped from the one, fell into the hands of the other. Moreover, mutinies (18) [spread throughout the country and reached] even Alexandria, so that we ourselves were besieged several times and the city was ruined; (19) . . . the end however *was good,* for the Sultan—may God bestow glory upon his victories—conquered the city (20) and caused justice to abound in it in a manner unprecedented in the (21) history of any king in the world; not even a dirham (22) was looted from anyone. Thus I had come to hope that because of his justice and strength God would give the (23) land into his hands, and I should thereupon go to Jerusalem in safety and tranquillity. For this reason I proceeded from Alexandria (24) to Cairo, in order to start [my journey] from there.

When, however, God had given Jerusalem, the blessed, into his hands (25) this state of affairs continued for too short a time to allow for making a journey there. (26) The Franks arrived and killed everybody in the city, whether of *Ishmael or of Israel;* (27) and the few who survived the slaughter were made prisoners. Some of these have been ransomed since, (28) while others are still in captivity in all parts of the world.

(29) Now, all of us had anticipated that our Sultan—may God bestow glory upon his victories—would set out against them [the Franks] with (30) his troops and chase them away. But time after time our hope failed. Yet, to this very (31) present moment we do hope that God will give his [the Sultan's] enemies into his hands. For it is inevitable that the armies will join in battle this year; (32)

and, if God grants us victory through him [the Sultan] and he conquers Jerusalem—and so it may be, with God's will—(33) I for one shall not be amongst those who will linger, but shall go there to behold the city; and shall afterwards return (34) straight to you—if God wills it. My salvation is in God, for this (35) [is unlike] the other previous occasions [of making a pilgrimage to Jerusalem]. God, indeed, will exonerate me, (36) since at my age I cannot afford to delay and wait any longer; (37) I want to return home under any circumstances, if I still remain alive—whether I shall have seen (38) Jerusalem or have given up the hope of doing it—both of which are possible.

(39) You know, of course, my Lord, what has happened to us in the course of the last five years: the plague, the illnesses, (40) and ailments have continued unabated for four successive years. As a result of this the wealthy became impoverished (41) and a great number of people died *of the plague,* so that entire families (42) perished in it. I, too, was affected with a grave illness, from which I recovered only (43) about a year ago; then I was taken ill the following year so that (on the margin) for four years I have remained [. . .]. He who has said: *The evil diseases of Egypt* [Deut. vii, 15] . . . he who hiccups does not live . . . ailments and will die . . . otherwise . . . will remain alive.

Notes

1. See S. Runciman, *History of the Crusades,* Cambridge, 1951, Vol. I, p. 333.

2. Runciman, *op. cit.,* p. 287. R. Grousset, *Histoire des Croisades,* I, p. 161.

3. *Year Book Zion,* Jerusalem, 1927, pp. 38-66.

4. Gilo, *Historia Gestorum,* vi, 264, quoted by Hagenmeyer, *Gesta Francorum* 1890, p. 477, note 7.

5. Baldricus, *Historia Jerosolimitana, Recueil, Occ.* iv, 103, note 7 (codex G of Blois Library, cf. Hagenmeyer, *op. cit.,* 476). Cf. R. Rohricht, *Geschichte des ersten Kreuzzuges,* 1901, 195-6.

6. Numbers not followed by the word "verso" refer to the first page of the letter.

7. Cf. J. Mann, *The Jews in Egypt and in Palestine under the Fatimids,* I, p. 232 and *passim.*

8. The problem of the sites of the Jewish quarters of Jerusalem at the eve of the Crusades was discussed in great detail by Y. Prawer in *Zion,* Vol. XII, pp. 136-148. PRAWER assumes that the southern quarter was relinquished in favour of the northern site. However, a Jewish letter, dated approximately 1054, has been recently published in the *Osaiah Press Jubilee Volume,* p. 121, which was dispatched from "Jerusalem, Gate of the Cave"=Damascus Gate. (The "Cave" is the one which is called to-day after Zedekiah and was called, in older times, after Qarun-Korah. Cf. Guy Le Strange, *Palestine under the Muslims,* p. 223.) This letter seems to indicate that the two quarters existed then side by side. In addition, the Jews would hardly have returned to the south of Jerusalem after 1187 had they not been living there before 1099.

9. See the title "The Manager of the Bedouin Levy" mentioned in the Cambridge Document, TS. Arabic I, xv, 111. This document is being published by me in the *Millas' Festschrift,* Barcelona.

10. Cf. J. Mann, *op. cit.,* I, pp. 87-90, and *passim.* When our letter (l. 45) says that three *Jewish* persons used to be ransomed for the sum of 100 dinars, it does not imply that the ransom price for non-Jews was different.

11. Most probably a member of the Tustari family, which occupied a leading position in Egypt in the eleventh century, cf. J. MANN, *op. cit., passim,* and W. J. FISCHEL, *The Jews in the Economic and Political Life of Mediæval Islam,* 68-69.

12. See MS. in the Jewish Theological Seminary Library, Adler Collection, No. 4010.

13. These documents were published with facsimiles by R. GOTTHEIL, in *Israel Abraham's Memorial Volume,* pp. 160-169.

14. I do not know exactly the difference between the two Arabic expressions used in the letter, *qahara* and *ittata gasban.* In Arab warfare, it was common practice to have intercourse with a captured woman without *ejaculatio seminis,* in which case a higher ransom was realised than after completed cohabitation. I do not know, however, whether the Franks made similar differentiations.

15. The writer of the letter uses the Hebrew expression *pelitim,* which has gained such sad fame in our own time. Although writing in Arabic, he denotes "captives" and "refugees" with Hebrew words, because of the religious duty to help them. As soon as religion comes in, Hebrew makes its appearance.

16. See J. Mann, *Texts and Studies in Jewish History and Literature,* I, 366-369.

17. The praise could refer also to al-Afdal.

18. See above, p. 62.

19. It is GROUSSET's theory that the extermination of the civilian population was due to military considerations. The elders of Ascalon in their letter, l. ll, ascribe the cruel killing of the captives to sheer lust of murder.

20. The detail, at the end of the letter, that "he who hiccups does not live" is found also in the Crusaders' descriptions of the epidemy (whose exact medical character will possibly never be known). As I understand from Dr. S. Muntner, this detail of medical knowledge was already a commonplace at Hippocrates' time and thus passed through Saracene mediation to the West.

21. This is reflected also in the Muslim sources which are amazingly reticent with regard to details about the fall of Jerusalem.

J. J. Saunders (essay date 1962)

SOURCE: "The Literature of the Crusades" in *Aspects of the Crusades,* University of Canterbury, 1962, pp. 10–16.

[*In the following essay, Saunders offers a brief overview of literature pertaining to the Crusades, beginning with the contemporary witness William of Tyre. Saunders discusses several other early accounts as well as later treatments of the Crusades through the twentieth century.*]

The Holy War seized on the imagination of Europe and called into being a wonderful literature of song and history. Almost every noble family of the West boasted crusaders among its ranks, and a large and growing public became avid for details of these deeds done beyond the seas. Nothing did more to stimulate the production of historical narratives, most of which were compiled in France. The best of the contemporary witnesses, William of Tyre, who was born in Frankish Syria, was one of the master-historians of the Middle Ages. His great work,[1] with its fascinating digressions on the manners and customs of the Turks and Arabs, the terrors of the desert, the usefulness of camels, and the sugar plantations of the Levant, was composed in Latin and carried the story down to 1184. It was continued by several hands in French, and one of the earliest books printed in England by Caxton was a translation of William's account of the siege and capture of Jerusalem in 1099.

When the Crusades had become a memory, the Italians in the days of the Renaissance were the first to attempt a general historical survey of the movement. Benedetto Accolti, a professor of law at Florence and secretary of the Republic in succession to Poggio, was joint author with his brother Leonardo of the ponderously titled *De bello a Christianis contra Barbaros gesto pro Christi sepulchro et Judaea recuperandis libri tres* (Venice, 1452), a history of the First Crusade written chiefly out of William of Tyre. As a work of scholarship the book was of small value, but in Italian and French translations it gained a wide popularity, being reprinted as late as 1731, and it is supposed to have inspired Tasso's immortal epic, *Jerusalem Delivered* (1574), the Christian *Iliad* of the Catholic Counter-Reformation.

Yet it was beyond the Alps that the Crusades attracted the most affectionate attention, since in France they were considered virtually as a national enterprise. Paulus Aemilius (Paolo Emilio), a reputable historian of Verona, was invited to Paris by Charles VIII and entrusted with the task of writing up the reigns of the French kings: the fourth book of his *De rebus gestis Francorum* (1517) treats of the Holy Wars and displays a more careful research than the superficial compilation of the Accolti brothers. As the level of French scholarship rose, it was but natural that efforts should be made to seek out and edit the original memorials of the Crusades. In 1611 Jacques Bongars, a learned diplomat who spent many years and much money in the service of Henry IV, brought out in two great folios,

under the patriotic title (borrowed from Guibert of Nogent) of *Gesta Dei per Francos,* 'the Deeds of God done through the Franks', a collection of all the principal contemporary writers of the Crusades. As a historical sourcebook of the Holy Wars it was quite unrivalled in its day and indeed kept its place for well over two hundred years. Here were conveniently gathered together the texts of William of Tyre, Albert of Aix, Fulcher of Chartres, James of Vitry, and almost all the other Latin writers who ranked as primary authorities. In the reign of Louis XIV a group of French savants published a splendid edition of the Byzantine historians, whose narratives so often supplement and correct the Western accounts of the Crusades. The Greek side could now be studied, and Sieur du Cange, best known for his marvellous and still unsurpassed Dictionary of Medieval Greek and Latin, edited with a wealth of learning Villehardouin's famous book on the capture of Constantinople in the Fourth Crusade of 1204.

Patriotism prevented the French from being harshly critical of the Crusades, but Protestant Europe was scornful of an enterprise planned and sponsored by the popes, to whom the most sordid motives were maliciously ascribed. Thomas Fuller, building on the Bongars collection, produced in his *Historie of the Holy Warre* (1639), the completest survey yet made in English, but its virulent anti-papalism deprived it of all claim to objectivity. 'This war', he wrote, 'would be the sewer of Christendom and drain all discords out of it', and elsewhere he described it as 'the pope's house of correction, whither he sent his sturdy and stubborn enemies to be tamed'.[2] Fuller's lively style and quaint conceits make him readable still, and he has the merit of being one of the first to discuss the ethics of the Crusades, the lawfulness, that is, of attempting to deprive the Muslims of the possession of Palestine. A century later the Lutheran church historian Mosheim, though severely critical of the popes, expressed a more moderate opinion: 'The Roman pontiffs and the European princes were engaged at first in these crusades by a principle of superstition only, but when in process of time they learnt by experience that these holy wars contributed much to increase their opulence and to extend their authority, by sacrificing their wealthy and powerful rivals, then new motives were presented to encourage these sacred expeditions into Palestine, and ambition and avarice seconded and enforced the dictates of fanaticism and superstition.'[3]

In the Age of Reason the Crusading studies suffered from the general depreciation of all things medieval. To men like Hume and Voltaire the Frankish expeditions to the Holy Land were nothing but orgies of superstitious militarism, unprovoked assaults by feudal barbarians on the richer and more sophisticated culture of the East. 'Parmi les Francs', says a historian of the period, 'une multitude de gens sans aveu et de libertins sortirent de l'Europe et ne passèrent en Asie que pour s'enrichir, se livrer de plus en plus à leurs vices et y trouver l'impunité; les crimes de ceux-ci, le fanatisme de quelques autres, et le mélange bizarre de religion et de chevalerie, ont fait désapprouver un siècle plus éclairé ces sortes de guerres.'⁴ Gibbon in his more balanced manner attempted to weigh the mixture of motives which impelled the Latin Christians in their thousands to take the cross: 'Of the chiefs and soldiers who marched to the holy sepulchre', he writes, 'I will dare to affirm that *all* were prompted by the spirit of enthusiasm, the belief of merit, the hope of reward, and the assurance of divine aid. But I am equally persuaded that in *many* it was not the sole, that in *some* it was not the leading principle of action', and in describing the frightful massacre of the Muslim population perpetrated in Jerusalem after its capture by the Crusaders, he characteristically adds: 'Nor shall I believe that the most ardent in slaughter and rapine were the foremost in the procession to the holy sepulchre.'⁵ But the rationalist historian is in general cool or tepid and inclined to treat the whole business as slightly absurd. Only with the coming of Romanticism in the early nineteenth century did the Crusades return to favour, and then they were studied with more enthusiasm than understanding. Once more the French took the lead; Napoleon's expedition to Egypt reawakened memories of St Louis and *Outremer,* and Chateaubriand's *Génie du Christianisme* drew a generation weary of the dry abstractions of the Enlightenment back in spirit to the ages of faith and chivalry.

In 1811 Joseph Michaud, a conservative and Catholic royalist who had narrowly escaped death during the Revolution, began the publication of a full length *Histoire des Croisades,* which was completed in six volumes in 1840. His aim was to show that the Crusades had been militarily necessary to save Christendom from being overwhelmed by Turkish Islam and that contact with the East had stimulated the growth of the arts and sciences in Europe. His German contemporary Wilken, who also brought out a history of the Crusades in seven volumes between 1807 and 1832, was the first to utilize Arabic and Syriac sources; this revealed to Michaud the necessity of exploring the libraries of the East, and in his later years he visited Palestine, not as he said to reform the errors of his life, but to correct the mistakes of his *History.*⁶ Partly because of his urging, the Academy of Inscriptions was induced to replace Bongars by a vast *Recueil des historiens des Croisades,* and under its auspices a series of texts ably edited and translated not only from Latin and Greek but from Arabic, Armenian, Syriac and other Oriental languages was issued between 1841 and 1906. It became at last possible for the student to view the whole Crusading movement from the Muslim and Byzantine, as well as from the Western standpoint. This great French collection of sources remains to this day an indispensable tool for all workers in the field, though its arrangement is awkward and its scholarship now (in part at least) antiquated.

Meanwhile the Crusades had attracted the attention of the new school of critical historiography which had gathered round Ranke and aimed to get at the truth of 'what had really happened' in the past by a severer and minuter scrutiny of the original sources than had hitherto been attempted.

One of Ranke's ablest pupils, Heinrich von Sybel, later to win fame by his studies of the French Revolution and the founding of the Bismarckian Reich, was assigned the task of re-examining the Crusading chronicles in the light of the new principles of criticism. He produced in 1841, at the age of twenty-four, a *History of the First Crusade,* which swept away the long-current legends of Peter the Hermit and Godfrey of Bouillon, and in particular destroyed the naïve notion that the whole movement was set going by the preaching of the eloquent Hermit of Amiens, an interpretation as childish as that which would explain the Reformation as the result of a quarrel between Dominican and Augustinian friars. Von Sybel's book, which went into a second edition in 1881, has not yet lost its value, and its penetrating critiques of William of Tyre, Albert of Aix and other historians, are still valid.⁷ Other German scholars built soundly on these foundations. Prutz published in 1883 a valuable *Kulturgeschichte der Kreuzzüge,* the first serious investigation of the non-military aspects of the Crusades, though marred by a tendency to ascribe to the Holy Wars almost all the changes that occurred in Western Europe between 1100 and 1300; and Röhricht, among numerous other writings on the subject, produced in 1898 a *History of the Kingdom of Jerusalem* which remains after more than sixty years the standard authority on the greatest of the Frankish principalities in the East.

The English-speaking world, notwithstanding the fame of Richard Lion-heart, was curiously backward in this field until the turn of the century. Archer and Kingsford's *The Crusades* (1895) was followed by Stanley Lane-Poole's *Saladin* (1898), still the best biography of the great Muslim hero; W. B. Stevenson's *The Crusaders in the East* (1907), a short but excellent survey, and Ernest Barker's admirable article, 'Crusades', in the 1910 edition of the *Encyclopedia Britannica,* reprinted in book form in 1923 and even now after fifty years the most illuminating brief introduction. In the United States an outstanding school of Crusading specialists sprang up under the inspiration of Dana C. Munro, who devoted close attention to the feudal institutions of the Frankish States in Syria. Munro himself wrote little, but a posthumous volume of lectures, published in 1935 under the title of *The Kingdom of the Crusaders,* challenges comparison with Barker for its mastery of the whole enormous field. His best-known pupil, LaMonte, was the author of a scholarly monograph, *Feudal Monarchy in the Latin Kingdom of Jerusalem* (1932), but he died prematurely in 1949, leaving behind an ambitious plan for a comprehensive, co-operative work which began to appear in 1955 from the press of the University of Pennsylvania. The first volume contains contributions from fifteen different scholars, three of them (Cahen, Gibb and Lewis) distinguished Orientalists. The whole work is planned to go far beyond the fall of Acre in 1291 and to cover the long Crusading epilogue of the fourteenth and fifteenth centuries, and the concluding volume will attempt an evaluation of the influence and consequences of the Crusades.

The Americans are specialists, each concentrating on his own minute piece of work in the great factory of history, but the Old World still brings forth men who are not afraid to take bold, Pisgah-like views of the subject and to adorn their narrative with the graces of a distinctive style. René Grousset, whose capacious and inquiring mind ranged over the whole vast expanse of Asian history from China to Armenia, composed, in the days when the French Mandate over Syria and the Lebanon had recalled the earlier 'France beyond the seas', a *Histoire des Croisades* (3 vols. 1934-6). This lively and fascinating work has the peculiar merit of enabling the reader to view the Western intruders into the Levant from the Muslim vantage-point. Grousset neglects the arts and has small interest in the constitutional history of the Frankish States, but no one has treated so thoroughly the Muslim reaction to the Crusades or the impact of the Mongol invasions on the situation in Syria. Since almost all previous accounts of the Crusades have been heavily weighted in favour of the West, it is good to have the balance redressed by a skilled Orientalist though the ardent French Catholic is not always fair to Islam.[8]

More recently, Sir Steven Runciman has published a *History of Crusades* (3 vols. 1951-4), a happy marriage of art and scholarship which is likely to remain for many years to come the principal source of information for the educated English-speaking reader. He also has abandoned the old-fashioned Western approach, but unlike Grousset, he takes his stand at Constantinople; and as befits one who made his reputation in Byzantine studies and possesses astonishing mastery over many Slavonic languages, his sympathies incline to the Greek East, and he rates the Fourth Crusade and the sack of the imperial city among the grossest crimes of history. The rude and barbarous Franks are often roughly handled, and we are never allowed to forget that the most permanent result of the Holy Wars was the ruin of the Byzantine Empire and the Christian Orient.

Despite this impressive mass of historical achievement, little has been done to familiarize the Western reader with the Muslim case. How did the Crusades look from the other side of the hill? What did the Muslims think of these sustained onslaughts from the West? How did they react? A good deal of material translated from the Arabic chronicles is embedded in the great French *Recueil,* five volumes of which are devoted to the Oriental sources, but this is likely to be read by none but specialists. Few Muslim historical writings of Crusading times are available to the general educated public, among them being the memoirs of Usamah b.Munqidh, a cultivated Syrian shaikh and friend of Saladin, who died in 1188,[9] the Chronicle of Ibn al-Qalanisi, a notable of Damascus whose story comes down to 1176,[10] and Baha al-Din's Life of Saladin, whose author died in 1234.[11] To these may be added brief references to the Franks and the Crusades in recently translated Arabic books such as Ibn Jubayr's *Travels,* which covers the years 1183-5,[12] and the famous *Muqaddima* or Introduction of Ibn Khaldun, the philosophic historian

who lived in the fourteenth century.[13] This is meagre enough. No more urgent need confronts workers in the field of Crusading historiography than the publication of sound and accurate translations of the leading Arabic chroniclers of the twelfth and thirteenth centuries. Only when we are provided with these will it be possible to get the Holy Wars into proper perspective: only then will we of the West be able to see the conflict from both sides.[14]

Notes

1. *Historia hierosolymitana,* or *Historia rerum in partibus transmarinis gestarum.* The first printed edition appeared at Basel in 1549. Eng. trans. by J. Badcock and A. C. Krey, *A History of Deeds done beyond the Sea,* New York, 1943. See also A. C. Krey, 'William of Tyre: the making of a historian of the Middle Ages', *Speculum,* XVI, 1941.

2. Fuller's *Historie,* 1840 reprint, pp. 16, 18.

3. Mosheim, *Eccles. History,* Eng. trans. Maclaine, 1790, III, 447-8.

4. De Guignes, *Hist. des Huns,* Paris, 1756, tom.I, part 1, p.13.

5. *Decline and Fall,* ch. 58.

6. Sainte-Beuve, *Causeries du Lundi,* tom. 7, p. 39. Michaud compiled a *Bibliothèque des Croisades,* 4 vols. 1829, a useful and meritorious collection of source-material which was, however, soon superseded by the fuller and richer *Recueil.*

7. There is an English translation by Lady Duff Gordon, *The History and Literature of the Crusades,* London, n.d. (c. 1865), published in Routledge's Universal Library series.

8. See a critique of Grousset in an article by T. S. R. Boase, 'Recent Developments in Crusading Historiography', *History,* Sept. 1937. Grousset's later and smaller work, *Les Croisades,* Paris, 1944, is perhaps more balanced and objective than his larger history.

9. *Usamáh ibn Murshid, called Ibn Munkidh, an Arab-Syrian Gentleman and Warrior in the period of the Crusades,* Eng. trans. P. K. Hitti, New York, 1929.

10. *The Damascus Chronicle of the Crusades,* Eng. trans. H. A. R. Gibb, London, 1932.

11. *The Life of Saladin by Behâ-ed-Dîn,* Eng. trans. C.R. Conder, Palestine Pilgrims' Text Soc., London, 1897.

12. *The Travels of Ibn Jubayr,* Eng. trans. R.J.C. Broadhurst, London, 1952. This book contains (p. 317) the oft-quoted passage in praise of the Frankish landlords in Syria.

13. Ibn Khaldun, *The Muqaddimah, an Introduction to History,* Eng. trans. F. Rosenthal, 3 vols., London, 1959.

14. The Italian Arabist F. Gabrieli has recently published a number of translated extracts from the

Arabic sources, *Storici arabi delle crociate,* Turin, 1957. See also, for further references, the art. 'Crusades' in the new *Enc. of Islam. . . .*

Alfred Foulet (essay date 1989)

SOURCE: "The Epic Cycle of the Crusades" in *A History of the Crusades, Vol. VI: The Impact of the Crusades on Europe,* edited by Kenneth M. Setton, University of Canterbury, 1989, pp. 98–115.

[*In the following essay, Foulet examines the content and form of two epic cycles about the Crusades—the first written at the end of the twelfth century, and the second composed during the 1350s.*]

"The Epic Cycle of the Crusades" is the name commonly given to two different cycles, composed in different centuries but related in subject matter, and both written in Old French dodecasyllabic verse. The first was apparently begun toward the end of the twelfth century by a versifier named Graindor of Douai, who rewrote and amalgamated three previously independent poems, *La Chanson d'Antioche, Les Chétifs* (the Captives), and *La Conquête de Jérusalem,* which dealt with the First Crusade. Graindor's compilation was later prefaced with an account of the fictitious youthful exploits of Godfrey of Bouillon and the story of his mythical grandfather, the swan-knight; at a later date (the middle of the thirteenth century) a sequel was added which carried the narrative from the end of the First Crusade down to the emergence of Saladin. The second cycle, composed, or at least begun, during the 1350's, comprises three separate poems, *Le Chevalier au Cygne et Godefroid de Bouillon, Baudouin de Sebourc,* and *Le Bâtard de Bouillon.*

The construction of an epic cycle over the years by different authors, usually belonging to different generations, but sometimes known to each other, conforms to a paradigm of which the best-known examples are the cycles of Charlemagne, William of Orange, and Doon of Mayence. At the center of a soon-proliferating cycle stands a martial figure whose prowess in many a combat has charmed a public never weary of hearing tales about prestigious heroes who fight and slay innumerable foes. At the beginning of the fourteenth century this avid interest was crystalized in the literary and iconographic cult of the "nine worthies" (three Jews: Joshua, David, and Judas Maccabeus; three pagans: Hector, Alexander, and Caesar; three Christians: Arthur, Charlemagne, and Godfrey of Bouillon). The epic hero is not allowed to remain in splendid isolation; he may be the brightest star within his family constellation, but the deeds of his father, grandfather, brothers, sons, nephews, and grandsons are likewise memorable and so must be praised in epic song. Just as Charlemagne's father Pepin and his nephew Roland are the protagonists of various *chansons de geste,* just so Godfrey of Bouillon's ancestors, brother, cousin, and their descendants

were celebrated in epics built around their persons and deeds, real or imaginary.

Superhuman strength and supernatural happenings endow the epic hero with a radiance that marks him as a man above other men, one of God's elect. When his fury is aroused he can with one mighty blow of his sword cleave an opponent and his steed in two, that is to say into four parts, two human and two equine. Miracles accompany him on his way, heavenly warriors battle at his side, his prayers stay the sun in its course so that the enemy may be pursued and annihilated, and archangels bear his soul to paradise, while devils precipitate slain Saracens into the nethermost regions of hell. How much of all this a medieval audience believed is somewhat beside the point. People of those days were certainly pleased with such tales, and being entertained were not unduly skeptical. Also, one of the fondest beliefs of the nobility was being catered to: blood will tell. Ancestors of a knight must of necessity have been brave and strong, qualities due to be possessed also by his relatives and descendants. Worth noticing is the explanation seemingly given in all seriousness for Eustace of Boulogne's failure to measure up to the worldly success of his brothers Godfrey and Baldwin: when he was an infant, during his mother's absence one day he had been suckled by a woman of low standing.

The ascription of a supernatural origin to Godfrey's family may perhaps be accounted for by many a nobleman's desire that his lineage should not be traced back to the common people. It is worth remembering that the Lusignans, who ruled over Cyprus and Jerusalem, claimed to be descended from the fairy Melusine. The legend of the Trojan origin of the Franks encouraged French and English feudal families to half believe that their forefathers, in the distant past, had come from the mysterious east.[1]

When compared with William of Tyre's *Historia rerum in partibus transmarinis gestarum* and its Old French sequels, the two epic cycles of the crusades have scant historical value, though they do not lack cultural significance. For three centuries, from the twelfth through the fourteenth, they fascinated the French-speaking and French-reading population of central and northern France, thus helping to nourish a lively interest in the Frankish east and in the crusades. A history of the crusades, therefore, should pay some attention to them.

To facilitate access to the first epic cycle I have deemed it advisable to give, for each of its three parts, a résumé of its contents, followed in each case by a few comments. The division into *chants* (cantos) of *Antioche* and *Jérusalem* is, of course, the invention of modern French editors, but as a means of reference it is a serviceable one.

A. THE FIRST CYCLE: GODFREY OF BOUILLON

SECTION 1: THE SWAN-CHILDREN[2]

King Orient rebukes his wife for saying that the birth of twins is proof of their mother's unfaithfulness to her husband, claiming that such a belief tends to limit God's power to act as he sees fit.[3] Soon afterward queen Beatrice gives birth to septuplets: six boys and a girl, each one wearing a silver necklace. Matabrune, the queen-mother, who hates her daugher-in-law, replaces the septuplets with a litter of seven pups and has Beatrice cast into prison by the outraged king. The seven infants are abandoned on the bank of a river, where they are found by a hermit who takes care of them. Ten years later the children are discovered by one of Matabrune's servants, who steals six of the necklaces. The children to whom they belong are transformed into swans; for several years they are fed by Elias, the seventh child, who has retained his human shape. Meanwhile Matabrune has one of the necklaces melted down by a silversmith. Young Elias succeeds in saving the life of his mother Beatrice, condemned after fifteen years' imprisonment to the stake. The swan-children, except the one whose necklace has been melted down, resume their human appearance and are christened Orient, Orion, Zacharias, John, and Rosette. Elias, whose father has abdicated in his favor, besieges Matabrune in her castle of Malbruiant. She is finally captured and burned at the stake. At the injunction of an angel Elias sets forth in a boat drawn by his brother the swan, after receiving from his mother the gift of a magic horn. On his way he slays Agolant, the dead Matabrune's brother. He enters the Rhine and reaches Nijmegen.

SECTION 2: THE SWAN-KNIGHT[4]

Duke Rainier of Saxony is laying claim before emperor Otto to the lands of the widowed duchess of Bouillon, who still lacks a champion willing to defend her rights and those of her young daughter Beatrice. The swan-knight proffers his services and succeeds in slaying Rainier, whose hostages are put to death. The Saxons seek revenge by sacking the castle of Florent, a nephew of the emperor. The swan-knight marries Beatrice, but cautions her never to ask him who he is nor whence he came, otherwise she will lose him forever. The vengeful Saxons kill Gelien, another nephew of the emperor, but the swan-knight rescues his wife from their hands. To them is born a girl, Ida, the future mother of duke Godfrey, count Eustace, and king Baldwin. The Saxons, still unappeased, besiege Bouillon but are finally routed by the emperor, whom the swanknight has called to his aid. On the seventh anniversary of her wedding Beatrice can no longer restrain her curiosity. The swan-knight takes sorrowful leave of his wife and daughter and departs in a swan-drawn boat which has suddenly come for him. As a farewell token, he entrusts his horn to Beatrice, recommending that she take good care of it. This she fails to do. One day at the hour of noon the ducal hall bursts into flames and, amid the general confusion, a swan is seen flying away with the neglected horn. Increasing in beauty every day, Ida reaches the age of fourteen.

SECTION 3: GODFREY OF BOUILLON[5]

Emperor Otto holds court at Cambrai. A newcomer, young count Eustace of Boulogne, waits upon him at table with such pleasing grace that Otto grants him a boon. Eustace asks for the hand of Ida of Bouillon, whose mother Beatrice does not oppose the match and retires to a nunnery. Within two and a half years Ida gives birth to three sons, Eustace, Godfrey, and Baldwin. She insists on suckling all three, for fear that another woman's milk might prove injurious to them. One day during Ida's absence one of the babies is given the breast by a nurse. On discovering this, the frantic mother shakes the infant till he regurgitates the debasing fluid, but alas!, in later days Eustace was never to equal his two brothers. At seventeen years of age Godfrey, having received knighthood at the hands of his father, is sent to the court of emperor Otto. He champions the rights of the orphaned daughter of a castellan against her cousin, whom he slays in judicial combat. Godfrey becomes duke of Bouillon.

The scene suddenly shifts to Mecca, where a great concourse of Saracen potentates and dignitaries is assembled. The spirits of the rejoicing Moslems are dampened when Calabre, mother of Corbaran (Kerbogha), prophesies that dire things are in store for the paynim world. She names Godfrey and his brothers as the leaders of an army that will conquer Syria and Palestine. Her nephew Cornumarant, son of Corbadas and lord of Jerusalem, decides to travel to France and discover for himself whether this Godfrey is the formidable adversary his soothsaying aunt proclaims him to be. He crosses the sea disguised as a palmer, with two razor-sharp knives hidden beneath his cloak. The abbot of Saint Trond recognizes Cornumarant, whom he has seen on a pilgrimage to the Holy Land, and warns Godfrey that he is in danger of being assassinated. Godfrey sends for all his friends and retainers. Cornumarant is greatly impressed by their number. He is told that within five years Godfrey will have conquered the Holy Land. Cornumarant replies that he will ready his kingdom to meet the Christian onslaught.

Comments: It is usually assumed that the three sections of part one came into being as separate poems and were later soldered together by a *remanieur* named Renaud. The legendary tales they embody were already known to William of Tyre, since in his *Historia* (IX, 6) he refers to the swan-knight and to countess Ida's prophecy that her three sons would grow up to become a duke (Godfrey), a king (Baldwin), and a count (Eustace). It should be noted here that through some curious transference the legend of the swan-knight became detached from the Godfrey epic cycle to fasten on the central figure of an entirely different cycle, that of Garin "le Lorrain", Wagner's Lohengrin (= Loherenc Garin).[6]

B. THE FIRST CYCLE: THE FIRST CRUSADE

SECTION 1: THE TAKING OF ANTIOCH[7]

I: Graindor of Douai will tell how the Christian host conquered Jerusalem. The liberation of the Holy Land was prophesied by Jesus on the cross. Peter the Hermit was praying at the tomb of the Redeemer in Jerusalem when God appeared to him, commanding him to return to the lands of Christendom and announce that the time had come to free his city. Sixty thousand men assemble at Peter's behest, among them Harpin of Bourges, Richard of Caumont, John of Alis, Baldwin of Beauvais, and his brother Ernoul. Peter and his followers begin the siege of Nicaea. Soliman (Kilij-Arslan), the lord of that city, has just received reinforcements, led by Corbaran (Kerbogha), from the sultan of Persia. The Christians are defeated on the slopes of Mount Civetot, the above-named knights being taken prisoner along with Fulcher of Meulan, Richard of Pavia, the bishop of Forez, and the abbot of Fécamp. Peter, who has escaped capture, betakes himself to Rome and then to France. The pope preaches a general crusade at Clermont in Auvergne. II: Godfrey of Bouillon takes command of the Christian host. Bohemond and Tancred join up with him at Constantinople. The crusaders have difficulties with the Greek emperor, which are smoothed away by Estatin the Noseless (Taticius) and Guy the seneschal. Soliman's army is defeated and Nicaea surrenders to Estatin. III: The crusaders resume their forward march. Bohemond and his men, who had outdistanced the main army, suffer a setback. Tancred and Baldwin quarrel about the possession of Tarsus. Tancred enters Mamistra and Choros (Corycus?). Baldwin accepts an invitation from the Old Man of the Mountain to go to Rohais (Edessa) and marry his daughter. Godfrey forces his way into Artais (Artāh). Thanks to Enguerrand of Saint Pol, the crusaders are able to seize two towers guarding the bridge over the river Far (Orontes). Emir Garsion (Yaghi-Siyan) prepares to defend Antioch.

IV: The crusaders encircle the city. Gontier of Aire gains possession of emir Fabur's steed. After several skirmishes, the besiegers erect a wooden tower. Dead Turks are dug up in a cemetery and decapitated, and their heads are catapulted into the city. The crusaders suffer from a shortage of food. Again the Turks attempt a sortie, again they are repulsed. At the height of the fray Godfrey cleaves one of his opponents in twain. Raimbaut Creton slaughters some two hundred Saracens who had sought refuge under the bridge over the Far. V: The Tafurs or riffraff of the army roast the bodies of the fallen Turks and eat the human flesh. When negotiations for a truce break down, the enraged Garsion orders Reginald Porquet, a recently captured Christian knight, to be hamstrung. Sansadoine (Shams-ad-Daulah), son of Garsion, is sent with a request for help to the sultan of Persia. Harldy has he arrived at the Persian court when Soliman of Nicaea shows up with a few battered stragglers. Corbaran takes command of the forces which will march to the rescue of Antioch. He is accompanied by Brohadas, one of the sultan's sons. Corbaran refuses to pay any heed to the warnings of his mother Calabre. VI: On his way to Antioch, Corbaran is unsuccessful in his attempt to storm Rohais. Meanwhile the crusaders repulse a sortie of the besieged during which the young son of emir Dacian (Fīrūz) falls into their hands. They send him back to his anxious father, who promises them his support. At this point count Stephen of Blois, having learned of Corbaran's approach, withdraws for greater security to Alexandretta. Emir Dacian informs Bo-

hemond that he will admit the Christians into Antioch. Bohemond demands of the other leaders that they yield their share of the city to him, but Raymond of Saint Gilles refuses to forgo his rights. Dacian slays his wife, who had become suspicious of his doings, and then lowers a rope ladder fastened to a merlon. Thirty-five knights scale the walls before the ladder collapses, but they are able to open one of the gates and let the rest of the army in. Antioch, with the exception of the citadel, is taken after two days of street fighting.

VII: Corbaran and his troops arrive in view of Antioch. He writes confidently to caliph Caifas and to the sultan of Persia, but again his mother Calabre informs him that he cannot hope to prevail against the soldiers of Christ. The Franks, whose turn it is to be besieged, are tormented by the lack of food. Count Stephen of Blois advises the Greek emperor not to help the beleaguered crusaders. Peter the Provençal (Peter Bartholomew) reveals that Saint Andrew has twice appeared to him in his sleep and has designated to him the exact place where is hidden the spear with which Jesus was struck on the cross. Amid general rejoicing the Holy Lance is unearthed. A fire destroys part of Antioch. Corbaran turns down an offer to decide the issue by means of champions chosen by both sides. Emir Amidelis, who has spied on the Christians, reports back to Corbaran. VIII: The bishop of Le Puy cannot find a knight willing to carry the Holy Lance into battle: Robert of Flanders, Robert of Normandy, Godfrey of Bouillon, Tancred, Bohemond, and Hugh of Vermandois decline each in his turn an honor which would keep them from the front ranks. Raymond of Saint Gilles consents to stay inside the city to prevent Garsion from breaking out of the citadel. As the Christian leaders ride out of Antioch emir Amidelis names each one to Corbaran. The battle begins. Among the first to fall are Reginald of Tor and Odo of Beauvais. The crusaders lay about them with lance, pike, and sword. Corbaran is knocked off his horse by Robert of Normandy and Brohadas is slain by Godfrey. The poet indulges in a lengthy enumeration of Christian and Moslem warriors, adducing as his authority Richard the Pilgrim. The Red Lion (Turkish: Kizil Arslan), Soliman, and Sansadoine succumb under the blows of Robert of Normandy, Godfrey, and Hugh of Vermandois. Several saints are seen fighting on the Christian side. The paynims are routed, but only after Godfrey has had a narrow escape. The defenders of the citadel surrender.

SECTION 2: CORBARAN'S CAPTIVES[8]

After his defeat at Antioch Corbaran flees to Sarmasane (Kermanshah), where he returns to the bereaved sultan of Persia the body of his son Brohadas. Accused of treachery, Corbaran agrees to be put to death if any Christian chosen by him cannot defeat any two Saracens selected by the sultan, thus failing to prove his contention that the Christians are better fighters than the Moslems. On the advice of his mother Calabre he calls upon the Christian knights he has held prisoner since the battle of Civetot. Richard of Caumont consents, in exchange for his freedom and that of his companions, to do battle with Goliath of Nicaea and Sorgalé of Mecca. He slays both. Goliath's son and Sorgalé's nephew attempt with their followers to murder Corbaran and Richard of Caumont, but they are defeated by Richard and his companions. Corbaran and his newly found friends are crossing the land of king Abraham when a dragon pounces on Ernoul of Beauvais and proceeds to devour him. His brother Baldwin finally pushes his sword through the heart of the monster. Corbaran is filled with admiration and can hardly restrain himself from becoming a Christian. His nephew, son of queen Florie, is carried off by a wolf. Harpin of Bourges, another of the Christian knights once held captive by Corbaran, gives chase, only to see a huge ape wrest the child from the wolf and clamber with it into a tree. Before he at last rescues the boy, Harpin has to beat off four lions. Then he is unable to prevent five highwaymen from kidnapping the young prince, but Corbaran, who has finally arrived on the scene, manages to obtain the release of his nephew. With Corbaran's approval, the Christian knights ride toward Jerusalem. On the way they join up with the other crusaders.

SECTION 3: THE TAKING OF JERUSALEM[9]

I: Godfrey of Bouillon, several other leaders, and ten thousand knights leave the main part of the army at La Mahomerie and ride close to the holy city. While they are foraging in the valley of Jehoshaphat, they are attacked by Cornumarant and fifty thousand Saracens. At this critical juncture they are joined by Richard of Caumont, Harpin of Bourges, and the other knights formerly held captive by Corbaran. A call is sent out for help, but the Turks are driven back into Jerusalem before the arrival of the rest of the crusaders. That night Tancred and Bohemond raid Caesarea and on their way back are attacked by the emir of Ascalon. Fortunately for them several saints enter the fray on their behalf. The following day the whole army resumes its advance and reaches the top of La Montjoie, a hill from which the holy city is plainly visible. II: Godfrey and the other leaders agree on the various sectors they will occupy facing Jerusalem. King Corbadas, watching the besiegers from a high tower, is dismayed when he sees Godfrey transfix three kites with a single arrow. That night Cornumarant sallies forth with ten thousand men, but Harpin of Bourges and his companions drive them back into the city. Exhorted by the king of the Tafurs and the bishop of Marturana, the crusaders prepare a general assault.

III. The king of the Tafurs is wounded, Pagan of Beauvais and Gontier of Aire are slain, and a rain of Greek fire forces the besiegers to retreat. Bohemond surprises an enemy column on its way to Acre. The Saracens send out carrier pigeons asking for assistance. These are intercepted by the Christians, who modify the terms of the messages. IV: A general assault is again attempted, but hostilities are soon suspended to allow for an exchange of prisoners. Cornumarant sets out to get help from the sultan of Persia. Baldwin of Edessa follows in hot pursuit, but is surrounded by Saracens and driven to take refuge in a marsh. His

armor proves insufficient protection against the leeches, and to add to his discomfort, the Turks set fire to the dry reeds. Cornumarant receives a promise of aid from the sultan of Persia. V: The besiegers are told when and how to assault Jerusalem. They attack between the Gates of St. Stephen and David, but are unsuccessful on the first day. On the following day, a Friday, Thomas of Marle has himself hoisted up to the battlements on the spears of thirty of his men and manages to open one of the gates. The crusaders pour into the city. Corbaran surrenders the Tower of David. Godfrey is chosen as ruler of the new kingdom but refuses to wear a crown. Most of the Christian lords are about to return to their native lands when they receive news that Cornumarant is advancing on Jerusalem at the head of a huge army. VI: Corbadas and his son meet in Barbais. While foraging in the valley of Jehoshaphat, Cornumarant is taken prisoner. Raymond of Saint Gilles falls into the hands of the Turks. Corbadas tells the sultan of Persia that his son is held captive within Jerusalem. Cornumarant is exchanged for Raymond. Before he is freed he is made to witness a parade of the Christian garrison in which Godfrey has the same men file by over and over again. The sultan's army approaches Jerusalem.

VII: On the caliph's advice, the Saracens display their treasures. Eager for booty, Peter the Hermit and his followers rush forth. He is taken prisoner. Threatened with death, Peter agrees to become a Moslem. The sultan sends an envoy to Godfrey ordering him to surrender Jerusalem and abjure the Christian faith. Wishing to impress the messenger, Godfrey repeats his previous stratagem of having the same men file by several times. To cap this show of strength, he cleaves a Turk in two. After failing to take the city by storm, the paynims withdraw to Ramla. While praying in the Temple Godfrey is reassured by several signs that God's help will be forthcoming. Hugh of Vermandois and the other chieftains arrive in Jerusalem. The crusaders ride forth in the direction of Ramla. As their battalions draw near, Peter the Hermit names the leaders to the sultan: Godfrey, Robert of Normandy, Hugh of Vermandois, Bohemond, Tancred, Rotrou of Perche, Stephen of Albermarle (Blois?), and the "king" of the Tafurs. VIII: The sultan of Persia exhorts his thirteen remaining sons to avenge the death of their brother Brohadas. The poet lists the many and sundry peoples comprising the sultan's army. The battle starts with Godfrey slaying Sinagon, the sultan's eldest son. There follows a series of jousts. Bohemond kills king Corbadas, and Lucabel, the king's brother, is slain by Tancred. Baldwin of Edessa lays low Cornumarant. Saint George and Saint Maurice are seen fighting the infidels. Peter the Hermit regains his freedom and promptly dispatches Sanguin, another of the sultan's sons. The paynims are routed. The bishop of Marturana's prayer is answered when the sun is stopped in its course and the light of day prolonged. During the pursuit, Baldwin of Edessa and Raimbaut Creton are cut off from the other knights, but are finally rescued. The sultan enters a boat at Acre and sails away to safety. Enguerrand of Saint Pol is solemnly buried. Funeral honors are also bestowed on

Cornumarant, the brave enemy whose heart, when cut out from his body, fills a helmet.

Comments: Part two of Cycle I is apparently the work of a versifier named Graindor of Douai, who amalgated the compositions of three earlier poets, no one of which survives in its original form. The first of these, written by a certain Richard le Pèlerin (Richard the Pilgrim), who may have taken part in the First Crusade, told of the taking of Antioch (*La Chanson d'Antioche*); the second (*Les Chétifs*), which in its present form contains a statement that it was composed at the request of Raymond of Antioch, narrated the fictitious adventures of six followers of Peter the Hermit who through their boldness and resourcefulness supposedly won the friendship of their captor Corbaran (Kerbogha); while the third related the siege and storming of Jerusalem (*La Conquête de Jérusalem*). In laisse 1 of section 1 Graindor of Douai names himself and implies that his song has for subject the First Crusade in its entirety:

> Sirs, pray be still and end your chatter,
> If you wish to hear a noble song.
> Never has a jongleur recited a better one;
> It tells of the holy city, so worthy of reverence,
> In which God allowed his body to be wounded and harmed,
> To be struck with a lance and nailed to the cross:
> Jerusalem it is called by its right name.
> Those newly fledged jongleurs who sing this song
> Leave out its opening part,
> But Graindor of Douai has no mind to do likewise,
> He who has rewritten all its verses.
> Now you will hear of Jerusalem
> And of those who went to adore the Sepulcher,
> How they assembled their armies,
> In France, in Berry, in neighboring Auvergne,
> Apulia, Calabria, down to Barletta on the sea,
> Far-away Wales; there they gathered their forces,
> And in many lands I know not by name;
> Of such a pilgrimage you never heard tell.
> For God they suffered many hardships;
> Thirst, heat, and cold, lack of food and sleep;
> Our Lord could not help but reward them
> And call their souls to him on high.

The beginning of Graindor's long narrative (about twenty thousand lines), with its emphasis on the six followers of Peter the Hermit taken prisoner by Kerbogha, is evidently borrowed from *Les Chétifs;* what follows is mostly based on Richard le Pèlerin's *Chanson d'Antioche;* the lifting of the siege of Antioch brought about by the battle the crusaders won on June 28, 1098, is followed by a very lengthy segment drawn from *Les Chétifs;* when the final section, which deals with the siege of Jerusalem, is reached, there is no clear indication as to the moment Graindor ceases using the *Chétifs* and starts to paraphrase the *Conquête de Jérusalem.* Although Graindor wrote in rhymed alexandrines, it is entirely possible that one or more of his predecessors composed in a different meter and was satisfied with assonance. Any historian of the First Crusade interested in assessing the factual value of Graindor's work should always remember that his "Song of Jerusa-

lem" represents an extensive *remaniement* of three poems which have not survived in their original form, undertaken in order to fuse their contents and thereby create the impression of a unified narrative. He should also bear in mind that Graindor's compilation has not been published as transcribed in the manuscripts, but was arbitrarily carved up in three different editions (1848, 1868, 1877) by two different editors (Paulin Paris, Célestin Hippeau).

Richard le Pèlerin must have written his *Chanson d'Antioche* not long after the First Crusade, if he is to be identified, as seems very likely, with the author of a song of Antioch who is taken to task by the chronicler Lambert of Ardres for not having included in his poem any mention of Arnold of Guines (d. 1138), presumably because that worthy had turned down the poet's request for a pair of shoes. The contents of Richard's poem can be reconstructed, at least in summary fashion, by comparing Graindor's *rifacimento* with the other accounts which derive from Richard: the Latin one by Albert of Aachen, the extant fragment from Gregory Bechada's Provençal *Canso d'Antiocha,* and the Spanish *Gran conquista de Ultramar.* Such a comparison shows that Graindor does not seem to have made any radical changes in Richard's narrative except in cantos VI and VII of his *Antioche,* for which Robert the Monk is the main source.[10]

The *Chétifs* may have been composed in Syria. According to a statement which appears in Graindor's revised version of the poem (Hippeau, II, 213), its author wrote at the request of Raymond, prince of Antioch (d. 1149), and was rewarded with a canonry at Saint Peter's in that city. Anouar Hatem claims that since the *Chétifs* manifests such intimate knowledge of Syria, its land, and its people, only a native of that country or a long-time resident could possibly be its author. Roger Goosens, though somewhat skeptical of all the local color which Hatem professes to find in the *Chétifs,* has nevertheless strengthened the case for a "Syrian" origin of the poem by pointing out that the themes, situations, and inspiration (struggles with wild animals, service of a Christian under a Saracen, desire to reconcile hostile peoples living side by side, and so forth) resemble similar material found in *Digenes Akritas* and other Byzantine epics. Urban T. Holmes and Claude Cahen, who also find themselves in general agreement with Hatem, believe that the adventures ascribed to Harpin of Bourges and his companions might well reflect the experiences of Bohemond I of Antioch and his cousin Richard of the Principate while they were prisoners of the Saracens.[11]

La Conquête de Jérusalem is the title that Hippeau chose for section 3 of Graindor of Douai's account of the First Crusade when he decided to publish it independently from the other two sections. Section 3, as is the case for the other two sections of part two, represents a revised version of older material, which at one time probably constituted an independent poem, though it may also have started as a sequel tacked on to Richard le Pèlerin's *Antioche.* The unrevised *Jérusalem,* still recognizable in the *Gran conquista de Ultramar,* was historically more accurate than its *rifaci-*

mento, which suffers from the injection of incidents and episodes similar to those found in *Antioche* and presumably borrowed from Richard le Pèlerin (or even possibly by Graindor from his own version of *Antioche*). Anouar Hatem has attempted to prove that the older *Jérusalem* was, like the original *Chétifs,* written in the Latin Orient, but Suzanne Duparc-Quioc's counterclaim that it was composed in northern France is based on more impressive evidence.[12]

C. The First Cycle: The Kings of Jerusalem

Raymond of Saint Gilles, Bohemond, Tancred, Harpin of Bourges, John of Alis, the king of the Tafurs, the bishop of Forez, and the abbot of Fécamp promise Godfrey that they will stay with him in the Holy Land. Corbaran receives baptism at the hands of the bishop of Marturana, and his sister Florie (also called Matroine) becomes the wife of Godfrey. Meanwhile the siege of Acre has begun. Tancred obtains possession of Caesarea. He jousts with the emir Dodekin (Tughtigin). The resistance of Acre ends when the besiegers start catapulting beehives onto the battlements. Godfrey angers Heraclius, the patriarch of Jerusalem, by asking for relics to send his mother, countess Ida. The irate prelate does not hesitate to poison the king. Heraclius conspires with Tancred to place Bohemond on the throne, but cannot prevent Baldwin of Edessa from taking his brother's place. Heraclius dies in prison and is succeeded by Henry, archbishop of Tyre. Death also claims John of Alis and Harpin of Bourges. Baldwin is taken prisoner. In order to guarantee the payment of his ransom to the sultan of Persia, he surrenders his younger daughter Beatrice (Yvette) as a hostage. When later she returns home, she reveals that she has been ravished by Blugadas, king of Aleppo, and becomes a sister of charity at the hospital at Acre. The elder daughter, Ida, had married Amalric of Auxerre, who succeeds Baldwin on the latter's death. Amalric is king of Jerusalem for only three years. His posthumous son Baldwin inherits the crown. The widowed Ida marries Baldwin of Sebourc (Le Bourg), a cousin of Hugh of Vermandois. With his own hand Baldwin of Sebourc kills the infamous Blugadas. At this point of the narrative Saladin makes his appearance. Son of king Eufrarin of Alexandria, he becomes master of all Egypt through the assassination of his overlord the Amulaine. At first, he makes little headway against young king Baldwin, who is ably assisted by three powerful lords, Baldwin of Falkenberg, count of Ramla, his brother Balian, count of Tripoli, and Reginald of Châtillon, castellan of Kerak. Unfortunately the young king is stricken with leprosy and cannot prevent Reginald from violating a truce both sides had promised to respect. Saladin besieges Kerak. King Baldwin manages to raise the siege and renew the truce. Soon afterward he dies without having named a successor.[13]

In the closing lines of part two of Cycle I reference is made to another poem in which the taking of Acre will be recounted, as well as the founding of the military orders. Part three does contain an account of the siege and capture of Acre, but nothing is said of the first appearance of either the Knights Templar or the Knights Hospitaller. As may be gathered from the summary given above, part three of Cycle I presents a very fanciful, yet not entirely unhistorical, recital of what took place in the Holy Land between the battle of Ascalon and the death of Baldwin IV. Godfrey of Bouillon's marriage to the fictitious Florie and the conversion of her supposed brother Corbaran are, of course, examples of unbridled fantasy. The drastic pruning down of the family tree of the kings of Jerusalem is worth noting: Godfrey's two immediate successors, his brother Baldwin I and his cousin Baldwin II, are telescoped into just one Baldwin; Baldwin II's son-in-law Fulk of Anjou and the latter's two sons, Baldwin III and Amalric, are replaced by the still more composite Amalric of Auxerre. Despite his disappearance from the roster of kings, Baldwin of Le Bourg is reborn as Baldwin of Sebourc, who will become the second husband of Ida, the supposed widow of Amalric of Auxerre. Baldwin II's eldest daughter, Melisend, and his youngest, Yvette, are now named Ida and Beatrice. Although it is historically true that Yvette was as a small child for a time a hostage in the hands of the Saracens, it is unlikely that she was sexually molested by them during her captivity, but it is indeed a fact that she later became a nun, abbess of Bethany. One may safely assume that patriarch Heraclius, who in the 1180's had for mistress the notorious Pasque de Riveti (*Madame la Patriarchesse*) and was rumored to have instigated the poisoning of William of Tyre, was the prototype of the nonhistorical patriarch Heraclius stated to have been the contemporary and poisoner of Godfrey of Bouillon. Finally, young king Baldwin IV's leprosy and Reginald of Kerak's misdeeds correspond to the historical accounts.

D. The First Cycle: An Evaluation

Cycle I, as a whole, is difficult to assess. Quite apart from the fact that it runs to well over thirty thousand lines, it suffers from having been edited piecemeal and in incomplete form. The editor of the *Chétifs* did not attempt to give the complete text of that poem, and part three (*The Kings of Jerusalem*) lies buried in the manuscripts; it is a very late addition to Cycle I. It is different in spirit from the first two parts, which do evince a certain amount of structural unity. Whereas part three is essentially a rhymed chronicle, however distorted its chronology and presentation of facts, parts one and two are epic in character; they celebrate the heroic deeds of one man, be he the swan-knight or his grandson Godfrey of Bouillon. It should also be noted that part one leads straight into part two. The prophecies foreshadowing the exploits of Godfrey and his brothers during the First Crusade are echoed in part two by reminders of the deeds of their supposed ancestor, the swan-knight. Cornumarant, the alleged leader of the Saracens during the siege of Jerusalem by the Christians, has already appeared as Godfrey's chief antagonist in part one. In addition, there is hardly any change of ethos between the two parts, at least from a medieval point of view. In part one first the swan-knight, then his grandson Godfrey, fight to protect damsels and ladies in distress; they are the

mah and other contemporaries write. The Christians preferred the Muslim doctors because of their greater skill in curing disease and less frequent use of the knife or axe. Common beliefs brought them together at some places of worship. Muslim as well as Christian venerated the spring where the Virgin had washed the clothes of the infant Jesus, the palm that bent its boughs so she could assuage her hunger, and the image near Damascus which healed Jews and Muslims as well as Christians.

With such conditions in the Holy Land, and with the constant going and coming of the pilgrims from the West and the building up of an active trade between the Orient and the Occident, the feeling about the Muslims became very different.

Possibly the feeling of hatred became less marked because the hatred was being transferred to the Byzantines. Mutual suspicion and frequent clashes in arms had marked the relations of the Byzantines and Crusaders during the First Crusade. When, after the capture of Nicaea, the Emperor gave great gifts to the leaders, Stephen of Blois waxes enthusiastic in a letter to his wife and tells her that he had received more from the Emperor than he got with her dowry; on the other hand, measures of brass coins had been distributed among the common people, and they felt aggrieved at being deprived of the pleasure of looting the city. Raymond the Chaplain expresses the feeling of many when he says that 'as long as they live the people will curse him and proclaim him a traitor' and, he continues, 'we recognized then that the Emperor had betrayed Peter the Hermit . . . for he compelled him . . . to cross the strait with his men and expose them to the Turks . . . who cut them down without effort and delay to the number of 60,000.'

The relations between the Emperor and the crusading leaders, especially Bohemund, became constantly more strained. Alexius was blamed for the failure of the Crusade of 1101, and a few years later Bohemund toured France denouncing the Emperor and raising a great army to attack the Byzantine Empire. From this time on until the capture of Constantinople in 1204, there was ever present an undercurrent of hostility to the Greeks. Consequently the Muslims were seldom execrated or ridiculed as had been the custom during the early years of the Crusades.

Accounts of atrocities may still have been used occasionally to inflame the minds of the Christians, but in the sermons that have been preserved only indefinite expressions are found. This is true, for example, of the writings of Bernard of Clairvaux, of the Abbot Martin, and of Innocent III.

The propaganda against Islam now took on a new form. Peter the Venerable, abbot of Cluny, felt it necessary to counteract the prevalent tendencies by a refutation of the beliefs of Islam and a portrayal of the character of the Prophet. Interest had been aroused in the beliefs and doctrines of the Muslim antagonists. Possibly some reports

had already come to the West of Christians who had been converted to the faith of Islam. But the more active influence seems to have been a visit to Spain by Peter the Venerable, made about 1141. There he witnessed 'the progress and power of the Saracens.' He determined to find out what the *Koran* contained so that its teaching might be refuted. He hired three Christian scholars and set them to work, together with an Arab, to translate the *Koran,* under the direction of his secretary. The translation cost Peter a large sum, and unfortunately it was very inaccurate and full of errors; but it was the only one known in the West until almost the end of the seventeenth century. Peter asked Bernard of Clairvaux to write a refutation of the *Koran.* When the latter refused, Peter himself undertook the task. He could not decide whether the Mohammedans were pagans or heretics, but in either case their teachings ought to be refuted and ridiculed. The portion of his work which has been preserved seems to be founded not only upon the translation of the *Koran* but also upon a life of Mohammed and a dialogue concerning the main points of his religion which Peter also had had translated from the Arabic. His work was frequently imitated, and polemical writings appeared in the various vernacular languages. As is to be expected in that age, they were frequently in verse. They did much to perpetuate the false beliefs about Mohammed and Islam which are so common in the literature of the thirteenth and the following centuries.

Such beliefs persisted in spite of the fact that more accurate information was given by Christians of approved faith even as early as the time of Saladin. Of especial interest is the account by Burchard, written about 1175 and incorporated in Arnold of Lübeck's *Chronicle.*[6] He had been sent by Frederick Barbarossa on a mission to Saladin. He gave a good statement of the beliefs of Islam, and lauded their tolerance. In Alexandria he reported that there were several Christian churches, and almost every village in Egypt had one. Every man was free to follow his own religion. He testified that most Moslems had only one wife. He told of their constancy in prayer and their belief that God was the creator of all things and Mohammed his most holy prophet and the author of their law, that the Blessed Virgin conceived by an Angel and after Christ's birth remained a Virgin; that the son of the Virgin was a prophet and was marvelously assumed by God into Heaven; and that they celebrate His birthday. They denied that he was the Son of God, that He was baptised, crucified, dead, and buried. They also believed, he declared, that the Apostles were prophets and they venerated many of the martyrs and confessors.

In spite of quoting this account by Burchard, Arnold of Lübeck elsewhere makes Saladin swear 'by the virtue of my god, Mohammed.' And he makes the Templar's reply to Saladin after the Battle of Hattin, 'We laugh at Maumath, the son of perdition, whom you call your god.'

Saladin was much admired in the west. His merciful conduct and generosity after the capture of Jerusalem, so different from that of the Crusaders in 1099, excited wonder. As was the custom among the Muslims, he was very tolerant. He allowed the Latin Christians to have two priests and two deacons at Jerusalem, at Bethlehem, and at Nazareth, and to carry on their services freely. He was noted for his courtesy. Between him and Richard the Lion-Hearted there were many friendly relations. Richard even proposed that his sister should marry the brother of Saladin and that the two should receive Jerusalem as a wedding present, thus ending the strife between Christians and Muslims. Many legends grew up about the name of the great Saracen leader, who was said to have received knighthood from a Christian. Tales of his mercy and generosity were spread to the west. It is interesting to note that earlier in the century the Crusaders had explained the greatness of Zangi by the belief that he was the son of the Countess Ida who had taken part in the Crusade of 1101; at the time of the Third Crusade, Qilig Arslam was supposed to be descended from the German nobility; but after the fame of Saladin had spread, a legend grew up to explain the greatness of Thomas à Becket by the fact that he had had a Saracen mother. All of these factors caused a very different feeling about the Muslims especially when, as has already been suggested, the hatred of the Byzantines became the dominant factor among many of the westerners.

A remarkable change was evident in the thirteenth century on the part of some Christians. The missionary journey of St Francis of Assisi to the Moslem countries is well known. St Louis of France is said to have directed the Crusade of 1270 to Tunis from the mistaken belief that the ruler of that country was ready to receive baptism, and he is reported to have said that he would love to be the god-father of such a god-son. This century saw the beginning of a period of great missionary activity. A plan was formed to have oriental languages taught in the University of Paris so that missionaries might be trained in the use of the necessary tongues. Later in the century, there was also a suggestion that Christian girls should be sent out as missionaries to marry Muslims and then convert their husbands.

Several writers of this period were influenced by the missionary movement. Oliver the Scholastic, in his *Historia Damiatina,* tells how the son of Saladin had destroyed Jerusalem in 1219, except the Temple of the Lord and the Tower of David. The Saracens considered destroying the Holy Sepulchre, but none dared to do so because of their reverence for the place. The book of the law, the *Koran,* says that Christ was conceived and born of the Virgin Mary and lived without sin that He was a Prophet and more than a Prophet; He restored sight to the blind, cleansed the lepers, and raised the dead. The Muslims believe, Oliver asserts, that He is the word and spirit of God and ascended alive into Heaven. They deny His passion and death, the union of the divine and human natures in Him, and the Trinity. Therefore, they should be called heretics rather than Saracens, but the usage of the false name has prevailed. When in the time of the Truce their learned men went up to Jerusalem, they asked to be shown

the Gospels and they kissed and venerated these because of the cleanliness of the doctrines which Christ taught and especially because of the verse in the Gospel of Luke, 'He sent His Angel Gabriel,' which the learned among them often repeat and discuss.

Oliver likewise declares that their book of the law which, at the dictation of the devil and through the agency of the monk Sergius, apostate and heretic, Mohammed gave to the Saracens, written in Arabic, has won its victories by the sword, holds its territory through the sword, and will be ended by the sword (this idea will be taken up more fully by later writers).

In 1221, Oliver wrote a letter to 'the King of Babylon' urging him to accept the Christian teaching, and in this letter he stressed the many points of belief common to the followers of the two religions. At the same time, he wrote a similar letter to the Doctors in Egypt, that is, the learned Mussulmen. In his letter to the King, he mentioned a debate which had taken place between a Christian, a Jew, and a Muslim in which the Christian placed the Mosaic above the Muslim law, the Jew preferred the Christian doctrines to the Muslim, and the Muslim placed the Christian above the Jewish. He argues from this circumstance the superiority of the Christian religion, since the two non-Christians praised it. This custom of debate between the adherents of the different religions seems to have been common, much as a St Louis might have condemned the practice. It is interesting to note that a century earlier it had not occurred to Abelard to introduce a Muslim into his debate where the Christian, the Jew, and the philosopher appear, although the Muslim would have fitted in well with the argument; but too little was known about the Muslim faith in the first half of the twelfth century.

Jacques de Vitry also attempted to convert the Muslims. He says in one of his letters, 'as I was not able to preach in the land of the Saracens, I showed the errors of their religion and the truth of ours by letters which I sent to them, written in the Saracen tongue.'[7] He may have had access to the work which William of Tyre had written about the Muslims. He certainly was acquainted with the writing of Peter the Venerable, who had also wished to convert them. His accounts of Mohammed and of Islam are very biased, but contain some accurate statements. He has the date for Mohammed approximately correct, he derives the name of the Saraceni from Sara and that of the Agarini from Agar. He tells correctly the Muslim belief about the Virgin and John the Baptist. He knows the books of the Bible which they receive. Most of those who did follow Jacques de Vitry chose his inaccurate statements rather than the true ones to quote. This is done by Matthew Paris, who uses both Jacques de Vitry and also another unnamed source, possibly Guibert; from the latter, he copies the story of Mohammed's being eaten by the pigs, and explains by this the Muslim's abhorrence of pork. Some others explains this in another way.

The accounts written in the second half of the thirteenth century are frequently more accurate. William of Tripoli, who wrote about 1271, wished to facilitate the task of the missionaries to the Muslims. He knew Arabic, and had been requested to write by Thedaldus, later Pope Gregory X. He first gives an account of Mohammed, and follows the Bahyra legend. He tells how Mohammed was appalled by the discovery that he had himself, while intoxicated, killed his teacher, and consequently forbade the use of wine to his followers. He believed that the power of Islam was nearing its end, and cited various alleged prophecies of the Mohammedans to show that the destruction of the Caliphate by Hulagu portended the end of the rule of the Saracens. He says that the *Koran* was compiled by learned Muslims; he states the Muslim belief that it contains the sayings of Mohammed transmitted by the Angel Gabriel, but he says that he has learned from Catholic Christians that this is not true, and that, fifteen years after the Prophet's death, a commission was appointed to draw up the book. As they found nothing worth while in Mohammed's teachings, they themselves composed the *Koran.* In discussing the contents of the letter, he says that it contains much praise of the Creator, lauding His power, knowledge, goodness, mercy, justice, and equity. It also commends those who believe in God and act justly. It praises and extols above all sons of men Jesus, the Son of Mary, and above all women Mary. It commends and praises all the Holy Fathers of the Old Testament. Four books the Muslim believes have come down from Heaven, the *Law,* the *Gospels,* the *Psalter,* the book of the Prophets, and a fifth, the *Koran.* The last mentions Mohammed only in two places and does not praise him at all. William gives other teachings of the *Koran* at considerable length, stressing those which are similar to the Christian doctrines, and concludes that the Muslims are close to the Christian faith and to the way of salvation. Then he describes briefly their marital customs and the Muslim paradise.

Humbert of Romans, Master-General of the Dominican order, wrote a pamphlet of advice for Pope Gregory X. As he had lived in the Holy Land, he possessed intimate knowledge, and his account is one of the most valuable. He says Mohammed's law is fraudulent, but the Saracens believe it was delivered by an angel. It pictures Paradise so that the most bestial man can understand it: full of delights of the flesh. The Muslim law, he continues, does not teach great austerity, but encourages lust and the enjoyment of many women. Mohammed does not threaten eternal punishment, but promises final salvation to true followers. He does not emphasize the disagreeable aspect of alms, prayers, and fasts. From this it is obvious that Mohammed's law was devised to destroy that of the Christians, whose religion is difficult in creed, as it is above reason, difficult in the austerities of this life, and difficult in its doctrine of eternal damnation for the wicked. For this reason, says Humbert, evil and foolish men are more easily turned from Christianity to Mohammedanism than vice versa. 'And thus it actually happens that many Christians are going over and have gone over to the Saracen faith. . . .' Some, he observes, object that it is wrong to attack the Saracens, as this does not make for conversion, but, on the contrary, incites them further against the Christian faith; when we conquer and kill them we send them to hell, which is contrary to Christian charity; and when we conquer their land, we have not obtained permanent power over those who cultivate and live on it, since our men do not wish to remain in those parts; in all there is no spiritual or temporal profit from this war.

The world, Humbert declares, was once converted to Christianity by preaching, miracles, and the holy example of the preachers. The Saracens exclude preachers, they decapitate anyone speaking against Mohammed's law or sect. The time of miracles is past; examples of Christian believers do not move the Saracens. They prefer their own prayers, fasts, pilgrimages, etc., to ours. What is more absurd, they prefer their own incontinence to our continence. Christian continence they call superstition, as may be seen in a letter of a Saracen to his Christian friend in which he invited the Christian to become a Saracen. There is no hope of converting them. They will always be in the world and multiply in increasing numbers unless they are destroyed by a Christian or barbarian power. Just as Mohammed acquired the world with the sword, Humbert concludes that he will likewise lose it by the sword.

Burchard of Mount Zion, who wrote about 1283, was often copied by later writers, for instance, by Marco Sanudo. Laurent calls Burchard the most noteworthy of all the mediaeval pilgrims. His account gives the beliefs of Islam accurately and concludes 'they are very hospitable, courteous, and kindly.'

Ricoldus, who wrote about 1294, says that 'we have been amazed that among the followers of so perfidious a law works of so great perfection are found.' He then records briefly some works of perfection on the part of the Saracens, more to reproach the Christians than to praise the Saracens. 'But who is not amazed by their zeal, devotion in prayer, mercy to the poor, reverence for the name of God, the prophets and holy places, their courtesy in manners, their affability to strangers, their concord and love for one another?'

Despite such testimony, the attitude of the majority of the clergy remained unchanged. They felt that it was impossible to convert the Muslims. They were alarmed at the number of Christians who had gone over to Islam. In 1274, Pope Gregory X felt it necessary to forbid giving any aid to apostate Templars. In a treaty made with the Muslims in 1283, the Franks were compelled to promise to protect the rights of renegades from the Christian faith. The Popes were working for a new Crusade and encouraged the propaganda against Islam.

Notes

1. Presidential address read at the Sixth Annual Meeting of the Mediaeval Academy of America, April 25, 1931.

2. H. Prutz, *Kulturgeschichte der Kreuzzüge* (Berlin, 1883), p. 72.

3. *The Crusades and other Historical Essays presented to Dana C. Munro* (New York: Crofts, 1928), p. 43.

4. Vienna Academy, *Sitzungsberichte,* XCVIII (1881), 354, note 1.

5. P. K. Hitti, *An Arab-Syrian Gentleman and Warrior* (New York: Columbia Univ. Press, 1929), p. 162

6. In the *Chronicle* he is called Gerhard; but as Laurent has shown in *Serapeum,* XIX (1858), no. 10, and XX (1859), no. 11, this is a mistake.

7. Philipp Funk, *Jakob von Vitry: Leben und Werke* (Leipzig: Teubner, 1909), p. 138.

Carl Erdmann (essay date 1977)

SOURCE: "The Further Development of the Popular Idea of Crusade" in *The Origin of the Idea of Crusade,* translated by Marshall W. Baldwin and Walter Goffart, Princeton University Press, 1977, pp. 269–305.

[*In the following essay, Erdmann analyzes the various elements—including religious and literary developments—that enabled the "general idea of crusade and war upon the heathen" to take the specific form of the Crusade to the Holy Land.*]

Gregory VII's idea of a hierarchical crusade brought general discord rather than united action; alongside it the popular idea of crusade led a life of its own.[1]

The socioeconomic conditions for the crusading movement were largely present in the second half of the eleventh century, as best illustrated by the fact that a free mercenary soldiery acquired increasing prominence at this time.[2] While mercenaries had been regularly used at Byzantium since late Antiquity, the West had rarely seen knights, or soldiers of lower rank, offering their services to lords outside the regular feudal relationship and in return for pay. From the middle of the eleventh century onward, however, the practice became common, an indication that a surplus of trained manpower was available. Mercenaries and crusaders obviously bear a close resemblance to one another, but they also offer a sharp contrast: cash payment for the former, and for the latter the church's call and the prospect of heavenly reward. As a result, it would be wrong to ascribe a mercenary character to all enterprises that went beyond local feudal combat.[3] Rather, a characteristic of the age was that crusaders existed side by side with mercenaries. The crusader is a volunteer; and even though military terminology may equate him with a mercenary, he must be distinguished from the latter if the historical forces motivating him are to be understood. On the other hand, a complete contrast between mercenaries and crusading knights would be historically and psychologically false, for troops had already been recruited for both money and spiritual rewards. The Germans whom Leo IX had led on his crusade against the Normans had streamed to his banner in return for pay, as well as for the sake of indulgences.[4] The skirmishes of the Roman schism of the 1060s were conducted largely as a holy war, but money payments played no slight role on both sides.[5] In the plans for a Jerusalem crusade drafted by Benzo of Alba for Henry IV—we will hear of them again—the needed troops were to be recruited with Byzantine gold.[6] Gregory VII, as we saw, relied as much on money payments as on crusading ideas to assemble armed forces. And even the warriors of the First Crusade, though certainly not mercenaries, did not wholly dispense with the prospect of earthly reward: the leaders of the crusade were to have great gifts from the Greek emperor, and the rank and file had the direct promise of pay.[7] In short, the crusading idea did not eliminate natural self-interest;[8] yet the fact that motives were mixed does not blot out the ideas of Christian knighthood and of crusade, and it in no way alters the autonomy of their development.

In our survey of this development up to the mid-eleventh century, we have encountered many individual incidents, but no system and no coherent plans for translating ideas into action. Conditions were basically the same in the second half of the century. The polemical literature, for all its divergences of opinion, discloses a gradual clarification of theoretical concepts and a certain agreement over fundamentals; but the authors who mention war only in passing express attitudes that are naive and generally confused. For example, a personage of the stature of Anselm of Canterbury still voiced a basic rejection of war, as being simply immoral.[9] At the opposite pole, it could still happen that none other than bishops won ecclesiastical praise for their exploits against an enemy of the Empire,[10] this at the very time when church doctrine took it for granted that bishops and abbots must not perform military service for the state.[11] Even the basic idea of Christian knighthood—namely, the consecration of the sword to ecclesiastical purposes—had by no means become the common property of all thinking men; and the contrast between secular and spiritual *militia,* though completely overcome by the popes and theoreticians, as we have seen, nevertheless retained its full primitive force in certain circles.[12] Now as before, different answers were given to the question whether a knight's piety should lie in good works alien to his military calling, or in military exploits performed for the church.[13] Meanwhile, the idea of service by knights to the church was not narrowly confined to the papacy. Around the monastery of La Sauve near Bordeaux, under Abbot Gerard (1079-1095), a company of ten dynasts was formed who allowed their swords to be consecrated in the monastery church and committed themselves by oath to avenge violence against the monks, to defend monastic property, and to protect pilgrims coming there.[14] This union recalls not only the Gregorian *militia s. Petri,* but also the beginnings of the Order of Templars; it represents a link between the old Peace of God unions and the later knighthood of the military orders. Such phenomena were isolated for the time being, since a variety of tendencies kept getting into one another's way; here as before we cannot hope to draw a complete picture. Nevertheless, we must elaborate upon a few aspects that were significant in future developments.

The first models in whose terms the religious idea of war was expressed were Old Testament figures, such as Joshua, Gideon, David, and Judas Maccabeus; throughout Christian history the military aspects of the Old Testament had a great impact. In the High Middle Ages, however, an even more important role was played by the saints to whom a special patronage of war and knights began to be ascribed. This was how the church's sanctification of the profession of arms was given its clearest expression. As was established before, the early medieval West knew nothing of such patronage.[15] When tendencies of this kind appeared, they were first related to saints who in life had been soldiers themselves, such as Maurice and Sebastian. The Pontifical of Cologne (probably from the beginning of the eleventh century) contains an order of service for the consecration of knights where the merits of the holy martyrs and soldiers Maurice, Sebastian, and George are already referred to.[16] Then Benzo of Alba, in relating the Roman schism (1062-1063), has St. Maurice make an appearance to fight for the cause of Cadalus.[17] Along different lines, Bernold compares Count Frederick of Mömpelgard to St. Sebastian and strikingly alters the older concept of this saint in doing so, for while the Acts of Sebastian contrast the Christianity of the saint to his military profession, Bernold praises Count Frederic precisely because his military prowess turned him into a courageous warrior of Christ and champion of the church.[18] The development of territorial patron saints was another element pointing in this direction. As early as the eleventh century, St. Denis was regarded as the patron saint of France;[19] without ever turning into a soldier-saint, he acquired the role of a protector in war, particularly as a result of the part played by the banner of St. Denis in French wars.[20] To some extent, St. Maurice and his lance had a comparable role in eleventh-century Germany,[21] and so did St. Martin and St. George in Hungary, though in a transitory way.[22] St. James, "Santiago," gained special importance as protector of Spain, where he would later be the patron of the greatest Spanish order of knighthood. Belief in the military efficacy of Santiago found its supreme expression in the legend of the battle with the Moors at Clavijo, where the saint was thought to have appeared on horseback, bearing a shining white flag to lead the Christians to victory.[23] The role of Santiago as patron of fighting knights is found fully developed only in the twelfth century; whether it antedates the First Crusade is not yet clear.[24]

The holy patrons of the crusading era, however, owe their development principally to a foreign source, namely the dominant ideas of Eastern Christendom, which now acquired currency in the West. For a long time, the Eastern church had known saints who brought victory, such as Demetrius, Theodore, Sergius, and George.[25] No later than the tenth century, the soldier-saints were venerated in the Byzantine army and portrayed on war banners.[26] A series of portraits of these saints, mostly dressed as soldiers, has survived to this day; they principally depict George, The-

odore (whom legend doubled and venerated as both Theodore the general and Theodore the recruit), and Demetrius, but also Procopius, Mercurius, Eustratius, and others.[27] These were explicitly Byzantine saints, who, except for George, were entirely unknown in the West or had only a local cult in Italy. As a result, the emergence of these same Greek saints as patrons of warfare in the West has considerable importance.[28] It is a process that may be satisfactorily traced in the liturgical acclamations of ecclesiastical and secular rulers, the so-called *Laudes,* most of which include a special appeal to a saint on behalf of the ruler and the army, or of the army alone.[29] No special patrons of war are indicated in the older Latin *Laudes,* of which the earliest dates from the eighth century; for the army, they simply mention saints whose cult could be regarded as popular.[30] The special soldier-saints who later appear are the Greek ones. Saints George, Theodore, and Mercurius are invoked on behalf of the ruler and army of the Christians in *Laudes* stemming from the kingdom of Burgundy,[31] and the *Laudes* for the imperial coronation also call on Theodore and Mercurius as saints for the army.[32] Since these acclamations are difficult to date, they do not definitely attest that the Greek soldiersaints were adopted in the West before the First Crusade.[33] Yet it is probable that they were, for in the crusade itself the heavenly assistance in battle of Sts. George, Theodore, Demetrius, and Mercurius was thought to have played a great role; the Latin accounts, which are numerous, introduce their names in so casual a way as to imply that their role as special patrons of war was familiar to Western readers.[34]

Saint George assumed a special place among the warrior saints. Though he too was an Eastern, more precisely a Palestinian, saint, he had been widely venerated even in the West ever since the beginning of the Middle Ages, but not as a patron of war; rather, he was a martyr for the faith, the greatest and most wonderful among the Christian confessors, for he was supposed to have risen again after three fatal martyrdoms and to have brought about the most incredible miracles.[35] He is a soldier as his legend begins, but this fact played as insignificant a part in his early cult in the West as it did in the cases of Sebastian, Maurice, or Martin.[36] The Greek East treated him differently. There the great triumphant martyr was chief of the soldier-saints and was celebrated as early as in the seventh century as a champion of the Empire.[37] Even at that date a legend in Constantinople told of the protection given by St. George to a cavalryman at war.[38] In the next centuries, the Greeks further developed the military versions of the legend of St. George, even though the most famous of them, the story of his fight with the dragon, cannot be traced before the twelfth century.[39] Other Greek miracles of St. George survive in manuscripts of the eleventh century and probably originated in the ninth or tenth. Their repeated motif is miraculous help, especially against heathens; the saint appears mounted and in arms to rescue prisoners or to defend his icon against pagan destructiveness.[40] Under Constantine Monomachos (1043-1055), St. George was the special patron of the war of the Empire against heathens: a Byzantine banner of the time depicts St. George with the emperor beside him, as he pursues the barbarians on horseback;[41] and a sermon on St. George, pronounced by John Euchaites, refers expressly to a victory over the wild Scyths, that is, the Petchenegs.[42]

Everyone knows that "the knight St. George" played a similar role in the West during the crusades and long after, as a heavenly helper in war and a patron of the Christian knight. The role is clearly attested as early as the First Crusade. As mentioned before, he was supposed to have appeared to the crusaders as a helper in battle, in company with Demetrius, Theodore, and Mercurius. He figured especially as standard-bearer of the crusading host and was thought to have referred to himself as such in a vision to a crusader.[43] The special veneration that the crusaders had for him found expression in the foundation of a bishopric at Ramleh, where the saint was supposedly buried.[44] To what extent the West regarded George as a special saint for war prior to the First Crusade is a more difficult question to answer. The age has left us neither Western images of St. George as a warrior nor reports of something like a banner of St. George.[45] Even the stories of the apparition of soldier-saints in eleventh-century battles belong to a later time.[46] The earliest of them is the account of Geoffrey Malaterra that St. George participated in the battle against the Saracens at Cerami (1063);[47] but since Geoffrey did not write until after the First Crusade, his testimony cannot prove that this motif existed prior to the 1090s. Yet one legend does antedate the crusade. A collection of miracles relates that a sacristan of San Giorgio in Velabro, on the coast near Rome, was seized by Saracens and taken to Palermo, but St. George appeared on a white horse and brought him back.[48] The context of this story imposes a date earlier than the First Crusade; by the end of the century, the Saracens could no longer make piratical descents upon the Roman coast, for they had been completely driven out of the Tyrrhenian Sea (they lost Palermo in 1072). To be sure, George does not appear in this legend as a real patron of knights and helper in battle; he intervenes on horseback and acts as a protector against the heathen, in the earlier Byzantine manner. But his future role is at least prefigured, and the process of transfering the image of George the warrior from the Greeks to the Latins had begun.

How the journey was completed is not known; the Normans and other mercenaries who served with the Byzantine army come to mind, but establishing the precise source of this motif hardly matters to our study. What counts instead is that the West had become receptive to such notions, which could now take root; this is what demonstrates the popularity gradually acquired by the idea of holy war.

The origin of the cult of warrior saints has another highly important aspect, namely the interconnection of legends of saints and chivalric poetry. A whole series of legendary warriors of the past came to be revered simultaneously as epic heroes and as saints of the church.[49] From at least the beginning of the twelfth century, heroic tales passed into clerical literature by taking on an edifying form;[50] reciprocally, the knightly epics of the twelfth century assumed many clerical features.

This combination of military fame and sanctity originated in the days preceding the crusades. In many cases, the first connection was the story that the heroes were converted in later life and entered a monastery. This edifying theme was of course quite old, the more so since the story often rested on historical fact. But earlier monastic legends of this kind hardly celebrated the antecedent feats of arms of their heroes; rather, they stressed only the contrast between secular and spiritual "guise [*habitus*]." Such is the case, for example, of the oldest version of the conversion of William of Gellone, a count from the circle of Charlemagne who ended his life as a monk.[51] Only later did the image change: legendary accounts of William's exploits in the Spanish campaign against the heathen began to be blended with the figure of the pious founder of monasteries. Thus the *Vita s. Wilhelmi* relates that William, before his monastic life, went forth into southern France as *triumphator* and standard-bearer of Christ to combat the Moslems, that he saved the people of God with his sword and enlarged the Christian *imperium*.[52] Such a story casts the light of sanctity even on William's warlike exploits. To be sure, this *Vita* seems to date from the twelfth century (*ca.* 1122),[53] but other conversion stories of the same kind are older. The *Conversio Othgerii militis* was certainly written before 1084, perhaps even in the tenth century; its subject is Ogier, another warrior of the heroic age to whose name knightly legends were attached, and it narrates his conversion at the monastery of St. Faro with marked emphasis upon his fame in war.[54] In fact, an epitaph of Ogier and his companion Benedict, composed about the middle of the eleventh century, stresses that the two men ranked first in both armies, temporal and spiritual; they were brave men of the emperor and brave agents of God.[55] Such parallelism of military and monastic exploits strikingly expresses the harmonization of warlike and ecclesiastical themes. Equally instructive is a section of the chronicle of Novalese that stems from the first half of the eleventh century. In relating that Walter of Aquitaine, the well-known hero of Ekkehard's poem, later became a monk in Novalese, the chronicle uses the expression *conversio militiae*, that is to say, a transformation of secular knighthood into spiritual.[56] Added to this is a poem that again celebrates the "dual combat" of Walter in elevated words,[57] and reports feats of arms that Walter performed even as a monk. Once, on the advice of the abbot, he allowed some robbers to despoil him of his clothes, but when they tried to take his loincloth as well, he killed them all and returned with great booty, for which he was of course obliged to do penance.[58] Besides, he reportedly triumphed over invading heathens three times, drove off some riders of King Desiderius who were devastating the monastic lands, and was then so filled with the exaltation of victory that he cut down with his sword a marble column that is still displayed.[59] Nothing is more apparent here than the admixture to a monastic legend of elements better known from French chivalric poetry.[60] In this way monasteries began to lay claim to heroic figures and ascribed a more positive value to warlike exploits than they formerly had. The typical conversion story continued to retain something of the old contrast between secular and monastic warfare and included a criticism of the bloody profession of arms. But the idea came forth quite spontaneously that a holy life and heroic warfare belonged together, especially in regard to war against the heathen.

The works just discussed were confined to clerical circles. More important were the repercussions of such ideas on real knightly poetry. Various opinions have been expressed for and against the role of clerics in the emergence of knightly epics, but the Christian element in these poems is beyond dispute.[61] Tenth-century poetry, such as the *Waltharius* of Ekkehard, lacked the theme of ecclesiastical war. The *Waltharius* definitely comes from a clerical hand; the poet blames greed as the cause of war, yet he knows no other ethos of war than the old Germanic one—the striving to measure one's own strength against that of the opponent, and the idea of revenge for the slain.[62] The Old French *Chanson de Guillaume,* which dates from the close of the eleventh century, is already different.[63] The poet has the knight Vivien swear an oath never to retreat; Vivien prays before battle that God might help him fulfill this oath, indeed he even compares death in battle with the sacrificial death of Christ.[64] This is possible because the enemy is Moslem, and the religious contrast is vividly felt.[65] Nevertheless, religion remains a personal matter and not yet an autonomous motive for war.

The ethical motivation is more developed in the French *Chanson de Roland,* which belongs to the same epoch. That the poem exudes the crusading spirit has often been stressed, and only the question whether it should be set shortly before or shortly after the First Crusade is disputed;[66] some say that "the *Chanson de Roland* would be impossible without the First Crusade," while others maintain that "the crusade would be incomprehensible without the *Chanson de Roland.*"[67] The poem assigns a dominant place to the idea of war upon heathens: battle is a judgment of God, the Christians are right, heathens wrong, and therefore Christians are victorious.[68] When Cordova falls to the emperor Charles, he causes all heathens who are not converted to Christianity to be killed. The emperor is in all respects the direct instrument of God, Who assists him with miracles and by His archangel delivers to him the commission to fight for the Christians. Yet only the ruler's person is portrayed in so starkly a Christian light.[69] The other warriors are handled differently: no trace is found of the specific ideal of Christian knighthood. Roland's exhortations before battle emphasize two ideas—feudal loyalty and fame in war.[70] He too has occasion to say that the heathens are in the wrong and the Christians right.[71] These words in context are meant essentially as a promise of victory, but everyone shares the basic idea. When Archbishop Turpin calls on the combatants to fight for king and Christendom, the words he uses make the war exactly resemble a crusade: "Confess your sins, pray God for mercy: I shall absolve you, to heal your souls. When you die you will be holy martyrs and have your place in the highest paradise." As the Franks thereupon cast themselves to the ground, the archbishop blesses them and prescribes sword thrusts as penance.[72] The idea of a crusading indulgence, which we find here in a crudely popular form, allows us to specify that the *Chanson* cannot antedate the time of Alexander II.[73] The popular character of the poem may also explain why, in spite of this date, the personal knightly ideal of Roland is still old-fashioned.[74] Above all, we are shown the decisive importance that war against the heathen assumed both earlier and later, as the popular form of holy war.

An original expression of the popular idea of knighthood is found in a quite different place. Among the rare remnants of Italian literature, a verse appeal to war has come to light under the title of "Exhortation to the Magnates of the Empire."[75] Written by an Italian partisan of the German king, it stems from the early years of Henry IV, probably from the days of the fighting over Cadalus in Rome (1062-1063).[76] The poet first appeals to the Romans, Italians, and Normans, calling on them to remain faithful to the young king, according to God's will and holy law, and to combat his enemies, especially "the duke" (Godfrey of Lorraine). Afterwards, however, those addressed are to fight against the Saracens and "Huns" (obviously the Hungarians or Balkan peoples) and to make Italy secure from heathens. In closing, the poet paints a coming utopia in which Rome will rule all peoples in union with Greece; Caesar, Augustus, and Charlemagne will rise again and renew the world according to the old laws, and simultaneously justice will reign under the keys of St. Peter. The prerequisite for all this is that those addressed should maintain fidelity and law; this is why the poem rings out in praise of "just service [*militia aequa*]." With knighthood thus subordinated to a higher idea, the poet proclaims a sort of holy war against the enemy of Rome as well as against heathens. He is far removed from hierarchical objectives. His originality lies rather in uninhibitedly mixing Christian themes with the idea of Eternal Rome. He is comparable in this to Benzo of Alba, with whose political standpoint he also agrees; possibly, Benzo himself is the poet. This particular formulation of the knightly ideal cannot have had much impact; yet the wide diffusion of the ideal itself is borne out when one finds it in so unexpected a combination of motifs.

This poem, as well as the hagiography and *chansons de geste* previously discussed, repeatedly feature war against the heathen. No additional proof is needed that war of this kind had the most important role in the popular sphere of the crusading idea. Equally characteristic are the reproaches that Lampert causes the rebellious Saxons to address to Henry IV: the king is blamed for being a heathen [*barbarus*] by persecuting the church and by permitting even the pagan Slavs to fall upon the Christian Saxons.[77] Although the idea of a chivalric crusade against heathens remained problematic until mid-century, it was then adopted by the reform papacy and, under its aegis, attained an initial peak in the early 1060s. The Curia then gave less encouragement to this tendency and preferred crusade within the church. But even in the age of Gregory VII the popular idea of crusade against heathens did not cease to play a role in battles on the frontiers of Christianity.

The most significant event of this kind was the crusade of Barbastro (1064),[78] prolonged in the next decades by a series of similar undertakings.[79] The Spanish campaign that Ebolus of Roucy began in agreement with Gregory VII has previously been mentioned.[80] The same pontificate witnessed the undertakings of Hugh I of Burgundy and William VI of Aquitaine in support of the king of Aragon. Additional bands of crusaders, especially from France, took part in the battle of Zallaca or Sagrajos against the Almoravids (1086). The severe defeat suffered there by the Christians brought new stimulus to the idea of a Spanish crusade. Alfonso VI of Castile sent to France for renewed support and was supposed to have threatened that, unless he received help, he would make an alliance with the Moslems and give up the Christian faith.[81] In the next year, substantial contingents of knights reached Spain from various parts of France under high-placed leadership. No lasting results were achieved on this occasion, but the bare fact that many French knights participated in the Spanish war against the Moors was very important, the more so as smaller groups of Frenchmen took part in the Spanish fighting both in 1086 and in the years to follow. These knights continued to attribute to the Moorish war the crusading character it had had in the Barbastro campaign. Before setting forth, Ebolus of Roucy promised his conquests to the pope. Hugh of Burgundy later proved his affection for the church by laying down his dukedom and entering the monastery of Cluny. William of Aquitaine is the man who placed himself at the disposal of Gregory VII in 1074 for the Eastern campaign; he was regarded as one of Gregory's most devoted adherents. As for the campaign of 1087, one of its leaders was the French knight Raimond of Saint-Gilles, who became famous ten years later in the First Crusade. Contemporaries were well aware that the great Eastern crusade was intimately related to the earlier Spanish wars;[82] Urban I! himself, as we shall later see, regarded the Moorish wars as a parallel undertaking to the First Crusade. The Spanish war was where the knighthood of France had manifested its crusading sentiments. This fact clearly explains why Gregory VII failed to obtain troops for papal war. Military forces were overabundant, and there was no lack of willingness for a pious crusade; but the special direction in which Gregory wished to drive chivalric combat found no response.

These observations apply only to the French who went to Spain, not to the Spaniards themselves. At mid-century, a new era of Christian opposition to Islamic rule opened in Spain, independently of the French crusaders; but the ensuing wars had a character of their own. As a rule, the Christian kings warred also with one another; the same was true of the Moorish kings, and in the crisscross of alliances, Moslems and Christians would often happen to fight shoulder to shoulder on both sides. Even at the battle

of Graus (1063), which occasioned the Barbastro campaign and where a Moslem fanatic killed Ramiro I of Aragon, the Castilians were allied to the Moorish king of Saragossa.[83] King Alfonso VI of Castile, who had made many Moorish districts pay him tribute, styled himself "emperor of both religions" in Arabic diplomas.[84] By clearly invoking Christian solidarity in his call for French help, Alfonso showed that the renewal of holy war by the Almoravids somewhat affected him; but the rumor that he took this occasion to threaten conversion to Islam suggests that he was scarcely regarded as a trustworthy champion of Christianity. The celebrated hero of Spain, the "Cid" Rodrigo Diaz, is a typical figure of this age. Many of his feats of arms were carried out on the Moorish side. The author of the Latin poem singing Rodrigo's deeds while he was still alive does not distinguish between his victories over Christians and over Moors; both are celebrated as gifts of God.[85] After taking Valencia, Rodrigo treated Christians and Moors as equals, and only the intransigent ways of the Almoravids gradually led him to a less tolerant attitude.[86] The Spanish rulers were always aware of religious differences,[87] but they did not yet treat their wars as crusades.

"Crusade" is even less appropriate as a term for the relations with pagans in Germany in the closing decades of the eleventh century. For one thing, the monarchy under Henry IV was far too embroiled in internal quarrels to be able to conduct wars against the pagan northeast; for another, the idea of a specifically knightly crusade came to Germany only later. France was far in advance in this field, as shown by the overwhelmingly negative response of the Germans to the First Crusade; Ekkehard of Aura tells us that, at first, the crusaders marching through Germany were ridiculed as fools.[88] Never before had there been so evident a difference in the collective conduct of the German and French peoples. To some extent, the difference may be traced to national character; the more emotional Romance peoples are more quickly influenced by inflammatory words than the Germans.[89] Perhaps one may detect even then the special form of German piety, which is inclined to set less value, from a religious standpoint, upon such "works" as pilgrimages and wars on pagans. This at least is suggested by the words that the Bamberg *scholasticus* Meinhard addressed to Gunther, his bishop, when the latter wished to depart for Jerusalem in 1063. Meinhard dismissed the earthly Jerusalem as "the domain where Herod murdered his father, the province where Pilate murdered God, and the homeland of Judas the traitor"; and far from praising pilgrimage itself as a pious work, he called for it to be used as the occasion for a renewal of spiritual life.[90] Just as it was Germany where the late medieval misuse of indulgences encountered opposition, so it may be that the earlier proclamation of a crusading indulgence found comparatively little German response. Besides, there was the reticent attitude adopted toward holy war. Although the imperial publicists left their views largely unvoiced, the crux of their teaching was that war and warriors had their own honor and their own ethics and that, on the other hand, religion was desecrated by the use of secular force. Both war and religion, therefore, offered arguments for the rejection of religious war. There may already have been something typically German to this attitude. Later on, admittedly, the idea of crusade won through in Germany, but it always remained problematic and called little blessing upon itself. Yet considerations of the kind we have just offered hardly acted in isolation. It must never be forgotten that the discrepancies in German and French development had particular historical causes, the principal among them being constitutional conditions and the history of church reform.[91] Moreover, as the contemporary Ekkehard of Aura rightly saw, there was the ecclesiastical schism of the Investiture Contest. This made many Germans question the authority of the pope who proclaimed the crusade, and it also compromised the idea of holy war, which had lost popularity by having been turned against the German king. That the crusading idea was a piece of church reform conceived by Romance peoples had in itself some effect in determining the attitude of Germany; an even greater deterrent was that this idea, as refashioned by Gregory VII, especially damaged the Germans. The deadlock broke only because the success of the First Crusade caused Gregory's plans to be forgotten.

France was not unique, though, in its early acceptance of the idea of crusade: Italy was equally precocious. The crusading aspect given by the Normans to their Sicilian conquests has previously been mentioned.[92] The Pisans briefly participated in this by launching an attack on the harbor of Palermo in 1063.[93] Besides, the Pisans periodically continued the maritime war against the Moslems that they had begun in the first half of the century.[94] With the Genoese, they entered the Spanish war in 1092, by joining Alfonso VI of Castile in a combined attack on Valencia; they then turned on Tortosa, but without success, since they arrived too late for the attack originally planned.[95] Their greatest feat in this period was the raid on Africa that they undertook in 1087, with the Genoese, Romans, and Amalfitans.[96] A relationship between this venture and the Spanish war is possible, for it took place simultaneously with the attempted counterattack against the advance of the African Almoravids upon the Iberian peninsula. In any case, the raid on Africa was conducted entirely as a crusade. Pope Victor III bestowed the banner of St. Peter upon the campaigners and granted them an indulgence.[97] After the Pisans had won and captured the city of Mahdia, they spent all their booty to adorn their cathedral and to build a church of St. Sixtus, on whose feast the main battle was won.[98] A rhythmical poem written in Pisa soon afterwards describes the war in lively colors.[99] The whole enterprise is depicted as a battle of Christ against the enemies of God; the reason for war is to liberate many Christian prisoners; during the battle Michael blows his trumpet, as in his fight with the dragon, and Peter appears with cross and sword; the warriors confess and take communion before the battle; a slain count is celebrated as a martyr; numerous Old Testament allusions are made, to Gideon and Judas Maccabeus, the capture of Jericho, David and Goliath, the slaughter of the hosts of Sennacherib by the angel, and the deliverance of Israel from Egypt.

Secular ideas also appear in comparisons with the wars of Rome with Carthage and in expressions of a new Pisan patriotism. A particularly interesting passage tells us that the defeated emir had to swear to hold the land from then on as a fief of St. Peter and to pay tribute to Rome.[100] No doubt this was a consequence of the Gregorian conception of the rights of St. Peter. But it would be false to consider the entire campaign from this standpoint, and to classify it as a "hierarchical" crusade; the subordination to St. Peter was a spur-of-the-moment decision, not originally intended.[101] Far from being papal, the Pisan poem is surely the clearest evidence we have for the popular idea of crusade as it then existed; hardly anything dating even from the days of the first Eastern crusade can equal it. One need only set the poem alongside Bonizo's set of commandments in order to obtain a true measure of its distance from the ecclesiastico-political idea of knighthood.

The East and its wars had a place apart. Long before the crusades, the Byzantine emperor had had Westerners fighting in his army against Arabs and Turks. Around 1040 Harald Hardrada, the later Norwegian king, achieved fame there,[102] and in the following decades the Normans were especially numerous in the fighting against the Turks, led by famed condottieri like Hervé, Robert Crispin, and Ursel of Bailleul.[103] Toward the end of the century, Germans regularly appeared alongside the Normans as auxiliaries of the Byzantines.[104] These mercenary bands should not be regarded as crusaders bent on war against the heathen.[105] Whenever they found more favorable conditions, they abandoned their employer and fought the Christian Byzantines as zealously as did the Turks, with whom they even entered into repeated alliances. Nevertheless, the connection between these wars and the later crusades is clear. The crusading plan of Gregory VII implied no more in practice than that auxiliaries would be supplied to the Byzantine emperor for his war against the Turks; and the efforts of Emperor Alexius to acquire Western mercenaries gave the direct impetus for the First Crusade.

Campaigning in the East could easily be combined with a pilgrimage to Jerusalem. Harald Hardrada was thought to have gone there during his Byzantine years, and others later did the same. Robert the Frisian, count of Flanders, was in Byzantium in 1089, returning from Jerusalem, when the emperor Alexius talked him into supplying an auxiliary contingent for the war on the Turks.[106] Circumstances like these are most clearly documented by a letter of Anselm of Canterbury, then still abbot of Bec (1079-1093), to a knight named William.[107] William wished to go far away to help his brother fighting in Byzantium, but Anselm tried to dissuade him: "Renounce the earthly Jerusalem and the treasures of Constantinople and Babylon which must be seized with bloodstained hands. . . ." The knight's intention must have been to fight in Byzantine and Arab lands and to visit Jerusalem at the same time. Passing from such plans to the decision to conquer Jerusalem itself was no longer a great step!

In the knight's case, the coincidence of campaigning with pilgrimage was external, based on geographical reasons alone. But there were many parallel cases. The idea of a Western expedition to Jerusalem was not unheard of in the eleventh century. Gerbert had expressed it, as we saw, but set it aside as impossible; after the destruction of the Holy Sepulcher, Sergius issued a regular call to crusade, though disapproving voices were heard even then. Gregory VII then made passing reference to Jerusalem in connection with the plan of a crusade in Asia Minor.[108] Bold as it was, the idea was not featured only in papal policy; we find it also in the emperor legends.

By the eleventh century, Charlemagne had assumed the role of the ideal emperor of the past, to whom poetry ascribed everything that seemed grandiose and worth striving for.[109] He was specially famed as the great champion of Christianity, not only in his own country but far afield. "The pious Charles, who, for fatherland and church, did not fear death, journeyed round the whole world and combated the enemies of God; and when he could not subdue with the words of Christ, he conquered with the sword," so wrote the priest Jocundus of Maastricht.[110] The authentic historical tradition contained reports that Charles sent embassies to Jerusalem and received them from there, that he made gifts to the Holy Sepulcher, and that he exercised protection over the holy places. Later times, in their exaggerated perspective, turned these facts into the belief that the emperor "had extended the empire as far as Jerusalem."[111] In relating that the patriarch of Jerusalem came in embassy to Charles, the Annals of Altaich attribute to him the intention of opening the city to the emperor "for the liberation of the Christian people"—and in so doing the Annals adopt almost the very words that would form Urban II's principal slogan in the call to crusade.[112] A parallel branch of the legend changed the embassy Charles sent to Jerusalem into a journey personally made by the emperor. The story appears as early as in the tenth-century Chronicle of Benedict of St. Andrea; according to it, Charles took a large following of Franks, Saxons, Bavarians, etc. with him to Jerusalem, Alexandria, and Constantinople, gave gifts to churches, and brought back relics, not as a conqueror, of course, but in friendly agreement with the caliph Haroun.[113] These various legendary themes presumably coalesced and resulted in the conception of a crusade of Charlemagne. We in fact have an extensive Latin account along these lines that scholars generally date to before the First Crusade.[114] As the story goes, the patriarch of Jerusalem was expelled by the heathens and begged the help of the emperor Charles in a letter specially stressing the defilement of the Holy Sepulcher; on this report, the Frankish warriors themselves pressed for a campaign, and Charles assembled a great army for a war upon the heathen, journeyed with it via Constantinople to Jerusalem, and after driving out the infidels, reinstated the Patriarch and the Christians; the Greek emperor wished to reward Charles with treasures, but he refused, accepting only relics, which he brought to Aachen.

Fantasies of this kind were not limited to the great emperor of the past, but were also predicted of the emperor of the future.[115] The Sibylline oracles, which had long been in circulation, predicted that the last emperor before the end of the world would conquer and convert the heathen, again unite the two halves of the empire, and finally go to Jerusalem, where he would lay down his crown and place the empire in the hands of God; after this the rule of antichrist would begin. In the original version of this prophecy, the journey to Jerusalem did not have the form of a crusade, but the story came to be altered in this sense. Two statements by the Italian bishop Benzo of Alba apply these predictions to Henry IV and expect him to undertake the journey to Jerusalem, not, however, to lay down the crown, but on the contrary to win it. In view of the imminent end of the world, the emperor was to restore Christian liberty after conquering his enemies and the pagans with his army; he would visit the Holy Sepulcher, which would then stand in the glory prophesied by Isaiah.[116] This is a regular plan for crusade, whose special importance consists in translating eschatological speculation into real policy. Benzo simultaneously combines his idea with the legend of Charlemagne: the banner that the patriarch of Jerusalem had sent to Charles prefigured Henry IV, who would be the standardbearer of the Christian religion in the planned crusade.[117]

What influence such stories and prophecies actually had is difficult to assess. We would hardly go wrong in assigning to them a comparatively marginal role in the First Crusade. Wholly disregarding them, however, would be a mistake, for we know that, when the crusade took place, many contemporaries looked upon it in the light of the imperial legend. The wars of Charlemagne against the heathens were cited as a model; the tale was told that the roads over which one journeyed to Constantinople had first been made by Charles for his army; some even believed that Charles himself rose again for the crusade.[118] A way was found to relate the capture of Jerusalem to the prophecy about the Jerusalem journey of the final emperor by altering the wording of the prophetic text and allowing the journey to be completed by the "kingdom" and the "people," in place of the emperor.[119] The bridges leading from these speculations to the idea of crusade were in fact crossed, and some spokesmen flatly connected the campaign to Jerusalem with the imminent end of the world.[120]

Though strange at first glance, such views may be explained by the unique position held by the city of Jerusalem in medieval thinking. The eleventh century must not be thought to have been gripped by enthusiasm for the "Holy Land"—a term that had not yet been coined.[121] Although Palestine was called the "land of promise [terra repromissionis]," this phrase related only to the ancient Israelites, not to the Christians, and was therefore of limited use; it was the crusade and the foundation of the kingdom of Jerusalem that turned Palestine into a holy land of the Christians. Aside from "holy places [loca sancta]"—a general concept without geographical localization[122]—only a Holy City [civitas sancta] had been known prior to the crusade. Jerusalem, however, obtained its special significance not just from Christ's suffering and

His tomb, but also from the mystical conception of the heavenly Jerusalem that dominated Christian literature on the basis of Paul and the Apocalypse.[123] These sources cast a shimmer of unreality upon the earthly Jerusalem and elevated it from the everyday world. Prophecies and legends about it could therefore have an effective influence that would have been inconceivable in regard to other localities.

In sum, several different elements prepared the ground that allowed the general idea of crusade and of war upon the heathen to assume the special form of a Jerusalem crusade. A few authors had in fact anticipated this very concept. We have yet to see what influence was exercised upon the Jerusalem crusade by the long-standing pilgrimages. It is well established that pilgrimages to Jerusalem had been popular long before the crusades and had attained great size in the eleventh century.[124] Neither does it need to be proved that these peaceful pilgrimages had at least a superficial relation to the crusades to Jerusalem. Sergius IV's call to a crusade was specifically connected with pilgrimages, and some versions of the emperor legend, as we saw, set the conquest of Jerusalem and the subjugation of the infidels in combination with a visit to the Holy Sepulcher and the acquisition of relics. Yet pilgrimage differed considerably from a crusade, especially in its rule that the pilgrim must be unarmed. What this meant in practice is best learned by examining the largest of the eleventh-century pilgrimages, the one of 1064 that some modern authors have regarded as a transitional step to the crusades, in which as many as 7,000 or even 12,000 pilgrims accompanied the archbishop of Mainz and the bishops of Bamberg, Regensburg, and Utrecht to Jerusalem.[125] The rule of being without weapons was scrupulously observed even in this passage.[126] When the pilgrims were attacked by robbers in Palestine, some refused for religious reasons to protect themselves from being robbed and maltreated.[127] The others resisted as best they could; but nearly all the chroniclers felt obliged to defend them against the reproach that they should not have fought at all.[128] Characteristically, the pilgrims had to be finally rescued from these robbers by none other than the Moslem authorities; for, as the Annals of Altaich specify, they feared that the stream of pilgrims would cease in the future, causing them to suffer a noticeable loss of revenue as a result.[129] This single episode illustrates the wide gap that then existed between pilgrimage and holy war.

Several questions come to mind nevertheless: Is it accidental that this largest pilgrimage took place in the very year when the idea of crusade against the heathen is found to have had its first surge, and particularly that it was contemporaneous with the first large crusade of the French knights in Spain? Is it also an accident that, three decades earlier, Radulf Glaber attests both to the attainment of high tide by the Peace of God movement and to the special prominence acquired by enthusiasm for the journey of Palestine?[130] Is it without significance that Erlembald of Milan, the first sainted knight of the West, had just returned from Jerusalem when the pope designated him as the champion of church reform?[131] Are deeper reasons irrelevant to the statement of Amatus of Monte Cassino that the first Normans—those who freed Salerno from the Moslems, whom he calls disinterested crusaders—reached Italy on the way home from a pilgrimage to Jerusalem?[132]

That these phenomena were interrelated seems to be beyond doubt.[133] To be sure, either pilgrimage or crusade could satisfy the desire to travel and could result from the need to abandon difficult circumstances at home; yet only a few of the coincidences listed above may be explained in this way. It is more appropriate to say that pilgrimage and crusade were equivalent ways of expressing the lay piety that characterized the knighthood of that period. Both pilgrimage and crusade show that the ecclesiastical ideal of life had spread beyond clerics and monks and had strongly affected the lay world; both had a special impact upon knights, by withdrawing them from everyday, secular fighting and subordinating their activity to a spiritual idea. Pilgrimages were therefore encouraged by the same Cluniac reformers who also promoted the Peace of God; Odilo of Cluny often helped travelers to Jerusalem, and Richard of St. Vannes personally accompanied 700 pilgrims on a journey to Palestine.[134] The view that long pilgrimages were unfitting and even detrimental to monks did not apply to laymen. It is no coincidence that several laymen who adhered to the reform movement, namely, the future abbot Poppo of Stablo and Count Frederick of Verdun, had previously been pilgrims to Jerusalem. Although Radulf Glaber, the Cluniac monk who relates their pilgrimage, sees in it an omen of antichrist coming from the East to lead even the elect into temptation, he nevertheless praises the pious zeal of the faithful, whom God will reward.[135]

From the standpoint of the ethic of knighthood, a pilgrimage was far less attractive than a crusade. It meant suspending one's martial profession, since the pilgrim stopped being a warrior for the duration of his travels. In its early development, the popular form of the idea of crusade did not at all coincide with the idea of a pilgrimage: its focus was war upon heathens. Pope Urban II was the first to unite pilgrimage and crusade in a synthesis—a synthesis that simultaneously renounced the application of the idea of crusade to hierarchical ends. His pontificate resolved the tensions and concentrated the forces that, for all their parallelism and contacts, had never before found a common resting place.[136]

Notes

1. The distinction between hierarchical and popular crusade stems from Ranke, *Weltgeschichte,* VIII, 71. It was adopted by O. Volk, *Kreuzzugsidee,* who also provides several useful comments.

2. The following is according to Schmitthenner, *Söldnertum,* whose survey must be corrected in details, since it is not based on first-hand study of the sources. Certain important sources may be added: the word *soldarius* in Hugh of Flavigny, *MGH SS.* 8.342, and in a letter from Lobbes, *MGH*

SS. 21.313; the Germans (*nemitzoi*) among the Byzantine mercenaries in a diploma of Alexius in 1088 (Dölger, *Regesten,* 1150, cf. C. Neumann, "Völkernamen," p. 374); Benzo of Alba's project of replacing the feudal levy by an army of mercenaries, with the help of an imperial tax, on which, H. Lehmgrübner, *Benzo von Alba,* pp. 122-25.

3. As does Schmitthenner, *Söldnertum,* p. 44 (Sardinian war of Benedict VIII); p. 51 (the latter's supposed mercenary treaty with the Normans); p. 55 ("afterwards, Rome often needed the support of Norman mercenaries," notably William of Montreuil); p. 56 (Eastern plan of Gregory VII); p. 25 (Beatrice and Mathilda of Tuscany); p. 20 (Gregory's request to the bishop of Trent); p. 68 (battle of Pleichfeld). In none of these cases do we have evidence that the relationship involved payment.

4. Hermann of Reichenau a. 1053, *MGH SS.* 5.132, see above, p. 122.

5. Above, pp. 130 and 152; Schmitthenner, pp. 52ff.

6. Benzo of Alba, II, 12 (*MGH SS.* 11.617). Cf. Erdmann, "Endkaiserglaube," pp. 403ff, and below, p. 299.

7. See R. Röhricht, *Geschichte,* pp. 65, 69, 81 n. 3, 88, 157f, 164.

[Erdmann's allusion to "an intermingling of motives" is, of course, correct, but his statement that "the rank and file had the direct promise of pay" seems too broad. The problem is obscure—as is also the question of numbers—and the reference to Röhricht does not fully answer the question. It is true that the leaders received gifts from the emperor, and in view of his request for aid, and presumed arrangements with the pope, probably expected recompense. But the emperor provided markets and, therefore, expected the crusaders to meet their own expenses en route. The leaders raised funds in various ways and doubtless equipped and paid foot-soldiers, but precisely what was expected of or provided for vassals, knights, etc. is not clear. Papal guarantees of freedom from debt and protection of property were presumably directed at less wealthy participants. Reports of prospective crusaders mortgaging their property, including followers of Peter the Hermit and Walter the Penniless, would seem to indicate need for personal financing. Moreover, Raimond of Toulouse's willingness to provide for poorer crusaders was certainly not pay in the ordinary sense of the word. On this, F. Duncalf, in *History of the Crusades,* ed. Setton, I, ch. VIII; S. Runciman, *History,* I, 121ff, and Appendix II; the comments of Bréhier in his review of Erdmann, p. 674. In addition, it is known that the journey was undertaken by a large number of noncombatants, for whom the pope apparently expected the leaders and knights to provide: W. Porges, "Non-combatants," pp. 1-23.]

8. Yet the idea was also voiced that true fighting for God was devalued by the acceptance of earthly reward; see the so-called *Descriptio* in G. Rauschen, *Legende,* p. 110.

9. Anselm of Canterbury, *Ep.* II, 19 (*MPL* 158.1168: *iniquitas est cruenta bellorum confusio,* etc.) See also Anselm's words to Diego of Compostela, *Ep.* IV, 19 (*MPL* 159.212).

10. The naive mixture of heterogeneous trains of thought in Rupert of Deutz, *Chronicon s. Laurentii,* c. 29, *MGH SS.* 8.272, is particularly interesting. See also Laurentius of Liège, *MGH SS.* 10.494-95.

11. Swabian Annalist a. 1077, *MGH SS.* 5.301. The old prohibition of armed service by clerics was renewed by the synod of Tours in 1060: *MPL* 142.1412, can. 7.

12. In addition to Anselm's letter (above, n. 9), see, for example, Sigebert, *Vita Wicberti,* c. 2 and 3 (*MGH SS.* 8.509, and above, p. 201).

13. A unique mixture of both points of view occurs in a biography of 1058, *Bouchard le Vénérable,* ed. de la Roncière, pp. 5, 6, 9, 26.

14. Cirot de la Ville, *Historie,* I, 297ff, 497f.

15. Above, p. 14, cf. p. 91.

16. See Exkurs I, sect. 6 [of the German edition]: A. Franz, *Benediktionen,* II, 297.

17. Benzo of Alba, II, 18 (*MGH SS.* 11.620f); see above, p. 130. The apostle Peter and Carpophorus appeared along with Maurice.

18. Bernold, a. 1102, *MGH SS.* 5.454; above, p. 14.

19. Lot, "Études," p. 340, maintains that these conceptions go back to the ninth century. But no more may be said with regard to the earlier period than that Denis was one of the greater saints of Gaul. Lot's direct evidence dates only from the twelfth century, though it testifies to a long-standing custom. The eleventh century provides the two reports of the translation of relics to Regensburg, the earlier (1049) in *MGH SS.* 30.823ff, the later one (prior to 1064, S. Rietschel, "Alter," pp. 641ff) in *SS.* 11.351ff.

[On the cult of St. Denis, B. Kötting, in *Lexikon für Theologie und Kirche;* E. H. Kantorowicz, *Laudes,* pp. 46, 116 n. 16, 117. The iconographical aspects of the cult are discussed in L. Réau, *Iconographie,* III, 374ff.]

20. See Erdmann, *Kaiserfahne,* pp. 892ff.

21. Cf. Hofmeister, *Heilige Lanze,* and Erdmann, "Heidenkrieg," pp. 135f n. 1. In Regensburg texts of the eleventh century (Arnold of St. Emmeram, *MGH SS.* 4.551; on the translation reports, above, n. 19), St. Emmeram plays the role of a military patron of the territory.

[On St. Maurice and the Holy Lance in Germany, Schramm, "Heilige Lanze," pp. 511ff. On the gift of the lance and the banner of St. Maurice to King Athelstan by Duke Hugh, L. H. Loomis, "Holy Relics," pp. 427-56.]

22. *Vita Stephani,* c. 6 and 8 (*MGH SS.* 11.232, 233); see also Meinhard of Bamberg in Erdmann, "Briefe," p. 406.

23. Cf. A. López Ferriero, *Historia,* II, 73ff, who still defends the authenticity of the Clavijo document.

    [On the origin of the cult of St. James at Compostela, see now José Guerra, "Notas," pp. 417-74, 559-90. There is also a brief summary with bibliography in V. and H. Hell, *Great Pilgrimage.* See also Sir Thomas Kendrick, *St. James,* ch. I, II.]

24. The history of the military cult of St. James is still a profitable field of research. Church historians of Spain (such as V. de la Fuente, *Historia,* III, 130ff, 230, 291ff, 458ff), as well as the richly documented but uncritical work of López Ferriero, may be taken as points of departure.

25. Above, p. 6.

26. Constantine Porphyrogenitus, *De ceremoniis,* I, 481, on the banners of the *martyres stratelatai;* Codinus. *De officiis,* pp. 47f.

    [See Bréhier, *Institutions,* p. 378.]

27. H. Delehaye, *Légendes grecques,* pp. 3ff; also C. Neumann, *Weltstellung,* pp. 36f.

28. It is interesting that Bernard of Angers (second half of the eleventh century) cites the killing of Julian the Apostate by St. Mercurius as illustrating a warlike deed by a saint (*Liber mirac. s. Fidis,* I, 26, ed. Bouillet, p. 68); but this is apparently book learning out of John of Damascus: Delehaye, *Légendes grecques,* pp. 98f.

29. Cf. A. Prost, "Caractère," pp. 167ff; K. Heldmann, *Kaisertum,* pp. 284ff; H. Leclercq, "Laudes Gallicanae," pp. 1898ff; Schramm, "Ordines," pp. 313f.

    [On the *laudes,* Kantorowicz, *Laudes,* who (p. 29 n. 48) maintains that Erdmann has suggested a rather late date for the reception of the Greek military saints. There are references to Theodore as early as the ninth century (pp. 105ff), and Michael, Maurice, Sebastian, and George were invoked by the Normans in the eleventh century (p. 167 n. 2). See also Réau, *Iconographie,* III, *passim.* On the Michael cult, above, Introduction, supplement to n. 46. For a survey of Eastern influences in the West, including the saints, G. Schreiber, "Christlicher Orient."]

30. Let me cite the following texts of *laudes,* each with the saints invoked for the army: (1) from 783-92 (Einhard, ed. Holder-Egger, Appendix, p. 47): Remigius (Rémi, the patron of Rheims); (2) from 796-800 (*Liber pontificalis,* ed. Duchesne, II, 37): Hilary, Martin, Maurice, Denys, Crispin and

Crispinian, Gereon (the patrons of Poitiers, Tours, St. Maurice, St. Denis, Soissons, and Cologne); (3) from 824-27 (C. Höffler, *Päpste,* I, 286, right-hand column): Andrew (the apostle); (4) from 858-67 (Prost, "Caractère," p. 176): Hilary, Martin, Maurice, Denys, Alban, Crispin, and Crispinian, Gereon (see no. 2; Alban was venerated at Mainz); (5) from about 880 (Prost, p. 238): Hilary, Martin, Maurice, Denys, Gereon (as no. 2); (6) from 1000-1002 (Prost, p. 181): Sylvester, Gregory, Leo, Ambrose (patrons of Rome and Milan); (7) eleventh century (Höffler, I, 287, left-hand column): John, Philip, Denys, Maurice, Hilary, Martin, Perpetuus, Paulinus (see no. 2; Perpetuus was venerated at Utrecht, Paulinus is surely the saint of Trier, while John and Philip are apostles). In nos. 1, 2, 4, and 5, the invocation is on behalf of the ruler and army of the Franks, in no. 3 only for the army of the Franks, in nos. 6 and 7 for the ruler and army of the Christians.

[J. R. in review of Erdmann, pp. 253-54, indicates that St. Mauritius does not refer here to the monastery of that name in Switzerland. Schramm, "Salische Kaiserordo," p. 400, mentions St. Maurice and the lance.]

31. Du Cange, *Glossarium,* s.v. *Laus* (and Prost, "Caractère," p. 179), after a MS of the church of Arles. The edition of Du Cange by the Benedictines of St. Maur adds that *similes litaniae* occur in a codex of St. Martial at Limoges (now Paris, Bibl. nat., MS lat. 1240, fol. 65-65ᵛ). According to Prost, pp. 177f., the Limoges text is unpublished, but it is also cited by Martène and dates from 923-36. Prost draws the incorrect conclusion that the Arles text belonged to about the same time as that of Limoges; the provenance of the MS and the saints' names (for the bishop: Ferreolus, Antidius, and Desideratus—all three from Besançon; for the king: Maurice, Sigismund, and Victor—the first two generally Burgundian, the third from Marseilles or Solothurn) render probable an origin in the united Burgundian kingdom, thus after 933; but a *terminus ante quem* cannot be supplied on this basis, since the Burgundian kingdom continued to exist after its union with the Empire.

[Also Kantorowicz, *Laudes,* p. 243 n. 31, mentioning the important relation between the Besançon MS and Arles.]

32. *Ordo* of the Codex Gemundensis (12th cent.?), *MGH Leg.* 2.78f (also in MS Vatican., lat. 7114, 13th-14th cent., E. Eichmann, *Quellensammlung,* I, 60); *Exercitui Francorum, Romanorum et Teutonicorum vitam et victoriam . . . sancte Theodore.* (Eichmann dates this text from the ninth century; see also Eichmann, "Ordines," p. 11; but it must be considerably later). The *laudes* of the *Ordo Cencius II* (Schramm, "Ordines," p. 384) align all the saints invoked; but since the army is in last place in the invocations, and since Mercurius is the

last of the saints invoked, there is no doubt that he is named in relation to the army.

33. This is also clearly apparent in Orderic Vitalis, VI, 2, ed. Le Prevost, III, 4, where the Greeks Demetrius, George, Theodore, and Eustace are named alongside the Westerners Sebastian and Maurice as ancient models for knights.

[See above, supplement to n. 29.]

34. See the sources in Röhricht, *Geschichte,* pp. 93 n. 1, 127 n. 1, 143f n. 5, 149 n. 4. Maurice and Blasius also appear but rather seldom.

35. Bibliography in K. Künstle, *Ikonographie der Heilingen,* pp. 263ff.

36. It suffices to mention the ninth-century German *Georgslied:* Ehrismann, *Literatur,* I, 212ff. The sermon on St. George by Peter Damiani (*MPL* 144.567ff) celebrates only the martyr and stresses the distinction between his former soldiering and his later *christiana militia,* i.e., martyrdom.

37. Arkadios of Cyprus in K. Krumbacher, *Georg,* p. 79: *tes basileias o promakos;* cf. pp. 206f.

38. Arculfus, III, 4, in T. Tobler and A. Molinier, *Itinera,* pp. 195ff.

39. J. B. Aufhauser, *Drachenwunder,* pp. 237ff. Add to this two further translations of the Greek dragon-miracle in twelfth-century manuscripts, published in John the Monk, ed. M. Huber, *Sammlung,* pp. 124ff. The editor conjectures (p. xxxi) that the translation stems from John the Monk. In this case, they would belong to the eleventh century; cf. Hofmeister, "Übersetzer," pp. 225ff. But I find no basis for this attribution.

40. Aufhauser, pp. 2ff, 28.

41. Psellos, *MPG* 122.531.

42. Krumbacher, p. 213.

43. Raymond of Aguilers, c. 32 (*RHC,* Occ., III, 290). There might be an echo here of the common Byzantine designation of George as *tropaiophoros.*

44. Röhricht, *Geschichte,* p. 182.

45. The earlier *Vita Stephani* (probably from the end of the eleventh century) has the king of Hungary win a victory "with the protection of the sign of the most glorious cross, the supporting merits of the ever virgin Mary, Mother of God, under the banner of Bishop Martin, dear to God, and of the holy martyr, George [*protegente gloriosissimae crucis signaculo, patrocinantibus Dei genetricis ac perpetuae virginis Mariae meritis, sub vexillo Deo dilecti pontificis Martini sanctique martyris Georgii*]" (*MGH SS.* 11.232); but this appears to be meant metaphorically; see above, n. 22.

[But see the remarks of Kantorowicz (cited above, supplement to n. 29) on earlier liturgical evidence.]

46. H. Günter, *Legendenstudien,* pp. 109f, sets the earliest appearance of St. George in the Slavic battle of 1004; but this comes from Adalbert's Life of Henry II, c. 4 (*MGH SS.* 4.793), a twelfth-century work. Much later still is the legend of the appearance of St. George at the battle of Alcoraz (1096; cf. Boissonnade, *Roland,* p. 37, Menéndez-Pidal, *España,* II, 563); it first occurs in the fourteenth-century *Chronica Pinnatensis* (*Historia de Aragon,* ed. Embun, p. 59), cf. Zurita, *Annales,* I, 32. (The statement that St. Victorian appeared at the same time stems from a gross misinterpretation of the words of Rodrigo of Toledo, VI, 1, in *Hispaniae Illustratae,* ed. Schott, II, 94.)

47. Geoffrey Malaterra, II, 33, ed. Pontieri, p. 44; cf. above, pp. 134-36.

48. Aufhauser, *Drachenwunder,* pp. 178f; A. Poncelet, "Catalogus hagiog. Rom.," p. 59. Both authors date the oldest manuscript containing this story (Rome, Lateran A 79) to the eleventh-twelfth century.

49. Bédier, *Légendes,* IV, 403-33; and *Roland commentée,* pp. 9f, 12ff.

50. E.g., the *Vita nobilissimi comitis Girardi de Rosselon,* ed. P. Meyer, *Romania* 7 (1878), 178ff. For the date, see most recently Lot, "Études," pp. 259f. It suffices, for further illustration, to mention Pseudo-Turpin; Bédier, *Légendes,* III, 42ff.

51. Ardo, *Vita Benedicti Anianensis,* c. 30 (*MGH SS.* 15.211-13).

52. *Vita s. Wilhelmi,* c. 5 and 7 (*AA. SS.* May, VI, 802). Otherwise, however, this Life holds fast to the contrast of *militia Dei* with *militia saecularis.*

53. Cf. Bédier, *Légendes,* I, 118.

[Around 1125, according to Riquer, *Chansons,* p. 138.]

54. J. Mabillon, *Acta sanctorum ordinis s. Benedicti,* saec. IV, I, 662-64; also Bédier, *Légendes,* II, 305ff.

55. Mabillon, p. 664: *Ite pares animae per quaelibet agmina primae, Fortes Caesarei, fortia membra Dei, Fortes athletae, per saecula cuncta valete.* On the date Bédier, *Légendes,* II, 307.

56. *Chronicon Novalic.,* II, 12 (*Monumenta Novalic.,* II, 156).

57. *Ibid.,* II, 7, p. 135.

58. *Ibid.,* II, 11, pp. 153ff.

59. *Ibid.,* pp. 155f.

60. See P. Rajna, "Contributi," pp. 36ff; Bédier, *Légendes,* II, 160ff.

61. According to Bédier (*Légendes* and *Roland commentée*), the *chansons de geste* owe their origins in the eleventh century to the cooperation of monks and jongleurs. But this theory has been sharply contested by the work of Lot, "Études"; R. Fawtier, *Roland,* and A. Pauphilet, "Roland."

[For more recent discussions of the entire problem, see Riquer, *Chansons;* I. Siciliano, *Chansons,* ch. x;

R. Menéndez-Pidal, *Roland*, tr. Cluzel. For the connection with crusade origins, see also A. Waas, *Kreuzzüge*, I, 41ff.]

62. See particularly the words of Hagen in Ekkehard, *Waltharius*, vv. 1276-78, ed. K. Strecker, p. 66.

[On the date, see P. Salmon, *Literature*, I, 25, 197-98.]

63. See now Lot, "Études," pp. 449ff.

64. *Chançun de Guillelme*, vv. 802-26.

65. See vv. 1198ff, where the wounded knight Guischart speaks of going to Cordova and giving up Christianity, but is fiercely scolded by William on this account.

66. See the recent works cited above, n. 61; add Boissonnade, *Roland*, W. Tavernier, *Vorgeschichte*, and E. Faral, *Roland*. Bédier, Boissonnade, Tavernier, and Faral set the *Chanson* after the First Crusade, Lot and Fawtier before it. I incline to the latter view.

[The controversy over all aspects of the *Song of Roland* still continues, but it seems now generally agreed that it was composed by a cleric in the form preserved in MS Bodleian Library, Digby 23, or at least in a form closely resembling this, in the latter decades of the eleventh century (according to most scholars), and certainly before 1124. See the literature cited above, supplement to n. 61, and also L. H. Loomis, "Relic," pp. 241-60; D. C. Douglas, "Song of Roland," pp. 99-116. A great deal of the modern discussion concerns the provenance of the complete text of the Bodleian MS. There seems to be general agreement that much of what was later included circulated in various forms before the First Crusade and reflects the eleventh-century holy war ethos.]

67. Cf. G. Paris, review of Marignan, p. 410.

68. Cf. A. M. Weiss, "Entwicklung," pp. 114ff (esp. 116f), also for what follows.

69. Cf. Pauphilet, "Roland," pp. 184ff.

70. *Chanson de Roland*, vv. 1008-16, 1053-58, 1113-23, 1456-66.

71. *Ibid.*, v. 1015.

72. *Ibid.*, vv. 1126-38; cf. vv. 1515-23 (1472-80).

73. Tavernier, *Vorgeschichte*, pp. 84-88, 98-100, claims that this and similar ideas would have been impossible before the First Crusade. This view is based in inadequate knowledge of the facts and is refuted throughout the present book.

[Two questions are raised by Erdmann's statement here: (1) what elements of the *Chanson* antedated the final version, and (2) the much-disputed question of the authenticity and/or meaning of Alexander's letter. See above, ch. IV, supplement to n. 72.]

74. See also Luchaire, *Premiers Capétiens*, p. 392.

75. *Exhortatio ad proceres regni*, ed. E. Dümmler, *NA* 1 (1876), 177. Cf. Schramm, *Renovatio*, I, 257; Menéndez-Pidal, *España*, I, 247. In vv. 5f (*Subdite Nortmanni iam colla ferocia regi, Imperio adsocii bella parate duci*), *Nortmanni* is not genitive singular but vocative plural; it parallels the *Romani* and *Itali* in the previous verses. For, to begin with, *colla* is plural; second, the expression *imperio adsocii* fits only the Normans, not the previously mentioned Romans and Italians; third, the further encouragements to war against the Saracens are evidently addressed to the Normans in particular.—After my book was in press, Mr. G. Radke (a doctoral candidate) drew my attention to certain points that invalidate the above argument and make it likely that the poet addresses only Romans and Italians and names the Normans as the first enemies to be combated. If so, there is in fact an astonishing similarity to Benzo of Alba's first plan of crusade, also drawn up in 1063 (Erdmann, "Endkaiserglaube," pp. 403f, and below, p. 299), whose expectation is that Henry IV will first triumph over the Normans and heathens and then undertake an eschatological journey to Jerusalem in company with the Byzantine emperor. I have left my statements in the text unchanged, on the understanding that Mr. Radke will publish his findings.

76. What makes this date likely is the appeal to war against the *dux*, which can only mean Godfrey of Lorraine, as well as the allusion to an alliance with the Greeks (v. 13: *Grecia iuncta aderit*).

77. Lampert a. 1073, 1076, ed. Holder-Egger, pp. 152, 277f. Cf. also Otloh, *Libellus*, c. 1 (*MPL* 146.246).

78. Above, pp. 136-40.

79. On what follows, Boissonnade, *Roland*, pp. 28ff, whose discussion can only be partially substantiated; also Menéndez-Pidal, *España*, pp. 370 n. 2, 563 n. 3, 679ff.

80. Above, pp. 155-56.

81. *Fragmentum historiae Francorum*, in *RHF*, XII, 2; Hugh of Fleury, *MGH SS.* 9·390.

[Dufourneaux, *français*, p. 141. On the reasons for the double designation of the battle, see Valdeavellano, *Historia*, pp. 831-32 and n. 1.]

82. See the spurious letter of Alexius in Hagenmeyer, *Kreuzzugsbriefe*, p. 133: "just as in the past year they freed for a time Galicia and the other Western kingdoms from the yoke of the pagans, so now, for the salvation of their souls, they attempt to free the kingdom of the Greeks [*sicut Galiciam et cetera Occidentalium regna anno praeterito a iugo paganorum aliquantulum liberaverunt, ita et nunc ob salutem animarum suarum regnum Graecorum liberare temptent*]." Further, the statements about William Carpentarius in the *Gesta Francorum*, c. 15, para. 2, ed. Hagenmeyer, p. 260 (ed. Bréhier, p. 78).

83. Menéndez-Pidal, *España,* I, 143ff; Boissonnade, "Cluny," pp. 266f.

84. Menéndez-Pidal, *España,* I, 347.

[Valdeavellano, *Historia,* pp. 833-34.]

85. *Carmen,* v. 90; Menéndez-Pidal, *España,* II, 892: "that God permitted him to vanquish [*quod Deus illi vincere permisit*]."

86. Menéndez-Pidal, *España,* II, 559.

[On Alfonso and the Cid, Valdeavellano, *Historia,* pp. 834-57. On the poem, see now C. Smith, *Poema,* esp. pp. xiii-xciii.]

87. For Rodrigo Diaz, see his charter for the bishop of Valencia, in Menéndez-Pidal, *España,* II, 877: "(God) roused up Rodrigo Campeador as the avenger of the disgrace of his servants and the defender of the Christian religion [(*Deus*) *Rudericum Campidoctorem obprobrii servorum suorum suscitavit ultorem et Christianae religionis propugnatorem*]." Similar expressions are found in the report of the consecration of Barcelona cathedral in 1058, in J. Mas, *Notes,* I, 192ff, e.g., on Raymond Berengar: "He was made the defender and the rampart of the Christian people [*factus est propugnator et murus christiani populi*]"; or on the institution of the feast of the holy Cross so that Christ, "as He did to King Constantine, might give us victory over the barbarians by the triumph of the cross [*sicut regi Constantino, sic nobis de barbaris per crucis triumphum det victoriam*]." Yet the same report quite calmly mentions charters of the Moorish rulers Mogehid and Ali subordinating the churches of Mallorca, Denia, and Orihuela to the bishopric of Barcelona.

88. *MGH SS.* 6.214, also Ekkehard, *Hierosolymita,* c. 9, pp. 109ff.

89. There is no need to refute the statements of Reynaud, *Origines,* I, 516, who offers as cause the "utilitarian realism" of the Germans.

90. Letter of Meinhard in Erdmann, "Briefe," p. 415. On earlier comments against overvaluing pilgrimages, Röhricht, *Pilgerfahrten,* pp. 327f.

91. Above, pp. 93-94.

92. Above, pp. 134-36.

93. Heinemann, *Geschichte,* I, 210f.

94. See above, p. 111.

95. Menéndez-Pidal, *España,* I, 441, 444f; II, 792, 795.

96. See now Hofmeister, "Übersetzer," pp. 269f.

[See also H. C. Kreuger, "Italian Cities," I, 52-53; Villey, *Croisade,* p. 61.]

97. Chronicle of Monte Cassino, III, 71 (*MGH SS.* 7·751). See below, pp. 306-7.

[Brundage, *Canon Law,* p. 28, and others question the crusade character of Victor III's summons.]

98. *Annales Pisani* a. 1088, ed. Gentile, p. 7.

99. Printed in W. Schneider, *Rythmen,* pp. 34ff, and elsewhere. I have not been able to see the new edition, with commentary by Biagi (1930) referred to in the *Annales Pisani,* ed. Gentile, p. 7 n. 1. H. Naumann, "Heide," p. 86, suggests that the poet "converts a presumably mercantile affair into a crusade." But the Chronicle of Monte Cassino proves that the "conversion" into a crusade does not stem from the poet but was envisaged from the start by the leaders of the enterprise.

100. Verse 60 (Schneider, *Rythmen,* p. 40): "He swears that the land belongs to St. Peter without question, And he now holds it of him without deception; Whence he will always send tributes and payments to Rome, He now commissions insignia of pure gold and silver [*Terram iurat sancti Petri esse sine dubio, Et ab eo tenet eam iam absque colludio; Unde semper mittet Roman tributa et praemia, Auri puri et argenti nunc mandat insignia*]," confirmed by Bernold a. 1088, *MGH SS.* 5·447: "they made the African king . . . tributary to the apostolic see [*Affricanum regem . . . apostolicae sedi tributarium fecerunt*]."

101. After capturing Mahdia, the Pisans realized that they could not retain permanent control of it. Geoffrey Malaterra, IV, 3, ed. Pontieri, pp. 86f, reports that they offered the city to Count Roger of Sicily, who refused it. Only then did they decide to leave Mahdia in the emir's possession and to impose upon him for the future (in addition to an immediate payment to the Pisans) only a tribute to Rome—without expecting that it would ever be paid.

102. See G. Schlumberger, *Épopée,* III, 228ff, 248; also Riant, *Expéditions,* pp. 123f.

103. Schlumberger, "Deux chefs," pp. 289ff; F. Brandileone, "Primi Normanni," pp. 227ff; also F. Hirsch, "Amatus," pp. 232ff, and C. Neumann, *Weltstellung,* pp. 115ff.

[J. Hussey in *CMH,* IV (2d ed.), pt. I, 197, 210. On Amatus's chronicle, W. Smidt, "Amatus," pp. 173-231.]

104. Charter of Alexius (1088): Dölger, *Regesten,* 1150; see also the reports about Robert the Frisian (below, n. 106).

105. Even Amatus of Monte Cassino does not give this aura to the deeds of Robert Crispin and Ursel of Bailleul in the East (Aimé, *Ystoire,* I, 8-15, ed. Delarc, pp. 13-18), whereas just before and just after he celebrates as crusades the fighting of the Normans in Spain and southern Italy.

106. Anna Comnena, *Alexiad,* VII, 6, and below, p. 322, Lampert a. 1071, ed. Holder-Egger, p. 122, claims that, long before, Robert made yet another Eastern journey, mingling among Jerusalem pilgrims in

order to reach the Norman auxiliary corps in Constantinople (on this, C. Verlinden, "Lambert," pp. 97ff).

[On Robert the Frisian, F. L. Ganshof, "Robert," pp. 57-74.]

107. Anselm, II, *Ep.* 19 (*MPL* 158.1167ff). As far as I know this significant letter has not been noticed hitherto.

108. Above, pp. 113-16, 168-69.

109. On the following, Hoffmann, *Karl,* pp. 97ff.

[On the Charlemagne legends, R. Folz, *Souvenir,* pp. 134ff. The impact of these legends on popular attitudes regarding Jerusalem and the crusade is emphasized by Alphandéry, *Chrétienté,* 1, 50ff.]

110. *Translatio s. Servatii* (1080s), *MGH SS.* 12.96. See also *Miracula s. Genulphi* (mid-eleventh century), *MGH SS.* 15.1206.

111. *Annales Elnonenses* (to 1061) a. 771, *MGH SS.* 5.18.

112. *Annales Altahenses* a. 800 (this part was written ca. 1032 or earlier), ed. ab Oefele, p. 4. The same theme is further elaborated in the Northumbrian annals reconstructed on the basis of Simeon of Durham, *MGH SS.* 13.156. What we have here and in the Annals of Altaich are merely late embroiderings upon the report of the Frankish Royal Annals; R. Pauli, "Karl," pp. 164, 165f.

113. *MGH SS.* 3.710f (also *Chronicon di Benedetto,* ed. Zuchetti, pp. 112ff). The later poem in Old French about Charles's journey is along the same lines.

114. The so-called *Descriptio,* printed in Rauschen, *Legende,* pp. 103ff; cf. the same author's "Untersuchungen," pp. 257ff and Hoffmann, *Karl,* pp. 112ff (to whose bibliography add Riant, "Inventaire," pp. 9ff). Hoffmann's idea that this journey was peaceful is contradicted by the text of the *Descriptio,* in which the statement (p. 119 line 4) that Charles rode a white mule refers only to the closing stages of the journey, when the emperor brings back relics from Constantinople (p. 118 line 3). I am not quite sure, however, that the *Descriptio* dates from before the First Crusade; also worth mentioning is the thesis of Bédier, *Légendes,* IV, 125ff, 139, who suggests the years 1110-24.

[On the *Descriptio,* Folz, *Souvenir,* pp. 138, 178ff.]

115. For the following, Erdmann, "Endkaiserglaube," pp. 384ff.

[On the Sibylline oracles, Folz, *Souvenir,* pp. 138ff; R. Konrad, "Jerusalem," pp. 537ff; S. Mähl, "Jerusalem," pp. 22 ff.]

116. Benzo of Alba, I, 15 and II, 12 (*MGH SS.* 11.605, 617); also Erdmann, "Endkaiserglaube," pp. 403ff.

117. Benzo of Alba, I, 17, p. 606.

118. Robert the Monk, I, 1 and 5 (*RHC,* Occ., III, 727 and 732); *Gesta Francorum,* c. 2, para. 1, ed.

Hagenmeyer, p. 109 (ed. Bréhier, p. 4); Ekkehard, *Chronicon, MGH SS.* 6.215; also Ekkehard, *Hierosolymita,* c. 11, para. 2, ed. Hagenmeyer, pp. 120f.

119. On the alteration of the interpolation in Adso, see Erdmann, "Endkaiserglaube," p. 412. There (p. 411) I dated the original text of this interpolation to before the First Crusade, but since this continues to be uncertain (*ibid.,* p. 412 n. 69), I shall not develop the point further.

[Folz, *Souvenir,* pp. 139ff, suggests a somewhat different interpretation, and notes that two new elements were superimposed on the original legend of the last emperor: (1) Benzo's idea of conquest and a new crown to be assumed in Jerusalem, and (2) the interpolation into the Adso text of an unknown conqueror, sometime before 1098, but perhaps reflecting the time of preparation for the crusade. See also Alphandéry, *Chrétienté,* I, 23-24; Konrad, "Jerusalem," p. 537; Mähl, "Jerusalem," p. 23; A. H. Bredero, "Jérusalem," pp. 23-24.]

120. Ekkehard, *Chronicon, MGH SS.* 6.212 (Ekkehard, *Hierosolymita,* c. 2, para. 1, ed. Hagenmeyer, pp. 55f); Guibert of Nogent, II, (*RHC,* Occ., IV, 138f). See also the reference to the Sibylline prophecies in the *Gesta Francorum,* c. 22, para. 8, ed. Hagenmeyer, pp. 327f (ed. Bréhier, p. 122).

121. I have looked in vain for the concept *Terra Sancta* in the eleventh-century sources. In Tobler-Molinier, *Itinera,* I find it only in Theodosius, *Terra Sancta;* but its occurrences are confined to the superscript (p. 63) which is a later trimming, and to ch. 40, which was added after the crusade had begun. The expression is also absent from the crusade letters and the earliest historians (*Gesta Francorum* and Raymond of Aguilers), but after 1100 it appears in many crusade historians (Fulcher, Ekkehard, Guibert, Baldric, etc.).

122. Bede, for example, includes Alexandria and Constantinople among the *loca sancta* (*Itinera,* ed. Geyer, pp. 301ff). Besides, the same term was also applied to all consecrated places, i.e., churches, as, for example, in Fulcher, I, 1, para. 2, ed. Hagenmeyer, p. 121.

123. Ekkehard, *Hierosolymita,* c. 34, para. 3, ed. Hagenmeyer, pp. 301ff. Cf. Röhricht, *Pilgerfahrten,* p. 376 n. 76. Benzo of Alba, who recommended a Jerusalem crusade, also spoke similarly about the heavenly Jerusalem (v, 6, *MGH SS.* 6.652: *Hierosolimam petamus*).

[The medieval eschatological fascination of Jerusalem is emphasized in most modern analyses of the popular religious ethos of the eleventh century. See, e.g., the works of Alphandéry, Konrad, Mähl, and Bredero, cited above, supplement to n. 119. The role of Jerusalem in the First Crusade is especially significant, and some have felt, e.g. Mayer,

Crusades, p. 12, that Alphandéry exaggerates the eschatological influence. But even he recognized that the question remains to what extent the emphasis on Jerusalem occurs in works written before the crusade.]

124. Still valuable, though containing some errors, is Röhricht, *Pilgerfahrten,* pp. 323ff; also Reynaud, *Origines,* I, 86, and Bréhier, *Église,* pp. 42ff.

[The relation between the Jerusalem pilgrimage and the First Crusade has long been debated, and many scholars feel that Erdmann in emphasizing holy war as the root of the crusade movement underplayed the impact of pilgrimage (see below, ch. x, supplement to n. 109; Appendix, supplement to n. 2; above, Translator's Foreword). For a summary of the Jerusalem pilgrimage, Runciman, *History,* I, ch. III, and in *History of the Crusades,* ed. Setton, I, 68-78; Alphandéry, *Chrétienté,* ch. I; Ebersolt, *Orient et Occident,* ch. VIII; E.-R. Labande, "Recherches," pp. 165, 339-47.]

125. On this pilgrimage, see now E. Joranson, "German Pilgrimage," pp. 3ff. New information on the preparation for the journey is provided by two letters of Meinhard of Bamberg, nos. 23 and 25, in Erdmann, "Briefe," pp. 345, 414, 418.

126. Joranson, "German Pilgrimage," pp. 14f., 22, 40.

127. Lampert a. 1065, ed. Holder-Egger, p. 94: "Many Christians thought it irreligious to protect themselves with the fist and to defend their safety, which they had vowed to God when setting forth abroad, with earthly weapons [*Plerique christianorum religiosum putantes manu sibi auxilium ferre et salutem suam, quam peregre proficiscentes Deo devoverant, armis corporalibus tueri*]." Cf. Joranson, p. 21.

[The meaning of *religiosum putantes* in the quotation is highly problematic. The excessively free translation given above—"thought it irreligious"—reflects Erdmann's apparent understanding of the passage and conforms to the currently authoritative German translation, "hielten es für nicht vereinbar mit ihrem Glauben" (Adolf Schmidt, *Ausgewählte Quellen zur deutschen Geschichte des Mittelalters,* ed. R. Buchner, XIII, Berlin, 1957, p. 97). A much more probable interpretation has been suggested to me by Mr. F. A. Mantello, a doctoral candidate at the Centre for Medieval Studies, University of Toronto: Lampert meant *religiosum putantes* ironically; the sense of the passage is, then, that many Christian pilgrims were foolish enough to "think it religious" to take up weapons in their own defense, and the appropriate retribution followed. Owing to the absence of any negation (even in the critical apparatus), Mr. Mantello's reading alone is faithful to the Latin and altogether preferable to the alternative. (W. G.)]

128. Joranson, p. 41.

129. *Annales Altahenses* a. 1065, ed. ab Oefele, p. 68.

130. Radulf Glaber, IV, 5 and 6, ed. Prou, pp. 103ff.

131. Above, p. 141.

132. Above, p. 109.

133. But A. Hatem, *Poèmes,* pp. 47ff and 58ff, goes too far. He finds connections between the Norman wars in Sicily and the pilgrimage to Mount Gargano (on the Adriatic coast; besides almost a half century passed between the pilgrimage described by William of Apulia and the Norman attack on Sicily), as well as between the Spanish crusades and the pilgrimage to Santiago de Compostela (in the far northwest of Spain; and he cannot adduce the slightest eleventh-century evidence for this pilgrimage). The thesis that the Cluniacs encouraged pilgrimages in order to bring about holy war is nebulous. To construct deliberate intentions out of what are merely significant correlations is an historical oversimplification.

[It now seems generally agreed that pilgrimage to Compostela was common in the eleventh century, especially during the second half. All this prompted the building of the new basilica. See the literature cited above, supplement to n. 23, and Kendrick's Introduction (p. 17) to the work of V. and H. Hell; Labande, "Recherches," p. 167. On Cluny and the Jerusalem pilgrimage, Cowdrey, *Cluniacs,* pp. 182-83.]

134. J.-H. Pignot, *Histoire,* II, 158f; E. Sackur, *Cluniacenser,* II, 231ff, also for what follows.

[On St. Odilo, Dom Hourlier, *Odilon de Cluny,* and his remarks in the discussion following Delaruelle, "Idée," pp. 439-40.]

135. Radulf Glaber, III, 6, ed. Prou, p. 109.

136. I was able to see E. Heisig, "Geschichtsmetaphysik," pp. 1-87, only after my book was printed. Heisig's discussion frequently touches upon the topics treated here, and he finds notable connections between eschatological conceptions and the idea of war against heathens—findings that accord well with those of the present chapter. Equally commendable is his reference (pp. 13ff) to the Spaniards Eulogius and Alvaro in the ninth century; but their role must be considered in the context of the total development, without making them the basis for ascribing a general primacy to Spain in the development of the idea of crusade. With regard to Cluny, Heisig endorses the doctrines rejected above, pp. 68-71 and below, p. 307 n. 4; he also amplifies them by confusing Hugh Candidus with Abbot Hugh of Cluny (p. 28).

Colin Morris (essay date 1998)

SOURCE: "Picturing the Crusades: The Uses of Visual Propaganda, c. 1095–1250" in *The Crusades and Their*

Sources: Essays Presented to Bernard Hamilton, edited by John France and William G. Zajac, Ashgate, 1998, pp. 195–209.

[*In the following essay, Morris examines the types of "visual propaganda"—such as placards and the windows and architecture of churches and halls—used to keep the crusading spirit alive.*]

Pictures, commented Gratian, are the 'literature of the laity'.[1] The idea had received its classic statement long before, in Gregory the Great's ruling to Bishop Serenus of Marseilles: 'pictures of images . . . were made for the instruction of the simple people, that those who do not know letters may understand the history'. Gregory's words provided the starting-point of medieval discussion of the use of images, and much modern commentary has followed the supposition that religious art was designed as a simple language for the laity.[2] Crusading was not a legal obligation, but depended on the ability to persuade. The popes were well aware of the power of visual imagery: the Romans, as Gerhoh of Reichersberg wrote, 'paint, speak and write, indoors and out' to communicate their message.[3] The use of images naturally took its place alongside sermons, songs and liturgy in the dissemination of crusading ideology.[4]

There are, however, complications in tracing the development of crusading propaganda in art and architecture. Much of the material survives only in copies, or has recently been uncovered in very imperfect form. There is every reason to suppose that a great deal has been lost without trace. More fundamentally, it is a mistake to assume that, in medieval art, every picture tells a story. The precept of Gregory must not be accepted in too uncritical a fashion.[5] It was quoted because of authority and because it conveniently allowed the use of images while sidestepping any suggestion that they were objects of worship in themselves, and not because his words really shaped the medieval attitude to symbolism. Christian images had never provided a simple narrative, but had from the beginning expressed levels of theological meaning: 'little medieval art is merely instructive'.[6] Images are ambiguous. Their power consists in their ability to present the viewer with several references at the same time, and it appears that artists and patrons were not rigidly controlled in the way they presented their themes. The idea of images as the direct translation of verbal teaching was based on belief in an 'all-powerful, encyclopedic, Christian intellectual atmosphere' dominating the Middle Ages. Few people would now see medieval culture in such a hierocratic way.[7]

It is true that the survival of illustrated vernacular manuscripts, including copies of the French translation of William of Tyre's history of Outremer, gives more confidence that we know what the higher aristocracy was reading. Such manuscripts become numerous from about 1250 onwards. Questions still remain about the true purpose of these luxurious books and the relationship of the images with the text which they supposedly clarify.[8] Still, the survival of vernacular manuscript evidence does open a new propaganda period. This is marked, too, by the loss of Latin Syria, and the dominance within the crusading movement of a new type of national state, especially France. In spite of the limitations in the earlier evidence, I shall concentrate here on what we know about visual propaganda during the twelfth and early thirteenth centuries.

It is difficult to find examples of art designed to advertise a particular expedition in the same way as the song, *Chevalier, mult estes guariz,* was written for the Second Crusade. Rather surprisingly, we hear from Muslim sources of placards carried around to advertise a crusade. Baha' al-Din reports that Conrad of Montferrat used one in the West:

> He had a picture of Jerusalem painted showing the ko-mama . . . Above the tomb the marquis had a horse painted, and mounted on it a Muslim knight who was trampling the tomb, over which his horse was urinating. This picture was sent abroad to the markets and meeting-places; priests carried it about, clothed in their habits, their heads covered, groaning, 'O the shame!'.[9]

Ibn al-Athir has a similar account of recruiting by Patriarch Eraclius, who led a group of clergy and knights, wearing mourning, and 'made a picture showing the Messiah, and an Arab striking him, showing blood on the face of Christ—blessings on him!—and they said to the crowds, "This is the Messiah, struck by Mahomet the prophet of the Muslims, who has wounded and killed him"'.[10] The themes are plausible ones for Christian propaganda, and placards of this sort may have been made familiar by the 'props' used in plays such as the *Jeu de St Nicholas* (c. 1202), itself possibly directed to recruiting for the Fourth Crusade. It would be unreasonable to hope for the survival of such transient objects, but there is also a lack of clear references to their use by preachers. When a Welsh prince joined the Third Crusade in 1188 with the words, 'I hasten to avenge the injury done to God the Father Almighty', he could indeed have been responding to such a placard, but there is no secure evidence that he was.[11]

There is, in fact, little proof of the use of any sort of visual aid by preachers, with the important exception of the Cross. This was regularly carried by crusade and other preachers, and of course the sign of the Cross was adopted by crusaders and became the badge of the movement. Taking the Cross became the standard expression for enlisting: 'A man should receive on his shoulder the sign of the holy Cross and say in his heart, "Lord, as you call upon me, I commend myself to you"'. The *Brevis ordinacio,* a collection of notes for the use of crusade preachers in England in 1216, strongly suggests that preachers were expected to use the Crucifix as a visual aid.[12]

Although it is hard to find works of art directly designed to recruit for a specific expedition, a few can plausibly be attached to its ceremonial departure. One of the ambulatory chapels in Suger's new church at St-Denis contained a set of panes devoted to the celebration of the glories of the First Crusade. They provided a narrative of its history, clearly based on chronicle accounts: the captures of Antioch and Jerusalem reflect a good knowledge of what actually happened, and the designer realized that the Saldjuks and Egyptians were different powers, indicated in the titles by *Parti* and *Arabes*. Charlemagne's legendary expedition to the East was celebrated in a second window, or in some panes within the Crusade window.[13] The occasion for which it was intended was perhaps the solemn departure of King Louis VII from St-Denis on 8 June 1147. The St-Denis glass does look like a special design for a unique occasion.

Another major artistic composition whose links with specific crusades are more obscure was the tympanum in the narthex at Vézelay. This was a great sculpture of the glorified Christ sending his power upon the apostles. In the outer bands of the composition are representations of the peoples of the world, including the distant dog-headed races of whom geographers had told them. The carving is a confident statement of the universal mission of the church, due, it has been suggested, to the influence of Abbot Peter the Venerable of Cluny. Vézelay was the site of Saint Bernard's preaching of the Second Crusade, and of the joint departure of the kings of France and England for the Third Crusade on 4 July 1190. It is more difficult to be sure that tympanum and crusade were genuinely connected. The tympanum looks like a depiction of the *divisio apostolorum,* when the apostles separated to take the gospel throughout the world, and does not contain overt references to crusading. On the other hand, the feast day of the *divisio* (15 July) was notable as being the very day when Jerusalem was liberated by the First Crusade, and contemporaries may have discerned a hidden pattern of references here. At all events, it was not a work of crusade propaganda in as obvious a sense as the St-Denis window.[14]

In the first 150 years of the movement we are able to find few single artistic compositions designed for raising troops for individual crusades. Almost every crusade produced a chronicle, or several chronicles, and it is tempting to look for narrative accounts on the walls of churches, designed for the glory of God and the encouragement of pilgrims. Here again, we almost draw a blank. Apart from the St-Denis window, there was a record of the history of the Fourth Crusade in the mosaic floor of the church of San Giovanni Evangelista at Ravenna. The floor was destroyed in the sixteenth century, but the few remaining panels can be best understood as part of a longer sequence. Unlike the glass at St-Denis, it would be readily accessible to the public, and is a very simple piece of work: crude representations in relatively cheap materials, and accompanied by other panels of popular proverbs, such as the story of the fox and goose.[15] Seen from our standpoint, it is difficult to believe that there were other major memorials which have disappeared without trace; but when we remember that there is no medieval mention of those at St-Denis and Ravenna, and that they survive only in copies or fragments, it is clear that nothing excludes the total disappearance of similar works at other major centres. We know, indeed, that in the 1250s the commitment of Henry III of England to the crusades, if it did not extend as far as a journey to the Holy Land, led him to have wall paintings made of their history on the walls of royal residences.[16]

Whatever may be the truth about extended historical narratives, there is little doubt that by 1200 the churches and great halls of the West had acquired allusions to the crusades, which would keep the fate of the Holy Land in the minds of the military classes, and, indeed, of the people as a whole. Enough remains to suggest that such paintings were once common. They were originally designed to fulfil a wide range of purposes: to give thanks for a victory or a safe return; to obtain the blessing of God on departure by an *ex voto* offering; to honour a king by displaying him as a warrior for Christendom; to celebrate the prowess of a Military Order and drum up support for its activities. A sequence of wall paintings was discovered after long obscurity in the little Templar chapel of Cressac in Charente where the whole chapel was once decorated. On the north wall we see a group of knights riding out from a Christian town to defeat a group of Saracen horsemen. The presence of a crowned Saracen has suggested that the decoration of the chapel commemorated a specific episode, the defeat of Nur al-Din in the battle of the Homs gap in September 1163. He was attacking Krak des Chevaliers, and in the Christian forces were a Templar contingent and two great nobles of western France—Hugh, count of Lusignan, and the brother of the count of Angoulême—who were returning from pilgrimage to Jerusalem. The decoration on the other walls is difficult or impossible to decipher, but it appears to include St George killing his dragon and a 'Romanesque rider'—two symbolic themes which I will discuss in a moment.[17] There are other sieges and battle scenes which may well have a crusade reference, but which cannot be firmly attributed. A bas-relief in the church of St-Nazaire, Carcassonne seems to commemorate the death of Simon of Montfort at Toulouse in 1218 during the Albigensian Crusade, although its purpose is obscure.[18] Often, we are left unsure of the exact subject which the designers had commissioned. It is natural to think that the scenes of battle on the Porta dei Leoni at San Nicola, Bari and the siege in the Salle d'Armes at Le Puy tell a crusade story, but there is no way of being certain.[19]

The rarity of funeral statues of the nobility in the twelfth century means that there are few commemorative portraits of crusaders. It is likely that a famous statue, formerly in the monastery of Belval, Lorraine, was an *ex voto,* an act of thanksgiving for a safe, if very delayed, return. It appears to show Count Hugh of Vaudémont, who came home from the Second Crusade after some fifteen years. His wife embraces her elderly husband, who has a cross on his breast and supports himself on a pilgrim staff.[20] Royal propaganda was beginning to present the ruler as a crusading hero. Frederick Barbarossa appears as a champion of the Cross and as a martyr, and a splendid English manuscript drawing of about 1250 shows a knight doing homage, conceivably Henry III making a commitment to a crusade.[21] A statue of St Louis and his wife, Marguerite of Provence, is a forceful statement of crusade ideology: Louis wears a robe with a cross, a sword and mail gauntlets, and carries a shield with the fleur-de-lys symbol. In his left hand, he holds a copy of the Holy Sepulchre.[22] Nobles, as well as kings, wanted to record their enthusiasm. It has been plausibly suggested that a group of knights on the wall at St-Jacques des Guérets in Loir et Cher is an *ex voto* for the departure of Count Peter I of Vendôme on crusade in 1248.[23] Problems of the survival and identification of works of art do not leave us with many specific references to crusades and crusaders before the middle of the thirteenth century. We can trace with more confidence the use of iconography to define the ideals of holy war, and conversely the invasion of Christian imagery by crusading themes. In art, as well as in its other expressions, crusading ideology cannot be isolated as a distinctive area within medieval culture. The word 'crusade' and its equivalents were slow to emerge, and were not much used. In canon law, Gratian was unaware of crusades as a distinct entity: crusading privileges were only defined legally in the thirteenth century, and then they were applied to a wide range of activities in the service of the church. Crusading settled like a cancer inside the body of medieval Christendom, adapting itself to its host in ways which the science of the time could not discern, and being carried to every part of the organism.

The image of the Christian life as a battle goes back at least to the injunction of Ephesians 6:10-20: 'Put on the whole armour of God'. In the visual arts, it was mediated to the West specially through the battle poem of Prudentius, the *Psychomachia,* composed about 400.[24] The warfare between individual virtues and their opposing vices, such as *largitas* and *avaritia,* was described there in very visual images, which tempted copyists to produce illuminated manuscripts. The first survives from the ninth century, but the archetype may well be much older than that. Prudentius was writing a psychological allegory about the triumph within the Christian soul of holiness over temptation, but once the imagery emerged into public life, the simplicity of his division between vice and virtue had drastic effects. It gave visual expression to the contemporary belief that, as *The Song of Roland* incisively put it, 'Christians are right and pagans are wrong'.

From the eleventh century onwards, there was a growing intensity in contemporary interest in the imagery of the *Psychomachia.* Illustrations were up-dated to show battles between modern knights. Single battles between a vice and a virtue were taken as subjects in the emerging art of figural sculpture. Joanne Norman has pointed to the capitals at Notre-Dame-du-Port, Clermont, as being 'an important example of the transition of the allegorical theme from manuscript to sculpture'.[25]

Given the probable use of model books in design, it was possible for images to travel both ways between Pruden-

tius's battles of virtue versus vice and pictures of contemporary warfare. 'Affronted knights' engaged in battle were a favourite theme in Saintonge, Poitou and south-western France generally, as well as in northern Spain, in the years around 1100. The purpose of these images varied. Some of the earliest ones have plausibly been interpreted as advertising the Peace of God or expressing the reliability of judicial combat.[26] These regions had a history marked by conflict with Muslim invaders, but it is difficult to be sure when 'affronted knights' first represented the battle between Christian and Muslim. There seems to be a convincing example on the 'screen' west front of Angoulême cathedral about 1130. On a capital at Cunault in Anjou, perhaps a few years later, a Christian knight is unquestionably confronted by a devilish Saracen.[27] The struggle of virtue against vice, having absorbed into itself the elements of war against the unbeliever, was further enriched by one of the great medieval epics, *The Song of Roland,* which began to be depicted all over Europe. Important examples are: the two knights (1139?) on the west front of Verona cathedral, one of them bearing the sword 'Durindarda'; the mosaic floor of Brindisi (1168?), which had the story of Roland at its margins; and the German manuscript of the *Ruolantes Liet,* illustrated perhaps about 1175. The wide dissemination of the theme suggests that there must have been earlier examples, but they are lost or cannot be conclusively identified.[28]

It was important to represent not only the conflict of faith with unbelief, but also its victory. In Saintonge and Poitou a clearly triumphant horseman, the 'Romanesque rider' as he is sometimes called, was a frequent figure. His majestic air has led to his identification with Constantine, himself a historic symbol of the triumph of the church over paganism.[29] Porches and west fronts began to incorporate another classical expression of triumph by adopting themes from Roman arches of victory. True, triumphalism is not necessarily directed against Islam, but at Moissac a carving showing the fall of the idols, and perhaps the entry into Jerusalem, underlines the crusade reference.

The first half of the twelfth century saw the abundant entrance of Islamic motifs, derived from buildings in the East and precious cloths brought back from the crusades, into the art of southern Europe. They were no doubt attractive as artistic novelties, but their presence was also part of the triumphal theme. Linda Seidel has suggested that façades were designed to celebrate the 'artistic piracy' practised in Spain and Syria by the lords who financed the building of the churches.[30] This view is confirmed by the presence of the themes in churches with special crusade associations, such as Le Puy, or Le Wast, near Boulogne, which was founded by Ida, the mother of Godfrey of Bouillon. The cathedral at Pisa seems to be an early example of this motif: an Islamic griffon, apparently captured in a raid on Palermo, was displayed prominently on its east end.[31] At San Nicola, Bari, the victory motif takes a rather different form in a splendid throne designed for Archbishop Elia (1098-1105), just after the victory of the First Crusade. The massive seat is upheld by distorted and exotic figures, which probably represent the pagan races who were being brought into obedience to Christendom.[32]

The artistic identification of Prudentius's virtues with crusaders is vividly illustrated in a carving at Civray (Vienne), where one of the virtues has a crusader cross on his sword.[33] It was confirmed by one of the most important steps towards an iconography of the crusades: the saints became Christian warriors. In all probability it was an irresistible tendency, but it had a historical basis. In the battle outside Antioch in June 1098 the Franks had been assisted by 'a countless host of men on white horses, whose banners were all white', led by Saints George, Mercurius and Demetrius.[34] The event is commemorated on the south doorway of the church at Fordington, near Dorchester, where the style of the figures suggests a date very shortly after 1100. George, with banner and lance, is overcoming the enemies of the faith, at the intercession of the knights kneeling behind him. The same episode is recorded in a painting at Poncé-sur-le-Loir, where Saracen soldiers are put to flight by white knights.[35] More commonly, artists loved to depict the victory of St George over the dragon, a theme which appeared in the West early in the twelfth century. There is a particularly triumphant one over the portal of the cathedral of St George at Ferrara, where George has already thrust his lance down the dragon's throat and is now brandishing his sword for the *coup de grâce*. The carving was designed by one of the greatest of the north Italian sculptors, Nicolà, about 1135.[36] By that time, George and the dragon had already appeared in another superb artwork, the Ganagobie mosaic (c. 1125) (Plate 5). The presence of George and the dragon among the holy war symbols at Cressac confirms that the legend was seen in a crusading context: in literature, it was located in Syria and linked to the conversion of a pagan king. By the 1160s, St Maurice too, on his home ground on a great reliquary in the treasury of Agaune in Switzerland, was bearing a cross on his shield and banner (Plate 7).

Chroniclers of the First Crusade readily adapted Biblical ideas to clarify God's work in the liberation of the Holy Land. Painters and sculptors did the same thing. Some of their devices were straightforward ones. On the central doorway of Autun cathedral, the last judgement (itself a new theme for grandiose sculpture) calls to their eternal reward two pilgrims, whose bags are marked with the cockleshell of Compostella and the cross of Jerusalem.[37] Other designs were more ambitious and original. The decoration of the south transept of Le Puy cathedral incorporates Biblical motifs quite rare in medieval churches: the life of Moses; three scenes from the life of Solomon, including his entry into Jerusalem; the building of the Temple after the return from exile(?); the entry of Christ into Jerusalem; and a scroll from Zephaniah 3:14: 'Rejoice and exult with all your heart, O daughter of Jerusalem!' Unfortunately the paintings are only recorded in a nineteenth-century copy, and are consequently difficult to date, but Anne Derbes has argued that they are best understood as a commemoration of the delivery of Jerusa-

lem in 1099, and a memorial to the great bishop Adhémar, who was the spiritual leader of the expedition until his death at Antioch.[38]

In Auxerre cathedral, the vaults of the apsidal crypt chapel are decorated with paintings of Christ, mounted on a white horse and carrying a jewelled cross, accompanied by four mounted angels. The reference is to Revelation 19:11-16, but the treatment is unusual. The design has been ascribed to Bishop Humbald (1092-1114), an assiduous decorator of the cathedral and enthusiast of the Holy Land; the suggestion is plausible, although less conclusive than the case of Le Puy.[39] Shortly after the Second Crusade, in 1151, the church of Schwarzrheindorf was consecrated. It was built by the archbishop of Cologne, Arnold of Wied, who had accompanied Conrad III to the Holy Land. The decorative scheme is very unusual indeed: twenty scenes from Ezekiel's visions of Jerusalem, concentrating mostly on the destruction of the city. Christ's purification of the Temple (itself, perhaps surprisingly, a very rare subject in Romanesque art) is prominent at the west end of the church. This concentration on Jerusalem must, one supposes, say something about expectations for the city in the aftermath of the failure in Palestine, but it is impossible for us to read the message: there may well be a strongly anti-Jewish element in this concentration on judgement. Perhaps the designer saw in the punishment of unfaithful Jerusalem a guarantee for the safety of the Christian city, in spite of the devastating setback which the Western armies had experienced.[40]

It was of course not necessary to find new Biblical iconography to express the holy war against Islam: ideas already established could be developed. The apocryphal gospel according to Matthew had told how, when the Holy Family fled to Egypt from Herod and entered a temple, 'all the idols fell to the ground so that all lay on their faces completely overturned and shattered'. It had long been believed, in defiance of reality, that Islam was idolatrous, and in the medieval mind its worship was not clearly distinguished from the paganism of the Greco-Roman world. This reputation was confirmed by the widely reported image of Antichrist discovered in the Temple by Tancred at the fall of Jerusalem.[41] One of the most dramatic presentations of the fall of the idols in face of the power of the Holy Family was on the portal at Moissac about 1125, as part of a rendering of the nativity stories from the Annunciation to the Flight into Egypt. Given the links between Moissac and Urban II, and imitation of classical triumphal architecture in its portal, one must agree with Michael Camille that 'the meaning of the Moissac image in its particular site has obvious bearings on the current concerns with Christian reconquest of the Holy Land'.[42] A few years before, the west front at Angoulême had shown a Saracen defeat in front, it seems, of an idol in a temple. The *Psychomachia* motif of the conflict of faith and idolatry obtains a full application to holy war in a poem written for the Second Crusade: *Fides cum idolatria pugnavit, teste gratia.* In Jean Bodin's play, the *Jeu de St Nicholas,* composed for performance at Amiens in 1202, a great deal of the action turns on the power struggle between the true image of St Nicholas and the false idol, and the action of the play suggests that the theme may have been far more familiar visually to contemporaries, from scenery and stage properties, than we would deduce from the surviving architectural fragments. Although there were Christian scholars who realized that Muslims did not worship idols, the obsession with the supposed idolatry of the enemy grew during the thirteenth century. A Parisian manuscript of William of Tyre, now in Baltimore, summarized the crusading movement in a diagram which consisted of the preaching of Urban II, the Crucifixion, a pilgrim at the Holy Sepulchre, and Muslims worshipping a naked idol on a column.[43]

It is increasingly accepted by historians that the primary and original purpose of Urban II in 1095 was the recovery of the Holy Sepulchre for Christendom. It is no accident that the crusades developed at a time when Western spirituality was placing increasing stress on the human life of Jesus, his suffering and death on the cross, and the apostolic life as a model of monastic discipline. This quest for the historical Jesus (if hardly in Albert Schweizer's sense of the words) was an authentic expression of contemporary attitudes, and involved an increased reverence for the sacred sites 'where his feet have trod'. Nativity sequences, 'majesties' of Mary and child, crucifixes, these and many other works of art could stimulate the imaginations of contemporaries and their love of the Holy Land, without the need to incorporate any specific allusion to the crusades. So, pre-eminently, could the arrival in the West of relics, of fragments of the True Cross and even soil from the Holy Sepulchre. The swelling pilgrimages of the eleventh and twelfth century brought such relics to parts of Europe which had not previously possessed them.

One aspect of this reverence for the Holy Places was the long-standing fascination of Christians with the actual form of the Holy Sepulchre. Its architecture seems to have been depicted, shortly after 400, in the great mosaic at Santa Pudenziana in Rome; just after 600 A.D. flasks designed for holy oil or earth were brought to the Lombard court, with diagrams of the Holy Places on them. Carolingian liturgy adopted Jerusalem ceremonial; the great churches incorporated areas which (symbolically at least) represented the Sepulchre; and manuscripts of the descriptions by Adomnan and Bede, which incorporated plans of the major Jerusalem churches, were widely distributed.[44] Attempts at a precise reproduction of the aedicule (or Sepulchre itself) or of the great fourth-century dome which overshadowed it, the Anastasis, preceded the crusades by more than a century. A diploma of Charles the Bald in 887 described the complex of churches at Santo Stefano, Bologna, as 'Jerusalem', although the significance of this is far from clear.[45] Bishop Konrad of Konstanz (935-75), assiduous pilgrim to the Holy Land and confidant of the Ottonian court, built a copy of the Sepulchre at his cathedral. It was entirely rebuilt *in situ* in the thirteenth century. The oldest such copy which survives intact is at Aquileia, built before 1077.

It is scarcely surprising that returning crusaders wanted to provide themselves with copies of the Sepulchre. The unusually fine version of the Anastasis at Holy Sepulchre, Northampton, was built by Simon of Senlis on his return from the First Crusade (Plate 8). The church of the Holy Sepulchre at Asti in Piemonte, long supposed to be a baptistery, is most naturally ascribed to Bishop Landulf after his return from the Holy Land in 1103.[46] In the distant Orkneys, the Jerusalem pilgrim Earl Hakon Paulsson (died 1122) built a small round church, of which the apse still remains, at his seat at Orphir (Plate 9). The site of the Round Church at Cambridge was granted by Abbot Reinald of Ramsey (1114-30) to the 'fraternity of the Holy Sepulchre' (probably an association of pilgrims) to build there 'in honour of God and the Holy Sepulchre'. At Pisa, which had close links with Jerusalem in the middle years of the twelfth century, the architect Diotisalvi produced two buildings inspired by the Anastasis: the delicate little church of Santo Sepolcro on the left bank of the Arno, and the majestic baptistery beside the cathedral, which was similarly designed as an imitation of the great rotunda at Jerusalem.[47] Bologna acquired a rather remarkable version of the Holy Sepulchre, and the Templars favoured round or polygonal buildings for some of their chapels. Along the same line of thinking, churches and chapels with crusading links were decorated with themes reminiscent of the Holy Sepulchre, such as the entombment of Christ.[48]

All these, and other such memorials, pointed to Jerusalem. Joshua Prawer commented that the Frankish rebuilding of the city was more ambitious than any other before the twentieth century. Logically, this survey should end with an examination of their work there, which in some senses was the supreme expression of the iconography of crusading. It is appropriate, however, that Bernard Hamilton himself has spared us the necessity, by illustrating in one of his most impressive articles how Jerusalem was rebuilt by its Latin rulers, not simply to provide pictures for the illiterate, but to form 'a visual expression of the faith of the crusaders, and indeed of that of the whole Christian west, and a symbol of their deep devotion to the humanity of Christ'.[49]

Notes

1. Gratian, 'Decretum', D. 3 de cons. c. 27, in E. Friedberg, ed., *Corpus iuris canonici,* 2nd edn, 2 vols (Leipzig, 1879), 1, col. 1360.

2. For abundant references to medieval statements based on Gregory, and their influence on modern thinkers, see the important article by L.G. Duggan, 'Was Art Really "the Book of the Illiterate"?', *Word and Image* 5 (1989), pp. 227-51.

3. Gerhoh, 'De investigatione Antichristi', *MGH Libelli,* 3.393.

4. For observations about crusading propaganda as a whole, see S. Menache, *The Vox Dei: Communication in the Middle Ages* (Oxford, 1990), chapters 5 and 8. Recent studies of crusade preaching include P.J. Cole, *The Preaching of the*

Crusades to the Holy Land, 1095-1270 (Cambridge, Mass., 1991), and C.T. Maier, *Preaching the Crusades: Mendicant Friars and the Cross in the Thirteenth Century* (Cambridge, 1994). For crusading songs, see the references in C. Morris, 'Propaganda for War: The Dissemination of the Crusading Ideal in the Twelfth Century', in *The Church and War,* ed. W.J. Sheils, *Studies in Church History* 21 (Oxford, 1983), pp. 79-101, and M. Routledge, 'Songs', in *The Oxford Illustrated History of the Crusades,* ed. J. Riley-Smith (Oxford, 1995), pp. 91-111. There is a discussion of liturgy as propaganda by A. Linder, '*Deus venerunt gentes:* Psalm 78 (79) in the Liturgical Commemoration of the Destruction of Latin Jerusalem', in *Medieval Studies in Honour of Avrom Saltman,* ed. B. Albert, Y. Friedman and S. Schwarzfuchs (Ramat-Gan, 1995), pp. 145-72.

5. See the introduction to *Iconography at the Crossroads,* ed. B. Cassidy (Princeton, 1993). There is an important analysis of the relation of text, image and orality by M. Camille, 'Seeing and Reading: Some Visual Implications of Medieval Literacy and Illiteracy', *Art History* 8 (1985), pp. 26-49.

6. A. Henry, ed., *Biblia pauperum* (Aldershot, 1987), pp. 17-18.

7. See, for this whole subject, J. Baschet, 'Inventivité et sérialité des images médiévales', *Annales: histoire, sciences sociales* 51 (1996), pp. 93-133.

8. There is a valuable summary of the discussion about the purpose of the miniatures, and their relation to the text, by L. Lawton, 'The Illustration of Late Medieval Secular Texts', in *Manuscripts and Readers in Fifteenth-Century England,* ed. D. Pearsall (Cambridge, 1983), pp. 41-69.

9. English translation in F. Gabrieli, *Arab Historians of the Crusades,* trans. E.J. Costello (Berkeley, 1969), pp. 208-9.

10. Gabrieli, *Arab Historians,* pp. 182-3. The Winchester Psalter of c. 1150 has precisely such a picture, with Jews and (seemingly) Muslims tormenting Christ: *The Oxford Illustrated History of Christianity,* ed. J. McManners (Oxford, 1990), p. 183.

11. Gerald of Wales, *The Journey through Wales and the Description of Wales,* trans. L. Thorpe (Harmondsworth, 1978), p. 76.

12. R. Röhricht, ed., *Quinti belli sacri scriptores minores, Société de l'Orient latin, série historique* 2 (Geneva, 1879), pp. 11-13, 19.

13. See Plates 1-2. The glass was lost at the time of the French Revolution, but had been copied by B. de Montfaucon, *Les monumens de la monarchie française,* 5 vols (Paris, 1729-33), 1.384-97. See also L. Grodecki, *Les vitraux de St-Denis* (Paris, 1976), pp. 115-21, and E.A.R. Brown and M.W. Cothren, 'The Twelfth-Century Crusading Window of the Abbey of St-Denis', *Journal of the Warburg and Courtauld Institutes* 49 (1986), pp. 1-40. This article suggests a possible date after the Second Crusade, which I do not myself find convincing.

14. See A. Katzenellenbogen, 'The Central Tympanum at Vézelay', *Art Bulletin* 26 (1944), pp. 141-51, and M.D. Taylor, 'The Pentecost at Vézelay', *Gesta* 19 (1980), pp. 9-15. There are photographs in these articles, and in M.F. Hearn, *Romanesque Sculpture* (Oxford, 1981), p. 168.

15. Plate 3. The date 1213 has been suggested for this pavement (G. Bovini, *Ravenna* [Ravenna, 1979]): under Innocent III the Latin conquest of Constantinople was being seen as an unambiguous victory and a great step towards the reunion of the Catholic church.

16. Two favourite themes were the capture of Antioch, and the legendary duel of Richard I and Saladin. See *The History of the King's Works,* gen. ed. H.M. Colvin, 6 vols (London, 1963-82), 1.128-9.

17. *Oxford Illustrated History of the Crusades,* p. 196 shows a Templar knight at Cressac, with motif on his shield and banner. See also P. Deschamps, 'Combats de cavalerie et épisodes de croisades dans les peintures murales du XIIe et du XIIIe siècle', *Orientalia christiana periodica* 13 (1947), pp. 454-74.

18. Photograph in H. Kraus, *The Living Theatre of Medieval Art* (London, 1967), p. 135.

19. There is a good account of the progressive investigation of this painting by F. Énaud, 'Peintures murales découvertes dans une dépendance de la cathédrale du Puy-en-Velay: problèmes d'interprétation', *Monuments historiques* 14/4 (1968), pp. 30-76, although the final interpretation is so complex that one wonders if viewers could understand it.

20. Illustration in *Oxford Illustrated History of the Crusades,* p. 69. It seems that Hugh returned about 1163 and died in 1165. See P. Deschamps, *Au temps des croisades* (Paris, 1972), pp. 81-3, and M. François, *Histoire des comtes et du comté de Vaudémont* (Nancy, 1935).

21. *Oxford Illustrated History of the Crusades,* pp. 38, 79 (for Barbarossa); 51 (Henry III?).

22. Illustrated in R. Delort, *Life in the Middle Ages* (London, 1974), p. 115.

23. Deschamps, 'Combats de cavalerie', p. 463.

24. See A. Katzenellenbogen, *Allegories of the Virtues and Vices in Medieval Art* (London, 1939), and J.S. Norman, *Metamorphoses of an Allegory: The Iconography of the Psychomachia in Medieval Art* (New York, 1988).

25. Norman, *Metamorphoses of an Allegory,* pp. 29-32. Unfortunately, it is impossible to date the capitals at Clermont, beyond saying that they must be roughly 1075/1125.

26. R. Lejeune and J. Stiennon, *La légende de Roland dans l'art du moyen âge,* 2nd edn (Brussels, 1967), pp. 19-25, on 'Peace of God' capitals. For the judicial combat theme at Cluny, see F. Cardini, *Le crociate tra il mito e la storia* (Rome, 1971), tav. XIIa; the correct text for this is under tav. XV.

27. Lejeune and Stiennon, *Roland,* pp. 29-30 and 88, and Hearn, *Romanesque Sculpture,* pp. 181-5. D.J.A. Ross, 'The Iconography of Roland', *Medium Aevum* 37 (1968), pp. 46-65, is sceptical about suggestions of earlier instances of warfare with Islam, but agrees that this is portrayed at Angoulême and Canault. For the capital at Cunault, see Plate 4. Anjou had very strong links with the kingdom of Jerusalem from 1129 onwards.

28. See Lejeune and Stiennon, *Roland,* passim, for possible earlier occurrences.

29. The most careful discussion of the 'Constantine thesis' is to be found in R. Crozet, 'Nouvelles remarques sur les cavaliers sculptés ou peints dans les églises romanes', *Cahiers de civilisation médiévale* 1 (1958), pp. 27-36. There are other studies of the teasing iconography of these façades in Saintonge and elsewhere by H. Le Roux, 'Figures équestres et personnages du nom de Constantin aux XIe et XIIe siècles', *Bulletin de la société des antiquaires de l'Ouest et des musées de Poitiers,* sér. 4, 12 (1974), pp. 379-94; L. Seidel, 'Holy Warriors: The Romanesque Rider and the Fight against Islam', in *The Holy War,* ed. T.P. Murphy (Columbus, 1976), pp. 33-54; and especially her *Songs of Glory: The Romanesque Façades of Aquitaine* (Chicago, 1981). See also A. Tcherikover, 'Une invention de XIXe siècle: les prétendus cavaliers de la cathédrale d'Angoulême', *Cahiers de civilisation médiévale* 38 (1995), pp. 275-8.

30. Seidel, *Songs of Glory,* pp. 79-82.

31. The cathedral was begun in 1063, financed by spoil from the raid on Palermo. We do not know when the decision was taken to put the captured article in its prominent position. The most striking example of display of booty is at San Marco, Venice, where the Pala d'Oro, the façade and the treasury proclaim victory over Byzantium rather than over Islam.

32. Hearn, *Romanesque Sculpture,* pp. 80-1. The statement by a later chronicler that the throne was a gift of Urban II in 1098 was probably a misunderstanding of the inscription.

33. Cardini, *Le crociate,* tav. XI.

34. *GF,* p. 69.

35. For the Fordington sculpture, see *Oxford Illustrated History of the Crusades,* p. 80. On Poncé see P. Deschamps, 'Combats de cavalerie', pp. 454-74. The St George wall paintings at Hardham in Sussex do not seem to allude to his appearance at the Battle of Antioch.

36. Plate 6. The statue is attributed to him by the inscription surrounding the tympanum. See S. Stocchi, *Italia Romanica 6: L'Emilia-Romagna* (Milan, 1984), pp. 342-50.

37. Cardini, *Le crociate,* tav. VIII.

38. A. Derbes, 'A Crusading Fresco Cycle at the Cathedral of Le Puy', *Art Bulletin* 73/4 (1991), pp. 561-76.

39. D. Denny, 'A Romanesque Fresco in Auxerre Cathedral', *Gesta* 25 (1986), pp. 197-202.

40. A. Derbes, 'The Frescoes of Schwarzrheindorf, Arnold of Wied and the Second Crusade', in *The Second Crusade and the Cistercians,* ed. M. Gervers (New York, 1992), pp. 141-54.

41. R.C. Schwinges, *Kreuzzugsideologie und Toleranz: Studien zu Wilhelm von Tyrus* (Stuttgart, 1977), Part II; M. Camille, *The Gothic Idol: Ideology and Image-Making in Medieval Art* (Cambridge, 1989), pp. 140ff.

42. Hearn, *Romanesque Sculpture,* with illustration at p. 175; Camille, *The Gothic Idol,* pp. 4-9; L. Seidel, 'Images of the Crusades in Western Art: Models and Metaphors', in *The Meeting of Two World: Cultural Exchange between East and West during the Period of the Crusades,* ed. V.P. Goss and C.V. Bornstein (Kalamazoo, 1986), pp. 377-91.

43. *Oxford Illustrated History of the Crusades,* p. 44.

44. A twelfth-century ground plan of the Holy Sepulchre still clearly reflects the influence of the Adomnan/Bede plans: *Oxford Illustrated History of the Crusades,* p. 115. The source and extent of the Jerusalem influence on Carolingian liturgy is disputed, but for a persuasive survey see C. Heitz, *Recherches sur les rapports entre architecture et liturgie à l'époque carolingienne* (Paris, 1963).

45. The Leverhulme Trust generously made it possible for me to visit some of the important sites in Italy and southern Germany. The issue of 'Jerusalem in the West' will be discussed in an article, 'Bringing Jerusalem to the West: S. Stefano, Bologna, from the Fifth to the Twentieth Century', in *Church Retrospective,* ed. R.N. Swanson, *Studies in Church History* 33. The cemetery chapel consecrated in 822 under Abbot Eigil at Fulda is sometimes listed as the first precise copy, but the inscription by Hrabanus Maurus probably meant simply that there was earth from the Holy Sepulchre there. See O. Ellger, *Die Michaelskirche zu Fulda als Zeugnis des Totensorge* (Fulda, 1988).

46. S. Casartelli-Novelli, 'L'église du St-Sépulchre ou le baptistère St-Pierre-Consavia', *Congrès archéologique* 129 (1977), pp. 358-63.

47. The photograph in *Oxford Illustrated History of Christianity,* p. 207, shows the baptistery at Pisa, to the front of the Piazza dei Miracoli. The gallery is a later substitution.

48. *Oxford Illustrated History of the Crusades,* p. 89, for the Holy Sepulchre chapel at Winchester

cathedral, which was perhaps painted on the occasion of Bishop Peter des Roches' crusade of 1227.

49. B. Hamilton, 'Rebuilding Zion: The Holy Places of Jerusalem in the Twelfth Century', in *Renaissance and Renewal in Christian History,* ed. D. Baker, *Studies in Church History* 14 (Oxford, 1977), pp. 105-16. More recently, the ideology of crusading art in the Holy Land itself has been magnificently examined by J. Folda, *The Art of the Crusaders in the Holy Land, 1098-1187* (Cambridge, 1995). The crusader buildings at the church of the Holy Sepulchre are illustrated in detail there, and much more briefly in *Oxford Illustrated History of the Crusades,* pp. 163, 212-13.

FURTHER READING

Criticism

Archer, T. A. *The Crusade of Richard I: 1189-92.* New York: G. P. Putnam's Sons, 1889, 395 p.

Collection of contemporary sources that discuss the history of the Third Crusade, and the involvement of King Richard I in it.

Atiya, Aziz Suryal. *The Crusade in the Later Middle Ages.* London: Methuen and Co. Ltd., 1938, 604 p.

Study of the crusading movement in the fourteenth and fifteenth centuries, offering a background of the earlier Crusades, the pilgrimages and propaganda leading up to the later Crusades, and an analysis of these later crusading expeditions.

————. *The Crusade: Historiography and Bibliography.* Bloomington: Indiana University Press, 1962, 170 p.

Provides a historiography and bibliography that stresses Arabic literature and sources. The material is arranged to support the author's distinction between the Crusade (as a movement) and the Crusades (as individual military expeditions).

Lamb, Harold. *The Crusades: The Whole Story of the Crusades Originally Published in Two Volumes as "Iron Men and Saints" and "The Flame of Islam."* New York: Doubleday & Company, 1930, 490 p.

History of the Crusades based on several eyewitness chronicles.

Newhall, Richard A. *The Crusades.* New York: Henry Holt and Company, 1927, 110 p.

Historical analyses covering the historical period leading up to the Crusades, the first four Crusades, and the social, commercial, and cultural effects in the aftermath of the Crusades.

Paetow, Louis J., ed. *The Crusades and Other Historical Essays.* 1928, Reprint. Freeport, N.Y.: Books for Libraries Press, 1968, 419 pages.

Collection of historical essays on the Crusades, including: studies of the German pilgrimage of 1064-65, Pope Urban II's conception of the First Crusade, and the *Gesta,* as well as examinations of various figures and events of the Crusades.

Peters, Edward, ed. *The First Crusade: The Chronicle of Fulcher of Chartres and Other Source Materials,* second ed. Philadelphia: University of Pennsylvania Press, 1971, 317 p.

Collection of source materials pertaining to the First Crusade, including: several versions of Pope Urban II's speech, various letters of Pope Urban II, letters of the Crusaders, Book I of Fulcher's chronicle, and several versions of the Peter the Hermit legend. Also included are accounts of the 1096-97 journey to and siege of Constantinople, the capture of Nicaea in 1097, the capture of Antioch in 1097-98, and the capture of Jerusalem in 1099.

Routledge, Michael. "Songs" in *The Oxford Illustrated History of the Crusades,* edited by Jonathan Riley–Smith, pp. 92–111. Oxford: Oxford University Press, 1995.

Demonstrates that the coinciding of the early Crusades with an evolution in both France and Germany of vernacular literature resulted in the creation of songs—written in the vernacular—dealing with or alluding to the Crusades.

Jean de Joinville
1225-1317

French crusader and chronicler.

INTRODUCTION

Joinville was a crusader turned chronicler. After fighting in the Seventh Crusade (1248-54) with King Louis IX of France, Joinville composed an account of his adventures with King Louis, who was canonized in 1297. The historical account, entitled *Vie de Saint Louis* (1309), or the *Life of Saint Louis,* is written more as an autobiographical account of Joinville's shared experiences with the King, rather than as an objective biography of Saint Louis. In the *Vie,* Joinville's reverence for his King is obvious, yet it is not blind; in some instances Joinville's criticism or questioning of King Louis is apparent. Joinville has been praised by critics for his vivid description of the era in which he lived and the war in which he fought with Saint Louis.

BIOGRAPHICAL INFORMATION

Born in Champagne to a noble, crusading family, Jean was the second son of Simon, Lord of Joinville. After the death of his father and older brother, Jean—still in his teens—became Lord of Joinville. As a youth he served as a vassal to his lord, the Comte de Champagne. In 1239, Joinville married Alix of Grandpré; the couple had two sons. Following the lead of King Louis IX, Joinville took the cross in 1244. Sailing with the fleet from southern France, Joinville joined the Seventh Crusade and followed King Louis to Cyprus. He fought in the battle of Mansourah in 1248 and along with King Louis was captured by the Bedouins. After the King paid a large ransom, he and Joinville were released from prison. From 1250 to 1254, Joinville lived near King Louis at Acre, Caesarea, and Jaffa, serving as the King's counselor. They returned to France in 1254 and Joinville retired to his estate. At some point, perhaps as early as 1272, it is believed that he began writing down an account of the events of 1248 through 1254. Around 1298, King Louis's Grandniece, Jeanne (Countess of Champagne and Queen of Navarre), requested that Joinville write an account of King Louis's life. Great interest in King Louis had been generated by his being canonized by Pope Boniface VIII in 1297. Joinville complied and began dictating the *Vie de Saint Louis.* Although there is some question of when different portions of the account were written, the work was completed by 1309. Joinville died in 1317.

MAJOR WORKS

Before writing the *Vie de Saint Louis,* Joinville composed a religious pamphlet in which both texts and illustrations are used to expound upon the Christian Creed. *Credo* was written between 1250 and 1251, although the only extant version is dated 1287.. There is some conjecture related to the nature of the revisions made in the later version. The *Vie de Saint Louis* covers the years 1248 through 1254, when Joinville accompanied King Louis on the Seventh Crusade. In general, Joinville speaks reverently of the king and emphasizes throughout the work the virtues of loyalty and *preudome.* (*Preudome* has been described as a religious interpretation of the concept of chivalry.) Filled with Joinville's anecdotes, descriptions of people, as well as moralizing, the *Vie de Saint Louis* is comprised of three sections: an introduction, which includes a dedicatory letter and the teachings of Saint Louis; the central section, which focuses on Saint Louis's early life, his reign as King, and his deeds during the crusade; and a closing section, which discusses the King's later years and also includes a postscript

TEXTUAL HISTORY

There are three primary extant manuscripts of the *Vie de Saint Louis*. The earliest, known as the Brussels manuscript, may date from as early as 1320, according to some scholars. The two others are believed to date from the sixteenth century. Most scholars agree that the two sixteenth-century manuscripts have a common source, but one which does not predate the Brussels manuscript. Although the first printed edition appeared in 1547, edited by Antoine de Rieux, the manuscript on which he based the edition has not been found and is believed to be corrupt. The first edition, which scholars believe may closely resemble Joinville's original, was printed in 1761, following the discovery of the Brussels manuscript and one of the sixteenth-century manuscripts. What has become the standard edition of the text appeared in 1874, in French, edited by Natalis De Wailly.

CRITICAL RECEPTION

Critical discussions of the *Vie de Saint Louis* are centered on two main areas: the dating of the work and Joinville's writing style. Alfred Foulet divides the work into five sections, and suggests dates of composition for each section. The five sections he identifies are: (1) the dedicatory letter; (2) the teachings of Saint Louis; (3) the life and reign of Louis IX including his later years; (4) the postscript; and (5) the final date of the book. After analyzing specific portions of the work, Foulet concludes that sections 1 and 5 were probably composed in 1309; sections 2 and 3 in 1305-06; and section 4 between 1306 and 1309. Foulet finds it highly unlikely that, as some scholars contend, approximately three-quarters of the book consist of personal recollections composed as early as 1272-73. Rene Hague, on the other hand, in his introduction to De Wailly's edition, suggests that Joinville had began writing his account in 1272. Maureen Slattery reviews the dating debate, summarizing the two schools of thought on the subject. Slattery notes that a large group of scholars maintain that the work was composed in two stages, with the main account of the Crusade having been written around 1272. In 1304-05, when Joinville was asked to compose a biography for the court, he officially dictated his original account and added sections to the beginning and end. Slattery explains that a smaller group of scholars, including Foulet, believe that the bulk of the work was composed around 1305-06, not earlier. Having outlined both views, Slattery emphasizes what both schools have in common: both use internal textual date references to date the work's final form (a method which Slattery finds to be inconclusive), and both agree that the work "emerged from stages of both oral and written development." Slattery stresses that the visual and oral sources deserve more weight than the written sources which informed Joinville's text, as the work is "one of a witness who saw and heard about the king, then dictated

his memories." Other critics have focused their attention on the style of Joinville's *Vie de Saint Louis*. In the introduction to her translation, Ethel Wedgwood praises the "directness and simplicity" of Joinville's style, although she also comments that he is neither an accomplished chronicler, nor a storyteller. In describing the anecdotal and moralizing tone of the book, Frank Marzials observes that Joinville's account is colored by the fact that he wrote about his days as young soldier when he was an elderly man. Helmut Hatzfeld examines both the style and language of the *Vie,* observing that Joinville's method of description employs the linkage of a "few well-observed features by a 'pale' line of action." In addition, Hatzfeld notes that Joinville avoids epithets, lengthy descriptions, and similes, but he does make use of exaggeration. Joinville prefers consecutive clauses, a habit characteristic of early French prose. Taking a different approach to Joinville's language, Newton S. Bement analyzes the way in which Latin remnants infused the French used at the time Joinville wrote the *Vie.* Bement explains that while such remnants are often viewed by modern critics as disorderly or confusing elements in the text, the remnants were common to thirteenth- and fourteenth-century speakers and writers of French.

PRINCIPAL WORKS

Credo (pamphlet) 1250–51
Vie de Saint Louis (memoirs) 1309

Principal English Translations

The Memoirs of the Lord of Joinville (translated by Ethel Wedgwood) 1906
Memoirs of the Crusades by Villehardouin and de Joinville (translated by Frank Marzials) 1908

CRITICISM

Ethel Wedgwood (essay date 1906)

SOURCE: A preface to *The Memoirs of the Lord of Joinville: A New English Version,* E. P. Dutton, 1906, pp. vi-ix.

[*In the following essay, Wedgwood comments on Joinville's life and his style in* Vie de Saint Louis. *Wedgwood observes that while Joinville was not a skilled chronicler, his work is characterized by "directness and simplicity."*]

Six hundred years ago, when the histories of Europe still lay buried among the Latin Charter Rolls of great abbeys,—before Piers Plowman had yet voiced the English conscience in the English tongue,—and when Dante was just turning to look back on half his life's journey,—John, Lord of Joinville, full of days and honours, began to write for his liege lady his recollections of her husband's grandfather, St. Louis.

Like many others of that line of great French memoir-writers which he heads,—such, for instance, as Commines, Sully, and Marbot,—Joinville was first of all a man of action, and only in the second place a man of letters; and for this very reason his book has that directness and simplicity which appeals to the common humanity of all ages. He is no skilled chronicler, like his compatriot the warrior and statesman Villehardouin; he is no born story-teller, like Villani or Froissart; but a hard-headed, plain-minded man to whom penmanship is no art, and who writes simply because he loved his friend and believes that he has a duty to his posterity.

John, Lord of Joinville, was hereditary Seneschal of Champagne and head of a family already illustrious for its Crusaders. By blood and old family friendship he was closely united with the great house of Brienne, and could claim cousinship with its famous cadet, John, King of Jerusalem, father-in-law to two emperors, and himself an emperor.[1] Born in 1225, Joinville was only twenty-three when he joined King Louis in the disastrous Seventh Crusade; and before he was thirty he was settled again on his estates, having escaped every conceivable peril by land and sea, to which nineteen out of every twenty men had succumbed. For the rest of his life he stayed at home, managing his estate and taking such part in public affairs as his position required. When, at nearly eighty years old, he began his Memoirs, he had lived beyond the reigns of three kings, and saw France, through the selfishness of her rulers, well advanced on that downward road that led to the coarse vice and brutality of the Hundred Years War, and to the corruption and luxurious bestiality of the last Valois kings. But Joinville, old, still keeps untainted the spirit of his youth. He writes in the mood of that golden age, the reign of the "Holy King," when still "from Courts men Courtesy did call"; and his book is a lasting witness to the influence of that master who thought it "a vile thing for a gentleman to get drunk," and who punished foul words as a crime.

His book brings us into some of the best company in the world. Joinville himself, as he appears through his narrative, is a fine sample of the great baron of feudal times. True to his word, firm in his justice, shrewd in business, intellectually limited, he approaches closely to the modern popular idea of an English squire. He is pious, not with the exalted visionary piety of the King, but with the practical morality that recognizes his duty to God in his duty to his own subjects.

The King, seen through Joinville's record, is a far nobler character than he is represented by his extravagant monkish eulogists,—Geoffrey de Beaulieu, Guillaume de Nangis, and the rest; and that he was a hero to his own commonplace intimates is a much greater testimony to his personality than any enumeration of his qualifications for saintship.

And of the rest of that circle of gallant and pious gentlemen of whom Joinville was the friend and comrade, there are many who deserve a lasting fame. Peter of Brittany, gashed and retreating, yet pausing to scoff at the disorderly rabble that jostle past him in panic; Walter of Brienne, like a second Regulus—tortured and helpless, exhorting his friends to resistance; Erard of Syverey, wounded to death, pausing to weigh the honour of his family against the chance of safety; Walter of Châtillon, crying his war-cry in the deserted street and turning single-handed to sweep away a horde of infidels; the good Bishop of Soissons, who, rather than turn his back on Jerusalem, "hastened his journey to God"; these are fit heroes for song and story through all time.

Historians laboriously bridge over the gulf that divides us from the past, and their bricks and mortar make but a long and dreary road; but in a narrative such as Joinville's, the spirit of the writer speaks direct to the spirit of the reader; their points of difference vanish away, leaving only what is common to both; and for a while the man of the thirteenth century joins hands with the man of the twentieth, and they stand side by side in the midst of that vast twilight of the unrecorded ages, compared with whose depths a thousand years are but as yesterday.

Notes

1. For what is known of the life of John of Joinville and the history of his family, see Delaborde's delightful book, "Jean de Joinville."

Frank Marzials (essay date 1908)

SOURCE: An introduction to *Memoirs of the Crusaders by Villehardouin and de Joinville,* translated by Frank Marzials, E. P. Dutton, 1908, pp. xxvii-xxxiii.

[*In the following essay, Marzials provides a brief biographical discussion of Joinville, followed by an overview of the style of* Vie de Saint Louis. *Marzials also analyzes Joinville's characterization of King Louis.*]

. . . Joinville was born, it is believed, in 1224. He embarked with St. Lewis for the Crusade on the 28th August 1248; he returned to France in the July of 1254. His Memoirs, as he himself tells us, were written, *i.e.* concluded, in the month of October, 1309, that is to say, when he was eighty-five years of age, and more than half a century after the events he had set himself to narrate. Thus while Villehardouin writes as a middle-aged soldier, succinctly, soberly, with eye intent on important events, and only casually alive to the passing show of things, Joinville writes as an old man looking lovingly, lingeringly, at the past—garrulous, discursive, glad of a listener. Nothing is beneath his attention. He lingers here, lingers there, picks up an anecdote as he goes along, tells how people looked, and what they wore, describes the manners and customs of the outlandish folk with whom he is brought into contact; has his innocent superstitions his suspicions of spiritualistic influence, stops to tell you about a tumbler's tricks, about a strange fossil that has struck his fancy; illustrates, discusses, moralises; reports at length his conversations, especially with the king; and would have a tendency to repeat himself in any case, even if he had not adopted, to begin with, a defective plan of narration, that involved much repetition. And with such a charm in it all! The man is so simple, so honest, so lovable. Fine fellow as he undoubtedly is, he makes claim to no heroic sentiments—tells you how he was afraid to turn his eyes towards his castle as he went away, leaving wife and children behind him—how he trembled, partly with fear, when he fell into the hands of the enemy. And his judgments upon his fellows are so essentially the judgments of a gentleman. Then he has the graphic gift: we see what he sees, and we know the people that he brings before us. All that world of the Crusade lives in his pages. Not even in Chaucer's immortal "Prologue" do we get so near to the life of the Middle Ages.

Yes, as one reads the chronicle, it is impossible not to love the chronicler. If a snob be, according to Thackeray's definition, one who meanly admires mean things, then surely one who grandly admires heroic things may be pronounced a hero. And Joinville had before him in St. Lewis a high ideal of Christian manhood, and all his heart went out in love and veneration for the friend, long dead when he wrote, who had been to him king and saint. He looks back with pride at that great figure which had loomed so large in his earlier manhood. He sees him once more as he rode in the field among his knights, flashing in arms, overtopping them all, the goodliest presence there.[1] He dwells upon his old chief's fearlessness, his courage before the enemy, his undaunted fortitude under the combined assault of disaster, defeat, and sickness unto death. He marks his refusal to selfishly abandon the people God had committed to his charge and secure his own safety. He notes that neither the prospect of death, nor torture, has power to move him one hair's-breadth from what he holds to be right, and notes also how, in his unswerving rectitude, he will keep to his word, even though that word has been given to the infidel, and though the infidel are far from keeping a reciprocal faith. Then, in more peaceful times, in the ordinary course of justice, he shows the king's determination that right shall be done, with no respect of persons, between man and man, and as between monarch and subject, and his passionate desire for a pure administration. And when, finally, St. Lewis is canonised—when Rome sets its seal and mark upon him for all time—then the loyal, loving servant seems to utter a kind of *Nunc dimittis*. Joinville feels that he himself may now depart in peace.

Not that there is any Boswellism about him. All that St. Lewis does is not of necessity good in Joinville's eyes.

The servant keeps his own judgment quite clear even when judging of his master's acts, and is unduly swayed neither by love nor reverence. Thus, when the Abbot of Cluny gives the king two costly palfreys as a preliminary to a discussion on certain business matters pending between them, Joinville does not hesitate to ask the king whether the gift had inclined him to listen with greater favour to what the abbot had to say, and to push home the obvious moral—a moral, be it said, in view of certain municipal facts, which the twentieth century might lay to heart with the same advantages as the contemporaries of St. Lewis.

Again, when some fifteen years after the return from Palestine, St. Lewis, prematurely old and broken in health, determines to turn Crusade once again (1270), Joinville not only refuses to accompany him, but evidently does all he can to dissuade his master from a policy so disastrous. "I thought that those committed a mortal sin who advised him to undertake that journey," says the upright counsellor, who was no parasite; and he thanks God he had no part or lot in that expedition.

And so too Joinville is not satisfied of the king's "good manners" in his relations with the queen. The queen, after being brought to bed of my lady Blanche, journeys by sea from Jaffa to rejoin the king at Sayette. Joinville goes to the shore to meet her—there is nothing to show why the king did not lovingly perform this office himself—and brings her up to the castle, reporting her arrival to the king, who is in his chapel. The king knew where Joinville was going, and has delayed the sermon till his return, and asks whether his wife and children are in good health. "And I bring these things to your notice," says Joinville, "because I had been in his company five years, and never yet had he spoken a word to me about the queen, or about his children—nor to any one else, so far as I ever heard. And, so it seems to me," adds the good chronicler, "there was some want of good manners" (*mores* in the Latin sense, I take it), "in being thus a stranger to one's wife and children."

To this the reader will, no doubt, be inclined to subscribe. Indeed, the want of more obviously cordial relations between the king and queen which may almost be inferred from Joinville's book, affords matter for surprise, seeing who and what that king and queen both were. For if Lewis was a hero and a saint, Margaret of Provence, the "falcon-hearted dove" of Mrs. Hemans' poem, was a heroine, and not all unfit, as men and women go, for canonisation. When she figures in Joinville's narrative it is as a woman altogether brave and lovable, and possessing a sense of humour withal. There are few more striking scenes in history than those in which she appears as a queen, about to become a mother, her husband and his host prisoners, the city in which she is, beleaguered and likely to fall—and kneels before the good old knight, and asks him to strike off her head or ever she falls into the enemy's hands; or that second scene, on the day after the birth of the child—Tristram they called him for sorrow—when she summons round her bed those who would basely surrender the city, and appealing to the babe's weakness and her own woman-hood, seeks to inspire them with her own courage.

One might have thought, *primâ facie,* that there would be some record of the meeting between king and queen after scenes like these, some written word to show how the queen greeted the king when he came out of captivity and sore peril, and how the king acknowledged her proud bearing in extreme danger. But the chronicler, who loved them both, is silent. And yet he stays to give us the picture of an earlier time, and not so much earlier, when the relations between the royal couple had been more loverlike. He tells how Blanche, the queen-mother, had tyrannised over them, as the *maîtresse-femme,* the woman accustomed to authority, will tyrannise in all stations of life, and how, to secure some privacy of intercourse, they had arranged a meeting-place on a hidden stairway, each scuttling back like a rabbit at the approach of the maternal enemy. And he tells of the younger woman's passionate appeal—one of those appeals that are so human that they ring through the ages, like the appeal of Marie Antoinette to her motherhood—tells how Margaret lay after child-birth, as all thought dying, and the king hung over her, and the queen-mother ordered him away, and the wife cried: "Alas! whether dead or alive, you will not suffer me to see my lord!" "Whereupon she fainted, and they thought she was dead, and the king, who thought she was dying, came back."[2]

It has been conjectured that politics came, to some extent, between the king and queen, and that the king wished to be unfettered by her influence in state affairs.[3] For Margaret was no lay-figure. She played a not unimportant part in the world's affairs. Failing the arbitration of Lewis himself, Henry III. and the English barons agreed to refer their differences to her. That arbitration proving abortive, she sided throughout and very actively with Henry, whose wife Eleanor was her younger sister. All her life long she passionately maintained her claims on Provence as against the king's brother. Possibly, therefore, St. Lewis may, while agreeing to allow her a certain independence of action, have preferred to remain outside the sphere of her activities. One cannot tell. The heart-relations between two human beings are always difficult to unravel—often too tangled to be unravelled even by the two persons most interested. At the same time, as I said, one cannot but agree with Joinville, that the king's "good manners" in relation to the queen are somewhat open to question. For myself I confess that I should have thought it better "manners," if, when the ship struck on the sand-bank, and death seemed imminent, he had gone to encourage his wife and children, instead of prostrating himself "crosswise, on the deck of the vessel . . . before the body of our Lord."

To a man of St. Lewis's temperament, the cloister must have offered attractions wellnigh irresistible; and it is recorded that, on one occasion at least, he expressed a determination to seek its retirement, when the queen effectually combated his resolution by silently fetching his children, and placing them before him. Had such monkish ideals anything to do with his attitude towards his wife?

Had he a kind of feeling that marriage acted as a restraint, not certainly on his passions, but on his piety? Was he swayed, in marriage, voluntarily or involuntarily, towards the celibate life? I scarcely think so. For the man, with all his religious fervour, was essentially sane of heart and head. His ethics were those of a saint, but they were also those of a supremely honest and upright man. Nor was he in the least priest-ridden. When the assembled bishops of France came to him, and proposed a course which his own conscience did not approve, he unhesitatingly refused to acquiesce, and give them powers they might misuse. He offers the example, rare at all times, and under every form of government, whether monarchic, aristocratic, or democratic, of a ruler bent on ruling according to the moral law alone.

With such a guiding spirit, with pure religious zeal and honesty at the helm, there can be no question as to the aims and objects of the Crusade, nor any necessity, or indeed excuse, for such a disquisition as that with which I introduced Villehardouin's chronicle. Dandolo, Montferrat, Baldwin, even Henry, nearly all the leading actors on Ville-hardouin's stage, may have been swayed this way and that, by motives not all avowable. St. Lewis had but one motive, and that open as the day, from the time when, in his sore sickness, and being then some thirty years of age (1244), he vowed to take the cross. Broadly, the condition of affairs in the Holy Land remained at that date pretty much what they had been when Montferrat's host embarked at Venice fifty-two years before (1202). (True, the intervening years had been crowded with action. Apart from the constantly-recurring local episodes of battle and siege, bloodshed and famine, and slaughter, there had been a descent into Egypt, with siege and sack of Damietta (1219), and a disastrous advance on Cairo, an expedition curiously similar in its incidents to that which St. Lewis was about to undertake. There had been the expedition to the Holy Land of the brilliant and cultured Frederick II. of Germany, who by treaty had obtained possession of Jerusalem (1229)—curiously enough he was at the time under ban of excommunication—and had been crowned there as king. There had been, also for a time, a recrudescence of Christian power and influence. But this had passed away. The tide had set against the West and against the Cross. A few strongholds on the shore of Judæa alone remained in Frank hands. As in 1202, so in 1248, when St. Lewis sailed from Aigues-Mortes, the task of reconquering Jerusalem still remained to be accomplished. That was the task to which St. Lewis set himself with all singleness of heart and aim,—and he failed. His generalship was clearly not on a level with his personal courage or self-devotion. Jerusalem had finally passed into Moslem hands. But the man himself, the story of him, the record of his loving follower and friend—these live for all time.

As to Joinville's style, why, I fear I have done him some wrong in speaking of his age and garrulity. No doubt he was eighty-five when he finished his book, and like most old men, he liked to hear himself talk. But those whom the gods love die young, and they die young not because their span of life is short, but because they carry into extreme age, nay to the very grave itself, the fresh youth of their spirit. And, in this sense, Joinville was young at four score years and five. With all his garrulity, his readiness to turn aside and be beguiled from the forward path by incident or episode, his love for going over the past lingeringly—with all this, his outlook is as keen, as full of interest, as blithe, as the outlook of a boy. He sees clearly, he describes well, and his touch is light and bright—not perhaps, to speak with perfect accuracy, the touch of a writer in the French tradition, because the French tradition was scarcely formed, but of a writer who occupies his due place in the formation of that tradition. Here again "the style is the man himself." . . .

Notes

1. Joinville is here quite lyrical. He brings to mind Sir Richard Vernon's speech on the royal army, in the first part of *King Henry IV.:*—

    "I saw young Harry with his beaver on,His cuisses on his thighs, gallantly arm'd,
    Rise from the ground like feather'd Mercury," etc.

2. Should one smile or sigh? The same Margaret, in after years, tried to exercise her influence most unduly over her own son Philip, and induced him to swear that he would remain subject to her authority till he had attained the age of thirty—with other like stipulations. See p. 422, *Revue des Questions Historiques,* 1867, Vol. III.

3. See the extremely interesting article entitled *Marguerite de Provence, son caractère, son rôle politique,* in the *Revue des Questions Historiques,* Vol. III., 1867, pp. 417-458.

Alfred Foulet (essay date 1941)

SOURCE: "When Did Joinville Write His *Vie de Saint Louis?*," *The Romantic Review,* Vol. XXXII, No. 3, October, 1941, pp. 233–43.

[*In the following essay, Foulet dates the various sections of Joinville's* Vie de Saint Louis, *and argues against the theory that a majority of the work consists of personal reminiscences composed as early as 1272-73.*]

While leading his second crusade against the Saracens, King Louis IX of France died of the plague near Carthage, August 25, 1270. Twenty-seven years later (August 1297), after three separate inquests into his saintly virtues and the miracles ascribed to him after his death, he was canonized by Pope Boniface VIII. Two Princesses of the Royal House, eager to spread the cult of the new saint, requested that his life be again made the subject of written accounts.[1] The first, Blanche de la Cerda, a daughter of Louis IX, commissioned her confessor, Guillaume de Saint-Pathus, who completed his task during the year 1303; the second, Countess Jeanne of Champagne,[2] who was both a grand-

niece of Saint Louis and the wife of his grandson (Philip IV), addressed herself to her Seneschal, Jean de Joinville, but she died (April 2, 1305) before her command had been carried out.

Any discussion of the dating of Joinville's book must be preceded by an outline of the several sections into which it may conveniently be divided. I have, of course, adopted the standard paragraph numbering introduced by Natalis de Wailly.[3]

> 1. Dedicatory letter to Louis, King of Navarre and Count of Champagne, later Louis X (§1-18).—2. Joinville's Part One: the teachings of Saint Louis (§19-67).—3. Joinville's Part Two: the life and reign of Louis IX (§68-765); a) §68-109: the youthful years (1214-1248), b) §110-663: The Seventh Crusade (1248-1254), c) §664-765: the later years (1254-1270).—4. Postscript to the book (§766-768).—5. Final date: *Ce fu escrit en l'an de grace mil CCC et IX, ou moys d'octovre* (§769).

Sections 1 and 5 may be considered together. In his dedicatory letter (section 1), Joinville addresses Louis as *fil dou roy de France, par la grace de Dieu roy de Navarre, de Champaigne et de Brie conte palazin.* Evidently he is writing after the death of Queen Jeanne of Navarre (April 2, 1305) and before Louis' accession to the throne of France (Nov. 29, 1314). Although the date of October 1309 given in §769 (section 5) is found in only one of the three manuscripts, it does not refer to MS *A*, the handwriting and language of which place it after 1350, but to an older manuscript now lost, presumably the presentation copy which Joinville offered to the future Louis X. This hypothesis seems all the more plausible when one is reminded that Louis, born October 4, 1289, was entering upon his twenty-first year in October 1309.[4] Before that time, the serious-minded old dedicator might have considered the royal dedicatee too immature in mind to appreciate at their proper value the moralizing features of the book he had composed.[5] It seems therefore fairly safe to assume that the date of October 1309 applies both to section 1 and to section 5.

Sections 2 and 3, which constitute the book proper, will also be examined together, at least at present. A reading of §19-765 of the *Vie de Saint Louis* yields the following data: §20 ignores the existence of §7-16 and consequently must have come into being before the composition of section 1; §35 was written before the death of Duke Jean of Brittany (Nov. 18, 1305); §108 was written after the death of Count Gui of Flanders (March 7, 1305); and §555 was written after the death of the Duke of Burgundy (March 21, 1306). It follows that Joinville composed the *Vie* over a period of at least six months, say between November 1, 1305 and April 30, 1306. Since Jeanne of Navarre was no longer among the living to speed her Seneschal on his commissioned task, it is quite natural to suppose that a *grand seigneur* like Joinville refused to let himself be rushed by his duties as a biographer.

Section 4 contains a reference to Louis of Navarre, but in the third person instead of the second as found in the dedicatory letter:

> Et ces choses ai je ramentues a mon signour le roy Looys, qui est heritiers de son non; et me semble que il fera le grei nostre saint roy Looys, s'i pourchassoit des reliques le vrai cors saint, et les envoioit a la dite chapelle de Saint Lorans a Joinville, par quoy cil qui venront a son autel que il y eussent plus grant devocion.[6]

Clearly section 4 must have been written before Joinville had decided to dedicate the book to Louis of Navarre, that is before sections 1 and 5, but, since it is a postscript, after the completion of sections 2 and 3, that is to say anywhere during the years 1306-1309.

Up till now I have been dating the composition of the *Vie* by what might be called *prima facie* evidence, evidence that was held satisfactory by Natalis de Wailly, the last editor of Joinville, although he has not, perhaps, presented it as precisely and as coherently as would have been desirable.[7] But the time has come to consider a theory that has gained wide and lasting acceptance, Gaston Paris' hypothesis of the "Memoirs" of Joinville.[8] According to G. Paris, Joinville composed section 3b as early as 1272 or 1273. He believes that §110-663, at the time they were written, were intended as an account of Joinville's personal share in the seventh crusade, their main purpose being not to glorify the late king, but to afford entertainment to the family and friends of the Seneschal of Champagne. Thirty years later (1305) when Joinville undertook to bring out a life of Saint Louis, he considerably expedited his task by incorporating with the saint's biography what may be termed chapters of his own autobiography, but with such trifling readjustments that section 3b remains hopelessly out of focus in the book that has come down to us. Gaston Paris offers five arguments in support of his theory, which I shall list before discussing their validity.

A literal interpretation of §555 shows that it was penned shortly after October 1272, and not shortly after March 1306. Talking of King Philip II of France and his departure from the Holy Land during the third crusade (1191), Joinville writes: *il lessa toute sa gent demourer en l'ost avec le duc Hugon de Bourgoingne, l'aioul cesti duc qui est mors nouvellement.* Since *aioul* means grandfather and not great-grandfather,[9] the recently deceased duke cannot be Robert II, who died on March 21, 1306, but must be Hugues IV, who died on October 27, 1272. If §555, which is part of section 3b, was written as early as 1272, presumably all of section 3b dates back to that year.

Section 3b is out of all proportion with the rest of Part Two: it devotes 554 paragraphs to six years (1248-1254) of a reign that lasted no less than forty-four (1226-1270); yet the balance, 38 years, is disposed of in a mere 144 paragraphs.

The central character of section 3b is quite evidently Joinville: concerning his adventures, his hardships, his everyday life, we are given details which in no way concern Louis IX; the king is never the protagonist and he appears in the narrative only when Joinville finds himself in his company.

One readily ascribes sections 1, 2, 3a, 3c and 4 to an hagiographer: in these 200 paragraphs Louis IX is referred to as "Saint Louis" at least thirty times. But in section 3b, which comprises over 550 paragraphs, only thrice does Louis appear as "Saint Louis," everywhere else he is merely "the King." These three cases of "Saint Louis" (§120, 207, 385) are so exceptional that they may be set down as haphazard changes or additions made at the time Joinville wedged his personal reminiscences into the *Vie.* Clearly section 3b was written before Louis IX had been canonized.

In 1272, Geoffroi de Joinville, the eldest son of the Seneschal, married Mabille de Villehardouin, a great-grand-daughter of the historian of the fourth crusade. Is it not tempting to imagine that one of the consequences of this alliance was that Joinville became acquainted with Villehardouin's account of the conquest of Constantinople and that he was spurred thereby to describe his own share in a later crusade? But argument 5 is advanced by G. Paris only as an interesting possibility.

Having thus stated the five arguments advanced by G. Paris in support of his theory, let us examine their validity.

Now as to the first argument. A perusal of other passages of the *Vie* suffices to show that G. Paris overemphasizes the significance of the word *aioul* in §555. Thus in §348 Joinville incorrectly describes Malik al-Sāalih Aiyūb, Sultan of Egypt, as the grandfather (*aious*) of Tūrān-Shāh, after having correctly called him his father (§288: *ses peres*). If in §348 Joinville has made a slip by using *aioul* instead of *pere,* it remains well within the realm of probability that in §555 he may have made a similar slip by saying *aioul* when he should have said *besaioul.*[10] Moreover it seems easier to postulate a slip of the author in §555 than to surmise instead with G. Paris[11] that §400, 600, 613 and 633, which contain references to events that occurred in the years 1275, 1291, 1295 and 1300, that is to say after 1272 (date of the assumed redaction of the "Memoirs"), were rewritten in 1305.

As to the second argument. If, instead of presenting it as an argument, G. Paris had formulated it as a question, we should discover that he himself comes very near providing us with a satisfactory answer. Why is section 3b out of all proportion to the rest of Part Two of the *Vie?* Let us turn to G. Paris. Speaking of the other two sections of Part Two, section 3a (§68-109) and section 3c (§664-765), he writes:[12]

> Là Joinville n'est plus le centre du récit; il n'écrit plus des mémoires personnels, dans lesquels le roi paraît lorsqu'il se trouve en contact avec lui; mais il ne faut pas croire non plus qu'il ait voulu écrire proprement une Histoire de saint Louis. Les "faiz" du saint roi,

dont il avait promis à la reine Jeanne de faire un livre, sont uniquement ceux dont il avait été témoin, comme les paroles sont celles qu'il lui avait entendu prononcer; il le déclare expressément au début: "Je . . . faz escrire la vie nostre saint roi Looïs, ce que je vi et oï par l'espace de sis anz que je fui en sa compaignie ou pelerinaige d'outre mer et puis que nous revenimes." Il a manqué à son plan quand il a cousu à la fin de son livre, faute de souvenirs personnels, des morceaux empruntés ailleurs, et il a pris soin de dire, en terminant, qu'il ne garantissait que ce qu'il avait "veü et oï." C'est en se plaçant à ce point de vue qu'il faut apprécier l'œuvre de joinville; autrement on la qualifierait d'incomplète et d'incohérente au delà de la mesure où elle mérite d'être ainsi qualifiée.

Very little elaboration of the words of G. Paris quoted above is needed to show the weakness of argument 2. As soon as we recognize that Joinville wished to set down concerning Saint Louis only what he had heard and seen, it becomes apparent that the years 1248-1254, during which he was frequently brought in contact with the King, are vastly more important than those that preceded or those that followed: before 1248 he was not yet on terms of friendship with Louis, after 1254 his duties as Seneschal of Champagne and Lord of Joinville did not allow him to spend much time at the Parisian court. Yes, there is a considerable disproportion between section 3b and the other two sections of Part Two, but this disproportion is justified by the attitude which the author has assumed from the very first, that of a reliable witness.

As to the third argument. There can be little doubt that G. Paris is right when he states that in section 3b the narrative sequence is provided by the succession of notable or curious events which took place in Joinville's life during the years of the seventh crusade. This fact is perhaps nowhere more strikingly illustrated than in the opening paragraphs of section 3b. Thus §110-113: Joinville confers with his men; §114: he obeys a summons of the king; §115-118: an example of Louis' justice is related to Joinville, while in Paris; §119-122: Joinville receives scrip and staff from a holy abbot; §123: he journeys down the valley of the Saône; §124: he sees a castle that has been pulled down by order of the king; §125-129: Joinville's sea voyage from Marseille to Cyprus; §130-131: he sees the supplies that have been gathered for the army; §132: Louis told him later in Syria how much he would have liked then to proceed immediately to Egypt. But does it follow that §110-663 could have been composed only as part of an autobiography and that they are out of focus in a purported biography? Before agreeing too hastily with G. Paris let us consider the problem which Joinville would have faced when he reached the year 1248 in Louis' reign, in case he had no "Memoirs" to fall back upon. Concerning the King's deeds, he had decided to narrate only what he had seen and heard, yet during those eventful years of the seventh crusade in which Joinville became a trusted friend of Louis IX he had not spent all his time, not even most of his time, at the King's side. How was he going to link the numerous, yet separate, occasions on which he was present at some action of the King? Joinville needed a

chronological thread to tie these events together, otherwise he would have given us a series of disconnected scenes loosely hanging in the air and we should have complained of the inartistic quality of the result.[13] What more truthful sequence could he have adopted than the accidents and incidents of his own odyssey? To these he could bear witness as well as to those of the King's. And if such was his decision, he has solved his problem of composition with outstanding success, because it is the now swift-flowing, now slow-moving narrative which finds its source in this autobiographical device that gives life and color to the deeds of Louis IX and prevents them from becoming a collection of "stills," to borrow a term from the language of the cinema. I believe that the autobiographical sequence which is present in section 3b was not only justifiable but desirable if Joinville was seeking to write artistically at the same time he was writing as an eye-witness.

As to the fourth argument. Could there be another reason than the one advocated by G. Paris which might account for the fact that Joinville, who makes a liberal use, but by no means an overwhelming use,[14] of the epithet "saint" in the rest of the book, is satisfied to use it only thrice in the 554 paragraphs of 3b? Joseph Bédier, perhaps the only critic so far who has refused to accept G. Paris' theory,[15] maintains that Joinville was consciously reacting against the monks and clerks who extolled only the ascetic virtues of the King, whereas our Seneschal, albeit he was a devout believer, wished to show that Louis before ever he became a "stained glass saint" had been richly endowed with virtues of this world, that he had been a knight both courteous and bold, a warm friend and a wise King. That Bédier offered a most plausible view is shown not only in §32 of section 2, which contains the well known "tenson" between Joinville and Robert de Sorbon,[16] but also by a passage in the very section under discussion, a passage which because of the light it sheds on Joinville's attitude I think worth quoting in full:

> Par nos journees, venimes ou sablon d'Acre, la ou li roys et li os nous lojames. Illec au lieu vint a moy uns grans peuples de la Grant Hermenie, qui aloit en pelerinaige en Jerusalem, par grant treu rendant aus Sarrazins qui les conduisoient. A un latimier qui savoit lour languaige et le nostre, il me firent prier que je lour monstrasse le saint roy. Je alai au roy la ou il se seoit en un paveillon, apuiez a l'estache dou paveillon; et seoit ou sablon, sans tapiz et sans nulle autre chose desouz li. Je li dis: "Sire, il a la hors un grant peuple de la Grant Hermenie qui vont en Jerusalem, et me proient, sire, que je lour face moustrer le saint roy; mais je ne bé ja a baisier vos os." Et il rist mout clerement, et me dist que je les alasse querre; et si fis je.[17]

The humorous quip upon which the anecdote ends should not blind us to its significance. Clearly there was a time when Joinville was in no hurry to see his royal friend enshrined and placed on an altar, and to let awe and veneration take the place of tenderer feelings, when the epithet "saint" struck a note of unwelcome estrangement. Is it so difficult to understand that Joinville, when he has effectively conjured up the past, tends quite naturally to discard a word that interposed barrier between himself and the friend of his youth? Notice how frequently—relatively speaking—that adjective is used at the start, how later it appears at wider and wider intervals, and after vanishing almost how it resumes its pristine frequency in the closing pages of the book.[18]

As to the fifth argument. Argument 5, based on evidence external to Joinville's book, is as tenuous as it is ingenious. It has really no intrinsic value and stands or falls according to the attitude one takes toward the first four arguments.

The preceding discussion should suffice to show that section 3b was not necessarily composed before 1305-1306, but we can, I believe, go farther and offer evidence indicating affirmatively that it was composed later than 1282. This evidence based on Joinville's deposition of 1282 and the 1287 redaction of his **Credo** I shall now present.

In 1282 Joinville was called before the ecclesiastical delegates who had been commissioned by the Pope to investigate the life, deeds and miracles of Louis IX, and he tells us that they questioned him for two whole days.[19] The text of Joinville's deposition has not come down to us, but, since it was utilized along with the testimony of 37 other witnesses by Guillaume de Saint-Pathus, we are able to reconstruct some parts of it. I shall list the fragments I have been able to recover from Guillaume de Saint-Pathus.[20] They will be arranged in the order in which Joinville later located them in the **Vie**. An asterisk before the abbreviation St-P means that Guillaume de Saint-Pathus acknowledges that he is drawing on Joinville at that place. The absence of an asterisk signifies that there is a close similarity between a passage of Guillaume de Saint-Pathus and Joinville's text, the presumption being that, although not mentioned by name, the Seneschal was the authority or at least one of the authorities consulted by Guillaume de Saint-Pathus.[21]

1. (§19) Joinville knew the King for 22 years: *St-P, pp. 72, 133.—2. (§22) Louis never spoke ill of anyone: *St-P, p. 133.—3. (§24) Invariably act and speak as if all could see and hear: *St-P, 72.—4. (§27-28) Mortal sin or leprosy, which is worse?: *St-P, p. 72.—5. (§38) Louis took the side of the weaker against the stronger: St-P, p. 78.—6. (§53) A knight's sword is his most telling argument against any miscreant: St-P, p. 25.—7. (§54) Every day Louis said the Office of the Dead: St-P, p. 37.—8. (§57-58) How Louis administered justice in person: St-P, p. 142.—9. (§71) Louis' mother would have preferred to see him dead than in a state of mortal sin: St-P, p. 13.—10. (§306) Louis refuses to leave his men during the retreat from Mansourah: St-P, pp. 74-75.—11. (§379, 386, 389) Louis refuses to sail till his brother is freed: St-P, pp. 76-77.—12. (§386-389) Louis insists on keeping his word to the Saracens: St-P, pp. 127-128.—13. (§517) Louis labors at the fortifications of Jaffa: St-P, p. 110.—14. (§582) Louis helps to bury the dead at Sidon: St-P, pp. 101-102.—15. (§617-629) Louis' composure during a narrowly averted shipwreck: St-P, pp. 77-78.—16. (§667) How

Louis clothed himself in the last part of his reign: St-P, 111.—17. (§682) Louis tried to keep peace between the neighboring princelings: St-P, pp. 73-74.—18. (§685) How Louis punished blasphemers in the Holy Land; St-P, p. 27.—19. (§686-687) Louis never swore: St-P, p. 124.—20. Louis taught that the saints were our intercessors in Heaven: *St-P, p. 73.—21. Louis criticized those who were ashamed to show their piety: *St-P, p. 73.—22. Joinville fully believed that the dead king could work miracles: *St-P, p. 133-134.

The last three items have no equivalent in the *Vie;* item 22 had become pointless after the canonization of Louis IX, but as items 21 and 22 would have found their way into Part One of the *Vie* had Joinville in 1305 been using a copy of his deposition, it may be assumed that he was not and that two teachings of Saint Louis escaped his memory at the time. But those minor items, present in the deposition and absent from the *Vie,* do not undermine the conclusion that for all practical purposes Joinville's deposition constitutes the first draft of the *Vie.* For the first time the Seneschal had been compelled to bring together and marshal all he knew about Louis; in the past he had doubtless narrated his memories of the King, but it must have been in piecemeal fashion, without plan or perspective. It so happens that several of the items listed above as belonging to this first draft of the *Vie* are to be found also in what G. Paris calls the "Memoirs" section of the 1305 redaction, which raises the suspicion that the said section is not essentially different from the other sections of the book, for those items are present in the Seneschal's sworn testimony about the King, and this suffices to show that section 3b existed in embryonic form in Joinville's deposition of 1282.

Joinville's conception of himself as a witness on oath is very noticeable in the *Vie.* Not only is this attitude proclaimed by the author in a general statement both at the beginning and the end of the book.[22] But it is apparent also in the care with which Joinville qualifies the nature of his information, when he is telling about things he has learned through hearsay. In §75, for instance, he refers only to people in general as his source for the reported item;[23] in §105 he is somewhat more specific: men who returned from the campaign of 1242 were his informants; in §390 and 392 he names two knights as his authorities for the way in which Gautier de Châtillon was killed in Egypt; in §562 his intimation of the stupendous sums Louis must have spent in fortifying Jaffa is based on a conversation Joinville had with the papal legate; in §756 and 757 his account of the last moments of the King is authenticated by a report made to him by Count Pierre of Alençon, a son of Louis who was present at the death of his father;[24] finally he relies on the word of Louis himself regarding facts such as the day on which the King was born, Louis' return from Montlhéry to Paris during an uprising of his nobles, the acquisition by the crown of fiefs sold by Thibaut IV of Champagne, the reaction of Blanche of Castille on being apprised that her son had taken the cross, Louis' impatience at being delayed in Cyprus, and the manner in which he was captured by the Saracens.[25] It should be noted that several of these guarantees of veracity are found in section 3b,[26] which proves that the attitude Joinville openly adopted in other sections of the book, the attitude of a witness on the stand, is also discernible in what G. Paris terms the "Memoirs," and strongly suggests that no part of the *Vie* antedates 1282, when Joinville's punctilious attitude must first have arisen.[27]

Between the deposition or "first draft of the *Vie*" of 1282 and the actual redaction of the *Vie* in the years 1305-1306, there exists one partial intermediate step, the second redaction of Joinville's *Credo*.[28] This little religious pamphlet, which emphasizes the paramount importance of the Creed in the matter of salvation, was first composed at Acre in 1250-1251; in 1287, when it had become plain to Joinville that Louis would soon be canonized, he revised the *Credo* by inserting at several places various teachings of the future saint.[29] A table of correspondences between the *Credo* and the *Vie* will enable the reader to see at a glance what passages of the *Credo* are paralleled by passages of similar content in the *Vie*.

> 1. (§24) Invariably act and speak as if all could see and hear: *Credo,* §774.—2. (§43) The Devil tries to make us doubt *in extremis: Credo,* §849.—3. (§44) How we should repulse him: *Credo,* §775.—4. (§45) Your parentage is a matter of faith: *Credo,* §771.—5. (§50) Count Amaury of Montfort needed no miracle to fortify his faith: *Credo,* §772-773.—6. (§334-339) Joinville takes courage during his captivity in Egypt: *Credo,* §801-815.—7. Louis claimed that the Christian religion alone had been prophesied and attested: *Credo,* §776.— 8. Friar Heinrich of Marburg's comment on the Creed: *Credo,* §777.—9. Why justice is represented by a double-edged sword: *Credo,* §825.

Items 7 and 9, which belong by rights to the teachings of Saint Louis, might very well have been introduced into Part One of the *Vie*. The fact that Joinville did not do so shows rather conclusively that he no more consulted the *Credo,* when he was at work on the *Vie,* than he did his deposition.[30] But it is more important for the present discussion to note that one long item of the *Credo* later found its way, with a few incidental changes, into the *Vie*. This item, item 6 of the above list, deals with a personal experience Joinville underwent in Egypt and which does not seem to concern Louis in any visible way, yet by this personal tale hangs a moral of such religious significance that Joinville deemed it worthy to find a place in the *Credo* along with the teachings of the King he inserted at the same time. Although the said experience had not happened to Louis, nor even to Joinville in the presence of Louis, it was of a type which the King enjoyed discussing and drawing upon for his teachings. That nearly all the personal experiences related by Joinville in section 3b lend themselves to the kind of serious moralizing Louis sought to induce and develop in his friends and that the community of views which existed between the proselytizing King and his zealous disciple results in at least didactic unity for the *Vie,* I hope to have shown in a previous article to which I refer the reader.[31]

So far the only open attack made upon the theory of Gaston Paris has come from Joseph Bédier, as has already been stated in the course of this article. In a history of French literature which appeared almost twenty years ago, Bédier made an eloquent plea in favor of the artistic unity of Joinville's book,[32] yet those brilliant pages have seemingly failed to bring about the overthrow of G. Paris' theory of the dual personality of the *Vie,* one-fourth biography and three-fourths autobiography. Because I have long felt that G. Paris was wrong and that Bédier was right, I have endeavored here to supplement the latter's demonstration with what it may have lacked, a point by point discussion of G. Paris's arguments and the reasons that can be adduced in favor of the unity of the *Vie* from a study of Joinville's deposition and *Credo.*

To sum up, Joinville's *Vie de Saint Louis* was written in 1305 and 1306 although the dedicatory letter did not come into existence till October 1309; the postscript is to be located in time somewhere between the book and the dedication. Gaston Paris's hypothesis that three-fourths of the book are personal reminiscences written as early as 1272-1273 appears untenable. Not these hypothetical "Memoirs," but Joinville's deposition during the canonization inquest of 1282, considered in conjunction with the 1287 redaction of his *Credo,* should be viewed as the initial step in the composition of the *Vie de Saint Louis.*

Notes

1. Pre-canonization biographies of Louis IX are those by Geoffroi de Beaulieu, Guillaume de Chartres, Guillaume de Nangis *et al.*

2. Jeanne was Countess of Champagne and Queen of Navarre in her own right.

3. *Histoire de Saint Louis,* par Jean, sire de Joinville, Paris, Firmin Didot, 1874, and subsequent small size editions published by Hachette from 1881 on.

4. It is true that Louis had been married to Marguerite of Burgundy as far back as Sept. 23, 1305, and that he had already been crowned King of Navarre on Oct. 1, 1307, but he was not to be dubbed a knight till June 3, 1313.

5. Notice the admonishment to Louis at the end of the dedication, §18.

6. *Vie,* §767.

7. See his edition of 1874, pp. i-x and 480-481.

8. Presented and expounded in *R,* XXIII (1894), 508-524, and also in *Histoire littéraire de la France,* XXXII (1898), 426-450. Among those who have subscribed to Paris' theory one may mention Molinier, see *Sources de l'histoire de France,* III, n° 2537, and Jeanroy, see Hanotaux, *Histoire de la nation française,* XII, pp. 441-444.

9. Which would be *besaioul* in Old French.

10. Joinville's error in §348 is pointed out by G. Paris, along with a dozen others, in *HLFr,* XXXII, 449-450.

11. See *HLFr,* XXXII, 428-429.

12. *HLFr,* XXXII, 439.

13. The lack of a connecting thread is at times painfully apparent in section 3c.

14. For a constant use of *benoiet* and *saint* see Guillaume de Saint-Pathus' life of Saint Louis.

15. In Bédier et Hazard, *Histoire de la littérature française illustrée,* 1, 82-85.

16. Subject of the debate: whether it is better to be a *preudome* (a gentleman) or a *beguin* (an ascetic).

17. *Vie,* §565-566.

18. Section 1: §2, 4. Section 2: §19, 20, 21, 35, 43, 50, 58. Section 3a: §68, 73, 87, 100. Section 3b: §120, 207, 385 (565-566). Section 3c: §678, 679, 685, 693, 757, 758, 760, 761, 762, 763, 765. Section 4: §766, 767, 768.

19. *Vie,* §760. He was questioned at Saint-Denis some time between June 12 and August 8, 1282.

20. *Vie de Saint Louis,* par Guillaume de Saint-Pathus, confesseur de la reine Marguerite, edited by H.-François Delaborde (Paris, 1899) in *Collection de textes pour servir à l'étude et de l'enseignement de l'histoire.*

21. Only about half of these corresponding passages have been pointed out by Delaborde in the foot-notes of his edition.

22. *Vie,* §19, 738, and 768.

23. See also *Vie,* §106 and 685.

24. See also *Vie,* §4.

25. *Vie,* §69, and 617, 73, 87, 107, 132, 308 and 404.

26. *Vie,* §132, 308, 390, 392, 404, 562, 617.

27. In 1298 Joinville was reminded of his deposition oath by one of the papal investigators.

28. Only this second redaction has survived; it has been edited by Natalis de Wailly in his 1874 edition of the *Vie.* De Wailly has numbered the paragraphs of the *Credo* from 770 to 852.

29. See Charles-Victor Langlois, *La Vie en France au Moyen âge du XIIᵉ au XIVᵉ siècle,* Paris, Hachette, 1928, IV, 13, note 3.

30. This conclusion is in perfect accord with G. Paris' assertion that Joinville always dictated from memory and never used material previously written or dictated by himself, see *HLFr,* XXXII, 446-448.

31. "Notes sur la *Vie de Saint Louis* de Joinville," *R,* LVIII (1932), 551-564.

32. The following sentence neatly summarizes Bédier's position: "Le sénéchal a écrit l'histoire du roi Louis, l'histoire de saint Louis et l'histoire de Jean de Joinville, et ces trois histoires forment un chef-d'oeuvre complexe, mais d'une seule venue, où tout est concerté pour que son ami revive tout entier."

Newton S. Bement (essay date 1947)

SOURCE: "Latin Remnants in Joinville's French," *Philological Quarterly,* Vol. XXVI, No. 4, October, 1947, pp. 289–301.

[*In the following essay, Bement analyzes the extant text of* Vie de Saint Louis *in order to determine how the French language of the time incorporated various remnants of Latin. Bement concludes that the text includes many such remnants that have led modern scholars to maintain that the text exhibits a certain "disorder" or "confusion." Such "orthographical variety," Bement argues, caused no confusion among thirteenth- and fourteenth-century writers and readers.*]

Definition of title is here not only a primary consideration but one which cannot at any point be relegated to a status of secondary importance.

The greater part of a century has elapsed since Charles Corrard's posthumous *Observations sur le texte de Joinville*[1] presented, in part unintentionally, the most scathing and impassioned criticism to which Joinville's composition has been subjected. In part unintentionally, because Corrard's criticism was directed at editors, calling upon the reader to judge between him and them, and because it dwelt at length upon the supposed unfaithfulness of the scribes responsible for MS fr. 13568 (ancien supplément 2016), which in his opinion had been based on an alteration or alterations of the original presented by Joinville to Louis X.

So far as they relate to the editing of MS fr. 13568, Corrard's criticisms appear largely to be justified, and may still be consulted with profit. However, unknown to Corrard, Natalis de Wailly had already met the majority of his objections, in an edition which appeared in 1867.[2] MS fr. 13568 had also been edited by Francisque Michel, in 1858. It is to the Michel edition published by Firmin-Didot, Paris, 1881, that all page references are made in the present article.

In 1868 Natalis de Wailly published a "restitution" of MS fr. 13568, that is, an edition conforming to the orthography of thirteenth-century *champenois.*[3] The validity of the product obtained by this process has been questioned by various crities, e.g., in *Encyclopaedia Britannica* (11ᵗʰ edition) and in Bédier and Hazard's *Histoire de la littérature française illustrée* (Paris, Larousse, 1923), I, 83. Although by definition its index of authenticity is zero, it is from this edition that examples have been drawn for citation by Brunot, Nyrop, and lesser scholars since. Both it and the Wailly edition of 1867 are indispensable aids to anyone using the Michel edition for purposes of linguistic research, and vice versa.

The composition of the ***Histoire de Saint Louis*** was begun after 1297 and completed in October, 1309. The dedicatory and introductory portion was probably completed by the same date, or in any case before 1314. Joinville's sole contributions were the vocabulary, the construction or word order, the organization of the whole, and the selection or retelling of facts drawn from older chronicles, which fill some nineteen pages of his own. The original presented to Louis X and the copy retained by the author represented Joinville's spoken French as recorded at the beginning of the fourteenth century by a secretary or secretaries well versed in clerical work. MS fr. 13568 was copied from the original during the decade 1354-1364 or perhaps slightly later.[4]

Consequently, Joinville's French as known to us through the medium of the Michel edition or MS fr. 13568 may be defined as the recording of a scribe of the first quarter of the fourteenth century, recopied by a scribe of the third quarter of the century. Its particular and peculiar authentic value resides in the fact that it presents a unique linguistic synthesis covering the first half of the fourteenth century, or the point of juncture between late Old French and early Middle French, with evidence of overlapping in both directions.

As for Latin remnants, they are to be found in whatever category one may choose to search for them, from orthography to modal syntax. The ancestral Latinity of our subject has long since been traced in considerable and well-ordered detail. And yet, to quote the opinion of Lucien Foulet, who found fourteenth-century French discouragingly chaotic as a subject of syntactical study, "dès qu'on se borne à décrire un état de la langue, il n'y a aucun avantage à regarder le français avec des lunettes latines."[5]

This is especially true with reference to the noun and the articles. Despite the Latin ancestry of their forms, the articles, as developed by usage, are almost exclusively French. In great degree the same is true of nouns, because their sense was controlled by the use or omission of an article, to denote the location, among the various levels of the user's consciousness, of whatever the noun served to name, and to specify, among all the potential representational capacities of a given noun, which one the user wished to convey.

At that stage of the language midway between Old French and early Middle French the degree of application, to the abstract nominal idea in the mind of the user, of a system involving the balanced use and non-use of the indefinite, definite, generic, and partitive articles, distinguishes the language to an observable extent from the language of the preceding and following periods. But any attempt to penetrate the processes underlying the syntactical definition of the sense-scope of nouns as practiced in Joinville's time brings one at once into contact with elements of Latin ancestry which can truly be called remnants because they persisted in a language which already possessed their semantic duplicates and could function perfectly in their absence.

To consider these remnants, let us begin with the use of the forms of the definite article, which was originally a

demonstrative (Latin *ille*) and in French became an indirect demonstrative by virtue of its commonest or anaphorical function in that language: to point out in the memory. Its force as an indirect demonstrative brought it at once into opposition with the direct demonstrative *ce* and resulted in a certain degree of confusion which is still evident in Joinville's prose:

> Et les hales sont faites à la guise des cloistres de *ces* (i.e., des) moinnes blans (31); unes manières de herberges que il [les Béduyns] font de cercles de tonniaus loiés à perches, aussi comme les chers à *ces* dames (i.e., les chars des dames) sont (78).

This usage, occasionally found in later authors (e.g., Commynes) and far more commonly in earlier ones, is exemplified at only two other points in Joinville's work (159, 181). There are also three borderline examples (25, 25, 205).

The reverse, or encroachment of the indirect demonstrative form on the domain of the direct demonstrative, occurs somewhat less rarely:

> je n'i vi cottes brodées, ne *les* roy ne *les* autrui (i.e., ni celles du roi ni celles des autres) (7); Au contraire, disoit-il que male chose estoit de prendre de *l'*autrui (i.e., le bien d'autrui) (9); en l'autre [bande] estoient les armes le soudanc de Haraphe; en l'autre bande estoient *les* au soudanc de Babiloine (63); et donnoit tout, et le sien et *l'*autrui (126); Et je li dis que oyl, se je puis ne du mien ne de *l'*autrui (130).

In the ***Histoire de Saint Louis*** there is no further occurrence of the specific construction just noted. Its form persists, however, in the sense that it had in Joinville's prose a mechanical counterpart, as may be noted in the two examples last cited or in the following ones:

> sa gent et *la moie* (celle de moi?) (37); ma robe touchoit *la* seue (celle de lui?) (11); je vous pri . . . que vous me donnés *du* vostre (29).

Compare:

> je prens le pechié sur l'ame de moy (110); La flebesce de li (236); à l'ame de vous (8); Et croient . . . que l' ame d'eulz en va en meilleur cours et en plus aaisié (78).

The forms *moie* and *seue,* showing agreement with an antecedent, obviously distinguish the nature of the preceding word from that of a demonstrative pronoun, although more frequently the function of these words is syntactically adjectival (e.g., La moy place, 181; un mien escuier, 37; avec les miens dix, 154; la seue bataille, 94; les seues couvenances, 117; la vostre merci, 53), just as it remains today in their secondary usage (e.g., un sien frère).

The total number of examples in which the form of the definite article serves in the capacity of a demonstrative pronoun is raised to an even score by sixteen occurrences of *la* in a usage which still persists (e.g., l'été de *la* Saint-Martin), followed by a genitive:

> Quant *la* Saint-Remy fut passé (57); après *la* Saint-Remy (59); ce fu entour *la* Saint-Jehan (131); contre *la* Saint-Remy (153).
>
> le jour de *la* Saint-Jehan (32, 167); le jour de *la* Penthecouste (46); le jour de *la* Saint-Nicholas (58); le jour de *la* Saint-Jaque (131); Le jour de *la* Touz-Sains (186); Le jour de *la* Saint-Marc (193).
>
> Lendemain de *la* Penthecouste (47); lendemain de *la* Saint-Berthelemi (243); le jeudi devant *l'*Ascension (105); le vendredi devant *la* Trinité (47); le samedi devant *l'*Ascension (105).

With identical syntactical function the form of the indefinite article occurs in a single instance:

> à la table le roy manjoit, emprès li, le conte de Poitiers, que il avoit fait chevalier nouvel à *une* Saint-Jehan (30).

Occasionally the word *fête* itself occurs in the construction, quite as any other noun may be followed by the genitive:

> le jour de *la feste* saint Sebastien (63); le soir de *la vegile* Nostre-Dame (234). le jour de *feste* Nostre-Dame (38); Lendemain de *feste* saint Berthemi (242: occurs in material taken from an earlier chronicle).
>
> le *jour* Noël (62).

Here as elsewhere the construction with the genitive is interchangeable with its analytical counterpart, e.g.,

> le jour *de* Penthecouste (47); la vegile *de* Saint-Marc (193).

In short, the use of the genitive, which as we shall presently note is rigidly restricted, is not only duplicated but at every point paralleled by that of the prepositional phrase:

> le jour *de quaresme-prenant* (67, 81, 84); le jour *d'un grand vendredi* (86); Le jeudi *après* Penthecouste (47); le vendredi *devant* Penthecouste (46); la semainne *devant Nouël* (61); le premier jour *de quaresme* (81).

During the perusal of the last few groups of examples it has no doubt been observed that they illustrate two common, diametrically opposed phenomena of the history of language: the leveling and unifying effect of usage on the syntax of semantic equivalents, and the persistence of semantically inalterable set phrases of proven linguistic economy. Elements of insufficient strength to remain in the latter category fall victims to analysis and disappear, while elements sufficiently strong to persist may nevertheless induce their analytical counterparts. What language, indeed, has grown otherwise than by analytical development and recomposition and has still remained webbed together completely within the capacity of its users to manipulate skilfully and comprehensively, or been capable of unlimited expansion to match the pace of civilization in tooling their minds and tongues? Of what happens when demand exceeds the semantic capacity of an exceptionally strong element Joinville offers the following example:

> Il s'esmut pour aler là le jour de la feste des apostres saint Pierre et saint Pol (174, no variant).

My observations concerning nouns relate chiefly to the persistence of the genitive standing after the noun it modifies. Of the genitive standing before the noun modified there are only eighteen examples in Joinville's work, involving only five different words: *Dieu* once, *autrui* seven times, *cui* (twice spelled *qui*) seven times, *laquelle* once, and *quel* twice. Parenthetically it may be added that *qui* is also spelled *cui,* with the result that *cui* likewise appears as a prepositional object (e.g., deux serjans le roy, . . . *à cui* les Turs . . . amenèrent . . . , 75; compare: entour son paveillon tenoient cil leur bordiaus *à qui* il avoit donné congié, 54). Examples:

> les bons executeurs . . . rendent l'*autrui* chatel (10); à tout *autrui* chatel (i.e., avec le bien d'autrui) (40); Les establissemens . . . furent tel, que nul n'i ravist *autrui* chose, . . . ne que nulz eust compaingnie à *autrui* femme ne à *autrui* fille (144).
>
> Je ving au conte de Soissons, *cui* cousine germainne j'avoie espousée (74); monseigneur Gobert d'Apremont son frère, en *qui* compaingnie, je, Jehan seigneur de Joinville, passames la mer en une nef que nous louames (35).
>
> «Seigneurs, pour *Dieu* merci, ne lessiés pas ceste ville . . . » (121).
>
> nulz chevaliers . . . ne peut revenir que il ne scet honni, se il laisse en la main des Sarrazins le peuple menu Nostre-Seigneur, en *laquelle* compaingnie il est alé (127); Saint-Jaque, *quel* pelerin je estoie et qui maint biens m'avoit fait (132).

Of the genitive standing after its noun there are some three hundred ten examples including one in which it stands in the predicate after *être.*[6] Well distributed over the 245 pages of the Michel edition or the 270 pages of the Wailly edition of 1868 they are not obtrusive, but collected for comparison and viewed *en masse* their effect is that of a constantly recurrent and all-pervasive obsession. It calls attention at once to the contrasting fact that there is barely a trace of persistence of the not less convenient other non-analytical oblique cases, e.g.,

> Et aucunes gens si disoient que le roy ne tenoit ces devant diz fiez que en gaje; mès ce n'est mie voir, car je le demandai *nostre saint roy Looys* outre-mer (28, no variant); monseigneur Giles le Brun, et bon chevalier et preudomme, *cui* li roys avoit donné la connestablie de France après la mort monseigneur Hymbert de Biaujeu le preudomme (132, no variant).

With a single exception which may be credited to force of habit, the genitive in Joinville's work is personal in the sense that it invariably represents a person, a saint, the devil (l'ennemi), God, or the Virgin:

Et ceste chose me ramenti le père *le roy* qui orendroit est (7); la fille *le conte* (26); «Cousin *le roi!*» (97); il avoit esté filz *saint Hélizabeth* (32); vous estes filz de vilain et de vilainne, et avez lessié l'abit *vostre père* et *vostre mère* (10); aus hoirs *la contesce* (21); le plus des serjans à armes *le roy* (55); la cote *le roy* à armer (81); Son nom estoit Scecedin le fils *Seic:* ce vaut autant à dire comme le veel le filz au veel (63).

Et lors je pris le pan de son seurcot et du seurcot *le roy* (10); ce sont des menaces *Nostre-Seigneur* (12); ce est des temptacions *l'ennemi* (14); à la table *le roy* (30); à l'ostel *le légat* (53); les armes *le soudanc* (63); la chambre *le soudanc* (105); le cors *le roy* et *les riches homes* (111); le chastel *mon oncle* (123); la terre *prestre Jehan* (145); la terre estoit *son frère* (205).

du tens *son père* et du temps *son ayoul* (34); au gue *le Béduyn* (67); ou servise *Dieu* (85); ou servise *le roy* (159); Tandis que le roy attendoit la délivrance *son frère* (121); dis que je feroie la clefz *le roy* (116); la cité des ennemis *Dieu* (173).

En non *Dieu* (15); «Or à eulz, de par *Dieu!*» (58); «Sèneschal, lessons huer ceste chiennaille; que, par la quoife *Dieu!* (ainsi comme il juroit,) encore en parlerons-nous de ceste journée ès chambres des dames» (76); Maintenant que mars entra, par le commandement *le roy,* le roy et les barons . . . comandèrent que . . . (46); «Voi! pour le chief *Dieu,* avez veu de ces ribaus!» (74); Jehan sire d'Apremont et conte de Salebruche de par *sa femme,* envoia à moy et . . . (37); et li dites, de par *moy,* que . . . (121).

The exception:

Et ainsi le roy acorda le conte *Champaingne* à la royne de Cypre, et fu la paiz faite en tel manière, que ledit conte de Champaingne donna à la royne de Cypre entour deux mille livrées de terre (28).

As may be noted in several of the examples cited above, the obvious or visible genitive in Joinville's work does not invariably express literal possession or relationship, but does relate rather exclusively to persons. Excepting *de par* (*de la part de*), this does not take into consideration the objects of certain prepositional locutions which had been formed earlier by agglutination. Such locutions either resist in various degrees subjection to the reverse process of semasiological deglutination under analytical pressure, or expand their structure to conform analytically with their function.

Those which best resist, or in other words those whose forms are either already fixed or in the process of becoming so, tend either to be replaced by their analytical synonyms or to persist with the form of the object already established, presumably because they have lost the sense of their component parts, with the result that their object which was primarily a genitive is no longer recognized as one. Such are *de par, entour, delez, en mi* and *enmi, par mi* and *parmi:*

et seront les baillifz puniz *par* nous [Louis IX], et les autres *par* les baillifz. Derechief, . . . les baillifs . . .

jureront que il ne donront ne n'envoieront nul don à home qui soit de nostre conseil, . . . ne à ceulz qui leurs contes retenront *de par* nous (221-222); un Sarrazin vint au roy et li presenta lait pris en pos et fleurs de diverses manières, *de par* les enfans de Nasac (119).

entour son paveillon (54); un hostel tout *delez* les bains (123); et le levèrent de *delez* le roy (110); ou il me menroient à terre, ou il me ancreroient *en mi* le flum (96); j'amoie miex que il m'ancrassent *enmi* le flum (96); Le roy ot conseil que il feroit faire une chauciée *par mi* la rivière (61); les Sarrazins . . . traioient à nous de visée *parmi* le flum (61); un de nos serjans tint son glaive *parmi le milieu,* et le lança à un des Turs (84).

Other old forms, less resistant, are submitting to expansion. Such are *encoste* and *encoste de, endroit* and *endroit de:*

et encore . . . mangoit *encoste* cele table la royne Blanche (31); Messire Gui d'Ybelin . . . s'agenoilla *encoste* moy et se confessa à moy (107); il me fist monter sus un palefroy, et me menoit *encoste de* li (100); il ot fait deffense *endroit* li des engins aus Sarrazins que nous avions gaaingnés (83); et dit que *endroit de* li avoit tué six de nos gens (112).

The *hors* group displays forms from all stages of growth from primary agglutination to analytical expansion and agglutinative recomposition, i.e., *hors* and *dehors* and *hors de, au dehors* and *au dehors de:*

il destruit quantque il trouvoit *hors* Chastel-Pèlerin, et *dehors* Acre, et *dehors* le Saffar et *dehors* Jaffe aussi (162); le moinne ne peut vivre *hors de* son cloistre sanz péché mortel (207); Et fist fère le bon roy la mèson des Chartriers *au dehors de* Paris (231); Assés tot après il fist fère une autre mèson *au dehors* Paris (231).

Newer locutions originating in the period of analytical expansion appear to be influenced by analogy in their behavior. Thus we find both *d'autre part de* and *d'autre part:*

Les cors aus Sarrazins, qui estoient retaillés, getoient *d'autre part du* pont et lessièrent aler *d'autre part* l'yaue (89).

The analogy in such instances is probably only apparent, resulting merely from the persistence of the genitive. Likewise, in view of this persistence, the assumption that the objects of prepositions such as *parmi* do not have genitive force in the mind of the user is subject to the same caution as an assumption that in the mind of the same user *lendemain* contains no article. Extreme linguistic flexibility is an obvious quality of the minds which produced this disordered and chaotic outgrowth of language, simultaneously continued to enjoy complete freedom of word order and to replace synthetic by analytic elements, and kept the language for two centuries in a turmoil precluding any premature state of equilibrium comparable to that of the preceding period.

The flexibility evident in *parmi* and *par mi,* in *en main, demain,* and *lendemain,* or in constructions such as *parmi le milieu,* is common among the prepositional locutions, and apparently the first prerequisite to growth. Based primarily on *contre,* for example, we find not only *encontre* but other prepositive formations, adverb, and noun:

> vous estes alés *contre* ma volenté (157); la royne . . . s'agenoilla *contre* li (188); nus ne nous osoit venir de Damiete . . . *contremont* l'yaue (90); vous . . . m'osastes loer ma demourée, *encontre* touz les grans hommes . . . qui me looient m'alée (130); Je estoie bien le quatorzième assis *encontre* le légat (128); nous tournames *encontremont* l'yaue (68); Un autre Sarrazin . . . disoit *encontre* et disoit ainsi: . . . (112); Quant j'oy dire qu'ele estoit venue, je me levay . . . et alai *encontre* li (186); Nous entrames en son paveillon, et son chamberlanc nous vint *à l'encontre* (55).

In recapitulation it may be noted that the objects of prepositions and prepositional locutions in many of the examples cited above include non-personal genitives incorporating the sense of unexpressed *de,* so that the term "possessive" or "possessive genitive" hardly covers the usage as a whole. In fact it is only the function of a genitive case that may be termed a Latin remnant. The form itself had been displaced by the dative in a possessive function in spoken Latin in the sixth century,[7] that is to say, by the ancestor of the "genitive" found in Joinville's work, while this dative in turn had in the seventh century encountered a rival in the use of the preposition *ad,*[8] in a construction appearing to be of Celtic origin.[9]

In the ***Histoire de Saint Louis*** the displacement of the genitive by *de,* as yet numerically far less complete than its displayed capacity would indicate, appears to be merely one of the phenomena of the infiltration of construction on a broad front by that preposition. Its power both to banish the genitive and to compete with *à* seems to be gathered from the ample foothold already achieved elsewhere in construction. Either despite or by virtue of its semantic breadth and consequent vagueness, *de* displaces the possessive genitive some two hundred twenty-six times in Joinville's work.

Or, to resort to comparative statistics: out of a total of some 646 instances of the expression of possession either by the possessive genitive, or by *de,* or by *à* (110 instances), the preposition *de* is used in about 35 per cent of the total instances, or more than twice as often as *à* (about 17 per cent), while the genitive is still used in about 48 per cent of the instances, or approximately half the time.

Of greater significance, perhaps, than that of the statistics, is the fact that the construction with *de* is completely interchangeable with the genitive and parallels it in every typical use:

> A son bon seigneur Looys, filz *du* roy de France, par la grace *de* Dieu roy de Navarre (1); En nom *de* Dieu (5); les piez *de* ces vilains ne laverai-je jà (8); et qu'elle

soit mère *de* Dieu (16); la royne de Cypre, qui estoit fille *de* l'ainsné filz *de* [Tybaut de] Champaingne (26); tout le pooir *du* soudanc (47); au tens *de* nos pères (52); les cités *des* ennemis (53); les armes *de* l'empereur (63); les autres terres *des* Sarrazins et *des* mescréans (79); la loy *des* Béduyns (79); Après la bataille au roy de Cézile, estoit la bataille *des* barons d'outre-mer (83); le cors *du* soudanc (89); pour délivrance de cors *de* homme (101); au pié *de* l'un d'eulz (107); la teste *du* patriarche (110); du serement le roy et *des* autres riches homes (111); ennemis *de* Dieu (127); en la main *des* Sarrazins (127); en hostel *de* roy (132); l'ostel *du* soudanc (134); la chemise *du* Vieil (137); testes *de* dyables (165); un serjant *du* mestre des arbalestriers (167); la cité *du* calife (183); en l'honneur du miracle que Dieu fist du dyable que il geta hors du cors *de* la fille à la veuve femme (184); le cors *de* vous, *de* vostre femme et *de* vos enfants (196); ce firent les filz *de* bourjois de Paris (202); La flebesce *de* li estoit si grant, que . . . (236).

As we have noted, the use of the personal genitive, as in *je . . . me séoie touzjours de coste le roy* (122), is paralleled by the use of a genitive object in numerous prepositional locutions where this genitive appears as an alternate of the construction with *de.* At the same time, in Joinville's work there seems to exist a definite consciousness of finely drawn limits of use of the personal genitive to express possession, relationship, or appurtenance. While examples of the type *au moustier Nostre-Dame* (57), *à la Fonteinne l'Arcevesque* (39), or even *au gue le Béduyn* (the ford known to the Bedouin) (67), are common, the limit appears to be reached in the type *des reliques le vrai cors saint [Louis]* (244). An example such as *Tandis que le roy attendoit la délivrance son frère* (121) is, by comparison with the whole body of examples of uses of the personal possessive genitive, a borderline case. Elsewhere, in the first mention of this matter, we find *le roy attendoit le paiement que sa gent fesoient aus Turs pour la délivrance de son frère* (119).

As successor to the possessive genitive, *de* naturally solved with ease the problem of the borderline case, and perhaps succeeded to them only the more naturally because it was already firmly entrenched in examples of the type *ce qui affiert au gouvernement du peuple* (2), where *de* expresses just the reverse of the genitive construction stressed and elaborated in Lincoln's Gettysburg address. *De* served with equal ease to indicate the opposite extremes of origin or possessor and destination or recipient:

> «Pour ce que je ne weil que nulz face jamès bien pour le guerredon *de* paradis avoir, ne pour la poour d'enfer; mès proprement pour l'amour *de* Dieu avoir, qui tant vaut et qui tout le bien nous peut faire» (134).

> «Si vous pri-je pour l'amour *de* Dieu, premier, et pour l'amour *de* moy, que vous les accoustumez à laver» (8);

or neither, although indirect or remote origin (but unrelated to possession) is implied in the following example:

> à ce que il craignent à encourre le vice de parjure, non pas tant seullement pour la paour *de* Dieu et *de* nous, mez pour la honte du monde (223).

Very rarely, habitual freedom of choice between the use of the genitive and the use of *de,* or in other words between the use and omission of *de,* appears to produce analogical repercussions in the syntax of other constructions concerned with the use of *de,* e.g.,

> *Les* grans deniers que le roy mist à fermer Jaffe ne convient-il pas *parler,* que c'est sanz nombre (174, no variant). Previously cited: Et ainsi le roy acorda *le conte Champaingne* à la royne *de* Cypre (28).

The language at this stage is both increasing and correcting a flexibility gained at a certain loss to semantic precision which in some instances of the use of *de* is never to be more than partially regained through the immense strides still to be taken in contextual clarification by restriction of the liberty of word order. On the other hand the language is gaining in unity and simplicity what it is losing in variety by the reduction of semantic duplicates such as the genitive and the construction with *à* which in the expression of possession or relationship duplicates every postpositive use of the genitive:

> le père *au* roy qui ore est (11); le cors Nostre-Seigneur, qui estoit devenuz en sanc et en char entre les mains *au* prestre (15); quant les enfans *aus* Sarrazins braioient (25); quant les chevaus *aus* Sarrazins et *aus* Béduins avoient poour d'un bysson (25); à Laingnes, qui estoit *au* conte de Nevers (28); qui estoit mère *au* roy d'Angleterre (32); devant la terre *aus* Sarrazins (41); il estoit prest . . . de délivrer Jhérusalem de la main *aus* Sarrazins (42); uns ferrais *au* soudanc du Coyne (45); en l'ostel *au* legat (53); Scecedine le filz *au* Seic (62); Or avint ainsi que je trouvai un gamboison d'estoupes *à* un Sarrazin (75); tout le pooir *au* soudanc de Babiloine (82); il venoit tant de char morte ès gencives *à* nostre gent (92); des chastiaus *aus* barons du païs (102); la sale *au* soudanc (105); pour li oster des mains *aus* Sarrazins (117); des péchiez *aus* Crestiens (134); au chevès du lit *au* Vieil (139); les os *au* conte Gautier (140); Le peuple *à* ce prince (147); ès hostiex des riches homes *à* qui il estoient (148); et fesoi temprer le vin *aus* vallés d'yaue, et ou vin des escuiers moin d'yaue (153).

> il en fist cuire le nez et le baleure *à* un bourjois de Paris (218).

I have set the last cited example apart as a near-borderline case. Similarly, in contrast with the main body of usage illustrated above, certain examples of less frequent occurrence contain semantic deviations which are either barely perceptible, or slight, or great, or even complete, including instances in which *en* appears as a locative alternate of *à:*

> pour l'amour que Dieu avoit *au* roy, qui la poour metoit ou cuer *à* nos ennemis (3); aussi comme Dieu morut pour l'amour que il avoit *en* son peuple, mist-il [Louis IX] son cors en avanture par pluseurs foiz pour l'amour que il avoit *à* son peuple (5); il avoit bien trois cens nageurs en sa galie, et *à* chascun de ses nageurs avoit une targe de ses armes, et *à* chascune targe avoit un penoncel de ses armes batu à or (50).

> c'est grant honte *au* royaume de France, et *au* roy . . ., que . . . (219); «Car ce seroit honte *aus* amiraus, se vous partiés de nos prisons à jeun» (113).

Il leur tournoit un foillet *ou* livre que il tenoit (113); et trouvai le roy qui estoit monté en l'eschaufaut *au* reliques, et fesoit aporter le vrai croiz aval (234).

Ferrais est cil qui tient les paveillons *au* soudanc et qui *li* nettoie ses mesons (45); il eust fait coper la teste *au* roy (108); il *vous* feront la teste coper, et *à* toute vostre gent (110); je ferai le roy jurer; car je *li* ferai la teste du patriarche voler en son geron (110).

Obviously from a comparison of these examples lying just outside of or far beyond the periphery of the usage of possessive *à* not the least remarkable quality of Joinville's prose is its spontaneously faithful reflection of the clarity maintained in French speech by and in spite of the homogenizing of its syntactical wealth.

The incipient abdication of *à* as successor to the possessive genitive, still far less complete today than that of the possessive genitive itself, is apparently related to its use in such examples as *Il me demanda se je lavoie les piez aux povres* (8) and to the syntax of the example last cited above. The object of possessive *à* tends broadly to be dispossessed, and simultaneously to be reinstated either as the indirect recipient of the action or with an ethical interest in its result, but without distinction as to which, so far as construction is concerned. It is to the ease with which, owing to syntactical homogeneity, this deviation of function could occur, that we should probably attribute the nearly complete absorption of the possessive genitive's succession by *de.*

Such instances of indirect causation should remind us that not only, as Foulet says, "il n'y a aucun avantage à regarder le français avec des lunettes latines," but, to paraphrase that opinion, *il n'y a non plus aucun avantage à regarder le français moyen avec des lunettes françaises modernes. Au contraire!* . . .

The "disorder" or confusion which observers (e.g., Brunot, *op. cit.,* I, 403) have noted in the language reflected by MS fr. 13568 is simply a modern view of the wealth of orthographical variety and indiscriminate word order which the thirteenth- and fourteenth-century creators of the foundations of modern French syntax enjoyed with no confusion to themselves while they continued to apply the same rule of syntactical economy that Constantine had applied to Caesar's Latin in the forum, but at this stage to a double series of conflicts arising between synthetic remnants and developed analytic elements on one hand, and on the other between conflicting developments of the analytic elements themselves.

All the repercussions of sporadic development and the exact details of the processes by which conflicts were resolved in the interests of syntactical economy will not be fully known until the entire body of fourteenth-century French prose has been subjected to minute comparative examination to establish the interrelations of linguistic phenomena, and perhaps not even then, in view of the paucity of authentic documents. Needless to add, observations in the present instance, being based on comparisons within the limits of a single document, have been made with no intention to generalize beyond those limits.

Notes

1. *Revue Archéologique, Nouvelle Série,* XV (1867), 169-193, 233-245.

2. Paris, Adrien Le Clère et Cie. Charles Corrard died Sept. 16, 1866.

3. Paris, Mme Ve Jules Renouard.

4. In *Linguistic Value of the Michel Edition of Joinville's Histoire de Saint Louis, RR,* XXXVIII (1947), 193-202, I have attempted, by comparison with the forms found in various documents of known date, and especially those found in the *Archives administratives de la ville de Reims* of the 14th century, to fix the date of MS fr. 13568.

5. Lucien Foulet, *Petite Syntaxe de l'ancien français* (Paris, Champion, 1923), p. 288.

6. This example (la terre estoit son frère) is so classified arbitrarily, in view of the preponderant use of the genitive construction in comparison with that of the construction with *à* (un chevalier qui estoit *à* monseigneur Erart de Brene, 48). In view of the community of sense in the two examples, the classification is possibly quite incorrect.

7. Ferdinand Brunot, *Histoire de la langue française des origines à 1900* (Paris, Armand Colin, 1905), I, 91.

8. *Id., ib.,* I, 95.

9. *Id., La Pensée et la langue* (Paris, Masson, 1922), p. 149.

Helmut Hatzfeld (essay date 1948)

SOURCE: "A Sketch of Joinville's Prose Style," in *Mediaeval Studies,* edited by Urban T. Holmes, Jr., Harvard University Press, 1948, pp. 71–80.

[*In the essay that follows, Hatzfeld provides a technical analysis of Joinville's style and descriptive methodology in* Vie de Saint Louis.]

Histories of Old French Literature of the future will present a new schema; besides the customary type and amount of information, they will include style sketches of the individual authors. These sketches will be objective if they are based on correct analysis, not on impressions. They will be unequivocal if they place in relief the nuances in the single forms of expression, and if they stress the uniqueness of the style elements in their constellation.

As a first attempt of the sort, I present, in the following lines, a sketch of Joinville's style. In contributing to this volume dedicated to Professor Ford, I should have preferred, however, to offer my whole material with examples and references. Since lack of space renders this impossible, the complete study is reserved for future publication elsewhere.

Joinville's descriptive method consists in linking a few well-observed features by a "pale" line of action. One means of effecting this is the avoidance of colors in particular and of epithets in general, of long descriptions and similes. He sometimes tries to develop the outline into a *tableau,* but because balance is lacking in the details which he selects to describe, he achieves only a disproportionate presentation. Most of his descriptions are interrupted by critical remarks. The visualizing power of the sentences is thereby weakened; the picture becomes less sharp.

A temporal circumstance, a modality, an intention, or a souvenir, inserted after the description has been initiated, interrupts the line of design precisely at the point where the eye is drawn to follow it. The inserted remarks are disturbing also because they stop the normal rhythmic flow of the sentence. We are, therefore, confronted with an element of rhythmical disproportion, even though the remark may be so "melted" with the described action as to belong to the action as much as to any critical or sentimental reflection.

"Pure" pictorial details themselves, if compressed in relative or conjunctional clauses, generally tend to accelerate the rhythm for this reason. The details given in these subordinate clauses are digressions in relation to the main action which has been expressed in the principal clause and is "waiting" to be resumed. This fact deprives the picture which appears in the subordinate clause of its importance and prevents the visualizing details from assuming their right proportions. The polysyndeton used for a description, in contradistinction to the acceleration in the dependent clauses, has a retarding effect as far as the rhythm is concerned. It is true that it gives the action poise by means of rhythmical onomatopoetic aid; but just this slow—too slow—progress in description reveals another defect in visualization—one which is due to lack of congruity in connecting the details. This hinders the polysyndeton from expanding into a frame to fit a *tableau.* The visualized parts appear, then, as though they were isolated and extraneous to the compound.

Only in his impressionistic "moving" pictures is Joinville able to keep the power of visualization on a high level because with verbs of vision (*voir, regarder, trouver*) he succeeds in creating a frame within which the picture develops stroke by stroke. Critical remarks have no room in this frame and consequently preserve their absolute, parenthetical character, which is less disturbing. However, even the pictorial impressionism of Joinville should be mistrusted, for his propensity to interpret and judge finds another way to throw the picture out of proportion. A hasty outline is only a pretext for a clever comparison or an anecdote. *Voir* is exchanged, then, for the more critical *sembler.* The anecdote underlines that another person saw (*vit*) or told (*conta*). The impression is metaphorically rendered and only added or retranslated; that is, it is rationally reconstructed almost as it was done by the point-illists of the nineteenth century.

There is only one example in Joinville where a *tableau,* or at least a *tableautin,* is large enough to absorb critical remarks and dialogue elements to the point of admitting them in full harmony and proportion with visualization. It is the famous scene where Joinville, standing in a corner near a window, is sulking because he thinks he has fallen into disgrace with the king, and is told after a time that the contrary is true. There is a colorful strip of pictorial cut-outs made more vivid by bits of scenic explanations and direct speeches: the railed window behind the king's bed, the pouting knight, the king placing his hands slowly on Joinville's shoulders, head, and eyes, the *sénéchal* deceived, thinking ("et je cuidai que ce fust") the blindfolding hands belong to Philip d'Anemos and shouting, "Lessiez moy en paiz!" until he notices the king's emerald ring, and his embarrassment which gives way to relief when the king begins to talk to him in a very friendly manner.

While disproportioned description is naïve as a composite with views and judgments put together at random, its single elements are not. But on the contrary, if Joinville, the *causeur,* evokes his youthful loves and hates, indigna-tions and irritations, jubilations and triumphs, the decisive word or expression at the beginning of the sentence is a single element of naïveté, created by his unrestrained emo-tion. If his desire to impress the "chambre des dames" with old warrior's adventures leads him into exaggerations that come from inadvertence to having said "so much that . . . ," the consequence has to be something naïvely gigantic contrived on the spur of the moment. If, in his extemporaneous talk, something is added like a patch or a tail, or if, in the attempt to report on strategic, diplomatic, scientific matters, he runs into a maze of anacolutha which finally obscure the meaning, we have, in these instances also, single elements of a naïve narration.

A preference for consecutive clauses seems symptomatic of early French prose and is found in Villehardouin as well as in Joinville. Even a propensity to exaggeration— the *gab* of the warrior—is found in Villehardouin. If with the latter, there appear, however, exaggerated comparisons in the *consecutio,* they are frozen; they belong to the *langue,* not to the *parole.* But Joinville, in his naïvely stressed consecutive clauses, makes of his exaggerations personal "visions." It is there that his most original comparisons appear. If they do not occur, at least a plastic situation is related in the *consecutio.*

One of the most naïve features of Joinville's *causerie* is the neglect to integrate his afterthoughts within the compound of his narration. This fact can be discerned from the manifold "patch-like" additions found at different points in the narration where they do not fit as far as

composition and rhythm are concerned. Joinville's "add as you write" language, more suitable for conversation than for "literature," follows, nevertheless, the same rules as does the "prose nombreuse" because the principle of rhythm must be taken into account in all types of prose. Therefore, we can say that the *cauda* in Joinville's prose deprives the sentence of a more effective clausula by add-ing unnecessary weight at the end. Or it deviates the normal *cursus* of the sentence by erecting "hurdles." A naïve emotional outburst is often responsible for this rhythmical damage. Syntactical proof for the existence of this *cauda* is the expression *et-aussi*—typical formula of the afterthought. It is the more indicative of an appendage since one would expect two or three substantives combined with *et* and followed by a verb in the plural. This exteriorly visible *et-aussi* is the key for the more hidden "sentimen-tal" or "pondering" *et* which is rhythmically different from the ordinary conjunctive or polysyndetic *et,* because it has a marked long pause before it. This pondering *et,* introduc-ing an emotional *cauda,* is very effective in its expression of hesitation, sorrow, repentance, indignation; love, melancholy, tenderness; irony, surprise; admiration, awe. The *cauda* can be, finally, of a deeper conceptual quality and comprehend a whole sentence. In this case an un-willed irony crowns the naïve report which aims at being complete.

The genuine polysyndeton, on the other hand, where the *et* (no longer *si*) links sentences through whole paragraphs, is the solemn expression of complicated diplomatic transac-tions like peace making. The report on juridical problems is underlined by long titles and appositions; strategic and other important actions are reported by the formula: "Il avint que." If the event is particularly important for Join-ville himself, he makes dramatic circumlocutions giving circumstances of time. Grave "faits divers" of a general interest are lengthily explained with *une aventure, manière, qui fut teix que,* or by the anacoluthon *teix, car . . . ,* or more expletively with *si est (fut, estoit) teix que.* This is the way in which he reports the fire which broke out in the cabin of the queen, the first discovery of the unusual weapon of the Saracens called *feu gregeois,* the trick of the Tartar king to deprive the host of the leaders by invit-ing them into his camp in order to conquer easily the town of Bagdad.

A naïve pseudoscientific presentation often buttresses an attempted explanation which is no explanation at all, but a mere statement; or it lends a scientific tone to a report which, although ostensibly focused on a juridical problem, is simply the play of a child-like imagination. Thus Join-ville, setting out to explain that earthen jars are bad heat conductors, explains rather that the water of the Nile is particularly cold. Or, wanting to discuss the juridical valid-ity of a letter the seal of which has been broken, he is car-ried away by the fantasy roused in his imagination by "the legs and the stool of the king," which are still visible on the broken seal.

Reducing the rich Old French linguistic material to a minimum, Joinville can not avoid repetitions. These repetitions, when used with variations, bring liveliness to the style. To the repetitive forms Joinville adds a lively dialogue which uses all types of speech to make the tone of the discussions and the report on the discussions animated.

Earlier critics intimate that Joinville's repetitions are awkward. This is out of the question. For we have many examples where he does not repeat the same noun after a short interval, but replaces it logically with a pronoun. From this we may conclude that, if Joinville repeats the noun, he does it for a specific reason. The first reason is clarity. The repetition of an expression, sometimes slightly varied, becomes the symbol of passionate complaint, of mournful pride, of ironical threat, of sarcastic indignation. Elevated to a witty *pointe,* repetition assumes the role of a spirited leitmotif, connected with word-play. Examples of longer parallelisms with repeated words have preferably a chiastic or half-chiastic character implying a lively satisfaction, or the spontaneous result of a premeditated action. Finally, Joinville in his repetitions is led by the delight he takes in echo sounds, a sign of his playfulness. These echo sounds range from a childish rhyme, or a more or less meaningful game with a *simplex* and *compositum,* to the repetition of a verb containing such wealth of connotations that the mere repetitive pondering on it creates new comparisons.

Half a century after all the words of the king, his counsellors, the military *chievetains* and other *prudhommes* have been spoken, Joinville makes bold to quote them. In this he is not different from other historians from Livy to Villehardouin who indulge so much in quoting direct speeches that in cases of uncertainty they even succumb to forgery. But Joinville's interest is centered more on a kaleidoscope of changing speech styles than on quotations. Whereas to our surprise he quotes direct speeches that were allegedly made by Saracens, Turks, Tartars, Egyptians, Bedouins and even their wives, he quotes words of the king and his close associates which he could possibly have known, in indirect, semidirect, or objective-narrative reports. But he does it in such a way that these different styles of speeches and reports constantly interchange and mingle, producing an extraordinary vividness. The direct answers to questions often consist of one or two words; the dialogues wax stichomythic; longer direct speeches are interspersed with secondary quotes of celebrities who are supposed to have said "this" or "that." Embryonic cases of the modern "style indirect libre" give certain passages an animated balance and serve as a spring board for new, direct, still livelier repartee between king and *sénéchaus—pièces de résistance* of the **Histoire de Saint Louis.**

The seemingly correct, but impossible, quotes from sayings of the enemies which were current in the French camp are all the more charmingly arrogant as they appear introduced by two *verba dicendi* instead of one. The indirect speeches of the French leaders are made savory by a kind of X-rayed quotations stemming from proverbs and popular comparisons which appear to have been taken directly from the mouth of the people. The direct speeches of the pagans do not transform sufficiently the French viewpoint, so that a Saracen carefully introduced as "qui avoit nom Sebreci qui estoit nez de Morentaigne" finally declares the French king to be "li plus forz ennemis que la loys paienime ait." The accelerato of lively dialogue is retarded to the moderato of indirect speech, when the subject matter takes a grave and serious turn. The "style indirect libre" is in Joinville's hand a fine means of distant empathy with the speaker whose problems, however, are not entirely his own. When the king asks the mariners whether they would abandon a ship loaded with precious merchandise simply for fear of death, Joinville, after beginning their answer in indirect form, continues and completes it in semidirect form. Joinville knows also the stronger type of the "style indirect libre"—that modern substitutionary report where the dividing lines between speaker and reporter are entirely effaced, because a general truth is shared by both of them—which leaves the reader to decide whose voice he is hearing. This occurs in the instructions on faith and morals given by the saintly king where the indirect speech is sometimes continued in a substitutionary way so that it could be understood also as the comment of the author.

There may be other features in the prose style of Joinville. Those mentioned certainly are original enough to make this early French writer the representative of a most personal "art de la prose."

Lionel J. Friedman (essay date 1953)

SOURCE: "A Mode of Medieval Thought in Joinville's *Credo,*" *Modern Language Notes,* Vol. LXVIII, No. 7, November, 1953, pp. 446–53.

[*In the following essay, Friedman discusses a particular mode of thought employed by Joinville in the* Credo. *This common medieval methodology was used to combine similar Biblical quotations into a new statement. Friedman maintains that critical ignorance of this mode of reasoning used by Joinville has caused some confusion regarding what constitutes a quotation in the* Credo.]

In the opening paragraph of the **Credo,** Joinville carefully warns those who will see and hear the work that the illustration is according to the humanity of Christ and to our own, since the Divinity and the Trinity cannot be known in themselves by mortal man, in witness whereof he invokes Holy Writ:

> . . . car ce est si grans choses, si com sains Pous et li autre saint le tesmoignent, que iex ne puet veoir, ne oreille oïr, ne lengue raconter, por les pechiez et les ordures don nous sumes plain et chargie en ceste mortel vie, qui nous tolent a veoir la clartei soveraine.[1]

This passage has been dutifully annotated with a reference to I Corinthians,[2] but that this text does not correspond precisely to the quotation of Joinville—explaining no more than the element *iex ne puet veoir, ne oreille oïr* of the romance, and containing no allusion to the element *ne lengue raconter*—appears not to have been found disturbing. Similar instances in the **Credo** have been shrugged off by Lozinski with the conclusion that Joinville *s'en rapportait à sa mémoire et celle-ci le trahissait*.[3]

The expression has already been treated by Gilson in connection with a similar one found in the *Queste del saint Graal: ce que cuers mortex ne porroit penser, ne langue d'ome terrien deviser.*[4] Gilson has demonstrated that we are dealing with a particular mode of medieval thought, common to hermeneutics and the sermon, called *auctoritates concordantes,* which consists of demonstrations made from separate elements of the Bible brought together as having some bearing upon the same point. The expression used by Joinville is not an inexact quotation, but a new statement, compounded of at least two scriptural texts, between which a concordance exists. The passages

> *Quod oculus non vidit, nec auris audivit,* nec in cor hominis ascendit, quae praeparavit Deus iis qui diligunt eum.[5]

and

> *A saeculo non audierunt, neque auribus perceperunt; oculus non vidit,* Deus, absque te, quae praeparasti expectantibus te.[6]

provide the two elements accounted for. A completely different text of John, concerning a man rapt into the third heaven, where *audivit arcana verba, quae non licet homini loqui,*[7] furnishes the *ne lengue raconter* of Joinville and the *ne langue d'ome terrien deviser* of the *Queste.* Other examples of this type of demonstration are easy to adduce.

The prophecy of the Crucifixion as prefigured in Isaac has been troublesome.[8]

> La profecie de l'evre sur la croiz, ce est de Ysaac, que vous verres ci apres point, qui fu obeissans a son pere jusques a la mort. A la mort fu livres Nostres Sires Ihesu Crist pour les felons Juis, et ausi honteuse mort comme de la crois, la u il pandoient alors les larons, ausi comme on fait orandroit les larons aus fourches. Entre dous larons le firent-il pandre en la crois, pour faire antendant au pueple que par son mesfait avoit mort deservie.[9]

The Middle Ages were constant in seeing in Isaac the figure of Christ for reasons mentioned quite accurately by Lozinski. However, this relationship once posited, Joinville develops a concordant statement of Paul—of important liturgical use during the Easter Season[10]—concerning Christ *factus obediens usque ad mortem.*[11] That this latter text is the one thought of by Joinville becomes patent when it is observed that the majority of the discussion is only an elucidation of the remainder of Paul's statement, *mortem autem crucis (ausi honteuse mort comme de la crois),* in which Joinville attempts to explain

the significance of this particular kind of death. This latter aspect of the problem is in no way concerned with the tale from Genesis but could arise only from the text of Philippians or from the liturgical formula. The appearance of the same grouping of ideas in Joinville and saint Bruno does not indicate either a source or an influence, but rather that the same method of scriptural concordance has produced a similar result, just as in the previous example. For the closing sentence, there is possible a further concordance with another traditional text for the Crucifixion, also of liturgical use: . . . *tradidit in mortem animam suam, et cum sceleratis reputatus est.*[12]

The prophecy of Christ by *la cote Joseph faite d'une pièce,* which gave Lozinski so much trouble since he was unable to find any authority for the fact that Joseph's coat was made in one piece, is amenable to the same sort of analysis. There has been a concordance between the *tunica polymita* or *tunica talaris* of Joseph and the *tunica inconsutilis, desuper contexta per totum* of Christ,[13] for which at the Crucifixion the soldiers cast lots rather than divide it. There is a further concordance with the awesome Psalm of the Crucifixion to which John specifically refers.[14]

An unawareness of this mode of reasoning has led also to a certain confusion as to what does or does not represent a quotation in the **Credo.** For the resurrection of the body, Joinville argues, in part:

> Là ne seroit pas la balance Nostre Seignor droite, se li cors de ceus (li cors aus pecheors) ne resuscitoient pour atandre lou jugemant et la joutise que Diex lour a appareillie en anfer, si com il meismes lou tesmoigne de sa bouche. Et lour maus vengera Diex seur les armes et seur les cors d'aus en l'autre siecle, pour ce que Diex ne fist nulle vangence d'aus en ce siecle.[15]

For some mysterious reason, Lozinski has chosen to believe that the specific allusion to the witness of God Himself refers to the words *et lour maus vengera Diex . . . en l'autre siecle* which *semblent viser*[16] John v, 29.[17] This requires some effort of the imagination, for the words of John refer only to the ultimate judgment of the righteous and the wicked, and have no bearing upon their being rewarded and punished in both body and soul, the very point to be made. The testimony alluded to by Joinville refers instead to the preceding portion of the text—*lou jugemant et la joutise que Diex lour a appareillie en anfer*—and is to be found in the statement of Christ concerning the Judgment and the separation of the sheep from the goats; the former to the right of the Son of Man, the latter to His left.

> Tunc dicet rex his qui a dextris erunt: Venite, benedicti Patris mei, possidete paratum vobis regnum a constitutione mundi . . . Tunc dicet et his qui a sinistris erunt: *Discedite a me, maledicti, in ignem aeternum, qui paratus est diabolo et angelis ejus.*[18]

There is here only an *allusio,* not a quotation. Similarly, in the same discussion:

Boneuree iert la resurrections des mors qui es euvres
Dieu morront, si com dist sainz Jehans en l'Apocalipse;
car lour joies et lour bieneurtez lour doubleront, ce est
a savoir en cors et en arme.[19]

A quite accurate identification has been made between the
first part of this development and the text of Revelation,[20]
but, as a synopsis and explanation of the Biblical text, the
words do not constitute a quotation, but an allusion. Lozinski, moreover, believes the following words *car lour
joies et lour bieneurtez lour doubleront* to be a quotation,
which he connects to several passages from Revelation.[21]

Testimony of the resurrection of the body was frequently
sought in references to duality, which were interpreted as
the specific duality *body-soul,* as in the line of Isaiah
glossed by Vincent de Beauvais, in this very context:

> *In terra sua,* quae est terra haereditatis aeternae, *dupli-
> cia possidebunt,* id est duplicem gloriam, in anima scil-
> icet et corpore.[22]

Again, Joinville has not given a quotation, but a conclusion based upon the text *Blessed are the dead which die in
the Lord,* concorded with either the line from Isaiah or
with the first of the possibilities mentioned by Lozinski,
and advanced at this point as a proof of the resurrection of
the body. The testimony of John concerning those who
have died in the Lord is meaningful of the resurrection
only when brought into concordance with pertinent
scriptural references to the two-fold, in answer to the question *why?* [23]

The texts examined do not show the activity of concordance, but its results, and indicate that the author has a
fund of theological knowledge which has been arrived at
by a specific mode of reasoning developed in medieval
exegesis and of common use in the sermon. Considering
the avowed purpose of the work—to confirm dying crusaders in the faith by proof of the articles of the Creed by
scriptural witness—it is not surprising that this mode of
thought was employed, but it should be realized that it has
a more extensive use than in the specific concordant activity of the Old Testament prophecies in words and works.

Notes

1. Joinville, *Histoire de Saint Louis, Credo, et Lettre à
   Louis X,* texte original, accompagné d'une
   traduction, par M. Natalis de Wailly. Paris, Didot,
   1874, p. 414.

2. I Corinthians, ii, 9.

3. Lozinski, "Recherches sur les Sources du *Credo* de
   Joinville," *Neuphilologische Mitteilungen.* 1930.
   XXXI, 189.

4. Gilson, "la Mystique de la grâce dans la *Queste del
   saint Graal," les Idées et les Lettres.* Paris, Vrin,
   1932, pp. 76-78.

5. I Corinthians, *loc. cit.*

6. Isaiah, lxiv, 4.

7. II Corinthians, xii, 4.

8. The search for a textual source has led Lozinski
   along the following perilous path: *La plupart des
   Pères ne font que noter la ressemblance qui existe
   entre Isaac portant le bois qui doit lui servir de
   bûcher, et le Christ qui porta lui-même la croix de
   sa passion. L'obéissance jusqu'à la mort n'est
   relevée que par saint Bruno, évêque de Segni:*
   obediens Patri usque ad mortem . . . *Joinville suit
   l'exemple de la minorité, et il a peutêtre tort, car la
   préfiguration s'arrête au bûcher, étant donné
   qu'Isaac ne périt pas et qu'il ne se doutait même
   pas du sort qui l'attendait.* (Lozinski, *op. cit.,* pp.
   194-195.)

9. Joinville, *op. cit.,* p. 422.

10. See use of the versicle *Christus factus est pro nobis
    obediens usque ad mortem, mortem autem crucis,*
    during Holy Week.

11. Philippians, ii, 8.

12. Isaiah, liii, 12. Versicle for the 1st Nocturn of Holy
    Saturday: *Tradidit in mortem animam suam; et inter
    sceleratos reputatus est.* For so much of the vast
    theological knowledge which Gaston Paris saw in
    the *Credo,* one does not have to go further than the
    Breviary to find a source. Beside the two instances
    noted, a third *prophecy* of the Crucifixion (the text
    of Jeremiah) serves as a Response for the second
    Nocturn of the same day: *O vos omnes qui transitis
    per viam, attendite et videte, si est dolor similis
    sicut dolor meus.* A fourth instance will be seen
    shortly. There is no reason to doubt Joinville's
    report of his assiduity at hearing his hours at the
    time he composed the *Credo.* A glimpse at the
    Joinville Breviary (and its illustrations?) could be
    very revealing.

13. John, xix, 23-24: *Milites ergo cum crucifixissent
    eum, acceperunt vestimenta ejus (et fecerunt quatuor
    partes, uniquique militi partem) et tunicam. Erat
    autem tunica inconsutilis, desuper contexta per
    totum. Dixerunt ergo ad invicem: Non scindamus
    eam, sed sortiamur de illa cujus sit. Ut Scriptura
    impleretur dicens: Partiti sunt vestimenta mea sibi,
    et in vestem meam miserunt sortem.*

14. Psalm xxi, 18: *Diviserunt sibi vestimenta mea, et
    super vestem meam miserunt sortem.* This line, too,
    has an extensive liturgical use.

15. Joinville, *op. cit.,* p. 438.

16. *Op. cit.,* p. 191. Lozinski has changed the
    punctuation supplied by Wailly. The manuscript is of
    little help here, the punctuation being very erratic.
    Wailly's division of the text into paragraphs, despite
    the paragraphing of the manuscript, which leaves
    this portion as a block, is of doubtful value.

17. Accordingly, the above would be Joinville's garbled
    version of *Et procedent qui bona fecerunt in
    resurrectionem vitae: qui vero male egerunt in
    resurrectionem judicii.*

18. Matthew, xxv, 31-34.

19. Joinville, *op. cit.,* pp. 438-440.

20. Revelation, xiv, 13, 13: *Beati mortui qui in Domino moriuntur. Amodo jam dicit Spiritus ut requiescat a laboribus suis; opera enim illorum sequuntur illos.*

21. Revelation, xviii, 6: *Reddite illi sicut et ipsa reddidit vobis: et duplicate duplicia secundum opera cjus: in poculo, quo miscuit, miseete illi duplum. Ibid.,* xx, 12-13. *Ibid.,* xxii, 12.

22. Vincent de Beauvais, *Speculum morale,* Douai, 1624, col. 770.

23. The other references given by Lozinski must be rejected, for Joinville is obviously working with the idea of *doubler,* and they refer to another type of witness, exemplified by *in qua mensura mensi fucritis, remetietur vobis.* (Matthew, vii, 2.)

Rene Hague (essay date 1955)

SOURCE: An introduction to *"The Life of St. Louis,"* by *John of Joinville,* translated by Rene Hague, Sheed and Ward, 1955, pp. 1–19.

[*In the following essay, Hague reviews the debate surrounding the dating of* Vie de Saint Louis, *comments on the content of the work, and offers an overview of the textual history of the extant manuscripts.*]

John of Joinville was a man whose generous spirit was easily moved to admiration; particularly was he moved when he saw a man of high rank sacrificing all that was dear and devoting even his life to what was to him the greatest of all causes: the armed fight against the enemies of the faith and the protection or rescue of the "humble folk of Our Lord", the poor nameless pilgrims who aided Christendom only by their suffering. When his King was canonised, there was but one thing that clouded John's joy—that Louis had not been enrolled among the martyrs. From a great family in Champagne, the house of Brienne, allied by marriage[1] to the family of Joinville, came at least two heroes to whom John extended an admiration something akin to that which he felt for Louis: John of Brienne, twelfth King of Jerusalem, whose disaster on the banks of the Nile in 1219 anticipated that of Louis' expedition thirty years later, and the "great Count Walter", on whom, murdered in prison at Cairo after the defeat at Gaza in 1244, Joinville looked as a martyr.

The connection between the two families, to both of which the pilgrimage of the Cross was a dear tradition, goes back to the first ancestor of John who is known to us.[2] Some time early in the eleventh century, before the Crusade was preached, there was a follower of Engelbert of Brienne, named Stephen. He married one of his leader's daughters, and built the "new castle" on the hill overlooking the town of Joinville.[3] It is interesting when we remember that five generations later his descendant, John, in his *Life of St.*

Louis, speaks of St. Louis' arguments with the clergy, and of his own troubles in connection with the Abbey of St. Urbain, that Stephen, too, was so high-handed in his demands on the local Abbey of Montiérender that King Robert the Pious ordered him to be excommunicated. Nor were these two the only Lords of Joinville who had similar disputes. Stephen's son, Geoffrey I, who succeeded his father in the lordship, was also threatened with excommunication by Pope Leo IX. His son, Geoffrey II, appears to have died childless, and it is with his nephew, Geoffrey III, who was Lord of Joinville after his father Roger, that the crusading tradition of the family is started.[4] This Geoffrey—"old Geoffrey" as he called himself to distinguish himself from his son, "young Geoffrey" ("Geoffrey le Valet")—was with the great Count Henry of Champagne in Palestine, where his conduct earned him the position, which was made hereditary in his family, of Seneschal of Champagne.[5] His son, Geoffrey IV, fought and died at Acre, where, after the fall of the city, he was buried; and it was this Geoffrey's son—Geoffrey V, Geoffrey "Trouillart" or "Trullard"[6]—who, in the eyes of our John, his nephew, was the hero of the family, and in whom appears something that reminds us of his nephew's character. He was twice overseas: first, with his father at Acre. King Richard of England was so impressed by his courage that he allowed him to quarter his arms with the Plantagenet lion.[7] It was this shield that John brought proudly and piously back from Palestine and hung in his chapel of Saint Lawrence at Joinville, where it remained until 1544, when it was stolen by Charles V's ruffians. After his father's death he returned to Champagne to settle his affairs. A little more than ten years later he takes the Cross again, at the tourney of Écry which gives a start to the Fourth Crusade,[8] and when the leader of the Crusade, the Count of Champagne, dies, he is one of the party of lords, which includes the historian Geoffrey of Villehardouin, Marshal of Champagne, which offers the leadership in turn to the Duke of Burgundy, the Count of Bar, and finally to the Marquis Boniface of Montferrat. Villehardouin sheds some hypocritical tears for those who refused the bait of Constantinople and took the road to Syria. Among these was Geoffrey. There is something of a pious sneer in Villehardouin's tone when he says that those who left the main body achieved little. It was little enough, indeed, but it cost Geoffrey his life, for in Syria he died, late in 1203, or early in 1204, at Krak, the huge castle of the Knights Hospitallers. I must confess that I like to share his nephew's admiration, and that it pleases me that Delaborde quotes Geoffrey's contemporary Guyot de Provins:

> *Queus estoit Joffrois de Joinvile?*
> *Meillors chevaliers par Saint Gille*
> *N'avoit de lui de ça lou Far.*[9]

He was unmarried, and the lordship of Joinville passed to his brother Simon, the father of our historian John. Simon also served overseas. He was with King John[10] at the taking of Damietta in November 1219, though he was home again a couple of months later, in January 1220; so that when John tells us that St. Louis' men were astounded that a city which their fathers had besieged for so long should fall to them so easily, his remark has behind it the memory of a familiar story. John was the first child born of his father's second wife, Beatrix; Delaborde fixes his birth as being after June 1224 and before May 1225. We know little of his youth except that he must have served as a squire at the Court of his overlord, Count Thibaut IV of Champagne, poet and Crusader. He tells us himself that in 1241 he accompanied his master and carved for him at the great feast given at Saumur by St. Louis. He tells us, too, that he took no part in the campaign of Taillebourg in 1242—he was not yet knighted—but in 1245 he and his brother learnt something of fighting under the Count of Chalon (see §277). About 1239 he was married to Alix of Grandpré. The marriage was not, presumably, consummated for several years; the date of the birth of his first son, Geoffrey, is not known, but he tells us that his second son, John, was born in 1248, just when he was on the eve of leaving with St. Louis on the crusading pilgrimage. He had taken the Cross at the same time as St. Louis, in 1244. It is the next six years of his life that are best known to us, from the account he gives of his experiences in Egypt and Palestine.

In 1254 he was back in France for good. He was now a man of considerable importance, a close friend of the King, and a high officer in the County of Champagne.[11] He was not infrequently at Court (he mentions several occasions) and he tells us (§665) of at least one important mission with which he was entrusted. But when St. Louis asked him to accompany him on his expedition to Tunis he not only refused but speaks very strongly of the folly and even wickedness of those who did not attempt to dissuade the King from his fruitless and unhappy journey.

Joinville was a very old man, ninety-two, when he died in 1317, on the eve of Christmas. He had lived under six Kings of France, from Louis VIII to Philip V. He was buried in his own chapel of St. Lawrence, but his grave was desecrated in 1793, and of castle and chapel nothing is left. A very touching document survives (see p. 238)—a letter he wrote in 1315 to Louis X, in which he says that "plus tost que je pourray, ma gent seront apparilié pour aleir ou il vous plaira"—in the MS. you can see that his secretary had first written "je et ma gent", but the first two words are struck out.

Not the least debt we owe to the poor pilgrims ("le peuple menu Nostre Signour") whose bones were scattered in the Balkan forests, in Asia Minor, in Syria, in Egypt, is the fresh youth of French prose.[12] The earliest chronicles of the Crusade, and the letters written home by Crusaders, were in Latin; the desire, however, for news of the pilgrims in a form that could be read by all created a demand for translations of the Latin chronicles and for original accounts in the vernacular—for books such as the "romant" (i.e. a book in French), to which Joinville refers at the end of his own book. William of Tyre's history, for example, was translated, and it was from a vernacular continuation of this translation that Joinville took the story of King Richard's being used as a bogey man to silence the Sa-

racen children when they cried.[13] His own book is sometimes spoken of as though it contained the memories of an old man, writing down his version of a story that had happened many years ago, and he has been both admired for the excellence of his memory and excused, when his memory failed him, on the ground that he is writing many years after the event. It is true that when he first wrote eighteen years (from 1254 to 1272) had elapsed since his return from overseas; but he was only twenty-three years old when he left home, and twenty-nine when he returned. He was even younger when he wrote the *Credo*. The date of this he fixes for us in §777—he wrote it at Acre after the King's brothers had left and before the King went to fortify Caesarea, i.e. between August 1250 and April 1251. It is apparent, however, from §820 that what we now have is a second edition, which was written in 1287.[14] There is nothing to show that much alteration was made in this later edition, as was done with the larger book. Joinville was interested in the physical production of books—in the *Credo* he attaches as much importance to the pictures as he does to the text, or even more; and when he wishes to describe St. Louis' foundations in France it is the metaphor of the illuminator which he uses—"Ainsi comme li escrivains qui a fait son livre, qui l'enlumine d'or et d'azur, enlumina lidiz roys son royaume de belles abbaies que il y fist".

It is different, however, with the book he wrote after his return. But, first, a word about the title. Joinville gives no definite title at the head of his book. He refers to it, however, first (§2) as "un livre des saintes paroles et des bon faiz nostre roy saint Looys", and later (§19) as "la vie nostre saint roy Looys". It is, perhaps, because as a life it is manifestly incomplete that the title "The History of St. Louis" or even "The Memoirs of John of Joinville" has been preferred to the author's own description. When you complete your first reading of it one thing cannot fail to strike you, that the book falls into three parts, and that the longest part is sandwiched between two shorter parts of a very different character. The middle section, indeed, appears to contain the memoirs of John of Joinville when he was overseas (though with special reference to St. Louis). At the beginning and end there appear to have been tacked on shorter sections which are concerned with the virtues of St. Louis. We have a good deal of evidence concerning the date at which the book, or the edition of it which we have, was written.[15] Joinville tells us that he made the book at the instance of Queen Jeanne of Navarre, who died on April 2nd, 1305, and that he was unable to finish it in her lifetime. From §35, we learn that John II, Duke of Brittany (the first to bear the title of Duke), was alive when he was writing, and John II died in November 1305. Finally, the last words of the book (though they do not apply to more than the particular copy in which they were first written) give us the date October 1309.

§555, however, mentions Hugh III, Duke of Burgundy (at Acre with King Richard), and speaks of him as being the grandfather of the Duke "recently dead",[16] and this would appear to refer to Hugh IV, who died in 1272. It appears likely, then, that when Queen Jeanne asked Joinville to write the book "des bons faiz et des saintes paroles" he already had by him his own account, written in 1272, of his companionship with St. Louis; and it may be suggested that this will appear more probable to one who considers some feats of memory (the yellow stripes on the servant's tunic in §407, the accuracy of most of the dates, Saracen names, the King's order in §389 to light the binnacle lamp) that would be astonishing in an octogenarian, unless he had kept very full notes, but would be no more than remarkable in a man of forty-seven writing eighteen years after the event. To this consideration might be added the differences in style and certainty of execution between what can be roughly described as the hagiographical and autobiographical sections, though we should remember that the difference in subject matter may possibly account for what we might attribute to a difference in time of composition. Joinville's six years overseas had obviously made a deep and lasting impression on him—and no doubt on his conversation—but he had little aptitude for the writing of history (in his historical digressions the facts are inclined to be muddled), and there is a distinct change of tone whenever, in the autobiographical section, he has occasion to speak of anything that was outside his personal experience. There is one further slight point that is worth considering, though it may be no more than a coincidence: the suggested date (1272) of a first edition of Joinville's memoirs of his years overseas with St. Louis is only two years from the date of the Saint's death, which was followed by a tremendous outburst of popular devotion. Of the sixty-five miracles recorded in Guillaume de Saint Pathus's *Les Miracles de St. Louis,* fourteen are dated 1271.[17]

Joinville has often been written of as though the chief interest which his book has to offer was the story of his adventures and the attractive picture it gives us of its author. But it is worth remembering that his avowed intention was to give a picture of St. Louis, and with this in mind it is interesting to see how that picture would have been affected had he confined himself to the overseas section of his book—roughly from chapters xxiv to cxxxiv inclusive. In the earlier part of the book we should not be troubled by missing the historical chapters xv-xxiv (though we should sacrifice the great feast at Saumur and the story of Queen Blanche's kissing the German boy on the forehead, because his mother, St. Elizabeth of Hungary, must have kissed it so often); the rather tedious sermon about God's threats in chapter vii will go; but much that is of great value would be lost (some of the most trifling and incidental stories are the ones that are the most illuminating): St. Louis' remark about clothes (§38) and his injunction to speak up at table; Joinville's preferring "thirty mortal sins" to leprosy; the argument between the Jew and the knight and St. Louis' rough-and-ready remedy for unbelief; the oak tree at Vincennes, dear to French tradition; the story of the broken seal.

This last in particular has a double interest, for it illustrates two points: that Joinville is at his best when he was present

at what he describes, and that the supreme kingly virtue which he wishes to emphasise is that of "loyalty"—loyalty in the sense of his word *léaultei,* a complete disregard of self-interest when faced with a question—even a political question—of right and wrong. Towards the end of the book, again, it is only Joinville's personal experiences that are of real interest; two of them are his dreams, and in one of these dreams (ch. cxlviii) the King, standing outside the chapel at Joinville, smiling and saying that he is not thinking of leaving just yet, not only has that sharpness and clarity which sometimes impress the mind so vividly in dreams, but speaks with the tone of intimacy and kindness which Joinville had the art of conveying in words.

When we come, again, to consider the central and much the longest section of the book there is one thing to note and one thing to bear in mind. We should bear in mind that, however enthralled Joinville was by the excitement and hardships and adventures of a campaign overseas and his taste of an Egyptian prisoner-of-war camp, he had constantly in his mind the character of his hero, and it is from love for Louis and a desire to describe his virtues that he writes. As, moreover, he wishes his book to provide examples which St. Louis' heirs may take to heart, a number of things are included as digressions simply because they illustrate a virtue which Joinville wishes his readers to imitate: the generosity of Count Henry of Champagne and of John the Armenian, for example; the long digression in praise of Count Walter of Brienne, the story of Amaury de Montfort and the unbelievers, the debate between the monks and the Jews; many such matters are introduced for the same reason.

It is noteworthy that Joinville is at his best when his own experience coincides with an opportunity to speak of Louis' courage, or charity, or humour; of his hasty temper, too; his "difficultness"; and even his harshness to or lack of consideration for his brave wife; his crossness to the unfortunate servant Ponce, who was late in bringing his horse; his extreme and even unreasonable severity, as experienced by the unhappy young men who made the journey from Lampedusa to Hyères towed in a boat behind the ship, as a punishment for delaying the fleet by guzzling fruit in the orchards on the island; even, a less dignified fault, that petulance which we hide from the world but do not, unhappily, scruple to display to those who are near to us—as when Louis complains (ch. lxxix) that his brother Robert would have been more assiduous in visiting him than was Alfonse: Louis is so much the mainspring of his work that it might well be argued that Joinville would not have written at all—even the *Credo* bears marks of Louis' tutorship; its very subject, faith, is at the root of Louis' teaching—had it not been the King who led the expedition to Egypt.

If one were able to question Joinville and ask him what sort of a character he had attempted to depict he might well have answered: the character of a *preudome.* That most difficult word sums up all the range of virtues that lie between personal courage and piety—discretion, determination, charity, prudence, justice—the quality of possessing just that particular virtue which is applicable to a given situation or emergency—courage, as when Walter of Châtillon, guarding the village street in the last march of the harassed French, rises in his stirrups and calls "ou sont mi preudome?"; piety (even among the infidels), as when the old man who visited Joinville and his companions in prison is described as a "preudome de sa loi". Joinville quotes an interesting remark of Philip Augustus, St. Louis' grandfather, about the difference between a *preux homme,* a man who was no more than physically brave, and a *preudome,* whose powers "li vient dou don Dieu".

Sainte-Beuve, whose essay on Joinville is full of understanding and sympathy, draws a contrast between the thirteenth-century notion of the *preudome* and the debased and more worldly standard we find in Froissart, and hints that Joinville fell a little short of the religious ideal of chivalry, as though he were halfway between St. Louis and Froissart. Although he readily applied the word to men of religion, it is true that he uses it freely for men of whom St. Louis would only have used the term *preux,* and that the military virtues and the virtues proper to a man in a high and responsible position were those which he recognised the most readily. "Par chevalerie", he tells us in the **Credo** (and the context makes it plain that he means more "fighting" or "soldiering" than what we mean by "chivalry"), "par chevalerie covient conquerre lou regne des ciex".

Nevertheless, the *preudome* represented to Joinville the summit of human virtue; it was he whom he naturally and without reflection admired. But when Queen Jeanne asked him to write of St. Louis' virtues and he looked again at his book he may have felt that he should make an attempt to write at least something of the more conventional details of hagiography—the details of prayers and devotions and fastings, of devotion to the Church and the religious Orders, of monastic foundations. Fortunately, he had little fluency in such composition, and though he praises the King for his frugality at table, for example, it is not difficult to see that he finds his hospitality and the fine manner in which he entertained his guests more attractive to describe. Joinville is the frankest and most honest of writers and, though he was also a most pious man, he does not mind admitting that for his own part there is a standard of sanctity at which he has no intention of aiming.

St. Louis was two things to Joinville; a very dear friend and master whose memory was to be cherished, and a saint to whom he had a great devotion. But the friendship was based on many years' comradeship and hardships shared, and it was to the description of that comradeship that his talents were naturally adapted. Not realising that in describing the comrade he was at the same time giving us the truest and most interesting picture of the saint, he might be surprised to find that, to a modern reader, his attempts to treat particularly of his friend's sanctity do little to increase the reader's knowledge. We might, in fact, go further and say that much of the impression we get of St.

Louis is obtained indirectly; it is obtained, that is, through the extremely vivid picture we have of the sort of man who admired him, and of the effect that admiration produced in Joinville's own conduct and ideas.

At the root of *léaultei* is truth, and Joinville is the most truthful of men. Little remains of the enquiries that were made as a prelude to St. Louis' canonisation,[18] and what Joinville tells us of them is doubly characteristic of him: he insists on Louis' love of truth (truth even to Saracens, and even "when a matter of ten thousand pounds was at stake") and at the same time he stresses the importance of his own evidence. There are biographies in which the character of the writer emerges even more clearly and attractively than that of the subject. In A. J. A. Symons' *The Quest for Corvo,* for example, the revelation of Symons' own character has a greater and more lasting attraction than his quest. This is not completely true of Joinville, because in his book both author and subject arouse our charity, but in his case there is the added interest that the virtues we see in the author were derived from, or at all events fostered by, the subject. Perhaps the most celebrated and certainly one of the most touching passages in the book provides an example not only of Joinville's devotion to truth but also of the way in which Louis and Joinville are so fused in the book that the most striking stories about Joinville are often the most revealing stories about the King; it is after the conference at Acre, where the question of returning to France has been discussed, and Joinville thinks that he is going to be left alone in Palestine. He tells us that as he put his arms through the little barred window he thought that, whatever happened, he would not go back on his word—he would not go home while there were still humble folk in Egyptian prisons—and there is no doubt but that he would, indeed, have taken service under one of the overseas barons.[19]

An even more striking instance, considering the freedom of modern speech (for we may say with Joinville that "a peinne puet l'on parler que on ne die 'que dyables y ait part'!"), is the occasion where Joinville dismissed a knight who, when they were pitching camp (§567), had struck another. In dismissing him, Joinville had said, "God help me, you shall stay in my company no longer"; and though the knight was repentant and Joinville was begged to have him back, he took his oath so seriously that he said that he could not reinstate him unless the Legate dispensed him from the oath—which, unfortunately, the Legate was unwilling to do.

One result of his love of truth is that we find no deliberate exaggeration or distortion in the facts he records, and he is careful to distinguish between what he saw and heard himself and what he knows (the journey to Tunis, for example) only by hearsay. This is not to say that there are not a few errors—minor errors in dates and names—where his memory is at fault, nor that there are not times where his concentration on his own experiences sets the facts somewhat out of focus. Thus in the account of the battle of Mansura on Shrove Tuesday his own private engagement at the little bridge he held (which is mentioned by no other writer) is given as much importance as the main battle. It is easy, however, to make allowance for such differences in emphasis, and it is to this personal preoccupation that we owe a host of vivid details which bring colour and depth to the black and white of historical writing.

At the same time Joinville is distinguished by his unwillingness to colour his story by the inclusion of idle and scandalous gossip. There are but few occasions on which he writes hardly of any man, and never does he do so without cause. (It would not, I think, be fair to hold against him his remark that when the envoys of Frederick II arrived in Palestine with letters to the Sultan and instructions to do what they could to hasten the release of the prisoners, many said that it was as well that they had come too late or they might secretly have hindered the release—for the anti-imperial Syrians may well have been so spiteful, and Joinville does not associate himself with the story.) About the battle of Mansura he felt very strongly, but he will not give the names of those he thought most worthy of censure, for they were dead when he wrote. John of Beaumont, again, was a man who was particularly offensive to Joinville—loud-mouthed and disobliging—but he no more than records his ill manners: he does not, as does the "Minstrel of Rheims" (who is little more than a gossip-monger), repeat the story that Beaumont was held responsible for the failure to keep the Nile open to traffic and for the consequent lack of provisions in the camp.[20] About the greatest mistake of all—Robert of Artois' foolish dash to Mansura—Joinville is just but not uncharitable. To the author of the *Eracles* it is an opportunity for the introduction of details possibly true but certainly discreditable; Matthew Paris seizes his chance to show his spite against the French.

It sometimes happens that we may have spent a long time in reading about a past event and have found difficulty in making the dead tale come to life in the imagination, when a chance remark will suddenly set the characters in motion like a film. We can read of the Crusaders starving in besieged Antioch during the First Crusade, but when William of Tyre tells us that food was so scarce that noble ladies stayed indoors and silently starved to death rather than face the shame of openly begging, and that the proudest knights were brought to spying out who had food for dinner that day and quietly walking in and sitting down uninvited, then even those who have not known poverty or hunger recognise what hunger was in the city. There are books which are first known to us by some such piercing remark, a quotation from a poem, a passage from an historian, but when we come to read the whole book we are disappointed to find that what all the world knows is pretty well the only thing worth knowing. It is here that the joy in Joinville is so constant. Every chapter has something which either gives the reader another delighted thrill of recognition or tells a little more of the endearing character of the author.

Many of our generation have sat in a tent in the North African sun and reached out to take a drink from the canvas water bottle or earthenware *gargoulette* hanging on the tent rope, as Joinville hung it; many have heard Mass in a stores tent, at one end a temporary altar, at the other piles of kit, tins of dehydrated potatoes, as Joinville heard it in a tent, with the corpse of his friend lying on a bier, and his jaunty comrades chatting in the background.[21] The C.O. of the neighbouring unit, with his taste for practical jokes, is known to us as the Count d'Eu was known; and many have queued, as Joinville did, at the entrance to the prisoner-of-war cage. You may read other historians, again—Matthew Paris, Jean Sarrasin, Makrisi's chronicle—and though you know that Louis' army was encumbered by women and children, it is not till Joinville tells us how he took the little ten-year-old boy Bartholomew by the hand, when they were captured, and kept hold of him so that he should not be taken and sold as a slave, and later, when they got back to Acre, had some dinner fetched for him, that you can visualise the children as little boys and girls with names we know.

Of the political history of St. Louis' reign, of his consolidation of the Capetian supremacy (the continuation of the work of his grandfather and of his mother), Joinville tells us little in detail; it lay outside the scope of his book. But his account of St. Louis' years in Syria shows us how he gave a new though short-lived vigour to the conception of a unified French state in that country. It is apparent from Joinville that his authority was unquestioned and that he was in effect, though not in name, the King of French Syria.[22] More generally, he succeeded admirably in describing how St. Louis' personal virtue, withstanding all those attacks of expediency and policy which bring corruption upon great power, was rewarded by a prestige that has never been enjoyed by another monarch.

THE TEXT OF JOINVILLE

See De Wailly, pp. xi-xxx; Gaston Paris in the *Histoire Littéraire de la France*, xxxii, and *Romania*, 1874 (in which he reviews De Wailly's edition and De Wailly answers his remarks); and Alfred Foulet, *Modern Language Quarterly*, 1945. Marius Sepet (*Revue des Questions historiques*, 1872, pp. 220-31) answers Père Cros, S.J., who maintained that the text of St. Louis' *Etablissements* given in the MSS. of Joinville had been tampered with in order to minimise St. Louis' respect for the Church; in the course of his refutation of Père Cros, Sepet describes the origin and value of the MSS. more clearly than De Wailly.

There are but three MSS.; the earliest in date (of the fourteenth century—perhaps, Foulet suggests, as early as 1320) is the Brussels MS. (A), brought back to France by Maurice of Saxony; the Lucca MS. (L), which was found at about the same time; and a MS. (B), which was first used by De Wailly and had been in the possession of M. Brissart-Binet. The two last belong to the sixteenth century. They have been "modernised", and in the modernisation the sense of the original has often been distorted. It is agreed that they have a common source, intermediate between them and the original, which is not shared by A. The chief value of B is that it fills in some gaps in L.

Printed editions. The first editor was Antoine de Rieux, whose edition was printed at Poitiers in 1547.[23] It was his boast that he had polished and given grace to the rude language of the original, which he found among some documents that had belonged to King René of Sicily, and he so fulfilled his boast that few editors have earned more obloquy. The MS. which he used has never been found, but it was undoubtedly already much corrupted, for many passages are complete nonsense and long sections bear no relation at all to our book. It must have been related to the MS. (also lost) used in 1617 by the next editor, Claude Ménard, who conscientiously printed the MS. as he had it; and it was Ménard's text that Du Cange printed (lacking any MS.) in his magnificent edition, enriched by his notes and lengthy dissertations, of 1668.

It was the discovery of two MSS. in the eighteenth century—the Brussels and Lucca MSS.—which made possible the first printed edition, that of 1761, which could hope to approach Joinville's original dictation. Three editors in turn were engaged in the work—Melot and Sallier, who both died before it was finished, and Capperonnier, who completed it. The book is a folio of great beauty, more elegant than Du Cange's; the text follows the Brussels MS., variants—though not all the variants—from L being printed at the foot of the page.

The edition (Daunou and Naudet's) in the twentieth volume of the *Recueil des Historiens des Gaules et de la France* (1840), admirable for its notes, is on the same lines, though B is at times corrected from L. Further corrections from L were included in Michel's edition of 1859, the text of which is reprinted in his edition of 1881.

It is to De Wailly, however, that we owe what has generally been accepted as the standard edition. His full edition, accompanied by notes and a translation into modern French, appeared in 1874.[24] De Wailly had the advantage of being able to use the MS. referred to above as B; in addition he was at pains to work the text back to the spelling current in Champagne at the time Joinville wrote. He believed that he had brought the reader as close as was humanly possible to the original text, and this belief has been commonly accepted, though it should be tempered by a reading of Gaston Paris's review in *Romania,* iii (1874), and (to obtain a very different view of the relation of the MSS. to Joinville's original) of Corrard's remarks in the *Revue Archéologique* of 1867. Corrard believed that the MSS. we have had already suffered the same sort of alterations as those which had been suffered by the lost MSS. of De Rieux and Ménard—repetitions, interpolations, glosses, etc.—and although most readers would agree that De Wailly gave a satisfactory answer to his arguments, enough remains to make it difficult to be quite as optimistic as De Wailly. Gaston Paris hints at another matter which deserves consideration: admitting that De Rieux' and Ménard's MSS. were corrupt, but remembering that a bad MS. may at times retain something which is lost in a better one, to what extent can we, arguing back from the printed text to the MS., use what we conclude must

have been the reading of the latter to correct our own MSS.? Two examples: in §354 the words "au col" in the first sentence are from Ménard's text (i.e. the Saracens came to the galley with Danish axes on their shoulders), and few, I believe, would say that De Wailly was wrong in admitting them, even though they are absent from our MSS. A further example, from §328, raises a more complicated question. Many, I believe, would agree that in the text of the MSS. the reason for the Legate's displeasure is by no means clear, and that if the reason was that he believed it to be foolish of Joinville to endanger his health by fasting, Joinville would have expressed himself more fully; and, moreover, that to explain the oddness of the sentence by Joinville's conversational style is to attribute to him altogether too great a degree of informality in his writing. The fuller version of the sentence (quoted in the note to this passage) found in De Rieux and Ménard is, to my mind, not only much clearer but also much more likely to have been written by Joinville. The complication arises from a conflict between a natural desire not to imitate De Rieux and try to improve upon Joinville, and the contrary desire to take an opportunity to remove from the MS. text, with justification, a carelessness and obscurity that were not present in the original. For my part, I think that the view of Joinville as a man who in his writing, or dictating, gaily rambled on with a charming but heedless inconsequence, has been exaggerated, and that both Ménard and De Rieux[25] call for more attention.

Translations. The first translation into English was that of Thomas Johnes (1748-1816) of Hafordychtryd, Cardiganshire, who printed his translation in 1807 at his own press ("at the Hafod Press by James Henderson"). He was also a translator of Sainte Palaye's Life of Froissart, of Froissart's Chronicle, of the Travels of Betrand de la Brocquière to Palestine, and of the Chronicle of Monstrelet. Unfortunately, although Capperonnier's edition was available to him (and he translated from it the extracts he included from Makrisi), he preferred to translate Du Cange's, on the ground that that of 1761 "would not be intelligible for three-fourths of its readers, who, unless perfectly well versed in the old French language, would be fatigued and disgusted with it". This translation was reprinted by Bohn in 1848 in a volume of *Chronicles of the Crusade,* which included also Richard of Devizes, and "Geoffrey of Vinsauf's" *Itinerarium Regis Ricardi.* James Hutton's translation of 1868 is abridged; so, too, is Ethel Wedgwood's of 1906, in which there is also some rearrangement of the contents. The translation by Sir Frank Marzials in Everyman's Library (*Memoirs of the Crusades*—it contains also his translation of Villehardouin) was first published in 1911. What he has to say in the introduction about translation is interesting, but I cannot agree that he was right in concluding that one should use "turns of speech, and a vocabulary, that are either archaic or suggest archaism". The translation by Dr. Joan Evans (1939) is more archaic in style and more consistently so. There is a typographic neatness and care in a modern, or modernised, French version by Henri Longnon (1928), which well become the quality of the work.

Notes

1. By the marriage of Felicity of Brienne to our Joinville's great-grandfather Geoffrey.

2. For John of Joinville's family see H. F. Delaborde, *Jean de Joinville et les Seigneurs de Joinville, suivi d'un catalogue de leurs actes,* 1894, in which is included a genealogical table. Du Cange also prints one, but it does not always agree with Delaborde, whose statements are supported by the deeds he catalogues. What I have written here I owe chiefly to Delaborde and to Gaston Paris in the *Histoire Littéraire de la France,* vol. xxxii.

3. There is a small, abridged and modernised, but well annotated edition of extracts from Joinville, by L.F. Flutre (1942), which contains a useful little map of the environs of Joinville.

4. A later tradition tried to connect the Joinville family with Godfrey of Bouillon; according to this, Stephen would have been a cousin of the great Duke. But Delaborde says that the story is not found before 1549, in Wassebourg's *Antiquités de la Gaule Belgique.*

5. The family maintained that the position was hereditary since the time of Geoffrey III; but their claim was not formally recognised till the time of John's father, Simon. (See Delaborde, p. 285, no. 189.)

6. For "Trouillart" see note to the *Epitaph,* p. 298.

7. See the *Epitaph:* King Richard did not arrive at Acre till June 1191, and Geoffrey Trouillart was back in Joinville by the end of 1190. He must, therefore, have been honoured by Richard for helping him in France against Philip Augustus. The "lion" in the difference was not the royal "leopards" we know, but the old Plantagenet lion.

8. Villehardouin, c. 2.

9. "And what a man was Geoffrey de Joinville! No better knight, by Saint Giles, was there this side the Strait" (*i.e.* of Messina). Guyot's editor, however, (Orr, *La Bible de Guiot de Provins,* Manchester, 1917), points out that he may refer to one of the other crusading Geoffreys.

10. John of Brienne had been suggested by Philip Augustus as a suitable husband for Mary, daughter of Isabella of Jerusalem and Conrad of Montferrat. He was an older man than Simon—past sixty when he married nineteen-year-old Mary—but a friend of his; the "Minstrel of Rheims" (§139 of De Wailly's edition) speaks of John's pleasure when he heard of the King's choice and how he shared it with his friends, including "le seigneur de Joinvile", *i.e.* Simon.

11. The Seneschal was in charge of arrangements for important functions at Court and was of necessity an authority on etiquette. I believe that on only three occasions does Joinville fail to give a knight his title, *mes sires* (monseigneur), and in each instance it is his friend Oliver of Termes. Antoine Thomas's *Francesco da Barberino et la littérature provençale en Italie* (1883) has a couple of stories about Joinville in his old age. Barberino was concerned by a question of table manners: when two persons of equal rank are seated side by side and there is no squire to cut the meat ("*écuyer tranchant*"), which of the two should do so? Meeting Joinville at Poissy, and being told that there was no greater authority on such matters, he asked him. "The one who has the knife on his right," was Joinville's answer, and it is for that reason that good servants are taught to lay the knife at the right hand.

12. "le χλγρόν des Grecs"—Sainte-Beuve, writing of Joinville.

13. Mas-Latrie's edition of the *Chronique d'Ernoul,* 1871, p. 282.

14. See De Wailly, 491.

15. See Gaston Paris in *Histoire Littéraire de la France,* vol. xxxii, pp. 291 ff.

16. "L'aioul cesti duc qui est mors nouvellement." But see De Wailly's argument (p. 480) on the rendering of "nouvellement" and the identification of "cestiduc" with Robert, who died in March 1306.

17. See, however, Alfred Foulet in the *Romanic Review,* 1941, pp. 233-43. Foulet argues that Gaston Paris's view—of two "editions"—is untenable. From a comparison of Joinville's testimony in the life by William of St. Pathus (and of other details which are common to that life and to Joinville) with Joinville's life, he concludes that "Joinville's deposition during the canonisation inquest of 1282, considered in conjunction with the 1287 redaction of the *Credo,* should be viewed as the initial step in the composition of the *Vie de S. Louis*". The date apart, the real point which Foulet makes is the unity of the *Vie;* as did Bédier, whom he quotes approvingly: "le sénéchal a écrit l'histoire du roi Louis, l'histoire de saint Louis, et l'histoire de Jean de Joinville, et ces trois histoires forment un chef d'oeuvre complet, mais d'une seule venue, où tout est concerté pour que son ami revive tout entier." (That men of the stature of Bédier and Paris should disagree on the point of the artistic unity of the work is a comfort to one who hesitates to disagree with either.) The most that Foulet will grant is that before Joinville had made his deposition "he had doubtless narrated his memoirs of the King, but it must have been in piecemeal fashion, without plan or perspective".

18. They are published, by H. F. Delaborde, in *Mémoires de la Société de l'Histoire de Paris et de l'Ile de France,* xxii, 1896, pp. 1-71. The Life of St. Louis by William of St. Pathus (Queen Margaret's confessor) appears, however, to be a translation of a Latin digest of the evidence (also edited by

Delaborde, 1899). Partly, I suppose, because it is based on the memories of different sorts of people, of different stations in life, from Counts to serving men, it is less conventional in tone, and enlivened by more real detail than the "official" lives of Geoffrey of Beaulieu (St. Louis' confessor), and William of Chartres (his chaplain). Gibbon sarcastically notes, "Read, if you can, the life and miracles of St.Louis, by the confessor of Queen Margaret"—advice that is better given as a serious compliment to two most interesting compilations.

19. It happens that this passage is the only one where Joinville's exact truthfulness has been suspected—his statement that he and William of Beaumont were the only two from France who voted for staying in Palestine appears to conflict with the King's own statement that the greater part of the barons were in favour of his staying, with which agrees the continuation of John Sarrasin's letter in the Rothelin. But Delaborde's suggestion in *Romania* (xxiii, p. 148) that the decision to stay was reached between the second and third of the three councils, when it was known that the Egyptians were not respecting their agreement with Louis, accounts for the discrepancy. Later, however, Foulet has shown (*Modern Language Notes,* 1934, 464-8) that there is no real contradiction between Louis and Joinville, who are the only first-hand authorities. Louis' letter reads as follows: "Quorum major pars concorditer asserebat, quod si nos recedere contingeret his diebus, praedictam terram dimitteremus omnino in admissionis articulo constitutam . . . His igitur consideratis attente, praedictae terrae sanctae compatientes miseris et pressuris, qui ad ejus subsidium veneremus, ac captivorum nostrorum captivitatibus et doloribus condolentes, licet nobis dissuaderetur a multis morari in partibus transmarinis, maluimus tamen adhuc differre passagium." The Count of Jaffa was present at the conference of which Joinville speaks, and was naturally in favour of the King's staying in Palestine. When, accordingly, the King writes of the "major pars" as being in favour of this stay, he must refer to the Syrian barons, who would outnumber the French—the "multi" who wished him to return to France immediately. It is interesting that the poem printed in *Romania,* xxii, 1893, p. 544 (it is quoted, except for the first stanza, in Dr. Evans' introduction), uses the same argument as Joinville—that the King still had the clergy's money and that it would be shameful to leave any poor men in the hands of the infidels—but such arguments might have occurred to many at Acre in 1250, and no one can be sure that Joinville was the author. Gaston Paris was inclined to believe that he was. Not so Bédier, who also prints the poem in his *Chansons de Croisade,* 1909.

20. *Récits d'un Ménestrel de Reims,* edited by De Wailly, 1876, §388.

21. Another similar and perhaps even more familiar reminiscence occurs from William of Tyre (ii, p. 332, in Paulin Paris's edition, 1879, of the old French translation), where King Amaury I was besieging Damietta: the rain was so heavy and continuous that they dug little trenches round their tents: "il covenoit à chascun entor sa tente faire fosse por recevoir la pluie, qu'ele n' entrast dedenz leur liz."

22. See Grousset, iii, p. 509, and De Wailly's notes *Sur le pouvoir royal* (pp. 454-9).

23. It is by error that a copy of the 1561 Poitiers edition is given in the British Museum catalogue as possibly having been printed in 1535.

24. It is this edition of De Wailly's that has been followed in this translation; references to Joinville in the introduction and notes are to the paragraphs in his edition, the numbering of which has been followed in the translation.

25. De Rieux included a number of passages omitted by Ménard—the capture of Bagdad, for example (ch. cxiv), the fossilised fish (§602), the harshness of Queen Blanche to Margaret (ch. cxix), etc. May we, too, grant him one phrase that savours more of the original than of his own refinement? Joinville compares the legs of those who suffered from "camp fever" to an old boot ("une vieille heuse"); De Rieux adds "stuffed away for ages behind a cupboard" ("vieilles bottes qui avoient esté cachées long temps derriere ung coffre").

Lionel J. Friedman (essay date 1958)

SOURCE: "Text and Iconography for Joinville's *Credo,*" in *Text and Iconography for Joinville's "Credo,"* The Mediaeval Academy of America, 1958, pp. 1–27.

[*In the following essay, Friedman analyzes the relationship between the extant versions of the text of the* Credo *and the extant versions of the work's iconography.*]

1. The account in the *Vie de saint Louis* of his life at Acre makes no mention of an activity which has assumed importance in Joinville's literary biography: the composition of the *Credo* between the months of August 1250 and April 1251. The lessons of Saint Louis reported in sections 43-45 of the *Vie* are generally believed to be the initial inspiration for this pious project to aid the moribund in their struggle with the devil.[1] The ancient enemy of mankind, no longer able to take away good works already performed, would seek to bring the dying to damnation by temptation in matters of faith. With the other bodily senses sinking at this moment, the only pathways left open to him would be those of the eyes and ears. The *Credo* found its utility in closing these last two entrances, for the patient could hear the words of the Creed read to him and see the illustrations of the faith shown to him. This use of the two

media of sight and hearing characterizes the *Credo* in which the miniatures are an integral part of the whole economy, not mere adornment. Both Perdrizet and Mâle have called attention to the interest offered by the *Credo* with its close interrelation of text and illumination for the study of mediaeval religious iconography.[2]

The only known text of the *Credo* is that preserved in *MS 4509* of the *nouvelles acquisitions du fonds français* (former 7857) of the Bibliothèque nationale in Paris. Its history has been adequately recorded.[3] After recognition by Paulin Paris that the work was by Joinville, a facsimile edition limited to twenty-five copies, with an accompanying translation, was published by Artaud de Montor in 1837. This in turn was reproduced in reduced format by Ambroise-Firmin Didot in 1870. The text was subsequently re-edited by Natalis de Wailly after a collation by Paul Meyer of the Montor edition with the original manuscript then at Ashburnham Place. Wailly appended line drawing reproductions of the miniatures—totally inadequate—from the earlier edition of Didot. The Montor edition was notably faulty and Wailly has not always indicated the changes he made. These are difficult to determine from a comparison of the two editions, since the latter editor applied to the *Credo* the technique he used on the *Vie* namely the modification of the orthography of the manuscript in accord with norms derived from other works from the chancellory of Joinville. For these reasons, as early as 1898, Gaston Paris indicated the utility of a new edition.[4]

As is apparent from the text, this version of the *Credo* can scarcely be the redaction of Acre in 1250-1251,[5] and 1287 is accepted as the date of the extant text.[6] That the only known copy is considerably posterior to the known date of composition has resulted in much conjecture about the changes which might have taken place between the two redactions.[7] Except for the passage concerning the old Saracen and the captive French crusaders, agreement is almost universal that such additions were limited to the introductory passages preceding the exposition of the Creed proper.

2. It is fortunate that two media were employed in the exposition of the *Credo,* for although the verbal text has been preserved in only one version, three versions of the iconographic text are extant. These three sets of miniatures will offer a third interest of the *Credo* for the study of problems and techniques of manuscript illumination. *MS 4509* is incomplete in its illumination, having only twenty-six miniatures although the text specifically announces eleven more scenes as depicted. Three blanks unfilled by miniatures have been left on the folios. Since the miniatures are introduced interruptively and directly into the text of this manuscript, it has been taken for granted by Delaborde and Langlois that this was the fashion in which the text ought to be illuminated. Considering that the specific indications for the placing of the miniatures given by the text rarely coincide with their actual placement, this assumption is less warranted than it has previ-

ously seemed to be. The miniatures have been here left in the positions they occupied in the manscript, even though this position may not be the one designed by the wording of the text.

The second set of illustrations comprises a series of outline drawings, inspired by the *Credo,* found on folios 231r°-232v° of *MS latin* 11907 of the Bibliothèque nationale, already reproduced photographically by Delaborde and Lauer in 1909.[8] At least one folio, possibly more, is missing, so that the series begins with the illustrations for the first part of Article V of the Creed. These drawings are here reproduced on Plates I-IV. At first glance, they give the impression of preliminary sketches to be used later by an illuminator, a hypothesis rejected by Delaborde on the grounds that the arrangement of the sketches in a continuous series does not reveal how they could be broken up to take their proper places in the text, that there are inversions in the order of the sketches compared to the text, and finally that all the legends with the exception of that for the scene of the captive crusaders are in Latin, which would not befit a work written in Romance. Hence the drawings were not the preliminary work for illuminating a text of the *Credo.*[9] Having arrived at these perhaps valid conclusions (based implicitly on the assumption that the illumination of the *Credo* was to have been as it appears in the extant text), the author then elaborated the hypothesis that the sketches were to serve for the mural decoration of the Maison-Dieu of Joinville. There is nothing easier than to fill a no longer extant building with murals. However, the subsequent discovery by W. Bakhtine of a 13th-century Breviary, ostensibly for the service of Saint-Nicaise of Rheims, executed before the canonization of Saint Louis, and preserved in the Public Library of Leningrad, offered a more plausible alternative which was not seized, probably because Delaborde's publication had been lost from sight.[10] The Breviary contains the only known complete set of illuminations for the *Credo,* which are here reproduced on Plates V-XXII.[11] Since these illustrations include the scene of the captive French crusaders (Pl. XVII), their origin in Joinville's work is beyond doubt. The Breviary fulfills all the conditions of the sketches, containing a set of miniatures not ostensibly subordinated to a Romance text, legends which, with the same exception as in the outline drawings, are in Latin, and a slight displacement in the order of the miniatures. The relation between the outline drawings and the Breviary will be examined at some length later.

3. Until now the main source of information on the Leningrad Breviary was a highly misleading report made by Ch.-V. Langlois to the Académie des Inscriptions et Belles-Lettres of a communication from W. Bakhtine of the Public Library of Leningrad. Langlois' inaccuracies were all the more regrettable since the Académie claimed to have lost Bakhtine's original. Among other things, Langlois stated that the scenes from the Old and New Testaments were brought together in symmetrical pairs on successive folios. The inaccuracy is patent from the most cursory glance at the illuminations. Plate VII brings together the Annuncia-

tion and Isaiah, the Nativity and Daniel, neither of which persons could be termed New Testament; plates VIII-IX contain both events of the Passion and of the "Estoire Joseph"; Plate X contains an event of the Passion and four Old Testament figures. Such examples could be further multiplied. What is the actual state of affairs?

In the body of the work, Joinville's task was to expound the Creed by the witness of Holy Writ. The tradition of scriptural testimony hardly requires review here, but its specific function in the *Credo* seemingly does. From his discussion in the second paragraph, it is clear that Joinville believed that faith was of things not manifest, concerning which we have certainty only through hearsay (*fides ex auditu*). In the category of hearsay is placed the witness of the Scriptures conceived as testimony from the mouth of the Almighty through the holy persons of both Testaments. As such, it transcends all other types of witness. The Scriptures are the *divina auctoritas* and in the *Credo* scriptural references are not the starting point of argumentation but the final proof.[12]

In the opening paragraph Joinville announces that "poez veoir ci aprés point et escrit les articles de nostre foi par letres et par ymages," from which it has been assumed that the expression "les articles de nostre foi" is equivalent to the twelve articles of the Creed. It is not, however, certain whether the author drew any careful distinction between the articles of faith construed specifically as the articles of the Creed or construed more generally as doctrinal points.[13] The concluding paragraphs of the work refer more precisely to the "romant qui devise et enseigne les poinz de nostre foi," for there can be no doubt that the term "les poinz de nostre foi" has an exact meaning not to be identified with the articles of the Creed as such but more generally with points of doctrine which the faithful are required to believe.[14] The situation in the *Credo* is that the articles of the Creed may serve as the fundamental basis representing the minimum required of the faithful for salvation, but the actual unit of composition is the "point of faith" seen to be contained in or derived from the article. These "points" have brought about the fragmentation of the articles and an expansion or development of each fragment.[15] More interesting is Joinville's identification as "points" of the faith of traditional scenes of mediaeval iconography: the Annunciation, the Nativity, the Baptism, "toute la Passion et l'Ascension et l'avenement dou Saint-Esperit." Mâle has indicated that the number of New Testament scenes treated in the middle ages was restricted and seldom varied. A partial explanation can perhaps be sought in the concept that they were explicit in some of the articles of the Creed. That the problem in the *Credo* was the application of this traditional material to the Creed is apparent in the iconography.

4. Although Delaborde was puzzled by it, there does exist a fairly obvious order in the arrangement of the outline drawings in registers. The portions of the articles of the Creed, in red letters, occur only in alternate registers, two of them side by side, inscribed over such scenes as the Harrowing of Hell, the Resurrection, the Ascension, Christ seated at the right of God, Christ of the Second Coming, Pentecost, and the Last Judgment. In the preceding, unfilled portion of the register and in the preceding register are found the illustrations for the prophecies in work and word for these "points," the prophecy in work on the left, in word on the right.[16] In almost all instances these prophetic scenes have the same order as in the text of the *Credo.* The prophecy in word is represented by a figure with an appropriately inscribed phylactery. If a prophecy occurs in the unfilled portion of a register containing the illustrations for the "points," it is always a prophecy in word. Lastly, for the portion of text concerned, the outline drawings adhere rigidly to the system of parallel prophecies in work and word.

The fragmentation into "points" is confirmed by the Leningrad Breviary which, by its ascription of each article to an Apostle opposed to a Prophet, permits definite identification of Joinville's division of the Articles and their subdivision into eighteen "points."

> Article I. Apostle, Peter. Prophet, Jeremiah.
> Point 1: *Credo in Deum Patrem omnipotentem . . .* (The Fall of the Angels).
> Point 2: *Creatorem celi et terre* (The Creation).
>
> Article II. Apostle, Andrew. Prophet, Nebuchadnezzar (?).
> (Joinville uses this article for the Advent and combines it with the following in his treatment, so only the prophecies occur.)
> A. *Credo in Jhesum Christum Filium Eius.*
> B. *Unicum Dominum nostrum.*
>
> Article III. Apostle, James. Prophet, Isaiah (?).
> Point 3: *Qui conceptus est de Spiritu Sancto* (The Annunciation).
> Point 4: *Natus ex Maria Virgine* (The Nativity).
>
> Article IV. Apostle, John. Prophet, Esdras.
> Point 5: *Passus sub Pontio Pilato* (The Passion):
> *a.* Pilate washes his hands, *b.* the Sale of Christ, *c.* the Flagellation, *d.* the Bearing of the Cross).
> Point 6: *Crucifixus* (Christ between the two thieves).
> Point 7: *Et mortuus* (Christ's death on the Cross with the accompanying prodigies).
> Point 8: *Et sepultus* (The Entombment).
>
> Article V. Apostle, Thomas. Prophet, Hosea (?).
> Point 9: *Descendit ad inferna* (The Harrowing of Hell).
> Point 10: *Tertia die resurrexit a mortuis* (The Resurrection).
>
> Article VI. Apostle, James the Less. Prophet, David.
> Point 11: *Ascendit ad celo* (The Ascension).
> Point 12: *Sedet ad dexteram Dei Patris omnipotentis* (Christ seated at the right of God).
>
> Article VII. Apostle, Philip. Prophet, Joel.
> Point 13: *Inde venturus judicare vivos et mortuos.* (Christ of the Second Coming).
>
> Article VIII. Apostle, Bartholomew. Prophet, Zachariah.
> Point 14: *Credo in Spiritum Sanctum* (Pentecost).

Article IX. Apostle, Matthew. Prophet, Solomon.
Point 15: *Sanctam Ecclesiam catholicam*
(The Church).

Article X. Apostle, Simon. Prophet, Micah.
Point 16: *Sanctorum communionem, remissionem pec catorum* (The Sacraments: *a.* Baptism, *b.* Marriage, *c.* Confession, *d.* the Eucharist).

Article XI. Apostle, Thaddeus (Jude). Prophet, Ezekiel.
Point 17: *Carnis ressurectionem* (The Resurrection Judgment).

Article XII. Apostle, Matthias. Prophet, Daniel.
Point 18: *Vitam eternam. Amen* (The Marriage Supper of the Lamb).

In the illumination of the Breviary, the prophecy in word for these "points" has frequently been incorporated into the miniature depicting the "point."

The described order does not obtain in the outline drawings after the first register of f. 232r° where the composition by prophecy undergoes considerable modification in the text. Another exception occurs with the first of the articles depicted (compartments 1-2, top register, Pl. I) where the red legend is placed over two drawings: the first, showing Samson opening the jaws of the lion, the other, the Harrowing of Hell. The usual symmetry is missing, the point appears also over the prophecy in work, and the prophecy in word is lacking, despite the fact that it, not Samson, should have appeared to the left of the Harrowing of Hell. In the corresponding miniatures in the Breviary (lower register, Pl. XIV), the portion of the Creed also covers both the prophecy of Samson and the Harrowing of Hell. In a previous publication attempting to demonstrate that the **Credo** was skillfully contrived, we indicated that the prophecy of Hosea, with its equivocation on the term "mors" concorded directly in *word* with Article IV of the Creed and the development on the Fishing of Leviathan, while it concorded directly in *idea* by its exegetic treatment with the exegesis of the Samson prophecy and the Harrowing of Hell.[17] It is gratifying to discover that the illumination of the Breviary confirms this by including the Hosea prophecy with the iconography for the Fishing of Leviathan (compartment 3, bottom register, Pl. XIII).

There is again an exception in the outline drawings for the point "Tertia die resurrexit a mortuis" (compartments 1-2, bottom register, Pl. I) where there is no separate illustration for the Resurrection, but where the red legend again appears over two compartments, the first of which contains a truncated Resurrection scene, with, inside its borders, the additional black legend "Resusitatio leunculi." The adjoining compartment shows the figure of David with his prophecy "Et refloruit caro mea." Both are Joinville's prophecies for the Resurrection. The remainder of the register is occupied by the illustration for the Ascension. In compartment 3 of the top register, where we should expect to find the prophecy in work for the Resurrection, occurs the prophecy in work for the Ascension, followed by a portion of the prophecy in word for the same event

(compartment 1, middle register). The remainder of this register contains one compartment depicting two different scenes: (1) Jonah coming forth from the whale, with the legend "Jonas exit de ventre ceti" and (2) the old Saracen talking to the captive crusaders, with the legend "Li Saradins dit au barons pris an Negite." This latter scene has suffered truncation of the young armed Saracens mentioned in the text. The Jonah scene is one of those believed by Delaborde to be out of order, since he thought it the Jonah prophecy for the Entombment given in the text. A different conclusion presents itself, however: the prophecy given is not for the Entombment but for the Resurrection. The middle ages distinguished three separate prophecies in the Jonah story: (1) his being cast into the sea: the Passion, (2) his being swallowed by the whale and the length of time passed in its belly: the Entombment, (3) his live return to shore: the Resurrection.[18] The *Speculum humanae salvationis* employs both Jonah's being swallowed and his being regurgitated with these different implications.[19] In the outline drawings, contrary to the extant text where the emphasis is placed upon a concordance of the time spent by Jonah in the whale's belly and by Christ in the tomb,[20] the reference is to Jonah's release (*Jonas* exit *de ventre ceti*) and it is, consequently, a prophecy for the Resurrection. There can be no doubt of Joinville's application of its accompanying illustration to the Resurrection.[21]

In the corresponding miniatures for the Breviary (Pl. XV) here too Elijah's being carried off in a fiery chariot, the prophecy in work for the Ascension, precedes the prophecies for the Resurrection, represented by Jonah coming forth from the whale (*Jonas exit de ventre cetis*) and David (*Et refloruit . . .*). The prophecy in word for the Ascension has been absorbed into the illumination for that point (upper register, Pl. XVI), the illumination for the Resurrection follows in the lower register, the resuscitation of the lion cub is neither depicted nor mentioned, and the scene of the captive crusaders appears out of place (compartment 1, upper register, Pl. XVII).

That the Jonah scene occurs here as a prophecy for the Resurrection is confirmed by the use in the Breviary of Jonah's being swallowed by the whale under the Entombment, with the legend "Jonas mittitur in mare" (compartment 1, upper register, Pl. XIII), so that the Breviary follows the same usage in this matter as the *Speculum humanae salvationis*. Langlois maintained that the appearance of the Jonah prophecy at this point demonstrated that the miniaturist had not servilely copied Joinville's text and had asserted his independence by substituting the more scriptural Jonah scene for the original lion cub.[22] This explanation, if it ever was satisfactory, certainly is no longer, since the same irregularity is found in the outline drawings (except that the resuscitation of the lion cub is there mentioned) and obviously stems from reasons more immediately discernible than an artist's strivings for independence and more readily discoverable by better methods than mindreading.

5. The hypothesis to be advanced is that the outline drawings stem from a version of the **Credo** in which the Resur-

rection was supported by the Jonah prophecy, the prophecy of the lion cub, the prophecy of David, and the personal exemplum (used as a prophecy?) of Joinville's experience in Egypt. This has resulted in overcrowding the space available for the illuminations, an artistic problem tentatively solved in the drawings by the pictorial suppression of the lion cub, and by the inclusion of the David prophecy in the illustration for the point. The Leningrad Breviary has solved the same problem in another fashion: the complete suppression of the lion cub, and the maintenance of a separate David prophecy. This still does not leave room for the captive crusaders, a scene which, in the Breviary, has been put in place of Jacob's rending his coat, the prophecy in work for the point "Sedet ad dexteram . . ." (compartment 1, top register, Pl. II). In the Breviary, the replaced prophecy has been moved back into position in the preceding cycle of the "Estoire Joseph" (compartment 2, upper register, Pl. X).[23] It seems apparent that both the outline drawings and the Breviary stem from a version of the *Credo* different from that conserved in *MS 4509*. Since the lion cub is still mentioned although pictorially suppressed in the outline drawings, the latter are perhaps intermediate between the original text and the Breviary, where the cub nowhere appears. A simple comparison between the order of the scenes in the drawings and the Breviary from this point on shows an identity of arrangement (except where the prophecy in word of pseudo-Job has been normally incorporated into the illustration for its point), including the inversion of the last two articles of the Creed which occur in the order "Vitam eternam. Amen" and "Carnis resurrexionem" (Pls. IV and XXII). The identity in anomalies and deviations from the extant text in both drawings and Breviary, the identity of treatment (except for the problems posed by the Resurrection), and the identity of order indicate a very direct relation between the sketches and the illuminations. The final purpose of the order of the sketches does not become apparent until the successive folios of the Breviary are brought into opposition. In opposing Plates IX and X, it is seen that the upper register of both folios contains the continuous exposition of the "Estoire Joseph" while the lower register carries the parallel story of the Passion. The opposition in this instance is not, as Langlois would have it, between folios, one devoted to New Testament scenes, the other to Old, but an opposition of Old and New Testament between upper and lower registers of two succeeding folios treated as a unit. If Plates XIII and XIV are opposed, the upper register of both pages contains the illuminations for the Entombment and its prophecies, while the lower contains the Harrowing of Hell with its materials. The opposition of Plates XV and XVI brings the prophecies for the Ascension into line with the illumination for the point in the upper register and the Resurrection material together in the lower. Plates XVII and XVIII appear to depart from this arrangement, unless it is recalled that the captive crusaders appear in place of a prophecy for the point "Sedet . . . ," and the lower register is consistent in its application to the point "Inde venturus. . . ." The same obtains for the remaining folios, so that it is only in this final opposition of the completed illumina-

tions of the Breviary that the rationale of the order of the outline drawings becomes apparent.

Although a direct relation between the sketches and the Breviary is demonstrable in this fashion, were the sketches actually the preliminary work for the illumination of the Breviary? The answer to this question is outside the competence of this writer and is best left to specialists in the field of mediaeval fine arts. The treatment of the individual scenes is not always identical, but certainly shows greater similarity than the treatment of the corresponding scenes in the extant version. On the other hand, it seems difficult to reconcile the rather wooden, stocky figures of the drawings with the graceful, svelte, elegant figures of the Breviary.[24] In the sketches, all the figures look alike; in the Breviary, they are highly individualized, with a particularly distinctive Christ and Virgin. All beards in the sketches receive the same treatment, which recurs only as one style among several in the Breviary. The compact crowns of the sketches have little resemblance to the flaring, elongated crowns of the Breviary. Many of these discrepancies may perhaps be attributed to the differences inherent between preliminary and finished work. There nevertheless remain differences of considerable importance. In the drawings, the scene of the captive crusaders depicts only the turbaned Saracen, leaning on one crutch, talking to the French captives in a pavillion (middle register, Pl. I). In the Breviary, the little old man, with a turban, leans on one crutch and appears in the company of the young Saracens with drawn swords. The French captives are within a tower or pavillion inside another enclosure (upper register, Pl. XVII). If the Breviary was illuminated from the drawings, a text was still necessary for the restoration of these details. Lastly, both these illustrations are far more faithful to the text than is the miniature of the extant version which merely opposes the band of armed Saracens with drawn swords and the little old man leaning on *two* crutches to the French captives (p. 40).[25]

Similarly the sketch for the Judgment of Solomon shows the king seated on a throne, the disputing women, and the executioner with the babe and a sword (compartment 3, top register, Pl. II). This treatment is similar to that of the extant version (p. 44) and both are adequate renderings of the Biblical scene. In the Breviary however these Biblical details have been relegated to the sides of the miniature, the center of which is occupied by Solomon, seated on a throne, holding a two-edged sword (lower register, Pl. XVII). A glance at the text shows that this is a complete rendering of Joinville's discussion centering chiefly around the two-edged sword of justice. The extant version and the sketches contain illustrations for the Biblical account of the Judgment of Solomon, while the miniature in the Breviary applies specifically to the use of this prophecy in Joinville's *Credo,* so that again a text would have been required for this highly particularized treatment.[26]

6. If the relation of the sketches to the Breviary is more or less clear, what is the relation of the extant version to

either or both of them? The declaration of the independence of the Breviary illuminations from the text of the **Credo** was made by Langlois. If he meant that the Breviary is not accompanied by a text, the statement is manifestly true. But if he referred to formal problems of the relation of the miniatures to a text, the statement is false, particularly as qualified by Langlois' explicitly stated opinion that the author intended the text to be illuminated in the manner of the extant version. In the author's statements of purpose there is nothing to warrant this sort of dependence: "Et devant lou malade façons lire le romant . . . si que par les eux et les oreilles mete l'on lou cuer dou malade si plain de la verraie cognoissance que li anemis . . . ne puisse riens metre ou malade dou sien . . ." (p. 51). This program calls for a text to be read to the patient and illustrations to be shown to him, but there is no necessity that the two occur together and in alternation. The opening lines of the body proper read: "Vous qui regardez cest livre troverez le **Credo** en letres vermeilles et les prophecies par euvres et par paroles en letres noires." No mention at all is made that the *reader* is going to encounter illuminations, since the indications apply only to the text. That a complete separation into a textual and pictorial series does not seem to have been the author's intent, however, is indicated in the opening lines of the preamble: "poez veoir ci aprés *point et escrit* les articles de nostre foi *par letres et par ymages* . . ." (italics ours) although it must be recalled that this preamble is considered an addition to the original version.

In regard to the formal problems of the relation of the miniatures to the text, the problem of "independence" appears to be the reverse of the position taken by Langlois. Indeed what mode of illumination could be more "independent" than that of the extant version, where the scribe or composer could interrupt the column of text wherever necessary or desired to insert an illustration? As many or as few as wished could be included, and they could all be placed with facility in their proper positions. Despite this maximal freedom, the specific textual references to the placement of the illuminations do not agree with the actual placing, nor do many of the scenes specifically announced appear at all. These discrepancies were evidence for Gaston Paris that the extant version was not executed under Joinville's eyes, the implication seemingly being that the 19th century critic found the work badly finished. In any event, it is evidence that the extant version was copied from a text, the redaction of 1287, in which the miniatures were placed according to the given indications. This view is confirmed by the pagination references in the text which do not refer to the actual pagination of the manuscript of the extant version. What information is supplied by the wording of these indications? They are, with the frequency of their occurrence: "Que vous veez ci aprés point" (3), "qui ci aprés sont point" (4), "ci aprés" (1), "que vous verrés ci aprés point" (2), "qui desus est point" (2), "que vous veez ci desuz point" (1), "que vous veez ci point" (4), "qui devant est point" (1), que vous veez ci devant pointes" (1). Aside from the expression "ci point," although the opposing terms "ci aprés" and "ci devant" occur, there is no

term opposed to "ci desuz." Such indications could conceivably apply to a page in which columns of text appeared *beneath* a group of miniatures.[27] The very use of these references in the text would seem applicable not to a system of illumination where the text could be opened wherever desired, but indicative of an attempt to synchronize a text with a series of miniatures which have to meet their own formal requirements of placement. The problem of overcrowding as witnessed for the Resurrection is a problem only if the formal arrangement of the miniatures must still be synchronized with a text. Completely liberated from the text, the artist could utilize as many or as few compartments as he wished.

Conversely, the method of illumination by opening the text leaves complete liberty to the author to modify his text as he wishes. Yet the extant version gives the appearance of having still another attempted solution to the problem of overcrowding in the iconography of the Resurrection—the textual suppression of the Jonah prophecy. At the point where it should occur, we find a discussion of the need of confession within a period of three days and a sentence of a pagan on sin. Neither of these requires illumination nor is consistent with the plan of the **Credo**. Are we dealing with a substitution for the Jonah prophecy? If so, such a substitution, rather than an outright deletion, is required only if a specific ratio between lines of text and iconography must be preserved.[28]

Are there other indications in the extant version to support this view? The miniatures for the Passion in the extant version contain a nimbed figure with a phylactery who has no relevance to the text (p. 33). Is he perchance a remnant of Saint John, the Apostle to whom the article is ascribed in the Breviary and whose nimbed head and phylactery appear there (compartment 1, lower register, Pl. IX)? Similarly the last miniature of the extant version (p. 50) applies to nothing in the text. Again is he the Prophet Daniel or Ezekiel, both of whom are opposed in the Breviary illuminations to Matthias and Jude respectively on the final folio (Pl. XXII)? The first of the two crucifixion scenes[29] contains a strange crowned figure holding a book in his left hand, with his right raised in the gesture of speech, who has no relevance to the Crucifixion. In all likelihood he is David, but the fusion of a prophecy in word with the illumination for the point is a technique of the Breviary.[30] Although the extant version has a miniature for the Jonah prophecy for the Entombment, it has the wrong scene from the cycle, unless we accept the iconographic peculiarity of Jonah's being swallowed feet first (p. 37). That the picture represents the Resurrection is quite conclusively proved by the presence of the tree, which figures only where Jonah is deposited by the whale on *terra firma* and not where he is being swallowed. At another sensitive spot (p. 42), the "Tunica Joseph" for the point "Sedet . . .," the extant version again has the wrong scene from the cycle (Joseph's coat presented to Jacob rather than Jacob's rending his own coat). Mere chance could hardly explain all these peculiarities, occurring only at the places which the sketches and Breviary have shown

pour aus atraire à nostre creance, il lour fist entaillier, en la chapelle, toute nostre creance, l'Annonciacion de l'angre, la Nativitei, le bauptesme dont Diex fu baptiziez, et toute la Passion et l'Ascension et l'avenement dou Saint Esperit . . ." (*Vie,* 471).

Outside Christianity, when speaking of the Assassins, he writes: "Li uns des poins de la loy Haali est que, quant uns hom se fait tuer pour le commandement son signour, que l'ame de li en va en plus aisié cors qu'elle n'estoit devant . . ." (*Vie,* 460). Speaking of the same group and of the Beduins, he writes: "Li autres poins si est teix, que il croient que nulz ne puet mourir que jusques au jour que il li est jugié . . . Et en cesti point croient li Beduin," (*Vie,* 461). The "points" patently refer to doctrinal beliefs and the expression "les poinz de nostre foi" refers to the general corpus of Christian doctrine rather than to the specific articles of the Creed.

15. L. J. Friedman, "On the Structure of Joinville's *Credo,*" *MP,* LI (1953), 1-8.

16. As noted, the separation of the articles and prophecies by the use of red and black ink respectively is a device of the text. Its preservation in the outline drawings may cast some doubt on Delaborde's assertion that the sketches are not subordinated to any text of the *Credo.*

   It has been generally assumed that Joinville's prophecies are Old Testament sayings or events intepreted as predictions of the events of the New Testament. The assumption will not bear examination, since the prophecy in word for the Ascension is the message which Christ enjoined Mary Magdalene to carry to the Disciples, the prophecy for the Entombment is Christ's answer to the wicked and adulterous generation seeking after a sign, and the prophecy in work for eternal life is the parable of the wise and foolish Virgins. The prophetic system is more extensive than the simple accommodation of the two Testaments.

17. Friedman, "Structure," pp. 5-6.

18. "Factis quoque praefiguratae sunt: projectio enim Jonae in mare Christi passionem, susceptio ejusdem in ventre ceti Christi sepulturam, redditio ejus vivi in littus Christi resurrectionem, aperte praefiguravit." Radulphus Ardens, *Homilia XXIV,* in Migne, *PL,* CLV, 2028.

19. *Op. cit.,* I, p. 57, 67, 145, 150 and II, Pls. 54 and 64.

20. Cf. p. 37.

21. Did Joinville intend it to serve as the prophecy in word? Or did the Jonah scene itself represent not only the prophecy in work of the Old Testament event but also the prophecy in word through the specific interpretation given it by Christ in the Gospels? Since the words of Christ have already

been used prophetically in connection with the Entombment, the latter seems improbable.

22. Langlois, "Observations," p. 366.

23. The Breviary shows another instance of overcrowding at the Crucifixion. A balance between prophecies in word and work is maintained by treating each of the prodigies accompanying the Crucifixion as a prophecy in work. The prophecies of Isaac, the pascal lamb, David, Caiaphas, and the Queen of Sheba appear on Pl. XI, with both David and the Queen of Sheba in one compartment. Habakkuk and the Centurion are absorbed into the illumination for the Crucifixion. Of the four prodigies, only the eclipse is illustrated by a scene from the legend of Saint Denis. Impossible to absorb into the point, this appears beneath the framework of dual registers. Pl. XII. It cannot be known whether Jeremiah or Saint Denis appeared in the outline drawings.

24. Delaborde, *les MSS à peintures:* "C'est l'art charmant et plein de noblesse des XIIIe et XIVe siècles dont Honoré est le représentant le plus connu. Les peintures de ce MS rappellent celles qui ornent le Bréviaire de Philippe le Bel, conservé à la Bibliothèque nationale à Paris sous le n° 1.023 du fonds latin."

25. "De sa resurrection vous dirai je que je en oï en la prison lou diemenche après ce que nous fumes pris, et ot on mis en un paveillon les riches homes . . . une grant foison de jeunes gens sarrasinz entrerent ou clos, la ou on nous tenoit pris, les espees traites . . . il amenerent un petit home si viel par samblant comme home poist estre . . . lors s'apoia li viex petit hom sor sa croce, et atout sa barbe et ses treces chenus . . ." (*Credo,* pp. 39-41).

26. Cf. p. 44.

27. As is clear by Joinville's use of the term, "ci aprés" does not mean "immediately following" but merely "following." An even larger interval might be indicated by the use of the future *verrés* for the present *veez.* It is futile to follow this track further, for a multitude of possible meanings opens up for these vague indications.

28. The only other possibility is that Joinville's remark "Au tiers jour vraiement Nostre Sires resuscita de mort a vie pour tenir covant a ses apostres et a ses deciples de sa resurrection . . ." is a reference to the Jonah prophecy. This hardly seems credible, since Christ gave the sign of Jonah not to his disciples and the Apostles but to the scribes and Pharisees, of which Joinville seems to be quite aware ("La profecie de la parole si dist Diex meesmes as Juis qui le requeroient qu'il lour feist aucum signe").

29. The substitution in the extant text of Jeremiah for Saint Denis could have two causes: the replacement of what was later realized to be a non-scriptural

quotation by an authentic one, or an attempt to solve the arrangement problems occasioned by overcrowding. In the extant text the eclipse is represented in the first Crucifixion scene at Jerusalem, rather than at Heliopolis as required by the Saint Denis prophecy. Once Saint Denis is removed, the eclipse may be absorbed in the existing illustration.

30. Even where prophet and point are juxtaposed elsewhere in the miniatures of the extant version, the two elements are isolated in separate frames (pp. 32, 33).

31. *Vie,* 45.

32. Friedman, "Structure," pp. 2-4.

33. Paris, "Joinville," pp. 367-368.

34. Lozinski, "Recherches," pp. 203-204.

35. Friedman, "Joinville, Job, and the Day of Wrath," *MLN,* LXVII (1952), 539-541.

36. Friedman, "A Mode of Medieval Thought in Joinville's *Credo,*" *MLN,* LXVIII (1953), 447-452.

37. *Vie,* 501.

Paul Archambault (essay date 1974)

SOURCE: "Joinville: History as Chivalric Code," in *Seven French Chroniclers: Witness to History,* Syracuse University Press, 1974, pp. 44–57, 129–31.

[*In the following essay, Archambault argues that critics have failed to recognize Joinville's criticism of King Louis in* Vie de Saint Louis. *The work is less about King Louis, Archambault maintains, than it is about the noble class and the nature of "preudome" as an institution in which Christian values, linked with the concept of nobility, are upheld to the best of one's ability.*]

Villehardouin's chronicle was composed a short time after the events narrated in order to justify a series of decisions the morality or the opportunity of which had been brought into question by some of his contemporaries. The circumstances surrounding the composition of Joinville's biography of Saint Louis are quite different. While Villehardouin was writing in a spirit of self-righteousness on a debatable subject, Joinville wrote in a spirit of reminiscence about a king whom the Roman Catholic Church, less than thirty years after his death, was in the process of canonizing.

Born in early 1225, Joinville was ten years younger than Saint Louis.[1] After the premature death of his oldest brother and of his father, Joinville inherited his ancestral home, which had belonged to his family since the eleventh century. When King Louis took the cross in 1244, after a prolonged illness, Joinville immediately and enthusiastically followed suit. He sailed with the crusading fleet from

the port of Hyères in southern France, followed the king to Cyprus, and took part in the landing at Damietta and in the battle of Mansourah in July 1248. Like King Louis, he was captured soon after this battle by the Bedouins and spent several months in a prison at Mansourah. Only by dint of a large ransom paid by the king did he and Louis avoid being decapitated.

After their release from prison, Joinville settled with the king on the Syrian coast. At Acre, in 1250, he argued vehemently against those barons in the king's council who favored an immediate return to France. For four years, from 1250 until 1254, he lived close to Louis at Acre, Caesarea, and Jaffa, served him as counselor and steward, and sailed with him back to France in July 1254. Back at his ancestral home, Joinville led a quiet, sedentary life until his death in 1317.

The Seventh Crusade had marked him for the rest of his life. His decision, in 1267, not to accompany Louis IX to Tunis for what was destined to be the king's final crusade was taken firmly and irrevocably. Religious though he was, Joinville found that the crusade of 1248 had been enough for his tastes. So alive were his memories of those cruel years that shortly after 1272 he began writing a personal account of the events of 1248-54. No doubt he did not realize at the time that he was in fact writing the body of what was later to become the *History of Saint Louis.* When, around 1298, Jeanne de Navarre, the young wife of King Philippe le Bel, begged Joinville to compose "a book containing the holy words and good deeds of Saint Louis," Joinville completed his manuscript, binding it at both ends with introductory and concluding chapters in praise of Saint Louis's Christian virtues, particularly his sense of charity and justice.

Joinville's vision of events has been described as laudatory, nostalgic, natural, sincere. Some of his critics have praised his extraordinary visual memory, while others say it already showed traces of senility. Rarely, perhaps, has a classic been so widely praised and so loosely analyzed. No one has ever paid attention to the negative side of Joinville's vision: the overt or implicit criticisms of Louis IX, the things left unsaid. Joinville's rhetorically modest claim in the opening passage to be writing merely in response to a pious queen's wish to revive the memory of her husband's grandfather has all too often been accepted at face value. The fact that he finished his book several years after the death of the queen whose request had set the work in motion should itself be an indication that Joinville's purpose transcended the vain wish to add yet another title to the list of the tediously flattering lives of Saint Louis that were published during the generation following the king's death.[2]

Readers of Joinville's *History of Saint Louis* like to recall the incidents in Chapter 4 as they do a familiar child's tale. Like a children's story, the scene might easily be represented with a series of Epinal pictures—those polychrome, heavily stylized images which for generations have provided French schoolchildren with an introduction to sweetened versions of their past. Chapter 4 of Joinville's chronicle seems to contain, as in a capsule, characteristic medieval attitudes toward social relationships, toward problems of dogmatic and moral theology, and toward the relative value of the present life in its relationship with the hereafter.

The actors perform with a curious mixture of flowing grace and puppetlike awkwardness; the liquidity of their gestures and words is sometimes broken up by gauche hesitations and trite pronouncements; like the smiling angel of the cathedral of Rheims, they strike a rigid pose, yet at the same time they give off flickers of warmth and sparks of humor. Louis IX has summoned his seneschal for a discussion of one of the most central of theological issues. He is aware of Joinville's dialectical subtlety ("I hesitate to speake to you of what touches God, for I know the subtlety of your mind"), and not entirely sure of his own capacities for argument and refutation; he has therefore chosen to protect himself by inviting a pair of friars to sustain him should he suffer a theological lapse in Joinville's presence. Louis's first question concerns the quiddity of God: "Tell me, Seneschal, what sort of a thing is God?" Joinville's reply amounts to a layman's version of Saint Anselm's ontological proof: "God is something so good that there cannot be any better." For his "excellent" answer, Joinville is rewarded with the king's unqualified approval, "for the very words in which you answered are written in this book I hold in my hand."[3]

Wishing to test Joinville further, Louis asks him two other questions, realizing perhaps that Joinville, with his distaste for every form of excess, will have trouble in providing a "correct" answer: whether Joinville would prefer to be a leper or to have committed a mortal sin; whether he washes the feet of the poor on Maundy Thursday. To the former question, Joinville retorts that he would rather commit thirty mortal sins than become a leper, and to the latter he answers simply: "God forbid!" The king dismisses the second answer as "wild and foolish" and the third as "poor."

For centuries readers have smiled or chortled over this confrontation and have assumed that Joinville is consciously playing the King's fool. One assumes that Joinville, as the king's seneschal, wants to act as a foil to what he considers the king's excessive seriousness. Upon closer examination, however, one sees Joinville and Louis IX differently. It is not at all certain that the seneschal wishes to play the fool. There are several scenes in the *History of Louis IX* when it is Joinville who has the last word, the punch line, the courageous piece of advice, or the word of reproval, where it is the king who ends up looking foolish. Any careful reader will notice that Joinville is as serious as is Louis himself about such matters as war, death, Christian piety, and salvation. Even in the scene just referred to, Joinville nowhere indicates that the king is right; nowhere does he say that Louis's answer is irrefutable or that he finds it convincing. Quite diplomatically, he

chooses to drop the matter and say nothing further. (Nevertheless one may imagine Joinville after the scene, feeling somewhat amused but undaunted.)

This scene is less comic, far more dramatic than French schoolmasters have traditionally presented it to their students over the centuries. The décor has all the plainness of a school or courtroom braced for theological or juridical debate. The characters belong to the only two social classes that might be expected to have a smattering of high culture: the nobility and the clergy. Each of the members present is aware of his social rank. Each knows that, no matter what the outcome of the debate, social stratification will under no circumstances be altered. The king, it will be noticed, has asserted his authority by calling the debate and even setting the rules by which the game will be played. The seneschal, a king's steward, has no other choice but to accept or reject the game. The friars, like the book on the king's knees, are symbolic of intellectual and spiritual authority. But how unobtrusive they are! They are dismissed as quickly as they had been summoned, without adding a word to the conversation, as if Louis IX simply wants to provide them (and perhaps his seneschal) with a physical reminder of their allegiance to him in social and temporal matters.

Suddenly, almost without warning, the scene becomes what Louis had from the start expected it to be: a personal confrontation, a testing of will rather than intellect, between himself and a subordinate, between a king and a member of the feudal nobility. Louis IX seems, in fact, to be consciously raising an issue that has obsessed all his Capetian forebears since Philip I: that in any confrontation between king and feudal nobility it is the principle of hereditary monarchy that must win.

Joinville has passed the test of intellect with an excellent answer. He is clearly intended to lose the test of will. Questions two and three cannot, in point of fact, be answered with a right or wrong answer. If he is to be sincere Joinville can only reply to both of these conundrums with a statement of personal preference or taste. Yet Louis IX reprimands him as if in both cases he has given a wrong answer. He mildly humiliates his seneschal by making him sit at his feet as he plays the role of severe master chastising a bad pupil. But Joinville is in no mood to be chastised. Sitting at the king's feet, after the dismissal of the friars, he tells Louis that he is "still of the same mind." When Louis insists that his is a "wild and roguish way of speaking" and lapses into a bland monologue about the relative merits of leprosy and mortal sin, Joinville does the only thing a civilized feudal lord can do when he is reduced to silence by the first noble in the kingdom: he speaks no further. But nowhere does Joinville concede that the king's answer is right.

The text of Chapter 4 first appears to the reader as just another illustration of the high sanctity of a man to whom Joinville's earthy humanity is supposed to act as foil. In fact it is a rapid encounter of clashing opinions, quickly followed by a troubled silence. Set up by Louis IX as a theological game in the presence of the clergy, the confrontation is quickly transformed into a symbolic test of will between a king and his seneschal in the solitude of the king's closet. After the seneschal has twice asserted an opinion that is diametrically opposed to the king's, he listens passively but refuses to capitulate as the king symbolically reminds him of his social inferiority and sternly reaffirms his moral authority.

Close inspection reveals the entire *History of Saint Louis* to be filled with ambiguities like these. The author's performance belies his stated intentions, and the hagiographical halo that has been placed above the book for centuries simply refuses to glow. For example, in the opening paragraphs Joinville claims that he has divided his book into two parts: "The first part tells how he ordered himself at all times by the will of God and of the Church, and for the well-being of his Kingdom; the second part of the book treats of the great things he did as a knight and a soldier" (1, 2). But the book is clearly divided into three sections: a first (chapters 1-24) highlighting some of the privileged moments of the king's life; a mammoth middle section (chapters 25-134), the main subject of which is Joinville's eyewitness account of the Seventh Crusade of 1248-54 and of his participation in that crusade alongside the king; and a final section (chapters 135-49), again dedicated to the highlights of Louis's life (especially after the Seventh Crusade), with much of the material being borrowed from contemporary biographies or chronicles.[4]

Structural analysis of the text has, to a certain extent, provided a satisfactory reason for Joinville's failure to live up to his intention of writing an edifying two-part biography of King Louis. Scholars now agree that Joinville stated his intentions long after most of the book had been written, as the body of the book was intended to be not so much hagiographical as autobiographical. Around 1272, perhaps on the occasion of the marriage of his eldest son to Mabile de Villehardouin, Joinville began to compose his personal reminiscences of the crusade of 1248-54, his model for which was the chronicle written by the scion of the illustrious family into which his son was marrying. No one knows what became of that early biography of Joinville, nor whether it was ever circulated. Several years later Queen Jeanne of Navarre begged Joinville to write a book on "the holy words and good deeds of our king Saint Louis." "It would seem likely," writes Joan Evans, "that she made this request at some time before 1297, when the King was canonized, from the desire to have all the possible evidence in favour of canonization that was to bring peculiar honour to the Royal House."[5] René Hague has argued that the autobiographical part of Joinville's history was written around or before 1272, and that the hagiographical part was written sometime between 1272 and 1309.[6]

Perhaps no one will ever know for sure what the original version of Joinville's autobiography looked like. The author is plainly the central character of the final version,

with Louis IX playing an essential but ancillary role. Yet Joinville's book has always been considered above all a book on the sanctity of King Louis. Why does this cleavage exist between what Joinville plainly says and what generations have always thought him to mean?

One might dismiss this as a pseudoproblem; or reply that, though Joinville allows himself more space, Louis IX remains the central figure; or assume that the discrepancy between intention and execution is largely a technical matter due to the fact that the author, not a professionally trained writer, completed his book without realizing that the bulk of its autobiographical materials all but succeeded in crowding the hagiographical materials out of the picture. Whether the asymmetry of the book and its failure to live up to the claims set forth in the preface can be ascribed to oversight, to old age, or to haste in completing the final product, one fact stands out: it is impossible to maintain that the book is what it purports to be, a book about the sanctity of Louis IX.

One thus remains inclined to assert that this is not a pseudoproblem and that the explanation does not reside in incompetence or old age or a hasty compilation of materials written several decades apart. If Joinville's book, as published, turns out to be anything but what the title and the prologue proclaim it to be, may it not be that Joinville's oversights, like his preteritions, are intended to be meaningful? May it not be that Joinville knew what he was about and that beneath the avowed purposes of the book he is in fact pointing obliquely toward an implicit conclusion?

The *History of Saint Louis* is a highly class-conscious book, none of the protagonists being more class-conscious than the author himself. Several anecdotes in the story illustrate to what extent Joinville was imbued with all the prejudices of his class, perhaps none more illuminating than Joinville's brief conversation with Robert de Sorbon, a member of the lower class who had managed to win his way into the king's entourage. To "Master Robert," who has just suggested to him that wearing finer clothes than the king is equivalent to "sitting above him on the bench," Joinville drily replies: "saving your grace, Master Robert, I am in no way to be blamed for wearing green and ermine. It was my father and mother who left me this gown. It is you who are in the wrong; you are the son of working folk [*vilains*] and you have given up the clothes your father and mother wore and are dressed in finer woolen cloth than the King." Louis IX, incidentally, is called to witness this dialogue, and his presence, characteristically, transforms it into a test of strength between the two nobles, "the King arguing in Robert's defence with the greatest vigour" (6, 36).

Joinville recalls admiringly how Count Henry the Generous of Champagne, having encountered a knight begging on the steps of Saint Stephen's Church at Troyes and not being able to express his fabled generosity in specie, did so in kind by giving away his companion, the burgher Artaud of Nogent. He did so, however, not without reminding the burgher of his inferior status: "Sir Villain," said the count, turning to Artaud, "you are wrong in saying that I have nothing more to give; I have you." Joinville adds, quite casually, that the knight took Artaud by the cloak and told him that he would not release him until the burgher had paid a ransom; "and before he was freed Artaud paid up to the tune of five hundred pounds" (20, 90-92).

In Egypt, and again in Caesarea, during the crusade of 1248-54, Joinville thought it natural that the common folk of the French army should set up a brothel at a stone's throw from the king's tent, and he expresses some measure of surprise that the king should dismiss them for having indulged in such sport. What, after all, are common yokels expected to do during their idle hours?[7] On the other hand, Joinville deems it "disgraceful" for a knight to talk and laugh while mass is being sung for the repose of the soul of a fellow knight (69, 297-98). He refuses adamantly and angrily to overlook the fact that one of his knights has been bullied by one of the king's men-at-arms and threatens to leave the king's service if he does not receive satisfaction, "seeing that . . . men-at-arms could push knights about" (99, 509). And Joinville's way of dispensing and rationing wine to his inferiors in Caesarea was directly related to their position on the social scale: "I bought a hundred barrels of wine, of which I always had the best drunk first. The servants' wine I had mixed with water, the squires' with less water. At my own table the knights were served with a large flask of wine and another of water, so that they could mix it to their taste" (98, 503-504).

Louis IX himself displays much the same caste prejudice as his seneschal. Though it may seem contentious to say so, the king's way of waiting upon "his poor" at table, giving them money before sending them on their way, and washing their feet on Maundy Thursday has a paternalistic and cloying odor about it. Other incidents in the narrative illustrate Louis's sense of social decorum and his belief in the unalterability of the orders of society. To the count of Montfort, who has been solidly outclassed in theological debate with a Jew, Louis suggests that lay noblemen should leave theological debates to the "learned clerks," the nobleman's business being, "as soon as he hears the Christian faith maligned, [to] defend it only by the sword, with a good thrust in the belly, as far as the sword will go" (10, 50-53). The king is refreshingly merciless when he is quibbling with the clergy or the hierarchy over social or political matters and uses the strongest language to remind them of their social rank.[8] Unfortunately, however, his strongest verbal lashings, his cruelest punishments, seem to be reserved for burghers or *vilains.* A knight caught in a brothel in Caesarea is allowed to choose either to forfeit his horse or to be led through the camp by his whore with a cord tied round his genitalia, but a goldsmith caught "uttering a filthy oath" is "put in the pillory, in his shirt and drawers, with the guts and lights of a pig round his neck, such a heap of them that came right up to his nose" (138, 685).[9] And it was a Parisian burgher whose nose and lips the king allegedly branded because he too had uttered a filthy oath.[10] Did Louis consider prostitution such a lesser sin than cursing that he should punish it so lightly, almost humorously? Or is the sin different according to whether the sinner is a noble, a knight, a burgher, a tradesman? And what is the reader to think of the king's harsh reply to Joinville's demand for indulgence toward Ponce, the old squire, who has served three generations of kings: "Seneschal . . . he has not served us. It is we that have served him, by allowing him to stay with us in spite of his bad habits" (133, 662)? The remainder of the king's reply sounds far less characteristic of a saint than of an advocate of free enterprise telling his son the secret of his family's success in business: "My grandfather King Philip told me that in rewarding your servants you should give one more and one less, according to their service. And he used to say also that no man could govern a country well if he could not refuse as boldly and bluntly as he could give. I tell you this . . . because people are now so greedy in their demands that there are few who look to the salvation of their souls and the honour of their persons, so long as they can by right or wrong lay their hands on other people's property."

For both Joinville and Saint Louis, in short, society was still pretty much composed of three basic orders: nobility, clergy, and peasant or burgher (*preudomes, clercs, vilains*). Ever since the time of Augustine, social orders had been described, and social duties apportioned, in such threefold terms. There are those who uphold the faith with the sword, the *defensores;* those who uphold it with discourses and prayer, the *clerici* or *oratores;* and those whose business is to work, both for self-preservation and for the perpetuation of the classes above them, the *laboratores.*[11] The vision of the social order held by Joinville and the king could have been held by any citizen of the later empire or of the feudal age: Augustine, Cassiodorus, Boethius, Charlemagne, Hugues Capet, Philip I, or Louis VII. The essential thing for a Christian, as Saint Paul had so clearly said, was to know his social *ordo* and stick to it: "in the state in which he was called" (*I Cor.* VII:20). For Joinville and Louis IX, class consciousness meant the art of holding one's rank as best one could; and living up to the highest ideal of that rank meant being a *preudome.*

What does it mean to be *preudome?*[12] The question is twice raised in Joinville's chronicle. On the first occasion (5, 32), the concept of *preudomie* is set apart from that of *beguinage,* the life of the devout layman living a religious life in community. For Louis, a *preudome* is "better than a beguin." That is to say, a lay Christian devoting himself heart and soul to the "defense and illustration" of the Christian religion in the world is better than a lay Christian who devotes himself to a life of surrogate monasticism: "When we had been disputing for a long time, the king gave his finding. . . . 'I would dearly love to have the name of being a *preudome* so long as I deserved it, and you would be welcome to the rest. For a *preudome* is so grand and good a thing that even to pronounce the word fills the mouth pleasantly'" (5, 32).

Later, in a digressive historical flashback, Joinville recalls a distinction once made, during the Third Crusade, by the "great King Philip" (Philip Augustus) about one of his men whom he considered physically brave but unworthy of the title of *preudome:*

> There is a world of difference [said King Philip] between a brave man [*preu home*] and a brave and good man [*preudome*]. There are, in Christians and Saracen lands, many brave knights, who have never believed in God and His Mother. And that is why I say that God gives a great gift and a great grace to the Christian knight whom he permits both to be bodily brave and to be His servant, preserving him from mortal sin; and it is the man who so orders himself that one should call *preudome,* since his prowess is a gift from God. But those of whom I spoke before, one should call *preuz homes,* since they are physically brave, but take no heed either of God or of sin. (109, 559-60)

Preudomie, therefore, appears to be a mean of excellence situated somewhere between an escapist piety and an impious audacity. The *preudome,* of necessity, is a layman, a Christian, an active and courageous participant in the affairs of the world, if need be a warrior and "defensor fidei"; he is not a *beguin* in that he eschews neither fine clothes nor gaiety nor the affairs of court nor worldly honor nor even the throne of his kingdom; but though he is physically brave, he "believes in God and His Mother" and is chary of committing mortal sins. He is "both bodily brave and a servant of God." One might say of him what Aristotle said of his proud men: "it is honour that they chiefly claim, but in accordance with their deserts," provided one adds that "he acknowledges God as the source of all honor and the end of all his service."[13]

Preudomie, it should be stressed, was a layman's ideal. Joinville realized that it was an ideal open to the Christian by the mere fact that he had not chosen the life of the cloister; and he certainly found it difficult (as Joan Evans suggests) "to accept the truth that the *prud'homme* was noble by character but not necessarily by birth."[14] I would go yet further and suggest that, so far as Joinville is concerned, the implicit conclusion to be drawn from his memoirs is that *preudomie* is an ideal open to the nobility alone. The *preudome* is a noble who has reached his peak of excellence. To Robert de Sorbon, the "son of working folk," Joinville concedes no more than "the great reputation he had for being a *preudome*" ("la grant renommée qu'il avoit d'estre preudome"), and for this the king allowed him to eat at his table (5, 37).[15] But it was only a matter of reputation, and Joinville was the first to remind Master Robert of his humble origins whenever the latter forgot the fact that at the king's board he was simply a *déclassé.* Never does Joinville ascribe the title of *preudome* to a clerk or a *vilain* (Master Robert being one only by adoption); but the king's eight counselors, as well as the lords who accompanied Louis and Joinville on the crusade are referred to as *preudomes* without qualification.[16]

A *preudome* simply because he belonged to the one class for which this ideal was conceivable, Joinville considered himself a social equal of Louis IX. *"Singulariter,"* he might have said, in scholastic discourse, "I am the king's seneschal; but *specialiter,* I am his social peer." As an individual, Joinville was the king's inferior; as a member of the nobility he was the king's class peer. Many times in his account the sentiment—one is almost tempted to say the resentment—of equality (a feudal resentment somewhat diluted by the middle of the thirteenth century, but never entirely repressed) is clearly implied.

Joinville's qualifications for the ideal of *preudomie* had a firm genealogical base. His first and last preoccupation before leaving for the crusade of 1248 is to spend a week with his family, "putting things right," as he describes it, and settling all matters of his estate (25, 111). For a full week before his departure, he plays the role of *paterfamilias,* feasting and dancing with his family, his brother the lord of Vaucouleurs, "and other great men." During that week, his first wife, the sister of the count of Grandpré, gives birth to Joinville's son John, lord of Ancerville, and Joinville is reassured by the thought that a male descendant will perpetuate the family name while he is abroad on his long and dangerous mission (25, 110). When he takes leave of his estate, having bequeathed most of his worldly possessions to his heirs, he does not dare look back, "lest my heart should weaken at the thought of the lovely castle I was leaving and of my two children" (28, 122).

The disasters and humiliations of the Egyptian campaign make Joinville no less conscious of his superior origin than before. In the full swing of his first landing on the shores of Damietta, in Egypt, he notes that the count of Jaffa "of the house of Joinville . . . made the finest landing of all" (34, 158). At Mansourah, where he is made captive, he is nearly assassinated by a Saracen who takes him for the king's cousin. When he succeeds in proving that he is related through his mother to Emperor Frederick of Germany, his life is spared. The Saracens are visibly impressed to hear that Joinville is a grandnephew of Frederick Barbarossa. "Otherwise," he comments with laconic grace, "we should all have been killed" (65, 326).

Joinville had every right to consider himself as the equal, in social class, of King Louis. He seems to have exercised that right unstintingly, as is obvious from his account of the occasions when he did not hesitate to speak up to his master; and when Saint Louis seems to have the last word, never will the reader find Joinville explicitly admitting defeat. Many are the occasions, on the other hand, when Joinville might have claimed to score a point, had his game of one-upmanship with Louis IX been explicitly declared. Why is he so emphatic in saying that, though he was severely outnumbered, it was he who prevailed upon Louis IX to remain in Caesarea rather than return prematurely to France (84-85)? Why the demeaning details about the king's dysentery at Mansourah ("so bad that it was necessary, so often was he obliged to go to the latrine, to cut away the lower part of his drawers"), while Joinville's illness from a throat tumor is described in dignified if melodramatic detail?[17] Why, within earshot of the king, does Joinville speak so compassionately with the renegade Christian who has converted to Islam, whom the king has just contemptuously told to be on his way (71, 418)? Why is Joinville so deliberately sanguine in telling of the gambling habits of the king's brothers at Acre (71, 418) while he stresses the king's intolerance and fury at the sight of their dicing (79, 405)? Why does Joinville address himself with such mock deference to the king when the pilgrims from Greater Armenia ask the seneschal to allow them into the king's tent, that they might see the "holy King": "I do not want to kiss your bones just yet" (110, 566)? Why does Joinville dwell on details such as the king's "estrangement" from his hapless wife Marguerite, his excessive and "senseless" grief after the death of his mother, his abnormal oedipal tendencies, his morbid and mother-inherited fear of sin (116, 594; 119, 604-608)?

Why? Because Louis IX answered only imperfectly to Joinville's mature and quite personal idea of Christian *preudomie*. One doubts whether such an intelligent writer as the old seneschal, whose experience of life was certainly as extensive as the king's, could fully admire the much-vaunted "sanctity" of a man for whom committing a mortal sin seems one and the same thing as desecrating his own mother. One doubts, too, whether Joinville truly admired the king's jejune way of presenting matters of faith in terms of conundrums and catechismal games ("Now, dear man, which would you prefer, leprosy or mortal sin?"). Such suspicions and doubts are perhaps not fully subject to proof. One cannot demonstrate what Joinville really thought about matters toward which he had to keep a diplomatic silence, even years after the king's canonization: or better, especially after the king's canonization, when the legend of the king's sanctity was rampant throughout the kingdom. One can only infer some of Joinville's authentic feeling toward Louis IX from his innuendos, his sallies of humor, and his silences. To pretend that Joinville's overt admiration for Louis IX was merely a cover for hostility would, of course, be overstating the case. It seems likely, however, that the seneschal considered his king as, at best, a *primus inter pares,* perhaps a "sanctus inter pares," but no more; and there are moments when he unquestionably considered himself more faithful to the canons of *preudomie* than the king himself.

This is not to say that Joinville ever thought of himself as a superior *preudome,* but simply that, to his mind, Louis occasionally betrayed that ideal either by excess or by default. Joinville's conception of *preudomie* is a balanced ideal, a mean of excellence, a state of moral equilibrium which, paradoxically, demands the fullest of the Christian lord's powers. Any excess in the striving for *preudomie* yields a lesser, not a greater sum of virtue. Any excess, even in the defense of the faith, yields less *preudomie,* therefore less sanctity. For *preudomie* is neither more nor less, in Joinville's mind, than lay Christian sanctity. Little wonder, then, that King Louis himself considered it far preferable to be a *preudome* than a *beguin: preudomie* simply corresponded better to the ideal of sanctity that a man of his class and station should aspire to. Little wonder,

too, that Joinville invariably praises Louis IX when the monarch remains within the guidelines of *preudomie* and takes him to task when he transgresses those guidelines. For in transgressing the boundaries of that ideal, even out of religious zeal, Louis IX is in fact prevaricating against himself, by falling short of the highest goal available both to him and to his social class.

Joinville has no choice, therefore, but to condemn with his silence any and all of the king's attempts to reduce the Christian faith to a number of adolescent riddles. He can boldly tell Louis that his coldness toward his wife is unbecoming to a man of sense and *preudomie* (116, 594). He can warn Louis sternly to beware his tendency to accept gifts from persons asking favors of him and can advise him in affairs of the world to "trust only those who knew most about them" (123, 628). Of the king's alleged decision to brand the nose and lips of a Parisian burgher who had been found guilty of blasphemy, Joinville can only respond with the dry disclaimer: "I did not see it myself" (138, 685). Of Louis's decision to embark on the last, fatal Eighth Crusade, Joinville can only remark that "those who advised him to go committed a mortal sin" (144, 736). These are matters in which the king was guilty either of excess or failure in matters of *preudomie,* a failure both to himself and to his class.

It is with undisguised pride, on the other hand, that Joinville tells of those occasions when the king acted like an unqualified *preudome.* Such occasions far outnumber those when King Louis lapses into an unfortunate *beguinage.*[18] When he tells Joinville and Robert de Sorbon that a man should dress according to his social degree (6, 38); when he refuses the demands of the bishops over matters of secular jurisdiction (13); when he tells his sailors, on the way back from *outremer,* that "there is perhaps no one on the ship who loves life any more than I do" (133, 628); when he is willing to treat with the Saracens at Mansourah, even to the point of paying a huge ransom for his own life and the lives of his men (71)—at moments like these King Louis is living according to the code of *preudomie.*

With regard to the last instance, it is noteworthy to contrast the king's attitude with that of Joinville's storekeeper, who proclaimed in Egypt that "we should allow ourselves to be killed and thus we shall go to Paradise."[19] While the Christian *preudome* will resort to all measures within reason to avoid martyrdom and prolong his life in the service of God and His Mother, only a *vilain* would be dimwitted enough to provoke death in order prematurely to win paradise. Joinville makes no attempt to conceal his feeling that such storekeepers are not to be listened to.

The Christian ideal of Saint Louis, in short, was conditioned and guided by the secular canons of his social class. The king's Christianity was far closer to Joinville's than to the storekeeper's. Otherwise stated, Joinville's sanctity is far closer to the king's than the seneschal has customarily been given credit for. Too long critics have spoken admiringly of the "foil" that Joinville provides for the holy king:

"Joinville is human whereas the king is saintly, and together they make a harmonious pair," so the argument runs in simplified terms.[20] Joinville was quite as serious about his piety as the king. As a member of the feudal nobility he had the right to aspire to the heights of *preudomie;* and there is nothing in his text to justify the mere suggestion that he considered himself any less a Christian, any less an *exemplum,* any less a *preudome* than the king he served.

In his attitude toward the faith Joinville has sometimes been dismissed as a lovable buffoon, principally because he seemed bent on appearing like a man who takes his Christianity with Gallic moderation. Readers usually think of Joinville as the man "who would rather commit thirty mortal sins than be a leper"; who did not so much as lend an ear to his storekeeper who tried to make martyrdom sound attractive; who, at the point of being decapitated at Mansourah, did not feel that confession was necessary, "for I could not remember any sin I had committed" (70, 354); who while in a Saracen prison found the prospect of the afterlife far less invigorating than the good news that he was about to be released (66, 337); who confessed and absolved a fellow lord while in prison and then admitted to having forgotten everything the man had said (70, 355). Joinville, in short, often strikes his critics as a man who takes his faith with a measure of humanistic skepticism—a Montaigne before his time, as it were.

In this matter, as in several others, Joinville's allusions are perhaps more eloquent than his words. His highly personal commentary on the Nicean Creed is the work of a deeply reflective mind.[21] A man of little faith would perhaps not have shown Joinville's high courage at Acre, when a vast majority of the French lords, including the king himself, were tempted to return prematurely to France. A spiritual buffoon would surely not have erected a chapel in honor of Saint Louis after seeing him in a dream and have provided that chapel with an endowment that would allow a mass to be sung "for ever in his honour" (148, 767).

Joinville very probably took matters of faith with the utmost seriousness. His was neither the unrelieved dullness of the professionally devout nor the prissiness of the king himself, who once observed that the Christian's harshest curse-word, at the peak of a fit of temper, should not exceed "In truth it was so" (138, 686). He seemed unafraid of letting joy intrude on his piety; he was not alarmed that cheerfulness kept getting in the way. Nietzsche once remarked of Jesus that "his disciples should look more redeemed."[22] One imagines Joinville as looking redeemed. His book is a record not merely of one saintly life but of a collective attempt at *preudomie,* including his own. Of his stay at Acre he wrote: "Now I must tell you of the many hardships and tribulations I suffered at Acre, from which God, in whom I trusted as I trust in Him now, delivered me. I shall have these written down that those who hear them may also put their trust in God when they suffer hardship and sorrow, and so God will help them as He helped me" (80, 406).

In Caesarea, Joinville regulated his days and nights with the same liturgical devotion as the king. He had with him in his tent two chaplains who recited hours for him, "one of them saying Mass for me as soon as the dawn appeared, the other waiting until my own knights and those of my division had risen. . . . My bed was so placed in my tent that no one could enter without seeing me in bed; this I did to avoid any scandal about women" (98, 501-502). Such, thought Joinville, is the responsibility of the lord and *preudome.* Without ever explicitly saying so, he interpreted his station in life, his personal and social vocation, as a call to bear the French nobleman's burden: to provide a religious model, to achieve *preudomie.*

The ***History of Saint Louis*** is a tribute to those saints and martyrs who accompanied Louis IX on the Seventh Crusade. Of them the king was certainly the best known, but he was not the only saint or the only martyr. Neither, so far as one can be sure, was he the most saintly of the martyrs. The king's style of sanctity, though communicable and highly personal, was neither the only nor necessarily the best. As members of the same peerage the king and the lords were equals. Each of them was entitled to his own style, each might serve as a model for others to imitate. The king is not exclusively worthy of imitation, and the possibilities of patterning one's life after his (if Joinville is to be taken at his word in the following passage) seem curiously restricted to members of the king's own family: "Great will be the honour to all those of his house who strive to resemble him in well doing, and . . . great reproach . . . to those of his house who seek to do ill, for fingers will be pointed at them and it will be said that the holy king from whom they are sprung would have scorned to do such wrong" (143, 761).

Joinville's intention was not to hold up the figure of Saint Louis for the Christian's imitation, but to write a manual of *preudomie* in which the king figures as one of two principal illustrations. The reader may identify more easily with the king; or with Joinville; or he may even choose to admire "all those who served as pilgrims and crusaders" with the king in Egypt and Palestine. Whatever the individual response, the ***History of Saint Louis*** is fundamentally a book about a class and an institution rather than about a man, a book written "that those who hear it may have full confidence in that part of it which is the very truth I saw and heard myself" (149, 768).

The subject of the book was *preudomie.* Insofar as the king lived by the code, he was doing no more than abiding by the canons prescribed for a member of his class. To the degree he lived by these canons the king was worthy of praise; inasmuch as he occasionally broke these humane canons with his excessive zeal, he was to be reprimanded, albeit posthumously. Such was the way Joinville might, in his old age, have justified his book to members of his family or peerage. But his reservations being expressed, Joinville ends his book on a conciliatory note. His last ghostly encounter with the king takes place in a dream, and it reads like a reunion between two members of the same peer group who immediately strike a common chord and a common language: "Now I must tell you some things about St. Louis which will be to his honour, and which I saw in my sleep. It seemed to me, then, in my dream, that I saw him in front of my chapel at Joinville, and he was, I thought, wonderfully gay and light of heart; and I, too, was happy to see him in my castle, and said to him, 'Sir, when you leave, I will entertain you in a house I have in a village of mine called Chevillon.' He answered me with a laugh, 'My Lord of Joinville, by the faith I owe you, I have no wish to leave this place so soon'" (148, 766).

The *History of Saint Louis* can be abstracted from its time and read as a revealing biography of two of the most engaging figures in thirteenth-century France. It can also be considered in its own right as a treatise on kingship wherein the figure of a great prince is held up for the admiration and the imitation of posterity. In both regards Joinville's chronicle is being read as a traditional piece of medeval historiography perpetuating the Graeco-Roman idea that history is above all a narration of the acts and deeds of great men for the purpose of moral edification.

We have attempted to consider the *History* not according to this timeless or traditional point of view, but as a product of the mental equipment of the thirteenth century. For one cannot disregard the intellectual structures of the period in which Joinville lived. Although he never engaged in the dialectical debates of the schools, Joinville was convinced, like most of his contemporaries, that there is a structural bond between a concept and its concrete representations. A concept like *preudomie* has real existence, both in its individual representations and, ultimately, in the mind of God. In that regard, the concept, the idea, the institution is both nobler and more real, in the order of being, than even the most authentic of its concrete representations.

Joinville's book might thus be read as the description of the dynamic structural relationship between a universal and a singular. There are moments when the singular lives up to the requirements of the universal; there are moments when it falls short. But the structural bond between them is a real one. By Froissart's time, the mid-fourteenth century, that bond has broken entirely.

Notes

1. Some biographical material on Joinville has been gathered from R. Bossuat, art., "Jean de Joinville," *Dictionnaire des lettres francaises: le moyen âge* (Paris: A. Fayard, 1964), pp. 417-19.

2. On August 6, 1297, Pope Boniface VIII summarized the canonization process of King Louis IX, begun in 1273, by saying that the last inquest alone had necessitated "more documents than an ass could carry." During the canonization process, all persons who had known Louis IX closely were invited to give their testimony. The written record of much of this testimony has been lost. However, two biographers, besides Joinville, expanded their testimony in the form of written memoirs: Geoffroi

de Beaulieu, Saint Louis's confessor; and Guillaume de Chartres, his chaplain. Between December 1302 and October 1303, Guillaume de Saint Pathus, who had been confessor to Queen Marguerite (Saint Louis's wife) for eighteen years, summarized most of the canonization testimony in a later biography of the king, translated into French as *Vie Monseigneur saint Loys,* ed. by Delaborde in 1899. These three pious biographies of Saint Louis contain some interesting materials; but on the whole they make for tedious reading and fail to achieve their edifying purpose.

3. John of Joinville, *The Life of Saint Louis,* translated by René Hague (London: Sheed and Ward, 1955), p. 26. Unless otherwise specified, all translated quotations from Joinville's text are taken from this source. References are cited in the text. For references to the original I have used Natalis de Wailly's edition of the *Histoire de Saint Louis* (Paris, 1874; reprinted in 1965 by the Johnson Reprint Corporation).

4. On this point, see Joan Evans' excellent introduction to her *History of Saint Louis* (Oxford: Oxford University Press, 1938), pp. xiii-xxviii, esp. pp. xxi-xxii.

5. Ibid., p. xx.

6. *The Life of Saint Louis,* p. 7.

7. Ibid., XXXVI, 171: "The common folk took up with loose women, for which . . . the King dismissed many of them. I asked him why he had done so."

8. See esp. Chapters XIII and CXXV.

9. *Life,* XCIX, 505: "The Knight chose to forfeit his horse and left the camp."

10. *Life,* CXXXVIII, 685. Joinville, who did not witness this incident and is somewhat reserved about telling it, derived this piece of information from Guillaume de Saint Pathus. In his biography of the king, this obsequious confessor of Queen Marguerite (the King's wife) applauds the king's zeal in this matter. Pope Clement IV had issued a bull in 1268 asking for moderation in punishing such offenders (according to Hague, *The Life of Saint Louis,* p. 293). Louis IX was literally trying to be *plus catholique que le pape.*

11. On the concept of tripartite society in medieval Europe, see Jacques Le Goff, *La Civilisation de l'occident médiéval* (Paris: Arthaud, 1965), ch. 5; W. J. Sedgefield, *King Alfred's Old English Version of Boethius* (Oxford: Clarendon Press, 1899); J. M. Wallace-Hadrill, *Early Germanic Kingship in England and on the Continent* (Oxford: Clarendon Press, 1971), ch. 6.

12. On *preudome* and *preudomie,* see A. R. Boysen, *Ueber den Begriff preu im Französischen (preu, prou, prouesse, prud'homme, prude, pruderie),* Inaugural-Dissertation, Westfälische

Wilhelms-Universität zu Munster, Lengerich, 1941; G. S. Burgess, *Contributions à l'étude du vocabulaire pré-courtois,* Publications Romanes et Francaises, 110 (Geneva: Droz, 1970); *Speculum* XLVI (1971): 363-64.

13. Aristotle, *Nicomachean Ethics,* 1123 b, in Richard McKeon, ed., *The Basic Works of Aristotle* (New York: Random House, 1941), p. 992.

14. *The History of Saint Louis,* p. xxiii. Joan Evans uses the modern French spelling of *prud'homme.* I have employed Joinville's spelling throughout.

15. I have translated the phrase myself, since René Hague does not specifically translate the word *renommée.*

16. This point is well taken by Evans, *The History of Saint Louis,* p. xxiii. In the original text the word *preudome* refers to someone with or above the rank of knight. (See de Wailly, *Histoire de Saint Louis,* p. 367, under the word *Preudom.*) On one occasion, however, Joinville uses the expression *cis preudom* of a greyfriar of extraordinary spiritual and humane qualities (de Wailly, *Histoire,* section 38d).

17. *Life,* LXIV, 324: "I sent for my people and told them I was a dead man, for I had a tumour in my throat. They asked me how I knew, and I showed them; as soon as they saw the water pouring out of my throat and nostrils they began to weep."

18. Here I disagree with Evans, *The History of Saint Louis,* p. xxiv: "It is with a conscious joy that he recounts the few occasions when Saint Louis acted rather as *prud'homme* than *dévot.*" I believe Joinville considered Louis's lapses into excessive piety as exceptional deviations from his usual *preudomie.*

19. *Life,* LXIII, 318-19: The storekeeper advises Joinville and his men to surrender to the Saracens on land rather than to the Sultan's galleys on the Nile, as the Saracens are sure to kill them or sell them to the Bedouins. "We paid no attention," comments Joinville, and the matter ends there.

20. Such, in substance, is the attitude shared by Sainte-Beuve, Joan Evans, Paul Guth, and other critics, although it has admittedly not been expressed in precisely these terms.

21. For the text of Joinville's *Credo,* see Hague, *The Life of Saint Louis,* pp. 223-37.

22. As quoted by Paul Tillich in *The New Being* (New York: Scribners, 1955), p. 142.

Maureen Slattery (essay date 1985)

SOURCE: An Introduction to *Myth, Man, and Sovereign Saint: King Louis IX in Jean de Joinville's Sources,* Peter Lang, 1985, pp. 1–31.

[In the following essay, Slattery offers an overview of the dating controversy surrounding Joinville's Vie de Saint Louis *and discusses the structure of the work, the sources from which Joinville may have drawn, the history of the early manuscripts, and the purpose of the work.]*

THE CRITICAL TRADITION ON JOINVILLE

Few would care to contest Bacon's observation that the invention of printing, gunpowder and the compass changed the form of civilization. But many of our medieval sources have been studied as if they had been written after the invention of the printing press. The majority of studies on Joinville's "Mémoires", as most historians persist in calling them, have succumbed to the magic of printing.[1] Depending on an historical method of a Langlois and Seignobos or even a Bernheim, these studies have taken the written document as the first if not the only criterion for our historical knowledge.

Before the accomplishment of the scientific edition of Natalis de Wailly, one read and reread Joinville's text as if it had been composed in the sixteenth century with Rieux's edition or the seventeenth century with Claude Menard's edition, or even the nineteenth century with Daunou and Naudet's edition of 1840. Rarely was it mentioned that Joinville could have composed his work from not only written sources but from what he had heard and seen. For Auguste Molinier, this master of Les Sources de l'Histoire de France, the work of Joinville was "un écrit un peu incohèrent au début et à la fin, et non exempt de redites, la partie centrale, la première rédigée, restant la meilleure."[2]

Other commentators have not ceased to call our attention to the 'special' language of Joinville, his familiar tone. Natalis de Wailly acknowledged the monotonous repetitions, the triviality of some details but saw Joinville's greater qualities. Gaston Paris referred to the opening section as a "laborieuse compilation de faits mal reliès entre eux." René Hague, Joinville's English translator, mentioned that his subject "had little aptitude to the writing of history."[3]

Critics have been puzzled that the opening and closing sections of Joinville's work present King Louis IX in short symbolic scenes with hagiographic style, while the central and longest sections describe him in running narrative form. Discussion has centred on dating the written composition of the dictated work. One eminent group of commentators, Gaston Paris, Molinier, Jeanroy and Bossuat, believe that the work was composed in two stages.[4] Paris maintains that the Crusade section (110-663) was an account of Joinville's adventures in the seventh Crusade with King Louis IX of France designed to entertain his family and friends of Champagne. Paris estimates that the tale was put to pen shortly after October, 1272, two years following the king's death. Thirty years later in 1304-5, Joinville was asked to write a life of Saint Louis for the royal court. At this time, he officially dictated his original Crusade story, adding appendages at the beginning and the end.

A smaller scholarly school, led by Bédier and supported by Alfred Foulet and Noel Corbett, believe that the book is a complex but single composition of 1305-6.[5] Alfred Foulet developed this hypothesis further in 1941, suggesting that the single composition of 1305-6 did develop in prior stages. He reasoned that Joinville's deposition during the canonization inquiry of 1282 together with the revision of Joinville's first written work, the **Credo,** in 1287, were initial steps in the composition of the finished product. Foulet even goes so far as to say that before 1282, Joinville "had doubtless narrated his memories of the king but it must have been in piecemeal fashion, without plan or perspective."[6]

Both schools have more in common than they have realized. Both groups of scholars stress the literary problem of dating the book's final rendering. Both teams date the work's final written form by internal textual date references. Apart from the fact that internal date references are not a conclusive method for dating the written composition of an orally dictated story, these critics have ignored the false anthropology of their literary priorities.

In our view, Paris and Foulet agree on the major character of the creation, but underestimate the fundamentally different consequences which such a character entails. Both scholars acknowledge that the work likely emerged from stages of both oral and written development. This common foundation merits our further attention and its takes us beyond our literary mind-sets.

It is simply in remembering that Joinville was first and foremost someone who saw bons faits and heard bonnes paroles long before the printing press that we can ask the question which is the subject of our study: is it possible to read Joinville's 'book' in the light of his visual and oral sources? Can we relegate to third rank his written sources without denying their place in his final text? The portrait which Joinville gives us of Louis IX is one of a witness who saw and who heard about the king, then dictated his memories. His borrowed written sources are auxiliary to this fundamental character of his work.

CLASSICAL WORKS ON KINGS AND SAINTS

Kings and saints have occupied the interest of many medieval studies. Both figures were prototypes of Christian symbolism in an age which gave them intriguing reverence. Louis IX of France, as king and saint, is a touchstone of two central medieval traditions.

As charming as Joinville is, it is his subject which occupies our curiousity because he reflects something so representative of the thirteenth century. Canonized seventeen years after his death, King Louis fulfilled his title: "most Christian of the Christian kings" and a Capetian quest for legitimacy through holiness.

Historical studies on the medieval monarchy have made excellent use of official documents surrounding the royal court. They have treated the administrative, liturgical, legal, political and financial aspects of its growth from theocratic to feudal to sovereign stages. During the reign of Louis IX, the French monarchy grew from feudal to more sovereign authority through the increasing territorial and legislative expansion of the crown. By the time of Louis' death in 1270, no part of the kingdom was without some tie to the royal government. Royal lawyers formed in the Roman law of Bologna and Montpellier began to affirm the imperium of the king.

Delisle, Wallon, Berger, Lavisse, Petit-Dutaillis, Kern, Luchaire, Lot, Langlois, Buisson, Glotz, Pfister, Funck-Brentano, Fawtier, David and Kantorowicz have contributed inestimably to our understanding of the French crown and Louis' reign. In a recent work, Jordan has illustrated the major role of the Crusade in Louis IX's self-understanding as a king and in his assumption of control after his mother's death in 1252. His meticulous and thorough application of his suzerainty upon his return from Crusade, coupled with his painfully won autonomy from his mother made him a forceful ruler of his kingdom. Increasingly, his provincial administration was controlled through his investigations of his baillis and seneschals and the strictly outlined their official duties in his ordinances of 1254 and 1256. Specialization of function began to develop his traditional feudal court into two bodies: a parlement who discussed judicial matters and a curia in compotis who dealt with financial affairs.

Louis continued the policy of his Capetian forbears by acquiring more land for the royal domain: Clermont-en-Beauvaisis, Mortain, Domfront and Mâcon. By the treaty of Paris in 1258, Louis recognized Henry III of England as Duke of Aquitaine but won back France's claim to Normandy, Maine, Anjou, Touraine and Poitou. He maintained neutrality in the struggle between Emperor Frederick II and the papacy, kept firm control over episcopal appointments in his territory and permitted complaints against papal taxes. These instititional aspects of Louis IX's reign have been extensively treated.

An important exception to this institutional emphasis on the French monarchy has been the study of Marc Bloch, Les rois thaumaturges which has unearthed the religious mentality and beliefs surrounding the medieval kings. His introduction explains the imbalance which his book attempts to right. Bloch says that it is not sufficient to understand the monarchy's administrative organization, judicial, financial or territorial changes. It is not sufficient to study the concepts of theoreticians which supported the divine right of kings or absolutism in the modern period:

> Il faut encore pénétrer les croyances et les fables qui fleurirent autour des maisons princières. Sur bien des points tout ce folklore nous en dit plus long que n'importe quel traité doctrinal.[7]

Marc Bloch's interest in the sacral beliefs surrounding medieval kings has been the inspiration for this study.

This work also takes its cue from a pioneer in medieval hagiography: Hippolyte Delehaye. Like kings, saints have also been studied in their legal, iconographic, homiletic, liturgical and pious aspects. Like kings, saints have been thoroughly documented as medieval events without much attention to the religious mentality surrounding them in their milieu. Rare is the study which treats the anthropology of sanctity in the medieval period.

The great contribution of Delehaye is that he presented the early medieval saint as an oral phenomena in a world of collective memory, symbolic representations and cultural rituals mirroring the divine. He illustrated how the oral memory retained simple, limited, similar incidents, describing saints who matched a type rather than an individual. Qualities and deeds which belonged to other local heros and heroines were often united under one head in the person of a saint. It was not uncommon to find exactly the same anecdote attributed to more than one saint. Delehaye explained how the oral memory relied on external signs to aid it: a monument, castle, feast-day or name-place preserved the tales attached to great people.[8] In analyzing the popular origins of medieval saints, Delehaye, like Bloch in his specific field, has enhanced our insight on the mentality of early medieval people, the way they thought about saints. Other scholars such as R. Aigrain, have built upon Delehaye's foundations. Aigrain has written on the methods and sources of hagiography in the esteemed Bollandist tradition.[9]

The cultivated perceptions and pioneering research of Bloch and Delehaye on medieval kings and saints form a basis from which to build. They show us the beginning of a methodology for studying the religious mentality surrounding the king-saint, Louis IX.

The Author

Jean de Joinville's portrait of Louis is the best contemporary account of the king. When he dictated the closing words of his "livre des saintes paroles et bon faiz nostre roy saint Looys", it was the month of October, 1309.[10] The courtly seneschal was eighty four years old. The extraordinary monarch with whom he had fought in the seventh Crusade (1248-1254) had been dead almost forty years, and a canonized saint for almost twelve years. Joinville had known him privately and loved him well.

Others had eulogized the king: the Dominicans, Geoffroi de Beaulieu and Guillaume de Chartres;[11] the monk of St. Denis, Guillaume de Nangis[12]—all had composed hagiographies of the monarch before his canonization. Guillaume de St. Pathus,[13] Franciscan confessor to the king's daughter, Blanche, had put the finishing touches on his hagiography in 1303. Joinville's product is a lay postscript to a clerical line. It is of particular value because it is the only lay biography on the lay king. Moreover, it is composed by a reliable first-hand participant witness of the events described. This also made it unique as the other works on the king compile their presentation of him through written sources.

Joinville was a member of the lesser nobility of Champagne, the north-west county of the French kingdom. Born

in 1225, eleven years after his royal subject, Louis, Joinville was the ninth lord of Joinville and likely served as a squire at the court of his overlord Thibaut IV, count of Champagne. Champagne had a proud and separate heritage from that of the direct royal domain of the French king. Joinville was very aware and proud of this distinct heritage.

His first known ancestor, Etienne de Vaux had founded the house of Joinville before 1027.[14] Since then, the house of Joinville had prospered by alliances with the families of Brienne and Broyes. John of Brienne twelfth king of Jerusalem was one of Joinville's family heroes. Joinville had a Crusading history to live up to in his family. Four generations of forbears had fought on Crusade before him: Geoffrey IV and V had won noble reputations on other Crusades and Joinville's own father, Simon, the son of Geoffrey V, had fought to take Damietta in 1219. Joinville inherited this Crusading tradition and eventually the title of seneschal of Champagne. This hereditary title made him an officer in the household of the count of Champagne, Thibaut.

Jean de Joinville received the courtly education of his time, learning to read and write with perhaps a bit of Latin. He was married at the age of fifteen and a year later accompanied his lord Thibaut to a great royal feast at Saumur, given by King Louis IX for his brother, the count of Poitiers. This was likely his first meeting with the king.

Joinville took the cross for the seventh Crusade at the same time as Louis IX in 1244. He set out in the summer of 1248 on the Crusading expedition for Egypt, from where the Crusaders planned to attack Syria from the south. He was captured and ransomed with Louis in Egypt. During the king's subsequent stay in the Holy Land, he became the king's closest confidante from 1250-1254. By an act of April, 1253, Joinville became a permanent vassal of the king with an annual income of 200 livres tournois.

While at Acre, Joinville composed a Scriptural elaboration of the Christian Creed known as the *Credo* and intended as an oral reading to solace the dying.[15] The *Credo* and his life of King Louis are the only two literary works we can positively attribute to him. Both reflect his serious moral character.

Upon his return to France in 1254, he divided his time between his fief, the Champagne court and the court of the king. He refused to go with Louis IX on his last Crusade, calling it folly. He never saw his royal friend again. Louis IX died of fever outside the walls of Tunis in 1270.

Early accounts of his Crusade experience were likely spoken to his peers upon his return to Champagne and possibly written during the 1270's. The final form of the work was composed at the request of his overlord, Jeanne of Navarre, heiress of Navarre and Champagne and wife of Philip IV of France. As she died in 1305, Joinville eventually dedicated the finished copy to her son, the future Louis X in 1309.

Joinville's officially recorded memories of Louis IX were politically pertinent. They gave prestige to the Capetian lineage and the dynasty which had produced a saint. Philippe IV and his wife Jeanne would not have been unaware of their political value.

Moreover, Joinville would have understood the possible moral value of his experience for future French kings. Philippe IV had ruthlessly departed from the ways of his grandfather Louis IX. Joinville's native province of Champagne had been acquired by Philippe III through the betrothal of Jeanne of Navarre to the future Philippe IV. Local administration in Champagne suffered under Philippe IV, whose political and ecclesiastical quarrels occupied his time.

As the seneschal closed his work on Saint Louis the Crusader, Philippe IV was proceeding against the Crusading Order of the Templars. He had ordered the arrest of every Templar in France, extracted an odious list of confessions and was bringing the Templars to trial to perjure themselves. Pope Clement V, at court in Avignon since 1308, was an impotent partner in the monarch's suppression.

Philippe le Bel's policies did not win him favour with the noble vassals of France. Joinville referred to him with distaste in his work:

> Si y preinge garde li roys qui ore est, car il est escha-
> pez de aussi grant peril ou de plus que nous ne feimes:
> si s'amende de ses mesfais en tel maniere que Dieu ne
> fiere en li ne en ses choses cruelment.[16]

THE WORK

As a biography of a lay royal saint composed by a contemporary lay knight, Joinville's work is unique. The knight from Champagne was proud that his subject was a lay-man: "on pourra venir tout cher que onques hom lays de nostre temps ne vesqui si saintement de tout son temps . . ."[17]

Like the almost contemporary roman in verse, le roman du Comte d'Anjoy, Joinville personified feudal personnages in himself and the king with secular biographical elements. However, his composition did not fall into any literary genre of exact definition. Sharing characteristics with the chronicles of Robert de Clari and his Champenois predecessor, Geoffroi de Villehardouin, Joinville nonetheless distinguished himself as both narrator and participant.[18]

The work consists of three basic sections:

1. Introductory section

a) dedicatory letter to Louis Hutin (1-18);

b) words and teachings of St. Louis (19-67);

2. Central section

a) early life and reign of the king (68-105);

b) deeds of the Crusade (106-664);

3. Closing section

a) later years of the king (665-767);

b) postscript to the book (767-769);

Both the opening and closing sections possess hagiographical elements. The opening section is based on Joinville's oral and visual sources, while the closing section is largely borrowed from the official hagiography of the king by Guillaume de Nangis, a Benedictine monk and official biographer of Louis IX for the dynasty. The central section is a narrative of the monarch and his trusty knight on Crusade. It is a blend of biography and autobiography.[19] Based on visual and oral witness, the central part is more chronological and eventful than the other two parts of the work which are divided into short symbolic scenes.

Joinville clearly designates when he uses augmenting oral report, borrows official written records and relies on his own first-hand witness throughout his work. For this reason, he makes an excellent choice for studying oral, visual and written reports on King Louis IX.

His primary source-material is his own inestimable witness of the monarch. His eye-witness account is part of a world in which visual witness was the beginning of a good oral tale. His evidence rings with the truth of his growing knowledge of the king and the unassuming details of human exchange inscribed in concrete examples.

His secondary evidence flows from the oral witnesses surrounding the king. The stories which Joinville heard about Louis illustrate the mentality of the milieu in which his own experience took shape and against which he measured his growing intimacy with the king. His oral sources are colourful anecdotes revealing the attitudes of the French noble Crusaders and their vassals towards the French king.

His tertiary sources are written material. He borrowed fairly long passages on law and short anecdotes on piety from Guillaume de Nangis' Chroniques de Saint-Denys and referred to at least one letter to refresh his memory. Joinville's major written source speaks for hagiographic and dynastic interests of a clerical milieu and its literary traditions quite distinct from Joinville's sociological grouping. Moreover, his written source relies on literary exemplars of sanctity and kingship which makes it an interesting point of comparison with Joinville's oral source-material.

Joinville's three sources are interwoven in refined discursive style with a careful choice of vocabulary.[20] We propose to separately examine the modes of perceiving the king in each source through a qualitative content-analysis.

HISTORY OF THE TEXT

Scholars rely on three manuscripts. The earliest, which dates from the fourteenth century, perhaps as early as

1320, is the Brussels MS., recovered by the Maréchal of Saxony in the eighteenth century. It is known as the Bibl. Nat. f. fr. Ms. 13568. The second is the Lucques MS. found by Saint-Palaye in the eighteenth century and known as Bibl. Nat. f. fr. MS. 10148. The third is the Rheims manuscript, discovered by M. Brissart-Binet in the nineteenth century known as Bibl. Nat. f. fr. 6273. The last two manuscripts date from the sixteenth century and have been 'modernized'. It is believed they have a common source, independent of the Brussels manuscript and intermediate between them and the original. They are valuable in that they serve to correct each other and to qualify the Brussels manuscript, which is the most authentic of the three manuscripts.

In 1547, Pierre-Antoine de Rieux published the first known edition of Joinville's life of Saint Louis, based on a document he had found among the belongings of King René of Sicily.

Rieux published it only after he had polished its style, orthography and illuminations to sparkle with sixteenth century tastes. The MS which he used was subsequently lost. His edition not only distorted the manuscript but changed what seems to have been a defective manuscript.[21] Rieux's edition depicted Joinville handing his book to a king of France called Louis, whose mother, the widow of Saint Louis, had requested the work. This same historical error appeared in the next edition which relied on a similar, apparently defective copy of the original. Claude Menard published this second edition in 1617 and dedicated it to Louis XIII. The MS which he utilized was also lost.[22]

It was a literary event when the Maréchal Maurice of Saxony found an early manuscript in Brussels in the eighteenth century. Its language, orthography and illuminations bore the unmistakable characteristics of the fourteenth century. This Brussels text, now acknowledged as the most authentic manuscript, was published in 1761 by Melot, Allier and Capperonnier. It brought the oldest, most authoritative version of Joinville's work to the public. Capperonnier also had at his disposal the sixteenth century Lucques manuscript, a freshly discovered document. He published its variations as foot-notes to his edition. The Brussels MS. 13568 was hailed as the original text. Several editions followed its first publication: Daunou and Naudet's in 1840, more fully foot-noted than Capperonnier's; Francisque Michel's in 1850 and Michaud and Poujoulat's in 1851.

These nineteenth century editions had recourse to both the Lucques and Brussels documents but gave preference to the most ancient one of the two.

In the last half of the nineteenth century, Natalis de Wailly found a third manuscript supplied through M. Brissart-Binet of Rheims. The Rheims document seemed to be a more complete version of the sixteenth century Lucques manuscript and to originate from a similar or identical source. Natalis de Wailly's published edition is the final and fullest publication. It has been accepted as the standard edition of Joinville's work.

Using all three manuscripts and comparing them to the language of Joinville's scribe in various original charters, de Wailly came to the conclusion that the Brussels manuscript was not the original text. He thought it to be a later fourteenth century copy of the original with minor grammatical alterations. He took it upon himself to edit a new and 'more original' text in a pseudo-champenois dialect. Despite the fact that his changes are minor, his edition is an altered version of the closest document we possess to Joinville's original manuscript. It should be studied in this cautionary light.

H. Moranvillé has made a good case for dating the Brussels MS. 13568 between 1320-1330, almost contemporary with Joinville's death in 1313.[23] He disagrees with de Wailly and maintains that it is an unaltered sister to the original text offered by Joinville to the future Louis X. Moranvillé reaches this conclusion for four reasons: 1) it alone of all three manuscripts contains this closing: "Ce fu escript l'an de grace mil CCC et IX au mois d'octovre"; 2) it alone contains a biting reference to Philippe le Bel quoted above; 3) it has several copying errors, many of which are carefully corrected by a contemporary hand; 4) the writing, illuminations etc., when carefully studied, date slightly later than the original manuscript of the *Vie de St. Louis* by Guillaume de St. Pathus which dates from approximately 1320. If this is indeed the case, the Brussels MS. 13568 may have been a Joinville family copy of the original text.[24]

THE ORIGINS OF JOINVILLE'S WORK

Joinville dedicated his work to the son of Philip IV of France, his future king. However, this king was to be the direct royal suzerain of Champagne, Joinville's native domain.

> A son bon signour Looys, fil dou roy de France, par la grace de Dieu roy de Navarre, de Champaigne et de Brie conte palazin, Jehans, sires de Joinville, ses seneschaus de Champaigne, salut et amour et honnour, et son servise appareillié.[25]

Joinville's work fulfilled a promise to his direct feudal suzerain, Jeanne de Navarre and de Champagne. Jeanne was the last independent feudal suzerain of Champagne. By Jeanne's marriage to Philip IV of France, Champagne came into the direct royal domain of the French monarchy:

> Chiers sire, je vous faiz à savoir que madame la royne vostre mere, qui mout m'amoit (à cui Dieu bone merci face!), me pria si à certes comme elle pot, que je li feisse faire un livre des saintes paroles et des bons faiz nostre roy saint Looys; je le li oi en couvenant, et à l'aide de Dieu li livres est assouvis en dous parties.[26]

This formal dedication at the opening of the seneschal's book was more than an external form such as we find employed in dedications of the fourteenth and fifteenth centuries. In the late thirteenth century, this dedication still represented the traditions of a feudal reality, tied to the heritage of Joinville's feudal service to the counts of Champagne and the honour of the royal service to Louis IX.

With his Crusading experience, Joinville represented a splendid Champenois history. The thirteenth century was the grand era of Champagne. The nobles of Champagne had married, fought and written well during this time. One can understand the influence such a glorious past might have on the imagination of the Champenois and the inspiration it might have given to Joinville's Crusading memories. One of Joinville's noble predecessors from Champagne had also written down his account of his Crusade experience. Like Joinville, this chronicler Ville-hardouin belonged to the noble ranks of Champagne society. Like the house of Joinville, the house of Villehardouin was well-connected by marriage or conquest in Europe:

> Les Chatillon devenaient comtes de Touraine, de Chartres et de Blois; les Dampierre héritaient du comté de Flandres. Les sires de Brenne allaient les uns conquérir le Sicile, les autres monter sur le trône de Jérusalem et sur celui de Constantinople: les Villehardouin se partageaient les débris de l'empire grec: Thibaut de Champagne ceignait la couronne de Navarre. On comprend l'influence que dut exercer sur l'imagination du peuple la splendeur de toutes les fortunes guerrières. L'honneur éveilla les muses, et la Champagne eut ses jours de gloire poétique et militaire.[27]

Joinville's work on King Louis was also feudal in the sense that it represented the antipathies and affections of an old and more independent Champagne before it came directly under the French crown. This heritage of territory and noble lineage, brought the customs, devotion, faith, independence and crusading spirit, to the service of the new seigneur of Champagne, the French monarch. The work of Joinville perpetuated the memory of Champagne's last independent seneschal, and the king who had been kindly to him.

The origins of Joinville's book lie not only in his Champenois traditions but in his family history. Joinville's kin-structure was one of distinction. Jean de Joinville was linked by the marriage of his great grandfather to the famed house of Brienne. In his work, he extolled at least two of the Brienne members as heroes: John of Brienne twelfth king of Jerusalem, whose glory ended in disaster on the banks of the Nile in 1219, and the "great count Walter" who was murdered in a Cairo prison after the Gaza defeat of 1244 and whom Joinville called a "martyr" as he likewise called Louis IX.[28]

Joinville was related to the Empress of Constantinople through the Brienne house. Mary, wife of Baldwin II was the daughter of John of Brienne. The Crusading seneschal devotes a telling passage of his work to her and recounts how the Empress of Constantinople chose Joinville and

Erard as her kinsmen. Nor did Joinville fail to mention that the chief emir of the Saracens queried him about his royal connections when he was captured:

> Et il me demanda se je tenoie riens de lignaige à l'empereour Ferri d'Allemaigne, qui lors vivoit; et je li respondi que je entendoie que madame ma mere estoit sa cousine germainne; et il me dist que de tant m'en amoit-il miex.[29]

Joinville's maternal great-aunt Beatrice had married Frederick Barbarossa, Frederick II's grandfather. This was a prestigious series of family connections for the seneschal from Champagne.

It seems that Joinville's work, particularly his central Crusade account, was at the service of this familial and feudal heritage. In this regard, it cannot be ignored that there were two heroes to Joinville's tale. For there was Joinville, his lineage and all the traditions of Champagne's noble chivalry to be defended, as well as the king to be honoured.[30] As we shall see in Joinville's eye-witness story, Louis IX was sometimes compared and contrasted to Joinville's feudal chivalry.

The dual allegiance and origin of Joinville's work emerges from the opening of his Crusade account. On the one hand, Joinville is proud to have served under the great and holy monarch, Louis IX. On the other hand, he does not fail to remind his audience of his own chivalry, and that of his family and Champenois nobles. For example, Joinville praises his father's defense of the Champenois city of Troyes against the forces of the Brittany allies:

> Li bourgois de Troies, quant il virent que il avoient perdu le secours de lour signour, il manderent à Symon Signour de Joinville, le pere au Signour de Joinville qui ore est, qu'i les venist se courre.[31]

Joinville recounts how Simon de Joinville saved Troyes, the capital of Champagne, from the destruction of its baronial enemies. Once the major defense of the city was accomplished, the King of France arrived to complete Simon's work:

> Li roys de France, qui sot que il estoient là, il s'adreça tout droit là pour combattre à aus . . .[32]

With this anecdote, Joinville accomplishes two things. While praising his father's noble bravery, he also illustrates the fruitful alliance which operated between his family and the French crown. This theme persists throughout Joinville's Crusade tale. The themes of the seneschal's Crusading memories were tied to the traditions of two lineages: that of the family and territory of Champagne and that of the Capetians to which Champagne was later joined.

Moreover, it is possible that Joinville recalled his memories through the oral traditions of his family and province.[33] Jeanne de Navarre and Champagne asked her seneschal to collect and write down the anecdotes she may have heard Joinville relate to his peers so that they could be offered as a book to the royal court. As we have seen, scholars agree that Joinville had orally recounted his Crusading experiences to his Champenois peers long before his book's composition.

As a noble of Thibaut de Champagne's homeland, as an official of his Champagne court, as a proud member of a Crusading family, Joinville was raised in an environment where epic legends, songs of troubadours, verses of poets and tales of returning Crusaders formed a familiar part of noble gatherings. His work emerges from this oral atmosphere and took its first origins within this Champenois culture. It was to this Champenois audience that Joinville first orally addressed his Crusading memories. Like the songs, romans and mises en prose of thirteenth century Champagne, Joinville's Crusading tales were addressed to a noble audience who wanted entertainment, adventure and glory. It is perhaps even possible that the general characteristics of the historical epic which we find in Ambroise, Ernould, Robert de Clari, Philipe de Novare, Villehardouin and Joinville originated from within noble oral traditions.

In his work on King Louis and the Crusade, Joinville indicates that his personal memories of the Crusade would have an informal oral destiny. This was quite apart from and prior to any thought of composing an official book for the royal court. The seneschal assumes that his experiences would find their way into noble oral traditions. For example, in his description of the battle of Mansurah, when he and the count of Soisson were holding a bridge against a Saracen onslaught against the king, the count reminds him that one day, they would speak of their adventures in noble halls:

> Li bons cuens de Soissons, en ce point là où nous estiens, se moquoit à moy et me disoit: "Seneschaus, lessons hiver ceste chiennaille; que par la quoife dieu: (ainsi comme il juroit) encore en parlerons - nous, entre vous et moi, de ceste journée es chambres des dames."[34]

Within this context of the familial, feudal and oral origins of the work, it is well to recall that Joinville's final book resulted from the oral mentality of his medieval culture. His book was an important honour and official achievement. But his final work was the literary adornment on the oral and visual experience and on the earlier story-telling of the proud and loyal seigneur of Joinville, seneschal of Champagne, a chivalrous but independent vassal of the great King Louis IX of France.

THE PURPOSE AND COMPOSITION OF JOINVILLE'S BOOK

In Joinville's *Credo,* the miniatures have been recognized as "an integral part of the whole economy, not mere adornment." Emile Mâle, in L'art religieux du XIIIe siècle en France called attention to the literal interrelation of its text and its illuminations. [35] The text was to be listened to and the miniatures were to be looked at. Since the *Credo* was designed for the religious exhortation of the dying, this work sought to bring the matters of faith to the victim through the two principal senses: the eyes and the ears.[36]

Although Joinville's memories of Louis on Crusade were designed for the living, there is a parallel to be drawn between this work and the *Credo.* While his book was to be read, it was to be read to others in a comparable fashion as the *Credo.* Joinville's portrait of Saint Louis was designed both for reading as well as for listening.

In his dedication of the royal portrait, Joinville tells the young and future king of twenty-one that he dictated King Louis' good deeds and words with the hope of influencing future kings and noble lords:

> pour ce que vous et vostre frere et li autre qui l'orront, y puissent penre bon exemple, et les exemples mettre à oevre, par quoy Diex lour en sache grei.[37]

The Champagne knight expected that his work on the king would be listened to both literally and figuratively. He thought that his book would be read aloud to members of the royal court. He hoped that it would offer good examples which would influence the future leaders of France.

In effect, Joinville was speaking through a book.[38] He was addressing an audience who would have the book read to them. In his work on King Louis, Joinville recalls that the monarch used to read stories of kings to his own children before bed-time:

> Avant que il se couchast en son lit, il fesoit venir ses enfans devant li, et tous recordoit les faiz des bons roys et des bons empereours, et tous disoit que à tiex gens devoient-il penre exemple.[39]

Along with the good kings, Louis recounted the deeds of the bad so that his children would learn that if they were not good, God would be angry and they could lose their kingdom for their misdeeds:

> "Et ces choses, fesoit-il, vous ramentoif-je pour ce que vous vous en gardez, par quoy Diex ne se courousse à vous."[40]

Was not this the function which Joinville envisioned for his own book: "pour edefier ceuz qui les orront"?

In a similar vein, Joinville records the tale of a sermon given to the king by the Grey Friar, Brother Hugh. It was delivered to Louis at Hyères when he first returned to France from his disastrous campaign in Egypt. The homily had a profound effect on Louis. It reminded the king that in all important books, no kingdom was ever lost to a lord or a king without some misdeed from its ruler:

> en la fin de son sermon dist ainsi, que il avoit leue la Bible et les livres qui vont encoste la Bible, ne onques n'avoit veu, ne ou livre des créans, ne ou livre des mescréans, que nus royaumes ne nulle signourie fust

onques perdue, ne changie de signourie en autre, ne de roy en autre, fors que par defaut de droit: "Or se gart, fist-il, li roys, puis que il en va en France, que il face te droiture à son peuple que en retiengne l'amour de Dieu, en tel maniere que Diex ne li toille le royaume de France à sa vie."[41]

While Joinville's **Credo** was composed to exhort the dying, Joinville dictated his book on Saint Louis to exhort the living. Like Brother Hugh's sermon which referred to authoritative books, Joinville's royal portrait had a homiletic purpose. This purpose was tied to the medieval custom of reading books aloud to appropriate audiences. Joinville's official audience for the final book was the royal court and its members.

In his book's final form, Joinville wished to primarily record what he had seen and heard during his six years in Palestine and Egypt with the king. To this central experience, he added other occasions on which he had seen the king at court. As such, he limited himself mainly to the roles of ear and eye-witness. At the very end of his composition, he included one major literary source. It consisted of several chapters from Guillaume de Nangis' life of the king. It is likely that Joinville added this official source on the Capetian monarchy to enhance the authoritative nature of his official book destined for the royal court. We shall evaluate this question further in the chapter on Joinville's written sources.

Finally, it must be acknowledged that the formal composition of Joinville's book was accomplished orally. He dictated it to a scribe: "Je . . . faiz escrire la vie notre saint roy Looys . . ."[42] He refers to his work as it "devise",[43] "parle",[44] "conte".[45]

Throughout Joinville's account, he uses expressions like:

> "or disons donc que . . ."[46]
> "je vous dirai . . ."[47]
> "je vous ai dit devant . . ."[48]
> "je vous avoie oublié à dire que . . ."[49]
> "après ces choses desus dites . . ."[50]
> "revenons à nostre matiere . . ."[51]
> "vous faiz-je à savoir . . ."[52]
> "je vous conteroie bien . . ."[53]
> "or di-je à vous . . ."[54]

Joinville is speaking in his book, in a way similar to that in which he spoke to his Champenois peers upon his return from Crusade. The audience was slightly different: this was royalty he was addressing in his book. The purpose was somewhat more serious, long-lasting and moral: this book could influence the destiny of the French kingdom. But the basic aim of the message was similar: this addressed a live audience of listeners. Its oral purpose was a constant characteristic of Joinville's tale, from its first to last telling.

In his composition, Joinville addresses his audience as if he expects them to hear his words:

or ces choses vous ramentoif-je pour vous faire entendant aucunes choses qui affierent à ma matiere . . .[55]

Joinville was utilizing a written vehicle for an oral tale to an audience of listeners. . . .

Notes

1. See R. Marichal, "Manuscrit", *Dictionnaire des lettres français, Le moyen âge*, ed. R. Bossuat, L. Pichard, G. de Lage (Paris, 1964).

2. Auguste Molinier, *Les sources de l'histoire de France* (Paris, 1903), 5: 28.

3. HSL, de Wailly, introduction; Gaston Paris, "La composition du livre de Joinville", *Romania* 23 (1894), p. 516; LSL, Hague, introduction.

4. Gaston Paris, "La Composition du livre de Joinville sur Saint Louis", *Romania* 23 (1894), p. 509; Molinier, *Les sources*, 3: 104-113; Robert Bossuat, "Jean de Joinville", *Dictionnaire des lettres françaises, Le moyen âge* (Paris, 1964), p. 418.

5. Joséph Bédier, "Jean de Joinville", *Histoire de la littérature française illustrée* (Paris, 1923), 1:83; Alfred Foulet, "Notes sur La Vie de Saint Louis de Joinville", *Romania* 58 (1932), pp. 551-565; Noel Lynn Corbett, *Joinville's Vie de Saint Louis, A Study of the Vocabulary, Syntax and Style* (Ottawa National Library, Public Archives Microfilms, no. 12937, 1968), p. 1.

6. Alfred Foulet, "When did Joinville write his Vie de Saint Louis?", *Romanic Review* 32 (1941), pp. 233-243; "Notes sur le texte de Joinville", *Mél. Ronques* 1(1951), pp. 59-62.

7. Marc Bloch, *Les rois thaumaturges* (Paris, 1924), p. 19. Recent scholarship which departs from the traditional conception of the Capetian monarchy to place it in touch with its socio-cultural matrix includes the excellent work of Andrew W. Lewis, *Royal Succession in Capetian France: Studies in Familial Order and the State* (Cambridge, Mass., 1981). In studying the Capetian dynasty in relation to its context of the royal family, Lewis treats royal holiness as an attribute of birth "de saint liu", pp. 122-133.

8. Hippolyte Delehaye, *Les passions des martyrs et les genres littéraires* (Brussels, 1921), p. 438.

9. Robert Aigrain, *L'hagiographie, ses sources, ses méthodes, son histoire* (Paris, 1953). Recent scholarship which treats the popular perceptions of saints includes: Weinstein, Donald and Bell, Rudolph M., *Saints and Society: The Two Worlds of Western Christendom, 1000-1700* (Chicago, 1982); Delooz, Pierre, *Sociologie et Canonisations* (Liège, 1969); Goodich, Michael, *Vita Perfecta: The Ideal of Sainthood in the Thirteenth Century* (Stuttgart, 1982); Vauchez, André, *La Sainteté en Occident aux derniers siècles du moyen âge: d'après les procès de canonisation et les documents hagiographiques* (Rome, 1981).

10. Joinville closed with the words: "Ce fu escrit en l'an de grace mil CCC et IX, ou moys d'octovre." Jean de Joinville, *Histoire de Saint Louis, Credo et Lettre à Louis IX*, ed. M. Natalis de Wailly (Paris, 1874), p. 412. (hereafter cited as HSL). A good readable version in the English language is by M.R.B. Shaw, as *Life of Saint Louis*, in *Chronicles of the Crusades* (London, 1963).

11. Geoffrey de Beaulieu, *Vita et sancta conversatio piae memoriae Ludovici regis*, HGF (Paris, 1840), pp. 3-27; Guillaume de Chartres, *De Vita et Actibus Regis Francorum Lucovici*, HGF (Paris, 1840), pp. 27-41. For background see: R.B. Brooke, *The Coming of the Friars* (London/N.Y., 1975); R.W. Emery, The Friars in Medieval France (London/N.Y., 1962).

12. Guillaume de Nangis, *Vita Sancti Ludovici*, HGF (Paris, 1840), pp. 58- 121. See N. de Wailly, "Examen de quelques questions relatives à l'origine des chroniques de Saint Denys", *Mém. Acad. Inscr.* 17 (1874), 403-407; L. Delisle, "Mémoire sur les ouvrages de Guillaume de Nangis", *Mém. Acad. Inscr.* 27.2 (1873), 342; H.-F. Delaborde, "Notes sur Guillaume de Nangis", *BEC* 44 (1883), 195-196; H. Moranvillé, "Le texte latin de la Chronique abrégée de Guillaume de Nangis", *BEC* 51 (1890), 652-659; A. Molinier, "Les Grandes Chroniques de France au XIIIe siècle", *Etudes d'histoire du moyen âge dédiées à Gabriel Monod* (Paris, 1896), pp. 311-313.

13. Guillaume de St. Pathus, *Vie de Saint Louis*, HGF (Paris, 1840), pp. 58-121. For background see: J. Moorman, *A History of the Franciscan Order from its origins to the year 1517* (Oxford, 1968); L.K. Little, "Saint Louis' Involvement with the Friars", *Church History* 33 (1964), 125-148; Elizabeth M. Hallam, "Aspects of the Monastic Patronage of the English and French Houses, c. 1130-1270" (unpublished doctoral dissertation, University of London, 1976), pp. 220-283.

14. Henri Delaborde, *Jean de Joinville et les Seigneurs de Joinville, suivi d'un catalogue de leurs actes* (Paris, 1894), p. 619; pp. 4-24 for Joinville's first known ancestors. On the period see: G. Sivéry, *Saint Louis et son siècle* (Paris, 1983); Elizabeth M. Hallam, Capetian France, 987-1328 (London, 1980), ch. 5.

15. Charles Langlois, "Le *Credo* de Joinville", *La vie au moyen âge* (Paris, 1928), 4: 1-22; also see D. O'Connell, *The Teachings of Saint Louis: A Critical Text* (Chapel Hill, 1972).

16. HSL 7.42, p. 24. On Philip IV see: J. Favier, *Philippe le Bel* (Paris, 1978); M. Barber, *The Trial of the Templars* (London, 1978).

17. HSL 1.1, p. 4.

18. Albert Pauphilet, "Introduction to Joinville's *Histoire de Saint Louis*", *Historiens et chroniqueurs du moyen âge* (Paris, 1952), p. 197.

19. Pauphilet emphasizes "deux portraits ou lieu d'un", in *Historiens et chroniqueurs*, p. 199. However, Georg Misch does not include Joinville in his autobiographers: *Geschichte der Autobiographie im Mittelalter* (Frankfurt, 1962).

20. Corbett, *Joinville's Vie*, p. 13.

21. HSL, p. 14, introduction.

22. John of Joinville, *The Life of St. Louis*, tr. René Hague (London, 1955), p. 16.

23. Henri Moranvillé, "Note sur le ms. français 13568 de la Bibl. Nat.: Histoire de saint Louis par le sire de Joinville" *BEC* 70 (1909), 303-312.

24. For the sense of heritage attached to the Joinville family see: Sachy de Fourdrinoy and P. Schouver, "Famille de Joinville", *Heraldique et Généalogie* 7 (1975), 108-109. For an interesting comparison to the sense of Capetian heritage see: B. Guenée, "Les généalogies entre l'histoire et la politique: la fierté d'être Capétien, en France au moyen âge", *Annales: Economies, Sociétés, Civilisations* 33 (1978), 461 and *passim*.

25. HSL 1.1, p. 2. On the prodigious uniformity of dedications in the Middle Ages and the presentation of a book as its formal time of publication see: K.J. Holzknecht, *Literary Patronage in the Middle Ages* (New York, 1966), ch. 8 and 9. MS. 13568 of Joinville's work contains an illumination which shows Joinville offering his book to Louis le Hutin, the future King of France.

26. HSL 1.2, p. 2. Joinville responded to the request of Countess Jeanne of Champagne, Queen of Navarre, a grand-niece of Saint Louis and wife of his grandson, Philip IV. Eager to spread the cult of the saint she addressed herself to her seneschal, Jean de Joinville, to solidify his memories. She died on April 2, 1305, before her command had been carried out. Another princess of the Royal House had made a similar request, Blanche de la Cerda, a daughter of Louis IX, had commissioned her confessor, Guillaume de Saint-Pathus, to write an account of her father, the king. Saint-Pathus had completed his task during the year 1303. Joinville dedicated his work to the Queen of Navarre's son, Louis le Hutin, sometime after her death in 1305 and before Louis' accession to the throne of France on Nov. 29, 1314. The date of October 1309 in par. 769 of Joinville's work: "Ce fu escrit en l'an de grace mil CCC et IX, ou moys d'octovre", is found in only one of the three manuscripts and presumably refers to the presentation copy to Louis. Louis was born on October 4, 1289 and entered his twenty-first year in October, 1309. It is possible that this birthday prompted Joinville's presentation of his work. Par. 767 again refers to Louis le Hutin of Navarre in the hopes that he will send some of King Louis IX's relics to Joinville's chapel of Saint Laurent.

27. P. Tarbe, *Les chansonniers de Champagne aux XIIe et XIIIe siècles* (Reims, 1850), p. VI. There was a

common bond of identity and loyalty among the knights of Champagne which Joinville reflected. As Alfred Foulet remarks: "Joinville a un orgueil de caste très net . . ." Foulet, "La Vie . . .", *Romania* 58 (1932), p. 560. Joinville's knightly solidarity extended in particular to the men of Champagne, who had a reputation of their own. Canon Ricardo in his chronicle of the Crusade of King Richard says: "Est quedam pars franciae quae campania dicitur, et cum regio tota studiis armorum floreat, haec quodam militae privilegio singularius excellit et praecellit." Ricardo, Canonico Sanctae Trinitatis Londoniensis, *Itinerarium Peregrinorum et Gesta Regis Ricardi*, ed. W. Stubbs (London: 1864), v. 1, liber 1, XXIX, p. 67. Thibaut de Champagne reflects this almost patriotic feeling at the end of a poem, when he cries: "salue nostre gent de Champaigne!" Thibaut was Joinville's literary count: Thibaut de Champagne, *Les Chansons de Thibaut de Champagne*, ed. A. Wallenskold (Paris, 1925), chanson V, p. 15, v. 44.

28. Joinville also mentions his kinsmen when he describes his landing at Damietta: "A nostre main senestre, ariva li cuens de Japhe, qui estoit cousins germains le conte de Monbeliart, et dou lignaige de Joinville . . .": HSL 34. 158, p. 86. Joinville's concern for his family heritage is also evident in his solicitude to have epitaphs composed for his ancestors, e.g. the epitaph of Clairvaux to Geoffrey III reads: "Pour les grands faits qu'il fist decâ mer et au delà." Consult: H. F. Delaborde, *Jean de Joinville et les Seigneurs de Joinville suivi d'un catalogue de leurs actes* (Paris, 1894). See also: A. Firmin-Didot, *Etudes sur la vie et les travaux de Jean Sire de Joinville* (Paris, 1870), v. 1, p. 106 on epitaphs. Joinville was proud of his family's Crusading heritage: five of his ancestors had preceded him to the Holy Land. Bédier asks of Joinville: "Pour quoi s'est il croisé, quand son suzerain de Champagne ne se croisait pas? Nulle raison temporelle ne l'y forçait. Il s'est croisé pour se conformer à une belle tradition de famille: cinq de ses aieux l'avaient précédé en terre sainte, dont il tenait à honneur de fouler les traces . . ." J. Bedier, "Jean de Joinville", *Histoire de la littérature française illustrée* (Paris, 1923), v. 1, p. 84.

29. HSL 65. 326, p. 178.

30. For the epic traditions of this theme see: W.T.H. Jackson, *The Hero and the King: an Epic Theme* (New York, 1982), pp. 1- 109, He examines "the conflict between hero and king" as a common epic theme. According to Jackson, the basic heroic conditions are sadness, loyalty, exile and desire for fame, none of which are absent from Joinville's self-account while runs parallel to his account of the king. For an innovative work on the creative nexus of medieval art, epics and chronicles see Stephen G. Nichols, Jr., *Romanesque Signs* (New Haven, Conn., 1983).

31. Apart from this anecdote on his father (HSL 19.84, p. 48), Joinville includes other tales from Champagne in his early life of the king. After a few initial stories on the early troubles of Louis' reign, Joinville recounts the war of Thibaut of Champagne against the barons of France. Learned through oral tradition, Joinville's account is not entirely accurate: e.g. he gives the rupture of Thibaut's marriage to Ioland of Brittany as a reason for the war, although this rupture occurred two years after the fact. He also digresses into the history of Count Henry I of Champagne and an anecdote concerning Henry and Artaud de Nogent (ch. 18 and 20). On one other occasion, Joinville refers to an earlier Crusade and seige of Damietta at which Simon de Joinville, Jean's father had assisted, Behind his remarks, undoubtedly lay the memory of familiar stories from his father about this long seige. (HSL 25. 165, p. 90)

32. HSL 19. 85, p. 48.

33. e.g. Joinville's departure from his native land for the glory of the Crusade is recounted with similar ardour and attachment to the land, similar sadness and sense of fidelity to a cause that we find in the thirteenth century poets of Champagne. Joinville recalls with sadness: "Et endementieres que je aloie à blehecourt et à saint-Urbain, je ne voz onques retourner mes yex vers Joinville, pour ce que li cuers ne me attendrisist dou biau chastel que je lessoie et de mes dous enfans." HSL 27. 122, p. 68. In *Girard de Vienne*, the work of the talented troubadour of Champagne, Bertrand de Bas-sur-Aube, the four sons of Garin leave their paternal château in a quest for glory in much the same fashion. See *Le roman de Girard de Viane, de Bertran de Bar-sur-Aube*, pub. P. Tarbe (Reims, 1850). Jean Misrahi, in "Girard de Vienne et la Geste de Guillaume", *Medium aevum* IV, 1 (1935), p. 14, comments on Girard: "Le héros n'est jamais un homme isolé; il fait toujours parti de son 'lignage'." When the abbot of Cluny receives Girard and Renier, the first thing he asks them is: ". . . dont estes vos enfant? De quel lingnaje? . . ." This observation is almost as apt for Joinville, the sixth of his lineage to go the Holy Land, a form of not only holy war but holy exile. Also consult: G. Doutrepont, *Les Mises en prose des épopées des romans chevaleresques* (Bruxelles, 1939) as the classic on the subject of the *mises en prose*. For a useful introduction to the differences between the auditory and visual memory and on the cultural transition from auditory to visual memory which started during Joinville's period, consult: H. J. Chaytor, *From Script to Print* (Cambridge, 1945), ch. II: "Reading and Writing", and ch. V, "Prose and Translation". Also refer to G. Chadwick, *The Growth of Literature* (Cambridge, 1936), for the transitions from script to print.

34. HSL 49. 242, p. 134. Gaston Paris' belief expounded in Romania 23 (1894), pp. 508-524, is that the central and longest section on the Crusade was composed of Joinville's personal Crusade memories, spoken "es chambres des dames" upon his return, and heard by the queen of Navarre and Champagne, his suzerain. Paris contends that the main purpose of Joinville's Crusade memories was not to glorify the king but to entertain the family and friends of the seneschal of Champagne. This is the part of Paris' hypothesis which seems most plausible. H. F. Delaborde, in his *Jean de Joinville*, p. 146 makes an interesting observation on the oral origins of Joinville's work. He notes Joinville mentions (3.25, pp. 12-14) that he advised Philippe le Hardi against spending so much money on his embroideried tunics. Joinville reminds the son of his father's simpler dress and greater charity. Delaborde comments: "Si Philippe le Hardi lui donnait déjà l'occasion d'opposer à sa conduite celle de son glorieux prédécesseur, combine de fois, sous le règne suivant, si différent de celui de Louis IX, à la cour de France comme dans la chambre de sa suzeraine, la comtesse de Champagne, reine de France, à Paris comme dans son château de Joinville, aux jeunes princes qui n'avaient pas connu leur grant aieul comme à ses propres enfants, combien de fois le sénéchal dut-il parler de la piété du saint roi, de sa fermeté dans ces dangers qu'il avait partagés, de son équité dans ces jugements dont il avait été le témoin."

35. Emile Male, *L'art religieux de XIIIᵉ siècle en France* (Paris, 1948), p. 177, n. 1. Perdrizet has also considered the *Credo* with its close relation of text and illumination as a source for the study of medieval religious iconography consult: *Speculum humanae salvationis, texte critique*, traduction inédite de Jean Mielot; J. Lutz et P. Perdrizet (Mulhouse, 1907), v. 1, p. 332.

36. Jean de Joinville, *Credo*, ed. L. Friedman (Cambridge, Mass., 1958), p. 1. While the verbal text has been preserved in only one version, three versions of the iconographic text are extant. This has led to a number of scholarly discussions on the fashion in which the text was to be illuminated and on the relation of the miniatures to the text. MS. 4509 is incomplete in its illuminations although it is the only known complete text of the *Credo*. The second group of illustrations is a series of outline drawings, inspired by the *Credo* and found on folios 231rᵒ - 232r⁰ of MS. Latin 11907 of the Bibliothèque nationale. At least one folio is missing. The third set of illustrations is complete and even includes the scene of the captive French crusaders which establishes their origin in Joinville's work. This group was discovered by W. Bakhtine in a thirteenth century Breviary for the service of Saint-Niçaise of Rheims, and was executed before the canonization of Saint Louis. Friedman reproduces the later findings of Bakhtine on plates v-xxii, and discusses the problem comprehensibly, highlighting the tradition of scriptural testimony which appears in the *Credo*. According to Joinville's mentality, faith was a form of belief in oral tradition, *fides ex auditus*: of things not manifest, concerning which we have certainty through oral report. Scripture was considered the divina auctoritas of oral report. Joinville offered his scriptural references as final proof of his arguments. Friedman's analysis points to an informal relation of the text and illuminations based on Joinville's purpose which calls for the text to be read to a dying victim and the illustrations shown to him: "Et devent lou malade façons lire le romant . . . si que par les eux et les oreilles mete l'on lou cuer dou malade si plain de la verraie cognoissance que li anemis . . . ne puisse riens metre ou malade dou sien . . ." (P. 51). See also L.J. Friedman, "On the structure of Joinville's *Credo*", *MP*, v. L1,(1953), pp. 1-8; G. Lozinski, "Recherches sur les sources du *Credo* de Joinville", *Neuphilologische Mitteilungen* 31 (1930), p. 200; Ch.-V. Langlois, "Observations sur un missel de Saint-Nicaise de Reims, conservé à la Bibliothèque de Leningrad", *Comptes-rendus de l'Académie des Inscriptions et Belles-Lettres* Bulletin de octobre-décembre (1928), pp. 362-368; H.F. Delaborde and Ph. Lauer, "Un projet de décoration murale inspiré du *Credo* de Joinville", *Monuments et mémoires publiés par l'Académie des inscriptions et Belles-Lettres* (Paris, 1909), t. XVI, pp. 61-84.

37. HSL 2.18, p. 10. Joinville's official purpose to influence the French crown to follow in the illustrious foot-steps of its great Saint Louis is found in this introductory section of his work, a second purpose which accured to his earlier oral purpose to glorify the deeds of the Champagne knights and the family of Joinville. Natalis de Wailly, in his 1868 edition of Joinville's work on Louis made a guess that Joinville dictated his memories of the king to "un des clercs de sa chancellerie, c'est-à-dire à un homme qui avait sa confiance, qui était toujours à sa disposition, et qui, sans doute, avait eu plus d'une fois l'occasion d'écrire, sous la dictée de son maître, des lettres-missive ou des chartes . . ." See Joinville, *Histoire de Saint Louis suivie du Credo et de la lettre à Louis X*, ed. N. de Wailly, (Paris, 1868), p. xxi. De Wailly believed that the work was composed as a whole for the final dictation and his estimate therefore refers to the last rendering of Joinville's book for Jeanne de Navarre. On the other hand, Gaston Paris believed that Joinville dictated his Crusade memories in 1272 from his head without referring either to notes or to the version of the *Credo* he had composed in 1250 at Acre. Paris maintained that in 1305, the Crusade section was merely recopied by a scribe, while the remainder of Joinville's memories were dictated by Joinville at that time and the concluding chapters of his work

were copied from the "romant" to which he referred at the end of the book. See G. Paris, "La Composition du Livre de Joinville sur Saint Louis", *Romania* 23 (1894), pp. 508-524. In his re-evaluation of the MS. 13568, H. Moranvillé defended the work's early orthography against de Wailly's and Paris' later dating of this MS. 13568. Moranvillé says: "rien ne pouvait que ce secrétaire eût fait partie de la chancellerie de Joinville . . ." He points out that secretaries travelled from house to house, château to château, and concludes that Joinville's scribe could have easily come from another part of France, hence with different grammar and orthography from a native Champenois of Joinville's region. See H. Moranvillé, "Note sur le MS français 13568 . . .", *BEC* 70 (1909), p. 305.

38. Ch.-V. Langlois, *La Vie en France au moyen âge* (Paris, 1928) t. IV, p. 3, describes it this way: "Dans le *Credo*, comme dans les *Mémories*, on entend pour ainsi dire, parler cet homme délicieux."

39. HSL 134. 689, p. 380.

40. HSL 134. 689, p. 380.

41. HSL 132. 659, p. 362.

42. HSL 3. 19, p. 10.

43. HSL 1.1, p. 2.

44. HSL 1.1, p. 4.

45. HSL 3.19, p. 10.

46. HSL 103.407, p. 222.

47. HSL 127.390, p. 212.

48. HSL 91. 194, p. 106.

49. HSL 34.160, p. 88.

50. HSL 24. 106, p. 60.

51. HSL 21. 93, p. 54.

52. HSL 20, 89, p. 50.

53. HSL 20. 89, p. 52.

54. HSL 2, 18, p. 10.

55. HSL 90. 189, p. 102. Joinville's oral style has been commented upon by H. Hatzfeld, "A Sketch of Joinville's prose style", Medieval Studies in honor of J.D.M. Ford (Cambridge, Mass., 1948), pp. 69-80. He describes Joinville's style as "'add as you write' language, more suitable for conversation than for literature", p. 75. This is one of the few articles which shows understanding of the oral nature of Joinville's style originating in his oral delivery. Another facet of Joinville's oral style is the manner in which his repetitions occur in his work: with the same themes and motifs but with an improvised variety of details. Gaston Paris noted this: "Le fait est particulièrement notable pour le récit, répété en tête du livre, des quatre occasions où saint Louis aventura sa vie pour son peuple: ici la répétition était légitime, et il semble que le sénéchal n'avait qu'à reprendre ce qu'il avait dit dans le corps du livre: mais il ne l'a pas fait, et tout en donnant au récit une forme beaucoup plus abrégée, il y a ajouté çà et là des détails qu'il avait omis dans la version plus ample (c'est ainsi que le nombre des 'notonier' que le roi consulta n'est indiqué que dans le résumé); ainsi sa mémoire lui fournissait les mêmes récits avec une admirable exactitude, mais,ce qui est bien naturel, avec quelques variantes de détail." G. Paris, "La Composition . . .", p. 522.

Abbreviations

Jean de Joinville's Edited Work

HSL *Histoire de Saint Louis*, Credo et Lettre à Louis IX, ed. Natalis de Wailly (Paris, 1874).

LSL *The Life of St. Louis*, tr. René Hague (London, 1955).

FURTHER READING

Criticism

Bement, Newton S. "Linguistic Value of the Michel Edition of Joinville's *Historie de Saint Louis." The Romantic Review* XXXVIII, No. 3 (October 1947): 193-202.

Examines the Michel edition of Joinville's *Historie de Saint Louis* and argues that Joinville's only contributions to the original dictated text were the vocabulary and construction or word order. Bement concludes that the Michel edition is valuable in that its language represents a synthesis between late Old French and early Middle French.

Foulet, Alfred. "The Archetype of Joinville's *Vie de Saint Louis." Modern Language Quarterly* 6, No. 1 (March 1945): 77-81.

Explains that the original dictation and presentation copy of the *Vie de Saint Louis* have not survived and questions the conclusions of Gaston Paris, who maintains that the five extant manuscripts all derive from a single archetype, an archetype that was not the original dictation. Foulet asserts that Paris's "identification of the archetype with the lost presentation copy" is based on a number of assumptions that require further examination.

Saladin
c. 1138-1193

Kurdish Muslim leader, Sultan of Egypt and Syria.

INTRODUCTION

Born in Tikrīt, Iraq, Saladin (also written as Salâh ed Dîn or Salah ed-Din Yusuf) rose to power during the time of the Second and Third Crusades. He gained a reputation as a superior general, and contemporary accounts by Frankish and Arabic sources credit Saladin with being merciful and fair. His name is most widely recognized among Westerners for his military engagement with King Richard I during the Third Crusade. Among Muslims, he has often been viewed as a hero of Islam for his efforts to unite the Islamic states culminating in the capture of Jerusalem in 1187. Others, Muslims and Westerners alike, believe that despite Saladin's devout claims, his actions were aimed at consolidating and increasing his personal power.

At age fourteen, Saladin entered into the service of Syrian ruler Nur ad-Din. In 1164, Nur ad-Din sent Saladin on a series of military expeditions aimed at assisting the Egyptian Fatmid rulers in defending themselves against the attacks of the Crusaders. Saladin's efforts in these campaigns were highly successful. By 1169, Saladin had become the commander in chief of the Syrian army, as well as the vizier of Egypt. Having defended Egypt against the Crusaders, Saladin now went on the attack against them. Following Nur ad-Din's death in 1174, Saladin expanded his power in both Syria and Mesopotamia. In 1187 Saladin's armies captured Jerusalem. Two years later, the Third Crusade was launched, forcing Saladin to defend his territory. King Richard I of England was successful in overtaking some of Saladin's strongholds, including Acre in 1191. In 1192, Saladin and Richard reached an armistice agreement that allowed the Crusaders control over cities along the Palestinian-Syrian coast. Saladin and the Muslims, however, retained control over the city the Crusaders most longed for—Jerusalem. Saladin died in 1193.

Saladin scholarship focuses largely on evaluations of the contemporary source material about Saladin's life, and assessments of Saladin's military efficacy, motivation, reputation, and legacy. Hamilton A. R. Gibb offers a ranking and analysis of contemporary Arabic sources that focus on the life of Saladin. Gibb maintains that the two best sources are the extant texts composed by 'Imâdeddîn of Isfahân, and the *Life of Saladin* by Bahâeddin Ibn Shaddad. Gibb also concludes that one of the most respected sources, the history *el-Kâmil* by 'Izzeddîn Ibn el-Athîr,

should no longer be regarded as the views "of a well-informed contemporary chronicler." Yaacov Lev examines how contemporary politics influenced Saladin's historian-admirers—Qadi al Fadil, 'Imad al-Din al-Isfahani, Ibn Shaddad, and Ibn el-Athîr—and affected their assessment of Saladin. Additionally, Lev discusses the cultural and religious biases that perhaps affected the biographers' views of Saladin. While Gibb and Lev study contemporary Arabic sources, C. R. Conder analyzes one such source—the account of Saladin's activities written by Saladin's friend Boha ed-Dîn—and Geoffrey de Vinsauf's account of the same events from the Frankish point of view. Both accounts, Conder observes, are in complete accordance on the main facts pertaining to the Third Crusade. Other critics have centered their studies on the way in which contemporary sources have been utilized or ignored by modern writers. An anonymous critic for the *Quarterly Review* argues that nineteenth-century English readers suffered from a lack of an accurate account of "Mohammedan history" written by a western author. The critic goes on to discuss the wealth of information about Saladin available from Arabic sources. Stanley Lane-Poole examines how Saladin legends, which appear in early French romances, influenced nineteenth-century romances such as Sir Walter Scott's *The Talisman* (1825). Lane-Poole demonstrates how Scott's and other literary treatments of Saladin include factual inaccuracies as well as insights into Saladin's character.

In evaluating and discussing Saladin's rise to power and his military and political achievements, some critics offer a favorable assessment of Saladin's character and motivations. Dana Carleton Munro offers a detailed account of Saladin's military conquests, and notes that Saladin treated Christian prisoners mercifully, and that he allowed Christian pilgrims access to Jerusalem. Steve Runciman characterizes Saladin as a devout Muslim, and comments that Saladin is as much admired in modern times as he was by his contemporaries. Like Munro, Runciman observes that Saladin showed "mercy and charity" to his defeated enemies. Similarly, Hamilton A. R. Gibb analyzes Saladin's activities and possible motivations. Gibb argues that Saladin's goals were to drive the Franks from Palestine and Syria, and to unite the Islamic states. Gibb praises Saladin as a man who stood for a "moral ideal"; Saladin expressed "this moral ideal in his own life and action," thereby creating "an impulse to unity." While these critics emphasize Saladin's religious motivation, his mercy, and his morality, others question—rather than praise—these qualities and impulses. Hilaire Belloc states that Saladin condemned enemies to torture and death, and remained "indifferent" to the suffering of these individuals. Belloc also describes Saladin as "fanatically anti-Christian." Malcolm Cameron Lyons and D. E. P. Jackson point out that Saladin was both admired and reviled by his Muslim contemporaries; some Muslims accused him of using the unification of Islam as a ruse for his quest for personal power. Still other critics have attempted analyses that avoid discussion of personal characteristics and motivation altogether. R. Stephen Humphreys offers a detailed examination of the political structure under which Saladin operated. Humphreys demonstrates how the territories brought together by Saladin functioned as a political system which was shaped by a network of loyalties Saladin had cultivated. Andrew S. Ehrenkreutz criticizes Gibb's and other "romantic" assessments of Saladin's achievements, and his own analysis of Saladin's early career does not focus on Saladin's devotion to Islam or to the holy war against the Crusaders. Ehrenkreutz goes on to discuss Saladin's military and diplomatic accomplishments, as well as his shortcomings as a leader. D. S. Richards in his study of Saladin's career, finds much to criticize in Ehrenkreutz's work. Richards claims that Ehrenkreutz's analysis is full of inaccuracies, as well as "slanted or unsupportable interpretations of texts." Richards concludes that while Gibb's portrait of Saladin may seem at first "too good to be true," it is preferable to Ehrenkreutz's faulty account.

REPRESENTATIVE WORKS

Bahâeddîn Ibn Shaddad
Life of Saladin (history) date unknown

'Imâddedîn of Isfahân
el-Barq el-Shâmî (history) date unknown

'Imâddedîn of Isfahân
el-Fath el-Qussî (history) date unknown

'Izzeddîn Ibn el-Athîr
el-Kâmil (history) unknown

Sir Walter Scott
The Talisman (novel) 1825

CRITICISM

The Quarterly Review (essay date 1896)

SOURCE: "The Age of Saladin," *The Quarterly Review*, Vol. CLXXXIII, No. CCCLXV, 1896, pp. 163–87.

[*In the following essay, the anonymous critic briefly reviews several nineteenth-century Western histories of the Crusades. The critic observes a lack of a thorough, accurate "Mohammedan history" by a Western writer and demonstrates that such information is available through Arabic sources.*]

. . . 1. *Ousama ibn Mounkidh, un Emir Syrien au premier siècle des Croisades* (1095-1188). Par Hartwig Derenbourg. Avec le texte arabe de l'Autobiographie d'Ousama, publié d'après le manuscrit de l'Escurial. Three Vols. Paris, 1886-1893.

2. *Siasset Nameh: Traité de Gouvernement.* Composé pour le Sultan Melik Shah par le Vizir Nizam oul-Moulk. Traduit par Charles Schefer, Membre de l'Institut. Paris, 1893.

3. *Recueil des Historiens des Croisades.* Publié par les soins de l'Académie des Inscriptions et Belles-Lettres. Historiens Orientaux, Tomes I.—III. Paris, 1872-1884.

4. *The Crusades: the Story of the Latin Kingdom of Jerusalem.* By T. A. Archer and C. L. Kingsford. London, 1894.

In reading any history of the Crusades, such as the sober and scholarly epitome which has recently appeared under the joint names of Mr. Archer and Mr. Kingsford, one cannot help being struck by the widely different presentment of the characters. The Crusaders stand out clearly enough in their heroic, if barbaric, qualities; many of them are living personalities in the reader's imagination; we can realize what manner of men they were, and understand the rude impulses which prompted their deeds. Of the Saracens, however, their foes in principle, but often their friends and allies in practice, our historians seem to have formed no distinct ideas. The 'swarthy painim' whom, as Milton has it,

> 'champions bold defyed
> To mortal combat or carriere with lance,'

are presented as misty impersonalities, vague 'types' possessed of no individual characteristics. Their outlandish names repel impatient readers, who find it impossible to take an interest in an unpronounceable person, destitute of qualities and passions—a sort of mechanical lay-figure without even an automaton's attribute of human likeness,—an actor, moreover, who plays an uncertain part in an historical drama whereof the very plot and scenes and *dramatis personæ* are not only unfamiliar but absolutely unknown. It would not be difficult to reckon up the number of Englishmen who possess a tolerable acquaintance with the internal history of the Mohammedan domination in Asia, Africa, and Europe; and, without some knowledge of the general conditions, it would be extravagant to expect an interest in individual developments. Some grasp of the nature and changes of Muslim civilization is necessary before one can understand the character and achievements of the men our ancestors vainly attempted to subdue.

It is true that a subject so unfamiliar, dealing with a civilization so unlike our own, with a religion so little understood even by the citizens of the greatest Mohammedan Empire of modern times, with names and events that certainly do not conciliate the student, demands exceptional gifts in its historian. The dryest History of England compels attention, simply because it is our own history; but the annals of the East do not bear obviously upon the problems of to-day, nor do they awaken the sentiments of patriotism or ancestral pride. Mohammedan history must be introduced to the Western reader with studied preparation of every allurement that may entice and chain his interest. The charm of style, the fascination of a vivid historical imagination, are never more needed than in the attempt to win adherents to a study which has hitherto been relegated to the dusty departments of 'research,' and has been systematically excluded from every course of academic teaching. There is no modern English history of the East, unfortunately, which can be recommended as literature, for its own sake; there is not even a general history of the Mohammedan period which can be said to atone for its dryness by the accuracy and completeness of its survey. The older historians are obsolete in view of the immense materials brought to hand by recent editors and translators of Arabic and Persian texts, and even among the veterans none but Gibbon—the universal exception—possessed the qualities of style and historical insight which are the preliminary conditions of popularizing an obscure

subject; and Gibbon, miraculously accurate as he is, in spite of the comparative poverty of his Oriental materials, could not anticipate the results of modern research. There is little solace in the reflection that we in England are not alone in the want of a worthy history of the mediæval East. Indeed it only makes the matter worse when we find that there is no adequate French or German work to fill the place left vacant in our own literature. One Dutch professor stood out conspicuous, richly endowed with the true historical insight, deeply versed in Oriental learning, and gifted with a rare charm of style in the French language he used; but the late Dr. Dozy devoted these remarkable qualities almost exclusively to the period of the Moors in Spain, which he illuminated with masterly research and painted with exquisite finish; and, save for a somewhat sketchy account of the growth of the Mohammedan religion, he did not touch upon the Eastern developments of the Muslim State. No other writer in French on Mohammedan history can be cited as an example. The Austrian Baron von Kremer compiled a singularly interesting, but fragmentary and disjointed, 'Culturgeschichte des Orients unter den Chalifen,' which makes no pretence to be a general survey of the Mohammedan Empire; and the standard German history of the Caliphate by Professor Weil, though a monument of Teutonic industry and learning, is at once restricted in scope and portentously dry in treatment.

Perhaps in few periods is the want of a really thorough Mohammedan history felt more keenly than in that of the Crusades, for it is obvious that a narrative of a war which inadequately appreciates the character and resources of the enemy can hardly be called a history. In Michaud's day there was little excuse for any such blindness to the other side of the shield; now there is none whatever. For it must not be supposed that the want of a good Mohammedan history is due to a lack of materials, least of all for the Crusading epoch: on the contrary, they abound. The splendid publications of the French Academy of Inscriptions have brought the records of the native chroniclers fairly, if cumbrously, within the grasp of all who are ignorant of Oriental languages. The old references to 'Abulfedæ Annales'—a noble work in its day, by which Reiske and Adler earned the gratitude of generations of students—may now be supplemented and corrected by citations from a number of other chroniclers and travellers who have been made accessible in French; and innumerable special monographs, scattered about the Transactions of learned societies, have thrown a flood of light upon what ought no longer to be termed an obscure period. Yet the majority of English readers are indubitably under the impression—if they are burdened by an impression at all—that the Saracens of the twelfth century were the same people living in much the same conditions as the Saracens whom the learned Cambridge Professor, Simon Ockley, introduced to an inappreciative public as they appeared in the first tumultuous wave of the new-born faith. All that the 'average schoolboy' knows on the subject—if he knows even that—is the imaginative portraiture of 'painim' chivalry in the 'Talisman.' If only Sir Walter Scott had possessed the materials which now lie ready to the hands of his unworthy successors, what a 'Talisman' there would have been!

Now the very first and commonest impression, that the Saracens of Saladin's age were Arabs, is a mistake. There were Arabs among them, undoubtedly, but the fighting element, the anti-crusading impulse, the tactical skill, came from a totally distinct race. The political world upon which the infant Saladin looked out in his cradle days in 1138 was widely different from the old empire of the Caliphate. The whole condition of Syria had vitally changed even in the lifetime of his father. The flaming zeal which had carried the victorious armies of Islam from their Arabian muster-ground to the desert of Sind on the east and the surge of the Atlantic on the west, had not availed to keep together, in the well-knit organization of a united State, the vast empire so suddenly, so amazingly, acquired. The Caliphate lasted indeed for over six hundred years, but it retained its imperial sway for scarcely a third of that time. In the seventh century the soldiers of the Arabian Prophet had rapidly subdued Egypt, Syria, Persia, and even the country beyond the Oxus, and early in the eighth they rounded off their conquest of the Barbary coast by the annexation of Spain. Such an empire, composed of contentious and rival races, and extending over remotely distant provinces, could not long be held in strict subjection to a central government issuing its patents of command from Damascus or Baghdad. The provincial 'proconsul' of the Mohammedan system was even more apt to acquire virtual independence than his Roman prototype. The very idea of the Caliphate, which was as much an ecclesiastical as an administrative authority, encouraged the local governors to assume powers which were not irreconcilable with the homage due to a spiritual chief; and the religious schisms of Islam, especially the strange and fanatical devotion inspired by the persecuted lineage of Aly, led by a different road to the dismemberment of the State. Already, in the ninth century, the extremities of the Mohammedan empire were in the hands of rulers who either repudiated the authority of the Abbasid Caliph of Baghdad, or at least tendered him, as Commander of the Faithful, a purely conventional homage. The Caliph's writ—or its Arabic equivalent—even in the days of the son of 'the good Harun er-Rashid,' did not run in Spain or Morocco, and met but a qualified respect in Tunis. Egypt on the one hand, and North-east Persia on the other, soon followed the lead of the extreme West, and by the middle of the tenth century the temporal power of the Caliph hardly extended beyond the walls of his own palace, within which his authority was grievously shackled by the guard of mercenaries whom he had imprudently imported in self-defence. This state of papal impotence continued with little change until the extinction of the Baghdad Caliphate by the Mongols in 1258. Now and again, by the weakness of their neighbours or the personal ascendency of an individual Caliph, the Abbasids temporarily recovered a part of their territorial power in the valleys of the Tigris and Euphrates; yet even then, although the Caliph had a larger army and possessed a wider dominion than his predecessors had enjoyed, his authority was restricted to a narrow territory in Mesopotamia, and his influence, save as pontiff of Islam, counted for almost nothing in Saladin's political world.

This political world was practically bounded by the Tigris on the east and the Libyan desert on the west. For a century and a half before Saladin began to mix in affairs of State, Egypt had been ruled by the Fatimid Caliphs, a schismatic dynasty claiming spiritual supremacy by right of descent from Aly, the son-in-law of the Prophet Mohammed, and therefore repudiating all recognition of the Abbasid Caliphate of Baghdad. Still more nearly affecting the politics of the Crusades was the situation in Syria and Mesopotamia. The whole of these districts, from the mountains of Kurdistan to the Lebanon, are in race and politics allied with Arabia. Large tribes of Arabs were settled from early times in the fertile valleys of Mesopotamia, where their names are still preserved in the geographical divisions. Bedawy tribes wandered annually from Arabia to the pasture-lands of the Euphrates, as they wander to this day; and many clans were, and are still, permanently settled in all parts of Syria. The decay of the Caliphate naturally encouraged the foundation of Arab kingdoms in the regions dominated by Arab tribes, and, in the tenth and eleventh centuries, the greater part of Syria and Mesopotamia owned the supremacy of Arab dynasties; but by the twelfth these had all passed away. The Arabs remained in their wonted seats, and camped over all the country to the upper valleys of Diyar Bekr, as they do now; but they no longer ruled the lands where they pastured their flocks. The supremacy of the Arab in those regions was gone for ever, and the rule of the Turk had begun.

The Turks who swept over Persia, Mesopotamia, and Syria in the course of the eleventh century were led by the descendants of Seljuk, a Turkoman chieftain from the Kirghiz steppes. In a rapid series of campaigns they first overran the greater part of Persia; other Turkish tribes came to swell their armies; and the whole of Western Asia, from the borders of Afghanistan to the frontier of the Greek Empire and the confines of Egypt, was gradually united under Seljuk rule. Persians, Arabs, and Kurds alike bowed before the overwhelming wave of conquest. But, wide as was their dominion, the significance of the Seljuk invasion lies deeper than mere territorial expansion. Their advent formed an epoch in Mohammedan history by creating a revival of the Muslim faith.

> At the time of their appearance the Empire of the Caliphate had vanished. What had once been a realm united under a sole Mohammedan ruler was now a collection of scattered dynasties, not one of which, save perhaps the Fatimids of Egypt (and they were schismatics), was capable of imperial sway. The prevalence of schism increased the disunion of the various provinces of the vanished Empire. A drastic remedy was needed, and it was found in the invasion of the Turks. These rude nomads, unspoilt by town life and civilized indifference to religion, embraced Islam with all the fervour of their uncouth souls. They came to the rescue of a dying State, and revived it. They swarmed over Persia, Mesopotamia, Syria, and Asia Minor,

devastating the country, and exterminating every dynasty that existed there; and, as the result, they once more reunited Mohammedan Asia, from the western frontier of Afghanistan to the Mediterranean, under one sovereign; they put a new life into the expiring zeal of the Muslims, drove back the re-encroaching Byzantines, and bred up a generation of fanatical Mohammedan warriors to whom, more than to anything else, the Crusaders owed their repeated failure. [S. Lane-Poole, 'The Mohammedan Dynasties,' pp. 149, 150.]

The Seljuk Empire did not long hold together. Less than half a century after they had entered Persia as conquerors, the vast fabric they had audaciously built and splendidly maintained split up into fragments. Seljuks continued to rule at Nishapur, Ispahan, and Kirman; Seljuks at Damascus and Aleppo; Seljuks in Asia Minor: but they were divided planks of the mighty bole, and did not long resist the new forces that pressed upon them. These new forces were indeed part of their system, and their own overthrow was the inevitable result of the organization of their State. For the Seljuk Empire was a purely military power; its authority rested on an army, composed to a large extent of hired or purchased soldiers, and officered by slaves of the royal household. Freemen were not trusted with high commands or the rule of distant provinces; native Persians and Arabs could not be expected to work loyally for the Turkish invader; and it was necessary to rely on the fidelity of slaves brought up at the Court in close relations of personal devotion to the Seljuk princes. These slaves or 'Mamluks,' natives for the most part of Kipchak and Tartary, formed the body-guard of the Sultan, filled the chief offices of the Court and camp, and rising step by step, according to their personal merits and graces, eventually won freedom and power. They were rewarded by grants of castles, cities, and provinces, which they held of their master on condition of military service. The whole empire was organized on this feudal basis, which seems to have been usual among Turkish races. Persia, Mesopotamia, and Syria were divided into military fiefs, and governed by Seljuk officers,—quondam slaves in the Mamluk body-guard,—who levied and lived on the taxes, and in return were expected to furnish troops at their Sultan's call.

The inevitable result was the supplanting of the enfeebled or corrupt master by the vigorous manly slave. As the Seljuks grew weak and their empire broke up into subdivisions, the great feudatories became independent; the Mamluks who had fought the battles of the conquest became the regents or guardians (Atabegs) of their masters' heirs; and the delegated function was presently exchanged for the full rights of sovereignty and the transmission of hereditary kingship. The twelfth century saw the greater part of the Seljuk Empire in the hands of petty sovereigns, who had risen from the ranks of the Mamluks and converted their fiefs into virtually independent States. In Persia, and beyond the Oxus, a cupbearer or a majordomo had founded powerful dynasties; and the slaves of these slaves, a generation of 'gentlemen's gentlemen,' had established minor principalities on the skirts of their masters' dominions. In this way a slave became regent

over his master's heir, and on his death assumed regal powers at Damascus: thus Zengy, founder of the long line of Atabegs of Mosil and Aleppo, was the son of a slave of the Seljuk Melik Shah; and the Ortukids and other local dynasts of Mesopotamia traced their fortunes to the same source. But, however servile in origin, the pedigree carried with it no sense of ignominy. In the East a slave is often held to be better than a son, and to have been the slave of Melik Shah was a special title to respect. The great slave feudatories of the Seljuks stood at least as high as the Bastards of mediæval aristocracy in Europe.

Melik Shah, the noblest of the Seljuk emperors, was indeed one of those rulers who possess the power of imposing their minds upon their epoch. To belong to his household, to hold his commands, was not merely an honour and a privilege; it was also an inculcation of principles. In serving the Sultan, one grew like him; and a standard of conduct was thus set up, modelled upon the life of the royal master, the pattern and exemplar of the age. It is recorded by an Arab historian that a chief or governor was esteemed by public opinion in strict accordance with the degree in which he conformed to the example of Melik Shah; and the standard thus adopted formed no ignoble ideal of a prince's duties. Justice was the first aim of Melik Shah; his chief effort was to promote his people's prosperity. Bridges, canals, and caravanserais bore witness to his enlightened encouragement of commerce and intercommunication throughout his dominions. The roads were safe, and it is stated that a couple of travellers might journey unguarded from Merv to Damascus. He punished robbery and looting with rigour, and the peasant could count on redress at the hands of an always accessible sovereign. Generous and brave, just and conscientious, he fulfilled the ideal of a Muslim Prince, and it is no wonder that his example impressed itself far and wide upon the minds of his followers.

Such is the picture of the great Mohammedan Emperor derived from the Arab biographers. Quite recently a new light has been thrown upon it by the labours of the learned director of the 'École spéciale des langues orientales vivantes' at Paris. M. Charles Schefer has translated from the Persian a treatise on the art of Government written by no less a personage than the celebrated Nizam-el-Mulk, who for thirty years (1063-1092) held the post of Chief Vezir or Prime Minister to the Seljuk Sultans. It sounds a little oddly for a prime minister to compete for a prize essay, yet that is precisely the origin of this interesting treatise. It appears that in 1091, the last year but one of his reign, Melik Shah addressed the elders and wise men of his Court somewhat in these terms:—

> Ye shall make the constitution of my government the subject of your thoughts; point out whatever undesirable principles have been sanctioned in my Court and administration; discover what has been hidden from me, and let me know any rules of my predecessors which I may have neglected. Ye shall write down, moreover, whatsoever ye may find among the laws and customs of preceding princes worthy to be introduced

into the imperial government. Submit your results to my judgment, that I may consider them and act upon them. Since God has awarded me the possession of the universe, covered me with his bounty, and subdued mine enemies before me, there must be no defect in my government, nothing that is not orderly in the management of public business, nor aught concealed from my regard.

A number of leading statesmen responded to this sensible invitation, but none of their essays was so much approved by the Sultan as that of Nizam-el-Mulk. 'All its chapters,' said Melik Shah, 'are drawn up to the height of my expectation; there is nothing to add. I shall make this book my guide, and it shall be the rule of my life.' This work, the *Siyaset Nameh* or 'Book of Government,' which was thus preferred by the Seljuk Emperor, is now before us, and, considering its source and section, it is a document of prime importance. Nizam-el-Mulk was unquestionably a great statesman. The Mohammedan writers dwell upon his spiritual virtues, and record with unction that he could repeat the entire Koran by heart at the age of twelve; but the chief testimony to his wisdom is seen in the prosperity and progress of the great empire for nearly a third of a century committed to his charge. His capacity for affairs was joined to a profound knowledge of jurisprudence and an enlightened support of learning and science. He it was who encouraged Omar Khayyam in his astronomical researches,—less celebrated to-day but far more important than his well-known 'Quatrains,'—and founded the famous Nizamiya College at Baghdad. The theory of government laid down by such a statesman in the full maturity of age, and approved by the greatest Asiatic ruler of the time, must necessarily be a work of unusual interest. Unfortunately it has been badly copied by ignorant Indian scribes, and the texts from which M. Schefer has produced his translation are full of errors. We must await the learned editor's promised volume of commentary before deciding on the exact trustworthiness of each detail; but in the meanwhile it is possible to trace the outline, at least, of the principles of government sanctioned by the high authority of Melik Shah and his Grand Vezir.

Those who expect to find in this work a systematic treatise on the functions of the various departments of State will, of course, be disappointed. It is not thus that an Oriental conceives political literature, and such an *aperçu* of an imperial systems as Abul-Fazl's marvellously minute and orderly account of India under Akbar [The 'Ain-i Akbari' has at length been worthily translated into English. In 1894 Colonel H. S. Jarrett completed, with laborious and praiseworthy fidelity, the version begun more than twenty years ago by the late Professor Blochmann. (Calcutta, Asiatic Society of Bengal, three vols., 1873, 1891, 1894.)] is a rare exception; nor is Abul-Fazl himself guiltless of the Oriental vices of discursiveness, exaggeration, and frequent omission of essential facts and conditions. In Nizam-el-Mulk's work, in the form in which it has come down, we perceive indeed a clear and philosophical arrangement; but the author is apt to run off the track in the pursuit of historical parallels and precedents, and some of

his sections appear to have been transposed, or inserted in the wrong place, as an afterthought in the process of revision. He states that he wrote thirty-nine chapters 'at one breath,' and then revised and added, which may account for occasional displacements and repetitions. But the chief fault to a Western critic is the truly Oriental preference for virtuous platitudes and vague generalizations, when one seeks for definite facts, statistics, and schedules. The actual opinions and precepts, moreover, of the great Vezir do not occupy a third of the volume; the rest is filled with traditions and anecdotes, derived from the ancient history of Persia or the annals of Mohammedan rulers, and forming a sort of 'case law' of precedents. Many of these are extremely characteristic, and their selection and adoption by the writer of course illustrate and confirm his personal views on government; but we could well have dispensed with a large proportion of his historical parallels—many of which are among the commonplaces of Oriental writers—in favour of a more detailed survey of the system which he elaborated, or at least sanctioned and supervised.

Nizam-el-Mulk's conception of a king is an embodiment of the doctrine of divine right: the sovereign is God's anointed; but the doctrine is tempered with a stern insistence upon the king's responsibility to God for every detail of his conduct towards the subjects entrusted to his protection. . . . [His] ideal of a true monarch savours of a counsel of perfection. He defines the character of a king by a quotation from an old Persian anecdote: 'He must subdue hatred, envy, pride, anger, lust, greed, false hopes, disputatiousness, lying, avarice, malice, violence, selfishness, impulsiveness, ingratitude, and frivolity; he must possess the qualities of modesty, equability of temper, gentleness, clemency, humility, generosity, staunchness, patience, gratitude, pity, love of knowledge, and justice.' One weighty judgment, it is alleged, is of more service to a king than a mighty army. He is cautioned to avoid favouritism and disproportionate rewards, to eschew excess in wine and unkingly levity, and recommended to be strict in fasting, prayer, alms-giving, and all religious exercises. In all circumstances he is to 'observe the mean,' for the blessed Prophet said, like Aristotle before him, that in all things the middle is the wisest place.

The most striking features in the system of government outlined by Nizam-el-Mulk are his constant insistence on the duties of the sovereign towards his subjects, and the elaborate checks suggested for the detection and punishment of official corruption and oppression. Twice a week the Sultan was obliged to hold public audience, when anybody, however humble and unknown, might come to present his grievances and demand justice. The Sultan must hear these petitions himself, without any go-between, listen patiently, and decide each case in accordance with equity. Various precautions are recommended to ensure the free access of the subject to the king. The precedent is cited of a Persian sovereign who held audience on horseback in the middle of a plain, so that all might see and approach him, and the obstacles of 'gates, barriers, vestibules, passages, curtains, and jealous chamberlains' might be removed. Another king made all petitioners wear red dresses, so that he might distinguish and take them aside for private audience; and the example is approvingly cited of a Samanid prince who sat on his horse all night during heavy snow, in the middle of the great square of Bokhara, without a single attendant, on the chance that some oppressed subject, who might have been turned away by his chamberlains, should see him and come for redress.

Extraordinary pains were to be taken lest the maladministration of local governors should escape detection. 'When an officer is appointed to a post, let him be benevolent to God's creatures. One must not exact from them more than is right, and one should demand it with gentleness and consideration. Taxes should never be claimed before the fixed legal day, . . . else the people, under pressure of need, will sell their goods at half-price, and become ruined and dispersed.' Constant inspection of the tax-gatherers and other officials is recommended, and severe punishment is to be meted out to the unjust. A vast body of secret spies was organized to watch the conduct of every public officer: *c'est là une des bases du gouvernement.* The great Vezir was aware of the drawbacks of this method,—the danger of fostering suspicion, and the risk of stimulating false evidence; but on the whole he cannot dispense with what, after all, has invariably been a conspicuous feature in Oriental administration. 'Spies,' he says, 'must perpetually traverse the roads of the various provinces, disguised as merchants, dervishes, &c., and send in reports of what they hear, so that nothing that passes shall remain unknown.' Another precaution (familiar in our own police system) was to transfer all tax-gatherers and agents every two or three years, so that they should not become rooted and overweening in their posts. Further, inspectors of high character, above suspicion, and paid by the treasury and not by local taxation, were appointed to watch the whole empire: 'The advantages which their uprightness brings will repay a hundredfold their salaries.' A prompt and regular system of post-messengers maintained rapid communications between the inspectors and the central government. Finally, the good behaviour of vassal chiefs was ensured by their sending hostages, to be relieved every year, to the Court, where 500 such captives were constantly detained. Various recommendations are also made in relation to the police, law courts, and method of rendering and auditing accounts.

These provisions for just administration affected the great and little feudatories quite as much as the ordinary local governors. It is laid down that the holders of fiefs must be made to understand that they are only allowed to raise from their lands such taxes as are legally assessed; that they must levy the taxes which are thus confided to them with mildness, and in no circumstances be permitted to distrain upon the subject's goods and chattels. Should a feudatory exceed these limits, he shall be deprived of his fief and be punished as a warning to others. 'It is imperative that these people should understand that the land and its inhabitants belong to the Sultan, and that the holders of fiefs, as well as the local governors, are but a guard ap-

pointed for their protection.' A special chapter is devoted to the means by which malpractices of feudatories are to be detected and proved. Nothing, unfortunately, is said about the conditions of military service and contributions in return for fiefs, beyond the stipulation that the feudatories must always keep the pay of their troops ready, set apart for the prompt settlement of each retainer's allowance. Incidentally, Nizam-el-Mulk seems to prefer the system of direct payment of all troops from the public treasury, without the intervention of feudatories. His reserve on the subject is, however, easily explained by a natural reluctance to attack a powerful body of men who had rendered immense services to the reigning dynasty. An interesting section describes the gradual process of promoting slaves from rank to rank, and mentions the age of thirty-five as the minimum at which a slave could receive a government, and hence, inferentially, a fief. The old feeling of the East is expressed in the saying that 'a good slave is more valuable than a son.' From the paragraphs relating to the army it appears that the body-guard, or *corps d'élite,* of the Sultan was reckoned at the low figure of 200 cavalry and 4,000 foot, whilst the whole army of the empire seems to have been estimated at 400,000. Care was taken to mix men of different nations in each regiment, in order to excite emulation and neutralize disaffection.

It has often been pointed out that one of the main characteristics of Seljuk civilization was the importance attached to education and learning. Although colleges existed previously in Mohammedan countries, we must ascribe to Seljuk patronage, above all to the influence of Nizam-el-Mulk, the great improvements in educational provision in the East during the eleventh and twelfth centuries. The celebrated Nizamiya *medresa* or university at Baghdad was the focus from which radiated an enthusiasm for learning all over Persia, Syria, and even Egypt, where it met a kindred stream of erudition within the *ribats* of the Azhar. To found a college was as much a pious act among Seljuk princes as to build a mosque, or conquer a city from the 'infidels.' The same spirit led the great feudatories and the numerous dynasties that sprang up on the decay of the Seljuk power to devote particular attention to questions of education, and by Saladin's time Damascus, Aleppo, Baalbekk, Emesa, Mosil, Baghdad, Cairo, and other cities had become so many centres of learned energy. Professors travelled from college to college, just as our own mediæval scholars wandered from university to university. Many of these learned men and ministers of State (the two were frequently united) were descendants of household officers of Seljuk Sultans. For example, the Atabeg Zengy, with all his vast energy and military talent, could scarcely have held the reins of his wide empire without the aid of his Vezir and right-hand man Jemal-ed-din, surnamed El-Jawad, 'the Bountiful,' whose grandfather had been keeper of the coursing leopards in Sultan Melik Shah's hunting stables. His father had risen to higher offices; and El-Jawad himself, after receiving a good education, had also been employed in the Seljuk service, where he attracted the notice of Zengy,

employed. He was a connoisseur in dogs and birds of prey, for his father, who was also a keen sportsman, annually imported the best that could be procured from Constantinople. Wherever he went, in Syria, Egypt, and Mesopotamia, his first thoughts were directed to the game of the district, and his notes form a curious sort of sportsman's calendar.

The passages in his Memoirs that possess the strongest interest for European readers are those which relate his experiences among the Franks. He draws a firm line of distinction between the settled Franks, the families of the first Crusaders, who had grown accustomed to Oriental life and become friendly with their Muslim neighbours, and the new arrivals, a set of bigoted pilgrims and needy adventurers, whose indiscreet zeal and greed of plunder embroiled the good understanding which had been established between the two creeds in Palestine. 'Those Franks,' he says, 'who have come and settled amongst us and cultivated he society of Muslims are much superior to the others who have lately joined them . . . The newcomers are invariably more inhuman than the older settlers who have become familiar with the Mohammedans.' Political alliances and personal friendships were frequent between the settled Crusaders and the neighbouring Muslims, and it was not unusual for a Mohammedan to enjoy the hospitality of a Christian knight. One of Osama's friends tells how he went to visit a distinguished cavalier of the First Crusade, and when dinner arrived his host removed all scruples by remarking, 'Eat; you will find it right. I do not eat Frankish food any more than you, but employ Egyptian cooks and eat only what they prepare. No pork ever comes into my house.' Osama himself had acquaintances among the Templars, whom he called his 'friends,' and whom he preferred to all other Franks. When he visited Jerusalem, they gave him one of their oratories, close to the Christianised mosque El-Aksa, to say his Muslim prayers in; he walked with them in the Haram Esh-Sherif, and was taken to the Dome of the Rock and House of the Chain. Of the hospitality of the Knights of St. John, too, he does not stint his praise. He was a witness of an ordeal by battle and ordeals by water, which did not increase his respect for Christian jurisprudence, and he cannot conceal his disgust for the want of proper surveillance over Frankish women, nor his indignation at the frequent breaches of sworn faith by the Crusaders, who seldom kept pact with the 'infidel.' Whilst generously admiring their valour, he lays especial stress upon their defensive tactics, their cautious orderly movements, their precautions against ambushes and surprises, and their self-control after victory in denying themselves the delights of a headlong pursuit. Like a grave Oriental, however, he cannot approve the idle merriment, jovial roars of laughter, and mad pursuit of pleasure, which he noticed among Franks of all degrees. An Eastern gentleman can never understand childish buffoonery or broad grins in men of sense and position.

It is a pity his notices of his contemporaries are not more complete and methodical, and that they seldom penetrate beneath the surface of things; but Osama was no philosopher, only a clever, sensitive, keen-eyed observer, and we must be grateful for such vivid pictures as the following account of a deal in ransoms:—

> 'The Franks brought before me their prisoners, one after the other, to be ransomed. I was about to buy back those whose deliverance God Most High had prepared, when there came up a devil of a Frank called William Jiba, mounted on his chariot of war, and just fresh from surprising a caravan of Magraby pilgrims, about four hundred men and women. Prisoners came in a flood towards me, with their owners, and I bought all I could. I noticed a man, still in his youth, who saluted and sat down in silence. I asked who he was—"An ascetic, belonging to a tanner." I asked the owner, how much? He answered, "By the virtue of my faith, I will not sell him except along with this old man—the two at cost price, forty-three dinars." I concluded the bargain . . . spent all I had with me, and gave my pledge for the balance. . . . On my return to Acre, there was William Jiba with twenty-eight prisoners still, one of them the wife of a man whom God Almighty had delivered by my means. I ransomed her, but did not pay on the spot. I went to the house of this scoundrel and said, "Will you sell me ten of these captives?" "By the virtue of my faith," said he, "I will only sell them *en bloc*." I went on, "The sum I have brought is not enough. I will buy some of them to start with, and the rest shall have their turn later." "I will only sell them *en bloc*," he repeated. So I went away. Now God (whose name be exalted!) decreed that the captives should every one escape that very night, and the country folk, being all Muslims round about Acre, concealed them. The rascal claimed them in vain, for God favoured their deliverance. Next day, William demanded of me the ransom of the woman I had bought back but not paid for. I said to him, "Hand her over and you shall have her price." "Nay," said he, "her price was due to me yesterday, before her flight," and he forced me to pay: which I did without regret, so delighted was I at the deliverance of these unhappy captives.'

Nothing could be more graphic than descriptions and stories like these, in which Osama's autobiography abounds. It throws a fresh and vivid light upon the people and life of his day. With the materials now accessible from the Oriental side, it should be possible to draw an accurate picture of men and manners of the time of Saladin as they appeared to contemporary witnesses. Few periods are more worthy to be distinguished in literature. The conflict of races and the tumult of tongues, the meeting of East and West on holy ground, the social revolution implied in the grafting of the feudal system of Tartary upon the democratic foundations of Islâm, the strong contrasts between the marauding life of the hill chieftains and the studious groups that hung upon the professors' lips in the cloisters of the city mosque, the unparalleled motley of creeds, systems, ideas, and languages, brought together from Asia, Africa, and Europe to fuse and mingle upon the sacred battlefield of faiths, offer rich occasions to the genius of a Froude or a Macaulay. The scene of the historical drama is laid in a land of moving associations; the air is full of the immemorial magic of the East; the romance of chivalry is joined to spiritual exaltation, the derring-do of battle to the quest of the Holy Grail. And the actors are not unworthy of their setting: among them are 'verray parfit gentil' knights, both Christian and Saracen, men of heroic deeds and generous magnanimity, standing out in fine relief from a crowd of truculent adventurers, whose word is as brittle as their sword is ready. Every condition that can lend glamour to a page of history seems to be fulfilled in the epoch of the Crusades—the Age of Saladin: only the illuminating insight is wanted to make the page shine among the great chapters of the world's literature. It is an office that should inspire the research, the eloquence, and the imagination of the highest historical genius.

C. R. Conder (essay date 1897)

SOURCE: "Saladin and King Richard: The Eastern Question in the Twelfth Century," *Blackwood's Edinburgh Magazine,* Vol. DCCCCLXXVII, No. CLXI, March, 1897, pp. 389–97.

[*In the following essay, Conder reviews the pre-history and military details of the Third Crusade, emphasizing the achievements of King Richard I. Conder notes that in accounts of the Crusade by Frankish and Muslim authors, both Saladin and Richard are praised and respected.*]

It is not often that so complete a double account of a great struggle can be found in medieval history as that which exists regarding the third crusade, of which the opposing heroes were Saladin and Richard Lion Heart. On the Frankish side Geoffrey de Vinsauf gives us a vivid description of the expedition in which he took part; and on the Moslem side Boha ed Dîn, Kâdy of Jerusalem, relates the life of his friend and patron, Salâh ed Dîn, the "honour of the Faith." Though tinged by admiration of their respective masters, these two works are so completely in accord as to the main facts that we are able to form an impartial estimate of events, while the details are in either case so full, and so easily understood by the light of recent exploration, that we can trace every movement on the ground, and are able to recognise the battle-fields of the hard-fought campaigns in which Palestine was lost to Christendom, and again recovered, in part, by English arms.

The personal characters of the chroniclers are unconsciously betrayed in an interesting manner by their incidental remarks. Geoffrey de Vinsauf was a monk to whom the grim facts of actual warfare were previously unknown. "Oh how different," he exclaims, "are the speculations of those who meditate amidst the columns of the cloister from the fearful exercise of war!" Boha ed Dîn was also a man of peace, unused to campaigning. He explains to us on each occasion why he was unable (through illness or other cause) to take part in the actual fighting; how he was terrified by the stormy sea of winter,

when he saw it first on the harbourless shores of Ascalon; and how he admired Saladin's determination to pursue the Franks over the waves "till not one unbeliever be left in the islands." He relates how he was unable to manage his mule, and dashed past Saladin on a rainy day of entry into Jerusalem, splashing the great Sultan with mud, and cannoning against him; and how Saladin only laughed good-naturedly at his awkward riding. The worthy scribe was respected for his intimate knowledge of Korân traditions, and Saladin had taken him into his service, after making his acquaintance during negotiations with the Khalif of Baghdad and the Atabek princes of Môsul on the Tigris. The charming picture which he draws of the champion of Islam is supported by the less partial accounts of Christian writers, and Saladin appears to have been distinguished by his sympathy, humility, and piety, not less than by his enormous energy, prudence, and daring. The chivalrous courtesy and valour of King Richard are equally admitted in the Moslem record, and the personal characters of these two great leaders took much from the bitterness of the struggle, and rendered possible a final agreement, which formed the *modus vivendi* in the East for nearly a century after.

The modern historian of European progress is apt to pass over the story of this English crusade with somewhat contemptuous curtness; and the general impression seems to be that King Richard would have been better employed in minding the affairs of his own kingdom, and that he failed notably to do any good in the Holy Land. It should not, however, be forgotten that King Richard wrested half his conquests from his great adversary, and that the Eastern Question in the twelfth century was as important and harassing to Europe as it is in our own times. The great families of "Outre Mer" were intimately connected, by birth and intermarriage, with the kings and princes of the West. The Courtenays of Edessa, the Italian Normans from Sicily in Antioch, the Ángevin and Lusignan houses in Jerusalem, had behind them strong family influences in France, England, and Italy; and an extensive trade with the East had been organised by Venice, Genoa, Pisa, and Marseilles during the ninety years in which the Holy Land was ruled by the Latin Christians. By his success in the East Richard became the hero of Christendom, and the most admired prince in Europe. He restored to the Templars and Hospitallers, and to the rulers of Lebanon, all their best lands in the shore plains, and to the great trading cities all their ports in the Levant. He added to the Latin possessions an island equal in area to the Syrian domains, by the conquest of Cyprus; and he made with Saladin a treaty which became the basis of many succeeding agreements. It was not merely from religious motives that the European princes spent their treasure on the Holy Land, for the spread of Moslem power was arrested, and ceased to menace the Mediterranean, while the commerce of the East continued to enrich the poorer lands of the West.

This episode of European history is thus worthy of greater consideration than it usually obtains, while the picturesque and romantic character of the events is brought vividly before us in the chronicles mentioned. The five years which intervened between the disastrous battle of Hattin and the final treaty with Saladin were full of wonderful events, and the struggle between France, England, and Germany on the one side, and Egypt, Syria, and Mesopotamia on the other, was of far-reaching influence on the immediate future.

For more than sixty years the kingdom won by the Latins under Godfrey de Bouillon in 1099 A.D. had grown stronger and more prosperous. It included the whole of Western Palestine, and the regions east of Jordan excepting Bashan; and its frontiers were guarded by a line of mighty castles. On the north the whole Lebanon as far as the Orontes was ruled by the allied Princes of Antioch and Counts of Tripoli; but the great province of Edessa, stretching over the Euphrates almost to the Tigris, which had been occupied in 1098 by Baldwin, brother of Godfrey de Bouillon, had fallen before Zanghi, the first Atabek Sultan of Môsul, in 1144 A.D. The native subjects of the Latins were partly oriental Christians and partly Sunnee Moslems. Both alike appear to have been content under the strong and wise rule of the Franks; and Islam was still divided by the internecine hatred of the Sunnees, who acknowledged the supremacy of the Khalif of Baghdad as a religious head, and of the Shi'ah or "sectaries" of 'Ali, who followed the Fatimite Khalif of Egypt. We hear little during this period of any internal troubles in Syria; and the frontiers west of the Euphrates had, so far, been successfully maintained, and were constantly strengthened by the building of new castles.

Yet there were already signs of danger on every side; and not only valour but wise statesmanship was greately needed, to preserve the Latin supremacy. The Egyptians were weak, and the communication with Europe might easily be threatened by any strong Moslem Power able to hold the Nile mouths, and to employ the fleets of the Delta. On the east the two sons of Zanghi were united in determination to wrest Palestine from the Franks; and Nûr ed Dîn, who inherited his father's power in Aleppo and Damascus, was a formidable foe. On the north the Christian kingdom of Lesser Armenia (in Cilicia) bordered on Antioch, but the Armenians looked coldly on the Latins, and were threatened themselves on the west by the Sultans of Iconium—the last representatives of the Seljuks who had founded the Turkish empire in the eleventh century under Melek Shah. The Greek Emperor of Byzantium (Manuel Comnenos) was friendly to the kings of Jerusalem, but the enmity of the Greek clergy to the Latins, who had set up their own Patriarch and bishops in the place of the Greeks, had become more and more bitter as time passed by; and the Greek populace shared the opinions of their priests. In Europe the wars had so distracted the various kingdoms that no armies had come for fourteen years to help the Franks against the Turks, nor did any such help reach Syria until Europe was roused, too late, by the news of Saladin's surprising success. Such briefly was the condition of the East when the unfortunate Amaury, second son of Fulk of Anjou, succeeded his brother on the throne of

Jerusalem in 1162 A.D. The former kings had been distinguished for gallantry and justice, but Amaury was half Armenian by birth, and was neither loved nor trusted by his subjects. The policy which he adopted of attempting to conquer Egypt weakened his kingdom, and failed as all other Frankish attempts on Cairo failed both before and after his time. He received no help from Europe, nor was his alliance with Manuel Comnenos of any use. Nûr ed Dîn despatched successive expeditions under Shirkoh (Saladin's uncle) to help the Egyptians, and on the death of the vizir of the last Fatimite Khalif (El 'Adid) in 1169, Shirkoh became Sultan of Egypt, and was succeeded two months later by his nephew. In 1171 El 'Adid died, and three years later Amaury was succeeded by his leper son Baldwin IV. Nûr ed Dîn also died in 1174, and left only a boy as his heir. By this rapid series of important changes Saladin became suddenly the greatest power in the Moslem world, and having proclaimed the religious supremacy of the Khalif of Baghdad at Cairo, he united the forces of Islam in Egypt, and in Syria east of the Jordan and of the Orontes.

Yusef Ibn Eyûb Salâh ed Dîn was born in 1137 A.D., the son of a Kurdish governor at Tekrit on the Tigris, named Eyûb, who was much trusted by Sultan Zanghi. Eyûb followed Nûr ed Dîn to Syria, and became governor of Baalbek. He defended Damascus against Louis VII. of France in 1148; and his brother Shirkoh, in 1163, took with him to Egypt his young nephew, whose ambition was not yet awakened, and who, according to his own statement, was very unwilling to leave Damascus. Succeeding Shirkoh as Sultan at Cairo, and becoming practically independent of his master Nûr ed Dîn, Saladin's reputation increased so rapidly that he was willingly received at Damascus in place of the youthful heir, Melek es Sâleh, who retreated to Aleppo in 1174. But the position of the popular usurper presented many difficulties, not only in Egypt, and in Yemen, which his brother Turan Shah subdued in the same year, but yet more on account of the jealousy of the earlier dynasties—the Seljuks of Iconium and the Atabeks of Môsul. The strong Castle of Kerak, on the cliffs east of the Dead Sea, was also held by Renaud of Châtillon, and barred the road from Damascus to Mecca and to Egypt. To attack the Christian kingdom was thus impossible until some arrangement had been made with the Atabek family, while the possession of Kerak—the great Eastern outpost of the Latins—was also one of the first objects of Saladin's campaigns. It is unnecessary to detail all the operations by which the great leader succeeded in securing his base, during more than twenty years of strenuous effort. He defeated the Atabeks, and finally entered into alliance with them. He attacked Kerak again and again, and he raided into the kingdom from the south and from the east, but he was defeated at Gezer in 1177, and near Tabor in 1183; and his assaults seemed to give little promise of the astonishing victory won four years later at Hattîn. In 1185 the leper King Baldwin IV. died, and was followed by his infant nephew Baldwin V. a year later, when the unfortunate Guy of Lusignan, second husband of Queen Sibyl—Amaury's eldest daughter—was very unwillingly accepted by the Latin barons as king. The loss of Palestine appears to have been mainly due to the weakness and incapacity of this last actual King of Jerusalem.

The character of Saladin, as depicted by Boha ed Din, was singularly noble and attractive. He was strict in all religious duties, and zealous in the collection of traditions concerning the Prophet. He was very temperate and abstemious, and his energy was such as to wear out his strength at the early age of fifty-three. His kindness to the poor, his modesty and simplicity, his justice and mercy, are attested by many anecdotes; and the advice which he gave to his son, Melekedh Dhâher, on sending him to rule in Aleppo, perhaps best summarises his character in his own words.

> "I commend you," he said, "to the Most High, the giver of all good. Do thou His will, for that is the way of peace. Beware of bloodshed, for spilt blood never sleeps; and seek the hearts of thy people, and care for them, for thou art sent by God and by me for their good. Try to gain the hearts of the emirs, the rulers, and the nobles. I have become great as I am because I won men's hearts by gentleness and kindness. Nourish no hatred against any one, for death spares none. Be prudent in dealing with men, for God will not pardon if they do not forgive; but between Him and thee He will pardon, if thou dost repent, for He is most gracious."

Since the days of Omar no such Moslem as Saladin had arisen, nor after him was there any other such. The simple tomb in the courtyard of the great mosque at Damascus enshrines the memory of one of the noblest natures that Islam ever knew. Those who charge against the Moslem faith all the cruelties which disgraced warriors like Bibars and Timur—forgetful of the cruelties which have been recorded against Christians also—should remember that Saladin's character was formed by the influence of the words of Muhammad, and on the example of Omar.

When Guy of Lusignan acceded, a truce had been made between Saladin and the Christians. It was broken by Renaud of Châtillon, lord of Kerak, who seized the pilgrims from Mecca and murdered them near Petra. A holy war was proclaimed, and forces from Môsul were sent to aid Saladin, in consequence of this outrage. Renaud, who had come from France with Louis VII., was ambitious and unscrupulous, embittered by seventeen years of captivity at Aleppo, and hated by Moslems already for his daring attempt to capture Medina—the city sacred as the Prophet's home—in 1183 A.D. His stepson, the younger Humphrey of Toron, had married Isabel, the second daughter of King Amaury, in the following year, and the wedding-feast was being held in the grim Castle of Kerak, when Saladin advanced to besiege the place. Renaud sent out meat and wine to the enemy, and Saladin in return gave orders that the tower in which the bride and bridegroom lived was not to be attacked during the assault. Such were the courtesies of war in this strange age; but Saladin never forgave the murder of the pilgrims travelling in faith of the truce, and Renaud paid the penalty of his treachery soon after.

An army of 50,000 men gathered to King Guy at the Fountain of Sepphoris, north-west of Nazareth. All the fortresses were denuded of troops: the Templars and Hospitallers gathered to the camp at Sepphoris; and the Patriarch brought the true cross. The advance-guard of the Moslems, under Saladin's son Melek el Afdal, met the Masters of the Temple and Hospital, who had only 150 knights, on the 1st May 1187 at Kefr Kenna, and defeated them. The Master of the Hospital and the Marshal of the Templars were slain; and on the 26th June the whole army of Saladin crossed the Jordan by the bridge south of the Sea of Galilee, and, turning north, sacked Tiberias and besieged the castle, also occupying the heights to the west, where the dark crags called "Horns of Hattîn" look down on the quiet lake to the east, and over the open corn-plain to the west. A march of ten miles thus separated the two armies; and though there was plenty of water both at Sepphoris to the west and at Hattîn to the east, between the two camps the country was dry and waterless. The position of Saladin was nevertheless one of great danger. On the south the basalt fortress of Belvoir, on the plateau south-west of Tiberias, threatened his line of retreat. On the north he could not cross the Jordan above the Sea of Galilee, for the only bridge was commanded by the recently built fort called Château Neuf. It would seem clear that if, while holding him in front, a strong force had been thrown into Belvoir and had attacked the southern bridges, all the Moslem army would have been cut off, and might have been driven into the lake; but this turning movement was for some reason never attempted.

On the 1st July a council was held at Sepphoris, and Raymond of Tripoli, whose wife was besieged in Tiberias, gave his opinion that it would be fatal to attempt an advance over the waterless plain. The Templars, furious at their defeat, advised an immediate attack; and in the night Gerard de Ridfort, the Grand Master, persuaded the vacillating king to sound his trumpets and call all his host to arms. In the early morning they set out on their fatal march, and crossed the plain harassed by the Moslem light horse, and surrounded by the smoke and flames of the burning stubble. In the afternoon they reached the village of Lûbieh, about a mile to the south-west of Hattîn—a small village without water, standing on a low limestone ridge. Watching all night in their armour, without water and surrounded by fire, the Christian host was utterly exhausted and unfit to fight, long before they came within striking distance of the foe, which awaited them covering the springs. The foot-soldiers threw away their arms, and went over to the Moslems to beg for water. The Knights were exhausted by fruitless charges against horsemen who fled whenever they rode out; and the Christian army melted away before any counter-attack was made. Raymond of Tripoli cut his way through the Turks with a few Knights, and escaped to Tyre, while the little group, which rallied on the "Horns of Hattîn" to protect the Cross, was gradually hemmed in and forced to surrender. Among them were King Guy and his brother, with Humphrey of Toron, Renaud of Châtillon, Odo of Gebal, and all the surviving Templars and Hospitallers. Thus, through the over-confidence of the Grand Master of the Templars and the weakness of Guy, and in spite of the wise advice of Raymond of Tripoli, a fatal defeat was inflicted on Christendom, and the kingdom so painfully built up during a century by the Latins was lost in a day.

Saladin sat before the tent which was being pitched near the village of Hattîn, and the prisoners were brought before him. Iced sherbet was offered to the king, who drank and passed it to Renaud of Châtillon. "Tell him," said Saladin to the interpreter, "that he, and not I, gives drink to that man." The customs of oriental hospitality were known to all, and the words sealed Renaud's fate. Saladin reproached him with his treachery and cruelty, and offered him the choice of infidels—the Korân or death. Renaud refused to abjure his faith, and Saladin with his own sword clove his shoulder. The guards cut off his head, and every Templar and every Hospitaller was likewise beheaded; but the rest were treated with courtesy and kindness, and sent prisoners to Damascus.

The news of this great victory sped fast to Moslem lands on every side, and the heavy tidings were carried over Europe, where a crusade was preached in haste. With overpowering energy Saladin swept over the whole of Syria and Palestine, denuded of its garrisons, and by the 3d May 1190 every city and castle had surrendered to, or had been taken by, Moslem assault, excepting only Antioch, Tripoli, and Tyre. Conrad of Montferrat—related to Philip II. of France—held Tyre, and caused a great picture to be painted, representing a Moslem horseman defiling the Holy Sepulchre. This was carried over the sea, and shown, amid tears and groans, in cities and markets of the West. All Europe armed for vengeance; but the German army, which was the first to set out, fell to pieces under the attacks of the Turks of Iconium; and Frederic Barbarossa the emperor was drowned in a small stream near Tarsus, on the borders of Lesser Armenia. Jerusalem surrendered on the 2d October 1189, when the Mosque was purified from the altars and pictures of the Templars, and became once more a Moslem place of prayer, the great gold cross being dragged from its dome. King Guy was released on promising not to fight again; but the Latin clergy absolved him from his oath, and at Tyre he gathered a force of 9000 men, and marched south along the shore to attempt the reconquest of Acre.

The two years' struggle which followed was one of extraordinary obstinacy. Acre was held by a garrison of 6000 Moslems, and the whole army of Saladin, including not only his own subjects in Syria and Egypt but also forces sent by the Atabeks of Môsul, advanced from upper Galilee to its support. The city, protected by double walls, stood on a promontory north of the broad shallow bay. To the south the Belus river ran through gardens to the sea; on the north were open plains under the rough Galilean hills; to the east and south-east were sanddunes and marshes, where the Moslems camped in winter on the Tells, surrounded with mud and water. The Christian army thrust itself between the city and Saladin's army, holding a hill on which in later times Napoleon placed his batteries to bombard the town; and here they made a rampart and ditch surrounding Acre and shutting out the relieving force. Reinforced from time to time by Germans, Flemish, French, and English, they clung to this strange position, in spite of defeat, famine, and sickness, from the 30th August 1189 to the middle of May 1191, trusting to the much-delayed appearance of the French and English armies. Thus, when King Richard landed at Pentecost of the latter year, he found all Palestine in Saladin's hands, and only a square mile of sand held by the Christians, between Acre and the Moslem host. The achievement of the Latins, in thus holding a landing-place in face of the united forces of Islam, was one of the most remarkable in the history of Crusades; but the final failure of their efforts was certain, if they had not been delivered by the large army brought to their assistance.

Richard was thirty four years of age, tall, strong, and ruddy, famous already for his gallantry and daring, and respected among European Princes for his masterful character. On his way to the East he had wrung from Tancred of Sicily the dower due to his sister Joan, who came with him in charge of Berengaria of Navarre. He had conquered Cyprus where Berengaria was wedded and crowned Queen of England; and he brought a fleet of 120 English galleys to Palestine, to find the French vainly attempting to mine the walls of Acre. His appearance gave new hope and new energy to the Franks, but his popularity roused the jealousy of Philip of France. On the 12th July, however, Acre surrendered to the united forces, after its walls had been ruined and the great tower Maledictum, at the north-east angle of the outer wall, had fallen. Saladin saw with dismay the Christian banners on the walls, but refused to recognise the terms on which the garrison was promised life—namely, the surrender of all his captives, and of the true cross, which he also held to ransom. King Richard executed all the prisoners taken, when the time granted had expired; and Saladin, retreating to Caymont, east of Carmel, was so infuriated by this massacre that in future he put to death all Christians who fell into his hands.

The contest was, however, yet undecided, since no great battle in the open had yet occurred. On the 1st of August the French king went home, and the Frenchmen were very unwilling to follow Richard; for he supported the claims of King Guy, who had helped him in Cyprus; while Philip advocated the claims of Conrad of Montferrat, who had married Isabel, divorced by the clergy from Humphrey de Toron. An army of 100,000 men, however, marched with Richard along the sea plains to occupy Cæsarea, Jaffa, and Ascalon; and on this march the crowning victory of the campaign was won. The chronicles enable us to trace each day's advance, and to recognise every halting-place by the streams which flow through the plain of Sharon to the sea. It was but four days' march, yet so slow and cautious was the advance that three weeks elapsed before Jaffa was reached. The Moslem forces gathered in the low hills south of Carmel, and camped at 'Ain el Asâwîr. Richard followed the shore road west of Carmel, marching in five great divisions, with a flanking force to his east under Henry of Champagne, who (through his grandmother, Eleanor of Guienne) was Richard's half-nephew, and also half-nephew of Philip of France. The Templars led the van; the Bretons and Angevins followed; King Guy in the centre led the men of Poitou; the Normans and English followed round the standard, which was dragged on a heavy truck; and the Knights Hospitallers brought up the rear. Harassed by the arrows of Saladin's light horsemen, the army moved on under the burning sun, until on the 7th September they found themselves on the sandy hills above the low cliffs, five miles north of the small fortress of Arsûf, in an open woodland of oaks called the Forest of Arsur.

It was here that the final contest was decided. Saladin is said to have had 300,000 men, but Richard's army was reduced by garrisons and desertions to about 50,000. The whole of Saladin's force burst upon him from the east, attacking the Hospitallers in rear. Troop after troop of the black-robed Knights charged inland, while Saladin's Guard, in yellow kaftans, strove to drive the Christians over the cliffs into the sea. King Richard, on his bay Cyprian steed, hewed a broad path through their ranks, and after an obstinate battle, lasting all day, the Moslems, already discouraged by their failure at Acre, fled to Mejdel Yaba on the way to Jerusalem, leaving King Guy to witness a victory yet greater than his defeat at Hattîn. Thus, by the winter of 1191 all the shore plains were recovered by the English, and Saladin, in utter dejection at Jerusalem, was daily expecting to see the Christians before its walls. Praying before the "Holy Rock" in the Mosque, he cast himself on the mercy of God, when suddenly the news came that the Franks had broken up their camp at Beit Nûba, within twelve miles of the Holy City, and had retreated to Ascalon and Jaffa.

This failure to push home the victory was due to many causes. The Templars wished to march to Egypt. The French refused to follow Richard unless he recognised Conrad of Montferrat. Richard himself was ill with fever; and bad news came from England; while no further funds could be raised to carry on the war. Saladin's resources were, however, equally exhausted, and intrigues of the Atabeks with his own nephew weakened his cause. During the winter Richard strove to reunite the various factions, and arranged to give Cyprus to King Guy, and to recognise Conrad of Montferrat, who was, however, killed by the Assassins at Tyre immediately after, on the 28th April 1192. Henry of Champagne, who then married Isabel, was chosen as his successor, being well regarded by both French and English, as being related to both kings. When, however, after Easter, the English again marched to the foot of the Jerusalem hills, the same discord broke out once more. The Syrian Franks said that no water could be found near the city, and again advised an advance on Egypt. Ill and disgusted, King Richard retired to Acre, and prepared to sail home; and Saladin was encouraged to march on Jaffa, which he took by assault. King Richard returned in haste, and, while the garrison of the citadel

were on the point of submitting, he leapt into the surf from his red galley, and fought his way on shore in his "sea-shoes." Aided by a few knights mounted on mules, he again drove Saladin to the hills, taking many important prisoners. The two champions thus confronted each other utterly exhausted, and both were willing to make peace.

The famous truce which was signed on 2d September 1192 was equally distasteful to Christians and Moslems, but it practically settled the Eastern Question for many years after. All the plains remained to the Latins, and the mountains to the Moslems. Jerusalem was recognised as a place of Christian pilgrimage, and priests were allowed in its cathedral, and at Nazareth and Bethlehem. Richard's success was not complete, but Saladin never won a battle against him. He recovered more than 3000 square miles of Syria for Christendom, and added an equal area to the Latin dominions in Cyprus. He defeated the greatest Moslem of the age in three battles—at Acre, Arsûf, and Jaffa—and stayed the Moslem advance on Europe which Saladin threatened. He not only made a mighty name in Europe, which strengthened him at home, but he re-established European trade in all the ports of the Levant. Those who pass over lightly his achievements, and speak of his failure, seem hardly to do justice to his memory, or to be in sympathy with the strong feelings of medieval Europe concerning the Holy Land.

Dana Carleton Munro (essay date 1935)

SOURCE: "Saladin and the Loss of the Kingdom" in *The Kingdom of the Crusaders,* Kennikat Press, 1935, pp. 147–73.

[*In the following essay, Munro offers an account of Saladin's rise to power and discusses his capture of Jerusalem and truce with the Christians.*]

From all those engaged in the crusading wars romance has singled out Saladin as its own particular hero, with Richard the Lion-Hearted as a poor second. The choice was a natural one, for Saladin had the qualities which commended him to both Christian and Muslim. He did not have the broad tolerance in religion with which Lessing endowed him in *Nathan der Weise:* no Muslim leader could have had this tolerance; some of the Christian leaders in the Crusades came nearer to it through their acquaintance with the many religions they found in the Holy Land, and through their disillusionment with their own narrow inherited faith. Saladin did have the virtues of generosity and courtesy, with which Scott, following the example of medieval Christian writers, depicted him in *The Talisman.* He won the admiration of followers and enemies by his bravery. He never broke his word, a virtue which his opponents made use of, but did not imitate. Although he could be stern in his vengeance on occasion, he was usually merciful, and in this respect his character shines brilliantly against the barbaric background of the age. Many examples are recorded of his compassion for those in tribulation, especially Christian women and children. He was so open-handed and generous that his servants had to secrete funds lest he leave himself without necessary resources. When he died, the most powerful ruler in the Muslim world, he was almost penniless. Saladin, which means Honor of the Faith, was a name prophetic of his character and success.

He was a Kurd, born in 1137 or 1138 at Takrit, a fortress on the River Tigris, which his father held for the sultan. A few years before his birth Zangi, fleeing after a defeat, reached the Tigris on the bank opposite Takrit. His only chance of safety from his pursuers was in reception into the impregnable fortress. Saladin's father rescued the fugitive and thus laid the foundation for the future greatness of his family, for Zangi never forgot his debt of gratitude. The sultan, at Bagdad, was annoyed at Zangi's escape, and, when later Saladin's uncle killed a Muslim in a private quarrel, the sultan seized the excuse to order the family to give up Takrit and leave his dominions in disgrace. While they were in the midst of their preparations for departure Saladin was born. His birth at such a time was regarded as a bad omen.

His father sought the protection of Zangi at Mosul and found a ready welcome. The following year he was made commander of Ba'labakk, which Zangi had just captured. This was then an important and prosperous city, and Zangi's outpost against Damascus, only thirty-five miles away. Everyone is familiar with the magnificent ruins of the temples at Ba'labakk; few people know that the temple ruins stand in the midst of a strong fortress, admirably adapted for defense in the days before cannon were invented; the walls with their subterranean passages are still well preserved and would be famous even if they did not contain the temple of Bacchus and the temple of the sun. There Saladin spent his early childhood.

When Zangi died the ruler of Damascus recovered Ba'labakk, but Saladin's father was given a fief near Damascus, and soon rose to be commander in chief of the army. When Nureddin secured Damascus in 1154 Saladin's father was made governor of the city, as he had prudently thrown in his lot with the son of his old patron. Nothing is known of Saladin's life during these years, although a Christian chronicler refers to a captivity which Saladin spent in Karak, the great fortress in the land of Moab. The Arab chroniclers record of him that he had "excellent qualities," and that he learned "to walk in the path of righteousness, to act virtuously, and to be zealous in fighting the infidels"—all commonplaces. Apparently there is nothing to tell until Saladin at the age of twenty-six took part in an expedition against Egypt, the land which later he ruled and loved better than any other. In the midst of one of his campaigns in Mesopotamia he wrote a poem, "Bear me a message to the Nile,—tell it that Euphrates can never quench my thirst."

Yet at first there was little hint of his future greatness or of his love for Egypt. He acquitted himself well on the first two expeditions to Egypt, but when his uncle was planning the third, which was destined to be the foundation of Saladin's fortunes, he was unwilling to go and was forced to do so only by the command of Nureddin. "'So I went,' said Saladin, recounting the scene in later years, 'I went like one driven to my death.' Thus were accomplished the words of the Koran: 'Perchance ye hate a thing although it is better for you, and perchance ye love a thing although it is worse for you: but God knoweth and ye know not.'" At thirty years of age Saladin was embarked on his life work. The remaining twenty-five years of his life were spent mainly in warfare. Only between the battles or in the intervals of truce could he find opportunity to engage in the theological discussions which he enjoyed.

The army sent by Nureddin was received by the Fatimite caliph of Egypt as an ally, and Saladin's uncle was soon made vizier and commander in chief of the Egyptian army. When he died, two months later, Saladin was appointed to succeed him. From this time on he "put aside the thought of pleasure and the love of ease, adopted a Spartan rule, and set it as an example to his troops. He devoted all his energies henceforth to one great object—to found a Muslim empire strong enough to drive the infidels out of the land. 'When God gave me the land of Egypt,' said he, 'I was sure that he meant Palestine for me also.'" "He had vowed himself to the Holy War." Many preliminary conquests were necessary, and many years were to intervene before he could address himself to this main task.

The next five years were spent in consolidating his position as ruler of Egypt. At first he was in great difficulties; the other emirs in Nureddin's army envied him and were insubordinate. The Egyptian officials plotted his murder. A revolt broke out in the Sudan and lasted for years. Damietta was attacked by an army of Crusaders and Greeks. By his prudence and by the aid of his father and brothers whom he had summoned to Egypt, Saladin overcame all obstacles. When the caliph died in 1171 Saladin took possession of the palace at Cairo and all its treasures, but he would not live in the palace, and he kept none of the treasures; part he distributed to his followers; part he sent to his overlord, Nureddin. The latter looked on Saladin's advancement with displeasure as he realized that the Kurd was becoming a rival power. Saladin used all deference to him but was unwilling to meet him, believing that his power and life would both be at stake if he fell into Nureddin's hands. He never felt safe until he received the news of Nureddin's death.

That opened to him his opportunity. His power was firmly established in Egypt. In Syria Nureddin's successor was a young boy, and his followers took advantage of his weakness to throw off their allegiance and to seize his lands. In the kingdom of Jerusalem the king died the same year, leaving as his heir a boy of thirteen. To a less sagacious ruler than Saladin the time might have seemed ripe to make war upon the Christians. He had already engaged in skirmishes with them and had besieged, usually in vain, some of their fortresses. But Saladin knew that if the Holy War was to be successful it must be waged with all the forces of the Muslims united. Even Nureddin had been able to accomplish comparatively little without the support of the Egyptian troops. Saladin needed the aid of the Syrian and Mesopotamian Muslims before he could undertake the Holy War.

He spent the next two years in getting control over the Muslims in Syria. There his greatest obstacles were the rulers of Aleppo, but he was especially annoyed by the sect of the Assassins, who were probably incited against him by the Muslim ruler of Aleppo. Saladin narrowly escaped assassination by the followers of the dreaded "Old Man of the Mountains." After two years he was master of Muslim Syria. He had some indecisive battles with the Christians, but as yet he was not able to put forth all his strength against them, for the Muslim chiefs in Mesopotamia were still hostile and ready to attack him at any time when it was safe to do so. In 1180 he succeeded in negotiating a truce by which he was recognized as the chief Muslim ruler from the Euphrates to the Nile. He then returned to his beloved Egypt and remained there for the two years of the truce. He had also made a truce with the Christians. But Saladin was the only one who had sworn the truces who kept them. In spite of many provocations he refused to fight until the time of the truce with the other Muslims had expired. Then he left Egypt, which he was fated never to see again, and went north to conquer Mesopotamia. By 1183 he had succeeded, and when he wrote to the pope at Rome he used the title "King of all the Oriental Kings." The only lands left to recover were those in the hands of the Christians.

After the death of the chivalrous King Amalric (possibly the most intelligent of all the kings of Jerusalem), the kingdom had been weakened by internal dissensions. His son and successor, Baldwin IV, had been carefully educated by William, later archbishop of Tyre, the historian, and gave great promise of both ability and character. But as a child he was partially paralyzed, and when his father borrowed the services of eminent native physicians they diagnosed the malady as leprosy. The ill-starred king who reigned only ten years is known as Baldwin the Leper. For his guardian the barons at first chose Raymond, count of Tripolis. He was descended both from Count Raymond of Toulouse, who participated in the First Crusade, and from King Baldwin II. He was the ablest among the crusading leaders. In addition to his hereditary county of Tripolis, he had secured by his marriage with the heiress the strongly fortified Tiberias on the Lake of Galilee. He was a friend of Saladin; this friendship later made him distrusted by many in the kingdom and has raised a question among historians of the Crusades as to his good faith. But he had the full confidence of William of Tyre and of other Christians who had been born in the Holy Land.

Inasmuch as the kingdom, like the fiefs in the Holy Land, was hereditary even in the female line, the illness of the king made it essential to find a husband for the king's elder sister Sibyl. The choice fell on William of Montferrat, who was a relative of both Philip Augustus of France and Frederick Barbarossa of Germany. But he lived less than a year and died before the birth of his son Baldwin, who was later to be king. Strangely enough, for three years no new husband was found for the widow. Then the king hastily married her to Guy of Lusignan, an adventurer from France. This marriage was much condemned by the native nobles because Guy was unpopular and considered stupid, but he was beautiful as a picture and had won the love of Sibyl. The unsuitableness of the marriage and the indecent haste with which Baldwin pushed it, celebrating the wedding, contrary to custom, in the midst of Lent, led to a report that the king had determined on the marriage only to cover up the guilty love of his sister. The more probable version of the marriage is that the king gave his consent to it and was induced to hasten the ceremony because of the imminent arrival of many of the barons in Jerusalem for the Easter festivities. It was a foregone conclusion that they would object to the princess' marrying a newcomer from the West, and if the marriage had the king's approval it would be better to confront the barons with a *fait accompli* than to allow time for their opposition to crystallize.

In 1183 Saladin made an invasion of the kingdom. To meet the threatened peril the Christians raised the largest force the kingdom had ever put into the field. They were joined by some great nobles, pilgrims from Europe, and the army moved against Saladin. But King Baldwin was too ill to lead the host,—too ill, even, to be carried in a litter to the field of battle, as was his custom,—and he had entrusted the command of the army to Guy. The other leaders refused to obey Guy, because, as they said, he was a man "unknown and of little skill in military matters." But even William of Tyre implies that Guy was not entirely to blame. The other barons resisted aggressive action, it was said, in order that Guy might not receive the credit of a victory. After the armies had faced one another for a week of inaction, Saladin withdrew, and the Christian army retired without striking a blow.

The dissatisfaction with Guy was so great that at a council held in Jerusalem it was determined to crown Baldwin, the king's nephew, son of Sibyl by her first husband, and to entrust the regency to Raymond of Tripolis for ten years. The boy was only six years old. To quote Ernoul, a contemporary: "When the matter was thus settled, the king bade crown the child. So they led him to the Sepulchre and crowned him. And because the child was small, they put him into the arms of a knight to be carried into the Temple of the Lord, to the end that he might not appear to be of less stature than the rest. This knight was a stalwart man and tall." The king also proposed to dissolve the marriage of Guy and his sister.

But the latter were safe in their city of Ascalon and were not without friends. While most of the nobles sided with Raymond, Guy and Sibyl had two devoted adherents; Reginald of Chatillon, lord of Karak, was on their side, and also Gerard of Ride-fort. The latter was a knight errant from England who had come to Syria. He had entered the service of Raymond of Tripolis and made himself so useful that he was promised the first wealthy heiress of whom Raymond had the disposal. Soon after, the lord of Botroun died, and his daughter was the coveted prize. Gerard expected to receive her and her fief. But a wealthy Italian merchant also coveted the prize and bought the heiress from Raymond. The girl is said to have been placed on the scale and balanced with her weight in gold, which the Italian paid for her. Gerard was very indignant, especially because a despised Italian merchant had been preferred to him. He left the count's service and, entering the Order of Templars, soon became grand master. His chief purpose in life was vengeance on Raymond.

Baldwin the Leper died before Easter of 1185, and the child king the following year. Unfortunately there is a gap in the amount and quality of historical evidence for the East between 1184 when William of Tyre ceased writing and 1190 when the Crusaders from the West reached the Holy Land. Ernoul, who continued the history of William of Tyre, was more inclined to accept rumor and gossip. Some account, however, of the events of 1186-87 can be pieced together from the various sources of the period. After the child's death, Gerard and Reginald of Chatillon saw their chance. They summoned Guy and Sibyl to come to Jerusalem; they closed the city gates and allowed no one to enter or leave. Their plan was to forestall Raymond and the native nobles by crowning Sibyl and Guy. They won over the patriarch of Jerusalem, who was said to be the lover of Sibyl's mother. The people were assembled in the Church of the Holy Sepulchre and two crowns were brought. Reginald proposed the choice of Sibyl as queen, and the pliant throng cheered for the daughter of Amalric, the mother of the late king, and the sister of the preceding one. After crowning her the patriarch said, "Lady, you are but a woman, wherefore it is fitting that you should have a man to support you in your rule. Take the crown before you and give it to him who can best help you to govern your realm." Sibyl then crowned Guy, saying: "My lord, receive this crown for I know not where I could bestow it better." Gerard of Ridefort is reported to have said: "This crown is well worth the marriage of Botroun."

Raymond and the native lords were very wroth and, rather than recognize Guy and Sibyl, chose as king, Humphrey, the step-son of Reginald and husband of Sibyl's younger sister. He was afraid to undertake the office and hastened to Jerusalem to seek Sibyl. She had heard nothing about the plan to make him king, but was angry with him and would not speak to him. "He stood before her," says the chronicler, "scratching his head like a shamefaced child," and muttering something about their wanting to make him king by force. When Sibyl understood what he was saying she quickly made him welcome.

After Humphrey had made his peace with Guy and Sibyl, almost all the other nobles recognized them as sovereigns,

because aside from Sibyl and Humphrey's wife there were no other legitimate heirs of Baldwin. Raymond of Tripolis remained obdurate. Gerard of Ridefort urged Guy to attack Raymond, and the king gathered a force to besiege him in Tiberias. But Raymond sought aid from Saladin, who sent troops, and the king did not dare to attack him. Raymond as regent had made a truce with Saladin which was very necessary to the Christians. New recruits were expected from the West, and Henry II of England had already sent large sums of money to the Holy Land for the expenses of the holy war. But all the Christians' hopes were shattered by an act of Reginald of Chatillon. During 1186 the caravans from Egypt and to Mecca had passed along the road under the walls of Karak, and Reginald had contented himself with levying tolls upon them. He had been absent from his fief much of the time, plotting for Guy's coronation or in attendance upon him. Toward the end of the year he was informed by his spies that an unusually large caravan was coming from Egypt. It was too much for Reginald's cupidity, and he again violated a truce by seizing all the treasures in the caravan and making the Muslims prisoners. It is reported that one of Saladin's sisters was travelling with the caravan under the escort of the merchants. "The taking of that caravan was the ruin of Jerusalem," says a Christian chronicler.

Saladin demanded satisfaction from King Guy, who attempted to make Reginald give up the booty. The latter replied that he was lord of his lands just as the king was of his, and that he had no truce with Saladin. He refused absolutely to return any of the prisoners or booty, and Guy was powerless to make him do so.

Saladin took a new oath that he would kill Reginald with his own hand and prepared for war. No attack could be attempted until the end of the rainy season. In the meantime Saladin summoned his forces from Egypt and the north coast of Africa, from Syria and Mesopotamia, determined upon a war which should make him master of all the Christian possessions. He would lead "the army of Paradise against the damned of Hell."

The danger to the Christians was imminent. All the resources of the kingdom were used to equip an army. Some of the money which Henry II had sent was taken to hire soldiers. Many pilgrims who came in the spring were pressed into the service. But as yet Raymond was not reconciled to Guy. His aid was absolutely necessary, and Guy sent ambassadors, the heads of the two military orders, the Hospital and the Temple, and others, to Tiberias to make peace with him.

In the meantime Saladin had sent a part of his army to the Lake of Tiberias under the command of one of his sons. This son asked permission from Raymond to cross the Jordan and make an expedition through his territory. The object of the excursion is not known. Raymond did not feel able to refuse, as Saladin's friendship was his best protection against Guy. He gave permission, provided that the Muslims should return the same day before sunset and should do no damage to any town or house. This was agreed upon, and Raymond gave orders that no Christian should venture outside the walls during the day. It happened that the king's ambassadors to Raymond entered his territory that very day and, learning from Raymond of the Muslim expedition, determined to attack it. Gathering what knights they could, some 130, without waiting for the foot-soldiers whom they had summoned, they fell upon the returning Muslims.

The grand master of the Hospitallers and all the other Christian knights were killed except Gerard of Ridefort and three of his Templars. The Muslims, carrying the heads of the Christians on their spears, passed exultantly under the walls of Tiberias and recrossed the Jordan at sunset. They had kept their promise to Raymond and had done no injury to any town or house.

The death of the grand master of the Hospital and of so many Christian knights spread dismay throughout the land. The feeling against Raymond was very bitter. Under the circumstances he thought it well to make his peace with Guy. His help was essential and was welcomed. It was agreed that all the available forces should be assembled at the Springs of Saffuriyah, just north of Nazareth, to repel the Saracen invasion. The host assembled, containing about 1200 knights, thousands of foot-soldiers, and many natives armed in the Saracen fashion. The whole may have numbered between twenty and thirty thousand men. The position at Saffuriyah was a strong one and, in particular, there was an abundant supply of water. This was especially necessary as it was June and the heat was great.

Saladin crossed the Jordan and besieged Tiberias, which was under the command of Raymond's wife. His purpose was to force the Christians to leave their strong position and march to attack him. He captured and sacked the city of Tiberias, but the citadel was still held by Raymond's wife. She sent an urgent appeal for aid to the Christian army. A council of war was held. Gerard of Ridefort, Reginald of Chatillon, and others urged an immediate march to relieve the countess. Raymond opposed this plan, pointing out that the country through which they must pass was destitute of water, that the ground was rocky, disadvantageous for the Christian cavalry, that their only chance of success was in maintaining their position until Saladin was forced to attack. He protested that this was the only wise course to pursue, although it was his own lands which Saladin was laying waste and his own wife and children who were besieged in the citadel. Gerard and Reginald insulted him repeatedly, arguing the cowardice of leaving the countess in peril. But Raymond's arguments were so weighty that the council decided to follow his advice. Late in the evening they separated, resolved to defend their position. But Gerard, knowing King Guy's weakness and hatred of Raymond, followed him to his tent and persuaded him to neglect the advice of the council and to order an immediate advance. This the king did, and at daybreak the army set out to attack Saladin at Tiberias. The distance was about twenty miles.

All day long the heavily armed warriors marched through a parched land; the heat was intense on the shadeless glaring limestone roads; their water bottles were soon emptied. They were surrounded by light-armed Saracens who poured on them a hail of arrows. The rear guard of Templars was so hard pressed that they could not keep up with the main host. Seeing their peril, King Guy ordered a halt, and they camped for the night, although only about half of the distance to Tiberias had been covered and there was no water. The Saracens surrounded the camp so closely that one chronicler says not even a cat could have gotten out. The Muslims were jubilant. It was the night of Qadr, the most holy night, the night of predestination when Gabriel and the angels descend to earth; the night that is better than a thousand months; the night of power. All night long the Muslims raised their cry, "Allah is great, there is no God but Allah."

The following morning, the fourth of July, 1187, the Christians again straggled onward, crazed with thirst. Their distress was aggravated by the smoke and flames from the fires which the Saracens had set in the dry grass and which a high wind carried over to the Christian lines. The knights and foot-soldiers became separated. Guy ordered Raymond to charge the enemy, hoping to break their line. As Raymond charged, according to one account, the Saracens opened their lines to let his men through; those with Raymond were the only ones to escape. Guy and some others took refuge on one of the Horns of Hattin, the site to which tradition assigns the Sermon on the Mount. The Horns are the remains of an ancient volcano and rise about two hundred feet above the level of the surrounding plain. The top was covered with boulders which made it impossible for the knights' horses to charge. The Lake of Galilee, or Tiberias, was in full sight to torture them in their thirst. The hot wind blew from the desert. The Christians fought bravely and desperately, but in vain. All except those who had been with Raymond and a few who became apostates were either killed or captured. A single Muslim soldier would be seen leading off thirty or more naked Christians, tied together with tent ropes.

Guy, Reginald, Gerard, and the other leaders were tied up and taken to Saladin's tent. First, all the Templars except the grand master, Gerard, were put to death. As King Guy was trembling and tortured with thirst, Saladin ordered brought to him rose water cooled with snow. Guy drank part and then handed the cup to Reginald, who emptied it. "But the Sultan," to quote the Muslim biographer, "turning toward the King, cried impetuously, 'You have not asked my permission to give a drink to that accursed one, the most criminal of the impious. I am not bound to spare his life. Do not give him another drink; I don't wish to have anything in common with this traitor. In giving him one drink you have not obtained my pardon for him and my protection does not extend to him.' He said that because of the rites of hospitality among the Mussulmans. It is one of the praiseworthy customs of the Arabs, one of their noble usages, that a captive has his life spared if he has eaten or drunk at the table of his captor, and it is to this generous custom that the Sultan made allusion."

While Saladin allowed the king and the others to be led away to refresh themselves, he left Reginald bound, lying in the vestibule of the tent. Later he summoned the king and the other chiefs. Then he heaped reproaches on Reginald for his crimes, enumerated his perfidies, saying, "Twice I have made a vow to God to kill you if I got hold of you, first when you tried to capture Mecca and Medina, second, when you treacherously seized the caravan." Then following the invariable custom, he commanded his prisoner to become a Muslim, and when Reginald refused he killed him. Guy was terrified, but Saladin comforted him saying, "Do not tremble,—a king does not kill a king." Reginald's head was carried to all the cities and castles in Egypt and Syria.

Then Saladin swept over the Holy Land. Only small garrisons had been left in the cities and castles. An anonymous letter writer tells what happened: "After this Saladin collected his army again and on Sunday came to *Saphora* [Saffuriyah] and took *Saphora* and Nazareth, and Mount Tabor, and on Monday came to *Acon* [Acre] which is also called *Acris;* and those in *Acon* surrendered. Likewise those of *Caifas* [Haifa] and those of *Cesarea* [Caesarea] and of *Jafa* [Joppa], and of *Naple* [Neapolis, Nabulus], and of *Ram* [Ramlah], and of St. George, and of *Ybelinon* [Ibelin], and of *Bellefort* [Belfort], and of Mirabel, and of *Tyron* [Tyre], and of Gwaler, and of *Gazer* [Gaza], and of *Audurum* [Darum], all surrendered." In three months he was master of most of them. Jerusalem had to surrender on October second. The commander there was Balian of Ibelin, who had escaped from Hattin, probably with Raymond. (The latter died, it is said by western writers, of shame shortly after the battle. Eastern writers give the cause of death as pleurisy.) But Balian, knowing Saladin's courtesy, sent to him asking for a safe conduct to go to Jerusalem, in order that he might take his wife and children away. Saladin gave the safe conduct on condition that Balian should remain only one night in Jerusalem and should never fight against him again. Balian took an oath that he would not. But when he reached Jerusalem, the people urged him to take command and the patriarch absolved him from his oath. Yet Saladin showed no anger against him and released him when he was again captured. The sultan did not expect the Christians to keep their oaths.

The city of Jerusalem had been defended with great valor but at length was forced to treat of surrender. Saladin granted very merciful terms. The well-to-do could ransom themselves; the poor were to be ransomed for a lump sum—forty days were allowed to collect the money. Then those who were not ransomed were to be slaves. "Never did Saladin show himself greater than during this memorable surrender." A Christian chronicler who was present says that Saladin's guards kept such order that no Christian suffered any ill-usage. Those who could, ransomed themselves. The remainder of King Henry II's treasure was used to ransom seven thousand of the poor. One of Saladin's emirs ransomed a thousand Armenians and sent them home. But the rich Christians took no thought for their poorer fellow-citizens and went away with all the treasure they could carry. The patriarch carried off all his own wealth, the treasures of the churches, and even the gold plate from the Holy Sepulchre. Saladin's officers remonstrated with him for letting the patriarch carry off so much treasure, but Saladin contemptuously let him do it. Thousands of the poor still remained unransomed. Then Saladin's brother begged the gift of a thousand and set them free. The patriarch and Balian also begged for some and were given another thousand to set free. Then Saladin said, "My brother has made his alms, and the patriarch and Balian have made theirs; now I would fain make mine." So he freed all the old people in the city. Ernoul, Balian's squire, the chronicler already quoted, says, "Such was the charity which Saladin did, of poor people without number." And he adds: "Then I shall tell you of the great courtesy which Saladin showed to the wives and daughters of knights, who had fled to Jerusalem when their lords were killed or made prisoners in battle. When these ladies were ransomed and had come forth from Jerusalem, they assembled and went before Saladin crying mercy. When Saladin saw them he asked who they were and what they sought. And it was told him that they were the dames and damsels of knights who had been taken or killed in battle. Then he asked what they wished, and they answered for God's sake have pity on them; for the husbands of some were in prison, and of others were dead, and they had lost their lands, and in the name of God let him counsel and help them. When Saladin saw them weeping, he had great compassion for them, and wept himself for pity. And he bade the ladies whose husbands were alive to tell him where they were captives, and as soon as he could go to the prisons he would set them free. (And all were released wherever they were found.) After that he commanded that to the dames and damsels whose lords were dead there should be handsomely distributed from his own treasure, to some more and others less, according to their estate. And he gave them so much that they gave praise to God and published abroad the kindness and honour which Saladin had done to them."

The contrast between this scene and the capture of Jerusalem by the Crusaders in 1099 offers some index of the difference in character and degree of civilization between Saladin and the Christian leaders. It is not even necessary to go back to the First Crusade for an example of the different standards. Balian's squire tells us that the refugees from Jerusalem were refused admittance to Tripolis and were robbed by their fellow-Christians of the property which Saladin had allowed them to carry away. Four years later Acre was captured by Richard the Lion-Hearted and Philip Augustus, and terms were granted to the Muslim inhabitants similar to those granted to the Christians at Jerusalem by Saladin. But when the ransom was not paid promptly Richard the Lion-Hearted ordered twenty-seven hundred of his hostages to be led out and slaughtered in cold blood before the eyes of the other Muslims—Richard was no Saladin. And his Christian chronicler added, "Nor was there any delay. The king's followers leapt forward eager to fulfill the commands, and thankful to the Divine Grace that permitted them to take such a vengeance."

Fortunately this example of Christian barbarity did not take place until after Saladin's conquests were over; otherwise he might have found it difficult to restrain his followers. At the surrender of the remaining positions held by the Christians he continued to show his accustomed clemency. At the siege of Ascalon Saladin promised Guy his freedom and that of the other leaders, if he would persuade the garrison to surrender. There was some delay on the part of the garrison, but they finally yielded. Whether Guy was at all influential in persuading them to capitulate is uncertain. At all events, Sibyl demanded that Saladin should fulfill his promise. Guy, Gerard, and the others were released and pledged their knightly honor that they would never again fight against Saladin. It is scarcely necessary to say that they did not keep their oath; as the Christian chronicler says, "The king was released by the sentence of the clergy from the enormity of this promise." The Saracens placed so little faith in an oath made by the Christians that on one occasion at least they would not accept an oath from the king unless it was sworn to by the Templars also. But in this case the grand master was equally guilty of perjury.

Saladin's conquest of the Holy Land was so nearly complete that Tyre was the only city that remained in the hands of the Christians. This Saladin began to besiege, but after a council of war raised the siege and dismissed most of his troops. They were weary of the long fighting and demanded a furlough, so that they might return to their homes and wives. Probably their unwillingness to continue the siege was the turning point in Saladin's victorious career. He had dreamed of driving all the Christians out of the Holy Land and then carrying the war into their country.

The kingdom of Jerusalem had been founded by Baldwin I in 1100; its power really ended with the capture of Jerusalem in 1187. For over a hundred years longer there was to be a nominal kingdom in the Holy Land. Jerusalem was to be recovered by the diplomacy of Frederick II and held for a period of fifteen years, from 1229 to 1244. The title of king of Jerusalem was to be used by one or more claimants continuously for centuries after the loss of the last Christian possessions in the Holy Land in 1291.

Except for Frederick II's Crusade the only serious attempt to recover the kingdom was the Third Crusade, in which Richard the Lion-Hearted, after the capture of Acre and after more than a year of fighting with alternate successes and reverses, was compelled to make a peace with Saladin by which the Christians retained the coast cities from Acre to Jaffa, which they had reconquered. Right of free passage was granted to both Muslim and Christian in the territory held by either party; and Christian pilgrims were allowed to visit the Holy Sepulchre at Jerusalem.

A year earlier Richard had suggested very different terms of peace. He proposed that Saladin's brother, Saphadin (Sayf al-Din), should marry his sister, the widowed queen of Sicily. Richard would give to his sister as a dowry Acre and the other cities which the Christians had taken. Sala-din should give his brother the rest of Palestine, and the couple should reign at Jerusalem. The True Cross which the Saracens had captured should be restored and prisoners should be freed. The knights of the Temple and of the Hospital should receive suitable establishments. Richard admitted to Saphadin that the Christians blamed him for wishing to see his sister married to a Muslim and that his sister objected to the match. Richard suggested that Saphadin might become a Christian. These propositions do not seem to have been taken seriously by Saladin, but his brother continued to visit Richard, and "On Palm Sunday, 1192," the Christian chronicler tells us, "King Richard, amid much splendor, girded with the belt of knighthood the son of Saphadin, who had been sent to him for that purpose." In this, Saladin's nephew was following his uncle's example, for years before Saladin had been admitted to the honor of knighthood by one of the Christian lords of Palestine.

Richard and Saladin never met, although they frequently fought against each other and long negotiations were carried on by them. Richard finally had to leave the Holy Land without seeing Jerusalem. Saladin died a few months later, at the age of fifty-five. His physician wrote that this was the only time that he knew of when a sovereign was truly mourned for by his people. The reason for their grief may be seen from the instructions which Saladin, shortly before his death, gave to his favorite son—"My son, I commend thee to the Most High God, the fountain of all goodness. Do His will, for that way lieth peace. Abstain from the shedding of blood; trust not to that; for blood that is spilt never slumbers. Seek to win the hearts of thy people, and watch over their prosperity; for it is to secure their happiness that thou art appointed by God and by me. Try to gain the hearts of thy emirs and ministers and nobles. I have become great as I am because I have won men's hearts by gentleness and kindness." The resemblance of this advice to the instructions which Saint Louis of France left, three-quarters of a century later, for his son, is very striking. In many respects Saint Louis and Saladin had much in common. Both were ascetic; Saladin may have shortened his life by his zeal in fasting in order to make up for the periods of fasting he had been compelled to neglect during his wars against the Christians. Both kings had the gift of tears, so highly prized by the Christians of the Middle Ages. Saladin would listen to the reading of the Koran until his ecstasy was so great that the tears would roll down his cheeks. The words of his biographers in relating this might well have been borrowed by a Christian chronicler to describe the devotion of his hero, e.g., Suger, abbot of S. Denis and regent of France, who during the office of the Mass "inundated the pavement with his tears."

Richard the Lion-Hearted prided himself upon being the best knight in Christendom. Saladin the Muslim surpassed him in some of the knightly virtues. His Christian opponents praised him especially for his courtesy. One of them, in recounting the story of Saladin's first siege of Karak, says that Reginald of Chatillon and his wife were celebrating the marriage of her son Humphrey with the younger daughter of King Amalric at the very time when Saladin invested the castle. Reginald's wife sent to Saladin some of the viands from the wedding banquet with a greeting and a reminder of how many times Saladin had carried her about in his arms when he was a captive at Karak and she was a little girl. Saladin was much pleased and thanked her for the gift. Then he asked in which part of the castle the newly wedded pair resided and forbade any attack upon that side of the castle. At the siege of Jaffa, Ernoul says that Saladin heard that Richard was in the town and had no horse on which to fight; consequently Saladin sent Richard a splendid charger. During the siege of Acre a Christian woman went to the Muslim camp begging for her baby, who had been carried off by the Saracens. The pickets let her pass and conducted her to Saladin, "for," they said, "he is very merciful." "Saladin was touched by her anguish; the tears stood in his eyes, and he had the camp searched" till the little girl was found. She was restored to her mother and both were escorted back to the enemy's camp. The act was characteristic of Saladin.

Hilaire Belloc (essay date 1937)

SOURCE: "The Encirclement" in *The Crusade: The World's Debate,* Cassell and Company Ltd., 1937, pp. 255–85.

[*In the following essay, Belloc analyzes Saladin's role in deciding the fate of the Christians in the Holy Land between the Second and Third Crusades. Belloc stresses that other scholars have made too much of Saladin's alleged respect for and fair treatment of his enemies.*]

I

THE ENCIRCLEMENT

The attack of Europe upon the Asiatic is over and has failed. The rest of the story is but one thing. It is the mortal sickness and death of the Crusading State.

The breakdown of the expedition against Damascus, "The Defeat of the Second Crusade," marks the outward visible manifestation of that inward ruin of the Christian Kingdom—the potential, impending ruin of it—which could be instinctively felt throughout the Holy Land ever since the fall of Edessa and even earlier: from the moment when the personality of Zengi had been thrown into the scales and when the unification of Moslem power against the now fated Christian effort had begun.

The retreat of the German Emperor and the French King to the coast, their departure just before the middle of the century, was a symbol that our high Western civilisation, pulsing higher year after year, was concentrated more and more upon its own life and would not nourish much longer the very difficult effort in the Orient.

From that day the whole character of the war was changed. The old episodes continued—the capture and the loss of strongholds, skirmishes and battles where victory falls to Islam or to Christendom, great men falling in disastrous fights, led away captive, ransomed again—all the refrain of all the Crusading time. But the *direction* has been reversed: and the Initiative. The tide is now on the ebb and racing out.

Before the fall of Edessa, the French action in Syria, based on the coast and fed from the sea, pointed inland and threatened further extension. After the fall of Edessa the minds of men were transformed. The confidence in further adventures disappeared, the fabric was shaken, and when, in that stifling Eastern night, the mixed host of half-breeds and of Western chivalry turned back from the orchards of Damascus, the whole spirit of the Holy War broke down. All now knew that Christendom in the Levant was on the defensive and all could feel that one issue dominated the future: whether, or rather when, the Mohammedan world of the Near East should achieve complete unity. By intrigue and policy that unity might be postponed. It might be delayed; it could not be avoided. When it fully appeared, when there was one Mohammedan command all around, Jerusalem was doomed.

Now whether Islam at the far end of the Mediterranean could achieve such unity or not depended on one thing: the linking up of Egypt with inland Syria, the linking up of Cairo and Bagdad, the putting of the wealthy and densely populated Nile delta and the tribute from the Upper Nile valley, under the same control as the revenues and government of Aleppo and of the Orontes and of Damascus and of Mesopotamia. The chance of life for the Frankish Christian Kingdom of Jerusalem depended on keeping apart the eastern from the western half of Islam, the country of the Euphrates and Orontes from the country of the Nile. The Kingdom of Jerusalem lay geographically between the two, the holding of the ports along the Syrian shore by the Christian power and the long belt of Crusading territory with its fortresses from the Dead Sea to the Lebanon and from the Lebanon northwards, physically separated the towns of the Orontes and the desert fringe, with great Damascus for its capital, and Mesopotamia, with its spiritual centre in Bagdad, from Egypt.

But of more importance than the physical situation was the spiritual situation. The spiritual head of Islam upon the Nile, the Caliph at Cairo, was Fatimite, irreconcilable with the orthodox Caliph to the east.

The whole business of the lifetime to come, the period between the Christian failure in front of Damascus in 1148 and the wiping out of the Christian power in 1187, lay in the struggle of the Moslem rulers of Syria to unite with themselves the wealth and the population of Egypt: the Christian kingship at Jerusalem could only live by preventing that annexation. Whenever Egypt—schismatic Egypt—should fall into the power of orthodox Islam, whenever the Nile should be governed by the same authority as Syria, it was certain that the end of the Crusading power had come. Though the sea-coast towns and the strip of Crusading territory physically intervened, it was possible for armies, and especially for native armies not too numerous, to turn the obstacle by the half-desert marches to the south of the Red Sea, and cross the neck of the Sinai peninsula. Spiritual unity having been achieved, physical unity would follow, and when physical unity was founded the Crusading State was encircled and could no longer permanently hold.

That encirclement ultimately took place. Moslem Syria and Moslem Egypt became one State under one control. The efforts of Christian Jerusalem and its feudatories to prevent such a coalescence failed, and when it had failed the end was clearly in sight. The Crusading State would be at the mercy of a surrounding Moslem world.

The stages of the disaster are clearly marked, and if we set them down here at the beginning of the story, that story will be the clearer.

The first stage is the unification of Syria.

Nureddin had not yet mastered Damascus. The city which withstood the Emperor and his Germans and Italians and the King of France and their armies was still an independent State; but after so great a peril, barely escaped, it was bound to take refuge with the main neighbouring Mohammedan power. That phase ended in 1154, when Nureddin rode in through the northern gate of the town, which acclaimed him and had not to be taken by force. It was just less than six years since Louis of France and Conrad of Germany had marched away.

There follow ten years in which the opponents, now eager Moslem, now anxious Christian, are watching each other with varied fortunes, ten years of balance, during which it is not certain whether Jerusalem will succeed in keeping Egypt free from Damascus or not. These ten years end in 1164, when the conquest of Egypt by Syria began. The Frankish influence was beaten back, Nureddin's officers commanded in Cairo; most important of all the schismatic Caliphate was suppressed, and in the great mosques the prayers were said no longer for the spiritual head of the Fatimites but only for the orthodox spiritual head, common now to Syria and Egypt alike. The King of Jerusalem, struggling for life, had lost the game. One common enemy lay all around. So ended the second ten years when, in 1174, Nureddin died.

With Nureddin's death comes the next phase, the mastery acquired by him who had been till then Nureddin's regent on the Nile, the man whose name will be associated for ever with the destruction of the Crusading power, Saladin.

On Nureddin's death Saladin proposes to make himself leader of all the newly united Syria. He succeeds in that effort, he becomes the master of the whole Mohammedan world in the Near East. It is a matter of a dozen years.

Then, all being accomplished, Saladin is free to strike the final blow and to achieve his great purpose. The whole power is concentrated in his hands, and against such power the desperate Kingdom of Jerusalem cannot stand. The decisive battle is fought at Hattin, right in the country wherein our religion arose, within sight of the Sea of Galilee, within a walk of Nazareth. At Hattin, in the summer of 1187, the Crusading State is killed in battle.

It is convenient to mark these steps by their place in the life of Saladin. He is a child of fifteen when his father Ayub (Job), Nureddin's right-hand man and Zengi's old captain, brings Nureddin into Damascus. He is a young man of twenty-five, still quite unknown, when the issue is joined on Egypt and Nureddin decides on the occupation of the Nile. He accompanies Nureddin's army, led by his uncle, and begins for the first time to show his strange quiet talent, *and* the good fortune to which he is predestined. He is a young man in his thirtieth year when he is given by Nureddin the command of Cairo itself. He is thirty-five years old when Nureddin dies. He is forty-seven when he has achieved complete rule, holding Mesopotamia with Syria and Egypt all in one hand. He is forty-eight when he wins his great victory over the last Christian army defending the Holy Places. Before he is fifty he has ridden in triumph through Jerusalem.

It behoves us, at the outset of that series, to understand what sort of man this was, he to whom such adventures happened.

Saladin was not of the type to which conform most great military leaders of history. Properly speaking, he did not achieve his results through the methods of a soldier so much as through the methods of a politician. He had in common with great soldiers of history two things only: First, his ambition seems to have arisen late and accidentally, aroused by unexpected original success; second, he acted in any crisis immediately. He decided on what he had to do and, having decided, moved at once—*that* quality never fails in those who achieve such things.

We must remember that, of a hundred decisions so taken and rapidly acted on, only a few bear fruit. The greater part lead to disaster and many more to nothingness. There was, therefore, a preponderant element of good luck in Saladin's achievement; also he was very cautious. He ran no risks.

Whether he should be accused of special cruelty it is difficult to say, so vilely cruel was the whole of his world. He was certainly quite indifferent to the sufferings of those whom he condemned to death and torture for the purposes of his policy.

He was, of course, fanatically anti-Christian: it is the character which has most recommended him to many of our modern historians. Islam always seems roused to a special anger against the organized religion of Christendom, but Saladin exceeded on this point. For him the Incarnation, the Priesthood, the Sacraments "polluted the air."

Like all other fighting men in that mixed world, the mounted leaders on either side in that Twelfth Century, whether Western or Oriental, he took a certain pleasure in the ritual practice of chivalry. Too much has been made of his supposed respect for opponents of equal valour or of equal power. He would, like his predecessor, destroy them without mercy when they were within his grasp, and he would personally murder one against whom his personal passion was roused, as he murdered Reginald of Chatillon, his prisoner. But he was not a man whose common characteristic was either violence or the love of revenge. His common characteristics were, oddly enough, those of the scholar. His devotion to all the details of his religion was a scholarly devotion rather than anything else, and had not accident led him into such high places he would rather have spent his life among books and listening to disquisitions on theology than in the saddle; and as for the sword he used it little himself—not from lack of courage, but from a preference for overseeing and managing. Mere fighting appealed little to him, but he enjoyed arranging the fighting of others.

His salient mark was a knowledge of man, and he loved to exercise this talent to the full. He was perpetually seeking out motives, and usually finding them accurately enough. He would deceive with skill and wait patiently, even for years, to reap the harvest of an intrigue. Yet he did not plan his own advancement: rather did he use it as it came, because all men, finding in themselves an aptitude, will naturally desire to express it and apply it.

One may sum him up by saying that he was a man upon whom most certainly a great part was thrust by fate; not a man who had sought it but a man who, finding himself called upon to play that part, played it consistently and well. He owed much to birth and accident, the rest to calculation.

Without a doubt he was sincere in his religion, not only negatively in his hatred of Christian things, but positively in his simple and profound attachment to Islam. When he declared the Holy War it was a personal, unmixed emotion that drove him. He was in this a mixture of integrity and of its opposite. No man was readier, in the chief moments of his life, to betray a bond of loyalty, to supplant one who had raised him, to oust the heirs of his benefactor or to lure men to their destruction by pretended mercy. Yet he was genuine in praising adhesion to a pledged word and he proved his honesty at times by foregoing advantages which he might have gained by betrayal.

To the major doctrines which the Mohammedan heresy had retained from Catholicism—the majesty of One Omnipotent and Beneficent God, the equal rights of His human creatures, the nature and destiny of man's immortal Soul—he maintained a profound and unswerving attachment. He stood erect in the presence of Life and Death.

It was the question of Egypt—the all-importance to Jerusalem of keeping up the quarrel between Cairo and Damascus, the all-importance to Damascus of acquiring Cairo and welding all Levantine Islam into one body for the encirclement and destruction of the Crusaders—that was to bring Saladin on to the stage of the world. But this struggle for Egypt began long before he was heard of.

His father, Job (Ayub), a Kurd of old family and distinction, Zengi's chief man, had ridden out to join that leader on the very night the boy was born—in 1138, the year before the capture of Baalbek whereof Ayub was made Governor. It was not till fifteen years later, after the failure of the Second Crusade and the consequent recasting of all Syrian politics, that the Egyptian question grew urgent; and the first manifestation of its importance appears indirectly in the taking of Ascalon by the King of Jerusalem, Baldwin III.

When, in diplomacy or warfare, there is a force which you both desire to have upon your side and to prevent from joining your enemy, there are two ways of going to work. You may plan for an alliance binding that force to your own side by an agreement, which at the same time divorces it from your opponent; or you may intimidate, coerce, master to the best of your ability, the element whose junction with your enemy you dread and whose support for yourself you need.

These two policies are not exclusive one of the other. They may be, and often are, worked side by side. So it was with the Egyptian Caliphate and the Kingdom of Jerusalem after the crash of Edessa and the lamentable failure in front of Damascus. The Kingdom of Jerusalem was now on the defensive and would be henceforward in permanent peril of destruction at the hands of the rapidly uniting Syrian and Mohammedan power which Zengi had formed and his son, Nureddin, was continuing. It was vital to Jerusalem that Cairo should be, if possible, an ally; if not an ally, a sort of dependant; and at all costs that Cairo should not be absorbed by the power of Nureddin.

With that object Jerusalem might cajole, or coerce, or both. As a fact, after the first phase of intrigue, it turned to coercion. It ultimately failed in both. Cairo fell into the hands of Syria, and the encirclement of the Christian Kingdom was accomplished. But it was a matter of sixteen or seventeen years before the failure of Jerusalem in this all-important point was complete.

The first sign, then, of the necessary new policy was Baldwin III's capture of Ascalon. It may seem farfetched to ascribe that feat of arms to so deliberate a policy as that just described; but even if the motive were not yet fully conscious, it was certainly present.

The Crusading State had left Ascalon unconquered for a lifetime. Divisions among leaders, hesitation, occupation elsewhere, had all contributed to save the town. But it was not an accident that now that should be done which might have been done earlier. Earlier it was not vital. Now it was vital. Ascalon was one point on the Crusading sea-coast still remaining as a landing-place and stronghold in Mohammedan hands, and a Mohammedan-Egyptian garrison had held it uninterruptedly for all these years, after Gaza, and Jaffa, and Cæsarea, and Haifa and Acre, and Beyrouth, and Tripoli, and Tyre and Sidon, and Tortosa and Byblos and Latakia—all the string of ports and roadsteads along the shore—had long been in Christian hands.

Within four years of the great change Ascalon was seized at last. It was well fortified, the semi-circle of its walls crowned heights stretching from the sea to the sea again. The garrison was permanently reinforced from Egypt by water and fresh contingents and relays arrived every three months. Its past immunity made its Egyptian owners think it impregnable. In this they were quite deceived, as people commonly are when they go by past form in military matters.

Ascalon being thus mastered, was a warning on the part of the Crusading King to the heretic Caliph at Cairo that he must regard Jerusalem as his superior. He might ally himself with Jerusalem if he would, or he might expect attack and compulsory subjection, which would serve the purpose as well or better than formal alliance. But by Ascalon he was both intimidated and warned.

The very next year, 1154, Damascus which had so long cherished its independence and stood out against the growing rule of Zengi and his son—even during its great peril in 1148—gave way. The agent of this change was again Ayub. Partly by argument, partly by bribes he got the Damascenes to admit Nureddin and thenceforward all the Moslem eastern half of the Syrian corridor was in one command with the wealth and central position of its chief city in hands of Zengi's son. On the 25th of April, 1154, Ayub's chief and lord, Nureddin of Aleppo, rode, acclaimed, into Damascus.

The second step in the "encirclement" had been taken.

It is typical of the military inferiority of the Crusading State, after the great change of 1144-48, that it dared not for some years provoke Nureddin on the main Egyptian question by a direct challenge: it was content to levy toll from the rival generals of the Caliph at Cairo and to make this a symbol of vague suzerainty.

Ascalon had, indeed, been seized, and there was of course throughout the ten years between the fall of that city and active operations in Egypt any amount of border warfare with varying fortunes between the two powers: Christian at Jerusalem, Moslem at Damascus. But during all these ten years neither Baldwin III nor his brother Amaury (Almeric) who succeeded him in 1162 attempted actual invasion. There was something like permanent or intermittent anarchy in the Egyptian government, the Vizirs succeeding each other by plot and counter-plot, and murder. There was therefore recurrent opportunity for action by Jerusalem; yet none was taken until the year after Amaury's accession, that is, in 1163.

At the beginning of that year an Arab Vizir, who had worked his way up to the chief power under the Fatimite Caliphate after having been governor of upper Egypt, was attacked by a rival general and driven out of Cairo. He had only held power for just over six months.

The man thus driven out, the Arab Vizir, was called Shawar. He took refuge with Nureddin at Damascus and offered fantastic terms for his support against his supplanter. He said that after his success, should it come about, he would pay all the costs of the Syrian King's campaign and pledged a third of the huge Egyptian revenues as a regular tribute to be paid thenceforward—for it must be remembered how in all this business the wealth of Egypt, which was on a different scale from that of all the rest of the Near East, played almost as great a part in the ambitions and rivalries of the two competing powers, Crusading-Christian and Mohammedan-Syrian, as did its strategic value.

It must not be supposed that during all these years the various competing, murderous, local commanders under the heretic Caliphate of Cairo had not thought of appealing to Damascus; but hitherto Damascus had not moved. It would be time enough to move (thought Nureddin) when Jerusalem moved—if then. Each was watching the other, as rival powers today in Europe watch each other before venturing on actual hostilities. Moreover, Nureddin was growing older and dreaded the ambition of his own generals.

An approach to Egypt could only be made by Damascus through the desert land beyond the Dead Sea, south of the Crusading Kingdom, which former lay right on the flank of such an advance.

The new King of Jerusalem, Amaury, then, moved first. Shawar's successful rival, Dirgham by name, was recalcitrant over the payment of that tribute which the King of Jerusalem regularly demanded as the symbol of his vague claims to protect the Caliph at Cairo. With the failure of the tribute as a pretext the King of Jerusalem at once invaded. He was checked by the flooding of the Delta. But the check came at that very moment when Dirgham heard that Shawar, whom he had expelled, was pressing Nureddin to strike. The King of Jerusalem had already retired; he was followed by passionate repentant pleadings from Dirgham.

Before these pleadings could be of effect, Nureddin had decided on war, six months after his rival, the Christian King, had first acted. He was persuaded to do so, rather against his will, by Ayub and by Ayub's brother, Shirkuh. Nureddin sent an army round by the south of the Kingdom of Jerusalem, through the desert land and across the neck of the Sinai peninsula. That army he confided to Shirkuh. Now Shirkuh was the brother of that same Job or Ayub who had been governor of Baalbek for Nureddin and had negotiated Nureddin's triumphal entry into Damascus ten years before, Shirkuh therefore was the uncle of the young

Saladin, now just past his twenty-fifth year: a modest, bookish lad whom no one had yet noted in connection with arms or indeed in any other fashion.

Later in life Saladin told in striking words the story of that chance summons into Egypt; how he hated going, having no sufficient equipage or position. How he only at last reluctantly obeyed the command of Nureddin himself, who bade him join his uncle without delay. [Or the second expedition. It matters not. The point is that Saladin did not seek his career but had it thrust upon him.]

Shirkuh then, took Saladin with him upon this expedition to Egypt which was to reinstate Shawar as Vizir, and with that setting forth, the story of Saladin begins.

Dirgham, hard pressed but not defeated, was turned upon by his own new subjects, thrown from his horse, and killed. Shawar, with the Damascene army at his back, was once more in power. It was the month of May, 1164.

Then came the habitual criss-cross of those purely personal intrigues among the rival Egyptian generals. Shawar, hoping to remain independent in spite of his ally, Shirkuh, being at the head of a conquering army, kept the Damascenes out of Cairo; or, at least, out of the fortifications. He refused to pay the sums of money he had promised. Shirkuh replied by occupying the eastern side of the Delta.

It is at this moment that Saladin first appears in an important position. His uncle Shirkuh gave him the command of the local occupation in this eastern province. Shawar appealed to the King of Jerusalem and Amaury marched against the Damascenes and their Egyptian entrenchments.

The thing ended in what was apparently a draw, but was really a preliminary defeat in this now open fighting for the possession of Egypt. Pressure having been put upon the far Damascene borders of Palestine by Nureddin, Amaury consented to a truce in Egypt. Shirkuh and his Syrian army, who were short of provision—they had been under a kind of siege at the hands of the Crusaders for three months—was ready enough for a temporary peace. The Syrian army went back to Damascus—but meanwhile Nureddin had taken the great castle at Banias, the Christian outpost against Damascus, and carried off as prisoners the Prince of Antioch and the Count of Tripoli as well.

That was towards the end of 1164. Three years later, Damascus, knowing its own power, once more took up the attack.

It is true that Nureddin again hesitated, but Shirkuh, feeling that his original expedition had been a success in spite of its inconclusive ending, pressed for a new campaign, and got his way. In the cold weather at the beginning of 1167, he made a desert march after a fashion in which the Mohammedans were ever superior to the Christians. It was only a small force of two thousand mounted men, but

carefully chosen. It turned the Dead Sea, gave a wide berth to the Christian power on the north, appeared upon the Nile, crossed the river, well south of Cairo, and began moving against that capital. Amaury, hearing of the movement, had promptly followed.

Thenceforward, for two years and rather more, went on a ding-dong struggle for Egypt. It was a struggle in which the two parties, Damascus and Jerusalem, might have seemed to some onlooker equal, and are treated as equal by more than one modern writer who fails to grasp the general sweep and outline of the time. They were not equal, and could never again be equal, because every factor of number, of time, of climate, of blood, was telling increasingly against the now beleaguered Western and half-Western Christian force in the Holy Land.

These campaigns, led by Amaury the King of Jerusalem, the successor of Baldwin III lately dead, were really sorties. Nothing could have made them true campaigns with a chance of final victory but sufficient and sustained external aid—best of all, large and recurrent reinforcement from the vigorous chivalry of Western Europe, particularly of France. The French nobles were the kinsmen of the men who governed in the now fatally imperilled garrisons of the Holy Land. The French language was still the language of all those commanders; but the French moved not. Those great recurrent but widely separated expeditions which are called each individually a "Crusade," needed strong news to launch them. For a lifetime there had been no such movement after the First, until the catastrophe of Edessa had stirred not only the French but the Germans to a Second—and we have seen how that ended.

Nothing short of the fall of Jerusalem could launch another such effort, and then, of course, it was too late.

The two years opened by an indecisive action, after which the French forces and the Egyptians with whom they were in alliance besieged Alexandria, which Saladin was to defend. The siege came to nothing. And once again (August, 1157) Damascus and Jerusalem consented to abandon the battle for the moment and leave Egypt to itself until they should return. Late in the next year (November, 1168), helped by the cold weather, the King of Jerusalem came back and this time the Caliph himself appealed to Nureddin at Damascus. Once more an army from Damascus set out. It was a small one, but it turned the King of Jerusalem's army, it entered Cairo, and the Christians went back to Palestine. For the second time they had retired before Shirkuh, but this time there was no truce—and no return. Shirkuh remained in Cairo as master. He died early the next year, and his death was the signal for the main opening of Saladin's career.

The Caliph, the Fatimite, the heretical Caliph, kept in fearful secluded pomp, a merely religious though still awful figure in his splendid palace, had taken Shirkuh, orthodox and emissary of Damascus, for his Vizir. Now that Shirkuh was dead, he, or rather his advisers, the clique within his palace (for the Cairene Caliph was quite young), chose Saladin to take his uncle's place, and to be Vizir in his turn. They chose him because Saladin "seemed to be unwarlike and easy to command."

Now there was here an element which had appeared more than once in the brief life of this young man (he was only thirty!), the element of chance, and what is more, of chance which, though favourable, the favoured one neither desired nor sought for.

But it was part of the complex character of Saladin, a character so difficult to grasp and therefore of such interest to follow, that an unexpected or even undesired opportunity being put into his hands he could not but apply to it not only his industry, which was of the scholar's sort and therefore detailed and continuous, but also that most unscholarly quality, his cunning.

He made himself popular—it was a thing he did all his life, and a thing he was fitted to do. Having selected whom he should cow, he was ruthless; but with the undecided mass whose support he desired he was a smiling, generous, and even just, figure. His first act on this elevation (he was appointed Vizir by the Cairene Caliph at the end of March, 1169) was to add to the prayers in the Mosque the name of his real master. Those prayers were still said for the heretical Caliph, his chief and nominator, but there was added to them the name of the orthodox Nureddin.

His next act was to destroy the armed guard of black Sudanese, who were the sole defence of the Caliph. He knew that they were secretly hostile. He discovered they were plotting against him, and he tortured, beheaded and burnt them after defeat without mercy. There he showed again another side of his character, a calculated bloodthirstiness, which pierces time after time through his suave and sober bearing. Perhaps bloodthirstiness is not quite the word. There is no doubt he loved the suffering of enemies. But he loved to do nothing that was not calculated. He was determined that an act of terror should make future armed resistance impossible. And in this he was successful.

Amaury tried one more throw. The quite insufficient forces of Palestine were joined by the fleet of the Byzantine Christians. They besieged Damietta, which, with Alexandria, was the twin town commanding the mouths of the Nile. As with Alexandria the siege came to nothing. Most of the Byzantine fleet was wrecked. A counter-attack was the only fruit of this last serious effort on the part of the Crusading State to check the now almost perfect encirclement of which Saladin in Cairo was the symbol. Saladin raided against Gaza, and the whole year after Damietta was filled with his activity for pressing in upon the threatened Crusaders.

That was 1170. The following year a last decisive step was taken. In September, 1171, the prayer was called in the Mosques of Cairo for the Caliph of Bagdad—it was as though prayers in the name of the Pope had been ordered by the Government of Belfast.

But the thing had been long prepared; the wrestling out of sight between the new-come Damascene power and the old unwarlike Egyptian State—very wealthy but unfitted for arms—had wearied out the less virile party, and they accepted their fate. Within a week the poor young Fatimite Caliph was dead.

The religious revolution, which was the decisive battle in all this affair, which put one spiritual force in command of all local Islam, to the south and to the west, as well as to the east of the Holy Land, which was to put all the revenues and all the recruitment from the wealthy Delta and valley of the Nile to wealthy Damascus and Aleppo and wealthy Mesopotamia in one hand, was accomplished.

Some thought that Saladin, with his old father Ayub still by him, might, in his triumph, attempt to supplant Nureddin—who was still their lord. But cunning was still the strongest force, and time was a sufficient ally.

Saladin, moreover, had been unsuccessful in following out Nureddin's own orders to attack that master castle, Kerak in Moab, south of the Dead Sea, which still interfered with the roundabout, half-desert way between Cairo and Damascus; and next Ayub was thrown from his horse and killed outside the gate of Cairo. All this made for delay.

There was one last insurrection by the relics of the black troops and of native Egyptians; it was put down with the usual complement of barbarity—everyone was crucified. It had been subsidised from Jerusalem, and on its failure Jerusalem was too weak to move. There was an abortive assault on Alexandria by the King of Sicily, who learnt the news of the plot's failure too late, and meanwhile that thing had happened which had been so patiently awaited—on the 15th of May, 1174, Nureddin, after a short illness, was dead.

II

KINGSHIP

The doomed Kingdom of Jerusalem being now encircled, the next progress towards its destruction would be the gathering of that encirclement into one military command.

For those who admire craft in public affairs a perfect spectacle is presented by Saladin immediately upon his hearing of Nureddin's death. Nureddin had left a little son, eleven years of age, to continue the dynasty of his grandfather, the great Zengi. Saladin at once had coins struck in the image of that royal boy and had prayers said in his name, public prayers in the Mosque at Cairo, which ceremonial act was the recognition of royalty.

He did more. He sent a letter to confirm and to make permanent the record of his loyalty to the great house which had made his father Ayub and his uncle Shirkuh and himself.

This letter he despatched straight to Damascus. In it he blamed other magnates for having taken over the guardianship of the young King and affirmed his own special devotion, saying that he saw with pain how they had arbitrarily taken over guardianship of "My Master, my Master's son." He went on to say that he, Saladin, was coming at once to do homage and to show his gratitude for the good things the boy's father had showered upon him.

Whereupon, dissension having arisen (as a matter of course) between Damascus and Aleppo, to which the young heir of Nureddin had been taken, he chose the best seven hundred out of his mounted men and made off across the desert fringe round by the south of Palestine, slipped through the widely separated posts and small thin garrisons of the Christians south of the Dead Sea, and rode into Damascus on the 27th of November, 1174.

He had come to break his word with that thoroughness and foresight which both belong to his inmost self.

To us of the West such hypocrisy is revolting; but then, we have difficulty in apprehending the Oriental mind.

Here let us note, in connection with that small column of seven hundred light-armed men on their light, swift Arab horses, what was one chief factor in all the success that lay before Saladin. *He now possessed the permanent nucleus of an army.* The troops whom he had maintained and drilled after regular fashion in Egypt had become, as it were, professional, and in that fluctuating fluid world of Islam such a solid kernel was of incalculable value.

It is something that appears fairly often throughout history in places and times where social habits and political institutions do not lend themselves to standing armies and trained bodies of soldiers. By having to maintain a prolonged uninterrupted effort a leader finds himself, without having perhaps at first intended it, possessed, at the end of some years, of a true army, a body of men steeped in the habits of military life and obedience: separate, increasingly superior in quality to the unorganised bodies, whether of civilians or of men temporarily armed, whom they have to meet. Of such a sort were Cromwell's cavalry regiments at the end of the Civil War, when the great Powers of Europe competed for his alliance. Of such a sort were the formations of the French Revolution within some few years of its outbreak; and especially after the campaign of Lombardy. Of such a sort now, in this late autumn of 1174, was the immediate command of Saladin.

He went forth at once to besiege Aleppo, and that young "My master, son of my old Master," to whom he had been so devoted on paper a few weeks before. He did not immediately succeed, but he beat off the young heir's cousin, another grandson of Zengi, who commanded in Mosul to the east, and was lord of Mesopotamia. The combined troops of Mesopotamia and Aleppo attacked Saladin near Hama. His veterans cut the attackers to pieces.

After that victory Saladin went the whole hog, a thing he never did in all his life until he felt certain. After such a period of intrigue he declared himself King, had his name put into the prayers as sovereign and struck coins whereon the name Nureddin's son no longer appeared, but only his own, 'Yussuf [Joseph], Ayub's son."

Though he felt himself so far secure he was still on the defensive, with enemies all around. They had already made an attempt upon his life by that strange sect of dissenting fanatics, the "hashish eaters," of whom we have made the word "assassin." These men were a small group, Ismailite in tradition, who hated both orthodoxy and a strong government in any hand. They were half brigands, half a secret society. They had come from the north to fix themselves in the difficult mountain tangle lying between Antioch and Latakia: a country difficult to penetrate, even today. Their castles were built on the peaks of those hills, inaccessible, reputed impregnable. They sent out men to murder Saladin, and in an attempted campaign against them in their own wild country he failed altogether. His failure had one good result, it produced fine dæmonic legends. In order to account for the ill-success, those about him spread supernatural stories which have about them the flavour of the Arabian Nights.

He was opposed also by sundry in Damascus itself, but his trained troops were invincible and were so dreaded that he counted confidently on his future. That future seemed specially prepared for him and for that scheme of a final Holy War against the Christians and their Faith, which had begun vaguely to take shape in his mind.

What made him thus confident was the disaster that had fallen on Jerusalem and the Crusading State. Less than two months after Nureddin's death his rival, the Christian champion, King Amaury, had died—on the 11th of July, 1174. Like Nureddin, Amaury had left no heir but a child: a boy of thirteen who was called King under the title of Baldwin IV. During all those two years, therefore, which were filled by Saladin's seizure of Damascus and successive attempts upon Aleppo, the hazarded Christian realm between him and the sea was stricken in its vital element, the element of monarchy.

For not only was the new king a boy under regency and in peril of political chaos thereby, but the East had done its work upon him, and he was known to be already a leper.

As against the enormous numbers of Islam, the masters of the Crusading State, the French nobility and the merchants of the seaports—themselves hampered by Mohammedan subjects and functionaries—had one force which Islam has never had: the Roman conception of a *State,* and with it the Roman inheritance of a continuous single command; the great legacy of the Empire to us Europeans. It did not suffice.

Islam did, indeed, know monarchy in fits and starts. Zengi had been an example of that, and now Saladin was already another. When Islam thus produced an ephemeral local dynasty it enjoyed single command, but it never conceived the political idea of political continuity. Just as its religion was all-pervading, so its lay controls were personal and passing. Leaders in Islam, warriors whom others would follow, rose like a wave of the sea, and they or their descendants sank again as do waves. So it had been with Zengi, so it was to be with Saladin.

As against such instability the Western tradition had rooted a dynasty at Jerusalem. The poor sick lad now on the throne was the fifth in succession from that first Baldwin who had made the monarchy more than seventy years before. It was but a spiritual force to set against the overwhelming masses that could be gathered against it from all around. It was not sufficient to save the Crusading State, but such as it was, it was a strength sufficient to bolster up the few last years of the Cross in Jerusalem.

At the end of the following year, 1177, there fell an incident which shows at once what the dying Christian monarchy could still do with its still superior type of fighting man, the mounted knights at its orders, *and* how pressing the power of Saladin had become.

On the 25th of November, 1177, Saladin, with something like twelve thousand behind him, led a raid right up to the sea-coast, pointing at Ascalon. Outside the walls of Ascalon, to the east, the young leper King, vastly outnumbered, won a victory against the raiders from which Saladin barely escaped on a fast camel.

But the significance of that fight, of that local Christian success which bore no fruit, was not the irresistible charge of a few Christian knights affirming itself once more over the Orientals. It was rather the fact that Saladin should take it for granted that he might at will ride at the head of troops right up to the coast of the Mediterranean. In the next year he won a victory in his turn against the Christians outside Hama, notable for the massacre in cold blood (by Saladin's orders) of the Crusading prisoners. The year after, 1179, he again rode right up to the sea-coast at the head of an army, passing through northern Galilee unchecked, and menacing Sidon itself. In the fighting he took prisoner the chiefs, the masters of the military orders, the young leper King himself, and netted enormous ransoms—Baldwin alone paying over 150,000 Tyrian pieces of gold.

Not only could the Mohammedan now almost at will pass through the whole breadth of the Christian kingdom and come up to the shore, but the rapidly uniting kingdom of Saladin could bring up the fleet from Egypt, and, a couple of years later, he nearly captured Beyrouth, after bombardment from the sea by machines mounted on the decks of his ships.

The whole story, then, is of continual increasing, and soon to be intolerable, pressure; and the end might have come even then, five years before it did, had not Saladin been diverted for the time by threats of attack from the East. The ever-swirling Mohammedan world of armed horsemen, changeful in allegiance, prepared to attack him from Mesopotamia. He turned his back to Palestine and rode for the great rivers.

He did not take Mosul, but he cowed it, and he exchanged with it as against such places as he had seized during his Mesopotamian invasion, the, to him, all-important fortress of Aleppo. He rode into that town on the 12th of June, 1183. It was the crown of his long effort, and yet he had to wait somewhat before he could deliver the final blow. For though Mesopotamia had bowed before him he did not feel that he could yet use it as a recruiting field, nor even that he was fully safe for the future against attack therefrom. Once more he marched against Mosul, fell ill and was on the point of death. Once more he avoided direct attack upon the walls, but this time he had no fears for what was to come. All Mesopotamia accepted him for suzerain, and the ruler of Mosul was ready to follow him in war. Therefore, by the spring of 1186, things were ready for the last phase.

During this eastern diversion there had been a truce patched up with the Kingdom of Jerusalem. That truce is yet another proof of the relation between all that was left of Christian power and the now consolidated Mohammedan organisation around it.

There was indeed among the vassals of the poor dying young leper king only one man left whom Saladin feared as a fighter and who for the vigour of his temperament, the determination to keep up the resistance, was feared upon the other side. That man was the savage, but most capable, soldier, Reginald of Chatillon. Other barons the Moslem knew and respected as great fighters still. Hugh of Toron, the Constable, who had fallen where the Damascus road crosses the Upper Jordan, where now the frontier bridge is, at Jacob's Ford; or that unfortunate but valiant lover and knight, the Lord of Ramleh, Saladin took him prisoner, too, and thereupon showed his chivalry by pulling out the Christian noble's teeth until he was ready to promise a fantastic ransom. There was the Master of the Templars, whom perhaps Saladin hated most of all for wearing the Cross and for his monastic vows. But the man whom he feared most was still Reginald of Chatillon.

He was that Reginald who had come as quite a young man from the Loire valley, sailing out East on quest, and had enjoyed and suffered such astonishing adventures, committed so many atrocious crimes and fought like a lion in the Marches of the North. He was that Reginald who in youth had mastered and married the heiress of Antioch and had ruled there. He had fallen prisoner to the Moslem twenty-five years ago, and of those twenty-five had spent sixteen as a prisoner in Aleppo Castle. After his release, and now elderly as the lives of fighting men in Syria then went, he had married the heiress of the Trans-Jordanian barony and had become lord of the strongest castle, and the one most boldly fronting Saladin's power, the great Kerak of Moab, the stumbling-block on the roundabout way from Damascus to Egypt.

Saladin would have given his left hand for Kerak. He besieged it on its precipice, once and once again, bringing all his power against it and the strongest siege-train men had yet seen. But the twenty-foot walls of stone stood on their height in that wilderness and still defied him, and Reginald carried on there, the chief menace, or at least challenger: a man who had actually dared to attempt a raid on Mecca, and who refused to despair even now of the Christian power. But he should have despaired, had he used his reason, a thing so wild a man would never use save immediately and tactically in the field. For, indeed, there was already no hope, and once the Mesopotamian affair was settled, once Saladin's hands were fully free and all Syria, all Egypt, mobilisable at his command, the final blow would fall.

In the midst of all this the poor young leper king died. He had been holy as well as gallant, and, in the midst of his fearful trial, constant in gallantry as a soldier and in cares as a king. He was not twenty-five when they buried him on Golgotha, by the side of the kings his forerunners, and now was Jerusalem abandoned and lacking all guidance.

Baldwin IV, dying, had pointed out as his successor the little child his nephew, the son of his sister Sibyl, a boy of five years old. The little fellow died after a few months, and what authority was to be found? What command over the predestined victims of the Holy Land? Who could rally them now?

In feudal law, by all the customs of France and of the West, the tall, fine young knight, Guy of Lusignan, was heir; for he was the new husband of Sibyl, the niece of Baldwin III and the sister of the dead leper King; the mother of the child who had just died in his turn.

But the strict law of heredity, if such an idea may be said to have already crystallised as early as 1184, did not hold in the Holy Land as it did in Western Europe, for the Holy Land was under siege, and needed the best soldier it could find. All the Lusignans were of good blood and proper soldiers, but a better leader was Raymond of Tripoli, the third of that name to rule the vassal State of the mid-coast, the Phœnician shore.

Moreover (what was of the highest moment in such a crisis) Lusignan was a newcomer. That would not have mattered a generation earlier, but the Syrian-born nobility was beginning to have a national feeling of its own. The great bulk of the lords of castles and of land were for Raymond.

What turned the scale was the intense will-power and thrust of two men, the Master of the Templars and Reginald of Chatillon: the first as an enemy of Tripoli, a violent personal enemy, the second because he desired to be

master, supported Guy. Guy was crowned, but crowned under the protection of Reginald, that is, of Kerak of Moab.

Raymond, persuading himself perhaps that it a was policy of a sort and a postponement of doom for the Christian kingdom, entered into a peace with Saladin upon his own initiative: a peace that might be called an alliance. Whereupon men called out treason upon him.

Against Guy, thus apparently isolated, Saladin still held his hand, but he was sending out his messengers to his vassals, his preparations were made, he only waited the occasion. Nor was occasion necessary to him. Yet occasion was afforded him: fortune gave him his excuse with both hands.

Sometime early in the year after Guy's coronation (or possibly a few days before the turn of the year), Reginald of Chatillon had issued from his stronghold and swooped, not for the first time, upon the caravan for Mecca, the largest and the richest of all. He held it to ransom prodigiously, and now the enemy could energise all his forces with moral indignation for the Holy War upon which he was determined, and the time for which was ripe.

The Lord of Kerak refused any compensation for his deed, though the King whom he had made begged him to yield. If he must go down, he would go down fighting. He said he was lord in his own house. The Count of Tripoli had made a truce with Saladin; he was free to do so if he willed; but Reginald thought nothing of such arrangements, and trusted them and Saladin not at all. Towards Easter, which fell in that year, 1187, on March 29th, Saladin, pleading virtue and honour and resenting in particular the detention of his sister by Reginald during that or some previous raid, mobilised all Islam from the Tigris to the Nile.

The spring days were full of the gathering. By the last week of June the Sultan could review a force of perhaps a hundred thousand men, such a force as none had seen since the First Crusade; and twelve thousand of them were fully-armed, mail-clad chiefs and leaders, corresponding to the knights of Christendom. In a crisis so mortal Raymond of Tripoli, who had a few weeks before allowed the entry and passage of Saladin's men through his lands, rallied to the common cause, whether from shame or from policy.

He, Reginald of Chatillon, the Master of the Templars, and the King, perhaps 1,000 knights, or at the most 1,200, some 15,000 to 20,000 all told with the footmen and mercenaries, began their concentration. By cutting to the bone all the garrisons and leaving walls almost defenceless, by spending all the money in the treasury of the Templars for the hire of Moslem troops as well as Christians, there may have been got together a fifth or a quarter in mere numbers of what Saladin was bringing against them; but in the decisive arm, the fully equipped mailed knights, they were only one to ten.

H. A. R. Gibb (essay date 1950)

SOURCE: "The Arabic Sources for the Life of Saladin," *Speculum,* Vol. XXV, No. 1, January, 1950, pp. 58–72.

[*In the following essay, Gibb examines the style, content, and historical accuracy and value of several contemporary Arabic sources of the life of Saladin.*]

All historians who have studied the life of Saladin have given the first place to two Arabic sources: the *Life of Saladin* by Bahâeddîn Ibn Shaddâd (translated in Volume III of the *Recueil des Historiens des Croisades: Historiens Orientaux*), and the universal history, *el-Kâmil,* of 'Izzeddîn Ibn el-Athîr (partially translated in Volumes I and II, 1, in the same series). As to the authority and reliability of the former, little can now be added to the testimony of Stanley Lane-Poole in his preface (p. vi) to *Saladin,* in the 'Heroes of the Nations' series (London and New York, 1898). Bahâeddîn (1145-1234) writes with the most sober good sense and honesty, and I can find in his work little even of that 'personal bias and oriental hyperbolism' which Lane-Poole thought it necessary to excuse. He first came into direct relation with Saladin, however, only in 1184, as one of the ambassadors from Mosul, and did not finally join him as Judge of the Army until 1188. From then onwards, i.e., during the whole period of the Third Crusade, he not only presents a faithful record of events as he saw them, but also, through his position as confidant and intimate friend of Saladin, gives us an insight (as no ordinary chronicle can do) into the motives by which Saladin was actuated in many critical decisions. For the nineteen years between 1169 and 1188, on the other hand, Bahâeddîn can only report at secondhand, and is not infrequently at fault over details of fact and chronology. Bahâeddîn's fellow-citizen, Ibn el-Athîr (1160-1234), has enjoyed for so many centuries the reputation of being one of the greatest historians of Islam that it may seem almost superfluous to discuss his qualifications and authority, especially when he was a contemporary of Saladin personally connected with the administration at Mosul, and therefore in a position to know at least the external facts. Though he had no doubt seen Saladin, both at Mosul and in Syria, there is no indication that he ever came into personal contact with him. His bias against Saladin is notorious; but, with some allowances made for that fact, his narratives have generally been accepted as those of a well-informed contemporary chronicler. That this view can no longer be maintained will be the main conclusion of the present article.

Two other important contemporary sources are known to have existed and were made partially available to students of the Crusades in the extracts or abstracts from them made by Abû Shâma (1203-1267) in his work known as *The Two Gardens* (partially translated in *R.H.C.Or.,* IV and V). One of these writers was a chronicler at Aleppo, Ibn Abî Taiy (*ca* 1160-1235, and therefore an exact contemporary of Ibn el-Athîr), who is distinguished by the fact that alone of the later chroniclers he was a Shi'ite,[1] a

fact which may have contributed to the disappearance of the original text of his works. The surviving extracts show him to have been an original writer, with a special interest in social and topographical details, but with a certain bias against Nûreddîn, who had exiled his father from Aleppo. Considerable portions of his history are found also in a later Arabic general chronicle, that of Ibn el-Furât (d. 1405), of which, however, the volume covering the years 1172 to 1190 is missing.

The second and much more important writer whose works were utilized by Abû Shâma was the 'Secretary' 'Imâdeddîn of Isfahân (1125-1200); indeed, the greater part of *The Two Gardens* may be described as an abridgement of the two works devoted by 'Imâdeddîn to the life of Saladin, with additional materials from other sources. The better-known of these two works, entitled *el-Fath el-Qussî,* opens with the preparations for the battle of Hattîn in 1187 and ends with the death of Saladin and division of his empire in 1193, thus covering much the same period as the firsthand part of Bahâeddîn's *Life.* Of this work several manuscripts have survived, and the text was published in 1888 by Count Carlo Landberg. Since 'Imâdeddîn had been Saladin's personal secretary since 1175, the authority of the work is not less than that of Bahâeddîn, yet the few historians who have made direct use of the text have with one voice complained of what Lane-Poole called his 'intolerable rhetoric.' For 'the Secretary' (*el-Kâtib*), as he is generally called, was one of the most famous of the classical exponents of that highly ornate and rhetorical rhyming-prose style of composition which was affected in the chanceries of the mediaeval Islamic kingdoms, and rivalled in his own time only by his official superior, Saladin's secretary of state, the kâdî el-Fâdil.

The *Fath* displays all the characteristics of this secretarial style, with its inclusion of rhetorical set-pieces on the seasons and other subjects, its inflated introductions to the narratives of events, and frequent excerpts from the author's own letters and despatches. This floridness of language, which is generally equated by western readers with emptiness of content and fulsome panegyric, largely accounts for the comparative neglect of this work, though its stylistic qualities obviously do not in themselves determine its quality as an historical source. It is also, however, difficult to read (even for Arab readers, as Abû Shâma himself points out), and it is scarcely surprising that few have been found to echo the judgment of its editor: 'Plus j'avançais dans mon travail, plus j'étais sous le charme de la parole du fameux Kâtib. Je n'avais rien lu de pareil, mais aussi n'avais-je rien lu de plus difficile au point de vue lexicographique. . . . Je suis rentré . . . plein d'enthousiasme pour mon auteur.'

The *Fath* was not, however, the principal work devoted by 'Imâdeddîn to the history of Saladin. This was a later and exhaustive history in seven volumes entitled *el-Barq el-Shâmî,* 'The Syrian Lightning,' which covered the whole period of the author's association with Saladin, including the early years when both were still in the service of

Nûreddîn. Like most of the voluminous Arabic chronicles of the Middle Ages, it soon dropped out of circulation in favor of the abridgement made by Abû Shâma. Apart from a vague indication of a manuscript or manuscripts at Leningrad, the only parts of it known to exist are two volumes in the Bodleian Library at Oxford: Vol. III, covering the years 573-575 A.H. (July 1177-May 1180), and Vol. V, covering 578 to the beginning of 580 (May 1182-July 1184). A detailed account of these volumes and their contents will be given elsewhere; here it is more important to indicate what light they throw upon the value of the *Barq* as an historical source and its relation to the other known sources.

The original text of the *Barq* makes it clear that (as might have been deduced from Abû Shâma's extracts and from the *Fath*) 'Imâdeddîn's history is in no sense an ordinary narrative chronicle. It is much more in the nature of a professional diary or record of the author's secretarial activities, copiously illustrated with copies of or extracts from his own despatches, his semi-private correspondence with the kâdî el-Fâdil, diplomas of appointment to various posts composed by him, his literary and poetic occasions, and (less frequently) details of his private affairs. But since 'Imâdeddîn accompanied Saladin almost without intermission from the summer of 1175 until his death, it is also a chronicle of events, with the remarkable feature that they are usually related in the first person plural, a practice which inevitably (but often, I think, mistakenly) gives an impression of vanity and self-importance on the writer's part. He does, however, include narratives of the few events at which he was not present, and occasionally relates events by reproducing one or more of his own or of the kâdî el-Fâdil's despatches instead of by a direct narrative.

The stylistic features of the work are not uniform, but vary considerably from section to section. In some passages the rhetorical structure is highly elaborated, in others it amounts to little more than a habit of expressing everything in rhyming-prose, which is upon occasions remarkably direct and unstilted. Saladin, for example, is represented as speaking in rhymed prose, but except in one or two short set discourses the impression is one of natural and unaffected speech. In the hands of so skilful a master of language and vocabulary, the fact that his narratives are cast throughout in this medium does not in the least detract from their clarity or their precision. The numerous excursus and introductions have a different literary function altogether and in no way interfere with the narrative passages, where the rhyming-prose style lends itself at most to the charge of redundancy or tautology.

On close examination 'Imâdeddîn's statements are remarkably sober. Leaving aside all questions of literary style, they are not unlike the minutes or reports of a conscientious civil servant (as indeed he was). There is a certain plainness of speech, an absence of comment either for or against, and even a kind of detachment which contrasts oddly with his official identification of himself with the

events by the constant use of the pronoun 'we.' It is almost a paradox that so solid and matter-of-fact a chronicle should be clothed in a garment of such literary and aesthetic exuberance. His reliability will be discussed later on; but a writer who tells of his own withdrawal because of cold feet from the expedition to Ramleh in 1177 and quotes the comments of his friends upon this action inspires us from the outset with some confidence in his truthfulness.

Although 'Imâdeddîn's literary elaboration in the long run detracted from the circulation of his writings, it is common knowledge that the generation of chroniclers after him fully realized their value and drew extensively upon them. Hitherto it has been difficult to determine the extent of their borrowings. In the following pages the narratives of the most celebrated of these histories, the *Kâmil* of Ibn el-Athîr, are analyzed for the years covered by the extant volumes of the *Barq,* and an attempt will be made to show the exact relation between them.

A.H. 573. Ibn el-Athîr begins with the narrative of Saladin's defeat at Ramleh (XI, 292-293 [I, 627-628]).[2] That this is taken entirely from the *Barq* is clear from the details included in the narrative, such as the gallantry of Taqîeddîn's son (reproducing the substance of one of 'Imâdeddîn's 'epic' passages: *Barq,* III, 13^v-14^r), and the capture and later ransom of 'Îsâ el-Hakkârî (15^r = Abû Shâma, I, 273, ll. 22-25 [IV, 187]). This is followed by an account of the attack on Hamâh by Philip of Flanders (XI, 294 [I, 630]), 'the reason for the attack being that one of the greatest of the Counts of the Franks had arrived in Palestine by sea, and on seeing that Saladin had returned to Egypt in defeat he seized the opportunity of the defenceless state of the country, because Shamseddawla [Tûrânshâh] was in Damascus as Saladin's lieutenant and had few troops with him, besides being absorbed in his pleasures and disinclined to action.'

Here too the dependence of Ibn el-Athîr upon the *Barq* seems clear from the fact that not only does the order of the statements follow precisely the order in *Barq,* III, 25^r, but the structure of events is practically the same (cf. Abû Shâma, I, 275 [IV, 191-2]). That this is not due to the quotation of an official despatch is clear from the description of Tûrânshâh's conduct, which would certainly have found no place in an official account. But Ibn el-Athîr does add something to his source, namely, the statement that the attack on Hamâh was occasioned by Saladin's defeat at Ramleh. This can only be ascribed either to carelessness, Ibn el-Athîr having been misled by the fact that in the *Barq* the attack on Hamâh follows the account of the Ramleh expedition, or else to deliberate falsehood, backed up by concealment of the dates of the two events. The *Barq* clearly states the date of the attack on Hamâh as 20 Jumâdâ I (14 November 1177) and that of Saladin's defeat at Ramleh as 1 Jumâdâ II (25 November), whereas Ibn el-Athîr mentions only Jumâdâ I in both entries and gives no precise date for the first.

The succeeding account of events in Aleppo (XI, 294-295 [I, 631-663]) again follows the order and the details of

Barq. 23^r-25^r, even to the extent of describing the torture of Gumushtegîn at Hârim in general terms instead of the precisions of his own earlier account in the *History of the Atâbegs* [II, 2, 325]. It is noteworthy that he ends this paragraph with the words 'When the Franks saw this, they left Hamâh and marched to Hârim in First Jumâdâ, as we shall relate.' But in fact he had given this relation on the previous page of the *Kâmil*, whereas in the *Barq* it follows immediately afterwards.

The only other event relating to Syria mentioned by Ibn el-Athîr in this year is an unconnected narrative of an unsuccessful raid by an undefined body of Franks on the territories of Hims (XI, 297 [I, 632]). The passage is taken entirely from a despatch to Baghdad, extracts from which are given in *Barq*, 43^v ff. The episode is mentioned on fol. 44^v and is couched in similar terms. But Ibn el-Athîr, finding it in this isolated form, failed to observe that it related to the same occasion as the abortive attack on Hamâh ('As they were passing by the frontier district of Hims,' in the words of the despatch), and the event itself is confirmed by William of Tyre (XXI, 19; trans., II, 425).

A. H. 574. The brief narratives on events in Syria which occupy nearly the whole entry for the year (Frankish attack on Hamâh, rebellion of Ibn el-Muqaddam and siege of Baalbek, other Frankish raids) all reproduce the substance of 'Imâdeddîn's narratives. It is arguable that they might have been derived from official circulars and other sources, however, and the very general terms which Ibn el-Athîr uses do not allow of any proof of direct dependence.

A. H. 575. The report of the battle at Merj 'Uyûn (9 June 1179) is certainly based on 'Imâdeddîn's account; the interpolated remark on the amount of Balian's ransom (XI, 301 [I, 636]) is taken from *Barq* III, 131 (Abû Shâma, II, 8 [IV, 199]), where it is one item in a longer list. The special attention given to the exploits of Farrukhshâh also reflects 'Imâdeddîn's special paragraph on the same subject (fol. 136) and quotes the same verse of poetry. The following account of the destruction of the Templars' castle at Jacob's Ford might have been taken from an official circular, but so closely follows the *Barq* that it is difficult to assume any other source, notably in the detail of the amir Chauli's appeal to Saladin to allow him to try the fortune of a *coup de main*, which is in *Barq*, 141^r, though missing from Abû Shâma's abridgement (II, 11). Ibn el-Athîr's reference at the end of his narrative to the large number of poems composed on the subject is certainly inspired by the poems (four in all) quoted in the *Barq*, and the verses which he cites are taken from the first two of these four poems.

The immediately following narrative of the battle between Taqîeddîn and the Seljuq Sultan of Konia (XI, 303 [I, 639]) is again obviously derived from 'Imâdeddîn. The latter begins his narrative with the remark that Taqîeddîn was absent from the operations at Jacob's Ford for this reason, a remark which Ibn el-Athir puts at the end; and a

still more definite indication is found in the figures given for the Seljuq army. 'Imâdeddîn (*Barq*, III, 138^r = Abû Shâma, II, 9*) puts it at 20,000 men; the parallel narrative of Ibn Abî Taiy at '3,000 cavalrymen' (Abû Shâma, *loc. cit.*); Ibn el-Athîr says 'a force said to have been 20,000 men.' In this instance the hypothesis of an official despatch can be excluded, since 'Imâdeddîn reproduces also the text of the despatch which was sent to Mosul on this occasion (*Barq*, 138^v-139^r), and in this document the Seljuq army is put at 30,000 men.

In the *miscellanea* with which, as usual, Ibn el-Athîr ends the events of the year, he includes (304-305 [I, 640]) a statement that Saladin, on Tûrânshâh's offer to exchange Baalbak for Alexandria, in the month of Dhu'l-Qa'da (i.e., April 1180) gave it to his nephew Farrukhshâh, who thereafter raided the lands of the Franks as far as Safed. He has here, as frequently, combined two passages in one, but the first one is a year out. Tûrânshâh left for Egypt at the end of Dhu'l-Qa'da 574 (May 1179) (*Barq*, 120^v-121^r =. bû Shâma, II, 6^3). Farrukhshâh's appointment to Baalbek was made in 575 and his raid on Safed in Dhu'l-Qa'da of that year ('Imâdeddîn dates it precisely to the 18th = 15 April; cf. Abû Shâma, II, 15*).

It will be seen from this summary that, in regard to the history of Syria during these three years, there is no fact mentioned in Ibn el-Athîr's chronicle which is not in 'Imâdeddîn's work, except for the misstatement relating to the attack on Hamâh in November 1177 and for a small personal reminiscence of seeing a letter of Saladin's (related in XI, 293). The only thing, in fact, which prevents us from asserting outright that every one of these narratives was derived from the *Barq* is Ibn el-Athîr's invariable habit of rewriting the content of the paragraphs which he uses in his own language, which excludes the final argument of identity of linguistic expression.

A. H. 578. The extant portion of Volume v of the *Barq* opens with Saladin's march into Upper Mesopotamia in the late summer of 1182. 'Imâdeddîn makes it clear that he had come north with the genuine intention of attacking Aleppo and that only after his arrival there were his plans unexpectedly changed by Geukburi's representations. Ibn el-Athîr (XI, 317 [I, 653-654]), on the other hand, declares that Geukburi had been in communication with Saladin during the abortive attack on Beirut in August and that the subsequent advance on Aleppo was a feint. The reason for his substitution of this version for the firsthand statement of 'Imâdeddîn is not clear. It may be that it was the version current in Mosul and that for that reason he preferred it, but it rather closely resembles a feature which is repeatedly found in his work, to be discussed later. The operations in Mesopotamia are described in both sources to much the same effect, Ibn el-Athîr's only addition being a small personal anecdote relating to the siege of Edessa. 'Imâdeddîn's narrative is elaborately ornamented, and Abû Shâma in his résumé reduced every page to a single line (II, 32*), but in doing so he omitted the reference to the siege of Edessa which is found in the original (fol. 20^r).

Thus, for the second time in these abstracts, what would have appeared, from Abû Shâma's abridgement, to be supplements by Ibn el-Athîr to 'Imâdeddîn's narratives, are seen to have been equally parts of the original text.

With the investment of Mosul Ibn el-Athîr is on his own ground, but it must be admitted that his narrative (XI, 319-320) makes no very favorable impression. His patriotism expends itself in trivial and imaginative anecdotes (which the editors of the *Recueil*, I, 656-657, mostly omit), to the exclusion of the general factors in the situation which are, on the contrary, so well brought out in the few lines of his fellow-citizen Bahâeddîn. His summary of the negotiations with Saladin, however, agrees, at least as to their outcome, with the account given by 'Imâdeddîn (*Barq*, V, 11-16), who was the actual negotiator on Saladin's behalf.

The immediately following narrative of operations in the Jezîra (XI, 321-323*) adds no positive information to the statements in the *Barq* (17 ff., 49 ff.), but, as in his account of the siege of Mosul, Ibn el Athîr introduces some anecdotal details and general reflections which have little or no historical validity. It should be remembered that it is one of the common forms of Arabic historiography to present a situation in terms of imaginary conversations or statements by the persons concerned, and there is no justification whatever for regarding them as records of actual events. Ibn el-Athîr carries this 'romantic' technique to excess, but 'Imâdeddîn too occasionally resorts to it, sometimes successfully, sometimes misleadingly, as, for example, in representing what he supposes to have been the policy or attitude of the Crusaders at a given moment.

The naval operations in the Red Sea called out by Reginald's exploits were certainly announced by despatches to all parts of the Muslim world. Ibn el-Athîr's statement (XI, 323 [I, 658]) combines, apparently, 'Imâdeddîn's preliminary account (V, 42^v = Abû Shâma, II, 35 [IV, 230 ff.]) with his despatch on Saladin's behalf to Baghdad (45^v-46^v = Abû Shâma, II, 37 [IV, 233-235]). The death of Farrukhshâh and his replacement as governor of Damascus by Ibn el-Muqaddam (XI, 324 [I, 659]) are, of course, described at much greater length in the *Barq* (36^r ff., 46^r).

A. H. 579. This opens with Saladin's siege and capture of Âmid (XI, 324-325*), to which 'Imâdeddîn had devoted one of the most finished sections of the *Barq* (49^r-65^r; Abû Shâma, II, 37-38*). There can be no reasonable doubt that this is the source of Ibn el-Athîr's narrative, which diverges from it in only one detail. In order to explain Saladin's unexpected success, Ibn el'Athîr, somewhat lamely, blames the governor's cupidity, in direct contradiction to the express statements of 'Imâdeddîn (fol. 60^r). The artificial nature of this device is thrown into greater relief by the fact that only a page or two later Ibn el-Athîr uses it again to explain away Saladin's success in capturing Aleppo.

The account of the capture of Tell Khâlid and 'Aintâb (XI, 325*) follows closely the lines of the *Barq* and the despatch of the kâdî el-Fâdil quoted there (V, 77^v-78^r). The immediately following account (*loc. cit.* [I, 660]) of the capture of a crusading galley and the repulse of a Frankish raid on Egypt is obviously taken from the despatches quoted in *Barq*, 105^r ff. (Abû Shâma, II, 47 [IV, 239]). The narrative of the capture of Aleppo (XI, 327 [I, 661]) contains little more than the bare facts and some resentful jibes at its prince, 'Imâdeddîn Zangi. But the following story of a prediction of the capture of Jerusalem (omitted in *Recueil*) comes straight out of the *Barq* (cf. Abû Shâma, II, 45*). Ibn el-Athîr then quotes two phrases taken from a despatch—not, however, from a public despatch, but from a private despatch sent by the kâdî el-Fâdil to el-'Âdil, Saladin's brother and governor in Egypt. Furthermore, by a method familiar to propagandists in all ages, he isolates one of these sentences from its context and interprets it in a manner which the quotation of the context would immediately show to be false.[4]

The story of the death of Saladin's brother appended to the narrative of the capture of Aleppo (XI, 328*) is also based upon 'Imâdeddîn's section in *Barq*, fol. 96^v (cf. Abû Shâma, II, 44*). Ibn el-Athîr has, however, worked it up in a more 'romantic' manner, with the dubious addition that Saladin had intended to give Aleppo to him. The following transfer of Hârim is again related on the same lines as in the *Barq* (89^v = Abû Shâma, II, 47 [IV, 238]), where it is described mainly by quotations from despatches.

The next entry is crucial for an estimate of Ibn el-Athîr's trustworthiness. After relating the transfer of their allegiance to Saladin by several vassals of Mosul, he briefly relates (XI, 230*) the negotiations which followed at Damascus between the envoys of the Caliphate, of Mosul, and Saladin. This episode is handled at length in the *Barq* (127^r-132^v), since 'Imâdeddîn played a leading part in it. By an exceptional chance, we have also a statement from the other side, since Bahâeddîn was a member of the Mosul delegation. His brief narrative (Schultens, 57 [III, 78-79]) confirms the accuracy and precision of 'Imâdeddîn's account. Nevertheless, Ibn el-Athîr substituted for the real point at issue a totally different formula, in order to present Saladin as unalterably hostile to any accommodation with Mosul.[5]

The year ended with an expedition to Beisan (end of September) in an endeavor to bring the Franks to battle, and an equally fruitless siege of Kerak. The former is described by 'Imâdeddîn in two parallel despatches (111^v-116^v; Abû Shâma, II, 50-51 [IV, 244-248]), of which Ibn el-Athîr's narrative (XI, 230 [I, 663]) is an abstract; the latter is described directly (118^r-119^r, 126^r, interrupted by the appointments of el-'Âdil to Aleppo and Taqîeddîn to Egypt, with their respective patents of appointment). A detail included in Ibn el-Athîr's narrative (XI, 231 [I, 664]), namely the excuse of insufficient siege equipment, clearly indicates his source, for it is taken directly from the narrative in the *Barq* (f. 126^r), although omitted by Abû Shâma (II, 51 [IV, 248]).

The extant portions of the *Barq* end at this point, but the preceding analysis is sufficient to show: (i) that it is the principal source used by Ibn el-Athîr for his accounts of Saladin's activities, which are, indeed, little more than short paraphrases of its main sections; (ii) that where Ibn el-Athîr supplies details not found in Abû Shâma's abstracts, they are nevertheless generally found in the original text; (iii) that Ibn el-Athîr occasionally changes the statements of his source or perverts their meaning out of hostility to Saladin. In the light of these conclusions, it is now possible to compare Ibn el-Athîr's narratives for the remaining years with Abû Shâma's abstracts from the *Barq,* and to estimate what value they have as independent historical sources. This is obviously too lengthy a task to be undertaken within the limits of an article, but from a number of examples it may be justifiable to reach some fairly definite results.

In regard to Saladin's early years in Egypt, before the death of Nûreddîn, i.e., from 1169 to 1174, Ibn el-Athîr has often reproduced in the *Kâmil* the relevant paragraphs of his earlier *History of the Atâbegs of Mosul.* These sections are presumably independent of 'Imâdeddîn's works, but like his previously-quoted independent section they are scrappy and anecdotal. 'Imâdeddîn, on the other hand, was at this time one of Nûreddîn's secretaries at Damascus, and of course well informed on Saladin's activities. His admiration of Nûreddîn was as sincere as that of Ibn el-Athîr, and at this period least of all can his statements be open to the charge of excessive partiality for Saladin. It is the more surprising, therefore, that although 'Imâdeddîn differs on many points from Ibn el-Athîr (notably in regard to the manner and date of the substitution of the 'Abbâsid for the Fâtimid allegiance in Egypt in 1171), his narratives should have been universally neglected by modern historians. Even Ibn el-Athîr himself did better than this; we shall see later that he did introduce, though with considerable adjustments, materials from 'Imâdeddîn into his history of these years, adapting them to his earlier imaginative and colorful picture of an ambitious Saladin thwarting Nûreddîn's plans for the Holy War.[6]

Before looking into these, however, we may examine Ibn el-Athîr's narratives of the two campaigns of Saladin against Aleppo in 1175 and 1176, which offer several interesting indications. There was, apparently, no account of these campaigns (in which the armies of Mosul were twice defeated) in the *History of the Atâbegs.* In each campaign Saladin was attacked by Assassins; Ibn el-Athîr's accounts of these two assaults (XI, 277, 285 [I, 618, 623-624]) are recognizably transcribed, in spite of the verbal paraphrases, from 'Imâdeddîn's narratives (Abû Shâma, I, 240* 258* cf. the parallel transcription of the first by Ibn Abî Taiy, I, 239). But it was only to be expected that the circumstances of the two battles in which Saladin routed the forces of Mosul would be presented by Ibn el-Athîr somewhat differently in detail, which is, indeed, carried to the last degree of absurdity by the assertion (XI, 283*) that in the second battle only one man was killed out of the two armies.

In an appendix to this narrative (omitted in the *Recueil*) Ibn el-Athîr refers directly for the one and only time to 'Imâdeddîn: 'El-'Imâd, the *Kâtib,* in the book of *el-Barq el-Shâmî* on the history of the reign of Saladin, has stated that Saifeddîn's army in this engagement included 20,000 cavalry.' That this statement is absurd he proceeds to demonstrate, very justly, on the basis of the army records at Mosul. 'Imâdeddîn does in fact share, though in a relatively moderate degree, the tendency of most mediaeval chroniclers to magnify the figures of opposing armies, and we have already seen (p. 62 above) an instance in which Ibn el-Athîr puts an implied question-mark to a similar estimate of his. In this instance, however, 'Imâdeddîn may be partially excused; he did not assert that Saifeddîn's army was 20,000 strong, but stated more cautiously that, as Saladin advanced northwards, 'the report came to us that they numbered 20,000 cavalry, exclusive of the train and the reinforcements behind them' (Abû Shâma, I, 255, ll. 1-2*). But apart from the controversy, Ibn el-Athîr here gives direct proof of his utilization of the *Barq,* even though he introduces it only by a casual reference—which is (as is well known) the most by which he ever acknowledges his literary debts; and it is not fanciful to discern in his remarks a certain pleasure at being able to find 'Imâdeddîn out for once in a misstatement of fact.

For the rest, it can be said generally that, apart from comment, there is little in Ibn el-Athîr's chronicle relating to the history of Saladin in these two years or in any of the other years not covered by the extant volumes of the *Barq,* which is not found in a fuller and more satisfactory presentation in Abû Shâma's extracts. We have already seen that in a number of cases Ibn el-Athîr by no means confined himself to shortening and paraphrasing 'Imâdeddîn's narratives, but arbitrarily rearranged them when it suited his purpose to do so. The comparison of the *Kâmil* with *The Two Gardens* (and with the *Fath* for the years after 1187) leaves little doubt that the same explanation is to be given in several passages where the two sources diverge in statements of fact.

Two particularly notable instances of this are furnished by the narratives of Saladin's siege of Mosul in 1185 and of Tyre in 1187. As related by Ibn el-Athîr, 'Izzeddîn sent out the ladies of the Zangid family to intercede with Saladin on his approach to the city in June 1185, but he refused their intercession and began to prosecute the siege (XI, 337*). 'Imâdeddîn, on the other hand, definitely places this incident towards the end of the conflict with Mosul when, after temporarily interrupting the siege, Saladin returned to Mosul in November of the same year (Abû Shâma, II, 64*). Both historians were at Mosul when these events took place, and the conflict of evidence seems to be absolute. But there can be no question that 'Imâdeddîn's narrative is the more natural and consistent in itself and with the circumstances, whereas Ibn el-Athîr, having transferred it in order to represent Saladin in the worst possible light, has rather lamely to explain away an action so extreme: 'It was not out of any weakness that they were sent, or inability to defend Mosul, but he sent them out of a desire to prevent the evil of war by a better course of action.' Moreover, 'Imâdeddîn asserts that in response to their appeal Saladin, though unable to grant all that they requested, agreed to accept the mediation of 'Imâdeddîn Zangi of Sinjâr, through which the conflict was in fact ultimately settled.

The second instance is still more obvious. In his account of the siege of Tyre in the winter of 1187, as of all the events in Palestine during that year, there can be no doubt that Ibn el-Athîr's source was 'Imâdeddîn's *Fath*. But when he presents the reasons for the discontinua ce of the siege (XI, 368 [I, 709-711]) he deliberately inverts the paragraphs in the *Fath* relating to Saladin's consultations with the amîrs and to his withdrawal (cf. Abû Shâma, II, 119-120 [IV, 343-344]). The result is that Saladin is represented as having taken the decision to give up the siege before the mutiny of the amîrs, and their action in refusing to fight and withdrawing their men thus becomes an absurdity. And Ibn el-Athîr, not content with distorting the facts and presenting a confused and inconsistent picture, proceeds to administer severe censure upon Saladin for an action for which his own fellow-soldiers of Mosul were largely responsible.

In analyzing Volume V of the *Barq*, two instances were found in which Ibn el-Athîr deliberately altered the facts related by 'Imâdeddîn. The total number of similar cases is fairly large, and two flagrant examples may be adduced here. The first is the passage relating to the relief of the garrison of Acre during the winter of 1190 (XII, 35-36 [II, 1, 32-33]). This paragraph is in its entirety a transcript of one in the *Fath* (cf. Abû Shâma, II, 181 [IV, 519-520]), and some of its details are not even fully intelligible without the aid of the fuller narrative of the *Fath*. 'Imâdeddîn, it should be noted, is critical of the wisdom of Saladin's action on this occasion, as on some other occasions, but plainly describes the vigor with which he conducted the operation and the energy with which he spurred on his agents and officers to greater efforts. All of this last passage is omitted by Ibn el-Athîr, who substitutes: 'Added to this was Saladin's inertia, and his throwing of all the responsibility upon his lieutenants.'[7]

The second is still more remarkable. On his return from the East in 1186 Saladin stopped for a time at Hims, where his nephew Nâsireddîn ibn Shîrkûh had just died, leaving a minor son. Saladin confirmed the boy in possession of his father's fiefs, under guardianship of an officer of Shîrkûh's old regiment, the Asadîya. 'We had an inventory made of Nâsireddîn's treasures (says 'Imâdeddîn, quoted by Abû Shâma, II, 69*), and we divided up his inheritance; the Sultan's sister el-Husâmîya, the wife of Nâsireddîn, was entitled to one-eighth, and the remainder was divided between his daughter and his son. The estate, in lands, specie, and furnishings, was beyond reckoning and in any case well over one million dinars. The Sultan did not give it a glance, but turned it all over to the lawful heirs.' Ibn el-Athîr begins his account of the episode (XI, 341*) by relating an intrigue on the part of Nâsireddîn with some of the Damascus troops during Saladin's illness, followed by his own sudden death. Then, without

mentioning his authorities, he proceeds: 'And they say—but the responsibility rests with them—that Saladin instigated a man called el-Nâsih b. el-'Amîd, of Damascus, who came to him, joined his drinking-party, and gave him a poisoned cup. . . . When he died Saladin gave the fief to his son Shîrkûh, who was twelve years old. Nâsireddîn left a vast fortune in moneys, horses and goods, and Saladin came to Hims, inventoried the estate, and took most of it for himself, leaving only what was of no use.' Finally the story is backed up by a piquant anonymous trailer: 'And I was told that. . . .' It may be observed that this is the one and only time in which Ibn el-Athîr finds an opportunity to charge Saladin with the practice of assassination and appropriation which features so prominently in the political annals of the age. He made the most of it, and the latter part of the story, at least, was repeated in almost all subsequent biographical notices of Saladin, even those of panegyrists like Ibn Khallikân and Tâjeddîn el-Subkî.[8] Indeed, so successful has Ibn el-Athîr's invention been in this instance that even the Baron de Slane, in translating the relevant paragraph of Bahâeddîn's *Life* (III, 87), rebuked the faithful kâdî for the 'blind admiration' of Saladin which had led him to conceal, in compiling his book, an event first published to the world in such dubious circumstances some years later.

In this last instance, it may be said that Ibn el-Athîr did not simply alter 'Imâdeddîn's narrative, but related a totally different version, which does not depend in any way upon 'Imâdeddîn. Yet it is set in a framework of chronology and events which is entirely derived from the *Barq,* and it is inconceivable that Ibn el-Athîr was unaware of 'Imâdeddîn's statement, made in the first person. Thus the account he gives must be regarded as a deliberate denial of 'Imâdeddîn's statement, and the substitution of another statement derived from sources which he does not care to name, with the object of making Saladin out to be no better than any other prince of his time.

Often, however, Ibn el-Athîr's distortions seem to be evolved out of passages and phrases from 'Imâdeddîn by combination or interpretation. An example can be found in his statement already referred to, attributing the surrender of Aleppo to the avarice of its prince 'Imâdeddîn Zangî (XI, 327 [I, 661]). Ibn el-Athîr expresses this, as usual, in the pictorial terms of an argument between the prince and his troops. But the basis for it appears to be 'Imâdeddîn's statement in the *Barq* (V, 84^V) that the prince 'found that he was paying out 30,000 dinars a month to the troops and amîrs, and if the siege were prolonged without hope of success he would lose all the gain and become utterly bankrupt,' after which calculation he opened negotiations with Saladin.

A single example does not, of course, constitute a proof, and owing to the loss of most of the *Barq* it may be difficult to detect other cases. In this very instance the passage quoted above is omitted from Abû Shâma's abstract (II, 42*). But a similar case is probably to be seen in Ibn el-Athîr's account of the Crusaders' siege of Damietta in

November-December 1169 (XI, 231 [I, 569]), although in this instance the 'correction' has not been made on the narrative of 'Imâdeddin, since the same account is given in the *History of the Atâbegs* [II, 2, 259]. According to this story, Nûreddin, on Saladin's appeal to him and representations that he could not risk sending his own troops to Damietta in view of the danger of a rising in Cairo, 'sent troops to him in successive contingents, one after another.' On the other hand, 'Imâdeddin (who, it may be recalled, was then in Damascus in Nûreddins service) states that 'Nûreddin sent a powerful army by sea . . . which arrived in the middle of Rabî I [*ca* 10 December], a week before the withdrawal of the Franks' (Abû Shâma, I, 181 [IV, 151⁹]). At the same time, he relates, Saladin remained in Cairo and 'kept sending reinforcement after reinforcement.' Both narratives are presumably based upon a circular despatch issued by Nûreddin, and the most likely explanation of the divergence is that Ibn el-Athîr transferred the statement about Saladin and applied it to Nûreddin, in order to draw a striking picture of Saladin's dependence upon him. William of Tyre (XX, 15-16; trans., II, 363-367), it will be noted, agrees, as usual, with 'Imâdeddin against Ibn el-Athîr.

A clearer instance of 'reinterpretation' occurs a few pages later (XI, 258 [I, 593]), when Ibn el-Athîr relates that—after failing to cooperate with Nûreddin in the siege of Kerak in September 1171—Saladin withdrew from a combined expedition to Kerak for the second time in July 1183, on receiving news of Nûreddin's approach. According to 'Imâdeddin, whose account is supported by the terms of an official report on the operations submitted by Saladin to Nûreddin, the purpose of Saladin's campaign was to drive out the bedouins who were serving the Franks of Kerak as guides, and thus to render communications between Egypt and Syria more secure (Abû Shâma, I, 206 [IV, 156-157]). This statement is again entirely confirmed by William of Tyre (XX, 28; trans., II, 389-390). When he wrote the *History of the Atâbegs* Ibn el-Athîr had no knowledge of this incident; and it can hardly be doubted that, finding it in 'Imâdeddin's work, he used it to build up his story of Saladin's persistent refusal to cooperate with Nûreddin in the Holy War, without regard to the fact that only a few lines earlier he had stated that at this very time Nûreddin was engaged in a campaign in Anatolia.

One final example should be sufficient. Ibn el-Athîr (XI, 347 [I, 674]) relates briefly the events following the death of Baldwin IV and the split between Raymond and Guy, leading up to the alliance between Raymond and Saladin. This is taken without any doubt from 'Imâdeddin's paragraph in the *Fath* (17-18), which concludes with the words: 'And he [Raymond] encouraged the Sultan's determination to attack them so that he might restore the kingdom to him' (Abû Shâma, II, 74 [IV, 257-258] omits this phrase). In place of these words Ibn el-Athîr substitutes: 'And Saladin promised to aid him and to strive to attain for him all that he desired, and guaranteed to make him future king of all the Franks.'

If the preceding argument is correct, the conclusion to which it points is rather a disconcerting one. Instead of a group of contemporary, firsthand, and largely independent sources for the history of Saladin on the Arabic side, we have, until Bahâeddin joined Saladin in 1188, only one major firsthand source, supplemented by fragmentary additions from other sources, the most important of which is Ibn Abî Taiy. Still worse, even of that major source, two-thirds have come down to us only in the form of Abû Shâma's abstract, to which we are indebted also for nearly all that has survived of the histories of Ibn Abî Taiy.

We are left therefore with two questions to answer. Firstly, how far can we rely upon the veracity and, so to speak, 'historical conscience' of our sole major source, the Secretary 'Imâdeddin? It has already been pointed out that when the verbiage is stripped away from his narratives, his statement of events is sober and free from extravagance. But it might be expected that he was to a considerable extent biassed in his statements by his admiration for Saladin. On this, it is possible to make two observations. While Ibn Abî Taiy is open to the suspicion of denigrating Nûreddin, and Ibn el-Athîr is certainly guilty of denigrating Saladin, 'Imâdeddin seems to have served both with an equal loyalty and shows no partiality between them. The second observation is that it would be a serious error to imagine that the rhetorical elaboration of the *Barq* is directed to mere eulogy of Saladin and fulsome flattery. There is scarcely a sentence, even in its loftiest flights, of direct panegyric of Saladin himself. Certainly 'Imâdeddin shows a deep admiration for Saladin, but his greatness appears wholly as a corollary from the facts themselves. Throughout the *Barq* he is presented in human and realistic terms, even more than in Bahâeddin's biography. While Bahâeddin's feeling for Saladin is that of a kindred spirit, the impression left by the *Barq* as a whole is that it is the work of a trained and self-controlled civil servant, familiar with the ways of Sultans and other officials, accustomed to dealing with them and, if need be, managing them, setting down their actions with the precision of his craft, and with all his fertility of verbal imagination never swept off his feet.

There is also another argument for 'Imâddedin's accuracy of statement which is less open to the charge of resting upon subjective impressions. When his narratives can be compared with other firsthand statements, whether those of Williamof Tyre, Ernoul, and other Latin chroniclers of the Third Crusade, or those in which Bahâeddin also writes from firsthand knowledge, there is an astonishing degree of identity in general substance, which often extends even into details. It is fortunate, therefore, that when we are reduced to a single original source for the greater part of Saladin's public career that source is both exceptionally authoritative in regard to its author's knowledge of the facts and trustworthy in regard to his presentation of them.

The second question is raised by the relation of Abû Shâma's abstract to the original text of the *Barq*. Since we have to rely on this for about two-thirds of the entire work,

Palestine would be conquered and divided, with the Byzantines receiving Jerusalem and the maritime cities except Ascalon. Asia Minor, if taken, would belong to the Eastern Empire, as far as Antioch and Armenia. In return for such assistance and territory, Andronicus doubtless promised aid to the Saracens in their struggle with the Latins of Syria. Saladin's exact response to these suggestions is unknown, but would seem to have been generally favorable; probably all territorial concessions were made dependent on the Byzantines' performance of their part of the treaty. Before Saladin's reply reached Constantinople, however, Andronicus was overthrown (12 September 1185) by a populace resentful over his failures in the Norman war.[2]

The demand of Andronicus, "that because he was emperor, he [Saladin] should do him homage,"[3] must have seemed both ridiculous and unacceptable to the ruler of Egypt and Syria. The weakness of the empire at that moment was everywhere manifest; not only were the Normans at Thessalonica, but also the Aegean was harried by Latin corsairs, Cyprus was in open and successful revolt, and the Turks and Hungarians were raiding across the frontiers. Saladin's power, on the other hand, was expanding, and his imminent triumph over the crusader states was perceptible to all. The subordination of the Arab world to the Byzantine, at this point, was unthinkable; yet the demand for it represented a traditional Byzantine view that for the emperor, God's earthly representative, to treat with anyone else on a basis of equality was inconceivable. That Andronicus was indulging in more than a rhetorical flourish is shown by his demand for Jerusalem and the coast of Palestine. Saladin apparently rejected the Byzantine claim to suzerainty.

Saladin's response to Andronicus was received by the new emperor, Isaac II Angelus, who, with the Normans threatening the capital itself, was delighted to find an ally. He confirmed the treaty (presumably as revised by Saladin) in a chrysobull and summoned his brother Alexius back from Saladin's court.[4]

Alexius Angelus was still a guest of the sultan, as Isaac had formerly been. When, about 1186, Isaac recalled his brother, he set out, but as rumor of the Byzantine-Muslim alliance had already reached the crusader states, when he was passing through Acre the count of Tripoli seized and imprisoned him. During his confinement the Pisans assisted him with loans, which he later neglected to repay.[5] On learning of this action, Isaac wrote to Saladin urging him to attack the Latin states in order to secure Alexius' release. In the spring of 1187 the Byzantines sent a fleet to attack Cyprus. In the Holy Land, this armada was interpreted as naval support for Saladin's offensive, but the Byzantine forces were defeated on Cyprus by Isaac Comnenus and the fleet was routed by the Sicilian Admiral Margaritone. In the meantime Saladin, motivated by Latin injuries rather than by Isaac's encouragements, attacked the kingdom of Jerusalem, capturing the capital and most of the coastal cities. At the fall of Acre, Alexius Angelus

was released from his prison and returned to Constantinople on a Genoese ship; in 1201 he had still not paid his fare.[6]

In one respect Isaac Angelus' friendship may have furthered Saladin's conquest of the Holy Land. The early surrender of Jerusalem was brought about by the knowledge that, out of hatred for the Latins, the Greek Orthodox residents (in Syria commonly called Melkites) were ready to betray the city. The Muslim ruler was in communication with them through one of his aides, Joseph Batit, a Melkite born in Jerusalem, who arranged for the opening of the gates by his coreligionists. The Latin leaders, aware of the Melkites' disaffection, and perhaps of the plot itself, made haste to yield the city. There is no known or necessary connection between Isaac Angelus and the Melkites' actions, but it may be noted that Saladin's alliance with the Byzantines involved the conversion of the existing Latin churches in the Holy Land to the Greek rite; the Melkites of Jerusalem were more than likely to be informed of Saladin's promise and they clearly had no love for their Frankish neighbors.[7]

Saladin, rejoicing in his successes over the crusaders, sent Isaac an embassy to announce his good fortune. As was customary in oriental diplomacy, the ambassadors brought splendid gifts for the Byzantine emperor: an elephant, fifty Turkish saddles, a jar of balsam, a hundred Turkish bows with quivers and arrows, a hundred captive Byzantines from Greece, a thousand and fifty Turkish or Turkoman horses, and a quantity of valuable spices. Isaac was delighted with the news and the gifts, housed the envoys in a splendid palace in the center of Constantinople, and renewed the alliance. He was particularly gratified by his brother's release from the crusaders' prison.[8]

Isaac replied to Saladin with a similar display of splendid gifts: four hundred breastplates, four thousand iron lances, five thousand swords (all of which arms he had taken in his defeat of William II's invading army), twelve samite cloths, two golden cups, two imperial robes, and three hundred beaver pelts; he made gifts of samite and imperial vestments to Saladin's brother and three sons. Most important of all, however, the envoys Sovestot (Sebastos?), Aspion, and the aged Arabic interpreter Constantius brought the sultan a gold crown and Isaac's declaration: "I send you this because in my opinion you now are and shall be rightfully a king, with my assistance and God willing,"[9] a symbol and words whereby (however unrealistically) the emperor sought to make evident his suzerainty over Saladin.

The envoys sailed to Acre, where on 6 January 1188 Saladin, abandoning the siege of Tyre, held a full court for them and in the presence of his sons, nobles, and officials confirmed anew the alliance. The messengers were especially eloquent in thanking Saladin for releasing Alexius Angelus: "Through you he has been saved and freed from the hands of the Latins, who held him in prison on your account."[10] Saladin inquired of the envoys concerning conditions in the empire, the war with the Vlachs, and the wars of other (evidently Western) rulers. The most important news which the Byzantines brought was that a new crusade was being summoned in the West to rescue the Holy Sepulchre.[11]

After some delay, during which Saladin probably received confirmation from elsewhere of the gathering of the Third Crusade, he determined to bind Isaac more closely to him in order to secure his support against any part of the crusade which might pass through the empire. He therefore sent back the Byzantine embassy, together with his own ambassadors charged to negotiate such an agreement. His gifts were more numerous than before: twenty Latin chargers, large boxes of gems and balsam, three hundred strings of jewels, a chest full of aloes, a hundred musk-sacs, twenty thousand bezants, a baby elephant, a musk-deer, an ostrich, five leopards, thirty quintals of pepper, numerous other spices, a huge silver jar of poisoned wine, and great quantities of poisoned flour and grain. These allegedly deadly foods (one whiff of the wine was said to have slain a Latin prisoner on whom it was tested) were apparently for distribution to Western crusaders passing through Byzantine lands; the chronicles of Frederick Barbarossa's crusade contain a number of stories concerning Byzantine attempts to destroy the Germans by such means.[12]

Among Saladin's gifts on this occasion also was a *maumeria,* which the emperor was to set up and cause to be venerated for the honor of the Saracens, as he had promised. The Latin word *maumeria* is clearly a rendering of the French *Mahomerie,* something connected with the Muslim religion; it seems to have been a *minbar* or pulpit with steps leading up to it. Throughout the ensuing negotiations with Isaac, Saladin's concern for maintenance of Islamic worship and the fittings of the mosque in Constantinople was manifest, as a counterpart to Isaac's desire to have the Greek rite practiced in the churches of the Holy Land. On this occasion, however, Saladin's pulpit did not reach Constantinople; the Genoese captured the ship taking this so-called "idol" to the Byzantine capital, and brought it to Tyre. Because the pulpit formed a concrete piece of evidence for the alliance between the emperor and the sultan, Conrad of Montferrat (who ruled in Tyre) circulated an announcement of its capture throughout Europe, and an embassy sent by Philip II of France to Constantinople incorporated the news in an information bulletin designed to encourage recruitment for the forthcoming crusade. In the autumn of 1188 Isaac's opposition to the crusade became public knowledge in Western Europe.[13]

By 20 September 1188, when Conrad of Montferrat wrote his letter reporting the pulpit's capture, he was sufficiently well-informed to be able to outline the principal provisions of the alliance. Saladin had turned over all churches in conquered Palestine to the Orthodox, and Isaac was to accept Saladin's form of Muslim worship in the Constantinopolitan mosque. In connection with the siege of Antioch, Isaac was to send a hundred galleys to assist Saladin,

so Conrad declared; this allegation may reflect a real promise of naval assistance, or be a mere recollection of the Byzantine fleet sent against Cyprus in 1187. To Saladin, however, opposition to the impending Third Crusade was vital: not only did Isaac, at his behest, seize and imprison Latins in Constantinople who took the Cross, but he also agreed to oppose any army which tried to pass through his dominions. In return Saladin promised to give him the entire Holy Land, a prize for which the Byzantines had struggled throughout the twelfth century, and for which Andronicus had also negotiated. The French embassy's report from Constantinople, written shortly after Conrad's letter, was able to add that the Muslim envoys were received in the emperor's palace with more honor than was accorded anyone else. The embassy also asserted that on the very day their messenger set out, Isaac ordered the expulsion of all Latins from the empire; if this proclamation, which is unconfirmed elsewhere, actually was issued, it was shortly rescinded or modified, for during the Third Crusade the presence of Venetian traders, Frankish mercenaries, and Latin civil servants in the Eastern Empire is well attested. Yet by imprisoning would-be crusaders in Constantinople, Isaac openly committed himself to a policy of hostility to the Western effort to recover Jerusalem.[14]

Whether the final terms of the military alliance were concluded by the embassy Saladin sent in 1188, or by one the following year, cannot be precisely determined. Emissaries of the Saracen ruler were in Constantinople in June 1189, at the moment of crisis in Isaac's relations with Frederick Barbarossa. When in 1188 the German emperor decided to participate in the Third Crusade, he announced to Isaac his intention of passing through the Byzantine Empire on the way to Syria. Isaac's envoys agreed to allow his passage, furnish markets for the crusaders, and make provision for transport across the Straits; at no time, however, did they ask for hostages to ensure the good behavior of the Germans. This omission, contrary to previous Byzantine practice, suggests that even then Isaac was meditating hostile action. Not only was he already deeply committed to Saladin, but he also feared lest Barbarossa's forces attack his capital to avenge the numerous affronts Manuel had offered their master and also the Latin Massacre of 1182. Shortly before Barbarossa set out (11 May 1189), he despatched the bishop of Münster with other leading German magnates to announce to Isaac his forthcoming arrival in Constantinople. About the middle of June, this embassy arrived and soon was imprisoned, probably at the insistence of Saladin's representatives; in any case, the envoys' horses and other possessions were given to the Saracens. By unlawfully seizing ambassadors, Isaac definitively committed himself against Barbarossa and his crusade.[15]

At the same moment that Isaac seized the bishop of Münster's embassy, he sent envoys to Saladin, evidently to confirm the alliance; they reached him in August-September 1189 at Merj 'Ayun in Syria. In addition to the terms already known to the Latins, a clause regarding a joint attack on Cyprus was included at this time or not long afterwards. It is probable that a future Byzantine subjugation of the sultanate of Rum (and perhaps even of Cilician Armenia and Antioch) was envisaged, since Isaac would scarcely have exposed himself to the certain ravages of the crusading army without specific promises of substantial territorial compensation. Saladin, who greatly feared Barbarossa, would have had no hesitation in giving away someone else's territory in return for the destruction of the German army. The Byzantines also invited Saladin to send a new religious embassy, in place of the one captured by the Genoese, to inaugurate the *khotba* (Muslim invocation) in the name of the Abbasid caliph at the mosque in Constantinople. Saladin was naturally eager to comply, and so, in addition to an ambassador, sent an imam, a pulpit, and several muezzins and readers of the Koran. They were well received, and the first *khotba* took place in the presence of a crowd of Muslim merchants and travellers.[16]

When Isaac's envoy died in Syria, probably during the latter part of the summer of 1189, he sent another to complete the negotiations. Isaac hoped to secure military assistance from Saladin, for Frederick Barbarossa was experiencing little difficulty in handling the Byzantine forces which opposed him, and the emperor thought news of these events would already be reaching Syria. Guerrilla opposition had harassed the German emperor from the moment he entered the Byzantine Empire at Branitchevo. Between Nish and Sofia he drove a Byzantine army from its fortifications; near Philippopolis he again defeated Isaac's forces. Having obtained definite information of the captivity of the bishop of Münster's embassy, Barbarossa undertook to compel its release by devastating Thrace from Enos to Thessalonica. Although the bishop and his companions were freed (about 20 October 1189), Isaac remained true to Saladin and refused to allow the Germans passage to Asia; in mid-November he wrote them that Thrace was a deathtrap from which they could never escape. Frederick thereupon extended his raids, seized Adrianople, and even planned a siege of Constantinople. Not until February 1190 did the Byzantine emperor finally give up hope of Saracen aid, admit defeat, and agree to the Treaty of Adrianople, which granted Frederick markets, passage to Asia Minor, and hostages to ensure Byzantine good behavior.[17]

In the light of Frederick's successes, Isaac's letter of about December 1189 carried by the replacement for the deceased envoy to Saladin, who was then at the siege of Acre, appeared a mixture of self-pity, bravado, and pleas for concrete acts on Saladin's part. A text of this letter, undoubtedly genuine and accompanied by a description of its appearance, has survived in a biography of Saladin by one of his companions; it vividly reveals Isaac's misgivings at a crucial moment of the alliance:

> This envoy brought a letter about the matter under consideration. We will describe this document, and give a copy of the translation. It was written in wide lines, but narrower than in the writing of Baghdad. The translation on both back and front was in the second section; between the two the seal had been affixed.

This seal was of gold, and had been stamped with a portrait of the King just as wax is impressed with a seal; it weighed fifteen dinars. The two sections of the letter ran as follows:

> "From Aīsākīūs [Isaac] the King, servant of the Messiah, crowned by the grace of God, ever glorious and victorious *Afghakūs* [imperial], ruling in the name of God, the invincible conqueror, the autocrat of the Greeks, Angelos, to His Excellency the Sultan of Egypt, Sālāh ed-Dīn, sincere affection and friendship.

> "The letter written by Your Excellency to My Empire [Byzantine diplomatic form, equivalent to "Our Majesty"] has been safely received. We have perused it, and have been informed thereby of the death of our ambassador. This has occasioned us great grief, more especially because he died in a strange land, leaving unfinished the business with which My Empire had charged him, and on which he was to confer with Your Excellency. Your Excellency doubtless intends sending us an ambassador to inform our Empire of the decision that has been made relative to the business with the arrangement of which we charged our late ambassador. The property he has left, or which may be recovered after his death, must be sent to My Empire, that it may be given to his children and relatives.

> "I cannot believe that Your Excellency will give ear to malicious reports of the march of the Germans through my dominions; it is not surprising that my enemies should propagate lies to serve their own ends. If you wish to know the truth, I will tell you. They suffered themselves more hardship and fatigue than they inflicted on my peasant population. Their losses in money, horses and men were considerable; they lost a great number of soldiers, and it was with great difficulty that they escaped my brave troops. They were so exhausted that they cannot reach your dominions; and even if they should succeed in reaching them, they could be of no assistance to their fellows, nor could they inflict any injury on Your Excellency. Considering these things, I am much astonished that you have forgotten our former [good] relations, and that you have not communicated any of your plans and projects to My Empire. It seems to My Empire, that the only result of my friendship with you has been to draw down upon me the hatred of the Franks and of all their kind. Your Excellency must fulfil the intention, announced in your letter, of sending me an ambassador to inform me of the decision in the business upon which I have corresponded with you for a long time past. Let this be done as soon as possible. I pray that the coming of the Germans, of which you have heard so many reports, may not weigh heavily on your hearts; the plans and purposes they entertain will work their own confusion. Written in the year 1501 [of the Seleucid era, equivalent to 1 September 1189-31 August 1190]."[18]

The querulous, frustrated tone of the letter, the repeated demands for a clear definition of Saladin's aims, the contradictory statements on whether the crusaders would succeed in reaching Syria, all betray Isaac's consciousness of his failure to destroy Barbarossa and his bitterness over Saladin's procrastination.

In February-April 1190, at the very moment he was making peace with Frederick and allowing him to cross the

Straits, Isaac wrote again reminding Saladin that he had re-established public prayer in the name of the Abbasid caliph in the mosque of Constantinople and affirming anew his friendship for the Muslims. He also explained that he had been forced to allow Frederick to pass, but declared that the German emperor and his army would be in no condition to fight when they did reach Syria alive:

> He has experienced every type of deception on the way; the sufferings he has endured and the shortage of his supplies have weakened and troubled him. He will not reach your country in any shape useful to himself or his army; he will find his grave there without being able to return and will fall victim to his own trap.[19]

Isaac repeated that he had done everything possible to destroy Barbarossa's army, and again pleaded with Saladin to send him an envoy with replies to the Byzantine requests. According to Saladin's secretary, Imad ed-Din, the sultan was favorably impressed and took action in accord with Isaac's desires; this probably means only that Saladin sent another embassy to Constantinople.[20]

Frederick Barbarossa, in the meantime, left the Byzantine Empire and marched through Asia Minor to Iconium, capital of the sultanate of Rum. This city, whose walls had withstood Manuel Comnenus, he stormed without difficulty—an achievement which must have shown to Saladin that Isaac Angelus' alleged decimation of the crusader army was largely fictitious. Frederick's own estimate of his losses in Thrace, somewhat over a hundred men up to 18 November 1189, after extensive guerrilla warfare, raids on Byzantine towns, and two engagements with Isaac's army, shows that Isaac had achieved little of his plan to destroy the crusaders; Barbarossa did, however, admit that his horses had been reduced in number. The ineffectiveness of Isaac's attacks on the German crusaders was made known to Saladin by reports of their progress through Asia Minor; the most notable of these bulletins was a letter from Basil, bishop of Ani and catholicos of Armenia, an Arsacid who favored Saladin out of hatred for the pro-Latin Roupenids of Cilician Armenia. The bishop gave an exaggerated account of the strength, discipline, and endurance of the Germans, and the Arabic historians of the period reflect the dread which Barbarossa's advance produced in their camp. In June 1190 Frederick drowned at the border of the Roupenid territory, and his army broke up almost immediately; Saladin, though, already knew enough to evaluate Isaac's deeds at their real worth. When, in the early summer of 1190, Isaac sent him word of Barbarossa's passage across the Straits and sufferings in Anatolia at the hands of the nomadic Turkomans who inhabited the fringes of the sultanate of Rum, Saladin did not even reply.[21]

In the summer of 1191 Isaac again sent Saladin a messenger equipped with gifts, a letter, and a verbal message; he was received by Saladin's brother, al-Adil. Saladin's foreign minister, al-Fadil, has preserved a résumé of the Byzantine statement. Isaac boasted that he had rejected repeated Western demands for assistance, declared that he had closed the passes and put his fortresses on guard against the crusaders, and alleged that he had excused to the Latins his failure to participate in the crusade by claiming that the ravages of pestilence and lack of supplies rendered postponement necessary. Al-Fadil then makes an appraisal of Isaac's motives and achievements which may represent a summary of al-Adil's reply. The Byzantine emperor, he declares, merely wished to defend his own lands against the crusaders, while pretending to act in the Muslims' interests. As to the patriarchate of Jerusalem, which now depended on him, Isaac was said to have told the Latins that his control lasted only until the Western ruler gave it to one of his own followers. By this excuse, Isaac had allegedly kept the Latins away from his own person, especially after Muslim prayer in the name of the Abbasid caliph had been established at Constantinople. Finally, according to al-Fadil, Saladin rejected all Byzantine requests which might damage the cause of Islam, a statement which suggests that the Byzantine emperor had again desired Saladin to give him control of the Holy Land or join in an attack on Iconium.[22]

The emperor, although once more beginning to seek allies in the West because of the growing strength of Henry VI of Hohenstaufen, did not yet despair entirely of the fulfillment of Saladin's promises. On 15 May 1192 an ambassador from Constantinople reached Jerusalem and two days later was admitted to Saladin's presence. His requests were a repetition of the clauses of the treaty alleged to have formerly existed; they included demands for the True Cross (that is, the fragments which Saladin had captured), for Orthodox possession of the churches of Jerusalem (which Saladin meditated yielding to Latin clergy as part of the price of Richard the Lion-Hearted's departure), for an offensive and defensive alliance between the two powers, and for a joint naval expedition against Cyprus. Although Saladin allegedly refused all these terms (actually, he may have given the envoy a piece of the True Cross), he despatched Ibn al-Bezzay, an Egyptian, as ambassador to Constantinople, to return with the Byzantine.[23]

As usual, Saladin sent rich gifts with his representative; these included horses, wild and tame animals from Egypt and Libya, aloe wood, balsam, and twenty-seven golden horse-trappings studded with gems and pearls. Isaac later evaluated these presents at 6675 hyperpers. In the late summer or early autumn the Byzantine and Saracen envoys sailed for Constantinople on a Venetian ship belonging to a certain Pordano. At sea, evidently near Rhodes, the vessel fell in with a fleet of Genoese and Pisan corsairs under the command of Guglielmo Grasso, who was rapidly making himself the terror of the region. The Venetian ship was pillaged, and Isaac's and Saladin's emissaries were all put to death. At this time, according to a later story, a Pisan named Forte seized the fragment of the True Cross which Saladin's envoys were carrying; he took it to the Pisan fortress of Bonifacio, on the coast of Corsica, where it was captured by the Genoese in 1195 and added to the relics treasured by the city. In November 1192 Isaac complained to Genoa and Pisa about this and other piratical outrages, and from Genoa he appears to have obtained some compensation for the financial losses he had sustained. The Byzantine emperor's relations with Saladin, however, were terminated by this event. Saladin was disillusioned with Isaac's military capabilities, while Isaac finally realized that Saladin was too distant to protect him from the Latins. By the time of Saladin's death in 1193 Isaac Angelus had reversed his policy and formed alliances with Genoa and Pisa, the pope, and the Sicilian Normans, which he hoped would relieve him of his former dependence upon the Muslims.[24]

From 1185 to 1192 the alliance with Saladin was the cornerstone of Byzantine foreign policy. In the face of the hostility of Normans, Pisans, Genoese, the German emperor, and the pope, the Eastern Empire leaned on the expanding Islamic power in Syria and Egypt. Isaac Angelus, in particular, derived a sense of confidence and security from it which ultimately led him into difficulties. His hostility to Barbarossa sprang largely from this cause; in order to fulfil his part of the treaty, he had to oppose any crusading army which entered the Byzantine domains. The rewards promised were goals Andronicus and the earlier Comneni had striven for, namely, recovery of rebellious Cyprus, repossession of the Holy Land, and re-establishment of the tenth century boundaries in Asia Minor. The failure of the alliance with Saladin forced a complete reversal of policy in the form of a rapproachement with the smaller Western powers in order to counter the growing ambitions of Henry VI.

That the alliance had any great effect on the course of events in the Levant appears doubtful. Isaac's relations with the Melkites may have speeded the surrender of Jerusalem, but the city was in no condition to hold out against the overwhelming force of the Muslims. Had Barbarossa's crusade actually reached the Holy Land in full strength and with undiminished discipline, it might have materially altered the situation, but its destruction was by no means the work of Isaac. His strongest attacks amounted to little more than pinpricks, and the crusaders suffered more from the terrain and climate than from the emperor. The Byzantines derived little tangible benefit from their alliance with Saladin; although some of the churches of the Holy Land came into the possession of the Orthodox, Cyprus, captured by the Latins, became an ally of Saladin before his death, and Iconium remained in Muslim hands. Isaac's alliance with Saladin, although fateful for the empire, altered little the situation in the Orient.

The evil effects of the tie with the Muslims on Byzantium's reputation were more enduring. The Latins of Syria were frankly alarmed at such a conjunction, and sought to stigmatize it throughout Europe. Frederick Barbarossa, while in Thrace, even instructed his son to urge the pope to preach a crusade against the Byzantines. The preference of Richard the Lion-Hearted, Philip Augustus, and later crusades for the sea-route is not unconnected with Isaac's

relations with the enemies of the Cross. Recollection of this policy surely influenced the men of the Fourth Crusade, and it had certainly served to discredit the Eastern Empire. Throughout the twelfth century, at the time of the crusades of 1101, during Bohemond's conflict with Alexius Comnenus, and after the Second Crusade, charges of Byzantine complicity with the Muslims had been levelled; in the present instance they were justified.[25]

The alliance produced a visible reduction in the empire's prestige and self-esteem. In the realm of political theory, Byzantium had scarcely admitted any nation to be its equal since the demise of Sassanid Persia; because the Roman Empire was God's chosen vehicle for the Christianization and governance of the world, no state could or should approach it except as a humble suppliant. While seeking the friendship of Saladin, the Byzantine emperors sought to perpetuate this image, as when Andronicus demanded Saladin's homage and Isaac sent a crown with a declaration intended to convey the idea that Byzantium retained the right of granting or withholding all legitimate titles. When Saladin ignored or repulsed these moves, the realities of the situation soon forced Byzantium into a decidedly subordinate position, for it was clearly the weaker partner. Isaac was forced to accept the humiliating devastation inflicted by the German crusaders in the hope that Saladin would eventually reward him for his loyal service. No reconciliation between Byzantine pretensions and the facts of politics was attempted; the claim to supremacy was quietly dropped as Andronicus' bluster subsided into Isaac's whine. The Byzantine historian, Nicetas Choniates, a high government official who could scarcely have been ignorant of something that was public knowledge in the West, never mentions the alliance with Saladin.[26]

In the end, the alliance between ancient enemies against the Latin interloper failed; Saladin was too distant to protect Isaac Angelus from his foes, and the Byzantines were in no condition to offer serious resistance to crusaders. The Muslim estimate of the value of the alliance is bluntly stated in a letter of al-Fadil, written while Guy of Cyprus was an ally of Saladin:

> You should attribute no importance to our negotiations with the ruler of Constantinople in regard to the aid we ought to lend him against Cyprus, for we promised it only when the country was in our enemies' hands. In truth, the Greek king has never succeeded in his enterprises; we gain nothing from his friendship, and need fear nothing from his enmity.[27]

Isaac's own appraisal was even gloomier: "It seems to My Empire, that the only result of my friendship with you has been to draw down upon me the hatred of the Franks and of all their kind."[28] The alliance with Saladin added much to the rising Western hostility for Byzantium which culminated in the diversion of the Fourth Crusade and the Latin capture of Constantinople. Isaac's acceptance of the necessity of playing a subordinate role in an alliance prepared the way for the once great empire's ultimate position as a minor power in the Eastern Mediterranean.

The question of the origin and reliability of the anonymous letter in Magnus deserves consideration. It has no address and perhaps began with other matters; it breaks off abruptly, after a mention of Saladin's determination to do something about the forthcoming Third Crusade and his embassy and gifts to Isaac, but without describing any of the terms Saladin proposed at this time. Magnus has interpolated this letter (with the notation: "Ut autem ordo historiae de qua agimus, ad notitiam posterorum manifestius perducatur, placuit hic interponere litteras eandem historiam continentes, scriptas siquidem in ultramarinis partibus et missas in partes nostras, sicque ad nos perlatas." Magnus, *Chron.*, pp. 510-511) after a narration of Barbarossa's difficulties in the Balkan peninsula, evidently with the purpose of explaining the Byzantine attacks, although the letter itself never reaches the point of making precise the agreement between Isaac and Saladin whereby Isaac undertook to destroy the crusade.

The last events mentioned in the letter occurred, apparently, in the summer of 1188; many of the same facts are mentioned in Conrad of Montferrat's letter of 20 September 1188 to Archbishop Baldwin of Canterbury, in Roger of Wendover, *Flores*, I, 153-154 (Röhricht, *Regesta*, No. 676), part of which is repeated verbatim in the report of the French embassy to Constantinople (commonly dated between September and November 1188), in Benedict of Peterborough, *Gesta regis Henrici*, II, 51-53 (mentioned by Röhricht, *Regesta*, under No. 688). Before coming to Palestine, Conrad of Montferrat had lived at Constantinople (spring and early summer 1187), as brother-in-law of the emperor Isaac, so that he had every opportunity of learning of Isaac's relations with Saladin. Among the other possible sources of his information, the writer of the anonymous letter mentions one: in 1186 the count of Tripoli and prince of Antioch learned of the alliance of Isaac and Saladin "a fidelibus suis et quibusdam Sarracenis nobilioribus, quorum consanguineos Saladinus suffocaverat" (Magnus, *Chron.*, p. 511). In addition, Conrad's letter (Roger of Wendover, *Flores*, I, 153) reports that the Mahomerie (*i.e.*, mosque-pulpit: see n. 13, above) sent by Saladin to Constantinople in 1188 and mentioned in the concluding sentence of the anonymous letter was captured by the Genoese at sea and brought to Tyre: probably much of the writer's precise information derived from captives taken on this occasion.

The letter's author was noticeably proud of the defense made at Tyre against Saladin: "Saladinus victus ignominiose ante Tyrum" (Magnus, *Chron.*, p. 512). The probable correctness of the gift lists in the anonymous letter is shown by the similar list of those sent Isaac in 1192 by Saladin, as stated in Isaac's complaint to the Genoese (November 1192), in Sanguineti and Bertolotto, "Doc. gen.," *loc. cit.*, p. 448-453 (Dölger, *Regesten*, No. 1612). These factors, together with the degree of precise detail contained therein, suggest that the anonymous letter is a genuine product of the late summer or fall 1188, from

Conrad or his circle at Tyre. That Magnus omitted something at the end also seems likely.

On the subject of this letter, see Riezler, "Kreuzzug," *loc. cit.*, p. 36, n. 8; Reinhold Röhricht, *Beiträge zur Geschichte der Kreuzzüge*, II (Berlin, 1878), 190-192; the same author's *Königreich Jerusalem*, p. 494, n. 1; Cognasso, "Isacco II," *loc. cit.*, p. 256, n. 4, and p. 257, n. 1-5.

Notes

1. For background on Andronicus' reign, see: Francesco Cognasso, "Parti politici e lotte dinastiche in Bisanzio alla morte di Manuele Comneno," *Memorie della Reale Accademia delle scienze di Torino*, 2nd Ser., LXII [Part 2] (1912), 213-317; John Danstrup, "Recherches critiques sur Andronicos Ier," Vetenskaps-Societeten i Lund, *Årsbok* (*Yearbook of the New Society of Letters at Lund*), 1944, pp. 69-101.

2. The sole source for Andronicus' embassy to Saladin (Franz Dölger, ed., *Regesten der Kaiserurkunden des oströmischen Reichs von 565-1453*, Corpus der griechischen Urkunden des Mittelalters und der neueren Zeit, Reihe A, Abt. I [Munich and Berlin, 1924-1960], No. 1563) is the anonymous letter from the East in Magnus Presbyterus Reicherspergensis, *Chronica collecta a Magno presbytero—1195*, W. Wattenbach, ed., MGH SS, XVII (Hanover, 1861), 511 (Reinhold Röhricht, ed., *Regesta Regni Hierosolymitani MXCVII-MCCXCI* [Innsbruck, 1893-1904], No. 688). The question of the authenticity of this letter is discussed in the Appendix to this article. See also Reinhold Röhricht, *Geschichte des Königreichs Jerusalem, 1100-1291* (Innsbruck, 1898), pp. 493-494; Cognasso, "Partiti pol.," *loc. cit.*, pp. 296-297; Claude Cahen, *La Syrie du Nord à l'époque des croisades et la principauté franque d'Antioche* (Paris, 1940), pp. 424-425; Danstrup, "Andronicos Ier," *loc. cit.*, p. 96, n. 119.

3. Magnus, *Chron.*, p. 511.

4. Magnus, *Chron.*, p. 511. Dölger, *Regesten*, No. 1579, dates this treaty to late 1187 (after the fall of Jerusalem), but the letter in Magnus, *Chron.*, pp. 511-512, makes a clear distinction between the two embassies.

5. The only detailed account of Isaac and Alexius' sojourn with Saladin is the letter in Magnus, *Chron.*, p. 511-512; the Pisans' loans are mentioned in Isaac's chrysobull to Pisa (February 1192), in Giuseppe Müller, ed., *Documenti sulle relazioni delle città toscane coll' Oriente cristiano e coi Turchi fino all' anno MDXXXI* (Florence, 1879), p. 41, 50 (Dölger, *Regesten*, No. 1607); Alexius' presence in Syria is also attested by: Nicetas Choniates, *Historia*, Immanuel Bekker, ed., Corpus Scriptorum Historiae Byzantinae (Bonn, 1835), p. 703; Geoffroi de Villehardouin, *Conquête de*

Constantinople, ed. Natalis de Wailly, 3rd ed. (Paris, 1882), p. 40; *idem,* ed. Edmond Faral (Paris, 1938-1939), I, 70; Robert de Clari, *La conquête de Constantinople,* ed. Philippe Lauer (Paris, 1924), p. 21, 28-29. Evidence for Isaac's visit to Syria is contained in John Kamateros, . . . W. Regel, ed., *Fontes Rerum Byzantinarum,* I (St Petersburg, 1892-1917), 250-252, which relates how Isaac fled from Andronicus through inhabited cities, desert places, and mountains torn by chasms (evidently the Taurus), how God made all smooth before him, and how he had a vision of Jacob's ladder while asleep in Harran (whose name, the orator declares, might be rendered "on the earth or on the ground" *loc. cit.,* p. 252). Harran is a town in Syria, near Edessa, on a route which might be used by one wishing to avoid Armenia and the Latin territories. This speech, which alludes to Andronicus' downfall and the defeat of the Normans, was probably delivered on 6 January 1186; the analysis of the part of the oration here referred to in Max Bachmann, *Die Rede des Joannes Syropulos an den Kaiser Isaak II. Angelos (1185-1195) (Text und Kommentar) nebst Beiträgen zur Geschichte des Kaisers aus zeitgenössischen rhetorischen Quellen* (Munich, 1935), pp. 43-46, omits the reference to Harran and apparently misconstrues this part of the speech: Isaac's flight across Constantinople (11 September 1185) would hardly be described in these terms. Isaac must have been in Syria during the early part of 1183 (he was at Nicaea, leading a revolt against Andronicus, by September 1183); see Nicetas, *Hist.,* pp. 345, 349. On Isaac and Alexius in Syria, see also Wilhelm Heyd, *Histoire du commerce du Levant au Moyen-Age,* trans. Furcy Raynaud, I (Leipzig, 1885), 230, n. 2; Francesco Cognasso, "Un imperatore bizantino della decadenza: Isacco II Angelo," *Bessarione,* XXXI (1915), 257. V. Laurent, "Rome et Byzance sous le pontificat de Célestin III (1191-1198)," *Echos d'Orient,* XXXIX (1940-1942), 49, 57, argues that Isaac's residence in Syria was the basis of his alliance with the Muslims; there is no evidence, however, for his view that the alliance persisted under Alexius III and caused hesitations in the papacy's dealings with that emperor.

6. Magnus, *Chron.,* pp. 511-512; Nicetas, *Hist.,* pp. 483-485; Isidoro La Lumia, *Storie siciliane,* I (Palermo, 1881), 535-537; Ferdinand Chalandon, *Histoire de la domination normande en Italie et en Sicile* (Paris, 1907; reprinted New York, 1960), II, 415; Cognasso, "Isacco II," *loc. cit.,* pp. 255, 257-258. The Genoese ship is mentioned in the instructions of 4 May 1201 to the Genoese envoys, in Angelo Sanguineti and Gerolamo Bertolotto, ed., "Nuovo serie di documenti sulle relazioni di Genova coll' Impero bizantino," *Atti della Società Ligure di Storia Patria,* XXVIII (1896-1898), 471 (see the textual emendation by Cognasso, "Isacco II," *loc. cit.,* p. 257, n. 5).

7. This information comes from an anonymous *History of the Patriachs of Alexandria* (*Siyar-al-abâ-al-Batarikah,* contained in Paris. MS. ar. 302), which has been partially published in translation in the notes to Edgar Blochet's "Histoire d'Egypte de Makrizi," *Revue de l'Orient Latin,* IX (1902), 29, n. 3 (p. 30 for the cited material)—the separate publication (Paris, 1908) is not available to me—, and in less complete form in Joseph T. Reinaud, ed., *Extraits des historiens arabes,* which forms Vol. IV of Joseph Michaud, ed., *Bibliothèque des Croisades* (Paris, 1829), p. 207, n. 1. On the author, an early thirteenth-century Jacobite Arab who is markedly favorable to Saladin, see Reinaud, p. xxii. See also René Grousset, *Histoire des Croisades et du Royaume franc de Jérusalem,* II (Paris, 1935), 811-812. Bar Hebraeus, *Chronography,* trans. E. A. Wallis Budge, I (London, 1932), 327, testifies that soon after the conquest of Jerusalem, Saladin let the Greek Patriarch administer the church.

8. Magnus, *Chron.,* pp. 511-512; Dölger, *Regesten,* No. 1579 (see above, n. 4).

9. Magnus, *Chron.,* p. 512.

10. Magnus, *Chron.,* p. 512.

11. Abd al-Rahmen ibn Isma'il, called Abu Šamah, *Le livre des deux jardins: Histoire des deux règnes, celui de Nour ed-Dîn et celui de Salah ed-Dîn* (A.-C. Barbier de Meynard, ed. and tr.), RHC HOr, IV (Paris, 1898), 389, quotes a letter of al-Fadil, Saladin's minister, to Seif al-Islam in Yemen, dated 584 A.H. (1188-89), reporting the receipt of news from the ruler of Constantinople, from Alexandria, and from North Africa concerning the gathering crusade. There is no reason to suppose a further embassy from Isaac to bring Saladin this news (as does Dölger, *Regesten,* No. 1584, dated about late 1188—by which time Saladin would have received plentiful news of this impending development), but such a Byzantine embassy is not out of the question. Dölger's only evidence is the letter of al-Fadil, cited above.

12. Magnus, *Chron.,* p. 512; on the alleged attempts to poison Barbarossa's troops, see Ansbert, *Historia de expeditione Friderici imperatoris,* ed. A. Chroust, in *Quellen zur Geschichte des Kreuzzuges Kaiser Friedrichs I.,* MGH SSRG, N.S., v (Berlin, 1928), 54-55, and *Historia peregrinorum,* A. Chroust, ed., *loc. cit.,* pp. 146-147.

13. The anonymous letter in Magnus, *Chron.,* p. 512; Conrad of Montferrat's letter (20 September 1188) to Archbishop Baldwin of Canterbury, in Roger of Wendover, *Liber qui dicitur Flores historiarum,* ed. Henry G. Hewlett, Rolls Series (London, 1886-1889), I, 153; the French embassy's report (autumn 1188), in Benedict of Peterborough, *Gesta regis Henrici,* ed. William Stubbs, Rolls Series (London, 1867), II, 52, as corrected by the version

included in Ralph of Diceto, *Opera historica,* ed. William Stubbs, Rolls Series, II (London, 1876), 60, which reads "Januensibus" for Benedict's "Venetiensibus."

The identity of the "maumeria" sent by Saladin and the "idolum" taken by the Genoese before 20 September 1188 rests on the fact that Saladin had to dispatch another religious embassy with a pulpit in the summer of 1189. The identification of the "maumeria" as a *minbar* or pulpit was made by Röhricht, *Königreich Jerusalem,* p. 496, n. 2 (he does, however, confuse this capture with the piracy of Guglielmo Grasso in 1192). The statement that this was a picture of Saladin, made by S. O. Riezler, "Der Kreuzzug Kaiser Friedrichs I.," *Forschungen zur deutschen Geschichte,* x (1870), 35, n. 4, is clearly incorrect. On the shape of the pulpit, see E. Diez, "Minbar," *Encyclopaedia of Islam,* III (Leiden and London, 1936), 499-500.

14. Benedict of Peterborough, *Gesta regis Henrici,* II, 51-53; Roger of Wendover, *Flores,* I, 153-154; Röhricht, *Regesta,* Nos. 676 and 688.

15. Ansbert, *Hist.,* pp. 15-16; *Hist. peregrinorum,* pp. 129-130; Bishop Dietpold of Passau's letter in Magnus, *Chron.,* p. 510. See also: Cognasso, "Isacco II," *loc. cit.,* pp. 260-263; K. Zimmert, "Der deutsch-byzantinische Konflikt vom Juli 1189 bis Februar 1190," *Byzantinische Zeitschrift,* XII (1903), 43-44.

A later Genoese source, the instructions issued in 1201 to Ottobono della Croce, in Sanguineti and Bertolotto, "Doc. gen.," *loc. cit.,* pp. 472-473, refers to the transportation of an embassy of Saladin to Constantinople, which may well have been the embassy of 1188 or 1189, by a ship belonging to Symon Musonus. In Constantinople the court seized 3000 hyperpers from him, and the Great Logothete and Sebastos Comanus (Comnenus? Chumnos?) threw him in prison. He was only released by giving his brother and nephew as hostages; they died of privations in prison. Meanwhile, the court forced him to carry some Hungarians overseas (*i.e.,* to the Holy Land), for which service the treasurer promised him thirteen hundred hyperpers, of which he received only six hundred petty bezants. The circumstance that Symon had to transport Hungarians (with whose king Isaac was allied by marriage and by policy) to the Holy Land suggests a date during the Third Crusade, and Saladin is not known to have sent any full-scale embassy to Constantinople between the religious one of August-September 1189 and the one destroyed by pirates in 1192. The reason for Symon Musonus' sufferings is not clear; was he held responsible for allowing the capture of the pulpit in 1188?

16. On the treaty and Isaac's embassy, see Dölger, *Regesten,* Nos. 1591 and 1593. On the arrival of the embassy and Saladin's religious embassy, see Baha ad-Din ibn Šaddad [Bohadin], *The Life of Saladin,* trans. C. R. Conder, Palestine Pilgrims' Text Society, No. 32 (London, 1897), pp. 198-199; Abu Šamah, *Livre des deux jardins,* pp. 471-472, who misdates the events to 1190; the genuineness of the clause respecting Cyprus is shown by al-Fadil's reference to it, quoted *ibid.,* p. 510.

17. On the death of Isaac's envoy, and the sending of a replacement, see Bohadin, *Life of Saladin,* pp. 199-201 (Dölger, *Regesten,* No. 1601). Frederick's successes are described in Bishop Dietpold's letter in Magnus, *Chron.,* pp. 509-510; Ansbert, *Hist.,* pp. 27-64; *Hist. peregrinorum,* pp. 131-149; Nicetas, *Hist.,* pp. 526-529, 533-536. See also Cognasso, "Isacco II," *loc. cit.,* pp. 253-269; Riezler, "Kreuzzug," *loc. cit.,* pp. 28-53; Zimmert, "Deutsch-byz. Konflikt," *loc. cit.,* pp. 43-72.

18. Bohadin, *Life of Saladin,* pp. 199-201 (Dölger, *Regesten,* No. 1601); the paragraphing is mine. The genuineness of this letter is beyond doubt; not only is the description of the letter convincing and the salutation characteristic (cf. for example Isaac's letter of November 1192 in Sanguineti and Bertolotto, "Doc. gen.," *loc. cit.,* p. 448), but the words and tone are pure Isaac Angelus. The Seleucid era was probably used in the dating clause as a system common to both cultures, without offensive religious connotations.

19. Isaac's letter (Dölger, *Regesten,* No. 1604) is quoted thus by Imad ed-Din, Saladin's secretary, in a fragment given by Abu Šamah, *Livre des deux jardins,* pp. 470-471. The alleged content of the other parts of this letter show it to have been different from the previous one, of about December 1189: Dölger, *Regesten,* No. 1601.

20. Abu Šamah, *Livre des deux jardins,* pp. 470-471.

21. On Frederick's advance and death, see Ansbert, *Hist.,* pp. 76-92; *Hist. peregrinorum,* pp. 155-172; Riezler, "Kreuzzug," *loc. cit.,* pp. 55-70. On Manuel I's attack on Iconium, see Ferdinand Chalandon, *Jean II Comnène (1118-1143) et Manuel I Comnène (1143-1180)* (Paris, 1912; reprinted New York, 1960), pp. 250-255. Frederick's losses are reported in a letter (Philippopolis, 18 November 1189) to Henry VI, in Ansbert, *Hist.,* p. 43. For reports on Barbarossa's progress, see Bohadin, *Life of Saladin,* pp. 170-171, 182-189 (including the Armenian Catholicos' letter), 198. On Isaac's letter, which is not mentioned by Dölger, and the date of which can only be conjectured, see the report of Imad ed-Din, quoted in Abu Šamah, *Livre des deux jardins,* pp. 437-438.

22. This embassy, Abu Šamah, *Livre des deux jardins,* pp. 508-509, is not mentioned by Dölger; Röhricht, *Königreich Jerusalem,* p. 497, n. 2, dates it summer 1191, on the basis of context.

23. Bohadin, *Life of Saladin,* pp. 334-335 (Dölger, *Regesten,* No. 1608); Cognasso, "Isacco II," *loc. cit.,*

pp. 275-276; Steven Runciman, *A History of the Crusades*, III (Cambridge, England, 1954), 63, 73-74.

24. Isaac retails the story of Grasso's attack in three different places: the letters of complaint to Genoa and Pisa (Sanguineti and Bertolotto, "Doc. gen.," *loc. cit.*, pp. 448-453; Müller, *Doc. tosc.*, p. 66), and the 1193 chrysobull to Genoa (Sanguineti and Bertolotto, "Doc. gen.," *loc. cit.*, pp. 454-464) (Dölger, *Regesten,* Nos 1612, 1616, and 1618). The story of Forte is in *Regni iherosolymitani brevis historia,* ed. Luigi Tommaso Belgrano, Annali genovesi di Caffaro e de' suoi continuatori dal MXCIX al MCCXCII, I [Fonti per la storia d'Italia, pubblicate dall' Istituto storico italiano, XI] (Genoa, 1890), 140-141; see J. K. Fotheringham, "Genoa and the Fourth Crusade," *English Historical Review,* XXV (1910), 28-29. A. Frolow, *Recherches sur la déviation de la IVᵉ Croisade vers Constantinople* (Paris, 1955), p. 68, in his survey of the histories of various fragments of the True Cross, mentions that Isaac's 1192 embassy requested it from Saladin, but does not include the story of Forte.

25. For the alarm of the Syrian Latins, see the anonymous letter from the East, Conrad of Montferrat's letter to Baldwin of Canterbury, and the French embassy's report, all frequently cited above. Frederick Barbarossa's appeal for a crusade is contained in his letter of 18 November 1189 to Henry VI, in Ansbert, *Hist.,* pp. 42-43. For Western knowledge of Isaac's alliance with Saladin, see, in addition to the sources for Barbarossa's crusade: *Continuatio weingartensis Chronici Hugonis a Sancto Victore,* ed. Ludwig Weiland, in Monumenta Welforum antiqua (SSRG in usum scholarum) (Hanover, 1869), p. 53; William of Newburgh, *Historia rerum anglicarum,* ed. Richard Howlett, in Chronicles of the Reigns of Stephen, Henry II, and Richard I, Rolls Series, I (London, 1884), 326; Richard of London, *Itinerarium peregrinorum et gesta regis Ricardi,* ed. William Stubbs, in Chronicles and Memorials of the Reign of Richard I, Rolls Series, I (London, 1864), 46; Ralph Niger, *Chronica,* ed. Robert Anstruther, Caxton Society Publications (London, 1851), p. 97; *Chronica regia coloniensis (Annales maximi colonienses),* ed. Georg Waitz, SSRG in usum scholarum (Hanover, 1880), p. 147; *Regni iher. hist. brevis,* pp. 140-141; *Chronicon Montis Sereni,* ed. Ernst Ehrenfeuchter, MGH SS, XXIII (Hanover, 1874), 161.

26. The only mention by Nicetas is an indirect quotation of what the Germans were saying about Isaac's conduct; in describing his own peace-making activities during the conflict with Barbarossa in Thrace, he says: "And we ourselves returning [to Constantinople] a little later related everything, declaring that the Germans said there was no difference between the faithful Emperor of the Romans' ignoring the treaties of the western

Christians and his making a treaty with the ruler of the Saracens . . ." (Nicetas, *Hist.,* p. 536). Even this statement treats the alliance with Saladin as a hypothetical alternative.

27. Abu Šamah, *Livre des deux jardins,* p. 510.

28. Bohadin, *Life of Saladin,* p. 201.

Hamilton A. R. Gibb (essay date 1962)

SOURCE: "The Achievement of Saladin" in *Studies in the Civilization of Islam,* edited by Stanford J. Shaw and William R. Polk, Princeton University Press, 1962, pp. 91–107.

[*In the following essay, Gibb assesses the motivation behind Saladin's achievements and addresses the theory that his successes were the result of his personal ambition and his exploitation of religious sentiments. Gibb maintains that Saladin's successes were the result of his "unselfishness, his humility and generosity, [and] his moral vindication of Islam."*]

In the effort to penetrate behind the external history of a person whose reputation rests upon some military achievement, the modern tendency is to analyse the complex of circumstances within which he acted, with the sometimes explicit suggestion that the individual is rather the creature than the creator of his circumstances, or, more justly, that his achievement is to be explained by a harmonious adjustment of his genius to the conditions within which it operated. That this is generally true calls for no argument. But history, especially the history of the Near East, is full of conquering kings, who seem to owe nothing to their circumstances except the possession of a powerful army and the weakness of their antagonists. The question posed by the career of Saladin is whether he was just another such conqueror, or whether his career involved distinctive moral elements which gave his initial victory and subsequent struggle with the Third Crusade a quality of its own. That he fought in the cause of Islam against the crusaders is not enough to justify an affirmative answer to the second question, and might even be irrelevant. To put the matter precisely: was Saladin one of those unscrupulous, but fortunate, generals whose motive was personal ambition and lust of conquest, and who merely exploited religious catchwords and sentiments to achieve their own ends?

The problem is thus one which involves a judgment upon interior questions of personality and motive. It is rarely indeed in medieval history that we have at our disposal authentic materials from which positive conclusions, that will stand up to rigorous historical criticism, can be drawn as to the motives of prominent historical figures. Before entering on the discussion at all, therefore, it is necessary to be assured that some at least of our sources are of a kind which offers some possibility of reaching an answer. For the life and achievements of Saladin we possess, by a fortunate conjunction, five contemporary sources in Arabic, in whole or in part, besides casual references in the writings of travelers and others. Of these five, one has survived only in fragments. This is the history of Ibn Abi Taiy, who, as a Shiite of Aleppo, one would expect to be hostile to Saladin (as he clearly was to his predecessor Nur ad-Din), but in fact shows himself, in the quotations from his works by other writers, to be rather favourably disposed to him.

The three other historical sources were all written by easterners, not Syrians. The most famous is the Mosul historian Ibn al-Athir, who belonged to a feudal family in close relations with the Zangid princes of Mosul and wrote a panegyrical history of their dynasty. His presentation of Saladin fairly reflects the original hostility and later wry admiration and grudging allegiance of the Zangid partisans. But except for this psychological attitude he is not a firsthand source. All, or almost all, his narratives relating to Saladin were taken from the works of Saladin's secretary Imad ad-Din and rewritten with an occasional twist or admixture of fiction.[1] Irrespective of his personal attitude, however, it is obvious that a chronicler, even if contemporary, cannot be relied upon to solve questions of interior personality and motive; if, therefore, we had nothing but Ibn Abi Taiy's and Ibn al-Athir's chronicles to go by, we should have no means at all of discovering the real quality of Saladin's achievement.

Equally well known is the biography of Saladin by his Judge of the Army, the qadi Baha ad-Din Ibn Shaddad, also of Mosul. From 1188 Baha ad-Din was the confidant and intimate friend of Saladin, and his history, written in a simple and straightforward style, portrays Saladin for us, as no ordinary chronicle can do, in his character as a man. Baha ad-Din may perhaps be called un-critical, but he was no deluded hero-worshipper. His admiration is that of an upright and honest friend from whom nothing was concealed, and there can be no question of deliberate suppression or deflection of the truth in his narrative of the last five years of Saladin's life. To have one such source for the history of any medieval prince is rare indeed. The portrait it gives us, however, is that of Saladin at his climax of success and in the desperate conflict of the Third Crusade; it supplies, therefore, little direct evidence on the long and hard struggle to build up his power.

In these circumstances it is a piece of incredibly good fortune that our fourth source, which covers (in the original text or in reliable summaries) the whole of his active career, is almost equally close and authoritative. This source is the works of "the secretary" (*al-Katib*) Imad ad-Din, a native of Isfahan. He belonged to the relatively new class of college-trained civil servants, entered the employment first of the Seljuk Sultans and the Caliphs in Iraq, then rose to high rank at Damascus in the service of Nur ad-Din, and finally became personal secretary to Saladin in 1175. In addition to his one-volume history of the campaigns of 1187-1188 and the Third Crusade,[2] he wrote a large work in seven volumes, entitled *al-Barq al-Shami*,

covering the period of his own career under Nur ad-Din and Saladin. Of this work only two volumes of the original are known to have survived, but the whole was carefully summarized by Abu Shama of Damascus (d. 1267).

Imad ad-Din was one of the most famous stylists of his age, and his works are composed in the elaborate and florid rhyming prose cultivated by the secretarial class; yet with all his display of verbal virtuosity, his actual narratives of events are invariably full, precise, and straightforward. He shows no sign of the twisting of facts, whether to cover up his own weaknesses or those of others or for the sake of a rhyme, nor of fanciful adulation, even of Saladin. To be sure he greatly admired Saladin, yet in his writings he criticizes at times his actions and judgment, and indeed seems to have done so to his face. He was on the best of terms with his official superior, the Chief Secretary al-Qadi al-Fadil, and he was clearly too conscious of his own merits and of the trust reposed in him to play the toady or to conceal the truth. His *Barq* is, one might say, almost as much an autobiography as it is a history of Saladin; and its importance is that it presents Saladin to us from the angle of a trained administrator, in close and daily contact with him, though on a less intimate footing than Baha ad-Din.

The fifth of our sources is in some respects the most valuable of all. These are the despatches and letters of his most trusted adviser and secretary of state, the Palestinian al-Qadi al-Fadil, preserved in full or in excerpts in the works of Imad ad-Din, Abu Shama, and various collections of documents. The intimacy of the relation between them can be felt in the loyal and affectionate letters addressed by al-Qadi al-Fadil to Saladin, especially during the Third Crusade, sustaining him in times of adversity and even admonishing him on occasions. While, therefore, the historian will treat with all necessary caution the more elaborate public despatches addressed by al-Qadi al-Fadil on Saladin's behalf to the caliphs and other potentates, yet the consistency with which certain themes and ideas are expressed in them must be taken to reflect some at least of Saladin's real purposes and ideals.

Saladin's fame, as has already been said, rests upon his miliary achievement in the battle of Hattin in 1187 and subsequent recapture of Jerusalem. Consequently, he is regarded by historical writers, both Muslim and Christian, as, first and foremost, a general, and secondly as the founder of a dynasty. The first is, naturally enough, the view taken in the western sources for the Third Crusade, and it is encouraged by Ibn al-Athir's presentation of him as a man who used his military talents to satisfy his dynastic ambitions and to build up a vast empire.

It is from the same angle that he is compared or contrasted with his predecessor Nur ad-Din. Unfortunately, we do not possess for an estimation of Nur ad-Din's personality anything comparable to the materials that exist for the study of Saladin. All the contemporary Muslim records (save for casual anecdotes) are chronicles, and their panegyrical tone reflects the attitude of Sunni circles to his services not only in organizing the defense of Syria against the Crusaders, but also (and perhaps even more) in propagating orthodoxy by the foundation and endowment of religious institutions (mosques, madrasas, oratories, sufi convents)[3] and by repression of the Shiites. Later chronicles, except for the extracts preserved from the works of the Aleppo Shiite writer Ibn Abi Taiy, are even more eulogistic. But when the judgment even of Christian writers like William of Tyre concords with their attitude, we can be sure that it is a faithful reflection of Nur ad-Din's *public* life; and it would be a gratuitous assumption, in the face of such evidence, that, inasmuch as these measures served the political interests of Nur ad-Din, they were not motivated by sincere personal attachment to their objects and ideals.

There are, however, some essential differences between the circumstances in which Nur ad-Din and Saladin carried out their tasks. Nur ad-Din operated *from within* the structure of politics of his age. Since the break-up of the Seljuk sultanate at the end of the eleventh century, Western Asia had been parceled out amongst a number of local dynasties, all of them (except a few remote baronies) founded by Turkish generals or Turcoman chiefs, and all of them characterized by two common features. One was the spirit of personal advantage and aggrandizement which determined their political actions and relationships. It seems well-nigh impossible to discover in the relations of the Turkish princes or the Turcoman chiefs with one another—even when they were members of the same family—any sense of loyalty or restraint in exploiting each other's weaknesses, let alone that solidarity shown, for example, by the Buwaihid brothers in Persia in the tenth century. The tale of plots, revolts, ephemeral alliances, treacheries, calculated perfidies, dethronements during the twelfth century is unending. In the general political demoralization even the most resolute and unscrupulous princes, a Zangi or a Takash, could scarcely keep their feet.

The other was the composition of their military forces. The foundation of each prince's power was a standing regiment of guards or *askar* of Turkish *mamluks,* consisting of Turkish slaves purchased in boyhood and trained as professional cavalrymen, freed in due course, and maintained by the grant of military fiefs, from which they drew their revenues in money and kind. The continual warfare between the principalities was carried on by these professional troops, whose intensely personal loyalty was given to their immediate commander, and who therefore followed him into rebellion or changes of allegiance with little regard to the interests of their prince. Being professional armies, they were expensive to maintain and therefore small in numbers; one of the reasons for the constant efforts of princes to seize their neighbors' territories was precisely in order to gain the means of enlarging their forces. Furthermore, they could not and would not remain on campaign longer than a certain period at a time; on the one hand, the prince could not afford a high

rate of wastage, and on the other the troops themselves, as soon as their period of campaign service (called in Arabic *baikar*) was over, had no thought but to return to enjoy the proceeds of their fiefs.[4] The Turcoman troops, though nomadic irregulars, were little different; they too went on campaign only for a limited time, for so long as they could subsist on plunder or were paid for their services in money and supplies.[5]

Nur ad-Din, the son of a Turkish professional soldier, not only understood this system, but himself formed a part of it. Assuming his object to have been the creation of a centralized military power strong enough to deal with the crusaders, rather than personal aggrandizement, nevertheless his military and political action conformed almost entirely to the practice of the time (even if at a higher moral level); while on the other hand his rivals and vassals accepted him as a natural representative of the system by reason of his family connections, and respected him because of the success with which he operated it, both as a diplomatist and as a commander of armies. Even his campaign of what we may call "moral rearmament" by giving every support to the religious leaders and revivalists was not in any way unprecedented; indeed, it was on the basis and example of what had already been accomplished in this way in the Seljuk empire that Nur ad-Din founded his own policy, and the most that can be claimed for him is greater honesty and deeper sincerity than some of his predecessors in adopting it.

Nur ad-Din, in fine, both as general and administrator, displayed an insight and a capacity which rose above the average of his time but without conflicting with the established system. There can be little doubt that, had he lived, and the temporary rift between him and Saladin been closed, the counterattack on the crusaders would have been quicker and more vigorously pressed than it actually proved to be. The fact of the rift with Saladin cannot be denied, but the causes of it are clear enough to anyone who studies the sources without the bias induced by Ibn al-Athir's malicious interpretations. To Nur ad-Din the conquest of Egypt meant only an immediate and substantial accretion of military and financial resources for the war in Syria; whereas Saladin, faced with a dangerous situation in Egypt, felt that his first responsibility was to build up the local forces to hold Egypt against the threat of collusion between pro-Fatimid elements within and Frankish attacks from without. Presumably, after the failure of the Sicilian expedition to Alexandria in 1174 the general situation in Egypt would have been sufficiently stabilized to restore full understanding between Nur ad-Din and Saladin, but even before it arrived Nur ad-Din had died.

The immediate consequence of Nur ad-Din's death was that the centralized military power which he had built up fell to pieces, under the normal operation of the politico-military system. His Mosul relations seized the Jazira provinces, and his Syrian forces split up under the rivalries of the generals surrounding his minor son al-Malik as-Salih. The whole task had to be begun again, and on a very different footing. Since there was no hope of finding a true successor to Nur ad-Din among the members of the Zangid house, any attempt to revive Nur ad-Din's structure, from whatever quarter it came, would have to begin by challenging the existing Zangid principalities; and while its leader, if he were of the right type, might eventually hope to gain the support of the "moral rearmament" movement, he would certainly be opposed by its representatives in the first instance, out of loyalty to the memory of Nur ad-Din.

As these circumstances, therefore, made the task of reconstructing a centralized military power in Syria a different, and in some respects harder, task than had been faced by Nur ad-Din, so also the methods and qualities of the man who undertook it would have to be different from those of Nur ad-Din. It might not have been done at all; but if it was to be done, there were, so far as one can judge, only two alternative methods. One was the absorption of the whole Zangid structure into a powerful military empire from outside (such as, say, an expanded Seljuk Sultanate of Anatolia, or a new empire in the East, had either been possible at the time). The other was to build upon the foundations of moral unity laid by Nur ad-Din, and so greatly strengthen them that the Zangid structure would be forced into the service of its ends. To purely outward appearances Saladin's way was the first; in reality, the secret of his success was that he adopted and carried through the second. To be sure, this involved the building up of a vast empire extending from Kurdistan and Diyar Bakr to Nubia and the Yemen; for whoso wills the end must will the means, and the circumstances of his task and time required nothing less than this. But Saladin's personal position and qualities, the spirit in which he approached his task, and the methods he employed were utterly different from those possessed and displayed by the founders of great military empires.

To begin with, Saladin was not a Turk but a Kurd. If the Turks, because of the sense of superiority bred in them by their military tradition and the all but universal monopolization of political power in Eastern Islam by Turkish princes, despised all the other Muslim races, those of Mosul and northern Syria regarded their Kurdish neighbours with special contempt.[6] The Mosul troops, marching out against Saladin for the first time in 1175, had[7] abused and mocked him, calling him "a dog that barks at his master." Seventeen years later, a Mosul officer, as he watched Saladin being assisted on to his horse during the defence of Jerusalem, is reported as saying: "Have a care, son of Ayyub, what sort of end you will come to—you who are helped to mount by a Seljuk prince and a descendant of Atabeg Zangi!"[8] The difference in tone between the two taunts may fairly enough represent the extent and the limits of the change of attitude towards him among the more race conscious and the more resistant to the ideals for which he stood.

Secondly, although Saladin's father, uncle, brothers, and he himself were enrolled in Nur ad-Din's feudal forces, he

was far from outstanding as a general or a strategist. This may seem a paradox in the victor of Hattin; but Saladin was a good tactician. Hattin, like his two early victories against the forces of Mosul, was won by good tactics, and these were his only successful battles in the open field. His most remarkable feat of arms was the capture of the reputedly impregnable fortress of Amid (Diyarbakr) in 1183 after a siege of only three weeks, an episode generally overlooked in Western histories. It is remarkable how often lack of confidence in his generalship was expressed by the officers in his own armies, and not always without reason, even if valuable opportunities were sometimes lost during the Third Crusade by their opposition to his tactics and plans of campaign.

Nor was he a good administrator. He seems to have taken little personal interest in details of administration beyond trying to suppress abuses. In his own territories he leaned heavily on his brother al-Adil Saif ad-Din and his secretary of state al-Qadi al-Fadil; the administration of the provinces was turned over entirely to their governors on two conditions, that they should follow his example in suppressing abuses and furnish him with troops (and if necessary with money) when he required them to do so for the Holy War.

The independent and concordant testimony furnished by the surviving documents of three of the men who stood closest to him, al-Qadi al-Fadil, Imad ad-Din and Baha ad-Din, supply us with the real explanation of his success. Himself neither warrior nor governor by training or inclination, he it was who inspired and gathered round himself all the elements and forces making for the unity of Islam against the invaders. And this he did, not so much by the example of his personal courage and resolution— which were undeniable—as by his unselfishness, his humility and generosity, his moral vindication of Islam against both its enemies and its professed adherents. He was no simpleton, but for all that an utterly simple and transparently honest man. He baffled his enemies, internal and external, because they expected to find him animated by the same motives as they were, and playing the political game as they played it. Guileless himself, he never expected and seldom understood guile in others—a weakness of which his own family and others sometimes took advantage, but only (as a general rule) to come up at the end against his singleminded devotion, which nobody and nothing could bend, to the service of his ideals.

The true nature of those ideals has not yet, in my opinion, been appreciated. The immediate task to which he found himself called was to drive the Franks out of Palestine and Syria. This was the part that his contemporaries saw, and that later generations assumed to have been his whole purpose. It is natural, when a masn accomplishes some great work, to imagine that this was what he had set as his goal. In reality, it is more often the case that what a man achieves is only a part of what he sets out to achieve; and perhaps it is only because his eyes are fixed on some more distant goal that he succeeds in doing as much as he does.

This was, in my view, eminently true of Saladin. His wider design was one which only a man of unbounded ambition or of unbounded simplicity would have entertained. In a certain sense, Saladin was both, but his ambition arose out of the simplicity of his character and the directness of his vision. He saw clearly that the weakness of the Muslim body politic, which had permitted the establishment and continued to permit the survival of the crusading states, was the result of political demoralization. It was against this that he revolted. There was only one way to end it: to restore and revive the political fabric of Islam as a single united empire, not under his own rule, but by restoring the rule of the revealed law, under the direction of the Abbasid Caliphate. The theory of the caliph's disposal of provinces by diploma, to the other princes of the time a convenient fiction, was to him a positive and necessary reality. He saw himself as simply the adjutant and commander of the armies of the Abbasids, as he had become for a brief time the wazir and commander of the armies of the Fatimid Caliphs. That he was called *sultan* was simply the title he had inherited as wazir of the Fatimids; it had nothing to do with the theory or claims of the Seljuk sultanate, and it never appears in his protocol or on his coins. Imad ad-Din relates an incident during the siege of Acre, which is particularly instructive because it is one of the occasions on which the secretary reproaches Saladin for his simplicity.[9] At the request of an envoy from the caliphate, he had consented to transfer the region of Shahrazur in Kurdistan to the Caliph's possession; when faced with the anger and scorn of his amirs at this decision, he replied: "The Caliph is the lord of mankind and the repository of the True Faith; if he were to join us here I should give him all these lands—so what of Shahrazur?"

But the argument does not rest on an incidental episode of this kind, however authentic it may be. This objective is the explicit theme of many of his despatches to Baghdad. "These three aims—*jihad* on the path of God, the restraining of actions hurtful to the servants of God, and submission to the caliph of God—are the sole desire of this servitor from the territories in his occupation and his sole gain from the worldly power granted to him. God is his witness that . . . he has no desire beyond these things and no aim beyond this aim."[10] It reappears in his bewilderment at the failure of the caliph and the caliph's officers at Baghdad to understand his motives and to give him at least moral support: "For let him consider, is there anyone else of the governors of Islam whose increase distresses the infidels?"[11] in the punctiliousness with which he supplicates for the caliph's diploma of investiture before operating in new territories, and his protests against the Zangids' claims to the Jazira on grounds of "inheritance" in default of a diploma, and their seizure of Aleppo;[12] in his attribution of the speedy capture of Amid to the influence of the caliph's authority;[13] and in his forthright message to sultan Qilij Arslan of Anatolia in 1178 that "he would not permit mutual warfare among Muslim princes instead of their uniting in the *jihad*."[14]

At the same time his idealism was yoked with a strong practical sense. The clarity with which he judged each step towards his objective and each situation as it arose supplies the clue to the steady expansion of his power. Knowing that the problem which he faced was not only political, but also or still more a moral and psychological one, and that to attack it merely on the political and military plane would fail to solve it, he realized that to gain effective results it was essential to cement political allegiance by moral and psychological stimulants and deterrents. The difficulty—even the apparent hopelessness—of this task in the circumstances of the time are evident, but Saladin found ways to meet it, often to the bewilderment or astonishment of his friends and counselors.

In dealing with the princes, whether friends or enemies, his first principle was sincerity and absolute loyalty to his word. Even with the crusaders a truce was a truce. There is no instance on record in which he broke faith with them, and to those who broke faith with him he was implacable, as Reginald of Chatillon and the Templars were to learn. Towards his Muslim rivals he supplemented loyalty with generosity. After the pact with al-Malik as-Salih in 1176 (and the famous incident of the return of Azaz), he left Aleppo alone until as-Salih's death, although he held the caliph's diploma for it.[15] The siege of Amid was undertaken because he had promised it to the Artuqid prince of Hisn Kaifa as the price of his alliance, and after capturing it he turned over all its immense treasures to his ally as they stood—an act of loyalty to his pledged word so unprecedented that it created a sensation.[16]

To achieve his object, however, he had to reinforce his own actions and example by creating a moral and psychological current in his favour so strong that it could not be resisted. For this he needed allies, and especially the influential class of "college men" who were the leaders of public opinion. This was one of his most serious difficulties since, as already noted, these were precisely the sections which Nur ad-Din had mobilized in his support. Since Saladin at first appeared to be a usurper who challenged the heirs of Nur ad-Din, they, with the people of Syria generally, were in the beginning opposed, or at least reserved, towards him. The Arabic sources give us little indication of the gradual change in their attitude, but that his sincerity finally gained their respect and admiration is amply evident, both from the chronicles and from the reports of other contemporaries.[17] His patronage of the sufis, again following the example of Nur ad-Din, was probably of particular importance for this "missionary" work, if the term may be used, among the population of Syria. The most effective appeal to the general population, however, was probably made by his insistence upon the removal of wrongful dues and burdens in all territories under his government and suzerainty, even if it is by no means certain that his subordinates were always prompt to carry out his instructions on this point. Finally, it is remarkable that the turbulent Shiites of Aleppo and northern Syria, who had remained unreconciled to Nur ad-Din, not only gave Saladin no trouble (after the early Assassin attempts on his life) but positively assisted him during the reconquest.[18]

The secretary Imad ad-Din supplies a striking example of this aspect of Saladin's diplomacy,[19] on an occasion when the Zangid atabek of Mosul and his advisors attempted to take advantage of his loyalty to the caliphate, by requesting the caliph's *diwan* to send the Shaikh ash-Shuyukh of Baghdad to intercede with Saladin in 1184, "because of their knowledge that we had no thought of anything but implicit obedience to the command that should be obeyed" (i.e., of the caliphate). Although the conduct of the envoy from Mosul made an accommodation next to impossible, Saladin finally placed himself unreservedly in the hands of the Shaikh ash-Shuyukh, only to be repulsed again by the envoy, who openly threatened an alliance between Mosul and the caliph's enemy, the Seljuk sultan of Persia, Tughril II. It was this, adds Imad ad-Din, which determined Saladin, who had hitherto been lukewarm in prosecuting the conflict with Mosul, to deal with it firmly. That Imad ad-Din's account is not exaggerated is proved by the fact that Saladin's conduct on this occasion was the starting-point of his friendship with the qadi Baha ad-Din, who was himself in the suite of the Mosul envoy and in his narrative confirms the main points of this statement.[20]

Apart from the capture of Amid (and perhaps even there as well), in fact, the extension of Saladin's empire in Asia between 1182 and 1186 was due far more to the influence of these factors than to military action. His campaigns before Mosul and Aleppo were demonstrations rather than sieges. The lesser princes of the Jazira, confident in the character of the man, voluntarily placed themselves under his protection. The leaders of Nur ad-Din's regiment at Aleppo, after little more than a show of battle,[21] came over *en masse* to give him the most loyal service. Even at Mosul, as Ibn al-Athir himself conveys in his narrative,[22] Saladin found supporters among the commanders, and it was they who eventually forced the Zangid atabek to yield in 1186. The extent of the influence exerted by the *fuqaha* over the troops should not perhaps be exaggerated; but there are several examples in our sources of their decisive intervention, and they certainly counted as a contributory factor. The most remarkable case of all is that of the powerful Shah-Arman of Khilat, who had been among the most tenacious of Saladin's adversaries but who, just before the end of the Third Crusade, voluntarily offered Saladin his allegiance and his troops.[23]

How much Saladin's reputation for absolute faithfulness to his word and generosity contributed to the recovery of Palestine and inner Syria during the year and a half that followed Hattin is well known. If it had been necessary to take every castle and fortified town by regular siege, not more than a tithe of them would have fallen before the opening of the Third Crusade, and the history of that crusade would have been very different if the crusaders had had the support of garrisons in Saladin's rear.

The stability of Saladin's structure was destined to be tried to the utmost limit by the Third Crusade. It was to prove a contest of a kind which he had never anticipated and for which he had made no preparations. Instead of pursuing his noble, if idealist, dream of restoring the reign of law in the Islamic world, he was involved in a struggle of the most painful actuality; but because he had sought to realize the former by unselfishness, justice and loyalty, and only because of these moral foundations, he was able to sustain the unprecedented task now thrust upon him. No Muslim prince had for centuries been confronted with the problem of maintaining an army continuously in the field for three years against an active and enterprising enemy. The military feudal system was entirely inadequate to such a campaign, even if it was possible to organize a limited system of reliefs between the Egyptian and the Mesopotamian regiments.

The contest uncovered one by one the material and even moral weaknesses in Saladin's empire which had remained concealed during the era of victory. He had never cared for money or for prudent management of his revenues. He had "spent the revenues of Egypt to gain Syria, the revenues of Syria to gain Mesopotamia, those of Mesopotamia to conquer Palestine,"[24] and now found himself without adequate resources to meet the cost of weapons, food, forage, equipment, and the pay of the auxiliary troops. In consequence, he could do little to ease the difficulties of the feudal troops, who were either forced into debt or into pressing their cultivators.[25] Perhaps this, even more than the survival of old rancors, may explain the reluctance of some of the Eastern contingents to sustain their part in the campaign. In addition, all the military equipment from Egypt and Syria had been locked up in Acre,[26] which Saladin had refortified as his main base for future operations; the siege and loss of Acre therefore seriously crippled the offensive power of the Muslim army.

Apart from this, however, the tactics and fighting traditions of the regular troops were baffled by the fortified trenches of the crusading besiegers. In open fighting on the plain against the western knights the Turkish regulars more than held their own, although Saladin's Kurdish guards proved less stable (as again at Arsuf). But when repeated success in the open field proved to be of no effect whatsoever in relieving the pressure on Acre, it was a natural reaction to slacken effort and to grumble against Saladin. Once it had started, grumbling became a habit and developed into criticism and opposition, especially in the later period of the campaign, when the fall of Acre seemed to have proved the weakness of Saladin's military leadership.

Yet this was after all a minor matter in comparison with the damage inflicted on Saladin and on the whole cause for which he stood by his own kinsmen. Here, if anywhere, was his most vulnerable point. The scarcely concealed appetites of several of his brothers and other relatives[27] had caused him much trouble in the past, but had been brought more or less under control. But at the very climax of his struggle with the crusaders his nephew Taqi ad-Din deliberately disobeyed his orders in Diyar Bakr, and by his disobedience opened up a series of conflicts and mutinies which grievously disabled Saladin during the campaign in

Palestine after the fall of Acre. Not only did they involve the absence of Taqi ad-Din's own troops and those of Diyar Bakr during the rest of the active fighting, but they led to further rifts within his family and to dissensions amongst his overstrained personal troops during the last crucial months.

These were the factors which robbed Saladin of the chance of complete victory in his struggle with Richard. But they only throw into stronger relief the most surprising and significant feature of the whole campaign—that year after year the Mosul contingents returned for active service, even if they sometimes lingered on the way. In the circumstances, there could have been no question of physical compulsion, nor could Saladin have restrained them (as the episode of Taqi ad-Din proves) from reoccupying the Jazira, as in fact they attempted to do immediately after his death. There can be no explanation of this except that the feeling of personal loyalty to Saladin, even in Mosul, was strong enough to overcome the reluctance or resistance of individuals. His own modestly-phrased remark to Baha ad-Din: "If I were to die, it is very unlikely that these *askars* would ever come together again,"[28] sums up the real nature of his achievement. For a brief but decisive moment, by sheer goodness and firmness of character, he raised Islam out of the rut of political demoralization. By standing out for a moral ideal, and expressing that ideal in his own life and action, he created around him an impulse to unity which, though never quite complete, sufficed to meet the unforeseen challenge flung down to him by destiny.

Notes

1. See "Arabic Sources for the Life of Saladin" in *Speculum*, xxv, no. i, pp. 58-72 (Cambridge, Mass., 1950).

2. *Conquête de la Syrie et de la Palestine,* ed. Carlo de Landberg (Leyden, 1888). This text has been little used so far by historians of the crusades.

3. See N. Elisséeff, "Les Monuments de Nur ad-Din" in *Bulletin d'Etudes Orientales,* t. xiii (Damascus, 1951), pp. 5-43.

4. This practice was dictated not only by personal considerations but also by sound economic reasons. The regular forces had to maintain themselves and their retainers on campaign with supplies and forage out of their own revenues, and a prolonged campaign involved them in considerable expense and even debt (cf. Imad ad-Din in Abu Shama, i. 271 foot, and *Fath* 392-3; Baha ad-Din (ed. Schultens) 200, 221).

5. Cf. Ibn al-Athir (ed. Tornberg), x. 400; Imad ad-Din, *Barq,* iii. 139b.

6. This is expressed vividly and with typical elaboration even by Imad ad-Din, who devotes more than a page to disparaging the unmilitary qualities of the Kurds in the Artuqid armies in contrast to the virtues and sobriety of Saladin's troops: *Barq,* v. 57b sq.

7. If Michael the Syrian is to be believed: ed. and trans. Chabot, iii. 365.

8. Ibn al-Athir, xii. 50.

9. *Fath* (ed. Landberg), 218-219.

10. From Abu Shama, ii. 48, after the occupation of Amid.

11. From Abu Shama, ii. 41, after the capture of Amid.

12. Cf. Abu Shama, ii. 24, 31 n. It might be claimed, and with truth, that such passages could be paralleled in the artificial correspondence of other princes with the caliphate. But it would be utterly inconsistent with all that we know of the character of Saladin to regard them as equally hypocritical; and if it all meant nothing more to him than mere playing with words, why should he have kept up such a stream of entreaties and expostulations to Baghdad?

13. Abu Shama, ii. 40-41.

14. *Barq,* iii. fol. 123a.

15. Abu Shama, ii. 34.

16. So consistent was his conduct in this respect, and so frightening to his enemies, that it was necessary to invent an incident to offset it, which is duly recorded (with a great show of impartiality) by Ibn al-Athir (xi. 341; see "Arabic Sources," *Speculum,* xxv, 67-68).

17. See Ibn Jubair, *Rihla,* pp. 297-298; Abd al-Latif al-Baghdadi in Ibn Abi Usaibia, *Uyun al-Anba,* ii. 206 (both translated in *R.H.C.Or.,* iii. 435 sqq.).

18. C. Cahen, *La Syrie du Nord à l'époque des croisades* (Paris, 1940), pp. 428-429.

19. *Barq,* v. fol. 129 sqq.

20. Ed. Schultens, p. 57.

21. Imad ad-Din, *Barq.* v. 79b sqq. (Abu Shama, ii. 43-44).

22. Ed. Tornberg, xi. 338, 340. See also the significant incident of the garrison of Harim (quoted by Grousset, ii. 720).

23. Baha ad-Din, 260.

24. Al-Qadi al-Fadil in Abu Shama, ii. 177.

25. Abu Shama, ii. 177, 178, 203; *Fath,* 207, 392-393, 443; Baha ad-Din, 200, 221, etc.

26. Baha ad-Din, 174.

27. Vividly portrayed by al-Qadi al-Fadil in a letter quoted by Abu Shama, ii. 178.

28. Baha ad-Din, 218.

Abbreviations

BEO *Bulletin d'études orientales*

BGA *Bibl. Geographorum Arabicorum*

BSOS *Bulletin of the School of Oriental Studies*

BSOAS *Bulletin of the School of Oriental and African Studies*

GJ *Geographical Journal*

IA *International Affairs*

IC *Islamic Culture*

JAOS *Journal of the American Oriental Society*

JCAS *Journal of the Central Asian Society*

JNES *Journal of Near Eastern Studies*

JRAS *Journal of the Royal Asiatic Society*

JRCAS *Journal of the Royal Central Asian Society*

JTS *Journal of Theological Studies*

MEJ *Middle East Journal*

MSOS *Mitteilungen des Seminars für orientalische Sprachen*

MW *Muslim World*

RAAD *Revue de l'Academie Arabe de Damas*

REI *Revue des études islamiques*

RMM *Revue du monde musulman*

RSO *Rivista degli studi orientali*

SI *Studia Islamica*

WI *Welt des Islams*

WZKM *Wiener Zeitschrift für die Kunde des Morgenlandes*

ZDMG *Zeitschrift der Deutschen morgenländischen Gesellschaft*

Andrew S. Ehrenkreutz (essay date 1972)

SOURCE: "The Showdown with the Crusader" in *Saladin,* State University of New York Press, 1972, pp. 195–261.

[*In the following essay, Ehrenkreutz offers an assessment of Saladin's career that focuses on his accomplishments as well as his shortcomings. Ehrenkreutz stresses that he does not, unlike many critics, conjecture about or romanticize Saladin's intentions.*]

> *"As for the claim of the Caliph that I've conquered Jerusalem with his army and under his banners—where were his banners and his army at the time? By God! I conquered Jerusalem with my own troops and under my own banners!"—Saladin to Caliph al-Nasir*

TRADITIONAL TREATMENT OF SALADIN'S CAREER IS OPEN TO QUESTION

To modern western readers Saladin is best known for his military battles with the Crusaders between 1187 and 1192.

This is understandable in view of the dramatic character of that struggle and the fact that it involved formidable naval and land forces and prominent leaders from Europe. The interest aroused by that brief climactic phase in Saladin's career is reflected in the arrangement of Lane-Poole's biography. The initial section of his book, entitled "Egypt" and covering the period from Saladin's birth to Nur al-Din's death (1138-74), is surveyed in sixty-three pages of rather diluted narrative. The second part, called "Empire" and dealing with the years of 1174-86, requires sixty-five pages. But to the third part, "The Holy War," covering 1187 to the signing of the peace agreement in 1192, Lane-Poole allocated one hundred sixty pages.

Does this traditional focus on Saladin's showdown with the Crusaders enable one to understand the real significance of his personality and the effects of his ambitions and accomplishments in history? According to Lane-Poole, "The Holy War had long been a fixed resolve with Saladin," so that following a series of provocations on the part of the notorious master of Kerak and Shaubak, the sultan "resolved to try no more half-measures, but to wage a war of extermination of the whole Christian kingdom."[1]

From the viewpoint of the history of the Crusades, Saladin's career is highly relevant to the story of European militaristic and economic penetration of the Near East during the Middle Ages. And that has been the main reason Saladin's personality and achievements have produced such an impact on the imagination of European writers from the Middle Ages down to modern times.

However, despite the dramatic and seemingly romantic nature of the "European" aspect of Saladin's career, both the Crusaders and, above all, Saladin himself belong integrally to Near Eastern history.

The history of the Crusades did not begin or end with Saladin, nor was the range of his historical accomplishments limited to his involvement with the Crusaders.

The validity of viewing Saladin's career solely in terms of his struggle with the Crusaders has been challenged by H. A. R. Gibb. In his article, "The Achievement of Saladin," Gibb proposed a new thesis concerning the ideological motivations and, consequently, the real historical role of the Ayyubid sultan.

> The immediate task to which he found himself called was to drive the Franks out of Palestine and Syria. This was the part that his contemporaries saw, and that later generations assumed to have been his whole purpose. It is natural, when a man accomplishes some great work, to imagine that this was what he had set as his goal. In reality, it is more often the case that what a man achieves is only a part of what he sets out to achieve; and perhaps it is only because his eyes are fixed on some more distant goal that he succeeds in doing as much as he does.

> This was, in my view eminently true of Saladin. His wider design was one which only a man of unbounded

ambition or of unbounded simplicity would have entertained. In a certain sense, Saladin was both, but his ambition arose out of the simplicity of his character and the directness of his vision. He saw clearly that the weakness of the Muslim body politic, which had permitted the establishment and continued to permit the survival of the crusading states, was the result of political demoralization. It was against this that he revolted. There was only one way to end it: to restore and revive the political fabric of Islam as a single united empire, not under his own rule, but by restoring the rule of the revealed law, under the direction of the Abbasid Caliphate. The theory of the Caliph's disposal of provinces by diploma, to the other princes of the time a convenient fiction, was to him a positive and necessary reality. He saw himself as simply the adjutant and commander of the armies of the Abbasids, as he had become for a brief time the wazir and commander of the armies of the Fatimid Caliphs. That he was called Sultan was simply the title he had inherited as wazir of the Fatimids; it had nothing to do with the theory of claims of the Seljuk Sultanate, and it never appears in his protocol or on his coins. Imad al-Din relates an incident during the siege of Acre, which is particularly instructive because it is one of the occasions on which the secretary reproaches Saladin for his simplicity. At the request of an envoy from the Caliphate, he had consented to transfer the region of Shahrazur in Kurdistan to the Caliph's possession; when faced with the anger and scorn of his amirs at his decision, he replied: "The Caliph is the lord of mankind and the repository of the True Faith; if he were to join us here I should give him all these lands—so what of Shahrazur?"[2]

If one considers that the total range of Crusader activities, even at their most expansive phase, affected a very limited area of the Near East, and, on the other hand, if one realizes that Saladin's alleged ideals aimed at reviving the political fabric of Islam under the auspices of the caliphate, then Gibb's thesis dramatically upgrades the significance of the great sultan in Near Eastern history.

For my part, I am happy neither with focusing on Saladin's Crusader struggle nor with attributing to him lofty devotion to "the true faith," which I am afraid are not borne out by the whole factual record. Historical phenomena are not finally assessed by the ideals of human protagonists, but by the effects these ideals or their implementation produce on society. The old saying that "the road to hell is paved with good intentions" is a handy maxim in drawing up the balance sheet of historical figures.

With Saladin one cannot be too certain concerning his real intentions at any stage of his colorful career, one can only assess his actual activities and accomplishments.

SALADIN'S DIPLOMATIC ARRANGEMENTS WITH THE CRUSADERS AND THE BYZANTINES

Although the conflict with Mosul was ended by 1186, Saladin showed no eagerness to prepare immediately for resumption of the Crusader war. His passivity may have been motivated by the fact that, even without his direct pressure, the Christian kingdom was moving toward self-destruction. The crowning of the unpopular Guy of Lusignan as King of Jerusalem, following the death of Baldwin IV in 1185 and Baldwin V in late summer 1186, resulted in a rebellious challenge from Count Raymund of Tripoli. The new king, advised by the master of the Templars, decided to correct this defiance by drastic military measures. But Raymund refused to be intimidated and to strengthen his own position requested assistance from Saladin. The Muslim sultan replied by sending him a number of troops and a promise of more.[3] By supplying fuel Saladin undoubtedly hoped to further the rapid disintegration of the Crusader kingdom, thus sparing himself the trouble of mobilizing troops and economic resources upon the expiration of his own truce.

At about that time Saladin concluded a formal treaty of alliance with the Christian Empire of Constantinople.[4] The policy of rapprochement between the Byzantines and Saladin, initiated by the last Comneni emperors, had been continued by their successors of the Angeli dynasty. Such a development was nothing new in the international politics of the eastern Mediterranean. Independent (Fatimids) and semi-independent (Tulunids and Ikhshidids) rulers of Islamic Egypt had engaged in diplomatic cooperation with Constantinople, even if such policy hurt both the interests of other Muslim leaders and the prestige of the Baghdad caliphate. In the last quarter of the twelfth century the Byzantines and the Ayyubids were drawn together by opposition to the same enemies. The Normans of Sicily were as dangerous to Egypt as to the Byzantines; the Saljuqids of Iconium had emerged from Myriokephalon as the strongest power in Asia Minor, capturing many Byzantine provinces and threatening Saladin's interests in the north; Cyprus, which had rebelled against Constantinople, was a possible adherent of the Crusaders; and finally, the Crusaders and their potential allies from Western Europe constituted a bloc as hostile to the Byzantines as to the Ayyubids.

There is no doubt that the last factor primarily induced Saladin to cooperate with Constantinople, though he may have been somewhat influenced by two Angeli princes, Alexius and Isaac, who stayed as guests at his court. Indeed, Alexius was still there when Isaac was raised to the Byzantine throne in September 1185.[5]

The first Greek embassy proposing a formal alliance had reached Saladin in the summer of 1185. However, the terms proved unacceptable to Saladin because Constantinople, besides arrogating to itself a suzerain status in respect of the Muslim warlord, claimed too many territorial concessions in Palestine, including Jerusalem and various maritime cities.[6]

Saladin proposed his own terms, rejecting the Byzantine claim to suzerainty, but offering to convert the existing Latin churches in the Holy Land to the Greek rite—a clever move, bound to promote pro-Ayyubid feelings among the Greek Christians in the Crusader kingdom. Saladin's counterproposals were favorably received by the Byzantines. With the Normans threatening the capital itself, Emperor Isaac II Angelus confirmed the revised version of the treaty and summoned his brother Alexius back from Saladin's court.[7]

Predictably, rumors of the Byzantine-Muslim alliance reached the Crusaders, so when Alexius Angelus was passing through Acre on his way to Constantinople, the Count of Tripoli seized and imprisoned him. Learning of that outrage, Isaac wrote to Saladin prodding him to attack the Crusaders in order to secure Alexius' release.[8] By then Saladin's relations with the Kingdom of Jerusalem had been brought to an explosive point of Reginald of Châtillon's blatant violation of the armistice. Early in 1187 Reginald attacked an important caravan passing between Cairo and Damascus, carried off considerable booty, and imprisoned its military escort. Breaking the truce was a serious matter, as even Reginald's friends realized. Saladin still tried negotiations to avert hostilities, but Reginald flatly refused to comply with the categorical requests of King Guy and ignored the Ayyubid ultimatum.[9] A showdown between the Muslim forces of the Ayyubids and the Crusaders could not be avoided.[10] Saladin proclaimed a *jihad,* to which the Muslim population in the areas affected by Reginald's recurrent bloody provocations responded with enthusiasm.[11] In addition to planning an all-out war against the Christians, Saladin vowed to take personal vengeance on Reginald.[12]

WAR WITH THE CRUSADERS AND VICTORY AT HATTIN

At the end of May 1187 Saladin's contingents completed their concentration. His cavalry alone reached an impressive total of 12,000 with possibly as many auxiliary troops and irregulars. Though they had come from different regions of his dominions—from Egypt and Syria, from al-Jazirah and Diyar Bakr, from Damascus, Aleppo, and Mosul—the warriors of the Ayyubid sultan were united by the idea of fighting the Frankish Infidels.[13] In spite of total mobilization of the fleet, however, the warships did not participate in the decisive expedition. Possibly the fiasco at Beirut caused Saladin to doubt the effectiveness of his fleet under real battle conditions. Or perhaps his decision was motivated by the knowledge that earlier in the spring the Byzantines had sent a fleet to attack Cyprus. Indeed, the Crusaders had interpreted the appearance of the Byzantine armada in Syrian waters as naval support for Saladin's offensive.[14] On Friday, 26 June 1187, Saladin set out for Palestine to start the momentous struggle[15] which was not terminated until five years later.

Aware of the all-out character of Saladin's new offensive, the Crusaders succeeded in collecting an army which numerically more or less equalled the Muslim force. The defeat of the Byzantine fleet off Cyprus by the Normans and the absence of the Egyptian navy allowed the Christian coastal fortresses to release all their fighting men for the main army. But they were internally disunited, they lacked confidence in Guy's leadership, and their tactics were greatly inferior to those of the experienced Ayyubid warlord. Although Raymund of Tripoli had insisted they should follow defensive tactics by using their castles, King Guy and some hawks in his entourage decided to march north to meet the Muslim army in open field. There they were out-maneuvered by Saladin, and after a few preliminary and costly skirmishes they had to accept battle under most unfavorable conditions on the plain of Hattin, overlooking the Lake of Tiberias. The Crusader army, exhausted by the summer heat and Muslim harassment, found access to the lake barred by fresh and confident contingents of Saladin.[16] There on 4 July 1187 occurred one of the most decisive military confrontations between the forces of Islam and the Latin Kingdom of Jerusalem. It was a battle which the Crusaders need not have fought at all and certainly should not have lost.[17] However, because of Saladin's superior tactics and especially because of renewed wrangling among the Christians on the eve of the battle, the Muslim forces won a smashing victory. It was Saladin's victory, it was Saladin's great day, from which he acquired the image of *jihad* leader *par excellence,* the Allah-inspired nemesis of the Frankish Infidels.

The emotions Saladin experienced during the battle were dramatically reported by his son al-Afdal:

> "It was my first set battle," said al-Afdal, at that time but sixteen-years old, "and I was at my father's side. When the King of the Franks had retired to the hill, his knights made a gallant charge, and drove the Moslems back upon my Father. I watched him, and I saw his dismay; he changed color, tugged at his beard, and rushed forward, shouting 'Give the devil the lie!' So the Moslems fell upon the enemy, who retreated up the hill. When I saw the Franks flying and the Moslems pursuing, I cried in my glee, 'We have routed them!' But the Franks charged again and drove our men back once more to where my Father was. Again he urged them forward, and they drove the enemy up the hill. Again I shouted, 'We have routed them!' But Father turned to me and said: 'Hold thy peace! We have *not* beaten them so long as that tent stands there.' At that instant the royal tent was overturned. Then the Sultan dismounted, and bowed himself to the earth, giving thanks to God, with tears of joy."[18]

It was indeed the end. In one single day Saladin routed virtually all local Christian forces capable of defending the Crusader establishment in the Near East. Only a small group led by Raymund of Tripoli managed to escape annihilation. Other Crusader leaders not killed in the battle were taken prisoner, including King Guy himself. Knights fared better than the foot soldiers, not only in escaping the bloodiest carnage but in receiving better care as captives. No code of chivalry or hope of ransom protected the lowly born. For Reginald of Châtillon Saladin reserved a special treatment.

SALADIN EXACTS BLOODY VENGEANCE

As soon as Saladin's tent had been pitched on the battlefield, he had the prisoners brought before him. He made King Guy sit down near himself, with Reginald next to him. Seeing the Christian king burning with thirst, the sultan ordered a cooling drink served to the royal prisoner. Guy drank and passed the cup to the lord of Kerak. At this, Saladin ominously remarked to Guy: "It is you who served him water. I, certainly, gave no water to him."[19] Saladin had never shown mercy to traitors or perjurers, Muslim and Christian alike. Reginald, who for over a decade had harassed the borders of Egypt and Arabia, who had dared to launch an expedition against Mecca, and who had caused the outbreak of war, the sultan had sworn to slay personally.[20] The prisoners were taken outside—all except Reginald. Saladin then proffered him the adoption of Islam, but the proud knight refused. Thereupon Saladin drew his scimitar and felled the defenseless prisoner with a blow that split his shoulder wide open. A coup de grace was then administered by a guard in attendance. Seeing Reginald's body dragged out of the tent, King Guy believed his own turn was coming. But Saladin reassured him: "It is not the custom of kings to slay kings; but that man had transgressed all bounds, so what happened—happened."[21]

Saladin's thirst for blood, however, had not been quenched by killing Reginald. He next ordered the execution of all captive Templar and Hospitaler knights, offering a reward of fifty dinars for every one brought to headquarters. In no time 200 prospective victims were led to the place of execution.[22] As on a similar occasion in 1178, Saladin personally watched the slaughter, with rows of soldiers sitting in front of him. His immediate entourage consisted of divines, jurists, and members of Muslim mystical orders. They asked the sultan to let each of them kill a prisoner of his choice. When permission was granted, they drew their swords and joined in the killing, though not all proved up to the grim task. "There were some whose strength gave out, so they backed out and were excused; there were others who did not hit strong enough and were laughed at by the crowds and had to be replaced by others; but there were some who revealed their noble descent in administering their blows."[23]

TRIUMPHANT BLITZKRIEG AND A STRATEGIC DILEMMA: TYRE OR JERUSALEM

So total and decisive was the victory at Hattin that Saladin followed it up immediately with a multipronged offensive against various Crusader cities and fortresses depleted of defenders. On 5 July he secured the capitulation of Tiberias, and on 9 July he received the surrender of Acre where, incidentally, he set free the Byzantine emperor's imprisoned brother.[24] After Acre the blitzkrieg gained such momentum that less than two months after Hattin all the major ports south of Tripoli, with the exception of Tyre and Ascalon, were in Muslim hands. In addition, virtually all the inland towns and castles south of Tiberias, except Shaubak and Kerak in Transjordan, capitulated. Only these two southern strongholds, and a few formidable castles in the north, such as Belvoir (Kaukab), Safad, and Belfort, managed to hold out.

It was to Tyre that Raymund of Tripoli had escaped from the battlefield of Hattin. And it was to Tyre that European reinforcements, led by the renowned Conrad of Montferrat, came following the fall of Acre. However, instead of attacking Tyre forthwith, Saladin marched south to Ascalon, the last Crusader outpost obstructing the direct coastal route between Egypt and Syria. This operation ended successfully on 5 September 1187 when Ascalon surrendered in exchange for the release of King Guy from captivity.[25]

Now Tyre, the last Crusader coastal fortress in that area, acquired great strategic significance. If it could repulse Saladin's troops, Tyre could become the rallying point for Crusader refugees and stragglers, military and civilian alike. Moreover, if it held out long enough, Tyre could serve as a beachhead for European reinforcements.

That chance Saladin provided himself. After the victory at Ascalon, he marched not against Tyre but against Jerusalem. This proved to be a strategic blunder which ultimately wiped out all the advantages achieved by the victory of Hattin. Experienced warlord as he was, Saladin must have realized the strategic implications of leaving Tyre alone. Certainly his troops, his miners, his naval contingents could have overpowered Tyre, animated as they were by an aggressive, dynamic mood. During his military career, Saladin had conquered many a difficult fortress, Ailah in 1171, Bait al-Ahzan in 1179, Amida in 1183, and all the coastal establishments captured that same summer of 1187.

On the other hand, Jerusalem, with but a handful of able-bodied defenders, completely cut off from both Crusader support and the coast itself and containing Greek inhabitants eager to shake off the Latin regime, presented neither a threat nor even a major military problem to Saladin. By then restoration of the holy city to Islam was merely a question of time, to be selected by the victorious sultan. And yet despite the strategic importance of Tyre, Saladin chose Jerusalem. What made him commit this grave strategic error? The answer seems to be that Saladin hoped to collect tremendous propaganda dividends from an easy occupation of the holy city.[26] He had already established his popularity as suppressor of the Shiite caliphate in Egypt; he had also been acclaimed as protector of the city of the Prophet. Now he could achieve a glory which in Islam's long and heroic history had been enjoyed only by Umar ibn al-Khattab, companion of Muhammad himself and chief architect of the seventh century Islamic ascendancy. And if some people were still skeptical about the real motivations behind his incessant campaigns, behind his staggering drive for power, behind his unrestricted investment of economic resources in military expenditure, their doubts must be dispelled by the reconquest of Jerusalem. Saladin's name had already been invoked in the *khutbah* all over Egypt, in North African regions, in Syria, in Jazirah, and in Mosul. Why should it not resound from the mosques of the liberated holy city? Ayyubid prestige would certainly be well served, even if failure to capture Tyre immediately risked inviting a new European invasion.

RECAPTURE OF JERUSALEM: THE CROWNING ACHIEVEMENT OF SALADIN'S CAREER

Predictably enough, Saladin had no trouble in forcing the garrison of Jerusalem into surrender. On 2 October 1197 the yellow banners of the Ayyubid conqueror appeared on the walls of the holy city which after eighty-eight years was finally returned to the fold of Islam. With this achievement the great sultan reached the apex of his political and military career. News of the dramatic event, stressing Saladin's role, spread quickly over the Muslim and Christian worlds. Jubilant letters were sent by his chancery to the caliph of Baghdad, to various Muslim princes and notables,[27] as well as to the Byzantine emperor.[28] When word of Jerusalem's fall reached Western Europe, it produced shock and grief—and calls for revenge.

Official celebrations honoring the liberation and purification of Jerusalem took place on Friday, 9 October 1187. An immense congregation assembled to pray with Saladin in the sanctuary of al-Aqsa. The chief qadi of Aleppo, Muhyi al-Din ibn al-Zaki, preached the main sermon. He praised God for the triumph of the faith and the cleansing of his holy house; he declared the pure creed of the Quran, and pronounced the blessings upon the Prophet and the caliphs, in the prescribed form of the Sunni bidding-prayer. He invoked the name of the reigning caliph, al-Nasir li-Din Allah. Finally, concluding his peroration, he declared:

> And prolong, O Almighty God, the reign of thy servant, humbly reverent, for thy favor thankful, grateful for thy gifts, thy sharp sword and shining torch, the champion of thy faith and defender of thy holy land, the firmly resisting, the great al-Malik al-Nasir, the unifier of the true religion, the vanquisher of the worshippers of the Cross, Salah al-Dunya wa al-Din. Saladin, Sultan of Islam and of the Moslems, purifier of the holy temple, Abu al-Muzaffar Yusuf, Son of Ayyub, reviver of the empire of the Commander of the Faithful. Grant, O God, that his empire may spread all over the earth, and that the angels may ever surround his standards, preserve him for the good of Islam; protect him for the profit of the Faith; and extend his dominion over the regions of the East and of the West. . . ."[29]

SALADIN'S CALAMITOUS FAILURE AT TYRE

Saladin's very belated action against Tyre proved disastrous. Only on 1 November 1187 did he dispatch an army against it. Twelve days later he arrived there to assume personal command.[30] One hundred nineteen days had elapsed since the battle of Hattin and fifty-six since the capture of Ascalon. During that crucial period the number of defenders in Tyre had been increased by refugees from all the places that had capitulated that summer. Conrad of Montferrat had worked intensively on strengthening fortifications, encouraging the defenders, and "directing them with superior ability." He had deepened and extended the moats till Tyre became "like a hand spread upon the sea, attached only by the wrist," an island approached by so narrow a spit that it would be easily defended by a small force, as well as covered by crossbows on the shielded Christian barges.[31] The Crusader garrison, knowing the momentous significance of the impending confrontation, was ready to resist or die.

The same was not true of Saladin's army. For nearly a month they had been celebrating their recapture of Jerusalem, proclaimed all over the Muslim world as the supreme and sacred objective of the *jihad*. And now, instead of being allowed to return home, covered with glory and rich in booty, they were being deployed against a spirited and tenacious Frankish garrison, well sheltered behind the strong defensive works of Tyre.

This imbalance in morale was the main reason that Saladin could neither intimidate nor overrun the Crusaders of Conrad of Montferrat. Saladin's attack against Tyre degenerated into a protracted siege in which the Egyptian fleet assumed an important function. Its duty was to blockade the port and deprive the defenders of relief by sea.[32] In December 1187 rain and snow converted the besiegers' camp into a sea of mud, and damp and cold bred sickness among the soldiers and horses. Exhausted by the strain of the siege some of Saladin's commanders voiced their pessimism regarding the outcome.[33]

To a large extent their doubts were caused by economic factors. Operating within the strictly defined feudal structure of military obligations and rights to regular compensation, Saladin's warriors had expected to return home, once their regular periodic campaign service was over, to collect the proceeds of their fiefs. One way of securing their extended participation in the campaign, beyond the prescribed duration, would be direct cash compensation from the coffers of the sultan. Unfortunately Saladin did not possess adequate monies. The long years of heavy military expenditure and of gold drain caused by extensive purchases of war material from Europeans had resulted in an acute cash crisis which his victories in Syria and Mesopotamia failed to alleviate.

Had Saladin been able to inspire his troops, had he been able to sustain the original enthusiasm for war which Reginald's outrageous provocations had generated and which the victories of Hattin, Acre, and Jerusalem later magnified, then the besieging generals and soldiers might have endured the extraordinary sacrifices required for the continuation of the siege. But Saladin was hardly the man to demand of his followers blind devotion to the holy war. After all, whatever his popular image among the Muslim masses, Saladin's personal and political conduct hardly served as an inspiring example of self-denial for the *jihad*.

Toward the very end of 1187, when Saladin experienced difficulties in maintaining discipline in his army, the Egyptian fleet suffered a humiliating setback. The Muslim ships blockading Tyre let themselves be taken by surprise—they were boarded during the night of 30 December by Christian raiders who succeeded in capturing five ships, together with their crews and the two top men in command. Saladin immediately ordered the remaining five ships to lift the blockade and proceed to their nearest base in Beirut. When the port of Tyre was thus opened, some Christian galleys, hitherto bottled up in the harbor, pursued the withdrawing Egyptian ships, whose crews had neither the courage to resist nor determination to bring the ships safely to Beirut. They simply abandoned the ships, jumping overboard and trying to save themselves by swimming ashore.[34]

This naval humiliation increased Saladin's trouble with his land forces. In spite of support from old associates such as Isa al-Hakkari and Izz al-Din Jurdiq, the sultan found it impossible to control the defeatist feelings pervading his camp. On 1 January 1188, he ordered a general retreat, dejectedly leaving all heavy equipment and armament behind.[35]

Lane-Poole rightly regards the ignominious retreat from Tyre as the "turning-point in Saladin's career of victory."[36] He also states that:

> Whatever the difficulties of the siege, *Delenda est Tyrus* should have been his immutable resolve. He should have built a new fleet, destroyed the Tyrian galleys, filled the moats, breached the walls, if he lost half his army in so doing. The only answer is that Saladin knew his men, and felt that he could not count upon their endurance. But even this does not explain his neglect to blockade the city by sea and land, to keep off reinforcements, and to starve its crowded population. However we look at it, Saladin's measures against Tyre appear neither soldierly nor statesmanlike. Tyre became the rallying point from which the Crusaders recovered part of their lost power and prestige along the coast of Palestine; and had this one city not held out, it is a question whether the Third Crusade would ever have been heard of at Acre.[37]

To this accurate assessment of Saladin's failure at Tyre one may add that not only did the sultan know his men, but his men, especially various military commanders, some of them his former rivals, were quite familiar with his previous record. They had recognized Saladin's consistent moves to strengthen and expand his own power, and they were aware of his political ambitions for the Ayyubid family. The disastrous siege of Tyre demonstrated that even the glorious reconquest of Jerusalem had not dispelled their doubts regarding Saladin's devotion to the holy war.

SERIOUS DETERIORATION OF RELATIONS WITH CALIPH AL-NASIR

The caliph of Baghdad also expressed skepticism about Saladin's political ideals during the difficult siege of Tyre. Unlike other congratulatory messages Saladin received from different quarters of the Muslim world, as well as from Constantinople, al-Nasir's letter contained nothing but sarcastic, insinuative questions and reproaches. Why had Saladin granted asylum to several political refugees from Baghdad? How dared he assume the honorific title of al-Nasir which was the official name of the Abbasid suzerain? And finally: "As to your jubilation over the capture of Jerusalem—had she not been conquered by the troops of the Caliph, under the banners of the Caliph?"[38]

Obviously the caliph had become deeply troubled by Saladin's staggering successes, especially the extension of his authority to northern Mesopotamia. There were people in Baghdad who accused Saladin of planning to finish off the Abbasids as he had the Fatimids.[39] The caliph's message was a warning; it was also an attempt to undermine the prestige of the sultan by refusing to recognize the mandate Saladin claimed destiny had entrusted to him to wage the holy war. The caliph's letter greatly shocked Saladin, who had been expecting expressions of thanks for his great accomplishments. He was not repentant. In talking to the envoy from Baghdad he rejected one after another of the caliph's points.

> The refugee knights who join my camp do it because a refugee is happy even with an old hut in the desert as long as it protects him from death. As for the alleged usurpation of the Caliph's honorific name—By God! I did neither choose it nor usurp it. It was given to me by Caliph al-Mustadi after I had destroyed the two-hundred-year-old regime of his Ismaili enemies.[40] This matter had been settled in a letter from Baghdad to Nur al-Din, before thine accession to the throne. I would not object if ten thousand Turkomans and Kurds in my army were called Saladin. As for the claim of the Caliph that I conquered Jerusalem with his army and under his banners—where were his banners and his army at the time? By God! I conquered Jerusalem with my own troops and under my own banners.[41]

Although Saladin refrained from public manifestion of his bitterness, al-Nasir's letter opened a rift between the two men. The caliph's first reprimand was followed by a much harsher lesson. An occasion was furnished when the official Syrian and Iraqi pilgrim caravans met at Arafat near Mecca on 9 February 1188, during a traditional celebration of the sacred pilgrimage month. The Iraqi ca`ravan and its military guard was led by Tashtigin, a prominent member of the Baghdad court. The caravan from Damascus was headed by Ibn al-Muqaddam, a man well known for his close political relations with Saladin. That year the Syrian caravan was unusually large, because it included crowds of pilgrims from Iraq, Mosul, Jazirah, Akhlat, Anatolia, and other regions, who had flocked to visit Jerusalem and other holy sites Saladin had newly liberated. The Ayyubid conqueror's popularity must have been at its highest point in the Hejaz and greater than that of other contemporary leaders. Perhaps for that very reason Ibn al-Muqaddam wanted his caravan to lead the procession of the pilgrims from Arafa to Mecca. This Tashtigin vigorously contested and when the leader from Damascus refused to yield, the caliph's representative signalled his men to attack. In the ensuing melee the Syrian caravan was ignominiously dispersed and its prominent leader bludgeoned to death.[42]

Relations between Saladin and the Abbasid caliph became colder than ever.

SHORTCOMINGS OF SALADIN'S LEADERSHIP

Despite his popular image following the great victory of Hattin and the glorious recovery of Jerusalem, Saladin's position as leader of the Muslim forces fighting the Crusaders was not too comfortable. As early as 1186, incidents with Nasir al-Din ibn Shirkuh and Taqi al-Din Umar had indicated that Saladin could not even trust his own relatives.[43] Events at Tyre in 1187 had revealed that the rank and file was not overwhelmingly inspired by the *jihad* ideal which Saladin publicly embraced, and this self-asserted mandate itself had been repudiated in no uncertain terms by the caliph of Baghdad. Nor did Saladin's successes evoke any enthusiasm from the powerful Almohad rulers of North Africa and Spain. This was because of the Ayyubid raids against their territories, which, however, the vigorous countermeasures of the great Yaqub al-Mansur[44] had ended in 1187.

It seems that Saladin's persistent expansionist policies in Egypt, Arabia, North Africa, Syria, and northern Mesopotamia had eroded confidence in the sincerity of his proclaimed devotion to the war against the Infidels. With his moral leadership open to doubts, Saladin might perhaps have impressed his followers with monetary inducements, but unfortunately his economic position precluded such a solution. Having earlier committed Egyptian resources to finance the relentless campaigns against his Muslim rivals, Saladin was now without substantial cash reserves. This proved an essential cause of failure in the attack against Tyre. It was also bound to create further complications if the war against the Crusaders escalated.

SALADIN'S ALLIANCE WITH THE BYZANTINE EMPIRE

On 6 January 1188—only a few days after his withdrawal from Tyre—Saladin received in Acre a Byzantine embassy bringing Emperor Isaac's thanks for the liberation of his brother and congratulations on the Muslim sultan's reconquest of Jerusalem. The Byzantine envoys also informed Saladin that a new Crusade was being summoned in the West to retrieve the holy sepulchre from the Muslims.[45]

Shocked by Saladin's capture of the holy city, Europeans reacted by mobilizing tremendous military and economic resources to reconquer Jerusalem. This mobilization produced numerous multinational armies and naval contingents ready to challenge Saladin's claim to supremacy in the holy land. In addition to a great many princes, barons, and prominent noblemen, the new Crusade included three mighty European sovereigns: Philip Augustus of France, Richard the Lionhearted of England, and the Holy Roman Emperor Frederick I Barbarossa.

The new European expedition was as disquieting to Saladin as to Isaac Angelus and dictated a tightening of military ties between the two rulers. Therefore, Saladin sent his own ambassadors back with the Byzantine embassy to negotiate an active military alliance to counter the invasion. Among the fabulous gifts dispatched to Isaac were two items attesting to Saladin's military imagination: a huge silver jar of poisoned wine and great quantities of poisoned flour and grain. These deadly foods (one whiff of the wine was said to have slain a Latin prisoner on whom it was tested) were apparently supplied for chemical warfare against the Crusaders passing through Byzantine lands; indeed, the chronicles of Frederick Barbarossa's Crusade contain a number of stories concerning Byzantine attempts to destroy the Germans by such means.[46]

Although the Ayyubid sultan and the Greek emperor firmly concluded an alliance in 1188 or 1189 and sustained it by regular exchanges of embassies, it proved of no essential military or political consequence. Apart from keeping Saladin informed about Crusader movements, Isaac proved incapable of helping Saladin during the Third Crusade. Frederick Barbarossa traversed Greek territory without meeting any serious Byzantine opposition. Only his accidental drowning in the Saleph River on 10 June 1190 prevented Frederick from reaching the holy land. As for Philip Augustus and Richard the Lionhearted, they elected to go to Acre by sea.

Disappointing though it was in military terms, the alliance with the Byzantines produced a significant diplomatic success: the emperor conferred on Saladin responsibility for the personnel and ritual activities in the mosque of Constantinople, an honor hitherto reserved for the Saljuqid sultans.[47] This act was tantamount to a formal recognition of Saladin as the official, legitimate champion of Sunni Islam.

THE BEGINNING OF THE THIRD CRUSADE

Following Saladin's victory of Hattin, the failure to capture Tyre was not his only strategic blunder. In 1188 he refrained from assaulting Tripoli, and that same year, instead of attacking Antioch, he concluded on 1 October an eight-month truce with its master, Bohemund.[48] No matter how impressive his numerous conquests in 1188-89, three crucial fortresses on the Syrian littoral remained in enemy hands. Not only had they survived the Muslim deluge, they now served as vital bases for renewed Frankish resistance which fresh troops from Europe gradually reinforced. Finally in August 1189 King Guy felt confident enough to lead his revitalized army, supported by a Pisan squadron, on an expedition against Acre.

In anticipation of the Crusader attack Saladin had ordered the fortifications of Acre strengthened and had committed to its defense his elite troops with abundant arms, food, and other supplies.[49] Finding Acre well prepared to meet a direct attack, King Guy's army was compelled to lay siege during which it in turn was surrounded on land by Muslim relief contingents which Saladin led. The action at Acre, where a Muslim garrison was first besieged by Crusader naval and land forces, which were in turn encompassed by Ayyubid land troops, gradually escalated into one of the most dramatic military confrontations between Islam and

Christianity—the famous Third Crusade. As a result of Saladin's ultimate failure to crush this new wave of European aggressors, the Crusader Kingdom in the Near East won a new lease on life which lasted for yet another century.

SALADIN'S LACK OF AUTHORITY OVER HIS
PRINCIPAL COMMANDERS

The battle of Acre lasted almost two years, 1189-91, during which the Crusaders, besieging and besieged, had to conduct difficult military operations, often under most adverse climatic, logistic, economic, and sanitary conditions. The situation in the Crusader camp became quite critical in the winter which rendered them more vulnerable to Muslim attacks. However, having survived the desperate winter of 1190-91, Crusader strength reached its peak in the spring of 1191 with the arrival of King Philip of France and King Richard of England and their forces.

The tremendous power the combined naval and land forces of the Third Crusade unleashed proved too much for the garrison of Acre, by then completely exhausted and cut off from any supplies. On 12 July 1191 the heroic defenders capitulated, having lost faith in Saladin's capacity to defeat the Crusaders. In addition to loss of the elite troops and huge quantities of war material, the fall of Acre was a terrible strategic and propaganda blow to Saladin, which threatened to wipe out all the advantages gained by the victory of Hattin.

A fundamental reason for Saladin's failure to defeat the Third Crusade, particularly in its initial winter stage, was his inability to sustain a rigorous campaign against the Europeans. On 4 October 1189 Saladin inflicted a bloody defeat on the Crusaders, but he was unable to follow it up, because his commanders insisted their troops deserved the rest to which they were formally entitled after fifty days of uninterrupted campaigning.[50] A year later, with the approach of winter, the Crusader situation had become so desperate that some prospects existed for an advantageous armistice agreement. However, Saladin's impatient regional commanders frustrated his plans by insisting on going home immediately. The Zangid prince of Sinjar, Imad al-Din, pressed the Ayyubid sultan to dismiss all troops for the winter. Another Zangid vassal, Sinjar of al-Jazirat al-Umar, attempted to lead his contingent home without even receiving permission. Finally, beginning mid-November 1190, Saladin gave in, and different contingents, preceded by the Zangid units, began to depart, leaving the sultan with only a few dedicated commanders and his own guard.[51]

Saladin's lack of a more forceful hold over his troops could be partly attributed to his deteriorating health. During the two-year siege of Acre, the sultan, who was over fifty, suffered violent attacks of what the Arab chroniclers called "colic," more probably the malignant Syrian fever.[52] This affliction handicapped his capacity to command undiminished loyalty of all his followers and especially the attachment of his Zangid vassals.

As Lane-Poole remarked, "It was not to be expected that the vanquished descendants of Zengy should show much enthusiasm in their supplanter's service."[53] Nor was this deplorable lack of enthusiasm limited to his Zangid vassals. In 1191 Taqi al-Din Umar, Saladin's nephew, failed to show up at the battle for Islam, because he was busy asserting his authority in his feudal possessions. This in turn caused the troops from Diyar Bakr to delay arrival, because their leaders had to protect their interests which Taqi al-Din imperiled. During the same spring, Izz al-Din of Mosul laid siege to al-Jazirat al-Umar, accusing its master, Sinjar Shah, of aiding his domestic enemies. This prevented Sinjar Shah from joining the battle of Acre. "This is the work of satan!" exclaimed Saladin when he learned about this shocking disobedience of his troop concentration orders.[54]

In June 1191 some of Saladin's men mutinied; they refused to attack the Christians and accused him of "ruining Islam."[55] Succumbing to defeatism, three leading amirs in the garrison of Acre deserted their posts in panic,[56] and finally, the garrison itself disobeyed the sultan's orders and surrendered to the Crusaders.[57]

MUSLIM RULERS INDIFFERENT TO SALADIN'S
STRUGGLE

In his efforts to protect Palestine from the Crusaders Saladin appealed in all directions for military and economic assistance. Swallowing his pride he kept sending urgent messages to the caliph of Baghdad,[58] to his own brother in the Yemen,[59] even to the Almohad sultan, Yaqub al-Mansur. In this last instance Saladin, cynically disavowing any responsibility for Qaragush's raids against North Africa, hoped that cooperation of the Moroccan fleet would slow down Christian shipping between the West and Acre.[60] But Saladin's anti-Crusader cause evoked little active support outside his own dominions. The caliph responded with two loads of *naftah* (a kind of twelfth century napalm), five specialists in the use of flame-throwers, and a promissory note of 20,000 dinars. This token aid so affronted Saladin that he returned the monetary portion.[61] Instead of receiving assistance from Yaqub al-Mansur, Saladin learned that North African ports had extended hospitality to the Genoese sailing to support the Crusaders at Acre.[62] One of the Saljuqid princes of Persia, instead of furnishing troops, asked for help against his own rivals.[63] Another Saljuqid prince, the master of Malatya, came to Saladin in 1191 and asked for support against his father and brothers in Anatolia.[64] Saladin's correspondence at the time of the battle of Acre contains many references to the caliph's indifference and the lack of outside assistance in his lonely struggle against the enemies of Islam. Obviously, Saladin's prestige as the champion of Islam did not rate high at the various Muslim courts. After all, had he not appealed to the same ideal during the entire period of 1174-86, while grabbing the lands of his Muslim neighbors? Furthermore, did not his earlier diplomatic arrangements with the Crusaders and his alliance with the Christian emperor of Constantinople darken his image as idealistic leader implacably dedicated to the *jihad?*

The successes of Richard the Lionhearted and the conclusion of the Third Crusade

In spite of their triumph at Acre the Crusaders did not pursue their original intention of liberating Jerusalem. Most of them, including the king of France, immediately returned home. Responsibility for continuing the war against Saladin was assumed by the intrepid king of England. Despite the small number of his troops and obvious logistic limitations, Richard maintained the strategic and tactical initiative. Skillfully exploiting available Christian naval support, he extended the Crusader beachhead southward: on 6 September 1191 Arsuf was captured; three days later—Jaffa; and on 20 January 1192 the Crusaders entered Ascalon. The acquisition of that gateway to Egypt allowed Richard to harass Saladin's communications lines with his main base of supply. Indeed, on 20 June Richard's troops intercepted a great caravan laden with supplies en route from Egypt to Saladin's camp in Jerusalem. According to an Arab chronicler, the Crusaders captured 3,000 camels, 3,000 horses, 500 prisoners, and a large amount of supplies.[65] Naturally, the presence of an aggressive Christian king in Ascalon brought back painful memories of Amalric and his Egyptian campaigns.

While inflicting humiliating reverses on the Muslim enemy, the English king did not rule out a negotiated end to the conflict. Following a series of diplomatic exchanges the belligerents agreed to suspend hostilities, and on 2 September 1192 they signed a three-year truce. The Crusaders were to hold a strip of coastal territory from Tyre to Jaffa; Ascalon was restored to Saladin, but its fortifications were to be demolished, so that it would cease function as a military base; finally, both Christians and Muslims were to have free passage through the whole of Palestine, which meant that Christian pilgrims could visit the holy sepulchre and other venerable sites in Jerusalem and elsewhere.[66]

Because Christian Europe had intervened, the kingdom of the Crusaders, which only five years earlier was threatened with total extinction, reestablished itself on the Syro-Palestinian littoral to serve as a focal point of aggressive plans against the Muslims for another century.

Saladin's leadership crisis

Modern accounts of the Third Crusade concentrate on the dramatic battle of Acre; and when discussing personalities, they emphasize both the bravery of Richard the Lionhearted and the chivalrous deportment of Saladin towards the Christian enemy, particularly in the last year of the historic confrontation.

Much less publicized is the shocking failure of the Muslim resistance. Although for two years the Crusaders were confined to a beachhead outside the walls of Acre, Muslim warriors proved incapable of crushing the aggressors or even effectively supporting the besieged garrison.

Later, after most of the Crusaders departed, the forces of Islam suffered further humiliations from a handful of Christians commanded by King Richard. In spite of overwhelming odds in their favor, the Muslims could neither outfight the Christian contingent nor simultaneously protect Ascalon and Jerusalem. Considering the military organization and defense-oriented economy of the Muslim countries and in view of the strategic advantages they secured in 1187-89, the terms of the 1192 armistice must be regarded as a humiliating concession the Christian invaders imposed on Islam.

This grievous failure of Islam during the Third Crusade must be attributed to lack of enthusiasm for the holy war. As at Acre, the Muslim leadership crisis was much in evidence during the 1191-92 campaign against Richard. The confidence Saladin originally enjoyed reached its low point in the final stage of the Third Crusade. Even one of Saladin's bravest and most experienced commanders, his impetuous nephew Taqi al-Din Umar, practically deserted the Sultan's cause. While his uncle was facing King Richard, Taqi al-Din was advancing into Armenia. His aim was the town of Akhlat on Lake Van; he succeeded in defeating the master of Akhlat, Sayf al-Din Bektumir, and seized much of his territory. Thereupon Bektumir appealed to Caliph al-Nasir who hastened to send a bitter letter to Saladin, reprimanding him for Taqi al-Din's attack. Moreover, the caliph requested that Saladin send to Baghdad al-Qadi al-Fadil, his experienced adviser and loyal friend. Predictably enough, Saladin paid little attention to his Abbasid suzerain. "Taqi al-Din went north," stated Saladin, "to collect troops, and he will return to participate in the *Jihad.* . . . As for al-Qadi al-Fadil, unfortunately he suffers from numerous physical indispositions and his lack of strength precludes a strenuous journey to Iraq."[67]

The callous pursuit of selfish territorial interests by Saladin's nephew came to an end when he died on the night of 9 October 1191 during his siege of Manzikert.[68] This gave rise to a dispute over his legacy between al-Afdal, Saladin's oldest son and al-Adil, Saladin's famous brother. At first the sultan conferred the disputed territories on his son, so on 19 February 1192 al-Afdal left the exposed area of Jerusalem with special diplomas and 20,000 dinars to help him get established. However, al-Adil put enough pressure on Saladin to cause him to rescind the earlier decision, which meant that al-Adil left Jerusalem to replace al-Afdal. News of his recall made al-Afdal so angry that upon his return to Damascus in May he refused to rejoin Saladin's service. Only the sultan's special persuasion made his defiant heir apparent return to action against the Crusaders.[69]

In addition to lack of family cooperation, Saladin ran into difficulties with his rank-and-file troops. It was their cowardice which forced him to give up defense of Ascalon.[70] Their defeatist feelings even caused them to doubt whether Jerusalem should be defended at all against Richard the Lionhearted.[71]

The most flagrant defiance of Saladin's authority on the battlefield occurred 5 August 1192, following the Muslim recapture of Jaffa. Doubting their chance of repelling the attack, the Crusader garrison had asked for terms and Saladin agreed to allow the Christians to leave the city with their goods, in exchange for money ransom. But the sultan could not control his troops, who had broken into the town, so the Christian garrison retired to the citadel while the Turks and Kurds pillaged. The angry sultan ordered his *mamluks* to stand at the city gates and take the booty away from the plunderers.[72]

Speeding to the rescue of Jaffa, Richard established his camp outside the city walls. As the Crusader relief contingent arrived by sea, the knights had no horses and could only fight as spearmen or bowmen. When Saladin realized the enemy's vulnerability, he decided to finish them off by a surprise night attack, which would avenge earlier humiliations and recover his prestige.

After dark on 5 August squadrons of Muslim cavalry moved against the Christian camp. But their movement had been detected and Richard warned. He drew up his little troop in battle array. When Saladin's warriors saw the solid line of the Crusaders, they lost all interest in battle. True, the *mamluks* made a few mounted charges, suffering heavily from the crossbow volleys, but the rest of the troops simply refused to attack. Saladin's famous biographer, Baha al-Din, who had become the sultan's secretary in June 1188, admitted the dismal performance of the Muslim soldiers. They were supposedly embittered by Saladin's protecting the Christians of Jaffa. Some of his troopers, observed Baha al-Din, had even taunted the sultan: "Make your own *mamluks* charge who beat off our people on the day we took Jaffa!"[73]

Whatever the cause, Saladin could not get his men to attack. To add insult to injury, Richard publicly exposed this total disobedience by riding along the whole front of Saladin's men, lance at rest, mocking them, and not a soldier attempted to touch him.[74] Saladin at last left the field in a fury and the next day was in Jerusalem ordering fresh fortifications.[75] A few weeks later, on 2 September, a formal armistice proclamation ended his long war against the Crusaders.

Certain developments in Damascus and Aleppo during that final stage of the war hinted at the rise of the antiestablishment sentiments on the homefront. In 1191 Saladin had to dismiss Muhammad ibn Abd Allah ibn Abi Asrun from his position as judge of Damascus, because of his harmful contacts and influence with the military. Nominated in his place was Muhyi al-Din ibn al-Zaki, the preacher who had delivered the famous sermon after the liberation of Jerusalem.[76]

Aleppo became the scene of the activities of al-Suhrawardi, one of the greatest mystics in the history of Islamic religious philosophy. The popularity which his unorthodox ideas began to enjoy with the traditionally liberal-minded population of Aleppo could not be tolerated by the Ayyubid regime. Saladin ordered this teacher of ideological devia-

tion put to death; so on 29 July 1191, to the roll of Muslim mystic martyrs was added al-Suhrawarti.[77]

EGYPT AND SALADIN'S WAR AGAINST THE CRUSADERS

If despite so many difficulties with his army and the apathy of various Muslim princes, Saladin succeeded in preventing the Third Crusade from reconquering Palestine, this was mainly due to the steady military and economic support received from Egypt. Egypt had once enabled Saladin to get established as a strong and independent ruler. Again, during his early bid in Syria, the troops based in Egypt had saved Saladin from imminent destruction. The Egyptian troops and resources had proved instrumental in annexing Aleppo and Mosul. And Egypt it was which supported Saladin's desperate struggle against the Third Crusade.

Besides providing him with means to maintain his own regiment of *mamluk* guards, Egypt supplied Saladin with about 4,000 cavalry for the offensive of 1187. As soon as he captured Acre in 1187, the sultan ordered al-Adil in Cairo to furnish more troops and to dispatch the Egyptian fleet. The opening of a direct coastal route between Egypt and Palestine had facilitated, of course, the movement of troops and supplies.

Still during the summer of 1187 when Saladin decided to transform Acre into an operational base for the war, he turned to Cairo to find personnel and money for that purpose. Baha al-Din Qaragush was recalled from overseeing the defense constructions in the Egyptian capital and came to Acre with architects, tools, and a prisoner-of-war labor force to fortify that town. The impressive results the Egyptian architects achieved allowed Saladin to conceive the strategy of containing the main forces of the Third Crusade on the beaches of Acre. He provided the fortress itself with experienced troops, equipment, and supplies, all of which Egypt furnished.

During the two-year battle of Acre, al-Adil or al-Qadi al-Fadil continued to send fresh troops and naval units from Egypt, either to supply the besieged garrison by breaking through the Frankish blockade or to join Saladin's army in the field. Beyond a doubt, Saladin's stand at Acre was made possible only because of Egypt's gigantic war effort. Later, during the struggle against the English king, Egyptian contributions in men, equipment, money, and naval support likewise sustained Saladin's operations. As a result of Egypt's essential support, most of the Europeans lost their crusading fervor following the capture of Acre, and Richard the Lionhearted's offensive operations fell short of the intended liberation of Jerusalem.

But the price Egypt had to pay was staggering. Besides the casualties suffered by units operating outside, the Egyptian land forces sustained their greatest losses from the fall of Acre. The surrender meant the loss of both experienced commanders such as Baha al-Din Qaragush and al-Mashtub and a great many Egyptian warriors, as well as large quantities of war material. Some of the commanders, including al-Mashtub, were later ransomed, but the king of England massacred the bulk of the rank and file.

The fall of Acre meant a disastrous blow to Egyptian naval power. During the siege of the city the superior naval forces of the Crusaders either captured or sunk many ships. Some of the Egyptian units had succeeded in breaking the blockade and penetrating the harbor, however, one of the surrender terms was that the Crusaders were to take all ships anchored in the harbor. Consequently the fall of Acre cost almost total loss of the Egyptian navy.[78]

Because of these disastrous naval developments, Saladin had to reckon with a possible invasion of Egypt. During the battle of Acre he had undertaken measures to prevent various towns in Palestine and the Lebanon from serving as fortified bases for the Crusaders in case they launched an inland offensive. In 1190 the sultan had ordered the walls destroyed at Tiberias, Jaffa, Arsuf, Caesarea, Sidon, and Jubail.[79] Following the loss of Acre, Ascalon once again emerged as the key to Egypt's safety. But Saladin's discouraged staff insisted that it would be impossible to defend Egypt and Palestine at the same time, so Saladin—placing the interests of the Holy Land above those of Egypt—ordered Ascalon abandoned and its walls dismantled, hoping to render it useless for a Christian invasion of the Delta.[80] This concern was not unwarranted, for Richard pushed as far south as Darum which had once served as a staging place for Amalric's invasion of Egypt.[81]

Saladin undertook other emergency measures in Egypt itself. He instructed his brother al-Adil to assume personal responsibility over the ministry of the fleet.[82] Fortifications of Damietta were refitted, while all women were ordered to leave. Tinnis was completely evacuated of its civil population—a measure which spelt the end of that once-flourishing urban center.[83]

Egypt's war effort also entailed considerable economic sacrifices. The need to produce costly replacements in personnel, equipment, and animals, as well as Saladin's recurrent demands for cash, strained to the utmost Egypt's financial resources. Saladin's administration in Cairo had traditionally been plagued with a gold shortage and its detrimental effect on the quality of the Egyptian dinars. In 1187—the year of the great triumph over the Crusaders—Saladin ordered a major monetary reform probably aimed at removing debased coins from circulation.[84] But the effects of that reform proved shortlived. During the critical struggle against the Third Crusade, production at the Egyptian mints decreased and their coins suffered from debasement.[85]

To finance the Third Crusade the faithful in Western Europe were called upon to pay a special tax, called Saladin's tithe.[86] For his part, Saladin—lacking economic and military support from other Muslim rulers—imposed special taxes on the Egyptian population. Among other

levies, al-Adil proposed an income tax of 1 percent, but Saladin found this absolutely inadequate considering the costs of the war.[87] Taxes on non-Muslim Egyptian minorities were also expanded.[88] In general, the Egyptian population suffered as more and more of its resources were absorbed. Egyptian ports witnessed a gradual increase of Turkish slaves, imported either to replace casualties or to beef up the regular cavalry units in anticipation of a Crusader attack against Egypt. Large-scale government purchases of foodstuffs caused prices of commodities to skyrocket, especially in the metropolitan area where the price of beans in 1192 increased by 100 percent.[89] Social malaise, if not outright discontent with developments in Egypt, found its expression in rumors and agitations affecting the life of Cairo and Fustat and even in a revival of Ismaili and pro-Fatimid propaganda. The first pro-Ismaili riots in Ayyubid Cairo occurred as early as 1188.[90] In 1192 a Fatimid pretender, supported by some surviving members of Shawar's family, staged an abortive revolt in Cairo. The administration found it necessary to remove the imprisoned members and followers of the Fatimid dynasty to a secure place from which they could neither engage in nor even inspire subversive activities.[91]

One of the lasting effects of Egyptian involvement in the Third Crusade was that the Christian leadership came to recognize Egypt as the key objective in efforts to recover the holy city. "The keys to Jerusalem are found in Cairo"[92] became the principle of Crusader strategy following the confrontation with Saladin. Continuous military pressure and two dangerous invasions by the Franks and their European allies, in 1218 and 1249, led to ever-increasing Egyptian defense efforts. Imports of costly slaves for the *mamluk* regiments had to be stepped up, and to finance this expansion it became necessary to expand governmental control over various areas of the Egyptian economy, including the transit and export trade. Egyptian political and economic systems underwent a process of militarization, which culminated in the middle of the thirteenth century, when a ruthless militaristic regime of the Mamluks took power. By then the delicate balance between Egypt's security needs and economic capacity had been decisively disturbed with prolonged and ruinous consequences for its society.

One of the main reasons precipitating that disastrous development in medieval Egypt was the costly expansionist policy of Saladin, his procrastination in launching a total war against the Crusaders, and his catastrophic failure to eliminate the Christian kingdom from Palestine.

Notes

1. *Saladin,* pp. 198, 199.

2. "The Achievement of Saladin," pp. 99-100.

3. Prawer, 1:637; M. W. Baldwin, art. cit., p. 605.

4. Ch. M. Brand, "The Byzantines and Saladin, 1185-1192: Opponents of the Third Crusade," *Speculum* 37 (1962): 168-169.

5. Ibid., p. 169.

6. Ibid., p. 168.

7. Ibid., p. 169.

8. Ibid., pp. 169-170.

9. M. W. Baldwin, art. cit., p. 606.

10. Prawer, 1:638-639.

11. IS, p. 75.

12. IS, p. 78.

13. "The Armies of Saladin," p. 81; "The Rise of Saladin," p. 585.

14. Ch. M. Brand, art. cit., p. 170.

15. IS, p. 75; IW, 2:187.

16. For an analysis of the tactical movements of the two opposing armies, see Prawer, 1:643-653; also idem, "La bataille de Hattin," *Israel Exploration Journal* 14 (1964): 160-179.

17. M. W. Baldwin, art. cit., p. 610.

18. *Saladin,* p. 213.

19. IS, p. 78.

20. Ibid.

21. IS, p. 79.

22. IW, 2:196.

23. Cf. 'Imād al-Dīn, *al Fath al-Quds,* in Francesco Gabrieli, *Arab Historians of the Crusades* (1969), p. 138.

24. Ch. M. Brand, art. cit., p. 170.

25. "The Rise of Saladin," p. 586.

26. E. Sivan, *L'Islam et la Croisade,* (Paris, 1968), p. 115 f.; idem, "Le caractère sacré de Jérusalem dans l'Islam aux XIIe-XIIIe siècles," *Studia Islamica* 27 (1967): 160 f.

27. IW, 2:238.

28. Ch. M. Brand, art. cit., p. 170.

29. Saladin, p. 237.

30. IW, 2:242.

31. *Saladin,* p. 239.

32. "The Place of Saladin," p. 111.

33. *Saladin,* p. 241.

34. "The Place of Saladin," p. 111.

35. IW, 2:246.

36. *Saladin,* p. 241.

37. Ibid., p. 243.

38. IW, 2:248. *TD,* fol. 20 r; IW, 2:248-249.

39. IW, 2:248-49.

40. In reality that title was given to Saladin by al-'Ādid, cf., above, p. 67.

41. *TD,* fol. 20 v.

42. IA, 11:212; IW, 2:250-252.

43. See above, pp. 191-93.

44. IA, 11:196; *Sulūk,* p. 99.

45. Ch. M. Brand, art. cit., p. 171.

46. Ibid., pp. 171-172.

47. Ibid., p. 172.

48. IS, p. 94; IA, 12:8.

49. IW, 2:253; *Sulūk,* p. 99.

50. *Saladin,* p. 266.

51. IS, p. 146; IW, 2:346.

52. *Saladin,* p. 266.

53. Ibid., p. 277.

54. IW, 2:354.

55. IS, p. 168; *Saladin,* p. 296.

56. IS, loc. cit.; *Saladin,* p. 297.

57. *Saladin,* p. 297.

58. IW, 2:306.

59. *Supra.*

60. ASh, *RHC, HO,* 4:497-505.

61. IW, 2:314; Sibt, p. 401.

62. "The Place of Saladin," p. 114.

63. IW, 2:306.

64. IW, 2:371.

65. IS, pp. 213-215; S. Painter, "The Third Crusade: Richard the Lionhearted and Philip Augustus," *A History of the Crusades* (Philadelphia, 1955-62), 2:82.

66. S. Painter, art. cit., p. 85.

67. IW, 2:375-376.

68. Ibid., 2:376.

69. Ibid., 2:378-379.

70. ASh, *RHC, HO,* 5:43.

71. IS, p. 216; IW, 2:387.

72. *Saladin,* pp. 344-347.

73. IS, p. 229; *Saladin,* pp. 352-354.

74. IS, loc. cit.; *Saladin,* p. 354.

75. IS, p. 230.

76. Sibt, p. 411.

77. IS, p. 10; H. Corbin, *Suhrawardî d' Alep (+1191) fondateur de la doctrine illuminative (ishrâqî)* (Paris, 1939) pp. 3, 9.

78. "The Place of Saladin," p. 115.

79. Ibid., p. 114.

80. *Saladin,* p. 326.

81. Ibid., pp. 338-339.

82. "The Place of Saladin," p. 115.

83. Ibid.

84. *Sulūk*, p. 99.

85. The low output is suggested by analysis of available numismatic evidence examined by the present author. For a recent treatment of the outflow of gold from the East, see H. L. Misbach, "Genoese commerce and the alleged flow of gold to the East, 1154-1253," *Revue internationale d'Histoire de la Banque* 3 (1970): 67-87.

86. Fr. A. Cazel, Jr., "The Tax of 1185 in Aid of the Holy Land." *Speculum* 30 (1955): 385-392; J. H. Round, "The Saladin Tithe," *English Historical Review* 31 (1916): 447-450.

87. Al-Nābulusī, *Kitāb luma' al-qawānīn*, ed, by Cl. Cahen, in *Bulletin d'Études Orientales* 16 (1958-1960): 12.

88. *Al-Nuzum al-mālīyah*, p. 46.

89. *Sulūk*, p. 110.

90. IA, 12:9-10.

91. *Sulūk*, pp. 110-111.

92. René Grousset, *Les Croisades* (Paris, 1848), p. 59.

Abbreviations

"The Achievement of Saladin": H. A. R. Gibb, "The Achievement of Saladin," in Stanford J. Shaw and William R. Polk, eds., *Studies of the Civilization of Islam* (Boston: Beacon Press, 1962) pp. 91-107.

"The Armies of Saladin": H. A. R. Gibb, "The Armies of Saladin," in Stanford J. Shaw and William R. Polk, eds., *Studies on the Civilization of Islam* (Boston: Beacon Press, 1962), pp. 74-90.

ASh: Abū Shāmah, *Kitāb alrawdatayn* (Cairo, 1956).

ASh, *RHC, HO*: Abū Shāmah, *op. cit.*, in *Recueil des Historiens des Croisades, Historiens Orientaux* (Paris, 1872-1906).

Ashtor: E. Ashtor, *Histoire des Prix et des Salaires dans l'Orient Médiéval* (Paris, 1969).

BJ: Claude Cahen, "Une Chronique Syrienne du VIe/XIIe siècle: Le *'Bustān al-Jāmi','* " *Bulletin d'Études Orientales* 7-8 (1937-38): 113-158.

EI: *The Encyclopaedia of Islam,* 2nd ed. (Leiden: E. J. Brill, 1960-).

Elisséeff: N. Elisséeff, *Nur al-Din* (Damascus, 1967).

Grousset: René Grousset, *Histoire des Croisades et du Royaume Franc de Jérusalem* (Paris, 1934-1936).

IA, *al-Atābakīyah*: Ibn al-Athīr, *al-Ta'rikh al-bāhir fī al-Dawlah al-Atābakīyah* (Cairo, 1963).

IA: Ibn al-Athīr, *Ta'rīkh al-kāmil* (Cairo, 1884).

IS: Bahā' al-Dīn Ibn Shaddād, *al-Nawādir al-sultānīyah* (Cairo, 1964).

Itt.: Ahmad ibn 'Alī *al-Maqrīzī, Itti'āz al-hunafā',* MS. AS 3013, Istanbul, Top Kapu Sarayi Library.

IW: Ibn Wāsil, *Mufarrij al-Kurūb (Cairo,* 1953-60).

Labib: Subhi Y. Labib, *Handelsgeschichte Ägyptens im Spätmitelalter (1171-1517)* (Wiesbaden, 1965).

al-Nuzum al-Mālīyah: H. M. Rabī', *al-Nuzum al-Mālīyah fī Misr zaman al-Ayyūbīyīn* (Cairo, 1964).

"The Place of Saladin": sAndrew S. Ehrenkreutz, "The Place of Saladin in the Naval History of the Mediterranean Sea in the Middle Ages," *Journal of the American Oriental Society* 75 (1955): 100–116.

Prawer: J. Prawer, *Histoire du Royaume Latin de Jérusalem* (Paris, 1969–70).

"The Rise of Saladin": H. A. R. Gibb, "The Rise of Saladin, 1169–1181," in Marshall W. Baldwin, Robert Lee Wolff, and Henry W. Hazard, eds., *A History of the Crusades,* 2 vols. (Philadelphia: University of Pennsylvania Press, 1958–1962), I: 563–589.

Saladin: Stanley Lane-Poole, *Saladin and the Fall of the Kingdom of Jerusalem* (London, 1906).

Sibt: Sibt ibn al-Jawzī, Mir'at al-zamān, VIII/I (Haydarabad, 1951).

Suluk: Ahmad ibn 'Alī al-Maqrīzī, *Kitāb al-sulūk*, vol. I, pt. I, ed. by M. M. Ziyādah (Cairo, 1956).

TD: Ibn al-Khazrajī, *Ta'rīkh Dawlat al-Akrād wa al-Atrak*, Ms, Hekimoglu Ali Pasa 695.

R. Stephen Humphreys (essay date 1977)

SOURCE: "The Structure of Politics in the Reign of Saladin" in *From Saladin to the Mongols: Ayyubids of Damascus, 1193–1260,* State University of New Yirk Press Albany, 1977, pp. 15–39, 414–21.

[In the following essay, Humphreys analyzes the political structure under which Saladin operated and discusses the ways in which he adapted this structure and established his authority. Humphreys emphasizes the system of loyalties cultivated by Saladin, and observes that such a system could not be sustained after his death. But overall, the political system that was prevalent during Saladin's reign "gave his immediate successors a framework of attitudes and behavior within which to define their own policies and goods."]

Saladin's legacy to his heirs was not merely a mass of territories brought together by force and diplomacy. It was a functioning political system—a structure of expectations, rights, and duties within which men sought power and influence. This political system had been shaped by Saladin's goals and imbued with his personality, but it did not evaporate upon his death. Indeed it gave his immediate successors a framework of attitudes and behavior within which to define their own policies and goals. It was also the initial point for the entire subsequent political evolution of the Ayyubid empire. From both points of view, then, the structure of politics under Saladin requires careful analysis—all the more as this task has not previously been undertaken in any systematic way.

Since in Muslim states politics begins with the throne, it seems best to base this analysis on an enquiry into the nature of Saladin's authority within his dominions. What measure of effective political authority did Saladin have, what powers of government was he personally able to exercise? By what means did he compel (or perhaps only encourage) obedience to his authority? And last, what groups did he enlist to support him and how did he try to bind them to himself?

By Saladin's political authority we mean specifically his capacity to control the crucial institutions of government, especially those (e.g., the army or the *iqta'* system) where there was a real possibility of resistance or rebellion. Most important in this regard were the regular armed forces. Although the bulk of his army was recruited and maintained by the princes and amirs on the basis of the revenues yielded by their appanages and *iqta's*[1], this did not imply *in principle* that there were intermediate loyalties separating him from the ordinary soldier. In Saladin's state, as in its Seljukid and Zangid antecedents, the *iqta'* system was meant to be an administrative device only, whose purpose was to relieve the financial strain on a state which had not the monetary resources to pay the regular cash salaries required by a standing army.[2] In the sultan's mind, the troops raised by an amir did not represent a private army for the latter's use, but simply the fulfillment of certain administrative obligations delegated to him.[3] The amirs' regiments could be used only for those purposes which Saladin had sanctioned in pursuit of his own political goals. Likewise when Saladin called out the army for a major campaign, the possibility of a refusal to participate was not entertained, and in the field he disposed forces and named unit commanders as he saw fit, with little concern to preserve the feudal identity of the army's component regiments.[4]

Obviously he suffered certain constraints. In Syria at least, a major *iqta'* implied territorial administration as well as troop supply; an amir or prince holding such a grant had to return (with his forces) to the lands under his administration for the autumn and winter. Only Saladin's personal guard could stay mobilized for extended periods of time. Saladin also had to contend with his amirs' discontent, especially after long or discouraging campaigns. Although this never degenerated into open mutiny, he could not ignore it; at crucial points in the wars of reconquest and the Third Crusade, he had to bring a hitherto promising campaign to an untimely end. But by and large, his authority among his amirs was such that he could manage campaigns of many months' duration for years on end without provoking serious dissension.

The second major aspect of Saladin's political control was that he retained exclusively in his own hands the authority to assign *iqta's* and princely appanages. Until his death all such assignments were subject to recall or modification, even those of such powerful subjects as his nephew Taqi al-Din 'Umar or his brother al-'Adil. Moreover, although the major *iqta's* and appanages seem normally to have been granted on the presumption that their holders would transmit them in hereditary succession, all new heirs were obliged to obtain a decree or diploma of confirmation from Saladin, which he sometimes refused to give. When al-Mansur Muhammad requested confirmation in all the possessions of his father, Taqi al-Din 'Umar (late 587/1191), Saladin permitted him to succeed only to that segment of them which was politically weakest and most restrictive.[5] Again, there were limits to Saladin's freedom of intervention; he could not afford to offend his more powerful relatives and *muqta's,* and any alteration in their status and holdings required a suitable *quid pro quo*. But the rule stands: under Saladin, all *iqta's* were held directly from him and at his discretion. There was no subinfeudation, nor any pattern of overlapping political loyalties.

Finally, in certain situations Saladin would interfere directly in the internal affairs of the appanages which he had established for the princes of his house, even though these were ordinarily considered to be self-contained and autonomous administrative units. This seems to have occurred when he doubted the prince's competence or in the case of newly conquered districts. Two examples will suffice. After recuperating from his near-fatal illness in Harran at the beginning of 582/1186, Saladin returned to Damascus, stopping in Homs to secure the administration of al-Mujahid Shirkuh, a youth of twelve who had just succeeded his father (and Saladin's cousin) Nasir al-Din Muhammad. He issued two decrees, one confirming Shirkuh in his father's territories and the second abolishing the *mukus* in al-Rahba (one of the towns included in Shirkuh's patrimony). In addition he named an amir from the Asadiyya regiment[6] to serve as regent during the young prince's minority and a second amir to be commandant of the citadel of Homs. Finally he oversaw the proper distribution of the legacy of Shirkuh's father. The second example is Palestine following Saladin's lightning reconquest of 583/1187. Although this region was assigned to the appanage (centered on Damascus) of Saladin's eldest son and heir-apparent as sultan, al-Afdal 'Ali, there is no evidence that al-Afdal ever had a word to say about its administration during his father's lifetime. It is not surprising that Saladin kept all these affairs in his own hands in 583/1187, when Palestine was still a military zone and his son but seventeen years of age. More worthy of note is that al-Afdal took no part in Saladin's administrative reorganization in Jerusalem and Galilee after the truce of 588/1192.[7]

By virtue of his capacity to control or at least supervise the army, the *iqta'* system, and local administration, Saladin was largely able to direct the policy-making process, whether on the scale of overall imperial evolution or of specific objectives. If there were cases where he felt it expedient to defer to the ambition and adventurism of some of his relatives or to the doubts and fears of his great amirs, it nevertheless seems clear that the empire developed according to his own ideas and purposes, and that no policy which did not contribute to his aims was long or seriously pursued.[8]

In view of the strength and comprehensiveness of Saladin's authority, which no other Ayyubid sultan, not even al-'Adil, would ever have, it is all the more remarkable that the institutional apparatus at his disposal was very weak. The *iqta'*-based organization of the Ayyubid armies meant that very few troops were under Saladin's direct command. It seems probable that the empire as a whole (excluding the Zangid and Artukid client states) could supply some 16,000 regular cavalry at the height of its expansion (ca. 582/1186). Of this figure, Saladin's guard (the *halqa*)—i.e., the troops recruited and supported from the revenues furnished by his personal estates (his *khassa*)—could never have surpassed 1000 men.[9] Beyond this tiny corps there simply was no royal force which could be used to police or garrison the provinces of his empire. In case of rebellion, Saladin would have had no effective instrument of coercion and repression.

Nor did the civilian institutions of government allow Saladin any real control over affairs in the provinces. It does not seem that he ever established a central financial administration which could collect and distribute in a rational manner revenues drawn from all parts of the empire. Nor did he subject the provincial financial organs to the constant and rigorous supervision which one would assume to be necessary in so vast an empire. Very probably he (or rather al-Qadi al-Fadil) did receive periodic reports from the provincial financial *diwans,* which provided him with some knowledge of the overall situation. But while this would allow him to discipline local officials if need be, the procedure still falls short of centralized financial control. Saladin apparently thought it good enough to rely on the established and internally autonomous fiscal administrations of Egypt (where the system was highly centralized and closely supervised by Cairo officials—a Fatimid legacy), Damascus, Aleppo, et al. And although we may suppose that Saladin had a privy purse (*bayt mal al-khassa*) whose revenues derived from his crown lands and could be spent at his discretion, the sources never specify anything like a true central treasury, established to supply funds for matters relevant to the empire as a whole. His practice was to have each provincial treasury meet the ordinary expenses of its region (military or otherwise). If some extraordinary need arose, Saladin simply took the necessary monies from the nearest source. When he undertook the siege of al-Karak in the autumn of 579/1183, for example, he instructed his brother al-'Adil (then his viceroy in Egypt) to join him, bringing with him his immediate family, his possessions, and his personal wealth. Saladin intended to assign his brother to the governorship of Aleppo, but when the latter arrived, he found Saladin lacking the funds to continue the siege. At his request, al-'Adil loaned him 150,000 *dinars* from his personal fortune until the situation should ease.[10]

In fact, the only organ of central control and surveillance at Saladin's disposal was his *diwan al-insha'*—the Chancery or Bureau of Official Correspondence. The role of this agency far surpassed the implications of its name, for (partly due to the prestige of its chief, al-Qadi al-Fadil) it functioned as a sort of combined ministry of foreign affairs and interior. And by keeping Saladin informed on the course of affairs and communicating his will to the provincial governments, it established the crucial foundation for policy-making. But while "knowledge is power," it is equally true that the Chancery could not supply Saladin with the material means to compel obedience to his policy.

If, as we have maintained, Saladin's regime was supported by such a weak institutional framework, what was the "glue" that held his empire together, not only during the years of expansion and triumph, but also through periods of stagnation and defeat? Two plausible answers present themselves: first, that Saladin's state had a profoundly ethical character, a sense of mission, which allowed it to overcome the rampant factionalism and petty ambition of the age; second, that Saladin's authority ultimately rested on a complex network of personal relationships by which the ambitions of his powerful subjects were inextricably bound to his own career. These two answers are by no means contradictory. Nevertheless, the degree to which either is felt to be the "fundamental" or "predominant" element in Saladin's success will condition our conception of the nature of politics in his time and of the relationship between his regime and that of his successors.

It is the efficacy of his political and religious idealism which has attracted by far the most scholarly attention. The strongest and most uncompromising statement of this hypothesis is Gibb's; Saladin's true and ultimate goal, says Gibb, was "to restore and revive the political fabric of Islam as a single united empire, not under his own rule, but by restoring the rule of the revealed law, under the direction of the Abbasid Caliphate."[11] As to the means he used in pursuit of this majestic goal, Gibb asserts:

> Himself neither warrior nor governor by training or inclination, he it was who inspired and gathered round himself all the elements and forces making for the unity of Islam against the invaders. And this he did . . . by his unselfishness, his humility and generosity, his moral vindication of Islam against both its enemies and professed adherents. . . . Guileless himself, he never expected and seldom understood guile in others—a weakness of which his own family and others sometimes took advantage, but only (as a general rule) to come up at the end against his single-minded devotion, which nobody and nothing could bend, to the service of his ideals.[12]

In fact Gibb was not so awed by Saladin's idealism that he failed to see some serious flaws in his statesmanship. He notes that the amirs' growing discontent after the fall of Acre (587/1191) had tarnished his charisma and—far worse—that the behavior of his own relatives more than once nearly destroyed all he had created.[13]

Other scholars have been less certain than Gibb of Saladin's moral leadership. Sivan's recent study of the ideology of the Muslim countercrusade demonstrates conclusively that the effects of a half century of intensive propaganda on behalf of the *jihad* by Nur al-Din and Saladin evaporated almost instantly upon the latter's death.[14] Though he reserves judgment as to the fundamental sincerity of these two leaders, he points out that no group, neither amirs nor '*ulama*', became independently committed to the countercrusade or made it of first importance in its scale of values. On the contrary, the amirs continued in their traditional pursuit of power and position, while the '*ulama*' concentrated on the Sunni renaissance within the lands of Islam. Interest in the countercrusade depended on the living presence of Nur al-Din and Saladin, either because of their personal examples, or, more realistically, because their policy compelled anyone who wanted political influence to go along with them.

The final step away from Gibb's apotheosis of Saladin has been taken by A. S. Ehrenkreutz, who presents Saladin as no more than another ambitious general, one whose activities left Syro-Egyptian society in a shambles from which it never entirely recovered. Far from ascribing any potency to Saladin's idealism, he asserts that "his alleged moral and religious attributes influenced neither the course of his public endeavours nor the conduct of his contemporaries" and concludes that Saladin's successes "should be attributed to his military and governmental experience, to his ruthless persecution and execution of political opponents and dissenters, to his vindictive belligerence and calculated opportunism, and to his readiness to compromise religious ideals to political expediency."[15]

The problem of Saladin's personal sincerity may well be insoluble. Motives are hard to fathom in any case, and with Saladin the difficulty is all the greater because the duty implied by his professed goals coincided so closely with the policies which mere selfish ambition might have suggested. Nor, although his propaganda changed little throughout his reign, should we assume that he did not alter in his devotion to his publicly proclaimed mission, for the same man who had been rather diffident about confronting the Franks in the earlier phases of his career proved a steadfast and unwavering soldier throughout the three-years' agony of the Third Crusade.

But whatever our answer to this difficult question, Sivan and Ehrenkreutz are certainly right in contending that political and religious idealism was not the major cohesive element in Saladin's state. This must be sought among those things which conditioned the patterns of ordinary political conduct in the twelfth century. Here two matters are especially important. First, Saladin's primary political problem was not the mobilization of mass opinion, however desirable that may have seemed in itself, but the satisfaction of the interests and ambitions of a tiny elite— and, indirectly, of the somewhat broader groups from which this elite was recruited. In simplest terms, the political elite consisted of those who had regular access to the

sultan and hence some capacity to affect both the formation and execution of state policy. More narrowly it might be restricted to those who could influence any change of government, whether it took place by coup d'état or by legitimate succession. If by political participation we mean the right and capacity to have a direct role in policy-making and in the choosing of leaders, then this elite was the only politically relevant group in Syro-Egyptian society. Only after satisfying its demands could Saladin—or any ruler—turn his attention to broader segments of society.

Second, the ruler could only ensure the long-term loyalty of this elite by establishing some network of personal ties between himself and its members. These might be bonds of personal alliance (family or marriage ties), personal dependence (master-slave or patron-client relationships), or what may be termed political dependence—i.e., where one's hopes of power and wealth were linked to the success or failure of a particular prince and would presumably be less well fulfilled under anyone else. Given the political assumptions of his age, it seems inconceivable that Saladin could have tried to rule without creating such a network of ties between himself and the disparate elements of his ruling elite. But in fact neither the composition of this elite nor his relationship to it has yet been the subject of serious study.

In Saladin's time the basic criterion for admission to the political elite was occupational; one had to be either an amir (i.e., a military officer) or a "man of the turban"—a term which included both scholars and officeholders in the civil or religious administrations.[16] One group often found in traditional Islamic power structures is conspicuously absent: the officers and servants of the royal household. The reason is probably that Saladin himself was a parvenu and a mature man when he first came to power; a palace establishment therefore had no role to play in the foundation of his regime. But it is worth nothing that the palace was a very important element in the government of his youthful rival in Aleppo, al-Salih Isma'il, and would likewise be so among many of the later Ayyubids.

Mere membership in the class of amirs or of *muta'ammimin* did not suffice; it merely made one part of the large pool from which the true political elite was selected. There is no way to give rigorously accurate figures in this matter, but some useful indications can be derived. Saladin's reformed Egyptian army of 577/1181 had 8640 regular cavalry, of whom 111 were amirs.[17] This yields an average of one amir for every seventy-eight troopers (a figure which happens to equal the minimum size of the basic combat formation, the *tulb*). If the whole Ayyubid army of Egypt, Syria, and the Jazira totaled some 16,000 regular cavalry, we can reasonably assume the presence of about 200 amirs at any given time, by no means a large body of men. But in fact for the entire twenty-four years of Saladin's rule we know only sixty to seventy of his amirs by name, and of these perhaps half appear to have been guiding forces in political life.

Information on the numbers of the men of the turban is necessarily even vaguer, but what we do know points to a very similar conclusion. During Saladin's regime there were 600 men of religion in Damascus alone who received some sort of official stipend. Damascus was very much the intellectual center of the empire at this time—it possessed half the *madrasas* in Nur al-Din's domains as of his death in 569/1174; thus a figure of 3000 "clergy" in Saladin's entire empire serves as a very rough guess as to the size of this body. But very few of the religious establishment could have entertained any real hope of ever getting into the political elite as such—only the *madrasa* professors and the *qadis* of the major towns, who together constituted the upper layer of the learned class. As to the civil bureaucracy, most are obscure figures of no name; only the *wazirs* of the larger Syrian towns and the chiefs of the more important Egyptian *diwans* could seriously hope to attain a position of real influence with the sultan. The whole of this elite group of scholars, jurists, and administrators could hardly have surpassed 150 persons.[18] And as in the case of the amirs, the number whom we can actually show to have had political influence is much smaller: a few close advisors, such as al-Qadi al-Fadil or Baha' al-Din ibn Shaddad; an occasional figure who had risen through the ranks of the bureaucracy, like Safi al-Din ibn al-Qabid; and some members of the great notable families of Damascus and Aleppo. At any one time no more than a score of the men of the turban had sufficient access to the throne to ensure that their opinions would carry weight in Saladin's councils.[19]

In sum, then, Saladin's political elite probably numbered some 50 individuals all told, out of the estimated 350 persons (amirs and highly placed *muta'ammimin*) who might be considered as direct candidates. As to the whole body of men—soldiers of all ranks, officials, and "clergy"—whom the elite represented and from which it was ultimately drawn, it equaled no more than 20,000.

The occupational division of the ruling group into amirs and *muta'ammimin* was paralleled by certain social and ethnic distinctions. But here we must begin with a *caveat*: it is commonly assumed that in Saladin's period the *muta'ammimin* were a long-established indigenous aristocracy, whose power was based on its religious leadership and its large-scale mercantile and landowning interests, while the amirs were aliens and parvenus—*mamluks,* or Kurdish or Türkmen interlopers. This view has some merit, of course. Examples of a deep-rooted native religious aristocracy can be seen in such families as the Banu al-'Adim and the Banu al-'Ajami of Aleppo, or the Qurashis, the Banu 'Asakir, the Shirazis, and the Banu al-Munajja of Damascus. Concerning the mercantile connections of the religious notables, we may note that the *faqih* Jamal al-Din ibn Rawaha, killed by the Franks outside Acre in 586/1190, was almost certainly a relative of the great merchant Zaki al-Din ibn Rawaha (d. 622/1225), who founded important *madrasas* in Aleppo and Damascus. Or, finally, it is interesting to learn that part of al-Qadi al-Fadil's vast income derived from his interests in the India and Maghribi trade.[20] As far as the amirs are concerned, there is absolutely no question that many of the most important in Saladin's time were indeed *mamluks* or Kurdish immigrants—the point is too clear to require specific documentation here.

Impressive as this evidence may seem, however, equally weighty proofs can be cited to suggest that the military class and the *muta'ammimin* were by no means sharply distinct entities during the second half of the twelfth century. Dominique Sourdel has already pointed out that a very large proportion of the *madrasa* professors in Aleppo between ca. 550/1155 and 650/1252 were "Easterners"— i.e., scholars from Kurdistan, upper Mesopotamia, and Iran—no less, in fact, than 57 out of 113, or 50.5 percent.[21] And every encouragement was given to such new arrivals by the state. Nur al-Din undertook the Madrasa 'Adiliyya Kubra expressly on behalf of the newly arrived Hanafi *faqih* Qutb ad-Din an-Nisaburi and built *madrasas* in Damascus, Aleppo, Homs, Hama, and Baalbek for Sharaf al-Din ibn Abi 'Asrun, a famed Shafi'i jurist of Mosul whom Nur al-Din invited to come to Aleppo in 545/1150-51.[22] The bulk of the new arrivals probably entered Syria in the time of Nur al-Din, but even if (as seems to be the case) the current did slow under Saladin, these men continued to represent a new element, only partly integrated into the established religious aristocracy of Syria and Egypt. They derived their social influence not from local family connections, but from their religious and intellectual prestige and from the official support which they received. It is true that many of these immigrants soon became ensconced in the local religious aristocracy, but that occurred after Saladin's generation.

The case of the civil bureaucracy is altogether less clear, so that we can only propose a few probable hypotheses. The great figures of the Egyptian bureaucracy all appear to have been Egyptians by birth and education, albeit there were men whose ancestors had come from Palestine in the days when that region was still a Fatimid province. The reason for this inbred character of the Egyptian bureaucracy probably lies in the unique intricacy of its procedures, which newcomers could not easily master, and perhaps also in an exceptionally strong hereditary tendency among its officials. It may be noted in contrast that Saladin's Egypt was certainly not resistant to outsiders in her *madrasas,* courts, and military establishment. Syria presents a rather more mixed profile, insofar as we can say anything definite about her administration. To some extent, clearly, the indigenous bureaucrats and notable families (e.g., the ubiquitous Banu al-'Ajami of Aleppo) continued to hold their own under the new regime. But there was also an influx of new men, some of them from Egypt, coming in Saladin's entourage as he occupied Syria, and some of them from the old Seljukid territories of Iraq and al-Jibal, who were both discouraged by the political and administrative decay of their homelands and attracted by the prospects of Nur al-Din's and Saladin's Syria. Unfortunately we can say nothing as to their numbers or the proportion of newcomers to native officials. One can only point out that Saladin's two highest-ranking administrators were both foreigners to Syria—al-Qadi al-Fadil of Egypt and 'Imad al-Din al-Katib al-Isfahani of southern Iraq. Presumably, the would-be bureaucrats attracted to each man's entourage included a number of his own relatives and countrymen.[23]

In dealing with the amirs we must make a sharp distinction between Egypt and Syria. The Ayyubid amirs—indeed the entire military establishment—constituted an unequivocally foreign body grafted onto Egyptian society. The Fatimid army which Saladin had inherited in 564/1169 was quickly disbanded, partly through brutal massacre, in order to make room for the Turco-Kurdish forces with whom he had come to Egypt and who had raised him to power.[24] The new army was at once smaller and more effective than the old. There is no reason to doubt that its chiefs administered their *iqta's* as well as had their Fatimid counterparts, but at least at the outset, during Saladin's reign, it had no roots or historical ties whatever with the country which it would henceforth defend and dominate.

The situation in Syria was far more complex, although Saladin's forces there were organized on much the same principles as his Egyptian army (for which Syria had in fact provided the model) and even included many of the same amirs at various times during their careers. The Syrian military structure dated back to the turn of the sixth/twelfth century and as an institution was thus well integrated into the life of the region.[25] Moreover the Syrian amirate of Saladin's day had a partially hereditary character: several were men whose ancestors had risen to prominence in the time of Zangi—as had, of course, Saladin's own forebears. One can say that there existed a small, fairly recent, but well-established hereditary military aristocracy in Syria, to which belonged Saladin himself, his relatives on both sides, and about a dozen other amirial families who held important administrative *iqta's* in Syria and the Jazira.[26]

These families were variously *mamluks,* Türkmen, or (less commonly) Kurdish. They did not constitute a closed caste by any means; rather, the assumption was that new amirs, whatever their origin, could expect to be assimilated to this class as they rose in status and influence. They too could bequeath to their descendents their rank and—in principle—their *iqta's* as well. While it is dangerous to exaggerate—this hereditary aristocracy was still in process of formation in Saladin's time, and its members remained closely dependent on the sultan—nevertheless it provided an instrument of assimilation for newcomers, and its existence meant that the military elite had long-term interests in and commitments to Syrian society. The army's ethnic composition provided another point of contact between it and the indigenous population, for it contained substantial numbers of Kurds, enrolled both as individual soldiers of fortune and as tribal units.[27] Many, of course, were rough tribesmen, mountaineers and pastoralists who could have had little in common with the agriculturalists and sophisticated townsmen of Syria. But it must be remem-

bered that the Kurds had been Islamized for centuries and that they had a sufficiently developed political tradition to have enabled them to found a series of successful dynasties in Diyar Bakr, Armenia, and Azerbayjan during the tenth and eleventh centuries. Moreover the existence of numerous Kurds in the Syrian religious establishment provided yet another bridge between Kurdish soldiers and local society. In short the Kurdish element in the military faced no real barriers to integration within the Syrian social and political structure.[28] Obviously the Syrian amirs did enjoy a unique status in the political system—not only because they held the monopoly of force, or because they were in effect the executive and police arm in urban and provincial government, but because Saladin's doctrine of *jihad* made them the very kernel of the state. Likewise the Turkish and Kurdish ethnic makeup of the amirate contrasted with that of the men of the turban, which was generally Arab (Syrian, Egyptian, and Jaziran) with a Kurdish and Iranian admixture. Nevertheless the Syrian amirs had too longstanding and widespread a connection with the indigenous society for us to call them a self-contained alien elite superimposed upon it.

Because Saladin's political elite was so disparate a body, he clearly could not ensure its loyalty by any one set of relationships, nor did every subgroup within it present the same problems for his authority. On the most general level of difference, that between the amirs and the *muta'ammimin,* the former group's control of the army meant that it would always pose a direct and immediate threat to his regime—not to mention his life. The men of the turban had by themselves no means to do this. Those in the religious establishment could seriously embarrass Saladin by publicly calling him to account for his actions; they could also undercut his claims to be the true spiritual heir of Nur al-Din by refusing him moral and propaganda support. But lacking access to military force, they were not a direct threat to his regime.[29]

The military class in itself was no more a unity than the political elite as a whole. Three subgroups in particular can be distinguished: 1) the free-born amirs, consisting of the Kurds, the Türkmen, and the hereditary amirial families (whose forebears of course were often of *mamluk* origin); 2) the *mamluk* amirs, usually Turkish freedmen who had been imported as youths from the pagan nations of Central Asia (most commonly the Kipchak),[30] but including a certain number of Rumis—i.e., Armenians and Anatolian Greeks—as well; 3) and Saladin's relatives. Had Saladin not become sultan, of course, his family would have enjoyed no particular importance, but since he did, they have a special status. Not only were they his most partisan adherents, they were also his intended heirs. The study of his relationships with them is thus the study of the origins of the Ayyubid constitution.

Among the free-born amirs the Kurds would seem the most dependent on Saladin's success for the progress of their own fortunes. He too was a Kurd, after all, and under his aegis they might hope for broader opportunities in rank, estates, and political influence than they could otherwise expect in the predominantly Turkish dynasties of the age. Conversely his regime might well have appeared to them a shield which could protect them against the ethnocentrism and racial prejudice of the Turks. That ethnic consciousness and friction did exist in Saladin's reign there can be no doubt. Saladin obtained the Fatimid vizierate partly on the strength of it. After Shirkuh's death, Saladin's close associate Diya' al-Din 'Isa al-Hakkari (a Kurd) visited the leaders of each faction contending for power to try to win them over to the election of Saladin, and to one Kurdish amir (Qutb al-Din Khusrau b. al-Talal) he used the following argument: "Verily, everybody is for Saladin except you and al-Yaruqi [a Türkmen amir from the north Syrian Yürük tribe]. What is needed now, above all, is an understanding between you and Saladin, especially because of his Kurdish origin, so that the command does not go from him to the Turks."[31] It is worth noting that within a few months of Saladin's elevation, all the Turkish amirs had returned to Syria save those in the late Shirkuh's Asadiyya corps.[32] There is more than this: Saladin was at least twice subjected to taunts about his origins by the Turkish soldiers of Mosul, and in one passage of his *al-Barq al-Shami* 'Imad al-Din indulges in a lengthy attack on the Kurdish troops of the Artukids. Treachery on the part of a group of Kurds among its defenders enabled Saladin to take Sinjar in 578/1182. Most indicative of all is the letter submitted to Saladin by his amirs as he was trying to prepare the defense of Jerusalem against the expected attack of Richard Coeur-de-Lion: "If you wish us to remain [here], then either you or one of your family should be present with us, so that we may rally together around him. Otherwise, the Kurds will not be subject to the Turks, nor the Turks to the Kurds."[33] None of this suggests deep-seated hatred; the Kurds did not have to worry about massacre or expulsion. But the undeniable mutual jealousy of Turk and Kurd suggests that the apparent Kurdish fear of being relegated to an inferior status was not unjustified.[34]

If the Kurds expected Saladin's patronage and protection, they had no reason to be disappointed. That he recruited them in considerable numbers appears not only from the numerous Kurdish amirs who appear in the chronicles, but also from the fact that in his later armies at least (the period 583/1187—588/1192) there were independently organized contingents from four tribes—the Hakkaris, the Humaydis, the Zarzaris, and the Mihranis. Among the Kurdish amirs Diya' al-Din 'Isa al-Hakkari, was one of his closest counselors, while another Hakkari, Sayf al-Din 'Ali b. Ahmad al-Mashtub, had been prominent since Saladin's election to the Fatimid vizierate—an office for which he himself had been a candidate for a brief time. Finally we may mention Husam al-Din Abu-l-Hayja' al-Hadhbani (called al-Samin, "the Obese"), the first commandant of Saladin's Salahiyya regiment and later a prominent figure in the defense of Acre.[35]

But one must be cautious. Even if Gibb is correct in asserting (for he cites no evidence) that Saladin's armies contained a much higher proportion of Kurds than had those of his master Nur al-Din,[36] it is still true that Saladin relied on other elements quite as much as on the Kurds and that he was no innovator either in recruiting large numbers of Kurds or in raising them to high rank. Indeed he even singled out his Kurdish troops for special punishment for their role in the humiliating defeat of Mont Gisard (573/1177).[37] As for favoritism in the distribution of *iqta's,* not only is there no evidence that the Kurds benefited from such a policy, but it even seems doubtful that any of them ever received *iqta's* to match the largest of those held by Turkish free-born amirs.[38] Large-scale recruitment of Kurds began in fact with Zangi, who even undertook to subjugate the mountainous Hakkari region north of Mosul to facilitate this object, and Nur al-Din continued his father's policy. Saladin's father Ayyub and uncle Shirkuh were considerable figures even under Zangi, while Nur al-Din established them in positions of immense power and influence. Even among the three Kurdish amirs most prominent in Saladin's time, two of them—Diya' al-Din 'Isa al-Hakkari and Sayf al-Din 'Ali al-Mashtub—were high-ranking and influential officers before the Egyptian expedition of 564/1168—9 which eventually brought Saladin to power.[39] Undoubtedly Saladin's relations with his Kurdish amirs were strengthened by common race and the broad role in affairs which he gave them. But since their rise to influence had begun and progressed nicely well before his time, this cannot be the whole story.

Something of the same problem faces us in dealing with the other groups comprising the free-born amirs: we can detect certain bonds between them and Saladin, but nothing that would in itself ensure their loyalty to his regime. Saladin's relationship to these free-born amirs (whether their ancestors had been *mamluks* or Türkmen) was particularly ticklish, not because they considered him in any sense an outsider, but precisely because he was one of them. He had no better right to the throne than any of them, nor any claim on their gratitude—they, like Saladin himself, owed all that they were to those same Zangids whom he had dispossessed. How, then, was he to justify his position and make himself acceptable as their master? To a limited extent, he availed himself of marriage alliances, which both created a familial bond (not always reliable) and constituted an open recognition of their high status. Among the most important examples are Saladin's own marriage in 572/1176 with 'Ismat al-Din, daughter of the former dictator of Damascus Mu'in al-Din Anar (d. 544/1149) and the sister of Saladin's leading supporter among the Syrian amirs, Sa'd al-Din Mas'ud b. Anar; and the marriage of Saladin's sister Rabi'a Khatun with the same Sa'd al-Din Mas'ud, and then after his death in 581/1185 with Muzaffar al-Din Gökböri, at that time lord of Harran and Edessa.[40] By itself, of course, such a policy was bound to be insufficient, not only because of a shortage of Ayyubid princesses, but also because it did not give the amirs the material rewards of power, on which political loyalty in twelfth-century Egypt and Syria ultimately depended. Saladin had to assure the Turkish free-born amirs (and many Kurdish and *mamluk* amirs as well) that they had nothing to fear and much to gain by supporting his regime.

In some cases his task could not have been a difficult one; others demanded the most tactful diplomacy. For the Banu al-Daya—and they were not alone—the rise of Saladin was in the nature of a deliverance rather than a threat. At the death of Nur al-Din, this group of three brothers had been one of the most powerful in Syria. They controlled the administration and police of Aleppo, while their *iqta's* included 'Ayntab, 'Azaz, Tall Bashir, Harim, Qal'at Ja'bar, and Shayzar—i.e., fortresses that stood astride the major roads leading to Aleppo from all four directions. But in the coup d'état of 569/1174 which made Sa'd al-Din Gümüshtigin the chief power in Aleppo, they were thrown into prison and stripped of all their lands. Only by virtue of Saladin's intervention did they obtain their release, for this was one of the conditions of peace in his treaty with Aleppo in 572/1176. The Banu al-Daya never entirely recovered their former grandeur, possibly because the two elder and more powerful (Shams al-Din 'Ali and Badr al-Din Hasan) may have died before Saladin gained control of their former territories in 579/1183. Nevertheless Shayzar was restored to the youngest, Sabiq al-Din 'Uthman, who also played a prominent role in the reconquest and the Third Crusade.[41]

The case of Shams al-Din ibn al-Muqaddam presented Saladin with a more delicate challenge. Soon after occupying Damascus in the autumn of 570/1174, Saladin awarded Shams al-Din the valuable *iqta'* of Baalbek, probably as a reward for his instrumental role in establishing the sultan in Syria. This *iqta'* seems not to have been the ordinary unilateral and revocable grant, but rather a kind of private treaty between the two men. In the summer of 574/1178 Saladin's older brother al-Mu'azzam Turanshah demanded the surrender of Baalbek to himself. The sultan felt obliged to accede to this awkward request, but Shams al-Din refused to step down despite Saladin's offer of a generous substitute. In the end Saladin was reduced to leading his army against Baalbek, and by the following winter Shams al-Din was compelled to surrender. The striking thing is that at this point the latter neither fled to the service of another sovereign nor stood trial as a rebel. He received a new *iqta'*, hardly less desirable than his old one (Barin, Kafartab, certain villages in the district of Ma'arrat al-Nu'man, and probably Apamea), and lost nothing of his high status and influence with the sultan. Indeed in 578/1182 he was given the sensitive position of viceroy in Damascus, a post which had been held exclusively by Saladin's relatives since 570/1174.[42] The rebellion of Shams al-Din was a crucial test for Saladin: on the one hand, he could not permit any amir to oppose his authority; on the other, he could not be seen to be penalizing a man to whom he owed much and who was merely defending his rights. Had he failed in either respect, he would have lost the loyalty of the hereditary amirs at least and perhaps of any who were in some sense independent of him.

A priori one might surmise that Saladin's authority vis-à-vis the *mamluk* amirs must have been far stronger and more immediate. As Ayalon has demonstrated, the ties binding the *mamluk* to his *ustadh* or *sayyid* are among the most powerful known to us in medieval Islamic societies, and they were in no way weakened by the act of manumission, but remained intact throughout the lifetimes of the two principals.[43] From a purely political point of view as well, the *mamluk* or freedman was heavily dependent on his master, for in him rested all his hopes of advancement. A *mamluk* who abandoned or betrayed his master was like a man without a country—no other patron could trust him, nor even admit him without injuring the prospects (and hence sapping the loyalty) of his own *mamluks*. On the other hand once a *mamluk's* master was dead, his loyalty was not necessarily transferred intact to the latter's son, let alone more distant relatives. In this situation *mamluks* and freedmen became much more unreliable, and their loyal service required suitable outlays of money and power.[44]

It is therefore surprising to learn that Saladin's own *mamluks* played a relatively small part in affairs of state until the very end of his reign; we do not find them awarded the major *iqta's* and governorships, nor used in sensitive diplomatic missions, nor assigned high field commands, nor appearing in the sultan's councils. One reason for this may be that Saladin purchased no *mamluks* on his own account until he became Fatimid *wazir* and undertook to form his own Salahiyya regiment. Thus even the slave youths entering his service at the outset (in 564/1169) would not have attained sufficient experience and maturity for high office until the last years of his regime. But even so, of the *fifteen* amirs who enjoyed the greatest long-term prominence in affairs under Saladin, only *one*—Husam al-Din Sungur al-Khilati—was his own *mamluk*.[45]

This is not tantamount to declaring that the *mamluk* amirs had no importance in Saladin's time, however, for among these fifteen amirs, six were originally *mamluks*. Two had been Nur al-Din's men, two Asad al-Din Shirkuh's, and one Najm al-Din Ayyub's. We have already noted that the relationship between a *mamluk* and his master's son was relatively weak, while the two Nuri amirs would have had no personal bond whatsoever with Saladin. Their loyalty was purely political in character. As for Baha' al-Din Karakush al-Asadi, he had been instrumental in obtaining for Saladin the Fatimid vizierate, so in a sense the sultan owed him an equal debt. And although Sayf al-Din Yazkuch attained his greatest prominence under Saladin's aegis, he was already a high-ranking and powerful figure at the time of his accession; he could have made his way in the world without him. Saladin was thus compelled to treat these *mamluk* amirs with much the same deference he showed to the hereditary group if he expected to retain their services.

In summarizing the bonds between Saladin and all the various classes of his amirs a curious fact emerges—none of them was entirely subject to those ties of personal dependence or alliance which, within the value system of his society, were thought most likely to induce loyalty and obedience. Moreover it seems unlikely that Saladin's personal status and prestige—at least in the opening years of his reign—was perceptibly greater than that of many of his great amirs; nor, as a usurper himself, could he hope to gain much from the majesty of his office. But despite this, all three amirial groups provided him with reliable and even devoted servants. There seems to be something of a paradox here, and it is only when one ceases to regard the groups of amirs as isolated entities and tries to see them as parts of a functioning political system that a satisfactory solution emerges. For viewed in this latter context Saladin's amirs were linked to him by very clear bonds of political dependence.

This political dependence proceeded in the first instance from Saladin's personal qualities and political skill. The sources (even Ibn al-Athir) unanimously attest his generosity, his patience, and his tact. How well these served him can be seen by recalling the affair of Shams al-Din ibn al-Muqaddam, and it only remains to add that they indicate less his simplicity and naiveté—as Gibb would have it[46]—than his astuteness. His extravagent generosity to those around him, though undoubtedly fiscally irresponsible, was also a widely used and much-esteemed political device for ensuring the loyalty of doubtful supporters; it had even received Koranic sanction under the name *ta'lif al-qulub*—"the winning-over of hearts."[47] His oftnoted reluctance to examine the activities of his provincial governors and administrators too closely was likewise more the product of calculation than of carelessness. Or at least even when he did learn of some malfeasance, he moved to punish the guilty official only in certain circumstances. Two anecdotes from 'Imad al-Din will establish the point:

> . . . at the beginning of my journey with him [Saladin] to Egypt in 572[1176], an accounting was demanded of his *sahib al-diwan* to cover the period of his term in office. The audit of his books indicated a deficit of 70,000 *dinars*. [The sultan] neither sought nor mentioned [this sum], and caused him to think that he knew nothing of it, although the *sahib al-diwan* did not deny it. . . . Nor was [the sultan] pleased to dismiss him, but put him in charge of the *diwan al-jaysh*.[48]

> Safi al-Din ibn al-Qabid [Saladin's Intendant of the Treasury in Damascus, 584/1188] had constructed for the sultan a residence in the Citadel overlooking the two *sharafs*. He had spent a great deal on it, and went to extremes in embellishing and beautifying it, supposing that the sultan would be most gratified. But he did not so much as glance at it, and did not think it a good thing. And this was but one of his offenses in the sultan's eyes which compelled his removal from the *diwan*. [The sultan] said, "What good are mansions to him who expects to die? We were created only for God's service and to strive for eternal joy. We did not come to Damascus to reside permanently, and we do not desire never to leave again."[49]

The first example concerns corruption or misadministration of a kind which only a few persons would ever know

about; by making little of it, Saladin could retain the services—and reinforce the sense of gratitude—of a presumably valued official. In the second case, however, Saladin's public image as the disinterested protagonist of the *jihad* and the Sunni faith stood to be seriously compromised by Safi al-Din's new palace. A warrior of God could not well appear to be a man devoted to luxury. Where Saladin's public reputation was at stake, in short, official misbehavior could not be condoned. This is not to say that Saladin was a cynic; the sources give us little direct insight into his motives. Nevertheless he was of necessity a politician and had to make a politician's choices. His generosity and forbearance were attractive qualities in themselves, but they were also of great political utility. Sometimes he had to decide whether to be guided by his natural inclinations or by the demands of strict justice, and his decision was at least partly conditioned by needs of state.

Saladin's personal qualities were important not only in dealing with individual cases, but also in handling his amirs as a body. He might have tried to exploit the latent rivalries between the disparate groups composing his amirate in order to neutralize the powers of each—a commonplace in the theory and practice of medieval Muslim states[50]—but the evidence is that he tried to tamp down such feelings. Each group could be confident that its chiefs were heard by the sultan, that it would receive a reasonable share of the *iqta's* and governorships, that it would not be shunted aside in favor of some other group. For Saladin the political benefits of such a policy were immense: his treatment of individuals meant that he had to face only a few cases of personal discontent, and even if some disgruntled amir had tried to mount a conspiracy against him, he would have found no faction at hand to support him.

It was of course much to Saladin's advantage that he was the only political leader in the region who had both the personality and the political insight to establish such a relationship with his amirs. Sa'd al-Din Gümüshtigin opened his brief career as dictator of Aleppo by imprisoning a number of amirs and alienating several others who should have been among the most loyal supporters of the Zangid house. By the same token when 'Izz al-Din Mas'ud of Mosul and his chief advisor Mujahid al-Din Kiymaz occupied Aleppo in 577/1182, they could not avoid favoring their own Mosul amirs over the Aleppan Nuriyya, with consequent discontent and at least one important defection to Saladin.[51] In the face of such treatment Saladin's generosity and equitableness were bound to seem more attractive than the duty of loyalty to the house of Zangi.

The political bond which Saladin's personal qualities created was a strong and effective one, but by itself it could not have sufficed. Saladin's amirs were ambitious men, after all, and like most professional soldiers in a position to choose their master, they would serve the man who assured them the richest rewards. Had Saladin been the chief of a small passive state—a comfortable but stagnant backwater—it is doubtful that he could long have retained the services of most of his amirs. The reality was quite the opposite, of course: from the outset his kingdom was clearly the most vigorous and dynamic power in the Nile Valley and Fertile Crescent. Even before Nur al-Din's death, he had undertaken important conquests in Nubia, Libya, and the Yemen, and within two years of that event, he was the master of all Syria save Aleppo, itself reduced nearly to the status of a client state. For a man of ambition, then, by far the brightest prospects lay with Saladin. There was little temptation, and it grew less with each passing year, to abandon Saladin's cause for that of Aleppo or Mosul, whose spheres of influence were constantly shrinking and were at last absorbed into the Ayyubid orbit.

But to participate in Saladin's success was to implicate oneself and one's whole future in it. By defecting or rebelling, one would not only cut oneself off from a constantly developing set of opportunities, but one would even threaten the entire edifice of newly secured interests (in land and political power) which the amirs now enjoyed. Having joined Saladin's service, an amir had no viable choice save to continue in it, at least during the years of imperial expansion. But if Saladin's success was his surest guarantee of the amirs' loyalty, would not failure and stagnation loosen the bond between them? If Saladin's service no longer seemed the only way—or even a very promising way—to attain one's ambitions, would not the inherent egotism and adventurism of most amirs resurface and lead to serious tensions and political breakdown? Certainly this is suggested by the events of the Third Crusade. The Armenian adventure of Taqi al-Din 'Umar in 587/1191 and the amirs' reluctance to commit themselves to Jerusalem's defense in the summer of 588/1192 both imply that the amirs were no longer so ready to identify their interests with those of Saladin. Although the sultan emerged from the struggle with his territorial possessions almost intact, the political bond woven by the years of triumph was already somewhat frayed.[52]

The system of loyalties created by Saladin thus rested equally on successful expansion and on his perceptiveness in dealing both with individuals and the disparate groups among his amirs. Expansion bound the amirs to his cause because it promised material reward, and this bond grew all the more effective as Saladin became the only prince in the region able to offer such inducements on a grand scale. But in the inevitable rivalries and disappointed hopes which accompany rapid imperial expansion, or in the face of frustration and defeat, a material tie of this kind was subject to quick dissolution. It was the cement of personal trust and mutual obligation which could (at least in part) sustain the commitment of his amirs under such circumstances.

But in this system of loyalties, remarkably solid and stable though it proved under Saladin himself, there was nothing which could be transmitted to a successor: events could not be ordered by an act of will into the favorable configuration of Saladin's reign, nor could his response to the needs, interests, and personalities of the amirs be duplicated by a man of necessarily different endowments. His death would inevitably cause the collapse of the particular set of loyalties which had heretofore bound the amirs to the throne. To create a new set would require new principles of loyalty. Given the political conceptions of the time, one would expect such principles to be quite as *ad hoc* and subjective as Saladin's, but there was also the possibility that his successors would begin to search for bonds of a more impersonal, institutional kind.

Notes

1. The Arabic texts use the term *"iqta'"* for both royal appanages and military land assignments. For its rull range of meanings, see Appendix B, "The Ayyubid Iqta'." For Seljukid practice, which is closely related to Ayyubid, see Lambton, *Landlord and Peasant,* 60-64.

2. On the financial problems of Egypt and Syria under Saladin, see Ehrenkreutz, "Dinar," 182; *idem, Saladin,* 103-104, 140, 142, 222-223. On the iqta' system, see Cahen, "Iqta'," 30, 32-33; Lambton, *Landlord and Peasant,* 49-52.

3. The amirs' troops in many such iqta'-based Muslim states did become private armies, of course, but not under Saladin. However, his success in this regard was due to the loyalty of his amirs, for one can assume almost *a priori* that the ordinary soldier felt more closely bound to the amir he served than to the sultan, especially if he were a mamluk of the former. On the bonds between master and slave recruit, see Ayalon, "Esclavage," 27-29.

4. The only one of Saladin's commanders to be tempted into a private war for his own benefit was his nephew Taqi al-Din 'Umar, in 582/1186 and again in 587/1191.

   As to Saladin's disposition of his forces in the field, the armies sent by allied or client states (Mosul, Mardin, etc.) did keep their commanders and identities, as one would expect. This point is further developed in my "Emergence of the Mamluk Army."

5. On the heritability of the Zangid and early Ayyubid *iqta',* see Cahen, "Iqta'," 44-45; Elisséeff, *Nur ad-Din,* II, 577-578; III, 727. Rabie, *Financial System of Egypt,* 58-60, argues that *iqta's* were not heritable. This may be true on the whole for Egypt, but the evidence for early Ayyubid Syria is all against him. As we shall see, there are several cases down to the death of al'Adil in 615/1218 of a minor succeeding to his father's *iqta'* under the guardianship of a tutor. And Rabie himself (pp. 29-30) cites similar evidence for Zangid Syria. The point is that an *iqta'* was heritable if the ruler chose to permit it, as he commonly did during this period, but men like Nur al-Din and Saladin were always strong enough to suspend this practice in particular cases.

Two clear cases of Saladin's confirmation of a succession: al-Amjad Bahramshah in Baalbek (578/1182)—*Raud. (Cairo),* II, 33; al-Mujahid Shirkuh in Homs (582/1186)—*Raud. (Cairo),* II, 69 (where part of the diploma is cited). The case of al-Mansur Muhammad of Hama is given in *Raud. (Cairo),* II, 194, 197; and *Mufarrij (Cairo),* II, 377-378. I know of one exception to the rule that Saladin kept all *iqta'* assignments in his own hands: in 571/1176 his brother al-Mu'azzam Turanshah appointed a new *muqta'* in Bosra and Salkhad—*Raud. (Cairo),* I, 260.

6. A significant detail. The Asadiyya was the *'askar* of al-Mujahid's grandfather Shirkuh; an amir chosen from it could thus be expected to be loyal to the interests of the young prince. On the other hand, Saladin had incorporated the Asadiyya into his own forces (though retaining its original identity and commanders) upon his uncle's death and had relied heavily upon this corps. Hence he could also rely on an Asadi amir to look after his own interests.

7. al-Mujahid Shirkuh: *Raud. (Cairo),* II, 69.

al-Afdal: *Raud. (Cairo),* II, 86, 137; *Mufarrij (Cairo),* II, 210, 247.

8. Gibb, "Achievement," 99, makes much the same point, albeit in a highly idealistic way: ". . . his singleminded devotion, which nobody and nothing could bend, to the service of his ideals."

9. These figures are derived from Gibb, "Armies," with some adjustments. Gibb submits the following figures (expressed here in round numbers) of regular cavalry: Egypt—9000; Mosul and the other Jaziran towns—6500; Syria—3500; Saladin's personal guard *(halqa),* supported from his *khassa* revenues—1000. The total is 20,000 regular cavalry. But if one excludes the troops from Mosul and the Artukid and Zangid client states, which were not directly subject to Saladin's commands, this would probably remove some 4000 troopers from the total.

10. Reports to al-Qadi al-Fadil: cf. Ehrenkreutz, *Saladin,* 221. A central *diwan al-istifa'* is never mentioned in the texts, though provincial ones are: e.g., Damascus—*Raud. (Cairo),* II, 125, 138, 195; Aleppo—*Zubda,* III, 75. Elisséeff, *Nur ad-Din,* III, 805-812, has considerable detail on administrative techniques, but nothing on the relations of the various financial departments to one another. He does speak as if Nur al-Din's state did have a central financial organism, but neglects to discuss this point explicitly. Ehrenkreutz, "Saladin in Naval History," 108, 115, states that the fleet was supported entirely by Egyptian revenues, in spite of its empire-wide role.

Al-'Adil's loan: *Raud. (Cairo),* II, 52, citing Ibn Abi Tayy, who relies on an anonymous informant. 'Imad al-Din's account says nothing of this. It is put in the context of a story which has a grateful Saladin

acceding to al-'Adil's request for Aleppo as a reward for his services. The brief account in *Zubda,* III, 75, is obviously an echo of Ibn Abi Tayy's original.

11. Gibb, "Achievement," 100.

12. Gibb, "Achievement," 99.

13. Gibb, "Achievement," 104-105.

14. Sivan, *L'Islam et la Croisade,* 120-124, *et passim.*

15. Ehrenkreutz, *Saladin,* 238. For the effect of Saladin's policies on local society, *Ibid.,* 11-12, 222-223, 226. On the absence of a higher moral order in Saladin's state, *Ibid.,* 191.

16. The Arabic term for this class is *"muta'ammimin."* Briefly it comprised all those who had received the religio-legal education provided by the *madrasas,* whatever the career lines they might afterwards follow. See Appendix C, "The Muta'ammimin: 'Ulama' and Bureaucracy."

17. Gibb, "Armies," 77.

18. The figure of 600 men of religion is from 'Imad al-Din al-Isfahani, *Conquête de la Syrie et de la Palestine par Saladin,* trans. by Henri Massé (Paris: Paul Geuthner for l'Académie des Inscriptions et Belles-letters, 1972), 431. This leads to the empire-wide total of 3000 through the following calculation: 600 each in Damascus, Cairo, and Aleppo; a total of 600 in all the other major towns of Syria; a total of 600 in the Ayyubid possessions in the Jazira.

The figure of 150 elite members of the *muta'ammimin* is derived as follows:

a) the number of *madrasas* in territories which Saladin ruled directly as of 582/1186 was roughly 50 (there were 40 in the same area exclusive of Egypt at Nur al-Din's death—see Elisséeff, *Nur ad-Din,* III, 915). This would give 50 *madrasa* professors, if every *madrasa* had had a different professor (which was not the case, as is easily confirmed by consulting Ibn Shaddad's *al-A'laq al-Khatira* for Damascus and Aleppo).

b) There were perhaps 15 major qadiships in Syria and the Jazira, and as many chiefs of local financial administrations in that area.

c) Egypt would have had as many as 10 major qadiships, and a maximum of 20 top-ranking administrative officials.

d) In Saladin's immediate entourage perhaps a half-dozen officials and men of religion were close to his councils—we shall arbitrarily name the figure of 10.

The total of the above is 120. To it should be added an indeterminate group of scholars and officials who were not of the highest ranks but were generally known and respected among the *muta'ammimin.*

19. There is no adequate study of the notable families of Aleppo and Damascus which supplied so many scholars and officials; provisionally see D. Sourdel, "Professeurs."

20. Ibn Rawaha: *Mufarrij (Cairo),* II, 300; *Daris,* I, 266-267; *Perles,* 113 and n. 2. Al-Qadi al-Fadil: *DD,* III (1894), 304 n. 66, citing 'Umara al-Yamani.

21. Sourdel, "Professeurs," 113-115. Not all of these men had been born in the east, but at least their families had first entered Syria in the time of Nur al-Din or Saladin.

22. *Daris,* I, 361; Elisséeff, *Nur ad-Din,* III, 929-930. Note also the lavish patronage extended by 'Izz al-Din Farrukhshah to the Hanafi *faqih* and grammarian Taj al-Din al-Kindi, a native of Baghdad: *Mufarrij,* II *(Cairo),* 125-126.

23. Explicit proof of this in 'Imad al-Din's case, who had introduced his kinsman Jamal al-Din Isma'il into the *Diwan al-Insha'* as a specialist in Persian correspondence: *Raud. (Cairo),* II, 195. As to the continuing role of the indigenous notables in the administration, we have no specific data on Damascus; for Aleppo a number of references in *Zubda,* III, show local figures in the administration (Shihab al-Din ibn al-'Ajami; Safi al-Din Tariq ibn al-Tarira).

24. Cahen, "Ayyubids," *EI²,* I, 797; Ehrenkreutz, *Saladin,* 73-79, 81-82.

25. The Syrian military system as the model for Saladin's reforms in Egypt: Cahen, "Note additionelle," 110. For the early development of the Syrian military system in the twelfth century, see H. A. R. Gibb, *Damascus Chronicle,* 32-40. (His discussion is based chiefly on Ibn al-Qalanisi and Usama b. Munqidh.)

26. We have used the term "administrative *iqta'*" following Lambton, *Landlord and Peasant,* 61-63.

Among the leading families of this hereditary aristocracy at the time of Saladin's rise to power are the following: the Banu al-Muqaddam, the Banu al-Daya, the Begtiginids of Irbil and Harran, the sons of Nasih al-Din Khumartigin in the Jabal Ansariyya, and the sons of Hassan al-Manbiji. The forebears of Saladin's Kurdish amir Sayf al-Din al-Mashtub had held castles around 'Imadiyya, north of Mosul, before Zangi's conquest of the area—Minorsky, *Caucasian History,* 144.

27. Minorsky, *Caucasian History,* 139-146. The orders of battle for the fighting around Acre during the Third Crusade, as given in *Raud.,* II, 144, 179, indicate at least four tribal contingents of Kurds.

28. On the Kurdish political tradition, see Bosworth, *Dynasties,* 53-54, 88-91; and Minorsky, *Caucasian History.* Minorsky, "Kurds," *EI¹,* II, 1135-1140, gives a detailed sketch of their history from the Arab conquest down to the Ayyubids; *ibid.,*

1150-1151, brief but useful notes on social structure. The most striking example of a man with connections both to the native religious notables and the military aristocracy is Diya' al-Din 'Isa al-Hakkari, on whom see below, pp. 30-31, and Minorsky, *Caucasian History,* 146.

There were perhaps a few Arab (*not* Bedouin) amirs in Saladin's forces as well. The only certain identification is Sayf al-Daula Mubarak b. Munqidh, who accompanied al-Mu'azzam Turanshah on his conquest of the Yemen and was Saladin's *na'ib* in Egypt in 588/1192—*Wafayat,* IV, 144-146. One other possibility, at least on the basis of his name (for nothing else is known about his background), is 'Izz al-Din Usama, *wali* of Beirut. The numbers involved are obviously insignificant, but the evidence at least suggests that Arab soldiers were not excluded *ipso facto* from high rank.

29. On their capacity to undercut Saladin's position, see the sharp criticism of Saladin's Jaziran campaigns by al-Qadi al-Fadil and others—Ehrenkreutz, *Saladin,* 187-188. Likewise Sivan, *L'Islam et la Croisade,* 104-106, shows that by 583/1187 Saladin was under strong pressure from his entourage to move against the Franks.

30. The Kipchak dwelt in regions easily accessible to slave raids from Khwarizm—between the Aral and Caspian Seas and north of the middle Jaxartes—and this fact probably accounts for their preponderance among the Turkish *mamluks.* They were widely used in the Khwarizmian army by the late twelfth century, both as *mamluks* and as pagan mercenaries. King David IV of Georgia had used Kipchak slave troops extensively early in the twelfth century. See Bosworth, "The Political and Dynastic History of the Iranian World (A.D. 1000-1217)," in *CHI,* 52, 141-142, 183; and Cahen, "The Turks in Iran and Anatolia before the Mongol Invasions," in Setton, *Crusades,* II, 670.

31. *Mufarrij (Cairo),* I, 169, cited in Ehrenkreutz, *Saladin,* 63.

32. On the other hand some of this related to political rather than properly ethnic tensions; it was an aspect of the struggle between Saladin and Nur al-Din. Ehrenkreutz, *Saladin,* 68, 72.

33. *Raud. (Cairo),* II, 199, citing Baha' al-Din. Capture of Sinjar: *Mufarrij (Cairo),* II, 124. See also Gibb, "Achievement," 98.

34. In less controlled situations, however, the fear of massacre or violence may well have been much more immediate and hatreds more inflammable—see Minorsky, *Caucasian History,* 138 and n. 3.

35. All three of these men appear in Ibn Khallikan, a solid testimony of their eminence. See also Minorsky, *Caucasian History,* 139-146; and Ehrenkreutz, *Saladin, index,* 274, 282, 283. On the Kurdish tribal units: *Raud. (Cairo),* II, 144, 179.

36. Gibb, "Rise of Saladin," in Setton, *Crusades,* I, 582.

37. Ehrenkreutz, *Saladin,* 159.

38. E.g., Muzaffar al-Din Gökböri's *iqta'* of Harran and Edessa—a principality in itself—or Shams al-Din ibn al-Muqaddam's of Baalbek. In 588/1192 Sayf al-Din al-Mashtub received Nablus, this being the largest Kurdish *iqta'* known to me.

39. Kurdish recruitment by the Zangids: Sourdel, "Professeurs," 113; Minorsky, *Caucasian History,* 144; Gibb, "The Career of Nur ad-Din," in Setton, *Crusades,* I, 520; Elisséeff, *Nur ad-Din,* II, 372-374; III, 729.

40. 'Ismat al-Din was also Nur al-Din's widow; Saladin's marriage to her thus underlined still further his claims to be the true heir of Nur al-Din—cf. Ehrenkreutz, *Saladin,* 153. Rabi'a Khatun: *Daris,* II, 80.

41. *Mufarrij (Cairo),* II, 9; *Raud. (Cairo),* II, 127; Berchem-Fatio, *Voyage,* 181-182, 232-234. On the earlier career of this family, see Elisséeff, *Nur ad-Din,* index (Magd al-Din Abu Bakr ibn al-Daya), 1008.

42. *Raud. (Cairo),* II, 2, 5; *Mufarrij (Cairo),* II, 71. Ibn al-Muqaddam's appointment as viceroy in Damascus: *Raud. (Cairo),* II, 33. See also Gibb, "Rise of Saladin," in Setton, *Crusades,* I, 572; Ehrenkreutz, *Saladin,* 160-161, 177.

43. Ayalon, "Esclavage," 27-29; a more general discussion of the problem in Forand, "Slave and Client."

44. Ayalon, "Structure," I, 206-213, 216-222.

45. The criteria for distinguishing the members of this elite are those mentioned at the beginning of the paragraph—in brief, an amir must appear in a variety of major roles and over at least a decade of Saladin's reign to be included. Obviously there is something arbitrary about defining any given number as "the elite"—why not one more? But even if we go beyond fifteen men whose status is indisputable to include ten or twelve borderline cases, we can place in this elite only one additional *mamluk* of Saladin's—Mujahid al-Din Ayaz al-Tawil. By such an extension, we also admit at least one Arab (Sayf al-Dawla b. Munqidh).

The amirs included in this elite as more narrowly defined are the following:

Kurds:

    1) Diya, al-Din 'Isa al-Hakkari

    2) Husam al-Din Abu'l-Hayja' al-Hadhbani al-Samin

    3) Sayf al-Din 'Ali b. Ahmad al-Mashtub

Türkmen and freeborn Turks:

    1) Badr al-Din Doldurum b. Baha' al-Daula b. Yürük

    2) Nasir al-Din Mengüverish b. Nasih al-Din Khumartigin

    3) Muzaffar al-Din Gökböri b. Zayn al-Din 'Ali Küchük b. Begtigin

    4) Shams al-Din Muhammad b. 'Abd al-Malik, called Ibn al-Muqaddam

    5) Sabiq al-Din 'Uthman ibn al-Daya

    6) 'Alam al-Din Sulayman b. Jandar (ethnic origins uncertain)

mamluks:

    1) Ghars al-Din Kilich al-Nuri

    2) 'Izz al-Din Jurdik al-Nuri

    3) Sayf al-Din Yazkuch al-Asadi

    4) Baha' al-Din Karakush al-Asadi

    5) Sarim al-Din Kiymaz al-Najmi

    6) Husam al-Din Sungur al-Khilati

In the last two or three years of Saladin's reign his own *mamluks* began to emerge into greater prominence. They received a number of important *iqta's* in Palestine and Lebanon, and they would play a crucial role in the decade after his death. But as of 589/1193 they were still far from dominating the high offices of state.

46. Gibb, "Achievement," 100.

47. Elisséeff, *Nur ad-Din,* III, 812.

48. *Raud. (Cairo),* II, 218.

49. *Raud. (Cairo),* II, 125. As the Barada River enters the walled city of Damascus from the west, it flows between two low parallel ridges lying north and south of it respectively. These two ridges, in the open air outside the walls and above the "flood plain" of the Barada, have been a popular place for suburban villas, *madrasas,* etc., since the early twelfth century at least. In Arabic they are called *sharaf,* or "overlook."

50. Bosworth, *Ghaznavids,* 107-108, has a good discussion of this point.

51. *Zubda,* III, 13-15, 17-19, 49-52. The defector was 'Alam al-Din Sulayman b. Jandar, a close friend of Saladin's from the time of Nur al-Din, but heretofore a loyal supporter of the Zangid succession in Aleppo. Moreover when Saladin appeared in Syria the following spring, he was invited across the Euphrates by Muzaffar al-Din Gökböri, who was annoyed with 'Izz al-Din of Mosul for different reasons (*Zubda,* III, 51-54, 57). This defection was serious in itself, in view of Gökböri's power and influence, but its real impact was to open the Jazira to penetration by Saladin. It thus counts as a major stage in the progressive collapse of Zangid resistance.

52. Cf. Ehrenkreutz, *Saladin,* 214-215, 217-220.

Malcolm Cameron Lyons and D. E. P. Jackson (essay date 1982)

SOURCE: "Conclusion" in *Saladin: Politics of the Holy War,* Cambridge University Press, 1982, pp. 365–85, 432–37.

[*In the following essay, Lyons and Jackson offer a brief assessment of Saladin's reputation, commenting that Saladin's Muslim contemporaries alternately viewed him as a hero of Islam or as a manipulator who used Islam to achieve personal power. Lyons and Jackson provide evidence of Saladin's strengths and weaknesses.*]

To his admirers, Saladin on his death-bed at Damascus can be seen as the hero of Islam, the destroyer of the Latin Kingdom and the restorer of the shrines in Jerusalem. Eulogy, however, must accommodate itself to the fact that such a view was not accepted by numbers of his Muslim contemporaries. He can be pictured by his detractors as manipulating Islam to win power for himself and his family and only then launching on an adventure which still left a Frankish state poised to strike, if Europe were willing to support it, at an overburdened and impoverished Muslim empire. The praise and blame implicit in such assessments may be irrelevant to a historical study, but the assessments themselves serve to underline the problem of Saladin's relationship to his background. In turn, this must be related to his own qualities, in so far as they can be seen to determine how far he controlled events, rather than merely reacted to them.

As a war leader, Saladin has to his credit two decisive victories in field actions against Muslim troops, at the Horns of Hama and at Tell al-Sultān, as well as his defeats of the Franks at Marj Uyūn and at Hattīn. In terms of the length of the action and its bearing on his career, an equally important success was his crushing of the Negroes in the street fighting in Cairo, while his reverses included the battle of Ramla, the loss of Acre, the battle of Arsūf and the debacle of Jaffa. His defeat at the battle of Ramla was caused primarily by his carelessness, but elsewhere his tactics and strategy were marked by caution against the Franks and daring against the Muslims.

It must be emphasised that at this period poor battlefield communications limited the tactical effectiveness of any commander when once battle had been joined, this being the reason for Saladin's nearly disastrous mistake in the battle of October 1189 at Acre and his failure to coordinate his ambush at Tibnīn earlier in the same year. In view of this, judgement should be based on the manipulation of time, distance and numbers. Of these, Saladin at his best handled time and numbers with remarkable economy, notably at the Horns of Hama and earlier in his first march on Damascus. Hattīn was the climax of a campaign conspicuous for the concentration of force at the critical moment, but Saladin's earlier delay at Kerak and his indecision in the orders sent to al-Afdal show a possible weakness of planning. It may be noted that in an almost identical position Napoleon criticised the son of the Pasha of Damascus, who reenacted al-Afdal's part and scattered his forces, for laying himself open to Murat's counter-blow.[1] At the siege of Acre Saladin was faced with an immensely complicated problem in his attempt to muster an army from the Nile, the Euphrates and the Tigris, and then to arrange for regular reliefs, while maintaining his offensive capacity. As has been shown, he had a number of failures, but these must be set against his overall success in keeping his men in the field.

He had an impressive record of success in siege warfare, but against this has to be set the time that he wasted at Aleppo and Mosul and his crucial failure at Tyre. It must also be remarked that he did not press home his attack at Baisān in 1182 or at 'Ain Jālūt in 1183. In part this can be explained in terms of razzia strategy, or it may be argued that the Baisān and 'Ain Jālūt campaigns were primarily political camouflage for the grand design against Mosul. A wider criticism can be directed against his apparent willingness to surrender the initiative to the Franks after Guy's march on Acre, and, in fact, his tactics throughout the Third Crusade can be seen as careful but unimaginative. Here again, however, the factors involved and, in particular, numbers, supplies and morale must not be forgotten, and although at times the Muslims were ineffective, Saladin's tenacity and organising ability allowed him to recover from what might have been a losing position.

A point in his favour was the excellence of his intelligence service. He was surprised by Baldwin at Marj 'Uyūn and he failed to save the Egyptian caravan from Richard, but, in general, he was able to base his plans on more or less accurate information. If this can be attributed to efficient organisation, the converse is true of his most conspicuous failure, which was at sea. The siege of Acre showed conclusively that he could not challenge Frankish naval supremacy and it appears that, in spite of his concern to improve his fleet, his administrators were unable to carry out his orders effectively.

The administrative machine itself consisted of an inherited bureaucracy, within whose framework operated a system of patronage with Saladin at its head. It was patronage, rather than formal administration, that appears to have occupied his own time and so many requests were forwarded to him that he was quoted as saying: "before me, subjects were afraid of kings and fled from them . . . but now they come on missions to me until they weary me".[2] Patronage was diffused through the social structure. Al-Fādil wrote that Saladin would have the (heavenly) reward for the difficulties that he had faced in collecting money, while his sons had to labour at giving it away.[3] Saladin's treasurer paid out money to Imād al-Dīn's protégés without asking for his master's authorisation[4] and as a gesture of respect for the emir Najm al-Dīn ibn Masāl payments recommended by him were continued after his death.[5]

The co-existence of bureaucracy and a patronage system is a common and often harmless phenomenon. Weaknesses are produced by the overlapping of particular interests and by the concentration of patronage in a way that interferes with efficiency. It is not surprising, then, to find at this period that money promised by patrons was withheld by administrators or that administrators ran foul of the system by ignoring the favoured position of its protégés. These difficulties were increased by the fragmentation of Saladin's empire. Tūrān-Shāh in Syria gave 'Imād al-Dīn a grant from the revenues of 'Aidhāb—"they told me: 'at least it is nearer than Aden'"[6]—after which he had to send the document in the diplomatic bag to al-Fādil, who was charged with taking it himself to 'Aidhāb on his way to Mecca.

A definition of administrative power given in a letter to Baghdad lists amongst its principal functions appointments and dismissals.[7] As has been shown, Saladin was quick to move his own family. His brother Būri was given the *iqtās* of the Fayyūm in the year 576 A.H. (1180/1 A.D.) and these were then transferred in the same year to Taqī al-Dīn.[8] Tūrān-Shāh was sent to Egypt almost immediately after Ibn al-Muqaddam's surrender of Baalbek and al-Zāhir was recalled in the winter of 1183 after less than six months in Aleppo. The motive for such moves seems generally to have been short-term advantage and Saladin did not make a habit of preventing the continued occupation of power bases within his lands. One example of this is the fact that Nāsir al-Dīn Muhammad ibn Shīrkūh was left in charge of Homs until his death and, more significantly, in spite of the embarrassment caused by Tughtekīn in Yemen, nothing positive was done to dislodge him.

Further down the scale, non-Ayyubid allies, such as Dildirim of Tell Bāshir and Mankūrus of Bū Qubais, were confirmed in the possession of their lands, presumably with a view to stability and good administration as well as out of reluctance to antagonise supporters. It should also be noted that a number of enforced appointments were made. A letter dated to 1179 reported that the emir 'Izz al-Dīn Mūsik had resigned from his position as governor of the eastern province of Egypt but had been reinstated against his will,[9] while the castle of Kaukab after its fall was forced on Sārim al-Dīn Qaimāz. Saladin's commanders were not always successful as civilian administrators—Abū'l-Haijā' had to be replaced in Nisībīn in 1183 and there were complaints about al-Mashtūb in Nablus in 1192[10]—and his conscription of the reluctant may, in part, reflect an absence of competent governors, just as the employment of Christian and Jewish clerks underlines a similar problem at a lower level. Money, however, is at least an equally obvious factor. Saladin's letter to Farrukh-Shāh about the fortifications and garrison of Damietta emphasised the point that the *iqtā* holder had to bear the expenses of the defence of his holding,[11] as did his orders to Taqī al-Dīn and al-Mashtūb in 1178-9 to "increase the number of their men and to employ the cream of the warriors".[12] This must have kept emirs from volunteering to take over places needing large garrisons and expensive repairs and 'Alam al-Dīn Sulaimān, whom 'Imād al-Dīn criticised for selling grain from Baghrās to the Franks,

should probably be seen as recouping losses rather than as making an illicit profit.

Saladin's own financial difficulties can be seen reflected in his own letters and in the complaints of al-Fādil and 'Imād al-Dīn. At the upper end of the scale, the link between power and borrowed money is shown in the huge sums owed by Tūrān-Shāh at his death. There was an ambivalent attitude towards extravagance. Generosity was one of the Bedouin virtues enshrined in the *Hamāsa,* which, as has been noted, supplied Saladin and his contemporaries with many of their conventions. Al-Fādil wrote that "debt is the disease of the generous",[13] and he quoted an anecdote about Hārūn al-Rashīd who was told by his treasurer that an expedition which he was planning would be expensive, to which he replied: "no money is wasted that leaves a legacy of praise".[14] On the other hand, there are al-Fādil's complaints about the overburdened economy of Egypt and in a letter to Saladin's treasurer in Damascus he pointed out that to mortgage more than the land could produce emptied the treasury and took wealth from the Muslims.[15]

Saladin himself subordinated money to men and, as al-Fādil reported, he used the wealth of Egypt for the conquest of Syria, that of Syria for the conquest of Jazīra and that of the Jazīra for the conquest of the Coast.[16] In such a process, however, as al-Fādil also noted, "hopes of expansion can never come to an end".[17] The difficulties that arose when expansion was halted can be seen in reports of violent disturbances amongst the peasants around Damascus at the end of the Third Crusade,[18] poverty in Jerusalem both in Saladin's lifetime and after his death and complaints after his death that "salaries in Egypt remain in name only and have no meaning".[19] To set against this it can be argued that the economy, which had to be flexible enough to cope with periods of famine and natural disasters, could accept short-term distortions. William of Tyre noted that liberality was one of Saladin's most dangerous weapons,[20] and, whatever strains and disappointments were involved, he unquestionably succeeded in his own main aim, the collecting of raw material for war in the form of men, money and supplies.

Liberality as a weapon in the power struggle was allied to diplomacy, both on a personal level and in dealings between states. Although Saladin prided himself on his ability to handle men, his record is not without blemish. The main—and insoluble—enigma remains his relationship with Nūr al-Dīn, where perhaps the fairest comment is that, whatever Nūr al-Dīn's feelings, no open breach was made. His early quarrel with the Qādī Kamāl al-Dīn was generously made up: it was unremarkable that a rival, such as Qut al-Dīn Ināl, should refuse to join his service or that al-Za'farānī should leave it, but the fact that he could not win over his old comrade, Jūrdīk, is surprising. Later in his career the arrest of Keukburī and the defection of Sanjar-Shāh were setbacks, but, on the other hand, considering the difficulties involved, his family relationships were generally successful. Admittedly, he was on the verge of a break with Taqī al-Dīn at the time of his recall from Egypt in 1186 and it was Taqī al-Dīn's quest for independence that later seduced him from the Holy War. Tūrān-Shāh was a source of embarrassment over the problem of Baalbek and Tughtekīn was both an embarrassment and a disappointment in Yemen. There were rumours of discontent on the part of Tūrān-Shāh and of Nāsir al-Dīn Muhammad ibn Shīrkūh, but in spite of this the Ayyubids as a family unit worked well together and it was not until after Taqī al-Dīn's death that there was a serious threat to their coherence.

On a wider front, Saladin's diplomatic manoeuvres are open to misinterpretation. It should be noted that the volume of diplomatic correspondence was very large indeed and the incompletely recorded exchanges must be seen as part of a continuous process, one of the main aims of which was the gathering of information. Illustrations of this can be seen in 'Isā's embassy to the camp of al-Pahlawān outside Khilāt and in exchanges of messages with the Crusaders. Further, the proposals made in Saladin's letters are not to be taken literally, but rather as fixing the limits of his bargaining position. He is found at various times negotiating with the Byzantines, Raymond of Tripoli. Conrad de Montferrat and, apparently, Guy de Lusignan against the Franks. The joint move on Mosul that he suggested to 'Imād al-Dīn Zangī matches what he wrote to the Emperor Isaac and to Conrad and it can be inferred that the offer of an offensive alliance was merely an opening gambit. He later dropped all mention of this when he settled terms with Conrad and his dismissal of both Isaac and Raymond as men whose friendship or enmity did not affect him can be taken as true to the extent that he was probably prepared to settle for neutrality. In view of this technique suggestions that he planned a far-reaching diplomatic campaign to isolate the Franks of the Coast by means of treaties with the Italian cities and with the Byzantines should not be pressed too far.

A similar interpretation should be applied to what appears to be the cynical opportunism of some of his letters. His references to Amalric's death, for instance, merely give the appropriate formulae for external and internal use and cannot be taken as showing any personal feelings. By the same token, congratulations sent him after the capture of Jerusalem must not be interpreted as showing that his success had won over his rivals. The Holy War propaganda and the continuous self-justification of his letters to Baghdad are examples of coloured rhetoric in which everything is shown in extremes and internal contradictions are glossed over or ignored. This too can be seen as a matter of convention. His claims were inflated and their justification dubious, but he should at least be acquitted of the charge of cynicism.

It is, course, true to say that Saladin blurred the distinctions of the Holy War by adding Muslims, such as the Almohades, to the list of possible enemies and, instead of being confined to the recovery of the Coast, the concept was thus almost infinitely extendable. In part, this may be accepted as the idealist's view of the obligation to fight

until the word of God is established, but it can also be linked to the fact that in the politics of expansion war appears as an integral part of a cyclic process, conditioning the expectations of society and the reactions of the holders of power. Seen in an internal Islamic context, the process involved was one of continuous realignment, either of the cells of a cellular society or of the classes and individuals who controlled the transmission of power. The fact that this power was based in the first instance on military force had the advantage of providing society with a ready-made defence against external threats, but the lack of balance, and in consequence the maladministration that it encouraged, can be seen in the loose organisation of Saladin's empire, where 'Aidhāb, formally part of his dominions since he first took power in Egypt, could be pictured by Ibn Jubair in 1183 as semi-independent[21] and where, for all Saladin's successes east of the Euphrates, in his illness al-Fādil could stress that he should be moved from Harrān to "his own lands".[22] This can, perhaps, be seen as an illustration of centrifugal force, balanced by the centripetal attraction of the centres of power, and it may be noted that to the old Byzantine-Arab world of parallel institutions, where schools, colleges, hospitals and careful bureaucratic supervision were duplicated on both sides, it was the hordes of "Franks", Turks and Kurds attracted to these centres who were the barbarians.[23] The accommodation to or assimilation of these war-bands by other groups could virtually monopolise the energies of a whole society, but although glimpses of this pattern can be seen almost throughout Saladin's career, his Holy War propaganda must be seen as an attempt, conscious or unconscious, to canalise energy and direct it outwards. The attempt failed and, together with the other problems whose roots lie in this period, notably the economic impact of Saladin's wars and the social consequences of the importance that they added to the military élite, the results of this failure must be studied further before a final judgement can be made of the effect of the Crusades on Islam.

In this, it is Saladin's actions rather than his personality that are of relevance, but the broader investigations required, which are outside the scope of a biography, must still take account of what lies beyond the balance sheet of success and failure, the quality of mind and, by extension, the measure of originality of the man himself. 'Imād al-Dīn paints a consistent picture of a hero whose life was based on contempt for the "spider's web" of the world[24]— "the old woman loved by young men"[25]—and on a devotion to the Holy War, "whose abandonment is a sin for which no excuse can be brought to God".[26] Satire's view of the Holy War can be seen in al-Wahrānī's recommendation to Taqī al-Dīn: "the servant's advice is that you should resign from this service, settle in the orchards of Damascus, turn from repentance and collect together the sinners of Damascus, the prostitutes of Mosul, the panders of Aleppo and the singing girls of Iraq, delighting the five senses . . . and relying on the forgiveness of the Forgiving and Merciful God". To ignore the existence of this type of humour is to distort the picture of Saladin's age, but it may fairly be argued that the conventional view of

Saladin is of importance, in spite of the details and attitudes that it obscures or ignores, specifically because it reflects a conventional mind.

Napoleon's secretary, Bourrienne, wrote:

> almost every day during the siege [of Acre] Bonaparte and myself used to walk together at a little distance from the sea-shore . . . He said to me: "Bourrienne, I see that this wretched place has cost me a number of men and wasted much time . . . If I succeed, as I expect, I shall find in the town the pacha's treasure and arms for 300,000 men. I will stir up and arm the people of Syria, who are disgusted at the ferocity of Djezzar . . . I shall then march upon Damascus and Aleppo. On [my] advancing into the country the discontented will flock around my standard and swell my army. I will announce to the people the abolition of servitude and of the tyrannical government of the pachas. I shall arrive at Constantinople with large masses of soldiery. I shall overturn the Turkish empire and found in the east a new and grand empire . . . Perhaps I shall return to Paris by Adrianople or Vienna, after having annihilated the house of Austria."[27]

In similar circumstances, Ibn Shaddād was in Saladin's company on a winter's day by the coast of Acre during the Frankish siege. Ibn Shaddād had only recently seen the sea and he was so awed by the waves that he wrote:

> were I to be offered the whole world to put out to sea for one mile, I would not do it . . . While I was thinking of this, Saladin turned to me and said: "Shall I tell you something?" "Certainly." "It is in my mind that when Almighty God facilitates the conquest of the rest of the Coast, I shall divide up the lands, give my instructions and take my leave. Then I shall cross this sea to the islands of the Franks and pursue them until no one remains on the face of the earth who does not acknowledge God or until I die."[28]

Al-Fādil knew perfectly well that, even if Saladin were able to take the Coast, he could never attack Europe and he wrote: "not one of the Franks beyond the seas fears that if Syria is conquered his own lands will be taken".[29] Saladin, in Ibn Shaddād's account, is merely painting a conventionally romantic picture of the future where inconvenient difficulties disappear in visions of death or glory. By contrast, Napoleon's plan, similarly grandiose and equally unsuccessful, was based on the logic of the possible. It might not have worked, even had Acre fallen, but unlike Saladin's day-dream it showed the practical imagination of genius.

Saladin, who objected to a poetic reference to silvery leaves, "because leaves are green",[30] clearly adopted "the plain man's" approach and his conventional quality reflects one aspect of Islam, in its capacity not as a religion but as an assimilative social force. Here the unconventional, such as the mystical philosophy of al-Suhrawardī, is dangerous and the common denominator is to be found not in reason but in emotion. Saladin himself, as has been seen, was an emotional man, who is shown weeping over the death of

Taqī al-Dīn and over the return of the baby to its Frankish mother at the siege of Acre. Perhaps significantly, he admired the line:

> "a year passes; another year follows it:
> a month returns, and then another month"[31]

The simple expression of this conventional idea skirts banality but is aimed at the common ground of emotion that can be identified without thought. It is the generosity of feeling derived from this common ground—co-existing with hypocrisy and brutality—that gave the Crusades their mythopoeic quality, where the Muslims admired the Franks who were fighting not for money or through fear or because of compulsion by a ruler, but "purely out of zeal for the object of their worship",[32] while, on the other hand, "had they [the Muslims] not been unbelievers", the Franks would have said that there were no better men born.[33] This, in turn, is the basis of the western legend that elevated Saladin from being a "patron of prostitutes" to the company of Hector, Aeneas and Caesar amongst the virtuous pagans of Dante's *Inferno*.

It is surely this that serves to explain much of what can be known about Saladin himself. He cannot be thought of as an innovator, but as a man who was content to act on ideas supplied him. He was a good, but not a great, strategist and tactician, an open-handed but not far-sighted administrator and a man with his share of faults, mixed motives and weaknesses. His reputation, however, in history and legend, is based on his identification with conventional emotion. He appears to have held instinctively to the middle ground. The conventional mind was matched by virtues that were no less attractive for being themselves conventional. He was not concerned to question the relevance of his ideals or even apparently, to check how far he was guilty of distorting them. They were part of the heritage of Islam, to be accepted emotionally, not intellectually, and with such an attitude he could be presumed to ignore contradictions. The attractiveness of such a position must depend largely on the fundamental sincerity, however intellectually muddled this may be, of its holder. This is a test that Saladin must be allowed to have passed. Not surprisingly, he failed to win over his Muslim enemies, but he impressed the Franks and, as for his friends, Ibn Shaddād wrote of his death: "I have heard people say that they would like to ransom those dear to them with their own lives, but this has only been said figuratively in my hearing, except on the day of his death. For I know that had our sacrifice been accepted, I and others would have given our lives for him."[34]

Notes

1. *Guerre d'Orient* 82.

2. Cit. A.S. Ra. 2.138.

3. 7307.21.

4. Bundārī 287.

5. *Ibid.* 306.

6. *Ibid.* 352.

7. Munich 113.

8. Abū Sālih 204.

9. Wahrānī 182.

10. Cf. I.S. 239.

11. See p. 88.

12. Bundārī 322.

13. Cit. Bundārī 298.

14. Cit. Bundārī 279.

15. TC. 75.

16. Cit. A.S. Ra. 2.177.

17. TC. 147.

18. See P. 361.

19. 7465.137.

20. See p. 83.

21. *Travels* 71.

22. See p. 236.

23. Cf. similiarities in detail and tone between the account of negotiations between Taqī al-Dīn's Turks and the inhabitants of Libyan Tripoli (A.S. Ra. 2.38) and Nicetas' description (397) of the capture of Thessalonica by the Latins.

24. 7307.98.

25. 7465.238.

26. 7465.222.

27. Bourienne, *Memoirs of Napoleon Bonaparte*, 85.

28. I.S. 22.

29. Cit. A.S. Ra. 2.148.

30. Cit. A.S. Ra. 2.210.

31. The author is Kamāl al-Dīn al-Shahrazūrī (cf. *Sanā* 398) and the line is based on one by al-Misjāh b. Sibā' cit. Abū Tammām, *Hamāsa*, 1.417.

32. 7465.81.

33. Ambroise, *L'Estoire*, 5069.

34. I.S. 246.

Abbreviations, etc, used in the Notes

A.S. = Abū Shāma, ed. Ahmad and Ziyāda, vol. 1.1.2.

A.S. 1 = Abū Shāma, Cairo, vol. 1.

A.S. Ra. 2 = Abū Shāma, Cairo, vol. 2.

B.A. = *Shifā 'l-qulūb;* see Anon.

Barq = al-Barq al-Shāmī; see under 'Imād al-Dīn.

Bundārī = *Sanā al-Barq;* see under 'Imād al-Dīn; references are to Seşen's edition.

Daulat al-Akrād; see Muhammad b. Ibrāhīm.

Ehrenkreutz = *Saladin.*

Fath = Kitāb al-faih al-Qussī; see under 'Imād al-Dīn.

Gibb = *The Life of Saladin.*

I.A. = Ibn al-Athīr, *al-Kāmil.*

I.F. = Ibn al-Furāt.

I.S. = Ibn Shaddād.

Kharīda; see under 'Imād al-Dīn.

Khitat; see under al-Maqrīzī.

Nur. = *Dīwān rasā'il;* see under 'Imād al-Dīn.

Q. = al-Qalqashandī.

Sanā = Sanā al-Barq; see under 'Imād al-Dīn; references are to F. El-Nabarawy's edition.

W.T. = William of Tyre.

For Berlin, Cairo (= *al-durr al-nazīma*), Cambridge, Leiden, Mosul, Munich, Paris, TC. (= Top Kapu), 7307, 25756, 25757; see al-Fādil.

Bibliography

BEO = Bulletin d'Études Orientales

BFA = Bulletin of the Faculty of Arts, Cairo University

JAOS = Journal of the American Oriental Society

JESHO = Journal of the Economic and Social History of the Orient

JRAS = Journal of the Royal Asiatic Society

MMIA = Majallat al-majma' al-'ilmī al-'arAbī

MMII = Majallat al majma 'al-'ilmī al-'irāqī

Works Referred to in the Notes: (A) Eastern (B) Others

(A) Eastern

Abū Sālih al-Armanī: *The churches and monasteries of Egypt and some neighbouring countries,* ed. and trans. B.T.A. Evetts, Oxford 1895.

Abū Shāma, 'Abd al-Rahmān b. Ismā'īl: *Kitāb al-raudatain fī akhbār al-daulatain,* vol. 1.1-2, ed M.H.M. Ahmad and M.M. Ziyāda, Cairo 1956, 1962; vols. 1 and 2, Cairo 1870. . . .

al-Fādil, 'Abd al-Rahīm b. 'Alī al-Baisānī: *al-durr al-nazīma min tarassul 'Abd al-Rahīm,* ed. A. Badawi, Cairo n.d.

MSS.:

Brit. Mus. Add. 7307

7465 . . .

Munich 402 . . .

Ibn Shaddād, Bahā' al-Dīn Yūsuf b. Rāfi': *al-Nawā dir al-sultānīya, sīrat Salāh al-Dīn,* ed. J. al-Shayyāl, Cairo 1962. . . .

'Imād al-Dīn, Muhammad b. Muhammad, al-Kātib al-Isfahānī: *al-Barq al-Shāmī,* sec. 3, MS. (Bodley) Bruce 11; sec. 5, MS. (Bodley) Marsh 425.

Sanā al-barq al-Shāmī, abridged by al-Bundārī, Fath b. 'Alī, pt 1, ed. R. Seşen, Beirut 1971; see also "A Critical Edition of the Abridgement by al-Bundārī of the *Kitāb al-Barq al-Shāmī* by 'Imād al-Dīn", by F. El-Nabarawy, unpublished thesis, Cambridge University Library [published Cairo, 1979, after this work was prepared]. . . .

al-Wahrānī, Zakī al-Dīn Muhammad b. Muhammad: *Maqāmāt al-Wahrānī wa-rasā'iluhu,* MS. Ayasofya (Istanbul) no. 4299, ed. Sha'lan, Cairo 1968. . . .

(B) Others

Ambroise: *L'Estoire de la Guerre Sainte,* ed. G. Paris, Paris 1897. . . .

Bourrienne, F. de: *Memoirs of Napoleon Bonaparte* (trans.), London 1905. . . .

C. P. Melville and M. C. Lyons (essay date 1992)

SOURCE: "Saladin's Hattin Letter" in *The Horns of Hattin,* edited by B. Z. Kedar, Yad Izhak Ben-Zvi, 1992, pp. 208–13.

[*In the following excerpt, Melville and Lyons note that Saladin's Hattin letter functions as a triumph song, rather than a factual account. Like most medieval Arabic diplomatic correspondence, the letter is "colored by metaphor and rhetorical exaggeration." The critics then offer an English translation of the letter.*]

The repetitive patterns of medieval Arabic diplomatic correspondence are colored by metaphor and rhetorical exaggeration. Here, facts are the one half-pennyworth of bread in an intolerable deal of sack, and to this general rule the Hattīn letter is no exception. Not surprisingly, it is a triumph song rather than a battlefield communiqué, but in spite of this it supplies a clue that is essential to an understanding of the battle. The letter tells us that the crusaders occupied "one of the waters" during their advance on Tiberias. If this is accepted as referring to the spring by the site of the village of Tur'ān, the detail transforms what is otherwise inexplicably foolish generalship into a militarily acceptable, if unfortunate, tactical plan.

What is given here is a transcription of MS. arabe 6024 in the Bibliothèque Nationale of Paris. A full critical study has yet to be made of the manuscript tradition of Saladin's letters and, until this has been done, individual transcrip-

tions must be treated with some reserve. The present state of research, however, suggests that, although individual words or phrases may be subject to alteration in a final edition, it is highly unlikely that the few facts presented here will be altered in any way. . . .

Another letter to the glorious *Dīwān,* giving an account of the capture of Tiberias.

May God perpetuate the days of the glorious Prophetic *Dīwān;* may its continuation ensure that Islamic precepts are fulfilled, while the armies of its enemies, seeing its victorious hosts, trail the skirts of defeat; may its horsemen continue to be amulets hung round the necks of fortresses; may its enemies not cease [90b] from finding the cup of death poured out where swords are flowers, whose calix is the scabbard, while its victorious army travels on eagles' wings under the clouds, with the birds of fate hovering around the streaming swords in the blazing fire of noon, while God's encompassing mercy is found where the sword hilts betray the swords.

The servant has sent this message of service from the outpost of Acre, may Almighty God preserve it, which has smiled at our arrival, as the night of unbelief cleared from around it. We came to it and it gave us to drink from what the Hanefite religion had shaken down for it of the saliva of satisfaction. The domain of Islam has expanded; its helpers and its warriors move freely, while the fears of the unbelievers are confirmed and their fate is near. The standards of clear victory are fluttering and the gleam of God's sword has terrified the polytheists. God has seen to the lifting up of the minaret of the Nāsirid *dawla,* the raising of its fire, and the bringing down of its enemies in disgrace, while its pens have recited its insignia on the pulpits of its fingers.

The servant advanced to the Wooden Bridge on such-and-such a day, having collected armies [91a] for which the vast plain was too narrow, darkening the eye of the sun with their dust cloud when they marched. He set off for the land of the foe with the army of Heraclius and the resolution of Alexander when the desertion of the Count, may God curse him, his hypocrisy and his breaking of covenants became clear, this being when his position became re-established and flourishing amongst his own damned people.

The servant attacked Tiberias in the morning, deflowering it with the sword and assaulting it in a rage. Its people were scattered, being either captured or killed, and they had no time to allow them to use deception and deceit. Stores, wealth, equipment and booty were seized, together with heaped piles of gold and silver,[1] fine horses and luxuries, in quantities past all counting, stirring up thoughts of gratitude and reliance (on God).

At noon, when God had deprived the unbelievers of help and assistance, the massed hosts of the Franks came in search of what had been lost by their misguidedness. The King came with his infidel companions, not knowing that dawn was about to break on the night of unbelief. When he saw [91b] that we had turned the town upside down,[2] rousing its sleepers by the sword and alerting the heedless, he set up the Cross, not realizing that whoever supports injustice will be cast down and that what he constructs in his error is more fragile than a spider's web.

The hawks of his infantry and the eagles of his cavalry hovered around the water and he took one of the waters by marching to it and turning aside. But the devil seduced him[3] into doing the opposite of what he had in mind and made to seem good to him what was not his (real) wish and intention. So he left the water and set out towards Tiberias, deciding, through pride and arrogance, to take his revenge.

The servant then sent his nephew, Taqī al-Dīn, and Muzaffar al-Dīn to the water, which they seized, and had they found him camped there, they would have dyed the water red with the blood of the damned infidels and seized him. He remained beleaguered, unable to flee and not allowed to stay. The servant kindled against him fire, giving off sparks, a reminder of what God has prepared for them in the next world. He then met them in battle, when the fires of thirst had tormented them and God had requited them for their past evils, assaulting them with His violence. The hooves of the horses [92a] produced a sky of dust, whose stars were lance points. The eagles of the (Muslim) horse flew at them, their fore-feathers being their legs, and the talons their bridles. The eyes of the spears were directed at their hearts, as though they were looking for their inmost parts. Rivers of swords sought out their livers, as though wanting to water what was diseased there. They drank the cup of fate when the sides of the sword blades came to water and the spears courted them. The horses' hooves massed dust clouds for them; showers of arrows, shooting out sparks, were sent down on them, merged together by the thunder of neighing horses, with the lightning of polished swords flashing alongside them.

When the Count, may God curse him, saw that fortune was revolving swiftly against them, he turned back, saying: "I have nothing to do with you. I see what you do not see."[4] Then the horses pounded them with their shoulders and the dusty sky hurled stars against them. God decreed the victory of the Hanefite faith and the triumph of its squadrons.

There now became clear to the King, may God curse him, what falsehood had concealed from him and the battle showed him what his foolish judgement had concealed from him. He and his companions dismounted from horseback and mounted a hill, hoping that [92b] it would save them from the heat of the sharp swords. They set up a red tent for the King, its pole resting on polytheism. Their men undertook to guard its ropes, but became its pegs. Our companions dismounted and climbed up to them, confident of obtaining the goal for which they hoped. The arrow birds were restored to the quiver nests; the eyes of the spears were directed to the stars (which gleamed) like

them, complaining of the drought of their joints. The horses neighed in anger where their legs were not stained with Frankish blood and the earth longed for their hoof prints to ornament it, as crescent moons ornament the sky, by circling over it. Sovereignty belonged to the sword-hilt and its blade did not pass beyond necessary justice.

The King was captured, and this was a hard day for the unbelievers.[5] The Prince, may God curse him, was taken and the servant harvested his seed, killing him with his own hand and so fulfilling his vow. A number of the leaders of his state and the great men of his false religion were taken prisoner, while the dead numbered more than forty thousand. Not one of the Templars survived. It was a day of grace, on which the wolf and the vulture kept company, while death and captivity followed in turns. The unbelievers [93a] were tied together in fetters, astride chains rather than stout horses.

On such-and-such a day we advanced against the outpost of Acre, coming up to fight its garrison. They sought refuge in a (request for) quarter, which we granted them, in accordance with Muslim custom. We entered the town on such-and-such a day, thanking God for this great gift and acknowledging to Him, the Great and Glorious, the extent of this vast and universal benefit.

Glory to God, who has raised up and exalted the word of faith and has preserved 'Abbāsid authority, taking it into His charge, adorning and gilding the career of al-Nāsir with these triumphs and blotting out the sign of the unbelief with that of Islam,[6] to which He has added sweetness.

Notes

1. Cf. Qur'ān 3.12.
2. Cf. Qur'ān 15.74.
3. Cf. Qur'ān 47.27.
4. Cf. Qur'ān 8.50.
5. Cf. Qur'ān 25.28.
6. Cf. Qur'ān 17.13.

Terry Jones and Alan Ereira (essay date 1995)

SOURCE: "Saladin the Upstart" in *Crusades,* Facts on File, 1995, pp. 135–47.

[*In the essay that follows, Jones and Ereira provide a brief overview of Saladin's gradual achievement of military power and comment on the reasons why some contemporary Muslims viewed Saladin as an "upstart." The critics' evaluation focuses on the apparent discrepancy between Saladin's expansionism (which involved fighting against fellow Muslims) and his claim that his activities were geared toward the conquest of Jerusalem and the goal of expelling Christians from the land.*]

'Upon the death of Shirkuh, the advisers of the Caliph al-Adid suggested that he name Yusuf the new Vizier, because he was the youngest, and seemingly the most inexperienced and weakest, of the emirs of the army.' This is how Ibn al-Athir interpreted Saladin's rise to power. In fact, at the risk of spoiling a good story, the idea that Saladin was a shy, retiring nobody who had suddenly been forced into the limelight is not really tenable. He had killed Shawar and put his uncle Shirkuh into power. He had demonstrated ability in the invasions of Egypt and proved himself in battle.

Even before the Egyptian campaign, the young Saladin must have shown promise for his uncle to have chosen him as his aide-de-camp in preference to Shirkuh's own sons. Before that, Nur ed-Din had himself appointed Saladin as chief of police in Damascus, a job in which Saladin was supposed to have levied a tax off the earnings of prostitutes. At any rate he seems to have earned a reputation for being pretty tough—a contemporary poet warns the thieves of Syria to 'go softly', for this Yusuf is prepared to cut off their hands.

There is a touch of Prince Hal in some of the Arab accounts of Saladin's assumption of power. They report that, on his appointment, he repented of 'wine-drinking and turned away from frivolity' so that he might in the future 'assume the dress of religion'.

There was certainly nothing uncertain, weak or inexperienced in the way Saladin handled his new situation. He was unexpectedly running an alien country of which he had little experience, amongst strangers, strange customs, and in the most dangerous job in a court celebrated for its intrigues and conspiracies. Some people might have come unstuck. Not Saladin. He immediately set about winning over the population by spending the money that his uncle had collected. He started moving Fatimid troops out of Cairo and the moment he got wind of a palace conspiracy, he acted ruthlessly and effectively.

One of his colleagues is supposed to have become suspicious of a ragged man carrying a new pair of shoes. On examination the shoes were discovered to contain a letter from a group of Egyptian emirs, headed by one of the palace eunuchs, requesting the Franks to come back and help destroy the Syrian interloper. This story is probably just an example of Saladin's propaganda, but however he learnt of the plot and whether or not there was a plot, Saladin had the eunuch killed.

This seems to have been the signal for a revolt by the Black Regiment of the Fatimids. Trouble had been brewing amongst them for some time, and they had made and broken Viziers. 'They thought that all white men were pieces of fat and that all black men were coals.' On the day after the eunuch's murder, the Black Regiment gathered in the main square and a pitched battle raged for the next two days. They were finally forced back to their own quarter and when this was burnt down, they sued for mercy. They were allowed to escape to Giza, presumably disarmed, and here they were set upon by Turanshah, Saladin's brother, and massacred virtually to a man.

THE RIFT BETWEEN SALADIN AND NUR ED-DIN

By the end of 1169 Saladin was the unchallenged master of Egypt. His wealth was vast. He gave his father and brother control of territories that brought them one million dinars a year. No matter how many times Saladin swore allegiance to Nur ed-Din, there was no disguising the situation: the former protégé was now in a position of almost equal power to his old master, and of greater wealth. This is not something that Nur ed-Din could have relished.

According to some accounts, Saladin's independence of action got up Nur ed-Din's nose. But the chronicler Abu Shama reports that Nur ed-Din was most irritated by the way that Saladin spent money without asking for his advice; the whole point of conquering Egypt was that it was rich and Nur ed-Din had good use for the money.

Nur ed-Din was also impatient for Saladin to abolish the Shi'ite Caliphate. But Saladin knew he could not move too fast without risking a popular revolt. In May 1170 he dismissed all Shi'ite judges and replaced them with orthodox *qadis,* but the circumspection of his efforts in this direction and his refusal to deal with the Fatimid Caliphate itself led Nur ed-Din 'to suspect and revile him'.

Finally, in June 1171, Nur ed-Din wrote to Saladin ordering him to remove the Caliph. Saladin still hesitated, but since this was a direct order he would have to obey or openly revoke his allegiance to Nur ed-Din. It was at this point that Saladin's amazing luck came to his rescue. The Caliph died. The timing was so perfect that it's hard to believe that poison was not involved, and yet only one source mentions such a possibility. Perhaps it's easier to believe it was just Saladin's luck.

The Caliph of Baghdad was now officially recognized in Egypt. Sunni orthodoxy had triumphed. But this did not smooth relations between Cairo and Damascus. On the contrary, the removal of the Fatimid Caliphate meant that Saladin simply became more independent. He was now absolute ruler of a state that was even larger and richer than Syria. Tensions with Nur ed-Din were bound to get even worse. For the next few years, Saladin was to execute an elaborate ballet in order to avoid confronting his 'master' head-on.

Egypt and Syria were separated by the Frankish fief of Transjordan. Shortly after the death of al-Adid, Saladin dutifully acted on a promise he had given Nur ed-Din that he would help capture this vital link. He boldly marched into southern Jordan and laid siege to the fortress of Kerak. After a few days, however, 'convinced that it was impregnable, Saladin gave the order to depart and returned to Egypt by the desert route'.

Ibn al-Athir says that the fortress was actually on the point of surrendering and that the real reason for Saladin's sudden departure was the imminent arrival of Nur ed-Din. The last thing Saladin wanted was a face-to-face meeting with his master, in which he would inevitably have to revert to being the subordinate. What if Nur ed-Din ordered him back to Damascus? It was safer to keep at a distance and maintain the fiction of submission whilst pursuing a policy of independence.

Another reason, says Ibn al-Athir, was that Saladin had no intention of removing the Franks from Palestine. A combined attack by the Syrians from the east and the Egyptians from the west might well annihilate the Frankish kingdom, but that would increase Nur ed-Din's power and, what is worse, remove the buffer between Cairo and Damascus. So Saladin pretended that he had to rush back to Egypt to suppress a Fatimid revolt. *'Nur ed-Din did not accept the excuse.'*

Indeed, Nur ed-Din was furious and threatened to invade Egypt. Saladin hastily summoned a family council. His nephew, Taki ed-Din, was all for war, but his father, Ayub, is quoted as telling Saladin, *'I am your father and if there is anyone here who loves you and wishes you well it is I. But know this: if Nur ed-Din came, nothing could ever prevent me from bowing down before him and kissing the ground at his feet. If he ordered me to lop off your head with my sabre, I would do it. For this land is his.'*

However, the story goes that when the council was over, Ayub told his son privately that if Nur ed-Din came he would not be allowed to touch a single sugar cane. But why provoke a confrontation? If Saladin continued to show submission and deference towards Nur ed-Din, his old master would have no excuse for invading. Saladin accepted the advice, and he continued to refer to himself, in their correspondence, as 'the servant' and to Nur ed-Din as 'the master'. He maintained the fiction that everything he did was in Nur ed-Din's name—whether it was ruling Egypt or annexing the Yemen.

Nur ed-Din, on the other hand, was expecting something a little more concrete: *'since the time when Egypt was taken Nur ed-Din had wanted an agreed sum of money to be contributed which would help him meet the expenses of the Holy War . . . He was waiting for Saladin to suggest this on his own account and did not ask him for it.'* Eventually Saladin sent him a gift, consisting of some of the Fatimid family treasures (confiscated after the death of al-Adid): 60 000 dinars, some 'manufactured goods', an ass and an elephant.

Nur ed-Din seems to have taken this present as a calculated insult. He was expecting the revenue due from his new state of Egypt and instead all he was being offered was a 'gift' from the nephew of his former lieutenant who now clearly regarded himself as his equal. *'We did not need this money . . . ,'* he retorted proudly, *'he [Saladin] knows that we did not spend money on the conquest of Egypt out of a need for [more] money'.*

But of course he needed the money badly. To assert his rights, Nur ed-Din ordered an audit of his newly acquired province. In fact his disenchantment with Saladin had become so bitter that no one in his court dared to mention Saladin's name any more. He was only referred to as 'the upstart', 'the disloyal', 'the ingrate' or 'the insolent'.

But before the auditor could make his report to Damascus, Nur ed-Din was dead—probably of a heart attack. Saladin's luck was infallible. The great atabeg had been out riding with one of his emirs who happened to say: *'God knows if we shall meet here again in a year's time,'* to which Nur ed-Din replied, *'who knows whether we shall meet here in a month's time?'* According to Ibn al-Athir, Nur ed-Din was actually in the midst of preparations to invade Egypt and take it from Saladin, when *'there came a command from God that he could not disobey'.*

MASTER OF DAMASCUS

Nur ed-Din left behind his ten year-old son, al-Salih, as his heir, with the inevitable result that there was a vicious scramble for power—for control of the boy—amongst the emirs. The Governor of Aleppo declared himself the boy's regent, but neither he nor any other Turk had the backing of the emirs of Damascus. They discussed their vulnerability to the Franks and decided that, like it or not, the only man who could successfully defend them was The Upstart. In one of the great U-turns in history Saladin *'was secretly summoned by the important men of Damascus'.*

In late October Saladin made his way across 'the desert wastes of Syria' and arrived at Damascus with a small army; the gates were thrown open to him. Saladin remembered the occasion in a roseate glow: *'We dawned on the people like light in darkness,'* he wrote. *'The people rushed to us both before and after we had entered the city in joy at the [coming of] our rule.'* In actual fact he had been met outside the gates by a not inconsiderable part of the Damascene army, over whom the emirs had lost control, but they had put up no serious resistance and dispersed without fighting. *'They knew that chaff is winnowed by the wind,'* as one of his qadis put it.

The take-over had been bloodless and Saladin immediately reassured the people of his good intentions towards them. He was anxious that his actions should be seen as legitimate by a population that had committed itself to Nur ed-Din. He cut taxes and claimed that he had taken the city as a step on the road to the conquest of Jerusalem. Everything he did was ostensibly for the Caliph in Baghdad and for the cause of *jihad*. He put himself forward as the only possible leader of the *jihad*—the only true *mujahid*. The unity of Syria under him was a simple necessity if the Franks were to be driven out.

'This Saladin . . . a man of humble antecedents and lowly station, now holds under his control all these kingdoms, for fortune has smiled too graciously upon him.' It is hardly surprising that Nur ed-Din should have looked upon Saladin as an upstart, but it is curious that the Frankish

historian William of Tyre should see him in exactly the same light. William continues: '*Saladin, in defiance of the laws of humanity, wholly regardless of his lowly condition, and ungrateful for the benefits that had been showered upon him by the father of that boy king, had risen against his rightful lord.*'

Within a couple of hundred years, Saladin's lowly birth was reckoned to be a point in his favour. '*Saladin was . . . a man of humble enough birth,*' wrote Boccaccio, '*but of great and loftiest spirit and highly trained in deeds of war . . . He was munificent in giving and of his magnificence one cannot say enough. He was a pious man and he marvellously loved and honoured good men.*'

But as he installed himself in Damascus in that October of 1174, his enemies in Aleppo saw Nur ed-Din's son as his true successor and Saladin as nothing but an ambitious adventurer who had betrayed his master: '*You go too far, Yusuf, you overstep all limits. You are but a servant of Nur ed-Din, and now you seek to grasp power for yourself alone? But make no mistake, for we who have raised you out of nothingness shall be able to return you to it.*'

The people of Damascus, on the other hand, were ready for a new leader. The combination of Nur ed-Din's Holy War propaganda and the continuing flow of refugees from Frankish lands had created a hotbed of religious fervour which was in a way similar to the energy that had launched the Crusades in Europe eighty years earlier.

JIHAD FEVER IN DAMASCUS

The centre of religious energy in Damascus was a suburb that had been founded by refugees from the Christian occupation in Palestine. In the region of Nablus, the Frankish overlord, Baldwin of Mirabel, had managed to generate an entire Islamic fundamentalist movement by himself.

Baldwin had been strapped for cash. A power struggle in Jerusalem between the forceful Queen Mother, Melisende, and her son, the boy-king Baldwin 111, had resulted in her setting up a luxurious but powerless shadow-court on Baldwin of Mirabel's doorstep. It was to be paid for out of income from the royal estate lands around it. Baldwin must have suddenly found himself being ordered to find large cash sums for the King's mother out of his own pocket, because his lands were part of that royal estate.

Desperately squeezed, he quadrupled the poll tax on his peasants. As this led to increased crime, he imposed draconian penalties; when people tried to run away, he ordered that they lose a foot. The peasants protested by attending religious services instead of working. There had been less Moslem emigration from this region than most, so the population was overwhelmingly Moslem. Every Friday became the equivalent of a strike day; fields emptied as peasants flocked to the village of Jama'il to listen to the midday Friday sermon of a religious teacher called Ahmad ibn Muhammad ibn Qudama.

Ibn Qudama was a strict orthodox firebrand who raged against the oppression taking place. In 1156 Baldwin decided to deal with him. That gentleman heard what was in store for him and organized a mass flight of over 130 families from Jama'il and the surrounding villages under cover of a pretended onion-planting expedition. They managed to get safely over the Jordan to Damascus, where they settled outside the walls. There the refugees founded a community dedicated to extreme religious orthodoxy and the vigorous teaching of *jihad*. Mosques and madrassas (schools) were founded and the suburb that resulted is to this day still called al-Salihiyya—'Purity'.

SALADIN AGAINST HIS FELLOW-MOSLEMS

Saladin's rhetoric may have been full of allegiance to the cause of *jihad*, but he actually spent most of the next ten years fighting Moslems rather than Franks. His first objective was Aleppo, where his nominal master and Nur ed-Din's rightful heir, al-Salih, was being kept under close guard by the emirs. Saladin was initially quite confident. When he wrote to his nephew he allowed himself a pun on the Arabic name for Aleppo, Halab, which means milk: '*We have only to do the milking and Aleppo will be ours.*' It was not that easy.

The moment Saladin first brought his army up to the walls of Aleppo, the thirteen year-old al-Salih appeared in the market place and made an impassioned appeal to the Aleppans. '*Behold this unjust and ungrateful man who wishes to take my country from me without regard to God or man! I am an orphan, and I rely upon you to defend me, in memory of my father who so loved you*'.

Never act with dogs or children, said W. C. Fields, and the same was true in medieval politics. After al-Salih's screen-stealing performance, it was difficult for Saladin to maintain the image of the faithful servant dutifully coming to the rescue of his master's son. The Aleppans were certainly not having any of it and decided to put a halt to the whole performance by calling in the services of the Assassins. Even while Saladin was encamped outside Aleppo, Assassins made a bold attempt on his life. One of his emirs was killed in the attack.

The next year Saladin defeated a combined Aleppan-Mosuli army just outside Aleppo. He gave the Lord of Mosul's tent to his nephew, and its contents were recorded by one of the chroniclers. It's rather extraordinary what a Syrian war-lord in the twelfth century took with him into battle: treasure-chests, wine, musical instruments, singing girls and a collection of birds including doves, nightingales and parrots. Saladin returned the latter to the Lord of Mosul with the note: '*Tell him to go back to playing with these birds, for they are safe and will not bring him into dangerous situations.*'

Saladin then turned to besiege Aleppo again and, once again, the Assassins struck. This time four of them actually managed to get right up to his tent. There was a violent struggle in which Saladin's cheek was gashed. Perhaps his life was saved by the fact that he had taken to wearing a mail coif under his head-dress. The Assassins were cut down and two of Saladin's protectors died.

Saladin himself retired a shaken man, blood streaming from his face. From then on he became understandably paranoid. His tent was henceforth surrounded by a stockade and he would not talk to anybody he did not recognize. Some say that he took to sleeping fully armed in a cage. In fact fear spread throughout the entire army and everyone became afraid of everyone else.

It was a situation that could not be allowed to continue. Saladin's answer was to go to the heart of the matter. In August of 1176 he set about besieging Masyaf—the Syrian stronghold of the Assassin's sect, and which is still to this day a centre of the Ismailis. But within a few days he had called the siege off. The reason why still remains a mystery.

The Assassins' own story was that Rashid ed-Din Sinan, 'the Old Man of the Mountains', was returning to his castle when Saladin's agents tried to capture him. As they approached him, however, a mysterious force suddenly rendered their limbs useless and the Old Man told them to tell Saladin he wished to see him in private. The agents rushed back and told Saladin, who was so frightened that he could hardly sleep. Nevertheless he woke up in the middle of the night to find some hot cakes of a type only backed by the Assassins on his pillow and a poisoned dagger to which was attached an insulting and threatening verse. Saladin lifted the siege the next day.

The more likely version is that Rashid al-Din Sinan had sent letters to Saladin's uncle, threatening to kill off members of the Ayub family, and it was this that persuaded Saladin to raise the siege. What is certain is that he never threatened them again.

In 1181 Nur ed-Din's heir, al-Salih, died. It was, of course, yet another staggering example of Saladin's amazing luck that al-Salih should have taken ill and died at such an early age—he was only nineteen; *'one of the most handsome of men'* and very popular in Aleppo. Of course there was talk of poison, but no one was able to prove anything. It might have been noticed, however, that one of the suspects later did very well for himself in Saladin's service.

Saladin certainly had his army all ready to move into Aleppo, but the lord of Mosul got there first. Saladin therefore redoubled his propaganda campaign, and claimed that he had been given Aleppo by the previous Caliph and had only left al-Salih in charge out of respect for his father—all of which was, of course, total eyewash.

During the next year Saladin stepped up his attacks east of the Euphrates and made an unsuccessful assault on Mosul. He still claimed, of course, that he was acting on behalf of the Caliph in Baghdad, even though the Caliph refused to legitimize his claims. He made some useful gains in the area that effectively reduced the power of Mosul. When he finally turned back to settle the score with Aleppo, in June 1183, the Governor realized the game was up and surrendered.

Saladin ensured that the take-over was bloodless; he needed to have the support of the Aleppans. For Saladin, Aleppo was *'the eye of Syria and its citadel was the pupil'.* Nor was the significance of its falling into Saladin's hands lost on William of Tyre: *'Redoubled fear took hold of our people on hearing this news, for the result most dreaded by them had come to pass. From the first it had been apparent to the Christians that if Saladin should succeed in adding Aleppo to his principality our territory would be as completely encompassed by his power and strength as if it were in a state of siege.'*

So perhaps Saladin's claims that his anti-Moslem campaigns were all part of *jihad* were not quite so ludicrous as his enemies would have us believe. His propaganda machine certainly went to work to emphasize the connection between his annexation of Aleppo and *jihad*. In letter after letter he stressed that the conquest of Aleppo was merely a milestone on the road to victory in the Holy War. Once he controlled Aleppo, Damascus and Egypt, he had the Franks in an unprecedented vice, and could attack as no-one had done before.

And—to do him justice—he did.

Yaacov Lev (essay date 1999)

SOURCE: "The Sources" in *Saladin in Egypt*, Constable London, 1976, pp. xii-xv.

[In the following essay, Lev reviews the main contemporary sources for Saladin's biography and examines the influence of the contemporary politics (as well as the biographers' attitudes and perceptions) on the biographers' assessments of Saladin.]

1. SETTING THE STAGE: THE TWELFTH CENTURY

A. CULTURAL AND RELIGIOUS TRENDS

I. The abundance of sources for Saladin's rise to power in Egypt should not mislead us as to our ability to fathom the deeper motives and aspirations of the main players on the political scene. We must be always aware that most of our information is derived from the writings of a small and well-defined group of Saladin's associates and admirers notably Qadi al-Fadil, 'Imad al-Din al-Isfahani and Ibn Shaddad. On the other hand stands Ibn al-Athir, who is mostly hostile to Saladin. To make things worse, only part of the original writings of Saladin's admirers has reached us directly. Therefore, we are dependent on later historians, who were familiar with those works and incorporated them in their own writings. Furthermore, Saladin's historian-admirers wrote their works after the death of Saladin. Their outlook must have been influenced by Saladin's later achievements; the victory at Hittin and the conquest of Jerusalem. In retrospect, they tended to idealize the personality of the man who became a hero of the Holy War. The events of Saladin's early life were remodelled and censored to fit in with his later fame.

In order to evaluate the writings of Saladin's historian-admirers and Ibn al-Athir as sources for the history of Saladin it is necessary to try to capture the mood of the time. Saladin's historians were a product of their age and their attitudes and perceptions were shaped by the political and cultural values of the twelfth century. Equally important are their personal biographies. Not only writing on Saladin, 'Imad al-Din and Qadi al-Fadil also wrote about themselves. To a lesser degree this is true in respect of other historians of Saladin, too. Although Qadi al-Fadil, 'Imad al-Din and Ibn Shaddad entered into Saladin's service at different times and circumstances they all became members of his inner circle. They have much in common in their educational and cultural backgrounds as well as in their professional careers. With the exception of Qadi al-Fadil, their world was shaped by the new institutions of learning that spread throughout the Middle East from the second half of the eleventh century. The cultural and religious life of the period was marked by traditionalism combined with mysticism, and focused on three institutions: *madrasa, khanqa* and *dar al-hadith*. In the *madrasa*, Sunni law and other auxiliary subjects were taught. *Dar al-Hadith* was an institution of a more narrow scope devoted to the study of the Prophetic traditions. The *khanqa* served the mystics (*sufis*) as a focal point of their social and religious life. The social life of the period was permeated to great extent by the zealous adherence of people, (*ta'assub*), to legal schools which were associated with theological schools of thought.[1]

The culture of Arabic-speaking lands of the twelfth-century Middle East was much influenced by developments in Iran. The Seljuks, who reached Baghadad in 1055, were instrumental in spreading religious trends and forms of social organization that had evolved in the Iranian world. Parallel with the movement to the west of the Seljuks, men of religion ('*ulama*'), jurists (*fuqaha*') and Sufis emigrated from Iran. They transplanted and disseminated Iranian Muslim culture to the Arabic-speaking Middle East and Egypt. The proliferation of *madrasas* in the Middle East is usually associated with the name of the Seljukid vizier, Nizam al-Mulk, the founder of the Nizamiyya *madrasa* at Baghdad, in 1063. However, as the works of C. E. Bosworth and Richard W. Bulliet have shown, *madrasas* were common in Nishapur and in other smaller towns of Khurasan before the second half of the eleventh century. Also the fusion of law (*fiqh*), theology (*kalam*) and moderate forms of Sufism took place in Khurasan of the tenth and eleventh centuries. In Nishapur two important developments took place; the adaption of Sufism by the Shafi'i jurists and the rise of the *khanqa* as a typical Sufi institu-

tion.[2] The personal contribution of Nizam al-Mulk, himself of Iranian origin, must not be underestimated. He created a network of law colleges and *khanqas* which covered the most important cities of Iran and Iraq. As an institution of learning the Nizamiyya was different in its educational character and the way it was administrated from other institutions of learning in eleventh century Baghdad. As for the motives of Nizam al-Mulk, the vizier, in the words of George Makdisi, "sought to control the '*ulama*' in order to control the masses".[3]

In the earlier periods, scholars and men of religion were to great extent economically independent and pursued a variety of different occupations. The process of learning itself was not rigidly structured and did not center on a specific educational institution. Most of the teaching took place at the mosque which was a multi-purpose institution for worship, learning and socializing. In the longer run, the spread of the law colleges in the Middle East (in the second half of the eleventh century and throughout the twelfth century) was instrumental for the institutionalization and professionalization of scholarship in medieval Islam.[4] At the law colleges, the students were financially supported during the period of their learning by incomes derived from pious endowments set up for the benefit of these institutions. Needless to say that the teaching staff of the college was paid too. Under the Seljuks the involvement of the government in the religious life, in the form of political backing of legal and theological schools of thought, was greatly intensified. The Turks adhered fanatically to the Hanafi legal system and objected to Ash'ari theology. In the lands under their rule in Iran and the Middle East these religious preferences were translated into more or less systematic state policies.[5]

When approaching the religious and cultural life of the twelfth century it would be misleading to focus only on the high culture of the jurists and law colleges or the learned Sufis in the *khanqas*. The Islam of the masses, urban and certainly rural, was differently oriented; more toward spiritualism and less concerned with texts. In popular Islam holy men were more central than learned men of religion. But the religion of the educated elite and that of the masses were not worlds entirely apart. Adherence to legal schools was important and central in the lives and outlook of the historians of the period as much as it was in the lives of their less renowned contemporaries.[6] Within Sunni Islam, a wide common ground can be discerned between high and popular forms of religion, and many religious practices were typical of both the Islam of the educated elite and of that of the people. Cross influences are discerned also between Shi'ite and Sunni Islam. The celebrations of *mawlid al-nabi*, Muhammad's Nativity, exemplify this trend. This festival was a Fatimid innovation and its beginnings go back to the first decades of the twelfth century. From Egypt it spread beyond Fatimid domains and was adopted by staunch Sunni rulers among them Nur al-Din.[7] In very much the same way the nights of mid-Sha'ban were widely celebrated in the Sunni world as well as in Fatimid Egypt. In Baghdad in the third decade of the ninth century these celebrations were opposed by the Hanbalis who considered them to be an unlawful innovation. But in the twelfth century, a Hanbali rural community in Syria adopted these rites without reservation. The visitation of the graves of holy men and women was an another religious practice common to urban and rural societies which crossed the boundaries of Shi'ite and Sunni Islam.[8]

II. Historians of Saladin were rather typical members of the Muslim civilian elite of the twelfth century, an elite which was composed of two distinct but partly overlapping groups: administrators and men of religion. Both 'Imad al-Din and Ibn Shaddad had been educated at law colleges and, like many of their colleagues, sought careers in the service of rulers and in state administration.[9] 'Imad al-Din, a jurist by education, an administrator by profession and a man of high culture, was exposed in the formative period of his live to Sufism and he had apparently some latent Sufi leanings. He chose as his burial place a Sufi cemetery.[10] The convergence of attitudes between rulers and men of religion is a familiar phenomenon in Islam of the high middle ages. The portrait of Saladin given by contemporary historians was much influenced by this trend. The biographical note on Nur al-Din (ruled 1146-1174) given by Ibn 'Asakir (1105-1176) in his biographical dictionary of people connected with Damascus—*Ta'rikh Dimashq*—epitomizes the prevailing political ideologies and the measure of co-operation between the civilian elite and rulers in the twelfth century. As Ibn 'Asakir himself states, his aim was to enumerate Nur al-Din's virtues (*manaqib*). But his note is more than just a dull list of virtues. Ibn 'Asakir provides a comprehensive account of Nur al-Din's military exploits and religious and social policies. Nonetheless, his account is a mixture of both virtues and policies and is dominated by the tendency to personify Nur al-Din's policies. Nur al-Din is described as a person with an aptitude for learning and religious learning in particular. He scrupulously followed religious observances such as prayers, alms-giving (*sadaqa*), and fasting, and was modest and restrained in his personal manners. He followed the example of the forefathers (*salaf*) and of men of religion and piety.[11]

Ibn 'Asakir's account begins with a brief history of the Zengid family mentioning Nur al-Din's grandfather, Ak Sungur, and Nur al-Din's father, 'Imad al-Din, and his exploits against the Christians—the Crusaders and the Byzantines.[12] The essential part of the text begins with the establishment of Nur al-Din's rule in Aleppo. At this point, Nur al-Din's credentials as a warrior of the Holy War are presented, and his struggle against the Shi'ites in Aleppo is described. Ibn 'Asakir states that under Nur al-Din's rule Sunni Islam prevailed in Aleppo. In this context, Ibn 'Asakir mentions the establishment of law colleges by Nur al-Din and the setting up of pious endowments for their support.[13]

In discussing Nur al-Din's seizure of Damascus, Ibn 'Asakir emphasizes that the town was peacefully surrendered to him by the population due to the high prices of foodstuffs and their fear of the Crusaders (literally infidels). This theme is elaborated elsewhere in Ibn 'Asakir's text, which emphasizes that Nur al-Din's wars did not result in the killing of Muslims and the cities that Nur al-Din conquered submitted themselves to his rule.[14] These remarks reflect the fact that internal wars between various Muslim potentates were the norm in the twelfth century and Nur al-Din in creating his state fought as much against fellow Muslims as against the Christians.

Nur al-Din's policies and deeds in Damascus are described in great detail. The walls of the town were improved and law colleges were set up. Nur al-Din brought economic prosperity to the town and illegal taxes were abolished. The taxation of wine was stopped and its consumption prohibited. Justice was administered by the judicial system and Nur al-Din established the Palace of Justice (*dar al-'adl*) personally presiding over the hearings. Men of religion were well treated and honored.[15] Ibn 'Asakir specifies Nur al-Din's acts of generosity toward the weak elements in the society. He lavished alms on the orphans and poor and established pious endowments for the treatment of the sick, insane and blind. Also those who taught orphans the Koran and writing were paid by pious endowments.[16] These deeds of Nur al-Din are part of what might in modern parlance be described as his social policy. However, Ibn 'Asakir uses the word *sadaqa*, alms-giving/charity, for both Nur al-Din's social policy and his personal religiosity. The lack of a distinction between public and personal aspects in the lives and activities of rulers is clearly and nicely illustrated here. This blurring of boundaries is behind the juxtaposition of Nur al-Din's virtues and policies in Ibn 'Asakir's account.

The same lack of distinction is revealed when Ibn 'Asakir mentions various building projects of Nur al-Din such as *ribats* (a multi-role institution; fortified outpost, inn for travellers or place for the Sufis and poor), *khanqas*, hospitals, bridges and *khans* (caravanserais). These policies, says Ibn 'Asakir, were implemented throughout Nur al-Din's territories.[17] This account lumps together two quite different categories of building; those which served commercial purposes and facilitated travel and trade (caravansaries and bridges), and buildings which had religious and social functions. In the same vein justice is equated with economic prosperity. The theme of justice appears several times in Ibn 'Asakir's text which asserts that in the lands conquered by Nur al-Din justice was administrated and illegal taxation and fiscal oppression were stopped. Nur al-Din listened to the complaints against his governors and ordered them to correct their ways. Ibn 'Asakir ascribes to Nur al-Din an aura of holiness by saying that Nur al-Din's *baraka* saved people from hardship and brought prosperity to his subjects.[18]

In various places throughout the whole text Nur al-Din is depicted as a warrior of the Holy War. His personal military prowess—his firmness in battles, archery and leadership—is praised. He led his men in attacks (*karra*) and covered them in retreat (*farra*). And his victories, achieved together with his brother, against the Crusaders, Byzantines and Armenians are specified. Ibn 'Asakir stresses the way Nur al-Din treated the families of those who died in the Holy War; they were given financial support and their sons appointed to the post of governor.[19] Another essential feature of Ibn 'Asakir's appreciation of Nur al-Din's rule is the extensive description of his policies toward the Holy Cities of Arabia. Nur al-Din is portrayed as adopting comprehensive long-term policies to improve the situation of the Holy Cities and this at a considerable cost to himself. According to Ibn 'Asakir, Nur al-Din showed respect to the emir of Medina and sent his troops to protect the town. He also improved the walls of the town and provided Medina with food. The emir of Mecca was granted fiefs (*iqta's*) and the taxes collected from pilgrims were abolished. The Bedouin were also given *iqta's* in exchange for ceasing their depredations against the pilgrims.[20]

Ibn 'Asakir, a scion of a leading family of learned men in Damascus, lived and wrote his huge biographical dictionary of people connected with the history of Damascus under the rule of Nur al-Din (who expressed interest in his work and encouraged him to finish it). Ibn 'Asakir, on his part, lent support to Nur al-Din's religious policies.[21] Thus Ibn 'Asakir's appraisal of Nur al-Din's rule, although not an official biography, is the product of a sympathizer. Ibn 'Asakir's text bears witness to the fact that the call for a Holy War turned into a powerful political and religious force in Syria of the second half of the twelfth century. Nur al-Din adopted the ideology of the Holy War and manipulated it for political ends. He assumed the title *mujahid,* warrior of the Holy War, early in his rule (1149). By comparison, Nur al-Din's father did not use this title, even not after the conquest of Edessa in 1144. In Nur al-Din's protocol the title *al-'adil*—the just (meaning the just ruler)—preceded even the title *mujahid.* Ibn 'Asakir's text reflects this presumption by stressing Nur al-Din's concern with the proper administration of justice by the cadi and the establishment of the Palace of Justice. In the Palace of Justice the hearing of grievances (*nazir fi 'l-mazalim*) took place. Basically, this was justice dispensed by the ruler himself: it had a long history in pre-Islamic Middle East and medieval Islam before Nur al-Din and was also perceived as a symbol of sovereignty and power. Nur al-Din's innovation was essentially instrumental: he set up the Palace of Justice to manifest his interest in the hearing of grievances and to emphasize his authority as a sovereign.[22]

Ibn 'Asakir's text must have been know to 'Imad al-Din who, about two decades later, also wrote an appraisal of Nur al-Din's reign. The similarities between the two texts are many and fundamental. 'Imad al-Din says that Nur al-Din was the one who restored the glory of Islam in Syria. His achievements were multitudinous; he defeated the Crusaders and repossessed lands that they had conquered from the Muslims. And he was responsible for the revival of religious science and the teaching of law. 'Imad al-Din praises Nur al-Din for the various building projects that were carried out during his rule. These included the construction of congregational mosques, law colleges and *khanqas,* all provided with generous pious endowments. 'Imad al-Din mentions also the building of fortifications, *khans* and *ribats.* Elsewhere in his writings, 'Imad al-Din discerns yet another positive aspect of Nur al-Din's rule: the abolition of taxes and custom duties unauthorized by the law. For instance, 'Imad al-Din says that in 569/1173-1174, the only taxes that were levied in Nur al-Din's territories were those prescribed by the law such as the land tax (*kharaj*) and poll-tax (*jizya*) imposed on non-Muslims.[23] The question of taxation posed a problem in relations between jurists and men of religion and rulers. The extent of taxation permitted by the law was very narrow and could not satisfy the needs of the state. Nur al-Din used to explain that the levying of taxes unauthorized by the law is necessary to cover the expenses of the Holy War.[24] These two texts give us a clear picture of what leading personalities of the civilian elite of the twelfth century sought and appreciated in their rulers: commitment to Holy War and Sunni orthodoxy, and what services they were ready to render them—to justify the wars that their patrons waged against fellow-Muslims.

B. POLITICAL LIFE

While Ibn 'Asakir's text is important for understanding the ideological dimension of relations between rulers and civilians, 'Umara's description of Fatimid politics reveals the real context in which these relations took place. 'Umara was a poet of Yemeni origin, who lived in Egypt during the closing years of the Fatimid period and the first years of Saladin's rule. 'Umara is a well-known personality. Hartwig Derenbourg has studied his life and edited his poetry and more recently Pieter Smoor discussed many of its aspects. Therefore I shall only discuss a few points directly pertinent to the purpose of the present work. Maqrizi (1364-1442) provides a concise but vivid account of 'Umara's early life and his career at the Najahid court in Zabid. 'Umara arrived in Zabid in 531/1136-1137 at the age of sixteen in search of further education. For about seven years he studied Shafi'i law in Zabid. From 538/1143-1144 'Umara was in the service of Hurra, the Queen mother, attaining a high position at her court and moving freely among the members of the ruling establishment. His social advancement went hand in hand with a great improvement in his economic position. He became a very wealthy merchant with commercial interests in Aden. His legal career also flourished; he taught law and issued legal opinions (*fatwas*), and his literary skills earned him recognition among members of the ruling circles. For ten years 'Umara thrived in Zabid. In 548/1153-1154 he became entangled in the complex politics of the region and, as a result, his position in Zabid was seriously undermined. A year later 'Umara found himself a fugitive in Mecca, but his reputation was great enough to secure for him a diplomatic mission to Cairo on behalf of the local ruler. 'Umara arrived in Egypt in 550/1155-1156 and was well received by the Fatimid ruling family and the vizier. He returned to Mecca and in 551/1156-1157, was again dispatched on a mision to Cairo choosing this time to settle in Egypt.

'Umara's book, entitled *Contemporary Observations on the History of the Egyptians Viziers,* is of an autobiographical character.[25] In it he recounts the circumstances in which he composed various poems. These background stories are intertwined with remarks and observations about the viziers and other people of the ruling circles whom 'Umara knew. It is true that 'Umara, in contrast to Qadi al-Fadil, 'Imad al-Din and Ibn Shaddad, was not an administrator, but his dealings with the ruling circles in the Holy Cities of Arabia, Yemen and Egypt were extensive. According to his own testimony, 'Umara served as an emissary, trader on behalf of rulers, keeper of deposits and above all as panegyrist.[26] He describes his relations with members of the ruling circles as based on payment in exchange of service (*khudma*) and panegyric (*madh*).[27] But some of his relations were based on friendship (*unsa*), too. For example, such were 'Umara's relations with the vizier Shawar.[28]

'Umara arrived in Egypt during the early years of the vizierate of Tala'i' ibn Ruzzik, called al-Malik al-Salih who, according to late medieval historians, was a Shi'ite of the Imami branch. Recently Seta B. Dadoyan has suggested that the family of Banu Ruzzik were Nusayris. 'Umara describes him as a fanatic, but he became a member of his circle. Out of what must have been many meetings with Tala'i' ibn Ruzzik, 'Umara chose to tell how in a session (*majlis*) that took place in the house of the vizier he protested against defamation of two of the Rightly Guided Caliphs of early Islam, Abu Bakr and 'Umar, whom the Shi'ites abhorred. Such sessions were both a pastime and a typical form in which cultural and religious life was conducted.[29] But 'Umara's choice to recount this event is not incidental; his aim is to portray himself as a person possessing values and integrity.

For seven years (1154-1161) Tala'i' ibn Ruzzik served as the vizier. He was assassinated by soldiers at the instigation of the aunt of the child-Imam, al-'Adid (19 Ramadan 556/10 September 1161). The reason behind the plot was the marriage between Tala'i' ibn Ruzzik's daughter and the Fatimid Imam. It was a forced marriage by which the vizier attempted to gain supreme power and legitimacy in the Fatimid state. 'Umara, a Fatimid sympathizer, says nothing about the background and the circumstances of Tala'i' ibn Ruzzik's death. But he provides a summary of his rule. Basically he describes him as a civilized ruler. Undoubtedly what appealed most to 'Umara was Tala'i' ibn Ruzzik's love of literature and literati and the fact that the vizier himself was a poet. 'Umara is even more enthusiastic about the short rule of Ruzzik ibn Tala'i', the vizier's son, who was entitled as al-Malik al-Nasir al-'Adil. He occupied the post of the vizier between 1161-1162. The new vizier abolished unlawful taxation, ceased financial extortions and was very generous toward the Holy Cities of Arabia. Ruzzik ibn Tala'i' was killed by Shawar, or his son Tayy, following a successful rebellion.

'Umara describes in vivid terms how in the vizierial palace he was shown by the conspirators the head of the slain vizier. 'Umara was shocked and says that it was a revolting killing. Although he condemns it, he is very positive in his appreciation of Shawar's first period as the vizier.[30]

'Umara tries to strike an objective tone when writing about Shawar whose friendship and financial support he fully acknowledges. During his second vizierate Shawar shed much blood and 'Umara holds him responsible for the invasion of Egypt by the Crusaders and Nur al-Din. 'Umara sums up his evaluation of the Fatimid viziers by saying that there was no one like Tala'i' ibn Ruzzik who advanced members of the ruling establishment while the vizier Dirgham excelled in killing them and the Shawar family impoverished them by financial extortions. The killings perpetrated by Dirgham were a result of factional power struggles within the army. Umara's remarks reveal the fear and the powerlessness of the civilians in the face of the unleashed violence.[31] Administrators and men of religion were politically and economically dependent on rulers. The rulers held a monopoly on administrative posts and they created vast and lucrative pious endowments through which religious and educational institutions were maintained. In this violent political environment the civilian elite had to struggle for survival and influence while trying to maintain at least a semblance of self-respect and integrity.[32] . . .

Notes

1. For the traditionalist trend, see G. Makdisi, "The Sunni Revival", in *Islamic Civilization, 950-1150,* (ed) D. S. Richards (Oxford, 1973), reprinted in his *History and Politics in Eleventh Century Baghdad,* (London, 1990). For the spread of Sufism, see G. Makdisi, "The Hanbali School and Sufism", *Humaniora Islamica,* 2(1974), 61-72. For Sufi institutions such as *khanqa, zawiya* and *ribat* see, D. Morray, *An Ayyubid Notable and His World,* (Leiden, 1994), 139-40. For the social significance of the adherence to legal schools, see R. W. Bulliet, *The Patricians of Nishapur,* (Cambridge Mass., 1972), 28-39; I. M. Lapidus, "Muslim Cities and Islamic Societies" in *Middle Eastern Cities,* (ed) I. M. Lapidus (Berkeley, 1969), 50, 53-4; W. Madelung, "The Spread of Maturidism and the Turks", reprinted in his, *Religious Schools and Sects in Medieval Islam,* (London, 1985), 135. I owe the last reference to the kindness of D. Talmon-Heller of the Hebrew University, Jerusalem.

2. For cultural and educational developments, see C. E. Bosworth, *The Ghaznavids. Their Empire in Afghanistan and Eastern Iran, 994-1040,* 2nd. ed. (Beirut, 1973), 173, 174-5; Bulliet, *The Patricians,* 39, n. 19, 249-55, and *Islam. The View from the Edge,* (N. Y., 1994), ch. 9; Madelung, 141; M. Malamud, "Sufi Organization and Structures of Authority in Medieval Nishapur", *IJMES,* 26 (1994), 427-9, 435, 436.

3. G. Makdisi, "Muslim Institutions of Learning in Eleventh Century Baghdad", *BSOAS,* XXIV (1961), 55, reprinted in his *Religion, Law and Learning in Classical Islam,* (London, 1991). In political terms, Bulliet sees the *madrasa* as one of the tools in the hands of the regime to control the patriciate. See, *The Patricians,* 73. The essence of the *madrasa* is much debated among the scholars. For a recent critical review of the prevailing views, see M. Chamberlain, *Knowledge and Social Practice in Medieval Damascus, 1190-1350,* (Cambridge, 1994), ch. 2. For his discussion of the political utility of the *madrasa,* see 51-3, esp., 52.

4. For scholars in the first centuries of Islam, see H. J. Cohen, "The Economic Background and the Secular Occupations of Muslim Jurisprudents and Traditionalists in the Classical Period of Islam", *JESHO,* 13(1970), 16-88, esp., 25, 39. For later periods, see J. E. Gilbert, "Institutionalization of Muslim Scholarship and Professionalization of the 'Ulama' in Medieval Damascus", *SI,* (1980), 105-34, esp., 114; Bulliet, *Islam,* 149. For the spread of *madrasas,* see D. Sourdel, "Réflexions sur la diffusion de la madrasa en Orient du XIè au XIIIè siècle", *REI,* XLIV (1976), 165-84. On the base of evidence drawn from Nishapur, Bulliet states that: "It was teaching rather than learning that was the object of system-atization" and "The central concern of the system was certification of teachers". See, *The Patricians,* 49, 50. To what extent these conclusions apply to the Arabic-speaking lands of the Middle East in the eleventh-twelfth centuries is, at this stage of the research, unclear.

5. Seljukid policies were not without precedent. For instance, the Shafi'i legal school enjoyed the support of the Ghaznavid rulers, see C. L. Klausner, *The Seljuk Vezirate,* (Cambridge Mass., 1973), 63-4. For other examples, see, Madelung, 126-7, 129, 130-3, 146-7.

6. Madelung, 132, n.59, 140.

7. For the Fatimid origin of *mawlid al-nabi,* see R. Shinar, "Traditional and Reformist Mawlid Celebrations in the Maghrib", in *Studies in Memory of Gaston Wiet,* (ed) M. Rosen-Ayalon (Jerusalem, 1977), 73; Y. Lev, *State and Society in Fatimid Egypt,* (Leiden, 1991), 146. For its adaptation by Nur al-Din, see N. J. G. Kaptein, *Muhammad's Birthday Festival,* (Leiden, 1993), 31-4.

8. For Sunni and Shi'ite traditions concerning Sha'ban, see M. Kister, "Sha'ban is My Month", in *Studia Oirentalia Memoriae D. H. Baneth Dedicata,* (Jerusalem, 1979), 15-37. For the celebrations of Sha'ban, see S. Sabari, *Mouvements populaires à Baghdad à l'époque abbasside IXè-XIè siècles,* (Paris, 1981), 106; D. Talmon-Heller, "The Shaykh and the Community. Popular Hanbalite Islam in 12th-13th Century Jabal Nablus and Jabal Qaysun", *SI,* (1995),116; Lev, *State,* 144-5. For fusion, on the

one hand, and antagonism, on the other hand, between "low" and "high" forms of Sufism in the late middle ages, see T. Khalidi, *Arabic Historical Thought in the Classical Period,* (Cambridge, 1994), 211-5.

9. For the connections between education at the *madrasas* and administrative careers, see Klausner, 62-3, 64-5, 66, who brings the examples of 'Imad al-Din and Ibn Hubayra. For men of religion and administrators, see R. S. Humphreys, *From Saladin to the Mongols,* (Albany, 1977), 377-80.

10. Al-Mundhiri, *Al-Takmila li-Wafayat al-Naqala,* (ed) B. A. Marouf (Najaf, 1968), II, 288. Separate Sufi cemeteries existed in twelfth-century Damascus and in late medieval Cairo. See, Ibn 'Asakir, *Ta'rikh Dimashq,* (ed) Muhibb al-Din 'Umar ibn Ghrama al-'Amrawi (Beirut, 1995), XV, 11; L. Fernandes, *The Evolution of a Sufi Institution in Mamluk Egypt: the Khanqah,* (Berlin, 1988), 22.

11. The text of Ibn 'Asakir's biography of Nur al-Din has been edited and translated into French by N. Elisséeff, see his "Un document contemporain de Nur al-Din, sa notice biographique par Ibn 'Asakir", *BEO,* XXV (1972), 125-40, esp., 139. I am grateful to Y. Frenkel of Haifa University who drew my attention to this article. A photocopy edition of the whole manuscript of Ibn 'Asakir's *Ta'rikh Dimashq* has been published in the Arab world (n. p., n. d.) in 19 volumes. Nur al-Din biography is included in volume sixteen.

12. My references are to both the published text and the manuscript, see Ibn 'Asakir, (ed) Elisséeff, 136, para. 1-3; MS, XVI, 293, 11, 4-12, 15-7.

13. Ibn 'Asakir (ed) Elisséeff, 137, para., 1-4; MS, XVI, 293, 11, 18-30.

14. Ibn 'Asakir (ed) Elisséeff, 137, para., 5; 140, para., 3; MS, XVI, 293, 1, 32; 296, 11, 6-7.

15. Ibn 'Asakir (ed) Elisséeff, 137, para., 5, 7; 138, para., 1; MS, XVI, 293, 1, 33; 294, 11, 3-4, 10-2.

16. Ibn 'Asakir (ed) Elisséeff, 138, para., 1-2; MS, XVI, 294, 11, 13, 21-2.

17. Ibn 'Asakir (ed) Elisséeff, 138, para., 1-2; MS, XVI, 294, 11, 21-3. For the spread of *ribats* from Khurasan to Baghdad and the association of *ribats* with Sufism, see J. Chabbi, "La fonction du ribat à Bagdad du Vè siècle au début du VIIè siècle", *REI,* XLII (1972), 101-21. According to Louis Pouzet, within the context of the Sufi world of thirteenth-century Damascus, *ribat* was an institution more associated with women. See, his *Damas au VIIè/XIIIè siècle. Vie et structures religieuses dans une métropole islamique,* (Beirut, 1991), 211. I owe the last reference to the kindness of Anne-Marie Eddé. For *ribats* designated for women in pre-Fatimid and Fatimid Egypt, see ch. 3.

18. Ibn 'Asakir (ed) Elisséeff, 137, para., 7, 140, para., 2, 6. Ibn 'Asakir's reference to Nur al-Din's

buildings does not cover the full extent of his building activities. For that, see N. Elisséeff, "Les monuments de Nur al-Din", *BEO,* XIII(1949-1951), 5-50.

19. Ibn 'Asakir (ed) Elisséeff, 137, para., 6, 138, para., 3-4, 140, para., 5; MS, XVI, 294, 1, 7, 296, ll, 8-9.

20. Ibn 'Asakir (ed) Elisséeff, 138, para., 1-2; MS, XVI, 294, ll, 15-6, 19.

21. For the cooperation between Nur al-Din and Ibn 'Asakir, see Elisséeff, "Une document", 126; Morray, 144-5; Jean-Michel Mouton, *Damas et sa Principauté sous les Saljoukides et les Bourides 468-549/1076-1154,* (Cairo, 1994), 4, 5, 6-7.

22. For Nur al-Din's titles, see Y. Tabbaa, "Monuments with Message: Propagation of Jihad under Nur al-Din (1146-1174)", in *The Meeting of Two Worlds,* (ed) V. P. Goss (Michigan, 1986), 224, 226; N. Elisséeff, "La titulature de Nur al-Din d'après ses inscriptions", *BEO,* XIV(1952-1954), 171-3, 181-2. For *dar al-'adl,* see J. S. Nielsen, *Secular Justice in the Islamic State,* (Istanbul, 1985), 13; N. O. Rabbat, "The Ideological Significance of Dar al-'Adl in the Medieval Islamic Orient", *IJMES,* 27(1995), 20-1.

23. Al-Bundari, *Sana al-Barq al-Shami,* (ed) R. Sesen (Beirut, 1971), 55-6, 143-4, 145. For 'Imad al-Din's admiration of Nur al-Din, see D. S. Richards, "'Imad al-Din al-Isfahani. Administrator, Litterateur and Historian", in *Crusaders and Muslims in Twelfth-Century Syria,* (ed) M. Shatzmiller (Leiden, 1993), 146.

24. E. Sivan, *L'Islam et la Croisade,* (Paris, 1968), 73.

25. For 'Umara's biography by Maqrizi, see his *Kitab al-Muqaffa al-Kabir,* (ed) M. Yalaoui (Beirut, 1991), VIII, 742. 'Umara's autobiography is entitled as *Al-Nukat al-'Asriyya fi Akhbar al-Wuzara' al-Misriyya,* (ed) H. Derenbourg (Paris, 1897). See, 93, where 'Umara explains the aim and the method which guided him in writing the book.

26. 'Umara, 41, 42, 142.

27. *Ibid,* 94. References to financial rewards and gifts that 'Umara received from people of the ruling class are frequently mentioned throughout 'Umara's book. For instance, from Shawar's brother 'Umara received a fief (*iqta'*) and he was on his payroll for three years receiving each month fifteen *dinars.* See, 135, and 43, 62-3, 88.

28. 'Umara, 69, 94, 135.

29. *Ibid,* 44-5. Tala'i' ibn Ruzzik associated himself with Shi'ites. For example, a member of his circle was the emir al-Zafari, who had served as the governor of Alexandria and Damietta. But, he became a Sufi and an expert on Shiism whom Ibn Ruzzik much respected. See Safadi, *Kitab al-Wafi bi-'l-Wafayat,* (ed) S. Dedering (Beirut, 1982), XIV, 8. In 1159, Tala'i' ibn Ruzzik established a large

pious endowment for the benefit of *ashraf* (i.e. the descendants of Hasan and Husayn, the two sons of 'Ali and Fatima) in Fustat, Cairo and Medina and its environs. For this *waqf,* see Cl. Cahen, Y. Ragib and M. A. Taher, "L'achat et le Waqf d'un grand domaine Égyptien par le vizir Fatimide Tala'i' b. Ruzzik", *AI,* XIV(1978), 113, ll, 22-3, 27, 114, ll, 29-30, 35, 115, ll, 43-4. For 'Umara's testimony about the Nusayri affiliation of Tala'i' ibn Ruzzik, see S. B. Dadoyan, *The Fatimid Armenians. Cultural and Political Interaction in the Near East,* (Leiden, 1977), 158, n. 22.

30. 'Umara, 66-7, 69. In many ways 'Umara's poetry is highly idiosyncratic verging on the blasphemous. The same is true with his exaggerated praises of the vizier Tala'i' ibn Ruzzik. See, P. Smoor, "'The Master of the Century': Fatimid Poets in Cairo", in *Egypt and Syria in the Fatimid, Ayyubid and Mamluk Eras,* (eds), U. Vermeulen and D. De Smet (Leuven, 1995), 148-52. For 'Umara's assessment of both the vizier Tala'i' ibn Ruzzik and his son, Ruzzik, see Dadoyan, 164-5, 168, 171-2.

31. 'Umara, 74, 77, 87, 88.

32. A different approach is adopted by D. E. P. Jackson, who sees the Muslim society of the twelfth century as vertically structured and cut across by professional and administrative classes which "tended to be relatively unaffected by the higher political turmoil of a given age". See, his "Some Preliminary Reflections on the Chancery Correspondence of the Qadi al-Fadil", in *Egypt and Syria,* 208.

Abbreviations

AAS: Asian and African Studies (Haifa)

Abu Shama (Beirut): Abu Shama, *Al-Rawdatayn fi Akhbar al-Dawlatayn,* (Beirut, n. d.), 2 vols

AI: Annales Islamologiques

BEO: Bulletin des Études Orientales

BIFAO: Bulletin de l'Institut Français d'Archéologie Orientale

BSOAS: Bulletin of the School of Oriental and African Studies

Crusaders and Muslims: Crusaders and Muslims in Twelfth-Century Syria, (ed) M. Shatzmiller (Leiden, 1993)

E.I.2.: Encyclopaedia of Islam, 2nd Edition

Egypt and Syria: Egypt and Syria in the Fatimid, Ayyubid and Mamluk Ears, (eds) U. Vermeulen and D. De Smet (Leuven, 1995)

JESHO: Journal of the Economic and Social History of the Orient

The Jihad and its Time: The Jihad and its Time, Dedicated to Andrew Stefan Ehrenkreutz, (eds) H. Dajani-Shakeel and R. A. Messier (Ann Arbor, 1991)

IJMES: International Journal of Middle East Studies

JAOS: Journal of the American Oriental Society

JARCE: Journal of the American Research Center in Egypt

JNES: Journal of Near Eastern Studies

JRAS: Journal of the Royal Asiatic Society

JSAI: Jerusalem Studies in Arabic and Islam

JSS: Journal of Semitic Studies

Maritime Aspects of Migration: Maritime Aspects of Migration, (ed) K. Friedland (Wien, 1989)

Medieval Historical Writings: Medieval Historical Writings in the Christian and Islamic Worlds, (ed) D. O. Morgan (London, 1982)

MM: The Mariner's Mirror

MW: The Muslim World

REI: Revue des Études Islamiques

SI: Studia Islamica

War and Society: War and Society in the Eastern Mediterranean, 7th-15th Centuries, (ed) Y. Lev (Leiden, 1997)

FURTHER READING

Criticism

Gabrieli, Francesco, ed. and trans. "Part Two: Saladin and the Third Crusade." In *Arab Historians of the Crusades,* selected and translated from Arabic by Francesco Gabrieli, translated from Italian by E. J. Costello, pp. 87-254. London: Routledge & Kegan Paul, 1957.

Translations of Arabic sources discussing Saladin's character—his generosity, courage, fairness, and "unfailing goodness"—as well as his military exploits, peace negotiations, and death.

————."The Arabic Historiography of the Crusades." In *Historians of the Middle East,* edited by Bernard Lewis and P. M. Holt, pp. 98-107. London: Oxford University Press, 1962.

Discusses the reasons why the Crusades were not treated as a specific historical phenomenon by Arabic historiographers, and analyzes the piecemeal manner in which the Crusades were treated among Muslim historians.

Gibb, Hamilton A. R. *"Al-Barq al-Shāmī:* The History of Saladin by the Kātib 'Imād ad-Dīn al Isfahānī." *Wiener Zeitschrift für die Kunde des Morgenlandes* 52. Band, Wien 1953, pp. 93-115.

Offers a summary of the contents of *Al-Barq al-Shāmī,* the history of Saladin composed by Saladin's secretary. Gibb also analyzes the literary style of the work.

————."The Rise of Saladin, 1169-1189." In *A History of the Crusades, Vol I, The First Hundred Years,* ed. by Marshall W. Baldwin, pp. 563-89. Madison: University of Wisconsin Press, 1969.

Biographical discussion of Saladin's rise to power. Gibb focuses not on Saladin's reign as "an episode in the history of the crusades," but on his achievement of a "moral unity" among Muslims.

————. *The Life of Saladin: From the works of 'Imād ad-Dīn and Bahā' ad-Dīn.* Oxford: Clarendon Press, 1973, 76 p.

Narrative tracing the episodes of Saladin's life, based on the accounts of two historians who were Saladin's close associates.

Hindley, Geoffrey. *Saladin* London: Constable, 1976.

Hindley offers an overview of Saladin's life, achievements, and historical importance. Hindley praises Saladin's (temporary) unification of Islam as well as his religious conviction and reputation for generosity and fairness.

Holt, P. M. "Saladin and His Admirers: A Biographical Reassessment." *Bulletin of the School of Oriental and African Studies, University of London* XLVI, Part 2 (June 1983): 235-39.

Examination of the biographical treatments of Saladin. Holt emphasizes that the idealistic view, which focuses on the Crusades, taken of Saladin by such biographers as Hamilton A. R. Gibb, does not give a properly balanced assessment, in that it centers on only a small part of Saladin's career.

Lamb, Harold. "Saladin." In *The Crusades: The Flame of Islam,* pp. 31-38. Gardn City, NY: Doubleday, Doran, & Company, Inc., 1930.

Brief, biographical discussion of Saladin's career through the year 1174.

Lane-Poole, Stanley. "Saladin in Romance." In *Saladin and the Fall of the Kingdom of Jerusalem,* pp. 140–159. Beirut: Khayats, 1964.

Lane-Poole examines the way Saladin is depicted in several romances, from early French romances to Sir Walter Scott's *The Talisman* (1825). Lane-Poole notes that such romances typically offer a favorable, but often fictionalized, portrayal of Saladin.

Lewis, Bernard. "Saladin and the Assassins." *Bulletin of the School of Oriental and African Studies, University of London* XV, Part 2 (June 1953): 239-45.

Analysis of the contemporary Arabic sources discussing Saladin's trouble with the Assassins, who were eventually killed after attempting to murder Saladin.

Minorsky, V. "Prehistory of Saladin." In *Studies in Caucasian History,* pp. 107-57. London: Taylor's Foreign Press, 1953.

Discusses how Saladin has been treated in Western histories, then turns to the historical events that occurred just prior to Saladin's birth and later emergence as a military leader.

Richards, D. S. "The Early History of Saladin." *The Islamic Quarterly* XVII, Nos. 3 and 4.

Richards criticizes Andrew S. Ehrenkreutz's assessment of Saladin's early career and offers his own discussion of this period in Saladin's life. Richards concludes that Ehrenkreutz's work contains numerous inaccuracies and is overly reliant upon the accounts of Ibn al-Athir (1160–1233,) a hostile source. Richards suggests that Hamilton A. R. Gibb's more positive depiction of Saladin is perhaps more reliable than Ehrenkreutz's account.

Richards, D. S. "A Consideration of Two Sources for the Life of Saladin." *Journal of Semitic Studies* 25, No. 1 (Spring 1980): 46-65.

Examines the dates of composition and relationship between two primary sources for the life of Saladin: the *Life of Saladin* by Bahā' ad-Dīn and *al-Fath al-Qussī* by 'Imād al-Din.

Stevenson, W. B. "Salah ed-Din Yusuf." In *The Crusaders in the East: A Brief History of the Wars of Islam with the Latins in Syria During the Twelfth and Thirteenth Centuries,* pp. 205-30. Cambridge: Cambridge University Press, 1907.

Assesses Saladin's character and career, and provides an overview of Saladin's military expeditions and achievements.

Geoffroi de Villehardouin
c. 1150-54-c.1212-18

French chronicler.

INTRODUCTION

An eyewitness observer of and participant in the Fourth Crusade, Villehardouin described his experiences in his *Conquête de Constantinople* (*The Conquest of Constantinople*). The work is believed to have been written in the early years of the thirteenth century, probably around 1207–12. Critical commentary on Villehardouin and his work centers on the author's style, often praised for being simple and direct, and on the debate regarding Villehardouin's motivation and honesty. Some critics believe that portions of *Conquête* attempt to conceal the truth about the diversion of the Fourth Crusade from Egypt to Constantinople. The work is frequently cited as the first French prose text of notable literary merit and as the first reliable account of the crusading expeditions written in French.

BIOGRAPHICAL INFORMATION

Villehardouin was born between 1150 and 1154 into an aristocratic family of French crusaders which presided over a court at Achaea. In 1185, he was given the title of "Maréchal," or Marshall, of Champagne, and in this capacity was selected in 1199 by the French barons as one of six delegates to travel to Venice and arrange with the Doge for the transportation of the crusaders to the Holy Land. The next years of Villehardouin's life are chronicled in *Conquête,* which takes the reader through the 1204 conquest of Constantinople and beyond, to 1207, when the baron Boniface de Montferrat was killed in Thrace. With the death of Matthieu de Montmorency, Villehardouin assumed the leadership of the Champagne faction of the French army, and in 1205 was named "Maréchal de Champagne et de Roumaine." While the time and place of Villehardouin's death are not known, it is believed that he died between 1212 and 1218.

MAJOR WORKS

Conquête de Constantinople begins in the year 1198, when a Fourth Crusade was being preached by Fulk of Neuilly, and ends in 1207, with the death of Boniface de Montferrat at the hand of Bulgars in Thrace. Villehardouin offers an explanation for the diversion of the crusade from the original destination—Egypt—to Constantinople. He maintains that the treaty with the Venetians, signed in

1201, had stipulated that the barons and their soldiers assemble in Venice in 1202. Many crusaders failed to meet this requirement, deciding to leave from ports other than Venice. Since they desired to honor their financial arrangements with the Venetians, the crusaders who had assembled in Venice, as agreed, were obliged to aid the Venetians in their attack on the city of Zara, and to help Prince Alexius Angelus restore his imprisoned father, Isaac, to the rightful position of Emperor of Constantinople. This accounting of events later became a source of debate among critics, Medieval through modern. The rest of the work goes on to describe, in simple, unencumbered language, Villehardouin's experiences as a crusader, and, as such, focuses primarily on military interests.

CRITICAL RECEPTION

From Medieval to modern times, many critics have questioned whether or not Villehardouin, in his treatment of the genesis of the Fourth Crusade, was acting in some way as an official apologist or propagandist. It has been argued that Villehardouin perhaps attempted in his account to conceal a plot devised from the beginning by military leaders to use the crusaders in an attack on Constantinople. Several modern critics have defended Villehardouin's veracity. Frank Marzials has expressed his belief in Villehardouin's "good faith and essential political honesty." Other critics, such as M. R. B. Shaw, have acknowledged that while Villehardouin was guilty of presenting a somewhat biased interpretation of the expedition, the work on the whole is "fair and honest." Colin Morris has agreed, maintaining that although some events are not treated fairly and may even be described as dishonest in their presentation, Villehardouin's reminiscences can safely be characterized as "substantially honest" and "accurate." Paul Archambault has taken a different approach to the controversy, examining the literary aspects of the work, rather than viewing *Conquête de Constantinople* as a historical document. Archambault argues that Villehardouin's writing lacks visual interest; that he sees his own viewpoint as an "enlightened" one, which he contrasts with his enemies' "dark" motivations; and that Villehardouin habitually highlights the events he seeks to dramatize while omitting "morally embarrassing" details.

Other critics have offered another view of Villehardouin's literary talents. Marzials has lauded his style as "simple, strong, and direct." Similarly, Shaw has argued that Villehardouin's work is notable for its "simplicity and lucidity," and has observed that Villehardouin does not obstruct the progress of his story with personal intrusions, "flights of the imagination," or lengthy, picturesque descriptions. In two separate essays, Jeanette M. A. Beer has provided detailed analyses of Villehardouin's style, taking a close look at the "clarity and brevity" for which Villehardouin is often praised, and observing how various stylistic devices, most notably repetition, antithesis, and tense usage, are used by Villehardouin in support of a simple and clear presentation of events. Beer has also examined the ways in which Villehardouin uses various features of the oral narrative tradition, including the use of stock conventions, the employment of "formulae of anticipation, recapitulation, and transition," and the usage of exaggeration and repetition.

PRINCIPAL WORKS

Conquête de Constantinople (chronicle) c. 1207-12

Principal English Translations

Memoirs of the Crusades by Villehardouin and de Joinville (translated by Frank Marzials) 1908

CRITICISM

Frank Marzials (essay date 1908)

SOURCE: An introduction to *Memoirs of the Crusades by Villehardouin and de Joinville*, translated by Sir Frank Marzials, J.M. Dent & Sons, 1908, pp. x-xxvii.

[*In the following excerpt, Marzials offers a brief review of Villehardouin's account of the first four crusades. He discusses the debate regarding Villehardouin's veracity, maintaining that he was essentially honest in his account of the Fourth Crusade. Marzials goes on to praise the simplicity and directness of Villehardouin's writing style.*]

Villehardouin's story opens with the closing years of the twelfth century. In those years, as he tells, Fulk of Neuilly, near Paris, a priest well known for his holiness and zeal, began to preach a new Crusade; and Fulk's words, so men thought, were confirmed by many signs and miracles; and even apart from such supernatural aid, it is not difficult, I think, to conjecture wherein lay the force of his appeal or to imagine its nature. But while he was descanting on the necessity for another attempt to recover the Holy Land, and setting forth the glories and spiritual advantages of the proposed adventure, did he ever dwell at all, one wonders, on the story of the Crusades that had already been undertaken? Did he unfold for his hearers that tragic and terrible scroll in the history of men—a scroll on which are recorded in strange, intermingled, fantastic characters, tales of saintly heroism, and fraud, and greed, and cruelty, and wrong—of sufferings at which one sickens, and foul deeds at which one sickens more, and acts of devotion and high courage that have found their place among the heirlooms and glories of mankind?

Did he tell them of the First Crusade—tell them how, a little more than a century before, the heart of Peter the Hermit had been moved to fiery indignation at the indignities offered to pilgrims at the sacred shrines, and he had made all Christendom resound to his angry eloquence; how at the Council of Clermont, in 1095, Pope Urban II. had re-echoed the hermit's cry; how the nations had responded to the call to arms in so holy a cause, the noble selling or mortgaging his land, the labourer abandoning his plough, the woman her hearth and distaff, the very children forsaking their play; how a great wave of humanity had thence been set rolling eastward—a wave of such mighty volume, and so impelled by fierce enthusiasm, that, notwithstanding every hindrance, dissension within, utter disorganisation, misrule, famine, plague, slaughter, wholesale desertions, treachery on every side, wild fanatical hostility—notwithstanding all this, it had yet rolled right across Europe, rolled on across the deserts and defiles of Asia Minor, and swept the infidel from Jerusalem and the fastnesses of Judæa? Did Fulk of Neuilly, one wonders, tell his hearers the story of that First Crusade, which, for all its miseries and horrors, accomplished the mission on which it started, and placed its great and saintly leader,

Godfrey of Bouillon on the throne of Jerusalem, and founded a Christian kingdom in the Holy Land? (1099).

Did he tell them the story of the Second Crusade? That was the Crusade preached by one of very different mould from Peter the Hermit, by one who was in many ways the master-spirit of his time, St. Bernard. For to St. Bernard it seemed a scandal and intolerable that the Christian kingdom of Judæa, prayed for with so many prayers, purchased with so much blood, should be dissolved. He held it as not to be borne that the place where our Lord had been cradled in the manger, the fields where He had taught, the hill where He had died for men, the sepulchre in which He had lain, should fall once more into the unholy possession of the infidel. And yet, ere fifty years had passed since the taking of Jerusalem, this seemed an approaching consummation, so weakened was the new kingdom by internal dissension, so fiercely attacked from without. Already the Moslem were prevailing on every side. The important position of Edessa had fallen into their hands. So St. Bernard came to the rescue. By his paramount personal influence, he induced Lewis VII. of France, and Conrad of Germany to take the cross. Again there was a march across Europe; again treachery on the part of the Greek Emperor at Constantinople; again most terrible slaughter in Asia Minor; again unheard-of sufferings; again folly, ineptitude, treachery. But not again the old ultimate success. This time the great human wave, though it did indeed reach Jerusalem, yet reached it spent and broken. Edessa was not retaken. Damascus was besieged, only to show the utter want of unity among the Crusaders. Conrad returned to Germany. Lewis, a year later, returned to France (1149); and of the Second Crusade there remained small immediate trace, save, in France and Germany, depopulated hamlets, and homes made desolate, and bones bleaching in the far Syrian deserts.

Could Fulk have turned, in the retrospect, with better heart to the Third Crusade?—Somewhat unquestionably. That Third Crusade is the one in which we Englishmen have most interest, for its central figure is our lion-hearted king, Richard. And it is, probably, the Crusade of which the main incidents are best known to the English reader, for they have been evoked from the past, and made, as it were, to reenact themselves before us, by the magic of Sir Walter Scott. What boy has not read the *Talisman?* And so it will not be necessary for me to dwell at length on the history of that Crusade: the rivalries of Richard and Philip Augustus; the siege and surrender of Acre; the return of Philip Augustus to France; the bitter feud with the Duke of Austria; the superb daring and personal prowess of Richard; the abortive march on Jerusalem—which must have been retaken save for the insane rivalries in the Christian host; the interchange of courtesies with the chivalrous Saladin; the abandonment of the Crusade; the return of the English king westward, and his imprisonment in an Austrian dungeon (1192).

Not a story of success, most certainly. Richard left the Holy Land pretty well where he found it. His object in go-ing thither had been the recovery of Jerusalem, which, in 1187, after being nearly ninety years in Christian hands, had fallen a prey to Saladin. And that object was as far as ever from attainment. But still there rested about the Third Crusade a glamour of courage and heroic deeds, so that when scarce nine years after its conclusion, Fulk went about preaching new efforts for the expulsion of the Saracens, he may possibly have sought to raise the courage of his warlike hearers by dwelling on the doughty deeds of Richard and his knights.

Otherwise, if he referred to the past at all—for the latest German expedition of 1196-1197 had just come to an inglorious close,—his message can scarcely have been one of confidence as he addressed the nobles and lesser men assembled at Ecri, towards the end of November 1199, to take part in the great tournament instituted by Thibaut III., Count of Champagne. No, the past was against them. It spoke little of success, and much of misery, disorganisation, disaster; while as to the future, if Fulk and his hearers had seen into *that,* one doubts if they could have been moved to much enthusiasm. Whatever admixture of worldly motives there may have been, the Fourth Crusade was vehemently advocated by Pope Innocent III., proclaimed by Fulk, joined by multitudes of devout pilgrims, for the express purpose of recapturing Jerusalem, and driving the heathen out of Palestine. But it never reached Palestine at all. It did far less than nothing towards the recovery of the Holy City. It delivered its blow with immense force and shattering effect upon a Christian, not a Moslem, state. It contributed not a little, in ultimate result, to break down Europe's barrier against the Turk. Thus, from the Crusading point of view, it was a gigantic failure; and, as such, denounced again and yet again by the great Pope who had done so much to give it life.

How did this come about? What were the real influences that led the Fourth Crusade to change its objective from Jerusalem to Constantinople? The question has been many times debated. It is, as one may almost say, one of the stock questions of history; and I can scarcely altogether give it the go-by here—as I should like to do—because in that question is involved the more personal question of Villehardouin's own good faith as a historian. If there were wire-pullers at work, almost from the beginning, who laboured to deflect the movement to their own ends; if the Venetians throughout played a double game,[1] and betrayed the Christian cause to the Saracens, then it is necessary, before we accept him altogether as a witness of truth, to inquire why he makes no mention of the Marquis of Montferrat's intrigues, or the Republic's duplicity. Did he write in ignorance? or did he, while possessing full knowledge, banish ugly facts from his narrative, and deliberately constitute himself, as has been said, the "official apologist" of the Crusade?

For, as he tells the story, all is simplicity itself. There is scarcely anything to explain. The Crusade has a purely religious origin: "Many took the cross because the indulgences were so great." Villehardouin himself, and his five brother delegates from the great lords assembled in parliament at Compiègne, go to Venice, and engage a fleet to take the host of the pilgrims "oversea"—an ambiguous term which meant Syria for the uninitiated, but "Babylon" or Cairo for the Venetian Council—"because it was in Babylon, rather than in any other land, that the Turks could best be destroyed." Then comes the death of Count Thibaut of Champagne, who would have been the natural leader of the Crusade, and the selection, in his stead, of the Marquis of Montferrat, "a right worthy man, and one of the most highly esteemed that were then alive." Afterwards the pilgrims begin to assemble in Venice; but owing to numerous defections, their number is so reduced that the stipulated passage money is not forthcoming, and the Venetians naturally refuse to move. The blame, up to this point, lies entirely with the pilgrims who had failed to keep their tryst. Meanwhile, what is to be done? Some, who in their heart of hearts wish not well to the cause, would break up the host and return to their own land. Others, who are better affected, would proceed at all hazards. Then the Doge proposes a compromise. If, says he, addressing his own people, we insist upon our pound of flesh, we can, no doubt, claim to keep the moneys already received, as some consideration for our great outlay; but, so doing, we shall be greatly blamed throughout Christendom. Let us rather agree to forego the unpaid balance and carry out our agreement, provided the pilgrims, on their part, will help us to recapture Zara, on the Adriatic, of which we have been wrongfully dispossessed by the King of Hungary. To this the Venetians consent, and likewise the Crusaders, notwithstanding the remonstrances of the evil-disposed party aforesaid. So the blind old Doge assumes the cross, with great solemnity, in the Church of St. Mark, and many Venetians assume it too, and all is got ready for departure.

Then, and not till then, do we get any hint of an attack on the Greek empire. "Now listen," says Villehardouin, "to one of the greatest marvels and greatest adventures that ever you heard tell of," and he proceeds to narrate how the young Greek prince Alexius, having escaped from the hands of that wicked usurper, his uncle, and being at Verona on the way to the court of his brother-in-law, "Philip of Germany," makes overtures to the Crusaders, and how the latter are not unprepared to help him to recover his father's throne, provided he in turn will help them to reconquer Jerusalem. Whereupon envoys are sent to accompany the youth into Germany, for further negotiation with Philip, and the host, Crusaders and Venetians together, set sail for their attack on Christian Zara.

And here for the first time Villehardouin makes mention of the religious objection to the course that the Crusade is taking. The inhabitants of Zara are prepared to capitulate, but are dissuaded by the party which, according to Villehardouin, were anxious to break up the host, and while the matter is under discussion, the abbot of Vaux, of the order of the Cistercians, rises in his place and says, "Lords, on behalf of the Apostle of Rome, I forbid you to attack this city, for it is a Christian city, and you are pilgrims."

Nevertheless the Doge insists that the Crusaders shall fulfil their contract, and Zara is besieged and taken.

While the host is waiting, after the capture, they are joined by the envoys from Philip, and from Philip's brother-in-law, Alexius, the son of the deposed Emperor of Constantinople. These envoys bring definite and very advantageous proposals. The Crusaders are to dispossess the treacherous and wicked emperor, also called Alexius, and reinstate the deposed Isaac; and in return for this great service, Alexius the younger promises, "in the very first place," that the Greek empire shall be brought back into obedience to Rome, and then—seeing that the pilgrims are poor—that they shall receive 200,000 marks of silver, and provisions for small and great, and further that substantial help shall be afforded towards the conquest of the "land of Babylon," oversea.

The hook was well baited. The reunion of Christendom, gold and stores in plenty, active co-operation from the near vantage ground of Constantinople in the dispossession of the infidel, a splendid adventure to be achieved—no wonder the Crusaders were tempted. Villehardouin himself never falters in his expressed conviction that the course proposed was the right course, that he and his companions did well in following, at this juncture, the fortunes of the younger Alexius. Nevertheless it is clear, even from his narrative, that a great, almost overwhelming, party in the host were unconvinced and bitterly opposed to the deflection of the Crusade. Hotly was the question debated. The laymen were divided. The clergy, even of the same religious order, were at bitter strife. When it came to the ratification of the convention with Alexius, only twelve French lords could be induced to swear. Thereafter came defection on defection—the deserters, as Villehardouin is always careful to note, not without a certain complacency, coming mainly to evil ends. "Now be it known to you, lords," says he, "that if God had not loved that host, it could never have kept together, seeing how many there were who wished evil to it." Even the Pope's forgiveness for the attack on Zara, and his exhortation to the pilgrims to remain united, did not avail to prevent further disintegration.

Nevertheless the host ultimately reaches Constantinople, routs the Greeks, who have no stomach for the fight, sends the usurping Emperor Alexius flying, reinstates the blinded Isaac, and seats the younger Alexius, by the side of Isaac, on the imperial throne. But naturally the position of Isaac and Alexius is precarious, and when the latter asks the Crusaders to delay their departure, the adverse party tries once more to obtain an immediate descent on Syria or Egypt. They are overborne. Soon, however, it becomes clear that Isaac and Alexius either cannot, or will not, fulful their promises. As a matter of fact Alexius has placed himself and his father in an impossible position, of which death, in cruel forms, is to be the outcome, and they become, in turn, the objects of attack, and their empire a field of plunder. Henceforward the die is cast. The Crusade ceases to be a Crusade, and becomes as purely an expedition of conquest as William's descent on England. Whatever may be their occasional qualms, Franks and Venetians have enough to do in the Greek Empire, without giving very much thought to Judæa.

But to all this there is another side. Thus, if we are to believe the chronicle[2] compiled in 1393, by order of Heredia, Grand Master of the Hospital of St. John of Jerusalem, Villehardouin first proposed the Crusade to his lord, the Count of Champagne, not on any specially religious grounds, but because, after the peace between the kings of France and England, there were a great many idle men-at-arms about, whom it would be desirable to employ. So also Ernoul, a contemporary, after telling how the barons of France, who had sided with Richard against Philip Augustus, cast off their armour at the tournament at Ecri, and ran to take the cross, adds: "There are certain persons who say that they thus took the cross for fear of the King of France, and so that he might not punish them because they had sided against him."[3]

This, however, is relatively unimportant. Mixed motives may at once be conceded as probable and natural. What is of greater significance is the attitude of the Venetians and the question of their good faith. Villehardouin here hints no doubt. According to him, the Republic made a bargain to provide freight and food for an expedition to the Holy Land or to "Babylon," and provided both amply, and it was only on the failure of the pilgrims to carry out their side of the bargain that the Venetians fell back on Zara. *They* were prepared to take the Crusade to its original destination. But the same Ernoul, from whom I have just quoted, tells another story. He relates how Saphardin, the brother of the deceased Saladin, hearing that the Crusaders had hired a fleet in Venice, sends envoys to the Venetians, with great gifts and promises of commercial adventage, and entreats them to "turn away the Christians," and how the Venetians accept the bribe, and use their influence accordingly;[4] while certain modern historians discover, or think they have discovered, that it was the Venetians who took the initiative in this act of treachery, and that after making the treaty with Villehardouin and his fellow delegates in 1201, they sent envoys to Saphardin and virtually gave the Crusaders away by a specific treaty—of which, however, the date, and with it the relevancy, has been contested.

So again, with regard to the evil influences at work within the host itself, certain historians have endeavoured to show that the misdirection of the Crusade was but an episode in the long struggle between Guelf and Ghibelline. For the Crusade was the pet child of Innocent III. It was the dearest object of his heart. It was to crown his pontificate. What more natural than that the Ghibelline, Philip of Swabia, the son of Barbarossa, himself just then lying under a solemn excommunication, should endeavour, by all the means in his power, to thwart the expedition, to turn it to his own ends—one of which was the conquest of Constantinople—for on Constantinople he had pretensions. Thus, according to this view, when Villehardouin suggested the

Marquis of Montferrat for the leadership, he was, indirectly indeed, acting as the mouthpiece of Philip. And the Marquis, from the date of his election, did but become Philip's agent, and had in view only one object—an attack on the Greek emperor.[5] All his actions and movements are to be explained on the grounds that he cared nothing about Jerusalem, and very much about Constantinople.

To go at length into all the pros and cons of this controversy, would take, not the comparatively short space allotted to an introduction, but a very considerable volume. And, indeed, the latest historian who has dealt with the subject, the very learned M. Luchaire, of the French Institute,[6] declares that, on the available data, the questions involved are insoluble. Having placed the two views before the reader, I shall not therefore go into the matter further here, beyond saying that after a great deal of reading, and research, I have come to the conclusion, Firstly, that the Venetians were not as bad as they have been painted. They were a commercial people, and they had made a bargain, and they kept to it. The Crusaders did not. To expect the Venetians, for the good of the cause, to forego repayment for the large sums expended on a superb fleet and what must have been, temporarily at least, a great disturbance of their commerce, is absurd. Why should the main expense of the expedition fall on them? As to the treacherous arrangements with the Saracens, they seem to me not proven. Therefore I hold myself justified in asking the reader to look, without a smile of sarcasm and incredulity, at the great scene in which Dandolo, the grand old Doge, blind and bearing gallantly his ninety years, goes up into the reading-desk of St. Mark, and there, before all the people—who wept seeing him—places the sign of the cross in his bonnet. Surely his bearing in council, and afterwards in battle, was not that of a vulpine old impostor.

Secondly, I own to very great doubts as to the elaborate Machiavellian schemes of Philip of Swabia, and the Marquis of Montferrat, and the after-participation therein, to a greater or less degree, of the leaders of the Crusade. Web-spinning so successful would imply gifts of foresight verging on prophesy. Let us "look at things more simply," as M. Luchaire says. And disbelieving, to a very great extent, in the plot, I am bound to exonerate Villehardouin from the charge of endeavouring to disguise its existence. Nay, I go further. What we see as the past was to Villehardouin the present and the future. We know that the Crusade came to nothing, ultimately "fizzled out," as one may say. But Villehardouin, looking forward from day to day, may quite honestly have believed that the course he consistently advocated was the course best calculated, all the circumstances being given, to ensure success. Shut up in the island of St. Nicholas, near Venice, without the necessary means for advance or retreat, or even for the provision of daily subsistence, the Crusading host was in helpless case. The advance on Zara had no alternative. Afterwards, leaders and men were without the sinews of war. When Alexius came with his definite proposals, one cannot wonder that men of strong political instinct, like our hero, should have thought that the best coign of vantage for an attack on Jerusalem, was Constantinople. The ignorant commonalty were for a direct descent on the Holy Land. The wiser chiefs would have preferred to first break the power of the Saracens in Egypt. The politicians of still larger outlook might naturally hold that with the Greek empire at their back, and with coffers full of Greek gold, they had the best chance of re-establishing the Christian kingdom of Jerusalem.

Nay, shall I go further still? The Franks defeated the Greeks with ease, defeated them as Pizarro and Cortes defeated the Peruvians and Mexicans, as Clive defeated the armies of India. What if they had not only conquered Roumania, but had also revivified the Greek empire; if, instead of giving themselves to the greed, and rapine, and unstatesmanlike oppression, which Villehardouin deplored, and so losing within sixty years (1261) what they had held unworthily—what if, instead of this, they had administered wisely and well, had mingled in blood and interest with the conquered, had breathed with the breath of a new life over the dry bones of that dead race and nationality, had created a virile state at this specially important point of the world's surface, and so barred the way against the entrance of the Turk into Europe? When the Frank fleet set sail from Venice, these things were on the knees of the gods. Should we have been misdoubting Villehardouin if they had come to pass?

And having said so much for Villehardouin's good faith and essential political honesty, one is the more free to admire the force and effectiveness of the man. What was his exact age at the date of the tournament at Ecri (November 1199), is not known. Probably he was then about forty, and in the fulness of his strength, and, as one may fairly conjecture, well-knit, and possessing a frame fitted to endure hardship and fatigue. Even if we regard as doubtful the statement of Heredia's chronicler, that it was he who first proposed the Crusade to Count Thibaut,[7] yet it is clear that, from the very beginning, he took a leading part in the enterprise, and *that,* as one may conclude, on purely personal grounds, for the Villehardouins were of no imposing *noblesse.* Thus he is chosen by the assembled chiefs as one of the six envoys sent to Venice to negotiate for the transport of the host; and it is he who stands forth as spokesman for the Crusaders in the first memorable assembly at St. Mark's. When Count Thibaut dies, he seems to take the most active part in the choice of a successor, and proposes the leader ultimately nominated. When, afterwards, the pilgrims begin to avoid Venice, and travel eastwards by other routes, he is one of the two delegates despatched to bring them to a better mind, succeeding, to some extent, by "comfort and prayers." To him is entrusted the task of explaining to the restored Emperor Isaac what are the conditions on which the Crusaders have consented to come to his help at Constantinople. Again he is selected for the perilous office of bearing to the Emperors Isaac and Alexius, in full court, the haughty defiance of the host. He is selected once more for the particularly delicate mission of reconciling the Marquis of Montferrat with the Emperor Baldwin, and he is afterwards deputed to bring the Marquis to Constantinople. Thus we see him taking a prominent part wherever there is a task of difficulty or danger to be undertaken; and finally, in one of the darkest, direst hours of the expedition, he stands forth heroically, and masters circumstance. The Crusaders, contrary to all preconcerted plans, have left their ranks and followed the lightly-armed Comans into the field, whereupon the Comans attack in turn, and cut the Crusaders to pieces, killing Count Lewis of Blois, and taking the Emperor Baldwin prisoner. A broken remnant of the host comes flying into the camp. "When he sees this, Geoffry, the Marshal of Champagne, who is keeping guard before one of the gates of the city, issues forth from the camp as quickly as he can, and with all his men, and sends word to Manasses of the Isle, who is keeping another gate, to follow." One can almost see it all, as he tells the story: the advance in serried ranks, rapid but in strict order, and with all the pomp of war—*à grande allure,*—and the long line of mailed riders forming across the plain; the fugitives in full flight, for the most part too panic-stricken to stop short of the camp itself, but those of better heart staying to strengthen the immovable breakwater of men. Towards that breakwater, but still keeping a respectful distance, surges the scattered host of Comans, Wallachians, Greeks, who do such mischief as they can with bows and arrows. It was between nones and vespers, as Villehardouin tells us, that the rout was stayed. It is not till nightfall that the enemy retire. Then, under cover of night, and in council with the Doge, he leads off the beaten remnant of the host, leaving, as he records with just pride, not one wounded man behind— and effects a masterly retreat to the sea and safety.

A man, evidently like Scott's William of Deloraine, "good at need"—a man trusted of all and trustworthy—honoured by the Doge, honoured by the Emperor Baldwin, honoured and beloved by the Marquis of Montferrat. Nor should it be imagined, because this is the impression left by a study of the chronicle, that Villehardouin's method of telling the story of the Crusade has in it anything of personal boastfulness or vainglory. When he speaks of himself, in the course of his narrative, he does so quite simply, and just as he speaks of others. There is no attempt to magnify his own deeds or influence. If he has taken part in any adventure or deliberation, he mentions the fact without false modesty, but does not dwell upon it unduly. And, indeed, as I read the man's character, a certain honourable straightforwardness seems to me one of its most important traits. He is a religious man, no doubt. The purely religious side of the Crusade has its influence upon him. He is not unaffected by the greatness of the pardon offered by the Pope. He believes that the expedition is righteous, and that God approves of it. He holds that God looks with a favouring eye upon all who are doing their best for its furtherance. "Listen," he cries after some great deliverance, "how great are the miracles of our Lord whenever it is his pleasure to perform them. . . . Well may we say that no man can harm those whom God favours." And he stands in no manner of doubt that the Divine justice will deal in a very exemplary manner with those who separate themselves from the host, and pursue their own paths to Palestine. But if he is a religious man, he is in no sense an enthusiast. He stands in marked contrast to such Crusaders as Godfrey of Bouillon and St. Lewis. The worldly side of the whole thing—its policy and business, and fighting and conquests—these are very habitually present to his thoughts. And withal, as I have said—and notwithstanding the doubts referred to in the earlier pages of this introduction—there is a ring about him of honesty and sincerity. His utterances are such as may be counted honourable to all time. He never forbears to inveigh against dishonesty, double-dealing, covetousness. It is not only as a politician, but as an upright man that he denounces the rapacious mishandling to which the Greeks are subjected.

Of such a man, as I repeat, one hesitates to believe that he lent himself to a long course of intrigue, and afterwards constituted himself the "official apologist" of what he knew to be indefensible.

And as the man is, so is his book. When judging that book, it has to be borne in mind that it is the first work of importance and sustained dignity written in the French tongue. At the time that he dictated it, therefore, Villehardouin had no precedents to go by, no models to imitate. He was in all respects—language, narrator's art, style—a pioneer. And this being so, it marks him as a born writer, and a writer of a very high order, that his narration should be so lucid and distinct. He marshals his facts well, proceeds from point to point with order and method, brings important matters into due prominence, keeps accessories properly in the background. Nor, notwithstanding the usual sobriety of his method, is he incapable, on due occasion, of rendering the moral aspect of a scene, or even the physical aspect of what has passed before his eyes. In proof of this I may refer to the two great scenes in St. Mark's, to the account of the attack on Constantinople, to the story of the battle in which Baldwin was taken prisoner.[8]

Still I admit that as a word-painter his powers are embryonic rather than fully developed—a fact which Sainte-Beuve, the great critic, accounts for by saying that "the descriptive style had not yet been invented." But here, I venture to think, Sainte-Beuve was nodding. For if Villehardouin himself depicts soberly, yet he had a contemporary and fellow-Crusader, Robert of Clari by name, who also wrote a chronicle, and Robert of Clari has left a description of the scene when the Crusading fleet set sail from Venice on the feast of St. Remigius, 1202, which is not wanting in picturesqueness and colour: "The Doge," he says, "had with him fifty galleys, all at his own charges. The galley in which he himself sailed was all vermilion, and there was a pavilion of red satin stretched above his head. And there were before him four trumpets of silver that trumpeted, and cymbals that made joy and merriment. And all the men of note, as well clerks as lay, and whether of small condition or great, made such joy at our departure, that never before had such joy been made, or so fine a fleet been seen. And then the pilgrims caused all the priests and clerks there present to get up into the castles of the

ships, and sing the *Veni Creator Spiritus,* and all, both the great and the small folk, wept for great joy and happiness. . . . It seemed as if the whole sea swarmed with ants, and the ships burned on the water, and the water itself were aflame with the great joy that they had."[9]

It was in colours like these that Turner saw Venice suffused when he painted such pictures as the Sun of Venice going out to sea. It was in terms almost identical that Shakespeare described Cleopatra's barge "burning" upon the Nile. Surely when Robert of Clari, a writer not otherwise comparable with Villehardouin, mixed such hues upon his palette, it cannot be said that the descriptive style was unborn. And if Villehardouin makes use of it but soberly, the reason is rather, I conceive, to be found in this, that his interest was but little concerned with the outward shows of things. He was a politician and soldier who had played an important part in the drama of history. What he cared to remember, in after days, was the deeds of the men who had played their parts with him, their passions and objects. Their dress, the pomp and circumstance by which they were surrounded, the look of the stage, and appearance of the side-scenes, all this had, comparatively, faded from his memory. His chronicle is that of a statesman, like the chronicle in which, some two centuries and a half later, Philippe de Commines enthroned, or gibbeted, the craft of his master Lewis XI.

As to his style, why style is the man's own self, according to Buffon's oft-quoted saying, and Villehardouin's style is simple, strong, and direct—like himself, and like his narration. Now and again, but very seldom, it bears a blossom, "puts forth a flower," as the French say when some bright image, some smiling fancy, breaks like a crocus or snowdrop through the cold aridity of prose. Thus, when the fleet is leaving Abydos—these vessels in full sail seem wonderfully to have stirred the hearts of the pilgrim host—he says that the Straits of St. George were "in flower" with ships. But expressions like this, which suffuse with imagination the plain statement of a fact, are rare with him. Usually he is sober in his use of image, as in his descriptions. He says what he has to say, and no more; and he says it in a short, plainly-constructed sentence which can be "construed," as a schoolboy would say, without difficulty. Compared with the sentence of most English and French writers of the fifteenth or sixteenth centuries, or even of most German writers of to-day, his sentence is simplicity itself.

"The modern literature of the West they might justly despise," says Gibbon, speaking of the Greeks of Villehardouin's time. Is that quite true? In Villehardouin we have a literature of the quite early spring—vigorous, full of sap, unforced, spontaneous, unsophisticated. Take, by way of contrast, and as illustrating the literature of autumn and decay, such a passage as the following from his contemporary, the Greek historian Nicetas: "What shall I say of the statue of Helen, of the perfection of her form, the alabaster of her arms and of her breast, of her perfect limbs?—of that Helen who brought all Greece beneath the walls of

Troy? Had she not softened the savage inhabitants of Laconia? All seemed possible to her whose looks enchained every heart. Her vesture was without artifice, but so ingeniously disposed that the greedy eye could see all the freshness of her charms scarce hidden by her light tunic, her veil, her crown, and the tresses of her hair. Her hair, bound only to her neck, floated according to the fancy of the winds, and fell to her feet in waving tresses; her mouth, half-opened like the calix of a young flower, seemed to offer a passage to the tender accents of her voice, and the sweet smile of her lips filled the soul of the spectator with delicious feeling. Never will it be possible to express, and posterity will seek vainly to feel or depict, the grace overspreading this divine statue. But, O daughter of Tyndareus, O masterpiece of love, O rival of Venus, where is the omnipotence of thy charms? Why didst thou not exercise them to subdue those barbarians as thou didst exercise them amiably of yore? Has Fate condemned thee to burn in the same fire with which thou wert wont to consume all hearts? Did the descendants of æneas wish to condemn thee to the same flames that thou didst light erewhile in Ilion?"[10] Was Nicetas, the author of this artificial rhetoric, really in a position to "despise" Villehardouin? In this matter, and with all due respect for Gibbon, one may say that the Frank represents the twilight of dawn, and the Greek the twilight of night.

And what became of Villehardouin at last? How and when did he die? All here is obscurity. We know, as I have said, next to nothing about his birth and earlier years. We know next to nothing about his later life and end. He emerges into the half-light of history with the beginning of his chronicle. He passes back into the darkness of the years with its close. Of what happened to him after the date in 1207, when, as he tells us—it is his latest record, as if his pen had faltered at that point—how the Marquis of Montferrat had been miserably slain—of what, I say, happened to him after that year we are almost ignorant. He had left his wife, his daughters, his two sons, to follow the cross. There is no evidence to suggest that he ever rejoined them in his native Champagne. M. Bouchet conjectures[11] that, replete with honour and rewards, weary of life's battle, saddened by the loss of so many of his old companions in arms, he retired to end his days in his castle of Messinopolis on the enemy's marches, and there composed his history; but much of this can be no more than conjecture. That the man lived to any great age is improbable, and indeed the year 1213 has usually been assigned as the year of his death. That he wrote, or rather dictated, his Chronicles when the hand of time lay heavy upon him seems to me, from the internal evidence of style and spirit, to be quite unlikely. Rather do I fancy that he composed them, in the halls of Messinopolis indeed, but with spirit unsubdued, and during some brief lull in the great strife between the Greeks and their Frank conquerors. . . .

Notes

1. "The unchristian cupidity of the banausically-minded Republic of St. Mark," is the quaint description given by Pope Innocent's latest biographer. *Innocent the Great,* by C. H. C. Pirie-Gordon, 1907.

2. *Libro de los Fechos et Conquistas del Principado de la Morea,* translated from Spanish into French by Alfred Morel-Fatio, and published at Geneva in 1885 for the *Société de l'Orient Latin.* See p. 1. I am bound, however, to say that this chronicle, which assigns to Villehardouin a very important part in the organisation of the Crusade, was compiled long after date, and seems clearly apocryphal in many of its details.

3. *Chronique d'Ernoul et de Bernard le Trésorier,* published by M. L. de Mas Latrie for the *Société de l'histoire de France.* Paris, 1871. See p. 337.

4. See *ibid.* pp. 345, 346, and 361, 362.

5. See M. Riant's articles quoted below. The curious reader who would follow this controversy is referred to the following works among many others, French and German. I place them, as will be seen, in the chronological order of publication:—

   Histoire de l'Isle de Chypre sous le Règne des Princes de la Maison de Lusignan, par M. L. de Mas Latrie, etc. Paris, 1861, Vol. I, pp. 161-165.—*Geoffroy de Villehardouin, Conquête de Constantinople,* etc., par M. Natalis de Wailly, etc. Second edition, Paris, 1874, pp. 429-439.

   Up to this point only the conduct of Venice is in question. With the following enters as protagonist Philip of Swabia, and we are asked to consider the part which he took in deflecting the Crusade from Egypt or the Holy Land to Constantinople, and the action taken, under his influence, by the Marquis Boniface of Montferrat.

   Innocent III., Philippe de Swabe et Boniface de Montferrat. Examen des Causes qui modifièrent au détriment de l'Empire Grec, le plan primitif de la 4e Croisade, published in *Revue des Questions Historiques,* Vol. XVII., April 1875, pp. 321-374, and Vol. XVIII., July 1875, pp. 5-75. Signed, Comte Riant.

   These two articles contain an elaborate and most learned indictment against Philip of Swabia and the Marquis of Montferrat, and, in a minor degree, against Villehardouin, as their accomplice and apologist. Comte Riant is most careful in giving reference to chapter and verse to support his conclusions, and so enable the student to verify and control, and—on occasion—to dissent.

   A short note, signed M. de Wailly, on the above articles of Comte Riant, expressing dissent. *Revue des Questions Historiques,* Vol. XVIII., October 1875, pp. 578 and 579 (not p. 576 as stated in index).

   Quatrième Croisade. La diversion sur Zara et Constantinople, par Jules Tessier, professeur à la faculté des lettres de Caen. Paris, 1884.

In this volume, with an equal learning, M. Tessier contests the position taken up by M. Riant, and defends Philip of Swabia and Venice.

The Fall of Constantinople, by Edwin Pears. London, 1885.

The *Notice,* extending to 300 pages in Vol. II. of M. Emile Bouchet's *Geoffroi de Villehardouin. La Conquête de Constantinople, texte et traduction nouvelle, avec notice, notes, et glossaire,* par Emile Bouchet. Paris, 1891.

M. Bouchet mainly accepts Comte Riant's facts and conclusions with regard to Philip and Venice, but exonerates Villehardouin, and defends him from the charge of having constituted himself the official apologist of the Crusade—pp. 289-297 and pp. 308, 309. M. Bouchet's manner is rather that of the historical narrator than of the erudite dissertator, and his notes are few. In this he differs from M. Riant and M. Tessier.

M. Luchaire, as I have noted in the text (1997) declares the questions raised to be insoluble on the available data.

The matter is referred to, but with no additional evidence or further discussion, in Sir Rennell Rodd's *The Principalities of Achaia and the Chronicles of Morea,* 1907, Chap. I, and Mr. Pirie-Gordon's *Innocent the Great, an Essay on his Life and Times,* 1907, Chap. IV.

6. *Innocent III.: La Question d'Orient.* 1907. See pp. 85, 86, 91, and 97.

7. See ante, p. xvi.

8. See pp. 7-8, 16-17, 37-44, and 94-96.

9. The reader may compare this passage with Villehardouin's description of the same event, p. 19, or of the departure from Corfu, p. 29.

10. I am translating from a French version which I happen to have before me—*Bibliothèque des Croisades,* by M. Michaud, third part, 1829, p. 428.

11. *La Conquête de Constantinople, texte et traduction nouvelle,* 1891, Vol. II., pp. 286 and following.

M. R. B. Shaw (essay date 1963)

SOURCE: An introduction to *Chronicles of the Crusades,* Penguin Books, 1963, pp. 7–25.

[*In the following essay, Shaw surveys the content, form, and style of Villehardouin's* Conquest of Constantinople. *Shaw commends the "simplicity and lucidity" of the work.*]

Few events in history have been more coloured by romantic imagination than that series of expeditions to the Holy Land known as the Crusades. The very name conjures up a vision of gallant knights inspired by pure religious zeal, leaving home and country to embark on a just and holy war against the enemies of the Christian faith. The two chronicles here presented, each composed by a man who took part in such an expedition, give a truer picture of an enterprise in which the darker as well as the brighter side of human nature is shown in the actions of those who took the cross. However, since these chronicles deal with only two of the Crusades, it is well perhaps in this introduction to place them in their context as giving part of a struggle between Christians and Moslems for possession of the Holy Land that lasted for nearly two hundred years.

Jerusalem, the Holy City, had been a centre of pilgrimage from very early times. Its capture in 638 by the Moslem Caliph Omar had left the Christians free to practise their religion. Conditions remained the same until 1076, when Jerusalem passed into the hands of the Seljukian Turks, who desecrated the holy places, and brutally treated the Christians in the city, throwing some into prison and massacring others. Pilgrims who managed to make their way to the Holy Land brought back pitiful tales of the plight of their co-religionists in the East.

The idea of a Holy War to avenge these wrongs occurred to Pope Gregory VII, and to his successor Victor III; but the peoples of Western Christendom, preoccupied with their own affairs at home, paid small attention to their pleas. However, little by little, to the north of the Alps, the preaching of Peter the Hermit did much to influence popular opinion in favour of a war against the infidel, and when, at the Council of Clermont in November 1095, Pope Urban II, a Frenchman born, appealed to his countrymen to join an international expedition to recover Jerusalem, he met with an enthusiastic response. In 1096 two expeditions started for the East. One, led by Peter the Hermit, consisted of an undisciplined mob, which was almost completely wiped out by the Turks in October of that year. The other, made up of properly organized troops in command of barons from Northern France and Flanders, Provence, and Southern Italy, arrived at Constantinople in December. Here they joined forces with the Byzantine Emperor. Passing through Asia Minor, where they helped the Greeks to capture Nicaea and defeated the Turks at Dorylaeum, they finally entered Syria. The people of the northern province of Edessa, in revolt against their Armenian ruler, invited Baudouin de Bouillon to take his place in March 1098. In June of that year the Crusaders captured Antioch; in July 1099 they took Jerusalem after a siege of only six weeks. This victory, one regrets to say, was followed by a merciless slaughter of Turks and Jews within the city. As a result of this first Crusade three Christian states were established in Syria: the principalities of Edessa and Antioch, and the kingdom of Jerusalem. The whole of this conquered territory was commonly known as Outremer (the land oversea).

For many years the barons of Outremer, by maintaining an offensive and defensive war against the surrounding enemy, managed to keep hold of the land they had gained without calling in aid from the West. In 1144, however, when the Turks overran the province of Edessa, the Queen-regent of Jerusalem, fearing lest, with Antioch now exposed on its northern border, the Turks might capture this province also, sent an urgent appeal to Pope Eugenius III to initiate a new Crusade. The Pope referred the matter to King Louis VII of France, a man of noted piety, who took the cross in 1146 at the Assembly of Vézelay, where Saint Bernard's eloquence moved many Frenchmen to follow their king's example. Travelling to Germany, the saint persuaded the Emperor Conrad to join the expedition. In 1147 an army led by the rulers of France and Germany set off on the Second Crusade, determined to do great things. In the end, however, instead of advancing on Edessa, the Crusaders made an unsuccessful attempt to capture Damascus, and returned home without accomplishing anything.

Meanwhile, in the East the Turks were increasing in strength, and the Christians growing weaker. Pilgrims who came to the Holy Land were often shocked by the luxury and license of life in Outremer. Internal disputes among the barons of the land wasted energy that might have been used in defending it. The death of King Amalric of Jerusalem in 1174, leaving the kingdom without a worthy successor, was shortly followed by Saladin's rise to power as head of a united Moslem Empire. In 1187 the Christians suffered their greatest disaster when, after Saladin had routed and destroyed their army at the Horns of Hattin on 3 July, he occupied Tiberias, Jaffa, Ascalon, and Gaza, and finally entered Jerusalem. The Moslem's humane treatment of its Christian population was in marked contrast to the conduct of those Crusaders who had captured the city in 1099.

Once again Western Christendom was roused to action. In 1189 a third Crusade, led by three sovereigns, Frederick Barbarossa of Germany, Philip Augustus of France, and Richard I of England, prepared to go oversea. Barbarossa, who started first, was drowned in a little river, on his way through Asia Minor, on 10 June 1190. His army, disheartened, dwindled away, till only a very small contingent was left. Early the next year Philip and Richard sailed from Messina to go to the help of the titular King of Jerusalem who, with a pitifully small army, was besieging Saladin in Acre. Theirs was an uneasy partnership from the first. Different in temperament—Richard hot-tempered, rash, and impetuous; Philip, cold and shrewd—their relations were still further complicated by the fact that the English king, as Duke of Normandy, was Philip's none too obedient vassal, while the French king, for his part, was jealous of Richard's power.

Philip arrived before Acre on 20 April 1191. Richard, delayed by a storm at sea, got there seven weeks later. When Acre surrendered on 12 July, the two kings raised their banners on the walls. Leopold of Austria, now in command of the German forces, had also placed his there, only to have it torn down and flung into the ditch, an insult for which a cruel vengeance was exacted later. Richard's slaughter of his Turkish prisoners after Acre surrendered casts a darker shadow on his name.

In August 1191, the French king, tired of crusading, and anxious about the state of things in his kingdom, returned to France. Richard took command of the remaining troops and continued the campaign. But although he defeated Saladin at Arsuf in September 1191, and successfully relieved Jaffa in August of the following year, he came within reach of Jerusalem only to veil his eyes from the sight of the city he dared not attempt to deliver. The sole achievement of this Crusade was a five years' truce with Saladin, which gave the Christians possession of the main coastal towns as far south as Jaffa, and allowed pilgrims free right of entry into Jerusalem.

So we come to the Fourth Crusade, the story of which is told by Villehardouin in his *Conquest of Constantinople,* a work distinguished among other things by the fact that it is the first reliable record of these expeditions to be written in French. The earlier Crusades, it is true, had their historians, but these, among whom we may particularly note William, Archbishop of Tyre, gave their accounts in Latin. There were not wanting certain effusions in verse concerning the exploits of Crusaders oversea; but none of these has any historical value. Graindor de Douai, writing in the first half of the twelfth century, gives lively accounts in the *Chanson d'Antioche* and the *Chanson de Jérusalem* of the taking of these two cities in the First Crusade; but, on the other hand, he has little conception of the motive behind the expedition, and a very imperfect knowledge of the main events. Less reliable still are those imitations of the Old French epics, such as *Godefroi de Bouillon* or the *Chevalier du Cygne,* in which fantasy takes the place of fact. The Norman Jongleur produces, in his *Histoire de la Guerre Sainte,* a straightforward record of the Third Crusade, but from his position as a humble pilgrim in the ranks he has no more than an outside view of the events he chronicles. It remained for a leading actor in the Fourth Crusade to present the first trustworthy and fully-informed history of such an expedition, in his own native tongue and in prose.

The author of the *Conquest of Constantinople* was born some time between 1150 and 1154. His father, Vilain de Villehardouin, was a nobleman of Champagne with estates in the southern part of the province, not far from its chief town Troyes. Geoffroy was not the eldest of Vilain's sons, but thanks to his connexions by birth, and later by marriage, with many noble families in Champagne and the neighbouring provinces, and no doubt also to his power of commanding confidence and respect, he became in 1185 Marshal of Champagne. In those days, when fighting between neighbouring barons was no remote contingency, a marshal's duty was to see that everything was in order to resist or make an attack; if war broke out, he had to make all necessary arrangements for a campaign, and in his lord's absence take over command. In addition to this, he was his lord's deputy in everything that concerned the administration of the province. Villehardouin, so far as we know, had not been an active service before he went oversea, but there is evidence of the important part he had played as arbiter in disputes within the province and representative of his lord in negotiations with the king of France. In the course of his duties he became familiar with many of those noble personages whose names are cited in his chronicle, and gained, as marshal of a province, experience that prepared him for the tasks that lay before him in a wider field.

His work, while it follows a chronological order, is not a record of events set down from day to day, but rather a kind of official history of the Fourth Crusade, compiled a few years after the close of this abortive expedition, by one who could supplement his own memories of it by reference to existing documents—letters, treaties, army lists, and so on—to which, as Marshal of Romania, he had free access. A man of mature years and ripe experience, and in the confidence of those who had organized and taken a leading part in the various campaigns and other incidents he chronicles, Villehardouin speaks with authority. Even if—as with all histories written before time has set events in their full perspective—his interpretation is sometimes biased, he gives on the whole a very fair and honest account of an enterprise that began so well and ended so disastrously.

All the same, the accuracy and fairness of Villehardouin's presentation of his story have not escaped challenge from certain quarters. Some of his critics, for instance, assert that in laying the responsibility for the diversion of the crusade to Zara, and later to Constantinople, on the men who failed to report at Venice he takes no account of certain machinations going on behind the scenes; others allege that in so doing he deliberately arranges his story so as to free the leaders of the expedition from blame. Such criticism can be easily answered. No doubt the Venetians welcomed a situation that gave them a chance of increasing their influence in the Mediterranean; no doubt Philip of Swabia was eager to have his brother-in-law Alexius restored to power. While this may be so, it is difficult to imagine that French Crusaders would have consented to further the aims of Venice and Germany if, in their straitened circumstances, they had seen any other way of succeeding in their own enterprise. As for the idea that Villehardouin acted as an official apologist, this can quickly be discounted, in view of his honest account of actions on the part of these same leaders at a later date.

Villehardouin has also been accused of undue harshness in his judgement on the men who failed to join or deserted from the army. Certainly he is severe; but we must consider the circumstances. The barons had bound themselves in full council to abide by any agreement their envoys made in Venice, and, by feudal custom, all those who had pledged themselves to go on the expedition were equally bound. A man of honour himself, with a high conception of his military duties, Villehardouin found it unthinkable that any man worthy of the name of knight should break his promise, or fail to go where his leader should command. Why then, he wondered, had so many knights defaulted? In his indignation at the harm their defection had caused to the enterprise, it seemed to him

that they must have thought it safer to go to Syria, where the Christians still held certain cities, than face the risks of campaigning in a country which was entirely in Moslem hands. None the less, with touching human inconsistency, in reporting the fate of those who went to Syria, it is not their want of courage but their lack of wisdom that Villehardouin blames. Speaking here in pity rather than in anger, he pays tribute to the memory of those good knights, regretting only that they made a bad choice, and paid the penalty for their sinful folly.

As for the allegation that Villehardouin, in his account of discord in the army and consequent desertions from it, makes no allowance for the religious scruples of those who protested against making war on Christians, it is difficult at this interval of time to determine how far such protestations were sincere, and how far they were put forward as a pretext for disbanding the army. In the case of the Abbot of Vaux there is some reason for suspicion; for this cleric, who was so active in stirring up dissension in the Crusaders' army, and who finally left it on the plea of religious scruples, showed no such squeamishness when in 1209 he played a leading part in the 'crusade' against the Albigenses, who were no less Christian than the Greeks.

All things considered, it is hardly to be wondered at that Villehardouin, convinced as he was that the only hope of delivering Jerusalem lay in keeping the army together, had little patience with those who wished to disband it and little sympathy with those who pleaded religious scruples. Had not the Pope himself, at first appalled by the attack on the Christian city of Zara, granted absolution to the Crusaders on the grounds that they had acted under constraint, and urged them to keep the army together? Moreover, at the very time that the Abbot of Vaux was making trouble, his Holiness, relying on the promise Alexius had given to bring the Greek Church under the authority of Rome, had finally, after some hesitation, let the Crusaders know that he would not oppose the expedition to Constantinople, provided it was managed in such a way as to bring about a reunion between the Roman and the Orthodox Church.

That hope was never to be fulfilled, nor did this army ever reach the Holy City. From the time that the Franks presented their ultimatum to the Emperor Alexius IV in February 1204 all thoughts of a Crusade were lost sight of in a series of contests between Franks and Greeks and the many troubles that followed the establishment of the Latin Empire of Romania by force of arms. In this latter part of the chronicle Villehardouin's bias must be taken into consideration. Recounting events from the French point of view, he interprets them, so far as he can, to the prejudice of the Greeks. What to them was the gallant attempt of a conquered nation to regain its lost independence was in his eyes a proof that they were by nature disloyal and treacherous. Apart from this bias, his chronicle gives a fair account of the long and tragic struggle between Christians of the East and West and one from which we can draw our own conclusions.

From the facts Villehardouin puts before us it is evident that, from their first assumption of power, the conquerors made the fatal mistake of underestimating the opposition they might have to meet. Confident, after the sudden collapse of resistance in Constantinople, that subduing the rest of the empire would be easy, and apparently unconscious of the bitter hatred aroused in a cultured race by insolent barbarians who had pillaged and wrecked their lovely city—one of the finest centres of civilization in the world—the Franks made no attempt to conciliate the Greeks.

At first it seemed as if their confidence was justified. Apart from a few isolated cities, still holding out against the conquerors, the whole of the land on the northern side of the straits submitted to foreign rule. The barons, however, as Villehardouin himself admits, instead of governing the lands allotted to them justly, thought only of what profit they could gain for themselves. This last provocation was too much for the Greeks. Rising in revolt, they drove the Franks out of Adrianople and Demotika, and took possession of these two important cities. In their eagerness to oust the conqueror by any possible means they entered into alliance with the powerful King of Wallachia and Bulgaria. In the end Johanitza proved even more unwelcome than the Franks. But if the Greeks had cause to regret his coming, so had their conquerors, as Johanitza's troops overran the empire, capturing and destroying the fine cities of Romania, till only two beside Constantinople remained in Frankish hands.

Meanwhile, on the other side of the straits, in Asia Minor, Theodore Lascaris, husband of Alexius III's daughter Anna, was doing his best to prevent the Franks from obtaining possession of th lands allotted to them, and finally, as Villehardouin tells us, succeeded in accomplishing his aim. Acknowledged from the first by Greeks in Asia Minor and those who rallied to his side from across the water as their legitimate ruler, he was crowned emperor in 1206. The Empire of Nicaea was to remain the headquarters of the Greek monarchy until, with the fall of the Latin Empire in 1261, a descendant of the Emperor Theodore returned to rule in Constantinople.

Villehardouin's chronicle ends somewhat abruptly with the death of the Marquis de Montferrat in 1207. The fact that Henri de Valenciennes, in his *Histoire de l'Empereur Henri,* continues the story of Romania from the very point at which Villehardouin's account breaks off suggests that the sudden ending of the ***Conquest of Constantinople*** was due to the author's death. The date of this is uncertain. There is evidence that Villehardouin was still alive in 1212, and still in Romania, where he probably remained for the rest of his life. Documents relating to donations in memory of himself and his wife afford proof that he died some time before June 1218. At all events, he lived long enough to see the Emperor Henri, wiser and more farsighted than his ill-fated brother, conciliating the Greeks by giving them a fair share of honours and offices, and establishing peace within that part of the empire still remaining to him.

The ***Conquest of Constantinople*** is one of our main sources of information on the course of the Fourth Crusade,[1] but it is also a fitting memorial of one whose constant practice of the knightly virtues of loyalty and courage gives him a place among the noblest characters of his day. A man of firm religious principles, Villehardouin's duty to God, as he sees it, is to serve Him as faithfully and devotedly as a good vassal serves his lord; and above and beyond all this to recognize that all events, whether as indications of God's pleasure or displeasure, are ordered by His will. Loyalty to God, moreover, entails complete integrity of conduct: all breaches of faith, all underhand dealings and acts of treachery, all covetousness and self-seeking, are not only contrary to the knightly code but violations of divine law. If the God Villehardouin serves is the 'God of Battles', if he accepts without question the legate's sanction of war against Greek Christians as just and holy, though we may regret the little place that love and mercy have in his religion, we cannot doubt the sincerity of his faith.

Equally loyal in his service of those to whom his earthly allegiance is due, Villehardouin interprets his duty as something more than blind obedience. A man of strong character and sound judgement, he does not fear to show his disapproval of the Emperor Baudouin's quarrel with the Marquis de Montferrat, but boldly intervenes to heal the breach. In this, as in other instances throughout the chronicle, his concern is to work for 'the common good of all'.

Courage, that other essential quality in a knight is, as he conceives it, a disciplined activity. It does not consist in shutting one's eyes to danger—there are many allusions in his work to the risks to which he and fellow-crusaders were exposed. Nor is it to be confused with rashness, which, as in the case of the disastrous fight at Adrianople, leads men to hazard not only their own lives but the enterprise to which they are committed. It is, in fact, an ability to make a cool and balanced appraisal of danger without giving way to fear. Such a courage is Villehardouin's; yet it comes to him so naturally that he takes it as nothing to boast about, relating each adventure that concerns himself as one in which his gallant companions have their full share.

A man of clear and balanced judgement, austere and reticent by nature, Villehardouin is distinguished for the simplicity and lucidity of his work. No obtrusion of his own personality, no flights of imagination, no long and picturesque descriptions such as his contemporary Robert de Clari[2] delights in, come in to break the clear line of a story that compels our interest by its masterly presentation of the facts. Statesmanlike in his approach to the vicissitudes of an expedition that began as a Crusade and ended as a war against Christians, he shows, by his skilful choice and treatment of his material, the political import of each turn of events as it leads on to further action, and that with no more comment than will set it in relief. He was a soldier as well as a statesman, and that sense of order and discipline ingrained in men of his profession is plainly apparent in his straightforward account of dissensions within the army, as also of the many engagements in the long contest between Franks and Greeks.

Yet for all the general sobriety of his exposition of the uneven course of the Fourth Crusade, his work is by no means lacking in animation. Whenever, for instance, his story moves from conferences and similar matters of routine to recollections of the army on campaign, the contrast between his lively, dramatic portrayal of its fortunes and his quieter presentation of other incidents in his work gives light and shade to a chronicle that never varies in its simplicity, but changes its tone and tempo as the occasion demands. Viewing this chronicle as a whole, and remembering that Villehardouin, as a pioneer among French historians, had no other guide save his own native genius, we can only marvel at the skill of this soldier-statesman, who marshals and deploys his facts as a good commander does his forces to bring this story of high hopes defeated so vividly before our eyes. . . .

Notes

1. Nicetas Choniates, a Greek historian whose own palace was burnt and plundered in the sack of Constantinople, gives a full account of the period up to 1206 from the Greek point of view. His interpretation of events has been taken into consideration in assessing Villehardouin's western bias.

2. Author of another eye-witness account of the Fourth Crusade, with the same title as Villehardouin's. His descriptions of what he saw for himself are not wanting in colour, but in his report of the expedition he relies too much on hearsay evidence—often incorrect—for his work to have any historical value.

Colin Morris (essay date 1968)

SOURCE: "Geoffroy de Villehardouin and the Conquest of Constantinople," *History,* Vol. LIII, No. 177, 1968, pp. 24-34.

[*In the essay that follows, Morris discusses the content and style of Villehardouin's* Conquest of Constantinople, *arguing that despite some omissions and the "unfair" treatment of certain subjects, Villehardouin's account is primarily an honest and accurate one.*]

The Conquest of Constantinople, by Geoffroy de Villehardouin, was much the most popular history of the fourth Crusade during the Middle Ages, and is still today the most easily available of the contemporary accounts.[1] It deserves its popularity. It gives a vivid description, told by one of the commanders, of the series of events by which a Crusade was turned to the destruction of the Christian Byzantine Empire. Villehardouin was in an unusually good position to give us a record of the decisions of the high

command and the reasons for them. The story, as we see it through his eyes, is of the progressive diversion of the expedition until it achieved what at the start had been in no way envisaged—the creation of a Latin Empire of Constantinople. When Villehardouin and his colleagues negotiated a treaty with Venice for the provision of a fleet in spring 1201, it was secretly specified that the objective was to be Egypt. The failure of the crusaders in the summer of 1202 to meet their obligations to Venice led to the capture of Zara in November of that year. During the following winter, a series of negotiations led to an agreement to go to Constantinople to restore the young Alexius to the throne from which his father had been deposed. Although this objective was achieved after the first siege of the city in the summer of 1203, it was followed by a rapid deterioration in relations between the Greeks and the Crusaders. In April 1204, the westerners succeeded, in a second siege, in breaking into the city. Its treasures were sacked; its provinces divided between the Franks and the Venetians; and a highly insecure Latin Empire was erected upon the ruins.

Edmond Faral, editor of the standard text of the work, took a high view of its historical merits, and was inclined to express himself with some force about those who doubted them:[2]

> It has become fashionable in recent years to accept immediately as true any evidence contrary to that of Villehardouin, and to welcome eagerly any assertion which can be set against him, no matter how unsupported or suspect it may be . . . Yet the criticisms which have been directed against Villehardouin according to this odd method disappear completely if only one studies them.

Critics of Villehardouin have tended to centre their criticism upon the idea that the book was a calculated piece of propaganda which deliberately distorted the events leading to the diversion of the Crusade:

> We know that Villehardouin wrote in order to justify this remarkable crusade; but it is a tribute to his high intelligence that he realized that an apology based on false statements would have been valueless; too many people had been involved in these startling events. So he told the truth; but he did not tell it *all.*[3]

What is the truth of the matter? To answer this question we must first examine the attitudes, both conscious and unconscious, which lie behind the work.

Villehardouin was in an excellent position to tell the story of the Crusade, for he was one of the small group of leaders, and involved in all the major decisions. Moreover, he took himself seriously as an historian, stating his claims in a passage unusual in so reticent a man:

> Geoffroy de Villehardouin, Marshal of Champagne, and the author of this work—who has never, to his knowledge, put anything in it contrary to the truth, and who was present, moreover, at all the conferences recorded in its pages . . . (p. 57)

The general atmosphere and spirit of the work suggests that he made this claim sincerely. His narrative is confined to events at which he himself had been present; when he has to fill in the background, he does so as briefly as possible. He shows little tendency to glorify himself or insist on his own importance. He probably wrote in 1207, reasonably close to the events concerned.[4] The high quality and reliability of the work may be seen by comparison with another eye-witness, Robert of Clari, who had little first-hand knowledge of anything before summer 1202, was outside the inner circle of leaders, was given to rambling accounts of a variety of matters on which he was not well informed, and wrote later than Villehardouin.[5] Nonetheless, it is important to check the work by reference to the mass of other eye-witness evidence, which (in spite of Faral's complaints about the use of remote and late evidence by Villehardouin's critics) is abundant. There are letters from the leaders who settled in the East;[6] reminiscences by returned Crusaders;[7] and descriptions by Greeks who were present at the fall of Constantinople.[8] Moreover, there is the further possibility of internal criticism of the work. Reticent as he was about himself, Villehardouin unconsciously revealed a good deal about his attitude to life, and this naturally shaped the work which he wrote.

He was a military commander above all else, in turn Marshal of Champagne and Marshal of Romania (the Latin Empire); an experienced soldier, probably a veteran of the third Crusade;[9] and his history is outstanding for the skill with which military events are described. The account of the first siege of Constantinople in July 1203 is a model of clarity, and it is common for him to pause in his narrative to bestow an accolade on someone who had performed a deed of special bravery. This strong military interest throws light on the literary form of the book. Villehardouin was influenced by the style and atmosphere of the *chansons de geste*. While he did not copy the fantasies of some of these, his sober account was governed by similar tastes and conventions. At exciting moments, he addresses his readers directly, in the manner of the *chansons:*

> Now let me tell you of an event so marvellous that it might be called a miracle. (p. 71)

He liked to present a formal debate or confrontation, as the epic writers did, and he preferred to state the terms of treaties, not by incorporating the text as a chronicler would have done, but by putting them into the mouths of one of the characters. This is not to say that Geoffroy is a careless writer, but only that he must be assessed, not as chronicler nor annalist nor modern historian, but as a writer of a real-life epic.

His keen military interests were accompanied by indifference to affairs which many Crusaders would have thought important. In the affairs of clerks, he has little interest. He took almost no notice of the relations of the papacy with the Crusade, and did not consult the papal letters to its leaders, of which he must have been aware. Partly, no doubt, this was due to his embarrassment at the turn of events, for Innocent III had persistently attempted to prevent the expedition from being turned against Christians. Villehardouin omits these prohibitions; wrongly states that Innocent 'very willingly' confirmed the Franco-Venetian treaty of spring 1201;[10] and he describes the sensational episode of the excommunication of an entire Crusade in such a roundabout way that it is hard to make out that the Crusaders were in fact excommunicated (p. 53). There is real evasion and suppression here, of a somewhat clumsy and naïve kind. There is genuine indifference, also, to ecclesiastical and spiritual matters. He expresses no interest in the moral condition of the Crusade, and, if he occasionally puts down a failure to the sins of the Crusaders, it is not a matter on which he wants to spill much ink. The relics of Constantinople, which moved other writers to raptures of enthusiasm, seemed to Villehardouin worth a sentence.[11] He had a simple theology of his own, consisting principally in an uncritical belief in divine providence. Several times we are told that, whatever the original intentions of the human actors, 'events turn out as God wills' (p. 36). While he does not argue the case, it seems clear that he thought that the supreme instance of providential over-ruling of human purposes was the fourth Crusade itself. It was a marvel that an operation designed for an attack on Egypt should end by attacking Constantinople; a greater marvel still that so small a force should overcome so great a city. The steps by which the diversion took place were neither foreseen nor intended by the participants, for the providence of God was directing them to the humbling of the Greeks at the hands of the Latins. Villehardouin's wonder at this is vividly expressed in a passage after the final fall of the city:

> So the troops of the Crusaders and the Venetians were duly housed. They all rejoiced and gave thanks to our Lord for the honour and the victory He had granted them, so that those who had been poor now lived in wealth and luxury. Thus they celebrated Palm Sunday and the Easter Day following, with hearts full of joy for the benefits our Lord and Saviour had bestowed on them. And well might they praise Him; since the whole of their army numbered no more than twenty thousand men, and with His help they had conquered four hundred thousand, or more, and that in the greatest, the most powerful, and most strongly fortified city in the world. (pp. 92-3)

These, then, are the presuppositions with which Villehardouin wrote. In spite of his first-hand knowledge, his circumstances were such as to make distortion easy. He probably had to depend largely on his own memory, and the lapse of about five years was sufficient to make this precarious. The weakness of his method is shown by his unsatisfactory handling of dates.[12] He very rarely gives a specific date, and one's impression is that he remembered very few, and did not care to seek information about them. Much of the narrative is wrapped in total chronological obscurity. From the beginning up to the treaty signed in spring 1201, it is not even possible to be sure what year he is talking about.[13] The stay at Venice in summer 1202 is completely without dates, and so is the first siege of Constantinople. The absolute dates given for the years 1202-3 suggest that they have been remembered accidentally because of their connection with a feast of the French church, and they form a very tenuous time-scheme.[14] These absolute dates are usually right, or at least fit quite well with dates given by other writers. Sometimes a well-meant effort to remember a date ends in misfortune. The Battle of Philia in 1204 is dated close on Candlemas and near Lent (p. 86); Candlemas is 2 February, and in that year Ash Wednesday was 10 March. Villehardouin is given to narratives which take events from day to day, and are studded with such notes of time as 'next day' or 'three days later'. They read like a lively account of an episode, remembered long after and decorated with a few suitable intervals of time; they are usually unclear, and when they can be checked they appear to be wrong.[15] There is, I think, no need to conclude from this that Villehardouin was suppressing some information for purposes of his own, nor even that he was careless about his history. The epic tradition in which he was writing had not taught him to pay attention to precise chronology, and it is not realistic to seek in his work an accuracy of dating which we might hope to find in a very good chronicler.

The whole spirit of the book is that of the reminiscences of a soldier and man of affairs. They are substantially honest and careful, and he is usually accurate on the main points. Unhappily, he shared with other writers of memoirs an inclination to omit painful facts. His evasion of the issues presented by papal policy, and clumsy attempt to skate round the excommunication, have already been noticed. After the establishment of the Latin Empire, in the midst of a detailed narrative of political events, there is at least one significant omission, for there is no mention of the rejection of the offer of alliance made by Ioannitsa, the Bulgarian king. The results of this foolish decision were so disastrous that Villehardouin perhaps found the episode too painful to record. His lack of frankness does not stop with the avoidance of a few awkward episodes. He was a man of strong and simple views, and did not have the sympathy and imagination to be fair to those with whom he disagreed.

The most striking instance of this appears in his treatment of the numerous Crusaders who opposed the successive diversions to Zara and Constantinople. For this group, Villehardouin has a standard description which becomes almost a technical term. They are 'those who wished the army to be disbanded'. He sets out to discredit them from their first appearance at Venice, when they protested at the plan to attack Zara:

> 'We've paid for our passage,' they said, 'and if the Venetians are willing to take us, we're quite ready to go. If not, we'll make shift for ourselves, and go some other way.' (They said this, in actual fact, because they would have liked the army to be disbanded.) (p. 42)

Geoffroy is rarely prepared to allow his opponents to state their views at all, and even when he mentions them, he at once repeats his accusation that they wanted to dissolve the army.[16] Interestingly enough, he does not libel them by inventing political or personal ambitions for them. He appears as unfair rather than dishonest, and as a result ends with an implausible picture of an opposition with a motive-less desire to destroy the Crusade on which it had come. His comments are in a sense close to the truth, for the leadership argued precisely that the policy of the dissentients would inevitably lead to the break-up of the expedition.[17] This uncritical hostility to Simon de Montfort and the other opponents of the diversion is matched by a strong admiration for Venice. Both of these attitudes must have become deeply ingrained over the years of fighting, in which the Venetians were his comrades-in-arms and the shortage of manpower deepened his resentment against those who abandoned the expedition. It is significant that Dandolo, the Doge of Venice, appears in these pages not as a subtle politician, but as a brave gentleman and faithful colleague in war. In part, indeed, one is bound to respect Geoffroy for his bias towards Venice. He showed no sign (as some other writers did) of wishing to shift the blame for the whole affair onto the shoulders of Venice. He gave full details of the Crusaders' obligations, and of their failure to meet them, in spite of the fact that he, as one of the envoys, was responsible for the acceptance of the unrealistic terms. Nonetheless, we are left with a completely unsatisfactory picture of the attitude of Venice, with no mention of the long-standing political and economic ambitions which the city had entertained in the eastern Mediterranean. In this connection, it will be useful to examine Villehardouin's account of his two stays at Venice, which illustrate a number of the weaknesses in his approach.

In the spring of 1201, he went with five other envoys to negotiate for shipping. They arrived, we are told, 'in the first week of Lent' (p. 31). Thereafter, they experienced a series of delays, the length of which is indicated, not always quite clearly, by Villehardouin. At the end of them he tells us, not very helpfully, that 'we were now in Lent' (p. 35). The treaty survives, and its date does not confirm this already confused chronology.[18] He is, however, largely correct about the terms of the treaty,[19] although his use of the document is odd. The treaty is not quoted in the text, but placed as a speech in the mouth of the Doge. A vivid conversation is set before us in grand epic style, but it is only created at the cost of historical plausibility. The negotiations, on this showing, followed an eccentric course. The envoys presented their credentials to the Doge, and four days later stated their errand to the Venetian Council. They gave no details, simply asking for the advice of the Venetians and for their help

> in any way that you care to advise or propose, so long as our lords can meet your conditions and bear the cost. (p. 33)

Thus it came about that the proposals were made by the Doge, speaking in language close to that of the treaty.[20] Although he had not been told how many Crusaders were expected, he promised transport for a specific number. The following day, the envoys signified their acceptance without any further negotiation. It is inconceivable that they did not supply some estimate of numbers, and highly unlikely that the terms were settled without argument; indeed, other writers mention disagreement over details. Villehardouin ends by recording papal confirmation, omitting to mention the condition that the Crusade must not proceed against Christians (p. 35). The whole account is characteristic. Much of it is accurate and careful, but the chronology is extremely vague, his desire to draw a picture of gentlemanly co-operation has led to implausibility, and he is evasive about the attitude of the Pope.

Similar features are apparent in his description of the stay at Veniçe in the summer of 1202. Again, there are no firm dates until the departure of the expedition after 1 October. The delay was caused by the failure of the Crusaders to produce the number of troops, and therefore the passage-money, to which their envoys had committed them. While Villlehardouin was an honest man to have admitted this so clearly, much of his handling of the episode is unfair and even dishonest. He tried to shift the blame upon the Crusaders who travelled from other ports. The case is a poor one, for there was no evident obligation upon the pilgrims as a whole to avail themselves of the travel arrangements prepared by Villehardouin and his associates. Moreover, his sympathy for Venice drew him into serious falsehoods designed to whitewash the citizens. Thus he described the generous provision made for the Crusaders during their stay there, on the Isle of St. Nicholas:

> The Venetians set up a market for them, as abundantly supplied as anyone could desire with everything necessary for the use of horses and men. (p. 42)

The author of the *Devastatio* gave a very different picture, asserting that the Crusaders were held on the Isle virtually as captives:[21]

> Moreover, there grew a great fear among the people, so that many returned to their own country, many hastened to Apulia to other ports and took ship; only a small part remained there, among whom a terrible plague raged to the point where the dead could scarcely be buried by the survivors.

It is interesting to find that this author thought that the shortage of numbers was partly due to maltreatment by Venice; and other eye-witnesses support the *Devastatio*.[22] The discrepancy is so great that it is hard to think that Villehardouin made an honest mistake.

The central drama in the history of the Crusade is that of the diversion from Egypt to Constantinople, and it is necessary to end by formulating a position on Villehardouin's handling of it. It has already been argued that he is not a fair witness. His whole method of writing history made it difficult to be objective. It gave him no firm chronological framework, and although his policy of confining himself to eye-witness experiences had much to commend it, it discouraged him from reporting the attitudes and interests

of his characters, as distinct from their public actions. He perhaps never had much perception about human character, and five stormy years had formed his prejudices firmly. Of Venice, he will record nothing ill; while the seceders do not receive the vestige of a fair hearing, and the papal policy (unacceptable as it was to the leaders of the Crusade) is given very little notice. Bias and unfairness, however, are substantially different from the deliberate re-writing of history in order to conceal what happened; and we must consider now the criticism that Villehardouin consciously re-told the story of the diversion so as to conceal the existence of a plot. It has been alleged that Geoffroy knew that Boniface of Montferrat and the Venetians intended, in advance of the Crusade, to deflect it to their own purposes; and that his profession to believe that the workings of providence had led the Crusade to Byzantium was intended to obscure the scandalous truth. Villehardouin tells us that the Crusaders were approached at Venice in the autumn of 1202 by the young Alexius with the proposal that they should restore him to the throne which he claimed (p. 45); that the leaders, against heavy opposition, came to terms with him at Zara in the winter of 1202-3 (pp. 51-2); and that the army as a whole agreed to go to Constantinople after a stormy discussion at Corfu (p. 56). So far as it goes, this seems to be the truth.[23] The question is what it omits. The young Alexius had arrived in the west during 1201, perhaps in the spring. He approached Innocent III, Philip of Suabia and Boniface of Montferrat for aid in recovering the throne from the usurper, Alexius III.[24] Villehardouin omits any mention of these negotiations, an his description of Alexius' approach to the Crusading leaders in the autumn of 1202 reads as if he had just arrived in Italy. Indeed, he goes out of his way to stress that the claimant's appearance was a complete surprise:

> Here let me tell you of one of the most remarkable and extraordinary events you have ever heard of. (p. 44)

Villehardouin must have heard of the negotiations of 1201, and the absence of any mention has given rise to the suspicion that he was deliberately concealing a plot. The suspicion is increased by the fact that he was closely associated with the two parties who had the strongest interest in intervening at Byzantium: Venice (with whom he had signed the treaty of 1201) and Boniface of Montferrat (whom he had proposed as leader of the expedition).

In spite of this, I find it hard to believe that one of the major purposes of the work was to remove all traces of the 'plot' from history. By 1207, when Villehardouin finished the book, the question of justifying the diversion was no longer a lively issue, for the Pope had accepted the consequences of the conquest.[25] Geoffroy's silence about the conversations of 1201 is probably the result of simple lack of interest in them. He always wrote supremely as an eye-witness, and avoided reporting episodes at which he had not been present. The conversations had in any case not been conclusive,[26] and he had only limited second-hand evidence about them.[27] In the circumstances, it would have been surprising if he had reported them. On the other hand, he is the only eye-witness to make it clear that Alexius had approached the Crusade before it left Venice—a very odd feature if it was his set purpose in writing to suppress traces of the early planning of the diversion.

We may doubt, indeed, whether Villehardouin measures up to the role of an adroit and skilful propagandist, for which he has sometimes been cast. He is both more honest, and more clumsy, than that. He is capable of distorting the facts, and he does so in largely omitting any consideration of papal policy, in his treatment of the opposition to the diversion, and in his presentation of Franco-Venetian relations. His blundering evasions and awkward omissions have left some fairly clear marks on his narrative, but I doubt if the absence of the 1201 negotiations is one of these. He can be faulted more severely for his failure to give any indication of the strong interests which both Venice and Boniface had in Byzantium—a failure characteristic of his whole method of writing. His work should be considered a rather special example of a familiar type of source: the reminiscences of a successful general. It is special in the sense that Villehardouin, although not unintelligent, was remarkably narrow in his outlook. In some ways, he is the perfect representative of the closed mind; his sympathies and interests were restricted, even by the standards of an age and class not given to breadth of vision. It is also special in a careful concentration upon what was actually seen and heard. The result is a rather curious mixture, the character of which perhaps explains the very divergent views which have been taken of its value. His judgements of men and motives are badly astray, for he saw his memories in the distorting mirrors of loyalty and resentment. The book in consequence shows signs of omission and evasion, often of a clumsy kind, and occasionally of deliberate falsehood. At the same time, he really knew the episodes he was describing, and basically had an honest intention to preserve for posterity the great events which he had witnessed. The greatness of the book, and the secret of its popularity, lie in this single-minded intention. Ignoring all complexities of policy and motive, it presents in dramatic simplicity the exciting chain of events which led to the conquest of Constantinople.

Notes

1. M. R. B. Shaw, *Joinville and Villehardouin: Chronicles of the Crusades,* Penguin Classics, 1963. References in the article are to this translation. I am grateful for the publishers' consent to the use of quotations from it.

2. Villehardouin, *La Conquête de Constantinople,* ed. E. Faral, Paris 1938-9, pp. xiv and xix.

3. A. Pauphilet, 'Robert de Clari et Villehardouin', in *Mélanges A. Jeanroy,* Paris 1928, p. 564. The same general position is stated by H. Grégoire, 'The question of the diversion of the Fourth Crusade', *Byzantion,* XV, p. 158, although Grégoire is concerned rather with the events themselves than with Villehardouin's sincerity.

4. The evidence for the date and method of composition is considered in Faral, *Conquête,* pp.

xiii-xvi. The most natural view is that it was certainly not started before the final fall of the city in 1204, and finished in 1207 (after the death of Boniface of Montferrat in September, but before hearing of the death of Ioannitsa of Bulgaria at about the same time).

5. *La Conquête de Constantinople,* ed. P. Lauer, Paris 1924. English translation by E. H. McNeal, Columbia 1936.

6. For example, the letters of Baldwin of Flanders (*Monumenta Germaniae Historica,* Scriptorum XXI, ed. G. E. Pertz, Hanover 1869, p. 224) and Hugh of St. Pol (G. L. Tafel and G. M. Thomas, *Urkunden zur . . . Staatsgeschichte der Republik Venedig,* Oesterreichische Geschichts-quellen XII, I, p. 304).

7. Robert of Clari has already been mentioned. Abbot Martin of Pairis is to be found in P. Riant, *Exuviae sacrae constantinopolitanae,* Geneva 1877, t. I. pp. 57-126. The memoirs of bishop Conrad of Halberstadt are incorporated in the *Gesta episcoporum Halberstadensium,* ed. L. Weiland, M.G.H. Script, xxiii, Hanover 1874, p. 116. The *Devastatio Constantinopolitana,* which may have been written by a follower of Boniface of Montferrat, is printed in C. Hopf, *Chroniques gréco-romanes inédites ou peu connues,* Berlin 1873, p. 86.

8. Nicetas Choniates was edited by I. Bekker in *Corpus Scriptorum Historiae Byzantinae,* Bonn 1835; and an anonymous account by Hopf, *op. cit.,* p. 93.

9. J. Longnon, *Recherches sur la vie de Geoffroy de Villehardouin* (Bibliothèque de l'École des Hautes Études 276, 1939) pp. 59-63.

10. p. 35. In fact, the pope attached the specific condition that the Crusade must not be diverted against Christians (*Gesta Innocentii III* c. 83) and Register VII, 18 (Migne P.L. 214 cols. cxxxi and 301).

11. His carelessness of ecclesiastical affairs was such that he failed to make out the best possible case for the diversion. One real advantage, in the eyes of contemporaries, was the opportunity it gave for a reunion of the Greek and Latin churches. Geoffroy fails to stress the point, and after the fall of the city never mentions the arrangements made to implement the union.

12. Faral was impressed by the 'precision and exactitude' of Villehardouin's chronology, and therefore believed that he 'perhaps' had personal notes or a diary on which it was based. On the following page, Faral became surer of this theory: he 'must have been using (notes) in all probability' (*op. cit.* pp. xiv-xv). As I am far from convinced that the chronology of the work is good, I assume, on the contrary, that Geoffroy had no diary.

13. The question is discussed by E. John, 'A note on the preliminaries of the Fourth Crusade', *Byzantion*, XXVIII, 1958, p. 95.

14. The absolute dates for 1202 are:

| Octave of Remigius | departure from Venice |
| St. Martin's eve and day | arrival at Zara |

In 1203 we have:

Easter Monday	departure from town of Zara
Pentecost eve	departure from Corfu
St. John Baptist eve and day	St. Stephen's and Chalcedon
St. Peter	coronation of Alexius
St. Martin	return of Alexius to Constantinople

An earlier date mentioned is the visit of Boniface of Montferrat to the general chapter at Cîteaux. The former Marshal of Champagne still remembered that 'this takes place every year on Holy Cross Day in September' (p. 38).

15. Faral admired these narratives, declaring that when added up the intervals agree rigorously with the absolute dates provided. I have been unable to find any instance where such time-schemes can be checked, for nowhere does the author provide a definite date at both the beginning and end of one of the sequences. The intervals mentioned for the siege of Zara certainly do not agree with the statements of other eye-witnesses. The *Gesta episcoporum* and *Devastatio* give the fall of the city as 24 or 25 November, and the arrival of Alexius' envoys as 1 January 1203; intervals different from those of Geoffroy.

16. 'The Cistercian Abbot of Vaux had something to say, in common with those who were eager to have the army disbanded. They all declared they would never give their consent, since it would mean marching against Christians' (p. 51).

17. The Crusade would not have been able to set out at all had not the leaders promised to recover Zara for Venice in payment of the outstanding debt. The only hope of continuing beyond Zara in the spring of 1203 (by which time only six months' supplies remained) was to accept Alexius' offer of assistance. To oppose the diversion was therefore arguably to want to disband the expedition.

18. The Venetian portion of the treaty is given in Tafel & Thomas, *op. cit.*, p. 369. It is dated 1 April, a week after Easter. Faral's suggestion (I, p. 219) that the official copy was written and dated after the departure of the envoys has a ring of desperation about it, for the sealing is described by Geoffroy, and the obvious meaning of the narrative places this in Lent (p. 35).

19. There are two significant mistakes. The Venetians are said to have promised supplies for nine months, as against the year specified in the treaty; and (according to the best manuscripts) the payment due is said to be 94,000 marks instead of 85,000. If Villehardouin had the text in front of him, he was using it carelessly.

20. As the treaty was drafted in the first and second persons, the Venetian section could easily be transformed into a speech by the Doge.

21. ed. Hopf, p. 87.

22. Bishop Conrad of Halberstadt (p. 117) and the Soissons account. The latter is not always reliable, but it owed something to Bishop Nivelon of Soissons, one of the leaders, and it appears well informed about conditions at Venice. See P. Riant, *op. cit.*, p. 5.

23. Other accounts differ in details, but in substance Villehardouin appears well informed about the facts, even if he is remarkably unfair to the opposition, who are given a better hearing by other writers.

24. The evidence and previous literature is well summarized by J. Folda, 'The Fourth Crusade, 1201-1204. Some Reconsiderations', in *Byzantino-Slavica*, 26, 1965, p. 177.

25. The letters of the leaders to the west in 1203-5 were obviously concerned with the justification of the diversion, for papal policy was still undecided. For Villehardouin, however, it is difficult to accept in a specific sense Pauphilet's judgement that 'he wrote in order to justify this remarkable Crusade'.

26. No contemporary suggested that an agreement had been reached before Zara. It may well be that Boniface and Venice were both hoping to deflect the Crusade, but there was no definite settlement with Alexius.

27. What information he had must have come from Boniface, who died shortly before the completion of the book. Alexius had been available as a source on the voyage from Corfu to Constantinople, but one suspects that he was not very intimate with Villehardouin.

Jeanette M. A. Beer (essay date 1968)

SOURCE: "*Le Conquette de Constantinople*—Its Style and Language" in *Villehardouin: Epic Historian*, Librarie Droz, 1968, pp. 67-81.

[In the following essay, Beer examines the two stylistic traits for which Villehardouin's work is most commonly praised: its clarity and brevity. Beer also investigates the way in which Villehardouin uses such devices as repetition and antitheses.]

The qualities most frequently praised in *La Conquête de Constantinople* are its clarity and its brevity.[1] Villehardouin's clarity could no doubt be unmediated—the result solely of a simple, orderly, perhaps even unimaginative conception of events. Nevertheless, a number of Villehardouin's stylistic devices suggest that he is taking pains to reinforce this particular tendency. His frequent exploitation of the epic habit of recapitulation in the form of a brief, summarizing résumé ("Ensi fu dessiegie Andrenople" [287]; "Et ensi cele chace fu recovree com vos avez oï [363]) is didactically useful, as are the attention-seeking formulae "Sachiez que" and "Oiez que." Since **La Conquête de Constantinople** was not, like the epic, an "article de foire," these tricks from the jongleur's oral technique had lost most of their original *raison d'être,* and Villehardouin's adoption of them acquires added significance. Of the epic techniques available, he has chosen to exploit most those that lend themselves to didacticism and persuasion.

The other feature commonly attributed to Villehardouin's style—its brevity—needs qualification. It is true that Villehardouin ignores completely the endless possibilities for embroidery or *amplificatio* afforded by his subject-matter. Neither is he tempted to abandon the narrative thread for incursions into anecdote. It is, however, noteworthy that his most frequent literary device is repetition in all its forms. Brevity should therefore be assumed a secondary consideration, perhaps even an unconscious habit for the most part, while clarity seems to be consistently cultivated, even at brevity's expense.

The work is structured upon a pattern of simple sentences. This is not to say that the sentence never extends itself. But its extensions generally consist of sub-divisions into self-contained simple sentence-units. The sentence length is, in these cases, arbitrarily determined by the punctuation rather than by internal necessity. In the following sentence from paragraph 182, for example, the only units which could not stand independently are the first two—the remaining clauses could be separated by stops without affecting the meaning: "Et traistrent a la prison ou l'emperere Sorsac estoit, qui avoit les ialz traiz, si le vestent emperialment; si l'emporterent el halt palais de Blaquerne, et l'asistrent en la halte chaiere, et l'obeïrent come lor seignor."

The lingering influence of epic versification with its predominance of self-contained lines might be suggested as a reason for this semi-staccato method of narration. But in that case, one might also expect a fairly standard sentence length reminiscent of the ten- or twelve-syllable line. In fact, the sentence length shows no such pattern, and presumably reflects no more than Villehardouin's personal taste and, possibly, the manner of the work's dictation.

The linking of these simple sentence units is made with overwhelming frequency by the conjunctions "et" and "si." As is often the case in Villehardouin's work, the constant repetition does not detract from the work's progress or simplicity but, on the contrary, enhances it:

"Cele nuit domaignement l'empereres Alexis de Costantinoble prist de son tresor ce qu'il en pot porter, et mena de ses genz avec lui qui aler s'en voldrent; si s'enfui, et laissa la cité. Et cil de la ville remestrent mult esbahi. Et traistrent a la prison ou l'emperere Sorsac estoit, qui avoit les ialz traiz, si le vestent emperialment; si l'emporterent el halt palais de Blaquerne, et l'asistrent en la halte chaiere, et l'obeïrent come lor seignor. Et dont pristrent messages par le conseil l'empereor Sursac et envoierent a l'ost, et manderent le fil l'empereor Sursac et les barons que l'empereres Alexis s'en ere fuiz et si avoient relevé a empereor l'empereor Sursac" (182). The swift succession of clauses in which "et" each time heralds a new event imparts speed to the narrative, underlines Villehardouin's orderly and chronological approach without which such a technique would not be possible, and at the same time suggests the directness of popular narrative.

Since the progression is largely from fact to fact without undue explanation or recapitulation within each episode, it is not surprising that Villehardouin makes no attempt to vary his opening conjunctions in a rhetorical interweaving of concessions, comparisons, or oppositions. This constant avoidance of variety extends beyond the conjunctions. The consistency with which Villehardouin maintains his modes of expression is almost formulaic. The fashionable rhetorical habit of padding out an idea by using it in several different forms[2] is not expressly[3] cultivated by Villehardouin. Indeed, there seems to be only one example, startling by its unexpected departure from Villehardouin's usual practice, in which Villehardouin studiously avoids repetition. In paragraph 479, Villehardouin persistently varies his choice of word for the concept "return": "si tornerent arriere, et revindrent en Equise, et troverent Perron de Braiecuel e Païen d'Orliens. Et Toldres li Ascres se fu deslogiez de devant et fu repariez arriere en sa terre. Ensi fu secorue Equise com vos oez. Et cil des galies s'en tornerent arrieres en Costantinoble et ratornerent lor oirre vers Andrenople." Since this isolated occurrence is so heavily outweighed by the constant examples of polyptoton, it would be rash to assume it was intentional. It is, of course, a valuable piece of internal evidence that Villehardouin had more lexical variants at his disposal than he generally chose to use.

Repetition was so much part of the medieval literary climate that its appearance in any work of the time seems almost inevitable. Repetitive patterns were cultivated both in the elaborating of a highly rhetorical style or in the jongleur's more practical task of projecting a story well—familiarity breeds satisfaction rather than contempt in a listening audience. The simplest type of repetition, the immediate repetition of single words (epizeuxis) reflects medieval habits of style and little more: "qui ainz ainz, qui mielz mielz" (174, 175, 243, 415, 466), "vis a vis" (180), "rez a rez" (204), "de respit en respit" (208), "lez a lez" (immediately followed by "delez aus" [212]), "coste a coste" (236), "main a main" (473). These are, without exception, stock phrases recurring constantly in contemporary literature, and presenting little individual interest. The more elaborate forms of epizeuxis involving the repetition of two predicates of identical form, two objects, or subject and object, offered possibilities for endless preciosity.[4] Significantly, however, Villehardouin's examples do not suggest stylistic polishing as much as the lack of it: "Enqui rendirent cil de la ville la ville a lor seignor" (111); "toz li gaainz qui i seroit seroit apportez ensemble" (234). It is only in the passages of direct speech perhaps[5] that epizeuxis seems in any degree calculated.

The repetition of the same word or phrase at the beginning of successive lines (anaphora) was a rhetorical habit which lent impact to a set of similarly constructed syllabic lines. Such impact is obviously lessened when the device is used for prose clauses of unequal length. Nevertheless, Villehardouin employs it in certain situations. Its purely utilitarian function may be seen if his usage is compared with that of Wace. F. W. Lorenz shows[6] that Wace uses a wide variety of anaphora types involving every part of speech, but with a preference for verbs. A distinctive feature of Villehardouin's use of anaphora is that it is almost entirely restricted to short, insignificant-sounding words, adverbs and pronouns whose repetition hardly serves for embellishment, but rather forms part of Villehardouin's didactism. Anaphora is thus used most frequently to stress expressions of quantity that, on account of their monosyllabic form or lack of distinctiveness, would gain little force from any other emphatic device (e.g. change of position within the sentence): "et *poi* mangierent, et *poi* burent, car *poi* avoient de viande" (181); "*Ensi* fu devisé et *ensi* fu fait" (193); "*la moitié* as Venisiens et *la moitié* a cels de l'ost" (234); "*En mains leus* descendirent a terre et allerent trosque as murs; et *en mains leus* refuirent les eschieles des nés si aprochies, que *cil des* tors et des murs et *cil des* eschieles s'entreferoient" (237); "*a pou de* gent et *a pou de* vïande" (353); "*Telx i ot qui* bien le fisent, et *telx i ot qui* le guerpirent" (360).[7]

The type of repetition which, to a modern reader, most readily suggests inattention to style in Villehardouin is *annominatio,* the use of words belonging to the same root in preference to unrelated alternatives. However, when this device was a recommended technique for embellishing a theme,[8] presupposing an author's delight in plays on words and an audience's aural sensitivity in registering them, Villehardouin's frequent use of it should not be regarded as an easy acceptance of the obvious. Ironically, it may be one of the more fashionably rhetorical (though not studied) features of his work to use, for example: "le plus perillous entrepris que onques genz entrepreïssent" (130) or "li venz venta" (217).[9]

The question of repetition of sounds i.e. alliteration, is not unrelated to Villehardouin's use of annominatio. It seems highly improbable that Villehardouin intended any onomatopeic suggestion when he uses a sound repeatedly. The alliteration of "pristrent proies assez et prisons" (486) is probably a function of his extreme fondness for annominatio, and no other explanation is necessary. Moreover, the frequency of such alliterative examples presumably

reinforced a tendency to repetition in other situations as well.[10] The phenomenon should therefore be regarded as semi-automatic assimilation rather than an attempt at impressionism.

The repetition of an idea through synonymic repetition was already so well-established a feature of French literary style[11] that Villehardouin's expression often is completely formulaic: "Des paroles . . . bones et belles" (30), "une meslee mult grant et mult fiere" (88). Certain individual preferences appear, however—the tendency, for example, to couple a common word with a more technical one from ecclesiastical or legal vocabulary: "si governer et si maïstrer" (65), "a grant travail et a grant martire" (89), "mort et malbailli" (159), "la concorde et la pais" (199), "par le conseil et par le consentment" (222), "le fist ensepellir com empereor honorablement et metre en terre" (223), "si com il ere asseüré et juré et faiz escomuniemenz" (252).

Villehardouin often couples words that are "pitched" at different levels. These synonymic formulae showing a downward progression are most foreign to modern literary style (unless it be humorous): "mort et malbailli" (159), "conmandoit et prioit" (107), "mortz et traïs" (422). One might be tempted to put "que mals ou ontes ne l'en venist" (231) in this category, were it not for reminiscences of the epic. Villehardouin's attitude to the verdict of posterity remains that of Oliver—"Mielz voeill murir que hunte nus seit retraite" (*Roland,* line 1701). He no doubt considered "li mals" in question, death at the hands of the Turks, as a lesser evil than the disgrace of an unfavorable mention in "li livers."

The order of the elements is not, however, fixed in all examples:[12] "fist la cité fondre et abatre" (416); "le fist abatre et fondre" (417); "la fist fondre et abatre" (418; twice). Although the composite expression "abatre-fondre" regularly imposes itself for the destruction of cities, the order of the two component parts seems often to be completely arbitrary.

One of the most stable repetitive patterns in Villehardouin (and, indeed, in Old French) is the reinforcement of an idea by "affirmation after negation."[13] The proposition is presented first in its negative aspect, then in its positive. The negative may be a true negative i.e. it may present the opposite facet of the second statement: "ne li ot mie bien tenues, ainz li ot fausees et brisies" (453). More frequently (in Villehardouin) the negative statement takes a litotic form: "ne repousa mie" (472) which is then "explained" by the positive element: "ainz gitterent ses perrieres as murs et aus tors."

The formula is occasionally used by Villehardouin in illogical form: "dist que il ne se lairoit ja laienz enfermer, ainz dist que il istroit fors" (323). The syntactic opposition is "dist: ainz dist," whereas the intended opposition in meaning is "il ne se lairoit ja laienz enfermer: ainz . . . il istroit fors."

In paragraph 394, the syntactic form is slightly varied with the use of the positive verb "menti" in the negative first element: "lor menti de quanque il lor ot couvent, ainz les fist prendre, et tolir tot lor avoir, et mener en Blakie nuz et deschauz et a pié" (394). However, the meaning is clearly negative: "failed to keep," even if the form is positive, so that the formula remains true to type, serving for re-inforcement and clarification of the elements Villehardouin wishes to emphasize.

Another rhetorical device that appears frequently in *La Conquête de Constantinople* is antithesis. Like repetition, it seems inevitable, both by its popularity in the contemporary literature of Villehardouin's day, but also by the nature of the subject-matter. The subject of the Fourth Crusade was as rich in inevitable oppositions as that of the *Roland*. The most obvious clash is between the French and the Greeks. This may be expressed by a positive-versus-negative statement: "Ensi se reposerent cil de l'ost cele nuit . . . Mais l'empereres Morchuflex ne reposa mie" (246), or by the coupling of different words of opposite meaning: "furent pesament armé, et cil legierement" (408); "si furent mult grant gent, et cil furent pou" (482). In addition, there are the two factions of the army: "l'une des parties se travailla a ce que li ost se departist et l'autre a ce que ele se tenist ensemble" (100), and the two nations making up the army, the French and the Venetians: the council scene in paragraph 162, for example, presents in detail the antithesis between land and sea interests.[14]

It is by antithesis that Villehardouin generally conveys the disagreement of a council scene, a process which results in exaggerated over-simplification. Were the deliberations of Boniface's council as devoid of meanderings as is suggested by: "Si i ot de cels qui li otroierent que il i alast, et de cels qui li loerent qu'il n'i alast mie" (298)? There is little doubt that by this elimination of all but the information Villehardouin considers relevant, the main issues are highlighted even if subsidiary ones blur slightly.

Although the device of antithesis would not appear to allow much subtlety, it can suggest more than its simple form would seem to contain. After a description of the Emperor Isaac's new wealth, a description that is expansive for *La Conquête de Constantinople,* Villehardouin remarks "Et tuit cil qui avoient esté le jor devant contre lui estoient cel jor tot a sa volonté" (185). This is more than an objective statement of fact. Placed in the context of Isaac's new, indescribable riches, it becomes a wry observation on human nature, and the importance of wealth and position. One may even detect Villehardouin's dislike of the corruptible.[15] And the antithesis in the study of the doge, an antithesis to which Villehardouin makes constant reference, is more original than are its component elements when considered separately. There is nothing particularly startling about a "viels hom qui gote ne veoit," but this is no longer the case when he possesses the qualities of Roland-cum-Oliver: "mais mult ere sages et preuz et vigueros" (364).

The vocabulary in *La Conquête de Constantinople* is exceptionally simple. It draws neither on Latinized variants nor on the language of the romance. It does not even assume occasionally the popular tones which are to be found in Robert de Clari.[16] If it were necessary to characterize *La Conquête de Constantinople* according to rhetorical labels, its style would presumably be "mediocris" rather than "gravis" or "humilis." It would, of course, be unfortunate to imply too much conscious striving on Villehardouin's part to maintain the narrative in a homogeneous style throughout. The process was doubtless automatic, and an impression of Villehardouin inevitably imposes itself from this narrative which is consistently simple without being trivial, and which continues uninterrupted by irrelevancies, never losing its dignity or sobriety.

If there is didactic intent, it is not that of apprizing the reader of miscellaneous unknown facts. Villehardouin does not, for example, employ technical explanations of warfare and strategy, which, incidentally, reveals as much about the nature of his audience as it does about the nature of his style. And when he uses learned vocabulary forms, they generally occur in conjunction with their more popular variants in synonymic doublets. The only learned form which induces anything resembling a parenthetical explanation is "mortalité": "La ot si grant mortalité de gent, qui furent occis, que ce ne fu se merveille non" (414). This barely resembles the elaborately informative interventions by the author of *Li Fet des Romains,* who is obviously aiming to introduce unfamiliar material to an interested but ignorant public. Thus, Villehardouin's parentheses are not used as glosses. They add precision to previously mentioned details: "lors se herberja en la ville, il et sa gent" (269). They repeat or re-define after the fashion of the oral style. They rarely expound.

A recurrent feature imported from the jongleur's narrative style is the tense usage. It had been a feature of the *chanson de geste* technique to employ present tenses for past time in passages involving the vivid representation of a set of events. This was so prominent a feature in the *Roland,* for example, that it is the present rather than the past tense which should there be regarded as the norm.[17] Villehardouin is nearer to modern tense usage,[18] preferring the past tense, but he reverts to the older narrative habits in certain circumstances.[19] A present tense is usually used for past time in conjunction with direct speech passages, presumably by assimilation: "Et li duc lor respont: 'Seignor, je ai veües vos letres'" (16); "Seignor, fait-il, escoltez" (41).

The verb "comencier" is very frequently used in the present tense, the notion of a process' duration in these cases taking precedence over the moment of its inception in Villehardouin's mind. In paragraph 323, for example, the narration is in the past tense, there has been no use of the epic present since paragraph 279 (again with "comencier"), but there is now a sudden switch with the occurrence of "comencent": "Et cil vint a tote s'ost et a granz batailles a pié et a cheval; et cil s'en issirent et comencent la bataille." The narration then continues again in the preterite: "Et i ot grant estor et grant melee." Similar occurrences are to be found in 61, 68, 157 (4 times), 172,

175, 176 (twice), 177, 180, 184, 217, 237, 243 (3 times), 244, 247, 279, 358 (twice), 359, 391, 407, 408, 424, and 499.

The present occurs frequently also in certain semi-fixed expressions: "Et (il) laissent aler les voilles al vent" (119, 133, 217); "lor tornent les dos" (140, 157); "li criz lieve en l'ost" (217, 355, 357). These are part of a wider pattern which may be seen in Villehardouin's work—the tendency to scatter present tenses in certain set scenes or *topoi,* mainly battle scenes, the landing or sailing of a fleet, and any generally imposing ceremony such as the arrival of envoys, the taking of the cross, or a coronation. The mere presence of a topos is presumably not sufficient. It must also have a more than usually dramatic impact for Villehardouin to represent it in this way. One of the most significant features in Villehardouin's tense usage is its changing pattern about halfway through the work. The number of "epic presents" sharply dwindles after the capture of Constantinople, as though the subjugation of Constantinople's outlying territories and the personal ambitions within the army no longer admit of epic presentation.

The assumption that the tense distribution is a rough index of Villehardouin's enthusiasm for his subject-matter would, by itself, be rash if there were not other noticeable changes in style. The incidence of direct speech declines in similar fashion,[20] and the descriptive development of each incident, which had originally been meagre, becomes in the second half so sparse that little evocative power remains in this interminable series of conquests.

Frappier interprets this as an increase in Villehardouin's historical approach to his subject-matter.[21] The question seems rather one of Villehardouin's enthusiasm. The qualities of style favoring an objective or historical presentation were, after all, noticeable from the beginning: clarity of exposition, simplicity of sentence structure and vocabulary, avoidance of rhetorical embellishment, and an orderly arrangement of a series of events. It is not here that Villehardouin changes so much as in his handling of potentially dramatic situations. The topoi are as frequent in the second part as in the first—it is their flatness that is new.

Notes

1. "Cette aversion pour tout ce qui sent l'homme de lettres, le rhéteur, est peut-être le trait le plus saillant du style de Villehardouin. C'est plus que de la simplicité, c'est la nudité voulue du style d'affaires" (*Extraits des chroniqueurs français,* ed. Gaston Paris et A. Jeanroy [Paris, 1927], p. 17); "Sa brièveté . . . est . . . le parti pris d'un auteur qui veut, non amuser la curiosité, mais satisfaire l'intelligence" (Ibid. p. 18); "Le style de l'écrivain, aussi éloigné que possible de la rhétorique, est dépourvu de tout ornement, strictement dépouillé, presque nu. Nul artifice, nulle recherche de l'effet: l'ignorance ou le dédain de ce que nous tenons pour les règles élémentaires de l'art d'écrire. Le mot est propre, juste, précis; mais, quand il le faut, il est répété à satiété, sans souci de varier l'expression. La phrase a la simplicité du style parlé" (E. Faral in his introduction to *La Conquête de Constantinople,* p. xxxvii).

2. "eamdem rem dicere, sed commutate" (E. Faral, *Les Arts poétiques du XIIe et du XIIIe siècle* [Paris, 1962], p. 63).

3. He does, of course, reflect the medieval practice of synonymic repetition (see, p. 73), but these are clichés, not a studied attempt at amplificatio.

4. "'Dame!' fet il, 'la force vient / De mon cuer, qui a vos se tient; / An cest voloir m'a mes cuers mis.' / 'Et qui le cuer, biaus douz amis?' / 'Dame! mi oel.'—'Et les iauz qui?' / 'La granz biautez, que an vos vi.' / 'Et la biautez qu'i a forfet?' / 'Dame! tant que amer me fet.' / 'Amer? Et cui'—'Vos, dame chiere.' / 'Moi!'—'Voire.'—'Voir? an quel meniere?'" (Chrestien de Troyes, *Yvain,* ed. T. B. W. Reid [Manchester, 1942], lines 2015-2024).

5. See below, p. 88.

6. F. W. Lorenz, *Der Stil in Maistre Wace's Roman de Rou* (Leipzig, 1885), pp. 54-59.

7. The adverbial class is the least exploited for anaphora by Wace, and is practically restricted to "tant" and "mult," with only sporadic appearances of other adverbs.

8. See, for example, E. Faral's edition of Matthieu de Vendôme, p. 178.

9. See Appendix I for further examples.

10. "autres *p*assages ne *p*ooit nul *p*reu tenir" (52) etc.

11. S. Pellegrini, "Iterazione sinonimiche nella 'Canzone di Rolando,'" *Studi mediolatini e volgari,* I (1953), 155-165.

12. The same applies to Villehardouin's contemporary, Robert de Clari, in whom most of the synonymic formulae are "reversible," rather than "irreversible binomials." See P. F. Dembowski's *La Chronique de Robert de Clari,* p. 94.

13. See Appendix II.

14. "Et donc pristrent cil de l'ost conseil ensemble por savoir quel chose il porroient faire: s'i assauroient la ville par mer ou par terre. Mult s'acorderent li Venisien que les eschieles fussent drecies es nés et que toz li assaus fust par devers la mer. Li François disoient que il ne se savoient mie si bien aider sor mer com il savoient; mais quant il aroient lor chevaus et lor armes, il se savoient miels aidier par terre. Ensi fu la fin del conseil que li Venisien assauroient par mer, et li baron et cil de l'ost par terre" (162).

15. Cf. "covoitise, qui est racine de toz mals" (253). The statement in paragraph 2 "Porce que cil pardons fu issi granz, si s'en esmurent mult li cuer des gens" also suggests to a modern reader that Villehardouin is satirizing the Crusaders' corruptibility. However,

such an interpretation is no doubt an anachronistic reading of a remark in which no overtones were intended. Apart from the fact that eternal salvation may well have ranked, in Villehardouin's mind, higher than an altruistic concern for others' physical safety, the attribution of cynicism to Villehardouin on such a basic subject as the motives of the Crusaders changes the interpretation of the whole work. It also removes Villehardouin from the epic generation, and suggests affinities with Commines and Machiavelli. The suggestion is not, of course, unprecedented. For a list and refutation of Villehardouin's harshest critics, see E. Faral, "Geoffroy de Villehardouin: La question de sa sincérité," *Revue historique,* CLXXVII (1936), 532.

16. "Garchons malvais; nous t'avons . . . geté de le merde et en le merde te remeterons" (ed. P. Lauer, p. 59).

17. See Anna Granville Hatcher, "Tenses in the *Roland,*" *Studies in Philology,* XXXIX (Oct. 1962), 599: "The preterite is used in the *Roland* to refer to events of the narrative about 325 times, the Perfect about 375, while the Present appears almost 1600 times."

18. See D. R. Sutherland, "Tenses in Old and Middle French" in *Studies in French Language and Medieval Literature Presented to M. K. Pope* (Manchester, 1939), p. 533: "Villehardouin seems to be moving towards the modern system, though he still has a fair proportion of present tenses, a usage which may be attributed again to his obviously oral style of narration."

19. It would, of course, be a mis-representation of the device to suggest that there were circumstances in which the use of present for past tense was absolutely fixed and inevitable. Its dramatic effectiveness depended precisely upon its flexibility, one might even say arbitrariness.

20. See below p. 92 for its distribution.

21. "Faut-il reconnaître dans cette suprématie accordée au style indirect la démarche d'un véritable historien? Je suis enclin à croire que oui dans une certaine mesure. Avant tout, Villehardouin a voulu donner dans sa chronique une idée claire des causes et des effets qui, par une sorte de nécessité interne, ont amené les Croisés à s'emparer de Constantinople et à s'y maintenir, sans qu'on puisse loyalement les accuser d'avoir jamais renoncé au fond d'eux-mêmes à la délivrance de la terre sainte; si cette conception de son œuvre n'est pas une garantie solide de son impartialité, puisqu'elle comporte une part d'apologie, elle avait le mérite éminent d'introduire dans le genre historique—au début du XIIIᵉ siècle—la recherche d'une explication morale et politique des événements" (Jean Frappier, "Les Discours chez Villehardouin," *Etudes romanes dédiées à Mario Roques* [Paris, 1946], p. 53).

Jeanette M. A. Beer (essay date 1970)

SOURCE: "Villehardouin and the Oral Narrative,"*Studies in Philology,* Vol. LXVII, No. 3, 1970, pp. 267-77.

[*In the following essay, Beer studies the way in which Villehardouin, in* Conquest of Constantinople, *utilizes elements of the oral narrative tradition. Beer observes that certain features, including Villehardouin's use of exclamations and his "fondness" for exaggeration and repetition, strongly demonstrate the influence of oral narration on Villehardouin's work.*]

Since Adolf Kressner's article "Über den epischen Charakter der Sprache Villehardouins,"[1] the transitional nature of Villehardouin's style has been accepted without question. However, the exact nature of his transitional features has not been clearly analyzed. Kressner labels "epic" many stylistic features which are not necessarily exclusive to that genre. E. H. McNeal, in a note on the narrative style of Villehardouin and Robert de Clari,[2] suggests more immediate sources, but again there is no intrinsic necessity binding the examples he cites to the *conte* rather than to the epic. Rather than highlighting a specific genre, this paper provides an analysis of the features which Villehardouin has imported from the oral narrative tradition, whether it be the oral style of the hagiographer, the epic jongleur, or the *conteör.* Villehardouin preferred prose over verse, thereby dissociating himself, like Baldwin VIII of Flanders, from fanciful epic inventions and rhyming amusements. But his prose retained from the popular literature preceding him a variety of stylistic features, of which not all were equally suited to a serious historical purpose. An analysis of these features not only aids in the appreciation of Villehardouin's achievement in moulding a new genre from available materials; it also provides certain standards by which to judge the reliability of Villehardouin the historian.

One of the most noticeable characteristics of *La Conquête de Constantinople* is the recurrence of stock conventions derived from the method of delivery of the popular narrative. Such formulae as "tel con je vos dirai," "com vos avez oï" make it clear that Villehardouin envisages for his work the same type of presentation as was used for earlier literary genres. In preference to the verb "escrire" he uses verbs proper to a story-teller's art: "cil Folques dont je vos di" (1); "ne vos puis tout *raconter*" (30); "del duel ne convient mie a *parler*" (37). This oral conception is both the strength and weakness of the history. Villehardouin shows to perfection the summary technique of the narrator who fears to burden his audience with undue elaboration. But he achieves this technique at the expense of analysis of motives and of background events. *La Conquête de Constantinople* was not, after all, an "article de foire"[3] like the *chanson de geste.* It was set down as a written record which would later be read for the enlightenment as much as for the amusement of the "Seignors" to whom Villehardouin appeals (104). He was therefore not obliged to attract, hold, and jolt to attention a motley crowd, but could concentrate upon the development of a subject in which his audience had been profoundly, if not personally, involved. Nevertheless, he employs the narrative methods to which he is acclimatized, despite their limitations.

The features which show the influence of the oral narrative most strongly are Villehardouin's formulae of anticipation, recapitulation, and transition, his frequent exclamations and personal interventions, his fondness for popular dicta, exaggeration, and repetition, his tense usage, and his alleging of an outside source.

The characteristically epic features of anticipation, recapitulation, and transitional devices were essentially a means of imparting shape to an oral narrative that was destined to be interrupted at constant intervals. Although the text of *La Conquête de Constantinople* was presumably unavailable to most of Villehardouin's audience, and a leisurely synthesis of its parts was therefore impossible, the need to signpost the direction in which the narrative moved was distinctly lessened through the more homogeneous audience, their already detailed knowledge of the Fourth Crusade's progress, and the less chaotic conditions under which they would listen to the work. But Villehardouin continues to use these rather mechanical devices (as does the medieval *conte*) more as a means of stress than because they are technically necessary. Before he describes the pardon offered to the Crusaders, he heightens its importance by an anticipatory formula "tel con je vos dirai" (2).[4] He precedes the retailing of an event with indications of its results or later significance. Thus he does not leave the audience to make its own verdict of an event, but anticipates both event and verdict with an advance classification of "mesavanture" or "domages": "et els en avint granz mesaventure, si com vos porroiz oïr avant" (55).

Formulae of foreboding predominate over favorable suggestion, a fact which may be explained either by the device's original function of stimulating interest in what is to come (disaster being always a more tempting bait), or by the very nature of the subject-matter—the vicissitudes of the Fourth Crusade. It is possibly this ambivalence that prevents Villehardouin's anticipatory clichés from appearing archaic. For, although he is following a traditional pattern for hints of impending disaster (*cf.* "Deus quel dulur que li Franceis nel sevent"[5]), his expression remains objective enough in appearance to resemble a rudimentary historical analysis of causes and effects. His exclamation "Ha! cum grant damages fu quant li autre qui alerent as autres porz ne vindrent illuec! Bien fust la crestïenté halcie et la terre des Turs abassie" (57) coincides so happily with the historical methods of several centuries later that it is easy to make anachronistic evaluations of it.

Recapitulation was a less dramatic but perhaps more vital technique than anticipation to the oral narrative. It counteracted fragmentation, and imposed a certain order upon the divagation of events. In Villehardouin straightforward chronological presentation has replaced the slow progression of the epic's paratactic episodes: his text must be the most satisfactory illustration available of "ordo naturalis."[6] Yet he uses recapitulation in vestigial form to clarify certain aspects of his account. Occasionally, he reconstructs the historical events leading to a certain political situation: paragraph 70 recounts the steps leading to Alexis' negotiations with the Crusaders, for example. He rarely repeats his own account,[7] and never refers to events from preceding Crusades (as did the cyclic epics). His favorite use of recapitulation is the short didactic résumé that sums up the contents of a paragraph. The more emphatic form of summary is "ensi" used correlatively with "con vos avez oï" or "com vos oez" (see, for example, 69, 76, 255, 394, 414, 479). But the formula may be reduced to the bare essentials that will keep the salient events ordered: "Ensi fu ceste trive asseüree et ces forteresces abatues" (489). In the economy of Villehardouin's vocabulary this formula recurs constantly to emphasize progressions in the narrative.

In the *chanson de geste,* transition from one theme to another was marked by a simple abrupt phrase. Kressner has listed the transitional formulae of various epics, and shows that the wording scarcely changes throughout. An example from *Amis et Amiles* (line 854) will suffice: "Ici lairons d'Amile le baron/ Si vos dirons d'Ami son compaignon."[8] It is this formula that Villehardouin has taken over without variation. He does not, however, use it indiscriminately for all scene-changes, but only for passages where his chronological method threatens clarity, *e.g.,* when he is obliged to move from place to place instead of completing the account of one particular operation. Thus, before the complicated pattern of combats with the Greeks, the 'Or vos lairons' formula occurs only once (*viz.* in par. 51), where a dissension in the expedition causes Villehardouin to record the names of those who deserted. After this record, he returns to his main theme with: "Or vos lairons de cels et dirons des pelerins." But from par. 229 onwards, the formula recurs frequently:

> Or vos lairons de cels qui devant Costantinople sunt, si parlerons de cels qui alerent as autres pors (229);
> Or vos lairons de cels, si parlerons de cels qui sunt devant Costantinople remés (232);
> Or vos lairons de cels devers Costantinople et revendrons al marchis Boniface de Montferrat (324);
> Or lairons de Renier de Trit, si revendrons a l'empereour Baudoin qui est[9] en Costantinople (347);
> Or lairons de cels de Costantinople . . . si revenrons al duc de Venise (369);
> Or vos lairons de cels, si dirons de Henri le frere l'empereor (380);
> Or lairons de Henri . . . si dirons de Johannisse (398);
> Or lairons de cez, si dirons de Tyerri de Los (455).

The crucial importance of these transitional formulae to an account of the involved network of Crusading operations would be immediately apparent if one were to experiment with their removal, for the course of events would then become incomprehensible. The usefulness of the oral narrative device is therefore not in question here; what is significant is that Villehardouin has again accepted a readily available device from the oral style without attempting to find other means to solve the specific problems involved in his historical method.

The exclamations and author's interventions which, in the oral narrative, were explicit appeals eliciting given responses from the audience, occur scattered throughout Villehardouin's text. Since such exclamations were a conventional means of suggesting that the audience share the emotions of the narrator, it is not surprising that in *La Conquête de Constantinople* they occur in passages that reflect particular interest or emotional involvement on Villehardouin's part. They are, for example, more frequent in the early chapters, while their overall total declines after the first three hundred paragraphs. Nevertheless, the paragraphs which deal with Villehardouin's role as rescuer of the army (362-84) show an unusual increase in phrases addressing or appealing to the audience: "com vos avez oï," "et sachiez," "or oiez," "veïssiez," "or vos lairons," "Ha! Diex!"[10]

The expressions are not identical, or even interchangeable, in their emotional intensity. Of the direct imperatives "sachiez" is by far the most frequent,[11] and contributes didactic rather than emotional emphasis. If "sachiez" reflects Villehardouin's desire (conscious or otherwise) to stress or prove a point, its repetition in par. 254 (four times in swift succession) becomes particularly revealing. Was there, in fact, some peculiarity about the booty distribution[12] to arouse such meticulous explanations?

The lesser-used "oiez" is, in Villehardouin, an emotional variant: it frequently introduces a startling piece of information or a miraculous turn of events. The opening sentence of par. 70 uses "oiez" to make up a hyperbolic introduction such as the eager story-teller might use to attract listeners: "Or oiez une des plus grant merveilles et des greignor aventures que vos onques oïsiez."[13] The paragraph to follow relates the incredible account (to Villehardouin) of Constantinople's dynastic treacheries and brutalities, and is exceptional in Villehardouin who generally avoids the anecdotic.

The hypothetical suggestion of such exclamations as "peüssiez veoir flori le braz Sain Jorge contremont de nés et de galies et de uissiers" (127), "veïssiez maint bon chevalier et maint bon serjant aler encontre et mener maint bel destrier" (112) was originally a most vivid form of address to the audience, since it appealed to them implicitly to exert their imaginations upon a certain set of events, and to co-operate in the joint re-creation of a tableau. Its use in Villehardouin's history is technically superfluous, in the sense that it adds no factual information. Stylistically, however, it marks the work as still of the epic mould, and indicates the type of audience Villehardouin still expected to inspire. It is not surprising that Villehardouin rarely encourages his audience to visualize the disasters of the Crusaders. The suggestion is generally reserved for scenes of exhilaration: the glorious departure of a fleet (127), the rich display of gold and silver contributed to the doge

(61), or the impressive attack upon Constantinople by the Venetians (172).[14]

Events that Villehardouin finds particularly distressing are introduced by the exclamations "Ha!" "Ha! las!" and "Ha! Deus!" which, apart from "Ha! Deus, tant bon destrier i ot mis!" (75), are consistently formulae of regret and foreboding. Again it is possible to see the influence of narrative techniques, which assumed warnings of disaster to be more productive of interest than warnings of its opposite—happiness and the satisfactory resolution of conflict.

Villehardouin's habit of applying a moral cliché to certain episodes is another form of author's intervention which allies him with the popular narrator. His moralizing is several times introduced by "Et por ce dit hom,"[15] a phrase which might seem to be the conclusion of a closely analyzed situation in which the thread of reasoning is visible throughout, but which is, in fact, completely formulaic in *La Conquête de Constantinople.* In 379, Villehardouin's statement about the deserters resolves itself into: they were much blamed ("Mult en reçurent grant blasme") and for this reason it is said to be a bad thing to be blamed ("Et por ce dit on que mult fait mal qui par paor de mort fait chose qui li est reprovee a toz jorz"). This is not a historical analysis of a situation. It is the re-iteration of an accepted epic truth that one must preserve one's *los* at all costs. The logic for the epigram was presumably self-evident to Villehardouin who lived in an epic climate. However, such formulaic moralizing emphasizes the transitional nature of Villehardouin's historical style. Its only value for the modern historian is that it constitutes evidence of attitudes current in the Crusading army. It does not provide a comment which would now be considered valid for the successful conduct of an expedition.

Hyperbole is a narrative technique that is little suited to the historian, and Villehardouin's examples, if they are not recognized as imports from the oral narrative, seem to inflate the Fourth Crusade to unrecognizable proportions.[16] They are, moreover, self-contradictory within the text.[17] For this reason Kressner has labelled them as "naïve Äusserungen,"[18] presuming that Villehardouin believes their literal accuracy each time he uses them. But it is stylistic "double-think" to expect that hyperbole be both hyperbolic and literally true. Villehardouin's use of hyperbole must be considered in the context of the oral style, and not in comparison with modern literary hyperbole, which is used sufficiently infrequently to enable it to fulfill specific stylistic ends. In the oral narrative (as in modern conversational style) the over-exploitation of hyperbole decreases its significance to the point where an interpretation of a superlative as restrictive or absolute would be ridiculous. This poses no problems provided that the techniques are recognized: there is no linguistic difficulty in assuming that the superlatives are not relative superlatives, but emphatic forms of the positive degree. Thus, the eulogy of Boniface[19] which closes Villehardouin's account of the Crusade is not a piece of objective information, but a reflection of Villehardouin's enthusiasm for his favorite candidate. Like so many features of the oral style, it is repetitive, illogical, conventional, and striking—for it is a feature of the oral style, both medieval and modern, that a figure may be repetitive or "conventional," and still arouse interest within its own context by its immediacy.

Since Villehardouin's style is frequently described as terse, without a useless word, it is surprising that repetition is his most frequent literary device. Much of this repetition must have been automatic. Epizeuxis, anaphora, polyptoton, annominatio, and synonymic repetition were stock habits of his literary contemporaries, and he reflects the same tastes.[20] However, his usage of repetitive devices is akin to that of the oral narrative, and not to the elaborations of the rhetorical manuals or even of a Chrétien de Troyes. Villehardouin's summation technique[21] is that of the story-teller who feels it necessary to underline each step in the progress of a lengthy narrative: "Ensi partirent del port de Venise con vos avez oï" (76); "Ensi mortel traïson fist li rois de Blakie com vos oez" (394). And his disinterest in varying his vocabulary ("*manderent* le conte . . . que il ivernoient a Marseille et que il lor *mandast* sa volenté, que il feroient ce que il lor *manderoit*. Et il lor *manda* . . ." [103]) should be interpreted as an automatic acceptance of oral narrative habits, not as a conscious pursuit of the rhetorical device of polyptoton. Repetition of this sort was inevitable and useful in the oral style: familiarity breeds satisfaction rather than contempt in a popular audience.

The tense usage in *La Conquête de Constantinople* is no longer that of the early epics. Professor Hatcher shows that in the *Roland* the present tense is the norm for the narration of past events,[22] while in Villehardouin the past tense (mainly the preterite) heavily outweighs the present by better than 32 to 1. A curious feature of Villehardouin's style is, however, his periodic lapse into the present tense in passages involving the vivid reproduction of certain sets of events. Thus, although the median figure for present tenses conveying past events is 2 per 10 paragraphs (the median figure for the past tense is 64½ per 10 paragraphs), the number of present tenses may rise steeply if a particularly dramatic situation is involved. Pars. 171-80 (the doge's "estrange proesce" in conveying the standard of St. Mark to land and initiating the capture of the towers of Constantinople) contain 23 present tenses—more than 11 times the normal proportion; pars. 151-60, or rather 156-60 (the capture of the tower of Galata) contain 15; pars. 241-50 (the defeat of Emperor Murzuphle and the capture of Constantinople) contain 14. It appears, therefore, that it is the situations which the epic would have developed into dramatic *topoi* that elicit an epic usage of tense in *La Conquête de Constantinople.*

Certain formulaic phrases are responsible for many other of Villehardouin's "epic presents": in pars. 271-80 (which show 8 present tenses for past action) it is not the blinding of Murzuphle that is described in the vivid present, despite the potential it contains for dramatic and horrifying tableaux. The present tenses occur in such battle clichés as "tornent en fuie," "lors comencent . . . a lui a torner," and similar automatic imports from the epic style.

The occurrence of a direct speech passage frequently induces a present tense by dramatic assimilation: "Sire, *font* il a Joffroi le mareschal, que volez que nos faciens?" (372). These time switches which plunge narrator and audience into the course of events were established features of the oral narrative tradition.[23] Their contribution to *La Conquête de Constantinople* is dramatic immediacy, their disadvantage is a blurring of historical perspective.

It was a frequent technique of the oral narrator to cite some source to which he claimed access, and which gave a stamp of authority to the most extravagant events. Villehardouin uses the same formula in his references to "li livres": "et maintes hautres bones gens dont li livres ne fait mie mention" (5); "et bien tesmoigne li livres que bien duroit demie liue Françoise li assals, si com il ere ordenez" (236). Edmond Faral interprets this "book" as "Non pas un livre que Villehardouin aurait consulté et exploité mais le livre même qu'il composait."[24] Certainly there is no reason to believe that Villehardouin needed to consult a written source to acquire his information. But the interpretation of "li livres" as Villehardouin's own work leaves out of account Villehardouin's traditionalism and formalism of style. Surely the frequency with which Villehardouin mentions "li livres" is another formulaic trait from the oral narrative. Without asserting that Villehardouin was wilfully fabricating additional sources, one may suggest that he used this formulaic cliché, as he used so many from the oral narrative, without undue thought for its precise meaning. This is, in fact, demonstrated by its use in 464: "et bien tesmoigne li livres que onques a plus grant meschief ne se defendirent.XL. chevalier a tant de gent: et bien i parut, que il n'en i ot mie.V. qui ne fuissent navré de toz les chevaliers qui i estoient." If Faral's interpretation of "li livres" as *La Conquête de Constantinople* is to be accepted here, which seems doubtful, Villehardouin first cites his book, and then corroborates it from his personal observations ("bien i parut"). Such a juxtaposition seems impossible, and one must interpret the passage in the light of similar formulae in the oral tradition. There the narrator posited an unnamed source merely to add emphasis and conviction to his statement, and Villehardouin, steeped in the oral tradition, repeats the narrative convention, despite the fact that it has outlived its usefulness: he, of all historians, was entitled to Aeneas' "Ipse vidi" as a guarantee of authenticity.

The fact that the stylistic habits of the oral narrative still permeate *La Conquête de Constantinople* is in no way surprising. Unfortunately, the story-telling aspects of Villehardouin's style have been inevitably obscured by his extraordinary status as the first French prose historian extant. A more detailed analysis of these narrative devices that he assumes so automatically should shed much light, not only on his understanding of existing literary conventions, but also on his attitude to his subject-matter.

Notes

1. Adolf Kressner, "Über den epischen Charakter der Sprache Villehardouins," *Archiv f. n. Sprachen,* LVII (1877), 1-16.

2. E. H. McNeal, "Chronicle and Conte; a Note on Narrative Style in Geoffrey of Villehardouin and Robert de Clari," *Festschrift für M. Blakemore Evans* (Columbus, 1945), pp. 110-3.

3. Jean Rychner, *La Chanson de geste* (Geneva, 1955), p. 22.

4. The tone of the whole paragraph is that of oral delivery. It opens with the injunction "sachiez," a customary address to a listening audience. And, in addition to the attention-getting "tel con je vos dirai," Villehardouin employs an emphatic repetition such as might occur in a popular narration: "Porce que cil pardons fu issi granz" and "porce que li pardons ere si granz."

5. *La Chanson de Roland,* ed. J. Bédier (Paris, 1924), line 716.

6. "Ordo bifurcat iter; tum limite nititur artis,/ Tum sequitur stratam naturae" (Geoffroi de Vinsauf, *Poetria Nova,* ed. E. Faral [Paris, 1924], p. 200, ll. 87-8).

7. *Cf.,* however, par. 398: "si dirons de Johannisse le roi de Blakie et de Bougrie, cui la Serre fu rendue si com vos l'avez oï retraire arriere, et qui ot occis cels en traïson qui s'erent rendu à lui, et ot chevauchié vers Salenike et ot sejorné longuement et gasté grant part de la terre." This relatively long recapitulation treats facts that were reported only four sections before in par. 394—an indication that Villehardouin is aware of the danger of confusion in these minor conquests and defeats.

8. Kressner, p. 7.

9. An interesting feature of this oral formula is the mixture of tenses that occurs in its wake. The preceding verbs are in the preterite, apart from the popular dictum "Et por ce si fait que sages qui se tient devers le mielz" in par. 231. Yet the oral formula seems sufficient to induce an automatic change of register in which the tense distribution becomes more dramatic and less predictable.

10. Nine occurrences in these 22 paragraphs alone, as opposed to 7 in pars. 300-62.

11. 47 occurrences as against 10 occurrences of "oiez." The variant "or poez savoir" occurs 7 times.

12. As Robert de Clari maintains. See *La Conquête de Constantinople,* ed. P. Lauer (Paris, 1924), par. LXXXI.

13. After this hyperbolic advertisement which could have been the opening sentence of a *cunte de fées,* the rest of the paragraph does not belie the introductory tone. The account continues with the vagueness of the *cunte*: "A cel tens ot un emperor en Costantinoble." "A cel tens" cannot be understood literally. It is not contemporaneous with the events in par. 70, but is one of those vague formulae of time that occur in an oral style. A résumé of events follows, with no time indications except the "longuement" of "Ensi le tint longuement en prison." Since in general Villehardouin is neither ignorant nor sparing of details he considers relevant to the account, his anecdotic approach here could again be interpreted as stylistic influence from the oral narrative induced by his credulous opening sentence.

14. *Cf.,* however, 371.

15. For example, "Et por ce dit hom que de mil males voies puet on retorner" (122).

16. See, for example, "onques si grant affaires ne fu empris de tant de gent puis que li monz fu estorez" (128).

17. "Et firent si grant essil que onques nus hom n'oï parler de si grant" (419) and "La rot si grant occision de gent que il n'avoit eü si grant en nulle ville ou il eüssent esté" (420).

18. Kressner, p. 5.

19. "Un des meillors barons et des plus larges et des meillors chevaliers qui fust el remanant del monde" (500).

20. The one notable omission among the various types of repetition is the intentional repetition of certain sounds either as a means of resonance, onomatopaeic suggestion, or simply as a "jeu d'esprit." The rare examples of alliteration are so heavily outweighed by non-alliterative formulae that they seem either unconscious *e. g.* "bones et belles," or else the accidental product of Villehardouin's fondness for other devices viz. annominatio: "pristrent proies assez et prisons" (486).

21. See above, pp. 269-70.

22. Anna G. Hatcher, "Tenses in the Roland," *SP* XXXIX (1942), 599.

23. In several vivid passages of direct speech in the first half of the work, Villehardouin introduces instructions resembling stage-directions for an oral narrator's purposes: "Maintenant li.VI. message s'agenoillent a lor piez mult plorant. Et li dux et tuit li autre s'escrierent tuit a une voiz, et tendent lor mains en halt, et distrent: 'Nos l'otrions! Nos l'otrions!'" (28); "li dux de Venise se dreça en estant et lor dist" (129); "Et li messages estoit devant les barons en estant et parla" (143); "se leva en piez Coenes" (144).

24. Geoffroy de Villehardouin, *La Conquête de Constantinople,* ed. E. Faral (Paris, 1938), I, 9, n. 4.

Paul Archambault (essay date 1974)

SOURCE: "Villehardouin: History in Black and White" in *Seven French Chroniclers: Witnesses to History,* Syracuse University Press, 1974, pp. 25-39, 127-29.

[In the following essay, Archambault summarizes the content of Villehardouin's Conquest of Constantinople *and reviews the debate concerning Villehardouin's motivation and sincerity. Archambault suggests that the work should be examined not as a historical document but as a work of literature "dictated by a certain vision of reality."]*

Villehardouin lived most of his life during the latter half of the twelfth century, but his ***Conquest of Constantinople,*** dictated in French from his castle in Thrace, belongs to the early thirteenth.[1] Born before 1150 at Valenciennes, about twenty miles from Troyes, Villehardouin came from one of the best-known aristocratic families of Champagne. The title of "Maréchal," which he bore from 1185 onwards, made him the grey eminence of Count Thibaud III of Champagne. When the count, along with several other French barons, annnounced at the tournament of Ecri in November 1199 that he was preparing a crusade *outremer,* it was only natural that Villehardouin should come along. Villehardouin was one of six delegates sent to Venice by the French barons in order to arrange with the doge, Enrico Dandolo, for the transportation of twenty thousand crusaders, with their horses and arms, to the Holy Land. The Fourth Crusade was in the making.

Villehardouin's activities during the entire expedition were as varied as they were essential. He was one of the barons who argued for the "necessity" of diverting the Franco-Venetian expedition to Constantinople in order to chase the usurper, Alexius Mourtzouphlos, from the Byzantine throne. When Mourtzouphlos, terrified by the presence of the fleet in the harbor of the city, abdicated and fled in June 1203, Villehardouin was delegated by the French army to obtain from the rightful emperor, Isaac II, a confirmation of the commitments that had been made to the crusaders by his son, the young Alexius Angelus. After the conquest and sack of Constantinople by the crusaders in April 1204, and the ensuing conquest of Thrace, Villehardouin almost single-handedly avoided a civil war between the two most powerful barons, Boniface de Montferrat and Baldwin of Flanders, and their factions over the question of the occupation of Thessalonica.

Villehardouin was both a distinguished negotiator and a courageous warrior. After the death of Matthieu de Montmorency, he became the leader of the Champagne faction of the French army, and (between 1205 and 1208) participated in several victorious campaigns in Thrace. In 1205 he was named "Maréchal de Champagne et de Roumaine." He died between 1212 and 1218. The exact time and place of his death are unknown.

Villehardouin's chronicle records the events he witnessed between the year 1198, when the hermit Fulk of Neuilly began preaching the Fourth Crusade, and the year 1207, when Boniface de Montferrat was killed by the Bulgars in Thrace. He does not seem to have divided his account into books or chapters, but it happens, quite naturally, to fall into two parts. In Part One (chapters 1-58 of Edmond Faral's edition) he relates the chain of events leading up to

the conquest of Constantinople in April 1204: Fulk of Neuilly's predication throughout the Ile de France; Villehardouin's trip to Venice; his agreement with the doge over the matter of maritime transportation; the assembly of the barons and knights at Venice; the conquest of Zara; the arrival of the fleet before Constantinople; the first conquest of the city; the restoration of the young Alexius Angelus after the capitulation of Alexius Mourtzouphlos; the conspiracy of Mourtzouphlos; the second conquest and the sack of the city by the crusaders and the coronation of Baldwin of Flanders as Latin emperor of Constantinople. The second part of the narrative (volume II of the Faral edition) is a frequently tedious but lucid account of the events that separate Baldwin's coronation from the death of Boniface de Montferrat (1204-1207): the conquest of Thrace; the dispute between Baldwin and Boniface over the possession of Thessalonica; Baldwin's death at the hands of Johanis of Bulgaria; the coronation of Henry of Flanders as second Latin emperor; Henry's war against Johanis; and the death of Boniface, killed by the Bulgars in September 1207.

Throughout his account, Villehardouin argues vigorously that the failure on the part of many crusading barons and their soldiers to assemble at Venice in 1202, as the treaty with the Venetians had stipulated a year earlier, set off an unavoidable chain of events that resulted in the change of course of the crusade from its original destination of Saracen Egypt to Constantinople. Impeded in their sincere attempt to honor their financial engagements with the Venetians because of the betrayal of "those who sailed from other ports," so the argument goes, the crusaders who sailed from Venice were compelled to help the Venetians in their conquest of Zara (a city on the Dalmatian coast long coveted by the doge) and to accept a plan submitted by the young refugee, prince Alexius Angelus, that would restore his imprisoned father, Isaac, to his rightful throne as emperor of Constantinople, provided Isaac were later to participate in the crusade.

More than a century ago Natalis de Wailly was the first to inquire whether Villehardouin was telling the story of the Fourth Crusade as he knew it, and much critical ink has flowed either to support or to challenge Villehardouin's sincerity.[2] Whether or not Villehardouin knew of a secret pact between the Venetians and the Sultan of Cairo; whether or not he knew, even before the Fourth Crusade was under way, that its real destination was Constantinople; whether or not he was aware of Dandolo's designs on the Byzantine city, no one has as yet been able to ascertain. The following pages will not resolve this problem, but they will attempt to detect concealed emotional charges, "blind spots," and unguarded revelations. In apologetic or confessional works of literature, verbal idiosyncracies and tones of voice can be as significant as the facts themselves—the most defensive part of the author's testimony.

No account of the Fourth Crusade can afford to overlook Robert de Clari (ca. 1170-after 1216), a footsoldier who accompanied Pierre d'Amiens and Hugues de Saint Pol on the Fourth Crusade. His brief account of the expedition, *Those Who Conquered Constantinople,* written from the fighting man's point of view, provides an important cross reference in order to verify or refute Villehardouin's account.[3] It is significant, perhaps even symbolic, that Robert brought back from his trip to Constantinople a number of religious relics to the artistic value of which he was totally indifferent—significant in that he managed to reduce his moral conscience to silence and justify, at least to himself, one of the most curious chapters in the history of medieval plunder; symbolic in that, unlike Villehardouin and other leaders of the expedition, Robert does not seem to have realized the importance or to have foreseen the consequences of his actions. His brief chronicle is wrapped in a shroud of insuperable ignorance. He participated in none of the great decisions; he did not know that the plan to attack Constantinople had been hatched since or before the departure of the expedition from Venice; he knew nothing about the military strategy that had preceded the battles in which he fought, a lackluster and solipsistic figure; he knew nothing, finally, about the art works he plundered or the cities he helped devastate.

Villehardouin was intelligent enough to be a scoundrel. Robert could never have been more than an amiable Boeotian. Of doubts, hesitations, and moral misgivings he seems to have had few; but neither his moral conscience nor his sense of logic was sufficiently honed to permit him to arrive at any significant conclusions. He described the palaces, homes, churches, and abbeys of Constantinople with an engaging stupidity, and seemed unable to tell one proper noun from another. He was fascinated by certain Byzantine objects which he had never seen in France—the *buhotian,* for example, which the Byzantines used as an oxygen mask. His account of those who conquered Constantinople might easily have fallen into oblivion, an energetic but jumbled tale, but its worth lies in its momentary flashes of conscience that offer an embarrassing refutation to Villehardouin's glib and all too symmetrical apologetics.

Medieval scholars are usually either hostile or favorable to Villehardouin, and the author of *The Conquest of Constantinople* might, to a certain extent, be to blame for the controversy that surrounds his name. He is that sort of military chronicler who is forever dividing the world into two camps: the attacker without the walls and the defender within; those "who sail from Venice" and those "who sail from other ports"; those "who wish to disband the army" and those "who wish to keep it together"; those "whom God loves" and those "whom He ceases to love."[4] The Manichaean Villehardouin elicits Manichaean responses: perhaps that is why scholars feel compelled to take up the gauntlet of the debate that bears his name, either to defend his sincerity or to accuse him of concealing part of the truth about the altered destination of the Fourth Crusade from Egypt to Constantinople.

But perhaps that is not the only way to read *The Conquest of Constantinople.* If Villehardouin's chronicle were to be judged not as a historical document but as a literary creation dictated by a certain vision of reality, then the value of the work might depend entirely upon the artistic, intellectual, and moral qualities of the mind that produced it.[5] Villehardouin's chronicle tells the reader a good deal about the Fourth Crusade, but it incidentally tells him even more about the author's way of structuring his inner and outer vision. The problem of Villehardouin's sincerity has both a historical and a psychological sense; and, though it may perhaps never be possible to know whether Villehardouin was sincere in a factual sense, his language betrays a highly selective visual technique enabling the man quite literally to disregard whatever he consciously or unwittingly decides to exclude from his field of vision.

He seems to have been an eye witness to those moving sermons preached by the hermit Fulk of Neuilly, which open the chronicle. They were being attended by large audiences throughout the Ile de France and surrounding provinces—a convincing indication of the man's popular appeal. Success, whatever the enterprise, is an unmistakable sign of divine favor: "God worked many miracles," and Frenchmen throughout the Ile de France decide to enlist in the crusade preached by the hermit because of the generous terms of the indulgence promised by the papal legate to France: "Because this indulgence was so great, the hearts of the people were quite moved; and many enlisted because the indulgence was so great."[6]

In the spring of 1199, the barons assembled at Compiègne in order to decide when and from which port they would depart for *outremer.* In a familiar phrase, Villehardouin relates that "many points of view were put forward," but the essential outcome of the gathering was that he was one of six "best messengers" chosen to make final arrangements for the expedition, "with full power to settle what should be done, exactly as if they were their lords in person."[7]

At the age of fifty or so, Villehardouin was thus fulfilling what it is not presumptuous to call a lifelong ambition: to act and speak with the full power of a count. Villehardouin, the Marshal of Champagne, had the temporary privilege of acting and speaking like his master Thibaut de Champagne! One imagines him during that scenic if arduous trip on horseback from Compiègne to Venice wrapped entirely in thoughts of power and prestige. One must perforce imagine him thus, as he does not seem to have paused to record a single visual detail. A Froissart in the same circumstances would have riddled every Alpine innkeeper with questions, described every landscape, and collected every folktale along the way. Not so with Villehardouin. On such an important mission as this, he cannot afford to waste his time or disperse his attention: "The six messengers departed, . . . conferred among themselves, and decided that in Venice they were likely to find a greater number of ships than in any other port. And they journeyed on horseback in stages until they arrived at their destination the first week in Lent."[8]

Villehardouin's account of the treaty signed in 1201 with the Venetians is one of his finest pieces of factual reporting. When the aged doge, Enrico Dandolo, tells Villehardouin and his companions that they must wait four days before he can summon the members of his council and present the French requests, Villehardouin notes quite simply that "the envoys waited until the fourth day, as the doge had appointed and then returned to the palace, which was a most beautiful building and very richly furnished."[9] Like so much of Villehardouin's "bridge material," such an incidental remark might reveal more about the narrator's psychological and visual equipment than many of his more consciously florid passages. Had Villehardouin been endowed with great esthetic interest, would he not have paused at this point of his account, even a dozen years later, to describe his impressions of Venice during that four-day waiting period? But Villehardouin's is a practical, rather than a visual or speculative temper. To him, the act of seeing is a selective process and a preamble to action. Like a man of action, Villehardouin considers visual description a waste of time and energy. One is attentive to reality not in order to see it, but to act upon it. Inactive moments are spent not in dreams but in expectations: "They waited until the day he had fixed."[10]

Although shorn of visual interest, Villehardouin's account of the mission to Venice has an abstract geometric pattern. The doge's attempts to persuade the Venetian citizenry to grant the requests of the French envoys are drawn in concentric circles. First the doge is alone; four days later he presents the French proposals to his privy council, which approves them; three days later he summons his Grand Council, composed of forty of the wisest and most influential Venetian citizens; finally, "he brought them all to . . . approve and agree to accept the proposed covenant, . . . persuading first a few, then more, then still more, till at last all the members of his council expressed their approval and consent. After this he assembled a good ten thousand of the common people in the church of San Marco—the most beautiful church in the world—where he invited them to hear a Mass of the Holy Spirit, and pray to God for guidance concerning the request the envoys had made to them."[11]

Villehardouin sees reality more like an architect than a painter; like a strategist, he draws not with a brush but with a chalk and compass. Indeed, one is impressed in general by the poverty of Villehardouin's coloring, the one tint that seems worthy of his attention being vermilion.[12]

In a moving discourse at San Marco Villehardouin implores the people of Venice to take pity on Jerusalem and to join the French barons in the crusade. Then the six French envoys kneel at the feet of the crowd in tears. The doge and all the others cry out in a single voice, "'We do agree! We do agree!' Then there was such a noise that it seemed as if the earth was falling. . . . When the great tumult had subsided, and this great show of pity, which surpassed anything that had ever been seen, the good duke of Venice, a very wise and courageous man, went up to the lectern and said to the people: 'My lords, see what an honor God has given us. . . .' I cannot recount all of the Duke's good and beautiful words."[13]

A memorable passage, but again how visually poor! How were the envoys dressed? Where were they kneeling? Where was the crowd standing? The reader must, like an imaginative archeologist, recreate the scene as if Villehardouin had provided a mere sketch or fragment. He must add epithets of color and sound to sentences that are almost entirely constructed with substantives and active verbs. Villehardouin's reluctance to recount "all of the duke's good words" reveals a distaste for digressive detail and an unquestionable talent for bringing out the inner meaning of an event, however biased the interpretation.

Villehardouin's habitual indifference to visual and intellectual nuance seems even more pronounced after the departure from Venice. The French barons have assembled at Venice in the spring of 1202, a year after the treaty with the Venetians. Of the eighty-five thousand marks requested by the Venetians for transporting the crusading army to Egypt, the barons have managed to a pay little better than fifty thousand, many of them having decided to sail from Flanders and Marseille. Perhaps Villehardouin is correct in arguing that it is the failure of all the barons to live up to the conditions of the treaty with Venice that compelled those who sailed from Venice to accept the altered course of the crusade.[14] His universe, in any case, is henceforth irrevocably divided between "those who sailed from Venice" and "those who sailed from other ports," and any action after the departure from Venice is motivated either by a treacherous desire to disband the army or by a patriotic attempt to keep it together. There can be no other way of seeing reality. Those who wish to disband the army are intended to resemble the fallen angels of a Manichaean heaven, even if their vision happens to have the greater number of adherents. Although the majority of the barons declare, at Venice, that they will shift for themselves and go some other way if the Venetians refuse to transport them to Egypt, Villehardouin suspects them of merely wishing to disband the army and return home. The enlightened, disinterested minority to which Villehardouin belongs is alone capable of acting nobly and in keeping with the divine mandates: "We'd much rather give all we have and go as poor men with the army than see it broken up and our enterprise a failure. For God will doubtless repay us in His own good time."[15]

As the chronicle progresses, Villehardouin's conscious selection of detail appears to grow more and more willfully systematic. One notices that he consistently views and represents reality in a contrast of light and shade which permits him to shape the contours of his narrative. His vision, in short, seems less a direct projection than a byproduct of contrasting light and shadow. With each advancing page, Villehardouin's "enlightened" viewpoint is forcefully, dogmatically projected against the foil of his adversaries' "dark" motives.

At Venice, in the summer of 1202, the leaders of the French army discover that, because many members of the crusading army have sailed from other ports, it will be impossible for them to pay the Venetians the full sum of money that was agreed upon at the treaty signed the year before. A few of the barons then propose that barons and foot-soldiers alike make up for the missing sum by contributing voluntarily of their money and goods. A majority of the crusaders argue against this proposal by stating that the sum they have already paid for their own passage is quite enough: "and if the Venetians are willing to take us, we're quite ready to go. If not we'll make shift for ourselves, and go some other way." Villehardouin cannot accept the good faith of such an argument and immediately accuses the majority of the crusaders of acting for some latent darker purpose: "They said this in actual fact, because they would have liked the army to be disbanded, and each man free to go home." Right after the meeting a few of the barons decide to set an example for the rest of the army by handing over all or most of their personal possessions to a common fund. Here Villehardouin describes the situation as a struggle between the niggling and destructive forces of darkness, who wish to disband the army, and the enlightened, disinterested few who share the narrator's opinion. And if it is the latter opinion that prevails, it is simply that God, "who gives hope to men in the depths of despair, was not willing" for the other side to have its way.[16]

Such a vision in black and white leads him to overdramatize the presence of the dark forces surrounding him and wishing him ill. Villehardouin is a master of the technique, well know to the professionally military, which consists of painting the darkest possible picture of what the enemy might do if he is not immediately wiped out. Hence the devastation and plunder of the Dalmatian city of Zara during the winter of 1203 is described as a "precaution" against the king of Hungary, to whom it belongs. Almost to reassure himself, Villehardouin adds dramatically "that the hearts of our people were not at peace, for one party was continually working to break up the army and the other to keep it together."[17] Surely such a "beautiful, prosperous and strongly defended" city as Zara could only be taken "with the help of God Himself!"[18]

Villehardouin's vision often loses all sense of perspective and proportion. Small objects are magnified and large ones made almost invisible. When Pope Innocent III excommunicates the barons for the crime of destroying the Christian city of Zara, his attitude is described merely as one of "displeasure."[19] The annihilation of the city by the Venetians, before the departure for Corfu, is described in a fleeting sentence: "The Venetians razed the city and its towers and walls."[20] Whereas the sight of a ravaged enemy city appears to be only a part of the logic of warfare, the defection from the army of several French barons is described much more strongly as "a great misfortune for the army, and a great disgrace to those who left it."[21] Villehardouin is adept at highlighting those events he wishes to dramatize. He is equally effective at blurring or dimming the reader's vision of an event that might prove embarrassing, the assembly of the French barons at Zara, for example. The barons have just proposed to the army that if they help the young Alexius Angelus reconquer the throne

of Constantinople from his uncle, the usurper Mourtzouphlos, he will bring the Byzantine empire back under the religious jurisdiction of Rome, pay the French barons two hundred thousand silver marks, and accompany the crusaders to Egypt with an army of ten thousand men.[22] There follows "a great divergence of opinion in the assembly. The Cistercian abbot of Vaux had something to say, in common with those who were eager to have the army disbanded. They all declared they would never give their consent, since it would mean marching against Christians. They had not left their home to do any such thing, and for their part wished to go to Syria."[23] The abbot's declaration makes one wonder why Villehardouin should then wish to blur the clarity of the issues involved by adding that "there was discord in the army. Nor can you wonder if the laymen were at loggerheads when the Cistercians accompanying the forces were equally at variance with each other."[24] The narrator thus subtly manages to blame the disarray of the army on the Cistercian abbots' confusion rather than on the moral untenability of the barons' proposal. Rather than reproducing reality, Villehardouin is creating an artificial windstorm of confusion, presumably to make the reader infer either that the moral issues are impossible to resolve or that the army is hopelessly divided.[25] The incidental minutiae will, Villehardouin seems to hope, blur the embarrassing conclusion that only twelve persons in all took the oaths on behalf of the French; no more could be persuaded to come forward.[26]

The reader is left wondering by what juridical ploy a party of twelve barons managed to decide the destiny of more than twenty thousand crusaders. Rather than be forced to answer such a question, Villehardouin chooses immediately to distract the reader's attention to the great number of desertions taking place: "During this time many men from the lower ranks deserted and escaped in merchant ships. About five hundred of them got away in one ship, but all of them lost their lives by drowning. Another group escaped by land, thinking to travel safely through Sclavonia; but the people of that country attacked them, killing a great number, and those who were left came flying back to the army. Thus our forces dwindled seriously from day to day."[27]

But the reader refuses to be distracted. How did the barons manage to convince the army that the altered course to Constantinople was morally acceptable? Strategists like Villehardouin know how useful tears can be in reducing logical structures. Whether or not they are historically factual, tears serve to blur description and provide the chronicler with an added excuse to heighten the dramatic nature of a critical moment: "The marquis [Boniface de Montferrat] and those with him fell at the feet of the other party, weeping bitterly, and said they would not get up again until these men had promised not to go away and leave them. . . . And when the others saw them they were filled with a great pity and wept sorely when they saw their lords, their relatives, and their friends fallen at their feet; and they said they would confer together and withdrew. Their decision was that they would remain with the army until Michaelmas, provided the leaders would solemnly swear on the gospels."[28]

Robert de Clari seems to have witnessed the same event with a drier eye:

> Then all the barons of the host were summoned by the Venetians. And when they were all assembled, the doge of Venice rose and spoke to them. "Lords," said the doge, "now we have a good excuse for going to Constantinople, if you approve of it, for we have the rightful heir." Now there were some who did not at all approve of going to Constantinople. Instead they said: "Bah! What shall we be doing in Constantinople? We have our pilgrimage to make, and also our plan of going to Babylon or Alexandria. Moreover, our navy is to follow us for only a year, and half of the year is already past." And the others said in answer: "What shall we do in Babylon or Alexandria when we have neither the provisions nor the money to enable us to go there? Better for us before we go there to secure provisions and money by some good excuse than to go there and die of hunger. . . ." And the marquis de Montferrat was at more pains to urge them to go to Constantinople than anyone else who was there, because he wanted to avenge himself for an injury for which the marquis hated the emperor of Constantinople. . . . Then the bishops answered that it would not be a sin but rather a righteous deed.[29]

The departure of the Franco-Venetian fleet from Corfu "on the eve of the Pentecost" (1203) is the most far-reaching and panoramic sight of Villehardouin's chronicle: "It seemed, indeed, that here was a fleet that might well conquer lands, for as far as the eye could reach there was nothing to be seen but sails outspread on all that vast array of ships, so that every man's heart was filled with joy at the sight."[30] Villehardouin, however, cannot help revealing himself even when enraptured. His visual attention is above all a process of exclusion ordained toward action; his joy at the sight of the fleet is neither an esthetic nor a moral response but an anticipation of action: "Here was a fleet that might well conquer lands." "There was nothing to be seen but sail outspread" is a curious admission that his visual field had excluded everything else. The common spectator like Robert de Clari knows that when a fleet like this lifts anchor, there is far more to be seen than sails outspread: "When the fleet left the port of Venice with its galleys, rich warships and so many other vessels, it was the most beautiful sight since the beginning of the world. For there were a hundred pairs of trumpets, made of silver as well as brass, sounding together at the weighing of the anchors, and so many bells and drums and other instruments that it was marvelous to behold. When the fleet was out to sea and had spread its sails and raised the banners and ensigns high on the masts, the whole sea seemed afire glittering with the ships upon it pouring out their joy."[31]

Villehardouin's exclusion of material unrelated to the action or purpose at hand applies to interior as well as exterior perceptions. At Cape Malia, in the southern Peloponnesus, the fleet happens to encounter two ships on their way back from Syria, "full of knights, sergeants, and pilgrims who were part of the company that had gone to that country by way of Marseille." Unwilling to trust the Venetians or to accept the mystifications of Boniface de Montferrat, these crusaders and the other barons had decided to sail directly for Syria. When they encountered the large fleet, a sergeant in one of the ships from Syria told his friends that he was going to join the expedition, "for it certainly seems to me they'll win some land for themselves."[32] Unable to resist the temptation to moralize, Villehardouin attributes the sergeant's gesture to a pious turn of heart: "And, after all, as people are wont to say, no matter how often a man can have gone astray, he can still come round to the right way in the end."[33] The comment does not seem to be made ironically, and it does not speak highly for Villehardouin's intuitions. It never seems to have occurred to the narrator that the sergeant's real motive might have been not to "come round to the right way" but to satisfy his appetite for gain. Such is one of the major paradoxes of Villehardouin's personality: his lucidity and intellectual rigor feed on truisms and reassuring platitudes. Even when he examines the human psyche he manages to exclude what he does not wish to see. Whether he is looking at the world or considering the arguments of those moral objectors "who wished to destroy the army," Villehardouin seems to see and hear only what his senses and his viewpoint care to admit.

When he first arrives within sight of Constantinople from the sea of Marmara, Villehardouin seems particularly impressed by such quantitative dimensions as the length, breadth, and height of the city: "I can assure you that all those who had never seen Constantinople before gazed very intently at the city, having never imagined there could be so fine a place in all the world. They noted the high walls and lofty towers encircling it, and its rich palaces and tall churches, of which there were so many that no one could have believed it to be true if he had not seen it with his own eyes, and viewed the length and breadth of that city which reigns supreme over all the others. There was indeed no man so brave and daring that his flesh did not shudder at the sight."[34]

Throughout his account of the siege and conquest of the city, Constantinople remains an object of eventual possession rather than of visual perception. One gathers the impression that the city is an abstract, two-dimensional configuration of lines being examined in headquarters, on a military map. Neither ships nor scaling ladders nor land nor sea nor horses are given any concrete dimensions; nor is the city viewed from a recognizable geographical perspective: "The Venetians were strongly of the opinion that the scaling ladders should be set up on the ships and the whole assault be made from the sea. The French, for their part, protested that they could not give such a good account of themselves on sea as the Venetians; but once on land, with their horses and their proper equipment, they could do much better service. So in the end it was decided that the Venetians would launch their attack from the sea while the barons and their army would tackle the enemy by land."[35]

Yet some of the scenes are recorded "live." The first of three great fires within the city's walls is observed from the shore opposite the port, near the tower of Galata, whence Villehardouin commands a broad and relatively close view of the city's walls: "The fire was so great and horrible that no one was able to extinguish or control it. When the barons in the camp on the other side of the port saw it, they were sorely afflicted, seeing the high churches and rich palaces crumble and collapse, and the great commercial quarters burn. . . . The fire spread beyond the port toward the most densely populated part of the city, until it reached the sea on one side near the church of Saint Sophia. . . . As it burned, the fire extended easily over a mile and a half of land."[36]

Villehardouin seems to be standing on the very same spot several months later as he watches the Venetians foil the Greeks' attempt to burn the crusading fleet:

> One night, at midnight, they set fire to their ships, hoisted the sails, and let the ships flame, so that it seemed as if the shore was on fire. The Greek ships floated toward the crusaders' fleet. The alarm went off in the camp. All ran to take up their arms. The Venetians and all those who owned ships scrambled to their ships and set about protecting them as best they could. And Geoffroy de Villehardouin, the Marshal of Champagne, who has composed this work, can testify that never did a seafaring people better manage than the Venetians. They leaped into the galleys and rowboats of their ships, grappled the Greek ships with hooks, and pulled them with all their strength (while their enemies looked on) into the current of the sea of Marmara, and let them sail in flames down toward the sea. There were so many Greeks on the far shore that it was impossible to count them; and the din was so great that it seemed as if the earth and the sky were falling.[37]

When Constantinople is sacked by the army in April 1204, however, the chronicler's eye is distracted by the various foci of action and dispersed ubiquitously throughout the city:

> The Marquis de Montferrat rode straight along the shore to the palace of Bucoleon. As soon as he arrived there the place was surrendered to him. . . . In the same way that the palace of Bucoleon was surrendered to the Marquis de Montferrat, so the palace of Blachernae was yielded to the Comte de Flandre's brother Henri, and on the same conditions. . . . There too was found a great store of treasure, not less than there had been in the palace of Bucoleon. . . . The rest of the army, scattered throughout the city, also gained much booty; so much, indeed, that no one could estimate its amount or its value. It included gold and silver, table-services and precious stones, satin and silk, mantles of squirrel fur, ermine and miniver, and every choicest thing to be found on this earth. Geoffroy de Villehardouin here declares that, to his knowledge, so much booty had never been gained in any city since the creation of the world. . . . So the troops of the crusaders and the Venetians . . . all rejoiced and gave thanks to our Lord for the honour and the victory he had granted them . . . so that those who had been poor now lived in wealth and luxury.[38]

But even this, one of the most large-scale of Villehardouin's pictures, excludes all embarrassing detail. Without going so far as to recall Delacroix's flamboyant recreation of the sack of the city, one has only to read the contemporary Byzantine chronicler Nicetas Choniates in order to realize that Villehardouin's picture is a whitened one indeed:

> The lust of the army spared neither maiden nor the virgin dedicated to God. Violence and debauchery were everywhere present; cries and lamentations and the groans of the pilgrims were heard throughout the city; for everywhere pillage was unrestrained and lust unbridled. The city was in wild confusion. Nobles, old men, women, and children ran to and fro trying to save their wealth, their honor, and their lives. Knights, foot-soldiers, and Venetian sailors jostled each other in a mad scramble for plunder. Threats of ill treatment, promises of safety if wealth were disgorged, mingled with the cries of many sufferers. These pious brigands . . . acted as if they had received a licence to commit every crime.[39]

So complex, so morally embarrassing is the event that Villehardouin must fall back upon his habitual defenses of selection and distraction to describe it. Selection of visual detail is a rather easy process: one simply excludes what one does not wish to see. But how does the writer distract the reader's attention when describing the climactic event of a chronicle? By overdramatizing the dangers of the situation and creating a "new enemy." To the ranks of those iniquitous sons of darkness who had "sailed from other ports," of those enemies "who wished to disband the army," of those Byzantine Greeks who did the French army so much harm by attempting to defend their own city, Villehardouin adds a fourth group of enemies, the soldiers within the crusading army who refused to surrender their plunder to the barons: "Some performed this duty conscientiously; others, prompted by covetousness, that never-failing source of all evil, proved less honest."[40]

His Manichaean world is henceforth divided between the "righteous" sackers of cities, who dutifully surrender their spoils, and the "unrighteous," who try to keep theirs: "From the very first, those who were prone to this vice began to keep some things back and became, in consequence, less pleasing to our Lord. Ah! God, how loyally they had behaved up to now! And up to now, in all their undertakings, our Lord had shown his gracious care for them and had exalted them above all people. But those who do right often have to suffer for the misdeeds of the unrighteous."[41]

The second half of Villehardouin's chronicle is a tedious recitation of the battles fought between those who do right and those who do wrong, of new enemies either defeated or victorious. "Such an arduous task it was to found the Latin empire in Greece," he might have concluded with a Vergilian turn of phrase, "when so many enemies were opposed to the designs of providence: Greeks, Wallachians, Bulgars, not to mention the dissident factions within the conquering army!" The chronicler's account of the events that occur between the election of Baldwin of Flanders as emperor of Constantinople (May 1204) and the death of Boniface de Montferrat (September 1207) is a dry enumeration of sieges, battles, and conquests in Thrace, on the Greek Mainland, in the Peloponnesus, and in Asia Minor. It is almost as if Villehardouin himself found the events that followed the sack of the city to be anticlimactic and hardly worth the reader's interest.

After the conquest Villehardouin never so much as alludes to the possibility of a departure for *outremer.* So much has happened since Venice that the reader will (one hopes) have forgotten that the expedition originally began as a crusade against the Infidel. The account of the events of 1204-1207 is but a prolonged distraction intended to discourage the reader from inquiring why, after conquering the city and liquidating their debt with the Venetians, the French barons thought it necessary to conquer the entire Greek empire rather than get down to the business of continuing the crusade.

Selection, discoloration, exclusion, dramatization, obfuscation of issues, distraction—such are a few of the major components of Villehardouin's narrative technique. Though it would be presumptuous to argue that a study of this technique allows one to bring a definitive answer to the "Villehardouin debate," it does seem to permit an evaluation of it. Historians will perhaps never know whether Villehardouin willfully concealed some facts as to the origins of the Fourth Crusade; but his visual and psychic makeup were such that, had he known these facts, he would probably have selected them carefully and rigorously. Can one conclude otherwise when one sees him so selective in depicting even harmless and unembarrassing events?

Approaching the problem of Villehardouin's sincerity by way of narrative technique serves the further purpose of providing a different opinion of the author's character. One fails to see that "mixture of simplicity and nobility that are characteristically his."[42] One finds it hard to respond to those "energetic, adventurous, rough and loyal spirits of the conquerors of Constantinople," or those "tears of pity" that Sainte-Beuve praises in a highly rhetorical passage.[43] One finds it impossible, finally, to agree with Edmond Faral's all too flattering picture of Villehardouin the loyal and courageous soldier.[44]

Such glorified images of Villehardouin are perhaps better discarded. Of his love of courage it can surely be said that he admired it selectively, in those who happened to share his views; and it might be argued that his "rough and loyal" character is largely the product of his selective perceptions. Villehardouin strikes some readers as a man of immoderate ambition whose talent for discourse and political compromise was largely self-serving. His fascination for wealth, plunder, and reputation impoverished his better impulses; despite his wealth of experience, his visual memory remains poor, rough, and discolored; the result is

a sketchy, unshaded, and curiously defensive picture of the most important event of his age.

Notes

1. Textual references are to G. de Villehardouin, *La Conquête de Constantinople,* edited by E. Faral (Paris: Les Belles Lettres, 1938). Biographical material on Villehardouin has been taken from R. Bossuat, art., "Geoffroi de Villehardouin," *Dictionnaire des lettres francaises* (Paris: A Fayard, 1964), pp. 304-307.

2. For a discussion of the problem of Villehardouin's sincerity, see Villehardouin, *La Conquête,* I, xvi-xxxvii; D. E. Queller and S. J. Stratton, "A Century of Controversy on the Fourth Crusade," in *Studies in Medieval and Renaissance History,* edited by William M. Bowsky (Lincoln: University of Nebraska Press, 1969), VI, 235-77.

3. Robert de Clari, *De chiaus qui conquistrent Constantinople,* edited by Philippe Lauer (Paris: H. Champion, 1924). Biographical material on Robert has been taken from U. T. Holmes, art., "Robert de Clari," *Dictionnaire des lettres francaises, Le Moyen âge,* p. 639.

4. For a summary of the controversy on the origins of the Fourth Crusade, see Queller and Stratton, "A Century of Controversy on the Fourth Crusade," in *Studies in Medieval and Renaissance History,* edited by Bowsky, 233-77. I have used M. R. B. Shaw's translation of Villehardouin, *Joinville and Villehardouin: Chronicles of the Crusades* (London: Penguin Books, 1963), and E. H. McNeal's edition and translation of Robert de Clari, *The Conquest of Constantinople* (New York: Columbia University Press, 1939). Whenever I have disagreed with these translations I have provided my own. On Villehardouin's habit of dividing the world into opposite camps, see *La Conquête,* I, par. 86, 87, 100, 234, 236.

5. A. Pauphilet, *Le Legs du moyen âge* (Melun: d'Argences, 1950), p. 219.

6. *La Conquête,* I, par. 2.

7. Ibid., par. 11.

8. Ibid., par. 14.

9. Ibid., par. 18.

10. Ibid.

11. Ibid., par. 25.

12. The one adjective of color that retains his attention is the *vermilion* of the Byzantine emperor's boots (ibid., par. 227, and again par. 245).

13. Ibid., par. 27-29.

14. Ibid., par. 57.

15. Ibid., par. 60.

16. E.g., ibid., par. 61: "Those who had retained their possessions were highly delighted and refused to

add anything of their own, since they were now quite confident that the army would be broken up and the troops dispersed. But God . . . was not willing for this to happen."

17. Ibid., par. 100.

18. Ibid., par. 77: "Comment porroit estre prise tel ville par force, se Diex meïsmes nel fait?"

19. Ibid., par. 105.

20. Ibid., par. 108.

21. Ibid., par. 110.

22. Ibid., par. 93.

23. Ibid., par. 95-97.

24. Ibid.

25. Villehardouin's clever game of obfuscation has succeeded down to the present. In his Introduction to *La Conquête,* I, xxii, Faral argues that the refusal of the Abbot of Vaux and Simon de Montfort to attack Constantinople did not prevent them, several years later, from destroying the Albigensians, "des hérétiques, mais pourtant des chrétiens." The point at issue is not whether the dissenters were contradictory in their conduct. One might simply remark that not unlike Villehardouin, Faral almost succeeds in distracting the reader's attention from the event at hand toward an ulterior and unrelated event.

26. Ibid., par. 99. Villehardouin attempts further to blur the embarrassing central issue by narrating it in an impersonal style as if it had been witnessed by someone else: "And the book says that there were only 12 who took the oath."

27. Ibid., par. 101.

28. Ibid., par. 116-17.

29. Robert de Clari, *The Conquest of Constantinople,* translated by E. H. McNeal (New York: Columbia University Press, 1939), pp. 59-66.

30. *La Conquête,* I, par. 120.

31. Robert de Clari, *La Conquête de Constantinople,* edited by Ph. Lauer (Paris, 1924), ch. XIII (my translation).

32. *La Conquête,* I, par. 122.

33. Ibid.: "Et por ce dit hom que de mil males voies puet on retorner."

34. Ibid., par. 128.

35. Ibid., par. 162.

36. Ibid., par. 204.

37. Ibid., II, par. 218.

38. Ibid., II, par. 249-51.

39. Nicetas Choniates, *Devastatio* quoted in E. Pears, *The Fall of Constantinople* (New York, 1886), pp. 354-55.

40. *La Conquête,* II, par. 253. One should note the Manichaean language of Villehardouin's text: "Li uns aporta *bien* et li autres *mauvaisement.*" Robert de Clari gives a less biased account of the event: "Afterwards it was ordered that all the wealth of the spoils should be brought to a certain church in the city. The wealth was brought there, and they took ten knights, high men, of the pilgrims, and ten of the Venetians who were thought to be honorable, and set them to guard the wealth. . . . And each one of the rich men took gold ornaments or cloth of silk and gold or anything else he wanted and carried it off. So in this way they began to rob the treasure, so that nothing was shared with the common people of the host or the poor knights or the sergeants who had helped to win the treasure" (McNeal translation, pp. 101-102).

41. *La Conquête,* II, par. 256-500.

42. Pauphilet, *Le Legs,* p. 95.

43. C. A. Sainte-Beuve, "G. de Villehardouin," *Causeries du lundi,* 6 février 1854, p. 412. Sainte-Beuve's portrait of Villehardouin ends on a dithyrambic note: "He has tears of pity beneath his visor, but he does not overuse them. He can get down on both knees, and without weakness, get up his feet again. His even temper and his common sense are equal to the situations in which he finds himself. In the breach to the very end of the battle, he carries his sword intrepidly and his pen simply. Among historians who also qualify as men of action, he is one of the most honorable and complete of his time."

44. *La Conquête,* I, xxx-xxxvii: "He was a lord. He belonged to the order of chivalry whose law was composed of two commandments: be faithful and be brave."

FURTHER READING

Criticism

Beer, Jeanette M. A. "Truth and Propaganda." In *Narrative Conventions of Truth in the Middle Ages,* pp. 109-13. Genève: Librairie Droz S. A., 1981.

Argues that the purpose of Villehardouin's *Conquête de Constantinople* was one of justification and persuasion, analyzing his language in the text to support this claim.

Grégoire, Henri. "The Question of the Diversion of the Fourth Crusade; or, An Old Controversy Solved by a Latin Adverb." *Byzantion* XV (1940-41): 158-66.

Maintains that the "diversion" of the Fourth Crusade from its original purposes to the conquest of Constantinople had been intended from the onset and was not a result of unplanned events.

How to Use This Index

Literary Criticism Series
Cumulative Author Index

Anderson, C. Farley
See Mencken, H(enry) L(ouis); Nathan, George Jean

Anderson, Jessica (Margaret) Queale 1916-
CLC 37
See also CA 9-12R; CANR 4, 62

Anderson, Jon (Victor) 1940- . **CLC 9; DAM POET**
See also CA 25-28R; CANR 20

Anderson, Lindsay (Gordon)
1923-1994 .... **CLC 20**
See also CA 125; 128; 146; CANR 77

Anderson, Maxwell 1888-1959 .... **TCLC 2; DAM DRAM**
See also CA 105; 152; DLB 7; MTCW 2

Anderson, Poul (William) 1926- .... **CLC 15**
See also AAYA 5; CA 1-4R, 181; CAAE 181; CAAS 2; CANR 2, 15, 34, 64; CLR 58; DLB 8; INT CANR-15; MTCW 1, 2; SATA 90; SATA-Brief 39; SATA-Essay 106

Anderson, Robert (Woodruff)
1917- .... **CLC 23; DAM DRAM**
See also AITN 1; CA 21-24R; CANR 32; DLB 7

Anderson, Sherwood 1876-1941 ..... **TCLC 1, 10, 24; DA; DAB; DAC; DAM MST, NOV; SSC 1; WLC**
See also AAYA 30; CA 104; 121; CANR 61; CDALB 1917-1929; DA3; DLB 4, 9, 86; DLBD 1; MTCW 1, 2

Andier, Pierre
See Desnos, Robert

Andouard
See Giraudoux, (Hippolyte) Jean

Andrade, Carlos Drummond de ...... **CLC 18**
See also Drummond de Andrade, Carlos

Andrade, Mario de 1893-1945 .... **TCLC 43**

Andreae, Johann V(alentin)
1586-1654 .... **LC 32**
See also DLB 164

Andreas-Salome, Lou 1861-1937 ... **TCLC 56**
See also CA 178; DLB 66

Andress, Lesley
See Sanders, Lawrence

Andrewes, Lancelot 1555-1626 .... **LC 5**
See also DLB 151, 172

Andrews, Cicily Fairfield
See West, Rebecca

Andrews, Elton V.
See Pohl, Frederik

Andreyev, Leonid (Nikolaevich) 1871-1919
TCLC 3
See also CA 104

Andric, Ivo 1892-1975 .... **CLC 8; SSC 36**
See also CA 81-84; 57-60; CANR 43, 60; DLB 147; MTCW 1

Androvar
See Prado (Calvo), Pedro

Angelique, Pierre
See Bataille, Georges

Angell, Roger 1920- .... **CLC 26**
See also CA 57-60; CANR 13, 44, 70; DLB 171, 185

Angelou, Maya 1928- .... **CLC 12, 35, 64, 77; BLC 1; DA; DAB; DAC; DAM MST, MULT, POET, POP; WLCS**
See also AAYA 7, 20; BW 2, 3; CA 65-68; CANR 19, 42, 65; CDALBS; CLR 53; DA3; DLB 38; MTCW 1, 2; SATA 49

Anna Comnena 1083-1153 .... **CMLC 25**

Annensky, Innokenty (Fyodorovich)
1856-1909 .... **TCLC 14**
See also CA 110; 155

Annunzio, Gabriele d'
See D'Annunzio, Gabriele

Anodos
See Coleridge, Mary E(lizabeth)

Anon, Charles Robert
See Pessoa, Fernando (Antonio Nogueira)

Anouilh, Jean (Marie Lucien Pierre)
1910-1987 .... **CLC 1, 3, 8, 13, 40, 50; DAM DRAM; DC 8**
See also CA 17-20R; 123; CANR 32; MTCW 1, 2

Anthony, Florence
See Ai

Anthony, John
See Ciardi, John (Anthony)

Anthony, Peter
See Shaffer, Anthony (Joshua); Shaffer, Peter (Levin)

Anthony, Piers 1934- .... **CLC 35; DAM POP**
See also AAYA 11; CA 21-24R; CANR 28, 56, 73; DLB 8; MTCW 1, 2; SAAS 22; SATA 84

Anthony, Susan B(rownell)
1916-1991 .... **TCLC 84**
See also CA 89-92; 134

Antoine, Marc
See Proust, (Valentin-Louis-George-Eugene-) Marcel

Antoninus, Brother
See Everson, William (Oliver)

Antonioni, Michelangelo 1912- .... **CLC 20**
See also CA 73-76; CANR 45, 77

Antschel, Paul 1920-1970
See Celan, Paul
See also CA 85-88; CANR 33, 61; MTCW 1

Anwar, Chairil 1922-1949 .... **TCLC 22**
See also CA 121

Anzaldua, Gloria 1942-
See also CA 175; DLB 122; HLCS 1

Apess, William 1798-1839(?) .... **NCLC 73; DAM MULT**
See also DLB 175; NNAL

Apollinaire, Guillaume 1880-1918 .. **TCLC 3, 8, 51; DAM POET; PC 7**
See also Kostrowitzki, Wilhelm Apollinaris de CA 152; MTCW 1

Appelfeld, Aharon 1932- .... **CLC 23, 47**
See also CA 112; 133; CANR 86

Apple, Max (Isaac) 1941- .... **CLC 9, 33**
See also CA 81-84; CANR 19, 54; DLB 130

Appleman, Philip (Dean) 1926- .... **CLC 51**
See also CA 13-16R; CAAS 18; CANR 6, 29, 56

Appleton, Lawrence
See Lovecraft, H(oward) P(hillips)

Apteryx
See Eliot, T(homas) S(tearns)

Apuleius, (Lucius Madaurensis)
125(?)-175(?) .... **CMLC 1**
See also DLB 211

Aquin, Hubert 1929-1977 .... **CLC 15**
See also CA 105; DLB 53

Aquinas, Thomas 1224(?)-1274 ..... **CMLC 33**
See also DLB 115

Aragon, Louis 1897-1982 .. **CLC 3, 22; DAM NOV, POET**
See also CA 69-72; 108; CANR 28, 71; DLB 72; MTCW 1, 2

Arany, Janos 1817-1882 .... **NCLC 34**

Aranyos, Kakay
See Mikszath, Kalman

Arbuthnot, John 1667-1735 .... **LC 1**
See also DLB 101

Archer, Herbert Winslow
See Mencken, H(enry) L(ouis)

Archer, Jeffrey (Howard) 1940- ...... **CLC 28; DAM POP**
See also AAYA 16; BEST 89:3; CA 77-80; CANR 22, 52; DA3; INT CANR-22

Archer, Jules 1915- .... **CLC 12**
See also CA 9-12R; CANR 6, 69; SAAS 5; SATA 4, 85

Archer, Lee
See Ellison, Harlan (Jay)

Arden, John 1930- .... **CLC 6, 13, 15; DAM DRAM**
See also CA 13-16R; CAAS 4; CANR 31, 65, 67; DLB 13; MTCW 1

Arenas, Reinaldo 1943-1990 . **CLC 41; DAM MULT; HLC 1**
See also CA 124; 128; 133; CANR 73; DLB 145; HW 1; MTCW 1

Arendt, Hannah 1906-1975 .... **CLC 66, 98**
See also CA 17-20R; 61-64; CANR 26, 60; MTCW 1, 2

Aretino, Pietro 1492-1556 .... **LC 12**

Arghezi, Tudor 1880-1967 .... **CLC 80**
See also Theodorescu, Ion N. CA 167

Arguedas, Jose Maria 1911-1969 .... **CLC 10, 18; HLCS 1**
See also CA 89-92; CANR 73; DLB 113; HW 1

Argueta, Manlio 1936- .... **CLC 31**
See also CA 131; CANR 73; DLB 145; HW 1

Arias, Ron(ald Francis) 1941-
See also CA 131; CANR 81; DAM MULT; DLB 82; HLC 1; HW 1, 2; MTCW 2

Ariosto, Ludovico 1474-1533 .... **LC 6**

Aristides
See Epstein, Joseph

Aristophanes 450B.C.-385B.C. .... **CMLC 4; DA; DAB; DAC; DAM DRAM, MST; DC 2; WLCS**
See also DA3; DLB 176

Aristotle 384B.C.-322B.C. .... **CMLC 31; DA; DAB; DAC; DAM MST; WLCS**
See also DA3; DLB 176

Arlt, Roberto (Godofredo Christophersen)
1900-1942 .... **TCLC 29; DAM MULT; HLC 1**
See also CA 123; 131; CANR 67; HW 1, 2

Armah, Ayi Kwei 1939- . **CLC 5, 33; BLC 1; DAM MULT, POET**
See also BW 1; CA 61-64; CANR 21, 64; DLB 117; MTCW 1

Armatrading, Joan 1950- .... **CLC 17**
See also CA 114

Arnette, Robert
See Silverberg, Robert

Arnim, Achim von (Ludwig Joachim von Arnim) 1781-1831 ..... **NCLC 5; SSC 29**
See also DLB 90

Arnim, Bettina von 1785-1859 .... **NCLC 38**
See also DLB 90

Arnold, Matthew 1822-1888 ..... **NCLC 6, 29; DA; DAB; DAC; DAM MST, POET; PC 5; WLC**
See also CDBLB 1832-1890; DLB 32, 57

Arnold, Thomas 1795-1842 .... **NCLC 18**
See also DLB 55

Arnow, Harriette (Louisa) Simpson
1908-1986 .... **CLC 2, 7, 18**
See also CA 9-12R; 118; CANR 14; DLB 6; MTCW 1, 2; SATA 42; SATA-Obit 47

Arouet, Francois-Marie
See Voltaire

Arp, Hans
See Arp, Jean

Arp, Jean 1887-1966 .... **CLC 5**
See also CA 81-84; 25-28R; CANR 42, 77

Arrabal
See Arrabal, Fernando

Arrabal, Fernando 1932- ... **CLC 2, 9, 18, 58**
See also CA 9-12R; CANR 15

Bakhtin, Mikhail Mikhailovich 1895-1975
  CLC 83
    See also CA 128; 113
Bakshi, Ralph 1938(?)- .... **CLC 26**
    See also CA 112; 138
Bakunin, Mikhail (Alexandrovich)
    1814-1876 .... **NCLC 25, 58**
Baldwin, James (Arthur) 1924-1987 . **CLC 1,
  2, 3, 4, 5, 8, 13, 15, 17, 42, 50, 67, 90,
  127; BLC 1; DA; DAB; DAC; DAM
  MST, MULT, NOV, POP; DC 1; SSC
  10, 33; WLC**
    See also AAYA 4; BW 1; CA 1-4R; 124;
      CABS 1; CANR 3, 24; CDALB 1941-
      1968; DA3; DLB 2, 7, 33; DLBY 87;
      MTCW 1, 2; SATA 9; SATA-Obit 54
Ballard, J(ames) G(raham) 1930- . **CLC 3, 6,
  14, 36; DAM NOV, POP; SSC 1**
    See also AAYA 3; CA 5-8R; CANR 15, 39,
      65; DA3; DLB 14, 207; MTCW 1, 2;
      SATA 93
Balmont, Konstantin (Dmitriyevich)
    1867-1943 .... **TCLC 11**
    See also CA 109; 155
Baltausis, Vincas
    See Mikszath, Kalman
Balzac, Honore de 1799-1850 ... **NCLC 5, 35,
  53; DA; DAB; DAC; DAM MST, NOV;
  SSC 5; WLC**
    See also DA3; DLB 119
Bambara, Toni Cade 1939-1995 ...... **CLC 19,
  88; BLC 1; DA; DAC; DAM MST,
  MULT; SSC 35; WLCS**
    See also AAYA 5; BW 2, 3; CA 29-32R;
      150; CANR 24, 49, 81; CDALBS; DA3;
      DLB 38; MTCW 1, 2; SATA 112
Bamdad, A.
    See Shamlu, Ahmad
Banat, D. R.
    See Bradbury, Ray (Douglas)
Bancroft, Laura
    See Baum, L(yman) Frank
Banim, John 1798-1842 .... **NCLC 13**
    See also DLB 116, 158, 159
Banim, Michael 1796-1874 .... **NCLC 13**
    See also DLB 158, 159
Banjo, The
    See Paterson, A(ndrew) B(arton)
Banks, Iain
    See Banks, Iain M(enzies)
Banks, Iain M(enzies) 1954- .... **CLC 34**
    See also CA 123; 128; CANR 61; DLB 194;
      INT 128
Banks, Lynne Reid .... **CLC 23**
    See also Reid Banks, Lynne AAYA 6
Banks, Russell 1940- .... **CLC 37, 72**
    See also CA 65-68; CAAS 15; CANR 19,
      52, 73; DLB 130
Banville, John 1945- .... **CLC 46, 118**
    See also CA 117; 128; DLB 14; INT 128
Banville, Theodore (Faullain) de 1832-1891
  NCLC 9
Baraka, Amiri 1934- . **CLC 1, 2, 3, 5, 10, 14,
  33, 115; BLC 1; DA; DAC; DAM MST,
  MULT, POET, POP; DC 6; PC 4;
  WLCS**
    See also Jones, LeRoi BW 2, 3; CA 21-24R;
      CABS 3; CANR 27, 38, 61; CDALB
      1941-1968; DA3; DLB 5, 7, 16, 38;
      DLBD 8; MTCW 1, 2
Barbauld, Anna Laetitia
    1743-1825 .... **NCLC 50**
    See also DLB 107, 109, 142, 158
Barbellion, W. N. P. .... **TCLC 24**
    See also Cummings, Bruce F(rederick)
Barbera, Jack (Vincent) 1945- .... **CLC 44**
    See also CA 110; CANR 45
Barbey d'Aurevilly, Jules Amedee 1808-1889
  NCLC 1; SSC 17

    See also DLB 119
Barbour, John c. 1316-1395 .... **CMLC 33**
    See also DLB 146
Barbusse, Henri 1873-1935 .... **TCLC 5**
    See also CA 105; 154; DLB 65
Barclay, Bill
    See Moorcock, Michael (John)
Barclay, William Ewert
    See Moorcock, Michael (John)
Barea, Arturo 1897-1957 .... **TCLC 14**
    See also CA 111
Barfoot, Joan 1946- .... **CLC 18**
    See also CA 105
Barham, Richard Harris
    1788-1845 .... **NCLC 77**
    See also DLB 159
Baring, Maurice 1874-1945 .... **TCLC 8**
    See also CA 105; 168; DLB 34
Baring-Gould, Sabine 1834-1924 ... **TCLC 88**
    See also DLB 156, 190
Barker, Clive 1952- ...... **CLC 52; DAM POP**
    See also AAYA 10; BEST 90:3; CA 121;
      129; CANR 71; DA3; INT 129; MTCW
      1, 2
Barker, George Granville
    1913-1991 .... **CLC 8, 48; DAM POET**
    See also CA 9-12R; 135; CANR 7, 38; DLB
      20; MTCW 1
Barker, Harley Granville
    See Granville-Barker, Harley
    See also DLB 10
Barker, Howard 1946- .... **CLC 37**
    See also CA 102; DLB 13
Barker, Jane 1652-1732 .... **LC 42**
Barker, Pat(ricia) 1943- .... **CLC 32, 94**
    See also CA 117; 122; CANR 50; INT 122
Barlach, Ernst (Heinrich)
    1870-1938 .... **TCLC 84**
    See also CA 178; DLB 56, 118
Barlow, Joel 1754-1812 .... **NCLC 23**
    See also DLB 37
Barnard, Mary (Ethel) 1909- .... **CLC 48**
    See also CA 21-22; CAP 2
Barnes, Djuna 1892-1982 .... **CLC 3, 4, 8, 11,
  29, 127; SSC 3**
    See also CA 9-12R; 107; CANR 16, 55;
      DLB 4, 9, 45; MTCW 1, 2
Barnes, Julian (Patrick) 1946- .... **CLC 42;
  DAB**
    See also CA 102; CANR 19, 54; DLB 194;
      DLBY 93; MTCW 1
Barnes, Peter 1931- .... **CLC 5, 56**
    See also CA 65-68; CAAS 12; CANR 33,
      34, 64; DLB 13; MTCW 1
Barnes, William 1801-1886 .... **NCLC 75**
    See also DLB 32
Baroja (y Nessi), Pio 1872-1956 ..... **TCLC 8;
  HLC 1**
    See also CA 104
Baron, David
    See Pinter, Harold
Baron Corvo
    See Rolfe, Frederick (William Serafino
      Austin Lewis Mary)
Barondess, Sue K(aufman)
    1926-1977 .... **CLC 8**
    See also Kaufman, Sue CA 1-4R; 69-72;
      CANR 1
Baron de Teive
    See Pessoa, Fernando (Antonio Nogueira)
Baroness Von S.
    See Zangwill, Israel
Barres, (Auguste-) Maurice
    1862-1923 .... **TCLC 47**
    See also CA 164; DLB 123
Barreto, Afonso Henrique de Lima
    See Lima Barreto, Afonso Henrique de

Barrett, (Roger) Syd 1946- .... **CLC 35**
Barrett, William (Christopher) 1913-1992
  CLC 27
    See also CA 13-16R; 139; CANR 11, 67;
      INT CANR-11
Barrie, J(ames) M(atthew)
    1860-1937 .... **TCLC 2; DAB; DAM
  DRAM**
    See also CA 104; 136; CANR 77; CDBLB
      1890-1914; CLR 16; DA3; DLB 10, 141,
      156; MAICYA; MTCW 1; SATA 100;
      YABC 1
Barrington, Michael
    See Moorcock, Michael (John)
Barrol, Grady
    See Bograd, Larry
Barry, Mike
    See Malzberg, Barry N(athaniel)
Barry, Philip 1896-1949 .... **TCLC 11**
    See also CA 109; DLB 7
Bart, Andre Schwarz
    See Schwarz-Bart, Andre
Barth, John (Simmons) 1930- ... **CLC 1, 2, 3,
  5, 7, 9, 10, 14, 27, 51, 89; DAM NOV;
  SSC 10**
    See also AITN 1, 2; CA 1-4R; CABS 1;
      CANR 5, 23, 49, 64; DLB 2; MTCW 1
Barthelme, Donald 1931-1989 ... **CLC 1, 2, 3,
  5, 6, 8, 13, 23, 46, 59, 115; DAM NOV;
  SSC 2**
    See also CA 21-24R; 129; CANR 20, 58;
      DA3; DLB 2; DLBY 80, 89; MTCW 1, 2;
      SATA 7; SATA-Obit 62
Barthelme, Frederick 1943- ...... **CLC 36, 117**
    See also CA 114; 122; CANR 77; DLBY
      85; INT 122
Barthes, Roland (Gerard)
    1915-1980 .... **CLC 24, 83**
    See also CA 130; 97-100; CANR 66;
      MTCW 1, 2
Barzun, Jacques (Martin) 1907- ...... **CLC 51**
    See also CA 61-64; CANR 22
Bashevis, Isaac
    See Singer, Isaac Bashevis
Bashkirtseff, Marie 1859-1884 .... **NCLC 27**
Basho
    See Matsuo Basho
Basil of Caesaria c. 330-379 .... **CMLC 35**
Bass, Kingsley B., Jr.
    See Bullins, Ed
Bass, Rick 1958- .... **CLC 79**
    See also CA 126; CANR 53; DLB 212
Bassani, Giorgio 1916- .... **CLC 9**
    See also CA 65-68; CANR 33; DLB 128,
      177; MTCW 1
Bastos, Augusto (Antonio) Roa
    See Roa Bastos, Augusto (Antonio)
Bataille, Georges 1897-1962 .... **CLC 29**
    See also CA 101; 89-92
Bates, H(erbert) E(rnest)
    1905-1974 . **CLC 46; DAB; DAM POP;
  SSC 10**
    See also CA 93-96; 45-48; CANR 34; DA3;
      DLB 162, 191; MTCW 1, 2
Bauchart
    See Camus, Albert
Baudelaire, Charles 1821-1867 . **NCLC 6, 29,
  55; DA; DAB; DAC; DAM MST,
  POET; PC 1; SSC 18; WLC**
    See also DA3
Baudrillard, Jean 1929- .... **CLC 60**
Baum, L(yman) Frank 1856-1919 ... **TCLC 7**
    See also CA 108; 133; CLR 15; DLB 22;
      JRDA; MAICYA; MTCW 1, 2; SATA 18,
      100
Baum, Louis F.
    See Baum, L(yman) Frank

Bennett, (Enoch) Arnold
1867-1931 .... **TCLC 5, 20**
See also CA 106; 155; CDBLB 1890-1914;
DLB 10, 34, 98, 135; MTCW 2

Bennett, Elizabeth
See Mitchell, Margaret (Munnerlyn)

Bennett, George Harold 1930-
See Bennett, Hal
See also BW 1; CA 97-100; CANR 87

Bennett, Hal .... **CLC 5**
See also Bennett, George Harold DLB 33

Bennett, Jay 1912- .... **CLC 35**
See also AAYA 10; CA 69-72; CANR 11,
42, 79; JRDA; SAAS 4; SATA 41, 87;
SATA-Brief 27

Bennett, Louise (Simone) 1919- ...... **CLC 28;
BLC 1; DAM MULT**
See also BW 2, 3; CA 151; DLB 117

Benson, E(dward) F(rederic) 1867-1940
TCLC 27
See also CA 114; 157; DLB 135, 153

Benson, Jackson J. 1930- .... **CLC 34**
See also CA 25-28R; DLB 111

Benson, Sally 1900-1972 .... **CLC 17**
See also CA 19-20; 37-40R; CAP 1; SATA
1, 35; SATA-Obit 27

Benson, Stella 1892-1933 .... **TCLC 17**
See also CA 117; 155; DLB 36, 162

Bentham, Jeremy 1748-1832 .... **NCLC 38**
See also DLB 107, 158

Bentley, E(dmund) C(lerihew) 1875-1956
TCLC 12
See also CA 108; DLB 70

Bentley, Eric (Russell) 1916- .... **CLC 24**
See also CA 5-8R; CANR 6, 67; INT
CANR-6

Beranger, Pierre Jean de
1780-1857 .... **NCLC 34**

Berdyaev, Nicolas
See Berdyaev, Nikolai (Aleksandrovich)

Berdyaev, Nikolai (Aleksandrovich)
1874-1948 .... **TCLC 67**
See also CA 120; 157

Berdyayev, Nikolai (Aleksandrovich)
See Berdyaev, Nikolai (Aleksandrovich)

Berendt, John (Lawrence) 1939- ...... **CLC 86**
See also CA 146; CANR 75; DA3; MTCW
1

Beresford, J(ohn) D(avys)
1873-1947 .... **TCLC 81**
See also CA 112; 155; DLB 162, 178, 197

Bergelson, David 1884-1952 .... **TCLC 81**

Berger, Colonel
See Malraux, (Georges-)Andre

Berger, John (Peter) 1926- .... **CLC 2, 19**
See also CA 81-84; CANR 51, 78; DLB 14,
207

Berger, Melvin H. 1927- .... **CLC 12**
See also CA 5-8R; CANR 4; CLR 32;
SAAS 2; SATA 5, 88

Berger, Thomas (Louis) 1924- .. **CLC 3, 5, 8,
11, 18, 38; DAM NOV**
See also CA 1-4R; CANR 5, 28, 51; DLB
2; DLBY 80; INT CANR-28; MTCW 1, 2

Bergman, (Ernst) Ingmar 1918- ...... **CLC 16,
72**
See also CA 81-84; CANR 33, 70; MTCW
2

Bergson, Henri(-Louis) 1859-1941 . **TCLC 32**
See also CA 164

Bergstein, Eleanor 1938- .... **CLC 4**
See also CA 53-56; CANR 5

Berkoff, Steven 1937- .... **CLC 56**
See also CA 104; CANR 72

Bermant, Chaim (Icyk) 1929- .... **CLC 40**
See also CA 57-60; CANR 6, 31, 57

Bern, Victoria
See Fisher, M(ary) F(rances) K(ennedy)

Bernanos, (Paul Louis) Georges 1888-1948
TCLC 3
See also CA 104; 130; DLB 72

Bernard, April 1956- .... **CLC 59**
See also CA 131

Berne, Victoria
See Fisher, M(ary) F(rances) K(ennedy)

Bernhard, Thomas 1931-1989 ..... **CLC 3, 32,
61**
See also CA 85-88; 127; CANR 32, 57;
DLB 85, 124; MTCW 1

Bernhardt, Sarah (Henriette Rosine)
1844-1923 .... **TCLC 75**
See also CA 157

Berriault, Gina 1926- . **CLC 54, 109; SSC 30**
See also CA 116; 129; CANR 66; DLB 130

Berrigan, Daniel 1921- .... **CLC 4**
See also CA 33-36R; CAAS 1; CANR 11,
43, 78; DLB 5

Berrigan, Edmund Joseph Michael, Jr.
1934-1983
See Berrigan, Ted
See also CA 61-64; 110; CANR 14

Berrigan, Ted .... **CLC 37**
See also Berrigan, Edmund Joseph Michael,
Jr. DLB 5, 169

Berry, Charles Edward Anderson 1931-
See Berry, Chuck
See also CA 115

Berry, Chuck .... **CLC 17**
See also Berry, Charles Edward Anderson

Berry, Jonas
See Ashbery, John (Lawrence)

Berry, Wendell (Erdman) 1934- ... **CLC 4, 6,
8, 27, 46; DAM POET; PC 28**
See also AITN 1; CA 73-76; CANR 50, 73;
DLB 5, 6; MTCW 1

Berryman, John 1914-1972 ... **CLC 1, 2, 3, 4,
6, 8, 10, 13, 25, 62; DAM POET**
See also CA 13-16; 33-36R; CABS 2;
CANR 35; CAP 1; CDALB 1941-1968;
DLB 48; MTCW 1, 2

Bertolucci, Bernardo 1940- .... **CLC 16**
See also CA 106

Berton, Pierre (Francis Demarigny) 1920-
CLC 104
See also CA 1-4R; CANR 2, 56; DLB 68;
SATA 99

Bertrand, Aloysius 1807-1841 .... **NCLC 31**

Bertran de Born c. 1140-1215 .... **CMLC 5**

Besant, Annie (Wood) 1847-1933 ..... **TCLC 9**
See also CA 105

Bessie, Alvah 1904-1985 .... **CLC 23**
See also CA 5-8R; 116; CANR 2, 80; DLB
26

Bethlen, T. D.
See Silverberg, Robert

Beti, Mongo . **CLC 27; BLC 1; DAM MULT**
See also Biyidi, Alexandre CANR 79

Betjeman, John 1906-1984 ...... **CLC 2, 6, 10,
34, 43; DAB; DAM MST, POET**
See also CA 9-12R; 112; CANR 33, 56;
CDBLB 1945-1960; DA3; DLB 20;
DLBY 84; MTCW 1, 2

Bettelheim, Bruno 1903-1990 .... **CLC 79**
See also CA 81-84; 131; CANR 23, 61;
DA3; MTCW 1, 2

Betti, Ugo 1892-1953 .... **TCLC 5**
See also CA 104; 155

Betts, Doris (Waugh) 1932- ...... **CLC 3, 6, 28**
See also CA 13-16R; CANR 9, 66, 77;
DLBY 82; INT CANR-9

Bevan, Alistair
See Roberts, Keith (John Kingston)

Bey, Pilaff
See Douglas, (George) Norman

Bialik, Chaim Nachman
1873-1934 .... **TCLC 25**
See also CA 170

Bickerstaff, Isaac
See Swift, Jonathan

Bidart, Frank 1939- .... **CLC 33**
See also CA 140

Bienek, Horst 1930- .... **CLC 7, 11**
See also CA 73-76; DLB 75

Bierce, Ambrose (Gwinett) 1842-1914(?)
**TCLC 1, 7, 44; DA; DAC; DAM MST;
SSC 9; WLC**
See also CA 104; 139; CANR 78; CDALB
1865-1917; DA3; DLB 11, 12, 23, 71, 74,
186

Biggers, Earl Derr 1884-1933 .... **TCLC 65**
See also CA 108; 153

Billings, Josh
See Shaw, Henry Wheeler

Billington, (Lady) Rachel (Mary)
1942- .... **CLC 43**
See also AITN 2; CA 33-36R; CANR 44

Binyon, T(imothy) J(ohn) 1936- .... **CLC 34**
See also CA 111; CANR 28

Bioy Casares, Adolfo 1914-1999 ... **CLC 4, 8,
13, 88; DAM MULT; HLC 1; SSC 17**
See also CA 29-32R; 177; CANR 19, 43,
66; DLB 113; HW 1, 2; MTCW 1, 2

Bird, Cordwainer
See Ellison, Harlan (Jay)

Bird, Robert Montgomery
1806-1854 .... **NCLC 1**
See also DLB 202

Birkerts, Sven 1951- .... **CLC 116**
See also CA 128; 133; 176; CAAE 176;
CAAS 29; INT 133

Birney, (Alfred) Earle 1904-1995 .. **CLC 1, 4,
6, 11; DAC; DAM MST, POET**
See also CA 1-4R; CANR 5, 20; DLB 88;
MTCW 1

Biruni, al 973-1048(?) .... **CMLC 28**

Bishop, Elizabeth 1911-1979 ..... **CLC 1, 4, 9,
13, 15, 32; DA; DAC; DAM MST,
POET; PC 3**
See also CA 5-8R; 89-92; CABS 2; CANR
26, 61; CDALB 1968-1988; DA3; DLB
5, 169; MTCW 1, 2; SATA-Obit 24

Bishop, John 1935- .... **CLC 10**
See also CA 105

Bissett, Bill 1939- .... **CLC 18; PC 14**
See also CA 69-72; CAAS 19; CANR 15;
DLB 53; MTCW 1

Bissoondath, Neil (Devindra)
1955- .... **CLC 120; DAC**
See also CA 136

Bitov, Andrei (Georgievich) 1937- ... **CLC 57**
See also CA 142

Biyidi, Alexandre 1932-
See Beti, Mongo
See also BW 1, 3; CA 114; 124; CANR 81;
DA3; MTCW 1, 2

Bjarme, Brynjolf
See Ibsen, Henrik (Johan)

Bjoernson, Bjoernstjerne (Martinius)
1832-1910 .... **TCLC 7, 37**
See also CA 104

Black, Robert
See Holdstock, Robert P.

Blackburn, Paul 1926-1971 .... **CLC 9, 43**
See also CA 81-84; 33-36R; CANR 34;
DLB 16; DLBY 81

Black Elk 1863-1950 .... **TCLC 33; DAM
MULT**
See also CA 144; MTCW 1; NNAL

Black Hobart
See Sanders, (James) Ed(ward)

Blacklin, Malcolm
See Chambers, Aidan

Blackmore, R(ichard) D(oddridge)
1825-1900 .... **TCLC 27**
See also CA 120; DLB 18

See also CA 17-18; 41-44R; CANR 35;
CAP 2; CDBLB 1945-1960; DA3; DLB
15, 162; MTCW 1, 2

Bowering, George 1935- .... **CLC 15, 47**
See also CA 21-24R; CAAS 16; CANR 10;
DLB 53

Bowering, Marilyn R(uthe) 1949- .... **CLC 32**
See also CA 101; CANR 49

Bowers, Edgar 1924- .... **CLC 9**
See also CA 5-8R; CANR 24; DLB 5

Bowie, David .... **CLC 17**
See also Jones, David Robert

Bowles, Jane (Sydney) 1917-1973 ..... **CLC 3,
68**
See also CA 19-20; 41-44R; CAP 2

Bowles, Paul (Frederick) 1910- ..... **CLC 1, 2,
19, 53; SSC 3**
See also CA 1-4R; CAAS 1; CANR 1, 19,
50, 75; DA3; DLB 5, 6; MTCW 1, 2

Box, Edgar
See Vidal, Gore

Boyd, Nancy
See Millay, Edna St. Vincent

Boyd, William 1952- .... **CLC 28, 53, 70**
See also CA 114; 120; CANR 51, 71

Boyle, Kay 1902-1992 .... **CLC 1, 5, 19, 58,
121; SSC 5**
See also CA 13-16R; 140; CAAS 1; CANR
29, 61; DLB 4, 9, 48, 86; DLBY 93;
MTCW 1, 2

Boyle, Mark
See Kienzle, William X(avier)

Boyle, Patrick 1905-1982 .... **CLC 19**
See also CA 127

Boyle, T. C. 1948-
See Boyle, T(homas) Coraghessan

Boyle, T(homas) Coraghessan
1948- .... **CLC 36, 55, 90; DAM POP;
SSC 16**
See also BEST 90:4; CA 120; CANR 44,
76; DA3; DLBY 86; MTCW 2

Boz
See Dickens, Charles (John Huffam)

Brackenridge, Hugh Henry
1748-1816 .... **NCLC 7**
See also DLB 11, 37

Bradbury, Edward P.
See Moorcock, Michael (John)
See also MTCW 2

Bradbury, Malcolm (Stanley)
1932- .... **CLC 32, 61; DAM NOV**
See also CA 1-4R; CANR 1, 33; DA3; DLB
14, 207; MTCW 1, 2

Bradbury, Ray (Douglas) 1920- .... **CLC 1, 3,
10, 15, 42, 98; DA; DAB; DAC; DAM
MST, NOV, POP; SSC 29; WLC**
See also AAYA 15; AITN 1, 2; CA 1-4R;
CANR 2, 30, 75; CDALB 1968-1988;
DA3; DLB 2, 8; MTCW 1, 2; SATA 11,
64

Bradford, Gamaliel 1863-1932 .... **TCLC 36**
See also CA 160; DLB 17

Bradley, David (Henry), Jr. 1950- ... **CLC 23,
118; BLC 1; DAM MULT**
See also BW 1, 3; CA 104; CANR 26, 81;
DLB 33

Bradley, John Ed(mund, Jr.) 1958- . **CLC 55**
See also CA 139

Bradley, Marion Zimmer 1930- ...... **CLC 30;
DAM POP**
See also AAYA 9; CA 57-60; CAAS 10;
CANR 7, 31, 51, 75; DA3; DLB 8;
MTCW 1, 2; SATA 90

Bradstreet, Anne 1612(?)-1672 ...... **LC 4, 30;
DA; DAC; DAM MST, POET; PC 10**
See also CDALB 1640-1865; DA3; DLB
24

Brady, Joan 1939- .... **CLC 86**
See also CA 141

Bragg, Melvyn 1939- .... **CLC 10**
See also BEST 89:3; CA 57-60; CANR 10,
48; DLB 14

Brahe, Tycho 1546-1601 .... **LC 45**

Braine, John (Gerard) 1922-1986 . **CLC 1, 3,
41**
See also CA 1-4R; 120; CANR 1, 33; CD-
BLB 1945-1960; DLB 15; DLBY 86;
MTCW 1

Bramah, Ernest 1868-1942 .... **TCLC 72**
See also CA 156; DLB 70

Brammer, William 1930(?)-1978 ...... **CLC 31**
See also CA 77-80

Brancati, Vitaliano 1907-1954 .... **TCLC 12**
See also CA 109

Brancato, Robin F(idler) 1936- .... **CLC 35**
See also AAYA 9; CA 69-72; CANR 11,
45; CLR 32; JRDA; SAAS 9; SATA 97

Brand, Max
See Faust, Frederick (Schiller)

Brand, Millen 1906-1980 .... **CLC 7**
See also CA 21-24R; 97-100; CANR 72

Branden, Barbara .... **CLC 44**
See also CA 148

Brandes, Georg (Morris Cohen) 1842-1927
TCLC 10
See also CA 105

Brandys, Kazimierz 1916- .... **CLC 62**

Branley, Franklyn M(ansfield)
1915- .... **CLC 21**
See also CA 33-36R; CANR 14, 39; CLR
13; MAICYA; SAAS 16; SATA 4, 68

Brathwaite, Edward (Kamau)
1930- ...... **CLC 11; BLCS; DAM POET**
See also BW 2, 3; CA 25-28R; CANR 11,
26, 47; DLB 125

Brautigan, Richard (Gary)
1935-1984 .... **CLC 1, 3, 5, 9, 12, 34, 42;
DAM NOV**
See also CA 53-56; 113; CANR 34; DA3;
DLB 2, 5, 206; DLBY 80, 84; MTCW 1;
SATA 56

Brave Bird, Mary 1953-
See Crow Dog, Mary (Ellen)
See also NNAL

Braverman, Kate 1950- .... **CLC 67**
See also CA 89-92

Brecht, (Eugen) Bertolt (Friedrich)
1898-1956 .... **TCLC 1, 6, 13, 35; DA;
DAB; DAC; DAM DRAM, MST; DC
3; WLC**
See also CA 104; 133; CANR 62; DA3;
DLB 56, 124; MTCW 1, 2

Brecht, Eugen Berthold Friedrich
See Brecht, (Eugen) Bertolt (Friedrich)

Bremer, Fredrika 1801-1865 .... **NCLC 11**

Brennan, Christopher John
1870-1932 .... **TCLC 17**
See also CA 117

Brennan, Maeve 1917-1993 .... **CLC 5**
See also CA 81-84; CANR 72

Brent, Linda
See Jacobs, Harriet A(nn)

Brentano, Clemens (Maria)
1778-1842 .... **NCLC 1**
See also DLB 90

Brent of Bin Bin
See Franklin, (Stella Maria Sarah) Miles
(Lampe)

Brenton, Howard 1942- .... **CLC 31**
See also CA 69-72; CANR 33, 67; DLB 13;
MTCW 1

Breslin, James 1930-1996
See Breslin, Jimmy
See also CA 73-76; CANR 31, 75; DAM
NOV; MTCW 1, 2

Breslin, Jimmy .... **CLC 4, 43**
See also Breslin, James AITN 1; DLB 185;
MTCW 2

Bresson, Robert 1901- .... **CLC 16**
See also CA 110; CANR 49

Breton, Andre 1896-1966 .. **CLC 2, 9, 15, 54;
PC 15**
See also CA 19-20; 25-28R; CANR 40, 60;
CAP 2; DLB 65; MTCW 1, 2

Breytenbach, Breyten 1939(?)- .. **CLC 23, 37,
126; DAM POET**
See also CA 113; 129; CANR 61

Bridgers, Sue Ellen 1942- .... **CLC 26**
See also AAYA 8; CA 65-68; CANR 11,
36; CLR 18; DLB 52; JRDA; MAICYA;
SAAS 1; SATA 22, 90; SATA-Essay 109

Bridges, Robert (Seymour)
1844-1930 ... **TCLC 1; DAM POET; PC
28**
See also CA 104; 152; CDBLB 1890-1914;
DLB 19, 98

Bridie, James .... **TCLC 3**
See also Mavor, Osborne Henry DLB 10

Brin, David 1950- .... **CLC 34**
See also AAYA 21; CA 102; CANR 24, 70;
INT CANR-24; SATA 65

Brink, Andre (Philippus) 1935- . **CLC 18, 36,
106**
See also CA 104; CANR 39, 62; INT 103;
MTCW 1, 2

Brinsmead, H(esba) F(ay) 1922- ...... **CLC 21**
See also CA 21-24R; CANR 10; CLR 47;
MAICYA; SAAS 5; SATA 18, 78

Brittain, Vera (Mary) 1893(?)-1970 . **CLC 23**
See also CA 13-16; 25-28R; CANR 58;
CAP 1; DLB 191; MTCW 1, 2

Broch, Hermann 1886-1951 .... **TCLC 20**
See also CA 117; DLB 85, 124

Brock, Rose
See Hansen, Joseph

Brodkey, Harold (Roy) 1930-1996 ... **CLC 56**
See also CA 111; 151; CANR 71; DLB 130

Brodskii, Iosif
See Brodsky, Joseph

Brodsky, Iosif Alexandrovich 1940-1996
See Brodsky, Joseph
See also AITN 1; CA 41-44R; 151; CANR
37; DAM POET; DA3; MTCW 1, 2

Brodsky, Joseph 1940-1996 ..... **CLC 4, 6, 13,
36, 100; PC 9**
See also Brodskii, Iosif; Brodsky, Iosif Alexandrovich MTCW 1

Brodsky, Michael (Mark) 1948- .... **CLC 19**
See also CA 102; CANR 18, 41, 58

Bromell, Henry 1947- .... **CLC 5**
See also CA 53-56; CANR 9

Bromfield, Louis (Brucker)
1896-1956 .... **TCLC 11**
See also CA 107; 155; DLB 4, 9, 86

Broner, E(sther) M(asserman)
1930- .... **CLC 19**
See also CA 17-20R; CANR 8, 25, 72; DLB
28

Bronk, William (M.) 1918-1999 .... **CLC 10**
See also CA 89-92; 177; CANR 23; DLB
165

Bronstein, Lev Davidovich
See Trotsky, Leon

Bronte, Anne 1820-1849 .... **NCLC 4, 71**
See also DA3; DLB 21, 199

Bronte, Charlotte 1816-1855 ...... **NCLC 3, 8,
33, 58; DA; DAB; DAC; DAM MST,
NOV; WLC**
See also AAYA 17; CDBLB 1832-1890;
DA3; DLB 21, 159, 199

Bronte, Emily (Jane) 1818-1848 ... **NCLC 16,
35; DA; DAB; DAC; DAM MST, NOV,
POET; PC 8; WLC**
See also AAYA 17; CDBLB 1832-1890;
DA3; DLB 21, 32, 199

Brooke, Frances 1724-1789 .... **LC 6, 48**
See also DLB 39, 99

Burgess, Anthony .. **CLC 1, 2, 4, 5, 8, 10, 13, 15, 22, 40, 62, 81, 94; DAB**
See also Wilson, John (Anthony) Burgess
AAYA 25; AITN 1; CDBLB 1960 to Present; DLB 14, 194; DLBY 98; MTCW 1

Burke, Edmund 1729(?)-1797 .... **LC 7, 36; DA; DAB; DAC; DAM MST; WLC**
See also DA3; DLB 104

Burke, Kenneth (Duva) 1897-1993 ... **CLC 2, 24**
See also CA 5-8R; 143; CANR 39, 74; DLB 45, 63; MTCW 1, 2

Burke, Leda
See Garnett, David

Burke, Ralph
See Silverberg, Robert

Burke, Thomas 1886-1945 .... **TCLC 63**
See also CA 113; 155; DLB 197

Burney, Fanny 1752-1840 .. **NCLC 12, 54, 81**
See also DLB 39

Burns, Robert 1759-1796 . **LC 3, 29, 40; DA; DAB; DAC; DAM MST, POET; PC 6; WLC**
See also CDBLB 1789-1832; DA3; DLB 109

Burns, Tex
See L'Amour, Louis (Dearborn)

Burnshaw, Stanley 1906- .... **CLC 3, 13, 44**
See also CA 9-12R; DLB 48; DLBY 97

Burr, Anne 1937- .... **CLC 6**
See also CA 25-28R

Burroughs, Edgar Rice 1875-1950 . **TCLC 2, 32; DAM NOV**
See also AAYA 11; CA 104; 132; DA3; DLB 8; MTCW 1, 2; SATA 41

Burroughs, William S(eward) 1914-1997 **CLC 1, 2, 5, 15, 22, 42, 75, 109; DA; DAB; DAC; DAM MST, NOV, POP; WLC**
See also AITN 2; CA 9-12R; 160; CANR 20, 52; DA3; DLB 2, 8, 16, 152; DLBY 81, 97; MTCW 1, 2

Burton, SirRichard F(rancis) 1821-1890 **NCLC 42**
See also DLB 55, 166, 184

Busch, Frederick 1941- .... **CLC 7, 10, 18, 47**
See also CA 33-36R; CAAS 1; CANR 45, 73; DLB 6

Bush, Ronald 1946- .... **CLC 34**
See also CA 136

Bustos, F(rancisco)
See Borges, Jorge Luis

Bustos Domecq, H(onorio)
See Bioy Casares, Adolfo; Borges, Jorge Luis

Butler, Octavia E(stelle) 1947- .... **CLC 38, 121; BLCS; DAM MULT, POP**
See also AAYA 18; BW 2, 3; CA 73-76; CANR 12, 24, 38, 73; DA3; DLB 33; MTCW 1, 2; SATA 84

Butler, Robert Olen (Jr.) 1945- .... **CLC 81; DAM POP**
See also CA 112; CANR 66; DLB 173; INT 112; MTCW 1

Butler, Samuel 1612-1680 .... **LC 16, 43**
See also DLB 101, 126

Butler, Samuel 1835-1902 . **TCLC 1, 33; DA; DAB; DAC; DAM MST, NOV; WLC**
See also CA 143; CDBLB 1890-1914; DA3; DLB 18, 57, 174

Butler, Walter C.
See Faust, Frederick (Schiller)

Butor, Michel (Marie Francois) 1926- .... **CLC 1, 3, 8, 11, 15**
See also CA 9-12R; CANR 33, 66; DLB 83; MTCW 1, 2

Butts, Mary 1892(?)-1937 .... **TCLC 77**
See also CA 148

Buzo, Alexander (John) 1944- .... **CLC 61**
See also CA 97-100; CANR 17, 39, 69

Buzzati, Dino 1906-1972 .... **CLC 36**
See also CA 160; 33-36R; DLB 177

Byars, Betsy (Cromer) 1928- .... **CLC 35**
See also AAYA 19; CA 33-36R, 183; CAAE 183; CANR 18, 36, 57; CLR 1, 16; DLB 52; INT CANR-18; JRDA; MAICYA; MTCW 1; SAAS 1; SATA 4, 46, 80; SATA-Essay 108

Byatt, A(ntonia) S(usan Drabble) 1936- ..... **CLC 19, 65; DAM NOV, POP**
See also CA 13-16R; CANR 13, 33, 50, 75; DA3; DLB 14, 194; MTCW 1, 2

Byrne, David 1952- .... **CLC 26**
See also CA 127

Byrne, John Keyes 1926-
See Leonard, Hugh
See also CA 102; CANR 78; INT 102

Byron, George Gordon (Noel) 1788-1824 **NCLC 2, 12; DA; DAB; DAC; DAM MST, POET; PC 16; WLC**
See also CDBLB 1789-1832; DA3; DLB 96, 110

Byron, Robert 1905-1941 .... **TCLC 67**
See also CA 160; DLB 195

C. 3. 3.
See Wilde, Oscar

Caballero, Fernan 1796-1877 .... **NCLC 10**

Cabell, Branch
See Cabell, James Branch

Cabell, James Branch 1879-1958 .... **TCLC 6**
See also CA 105; 152; DLB 9, 78; MTCW 1

Cable, George Washington 1844-1925 .... **TCLC 4; SSC 4**
See also CA 104; 155; DLB 12, 74; DLBD 13

Cabral de Melo Neto, Joao 1920- ... **CLC 76; DAM MULT**
See also CA 151

Cabrera Infante, G(uillermo) 1929- . **CLC 5, 25, 45, 120; DAM MULT; HLC 1**
See also CA 85-88; CANR 29, 65; DA3; DLB 113; HW 1, 2; MTCW 1, 2

Cade, Toni
See Bambara, Toni Cade

Cadmus and Harmonia
See Buchan, John

Caedmon fl. 658-680 .... **CMLC 7**
See also DLB 146

Caeiro, Alberto
See Pessoa, Fernando (Antonio Nogueira)

Cage, John (Milton, Jr.) 1912-1992 . **CLC 41**
See also CA 13-16R; 169; CANR 9, 78; DLB 193; INT CANR-9

Cahan, Abraham 1860-1951 .... **TCLC 71**
See also CA 108; 154; DLB 9, 25, 28

Cain, G.
See Cabrera Infante, G(uillermo)

Cain, Guillermo
See Cabrera Infante, G(uillermo)

Cain, James M(allahan) 1892-1977 .. **CLC 3, 11, 28**
See also AITN 1; CA 17-20R; 73-76; CANR 8, 34, 61; MTCW 1

Caine, Hall 1853-1931 .... **TCLC 99**

Caine, Mark
See Raphael, Frederic (Michael)

Calasso, Roberto 1941- .... **CLC 81**
See also CA 143

Calderon de la Barca, Pedro 1600-1681 .... **LC 23; DC 3; HLCS 1**

Caldwell, Erskine (Preston) 1903-1987 .. **CLC 1, 8, 14, 50, 60; DAM NOV; SSC 19**
See also AITN 1; CA 1-4R; 121; CAAS 1; CANR 2, 33; DA3; DLB 9, 86; MTCW 1, 2

Caldwell, (Janet Miriam) Taylor (Holland) 1900-1985 .. **CLC 2, 28, 39; DAM NOV, POP**
See also CA 5-8R; 116; CANR 5; DA3; DLBD 17

Calhoun, John Caldwell 1782-1850 .... **NCLC 15**
See also DLB 3

Calisher, Hortense 1911- ..... **CLC 2, 4, 8, 38; DAM NOV; SSC 15**
See also CA 1-4R; CANR 1, 22, 67; DA3; DLB 2; INT CANR-22; MTCW 1, 2

Callaghan, Morley Edward 1903-1990 ...... **CLC 3, 14, 41, 65; DAC; DAM MST**
See also CA 9-12R; 132; CANR 33, 73; DLB 68; MTCW 1, 2

Callimachus c. 305B.C.-c. 240B.C. .... **CMLC 18**
See also DLB 176

Calvin, John 1509-1564 .... **LC 37**

Calvino, Italo 1923-1985 .... **CLC 5, 8, 11, 22, 33, 39, 73; DAM NOV; SSC 3**
See also CA 85-88; 116; CANR 23, 61; DLB 196; MTCW 1, 2

Cameron, Carey 1952- .... **CLC 59**
See also CA 135

Cameron, Peter 1959- .... **CLC 44**
See also CA 125; CANR 50

Camoens, Luis Vaz de 1524(?)-1580
See also HLCS 1

Camoes, Luis de 1524(?)-1580
See also HLCS 1

Campana, Dino 1885-1932 .... **TCLC 20**
See also CA 117; DLB 114

Campanella, Tommaso 1568-1639 .... **LC 32**

Campbell, John W(ood, Jr.) 1910-1971 .... **CLC 32**
See also CA 21-22; 29-32R; CANR 34; CAP 2; DLB 8; MTCW 1

Campbell, Joseph 1904-1987 .... **CLC 69**
See also AAYA 3; BEST 89:2; CA 1-4R; 124; CANR 3, 28, 61; DA3; MTCW 1, 2

Campbell, Maria 1940- .... **CLC 85; DAC**
See also CA 102; CANR 54; NNAL

Campbell, (John) Ramsey 1946- ..... **CLC 42; SSC 19**
See also CA 57-60; CANR 7; INT CANR-7

Campbell, (Ignatius) Roy (Dunnachie) 1901-1957 .... **TCLC 5**
See also CA 104; 155; DLB 20; MTCW 2

Campbell, Thomas 1777-1844 .... **NCLC 19**
See also DLB 93; 144

Campbell, Wilfred .... **TCLC 9**
See also Campbell, William

Campbell, William 1858(?)-1918
See Campbell, Wilfred
See also CA 106; DLB 92

Campion, Jane .... **CLC 95**
See also CA 138; CANR 87

Camus, Albert 1913-1960 ...... **CLC 1, 2, 4, 9, 11, 14, 32, 63, 69, 124; DA; DAB; DAC; DAM DRAM, MST, NOV; DC 2; SSC 9; WLC**
See also CA 89-92; DA3; DLB 72; MTCW 1, 2

Canby, Vincent 1924- .... **CLC 13**
See also CA 81-84

Cancale
See Desnos, Robert

Canetti, Elias 1905-1994 .. **CLC 3, 14, 25, 75, 86**
See also CA 21-24R; 146; CANR 23, 61, 79; DA3; DLB 85, 124; MTCW 1, 2

Canfield, Dorothea F.
See Fisher, Dorothy (Frances) Canfield

Canfield, Dorothea Frances
See Fisher, Dorothy (Frances) Canfield

Celan, Paul .... **CLC 10, 19, 53, 82; PC 10**
  See also Antschel, Paul DLB 69
Celine, Louis-Ferdinand ... **CLC 1, 3, 4, 7, 9, 15, 47, 124**
  See also Destouches, Louis-Ferdinand DLB 72
Cellini, Benvenuto 1500-1571 .... **LC 7**
Cendrars, Blaise 1887-1961 ...... **CLC 18, 106**
  See also Sauser-Hall, Frederic
Cernuda (y Bidon), Luis
  1902-1963 .... **CLC 54; DAM POET**
  See also CA 131; 89-92; DLB 134; HW 1
Cervantes, Lorna Dee 1954-
  See also CA 131; CANR 80; DLB 82; HLCS 1; HW 1
Cervantes (Saavedra), Miguel de 1547-1616
  LC 6, 23; DA; DAB; DAC; DAM MST, NOV; SSC 12; WLC
Cesaire, Aime (Fernand) 1913- .. **CLC 19, 32, 112; BLC 1; DAM MULT, POET; PC 25**
  See also BW 2, 3; CA 65-68; CANR 24, 43, 81; DA3; MTCW 1, 2
Chabon, Michael 1963- .... **CLC 55**
  See also CA 139; CANR 57
Chabrol, Claude 1930- .... **CLC 16**
  See also CA 110
Challans, Mary 1905-1983
  See Renault, Mary
  See also CA 81-84; 111; CANR 74; DA3; MTCW 2; SATA 23; SATA-Obit 36
Challis, George
  See Faust, Frederick (Schiller)
Chambers, Aidan 1934- .... **CLC 35**
  See also AAYA 27; CA 25-28R; CANR 12, 31, 58; JRDA; MAICYA; SAAS 12; SATA 1, 69, 108
Chambers, James 1948-
  See Cliff, Jimmy
  See also CA 124
Chambers, Jessie
  See Lawrence, D(avid) H(erbert Richards)
Chambers, Robert W(illiam) 1865-1933
  TCLC 41
  See also CA 165; DLB 202; SATA 107
Chamisso, Adelbert von
  1781-1838 .... **NCLC 82**
  See also DLB 90
Chandler, Raymond (Thornton) 1888-1959
  TCLC 1, 7; SSC 23
  See also AAYA 25; CA 104; 129; CANR 60; CDALB 1929-1941; DA3; DLBD 6; MTCW 1, 2
Chang, Eileen 1920-1995 .... **SSC 28**
  See also CA 166
Chang, Jung 1952- .... **CLC 71**
  See also CA 142
Chang Ai-Ling
  See Chang, Eileen
Channing, William Ellery
  1780-1842 .... **NCLC 17**
  See also DLB 1, 59
Chao, Patricia 1955- .... **CLC 119**
  See also CA 163
Chaplin, Charles Spencer
  1889-1977 .... **CLC 16**
  See also Chaplin, Charlie CA 81-84; 73-76
Chaplin, Charlie
  See Chaplin, Charles Spencer
  See also DLB 44
Chapman, George 1559(?)-1634 .... **LC 22; DAM DRAM**
  See also DLB 62, 121
Chapman, Graham 1941-1989 .... **CLC 21**
  See also Monty Python CA 116; 129; CANR 35
Chapman, John Jay 1862-1933 .... **TCLC 7**
  See also CA 104

Chapman, Lee
  See Bradley, Marion Zimmer
Chapman, Walker
  See Silverberg, Robert
Chappell, Fred (Davis) 1936- ..... **CLC 40, 78**
  See also CA 5-8R; CAAS 4; CANR 8, 33, 67; DLB 6, 105
Char, Rene(-Emile) 1907-1988 .... **CLC 9, 11, 14, 55; DAM POET**
  See also CA 13-16R; 124; CANR 32; MTCW 1, 2
Charby, Jay
  See Ellison, Harlan (Jay)
Chardin, Pierre Teilhard de
  See Teilhard de Chardin, (Marie Joseph) Pierre
Charlemagne 742-814 .... **CMLC 37**
Charles I 1600-1649 .... **LC 13**
Charriere, Isabelle de 1740-1805 .. **NCLC 66**
Charyn, Jerome 1937- .... **CLC 5, 8, 18**
  See also CA 5-8R; CAAS 1; CANR 7, 61; DLBY 83; MTCW 1
Chase, Mary (Coyle) 1907-1981 .... **DC 1**
  See also CA 77-80; 105; SATA 17; SATA-Obit 29
Chase, Mary Ellen 1887-1973 .... **CLC 2**
  See also CA 13-16; 41-44R; CAP 1; SATA 10
Chase, Nicholas
  See Hyde, Anthony
Chateaubriand, Francois Rene de 1768-1848
  NCLC 3
  See also DLB 119
Chatterje, Sarat Chandra 1876-1936(?)
  See Chatterji, Saratchandra
  See also CA 109
Chatterji, Bankim Chandra 1838-1894
  NCLC 19
Chatterji, Saratchandra .... **TCLC 13**
  See also Chatterje, Sarat Chandra
Chatterton, Thomas 1752-1770 ..... **LC 3, 54; DAM POET**
  See also DLB 109
Chatwin, (Charles) Bruce
  1940-1989 . **CLC 28, 57, 59; DAM POP**
  See also AAYA 4; BEST 90:1; CA 85-88; 127; DLB 194, 204
Chaucer, Daniel
  See Ford, Ford Madox
Chaucer, Geoffrey 1340(?)-1400 .... **LC 17; DA; DAB; DAC; DAM MST, POET; PC 19; WLCS**
  See also CDBLB Before 1660; DA3; DLB 146
Chavez, Denise (Elia) 1948-
  See also CA 131; CANR 56, 81; DAM MULT; DLB 122; HLC 1; HW 1, 2; MTCW 2
Chaviaras, Strates 1935-
  See Haviaras, Stratis
  See also CA 105
Chayefsky, Paddy .... **CLC 23**
  See also Chayefsky, Sidney DLB 7, 44; DLBY 81
Chayefsky, Sidney 1923-1981
  See Chayefsky, Paddy
  See also CA 9-12R; 104; CANR 18; DAM DRAM
Chedid, Andree 1920- .... **CLC 47**
  See also CA 145
Cheever, John 1912-1982 ..... **CLC 3, 7, 8, 11, 15, 25, 64; DA; DAB; DAC; DAM MST, NOV, POP; SSC 1, 38; WLC**
  See also CA 5-8R; 106; CABS 1; CANR 5, 27, 76; CDALB 1941-1968; DA3; DLB 2, 102; DLBY 80, 82; INT CANR-5; MTCW 1, 2

Cheever, Susan 1943- .... **CLC 18, 48**
  See also CA 103; CANR 27, 51; DLBY 82; INT CANR-27
Chekhonte, Antosha
  See Chekhov, Anton (Pavlovich)
Chekhov, Anton (Pavlovich) 1860-1904
  TCLC 3, 10, 31, 55, 96; DA; DAB; DAC; DAM DRAM, MST; DC 9; SSC 2, 28; WLC
  See also CA 104; 124; DA3; SATA 90
Chernyshevsky, Nikolay Gavrilovich
  1828-1889 .... **NCLC 1**
Cherry, Carolyn Janice 1942-
  See Cherryh, C. J.
  See also CA 65-68; CANR 10
Cherryh, C. J. .... **CLC 35**
  See also Cherry, Carolyn Janice AAYA 24; DLBY 80; SATA 93
Chesnutt, Charles W(addell) 1858-1932
  TCLC 5, 39; BLC 1; DAM MULT; SSC 7
  See also BW 1, 3; CA 106; 125; CANR 76; DLB 12, 50, 78; MTCW 1, 2
Chester, Alfred 1929(?)-1971 .... **CLC 49**
  See also CA 33-36R; DLB 130
Chesterton, G(ilbert) K(eith) 1874-1936
  TCLC 1, 6, 64; DAM NOV, POET; PC 28; SSC 1
  See also CA 104; 132; CANR 73; CDBLB 1914-1945; DLB 10, 19, 34, 70, 98, 149, 178; MTCW 1, 2; SATA 27
Chiang, Pin-chin 1904-1986
  See Ding Ling
  See also CA 118
Ch'ien Chung-shu 1910- .... **CLC 22**
  See also CA 130; CANR 73; MTCW 1, 2
Child, L. Maria
  See Child, Lydia Maria
Child, Lydia Maria 1802-1880 .. **NCLC 6, 73**
  See also DLB 1, 74; SATA 67
Child, Mrs.
  See Child, Lydia Maria
Child, Philip 1898-1978 .... **CLC 19, 68**
  See also CA 13-14; CAP 1; SATA 47
Childers, (Robert) Erskine
  1870-1922 .... **TCLC 65**
  See also CA 113; 153; DLB 70
Childress, Alice 1920-1994 .. **CLC 12, 15, 86, 96; BLC 1; DAM DRAM, MULT, NOV; DC 4**
  See also AAYA 8; BW 2, 3; CA 45-48; 146; CANR 3, 27, 50, 74; CLR 14; DA3; DLB 7, 38; JRDA; MAICYA; MTCW 1, 2; SATA 7, 48, 81
Chin, Frank (Chew, Jr.) 1940- .... **DC 7**
  See also CA 33-36R; CANR 71; DAM MULT; DLB 206
Chislett, (Margaret) Anne 1943- ...... **CLC 34**
  See also CA 151
Chitty, Thomas Willes 1926- .... **CLC 11**
  See also Hinde, Thomas CA 5-8R
Chivers, Thomas Holley
  1809-1858 .... **NCLC 49**
  See also DLB 3
Choi, Susan .... **CLC 119**
Chomette, Rene Lucien 1898-1981
  See Clair, Rene
  See also CA 103
Chopin, Kate .. **TCLC 5, 14; DA; DAB; SSC 8; WLCS**
  See also Chopin, Katherine CDALB 1865-1917; DLB 12, 78
Chopin, Katherine 1851-1904
  See Chopin, Kate
  See also CA 104; 122; DAC; DAM MST, NOV; DA3
Chretien de Troyes c. 12th cent. - . **CMLC 10**
  See also DLB 208

Coles, Don 1928- .... **CLC 46**
    See also CA 115; CANR 38
Coles, Robert (Martin) 1929- .... **CLC 108**
    See also CA 45-48; CANR 3, 32, 66, 70;
    INT CANR-32; SATA 23
Colette, (Sidonie-Gabrielle)
    1873-1954 . **TCLC 1, 5, 16; DAM NOV;**
    SSC 10
    See also CA 104; 131; DA3; DLB 65;
    MTCW 1, 2
Collett, (Jacobine) Camilla (Wergeland)
    1813-1895 .... **NCLC 22**
Collier, Christopher 1930- .... **CLC 30**
    See also AAYA 13; CA 33-36R; CANR 13,
    33; JRDA; MAICYA; SATA 16, 70
Collier, James L(incoln) 1928- .... **CLC 30;**
    DAM POP
    See also AAYA 13; CA 9-12R; CANR 4,
    33, 60; CLR 3; JRDA; MAICYA; SAAS
    21; SATA 8, 70
Collier, Jeremy 1650-1726 .... **LC 6**
Collier, John 1901-1980 .... **SSC 19**
    See also CA 65-68; 97-100; CANR 10;
    DLB 77
Collingwood, R(obin) G(eorge) 1889(?)-1943
    TCLC 67
    See also CA 117; 155
Collins, Hunt
    See Hunter, Evan
Collins, Linda 1931- .... **CLC 44**
    See also CA 125
Collins, (William) Wilkie
    1824-1889 .... **NCLC 1, 18**
    See also CDBLB 1832-1890; DLB 18, 70,
    159
Collins, William 1721-1759 . **LC 4, 40; DAM**
    POET
    See also DLB 109
Collodi, Carlo 1826-1890 .... **NCLC 54**
    See also Lorenzini, Carlo CLR 5
Colman, George 1732-1794
    See Glassco, John
Colt, Winchester Remington
    See Hubbard, L(afayette) Ron(ald)
Colter, Cyrus 1910- .... **CLC 58**
    See also BW 1; CA 65-68; CANR 10, 66;
    DLB 33
Colton, James
    See Hansen, Joseph
Colum, Padraic 1881-1972 .... **CLC 28**
    See also CA 73-76; 33-36R; CANR 35;
    CLR 36; MAICYA; MTCW 1; SATA 15
Colvin, James
    See Moorcock, Michael (John)
Colwin, Laurie (E.) 1944-1992 .... **CLC 5, 13,**
    23, 84
    See also CA 89-92; 139; CANR 20, 46;
    DLBY 80; MTCW 1
Comfort, Alex(ander) 1920- .... **CLC 7; DAM**
    POP
    See also CA 1-4R; CANR 1, 45; MTCW 1
Comfort, Montgomery
    See Campbell, (John) Ramsey
Compton-Burnett, I(vy)
    1884(?)-1969 .... **CLC 1, 3, 10, 15, 34;**
    DAM NOV
    See also CA 1-4R; 25-28R; CANR 4; DLB
    36; MTCW 1
Comstock, Anthony 1844-1915 ...... **TCLC 13**
    See also CA 110; 169
Comte, Auguste 1798-1857 .... **NCLC 54**
Conan Doyle, Arthur
    See Doyle, Arthur Conan
Conde (Abellan), Carmen 1901-
    See also CA 177; DLB 108; HLCS 1; HW
    2

Conde, Maryse 1937- .... **CLC 52, 92; BLCS;**
    DAM MULT
    See also Boucolon, Maryse BW 2; MTCW
    1
Condillac, Etienne Bonnot de
    1714-1780 .... **LC 26**
Condon, Richard (Thomas)
    1915-1996 ...... **CLC 4, 6, 8, 10, 45, 100;**
    DAM NOV
    See also BEST 90:3; CA 1-4R; 151; CAAS
    1; CANR 2, 23; INT CANR-23; MTCW
    1, 2
Confucius 551B.C.-479B.C. .. **CMLC 19; DA;**
    DAB; DAC; DAM MST; WLCS
    See also DA3
Congreve, William 1670-1729 .... **LC 5, 21;**
    DA; DAB; DAC; DAM DRAM, MST,
    POET; DC 2; WLC
    See also CDBLB 1660-1789; DLB 39, 84
Connell, Evan S(helby), Jr. 1924- . **CLC 4, 6,**
    45; DAM NOV
    See also AAYA 7; CA 1-4R; CAAS 2;
    CANR 2, 39, 76; DLB 2; DLBY 81;
    MTCW 1, 2
Connelly, Marc(us Cook) 1890-1980 . **CLC 7**
    See also CA 85-88; 102; CANR 30; DLB
    7; DLBY 80; SATA-Obit 25
Connor, Ralph .... **TCLC 31**
    See also Gordon, Charles William DLB 92
Conrad, Joseph 1857-1924 .... **TCLC 1, 6, 13,**
    25, 43, 57; DA; DAB; DAC; DAM
    MST, NOV; SSC 9; WLC
    See also AAYA 26; CA 104; 131; CANR
    60; CDBLB 1890-1914; DA3; DLB 10,
    34, 98, 156; MTCW 1, 2; SATA 27
Conrad, Robert Arnold
    See Hart, Moss
Conroy, Pat
    See Conroy, (Donald) Pat(rick)
    See also MTCW 2
Conroy, (Donald) Pat(rick) 1945- ... **CLC 30,**
    74; DAM NOV, POP
    See also Conroy, Pat AAYA 8; AITN 1; CA
    85-88; CANR 24, 53; DA3; DLB 6;
    MTCW 1
Constant (de Rebecque), (Henri) Benjamin
    1767-1830 .... **NCLC 6**
    See also DLB 119
Conybeare, Charles Augustus
    See Eliot, T(homas) S(tearns)
Cook, Michael 1933- .... **CLC 58**
    See also CA 93-96; CANR 68; DLB 53
Cook, Robin 1940- .... **CLC 14; DAM POP**
    See also AAYA 32; BEST 90:2; CA 108;
    111; CANR 41; DA3; INT 111
Cook, Roy
    See Silverberg, Robert
Cooke, Elizabeth 1948- .... **CLC 55**
    See also CA 129
Cooke, John Esten 1830-1886 .... **NCLC 5**
    See also DLB 3
Cooke, John Estes
    See Baum, L(yman) Frank
Cooke, M. E.
    See Creasey, John
Cooke, Margaret
    See Creasey, John
Cook-Lynn, Elizabeth 1930- . **CLC 93; DAM**
    MULT
    See also CA 133; DLB 175; NNAL
Cooney, Ray .... **CLC 62**
Cooper, Douglas 1960- .... **CLC 86**
Cooper, Henry St. John
    See Creasey, John
Cooper, J(oan) California (?)- .... **CLC 56;**
    DAM MULT
    See also AAYA 12; BW 1; CA 125; CANR
    55; DLB 212

Cooper, James Fenimore
    1789-1851 .... **NCLC 1, 27, 54**
    See also AAYA 22; CDALB 1640-1865;
    DA3; DLB 3; SATA 19
Coover, Robert (Lowell) 1932- ...... **CLC 3, 7,**
    15, 32, 46, 87; DAM NOV; SSC 15
    See also CA 45-48; CANR 3, 37, 58; DLB
    2; DLBY 81; MTCW 1, 2
Copeland, Stewart (Armstrong)
    1952- .... **CLC 26**
Copernicus, Nicolaus 1473-1543 .... **LC 45**
Coppard, A(lfred) E(dgar)
    1878-1957 .... **TCLC 5; SSC 21**
    See also CA 114; 167; DLB 162; YABC 1
Coppee, Francois 1842-1908 .... **TCLC 25**
    See also CA 170
Coppola, Francis Ford 1939- ... **CLC 16, 126**
    See also CA 77-80; CANR 40, 78; DLB 44
Corbiere, Tristan 1845-1875 .... **NCLC 43**
Corcoran, Barbara 1911- .... **CLC 17**
    See also AAYA 14; CA 21-24R; CAAS 2;
    CANR 11, 28, 48; CLR 50; DLB 52;
    JRDA; SAAS 20; SATA 3, 77
Cordelier, Maurice
    See Giraudoux, (Hippolyte) Jean
Corelli, Marie 1855-1924 .... **TCLC 51**
    See also Mackay, Mary DLB 34, 156
Corman, Cid 1924- .... **CLC 9**
    See also Corman, Sidney CAAS 2; DLB 5,
    193
Corman, Sidney 1924-
    See Corman, Cid
    See also CA 85-88; CANR 44; DAM POET
Cormier, Robert (Edmund) 1925- ... **CLC 12,**
    30; DA; DAB; DAC; DAM MST, NOV
    See also AAYA 3, 19; CA 1-4R; CANR 5,
    23, 76; CDALB 1968-1988; CLR 12, 55;
    DLB 52; INT CANR-23; JRDA; MAI-
    CYA; MTCW 1, 2; SATA 10, 45, 83
Corn, Alfred (DeWitt III) 1943- .... **CLC 33**
    See also CA 179; CAAE 179; CAAS 25;
    CANR 44; DLB 120; DLBY 80
Corneille, Pierre 1606-1684 ..... **LC 28; DAB;**
    DAM MST
Cornwell, David (John Moore)
    1931- .... **CLC 9, 15; DAM POP**
    See also le Carre, John CA 5-8R; CANR
    13, 33, 59; DA3; MTCW 1, 2
Corso, (Nunzio) Gregory 1930- .... **CLC 1, 11**
    See also CA 5-8R; CANR 41, 76; DA3;
    DLB 5, 16; MTCW 1, 2
Cortazar, Julio 1914-1984 ... **CLC 2, 3, 5, 10,**
    13, 15, 33, 34, 92; DAM MULT, NOV;
    HLC 1; SSC 7
    See also CA 21-24R; CANR 12, 32, 81;
    DA3; DLB 113; HW 1, 2; MTCW 1, 2
CORTES, HERNAN 1484-1547 .... **LC 31**
Corvinus, Jakob
    See Raabe, Wilhelm (Karl)
Corwin, Cecil
    See Kornbluth, C(yril) M.
Cosic, Dobrica 1921- .... **CLC 14**
    See also CA 122; 138; DLB 181
Costain, Thomas B(ertram)
    1885-1965 .... **CLC 30**
    See also CA 5-8R; 25-28R; DLB 9
Costantini, Humberto 1924(?)-1987 . **CLC 49**
    See also CA 131; 122; HW 1
Costello, Elvis 1955- .... **CLC 21**
Costenoble, Philostene
    See Ghelderode, Michel de
Cotes, Cecil V.
    See Duncan, Sara Jeannette
Cotter, Joseph Seamon Sr.
    1861-1949 ...... **TCLC 28; BLC 1; DAM**
    MULT
    See also BW 1; CA 124; DLB 50

Ferguson, Helen
See Kavan, Anna
Ferguson, Samuel 1810-1886 .... **NCLC 33**
See also DLB 32
Fergusson, Robert 1750-1774 .... **LC 29**
See also DLB 109
Ferling, Lawrence
See Ferlinghetti, Lawrence (Monsanto)
Ferlinghetti, Lawrence (Monsanto) 1919(?)-
**CLC 2, 6, 10, 27, 111; DAM POET; PC
1**
See also CA 5-8R; CANR 3, 41, 73;
CDALB 1941-1968; DA3; DLB 5, 16;
MTCW 1, 2
Fernandez, Vicente Garcia Huidobro
See Huidobro Fernandez, Vicente Garcia
Ferre, Rosario 1942- .... **SSC 36; HLCS 1**
See also CA 131; CANR 55, 81; DLB 145;
HW 1, 2; MTCW 1
Ferrer, Gabriel (Francisco Victor) Miro
See Miro (Ferrer), Gabriel (Francisco
Victor)
Ferrier, Susan (Edmonstone) 1782-1854
NCLC 8
See also DLB 116
Ferrigno, Robert 1948(?)- .... **CLC 65**
See also CA 140
Ferron, Jacques 1921-1985 .... **CLC 94; DAC**
See also CA 117; 129; DLB 60
Feuchtwanger, Lion 1884-1958 .... **TCLC 3**
See also CA 104; DLB 66
Feuillet, Octave 1821-1890 .... **NCLC 45**
See also DLB 192
Feydeau, Georges (Leon Jules Marie)
1862-1921 .... **TCLC 22; DAM DRAM**
See also CA 113; 152; CANR 84; DLB 192
Fichte, Johann Gottlieb
1762-1814 .... **NCLC 62**
See also DLB 90
Ficino, Marsilio 1433-1499 .... **LC 12**
Fiedeler, Hans
See Doeblin, Alfred
Fiedler, Leslie A(aron) 1917- .. **CLC 4, 13, 24**
See also CA 9-12R; CANR 7, 63; DLB 28,
67; MTCW 1, 2
Field, Andrew 1938- .... **CLC 44**
See also CA 97-100; CANR 25
Field, Eugene 1850-1895 .... **NCLC 3**
See also DLB 23, 42, 140; DLBD 13; MAI-
CYA; SATA 16
Field, Gans T.
See Wellman, Manly Wade
Field, Michael 1915-1971 .... **TCLC 43**
See also CA 29-32R
Field, Peter
See Hobson, Laura Z(ametkin)
Fielding, Henry 1707-1754 ..... **LC 1, 46; DA;
DAB; DAC; DAM DRAM, MST, NOV;
WLC**
See also CDBLB 1660-1789; DA3; DLB
39, 84, 101
Fielding, Sarah 1710-1768 .... **LC 1, 44**
See also DLB 39
Fields, W. C. 1880-1946 .... **TCLC 80**
See also DLB 44
Fierstein, Harvey (Forbes) 1954- .... **CLC 33;
DAM DRAM, POP**
See also CA 123; 129; DA3
Figes, Eva 1932- .... **CLC 31**
See also CA 53-56; CANR 4, 44, 83; DLB
14
Finch, Anne 1661-1720 .... **LC 3; PC 21**
See also DLB 95
Finch, Robert (Duer Claydon)
1900- .... **CLC 18**
See also CA 57-60; CANR 9, 24, 49; DLB
88

Findley, Timothy 1930- . **CLC 27, 102; DAC;
DAM MST**
See also CA 25-28R; CANR 12, 42, 69;
DLB 53
Fink, William
See Mencken, H(enry) L(ouis)
Firbank, Louis 1942-
See Reed, Lou
See also CA 117
Firbank, (Arthur Annesley) Ronald
1886-1926 .... **TCLC 1**
See also CA 104; 177; DLB 36
Fisher, Dorothy (Frances) Canfield
1879-1958 .... **TCLC 87**
See also CA 114; 136; CANR 80; DLB 9,
102; MAICYA; YABC 1
Fisher, M(ary) F(rances) K(ennedy)
1908-1992 .... **CLC 76, 87**
See also CA 77-80; 138; CANR 44; MTCW
1
Fisher, Roy 1930- .... **CLC 25**
See also CA 81-84; CAAS 10; CANR 16;
DLB 40
Fisher, Rudolph 1897-1934 .. **TCLC 11; BLC
2; DAM MULT; SSC 25**
See also BW 1, 3; CA 107; 124; CANR 80;
DLB 51, 102
Fisher, Vardis (Alvero) 1895-1968 ...... **CLC 7**
See also CA 5-8R; 25-28R; CANR 68; DLB
9, 206
Fiske, Tarleton
See Bloch, Robert (Albert)
Fitch, Clarke
See Sinclair, Upton (Beall)
Fitch, John IV
See Cormier, Robert (Edmund)
Fitzgerald, Captain Hugh
See Baum, L(yman) Frank
FitzGerald, Edward 1809-1883 .... **NCLC 9**
See also DLB 32
Fitzgerald, F(rancis) Scott (Key) 1896-1940
**TCLC 1, 6, 14, 28, 55; DA; DAB; DAC;
DAM MST, NOV; SSC 6, 31; WLC**
See also AAYA 24; AITN 1; CA 110; 123;
CDALB 1917-1929; DA3; DLB 4, 9, 86;
DLBD 1, 15, 16; DLBY 81, 96; MTCW
1, 2
Fitzgerald, Penelope 1916- ... **CLC 19, 51, 61**
See also CA 85-88; CAAS 10; CANR 56,
86; DLB 14, 194; MTCW 2
Fitzgerald, Robert (Stuart)
1910-1985 .... **CLC 39**
See also CA 1-4R; 114; CANR 1; DLBY
80
FitzGerald, Robert D(avid)
1902-1987 .... **CLC 19**
See also CA 17-20R
Fitzgerald, Zelda (Sayre)
1900-1948 .... **TCLC 52**
See also CA 117; 126; DLBY 84
Flanagan, Thomas (James Bonner) 1923-
CLC 25, 52
See also CA 108; CANR 55; DLBY 80; INT
108; MTCW 1
Flaubert, Gustave 1821-1880 .... **NCLC 2, 10,
19, 62, 66; DA; DAB; DAC; DAM
MST, NOV; SSC 11; WLC**
See also DA3; DLB 119
Flecker, Herman Elroy
See Flecker, (Herman) James Elroy
Flecker, (Herman) James Elroy 1884-1915
TCLC 43
See also CA 109; 150; DLB 10, 19
Fleming, Ian (Lancaster) 1908-1964 . **CLC 3,
30; DAM POP**
See also AAYA 26; CA 5-8R; CANR 59;
CDBLB 1945-1960; DA3; DLB 87, 201;
MTCW 1, 2; SATA 9

Fleming, Thomas (James) 1927- ...... **CLC 37**
See also CA 5-8R; CANR 10; INT CANR-
10; SATA 8
Fletcher, John 1579-1625 .... **LC 33; DC 6**
See also CDBLB Before 1660; DLB 58
Fletcher, John Gould 1886-1950 .... **TCLC 35**
See also CA 107; 167; DLB 4, 45
Fleur, Paul
See Pohl, Frederik
Flooglebuckle, Al
See Spiegelman, Art
Flying Officer X
See Bates, H(erbert) E(rnest)
Fo, Dario 1926- .... **CLC 32, 109; DAM
DRAM; DC 10**
See also CA 116; 128; CANR 68; DA3;
DLBY 97; MTCW 1, 2
Fogarty, Jonathan Titulescu Esq.
See Farrell, James T(homas)
Follett, Ken(neth Martin) 1949- ..... **CLC 18;
DAM NOV, POP**
See also AAYA 6; BEST 89:4; CA 81-84;
CANR 13, 33, 54; DA3; DLB 87; DLBY
81; INT CANR-33; MTCW 1
Fontane, Theodor 1819-1898 .... **NCLC 26**
See also DLB 129
Foote, Horton 1916- .... **CLC 51, 91; DAM
DRAM**
See also CA 73-76; CANR 34, 51; DA3;
DLB 26; INT CANR-34
Foote, Shelby 1916- ..... **CLC 75; DAM NOV,
POP**
See also CA 5-8R; CANR 3, 45, 74; DA3;
DLB 2, 17; MTCW 2
Forbes, Esther 1891-1967 .... **CLC 12**
See also AAYA 17; CA 13-14; 25-28R; CAP
1; CLR 27; DLB 22; JRDA; MAICYA;
SATA 2, 100
Forche, Carolyn (Louise) 1950- .... **CLC 25,
83, 86; DAM POET; PC 10**
See also CA 109; 117; CANR 50, 74; DA3;
DLB 5, 193; INT 117; MTCW 1
Ford, Elbur
See Hibbert, Eleanor Alice Burford
Ford, Ford Madox 1873-1939 ... **TCLC 1, 15,
39, 57; DAM NOV**
See also CA 104; 132; CANR 74; CDBLB
1914-1945; DA3; DLB 162; MTCW 1, 2
Ford, Henry 1863-1947 .... **TCLC 73**
See also CA 115; 148
Ford, John 1586-(?) .... **DC 8**
See also CDBLB Before 1660; DAM
DRAM; DA3; DLB 58
Ford, John 1895-1973 .... **CLC 16**
See also CA 45-48
Ford, Richard 1944- .... **CLC 46, 99**
See also CA 69-72; CANR 11, 47, 86;
MTCW 1
Ford, Webster
See Masters, Edgar Lee
Foreman, Richard 1937- .... **CLC 50**
See also CA 65-68; CANR 32, 63
Forester, C(ecil) S(cott) 1899-1966 ... **CLC 35**
See also CA 73-76; 25-28R; CANR 83;
DLB 191; SATA 13
Forez
See Mauriac, Francois (Charles)
Forman, James Douglas 1932- .... **CLC 21**
See also AAYA 17; CA 9-12R; CANR 4,
19, 42; JRDA; MAICYA; SATA 8, 70
Fornes, Maria Irene 1930- . **CLC 39, 61; DC
10; HLCS 1**
See also CA 25-28R; CANR 28, 81; DLB
7; HW 1, 2; INT CANR-28; MTCW 1
Forrest, Leon (Richard) 1937-1997 .. **CLC 4;
BLCS**
See also BW 2; CA 89-92; 162; CAAS 7;
CANR 25, 52, 87; DLB 33

Goldman, Francisco 1954- .... **CLC 76**
See also CA 162

Goldman, William (W.) 1931- ...... **CLC 1, 48**
See also CA 9-12R; CANR 29, 69; DLB 44

Goldmann, Lucien 1913-1970 .... **CLC 24**
See also CA 25-28; CAP 2

Goldoni, Carlo 1707-1793 .... **LC 4; DAM DRAM**

Goldsberry, Steven 1949- .... **CLC 34**
See also CA 131

Goldsmith, Oliver 1728-1774 . **LC 2, 48; DA; DAB; DAC; DAM DRAM, MST, NOV, POET; DC 8; WLC**
See also CDBLB 1660-1789; DLB 39, 89, 104, 109, 142; SATA 26

Goldsmith, Peter
See Priestley, J(ohn) B(oynton)

Gombrowicz, Witold 1904-1969 .... **CLC 4, 7, 11, 49; DAM DRAM**
See also CA 19-20; 25-28R; CAP 2

Gomez de la Serna, Ramon 1888-1963 .... **CLC 9**
See also CA 153; 116; CANR 79; HW 1, 2

Goncharov, Ivan Alexandrovich 1812-1891 **NCLC 1, 63**

Goncourt, Edmond (Louis Antoine Huot) de 1822-1896 .... **NCLC 7**
See also DLB 123

Goncourt, Jules (Alfred Huot) de 1830-1870 **NCLC 7**
See also DLB 123

Gontier, Fernande 19(?)- .... **CLC 50**

Gonzalez Martinez, Enrique 1871-1952 **TCLC 72**
See also CA 166; CANR 81; HW 1, 2

Goodman, Paul 1911-1972 ..... **CLC 1, 2, 4, 7**
See also CA 19-20; 37-40R; CANR 34; CAP 2; DLB 130; MTCW 1

Gordimer, Nadine 1923- ...... **CLC 3, 5, 7, 10, 18, 33, 51, 70; DA; DAB; DAC; DAM MST, NOV; SSC 17; WLCS**
See also CA 5-8R; CANR 3, 28, 56; DA3; INT CANR-28; MTCW 1, 2

Gordon, Adam Lindsay 1833-1870 .... **NCLC 21**

Gordon, Caroline 1895-1981 . **CLC 6, 13, 29, 83; SSC 15**
See also CA 11-12; 103; CANR 36; CAP 1; DLB 4, 9, 102; DLBD 17; DLBY 81; MTCW 1, 2

Gordon, Charles William 1860-1937
See Connor, Ralph
See also CA 109

Gordon, Mary (Catherine) 1949- .... **CLC 13, 22, 128**
See also CA 102; CANR 44; DLB 6; DLBY 81; INT 102; MTCW 1

Gordon, N. J.
See Bosman, Herman Charles

Gordon, Sol 1923- .... **CLC 26**
See also CA 53-56; CANR 4; SATA 11

Gordone, Charles 1925-1995 .... **CLC 1, 4; DAM DRAM; DC 8**
See also BW 1, 3; CA 93-96; 180; 150; CAAE 180; CANR 55; DLB 7; INT 93-96; MTCW 1

Gore, Catherine 1800-1861 .... **NCLC 65**
See also DLB 116

Gorenko, Anna Andreevna
See Akhmatova, Anna

Gorky, Maxim 1868-1936 ..... **TCLC 8; DAB; SSC 28; WLC**
See also Peshkov, Alexei Maximovich MTCW 2

Goryan, Sirak
See Saroyan, William

Gosse, Edmund (William) 1849-1928 .... **TCLC 28**
See also CA 117; DLB 57, 144, 184

Gotlieb, Phyllis Fay (Bloom) 1926- .. **CLC 18**
See also CA 13-16R; CANR 7; DLB 88

Gottesman, S. D.
See Kornbluth, C(yril) M.; Pohl, Frederik

Gottfried von Strassburg fl. c. 1210- .... **CMLC 10**
See also DLB 138

Gould, Lois .... **CLC 4, 10**
See also CA 77-80; CANR 29; MTCW 1

Gourmont, Remy (-Marie-Charles) de 1858-1915 .... **TCLC 17**
See also CA 109; 150; MTCW 2

Govier, Katherine 1948- .... **CLC 51**
See also CA 101; CANR 18, 40

Goyen, (Charles) William 1915-1983 .... **CLC 5, 8, 14, 40**
See also AITN 2; CA 5-8R; 110; CANR 6, 71; DLB 2; DLBY 83; INT CANR-6

Goytisolo, Juan 1931- . **CLC 5, 10, 23; DAM MULT; HLC 1**
See also CA 85-88; CANR 32, 61; HW 1, 2; MTCW 1, 2

Gozzano, Guido 1883-1916 .... **PC 10**
See also CA 154; DLB 114

Gozzi, (Conte) Carlo 1720-1806 .... **NCLC 23**

Grabbe, Christian Dietrich 1801-1836 .... **NCLC 2**
See also DLB 133

Grace, Patricia Frances 1937- .... **CLC 56**
See also CA 176

Gracian y Morales, Baltasar 1601-1658 .... **LC 15**

Gracq, Julien .... **CLC 11, 48**
See also Poirier, Louis DLB 83

Grade, Chaim 1910-1982 .... **CLC 10**
See also CA 93-96; 107

Graduate of Oxford, A
See Ruskin, John

Grafton, Garth
See Duncan, Sara Jeannette

Graham, John
See Phillips, David Graham

Graham, Jorie 1951- .... **CLC 48, 118**
See also CA 111; CANR 63; DLB 120

Graham, R(obert) B(ontine) Cunninghame
See Cunninghame Graham, R(obert) B(ontine)
See also DLB 98, 135, 174

Graham, Robert
See Haldeman, Joe (William)

Graham, Tom
See Lewis, (Harry) Sinclair

Graham, W(illiam) S(ydney) 1918-1986 .... **CLC 29**
See also CA 73-76; 118; DLB 20

Graham, Winston (Mawdsley) 1910- .... **CLC 23**
See also CA 49-52; CANR 2, 22, 45, 66; DLB 77

Grahame, Kenneth 1859-1932 ...... **TCLC 64; DAB**
See also CA 108; 136; CANR 80; CLR 5; DA3; DLB 34, 141, 178; MAICYA; MTCW 2; SATA 100; YABC 1

Granovsky, Timofei Nikolaevich 1813-1855 **NCLC 75**
See also DLB 198

Grant, Skeeter
See Spiegelman, Art

Granville-Barker, Harley 1877-1946 .... **TCLC 2; DAM DRAM**
See also Barker, Harley Granville CA 104

Grass, Guenter (Wilhelm) 1927- ... **CLC 1, 2, 4, 6, 11, 15, 22, 32, 49, 88; DA; DAB; DAC; DAM MST, NOV; WLC**
See also CA 13-16R; CANR 20, 75; DA3; DLB 75, 124; MTCW 1, 2

Gratton, Thomas
See Hulme, T(homas) E(rnest)

Grau, Shirley Ann 1929- . **CLC 4, 9; SSC 15**
See also CA 89-92; CANR 22, 69; DLB 2; INT CANR-22; MTCW 1

Gravel, Fern
See Hall, James Norman

Graver, Elizabeth 1964- .... **CLC 70**
See also CA 135; CANR 71

Graves, Richard Perceval 1945- .... **CLC 44**
See also CA 65-68; CANR 9, 26, 51

Graves, Robert (von Ranke) 1895-1985 .. **CLC 1, 2, 6, 11, 39, 44, 45; DAB; DAC; DAM MST, POET; PC 6**
See also CA 5-8R; 117; CANR 5, 36; CD-BLB 1914-1945; DA3; DLB 20, 100, 191; DLBD 18; DLBY 85; MTCW 1, 2; SATA 45

Graves, Valerie
See Bradley, Marion Zimmer

Gray, Alasdair (James) 1934- .... **CLC 41**
See also CA 126; CANR 47, 69; DLB 194; INT 126; MTCW 1, 2

Gray, Amlin 1946- .... **CLC 29**
See also CA 138

Gray, Francine du Plessix 1930- ..... **CLC 22; DAM NOV**
See also BEST 90:3; CA 61-64; CAAS 2; CANR 11, 33, 75, 81; INT CANR-11; MTCW 1, 2

Gray, John (Henry) 1866-1934 ...... **TCLC 19**
See also CA 119; 162

Gray, Simon (James Holliday) 1936- .... **CLC 9, 14, 36**
See also AITN 1; CA 21-24R; CAAS 3; CANR 32, 69; DLB 13; MTCW 1

Gray, Spalding 1941- ..... **CLC 49, 112; DAM POP; DC 7**
See also CA 128; CANR 74; MTCW 2

Gray, Thomas 1716-1771 .... **LC 4, 40; DA; DAB; DAC; DAM MST; PC 2; WLC**
See also CDBLB 1660-1789; DA3; DLB 109

Grayson, David
See Baker, Ray Stannard

Grayson, Richard (A.) 1951- .... **CLC 38**
See also CA 85-88; CANR 14, 31, 57

Greeley, Andrew M(oran) 1928- ..... **CLC 28; DAM POP**
See also CA 5-8R; CAAS 7; CANR 7, 43, 69; DA3; MTCW 1, 2

Green, Anna Katharine 1846-1935 .... **TCLC 63**
See also CA 112; 159; DLB 202

Green, Brian
See Card, Orson Scott

Green, Hannah
See Greenberg, Joanne (Goldenberg)

Green, Hannah 1927(?)-1996 .... **CLC 3**
See also CA 73-76; CANR 59

Green, Henry 1905-1973 .... **CLC 2, 13, 97**
See also Yorke, Henry Vincent CA 175; DLB 15

Green, Julian (Hartridge) 1900-1998
See Green, Julien
See also CA 21-24R; 169; CANR 33, 87; DLB 4, 72; MTCW 1

Green, Julien .... **CLC 3, 11, 77**
See also Green, Julian (Hartridge) MTCW 2

Green, Paul (Eliot) 1894-1981 .... **CLC 25; DAM DRAM**
See also AITN 1; CA 5-8R; 103; CANR 3; DLB 7, 9; DLBY 81

Greenberg, Ivan 1908-1973
See Rahv, Philip
See also CA 85-88

Hemingway, Ernest (Miller)
1899-1961 .... **CLC 1, 3, 6, 8, 10, 13, 19, 30, 34, 39, 41, 44, 50, 61, 80; DA; DAB; DAC; DAM MST, NOV; SSC 1, 25, 36; WLC**
See also AAYA 19; CA 77-80; CANR 34; CDALB 1917-1929; DA3; DLB 4, 9, 102, 210; DLBD 1, 15, 16; DLBY 81, 87, 96, 98; MTCW 1, 2

Hempel, Amy 1951- .... **CLC 39**
See also CA 118; 137; CANR 70; DA3; MTCW 2

Henderson, F. C.
See Mencken, H(enry) L(ouis)

Henderson, Sylvia
See Ashton-Warner, Sylvia (Constance)

Henderson, Zenna (Chlarson)
1917-1983 .... **SSC 29**
See also CA 1-4R; 133; CANR 1, 84; DLB 8; SATA 5

Henkin, Joshua .... **CLC 119**
See also CA 161

Henley, Beth .... **CLC 23; DC 6**
See also Henley, Elizabeth Becker CABS 3; DLBY 86

Henley, Elizabeth Becker 1952-
See Henley, Beth
See also CA 107; CANR 32, 73; DAM DRAM, MST; DA3; MTCW 1, 2

Henley, William Ernest 1849-1903 .. **TCLC 8**
See also CA 105; DLB 19

Hennissart, Martha
See Lathen, Emma
See also CA 85-88; CANR 64

Henry, O. .... **TCLC 1, 19; SSC 5; WLC**
See also Porter, William Sydney

Henry, Patrick 1736-1799 .... **LC 25**

Henryson, Robert 1430(?)-1506(?) ...... **LC 20**
See also DLB 146

Henry VIII 1491-1547 .... **LC 10**
See also DLB 132

Henschke, Alfred
See Klabund

Hentoff, Nat(han Irving) 1925- .... **CLC 26**
See also AAYA 4; CA 1-4R; CAAS 6; CANR 5, 25, 77; CLR 1, 52; INT CANR-25; JRDA; MAICYA; SATA 42, 69; SATA-Brief 27

Heppenstall, (John) Rayner
1911-1981 .... **CLC 10**
See also CA 1-4R; 103; CANR 29

Heraclitus c. 540B.C.-c. 450B.C. ... **CMLC 22**
See also DLB 176

Herbert, Frank (Patrick)
1920-1986 .... **CLC 12, 23, 35, 44, 85; DAM POP**
See also AAYA 21; CA 53-56; 118; CANR 5, 43; CDALBS; DLB 8; INT CANR-5; MTCW 1, 2; SATA 9, 37; SATA-Obit 47

Herbert, George 1593-1633 ..... **LC 24; DAB; DAM POET; PC 4**
See also CDBLB Before 1660; DLB 126

Herbert, Zbigniew 1924-1998 ..... **CLC 9, 43; DAM POET**
See also CA 89-92; 169; CANR 36, 74; MTCW 1

Herbst, Josephine (Frey)
1897-1969 .... **CLC 34**
See also CA 5-8R; 25-28R; DLB 9

Heredia, Jose Maria 1803-1839
See also HLCS 2

Hergesheimer, Joseph 1880-1954 ... **TCLC 11**
See also CA 109; DLB 102, 9

Herlihy, James Leo 1927-1993 .... **CLC 6**
See also CA 1-4R; 143; CANR 2

Hermogenes fl. c. 175- .... **CMLC 6**

Hernandez, Jose 1834-1886 .... **NCLC 17**

Herodotus c. 484B.C.-429B.C. .... **CMLC 17**
See also DLB 176

Herrick, Robert 1591-1674 .... **LC 13; DA; DAB; DAC; DAM MST, POP; PC 9**
See also DLB 126

Herring, Guilles
See Somerville, Edith

Herriot, James 1916-1995 ..... **CLC 12; DAM POP**
See also Wight, James Alfred AAYA 1; CA 148; CANR 40; MTCW 2; SATA 86

Herrmann, Dorothy 1941- .... **CLC 44**
See also CA 107

Herrmann, Taffy
See Herrmann, Dorothy

Hersey, John (Richard) 1914-1993 .... **CLC 1, 2, 7, 9, 40, 81, 97; DAM POP**
See also AAYA 29; CA 17-20R; 140; CANR 33; CDALBS; DLB 6, 185; MTCW 1, 2; SATA 25; SATA-Obit 76

Herzen, Aleksandr Ivanovich 1812-1870 **NCLC 10, 61**

Herzl, Theodor 1860-1904 .... **TCLC 36**
See also CA 168

Herzog, Werner 1942- .... **CLC 16**
See also CA 89-92

Hesiod c. 8th cent. B.C.- .... **CMLC 5**
See also DLB 176

Hesse, Hermann 1877-1962 ... **CLC 1, 2, 3, 6, 11, 17, 25, 69; DA; DAB; DAC; DAM MST, NOV; SSC 9; WLC**
See also CA 17-18; CAP 2; DA3; DLB 66; MTCW 1, 2; SATA 50

Hewes, Cady
See De Voto, Bernard (Augustine)

Heyen, William 1940- .... **CLC 13, 18**
See also CA 33-36R; CAAS 9; DLB 5

Heyerdahl, Thor 1914- .... **CLC 26**
See also CA 5-8R; CANR 5, 22, 66, 73; MTCW 1, 2; SATA 2, 52

Heym, Georg (Theodor Franz Arthur)
1887-1912 .... **TCLC 9**
See also CA 106; 181

Heym, Stefan 1913- .... **CLC 41**
See also CA 9-12R; CANR 4; DLB 69

Heyse, Paul (Johann Ludwig von) 1830-1914 **TCLC 8**
See also CA 104; DLB 129

Heyward, (Edwin) DuBose
1885-1940 .... **TCLC 59**
See also CA 108; 157; DLB 7, 9, 45; SATA 21

Hibbert, Eleanor Alice Burford 1906-1993 **CLC 7; DAM POP**
See also BEST 90:4; CA 17-20R; 140; CANR 9, 28, 59; MTCW 2; SATA 2; SATA-Obit 74

Hichens, Robert (Smythe)
1864-1950 .... **TCLC 64**
See also CA 162; DLB 153

Higgins, George V(incent) 1939- ... **CLC 4, 7, 10, 18**
See also CA 77-80; CAAS 5; CANR 17, 51; DLB 2; DLBY 81, 98; INT CANR-17; MTCW 1

Higginson, Thomas Wentworth 1823-1911 **TCLC 36**
See also CA 162; DLB 1, 64

Highet, Helen
See MacInnes, Helen (Clark)

Highsmith, (Mary) Patricia
1921-1995 .... **CLC 2, 4, 14, 42, 102; DAM NOV, POP**
See also CA 1-4R; 147; CANR 1, 20, 48, 62; DA3; MTCW 1, 2

Highwater, Jamake (Mamake)
1942(?)- .... **CLC 12**
See also AAYA 7; CA 65-68; CAAS 7; CANR 10, 34, 84; CLR 17; DLB 52; DLBY 85; JRDA; MAICYA; SATA 32, 69; SATA-Brief 30

Highway, Tomson 1951- .... **CLC 92; DAC; DAM MULT**
See also CA 151; CANR 75; MTCW 2; NNAL

Higuchi, Ichiyo 1872-1896 .... **NCLC 49**

Hijuelos, Oscar 1951- .... **CLC 65; DAM MULT, POP; HLC 1**
See also AAYA 25; BEST 90:1; CA 123; CANR 50, 75; DA3; DLB 145; HW 1, 2; MTCW 2

Hikmet, Nazim 1902(?)-1963 .... **CLC 40**
See also CA 141; 93-96

Hildegard von Bingen 1098-1179 . **CMLC 20**
See also DLB 148

Hildesheimer, Wolfgang 1916-1991 .. **CLC 49**
See also CA 101; 135; DLB 69, 124

Hill, Geoffrey (William) 1932- ...... **CLC 5, 8, 18, 45; DAM POET**
See also CA 81-84; CANR 21; CDBLB 1960 to Present; DLB 40; MTCW 1

Hill, George Roy 1921- .... **CLC 26**
See also CA 110; 122

Hill, John
See Koontz, Dean R(ay)

Hill, Susan (Elizabeth) 1942- .... **CLC 4, 113; DAB; DAM MST, NOV**
See also CA 33-36R; CANR 29, 69; DLB 14, 139; MTCW 1

Hillerman, Tony 1925- . **CLC 62; DAM POP**
See also AAYA 6; BEST 89:1; CA 29-32R; CANR 21, 42, 65; DA3; DLB 206; SATA 6

Hillesum, Etty 1914-1943 .... **TCLC 49**
See also CA 137

Hilliard, Noel (Harvey) 1929- .... **CLC 15**
See also CA 9-12R; CANR 7, 69

Hillis, Rick 1956- .... **CLC 66**
See also CA 134

Hilton, James 1900-1954 .... **TCLC 21**
See also CA 108; 169; DLB 34, 77; SATA 34

Himes, Chester (Bomar) 1909-1984 .. **CLC 2, 4, 7, 18, 58, 108; BLC 2; DAM MULT**
See also BW 2; CA 25-28R; 114; CANR 22; DLB 2, 76, 143; MTCW 1, 2

Hinde, Thomas .... **CLC 6, 11**
See also Chitty, Thomas Willes

Hine, (William) Daryl 1936- .... **CLC 15**
See also CA 1-4R; CAAS 15; CANR 1, 20; DLB 60

Hinkson, Katharine Tynan
See Tynan, Katharine

Hinojosa(-Smith), Rolando (R.) 1929-
See Hinojosa-Smith, Rolando
See also CA 131; CAAS 16; CANR 62; DAM MULT; DLB 82; HLC 1; HW 1, 2; MTCW 2

Hinojosa-Smith, Rolando 1929-
See Hinojosa(-Smith), Rolando (R.)
See also CAAS 16; HLC 1; MTCW 2

Hinton, S(usan) E(loise) 1950- .... **CLC 30, 111; DA; DAB; DAC; DAM MST, NOV**
See also AAYA 2; CA 81-84; CANR 32, 62; CDALBS; CLR 3, 23; DA3; JRDA; MAICYA; MTCW 1, 2; SATA 19, 58

Hippius, Zinaida .... **TCLC 9**
See also Gippius, Zinaida (Nikolayevna)

Hiraoka, Kimitake 1925-1970
See Mishima, Yukio
See also CA 97-100; 29-32R; DAM DRAM; DA3; MTCW 1, 2

Hirsch, E(ric) D(onald), Jr. 1928- .... **CLC 79**
See also CA 25-28R; CANR 27, 51; DLB 67; INT CANR-27; MTCW 1

Hirsch, Edward 1950- .... **CLC 31, 50**
See also CA 104; CANR 20, 42; DLB 120

Hitchcock, Alfred (Joseph)
1899-1980 .... **CLC 16**
See also AAYA 22; CA 159; 97-100; SATA 27; SATA-Obit 24

Hitler, Adolf 1889-1945 .... **TCLC 53**
See also CA 117; 147

Hoagland, Edward 1932- .... **CLC 28**
See also CA 1-4R; CANR 2, 31, 57; DLB 6; SATA 51

Hoban, Russell (Conwell) 1925- . **CLC 7, 25; DAM NOV**
See also CA 5-8R; CANR 23, 37, 66; CLR 3; DLB 52; MAICYA; MTCW 1, 2; SATA 1, 40, 78

Hobbes, Thomas 1588-1679 .... **LC 36**
See also DLB 151

Hobbs, Perry
See Blackmur, R(ichard) P(almer)

Hobson, Laura Z(ametkin)
1900-1986 .... **CLC 7, 25**
See also CA 17-20R; 118; CANR 55; DLB 28; SATA 52

Hochhuth, Rolf 1931- .. **CLC 4, 11, 18; DAM DRAM**
See also CA 5-8R; CANR 33, 75; DLB 124; MTCW 1, 2

Hochman, Sandra 1936- .... **CLC 3, 8**
See also CA 5-8R; DLB 5

Hochwaelder, Fritz 1911-1986 .... **CLC 36; DAM DRAM**
See also CA 29-32R; 120; CANR 42; MTCW 1

Hochwalder, Fritz
See Hochwaelder, Fritz

Hocking, Mary (Eunice) 1921- .... **CLC 13**
See also CA 101; CANR 18, 40

Hodgins, Jack 1938- .... **CLC 23**
See also CA 93-96; DLB 60

Hodgson, William Hope
1877(?)-1918 .... **TCLC 13**
See also CA 111; 164; DLB 70, 153, 156, 178; MTCW 2

Hoeg, Peter 1957- .... **CLC 95**
See also CA 151; CANR 75; DA3; MTCW 2

Hoffman, Alice 1952- ... **CLC 51; DAM NOV**
See also CA 77-80; CANR 34, 66; MTCW 1, 2

Hoffman, Daniel (Gerard) 1923- . **CLC 6, 13, 23**
See also CA 1-4R; CANR 4; DLB 5

Hoffman, Stanley 1944- .... **CLC 5**
See also CA 77-80

Hoffman, William M(oses) 1939- ..... **CLC 40**
See also CA 57-60; CANR 11, 71

Hoffmann, E(rnst) T(heodor) A(madeus)
1776-1822 .... **NCLC 2; SSC 13**
See also DLB 90; SATA 27

Hofmann, Gert 1931- .... **CLC 54**
See also CA 128

Hofmannsthal, Hugo von
1874-1929 ...... **TCLC 11; DAM DRAM; DC 4**
See also CA 106; 153; DLB 81, 118

Hogan, Linda 1947- .. **CLC 73; DAM MULT**
See also CA 120; CANR 45, 73; DLB 175; NNAL

Hogarth, Charles
See Creasey, John

Hogarth, Emmett
See Polonsky, Abraham (Lincoln)

Hogg, James 1770-1835 .... **NCLC 4**
See also DLB 93, 116, 159

Holbach, Paul Henri Thiry Baron 1723-1789 **LC 14**

Holberg, Ludvig 1684-1754 .... **LC 6**

Holden, Ursula 1921- .... **CLC 18**
See also CA 101; CAAS 8; CANR 22

Holderlin, (Johann Christian) Friedrich
1770-1843 .... **NCLC 16; PC 4**

Holdstock, Robert
See Holdstock, Robert P.

Holdstock, Robert P. 1948- .... **CLC 39**
See also CA 131; CANR 81

Holland, Isabelle 1920- .... **CLC 21**
See also AAYA 11; CA 21-24R; 181; CAAE 181; CANR 10, 25, 47; CLR 57; JRDA; MAICYA; SATA 8, 70; SATA-Essay 103

Holland, Marcus
See Caldwell, (Janet Miriam) Taylor (Holland)

Hollander, John 1929- .... **CLC 2, 5, 8, 14**
See also CA 1-4R; CANR 1, 52; DLB 5; SATA 13

Hollander, Paul
See Silverberg, Robert

Holleran, Andrew 1943(?)- .... **CLC 38**
See also CA 144

Holley, Marietta 1836(?)-1926 ...... **TCLC 99**
See also CA 118; DLB 11

Hollinghurst, Alan 1954- .... **CLC 55, 91**
See also CA 114; DLB 207

Hollis, Jim
See Summers, Hollis (Spurgeon, Jr.)

Holly, Buddy 1936-1959 .... **TCLC 65**

Holmes, Gordon
See Shiel, M(atthew) P(hipps)

Holmes, John
See Souster, (Holmes) Raymond

Holmes, John Clellon 1926-1988 ...... **CLC 56**
See also CA 9-12R; 125; CANR 4; DLB 16

Holmes, Oliver Wendell, Jr.
1841-1935 .... **TCLC 77**
See also CA 114

Holmes, Oliver Wendell
1809-1894 .... **NCLC 14, 81**
See also CDALB 1640-1865; DLB 1, 189; SATA 34

Holmes, Raymond
See Souster, (Holmes) Raymond

Holt, Victoria
See Hibbert, Eleanor Alice Burford

Holub, Miroslav 1923-1998 .... **CLC 4**
See also CA 21-24R; 169; CANR 10

Homer c. 8th cent. B.C.- .. **CMLC 1, 16; DA; DAB; DAC; DAM MST, POET; PC 23; WLCS**
See also DA3; DLB 176

Hongo, Garrett Kaoru 1951- .... **PC 23**
See also CA 133; CAAS 22; DLB 120

Honig, Edwin 1919- .... **CLC 33**
See also CA 5-8R; CAAS 8; CANR 4, 45; DLB 5

Hood, Hugh (John Blagdon) 1928- . **CLC 15, 28**
See also CA 49-52; CAAS 17; CANR 1, 33, 87; DLB 53

Hood, Thomas 1799-1845 .... **NCLC 16**
See also DLB 96

Hooker, (Peter) Jeremy 1941- .... **CLC 43**
See also CA 77-80; CANR 22; DLB 40

hooks, bell .... **CLC 94; BLCS**
See also Watkins, Gloria Jean MTCW 2

Hope, A(lec) D(erwent) 1907- .... **CLC 3, 51**
See also CA 21-24R; CANR 33, 74; MTCW 1, 2

Hope, Anthony 1863-1933 .... **TCLC 83**
See also CA 157; DLB 153, 156

Hope, Brian
See Creasey, John

Hope, Christopher (David Tully)
1944- .... **CLC 52**
See also CA 106; CANR 47; SATA 62

Hopkins, Gerard Manley
1844-1889 .... **NCLC 17; DA; DAB; DAC; DAM MST, POET; PC 15; WLC**
See also CDBLB 1890-1914; DA3; DLB 35, 57

Hopkins, John (Richard) 1931-1998 .. **CLC 4**
See also CA 85-88; 169

Hopkins, Pauline Elizabeth
1859-1930 ...... **TCLC 28; BLC 2; DAM MULT**
See also BW 2, 3; CA 141; CANR 82; DLB 50

Hopkinson, Francis 1737-1791 .... **LC 25**
See also DLB 31

Hopley-Woolrich, Cornell George 1903-1968
See Woolrich, Cornell
See also CA 13-14; CANR 58; CAP 1; MTCW 2

Horatio
See Proust, (Valentin-Louis-George-Eugene-) Marcel

Horgan, Paul (George Vincent O'Shaughnessy) 1903-1995 . **CLC 9, 53; DAM NOV**
See also CA 13-16R; 147; CANR 9, 35; DLB 212; DLBY 85; INT CANR-9; MTCW 1, 2; SATA 13; SATA-Obit 84

Horn, Peter
See Kuttner, Henry

Hornem, Horace Esq.
See Byron, George Gordon (Noel)

Horney, Karen (Clementine Theodore Danielsen) 1885-1952 .... **TCLC 71**
See also CA 114; 165

Hornung, E(rnest) W(illiam) 1866-1921 **TCLC 59**
See also CA 108; 160; DLB 70

Horovitz, Israel (Arthur) 1939- ...... **CLC 56; DAM DRAM**
See also CA 33-36R; CANR 46, 59; DLB 7

Horvath, Odon von
See Horvath, Oedoen von
See also DLB 85, 124

Horvath, Oedoen von 1901-1938 ... **TCLC 45**
See also Horvath, Odon von CA 118

Horwitz, Julius 1920-1986 .... **CLC 14**
See also CA 9-12R; 119; CANR 12

Hospital, Janette Turner 1942- .... **CLC 42**
See also CA 108; CANR 48

Hostos, E. M. de
See Hostos (y Bonilla), Eugenio Maria de

Hostos, Eugenio M. de
See Hostos (y Bonilla), Eugenio Maria de

Hostos, Eugenio Maria
See Hostos (y Bonilla), Eugenio Maria de

Hostos (y Bonilla), Eugenio Maria de
1839-1903 .... **TCLC 24**
See also CA 123; 131; HW 1

Houdini
See Lovecraft, H(oward) P(hillips)

Hougan, Carolyn 1943- .... **CLC 34**
See also CA 139

Household, Geoffrey (Edward West)
1900-1988 .... **CLC 11**
See also CA 77-80; 126; CANR 58; DLB 87; SATA 14; SATA-Obit 59

Housman, A(lfred) E(dward) 1859-1936 **TCLC 1, 10; DA; DAB; DAC; DAM MST, POET; PC 2; WLCS**
See also CA 104; 125; DA3; DLB 19; MTCW 1, 2

Housman, Laurence 1865-1959 .... **TCLC 7**
See also CA 106; 155; DLB 10; SATA 25

Howard, Elizabeth Jane 1923- ..... **CLC 7, 29**
See also CA 5-8R; CANR 8, 62

Howard, Maureen 1930- .... **CLC 5, 14, 46**
See also CA 53-56; CANR 31, 75; DLBY 83; INT CANR-31; MTCW 1, 2

Howard, Richard 1929- .... **CLC 7, 10, 47**
See also AITN 1; CA 85-88; CANR 25, 80; DLB 5; INT CANR-25

Howard, Robert E(rvin)
1906-1936 .... **TCLC 8**
See also CA 105; 157

Howard, Warren F.
See Pohl, Frederik

Howe, Fanny (Quincy) 1940- .... **CLC 47**
See also CA 117; CAAS 27; CANR 70; SATA-Brief 52

Howe, Irving 1920-1993 .... **CLC 85**
See also CA 9-12R; 141; CANR 21, 50; DLB 67; MTCW 1, 2

Howe, Julia Ward 1819-1910 .... **TCLC 21**
See also CA 117; DLB 1, 189

Howe, Susan 1937- .... **CLC 72**
See also CA 160; DLB 120

Howe, Tina 1937- .... **CLC 48**
See also CA 109

Howell, James 1594(?)-1666 .... **LC 13**
See also DLB 151

Howell, W. D.
See Howells, William Dean

Howells, William D.
See Howells, William Dean

Howells, William Dean 1837-1920 .. **TCLC 7, 17, 41; SSC 36**
See also CA 104; 134; CDALB 1865-1917; DLB 12, 64, 74, 79, 189; MTCW 2

Howes, Barbara 1914-1996 .... **CLC 15**
See also CA 9-12R; 151; CAAS 3; CANR 53; SATA 5

Hrabal, Bohumil 1914-1997 .... **CLC 13, 67**
See also CA 106; 156; CAAS 12; CANR 57

Hroswitha of Gandersheim c. 935-c. 1002
CMLC 29
See also DLB 148

Hsun, Lu
See Lu Hsun

Hubbard, L(afayette) Ron(ald) 1911-1986
CLC 43; DAM POP
See also CA 77-80; 118; CANR 52; DA3; MTCW 2

Huch, Ricarda (Octavia)
1864-1947 .... **TCLC 13**
See also CA 111; DLB 66

Huddle, David 1942- .... **CLC 49**
See also CA 57-60; CAAS 20; DLB 130

Hudson, Jeffrey
See Crichton, (John) Michael

Hudson, W(illiam) H(enry)
1841-1922 .... **TCLC 29**
See also CA 115; DLB 98, 153, 174; SATA 35

Hueffer, Ford Madox
See Ford, Ford Madox

Hughart, Barry 1934- .... **CLC 39**
See also CA 137

Hughes, Colin
See Creasey, John

Hughes, David (John) 1930- .... **CLC 48**
See also CA 116; 129; DLB 14

Hughes, Edward James
See Hughes, Ted
See also DAM MST, POET; DA3

Hughes, (James) Langston
1902-1967 .... **CLC 1, 5, 10, 15, 35, 44, 108; BLC 2; DA; DAB; DAC; DAM DRAM, MST, MULT, POET; DC 3; PC 1; SSC 6; WLC**
See also AAYA 12; BW 1, 3; CA 1-4R; 25-28R; CANR 1, 34, 82; CDALB 1929-1941; CLR 17; DA3; DLB 4, 7, 48, 51, 86; JRDA; MAICYA; MTCW 1, 2; SATA 4, 33

Hughes, Richard (Arthur Warren)
1900-1976 .... **CLC 1, 11; DAM NOV**
See also CA 5-8R; 65-68; CANR 4; DLB 15, 161; MTCW 1; SATA 8; SATA-Obit 25

Hughes, Ted 1930-1998 . **CLC 2, 4, 9, 14, 37, 119; DAB; DAC; PC 7**
See also Hughes, Edward James CA 1-4R; 171; CANR 1, 33, 66; CLR 3; DLB 40, 161; MAICYA; MTCW 1, 2; SATA 49; SATA-Brief 27; SATA-Obit 107

Hugo, Richard F(ranklin)
1923-1982 .... **CLC 6, 18, 32; DAM POET**
See also CA 49-52; 108; CANR 3; DLB 5, 206

Hugo, Victor (Marie) 1802-1885 .... **NCLC 3, 10, 21; DA; DAB; DAC; DAM DRAM, MST, NOV, POET; PC 17; WLC**
See also AAYA 28; DA3; DLB 119, 192; SATA 47

Huidobro, Vicente
See Huidobro Fernandez, Vicente Garcia

Huidobro Fernandez, Vicente Garcia
1893-1948 .... **TCLC 31**
See also CA 131; HW 1

Hulme, Keri 1947- .... **CLC 39**
See also CA 125; CANR 69; INT 125

Hulme, T(homas) E(rnest)
1883-1917 .... **TCLC 21**
See also CA 117; DLB 19

Hume, David 1711-1776 .... **LC 7**
See also DLB 104

Humphrey, William 1924-1997 .... **CLC 45**
See also CA 77-80; 160; CANR 68; DLB 212

Humphreys, Emyr Owen 1919- .... **CLC 47**
See also CA 5-8R; CANR 3, 24; DLB 15

Humphreys, Josephine 1945- ..... **CLC 34, 57**
See also CA 121; 127; INT 127

Huneker, James Gibbons
1857-1921 .... **TCLC 65**
See also DLB 71

Hungerford, Pixie
See Brinsmead, H(esba) F(ay)

Hunt, E(verette) Howard, (Jr.)
1918- .... **CLC 3**
See also AITN 1; CA 45-48; CANR 2, 47

Hunt, Francesca
See Holland, Isabelle

Hunt, Kyle
See Creasey, John

Hunt, (James Henry) Leigh
1784-1859 .... **NCLC 1, 70; DAM POET**
See also DLB 96, 110, 144

Hunt, Marsha 1946- .... **CLC 70**
See also BW 2, 3; CA 143; CANR 79

Hunt, Violet 1866(?)-1942 .... **TCLC 53**
See also DLB 162, 197

Hunter, E. Waldo
See Sturgeon, Theodore (Hamilton)

Hunter, Evan 1926- .... **CLC 11, 31; DAM POP**
See also CA 5-8R; CANR 5, 38, 62; DLBY 82; INT CANR-5; MTCW 1; SATA 25

Hunter, Kristin (Eggleston) 1931- .... **CLC 35**
See also AITN 1; BW 1; CA 13-16R; CANR 13; CLR 3; DLB 33; INT CANR-13; MAICYA; SAAS 10; SATA 12

Hunter, Mary
See Austin, Mary (Hunter)

Hunter, Mollie 1922- .... **CLC 21**
See also McIlwraith, Maureen Mollie Hunter AAYA 13; CANR 37, 78; CLR 25; DLB 161; JRDA; MAICYA; SAAS 7; SATA 54, 106

Hunter, Robert (?)-1734 .... **LC 7**

Hurston, Zora Neale 1903-1960 .. **CLC 7, 30, 61; BLC 2; DA; DAC; DAM MST, MULT, NOV; SSC 4; WLCS**
See also AAYA 15; BW 1, 3; CA 85-88; CANR 61; CDALBS; DA3; DLB 51, 86; MTCW 1, 2

Husserl, E. G.
See Husserl, Edmund (Gustav Albrecht)

Husserl, Edmund (Gustav Albrecht)
1859-1938 .... **TCLC 100**
See also CA 116; 133

Huston, John (Marcellus)
1906-1987 .... **CLC 20**
See also CA 73-76; 123; CANR 34; DLB 26

Hustvedt, Siri 1955- .... **CLC 76**
See also CA 137

Hutten, Ulrich von 1488-1523 .... **LC 16**
See also DLB 179

Huxley, Aldous (Leonard)
1894-1963 .... **CLC 1, 3, 4, 5, 8, 11, 18, 35, 79; DA; DAB; DAC; DAM MST, NOV; WLC**
See also AAYA 11; CA 85-88; CANR 44; CDBLB 1914-1945; DA3; DLB 36, 100, 162, 195; MTCW 1, 2; SATA 63

Huxley, T(homas) H(enry)
1825-1895 .... **NCLC 67**
See also DLB 57

Huysmans, Joris-Karl 1848-1907 ... **TCLC 7, 69**
See also CA 104; 165; DLB 123

Hwang, David Henry 1957- .. **CLC 55; DAM DRAM; DC 4**
See also CA 127; 132; CANR 76; DA3; DLB 212; INT 132; MTCW 2

Hyde, Anthony 1946- .... **CLC 42**
See also CA 136

Hyde, Margaret O(ldroyd) 1917- ..... **CLC 21**
See also CA 1-4R; CANR 1, 36; CLR 23; JRDA; MAICYA; SAAS 8; SATA 1, 42, 76

Hynes, James 1956(?)- .... **CLC 65**
See also CA 164

Hypatia c. 370-415 .... **CMLC 35**

Ian, Janis 1951- .... **CLC 21**
See also CA 105

Ibanez, Vicente Blasco
See Blasco Ibanez, Vicente

Ibarbourou, Juana de 1895-1979
See also HLCS 2; HW 1

Ibarguengoitia, Jorge 1928-1983 ...... **CLC 37**
See also CA 124; 113; HW 1

Ibsen, Henrik (Johan) 1828-1906 ... **TCLC 2, 8, 16, 37, 52; DA; DAB; DAC; DAM DRAM, MST; DC 2; WLC**
See also CA 104; 141; DA3

Ibuse, Masuji 1898-1993 .... **CLC 22**
See also CA 127; 141; DLB 180

Ichikawa, Kon 1915- .... **CLC 20**
See also CA 121

Idle, Eric 1943- .... **CLC 21**
See also Monty Python CA 116; CANR 35

Ignatow, David 1914-1997 .. **CLC 4, 7, 14, 40**
See also CA 9-12R; 162; CAAS 3; CANR 31, 57; DLB 5

Ignotus
See Strachey, (Giles) Lytton

Ihimaera, Witi 1944- .... **CLC 46**
See also CA 77-80

Ilf, Ilya .... **TCLC 21**
See also Fainzilberg, Ilya Arnoldovich

Illyes, Gyula 1902-1983 .... **PC 16**
See also CA 114; 109

Immermann, Karl (Lebrecht) 1796-1840
NCLC 4, 49
See also DLB 133

Kessler, Jascha (Frederick) 1929- ...... **CLC 4**
See also CA 17-20R; CANR 8, 48
Kettelkamp, Larry (Dale) 1933- .... **CLC 12**
See also CA 29-32R; CANR 16; SAAS 3;
SATA 2
Key, Ellen 1849-1926 .... **TCLC 65**
Keyber, Conny
See Fielding, Henry
Keyes, Daniel 1927- ...... **CLC 80; DA; DAC;**
DAM MST, NOV
See also AAYA 23; CA 17-20R, 181; CAAE
181; CANR 10, 26, 54, 74; DA3; MTCW
2; SATA 37
Keynes, John Maynard
1883-1946 .... **TCLC 64**
See also CA 114; 162, 163; DLBD 10;
MTCW 2
Khanshendel, Chiron
See Rose, Wendy
Khayyam, Omar 1048-1131 .... **CMLC 11;**
DAM POET; PC 8
See also DA3
Kherdian, David 1931- .... **CLC 6, 9**
See also CA 21-24R; CAAS 2; CANR 39,
78; CLR 24; JRDA; MAICYA; SATA 16,
74
Khlebnikov, Velimir .... **TCLC 20**
See also Khlebnikov, Viktor Vladimirovich
Khlebnikov, Viktor Vladimirovich 1885-1922
See Khlebnikov, Velimir
See also CA 117
Khodasevich, Vladislav (Felitsianovich)
1886-1939 .... **TCLC 15**
See also CA 115
Kielland, Alexander Lange
1849-1906 .... **TCLC 5**
See also CA 104
Kiely, Benedict 1919- .... **CLC 23, 43**
See also CA 1-4R; CANR 2, 84; DLB 15
Kienzle, William X(avier) 1928- ..... **CLC 25;**
DAM POP
See also CA 93-96; CAAS 1; CANR 9, 31,
59; DA3; INT CANR-31; MTCW 1, 2
Kierkegaard, Soren 1813-1855 ..... **NCLC 34,**
78
Kieslowski, Krzysztof 1941-1996 .... **CLC 120**
See also CA 147; 151
Killens, John Oliver 1916-1987 .... **CLC 10**
See also BW 2; CA 77-80; 123; CAAS 2;
CANR 26; DLB 33
Killigrew, Anne 1660-1685 .... **LC 4**
See also DLB 131
Kim
See Simenon, Georges (Jacques Christian)
Kincaid, Jamaica 1949- .... **CLC 43, 68; BLC**
2; DAM MULT, NOV
See also AAYA 13; BW 2, 3; CA 125;
CANR 47, 59; CDALBS; DA3; DLB 157;
MTCW 2
King, Francis (Henry) 1923- .... **CLC 8, 53;**
DAM NOV
See also CA 1-4R; CANR 1, 33, 86; DLB
15, 139; MTCW 1
King, Kennedy
See Brown, George Douglas
King, Martin Luther, Jr.
1929-1968 .... **CLC 83; BLC 2; DA;**
DAB; DAC; DAM MST, MULT;
WLCS
See also BW 2, 3; CA 25-28; CANR 27,
44; CAP 2; DA3; MTCW 1, 2; SATA 14
King, Stephen (Edwin) 1947- .... **CLC 12, 26,**
37, 61, 113; DAM NOV, POP; SSC 17
See also AAYA 1, 17; BEST 90:1; CA 61-
64; CANR 1, 30, 52, 76; DA3; DLB 143;
DLBY 80; JRDA; MTCW 1, 2; SATA 9,
55
King, Steve
See King, Stephen (Edwin)

King, Thomas 1943- ... **CLC 89; DAC; DAM**
MULT
See also CA 144; DLB 175; NNAL; SATA
96
Kingman, Lee .... **CLC 17**
See also Natti, (Mary) Lee SAAS 3; SATA
1, 67
Kingsley, Charles 1819-1875 .... **NCLC 35**
See also DLB 21, 32, 163, 190; YABC 2
Kingsley, Sidney 1906-1995 .... **CLC 44**
See also CA 85-88; 147; DLB 7
Kingsolver, Barbara 1955- ...., **CLC 55, 81;**
DAM POP
See also AAYA 15; CA 129; 134; CANR
60; CDALBS; DA3; DLB 206; INT 134;
MTCW 2
Kingston, Maxine (Ting Ting) Hong 1940-
CLC 12, 19, 58, 121; DAM MULT,
NOV; WLCS
See also AAYA 8; CA 69-72; CANR 13,
38, 74, 87; CDALBS; DA3; DLB 173,
212; DLBY 80; INT CANR-13; MTCW
1, 2; SATA 53
Kinnell, Galway 1927- ..... **CLC 1, 2, 3, 5, 13,**
29; PC 26
See also CA 9-12R; CANR 10, 34, 66; DLB
5; DLBY 87; INT CANR-34; MTCW 1, 2
Kinsella, Thomas 1928- .... **CLC 4, 19**
See also CA 17-20R; CANR 15; DLB 27;
MTCW 1, 2
Kinsella, W(illiam) P(atrick) 1935- . **CLC 27,**
43; DAC; DAM NOV, POP
See also AAYA 7; CA 97-100; CAAS 7;
CANR 21, 35, 66, 75; INT CANR-21;
MTCW 1, 2
Kinsey, Alfred C(harles)
1894-1956 .... **TCLC 91**
See also CA 115; 170; MTCW 2
Kipling, (Joseph) Rudyard
1865-1936 .... **TCLC 8, 17; DA; DAB;**
DAC; DAM MST, POET; PC 3; SSC
5; WLC
See also AAYA 32; CA 105; 120; CANR
33; CDBLB 1890-1914; CLR 39; DA3;
DLB 19, 34, 141, 156; MAICYA; MTCW
1, 2; SATA 100; YABC 2
Kirkup, James 1918- .... **CLC 1**
See also CA 1-4R; CAAS 4; CANR 2; DLB
27; SATA 12
Kirkwood, James 1930(?)-1989 .... **CLC 9**
See also AITN 2; CA 1-4R; 128; CANR 6,
40
Kirshner, Sidney
See Kingsley, Sidney
Kis, Danilo 1935-1989 .... **CLC 57**
See also CA 109; 118; 129; CANR 61; DLB
181; MTCW 1
Kivi, Aleksis 1834-1872 .... **NCLC 30**
Kizer, Carolyn (Ashley) 1925- ... **CLC 15, 39,**
80; DAM POET
See also CA 65-68; CAAS 5; CANR 24,
70; DLB 5, 169; MTCW 2
Klabund 1890-1928 .... **TCLC 44**
See also CA 162; DLB 66
Klappert, Peter 1942- .... **CLC 57**
See also CA 33-36R; DLB 5
Klein, A(braham) M(oses)
1909-1972 . **CLC 19; DAB; DAC; DAM**
MST
See also CA 101; 37-40R; DLB 68
Klein, Norma 1938-1989 .... **CLC 30**
See also AAYA 2; CA 41-44R; 128; CANR
15, 37; CLR 2, 19; INT CANR-15; JRDA;
MAICYA; SAAS 1; SATA 7, 57
Klein, T(heodore) E(ibon) D(onald) 1947-
CLC 34
See also CA 119; CANR 44, 75

Kleist, Heinrich von 1777-1811 ...... **NCLC 2,**
37; DAM DRAM; SSC 22
See also DLB 90
Klima, Ivan 1931- .... **CLC 56; DAM NOV**
See also CA 25-28R; CANR 17, 50
Klimentov, Andrei Platonovich 1899-1951
See Platonov, Andrei
See also CA 108
Klinger, Friedrich Maximilian von
1752-1831 .... **NCLC 1**
See also DLB 94
Klingsor the Magician
See Hartmann, Sadakichi
Klopstock, Friedrich Gottlieb 1724-1803
NCLC 11
See also DLB 97
Knapp, Caroline 1959- .... **CLC 99**
See also CA 154
Knebel, Fletcher 1911-1993 .... **CLC 14**
See also AITN 1; CA 1-4R; 140; CAAS 3;
CANR 1, 36; SATA 36; SATA-Obit 75
Knickerbocker, Diedrich
See Irving, Washington
Knight, Etheridge 1931-1991 . **CLC 40; BLC**
2; DAM POET; PC 14
See also BW 1, 3; CA 21-24R; 133; CANR
23, 82; DLB 41; MTCW 2
Knight, Sarah Kemble 1666-1727 .... **LC 7**
See also DLB 24, 200
Knister, Raymond 1899-1932 .... **TCLC 56**
See also DLB 68
Knowles, John 1926- . **CLC 1, 4, 10, 26; DA;**
DAC; DAM MST, NOV
See also AAYA 10; CA 17-20R; CANR 40,
74, 76; CDALB 1968-1988; DLB 6;
MTCW 1, 2; SATA 8, 89
Knox, Calvin M.
See Silverberg, Robert
Knox, John c. 1505-1572 .... **LC 37**
See also DLB 132
Knye, Cassandra
See Disch, Thomas M(ichael)
Koch, C(hristopher) J(ohn) 1932- .... **CLC 42**
See also CA 127; CANR 84
Koch, Christopher
See Koch, C(hristopher) J(ohn)
Koch, Kenneth 1925- .... **CLC 5, 8, 44; DAM**
POET
See also CA 1-4R; CANR 6, 36, 57; DLB
5; INT CANR-36; MTCW 2; SATA 65
Kochanowski, Jan 1530-1584 .... **LC 10**
Kock, Charles Paul de 1794-1871 . **NCLC 16**
Koda Shigeyuki 1867-1947
See Rohan, Koda
See also CA 121; 183
Koestler, Arthur 1905-1983 ... **CLC 1, 3, 6, 8,**
15, 33
See also CA 1-4R; 109; CANR 1, 33; CD-
BLB 1945-1960; DLBY 83; MTCW 1, 2
Kogawa, Joy Nozomi 1935- .. **CLC 78; DAC;**
DAM MST, MULT
See also CA 101; CANR 19, 62; MTCW 2;
SATA 99
Kohout, Pavel 1928- .... **CLC 13**
See also CA 45-48; CANR 3
Koizumi, Yakumo
See Hearn, (Patricio) Lafcadio (Tessima
Carlos)
Kolmar, Gertrud 1894-1943 .... **TCLC 40**
See also CA 167
Komunyakaa, Yusef 1947- .... **CLC 86, 94;**
BLCS
See also CA 147; CANR 83; DLB 120
Konrad, George
See Konrad, Gyoergy
Konrad, Gyoergy 1933- .... **CLC 4, 10, 73**
See also CA 85-88

Author Index

MacNeice, (Frederick) Louis
    1907-1963 .... **CLC 1, 4, 10, 53; DAB;
    DAM POET**
    See also CA 85-88; CANR 61; DLB 10, 20;
    MTCW 1, 2
MacNeill, Dand
    See Fraser, George MacDonald
Macpherson, James 1736-1796 .... **LC 29**
    See also Ossian DLB 109
Macpherson, (Jean) Jay 1931- .... **CLC 14**
    See also CA 5-8R; DLB 53
MacShane, Frank 1927- .... **CLC 39**
    See also CA 9-12R; CANR 3, 33; DLB 111
Macumber, Mari
    See Sandoz, Mari(e Susette)
Madach, Imre 1823-1864 .... **NCLC 19**
Madden, (Jerry) David 1933- .... **CLC 5, 15**
    See also CA 1-4R; CAAS 3; CANR 4, 45;
    DLB 6; MTCW 1
Maddern, Al(an)
    See Ellison, Harlan (Jay)
Madhubuti, Haki R. 1942- . **CLC 6, 73; BLC
    2; DAM MULT, POET; PC 5**
    See also Lee, Don L. BW 2, 3; CA 73-76;
    CANR 24, 51, 73; DLB 5, 41; DLBD 8;
    MTCW 2
Maepenn, Hugh
    See Kuttner, Henry
Maepenn, K. H.
    See Kuttner, Henry
Maeterlinck, Maurice 1862-1949 ... **TCLC 3;
    DAM DRAM**
    See also CA 104; 136; CANR 80; DLB 192;
    SATA 66
Maginn, William 1794-1842 .... **NCLC 8**
    See also DLB 110, 159
Mahapatra, Jayanta 1928- .... **CLC 33; DAM
    MULT**
    See also CA 73-76; CAAS 9; CANR 15,
    33, 66, 87
Mahfouz, Naguib (Abdel Aziz Al-Sabilgi)
    1911(?)-
    See Mahfuz, Najib
    See also BEST 89:2; CA 128; CANR 55;
    DAM NOV; DA3; MTCW 1, 2
Mahfuz, Najib .... **CLC 52, 55**
    See also Mahfouz, Naguib (Abdel Aziz Al-
    Sabilgi) DLBY 88
Mahon, Derek 1941- .... **CLC 27**
    See also CA 113; 128; DLB 40
Mailer, Norman 1923- .. **CLC 1, 2, 3, 4, 5, 8,
    11, 14, 28, 39, 74, 111; DA; DAB;
    DAC; DAM MST, NOV, POP**
    See also AAYA 31; AITN 2; CA 9-12R;
    CABS 1; CANR 28, 74, 77; CDALB
    1968-1988; DA3; DLB 2, 16, 28, 185;
    DLBD 3; DLBY 80, 83; MTCW 1, 2
Maillet, Antonine 1929- .. **CLC 54, 118; DAC**
    See also CA 115; 120; CANR 46, 74, 77;
    DLB 60; INT 120; MTCW 2
Mais, Roger 1905-1955 .... **TCLC 8**
    See also BW 1, 3; CA 105; 124; CANR 82;
    DLB 125; MTCW 1
Maistre, Joseph de 1753-1821 .... **NCLC 37**
Maitland, Frederic 1850-1906 .... **TCLC 65**
Maitland, Sara (Louise) 1950- .... **CLC 49**
    See also CA 69-72; CANR 13, 59
Major, Clarence 1936- . **CLC 3, 19, 48; BLC
    2; DAM MULT**
    See also BW 2, 3; CA 21-24R; CAAS 6;
    CANR 13, 25, 53, 82; DLB 33
Major, Kevin (Gerald) 1949- . **CLC 26; DAC**
    See also AAYA 16; CA 97-100; CANR 21,
    38; CLR 11; DLB 60; INT CANR-21;
    JRDA; MAICYA; SATA 32, 82
Maki, James
    See Ozu, Yasujiro
Malabaila, Damiano
    See Levi, Primo

Malamud, Bernard 1914-1986 .. **CLC 1, 2, 3,
    5, 8, 9, 11, 18, 27, 44, 78, 85; DA;
    DAB; DAC; DAM MST, NOV, POP;
    SSC 15; WLC**
    See also AAYA 16; CA 5-8R; 118; CABS
    1; CANR 28, 62; CDALB 1941-1968;
    DA3; DLB 2, 28, 152; DLBY 80, 86;
    MTCW 1, 2
Malan, Herman
    See Bosman, Herman Charles; Bosman,
    Herman Charles
Malaparte, Curzio 1898-1957 .... **TCLC 52**
Malcolm, Dan
    See Silverberg, Robert
Malcolm X ...... **CLC 82, 117; BLC 2; WLCS**
    See also Little, Malcolm
Malherbe, Francois de 1555-1628 .... **LC 5**
Mallarme, Stephane 1842-1898 ...... **NCLC 4,
    41; DAM POET; PC 4**
Mallet-Joris, Francoise 1930- .... **CLC 11**
    See also CA 65-68; CANR 17; DLB 83
Malley, Ern
    See McAuley, James Phillip
Mallowan, Agatha Christie
    See Christie, Agatha (Mary Clarissa)
Maloff, Saul 1922- .... **CLC 5**
    See also CA 33-36R
Malone, Louis
    See MacNeice, (Frederick) Louis
Malone, Michael (Christopher)
    1942- .... **CLC 43**
    See also CA 77-80; CANR 14, 32, 57
Malory, (Sir) Thomas
    1410(?)-1471(?) .... **LC 11; DA; DAB;
    DAC; DAM MST; WLCS**
    See also CDBLB Before 1660; DLB 146;
    SATA 59; SATA-Brief 33
Malouf, (George Joseph) David
    1934- .... **CLC 28, 86**
    See also CA 124; CANR 50, 76; MTCW 2
Malraux, (Georges-)Andre
    1901-1976 .... **CLC 1, 4, 9, 13, 15, 57;
    DAM NOV**
    See also CA 21-22; 69-72; CANR 34, 58;
    CAP 2; DA3; DLB 72; MTCW 1, 2
Malzberg, Barry N(athaniel) 1939- ... **CLC 7**
    See also CA 61-64; CAAS 4; CANR 16;
    DLB 8
Mamet, David (Alan) 1947- .. **CLC 9, 15, 34,
    46, 91; DAM DRAM; DC 4**
    See also AAYA 3; CA 81-84; CABS 3;
    CANR 15, 41, 67, 72; DA3; DLB 7;
    MTCW 1, 2
Mamoulian, Rouben (Zachary) 1897-1987
    CLC 16
    See also CA 25-28R; 124; CANR 85
Mandelstam, Osip (Emilievich)
    1891(?)-1938(?) .... **TCLC 2, 6; PC 14**
    See also CA 104; 150; MTCW 2
Mander, (Mary) Jane 1877-1949 ... **TCLC 31**
    See also CA 162
Mandeville, John fl. 1350- .... **CMLC 19**
    See also DLB 146
Mandiargues, Andre Pieyre de .... **CLC 41**
    See also Pieyre de Mandiargues, Andre
    DLB 83
Mandrake, Ethel Belle
    See Thurman, Wallace (Henry)
Mangan, James Clarence
    1803-1849 .... **NCLC 27**
Maniere, J.-E.
    See Giraudoux, (Hippolyte) Jean
Mankiewicz, Herman (Jacob) 1897-1953
    TCLC 85
    See also CA 120; 169; DLB 26
Manley, (Mary) Delariviere
    1672(?)-1724 .... **LC 1, 42**
    See also DLB 39, 80

Mann, Abel
    See Creasey, John
Mann, Emily 1952- .... **DC 7**
    See also CA 130; CANR 55
Mann, (Luiz) Heinrich 1871-1950 ... **TCLC 9**
    See also CA 106; 164, 181; DLB 66, 118
Mann, (Paul) Thomas 1875-1955 ... **TCLC 2,
    8, 14, 21, 35, 44, 60; DA; DAB; DAC;
    DAM MST, NOV; SSC 5; WLC**
    See also CA 104; 128; DA3; DLB 66;
    MTCW 1, 2
Mannheim, Karl 1893-1947 .... **TCLC 65**
Manning, David
    See Faust, Frederick (Schiller)
Manning, Frederic 1887(?)-1935 ... **TCLC 25**
    See also CA 124
Manning, Olivia 1915-1980 .... **CLC 5, 19**
    See also CA 5-8R; 101; CANR 29; MTCW
    1
Mano, D. Keith 1942- .... **CLC 2, 10**
    See also CA 25-28R; CAAS 6; CANR 26,
    57; DLB 6
Mansfield, Katherine . **TCLC 2, 8, 39; DAB;
    SSC 9, 23, 38; WLC**
    See also Beauchamp, Kathleen Mansfield
    DLB 162
Manso, Peter 1940- .... **CLC 39**
    See also CA 29-32R; CANR 44
Mantecon, Juan Jimenez
    See Jimenez (Mantecon), Juan Ramon
Manton, Peter
    See Creasey, John
Man Without a Spleen, A
    See Chekhov, Anton (Pavlovich)
Manzoni, Alessandro 1785-1873 .... **NCLC 29**
Map, Walter 1140-1209 .... **CMLC 32**
Mapu, Abraham (ben Jekutiel) 1808-1867
    NCLC 18
Mara, Sally
    See Queneau, Raymond
Marat, Jean Paul 1743-1793 .... **LC 10**
Marcel, Gabriel Honore 1889-1973 . **CLC 15**
    See also CA 102; 45-48; MTCW 1, 2
March, William 1893-1954 .... **TCLC 96**
Marchbanks, Samuel
    See Davies, (William) Robertson
Marchi, Giacomo
    See Bassani, Giorgio
Margulies, Donald .... **CLC 76**
Marie de France c. 12th cent. - ..... **CMLC 8;
    PC 22**
    See also DLB 208
Marie de l'Incarnation 1599-1672 ...... **LC 10**
Marier, Captain Victor
    See Griffith, D(avid Lewelyn) W(ark)
Mariner, Scott
    See Pohl, Frederik
Marinetti, Filippo Tommaso 1876-1944
    TCLC 10
    See also CA 107; DLB 114
Marivaux, Pierre Carlet de Chamblain de
    1688-1763 .... **LC 4; DC 7**
Markandaya, Kamala .... **CLC 8, 38**
    See also Taylor, Kamala (Purnaiya)
Markfield, Wallace 1926- .... **CLC 8**
    See also CA 69-72; CAAS 3; DLB 2, 28
Markham, Edwin 1852-1940 .... **TCLC 47**
    See also CA 160; DLB 54, 186
Markham, Robert
    See Amis, Kingsley (William)
Marks, J
    See Highwater, Jamake (Mamake)
Marks-Highwater, J
    See Highwater, Jamake (Mamake)
Markson, David M(errill) 1927- .... **CLC 67**
    See also CA 49-52; CANR 1

Maynard, Joyce 1953- .... **CLC 23**
See also CA 111; 129; CANR 64
Mayne, William (James Carter)
1928- .... **CLC 12**
See also AAYA 20; CA 9-12R; CANR 37,
80; CLR 25; JRDA; MAICYA; SAAS 11;
SATA 6, 68
Mayo, Jim
See L'Amour, Louis (Dearborn)
Maysles, Albert 1926- .... **CLC 16**
See also CA 29-32R
Maysles, David 1932- .... **CLC 16**
Mazer, Norma Fox 1931- .... **CLC 26**
See also AAYA 5; CA 69-72; CANR 12,
32, 66; CLR 23; JRDA; MAICYA; SAAS
1; SATA 24, 67, 105
Mazzini, Guiseppe 1805-1872 .... **NCLC 34**
McAlmon, Robert (Menzies) 1895-1956
TCLC 97
See also CA 107; 168; DLB 4, 45; DLBD
15
McAuley, James Phillip 1917-1976 .. **CLC 45**
See also CA 97-100
McBain, Ed
See Hunter, Evan
McBrien, William Augustine 1930- .. **CLC 44**
See also CA 107
McCaffrey, Anne (Inez) 1926- .... **CLC 17;**
DAM NOV, POP
See also AAYA 6; AITN 2; BEST 89:2; CA
25-28R; CANR 15, 35, 55; CLR 49; DA3;
DLB 8; JRDA; MAICYA; MTCW 1, 2;
SAAS 11; SATA 8, 70
McCall, Nathan 1955(?)- .... **CLC 86**
See also BW 3; CA 146
McCann, Arthur
See Campbell, John W(ood, Jr.)
McCann, Edson
See Pohl, Frederik
McCarthy, Charles, Jr. 1933-
See McCarthy, Cormac
See also CANR 42, 69; DAM POP; DA3;
MTCW 2
McCarthy, Cormac 1933- ...... **CLC 4, 57, 59,**
101
See also McCarthy, Charles, Jr. DLB 6, 143;
MTCW 2
McCarthy, Mary (Therese)
1912-1989 .. **CLC 1, 3, 5, 14, 24, 39, 59;**
SSC 24
See also CA 5-8R; 129; CANR 16, 50, 64;
DA3; DLB 2; DLBY 81; INT CANR-16;
MTCW 1, 2
McCartney, (James) Paul 1942- . **CLC 12, 35**
See also CA 146
McCauley, Stephen (D.) 1955- .... **CLC 50**
See also CA 141
McClure, Michael (Thomas) 1932- ... **CLC 6,**
10
See also CA 21-24R; CANR 17, 46, 77;
DLB 16
McCorkle, Jill (Collins) 1958- .... **CLC 51**
See also CA 121; DLBY 87
McCourt, Frank 1930- .... **CLC 109**
See also CA 157
McCourt, James 1941- .... **CLC 5**
See also CA 57-60
McCourt, Malachy 1932- .... **CLC 119**
McCoy, Horace (Stanley)
1897-1955 .... **TCLC 28**
See also CA 108; 155; DLB 9
McCrae, John 1872-1918 .... **TCLC 12**
See also CA 109; DLB 92
McCreigh, James
See Pohl, Frederik
McCullers, (Lula) Carson (Smith) 1917-1967
CLC 1, 4, 10, 12, 48, 100; DA; DAB;
DAC; DAM MST, NOV; SSC 9, 24;
WLC

See also AAYA 21; CA 5-8R; 25-28R;
CABS 1, 3; CANR 18; CDALB 1941-
1968; DA3; DLB 2, 7, 173; MTCW 1, 2;
SATA 27
McCulloch, John Tyler
See Burroughs, Edgar Rice
McCullough, Colleen 1938(?)- .... **CLC 27,**
107; DAM NOV, POP
See also CA 81-84; CANR 17, 46, 67; DA3;
MTCW 1, 2
McDermott, Alice 1953- .... **CLC 90**
See also CA 109; CANR 40
McElroy, Joseph 1930- .... **CLC 5, 47**
See also CA 17-20R
McEwan, Ian (Russell) 1948- .... **CLC 13, 66;**
DAM NOV
See also BEST 90:4; CA 61-64; CANR 14,
41, 69, 87; DLB 14, 194; MTCW 1, 2
McFadden, David 1940- .... **CLC 48**
See also CA 104; DLB 60; INT 104
McFarland, Dennis 1950- .... **CLC 65**
See also CA 165
McGahern, John 1934- ... **CLC 5, 9, 48; SSC**
17
See also CA 17-20R; CANR 29, 68; DLB
14; MTCW 1
McGinley, Patrick (Anthony) 1937- . **CLC 41**
See also CA 120; 127; CANR 56; INT 127
McGinley, Phyllis 1905-1978 .... **CLC 14**
See also CA 9-12R; 77-80; CANR 19; DLB
11, 48; SATA 2, 44; SATA-Obit 24
McGinniss, Joe 1942- .... **CLC 32**
See also AITN 2; BEST 89:2; CA 25-28R;
CANR 26, 70; DLB 185; INT CANR-26
McGivern, Maureen Daly
See Daly, Maureen
McGrath, Patrick 1950- .... **CLC 55**
See also CA 136; CANR 65
McGrath, Thomas (Matthew) 1916-1990
CLC 28, 59; DAM POET
See also CA 9-12R; 132; CANR 6, 33;
MTCW 1; SATA 41; SATA-Obit 66
McGuane, Thomas (Francis III)
1939- .... **CLC 3, 7, 18, 45, 127**
See also AITN 2; CA 49-52; CANR 5, 24,
49; DLB 2, 212; DLBY 80; INT CANR-
24; MTCW 1
McGuckian, Medbh 1950- .... **CLC 48; DAM**
POET; PC 27
See also CA 143; DLB 40
McHale, Tom 1942(?)-1982 .... **CLC 3, 5**
See also AITN 1; CA 77-80; 106
McIlvanney, William 1936- .... **CLC 42**
See also CA 25-28R; CANR 61; DLB 14,
207
McIlwraith, Maureen Mollie Hunter
See Hunter, Mollie
See also SATA 2
McInerney, Jay 1955- .... **CLC 34, 112; DAM**
POP
See also AAYA 18; CA 116; 123; CANR
45, 68; DA3; INT 123; MTCW 2
McIntyre, Vonda N(eel) 1948- .... **CLC 18**
See also CA 81-84; CANR 17, 34, 69;
MTCW 1
McKay, Claude . **TCLC 7, 41; BLC 3; DAB;**
PC 2
See also McKay, Festus Claudius DLB 4,
45, 51, 117
McKay, Festus Claudius 1889-1948
See McKay, Claude
See also BW 1, 3; CA 104; 124; CANR 73;
DA; DAC; DAM MST, MULT, NOV,
POET; MTCW 1, 2; WLC
McKuen, Rod 1933- .... **CLC 1, 3**
See also AITN 1; CA 41-44R; CANR 40
McLoughlin, R. B.
See Mencken, H(enry) L(ouis)

McLuhan, (Herbert) Marshall 1911-1980
CLC 37, 83
See also CA 9-12R; 102; CANR 12, 34, 61;
DLB 88; INT CANR-12; MTCW 1, 2
McMillan, Terry (L.) 1951- .... **CLC 50, 61,**
112; BLCS; DAM MULT, NOV, POP
See also AAYA 21; BW 2, 3; CA 140;
CANR 60; DA3; MTCW 2
McMurtry, Larry (Jeff) 1936- .. **CLC 2, 3, 7,**
11, 27, 44, 127; DAM NOV, POP
See also AAYA 15; AITN 2; BEST 89:2;
CA 5-8R; CANR 19, 43, 64; CDALB
1968-1988; DA3; DLB 2, 143; DLBY 80,
87; MTCW 1, 2
McNally, T. M. 1961- .... **CLC 82**
McNally, Terrence 1939- ... **CLC 4, 7, 41, 91;**
DAM DRAM
See also CA 45-48; CANR 2, 56; DA3;
DLB 7; MTCW 2
McNamer, Deirdre 1950- .... **CLC 70**
McNeal, Tom .... **CLC 119**
McNeile, Herman Cyril 1888-1937
See Sapper
See also DLB 77
McNickle, (William) D'Arcy
1904-1977 .... **CLC 89; DAM MULT**
See also CA 9-12R; 85-88; CANR 5, 45;
DLB 175, 212; NNAL; SATA-Obit 22
McPhee, John (Angus) 1931- .... **CLC 36**
See also BEST 90:1; CA 65-68; CANR 20,
46, 64, 69; DLB 185; MTCW 1, 2
McPherson, James Alan 1943- .. **CLC 19, 77;**
BLCS
See also BW 1, 3; CA 25-28R; CAAS 17;
CANR 24, 74; DLB 38; MTCW 1, 2
McPherson, William (Alexander)
1933- .... **CLC 34**
See also CA 69-72; CANR 28; INT
CANR-28
Mead, George Herbert 1873-1958 . **TCLC 89**
Mead, Margaret 1901-1978 .... **CLC 37**
See also AITN 1; CA 1-4R; 81-84; CANR
4; DA3; MTCW 1, 2; SATA-Obit 20
Meaker, Marijane (Agnes) 1927-
See Kerr, M. E.
See also CA 107; CANR 37, 63; INT 107;
JRDA; MAICYA; MTCW 1; SATA 20,
61, 99; SATA-Essay 111
Medoff, Mark (Howard) 1940- ... **CLC 6, 23;**
DAM DRAM
See also AITN 1; CA 53-56; CANR 5; DLB
7; INT CANR-5
Medvedev, P. N.
See Bakhtin, Mikhail Mikhailovich
Meged, Aharon
See Megged, Aharon
Meged, Aron
See Megged, Aharon
Megged, Aharon 1920- .... **CLC 9**
See also CA 49-52; CAAS 13; CANR 1
Mehta, Ved (Parkash) 1934- .... **CLC 37**
See also CA 1-4R; CANR 2, 23, 69; MTCW
1
Melanter
See Blackmore, R(ichard) D(oddridge)
Melies, Georges 1861-1938 .... **TCLC 81**
Melikow, Loris
See Hofmannsthal, Hugo von
Melmoth, Sebastian
See Wilde, Oscar
Meltzer, Milton 1915- .... **CLC 26**
See also AAYA 8; CA 13-16R; CANR 38;
CLR 13; DLB 61; JRDA; MAICYA;
SAAS 1; SATA 1, 50, 80
Melville, Herman 1819-1891 ..... **NCLC 3, 12,**
29, 45, 49; DA; DAB; DAC; DAM
MST, NOV; SSC 1, 17; WLC
See also AAYA 25; CDALB 1640-1865;
DA3; DLB 3, 74; SATA 59

See also AAYA 23; CA 109; 125; CANR 55; CDALBS; DA3; DLB 9; MTCW 1, 2

Mitchell, Peggy
See Mitchell, Margaret (Munnerlyn)

Mitchell, S(ilas) Weir 1829-1914 .... **TCLC 36**
See also CA 165; DLB 202

Mitchell, W(illiam) O(rmond) 1914-1998
CLC 25; DAC; DAM MST
See also CA 77-80; 165; CANR 15, 43; DLB 88

Mitchell, William 1879-1936 .... **TCLC 81**

Mitford, Mary Russell 1787-1855 ... **NCLC 4**
See also DLB 110, 116

Mitford, Nancy 1904-1973 .... **CLC 44**
See also CA 9-12R; DLB 191

Miyamoto, (Chujo) Yuriko
1899-1951 .... **TCLC 37**
See also CA 170, 174; DLB 180

Miyazawa, Kenji 1896-1933 .... **TCLC 76**
See also CA 157

Mizoguchi, Kenji 1898-1956 .... **TCLC 72**
See also CA 167

Mo, Timothy (Peter) 1950(?)- .... **CLC 46**
See also CA 117; DLB 194; MTCW 1

Modarressi, Taghi (M.) 1931- .... **CLC 44**
See also CA 121; 134; INT 134

Modiano, Patrick (Jean) 1945- .... **CLC 18**
See also CA 85-88; CANR 17, 40; DLB 83

Moerck, Paal
See Roelvaag, O(le) E(dvart)

Mofolo, Thomas (Mokopu) 1875(?)-1948
TCLC 22; BLC 3; DAM MULT
See also CA 121; 153; CANR 83; MTCW 2

Mohr, Nicholasa 1938- .... **CLC 12; DAM MULT; HLC 2**
See also AAYA 8; CA 49-52; CANR 1, 32, 64; CLR 22; DLB 145; HW 1, 2; JRDA; SAAS 8; SATA 8, 97; SATA-Essay 113

Mojtabai, A(nn) G(race) 1938- ..... **CLC 5, 9, 15, 29**
See also CA 85-88

Moliere 1622-1673 ..... **LC 10, 28; DA; DAB; DAC; DAM DRAM, MST; WLC**
See also DA3

Molin, Charles
See Mayne, William (James Carter)

Molnar, Ferenc 1878-1952 .. **TCLC 20; DAM DRAM**
See also CA 109; 153; CANR 83

Momaday, N(avarre) Scott 1934- ...... **CLC 2, 19, 85, 95; DA; DAB; DAC; DAM MST, MULT, NOV, POP; PC 25; WLCS**
See also AAYA 11; CA 25-28R; CANR 14, 34, 68; CDALBS; DA3; DLB 143, 175; INT CANR-14; MTCW 1, 2; NNAL; SATA 48; SATA-Brief 30

Monette, Paul 1945-1995 .... **CLC 82**
See also CA 139; 147

Monroe, Harriet 1860-1936 .... **TCLC 12**
See also CA 109; DLB 54, 91

Monroe, Lyle
See Heinlein, Robert A(nson)

Montagu, Elizabeth 1720-1800 .... **NCLC 7**

Montagu, Elizabeth 1917- .... **NCLC 7**
See also CA 9-12R

Montagu, Mary (Pierrepont) Wortley
1689-1762 .... **LC 9; PC 16**
See also DLB 95, 101

Montagu, W. H.
See Coleridge, Samuel Taylor

Montague, John (Patrick) 1929- ..... **CLC 13, 46**
See also CA 9-12R; CANR 9, 69; DLB 40; MTCW 1

Montaigne, Michel (Eyquem) de 1533-1592
LC 8; DA; DAB; DAC; DAM MST; WLC

Montale, Eugenio 1896-1981 ... **CLC 7, 9, 18; PC 13**
See also CA 17-20R; 104; CANR 30; DLB 114; MTCW 1

Montesquieu, Charles-Louis de Secondat
1689-1755 .... **LC 7**

Montgomery, (Robert) Bruce 1921(?)-1978
See Crispin, Edmund
See also CA 179; 104

Montgomery, L(ucy) M(aud) 1874-1942
TCLC 51; DAC; DAM MST
See also AAYA 12; CA 108; 137; CLR 8; DA3; DLB 92; DLBD 14; JRDA; MAI-CYA; MTCW 2; SATA 100; YABC 1

Montgomery, Marion H., Jr. 1925- .... **CLC 7**
See also AITN 1; CA 1-4R; CANR 3, 48; DLB 6

Montgomery, Max
See Davenport, Guy (Mattison, Jr.)

Montherlant, Henry (Milon) de 1896-1972
CLC 8, 19; DAM DRAM
See also CA 85-88; 37-40R; DLB 72; MTCW 1

Monty Python
See Chapman, Graham; Cleese, John (Marwood); Gilliam, Terry (Vance); Idle, Eric; Jones, Terence Graham Parry; Palin, Michael (Edward)
See also AAYA 7

Moodie, Susanna (Strickland) 1803-1885
NCLC 14
See also DLB 99

Mooney, Edward 1951-
See Mooney, Ted
See also CA 130

Mooney, Ted .... **CLC 25**
See also Mooney, Edward

Moorcock, Michael (John) 1939- ...... **CLC 5, 27, 58**
See also Bradbury, Edward P. AAYA 26; CA 45-48; CAAS 5; CANR 2, 17, 38, 64; DLB 14; MTCW 1, 2; SATA 93

Moore, Brian 1921-1999 ... **CLC 1, 3, 5, 7, 8, 19, 32, 90; DAB; DAC; DAM MST**
See also CA 1-4R; 174; CANR 1, 25, 42, 63; MTCW 1, 2

Moore, Edward
See Muir, Edwin

Moore, G. E. 1873-1958 .... **TCLC 89**

Moore, George Augustus
1852-1933 .... **TCLC 7; SSC 19**
See also CA 104; 177; DLB 10, 18, 57, 135

Moore, Lorrie .... **CLC 39, 45, 68**
See also Moore, Marie Lorena

Moore, Marianne (Craig)
1887-1972 ... **CLC 1, 2, 4, 8, 10, 13, 19, 47; DA; DAB; DAC; DAM MST, POET; PC 4; WLCS**
See also CA 1-4R; 33-36R; CANR 3, 61; CDALB 1929-1941; DA3; DLB 45; DLBD 7; MTCW 1, 2; SATA 20

Moore, Marie Lorena 1957-
See Moore, Lorrie
See also CA 116; CANR 39, 83

Moore, Thomas 1779-1852 .... **NCLC 6**
See also DLB 96, 144

Mora, Pat(ricia) 1942-
See also CA 129; CANR 57, 81; CLR 58; DAM MULT; DLB 209; HLC 2; HW 1, 2; SATA 92

Moraga, Cherrie 1952- .... **CLC 126; DAM MULT**
See also CA 131; CANR 66; DLB 82; HW 1, 2

Morand, Paul 1888-1976 .... **CLC 41; SSC 22**
See also CA 69-72; DLB 65

Morante, Elsa 1918-1985 .... **CLC 8, 47**
See also CA 85-88; 117; CANR 35; DLB 177; MTCW 1, 2

Moravia, Alberto 1907-1990 .... **CLC 2, 7, 11, 27, 46; SSC 26**
See also Pincherle, Alberto DLB 177; MTCW 2

More, Hannah 1745-1833 .... **NCLC 27**
See also DLB 107, 109, 116, 158

More, Henry 1614-1687 .... **LC 9**
See also DLB 126

More, Sir Thomas 1478-1535 .... **LC 10, 32**

Moreas, Jean .... **TCLC 18**
See also Papadiamantopoulos, Johannes

Morgan, Berry 1919- .... **CLC 6**
See also CA 49-52; DLB 6

Morgan, Claire
See Highsmith, (Mary) Patricia

Morgan, Edwin (George) 1920- .... **CLC 31**
See also CA 5-8R; CANR 3, 43; DLB 27

Morgan, (George) Frederick 1922- .. **CLC 23**
See also CA 17-20R; CANR 21

Morgan, Harriet
See Mencken, H(enry) L(ouis)

Morgan, Jane
See Cooper, James Fenimore

Morgan, Janet 1945- .... **CLC 39**
See also CA 65-68

Morgan, Lady 1776(?)-1859 .... **NCLC 29**
See also DLB 116, 158

Morgan, Robin (Evonne) 1941- .... **CLC 2**
See also CA 69-72; CANR 29, 68; MTCW 1; SATA 80

Morgan, Scott
See Kuttner, Henry

Morgan, Seth 1949(?)-1990 .... **CLC 65**
See also CA 132

Morgenstern, Christian 1871-1914 .. **TCLC 8**
See also CA 105

Morgenstern, S.
See Goldman, William (W.)

Moricz, Zsigmond 1879-1942 .... **TCLC 33**
See also CA 165

Morike, Eduard (Friedrich) 1804-1875
NCLC 10
See also DLB 133

Moritz, Karl Philipp 1756-1793 .... **LC 2**
See also DLB 94

Morland, Peter Henry
See Faust, Frederick (Schiller)

Morley, Christopher (Darlington) 1890-1957
TCLC 87
See also CA 112; DLB 9

Morren, Theophil
See Hofmannsthal, Hugo von

Morris, Bill 1952- .... **CLC 76**

Morris, Julian
See West, Morris L(anglo)

Morris, Steveland Judkins 1950(?)-
See Wonder, Stevie
See also CA 111

Morris, William 1834-1896 .... **NCLC 4**
See also CDBLB 1832-1890; DLB 18, 35, 57, 156, 178, 184

Morris, Wright 1910-1998 .. **CLC 1, 3, 7, 18, 37**
See also CA 9-12R; 167; CANR 21, 81; DLB 2, 206; DLBY 81; MTCW 1, 2

Morrison, Arthur 1863-1945 .... **TCLC 72**
See also CA 120; 157; DLB 70, 135, 197

Morrison, Chloe Anthony Wofford
See Morrison, Toni

Morrison, James Douglas 1943-1971
See Morrison, Jim
See also CA 73-76; CANR 40

Morrison, Jim .... **CLC 17**
See also Morrison, James Douglas

Neihardt, John Gneisenau 1881-1973 .... **CLC 32**
See also CA 13-14; CANR 65; CAP 1; DLB 9, 54

Nekrasov, Nikolai Alekseevich 1821-1878 **NCLC 11**

Nelligan, Emile 1879-1941 .... **TCLC 14**
See also CA 114; DLB 92

Nelson, Willie 1933- .... **CLC 17**
See also CA 107

Nemerov, Howard (Stanley) 1920-1991 .... **CLC 2, 6, 9, 36; DAM POET; PC 24**
See also CA 1-4R; 134; CABS 2; CANR 1, 27, 53; DLB 5, 6; DLBY 83; INT CANR-27; MTCW 1, 2

Neruda, Pablo 1904-1973 .. **CLC 1, 2, 5, 7, 9, 28, 62; DA; DAB; DAC; DAM MST, MULT, POET; HLC 2; PC 4; WLC**
See also CA 19-20; 45-48; CAP 2; DA3; HW 1; MTCW 1, 2

Nerval, Gerard de 1808-1855 ... **NCLC 1, 67; PC 13; SSC 18**

Nervo, (Jose) Amado (Ruiz de) 1870-1919 **TCLC 11; HLCS 2**
See also CA 109; 131; HW 1

Nessi, Pio Baroja y
See Baroja (y Nessi), Pio

Nestroy, Johann 1801-1862 .... **NCLC 42**
See also DLB 133

Netterville, Luke
See O'Grady, Standish (James)

Neufeld, John (Arthur) 1938- .... **CLC 17**
See also AAYA 11; CA 25-28R; CANR 11, 37, 56; CLR 52; MAICYA; SAAS 3; SATA 6, 81

Neumann, Alfred 1895-1952 .... **TCLC 100**
See also CA 183; DLB 56

Neville, Emily Cheney 1919- .... **CLC 12**
See also CA 5-8R; CANR 3, 37, 85; JRDA; MAICYA; SAAS 2; SATA 1

Newbound, Bernard Slade 1930-
See Slade, Bernard
See also CA 81-84; CANR 49; DAM DRAM

Newby, P(ercy) H(oward) 1918-1997 .... **CLC 2, 13; DAM NOV**
See also CA 5-8R; 161; CANR 32, 67; DLB 15; MTCW 1

Newlove, Donald 1928- .... **CLC 6**
See also CA 29-32R; CANR 25

Newlove, John (Herbert) 1938- .... **CLC 14**
See also CA 21-24R; CANR 9, 25

Newman, Charles 1938- .... **CLC 2, 8**
See also CA 21-24R; CANR 84

Newman, Edwin (Harold) 1919- ...... **CLC 14**
See also AITN 1; CA 69-72; CANR 5

Newman, John Henry 1801-1890 .. **NCLC 38**
See also DLB 18, 32, 55

Newton, (Sir)Isaac 1642-1727 .... **LC 35, 52**

Newton, Suzanne 1936- .... **CLC 35**
See also CA 41-44R; CANR 14; JRDA; SATA 5, 77

Nexo, Martin Andersen 1869-1954 .... **TCLC 43**

Nezval, Vitezslav 1900-1958 .... **TCLC 44**
See also CA 123

Ng, Fae Myenne 1957(?)- .... **CLC 81**
See also CA 146

Ngema, Mbongeni 1955- .... **CLC 57**
See also BW 2; CA 143; CANR 84

Ngugi, James T(hiong'o) .... **CLC 3, 7, 13**
See also Ngugi wa Thiong'o

Ngugi wa Thiong'o 1938- .. **CLC 36; BLC 3; DAM MULT, NOV**
See also Ngugi, James T(hiong'o) BW 2; CA 81-84; CANR 27, 58; DLB 125; MTCW 1, 2

Nichol, B(arrie) P(hillip) 1944-1988 . **CLC 18**
See also CA 53-56; DLB 53; SATA 66

Nichols, John (Treadwell) 1940- ...... **CLC 38**
See also CA 9-12R; CAAS 2; CANR 6, 70; DLBY 82

Nichols, Leigh
See Koontz, Dean R(ay)

Nichols, Peter (Richard) 1927- .... **CLC 5, 36, 65**
See also CA 104; CANR 33, 86; DLB 13; MTCW 1

Nicolas, F. R. E.
See Freeling, Nicolas

Niedecker, Lorine 1903-1970 ..... **CLC 10, 42; DAM POET**
See also CA 25-28; CAP 2; DLB 48

Nietzsche, Friedrich (Wilhelm) 1844-1900 **TCLC 10, 18, 55**
See also CA 107; 121; DLB 129

Nievo, Ippolito 1831-1861 .... **NCLC 22**

Nightingale, Anne Redmon 1943-
See Redmon, Anne
See also CA 103

Nightingale, Florence 1820-1910 ... **TCLC 85**
See also DLB 166

Nik. T. O.
See Annensky, Innokenty (Fyodorovich)

Nin, Anais 1903-1977 ..... **CLC 1, 4, 8, 11, 14, 60, 127; DAM NOV, POP; SSC 10**
See also AITN 2; CA 13-16R; 69-72; CANR 22, 53; DLB 2, 4, 152; MTCW 1, 2

Nishida, Kitaro 1870-1945 .... **TCLC 83**

Nishiwaki, Junzaburo 1894-1982 .... **PC 15**
See also CA 107

Nissenson, Hugh 1933- .... **CLC 4, 9**
See also CA 17-20R; CANR 27; DLB 28

Niven, Larry .... **CLC 8**
See also Niven, Laurence Van Cott AAYA 27; DLB 8

Niven, Laurence Van Cott 1938-
See Niven, Larry
See also CA 21-24R; CAAS 12; CANR 14, 44, 66; DAM POP; MTCW 1, 2; SATA 95

Nixon, Agnes Eckhardt 1927- .... **CLC 21**
See also CA 110

Nizan, Paul 1905-1940 .... **TCLC 40**
See also CA 161; DLB 72

Nkosi, Lewis 1936- ... **CLC 45; BLC 3; DAM MULT**
See also BW 1, 3; CA 65-68; CANR 27, 81; DLB 157

Nodier, (Jean) Charles (Emmanuel) 1780-1844 .... **NCLC 19**
See also DLB 119

Noguchi, Yone 1875-1947 .... **TCLC 80**

Nolan, Christopher 1965- .... **CLC 58**
See also CA 111

Noon, Jeff 1957- .... **CLC 91**
See also CA 148; CANR 83

Norden, Charles
See Durrell, Lawrence (George)

Nordhoff, Charles (Bernard) 1887-1947 **TCLC 23**
See also CA 108; DLB 9; SATA 23

Norfolk, Lawrence 1963- .... **CLC 76**
See also CA 144; CANR 85

Norman, Marsha 1947- .... **CLC 28; DAM DRAM; DC 8**
See also CA 105; CABS 3; CANR 41; DLBY 84

Normyx
See Douglas, (George) Norman

Norris, Frank 1870-1902 .... **SSC 28**
See also Norris, (Benjamin) Frank(lin, Jr.) CDALB 1865-1917; DLB 12, 71, 186

Norris, (Benjamin) Frank(lin, Jr.) 1870-1902 **TCLC 24**
See also Norris, Frank CA 110; 160

Norris, Leslie 1921- .... **CLC 14**
See also CA 11-12; CANR 14; CAP 1; DLB 27

North, Andrew
See Norton, Andre

North, Anthony
See Koontz, Dean R(ay)

North, Captain George
See Stevenson, Robert Louis (Balfour)

North, Milou
See Erdrich, Louise

Northrup, B. A.
See Hubbard, L(afayette) Ron(ald)

North Staffs
See Hulme, T(homas) E(rnest)

Norton, Alice Mary
See Norton, Andre
See also MAICYA; SATA 1, 43

Norton, Andre 1912- .... **CLC 12**
See also Norton, Alice Mary AAYA 14; CA 1-4R; CANR 68; CLR 50; DLB 8, 52; JRDA; MTCW 1; SATA 91

Norton, Caroline 1808-1877 .... **NCLC 47**
See also DLB 21, 159, 199

Norway, Nevil Shute 1899-1960
See Shute, Nevil
See also CA 102; 93-96; CANR 85; MTCW 2

Norwid, Cyprian Kamil 1821-1883 .... **NCLC 17**

Nosille, Nabrah
See Ellison, Harlan (Jay)

Nossack, Hans Erich 1901-1978 .... **CLC 6**
See also CA 93-96; 85-88; DLB 69

Nostradamus 1503-1566 .... **LC 27**

Nosu, Chuji
See Ozu, Yasujiro

Notenburg, Eleanora (Genrikhovna) von
See Guro, Elena

Nova, Craig 1945- .... **CLC 7, 31**
See also CA 45-48; CANR 2, 53

Novak, Joseph
See Kosinski, Jerzy (Nikodem)

Novalis 1772-1801 .... **NCLC 13**
See also DLB 90

Novis, Emile
See Weil, Simone (Adolphine)

Nowlan, Alden (Albert) 1933-1983 . **CLC 15; DAC; DAM MST**
See also CA 9-12R; CANR 5; DLB 53

Noyes, Alfred 1880-1958 ...... **TCLC 7; PC 27**
See also CA 104; DLB 20

Nunn, Kem .... **CLC 34**
See also CA 159

Nye, Robert 1939- . **CLC 13, 42; DAM NOV**
See also CA 33-36R; CANR 29, 67; DLB 14; MTCW 1; SATA 6

Nyro, Laura 1947- .... **CLC 17**

Oates, Joyce Carol 1938- .. **CLC 1, 2, 3, 6, 9, 11, 15, 19, 33, 52, 108; DA; DAB; DAC; DAM MST, NOV, POP; SSC 6; WLC**
See also AAYA 15; AITN 1; BEST 89:2; CA 5-8R; CANR 25, 45, 74; CDALB 1968-1988; DA3; DLB 2, 5, 130; DLBY 81; INT CANR-25; MTCW 1, 2

O'Brien, Darcy 1939-1998 .... **CLC 11**
See also CA 21-24R; 167; CANR 8, 59

O'Brien, E. G.
See Clarke, Arthur C(harles)

O'Brien, Edna 1936- ... **CLC 3, 5, 8, 13, 36, 65, 116; DAM NOV; SSC 10**
See also CA 1-4R; CANR 6, 41, 65; CD-BLB 1960 to Present; DA3; DLB 14; MTCW 1, 2

Owens, Rochelle 1936- .... CLC 8
  See also CA 17-20R; CAAS 2; CANR 39

Oz, Amos 1939- ...... CLC 5, 8, 11, 27, 33, 54;
    DAM NOV
  See also CA 53-56; CANR 27, 47, 65;
    MTCW 1, 2

Ozick, Cynthia 1928- .... CLC 3, 7, 28, 62;
    DAM NOV, POP; SSC 15
  See also BEST 90:1; CA 17-20R; CANR
    23, 58; DA3; DLB 28, 152; DLBY 82;
    INT CANR-23; MTCW 1, 2

Ozu, Yasujiro 1903-1963 .... CLC 16
  See also CA 112

Pacheco, C.
  See Pessoa, Fernando (Antonio Nogueira)

Pacheco, Jose Emilio 1939-
  See also CA 111; 131; CANR 65; DAM
    MULT; HLC 2; HW 1, 2

Pa Chin .... CLC 18
  See also Li Fei-kan

Pack, Robert 1929- .... CLC 13
  See also CA 1-4R; CANR 3, 44, 82; DLB 5

Padgett, Lewis
  See Kuttner, Henry

Padilla (Lorenzo), Heberto 1932- ..... CLC 38
  See also AITN 1; CA 123; 131; HW 1

Page, Jimmy 1944- .... CLC 12

Page, Louise 1955- .... CLC 40
  See also CA 140; CANR 76

Page, P(atricia) K(athleen) 1916- ...... CLC 7,
    18; DAC; DAM MST; PC 12
  See also CA 53-56; CANR 4, 22, 65; DLB
    68; MTCW 1

Page, Thomas Nelson 1853-1922 .... SSC 23
  See also CA 118; 177; DLB 12, 78; DLBD
    13

Pagels, Elaine Hiesey 1943- .... CLC 104
  See also CA 45-48; CANR 2, 24, 51

Paget, Violet 1856-1935
  See Lee, Vernon
  See also CA 104; 166

Paget-Lowe, Henry
  See Lovecraft, H(oward) P(hillips)

Paglia, Camille (Anna) 1947- .... CLC 68
  See also CA 140; CANR 72; MTCW 2

Paige, Richard
  See Koontz, Dean R(ay)

Paine, Thomas 1737-1809 .... NCLC 62
  See also CDALB 1640-1865; DLB 31, 43,
    73, 158

Pakenham, Antonia
  See Fraser, (Lady) Antonia (Pakenham)

Palamas, Kostes 1859-1943 .... TCLC 5
  See also CA 105

Palazzeschi, Aldo 1885-1974 .... CLC 11
  See also CA 89-92; 53-56; DLB 114

Pales Matos, Luis 1898-1959
  See also HLCS 2; HW 1

Paley, Grace 1922- .... CLC 4, 6, 37; DAM
    POP; SSC 8
  See also CA 25-28R; CANR 13, 46, 74;
    DA3; DLB 28; INT CANR-13; MTCW 1,
    2

Palin, Michael (Edward) 1943- .... CLC 21
  See also Monty Python CA 107; CANR 35;
    SATA 67

Palliser, Charles 1947- .... CLC 65
  See also CA 136; CANR 76

Palma, Ricardo 1833-1919 .... TCLC 29
  See also CA 168

Pancake, Breece Dexter 1952-1979
  See Pancake, Breece D'J
  See also CA 123; 109

Pancake, Breece D'J .... CLC 29
  See also Pancake, Breece Dexter DLB 130

Panko, Rudy
  See Gogol, Nikolai (Vasilyevich)

Papadiamantis, Alexandros
    1851-1911 .... TCLC 29
  See also CA 168

Papadiamantopoulos, Johannes 1856-1910
  See Moreas, Jean
  See also CA 117

Papini, Giovanni 1881-1956 .... TCLC 22
  See also CA 121; 180

Paracelsus 1493-1541 .... LC 14
  See also DLB 179

Parasol, Peter
  See Stevens, Wallace

Pardo Bazan, Emilia 1851-1921 .... SSC 30

Pareto, Vilfredo 1848-1923 .... TCLC 69
  See also CA 175

Parfenie, Maria
  See Codrescu, Andrei

Parini, Jay (Lee) 1948- .... CLC 54
  See also CA 97-100; CAAS 16; CANR 32,
    87

Park, Jordan
  See Kornbluth, C(yril) M.; Pohl, Frederik

Park, Robert E(zra) 1864-1944 ..... TCLC 73
  See also CA 122; 165

Parker, Bert
  See Ellison, Harlan (Jay)

Parker, Dorothy (Rothschild)
    1893-1967 .... CLC 15, 68; DAM POET;
    PC 28; SSC 2
  See also CA 19-20; 25-28R; CAP 2; DA3;
    DLB 11, 45, 86; MTCW 1, 2

Parker, Robert B(rown) 1932- .... CLC 27;
    DAM NOV, POP
  See also AAYA 28; BEST 89:4; CA 49-52;
    CANR 1, 26, 52; INT CANR-26; MTCW
    1

Parkin, Frank 1940- .... CLC 43
  See also CA 147

Parkman, Francis Jr., Jr.
    1823-1893 .... NCLC 12
  See also DLB 1, 30, 186

Parks, Gordon (Alexander Buchanan) 1912-
    CLC 1, 16; BLC 3; DAM MULT
  See also AITN 2; BW 2, 3; CA 41-44R;
    CANR 26, 66; DA3; DLB 33; MTCW 2;
    SATA 8, 108

Parmenides c. 515B.C.-c.
    450B.C. .... CMLC 22
  See also DLB 176

Parnell, Thomas 1679-1718 .... LC 3
  See also DLB 94

Parra, Nicanor 1914- ...... CLC 2, 102; DAM
    MULT; HLC 2
  See also CA 85-88; CANR 32; HW 1;
    MTCW 1

Parra Sanojo, Ana Teresa de la 1890-1936
  See also HLCS 2

Parrish, Mary Frances
  See Fisher, M(ary) F(rances) K(ennedy)

Parson
  See Coleridge, Samuel Taylor

Parson Lot
  See Kingsley, Charles

Partridge, Anthony
  See Oppenheim, E(dward) Phillips

Pascal, Blaise 1623-1662 .... LC 35

Pascoli, Giovanni 1855-1912 .... TCLC 45
  See also CA 170

Pasolini, Pier Paolo 1922-1975 .. CLC 20, 37,
    106; PC 17
  See also CA 93-96; 61-64; CANR 63; DLB
    128, 177; MTCW 1

Pasquini
  See Silone, Ignazio

Pastan, Linda (Olenik) 1932- .... CLC 27;
    DAM POET
  See also CA 61-64; CANR 18, 40, 61; DLB
    5

Pasternak, Boris (Leonidovich) 1890-1960
    CLC 7, 10, 18, 63; DA; DAB; DAC;
    DAM MST, NOV, POET; PC 6; SSC 31;
    WLC
  See also CA 127; 116; DA3; MTCW 1, 2

Patchen, Kenneth 1911-1972 .. CLC 1, 2, 18;
    DAM POET
  See also CA 1-4R; 33-36R; CANR 3, 35;
    DLB 16, 48; MTCW 1

Pater, Walter (Horatio) 1839-1894 .. NCLC 7
  See also CDBLB 1832-1890; DLB 57, 156

Paterson, A(ndrew) B(arton) 1864-1941
    TCLC 32
  See also CA 155; SATA 97

Paterson, Katherine (Womeldorf)
    1932- .... CLC 12, 30
  See also AAYA 1, 31; CA 21-24R; CANR
    28, 59; CLR 7, 50; DLB 52; JRDA; MAI-
    CYA; MTCW 1; SATA 13, 53, 92

Patmore, Coventry Kersey Dighton
    1823-1896 .... NCLC 9
  See also DLB 35, 98

Paton, Alan (Stewart) 1903-1988 ...... CLC 4,
    10, 25, 55, 106; DA; DAB; DAC; DAM
    MST, NOV; WLC
  See also AAYA 26; CA 13-16; 125; CANR
    22; CAP 1; DA3; DLBD 17; MTCW 1, 2;
    SATA 11; SATA-Obit 56

Paton Walsh, Gillian 1937-
  See Walsh, Jill Paton
  See also AAYA 11; CANR 38, 83; DLB
    161; JRDA; MAICYA; SAAS 3; SATA 4,
    72, 109

Patton, George S. 1885-1945 .... TCLC 79

Paulding, James Kirke 1778-1860 ... NCLC 2
  See also DLB 3, 59, 74

Paulin, Thomas Neilson 1949-
  See Paulin, Tom
  See also CA 123; 128

Paulin, Tom .... CLC 37
  See also Paulin, Thomas Neilson DLB 40

Pausanias c. 1st cent. - .... CMLC 36

Paustovsky, Konstantin (Georgievich)
    1892-1968 .... CLC 40
  See also CA 93-96; 25-28R

Pavese, Cesare 1908-1950 .. TCLC 3; PC 13;
    SSC 19
  See also CA 104; 169; DLB 128, 177

Pavic, Milorad 1929- .... CLC 60
  See also CA 136; DLB 181

Pavlov, Ivan Petrovich 1849-1936 . TCLC 91
  See also CA 118; 180

Payne, Alan
  See Jakes, John (William)

Paz, Gil
  See Lugones, Leopoldo

Paz, Octavio 1914-1998 . CLC 3, 4, 6, 10, 19,
    51, 65, 119; DA; DAB; DAC; DAM
    MST, MULT, POET; HLC 2; PC 1;
    WLC
  See also CA 73-76; 165; CANR 32, 65;
    DA3; DLBY 90, 98; HW 1, 2; MTCW 1,
    2

p'Bitek, Okot 1931-1982 .... CLC 96; BLC 3;
    DAM MULT
  See also BW 2, 3; CA 124; 107; CANR 82;
    DLB 125; MTCW 1, 2

Peacock, Molly 1947- .... CLC 60
  See also CA 103; CAAS 21; CANR 52, 84;
    DLB 120

Peacock, Thomas Love
    1785-1866 .... NCLC 22
  See also DLB 96, 116

Peake, Mervyn 1911-1968 .... CLC 7, 54
  See also CA 5-8R; 25-28R; CANR 3; DLB
    15, 160; MTCW 1; SATA 23

Pearce, Philippa .... CLC 21
  See also Christie, (Ann) Philippa CLR 9;
    DLB 161; MAICYA; SATA 1, 67

See also BW 2, 3; CA 141; CANR 79

Plaidy, Jean
  See Hibbert, Eleanor Alice Burford

Planche, James Robinson
  1796-1880 .... NCLC 42

Plant, Robert 1948- .... CLC 12

Plante, David (Robert) 1940- ...... CLC 7, 23, 38; DAM NOV
  See also CA 37-40R; CANR 12, 36, 58, 82; DLBY 83; INT CANR-12; MTCW 1

Plath, Sylvia 1932-1963 ..... CLC 1, 2, 3, 5, 9, 11, 14, 17, 50, 51, 62, 111; DA; DAB; DAC; DAM MST, POET; PC 1; WLC
  See also AAYA 13; CA 19-20; CANR 34; CAP 2; CDALB 1941-1968; DA3; DLB 5, 6, 152; MTCW 1, 2; SATA 96

Plato 428(?)B.C.-348(?)B.C. ... CMLC 8; DA; DAB; DAC; DAM MST; WLCS
  See also DA3; DLB 176

Platonov, Andrei .... TCLC 14
  See also Klimentov, Andrei Platonovich

Platt, Kin 1911- .... CLC 26
  See also AAYA 11; CA 17-20R; CANR 11; JRDA; SAAS 17; SATA 21, 86

Plautus c. 251B.C.-184B.C. ... CMLC 24; DC 6
  See also DLB 211

Plick et Plock
  See Simenon, Georges (Jacques Christian)

Plimpton, George (Ames) 1927- .... CLC 36
  See also AITN 1; CA 21-24R; CANR 32, 70; DLB 185; MTCW 1, 2; SATA 10

Pliny the Elder c. 23-79 .... CMLC 23
  See also DLB 211

Plomer, William Charles Franklin 1903-1973 CLC 4, 8
  See also CA 21-22; CANR 34; CAP 2; DLB 20, 162, 191; MTCW 1; SATA 24

Plowman, Piers
  See Kavanagh, Patrick (Joseph)

Plum, J.
  See Wodehouse, P(elham) G(renville)

Plumly, Stanley (Ross) 1939- .... CLC 33
  See also CA 108; 110; DLB 5, 193; INT 110

Plumpe, Friedrich Wilhelm
  1888-1931 .... TCLC 53
  See also CA 112

Po Chu-i 772-846 .... CMLC 24

Poe, Edgar Allan 1809-1849 ..... NCLC 1, 16, 55, 78; DA; DAB; DAC; DAM MST, POET; PC 1; SSC 34; WLC
  See also AAYA 14; CDALB 1640-1865; DA3; DLB 3, 59, 73, 74; SATA 23

Poet of Titchfield Street, The
  See Pound, Ezra (Weston Loomis)

Pohl, Frederik 1919- .... CLC 18; SSC 25
  See also AAYA 24; CA 61-64; CAAS 1; CANR 11, 37, 81; DLB 8; INT CANR-11; MTCW 1, 2; SATA 24

Poirier, Louis 1910-
  See Gracq, Julien
  See also CA 122; 126

Poitier, Sidney 1927- .... CLC 26
  See also BW 1; CA 117

Polanski, Roman 1933- .... CLC 16
  See also CA 77-80

Poliakoff, Stephen 1952- .... CLC 38
  See also CA 106; DLB 13

Police, The
  See Copeland, Stewart (Armstrong); Summers, Andrew James; Sumner, Gordon Matthew

Polidori, John William 1795-1821 . NCLC 51
  See also DLB 116

Pollitt, Katha 1949- .... CLC 28, 122
  See also CA 120; 122; CANR 66; MTCW 1, 2

Pollock, (Mary) Sharon 1936- .... CLC 50; DAC; DAM DRAM, MST
  See also CA 141; DLB 60

Polo, Marco 1254-1324 .... CMLC 15

Polonsky, Abraham (Lincoln)
  1910- .... CLC 92
  See also CA 104; DLB 26; INT 104

Polybius c. 200B.C.-c. 118B.C. ...... CMLC 17
  See also DLB 176

Pomerance, Bernard 1940- ... CLC 13; DAM DRAM
  See also CA 101; CANR 49

Ponge, Francis 1899-1988 . CLC 6, 18; DAM POET
  See also CA 85-88; 126; CANR 40, 86

Poniatowska, Elena 1933-
  See also CA 101; CANR 32, 66; DAM MULT; DLB 113; HLC 2; HW 1, 2

Pontoppidan, Henrik 1857-1943 .... TCLC 29
  See also CA 170

Poole, Josephine .... CLC 17
  See also Helyar, Jane Penelope Josephine
  SAAS 2; SATA 5

Popa, Vasko 1922-1991 .... CLC 19
  See also CA 112; 148; DLB 181

Pope, Alexander 1688-1744 .... LC 3; DA; DAB; DAC; DAM MST, POET; PC 26; WLC
  See also CDBLB 1660-1789; DA3; DLB 95, 101

Porter, Connie (Rose) 1959(?)- .... CLC 70
  See also BW 2, 3; CA 142; SATA 81

Porter, Gene(va Grace) Stratton
  1863(?)-1924 .... TCLC 21
  See also CA 112

Porter, Katherine Anne 1890-1980 ... CLC 1, 3, 7, 10, 13, 15, 27, 101; DA; DAB; DAC; DAM MST, NOV; SSC 4, 31
  See also AITN 2; CA 1-4R; 101; CANR 1, 65; CDALBS; DA3; DLB 4, 9, 102; DLBD 12; DLBY 80; MTCW 1, 2; SATA 39; SATA-Obit 23

Porter, Peter (Neville Frederick)
  1929- .... CLC 5, 13, 33
  See also CA 85-88; DLB 40

Porter, William Sydney 1862-1910
  See Henry, O.
  See also CA 104; 131; CDALB 1865-1917; DA; DAB; DAC; DAM MST; DA3; DLB 12, 78, 79; MTCW 1, 2; YABC 2

Portillo (y Pacheco), Jose Lopez
  See Lopez Portillo (y Pacheco), Jose

Portillo Trambley, Estela 1927-1998
  See also CANR 32; DAM MULT; DLB 209; HLC 2; HW 1

Post, Melville Davisson
  1869-1930 .... TCLC 39
  See also CA 110

Potok, Chaim 1929- ... CLC 2, 7, 14, 26, 112; DAM NOV
  See also AAYA 15; AITN 1, 2; CA 17-20R; CANR 19, 35, 64; DA3; DLB 28, 152; INT CANR-19; MTCW 1, 2; SATA 33, 106

Potter, Dennis (Christopher George)
  1935-1994 .... CLC 58, 86
  See also CA 107; 145; CANR 33, 61; MTCW 1

Pound, Ezra (Weston Loomis) 1885-1972
  CLC 1, 2, 3, 4, 5, 7, 10, 13, 18, 34, 48, 50, 112; DA; DAB; DAC; DAM MST, POET; PC 4; WLC
  See also CA 5-8R; 37-40R; CANR 40; CDALB 1917-1929; DA3; DLB 4, 45, 63; DLBD 15; MTCW 1, 2

Povod, Reinaldo 1959-1994 .... CLC 44
  See also CA 136; 146; CANR 83

Powell, Adam Clayton, Jr.
  1908-1972 .... CLC 89; BLC 3; DAM MULT
  See also BW 1, 3; CA 102; 33-36R; CANR 86

Powell, Anthony (Dymoke) 1905- . CLC 1, 3, 7, 9, 10, 31
  See also CA 1-4R; CANR 1, 32, 62; CD-BLB 1945-1960; DLB 15; MTCW 1, 2

Powell, Dawn 1897-1965 .... CLC 66
  See also CA 5-8R; DLBY 97

Powell, Padgett 1952- .... CLC 34
  See also CA 126; CANR 63

Power, Susan 1961- .... CLC 91

Powers, J(ames) F(arl) 1917-1999 ..... CLC 1, 4, 8, 57; SSC 4
  See also CA 1-4R; 181; CANR 2, 61; DLB 130; MTCW 1

Powers, John J(ames) 1945-
  See Powers, John R.
  See also CA 69-72

Powers, John R. .... CLC 66
  See also Powers, John J(ames)

Powers, Richard (S.) 1957- .... CLC 93
  See also CA 148; CANR 80

Pownall, David 1938- .... CLC 10
  See also CA 89-92; 180; CAAS 18; CANR 49; DLB 14

Powys, John Cowper 1872-1963 ... CLC 7, 9, 15, 46, 125
  See also CA 85-88; DLB 15; MTCW 1, 2

Powys, T(heodore) F(rancis) 1875-1953
  TCLC 9
  See also CA 106; DLB 36, 162

Prado (Calvo), Pedro 1886-1952 ... TCLC 75
  See also CA 131; HW 1

Prager, Emily 1952- .... CLC 56

Pratt, E(dwin) J(ohn)
  1883(?)-1964 .... CLC 19; DAC; DAM POET
  See also CA 141; 93-96; CANR 77; DLB 92

Premchand .... TCLC 21
  See also Srivastava, Dhanpat Rai

Preussler, Otfried 1923- .... CLC 17
  See also CA 77-80; SATA 24

Prevert, Jacques (Henri Marie) 1900-1977
  CLC 15
  See also CA 77-80; 69-72; CANR 29, 61; MTCW 1; SATA-Obit 30

Prevost, Abbe (Antoine Francois) 1697-1763
  LC 1

Price, (Edward) Reynolds 1933- ... CLC 3, 6, 13, 43, 50, 63; DAM NOV; SSC 22
  See also CA 1-4R; CANR 1, 37, 57, 87; DLB 2; INT CANR-37

Price, Richard 1949- .... CLC 6, 12
  See also CA 49-52; CANR 3; DLBY 81

Prichard, Katharine Susannah 1883-1969
  CLC 46
  See also CA 11-12; CANR 33; CAP 1; MTCW 1; SATA 66

Priestley, J(ohn) B(oynton)
  1894-1984 .... CLC 2, 5, 9, 34; DAM DRAM, NOV
  See also CA 9-12R; 113; CANR 33; CD-BLB 1914-1945; DA3; DLB 10, 34, 77, 100, 139; DLBY 84; MTCW 1, 2

Prince 1958(?)- .... CLC 35

Prince, F(rank) T(empleton) 1912- .. CLC 22
  See also CA 101; CANR 43, 79; DLB 20

Prince Kropotkin
  See Kropotkin, Peter (Alekseievich)

Prior, Matthew 1664-1721 .... LC 4
  See also DLB 95

Prishvin, Mikhail 1873-1954 .... TCLC 75

Pritchard, William H(arrison)
  1932- .... CLC 34
  See also CA 65-68; CANR 23; DLB 111

Pritchett, V(ictor) S(awdon)
1900-1997 ...... **CLC 5, 13, 15, 41; DAM NOV; SSC 14**
See also CA 61-64; 157; CANR 31, 63; DA3; DLB 15, 139; MTCW 1, 2

Private 19022
See Manning, Frederic

Probst, Mark 1925- .... **CLC 59**
See also CA 130

Prokosch, Frederic 1908-1989 ...... **CLC 4, 48**
See also CA 73-76; 128; CANR 82; DLB 48; MTCW 2

Propertius, Sextus c. 50B.C.-c. 16B.C. .... **CMLC 32**
See also DLB 211

Prophet, The
See Dreiser, Theodore (Herman Albert)

Prose, Francine 1947- .... **CLC 45**
See also CA 109; 112; CANR 46; SATA 101

Proudhon
See Cunha, Euclides (Rodrigues Pimenta) da

Proulx, Annie
See Proulx, E(dna) Annie

Proulx, E(dna) Annie 1935- .. **CLC 81; DAM POP**
See also CA 145; CANR 65; DA3; MTCW 2

Proust, (Valentin-Louis-George-Eugene-) Marcel 1871-1922 .... **TCLC 7, 13, 33; DA; DAB; DAC; DAM MST, NOV; WLC**
See also CA 104; 120; DA3; DLB 65; MTCW 1, 2

Prowler, Harley
See Masters, Edgar Lee

Prus, Boleslaw 1845-1912 .... **TCLC 48**

Pryor, Richard (Franklin Lenox Thomas) 1940- .... **CLC 26**
See also CA 122; 152

Przybyszewski, Stanislaw 1868-1927 .... **TCLC 36**
See also CA 160; DLB 66

Pteleon
See Grieve, C(hristopher) M(urray)
See also DAM POET

Puckett, Lute
See Masters, Edgar Lee

Puig, Manuel 1932-1990 .... **CLC 3, 5, 10, 28, 65; DAM MULT; HLC 2**
See also CA 45-48; CANR 2, 32, 63; DA3; DLB 113; HW 1, 2; MTCW 1, 2

Pulitzer, Joseph 1847-1911 .... **TCLC 76**
See also CA 114; DLB 23

Purdy, A(lfred) W(ellington) 1918- ... **CLC 3, 6, 14, 50; DAC; DAM MST, POET**
See also CA 81-84; CAAS 17; CANR 42, 66; DLB 88

Purdy, James (Amos) 1923- .... **CLC 2, 4, 10, 28, 52**
See also CA 33-36R; CAAS 1; CANR 19, 51; DLB 2; INT CANR-19; MTCW 1

Pure, Simon
See Swinnerton, Frank Arthur

Pushkin, Alexander (Sergeyevich) 1799-1837 **NCLC 3, 27, 83; DA; DAB; DAC; DAM DRAM, MST, POET; PC 10; SSC 27; WLC**
See also DA3; DLB 205; SATA 61

P'u Sung-ling 1640-1715 .... **LC 49; SSC 31**

Putnam, Arthur Lee
See Alger, Horatio Jr., Jr.

Puzo, Mario 1920-1999 .... **CLC 1, 2, 6, 36, 107; DAM NOV, POP**
See also CA 65-68; CANR 4, 42, 65; DA3; DLB 6; MTCW 1, 2

Pygge, Edward
See Barnes, Julian (Patrick)

Pyle, Ernest Taylor 1900-1945
See Pyle, Ernie
See also CA 115; 160

Pyle, Ernie 1900-1945 .... **TCLC 75**
See also Pyle, Ernest Taylor DLB 29; MTCW 2

Pyle, Howard 1853-1911 .... **TCLC 81**
See also CA 109; 137; CLR 22; DLB 42, 188; DLBD 13; MAICYA; SATA 16, 100

Pym, Barbara (Mary Crampton) 1913-1980 **CLC 13, 19, 37, 111**
See also CA 13-14; 97-100; CANR 13, 34; CAP 1; DLB 14, 207; DLBY 87; MTCW 1, 2

Pynchon, Thomas (Ruggles, Jr.) 1937- ...... **CLC 2, 3, 6, 9, 11, 18, 33, 62, 72; DA; DAB; DAC; DAM MST, NOV, POP; SSC 14; WLC**
See also BEST 90:2; CA 17-20R; CANR 22, 46, 73; DA3; DLB 2, 173; MTCW 1, 2

Pythagoras c. 570B.C.-c. 500B.C. . **CMLC 22**
See also DLB 176

Q
See Quiller-Couch, SirArthur (Thomas)

Qian Zhongshu
See Ch'ien Chung-shu

Qroll
See Dagerman, Stig (Halvard)

Quarrington, Paul (Lewis) 1953- ..... **CLC 65**
See also CA 129; CANR 62

Quasimodo, Salvatore 1901-1968 ..... **CLC 10**
See also CA 13-16; 25-28R; CAP 1; DLB 114; MTCW 1

Quay, Stephen 1947- .... **CLC 95**

Quay, Timothy 1947- .... **CLC 95**

Queen, Ellery .... **CLC 3, 11**
See also Dannay, Frederic; Davidson, Avram (James); Lee, Manfred B(ennington); Marlowe, Stephen; Sturgeon, Theodore (Hamilton); Vance, John Holbrook

Queen, Ellery, Jr.
See Dannay, Frederic; Lee, Manfred B(ennington)

Queneau, Raymond 1903-1976 ..... **CLC 2, 5, 10, 42**
See also CA 77-80; 69-72; CANR 32; DLB 72; MTCW 1, 2

Quevedo, Francisco de 1580-1645 .... **LC 23**

Quiller-Couch, SirArthur (Thomas) 1863-1944 .... **TCLC 53**
See also CA 118; 166; DLB 135, 153, 190

Quin, Ann (Marie) 1936-1973 .... **CLC 6**
See also CA 9-12R; 45-48; DLB 14

Quinn, Martin
See Smith, Martin Cruz

Quinn, Peter 1947- .... **CLC 91**

Quinn, Simon
See Smith, Martin Cruz

Quintana, Leroy V. 1944-
See also CA 131; CANR 65; DAM MULT; DLB 82; HLC 2; HW 1, 2

Quiroga, Horacio (Sylvestre) 1878-1937 **TCLC 20; DAM MULT; HLC 2**
See also CA 117; 131; HW 1; MTCW 1

Quoirez, Francoise 1935- .... **CLC 9**
See also Sagan, Francoise CA 49-52; CANR 6, 39, 73; MTCW 1, 2

Raabe, Wilhelm (Karl) 1831-1910 . **TCLC 45**
See also CA 167; DLB 129

Rabe, David (William) 1940- .. **CLC 4, 8, 33; DAM DRAM**
See also CA 85-88; CABS 3; CANR 59; DLB 7

Rabelais, Francois 1483-1553 ...... **LC 5; DA; DAB; DAC; DAM MST; WLC**

Rabinovitch, Sholem 1859-1916
See Aleichem, Sholom
See also CA 104

Rabinyan, Dorit 1972- .... **CLC 119**
See also CA 170

Rachilde
See Vallette, Marguerite Eymery

Racine, Jean 1639-1699 . **LC 28; DAB; DAM MST**
See also DA3

Radcliffe, Ann (Ward) 1764-1823 ... **NCLC 6, 55**
See also DLB 39, 178

Radiguet, Raymond 1903-1923 ...... **TCLC 29**
See also CA 162; DLB 65

Radnoti, Miklos 1909-1944 .... **TCLC 16**
See also CA 118

Rado, James 1939- .... **CLC 17**
See also CA 105

Radvanyi, Netty 1900-1983
See Seghers, Anna
See also CA 85-88; 110; CANR 82

Rae, Ben
See Griffiths, Trevor

Raeburn, John (Hay) 1941- .... **CLC 34**
See also CA 57-60

Ragni, Gerome 1942-1991 .... **CLC 17**
See also CA 105; 134

Rahv, Philip 1908-1973 .... **CLC 24**
See also Greenberg, Ivan DLB 137

Raimund, Ferdinand Jakob 1790-1836 **NCLC 69**
See also DLB 90

Raine, Craig 1944- .... **CLC 32, 103**
See also CA 108; CANR 29, 51; DLB 40

Raine, Kathleen (Jessie) 1908- ..... **CLC 7, 45**
See also CA 85-88; CANR 46; DLB 20; MTCW 1

Rainis, Janis 1865-1929 .... **TCLC 29**
See also CA 170

Rakosi, Carl 1903- .... **CLC 47**
See also Rawley, Callman CAAS 5; DLB 193

Raleigh, Richard
See Lovecraft, H(oward) P(hillips)

Raleigh, Sir Walter 1554(?)-1618 .. **LC 31, 39**
See also CDBLB Before 1660; DLB 172

Rallentando, H. P.
See Sayers, Dorothy L(eigh)

Ramal, Walter
See de la Mare, Walter (John)

Ramana Maharshi 1879-1950 .... **TCLC 84**

Ramoacn y Cajal, Santiago 1852-1934 .... **TCLC 93**

Ramon, Juan
See Jimenez (Mantecon), Juan Ramon

Ramos, Graciliano 1892-1953 .... **TCLC 32**
See also CA 167; HW 2

Rampersad, Arnold 1941- .... **CLC 44**
See also BW 2, 3; CA 127; 133; CANR 81; DLB 111; INT 133

Rampling, Anne
See Rice, Anne

Ramsay, Allan 1684(?)-1758 .... **LC 29**
See also DLB 95

Ramuz, Charles-Ferdinand 1878-1947 .... **TCLC 33**
See also CA 165

Rand, Ayn 1905-1982 ...... **CLC 3, 30, 44, 79; DA; DAC; DAM MST, NOV, POP; WLC**
See also AAYA 10; CA 13-16R; 105; CANR 27, 73; CDALBS; DA3; MTCW 1, 2

Silone, Ignazio 1900-1978 .... **CLC 4**
See also CA 25-28; 81-84; CANR 34; CAP 2; MTCW 1

Silver, Joan Micklin 1935- .... **CLC 20**
See also CA 114; 121; INT 121

Silver, Nicholas
See Faust, Frederick (Schiller)

Silverberg, Robert 1935- .... **CLC 7; DAM POP**
See also AAYA 24; CA 1-4R; CAAS 3; CANR 1, 20, 36, 85; CLR 59; DLB 8; INT CANR-20; MAICYA; MTCW 1, 2; SATA 13, 91; SATA-Essay 104

Silverstein, Alvin 1933- .... **CLC 17**
See also CA 49-52; CANR 2; CLR 25; JRDA; MAICYA; SATA 8, 69

Silverstein, Virginia B(arbara Opshelor) 1937- .... **CLC 17**
See also CA 49-52; CANR 2; CLR 25; JRDA; MAICYA; SATA 8, 69

Sim, Georges
See Simenon, Georges (Jacques Christian)

Simak, Clifford D(onald) 1904-1988 . **CLC 1, 55**
See also CA 1-4R; 125; CANR 1, 35; DLB 8; MTCW 1; SATA-Obit 56

Simenon, Georges (Jacques Christian) 1903-1989 .... **CLC 1, 2, 3, 8, 18, 47; DAM POP**
See also CA 85-88; 129; CANR 35; DA3; DLB 72; DLBY 89; MTCW 1, 2

Simic, Charles 1938- ... **CLC 6, 9, 22, 49, 68; DAM POET**
See also CA 29-32R; CAAS 4; CANR 12, 33, 52, 61; DA3; DLB 105; MTCW 2

Simmel, Georg 1858-1918 .... **TCLC 64**
See also CA 157

Simmons, Charles (Paul) 1924- .... **CLC 57**
See also CA 89-92; INT 89-92

Simmons, Dan 1948- .... **CLC 44; DAM POP**
See also AAYA 16; CA 138; CANR 53, 81

Simmons, James (Stewart Alexander) 1933- **CLC 43**
See also CA 105; CAAS 21; DLB 40

Simms, William Gilmore 1806-1870 .... **NCLC 3**
See also DLB 3, 30, 59, 73

Simon, Carly 1945- .... **CLC 26**
See also CA 105

Simon, Claude 1913-1984 . **CLC 4, 9, 15, 39; DAM NOV**
See also CA 89-92; CANR 33; DLB 83; MTCW 1

Simon, (Marvin) Neil 1927- ... **CLC 6, 11, 31, 39, 70; DAM DRAM**
See also AAYA 32; AITN 1; CA 21-24R; CANR 26, 54, 87; DA3; DLB 7; MTCW 1, 2

Simon, Paul (Frederick) 1941(?)- ..... **CLC 17**
See also CA 116; 153

Simonon, Paul 1956(?)- .... **CLC 30**

Simpson, Harriette
See Arnow, Harriette (Louisa) Simpson

Simpson, Louis (Aston Marantz) 1923- ...... **CLC 4, 7, 9, 32; DAM POET**
See also CA 1-4R; CAAS 4; CANR 1, 61; DLB 5; MTCW 1, 2

Simpson, Mona (Elizabeth) 1957- .... **CLC 44**
See also CA 122; 135; CANR 68

Simpson, N(orman) F(rederick) 1919- .... **CLC 29**
See also CA 13-16R; DLB 13

Sinclair, Andrew (Annandale) 1935- . **CLC 2, 14**
See also CA 9-12R; CAAS 5; CANR 14, 38; DLB 14; MTCW 1

Sinclair, Emil
See Hesse, Hermann

Sinclair, Iain 1943- .... **CLC 76**
See also CA 132; CANR 81

Sinclair, Iain MacGregor
See Sinclair, Iain

Sinclair, Irene
See Griffith, D(avid Lewelyn) W(ark)

Sinclair, Mary Amelia St. Clair 1865(?)-1946
See Sinclair, May
See also CA 104

Sinclair, May 1863-1946 .... **TCLC 3, 11**
See also Sinclair, Mary Amelia St. Clair CA 166; DLB 36, 135

Sinclair, Roy
See Griffith, D(avid Lewelyn) W(ark)

Sinclair, Upton (Beall) 1878-1968 ..... **CLC 1, 11, 15, 63; DA; DAB; DAC; DAM MST, NOV; WLC**
See also CA 5-8R; 25-28R; CANR 7; CDALB 1929-1941; DA3; DLB 9; INT CANR-7; MTCW 1, 2; SATA 9

Singer, Isaac
See Singer, Isaac Bashevis

Singer, Isaac Bashevis 1904-1991 .. **CLC 1, 3, 6, 9, 11, 15, 23, 38, 69, 111; DA; DAB; DAC; DAM MST, NOV; SSC 3; WLC**
See also AAYA 32; AITN 1, 2; CA 1-4R; 134; CANR 1, 39; CDALB 1941-1968; CLR 1; DA3; DLB 6, 28, 52; DLBY 91; JRDA; MAICYA; MTCW 1, 2; SATA 3, 27; SATA-Obit 68

Singer, Israel Joshua 1893-1944 .... **TCLC 33**
See also CA 169

Singh, Khushwant 1915- .... **CLC 11**
See also CA 9-12R; CAAS 9; CANR 6, 84

Singleton, Ann
See Benedict, Ruth (Fulton)

Sinjohn, John
See Galsworthy, John

Sinyavsky, Andrei (Donatevich) 1925-1997 **CLC 8**
See also CA 85-88; 159

Sirin, V.
See Nabokov, Vladimir (Vladimirovich)

Sissman, L(ouis) E(dward) 1928-1976 .... **CLC 9, 18**
See also CA 21-24R; 65-68; CANR 13; DLB 5

Sisson, C(harles) H(ubert) 1914- .... **CLC 8**
See also CA 1-4R; CAAS 3; CANR 3, 48, 84; DLB 27

Sitwell, Dame Edith 1887-1964 ..... **CLC 2, 9, 67; DAM POET; PC 3**
See also CA 9-12R; CANR 35; CDBLB 1945-1960; DLB 20; MTCW 1, 2

Siwaarmill, H. P.
See Sharp, William

Sjoewall, Maj 1935- .... **CLC 7**
See also CA 65-68; CANR 73

Sjowall, Maj
See Sjoewall, Maj

Skelton, John 1463-1529 .... **PC 25**

Skelton, Robin 1925-1997 .... **CLC 13**
See also AITN 2; CA 5-8R; 160; CAAS 5; CANR 28; DLB 27, 53

Skolimowski, Jerzy 1938- .... **CLC 20**
See also CA 128

Skram, Amalie (Bertha) 1847-1905 .... **TCLC 25**
See also CA 165

Skvorecky, Josef (Vaclav) 1924- ...... **CLC 15, 39, 69; DAC; DAM NOV**
See also CA 61-64; CAAS 1; CANR 10, 34, 63; DA3; MTCW 1, 2

Slade, Bernard .... **CLC 11, 46**
See also Newbound, Bernard Slade CAAS 9; DLB 53

Slaughter, Carolyn 1946- .... **CLC 56**
See also CA 85-88; CANR 85

Slaughter, Frank G(ill) 1908- .... **CLC 29**
See also AITN 2; CA 5-8R; CANR 5, 85; INT CANR-5

Slavitt, David R(ytman) 1935- ..... **CLC 5, 14**
See also CA 21-24R; CAAS 3; CANR 41, 83; DLB 5, 6

Slesinger, Tess 1905-1945 .... **TCLC 10**
See also CA 107; DLB 102

Slessor, Kenneth 1901-1971 .... **CLC 14**
See also CA 102; 89-92

Slowacki, Juliusz 1809-1849 .... **NCLC 15**

Smart, Christopher 1722-1771 .. **LC 3; DAM POET; PC 13**
See also DLB 109

Smart, Elizabeth 1913-1986 .... **CLC 54**
See also CA 81-84; 118; DLB 88

Smiley, Jane (Graves) 1949- ...... **CLC 53, 76; DAM POP**
See also CA 104; CANR 30, 50, 74; DA3; INT CANR-30

Smith, A(rthur) J(ames) M(arshall) 1902-1980 .... **CLC 15; DAC**
See also CA 1-4R; 102; CANR 4; DLB 88

Smith, Adam 1723-1790 .... **LC 36**
See also DLB 104

Smith, Alexander 1829-1867 .... **NCLC 59**
See also DLB 32, 55

Smith, Anna Deavere 1950- .... **CLC 86**
See also CA 133

Smith, Betty (Wehner) 1896-1972 .... **CLC 19**
See also CA 5-8R; 33-36R; DLBY 82; SATA 6

Smith, Charlotte (Turner) 1749-1806 .... **NCLC 23**
See also DLB 39, 109

Smith, Clark Ashton 1893-1961 .... **CLC 43**
See also CA 143; CANR 81; MTCW 2

Smith, Dave .... **CLC 22, 42**
See also Smith, David (Jeddie) CAAS 7; DLB 5

Smith, David (Jeddie) 1942-
See Smith, Dave
See also CA 49-52; CANR 1, 59; DAM POET

Smith, Florence Margaret 1902-1971
See Smith, Stevie
See also CA 17-18; 29-32R; CANR 35; CAP 2; DAM POET; MTCW 1, 2

Smith, Iain Crichton 1928-1998 .... **CLC 64**
See also CA 21-24R; 171; DLB 40, 139

Smith, John 1580(?)-1631 .... **LC 9**
See also DLB 24, 30

Smith, Johnston
See Crane, Stephen (Townley)

Smith, Joseph, Jr. 1805-1844 .... **NCLC 53**

Smith, Lee 1944- .... **CLC 25, 73**
See also CA 114; 119; CANR 46; DLB 143; DLBY 83; INT 119

Smith, Martin
See Smith, Martin Cruz

Smith, Martin Cruz 1942- .... **CLC 25; DAM MULT, POP**
See also BEST 89:4; CA 85-88; CANR 6, 23, 43, 65; INT CANR-23; MTCW 2; NNAL

Smith, Mary-Ann Tirone 1944- .... **CLC 39**
See also CA 118; 136

Smith, Patti 1946- .... **CLC 12**
See also CA 93-96; CANR 63

Smith, Pauline (Urmson) 1882-1959 .... **TCLC 25**

Smith, Rosamond
See Oates, Joyce Carol

Smith, Sheila Kaye
See Kaye-Smith, Sheila

Smith, Stevie .... **CLC 3, 8, 25, 44; PC 12**
See also Smith, Florence Margaret DLB 20; MTCW 2

Tate, Ellalice
See Hibbert, Eleanor Alice Burford

Tate, James (Vincent) 1943- ..... **CLC 2, 6, 25**
See also CA 21-24R; CANR 29, 57; DLB
5, 169

Tauler, Johannes c. 1300-1361 ...... **CMLC 37**
See also DLB 179

Tavel, Ronald 1940- .... **CLC 6**
See also CA 21-24R; CANR 33

Taylor, C(ecil) P(hilip) 1929-1981 .... **CLC 27**
See also CA 25-28R; 105; CANR 47

Taylor, Edward 1642(?)-1729 ..... **LC 11; DA;**
DAB; DAC; DAM MST, POET
See also DLB 24

Taylor, Eleanor Ross 1920- .... **CLC 5**
See also CA 81-84; CANR 70

Taylor, Elizabeth 1912-1975 ..... **CLC 2, 4, 29**
See also CA 13-16R; CANR 9, 70; DLB
139; MTCW 1; SATA 13

Taylor, Frederick Winslow
1856-1915 .... **TCLC 76**

Taylor, Henry (Splawn) 1942- .... **CLC 44**
See also CA 33-36R; CAAS 7; CANR 31;
DLB 5

Taylor, Kamala (Purnaiya) 1924-
See Markandaya, Kamala
See also CA 77-80

Taylor, Mildred D. .... **CLC 21**
See also AAYA 10; BW 1; CA 85-88;
CANR 25; CLR 9, 59; DLB 52; JRDA;
MAICYA; SAAS 5; SATA 15, 70

Taylor, Peter (Hillsman) 1917-1994 .. **CLC 1,**
4, 18, 37, 44, 50, 71; SSC 10
See also CA 13-16R; 147; CANR 9, 50;
DLBY 81, 94; INT CANR-9; MTCW 1, 2

Taylor, Robert Lewis 1912-1998 .... **CLC 14**
See also CA 1-4R; 170; CANR 3, 64; SATA
10

Tchekhov, Anton
See Chekhov, Anton (Pavlovich)

Tchicaya, Gerald Felix 1931-1988 .. **CLC 101**
See also CA 129; 125; CANR 81

Tchicaya U Tam'si
See Tchicaya, Gerald Felix

Teasdale, Sara 1884-1933 .... **TCLC 4**
See also CA 104; 163; DLB 45; SATA 32

Tegner, Esaias 1782-1846 .... **NCLC 2**

Teilhard de Chardin, (Marie Joseph) Pierre
1881-1955 .... **TCLC 9**
See also CA 105

Temple, Ann
See Mortimer, Penelope (Ruth)

Tennant, Emma (Christina) 1937- .. **CLC 13,**
52
See also CA 65-68; CAAS 9; CANR 10,
38, 59; DLB 14

Tenneshaw, S. M.
See Silverberg, Robert

Tennyson, Alfred 1809-1892 ... **NCLC 30, 65;**
DA; DAB; DAC; DAM MST, POET;
PC 6; WLC
See also CDBLB 1832-1890; DA3; DLB
32

Teran, Lisa St. Aubin de .... **CLC 36**
See also St. Aubin de Teran, Lisa

Terence c. 184B.C.-c. 159B.C. ...... **CMLC 14;**
DC 7
See also DLB 211

Teresa de Jesus, St. 1515-1582 .... **LC 18**

Terkel, Louis 1912-
See Terkel, Studs
See also CA 57-60; CANR 18, 45, 67; DA3;
MTCW 1, 2

Terkel, Studs .... **CLC 38**
See also Terkel, Louis AAYA 32; AITN 1;
MTCW 2

Terry, C. V.
See Slaughter, Frank G(ill)

Terry, Megan 1932- .... **CLC 19**
See also CA 77-80; CABS 3; CANR 43;
DLB 7

Tertullian c. 155-c. 245 .... **CMLC 29**

Tertz, Abram
See Sinyavsky, Andrei (Donatevich)

Tesich, Steve 1943(?)-1996 .... **CLC 40, 69**
See also CA 105; 152; DLBY 83

Tesla, Nikola 1856-1943 .... **TCLC 88**

Teternikov, Fyodor Kuzmich 1863-1927
See Sologub, Fyodor
See also CA 104

Tevis, Walter 1928-1984 .... **CLC 42**
See also CA 113

Tey, Josephine .... **TCLC 14**
See also Mackintosh, Elizabeth DLB 77

Thackeray, William Makepeace 1811-1863
NCLC 5, 14, 22, 43; DA; DAB; DAC;
DAM MST, NOV; WLC
See also CDBLB 1832-1890; DA3; DLB
21, 55, 159, 163; SATA 23

Thakura, Ravindranatha
See Tagore, Rabindranath

Tharoor, Shashi 1956- .... **CLC 70**
See also CA 141

Thelwell, Michael Miles 1939- .... **CLC 22**
See also BW 2; CA 101

Theobald, Lewis, Jr.
See Lovecraft, H(oward) P(hillips)

Theodorescu, Ion N. 1880-1967
See Arghezi, Tudor
See also CA 116

Theriault, Yves 1915-1983 .... **CLC 79; DAC;**
DAM MST
See also CA 102; DLB 88

Theroux, Alexander (Louis) 1939- .... **CLC 2,**
25
See also CA 85-88; CANR 20, 63

Theroux, Paul (Edward) 1941- ..... **CLC 5, 8,**
11, 15, 28, 46; DAM POP
See also AAYA 28; BEST 89:4; CA 33-36R;
CANR 20, 45, 74; CDALBS; DA3; DLB
2; MTCW 1, 2; SATA 44, 109

Thesen, Sharon 1946- .... **CLC 56**
See also CA 163

Thevenin, Denis
See Duhamel, Georges

Thibault, Jacques Anatole Francois
1844-1924
See France, Anatole
See also CA 106; 127; DAM NOV; DA3;
MTCW 1, 2

Thiele, Colin (Milton) 1920- .... **CLC 17**
See also CA 29-32R; CANR 12, 28, 53;
CLR 27; MAICYA; SAAS 2; SATA 14,
72

Thomas, Audrey (Callahan) 1935- .... **CLC 7,**
13, 37, 107; SSC 20
See also AITN 2; CA 21-24R; CAAS 19;
CANR 36, 58; DLB 60; MTCW 1

Thomas, Augustus 1857-1934 .... **TCLC 97**

Thomas, D(onald) M(ichael) 1935- . **CLC 13,**
22, 31
See also CA 61-64; CAAS 11; CANR 17,
45, 75; CDBLB 1960 to Present; DA3;
DLB 40, 207; INT CANR-17; MTCW 1,
2

Thomas, Dylan (Marlais)
1914-1953 ... **TCLC 1, 8, 45; DA; DAB;**
DAC; DAM DRAM, MST, POET; PC
2; SSC 3; WLC
See also CA 104; 120; CANR 65; CDBLB
1945-1960; DA3; DLB 13, 20, 139;
MTCW 1, 2; SATA 60

Thomas, (Philip) Edward
1878-1917 .... **TCLC 10; DAM POET**
See also CA 106; 153; DLB 98

Thomas, Joyce Carol 1938- .... **CLC 35**
See also AAYA 12; BW 2, 3; CA 113; 116;
CANR 48; CLR 19; DLB 33; INT 116;
JRDA; MAICYA; MTCW 1, 2; SAAS 7;
SATA 40, 78

Thomas, Lewis 1913-1993 .... **CLC 35**
See also CA 85-88; 143; CANR 38, 60;
MTCW 1, 2

Thomas, M. Carey 1857-1935 .... **TCLC 89**

Thomas, Paul
See Mann, (Paul) Thomas

Thomas, Piri 1928- .... **CLC 17; HLCS 2**
See also CA 73-76; HW 1

Thomas, R(onald) S(tuart) 1913- ...... **CLC 6,**
13, 48; DAB; DAM POET
See also CA 89-92; CAAS 4; CANR 30;
CDBLB 1960 to Present; DLB 27; MTCW
1

Thomas, Ross (Elmore) 1926-1995 .. **CLC 39**
See also CA 33-36R; 150; CANR 22, 63

Thompson, Francis Clegg
See Mencken, H(enry) L(ouis)

Thompson, Francis Joseph
1859-1907 .... **TCLC 4**
See also CA 104; CDBLB 1890-1914; DLB
19

Thompson, Hunter S(tockton)
1939- ... **CLC 9, 17, 40, 104; DAM POP**
See also BEST 89:1; CA 17-20R; CANR
23, 46, 74, 77; DA3; DLB 185; MTCW
1, 2

Thompson, James Myers
See Thompson, Jim (Myers)

Thompson, Jim (Myers)
1906-1977(?) .... **CLC 69**
See also CA 140

Thompson, Judith .... **CLC 39**

Thomson, James 1700-1748 ... **LC 16, 29, 40;**
DAM POET
See also DLB 95

Thomson, James 1834-1882 .... **NCLC 18;**
DAM POET
See also DLB 35

Thoreau, Henry David 1817-1862 .. **NCLC 7,**
21, 61; DA; DAB; DAC; DAM MST;
WLC
See also CDALB 1640-1865; DA3; DLB 1

Thornton, Hall
See Silverberg, Robert

Thucydides c. 455B.C.-399B.C. ..... **CMLC 17**
See also DLB 176

Thumboo, Edwin 1933- .... **PC 29**

Thurber, James (Grover)
1894-1961 .... **CLC 5, 11, 25, 125; DA;**
DAB; DAC; DAM DRAM, MST, NOV;
SSC 1
See also CA 73-76; CANR 17, 39; CDALB
1929-1941; DA3; DLB 4, 11, 22, 102;
MAICYA; MTCW 1, 2; SATA 13

Thurman, Wallace (Henry)
1902-1934 .... **TCLC 6; BLC 3; DAM**
MULT
See also BW 1, 3; CA 104; 124; CANR 81;
DLB 51

Tibullus, Albius c. 54B.C.-c.
19B.C. .... **CMLC 36**
See also DLB 211

Ticheburn, Cheviot
See Ainsworth, William Harrison

Tieck, (Johann) Ludwig
1773-1853 .... **NCLC 5, 46; SSC 31**
See also DLB 90

Tiger, Derry
See Ellison, Harlan (Jay)

Tilghman, Christopher 1948(?)- .... **CLC 65**
See also CA 159

Tutuola, Amos 1920-1997 ...... **CLC 5, 14, 29; BLC 3; DAM MULT**
See also BW 2, 3; CA 9-12R; 159; CANR 27, 66; DA3; DLB 125; MTCW 1, 2

Twain, Mark ..... **TCLC 6, 12, 19, 36, 48, 59; SSC 34; WLC**
See also Clemens, Samuel Langhorne AAYA 20; CLR 58, 60; DLB 11, 12, 23, 64, 74

Tyler, Anne 1941- . **CLC 7, 11, 18, 28, 44, 59, 103; DAM NOV, POP**
See also AAYA 18; BEST 89:1; CA 9-12R; CANR 11, 33, 53; CDALBS; DLB 6, 143; DLBY 82; MTCW 1, 2; SATA 7, 90

Tyler, Royall 1757-1826 .... **NCLC 3**
See also DLB 37

Tynan, Katharine 1861-1931 .... **TCLC 3**
See also CA 104; 167; DLB 153

Tyutchev, Fyodor 1803-1873 .... **NCLC 34**

Tzara, Tristan 1896-1963 ...... **CLC 47; DAM POET; PC 27**
See also CA 153; 89-92; MTCW 2

Uhry, Alfred 1936- .. **CLC 55; DAM DRAM, POP**
See also CA 127; 133; DA3; INT 133

Ulf, Haerved
See Strindberg, (Johan) August

Ulf, Harved
See Strindberg, (Johan) August

Ulibarri, Sabine R(eyes) 1919- .... **CLC 83; DAM MULT; HLCS 2**
See also CA 131; CANR 81; DLB 82; HW 1, 2

Unamuno (y Jugo), Miguel de 1864-1936 **TCLC 2, 9; DAM MULT, NOV; HLC 2; SSC 11**
See also CA 104; 131; CANR 81; DLB 108; HW 1, 2; MTCW 1, 2

Undercliffe, Errol
See Campbell, (John) Ramsey

Underwood, Miles
See Glassco, John

Undset, Sigrid 1882-1949 .... **TCLC 3; DA; DAB; DAC; DAM MST, NOV; WLC**
See also CA 104; 129; DA3; MTCW 1, 2

Ungaretti, Giuseppe 1888-1970 ... **CLC 7, 11, 15**
See also CA 19-20; 25-28R; CAP 2; DLB 114

Unger, Douglas 1952- .... **CLC 34**
See also CA 130

Unsworth, Barry (Forster) 1930- .... **CLC 76, 127**
See also CA 25-28R; CANR 30, 54; DLB 194

Updike, John (Hoyer) 1932- . **CLC 1, 2, 3, 5, 7, 9, 13, 15, 23, 34, 43, 70; DA; DAB; DAC; DAM MST, NOV, POET, POP; SSC 13, 27; WLC**
See also CA 1-4R; CABS 1; CANR 4, 33, 51; CDALB 1968-1988; DA3; DLB 2, 5, 143; DLBD 3; DLBY 80, 82, 97; MTCW 1, 2

Upshaw, Margaret Mitchell
See Mitchell, Margaret (Munnerlyn)

Upton, Mark
See Sanders, Lawrence

Upward, Allen 1863-1926 .... **TCLC 85**
See also CA 117; DLB 36

Urdang, Constance (Henriette) 1922- .... **CLC 47**
See also CA 21-24R; CANR 9, 24

Uriel, Henry
See Faust, Frederick (Schiller)

Uris, Leon (Marcus) 1924- .... **CLC 7, 32; DAM NOV, POP**
See also AITN 1, 2; BEST 89:2; CA 1-4R; CANR 1, 40, 65; DA3; MTCW 1, 2; SATA 49

Urista, Alberto H. 1947-
See Alurista
See also CA 45-48, 182; CANR 2, 32; HLCS 1; HW 1

Urmuz
See Codrescu, Andrei

Urquhart, Guy
See McAlmon, Robert (Menzies)

Urquhart, Jane 1949- .... **CLC 90; DAC**
See also CA 113; CANR 32, 68

Usigli, Rodolfo 1905-1979
See also CA 131; HLCS 1; HW 1

Ustinov, Peter (Alexander) 1921- .... **CLC 1**
See also AITN 1; CA 13-16R; CANR 25, 51; DLB 13; MTCW 2

U Tam'si, Gerald Felix Tchicaya
See Tchicaya, Gerald Felix

U Tam'si, Tchicaya
See Tchicaya, Gerald Felix

Vachss, Andrew (Henry) 1942- .... **CLC 106**
See also CA 118; CANR 44

Vachss, Andrew H.
See Vachss, Andrew (Henry)

Vaculik, Ludvik 1926- .... **CLC 7**
See also CA 53-56; CANR 72

Vaihinger, Hans 1852-1933 .... **TCLC 71**
See also CA 116; 166

Valdez, Luis (Miguel) 1940- .. **CLC 84; DAM MULT; DC 10; HLC 2**
See also CA 101; CANR 32, 81; DLB 122; HW 1

Valenzuela, Luisa 1938- .... **CLC 31, 104; DAM MULT; HLCS 2; SSC 14**
See also CA 101; CANR 32, 65; DLB 113; HW 1, 2

Valera y Alcala-Galiano, Juan 1824-1905 **TCLC 10**
See also CA 106

Valery, (Ambroise) Paul (Toussaint Jules) 1871-1945 ... **TCLC 4, 15; DAM POET; PC 9**
See also CA 104; 122; DA3; MTCW 1, 2

Valle-Inclan, Ramon (Maria) del 1866-1936 **TCLC 5; DAM MULT; HLC 2**
See also CA 106; 153; CANR 80; DLB 134; HW 2

Vallejo, Antonio Buero
See Buero Vallejo, Antonio

Vallejo, Cesar (Abraham) 1892-1938 .. **TCLC 3, 56; DAM MULT; HLC 2**
See also CA 105; 153; HW 1

Valles, Jules 1832-1885 .... **NCLC 71**
See also DLB 123

Vallette, Marguerite Eymery 1860-1953 **TCLC 67**
See also CA 182; DLB 123, 192

Valle Y Pena, Ramon del
See Valle-Inclan, Ramon (Maria) del

Van Ash, Cay 1918- .... **CLC 34**

Vanbrugh, Sir John 1664-1726 .... **LC 21; DAM DRAM**
See also DLB 80

Van Campen, Karl
See Campbell, John W(ood, Jr.)

Vance, Gerald
See Silverberg, Robert

Vance, Jack .... **CLC 35**
See also Vance, John Holbrook DLB 8

Vance, John Holbrook 1916-
See Queen, Ellery; Vance, Jack
See also CA 29-32R; CANR 17, 65; MTCW 1

Van Den Bogarde, Derek Jules Gaspard Ulric Niven 1921-1999
See Bogarde, Dirk
See also CA 77-80; 179

Vandenburgh, Jane .... **CLC 59**
See also CA 168

Vanderhaeghe, Guy 1951- .... **CLC 41**
See also CA 113; CANR 72

van der Post, Laurens (Jan) 1906-1996 .... **CLC 5**
See also CA 5-8R; 155; CANR 35; DLB 204

van de Wetering, Janwillem 1931- ... **CLC 47**
See also CA 49-52; CANR 4, 62

Van Dine, S. S. .... **TCLC 23**
See also Wright, Willard Huntington

Van Doren, Carl (Clinton) 1885-1950 .... **TCLC 18**
See also CA 111; 168

Van Doren, Mark 1894-1972 .... **CLC 6, 10**
See also CA 1-4R; 37-40R; CANR 3; DLB 45; MTCW 1, 2

Van Druten, John (William) 1901-1957 **TCLC 2**
See also CA 104; 161; DLB 10

Van Duyn, Mona (Jane) 1921- ...... **CLC 3, 7, 63, 116; DAM POET**
See also CA 9-12R; CANR 7, 38, 60; DLB 5

Van Dyne, Edith
See Baum, L(yman) Frank

van Itallie, Jean-Claude 1936- .... **CLC 3**
See also CA 45-48; CAAS 2; CANR 1, 48; DLB 7

van Ostaijen, Paul 1896-1928 .... **TCLC 33**
See also CA 163

Van Peebles, Melvin 1932- .... **CLC 2, 20; DAM MULT**
See also BW 2, 3; CA 85-88; CANR 27, 67, 82

Vansittart, Peter 1920- .... **CLC 42**
See also CA 1-4R; CANR 3, 49

Van Vechten, Carl 1880-1964 .... **CLC 33**
See also CA 183; 89-92; DLB 4, 9, 51

Van Vogt, A(lfred) E(lton) 1912- .... **CLC 1**
See also CA 21-24R; CANR 28; DLB 8; SATA 14

Varda, Agnes 1928- .... **CLC 16**
See also CA 116; 122

Vargas Llosa, (Jorge) Mario (Pedro) 1936- **CLC 3, 6, 9, 10, 15, 31, 42, 85; DA; DAB; DAC; DAM MST, MULT, NOV; HLC 2**
See also CA 73-76; CANR 18, 32, 42, 67; DA3; DLB 145; HW 1, 2; MTCW 1, 2

Vasiliu, Gheorghe 1881-1957
See Bacovia, George
See also CA 123

Vassa, Gustavus
See Equiano, Olaudah

Vassilikos, Vassilis 1933- .... **CLC 4, 8**
See also CA 81-84; CANR 75

Vaughan, Henry 1621-1695 .... **LC 27**
See also DLB 131

Vaughn, Stephanie .... **CLC 62**

Vazov, Ivan (Minchov) 1850-1921 . **TCLC 25**
See also CA 121; 167; DLB 147

Veblen, Thorstein B(unde) 1857-1929 .... **TCLC 31**
See also CA 115; 165

Vega, Lope de 1562-1635 .... **LC 23; HLCS 2**

Venison, Alfred
See Pound, Ezra (Weston Loomis)

Verdi, Marie de
See Mencken, H(enry) L(ouis)

Verdu, Matilde
See Cela, Camilo Jose

Verga, Giovanni (Carmelo) 1840-1922 .... **TCLC 3; SSC 21**
See also CA 104; 123

Wilder, Billy .... CLC **20**
   See also Wilder, Samuel DLB 26
Wilder, Samuel 1906-
   See Wilder, Billy
   See also CA 89-92
Wilder, Thornton (Niven)
   1897-1975 ... CLC **1, 5, 6, 10, 15, 35, 82;**
   DA; DAB; DAC; DAM DRAM, MST,
   NOV; DC 1; WLC
      See also AAYA 29; AITN 2; CA 13-16R;
      61-64; CANR 40; CDALBS; DA3; DLB
      4, 7, 9; DLBY 97; MTCW 1, 2
Wilding, Michael 1942- .... CLC **73**
   See also CA 104; CANR 24, 49
Wiley, Richard 1944- .... CLC **44**
   See also CA 121; 129; CANR 71
Wilhelm, Kate .... CLC **7**
   See also Wilhelm, Katie Gertrude AAYA
   20; CAAS 5; DLB 8; INT CANR-17
Wilhelm, Katie Gertrude 1928-
   See Wilhelm, Kate
   See also CA 37-40R; CANR 17, 36, 60;
   MTCW 1
Wilkins, Mary
   See Freeman, Mary E(leanor) Wilkins
Willard, Nancy 1936- .... CLC **7, 37**
   See also CA 89-92; CANR 10, 39, 68; CLR
   5; DLB 5, 52; MAICYA; MTCW 1; SATA
   37, 71; SATA-Brief 30
William of Ockham 1285-1347 ..... CMLC **32**
Williams, Ben Ames 1889-1953 ..... TCLC **89**
   See also CA 183; DLB 102
Williams, C(harles) K(enneth)
   1936- .... CLC **33, 56; DAM POET**
   See also CA 37-40R; CAAS 26; CANR 57;
   DLB 5
Williams, Charles
   See Collier, James L(incoln)
Williams, Charles (Walter Stansby)
   1886-1945 .... TCLC **1, 11**
   See also CA 104; 163; DLB 100, 153
Williams, (George) Emlyn
   1905-1987 .... CLC **15; DAM DRAM**
   See also CA 104; 123; CANR 36; DLB 10,
   77; MTCW 1
Williams, Hank 1923-1953 .... TCLC **81**
Williams, Hugo 1942- .... CLC **42**
   See also CA 17-20R; CANR 45; DLB 40
Williams, J. Walker
   See Wodehouse, P(elham) G(renville)
Williams, John A(lfred) 1925- ..... CLC **5, 13;**
   BLC 3; DAM MULT
   See also BW 2, 3; CA 53-56; CAAS 3;
   CANR 6, 26, 51; DLB 2, 33; INT
   CANR-6
Williams, Jonathan (Chamberlain) 1929-
   CLC **13**
   See also CA 9-12R; CAAS 12; CANR 8;
   DLB 5
Williams, Joy 1944- .... CLC **31**
   See also CA 41-44R; CANR 22, 48
Williams, Norman 1952- .... CLC **39**
   See also CA 118
Williams, Sherley Anne 1944- .... CLC **89;**
   BLC 3; DAM MULT, POET
   See also BW 2, 3; CA 73-76; CANR 25,
   82; DLB 41; INT CANR-25; SATA 78
Williams, Shirley
   See Williams, Sherley Anne
Williams, Tennessee 1911-1983 . CLC **1, 2, 5,**
   7, 8, 11, 15, 19, 30, 39, 45, 71, 111; DA;
   DAB; DAC; DAM DRAM, MST; DC
   4; WLC
      See also AAYA 31; AITN 1, 2; CA 5-8R;
      108; CABS 3; CANR 31; CDALB 1941-
      1968; DA3; DLB 7; DLBD 4; DLBY 83;
      MTCW 1, 2

Williams, Thomas (Alonzo)
   1926-1990 .... CLC **14**
   See also CA 1-4R; 132; CANR 2
Williams, William C.
   See Williams, William Carlos
Williams, William Carlos
   1883-1963 ... CLC **1, 2, 5, 9, 13, 22, 42,**
   67; DA; DAB; DAC; DAM MST,
   POET; PC 7; SSC 31
      See also CA 89-92; CANR 34; CDALB
      1917-1929; DA3; DLB 4, 16, 54, 86;
      MTCW 1, 2
Williamson, David (Keith) 1942- ..... CLC **56**
   See also CA 103; CANR 41
Williamson, Ellen Douglas 1905-1984
   See Douglas, Ellen
   See also CA 17-20R; 114; CANR 39
Williamson, Jack .... CLC **29**
   See also Williamson, John Stewart CAAS
   8; DLB 8
Williamson, John Stewart 1908-
   See Williamson, Jack
   See also CA 17-20R; CANR 23, 70
Willie, Frederick
   See Lovecraft, H(oward) P(hillips)
Willingham, Calder (Baynard, Jr.)
   1922-1995 .... CLC **5, 51**
   See also CA 5-8R; 147; CANR 3; DLB 2,
   44; MTCW 1
Willis, Charles
   See Clarke, Arthur C(harles)
Willis, Fingal O'Flahertie
   See Wilde, Oscar
Willy
   See Colette, (Sidonie-Gabrielle)
Willy, Colette
   See Colette, (Sidonie-Gabrielle)
Wilson, A(ndrew) N(orman) 1950- .. CLC **33**
   See also CA 112; 122; DLB 14, 155, 194;
   MTCW 2
Wilson, Angus (Frank Johnstone) 1913-1991
   CLC **2, 3, 5, 25, 34; SSC 21**
   See also CA 5-8R; 134; CANR 21; DLB
   15, 139, 155; MTCW 1, 2
Wilson, August 1945- ... CLC **39, 50, 63, 118;**
   BLC 3; DA; DAB; DAC; DAM
   DRAM, MST, MULT; DC 2; WLCS
      See also AAYA 16; BW 2, 3; CA 115; 122;
      CANR 42, 54, 76; DA3; MTCW 1, 2
Wilson, Brian 1942- .... CLC **12**
Wilson, Colin 1931- .... CLC **3, 14**
   See also CA 1-4R; CAAS 5; CANR 1, 22,
   33, 77; DLB 14, 194; MTCW 1
Wilson, Dirk
   See Pohl, Frederik
Wilson, Edmund 1895-1972 .. CLC **1, 2, 3, 8,**
   24
      See also CA 1-4R; 37-40R; CANR 1, 46;
      DLB 63; MTCW 1, 2
Wilson, Ethel Davis (Bryant) 1888(?)-1980
   CLC **13; DAC; DAM POET**
   See also CA 102; DLB 68; MTCW 1
Wilson, John 1785-1854 .... NCLC **5**
Wilson, John (Anthony) Burgess 1917-1993
   See Burgess, Anthony
   See also CA 1-4R; 143; CANR 2, 46; DAC;
   DAM NOV; DA3; MTCW 1, 2
Wilson, Lanford 1937- .... CLC **7, 14, 36;**
   DAM DRAM
   See also CA 17-20R; CABS 3; CANR 45;
   DLB 7
Wilson, Robert M. 1944- .... CLC **7, 9**
   See also CA 49-52; CANR 2, 41; MTCW 1
Wilson, Robert McLiam 1964- .... CLC **59**
   See also CA 132
Wilson, Sloan 1920- .... CLC **32**
   See also CA 1-4R; CANR 1, 44
Wilson, Snoo 1948- .... CLC **33**
   See also CA 69-72

Wilson, William S(mith) 1932- .... CLC **49**
   See also CA 81-84
Wilson, (Thomas) Woodrow 1856-1924
   TCLC **79**
   See also CA 166; DLB 47
Winchilsea, Anne (Kingsmill) Finch Counte
   1661-1720
   See Finch, Anne
Windham, Basil
   See Wodehouse, P(elham) G(renville)
Wingrove, David (John) 1954- .... CLC **68**
   See also CA 133
Winnemucca, Sarah 1844-1891 ..... NCLC **79**
Winstanley, Gerrard 1609-1676 .... LC **52**
Wintergreen, Jane
   See Duncan, Sara Jeannette
Winters, Janet Lewis .... CLC **41**
   See also Lewis, Janet DLBY 87
Winters, (Arthur) Yvor 1900-1968 .... CLC **4,**
   8, 32
      See also CA 11-12; 25-28R; CAP 1; DLB
      48; MTCW 1
Winterson, Jeanette 1959- .... CLC **64; DAM**
   POP
   See also CA 136; CANR 58; DA3; DLB
   207; MTCW 2
Winthrop, John 1588-1649 .... LC **31**
   See also DLB 24, 30
Wirth, Louis 1897-1952 .... TCLC **92**
Wiseman, Frederick 1930- .... CLC **20**
   See also CA 159
Wister, Owen 1860-1938 .... TCLC **21**
   See also CA 108; 162; DLB 9, 78, 186;
   SATA 62
Witkacy
   See Witkiewicz, Stanislaw Ignacy
Witkiewicz, Stanislaw Ignacy 1885-1939
   TCLC **8**
   See also CA 105; 162
Wittgenstein, Ludwig (Josef Johann)
   1889-1951 .... TCLC **59**
   See also CA 113; 164; MTCW 2
Wittig, Monique 1935(?)- .... CLC **22**
   See also CA 116; 135; DLB 83
Wittlin, Jozef 1896-1976 .... CLC **25**
   See also CA 49-52; 65-68; CANR 3
Wodehouse, P(elham) G(renville) 1881-1975
   CLC **1, 2, 5, 10, 22; DAB; DAC; DAM**
   NOV; SSC 2
      See also AITN 2; CA 45-48; 57-60; CANR
      3, 33; CDBLB 1914-1945; DA3; DLB 34,
      162; MTCW 1, 2; SATA 22
Woiwode, L.
   See Woiwode, Larry (Alfred)
Woiwode, Larry (Alfred) 1941- ... CLC **6, 10**
   See also CA 73-76; CANR 16; DLB 6; INT
   CANR-16
Wojciechowska, Maia (Teresa)
   1927- .... CLC **26**
   See also AAYA 8; CA 9-12R, 183; CAAE
   183; CANR 4, 41; CLR 1; JRDA; MAI-
   CYA; SAAS 1; SATA 1, 28, 83; SATA-
   Essay 104
Wojtyla, Karol
   See John Paul II, Pope
Wolf, Christa 1929- .... CLC **14, 29, 58**
   See also CA 85-88; CANR 45; DLB 75;
   MTCW 1
Wolfe, Gene (Rodman) 1931- .... CLC **25;**
   DAM POP
   See also CA 57-60; CAAS 9; CANR 6, 32,
   60; DLB 8; MTCW 2
Wolfe, George C. 1954- .... CLC **49; BLCS**
   See also CA 149

Author Index

Literary Criticism Series
Cumulative Topic Index

This index lists all topic entries in Gale's *Classical and Medieval Literature Criticism, Contemporary Literary Criticism, Literature Criticism from 1400 to 1800, Nineteenth-Century Literature Criticism,* and *Twentieth-Century Literary Criticism.*

Topic Index

CMLC Cumulative Nationality Index

CMLC Cumulative Title Index

Title Index